W9-CTX-060

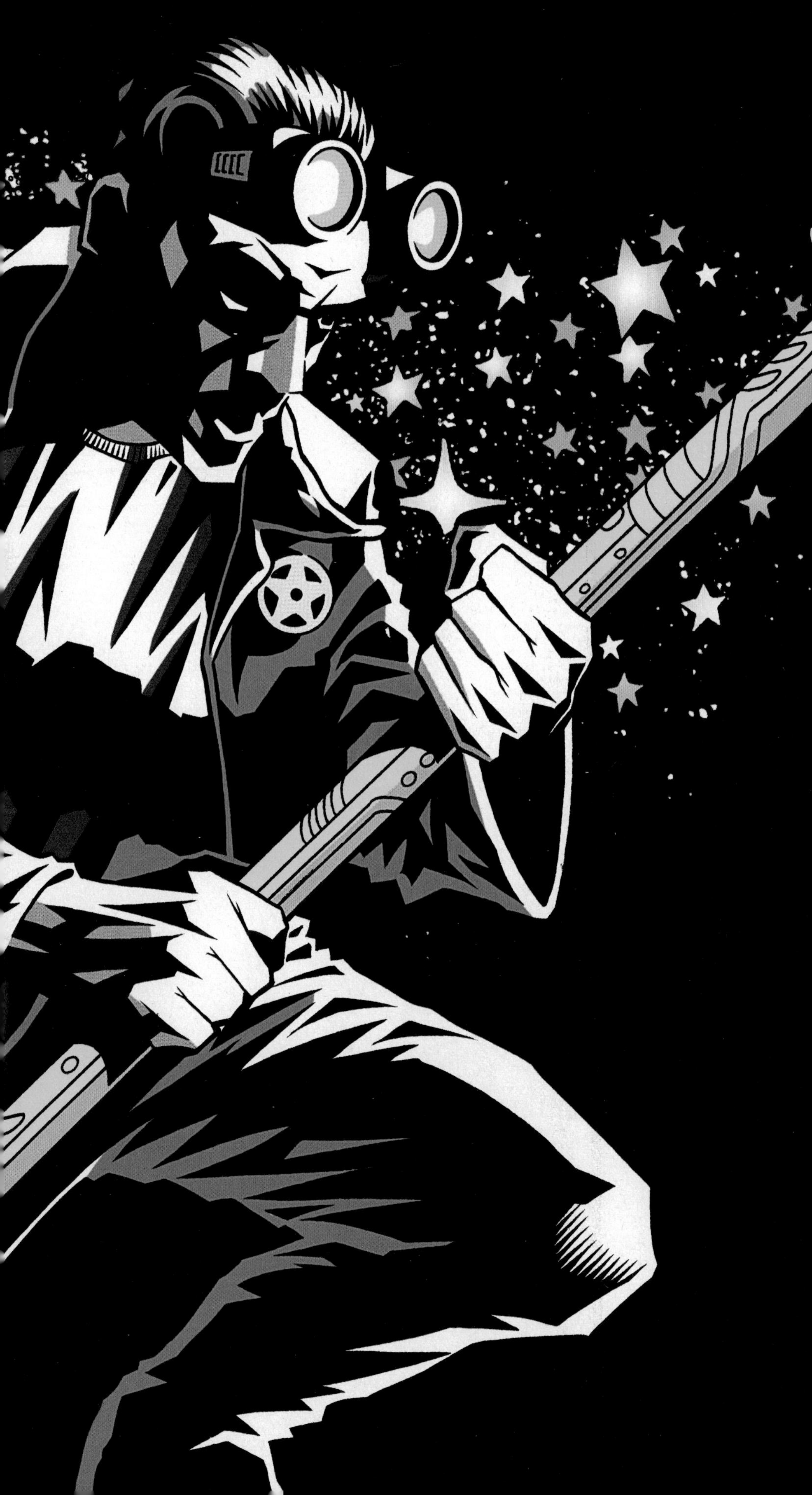

THE STARMAN OMNIBUS

VOLUME ONE

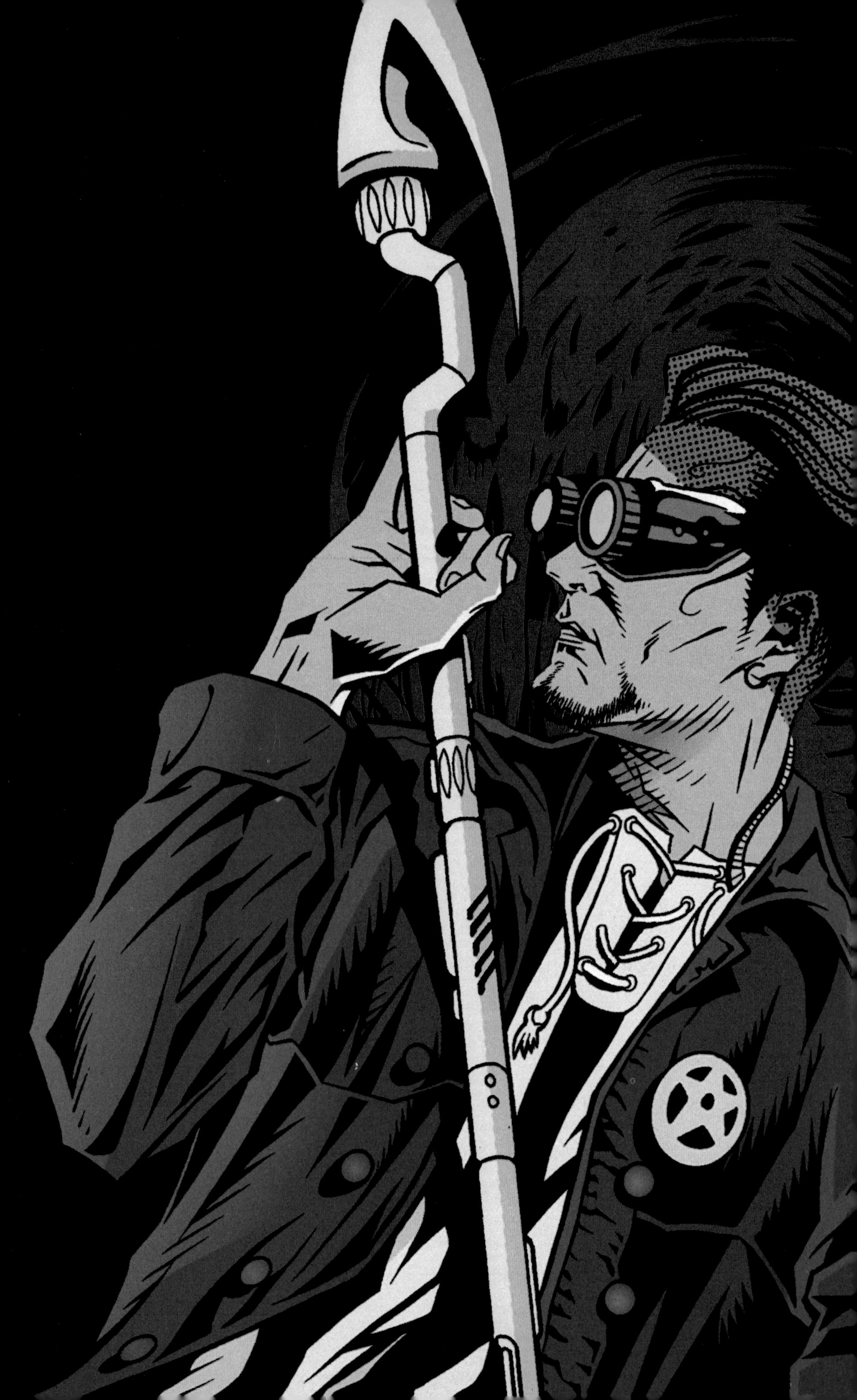

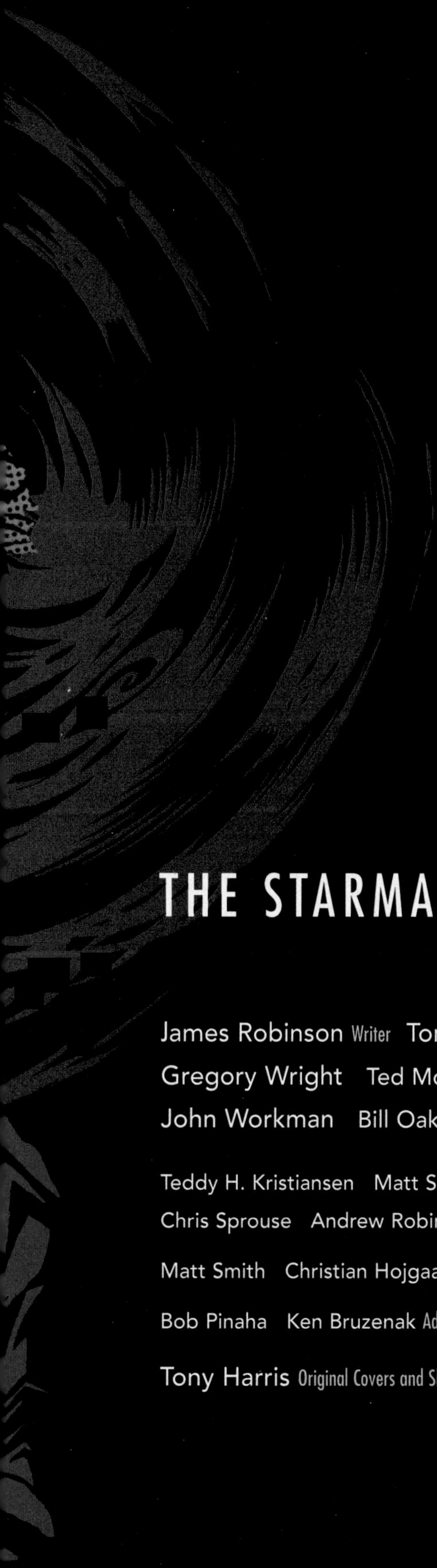

THE STARMAN OMNIBUS VOLUME ONE

James Robinson Writer   Tony Harris Penciller   Wade von Grawbadger Inker
Gregory Wright   Ted McKeever Colorists
John Workman   Bill Oakley   Gaspar Saladino Letterers

Teddy H. Kristiansen   Matt Smith   Tommy Lee Edwards   Stuart Immonen
Chris Sprouse   Andrew Robinson   Gary Erskine   Amanda Conner Additional Pencillers

Matt Smith   Christian Hojgaard   Bjarne Hansen   Kim Hagen   Gary Erskine Additional Inkers

Bob Pinaha   Ken Bruzenak Additional Letterers

Tony Harris Original Covers and Sketches

Dan DiDio
Senior VP-Executive Editor

Archie Goodwin
Editor-original series

Chuck Kim
Assistant Editor-original series

Anton Kawasaki
Editor-collected edition

Robbin Brosterman
Senior Art Director

Paul Levitz
President & Publisher

Georg Brewer
VP-Design & DC Direct Creative

Richard Bruning
Senior VP-Creative Director

Patrick Caldon
Executive VP-Finance & Operations

Chris Caramalis
VP-Finance

John Cunningham
VP-Marketing

Terri Cunningham
VP-Managing Editor

Alison Gill
VP-Manufacturing

David Hyde
VP-Publicity

Hank Kanalz
VP-General Manager, WildStorm

Jim Lee
Editorial Director-WildStorm

Paula Lowitt
Senior VP-Business & Legal Affairs

MaryEllen McLaughlin
VP-Advertising & Custom Publishing

John Nee
Senior VP-Business Development

Gregory Noveck
Senior VP-Creative Affairs

Sue Pohja
VP-Book Trade Sales

Steve Rotterdam
Senior VP-Sales & Marketing

Cheryl Rubin
Senior VP-Brand Management

Jeff Trojan
VP-Business Development, DC Direct

Bob Wayne
VP-Sales

Cover by Tony Harris

THE STARMAN OMNIBUS
Volume One

Published by DC Comics.
Cover, introduction, afterword, and
compilation Copyright © 2008 DC Comics.
All Rights Reserved.

Originally published in single
magazine form in STARMAN #0, 1-16.
Copyright © 1994, 1995 DC Comics.
All Rights Reserved. All characters, their
distinctive likenesses and related elements
featured in this publication are trademarks
of DC Comics.
The stories, characters and incidents
featured in this publication are
entirely fictional. DC Comics does
not read or accept unsolicited
submissions of ideas, stories
or artwork.

DC Comics, 1700 Broadway,
New York, NY 10019
A Warner Bros. Entertainment Company
Printed in Canada. First Printing.

HC ISBN: 978-1-4012-1699-3
SC ISBN: 978-1-4012-1937-6

REMEMBERING THE STARS, OH HOW THEY SHONE—

JAMES ROBINSON

This is my second go around at writing this intro. The first was a long piece, digging into everything I could think of about Jack Knight, Opal City, their creation and all that. It was long — way, way long — and somewhat over-aggrandizing regarding my genius as a writer.

...At least that's what the powers that be at DC said.

"It's too much," said the powers that be at DC.

"Too much, how so?" I asked, oh so innocently.

"Are you insane?" the powers at DC screamed. "The thing weighs in at thirteen odd pages and you aren't even half done. And," they added, I thought overly cruelly, "they were very odd pages indeed."

Brushing off a tear, I convinced them to compromise. As such, my initial intro (or as the powers at DC like to refer to it — "James Robinson's ode to the wonder of himself") will be an aftermath in this and the other volumes where hopefully I can fill you in on more of the backstory — arc by arc, plot twist by twist (both in the book and in the real world of those working on it).

So, with the instruction that I could again write what I like as long as "for God's sake, Robinson — keep it brief," I begin again.

I begin.

I...am at a loss.

No. I've got something. Here we go...

Back in the day, writing the first text piece for the comic prior to letters coming in for it, I spoke of my youth, in England, learning the wonders of alcohol, staggering home from the underground (subway) warm with booze, looking skyward, gazing at/counting the stars. Enjoying the night. I mused then that perhaps this might be where the first seed of Jack Knight took root within my imagination.

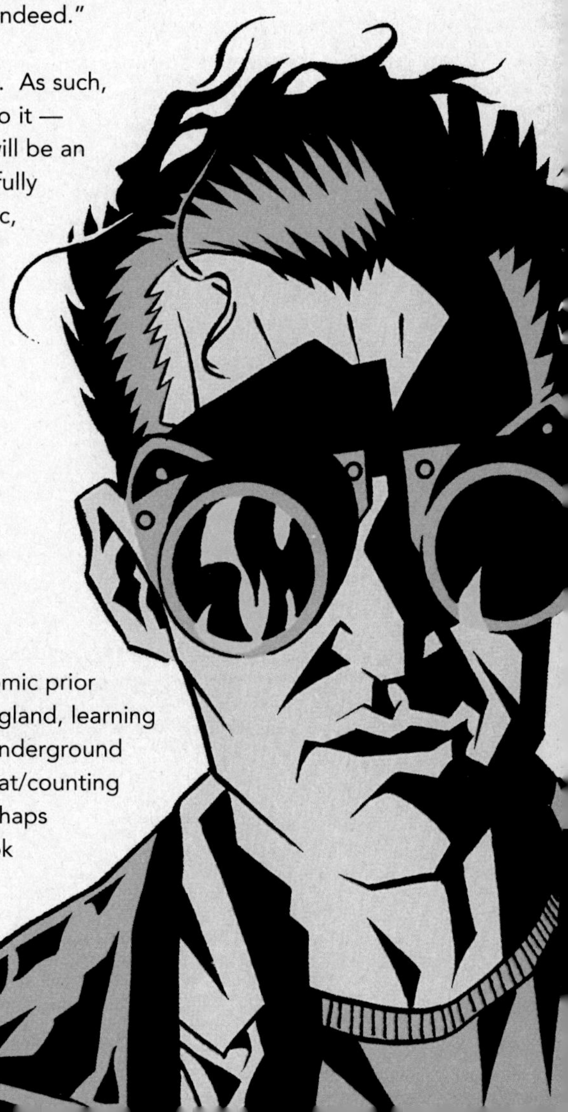

Now, looking back, trying to recall, all I'm aware of is time passing.

It was 1994 when Jack Knight first appeared. The series lasted for 80 issues plus Annuals, Specials and the odd guest appearance. It flew by, the time. And yet it was such a part of my life.

In my time working month after month with Tony Harris, our personalities were never quite on the same page, yet our differences combined to make something far more interesting than either of us, at that time, could have done on our own. (Do you think I would have had one pirate reference, if Tony hadn't been on board? His version of Grundy — thin, gentle Grundy — led to my revising/explaining Grundy's various incarnations/personalities to the point that that's become a part of DC lore. Grundy would have been a one-appearance villain if Tony hadn't "gotten all creative on me" — but again to the betterment of the opus as a whole.) Two examples of many, many where Tony added and changed my thoughts and changed my mind and made Jack's world the better for it.

I used the term "opus" just now. And that's what this is. An opus. I loved this book. I put all I could into it. And in return, a loyal body of fans kept the book alive in terms of sales and allowed Jack to enjoy his story from start to finish.

The plan is that Jack's arc will be told, complete with text pieces, Shade Journals, the Shade miniseries and sundry other bits and bobs over six volumes. I am as proud of this as can be. And as we go, through the meandering garbage DC has allowed me to write at the back of the book each volume, I can fill you in on things as we go — the guidance of Archie Goodwin, the faith in the book of Paul Levitz, the ever growing skills of Tony Harris, the bravery of Chuck Kim and ultimately the second life of Jack Knight under the helm of Peter Tomasi, Peter Snejbjerg and myself. I can tell you of colorist Greg Wright, whose commitment to the book I will be forever indebted to. All of that and more.

But for now, let me merely welcome you. For some this is the collecting of old memories; for others it's a new find. Either way you put down hard-earned dough, so thank you, thank you, thank you. I hope you enjoy the ride. I hope comes the time, you're proud to have six volumes on your bookshelves that encompass seven years of my life.

Times have changed from when I was that young drunk, staggering home, looking starward. Now I am an accomplished drunk with the money to pay for cabs instead of walking. And living in Los Angeles, the smog means I rarely see the stars anymore at all.

But in my memories I do. Remembering then. And the excitement and fun and fear I felt each time I added another beat, another issue, another adventure to the life of Jack Knight.

Thanks for being a part of this revisit. Enjoy. Enjoy. And thanks again.

James Robinson
Hollywood, California
March, 2008

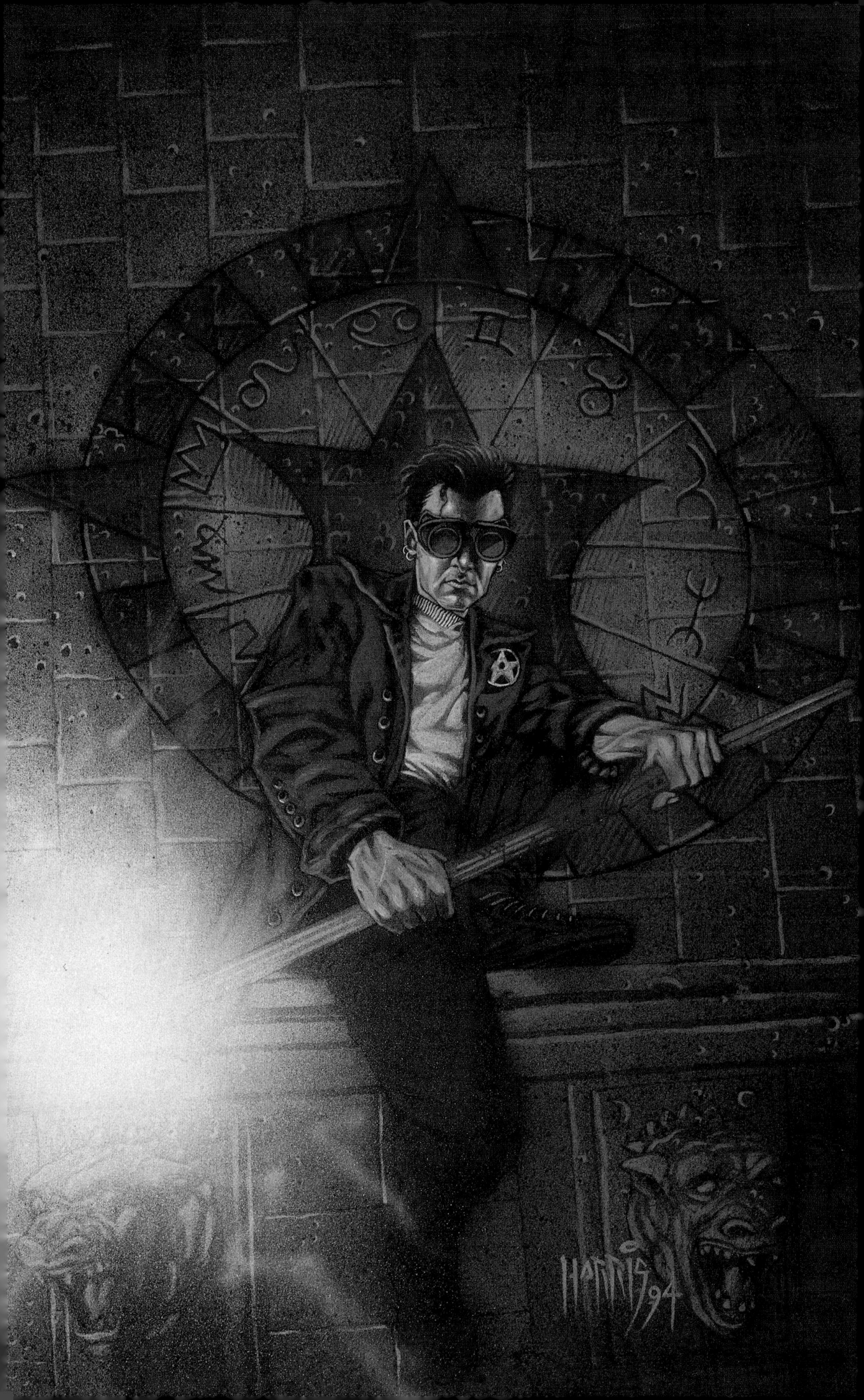
HARRIS 94

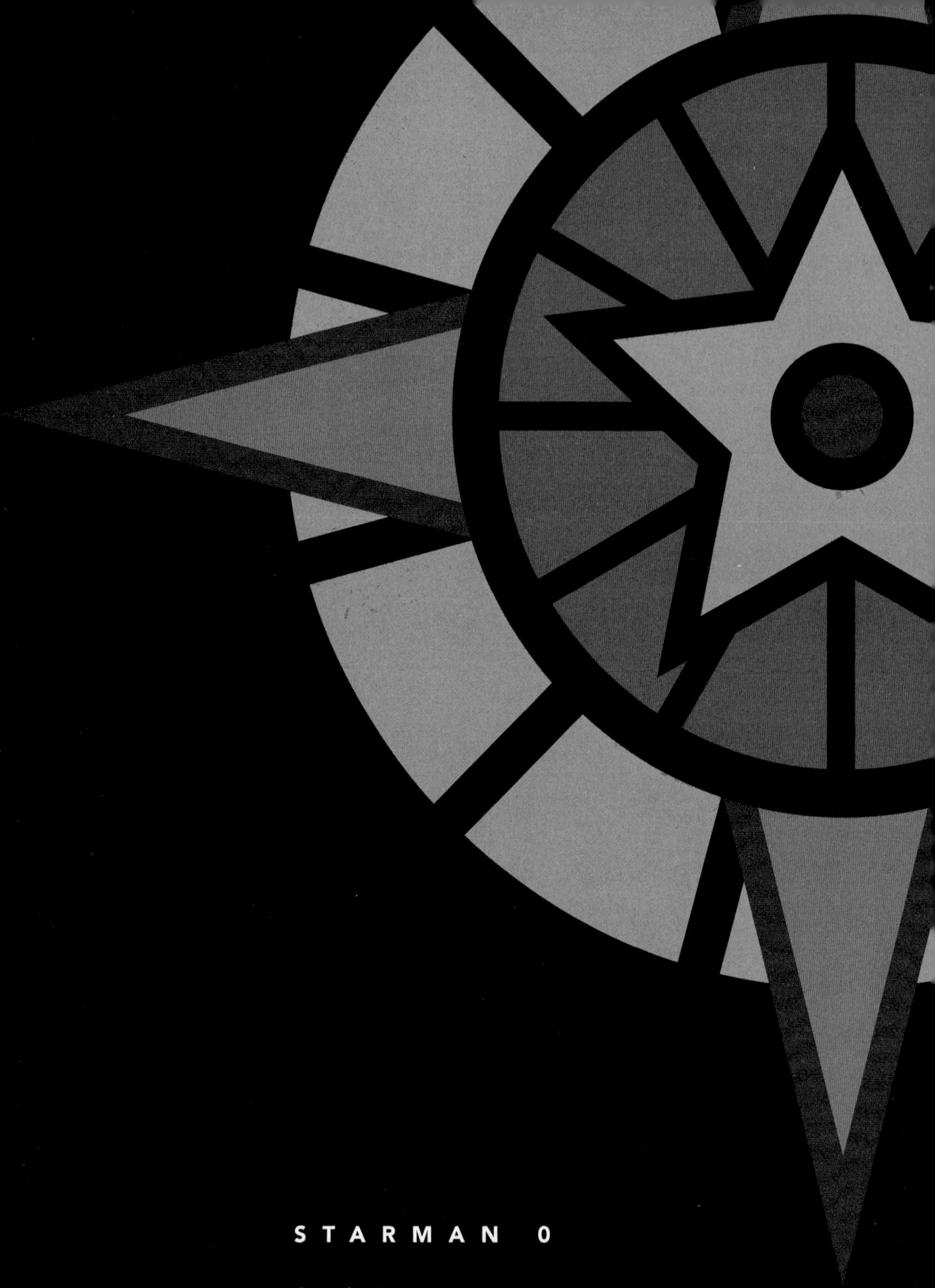

S T A R M A N 0

Cover by Tony Harris

Written by James Robinson

Pencils by Tony Harris,

with inks by Wade von Grawbadger

and colors by Gregory Wright

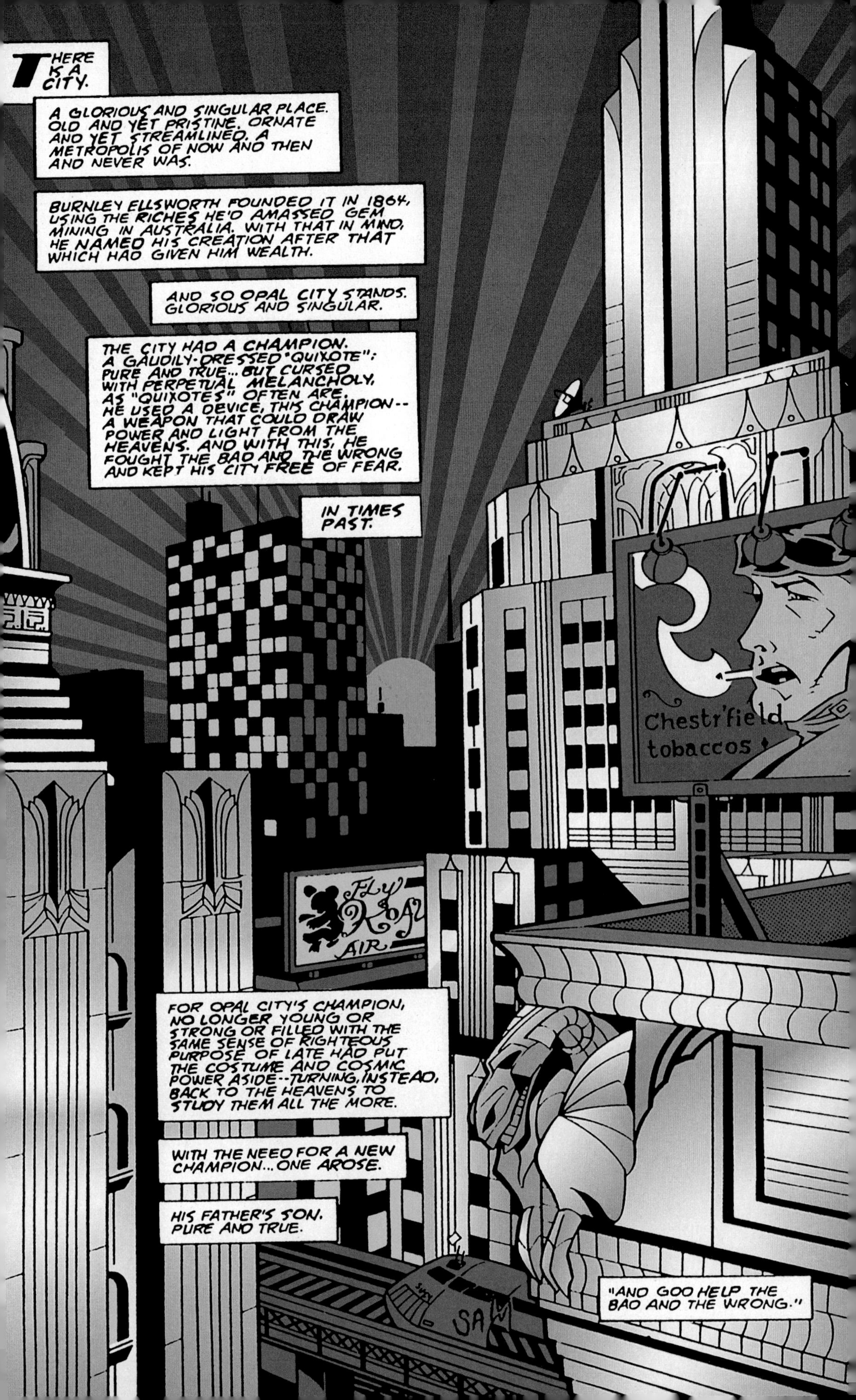
THERE IS A CITY.
A GLORIOUS AND SINGULAR PLACE. OLD AND YET PRISTINE. ORNATE AND YET STREAMLINED. A METROPOLIS OF NOW AND THEN AND NEVER WAS.
BURNLEY ELLSWORTH FOUNDED IT IN 1864, USING THE RICHES HE'D AMASSED GEM MINING IN AUSTRALIA. WITH THAT IN MIND, HE NAMED HIS CREATION AFTER THAT WHICH HAD GIVEN HIM WEALTH.
AND SO OPAL CITY STANDS. GLORIOUS AND SINGULAR.
THE CITY HAD A CHAMPION. A GAUDILY-DRESSED "QUIXOTE": PURE AND TRUE... BUT CURSED WITH PERPETUAL MELANCHOLY, AS "QUIXOTES" OFTEN ARE. HE USED A DEVICE, THIS CHAMPION-- A WEAPON THAT COULD DRAW POWER AND LIGHT FROM THE HEAVENS. AND WITH THIS, HE FOUGHT THE BAD AND THE WRONG AND KEPT HIS CITY FREE OF FEAR.
IN TIMES PAST.
Chestr'field tobaccos
FLY ROYAL AIR
FOR OPAL CITY'S CHAMPION, NO LONGER YOUNG OR STRONG OR FILLED WITH THE SAME SENSE OF RIGHTEOUS PURPOSE OF LATE HAD PUT THE COSTUME AND COSMIC POWER ASIDE--TURNING, INSTEAD, BACK TO THE HEAVENS TO STUDY THEM ALL THE MORE.
WITH THE NEED FOR A NEW CHAMPION... ONE AROSE.
HIS FATHER'S SON. PURE AND TRUE.
"AND GOD HELP THE BAD AND THE WRONG."

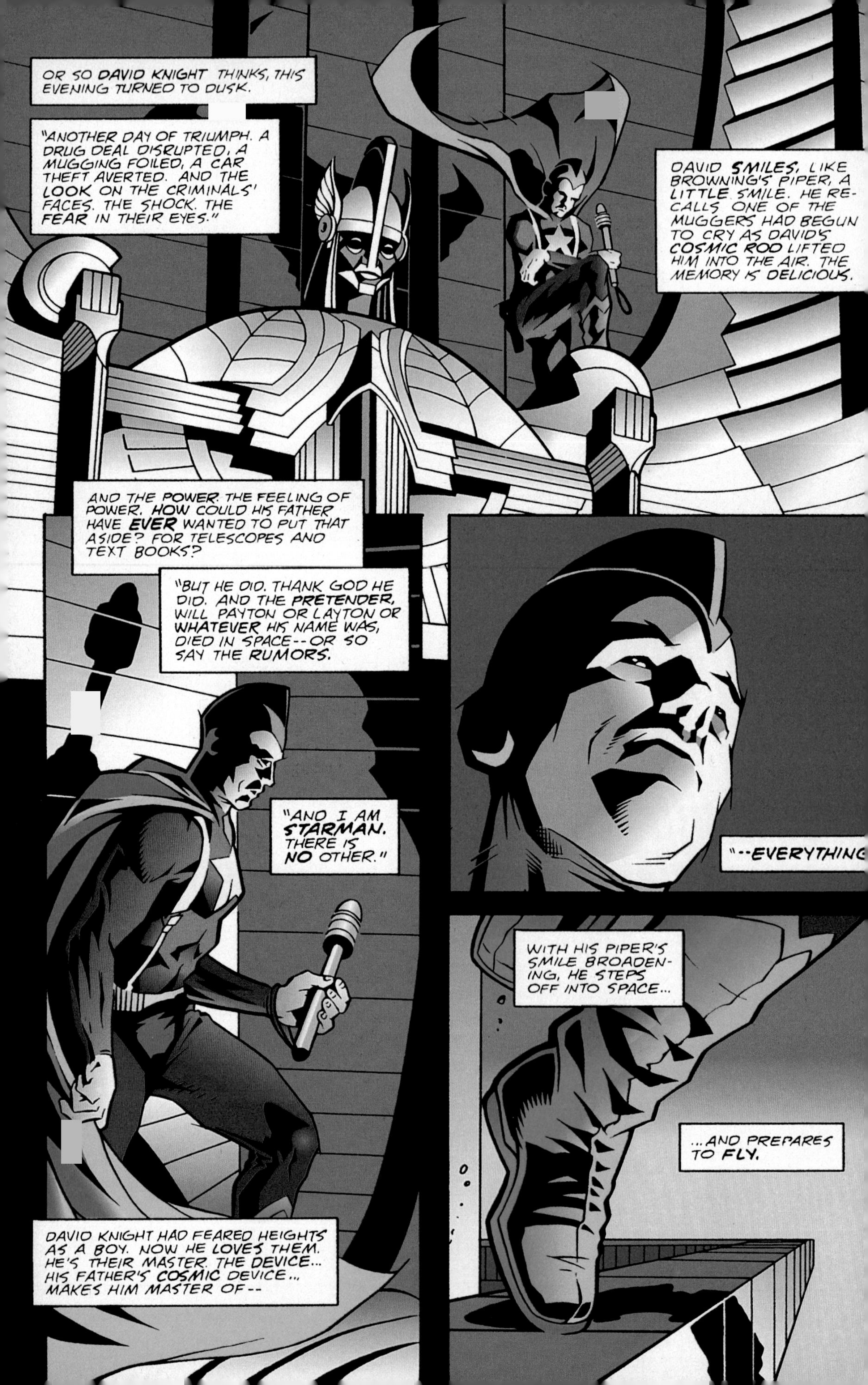
OR SO DAVID KNIGHT THINKS, THIS EVENING TURNED TO DUSK.
"ANOTHER DAY OF TRIUMPH. A DRUG DEAL DISRUPTED, A MUGGING FOILED, A CAR THEFT AVERTED. AND THE LOOK ON THE CRIMINALS' FACES. THE SHOCK. THE FEAR IN THEIR EYES."
DAVID SMILES, LIKE BROWNING'S PIPER, A LITTLE SMILE. HE RECALLS ONE OF THE MUGGERS HAD BEGUN TO CRY AS DAVID'S COSMIC ROD LIFTED HIM INTO THE AIR. THE MEMORY IS DELICIOUS.
AND THE POWER. THE FEELING OF POWER. HOW COULD HIS FATHER HAVE EVER WANTED TO PUT THAT ASIDE? FOR TELESCOPES AND TEXT BOOKS?
"BUT HE DID. THANK GOD HE DID. AND THE PRETENDER, WILL PAYTON OR LAYTON OR WHATEVER HIS NAME WAS, DIED IN SPACE--OR SO SAY THE RUMORS.
"AND I AM STARMAN. THERE IS NO OTHER."
DAVID KNIGHT HAD FEARED HEIGHTS AS A BOY. NOW HE LOVES THEM. HE'S THEIR MASTER. THE DEVICE... HIS FATHER'S COSMIC DEVICE... MAKES HIM MASTER OF--
"--EVERYTHING
WITH HIS PIPER'S SMILE BROADENING, HE STEPS OFF INTO SPACE...
...AND PREPARES TO FLY.

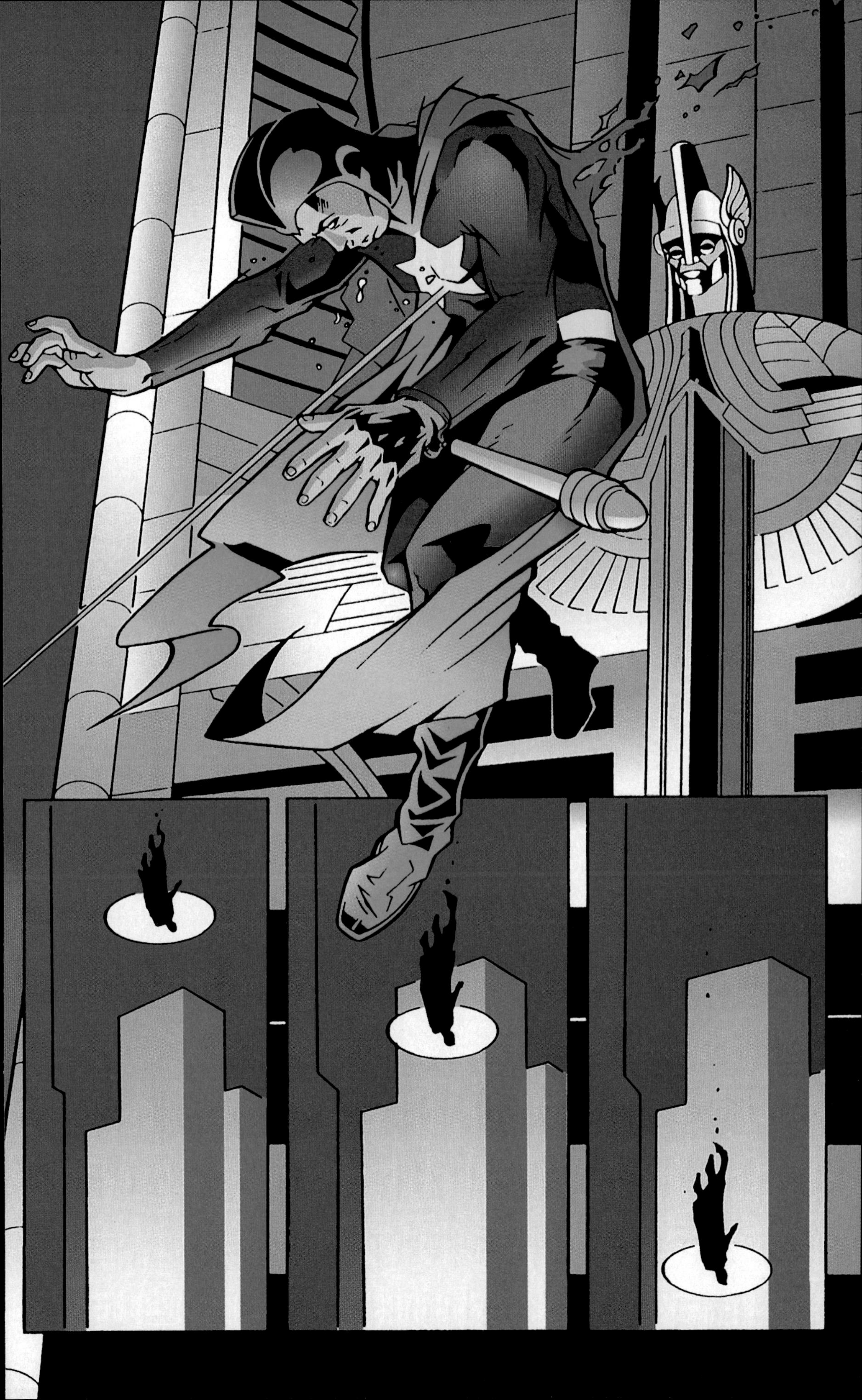

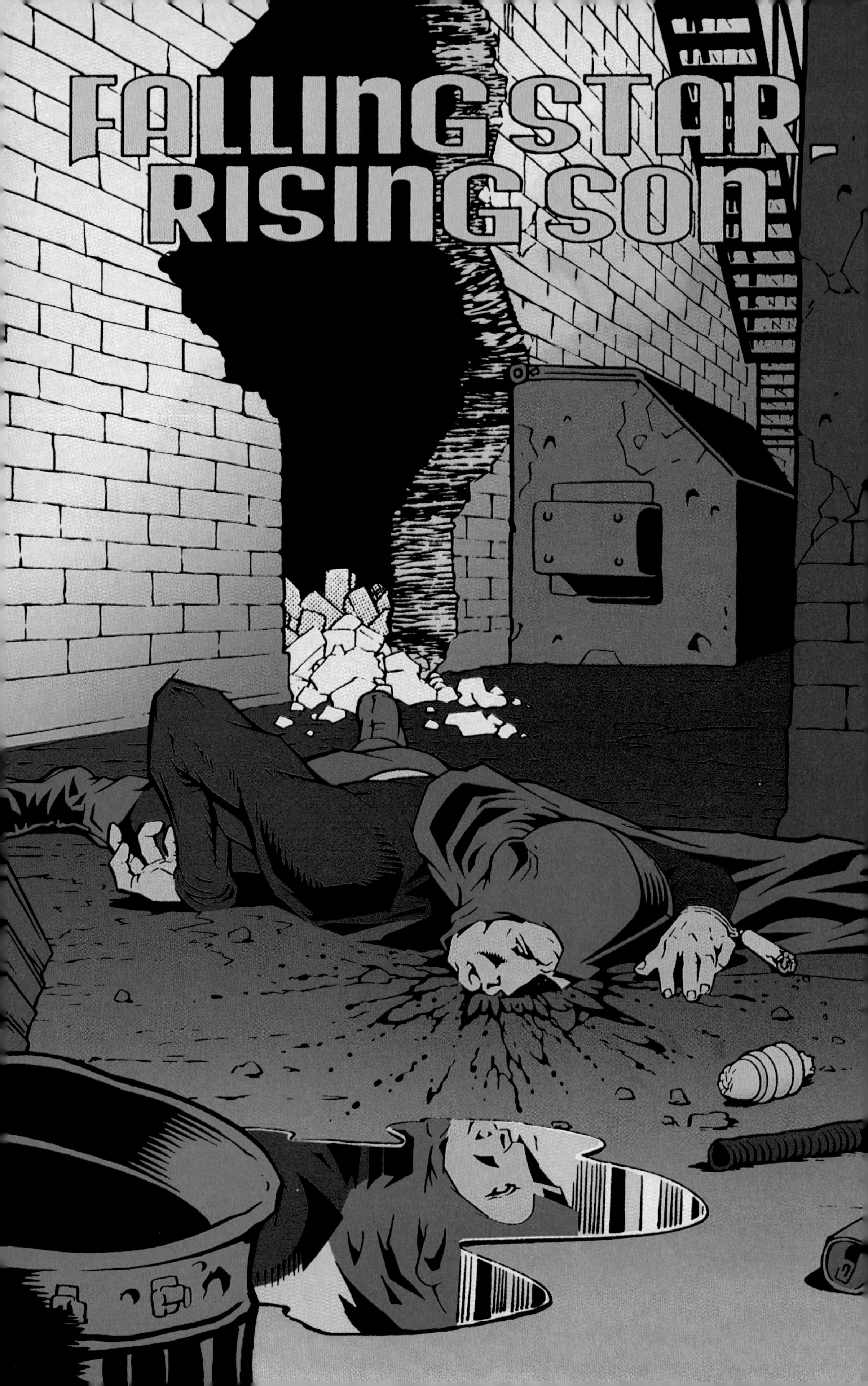
FALLING STAR, RISING SON

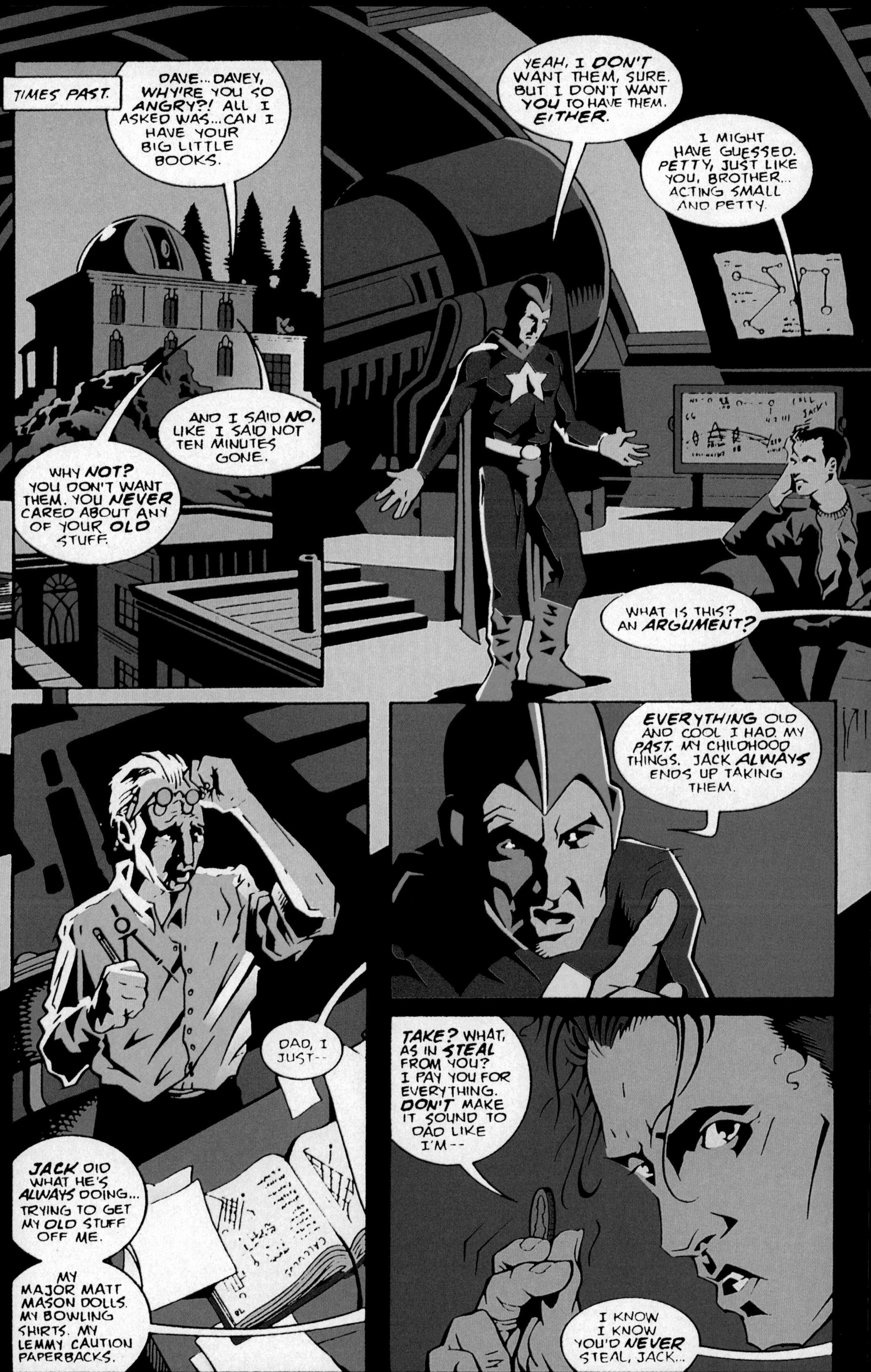

TIMES PAST.
DAVE... DAVEY, WHY'RE YOU SO ANGRY?! ALL I ASKED WAS... CAN I HAVE YOUR BIG LITTLE BOOKS.
AND I SAID NO. LIKE I SAID NOT TEN MINUTES GONE.
WHY NOT? YOU DON'T WANT THEM. YOU NEVER CARED ABOUT ANY OF YOUR OLD STUFF.
YEAH, I DON'T WANT THEM, SURE. BUT I DON'T WANT YOU TO HAVE THEM. EITHER.
I MIGHT HAVE GUESSED. PETTY, JUST LIKE YOU, BROTHER... ACTING SMALL AND PETTY.
WHAT IS THIS? AN ARGUMENT?
EVERYTHING OLD AND COOL I HAD. MY PAST. MY CHILDHOOD THINGS. JACK ALWAYS ENDS UP TAKING THEM.
DAD, I JUST--
JACK DID WHAT HE'S ALWAYS DOING... TRYING TO GET MY OLD STUFF OFF ME.
MY MAJOR MATT MASON DOLLS. MY BOWLING SHIRTS. MY LEMMY CAUTION PAPERBACKS.
TAKE? WHAT, AS IN STEAL FROM YOU? I PAY YOU FOR EVERYTHING. DON'T MAKE IT SOUND TO DAD LIKE I'M--
I KNOW I KNOW YOU'D NEVER STEAL, JACK...

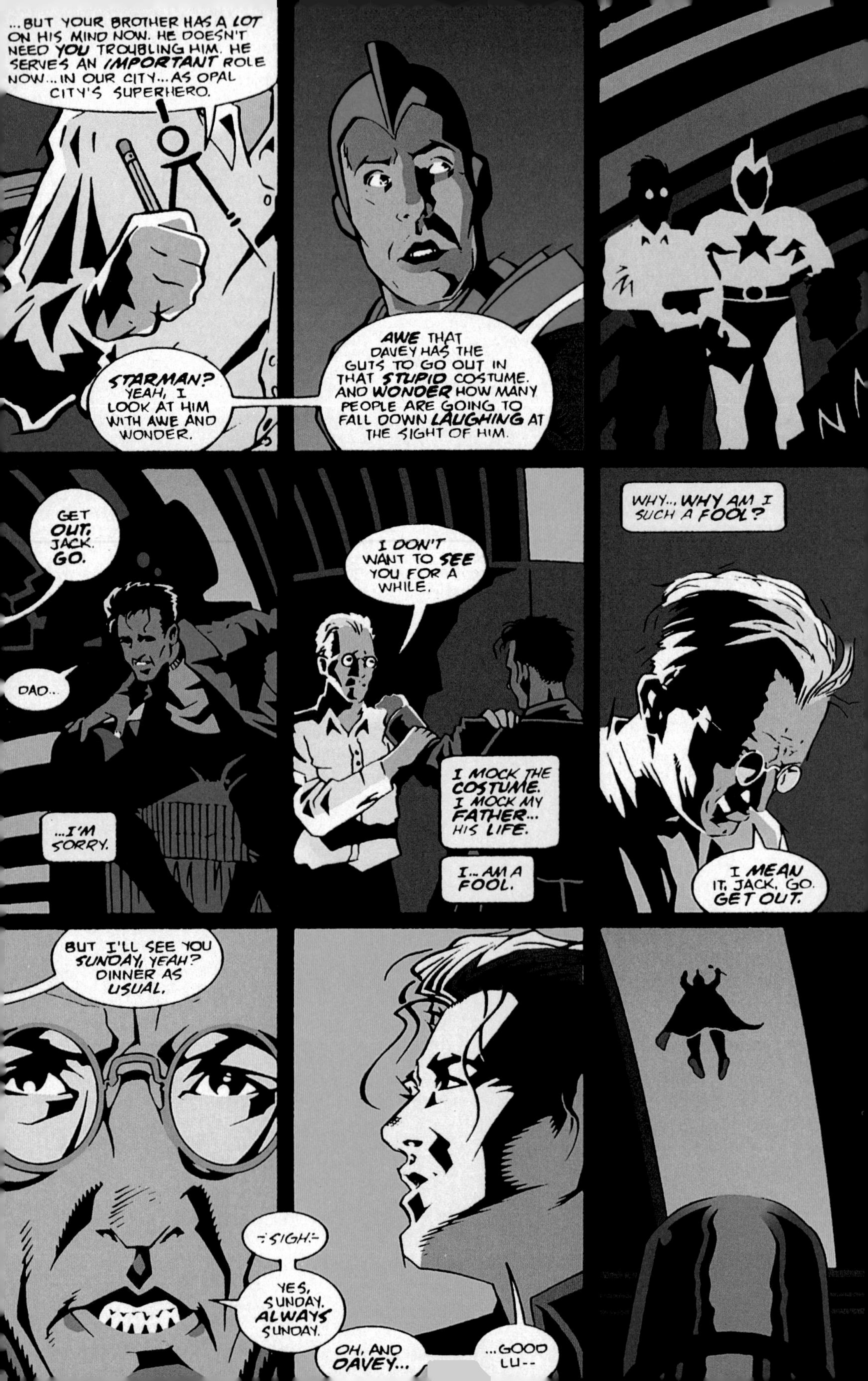
...BUT YOUR BROTHER HAS A LOT ON HIS MIND NOW. HE DOESN'T NEED YOU TROUBLING HIM. HE SERVES AN IMPORTANT ROLE NOW... IN OUR CITY... AS OPAL CITY'S SUPERHERO.
STARMAN? YEAH, I LOOK AT HIM WITH AWE AND WONDER.
AWE THAT DAVEY HAS THE GUTS TO GO OUT IN THAT STUPID COSTUME. AND WONDER HOW MANY PEOPLE ARE GOING TO FALL DOWN LAUGHING AT THE SIGHT OF HIM.
GET OUT, JACK. GO.
DAD..
...I'M SORRY.
I DON'T WANT TO SEE YOU FOR A WHILE.
I MOCK THE COSTUME. I MOCK MY FATHER... HIS LIFE.
I... AM A FOOL.
WHY... WHY AM I SUCH A FOOL?
I MEAN IT, JACK. GO. GET OUT.
BUT I'LL SEE YOU SUNDAY, YEAH? DINNER AS USUAL.
-SIGH-
YES, SUNDAY. ALWAYS SUNDAY.
OH, AND DAVEY...
...GOOD LU--

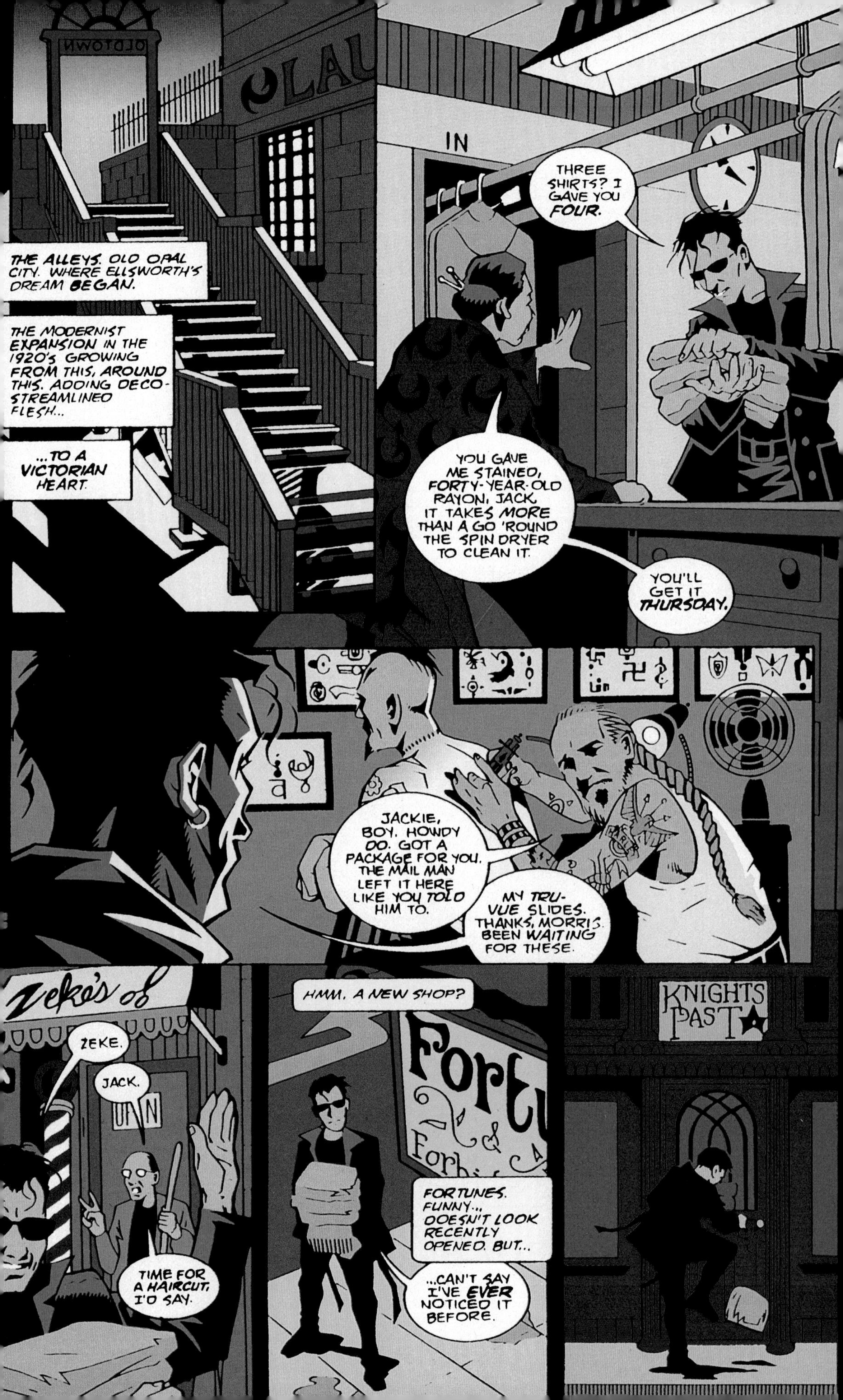
OLDTOWN
LAU
THE ALLEYS. OLD OPAL CITY. WHERE ELLSWORTH'S DREAM BEGAN.
THE MODERNIST EXPANSION IN THE 1920'S GROWING FROM THIS, AROUND THIS. ADDING DECO-STREAMLINED FLESH...
...TO A VICTORIAN HEART.
IN
THREE SHIRTS? I GAVE YOU FOUR.
YOU GAVE ME STAINED, FORTY-YEAR-OLD RAYON, JACK. IT TAKES MORE THAN A GO 'ROUND THE SPIN DRYER TO CLEAN IT.
YOU'LL GET IT THURSDAY.
JACKIE, BOY. HOWDY DO. GOT A PACKAGE FOR YOU. THE MAIL MAN LEFT IT HERE LIKE YOU TOLD HIM TO.
MY TRU-VUE SLIDES. THANKS, MORRIS. BEEN WAITING FOR THESE.
Zeke's
ZEKE.
JACK.
TIME FOR A HAIRCUT, I'D SAY.
HMM. A NEW SHOP?
Fort
FORTUNES. FUNNY... DOESN'T LOOK RECENTLY OPENED. BUT...
...CAN'T SAY I'VE EVER NOTICED IT BEFORE.
KNIGHTS PAST

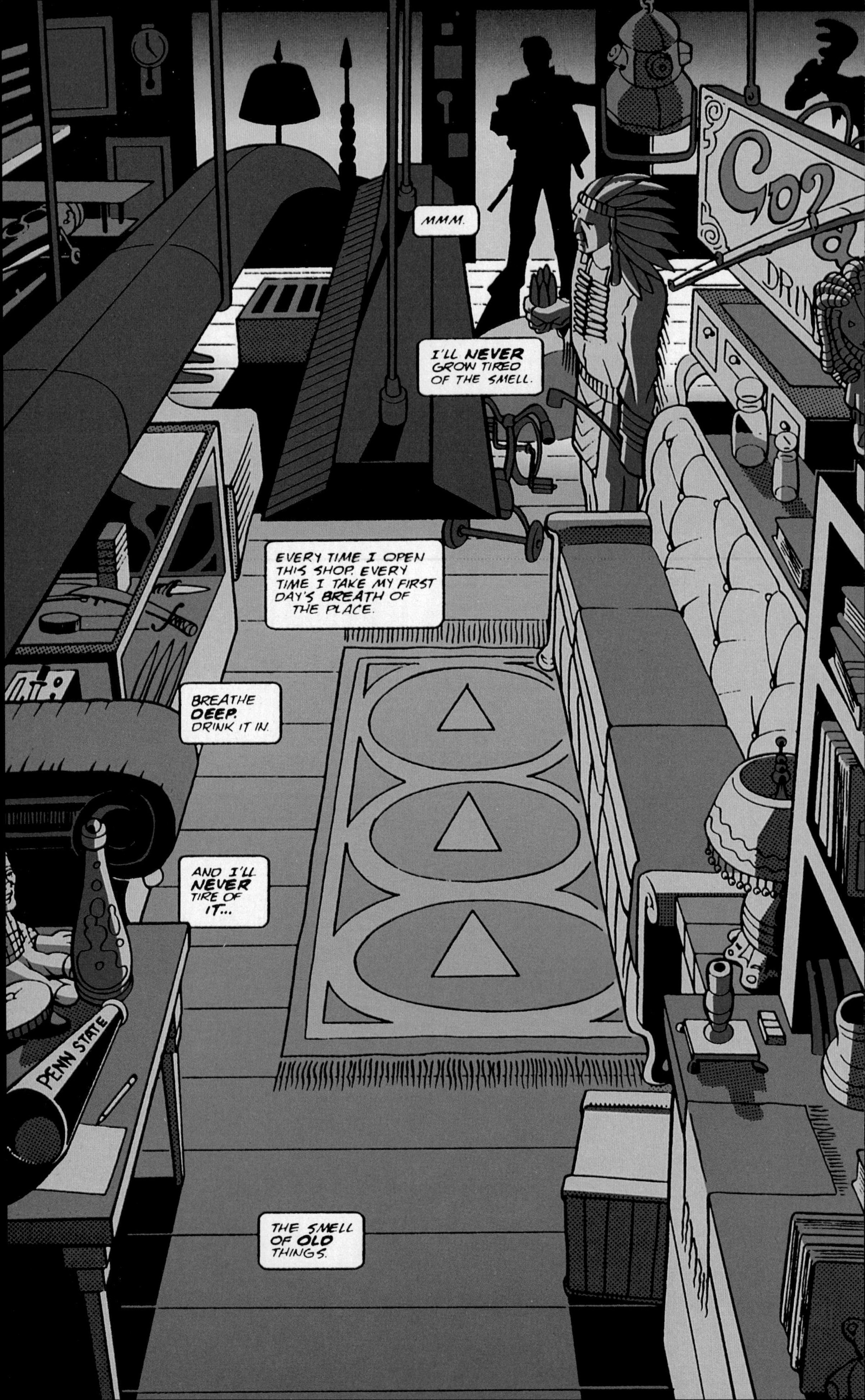
MMM.
I'LL NEVER GROW TIRED OF THE SMELL.
EVERY TIME I OPEN THIS SHOP. EVERY TIME I TAKE MY FIRST DAY'S BREATH OF THE PLACE.
BREATHE DEEP. DRINK IT IN.
AND I'LL NEVER TIRE OF IT...
THE SMELL OF OLD THINGS.
PENN STATE

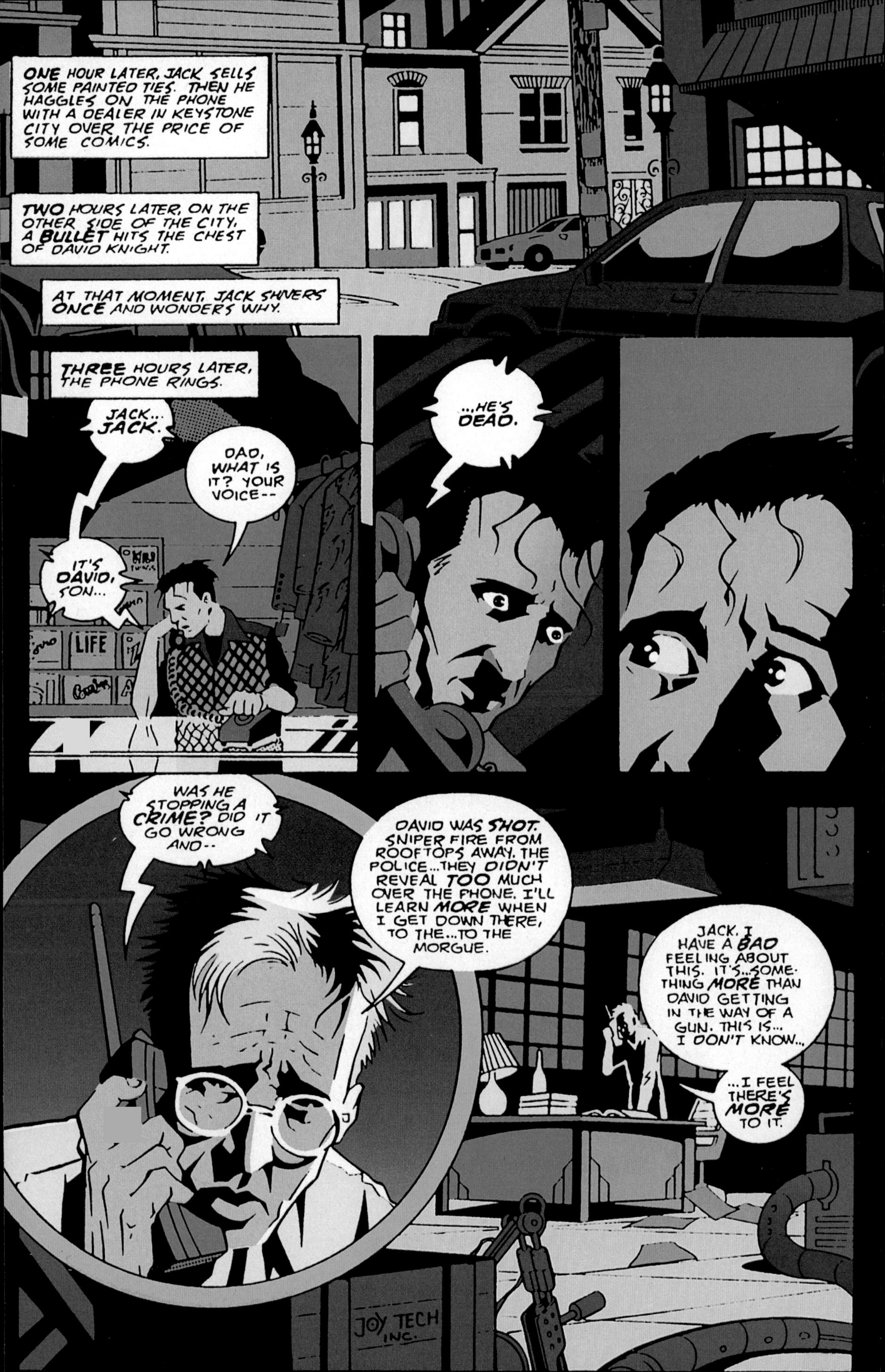
ONE HOUR LATER, JACK SELLS SOME PAINTED TIES. THEN HE HAGGLES ON THE PHONE WITH A DEALER IN KEYSTONE CITY OVER THE PRICE OF SOME COMICS.
TWO HOURS LATER, ON THE OTHER SIDE OF THE CITY, A BULLET HITS THE CHEST OF DAVID KNIGHT.
AT THAT MOMENT, JACK SHIVERS ONCE AND WONDERS WHY.
THREE HOURS LATER, THE PHONE RINGS.
JACK... JACK.
DAD, WHAT IS IT? YOUR VOICE--
IT'S DAVID, SON...
LIFE
...HE'S DEAD.
WAS HE STOPPING A CRIME? DID IT GO WRONG AND--
DAVID WAS SHOT. SNIPER FIRE FROM ROOFTOPS AWAY. THE POLICE...THEY DIDN'T REVEAL TOO MUCH OVER THE PHONE. I'LL LEARN MORE WHEN I GET DOWN THERE, TO THE...TO THE MORGUE.
JACK, I HAVE A BAD FEELING ABOUT THIS. IT'S...SOME-THING MORE THAN DAVID GETTING IN THE WAY OF A GUN. THIS IS... I DON'T KNOW...
...I FEEL THERE'S MORE TO IT.
JOY TECH INC.

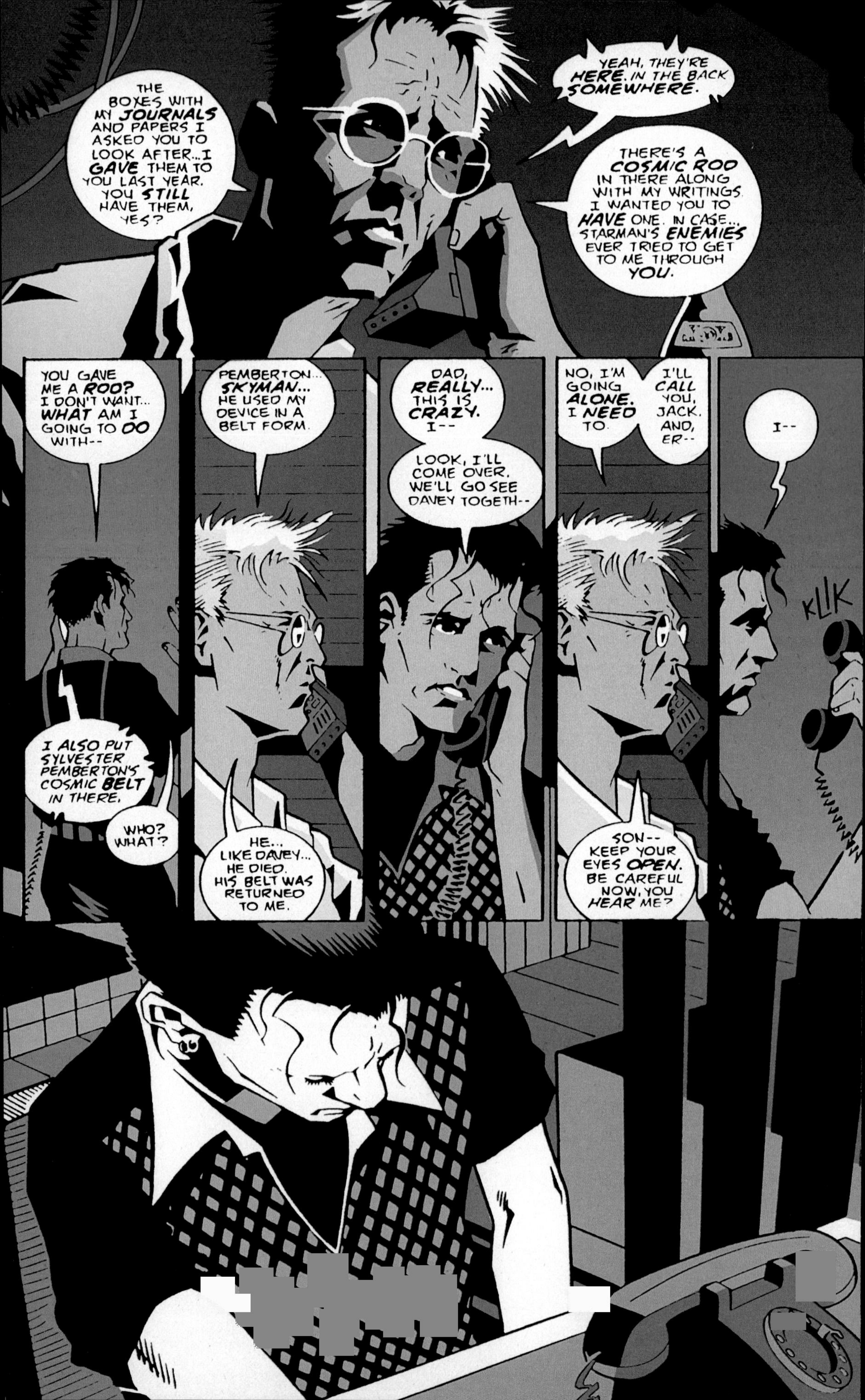
THE BOXES WITH MY JOURNALS AND PAPERS I ASKED YOU TO LOOK AFTER... I GAVE THEM TO YOU LAST YEAR. YOU STILL HAVE THEM, YES?
YEAH, THEY'RE HERE. IN THE BACK SOMEWHERE.
THERE'S A COSMIC ROD IN THERE ALONG WITH MY WRITINGS. I WANTED YOU TO HAVE ONE. IN CASE... STARMAN'S ENEMIES EVER TRIED TO GET TO ME THROUGH YOU.
YOU GAVE ME A ROD? I DON'T WANT... WHAT AM I GOING TO DO WITH--
I ALSO PUT SYLVESTER PEMBERTON'S COSMIC BELT IN THERE.
WHO? WHAT?
PEMBERTON... SKYMAN... HE USED MY DEVICE IN A BELT FORM.
HE... LIKE DAVEY... HE DIED. HIS BELT WAS RETURNED TO ME.
DAD, REALLY... THIS IS CRAZY. I--
LOOK, I'LL COME OVER. WE'LL GO SEE DAVEY TOGETH--
NO, I'M GOING ALONE. I NEED TO.
I'LL CALL YOU, JACK. AND, ER--
SON-- KEEP YOUR EYES OPEN. BE CAREFUL NOW, YOU HEAR ME?
I--
KLIK

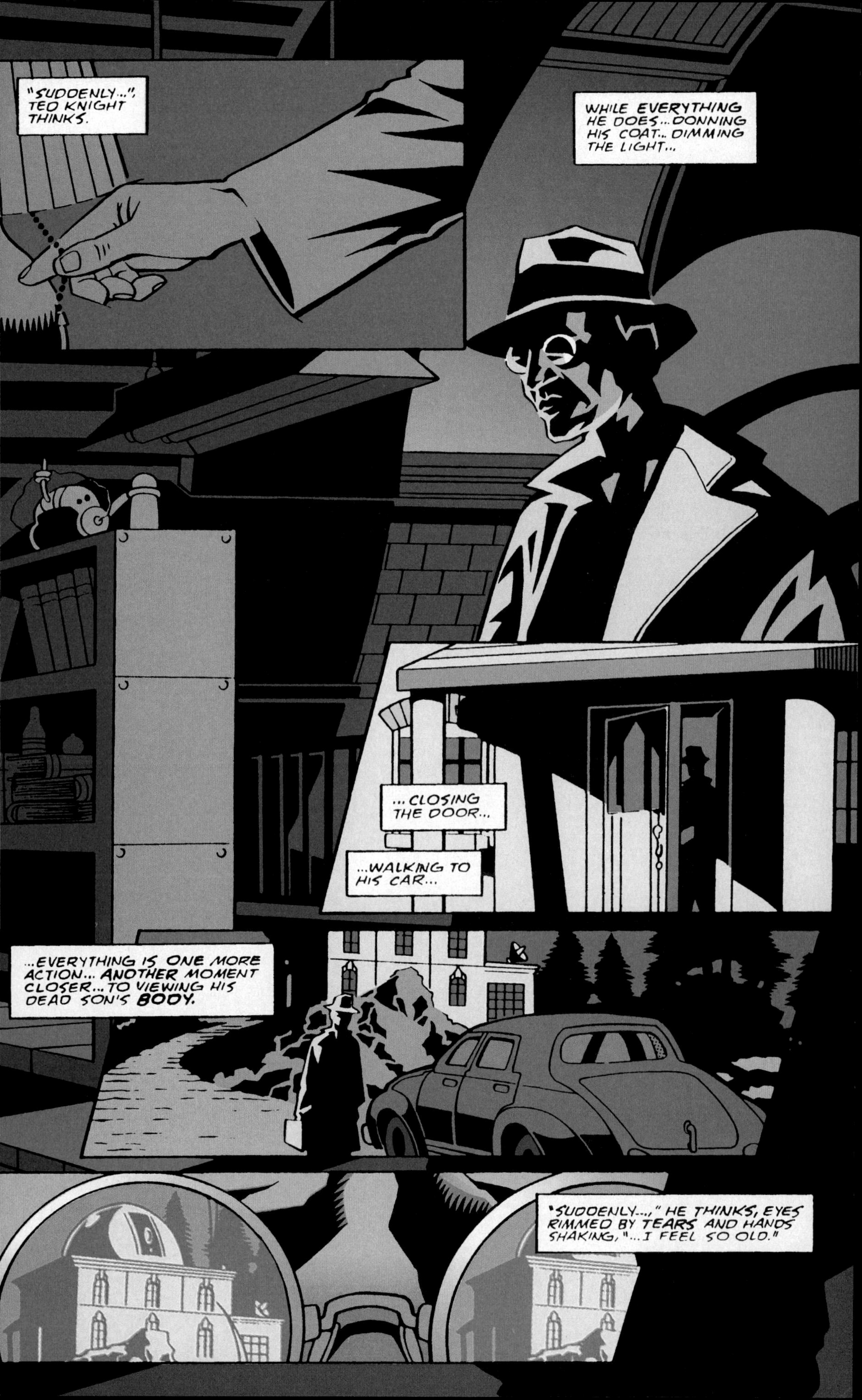
"SUDDENLY...", TED KNIGHT THINKS.
WHILE EVERYTHING HE DOES... DONNING HIS COAT... DIMMING THE LIGHT...
...CLOSING THE DOOR...
...WALKING TO HIS CAR...
...EVERYTHING IS ONE MORE ACTION... ANOTHER MOMENT CLOSER... TO VIEWING HIS DEAD SON'S BODY.
"SUDDENLY...," HE THINKS, EYES RIMMED BY TEARS AND HANDS SHAKING, "...I FEEL SO OLD."

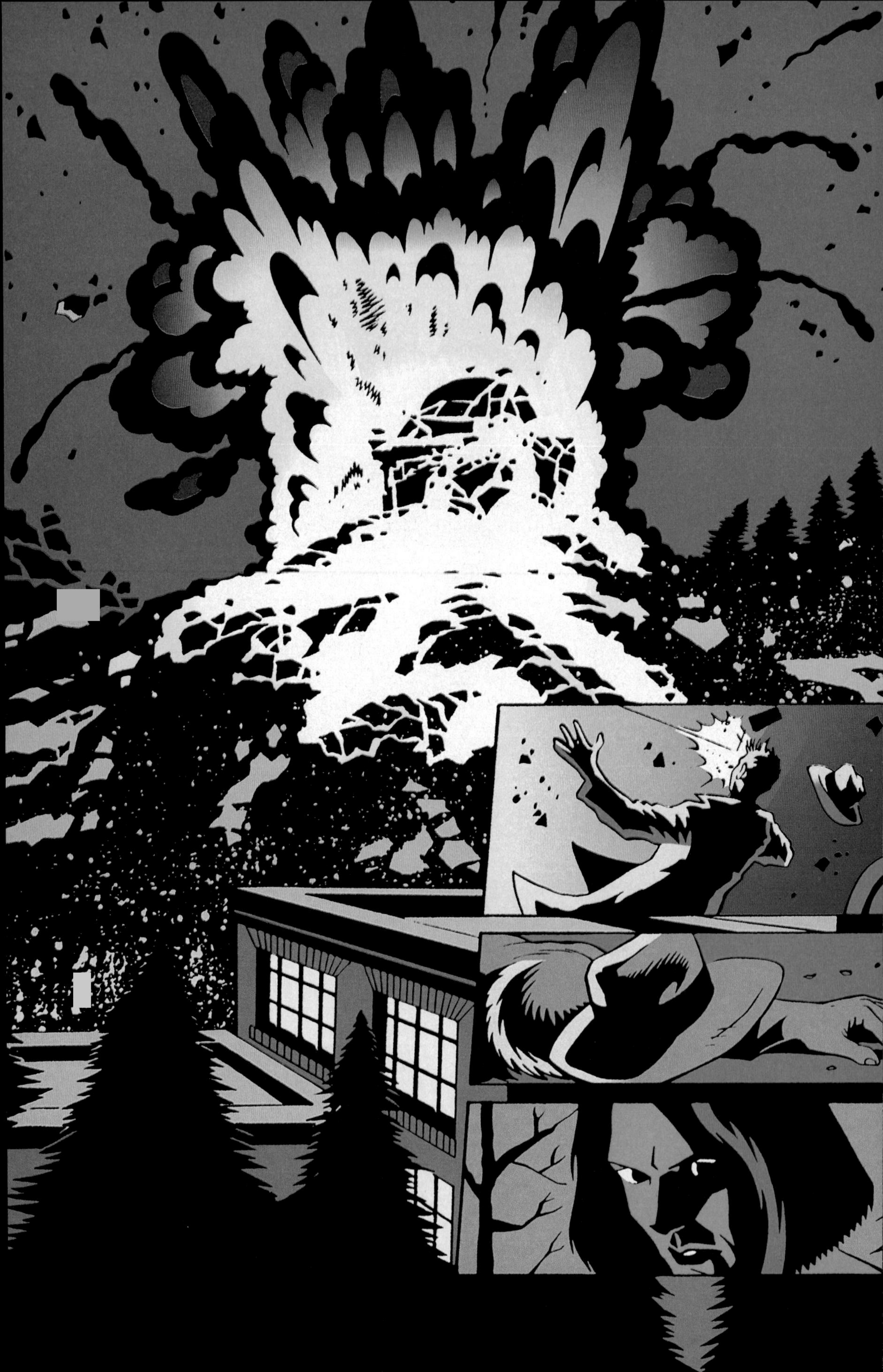

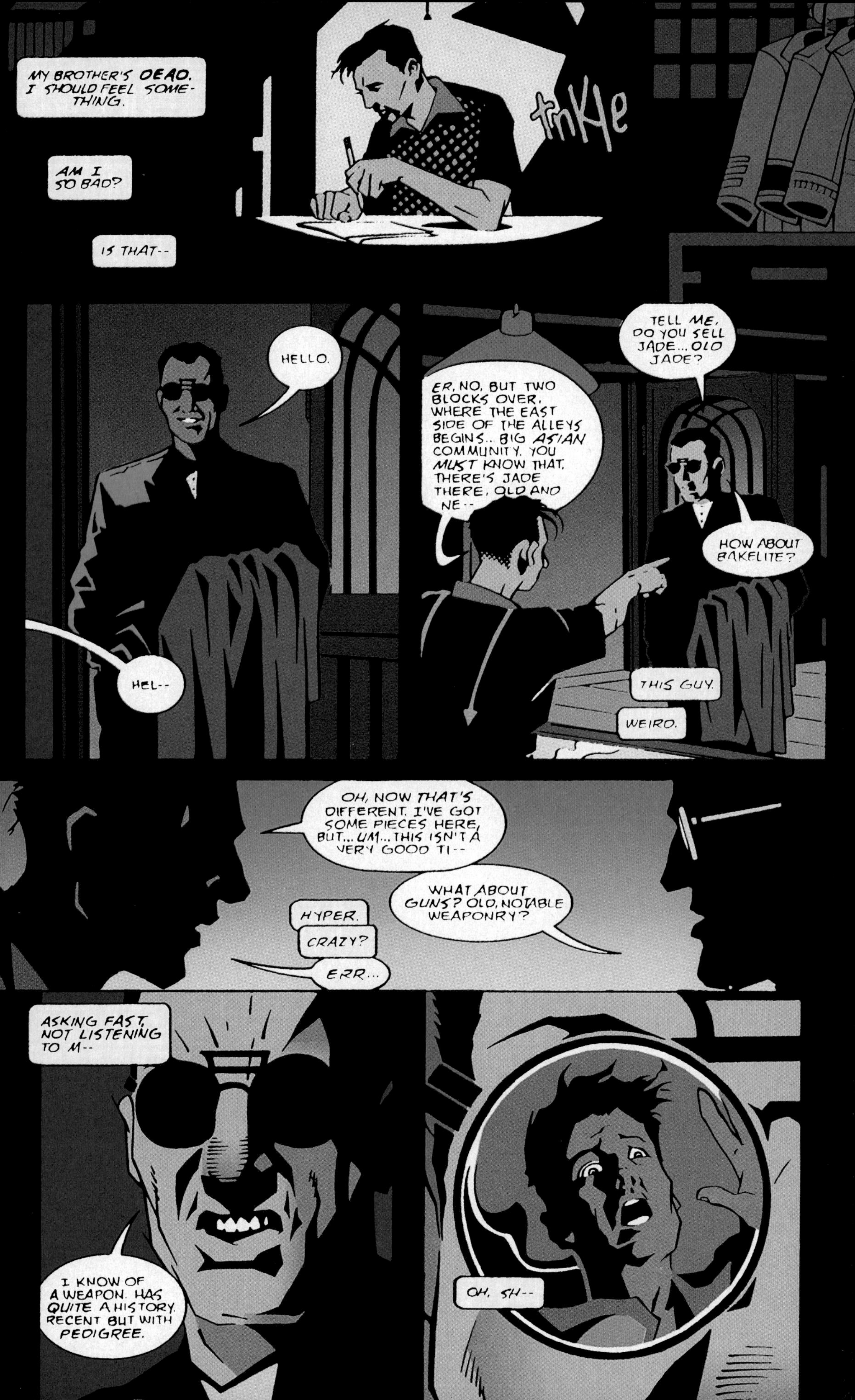
MY BROTHER'S DEAD. I SHOULD FEEL SOME-THING.
AM I SO BAD?
IS THAT--
tnKle
HELLO.
HEL--
TELL ME, DO YOU SELL JADE... OLD JADE?
ER, NO, BUT TWO BLOCKS OVER, WHERE THE EAST SIDE OF THE ALLEYS BEGINS... BIG ASIAN COMMUNITY. YOU MUST KNOW THAT. THERE'S JADE THERE, OLD AND NE--
HOW ABOUT BAKELITE?
THIS GUY.
WEIRD.
OH, NOW THAT'S DIFFERENT. I'VE GOT SOME PIECES HERE, BUT... UM... THIS ISN'T A VERY GOOD TI--
WHAT ABOUT GUNS? OLD, NOTABLE WEAPONRY?
HYPER.
CRAZY?
ERR...
ASKING FAST, NOT LISTENING TO M--
I KNOW OF A WEAPON. HAS QUITE A HISTORY. RECENT BUT WITH PEDIGREE.
OH, SH--

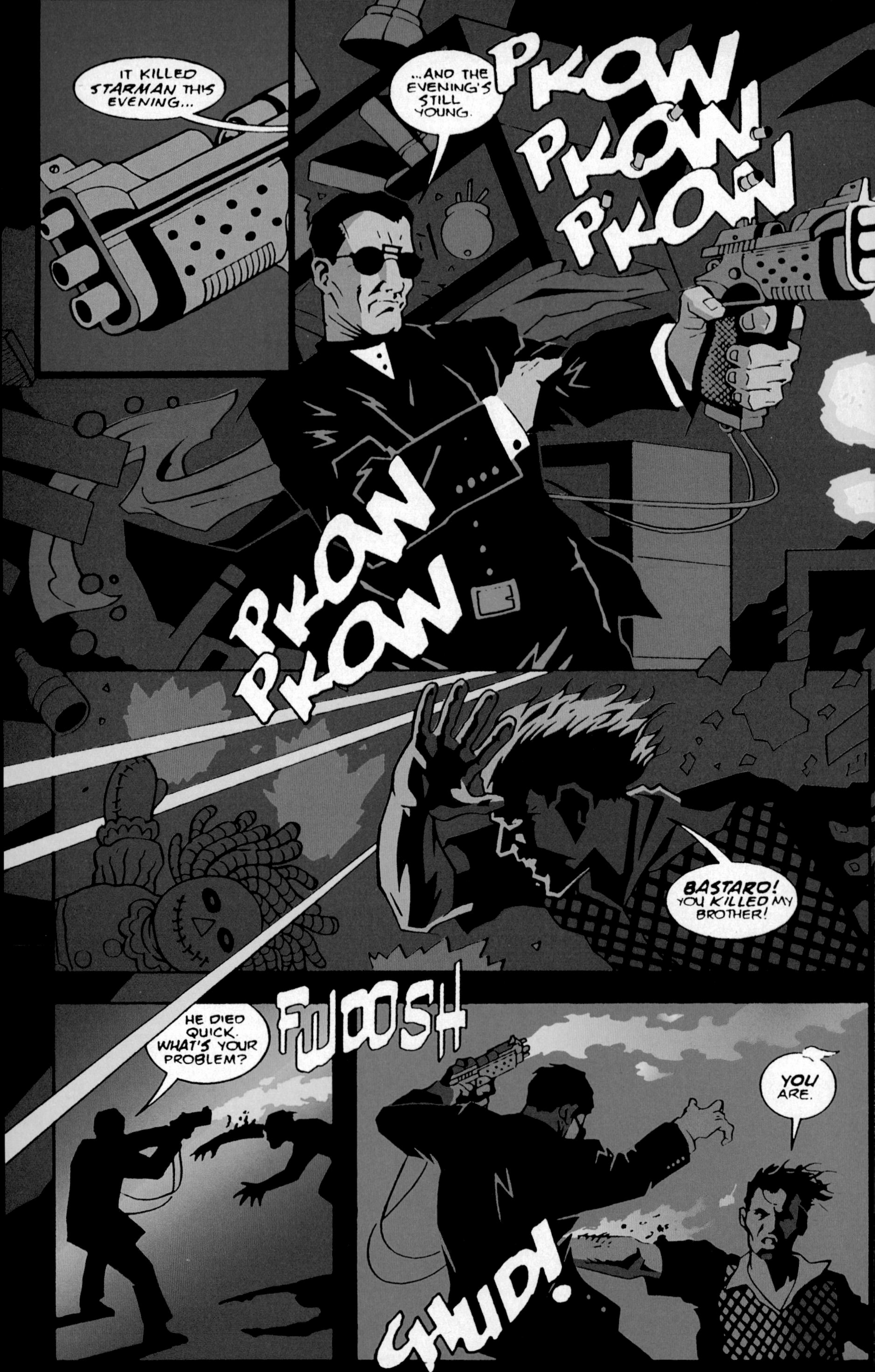
IT KILLED STARMAN THIS EVENING...
...AND THE EVENING'S STILL YOUNG.
PKOW PKOW PKOW
PKOW PKOW
BASTARO! YOU KILLED MY BROTHER!
HE DIED QUICK. WHAT'S YOUR PROBLEM?
FWOOSH
YOU ARE.
CHUD!

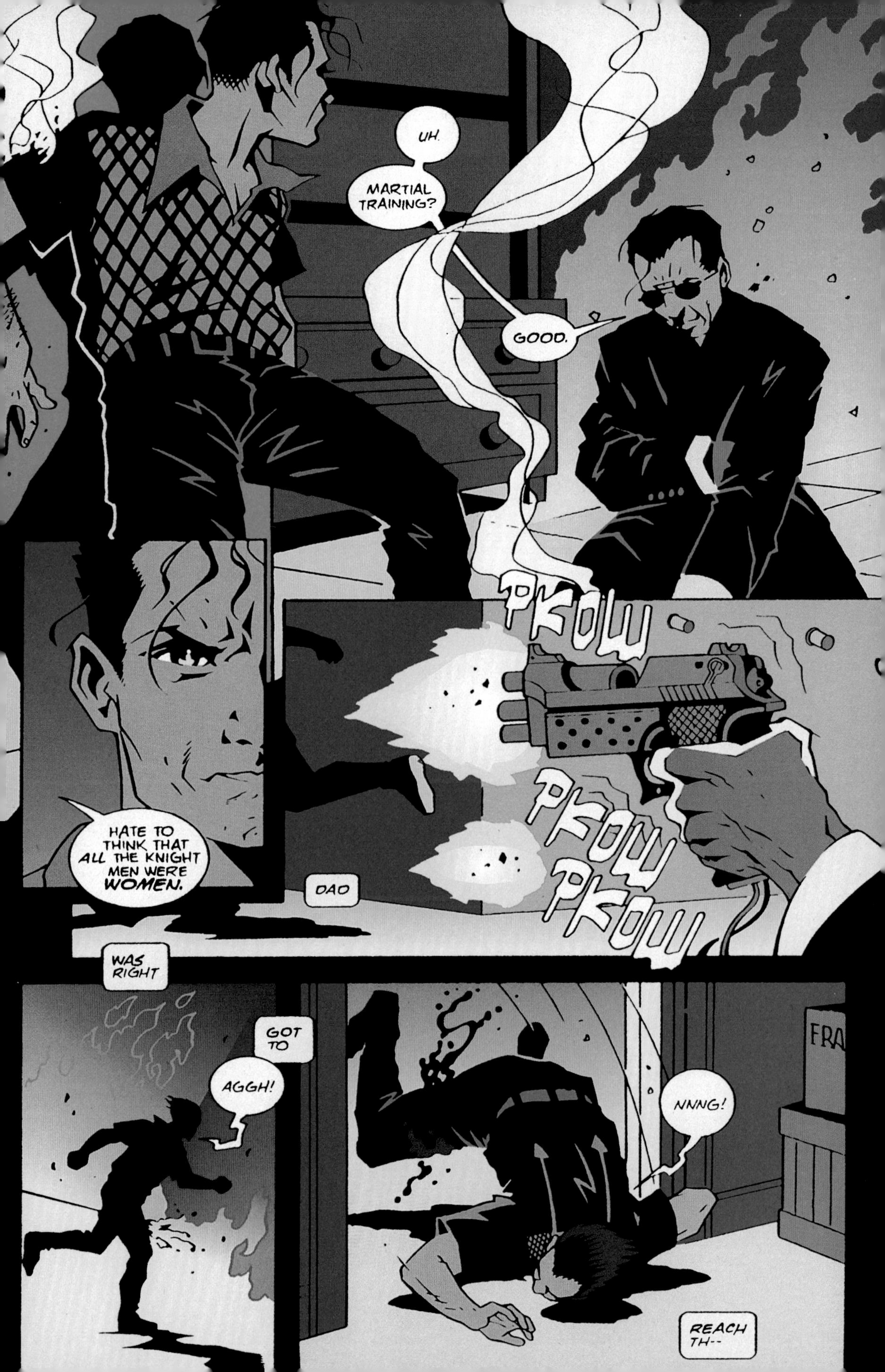
UH.
MARTIAL TRAINING?
GOOD.
HATE TO THINK THAT ALL THE KNIGHT MEN WERE WOMEN.
PKOW
PKOW PKOW PKOW
DAO
WAS RIGHT
GOT TO
AGGH!
NNNG!
REACH TH--

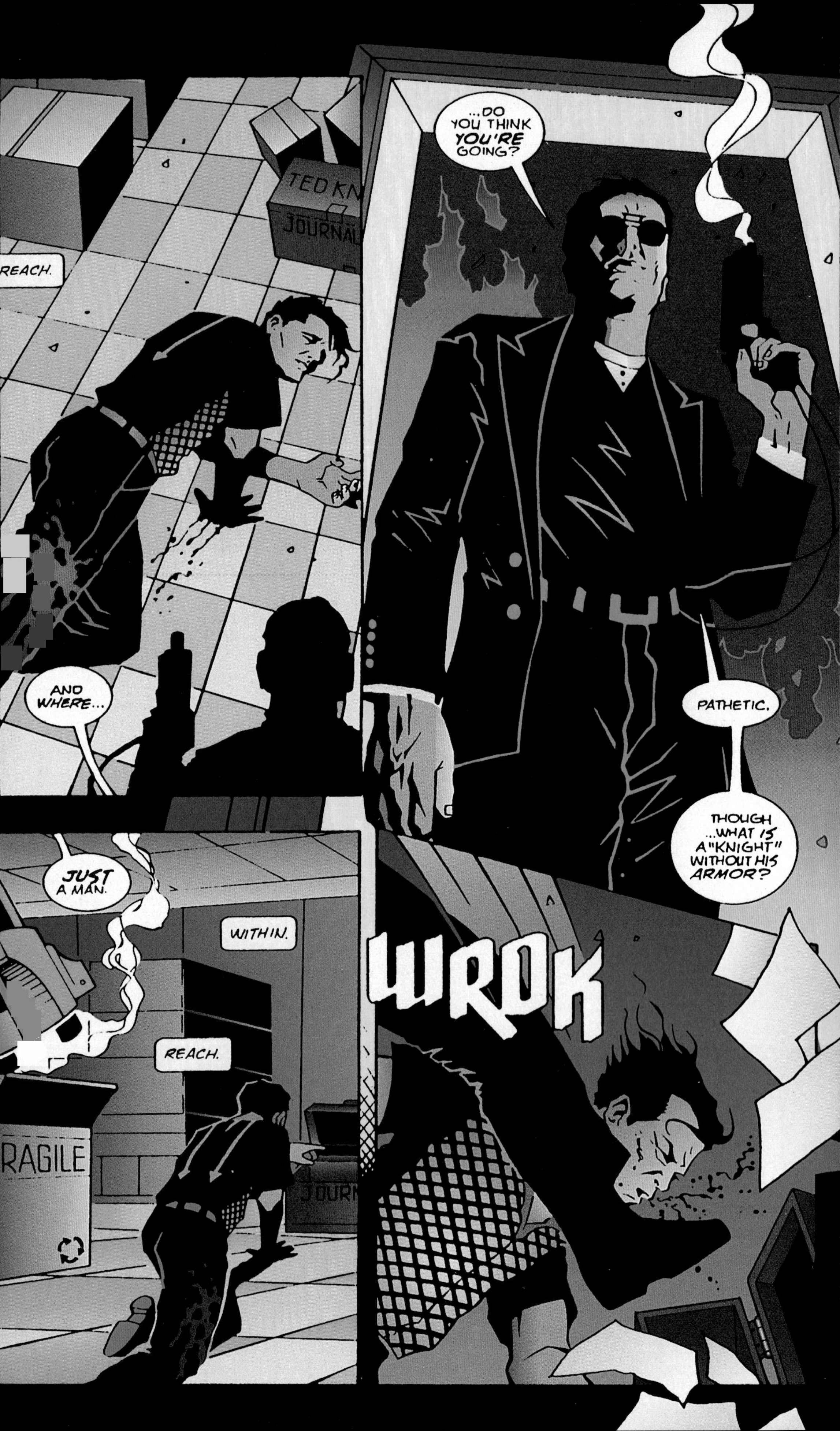

TED KN
JOURNAL
REACH.
AND WHERE...
...DO YOU THINK YOU'RE GOING?
PATHETIC.
THOUGH ...WHAT IS A "KNIGHT" WITHOUT HIS ARMOR?
JUST A MAN.
WITHIN.
REACH.
RAGILE
JOURN
WROK

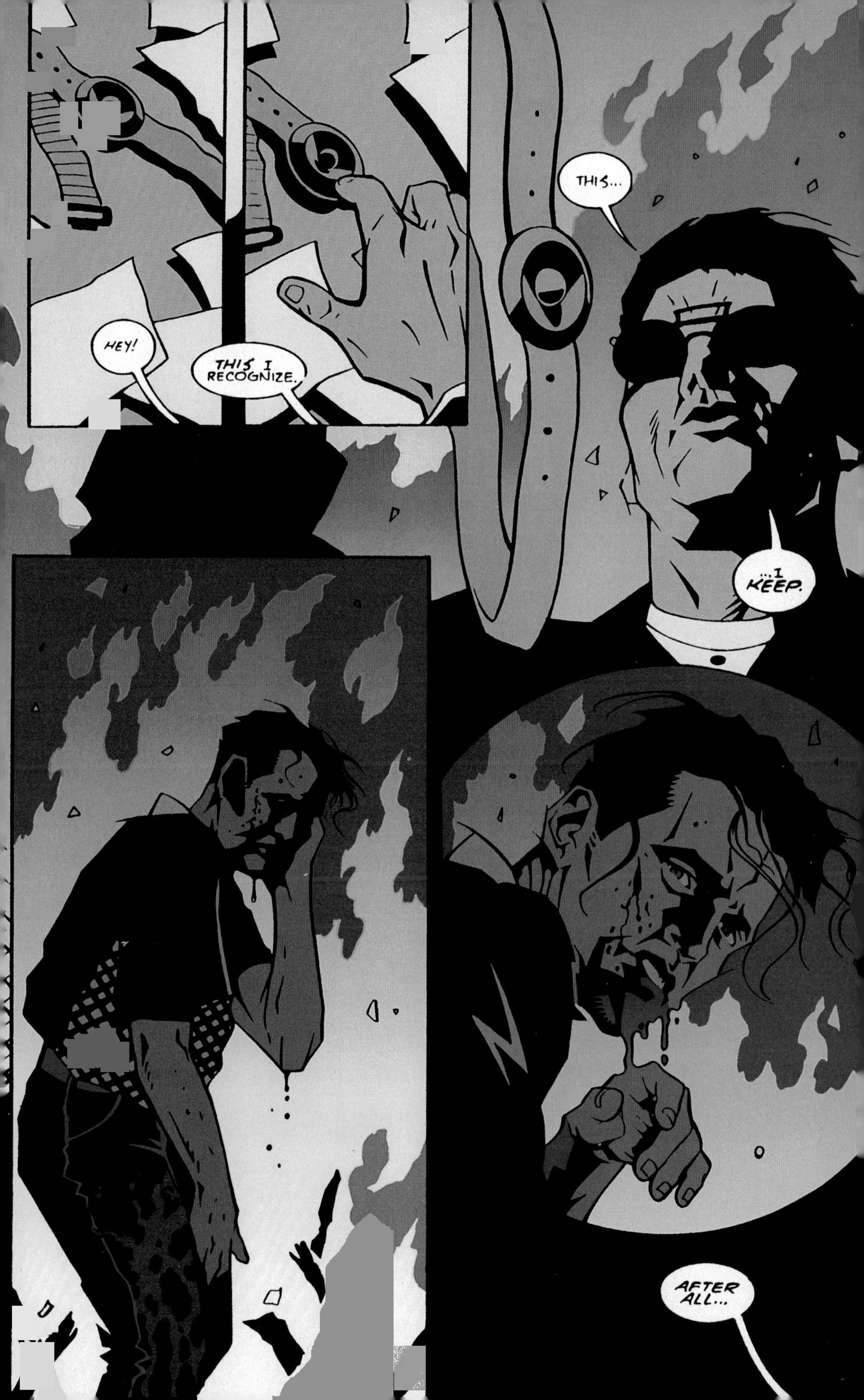
HEY!
THIS I RECOGNIZE..
THIS...
...I KEEP.
AFTER ALL...

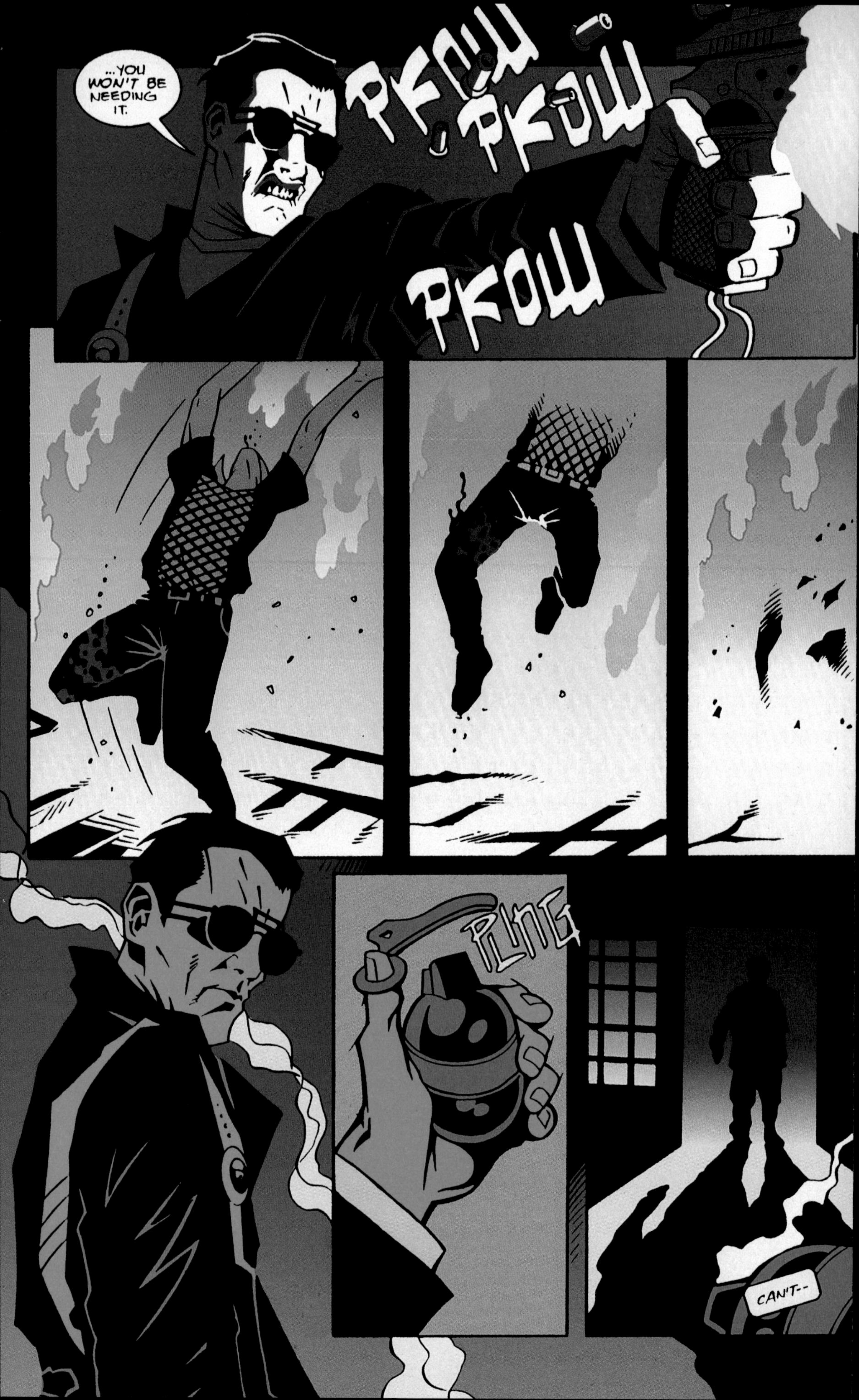
...YOU WON'T BE NEEDING IT.
PKOW PKOW
PKOW
PLING
CAN'T--

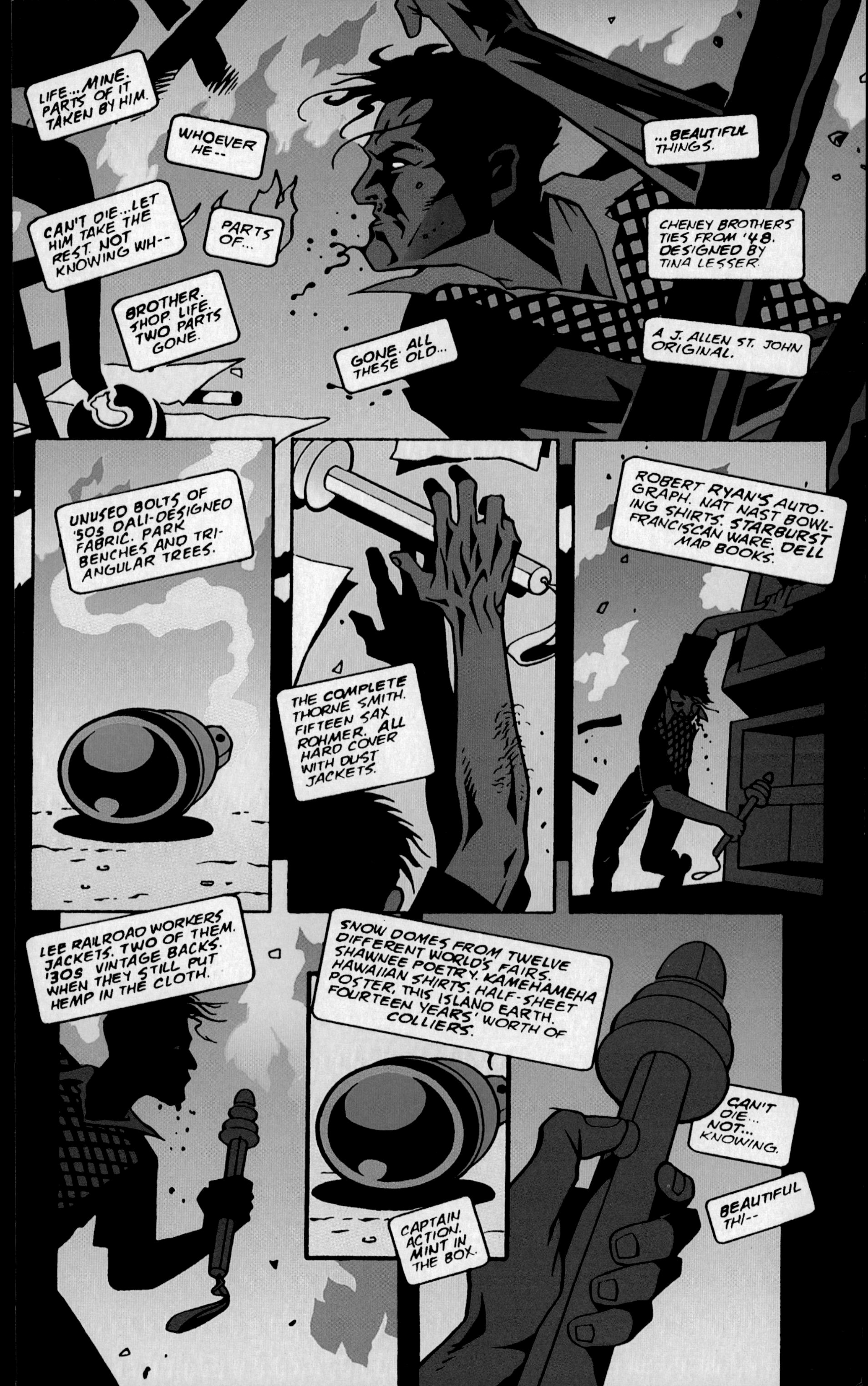
LIFE... MINE. PARTS OF IT TAKEN BY HIM.
WHOEVER HE--
CAN'T DIE... LET HIM TAKE THE REST. NOT KNOWING WH--
PARTS OF...
BROTHER. SHOP. LIFE. TWO PARTS GONE.
GONE. ALL THESE OLD...
...BEAUTIFUL THINGS.
CHENEY BROTHERS TIES FROM '48. DESIGNED BY TINA LESSER.
A J. ALLEN ST. JOHN ORIGINAL.
UNUSED BOLTS OF '50S DALI-DESIGNED FABRIC. PARK BENCHES AND TRI-ANGULAR TREES.
THE COMPLETE THORNE SMITH. FIFTEEN SAX ROHMER. ALL HARD COVER WITH DUST JACKETS.
ROBERT RYAN'S AUTO-GRAPH. NAT NAST BOWL-ING SHIRTS. STARBURST FRANCISCAN WARE. DELL MAP BOOKS.
LEE RAILROAD WORKERS JACKETS. TWO OF THEM. '30S VINTAGE BACKS. WHEN THEY STILL PUT HEMP IN THE CLOTH.
SNOW DOMES FROM TWELVE DIFFERENT WORLD'S FAIRS. SHAWNEE POETRY. KAMEHAMEHA HAWAIIAN SHIRTS. HALF-SHEET POSTER, THIS ISLAND EARTH. FOURTEEN YEARS' WORTH OF COLLIERS.
CAPTAIN ACTION. MINT IN THE BOX.
CAN'T DIE... NOT... KNOWING.
BEAUTIFUL THI--

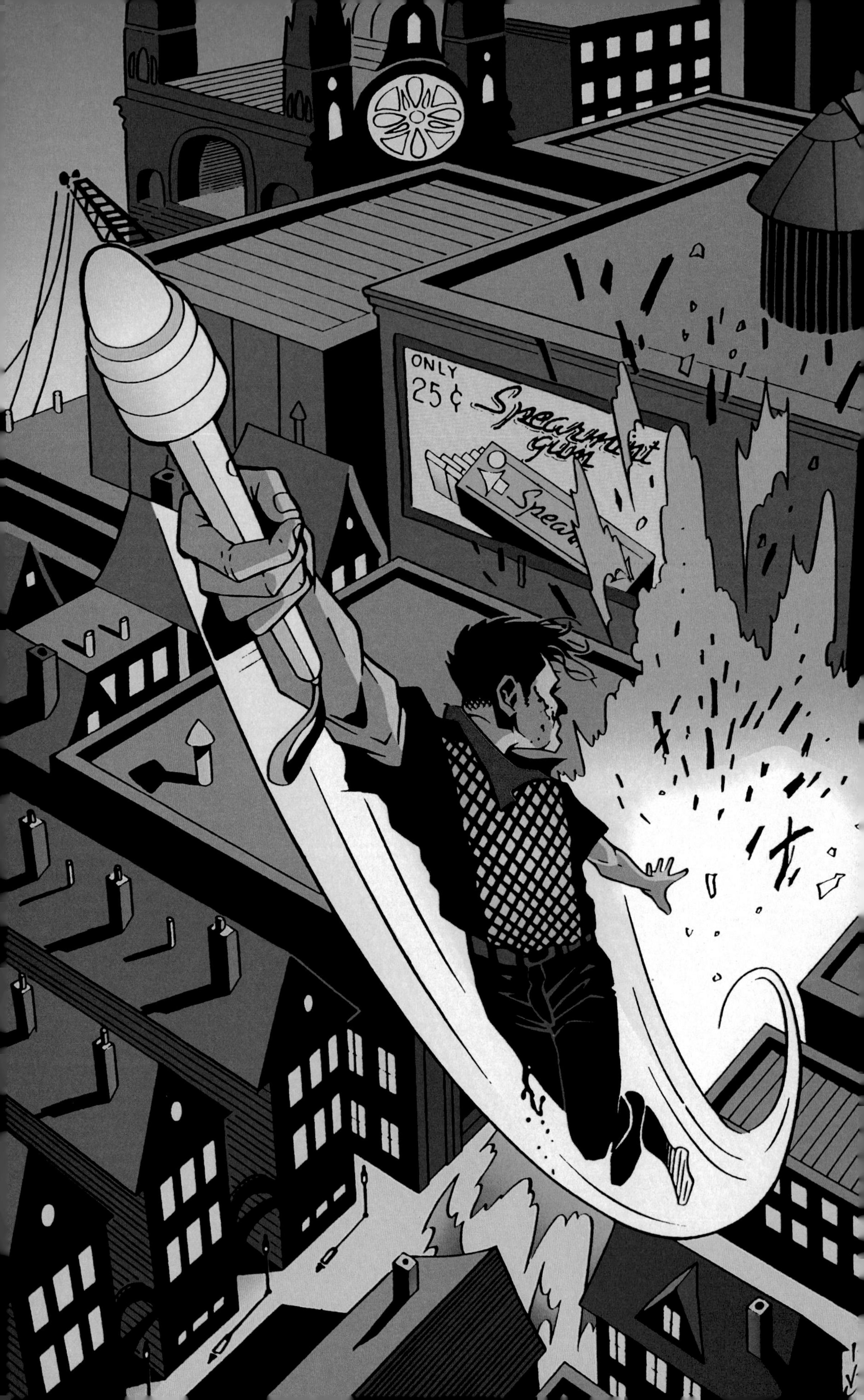
ONLY
25¢
Gum

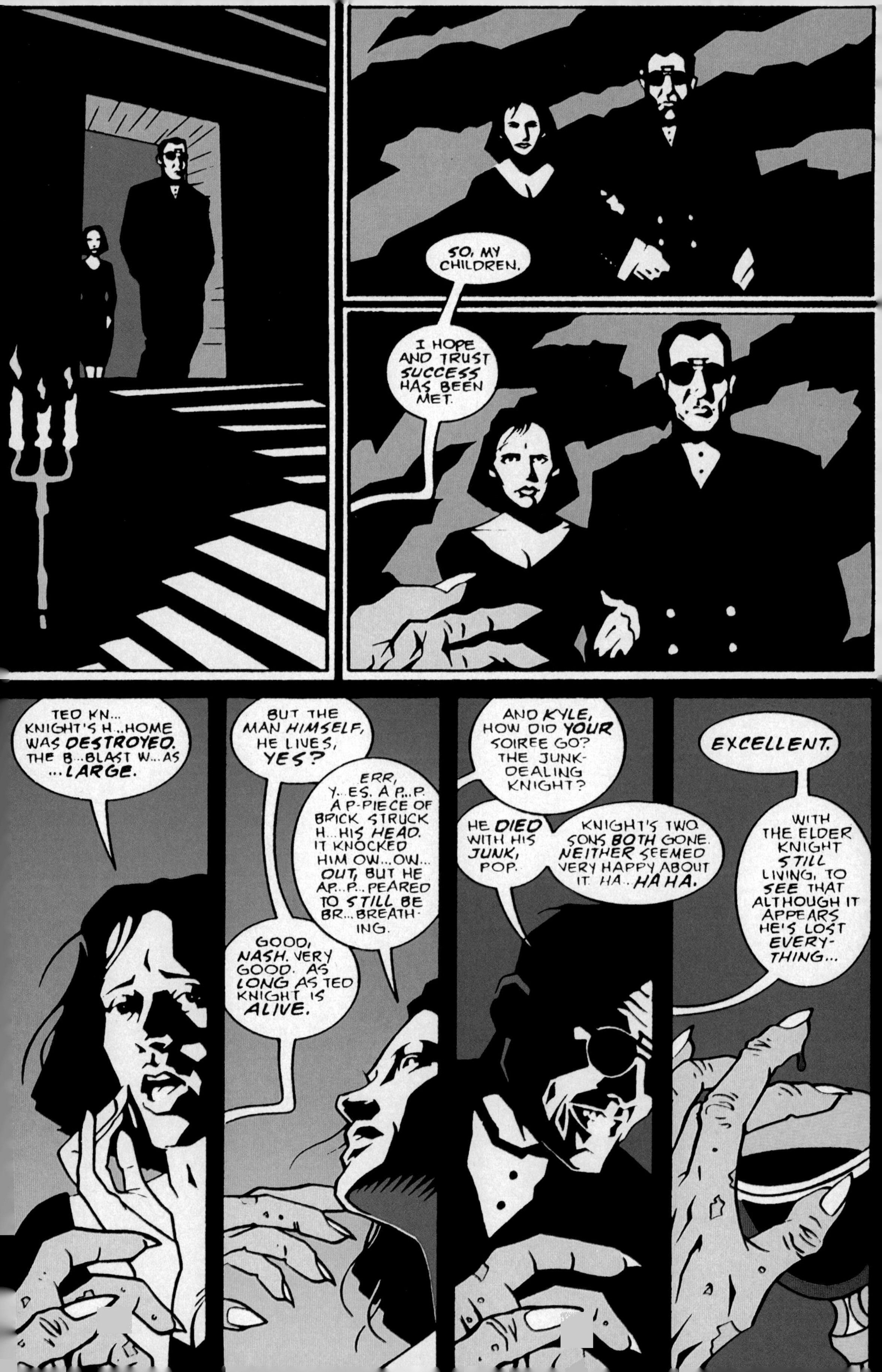
SO, MY CHILDREN.
I HOPE AND TRUST SUCCESS HAS BEEN MET.
TED KN... KNIGHT'S H...HOME WAS DESTROYED. THE B...BLAST W...AS ...LARGE.
BUT THE MAN HIMSELF, HE LIVES, YES?
ERR, Y...ES. A P...P. A P-PIECE OF BRICK STRUCK H...HIS HEAD. IT KNOCKED HIM OW...OW... OUT, BUT HE AP...P...PEARED TO STILL BE BR...BREATH-ING.
GOOD, NASH. VERY GOOD. AS LONG AS TED KNIGHT IS ALIVE.
AND KYLE, HOW DID YOUR SOIREE GO? THE JUNK-DEALING KNIGHT?
HE DIED WITH HIS JUNK, POP.
KNIGHT'S TWO SONS BOTH GONE. NEITHER SEEMED VERY HAPPY ABOUT IT. HA...HAHA.
EXCELLENT.
WITH THE ELDER KNIGHT STILL LIVING, TO SEE THAT ALTHOUGH IT APPEARS HE'S LOST EVERY-THING...

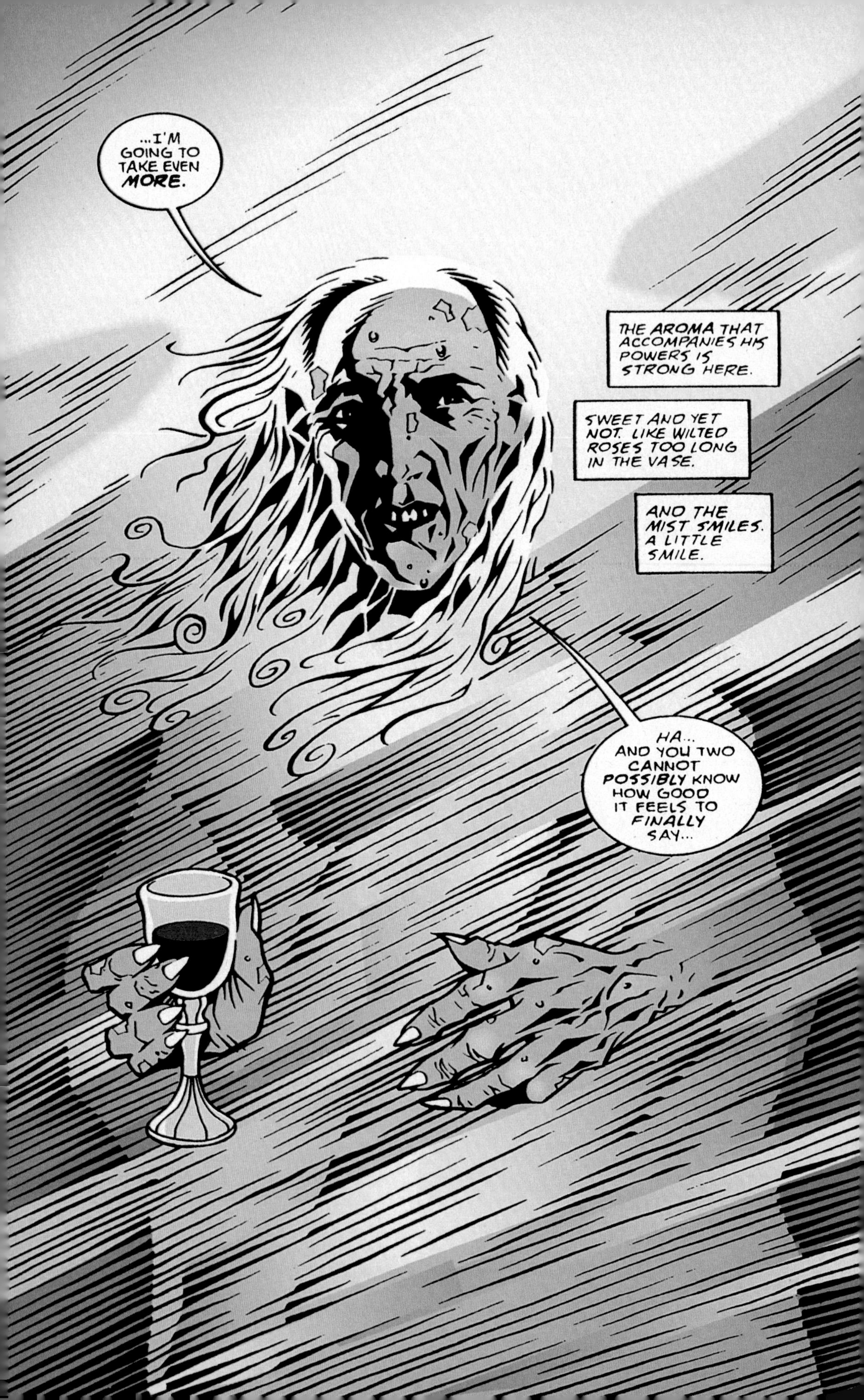
...I'M GOING TO TAKE EVEN MORE.
THE AROMA THAT ACCOMPANIES HIS POWERS IS STRONG HERE.
SWEET AND YET NOT. LIKE WILTED ROSES TOO LONG IN THE VASE.
AND THE MIST SMILES. A LITTLE SMILE.
HA... AND YOU TWO CANNOT POSSIBLY KNOW HOW GOOD IT FEELS TO FINALLY SAY...

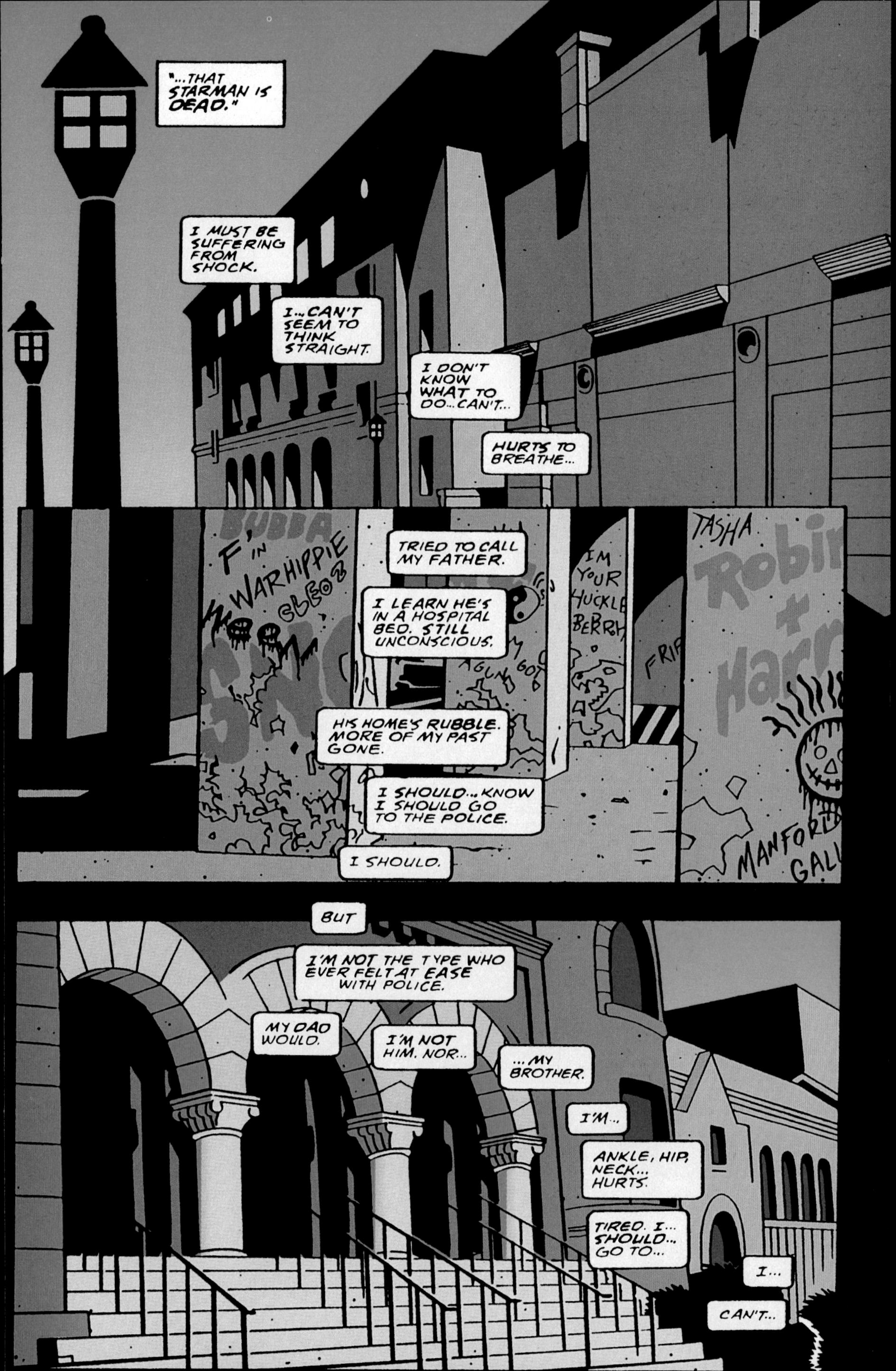
"...THAT STARMAN IS DEAD."
I MUST BE SUFFERING FROM SHOCK.
I...CAN'T SEEM TO THINK STRAIGHT.
I DON'T KNOW WHAT TO DO...CAN'T...
HURTS TO BREATHE...
TRIED TO CALL MY FATHER.
I LEARN HE'S IN A HOSPITAL BED. STILL UNCONSCIOUS.
HIS HOME'S RUBBLE. MORE OF MY PAST GONE.
I SHOULD...KNOW I SHOULD GO TO THE POLICE.
I SHOULD.
BUT
I'M NOT THE TYPE WHO EVER FELT AT EASE WITH POLICE.
MY DAD WOULD.
I'M NOT HIM. NOR...
...MY BROTHER.
I'M...
ANKLE, HIP, NECK... HURTS.
TIRED. I... SHOULD... GO TO...
I...
CAN'T...

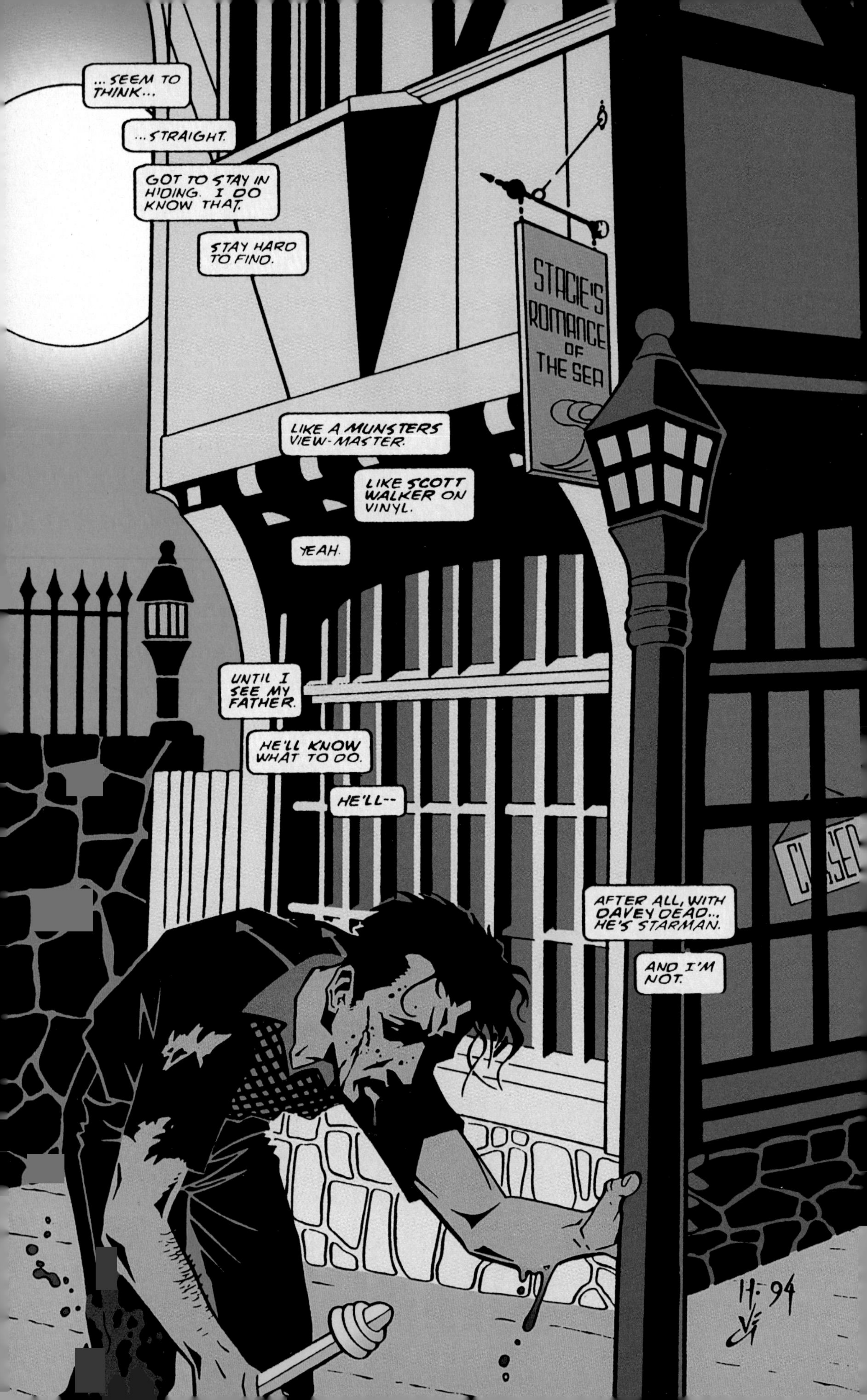
...SEEM TO THINK...
...STRAIGHT.
GOT TO STAY IN HIDING. I DO KNOW THAT.
STAY HARD TO FIND.
STACIE'S ROMANCE OF THE SEA
LIKE A MUNSTERS VIEW-MASTER.
LIKE SCOTT WALKER ON VINYL.
YEAH.
UNTIL I SEE MY FATHER.
HE'LL KNOW WHAT TO DO.
HE'LL--
AFTER ALL, WITH DAVEY DEAD... HE'S STARMAN.
AND I'M NOT.
H. 94

THE FOLLOWING TEXT APPEARED IN
THE LETTER COLUMN PAGES OF STARMAN #0

Hello, I'm James Robinson, writer of STARMAN. I have to rush to get this column in. I'm leaving town for a few days in search of my one favorite collectible, so I have to hammer this out and get it to DC before my evening flight. For this reason, this page is going to be a tad scattershot. I'll be jumping from topic to topic as stuff enters my head. It's all going to be a bit bumpy and free-form, so bear with me.

⭐

When I lived in England, I was quite a drinker (like most of my countrymen). I remember walking home from the tube station completely blitzed more than once, with my head raised high to the night sky. I loved to gaze at the stars in my drunken state, with my senses numbed to the point where I could almost imagine I was floating...that the houses around me and the pavement under my feet weren't there and I was floating among the stars.

It was at my most rapturous moment, usually, that I'd walk into a lamppost, but that's by the by. The thing is...I recall thinking of those nighttime travels through the heavens when I asked Archie if I could do STARMAN.

⭐

Another thing on my mind was how DC characters have been changed. Barry Allen's dead, Hal Jordan's a bad guy, the Teen Titans are no longer teens, etc., etc. Now, I'm not saying that this is good or bad; it's merely the way ongoing continuity changes stuff. Every generation wants a different set of heroes. But...the DC characters that are around now aren't the ones I grew up with. I'm not saying that's good or bad either. Again, it's just the way things are.

With STARMAN, however, we have a name and a Golden Age heritage that have been left pretty much untouched. People are familiar with the character and his powers and his green and red costume, and yet they're not. In fact, I'd brazenly hazard a guess that I developed the character of Ted Knight more within the pages of the GOLDEN AGE miniseries than was ever done before. And that's not saying much. But, at the same time, his appearances in the Justice Society crossovers of yore, and the fact that although he was never a first-rung hero, his powers are far, far greater than those of the acrobatic masked men who comprised about half of the 1940s super-hero roll call, have meant that people sort of know him.

I intend to make use of that.

If there is a flaw in the past incarnations of Starman, I see it being that they've all been a bit insular. None of them interacted to any degree with any of the other Starmen. There was no overriding hook that anchored them to the DC Universe other than the fact that they shared the name with Ted Knight. In this book, there *will* be a sense of lineage and history. (History: a very important word I'll be getting back to later.) Every person alive or dead who bore the name of Starman will have some resonance and bearing on this new ongoing comic, even David Knight, the poor schmuck who gets blown away on page four.

So...I can't have the heroes of my childhood the way they were then, but perhaps I get something even better: a chance to create/hone/perfect a DC character all my own. And I want to imagine that while Barry Allen and Hal Jordan and Ray Palmer were off having their Silver Age adventures, Ted Knight was too; older, but still active. Starman has always been around, a light in the darkness, in his own little corner of the DC Universe.

Now let's talk about where that "corner" is.

Some people find DC's fictional cities annoying, a holdover from a bygone era. I, on the other hand, find them utterly charming. Comics are an expressionistic medium, after all, a world of gaudy gods and dynamic demons. Who wants this set in a place you can hop on a plane to and see firsthand? Not I. Who wants Chicago when you can have Gotham? Or Philadelphia when you can have Metropolis? Or Boston when you can have... Opal City?

In the course of this book, I intend to create this city — give it streets you recognize by the landmarks; give it a design sense all its own. Fortunately, I'm collaborating with Tony Harris, an artist who not only shares that vision, but has the visual talent and skill to bring off the architectural diversity we have in mind. We want the Opal City skyline to be so distinctive that you'll recognize it without a caption or any verbal indication of where you are. Starman's home. You'll have gathered it's a stylized place, but then again, I ask, who wants the everyday in a comic book?

(Actually, I'm being both presumptuous and a bit sweeping by saying that. The everyday in a comic book is wonderful.)

(But not here.)

Which brings me around to history.

In the course of this book, we're going to have an irregular series of single tales loosely grouped together under the banner of TIMES PAST. Don't worry, the first of these won't be for a while yet, but when they appear, they'll focus on different moments/events/singular occurrences in Opal City's history and the surrounding Turk County (why, for instance, its original name was DEAD TURK COUNTY). They'll feature guest artists and be little sojourns away from Jack's adventures in the present. Any excuse to get back to my history books.

But I don't want you to think this is going to be just a retread through a lot of old continuity. I really am going to try, in my own inept way, to make this book different, focusing on a character more interested in second-hand collectibles than in fighting crime, whose idea of a costume is goggles and a jacket. I also intend to deliver one of the more interesting supporting casts.

I hope you'll stick around to see how I do.

★

I'm jumping topics here, but it occurs to me that Starman has always been a character I've been interested in. The first time I encountered him was in a Justice Society crossover. It was the first part of the two issues that end with Black Canary's husband dying. I forget the number of the issue. What I do remember is that the story began with Starman. He sees a menace in the sky. He goes up to fight it. He's defeated and plummets back to Earth.

Now, this is all a bit sketchy in my memory, so if I've gotten the exact facts wrong, forgive me. But what I liked then was this new (to me) hero with a green and red costume and his hood with a fin on the top. I always looked out for appearances by the character after that. (Yeah, yeah, I know they're simplistic reasons for liking him, but I was like six or seven at the time. What do you want?)

From there I discovered Jack Burnley. Now, if ever there was an underrated creator, it's this guy. With a few notable exceptions, the artists from the Golden Age of comics were not that great. I know, I know, there was Kirby, Robinson, Crandall, Fine, Sprang, Eisner, Raboy, Beck, Everett, etc. I know you can give me a list of the great ones. And I can turn around and show you three times as many artists who were terrible. It was a simpler time. Kids wanted colors and characters then. They didn't care about anatomy. (Actually, maybe things haven't changed so radically at that, eh?) Anyways, of the great artists back then, of the ones known and revered today, I'm always aware that Jack Burnley's name is absent. And yet he was an amazing draftsman; his work had a realistic quality that was missing from many of his peers. There was a delightfully expressionistic, surreal feel to elements with his work that I think is incredible.

It was in the pages of WANTED, the DC reprint book, that I first encountered Burnley's work. I then went on to find other examples from the 100-page reprints and the like. All his work was of the same high standard. And, together with Gardner Fox, he created Starman.

The other memory that stands out was a comics purchase at the age of twelve. Eleven, maybe, around about then. A Justice League 10-pager. Blue cover. Amazo was the villain of the new story. And in the back was an old Starman reprint by Mort Meskin.

Now, all I know about Meskin is what I've read in Steranko's History of Comics. But as Steranko was quick to point out, and as you can see at a glance, even back then, the guy was cooking. The story is layered in shadows and drama. The plot is simple enough. It's eight or ten pages at best, but the use of angles and mood and tone by Meskin makes the tale wonderful. (Funnily enough, the tale, about a poor boy who's kidnapped by mistake instead of his wealthy friend, has almost the exact same plot as the one used by Ed McBain in the 87th Precinct novel King's Ransom...which in turn was adapted to film by Japanese cinema genius Akira Kurosawa as High and Low.)

And in all appearances I found, there was the garish green and red costume. And always with the fin on the top of his hood.

I should also mention here that I will be answering the letter columns personally for the foreseeable future. I want to relate with the readers of this book and I feel this is a good way to begin going about it. Some of you who follow my work may know that I've already begun this practice in the Firearm comic I do for Malibu.

I stated in there something I'll reiterate now: this being that I would prefer not every letter be about the issue at hand. STARMAN is about superheroics and shadows and nighttime horrors and all that, but it's also about old books and records and collectibles and all the odd facts and details that drift through and around the mind of a fellow such as Jack. How different is he from me...or any of you, for that matter, with your comics collections and your Sandman hologram cards and your Otis Redding boxed sets and signed Ray Bradbury hardcovers and vintage Levi red tags and/or whatever else is the rarity/oddity you hold near and dear to your heart?

I'd like some of the letter column to be about this. Collections. All of the weird junk that's out there to be found and hoarded away. I'd also like you to write in about anything else that might pop into your head. All the weird junk that you've hoarded away there, too. If it pertains to an issue of STARMAN, great. If not, then that's cool also. Just write in one way or the other.

And with collectibles in mind...finally I'm left to ask...

...If anyone out there has a Munsters or an Addams Family View-Master, or the Japanese import CD by Jump with Joey that they'd like to sell, please, please, please write in.

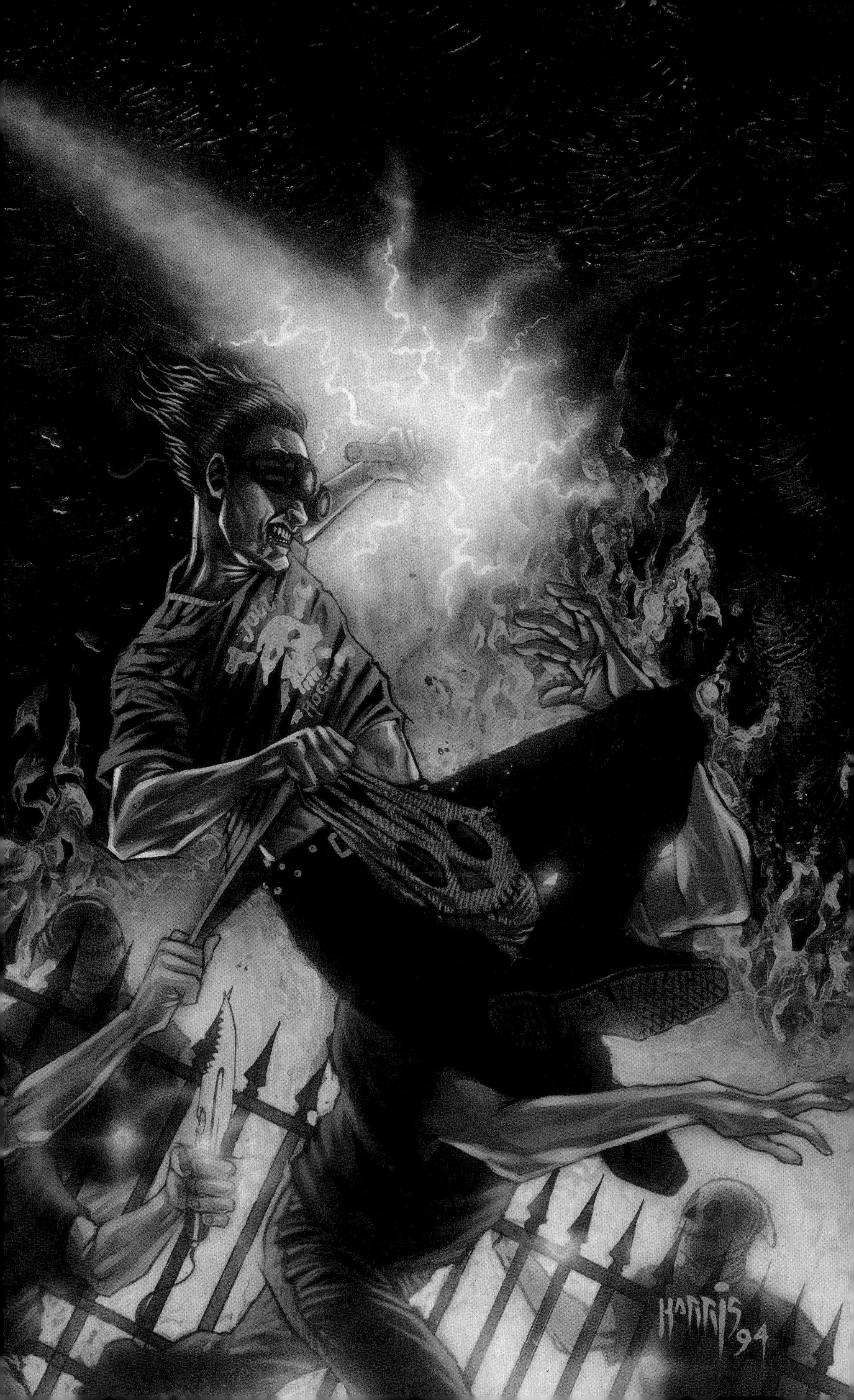
HARRIS 94

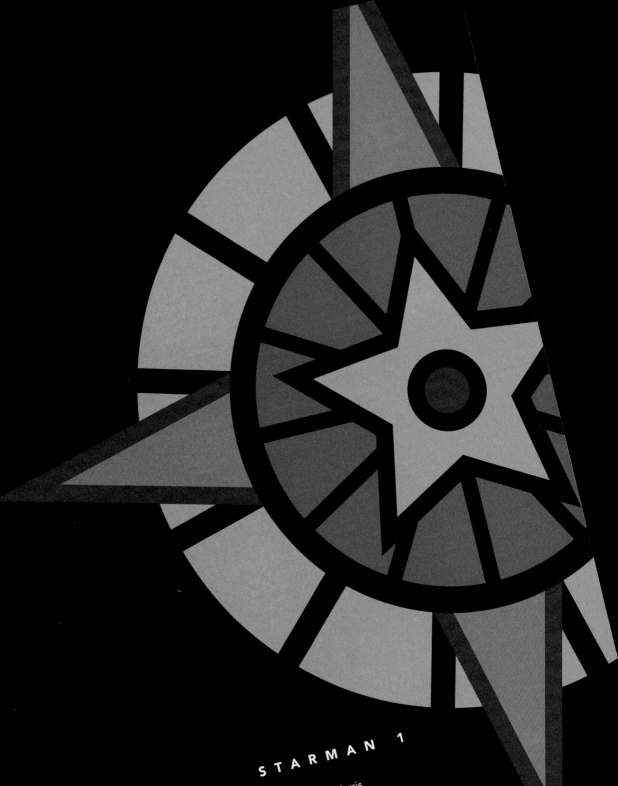

S T A R M A N 1

Cover by Tony Harris

Written by James Robinson

Pencils by Tony Harris,

with inks by Wade von Grawbadger

and colors by Gregory Wright

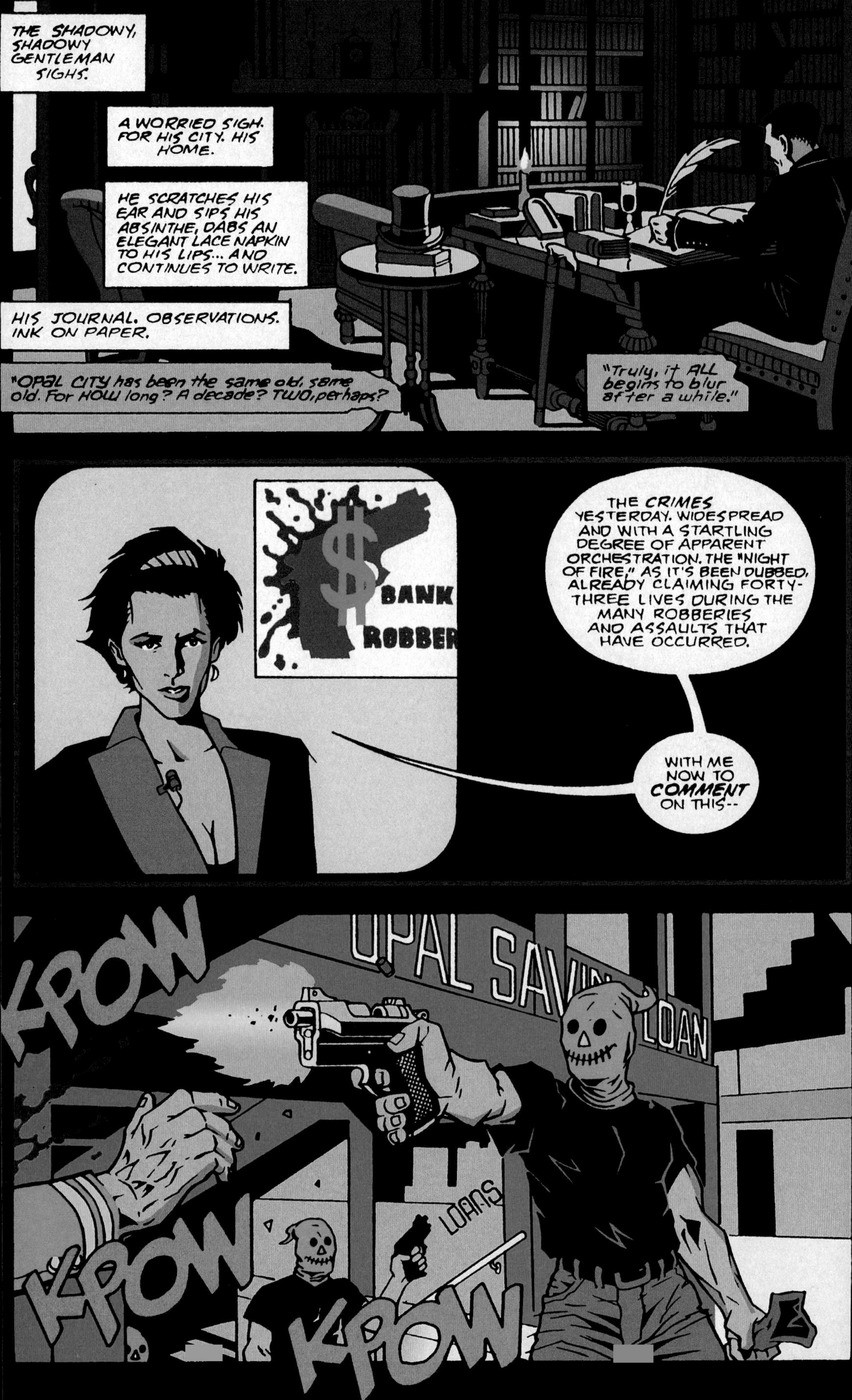
THE SHADOWY, SHADOWY GENTLEMAN SIGHS.
A WORRIED SIGH. FOR HIS CITY. HIS HOME.
HE SCRATCHES HIS EAR AND SIPS HIS ABSINTHE, DABS AN ELEGANT LACE NAPKIN TO HIS LIPS... AND CONTINUES TO WRITE.
HIS JOURNAL. OBSERVATIONS. INK ON PAPER.
"OPAL CITY has been the same old, same old. For HOW long? A decade? TWO, perhaps?
"Truly, it ALL begins to blur after a while."
BANK ROBBER
THE CRIMES YESTERDAY. WIDESPREAD AND WITH A STARTLING DEGREE OF APPARENT ORCHESTRATION. THE "NIGHT OF FIRE," AS IT'S BEEN DUBBED, ALREADY CLAIMING FORTY-THREE LIVES DURING THE MANY ROBBERIES AND ASSAULTS THAT HAVE OCCURRED.
WITH ME NOW TO COMMENT ON THIS--
KPOW
OPAL SAVIN
LOAN
LOANS
KPOW
KPOW

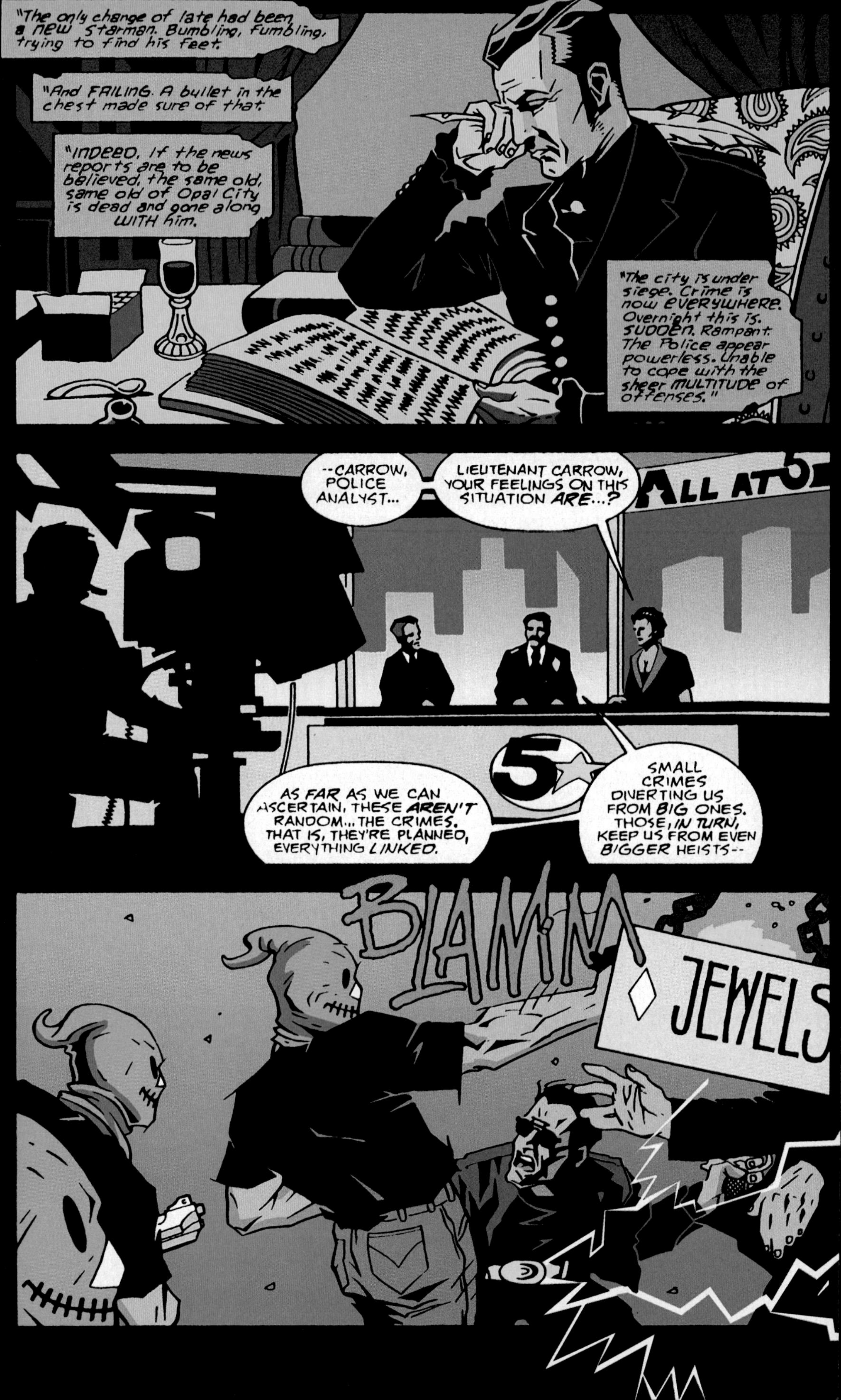
"The only change of late had been a new Starman. Bumbling, fumbling, trying to find his feet.
"And FAILING. A bullet in the chest made sure of that.
"INDEED. If the news reports are to be believed, the same old, same old of Opal City is dead and gone along WITH him.
"The city is under siege. Crime is now EVERYWHERE. Overnight this is. SUDDEN. Rampant. The Police appear powerless. Unable to cope with the sheer MULTITUDE of offenses."
--CARROW, POLICE ANALYST...
LIEUTENANT CARROW, YOUR FEELINGS ON THIS SITUATION ARE...?
AS FAR AS WE CAN ASCERTAIN, THESE AREN'T RANDOM... THE CRIMES. THAT IS, THEY'RE PLANNED, EVERYTHING LINKED.
SMALL CRIMES DIVERTING US FROM BIG ONES. THOSE, IN TURN, KEEP US FROM EVEN BIGGER HEISTS--
BLAMM
JEWELS

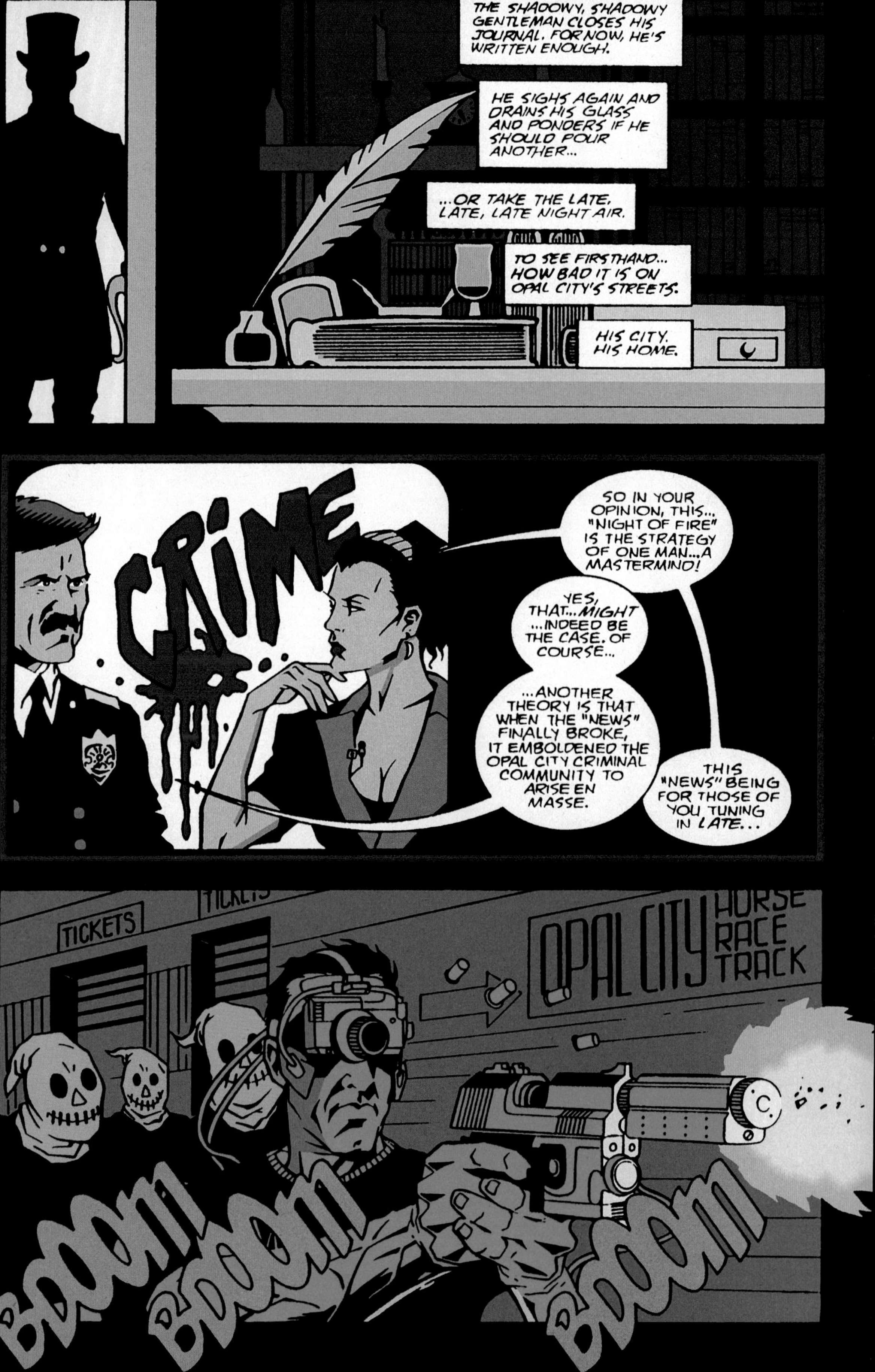
THE SHADOWY, SHADOWY GENTLEMAN CLOSES HIS JOURNAL. FOR NOW, HE'S WRITTEN ENOUGH.
HE SIGHS AGAIN AND DRAINS HIS GLASS AND PONDERS IF HE SHOULD POUR ANOTHER...
...OR TAKE THE LATE, LATE, LATE NIGHT AIR.
TO SEE FIRSTHAND... HOW BAD IT IS ON OPAL CITY'S STREETS.
HIS CITY. HIS HOME.
CRIME
SO IN YOUR OPINION, THIS... "NIGHT OF FIRE" IS THE STRATEGY OF ONE MAN...A MASTERMIND!
YES, THAT...MIGHT ...INDEED BE THE CASE. OF COURSE...
...ANOTHER THEORY IS THAT WHEN THE "NEWS" FINALLY BROKE, IT EMBOLDENED THE OPAL CITY CRIMINAL COMMUNITY TO ARISE EN MASSE.
THIS "NEWS" BEING FOR THOSE OF YOU TUNING IN LATE...
TICKETS
TICKETS
OPAL CITY HORSE RACE TRACK
BDOOM
BDOOM
BDOOM

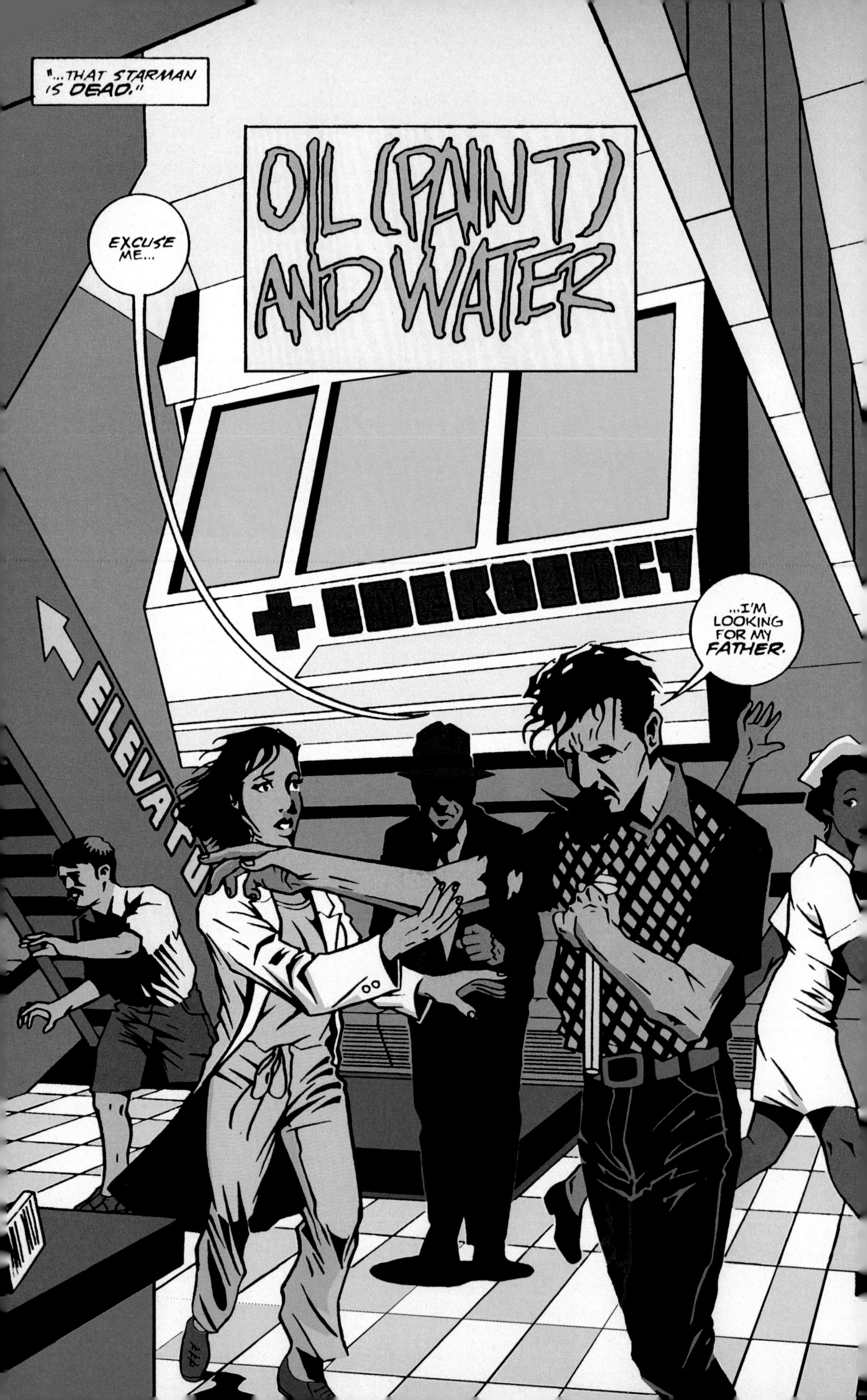
"...THAT STARMAN IS DEAD."
OIL (PAINT) AND WATER
EXCUSE ME...
...I'M LOOKING FOR MY FATHER.
EMERGENCY
ELEVATO

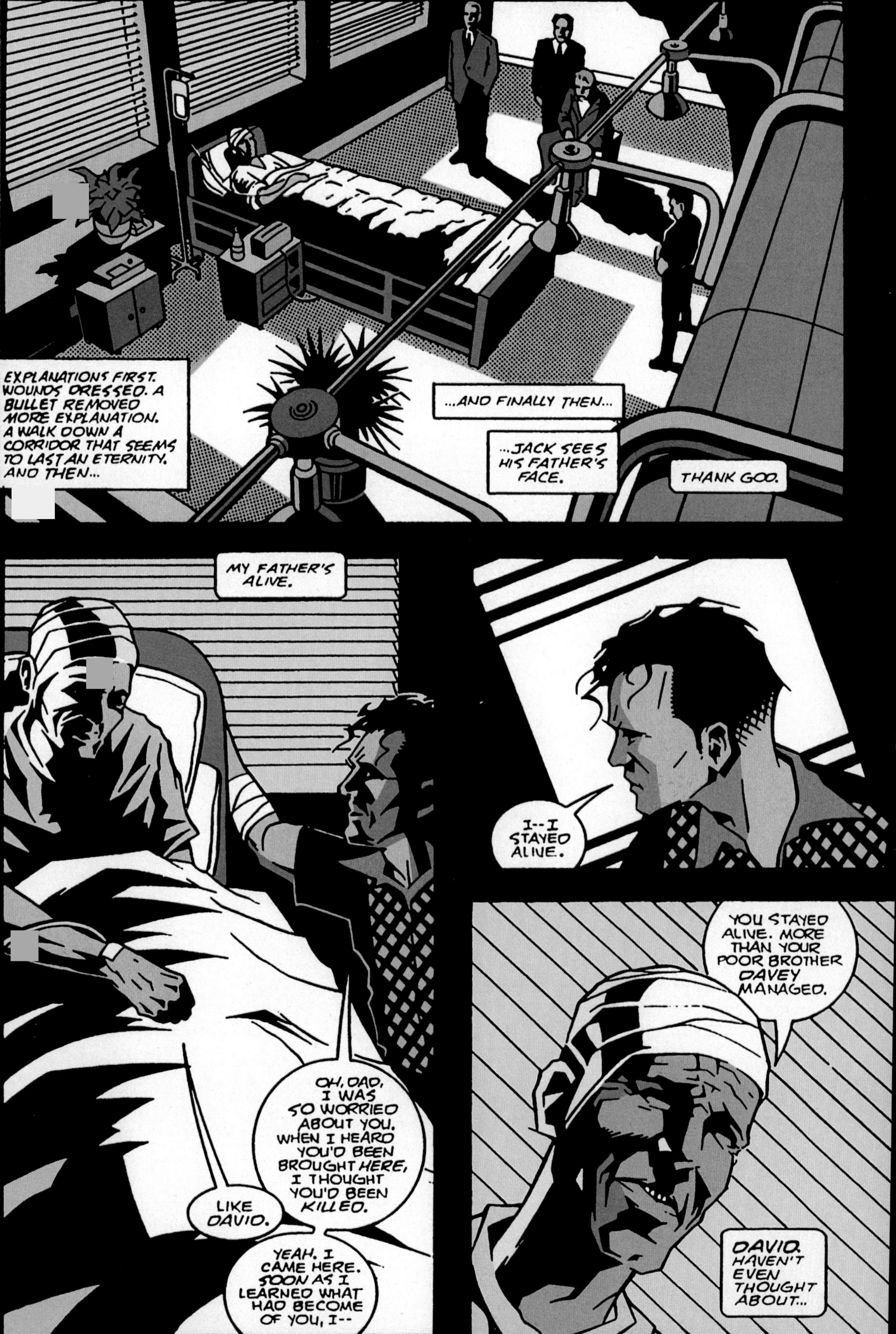

EXPLANATIONS FIRST. WOUNDS DRESSED. A BULLET REMOVED MORE EXPLANATION. A WALK DOWN A CORRIDOR THAT SEEMS TO LAST AN ETERNITY. AND THEN...
...AND FINALLY THEN...
...JACK SEES HIS FATHER'S FACE.
THANK GOD.
MY FATHER'S ALIVE.
OH, DAD, I WAS SO WORRIED ABOUT YOU. WHEN I HEARD YOU'D BEEN BROUGHT HERE, I THOUGHT YOU'D BEEN KILLED.
LIKE DAVID.
YEAH. I CAME HERE. SOON AS I LEARNED WHAT HAD BECOME OF YOU, I--
I--I STAYED ALIVE.
YOU STAYED ALIVE. MORE THAN YOUR POOR BROTHER DAVEY MANAGED.
DAVID. HAVEN'T EVEN THOUGHT ABOUT...

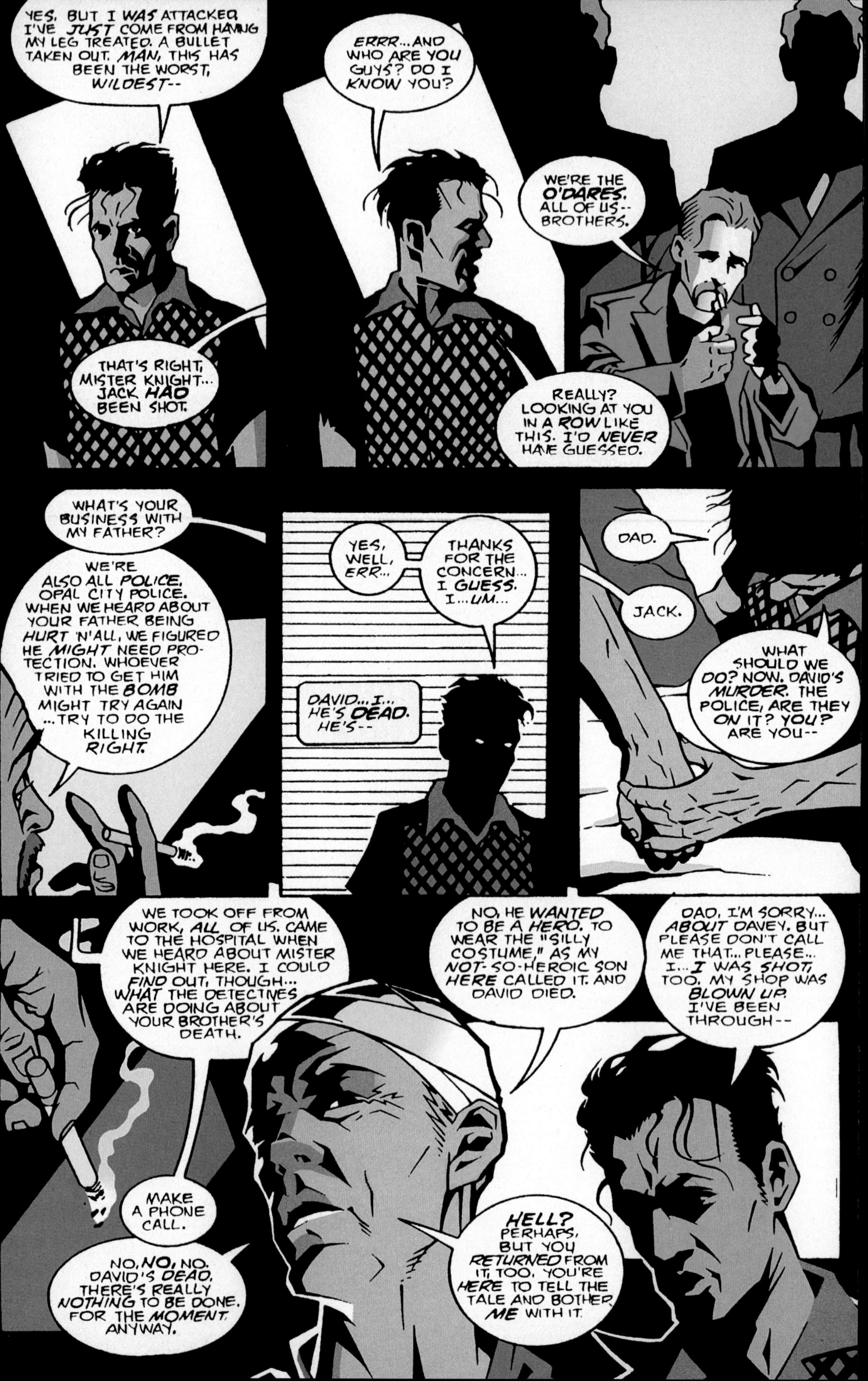
YES, BUT I WAS ATTACKED. I'VE JUST COME FROM HAVING MY LEG TREATED. A BULLET TAKEN OUT. MAN, THIS HAS BEEN THE WORST, WILDEST--
THAT'S RIGHT, MISTER KNIGHT... JACK HAD BEEN SHOT.
ERRR... AND WHO ARE YOU GUYS? DO I KNOW YOU?
WE'RE THE O'DARES. ALL OF US-- BROTHERS.
REALLY? LOOKING AT YOU IN A ROW LIKE THIS, I'D NEVER HAVE GUESSED.
WHAT'S YOUR BUSINESS WITH MY FATHER?
WE'RE ALSO ALL POLICE. OPAL CITY POLICE. WHEN WE HEARD ABOUT YOUR FATHER BEING HURT 'N'ALL, WE FIGURED HE MIGHT NEED PROTECTION. WHOEVER TRIED TO GET HIM WITH THE BOMB MIGHT TRY AGAIN ...TRY TO DO THE KILLING RIGHT.
YES, WELL, ERR...
THANKS FOR THE CONCERN... I GUESS. I...UM...
DAVID...I... HE'S DEAD. HE'S--
DAD.
JACK.
WHAT SHOULD WE DO? NOW. DAVID'S MURDER. THE POLICE, ARE THEY ON IT? YOU? ARE YOU--
WE TOOK OFF FROM WORK, ALL OF US. CAME TO THE HOSPITAL WHEN WE HEARD ABOUT MISTER KNIGHT HERE. I COULD FIND OUT, THOUGH... WHAT THE DETECTIVES ARE DOING ABOUT YOUR BROTHER'S DEATH.
MAKE A PHONE CALL.
NO, NO, NO. DAVID'S DEAD. THERE'S REALLY NOTHING TO BE DONE. FOR THE MOMENT, ANYWAY.
NO, HE WANTED TO BE A HERO. TO WEAR THE "SILLY COSTUME," AS MY NOT-SO-HEROIC SON HERE CALLED IT. AND DAVID DIED.
DAD, I'M SORRY... ABOUT DAVEY. BUT PLEASE DON'T CALL ME THAT... PLEASE... I...I WAS SHOT, TOO. MY SHOP WAS BLOWN UP. I'VE BEEN THROUGH--
HELL? PERHAPS, BUT YOU RETURNED FROM IT, TOO. YOU'RE HERE TO TELL THE TALE AND BOTHER ME WITH IT.

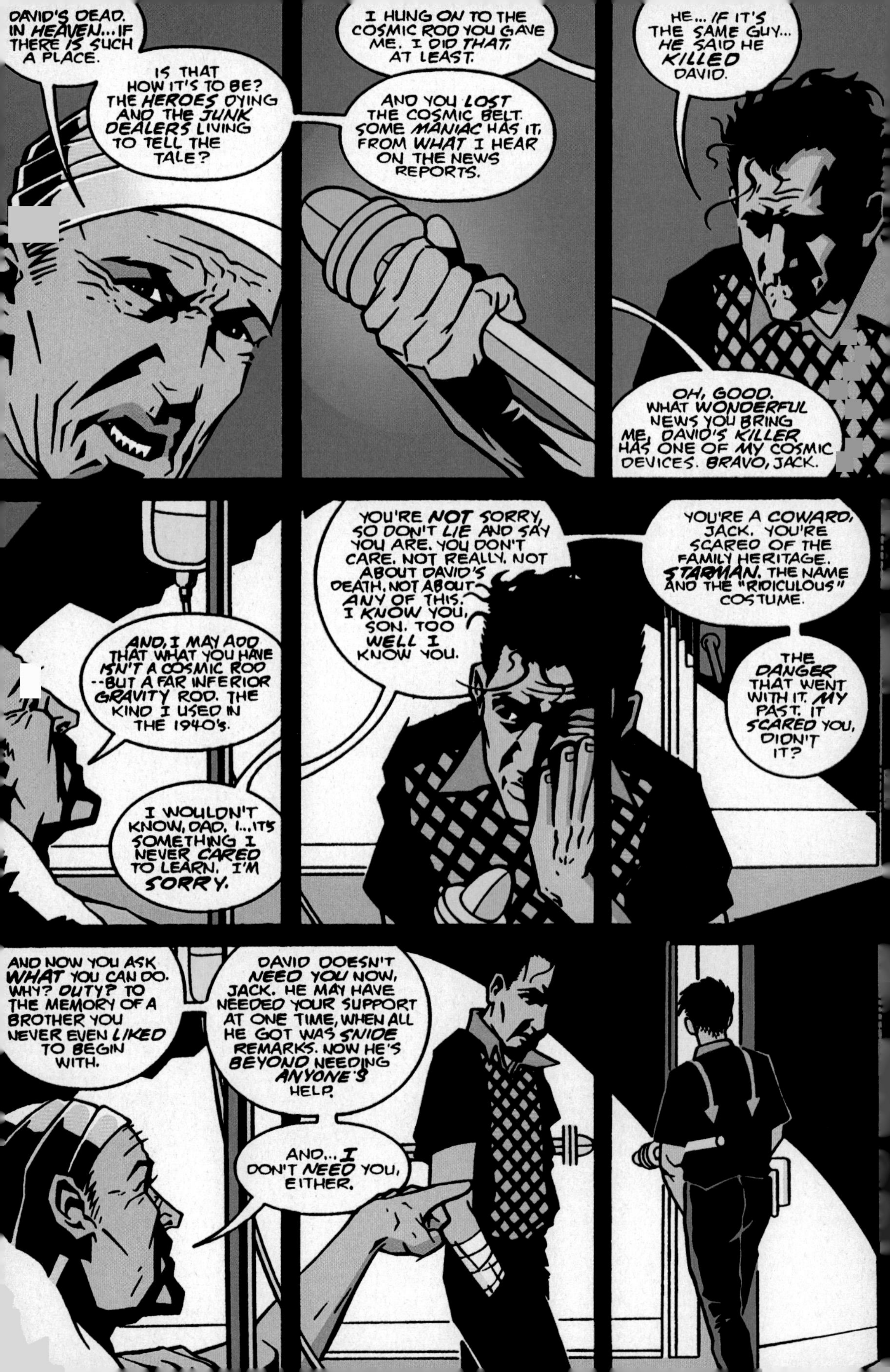
DAVID'S DEAD. IN HEAVEN... IF THERE IS SUCH A PLACE.
IS THAT HOW IT'S TO BE? THE HEROES DYING AND THE JUNK DEALERS LIVING TO TELL THE TALE?
I HUNG ON TO THE COSMIC ROD YOU GAVE ME. I DID THAT, AT LEAST.
AND YOU LOST THE COSMIC BELT. SOME MANIAC HAS IT, FROM WHAT I HEAR ON THE NEWS REPORTS.
HE... IF IT'S THE SAME GUY... HE SAID HE KILLED DAVID.
OH, GOOD. WHAT WONDERFUL NEWS YOU BRING ME. DAVID'S KILLER HAS ONE OF MY COSMIC DEVICES. BRAVO, JACK.
AND, I MAY ADD THAT WHAT YOU HAVE ISN'T A COSMIC ROD --BUT A FAR INFERIOR GRAVITY ROD. THE KIND I USED IN THE 1940'S.
I WOULDN'T KNOW, DAD. I...IT'S SOMETHING I NEVER CARED TO LEARN. I'M SORRY.
YOU'RE NOT SORRY, SO DON'T LIE AND SAY YOU ARE. YOU DON'T CARE. NOT REALLY. NOT ABOUT DAVID'S DEATH, NOT ABOUT ANY OF THIS. I KNOW YOU, SON. TOO WELL I KNOW YOU.
YOU'RE A COWARD, JACK. YOU'RE SCARED OF THE FAMILY HERITAGE. STARMAN. THE NAME AND THE "RIDICULOUS" COSTUME.
THE DANGER THAT WENT WITH IT. MY PAST. IT SCARED YOU, DIDN'T IT?
AND NOW YOU ASK WHAT YOU CAN DO. WHY? DUTY? TO THE MEMORY OF A BROTHER YOU NEVER EVEN LIKED TO BEGIN WITH.
DAVID DOESN'T NEED YOU NOW, JACK. HE MAY HAVE NEEDED YOUR SUPPORT AT ONE TIME, WHEN ALL HE GOT WAS SNIDE REMARKS. NOW HE'S BEYOND NEEDING ANYONE'S HELP.
AND... I DON'T NEED YOU, EITHER.

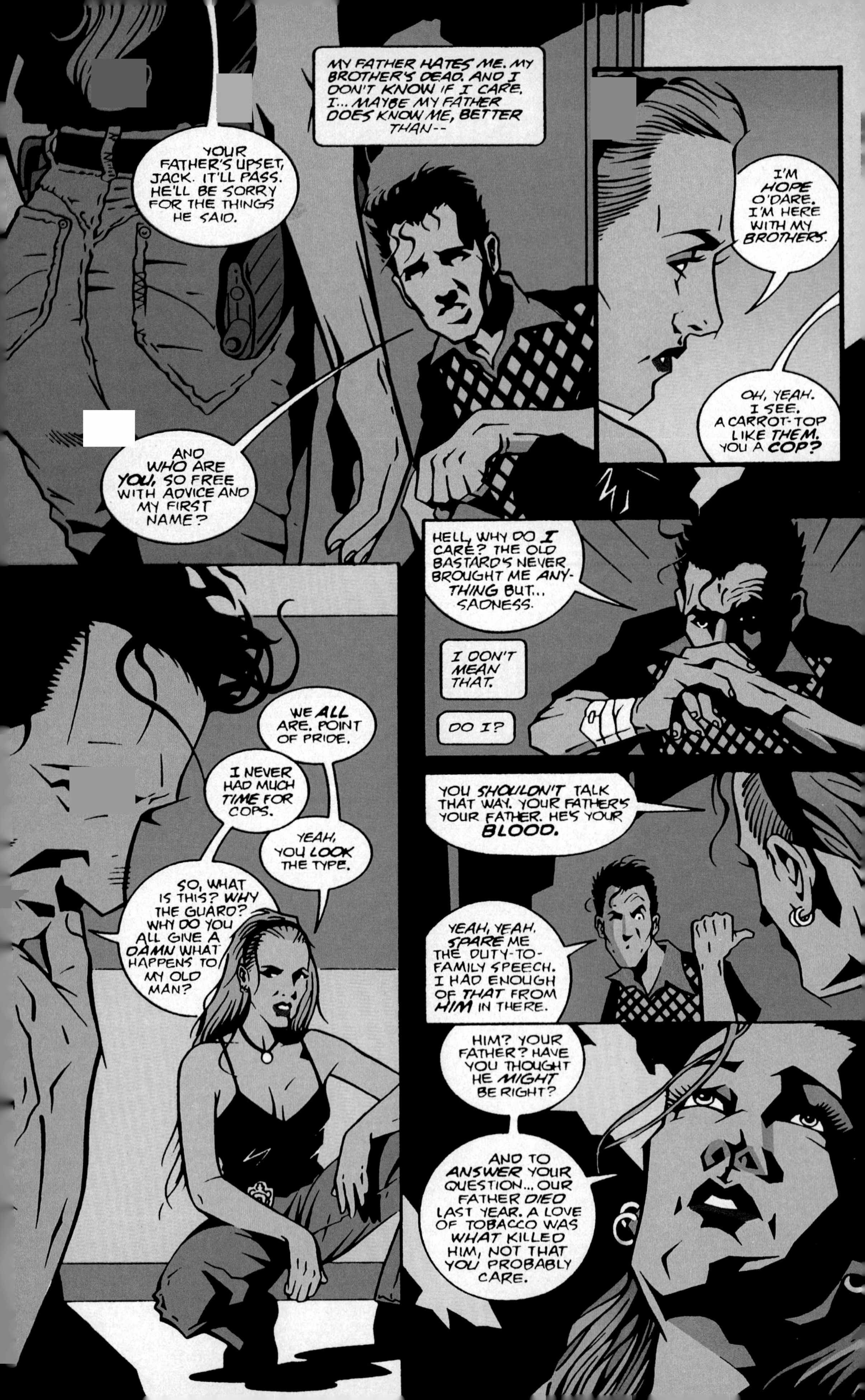
YOUR FATHER'S UPSET, JACK. IT'LL PASS. HE'LL BE SORRY FOR THE THINGS HE SAID.
MY FATHER HATES ME. MY BROTHER'S DEAD. AND I DON'T KNOW IF I CARE. I... MAYBE MY FATHER DOES KNOW ME, BETTER THAN--
AND WHO ARE YOU, SO FREE WITH ADVICE AND MY FIRST NAME?
I'M HOPE O'DARE. I'M HERE WITH MY BROTHERS.
OH, YEAH. I SEE. A CARROT-TOP LIKE THEM. YOU A COP?
WE ALL ARE. POINT OF PRIDE.
I NEVER HAD MUCH TIME FOR COPS.
YEAH, YOU LOOK THE TYPE.
SO, WHAT IS THIS? WHY THE GUARD? WHY DO YOU ALL GIVE A DAMN WHAT HAPPENS TO MY OLD MAN?
HELL, WHY DO I CARE? THE OLD BASTARD'S NEVER BROUGHT ME ANYTHING BUT... SADNESS.
I DON'T MEAN THAT.
DO I?
YOU SHOULDN'T TALK THAT WAY. YOUR FATHER'S YOUR FATHER. HE'S YOUR BLOOD.
YEAH, YEAH. SPARE ME THE DUTY-TO-FAMILY SPEECH. I HAD ENOUGH OF THAT FROM HIM IN THERE.
HIM? YOUR FATHER? HAVE YOU THOUGHT HE MIGHT BE RIGHT?
AND TO ANSWER YOUR QUESTION... OUR FATHER DIED LAST YEAR. A LOVE OF TOBACCO WAS WHAT KILLED HIM, NOT THAT YOU PROBABLY CARE.

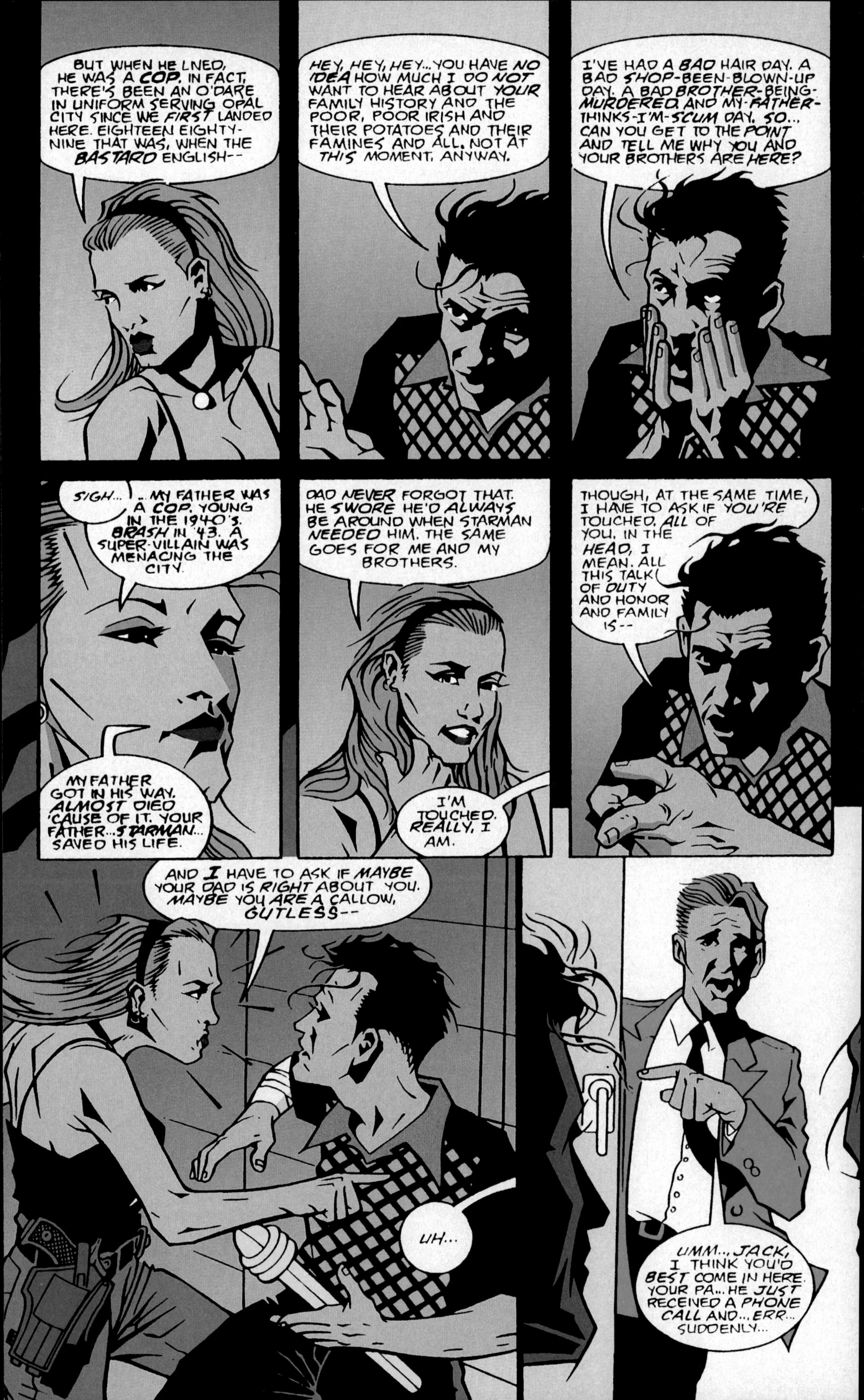
BUT WHEN HE LIVED, HE WAS A COP. IN FACT, THERE'S BEEN AN O'DARE IN UNIFORM SERVING OPAL CITY SINCE WE FIRST LANDED HERE. EIGHTEEN EIGHTY-NINE THAT WAS, WHEN THE BASTARD ENGLISH--
HEY, HEY, HEY... YOU HAVE NO IDEA HOW MUCH I DO NOT WANT TO HEAR ABOUT YOUR FAMILY HISTORY AND THE POOR, POOR IRISH AND THEIR POTATOES AND THEIR FAMINES AND ALL. NOT AT THIS MOMENT, ANYWAY.
I'VE HAD A BAD HAIR DAY. A BAD SHOP-BEEN-BLOWN-UP DAY. A BAD BROTHER-BEING-MURDERED. AND MY-FATHER-THINKS-I'M-SCUM DAY. SO... CAN YOU GET TO THE POINT AND TELL ME WHY YOU AND YOUR BROTHERS ARE HERE?
SIGH...
...MY FATHER WAS A COP, YOUNG IN THE 1940'S. BRASH IN '43. A SUPER-VILLAIN WAS MENACING THE CITY.
MY FATHER GOT IN HIS WAY. ALMOST DIED 'CAUSE OF IT. YOUR FATHER... STARMAN... SAVED HIS LIFE.
DAD NEVER FORGOT THAT. HE SWORE HE'D ALWAYS BE AROUND WHEN STARMAN NEEDED HIM. THE SAME GOES FOR ME AND MY BROTHERS.
I'M TOUCHED. REALLY, I AM.
THOUGH, AT THE SAME TIME, I HAVE TO ASK IF YOU'RE TOUCHED, ALL OF YOU. IN THE HEAD, I MEAN. ALL THIS TALK OF DUTY AND HONOR AND FAMILY IS--
AND I HAVE TO ASK IF MAYBE YOUR DAD IS RIGHT ABOUT YOU. MAYBE YOU ARE A CALLOW, GUTLESS--
UH...
UMM... JACK, I THINK YOU'D BEST COME IN HERE. YOUR PA... HE JUST RECEIVED A PHONE CALL AND... ERR... SUDDENLY...

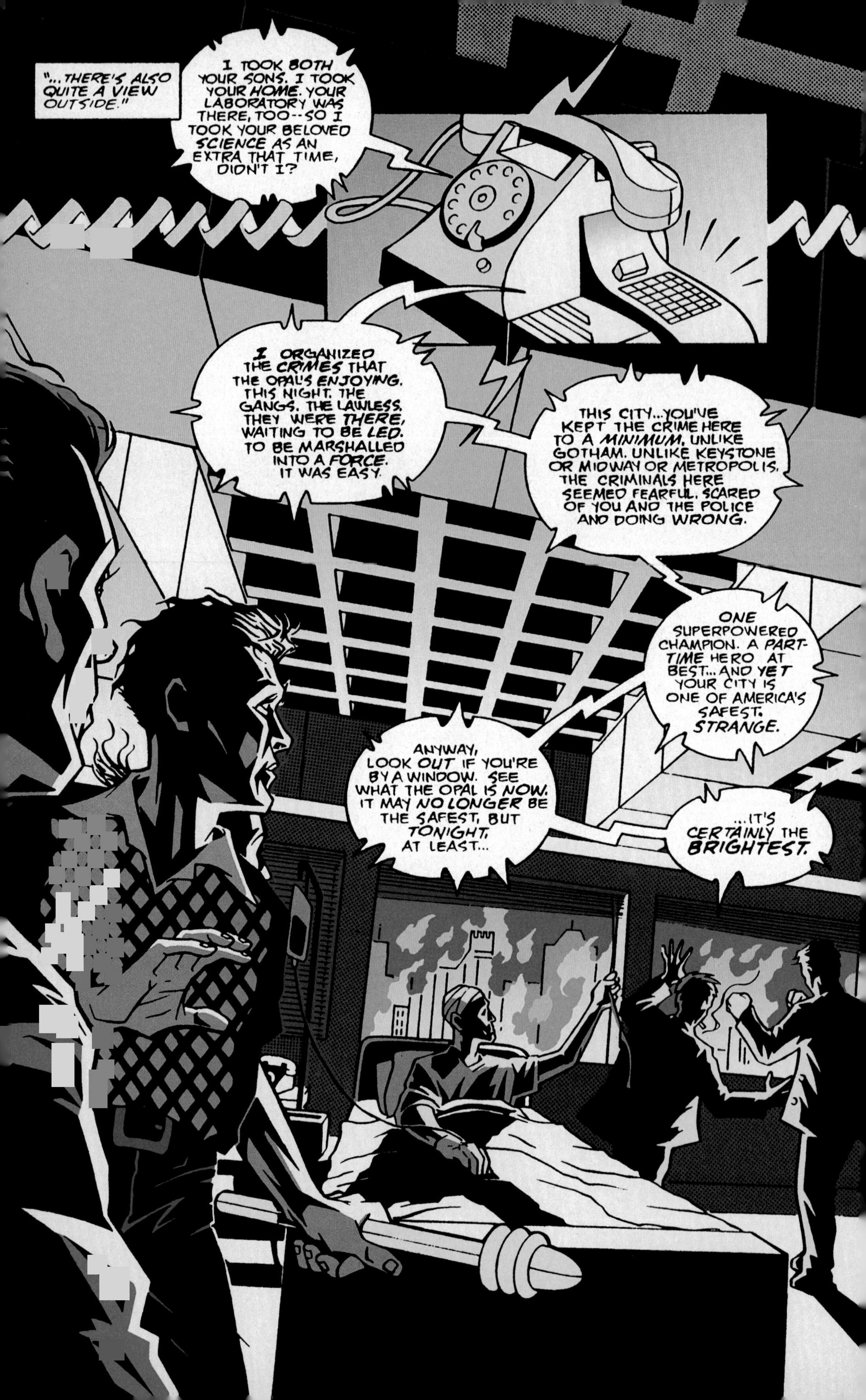
"...THERE'S ALSO QUITE A VIEW OUTSIDE."
I TOOK BOTH YOUR SONS. I TOOK YOUR HOME. YOUR LABORATORY WAS THERE, TOO--SO I TOOK YOUR BELOVED SCIENCE AS AN EXTRA THAT TIME, DIDN'T I?
I ORGANIZED THE CRIMES THAT THE OPAL'S ENJOYING. THIS NIGHT. THE GANGS. THE LAWLESS. THEY WERE THERE, WAITING TO BE LED. TO BE MARSHALLED INTO A FORCE. IT WAS EASY.
THIS CITY...YOU'VE KEPT THE CRIME HERE TO A MINIMUM, UNLIKE GOTHAM. UNLIKE KEYSTONE OR MIDWAY OR METROPOLIS. THE CRIMINALS HERE SEEMED FEARFUL. SCARED OF YOU AND THE POLICE AND DOING WRONG.
ONE SUPERPOWERED CHAMPION. A PART-TIME HERO AT BEST... AND YET YOUR CITY IS ONE OF AMERICA'S SAFEST. STRANGE.
ANYWAY, LOOK OUT IF YOU'RE BY A WINDOW. SEE WHAT THE OPAL IS NOW. IT MAY NO LONGER BE THE SAFEST, BUT TONIGHT, AT LEAST...
...IT'S CERTAINLY THE BRIGHTEST.

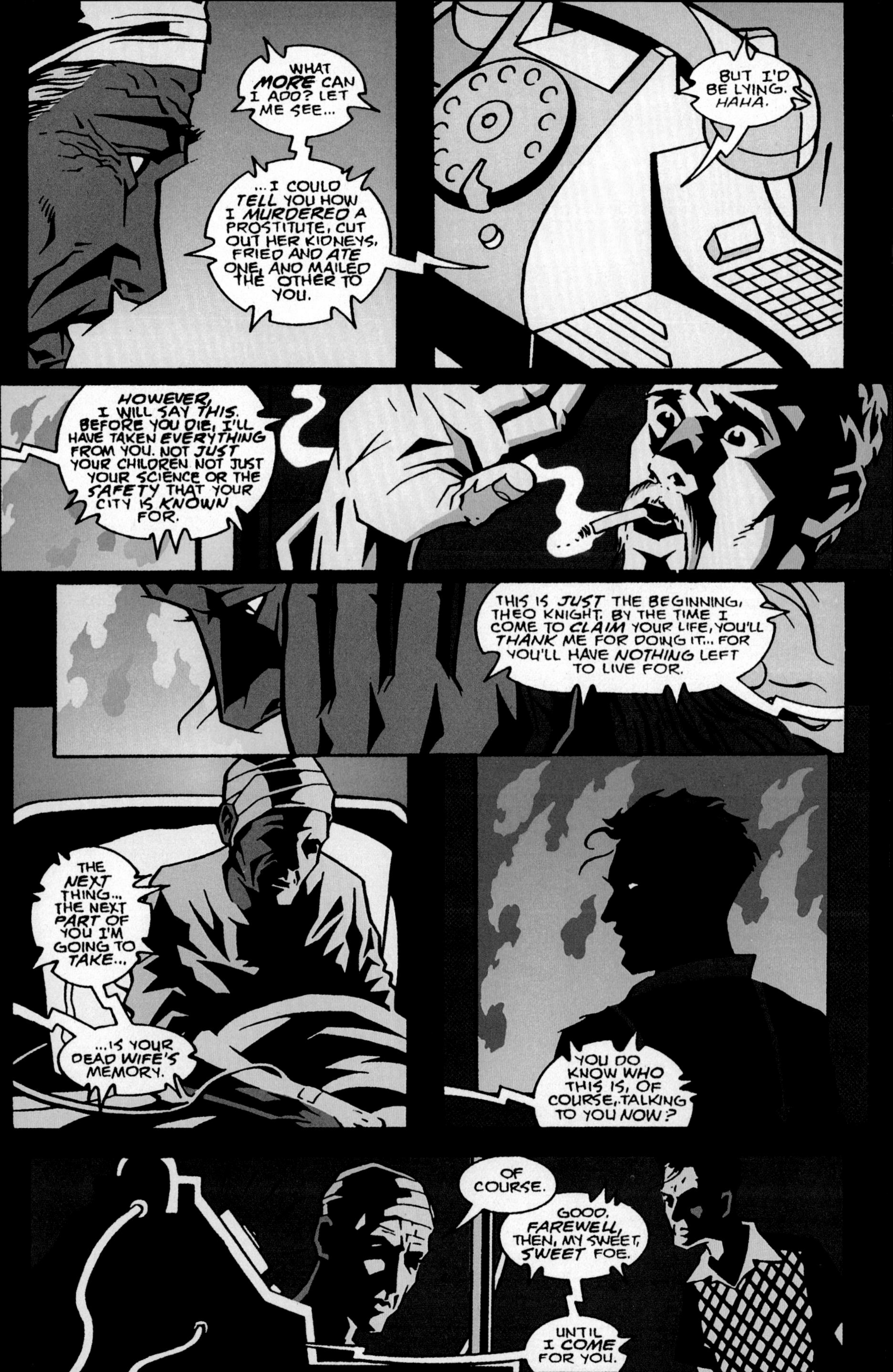
WHAT MORE CAN I ADD? LET ME SEE...
...I COULD TELL YOU HOW I MURDERED A PROSTITUTE, CUT OUT HER KIDNEYS, FRIED AND ATE ONE, AND MAILED THE OTHER TO YOU.
BUT I'D BE LYING. HAHA.
HOWEVER, I WILL SAY THIS. BEFORE YOU DIE, I'LL HAVE TAKEN EVERYTHING FROM YOU. NOT JUST YOUR CHILDREN. NOT JUST YOUR SCIENCE OR THE SAFETY THAT YOUR CITY IS KNOWN FOR.
THIS IS JUST THE BEGINNING, THEO KNIGHT. BY THE TIME I COME TO CLAIM YOUR LIFE, YOU'LL THANK ME FOR DOING IT... FOR YOU'LL HAVE NOTHING LEFT TO LIVE FOR.
THE NEXT THING... THE NEXT PART OF YOU I'M GOING TO TAKE...
...IS YOUR DEAD WIFE'S MEMORY.
YOU DO KNOW WHO THIS IS, OF COURSE, TALKING TO YOU NOW?
OF COURSE.
GOOD. FAREWELL, THEN, MY SWEET, SWEET FOE.
UNTIL I COME FOR YOU.

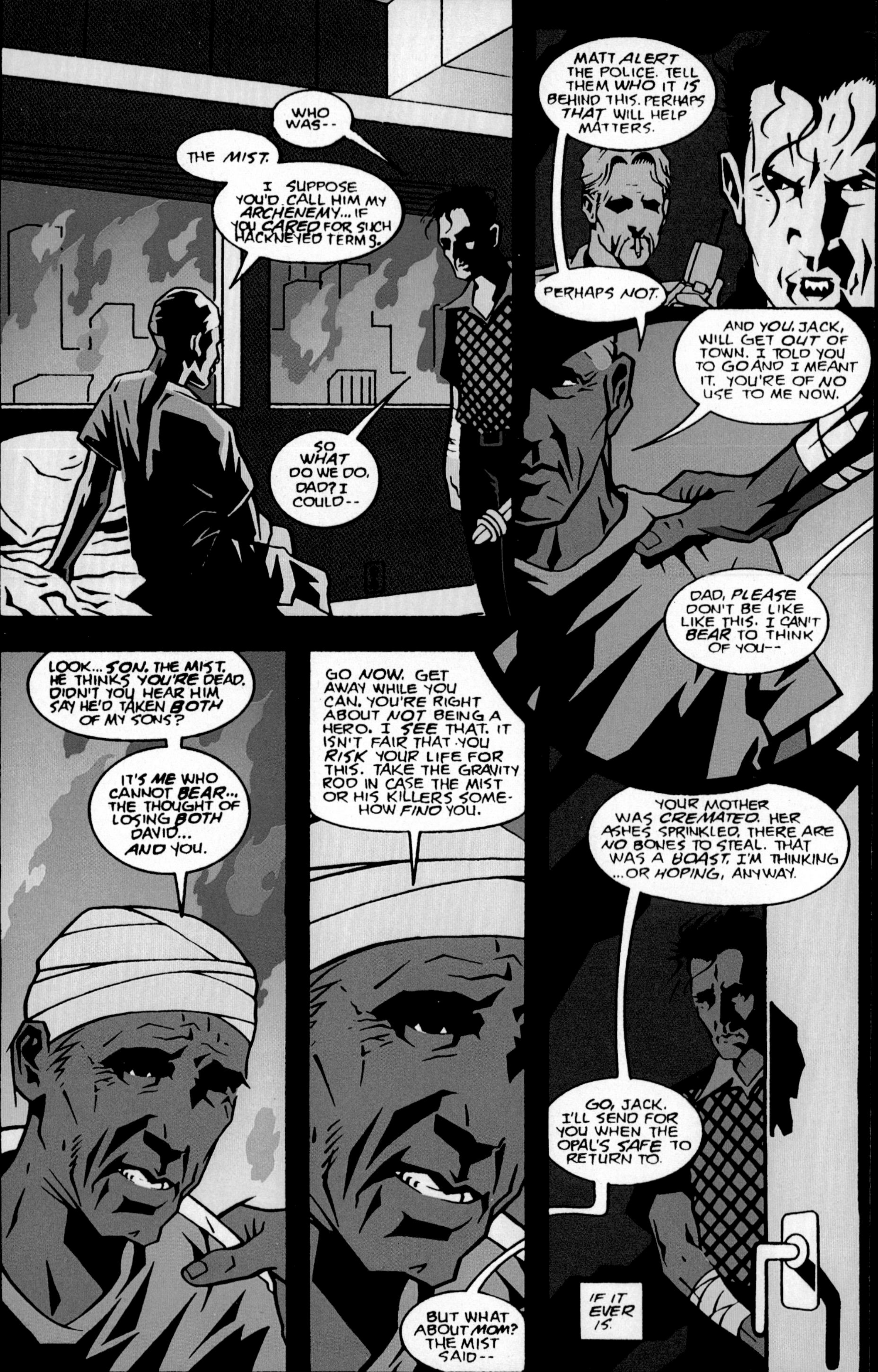
WHO WAS--
THE MIST.
I SUPPOSE YOU'D CALL HIM MY ARCHENEMY... IF YOU CARED FOR SUCH HACKNEYED TERMS.
SO WHAT DO WE DO, DAD? I COULD--
MATT ALERT THE POLICE. TELL THEM WHO IT IS BEHIND THIS. PERHAPS THAT WILL HELP MATTERS.
PERHAPS NOT.
AND YOU, JACK, WILL GET OUT OF TOWN. I TOLD YOU TO GO AND I MEANT IT. YOU'RE OF NO USE TO ME NOW.
DAD, PLEASE DON'T BE LIKE LIKE THIS. I CAN'T BEAR TO THINK OF YOU--
LOOK... SON. THE MIST. HE THINKS YOU'RE DEAD. DIDN'T YOU HEAR HIM SAY HE'D TAKEN BOTH OF MY SONS?
IT'S ME WHO CANNOT BEAR... THE THOUGHT OF LOSING BOTH DAVID... AND YOU.
GO NOW. GET AWAY WHILE YOU CAN. YOU'RE RIGHT ABOUT NOT BEING A HERO. I SEE THAT. IT ISN'T FAIR THAT YOU RISK YOUR LIFE FOR THIS. TAKE THE GRAVITY ROD IN CASE THE MIST OR HIS KILLERS SOMEHOW FIND YOU.
BUT WHAT ABOUT MOM? THE MIST SAID--
YOUR MOTHER WAS CREMATED. HER ASHES SPRINKLED. THERE ARE NO BONES TO STEAL. THAT WAS A BOAST, I'M THINKING ...OR HOPING, ANYWAY.
GO, JACK. I'LL SEND FOR YOU WHEN THE OPAL'S SAFE TO RETURN TO.
IF IT EVER IS.

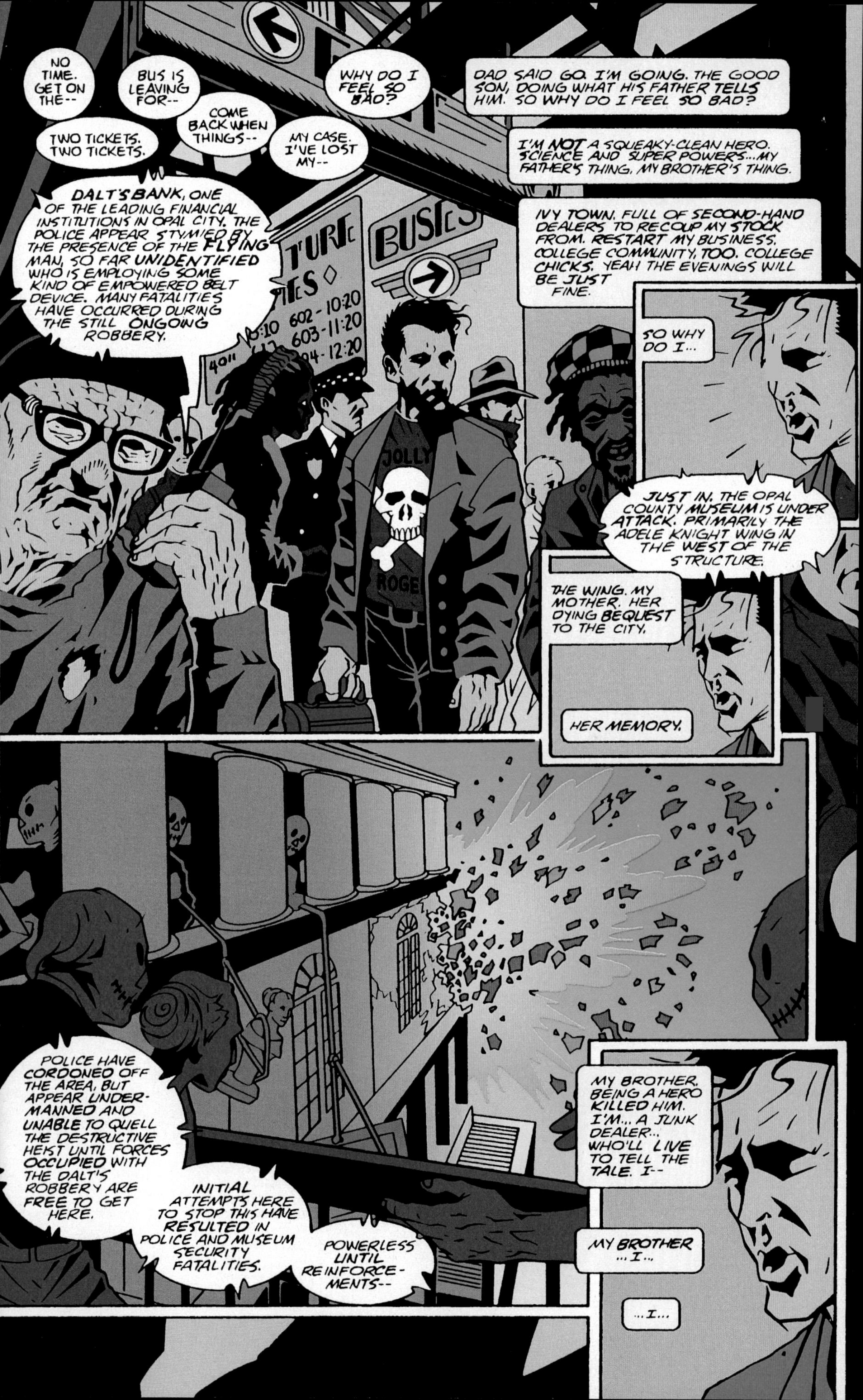
NO TIME. GET ON THE--
BUS IS LEAVING FOR--
COME BACK WHEN THINGS--
TWO TICKETS. TWO TICKETS.
WHY DO I FEEL SO BAD?
MY CASE. I'VE LOST MY--
DAD SAID GO. I'M GOING. THE GOOD SON, DOING WHAT HIS FATHER TELLS HIM. SO WHY DO I FEEL SO BAD?
I'M NOT A SQUEAKY-CLEAN HERO. SCIENCE AND SUPER POWERS...MY FATHER'S THING. MY BROTHER'S THING.
DALT'S BANK, ONE OF THE LEADING FINANCIAL INSTITUTIONS IN OPAL CITY. THE POLICE APPEAR STYMIED BY THE PRESENCE OF THE FLYING MAN, SO FAR UNIDENTIFIED WHO IS EMPLOYING SOME KIND OF EMPOWERED BELT DEVICE. MANY FATALITIES HAVE OCCURRED DURING THE STILL ONGOING ROBBERY.
IVY TOWN. FULL OF SECOND-HAND DEALERS TO RECOUP MY STOCK FROM. RESTART MY BUSINESS. COLLEGE COMMUNITY, TOO. COLLEGE CHICKS. YEAH THE EVENINGS WILL BE JUST FINE.
BUSES
602-10:20
603-11:20
SO WHY DO I...
JUST IN. THE OPAL COUNTY MUSEUM IS UNDER ATTACK. PRIMARILY THE ADELE KNIGHT WING IN THE WEST OF THE STRUCTURE.
THE WING. MY MOTHER. HER DYING BEQUEST TO THE CITY.
HER MEMORY.
POLICE HAVE CORDONED OFF THE AREA, BUT APPEAR UNDER-MANNED AND UNABLE TO QUELL THE DESTRUCTIVE HEIST UNTIL FORCES OCCUPIED WITH THE DALT'S ROBBERY ARE FREE TO GET HERE.
INITIAL ATTEMPTS HERE TO STOP THIS HAVE RESULTED IN POLICE AND MUSEUM SECURITY FATALITIES.
POWERLESS UNTIL REINFORCE-MENTS--
MY BROTHER. BEING A HERO KILLED HIM. I'M... A JUNK DEALER... WHO'LL LIVE TO TELL THE TALE. I--
MY BROTHER ...I...
...I...

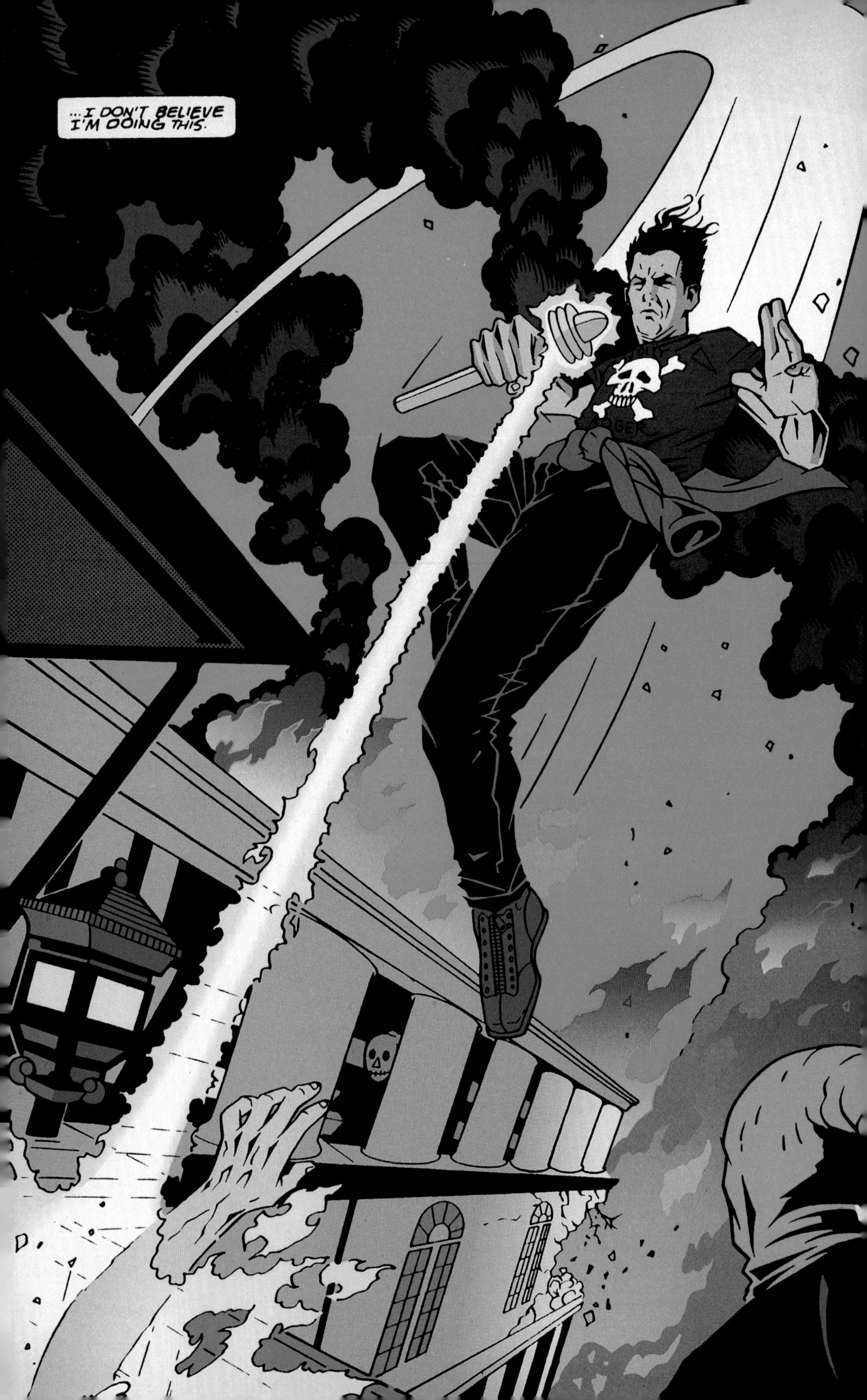
...I DON'T BELIEVE I'M DOING THIS.

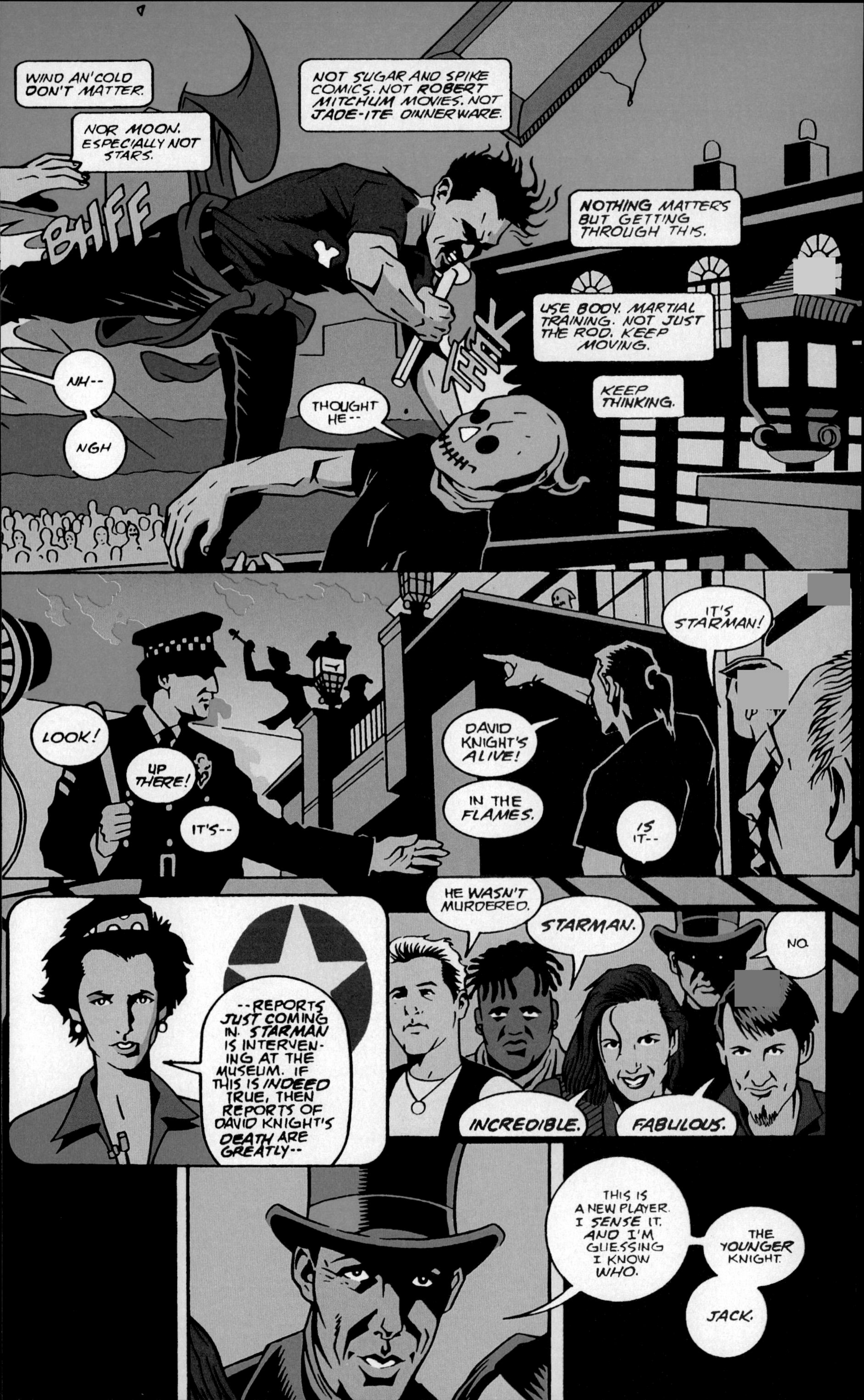
WIND AN' COLD DON'T MATTER.
NOR MOON. ESPECIALLY NOT STARS.
NOT SUGAR AND SPIKE COMICS. NOT ROBERT MITCHUM MOVIES. NOT JADE-ITE DINNERWARE.
BHFF
NOTHING MATTERS BUT GETTING THROUGH THIS.
USE BODY. MARTIAL TRAINING. NOT JUST THE ROD. KEEP MOVING.
THAK
KEEP THINKING.
NH--
NGH
THOUGHT HE--
LOOK!
UP THERE!
IT'S--
DAVID KNIGHT'S ALIVE!
IN THE FLAMES.
IS IT--
IT'S STARMAN!
--REPORTS JUST COMING IN. STARMAN IS INTERVENING AT THE MUSEUM. IF THIS IS INDEED TRUE, THEN REPORTS OF DAVID KNIGHT'S DEATH ARE GREATLY--
HE WASN'T MURDERED.
STARMAN.
NO.
INCREDIBLE.
FABULOUS.
THIS IS A NEW PLAYER. I SENSE IT. AND I'M GUESSING I KNOW WHO.
THE YOUNGER KNIGHT.
JACK.

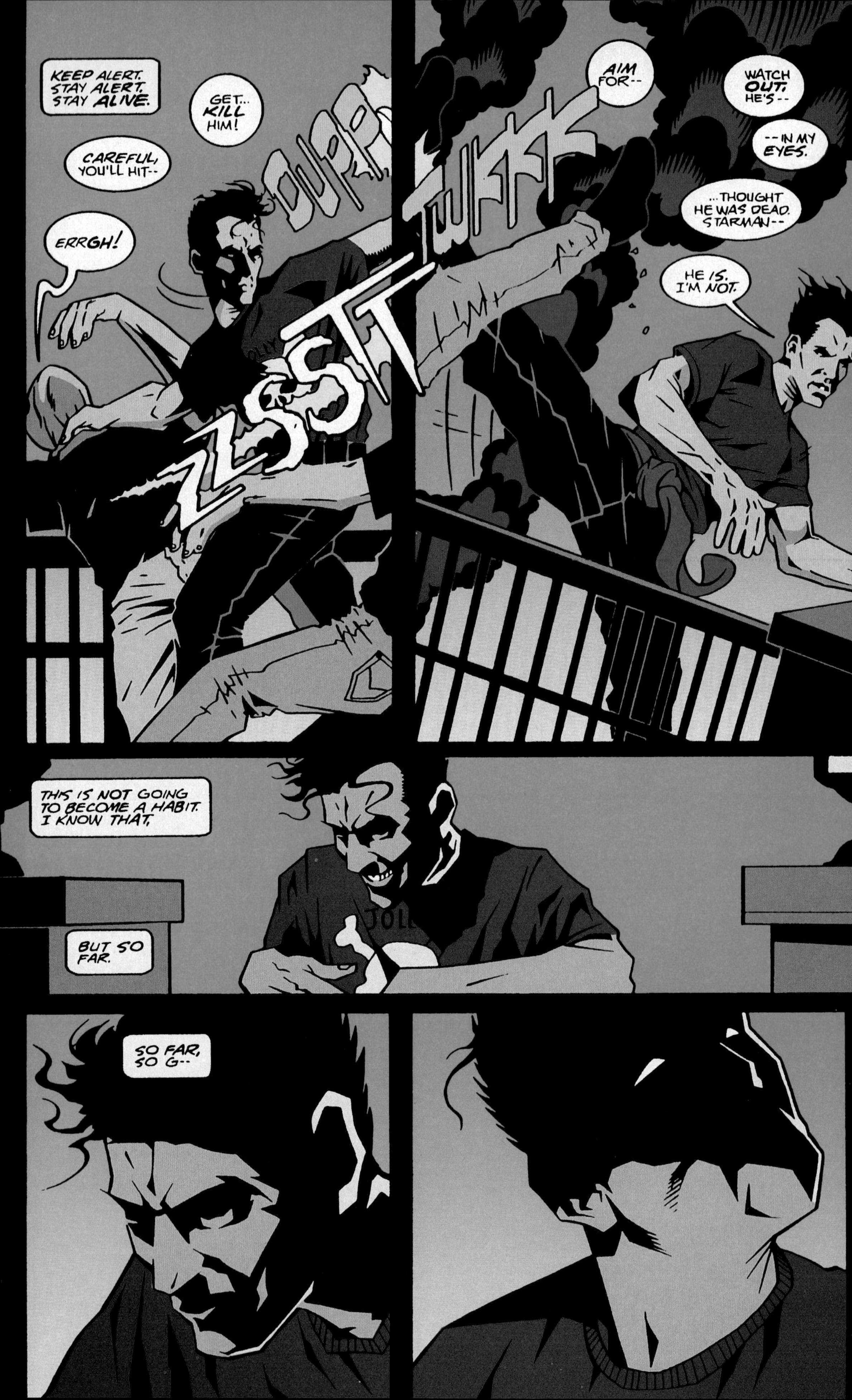
KEEP ALERT. STAY ALERT. STAY ALIVE.
GET... KILL HIM!
CAREFUL, YOU'LL HIT--
DUPP
ERRGH!
ZZSSTT
TWFFF
AIM FOR--
WATCH OUT, HE'S--
--IN MY EYES.
...THOUGHT HE WAS DEAD. STARMAN--
HE IS. I'M NOT.
THIS IS NOT GOING TO BECOME A HABIT. I KNOW THAT.
BUT SO FAR.
SO FAR, SO G--

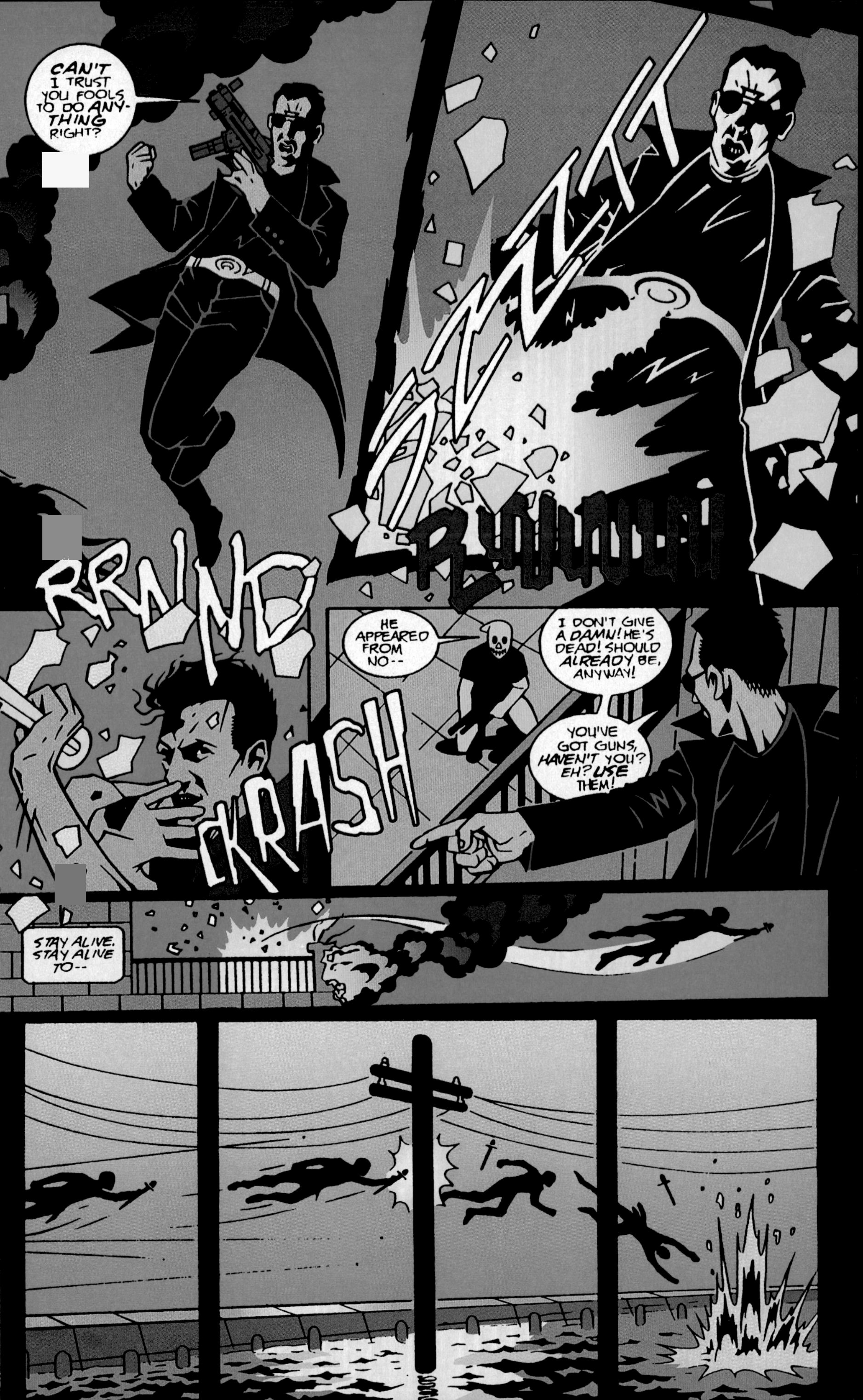

CAN'T I TRUST YOU FOOLS TO DO ANYTHING RIGHT?
HE APPEARED FROM NO--
I DON'T GIVE A DAMN! HE'S DEAD! SHOULD ALREADY BE, ANYWAY!
YOU'VE GOT GUNS, HAVEN'T YOU? EH? USE THEM!
CKRASH
STAY ALIVE. STAY ALIVE TO--

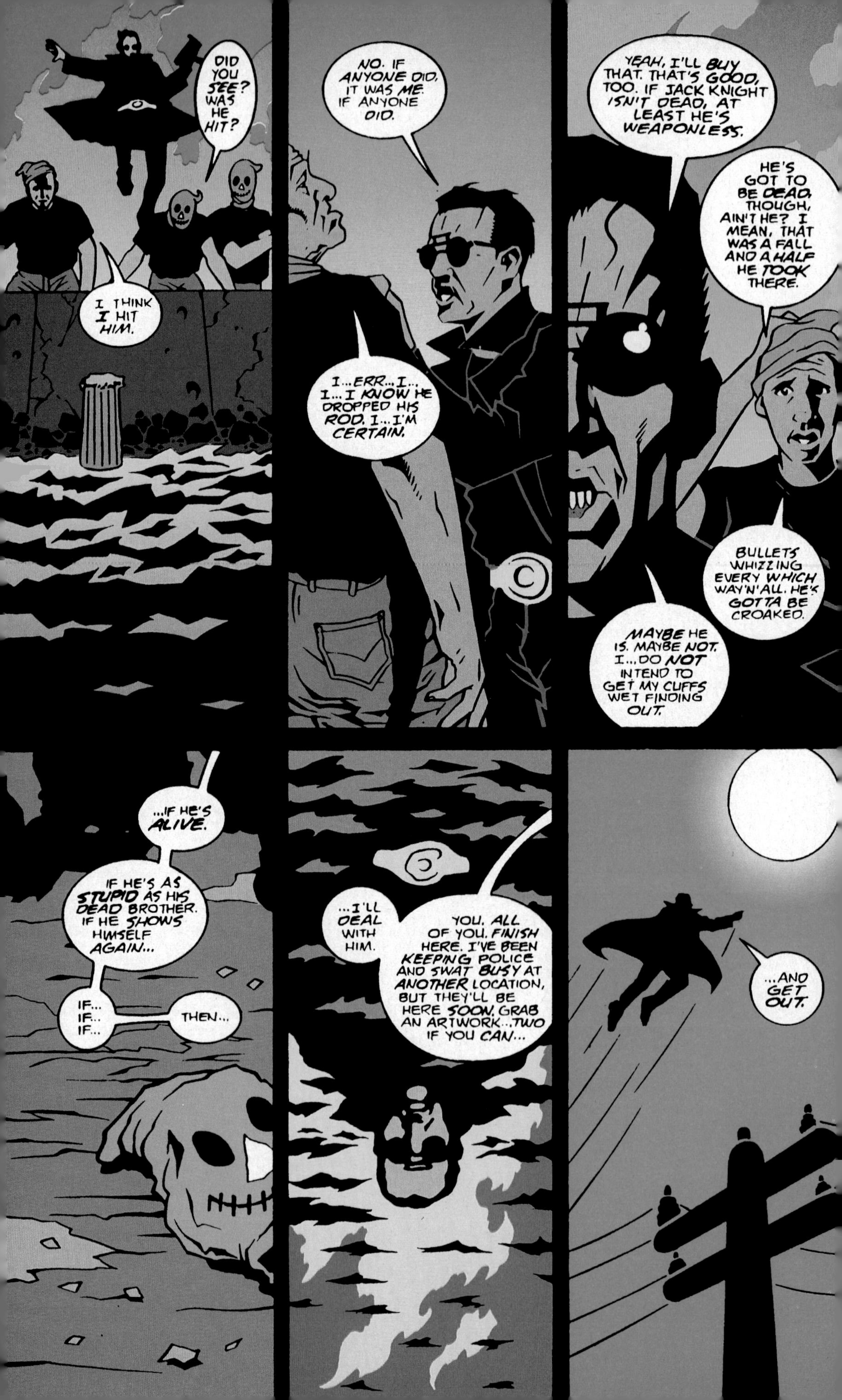
DID YOU SEE? WAS HE HIT?
I THINK I HIT HIM.
NO. IF ANYONE DID, IT WAS ME. IF ANYONE DID.
I...ERR...I... I...I KNOW HE DROPPED HIS ROD. I...I'M CERTAIN.
YEAH, I'LL BUY THAT. THAT'S GOOD, TOO. IF JACK KNIGHT ISN'T DEAD, AT LEAST HE'S WEAPONLESS.
HE'S GOT TO BE DEAD, THOUGH, AIN'T HE? I MEAN, THAT WAS A FALL AND A HALF HE TOOK THERE.
BULLETS WHIZZING EVERY WHICH WAY'N'ALL. HE'S GOTTA BE CROAKED.
MAYBE HE IS. MAYBE NOT. I...DO NOT INTEND TO GET MY CUFFS WET FINDING OUT.
...IF HE'S ALIVE.
IF HE'S AS STUPID AS HIS DEAD BROTHER. IF HE SHOWS HIMSELF AGAIN...
IF... IF... IF...
THEN...
...I'LL DEAL WITH HIM.
YOU. ALL OF YOU. FINISH HERE. I'VE BEEN KEEPING POLICE AND SWAT BUSY AT ANOTHER LOCATION, BUT THEY'LL BE HERE SOON. GRAB AN ARTWORK...TWO IF YOU CAN...
...AND GET OUT.

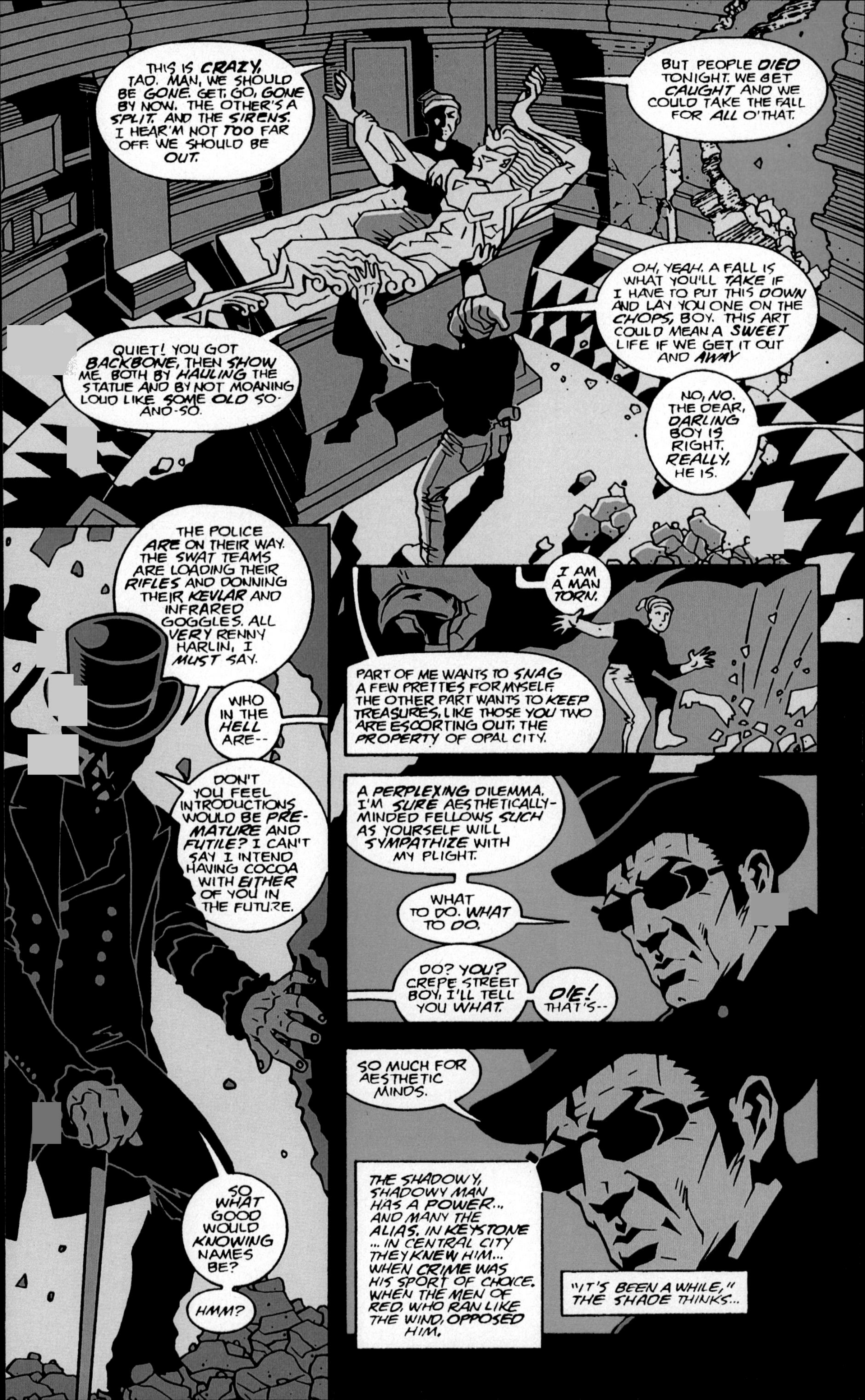
THIS IS CRAZY, TAO. MAN, WE SHOULD BE GONE. GET, GO, GONE BY NOW. THE OTHER'S A SPLIT, AND THE SIRENS. I HEAR'M NOT TOO FAR OFF. WE SHOULD BE OUT.
BUT PEOPLE DIED TONIGHT. WE GET CAUGHT AND WE COULD TAKE THE FALL FOR ALL O'THAT.
QUIET! YOU GOT BACKBONE, THEN SHOW ME. BOTH BY HAULING THE STATUE AND BY NOT MOANING LOUD LIKE SOME OLD SO-AND-SO.
OH, YEAH. A FALL IS WHAT YOU'LL TAKE IF I HAVE TO PUT THIS DOWN AND LAY YOU ONE ON THE CHOPS, BOY. THIS ART COULD MEAN A SWEET LIFE IF WE GET IT OUT AND AWAY.
NO, NO. THE DEAR, DARLING BOY IS RIGHT. REALLY, HE IS.
THE POLICE ARE ON THEIR WAY. THE SWAT TEAMS ARE LOADING THEIR RIFLES AND DONNING THEIR KEVLAR AND INFRARED GOGGLES. ALL VERY RENNY HARLIN, I MUST SAY.
WHO IN THE HELL ARE--
DON'T YOU FEEL INTRODUCTIONS WOULD BE PREMATURE AND FUTILE? I CAN'T SAY I INTEND HAVING COCOA WITH EITHER OF YOU IN THE FUTURE.
SO WHAT GOOD WOULD KNOWING NAMES BE?
HMM?
I AM A MAN TORN.
PART OF ME WANTS TO SNAG A FEW PRETTIES FOR MYSELF. THE OTHER PART WANTS TO KEEP TREASURES, LIKE THOSE YOU TWO ARE ESCORTING OUT, THE PROPERTY OF OPAL CITY.
A PERPLEXING DILEMMA. I'M SURE AESTHETICALLY-MINDED FELLOWS SUCH AS YOURSELF WILL SYMPATHIZE WITH MY PLIGHT.
WHAT TO DO. WHAT TO DO.
DO? YOU? CREPE STREET BOY, I'LL TELL YOU WHAT.
DIE! THAT'S--
SO MUCH FOR AESTHETIC MINDS.
THE SHADOWY, SHADOWY MAN HAS A POWER... AND MANY THE ALIAS. IN KEYSTONE ... IN CENTRAL CITY THEY KNEW HIM... WHEN CRIME WAS HIS SPORT OF CHOICE. WHEN THE MEN OF RED, WHO RAN LIKE THE WIND, OPPOSED HIM.
"IT'S BEEN A WHILE," THE SHADE THINKS...

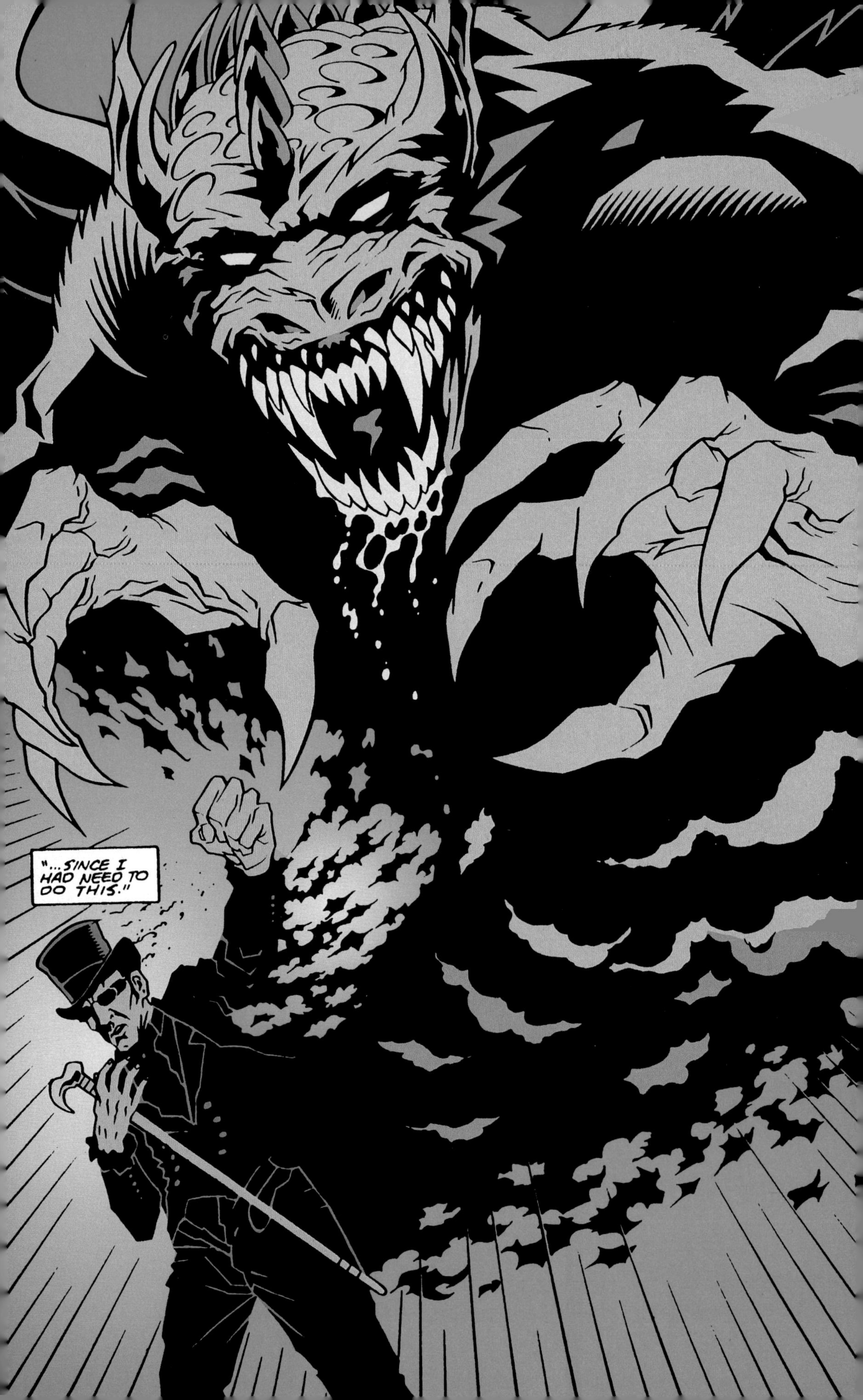
"...SINCE I HAD NEED TO DO THIS."

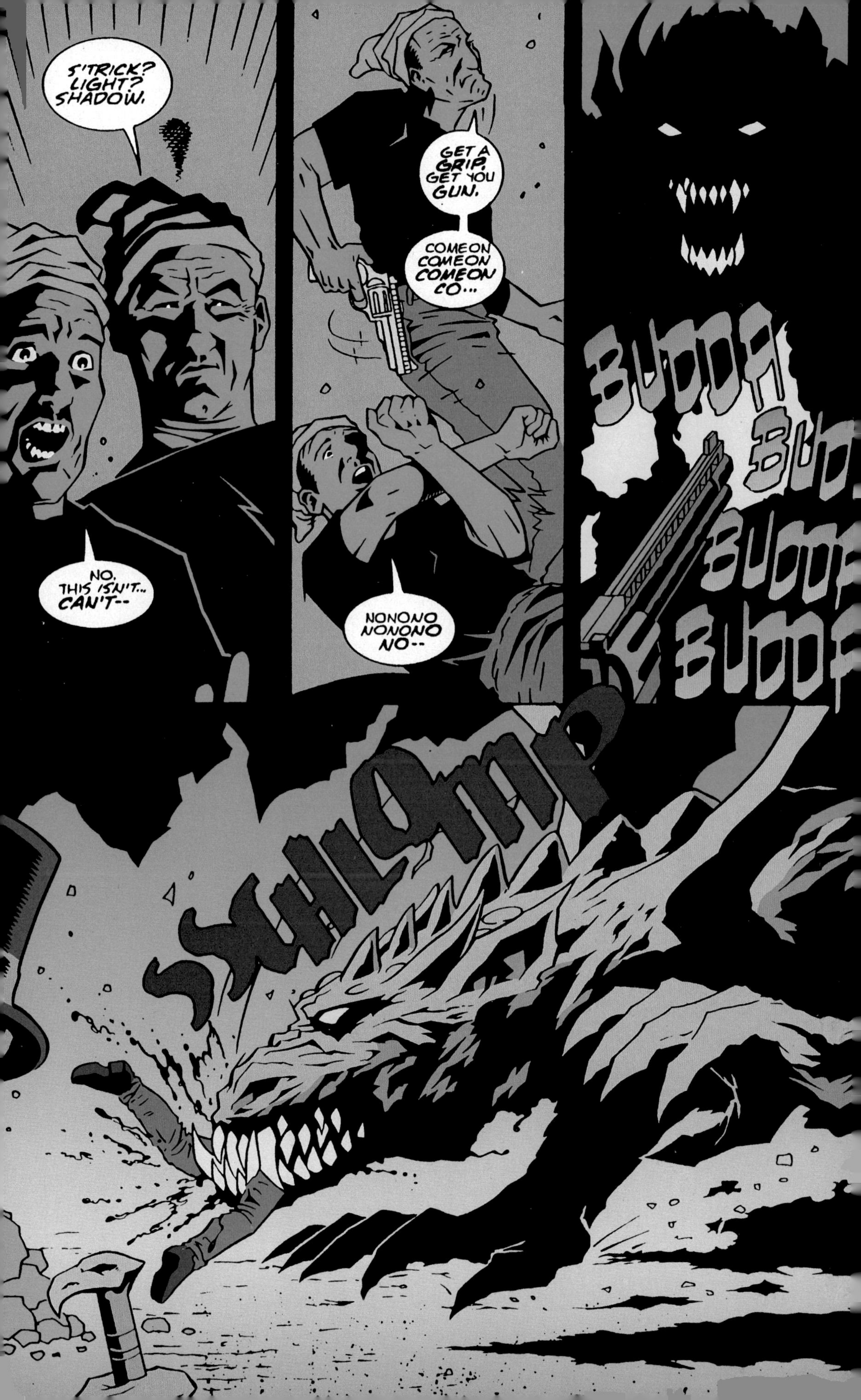
S'TRICK? LIGHT? SHADOW.
NO. THIS ISN'T... CAN'T--
GET A GRIP. GET YOU GUN.
COMEON COMEON COMEON CO...
NONONO NONONO NO--
BUDDA

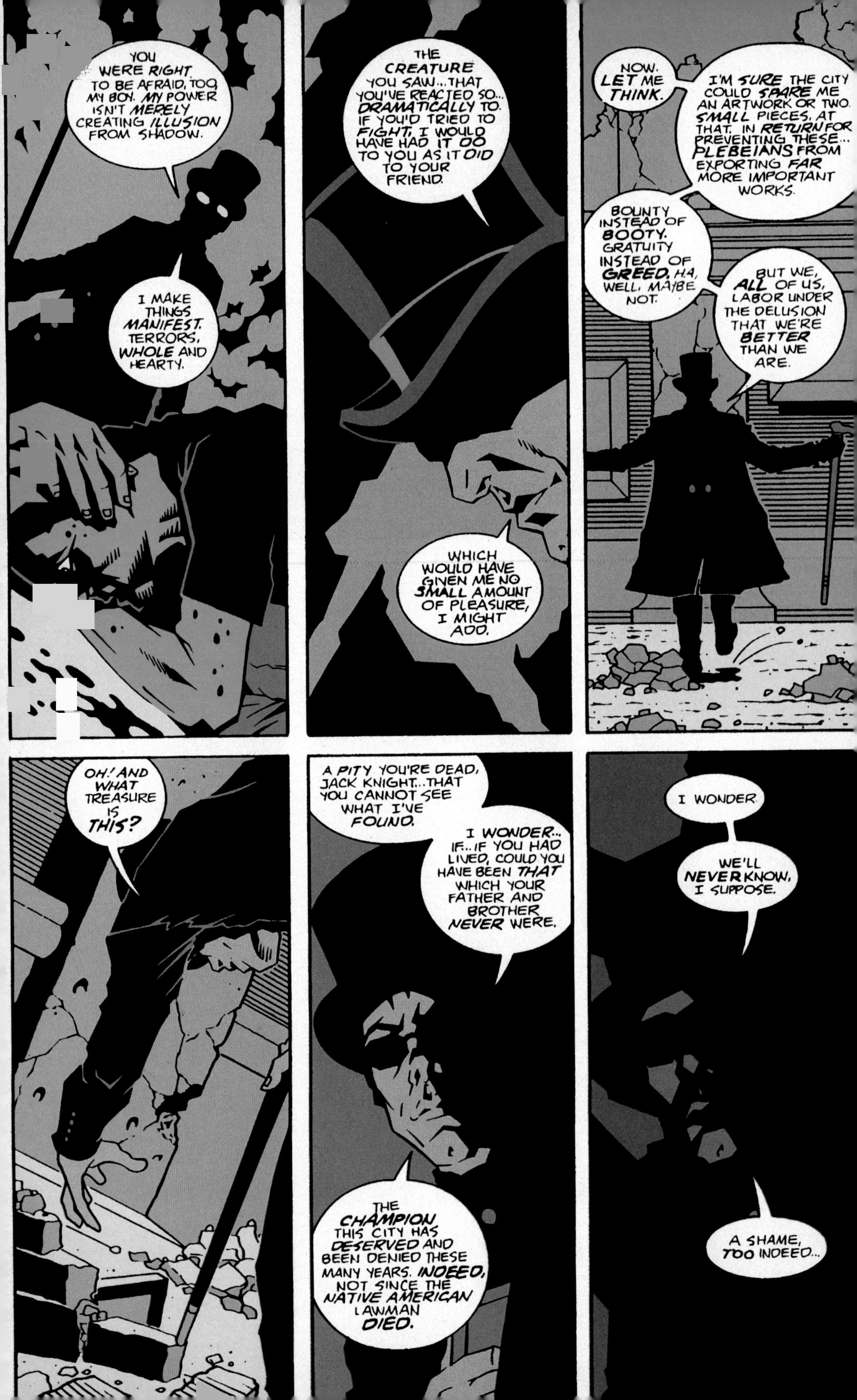
YOU WERE RIGHT TO BE AFRAID, TOO, MY BOY. MY POWER ISN'T MERELY CREATING ILLUSION FROM SHADOW.
I MAKE THINGS MANIFEST. TERRORS, WHOLE AND HEARTY.
THE CREATURE YOU SAW... THAT YOU'VE REACTED SO... DRAMATICALLY TO. IF YOU'D TRIED TO FIGHT, I WOULD HAVE HAD IT DO TO YOU AS IT DID TO YOUR FRIEND.
WHICH WOULD HAVE GIVEN ME NO SMALL AMOUNT OF PLEASURE, I MIGHT ADD.
NOW. LET ME THINK.
I'M SURE THE CITY COULD SPARE ME AN ARTWORK OR TWO. SMALL PIECES, AT THAT. IN RETURN FOR PREVENTING THESE... PLEBEIANS FROM EXPORTING FAR MORE IMPORTANT WORKS.
BOUNTY INSTEAD OF BOOTY. GRATUITY INSTEAD OF GREED. HA, WELL, MAYBE NOT.
BUT WE, ALL OF US, LABOR UNDER THE DELUSION THAT WE'RE BETTER THAN WE ARE.
OH! AND WHAT TREASURE IS THIS?
A PITY YOU'RE DEAD, JACK KNIGHT... THAT YOU CANNOT SEE WHAT I'VE FOUND.
I WONDER... IF... IF YOU HAD LIVED, COULD YOU HAVE BEEN THAT WHICH YOUR FATHER AND BROTHER NEVER WERE.
THE CHAMPION THIS CITY HAS DESERVED AND BEEN DENIED THESE MANY YEARS. INDEED, NOT SINCE THE NATIVE AMERICAN LAWMAN DIED.
I WONDER.
WE'LL NEVER KNOW, I SUPPOSE.
A SHAME, TOO INDEED...

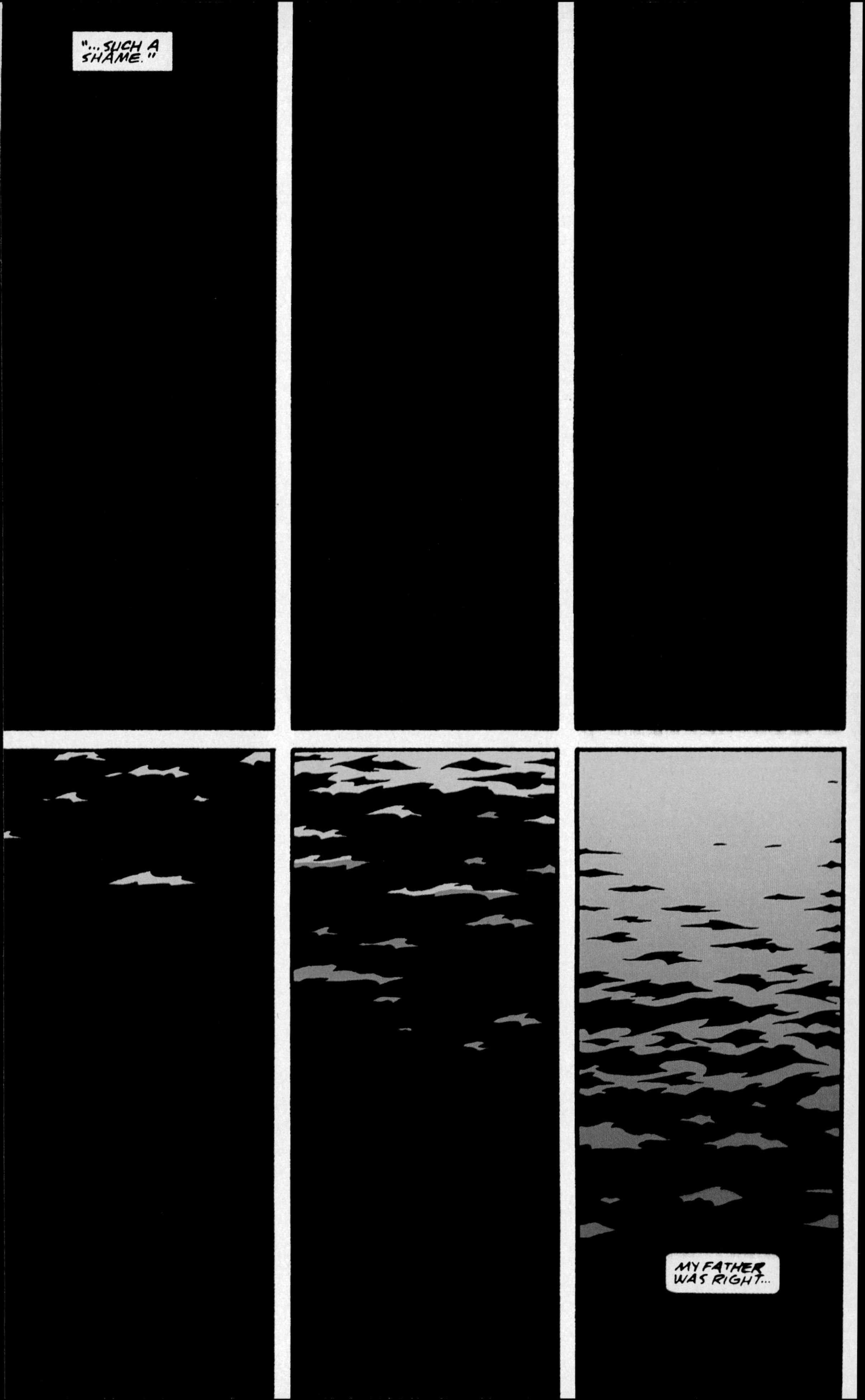
"...SUCH A SHAME."
MY FATHER WAS RIGHT...

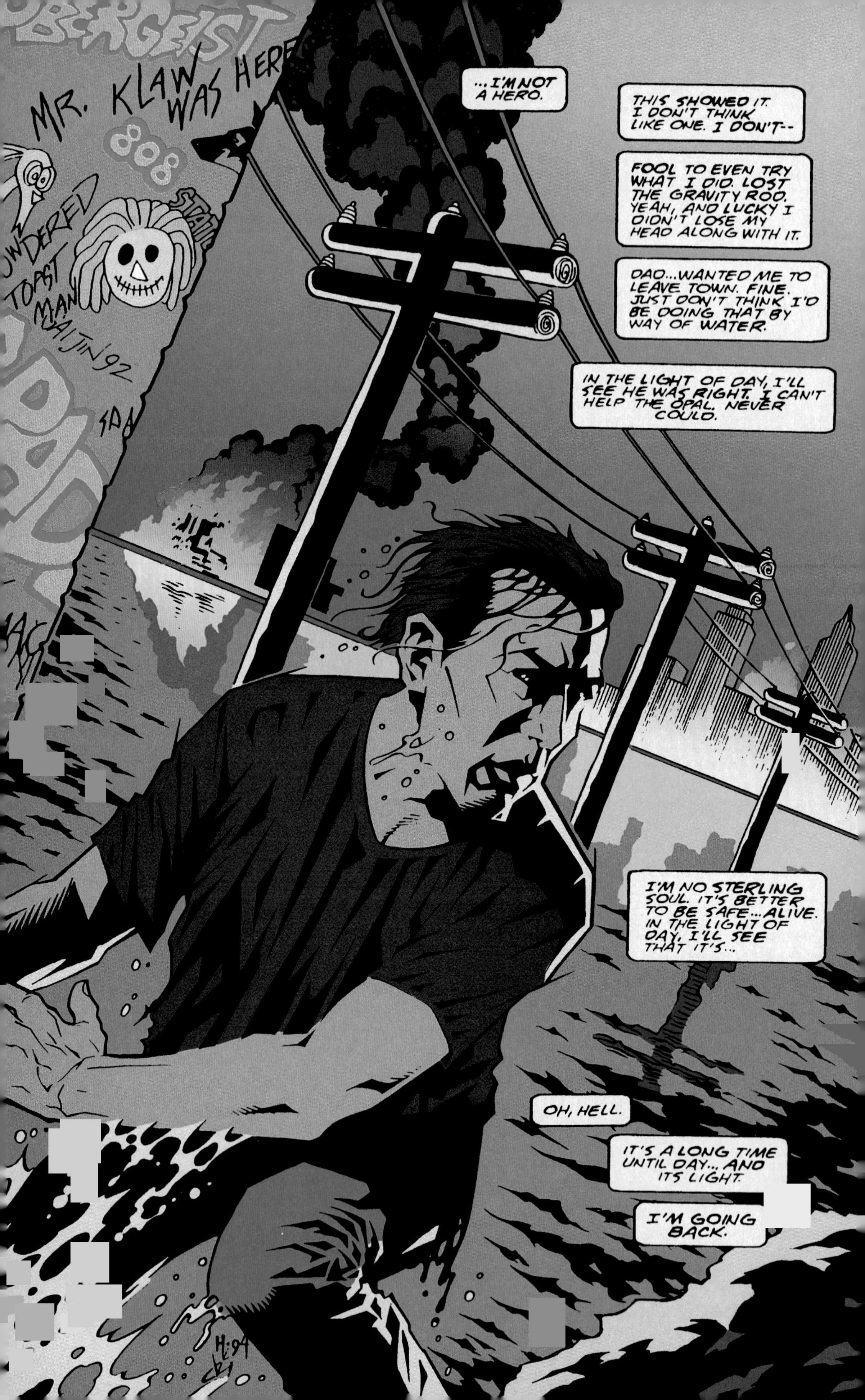
MR. KLAW WAS HERE
...I'M NOT A HERO.
THIS SHOWED IT. I DON'T THINK LIKE ONE. I DON'T--
FOOL TO EVEN TRY WHAT I DID. LOST THE GRAVITY ROD. YEAH, AND LUCKY I DIDN'T LOSE MY HEAD ALONG WITH IT.
DAD...WANTED ME TO LEAVE TOWN. FINE. JUST DON'T THINK I'D BE DOING THAT BY WAY OF WATER.
IN THE LIGHT OF DAY, I'LL SEE HE WAS RIGHT. I CAN'T HELP THE OPAL. NEVER COULD.
I'M NO STERLING SOUL. IT'S BETTER TO BE SAFE...ALIVE. IN THE LIGHT OF DAY, I'LL SEE THAT IT'S...
OH, HELL.
IT'S A LONG TIME UNTIL DAY... AND ITS LIGHT.
I'M GOING BACK.

THE FOLLOWING TEXT APPEARED IN THE LETTER COLUMN PAGES OF STARMAN #1

Hello again.

This one really is down to the wire. I got the call yesterday telling me that this piece was needed pronto. So here I am writing, yet not really certain what I'm writing about or where this is going or any of that. Hell, some writers win Pulitzers doing the same. Let's see where we end up, shall we?

This whole thing will become much easier when you start sending in letters. Then the onus is on you to think of something cool. Me, I just have to read your thoughts, and answer with witty/sage/inane snippets. Money for jam. So hurry up and get the answers in. Not necessarily about the comic either, as I said last month. Whatever comes to mind. If you want to impart thoughts on collectibles and the wonder of old things, definitely drop in a line.

What do I collect? I guess I'll tell you now, so you'll know when I decide to have Jack Knight wax lyrical about one of these subjects in the issues to come.

First, I have to say that I don't really collect comics to the degree I did, say, ten years ago. I read them...some of them, sure, but I'm not a manic collector in the way I was in my teen years. If there's one artist's work I look out for, it's probably Alex Toth. I still buy his books when they pass my way. I'll always love his work. And there are modern creators whose work I follow: Miller, Gaiman, Mignola, Allred, Jeff Smith, Stan Sakai — you know, the same old codgers everyone enjoys. But that isn't really collecting, is it? Buying the latest issue of something is no more a challenge than buying the Sunday paper. At least as far as I'm concerned.

I think there lies the root of my feeling about collecting anything...it's not the same unless the collecting involves some small degree of hunting too. There is nothing quite like getting the dust of a second-hand store under your fingers as you search for things. Or the thrill of the find — ahh, so sweet.

My big interest is View-Masters. I love them. I'm especially interested in the old clay figure children's tales, but I collect and enjoy all the other kinds too. Travel packets. Television shows. Special interest obscure stuff. You name it. I'm always looking out for packets I don't have or earlier versions of packets I already own. View-Masters are my passion.

My wife and I collect Heywood Wakefield furniture. This is blond wood, with 1950s lines. Minimal and yet elegant. It costs a lot, but a home full of the stuff looks amazing.

I also love VW Karmann Ghias. I had one for a few years. Got rid of it and immediately regretted it. At the moment, I'm driving a '65 Barracuda, but I'm buying another Ghia as soon as I find one that's the right year and model that I'm looking for.

Now, it never ceases to amaze me, the bizarre extent of the things people collect. Everybody has no doubt heard about barbed wire collectors and laughed at the strangeness of it. But think about it for a moment...the first brave lonely soul who decided that he'd gather different pieces of barbed wire. And then others joined him, and before you knew it, they were holding barbed wire conventions. That is absolutely wild. Even I, lover of old things that I am, am astounded by the concept. But at the same time, that's what I find incredibly romantic and heroic about collecting. Daring to announce your interests, no matter how lame they seem to the general public.

Or maybe I'm wrong. Maybe it's the compulsive obsessive tendencies of a seriously damaged individual. What do you think? How healthy is it to obsess about things past?

I think that to a degree, we follow the dictates of a society governing what is acceptable and what is not. The Beatles are renowned and loved throughout the world, and someone who collected their memorabilia wouldn't be thought too strange. Someone who collected the memorabilia of Pinky Lee, on the other hand, might be viewed with a tad more concern.

Hey, I'd love to hear your point of view about whatever comes to mind. Write in. Reading a good book? Write in. Seen a good film or museum exhibition? Eaten a good meal?

Or...maybe you've just bought the collectible of your dreams at a swap meet.

James Robinson

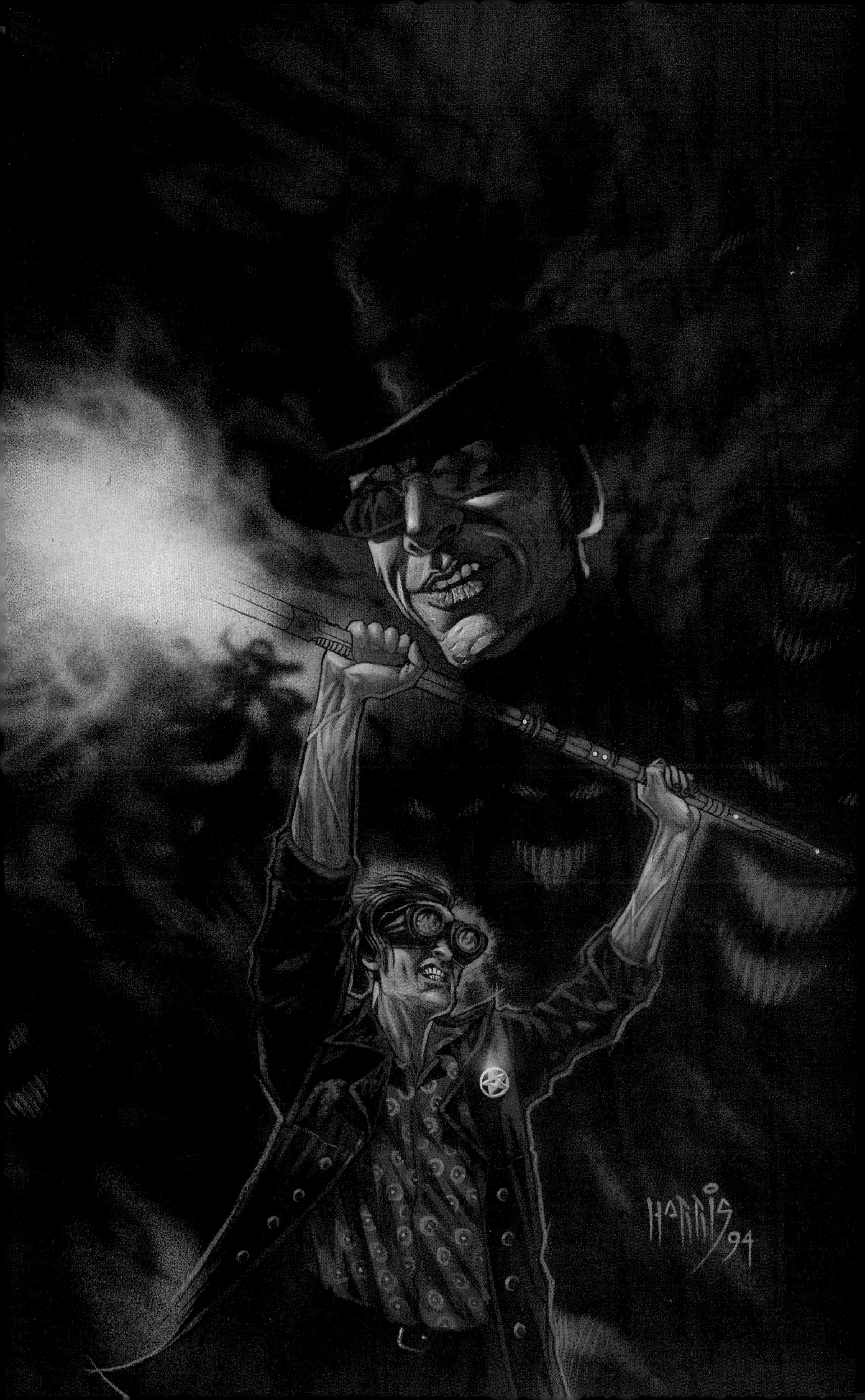
HARRIS 94

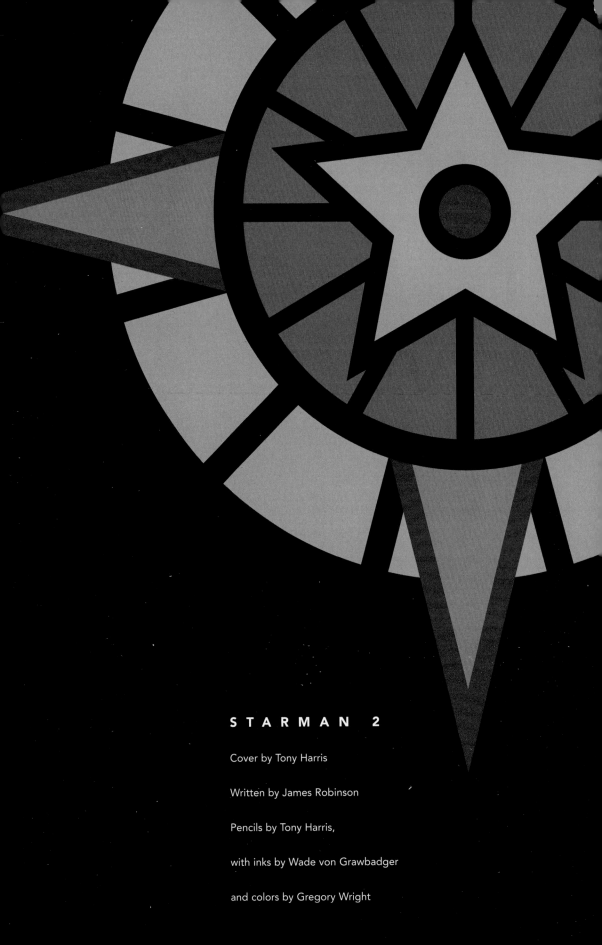

STARMAN 2

Cover by Tony Harris

Written by James Robinson

Pencils by Tony Harris,

with inks by Wade von Grawbadger

and colors by Gregory Wright

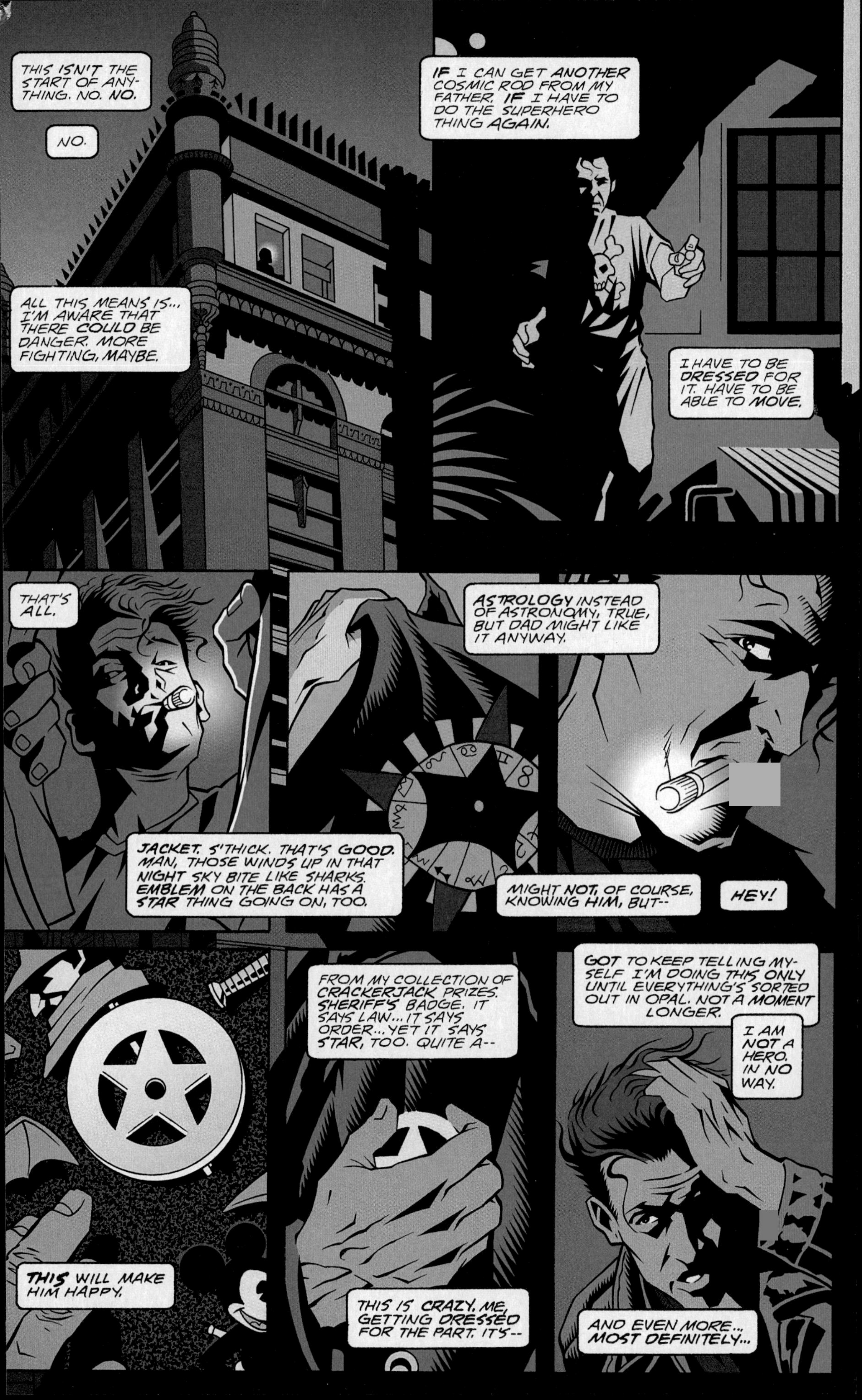
THIS ISN'T THE START OF ANY-THING. NO. NO.
NO.
IF I CAN GET ANOTHER COSMIC ROD FROM MY FATHER. IF I HAVE TO DO THE SUPERHERO THING AGAIN.
ALL THIS MEANS IS... I'M AWARE THAT THERE COULD BE DANGER. MORE FIGHTING, MAYBE.
I HAVE TO BE DRESSED FOR IT. HAVE TO BE ABLE TO MOVE.
THAT'S ALL.
ASTROLOGY INSTEAD OF ASTRONOMY, TRUE, BUT DAD MIGHT LIKE IT ANYWAY.
JACKET. S'THICK. THAT'S GOOD. MAN, THOSE WINDS UP IN THAT NIGHT SKY BITE LIKE SHARKS. EMBLEM ON THE BACK HAS A STAR THING GOING ON, TOO.
MIGHT NOT, OF COURSE, KNOWING HIM, BUT--
HEY!
THIS WILL MAKE HIM HAPPY.
FROM MY COLLECTION OF CRACKERJACK PRIZES. SHERIFF'S BADGE. IT SAYS LAW... IT SAYS ORDER... YET IT SAYS STAR, TOO. QUITE A--
THIS IS CRAZY. ME, GETTING DRESSED FOR THE PART. IT'S--
GOT TO KEEP TELLING MY-SELF I'M DOING THIS ONLY UNTIL EVERYTHING'S SORTED OUT IN OPAL. NOT A MOMENT LONGER.
I AM NOT A HERO. IN NO WAY.
AND EVEN MORE... MOST DEFINITELY...

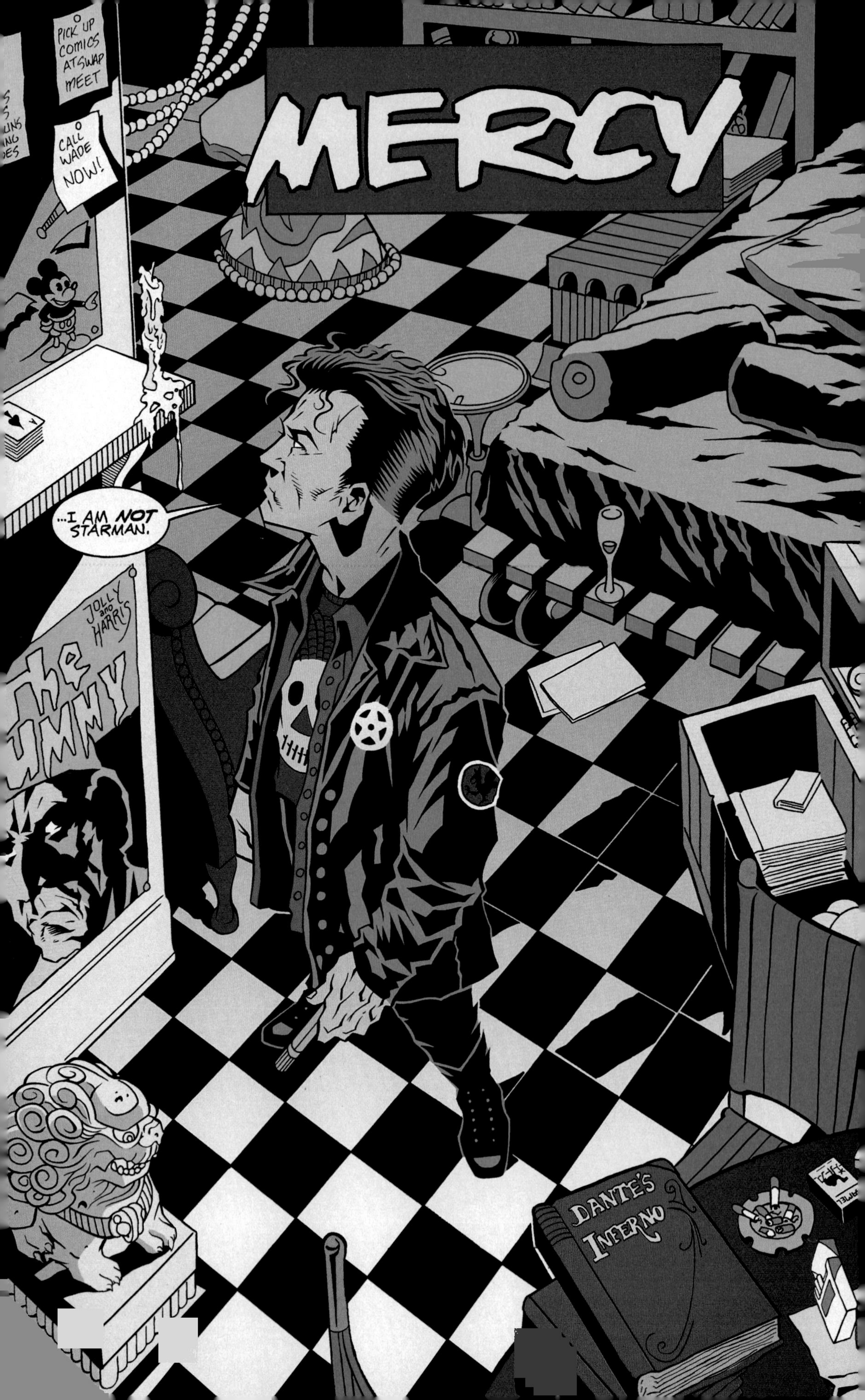
MERCY
PICK UP COMICS AT SWAP MEET
CALL WADE NOW!
...I AM *NOT* STARMAN.
JOLLY AND HARRIS
DANTE'S INFERNO

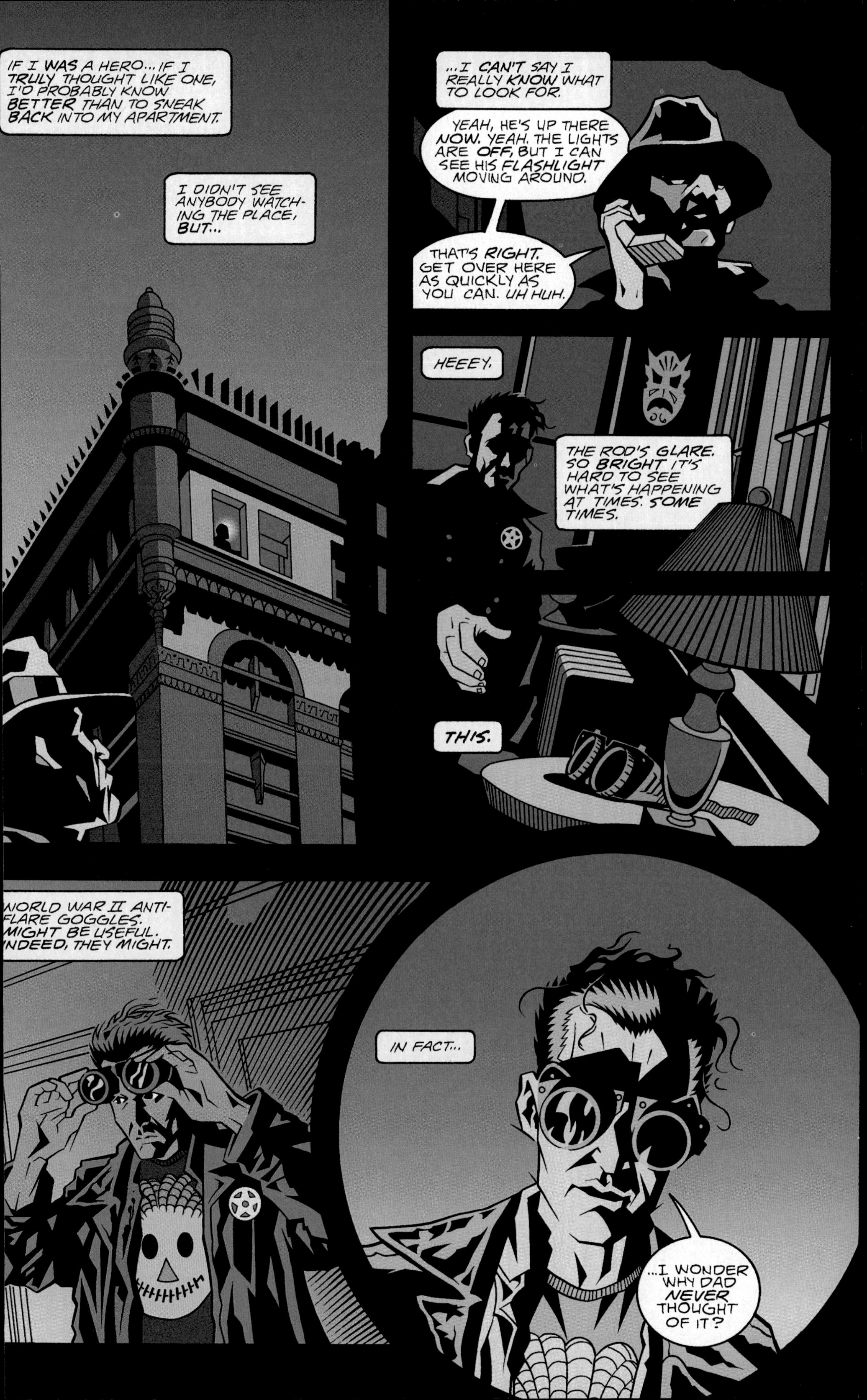
IF I WAS A HERO... IF I TRULY THOUGHT LIKE ONE, I'D PROBABLY KNOW BETTER THAN TO SNEAK BACK INTO MY APARTMENT.
I DIDN'T SEE ANYBODY WATCHING THE PLACE, BUT...
...I CAN'T SAY I REALLY KNOW WHAT TO LOOK FOR.
YEAH, HE'S UP THERE NOW. YEAH. THE LIGHTS ARE OFF, BUT I CAN SEE HIS FLASHLIGHT MOVING AROUND.
THAT'S RIGHT. GET OVER HERE AS QUICKLY AS YOU CAN. UH HUH.
HEEEY.
THE ROD'S GLARE. SO BRIGHT IT'S HARD TO SEE WHAT'S HAPPENING AT TIMES. SOME TIMES.
THIS.
WORLD WAR II ANTI-FLARE GOGGLES. MIGHT BE USEFUL. INDEED, THEY MIGHT.
IN FACT...
...I WONDER WHY DAD NEVER THOUGHT OF IT?

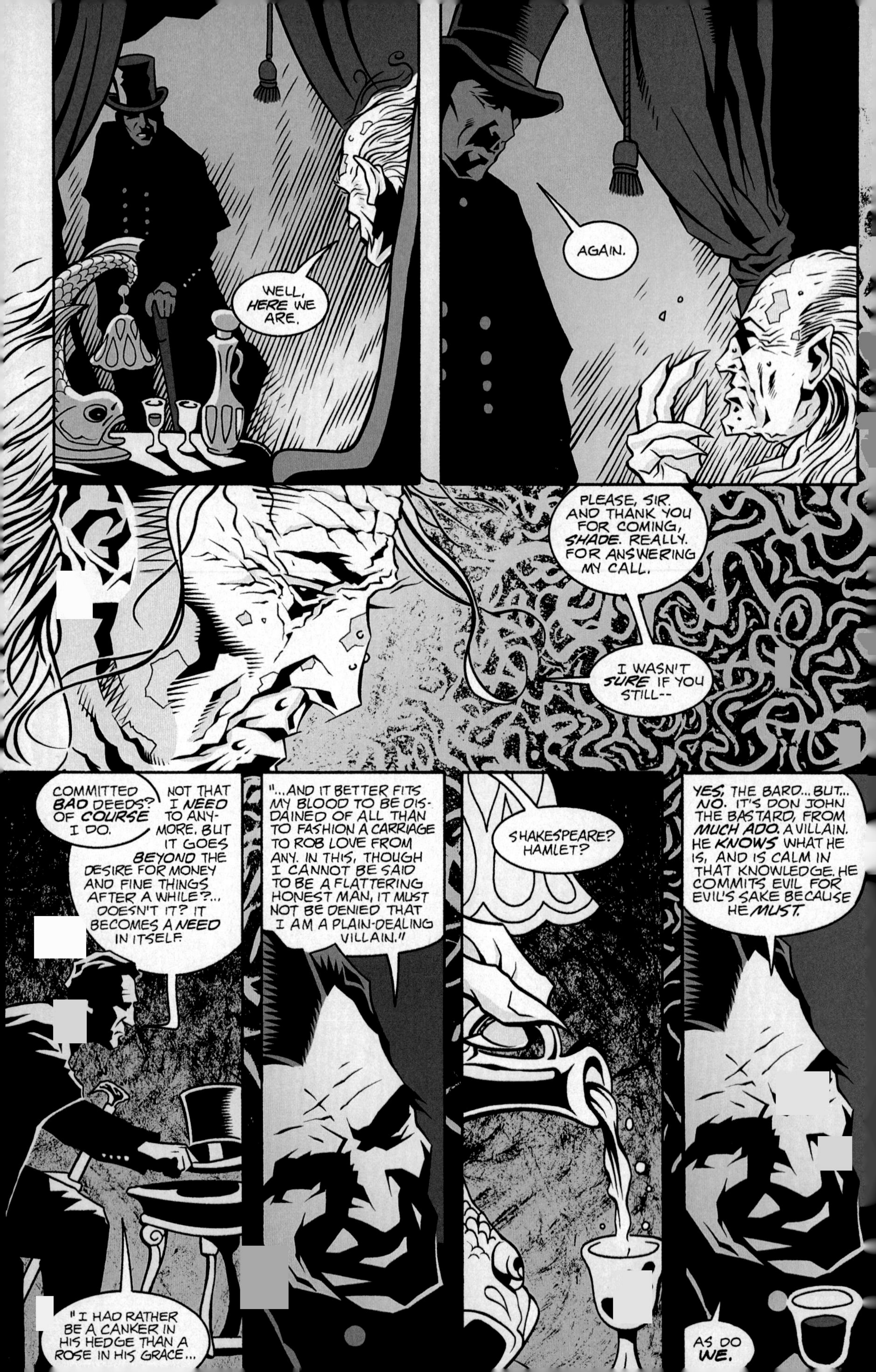
WELL, HERE WE ARE.
AGAIN.
PLEASE, SIR. AND THANK YOU FOR COMING, SHADE. REALLY. FOR ANSWERING MY CALL.
I WASN'T SURE IF YOU STILL--
COMMITTED BAD DEEDS? OF COURSE I DO.
NOT THAT I NEED TO ANYMORE. BUT IT GOES BEYOND THE DESIRE FOR MONEY AND FINE THINGS AFTER A WHILE?... DOESN'T IT? IT BECOMES A NEED IN ITSELF.
"I HAD RATHER BE A CANKER IN HIS HEDGE THAN A ROSE IN HIS GRACE...
"...AND IT BETTER FITS MY BLOOD TO BE DISDAINED OF ALL THAN TO FASHION A CARRIAGE TO ROB LOVE FROM ANY. IN THIS, THOUGH I CANNOT BE SAID TO BE A FLATTERING HONEST MAN, IT MUST NOT BE DENIED THAT I AM A PLAIN-DEALING VILLAIN."
SHAKESPEARE? HAMLET?
YES, THE BARD... BUT... NO. IT'S DON JOHN THE BASTARD, FROM MUCH ADO. A VILLAIN. HE KNOWS WHAT HE IS, AND IS CALM IN THAT KNOWLEDGE. HE COMMITS EVIL FOR EVIL'S SAKE BECAUSE HE MUST.
AS DO WE.

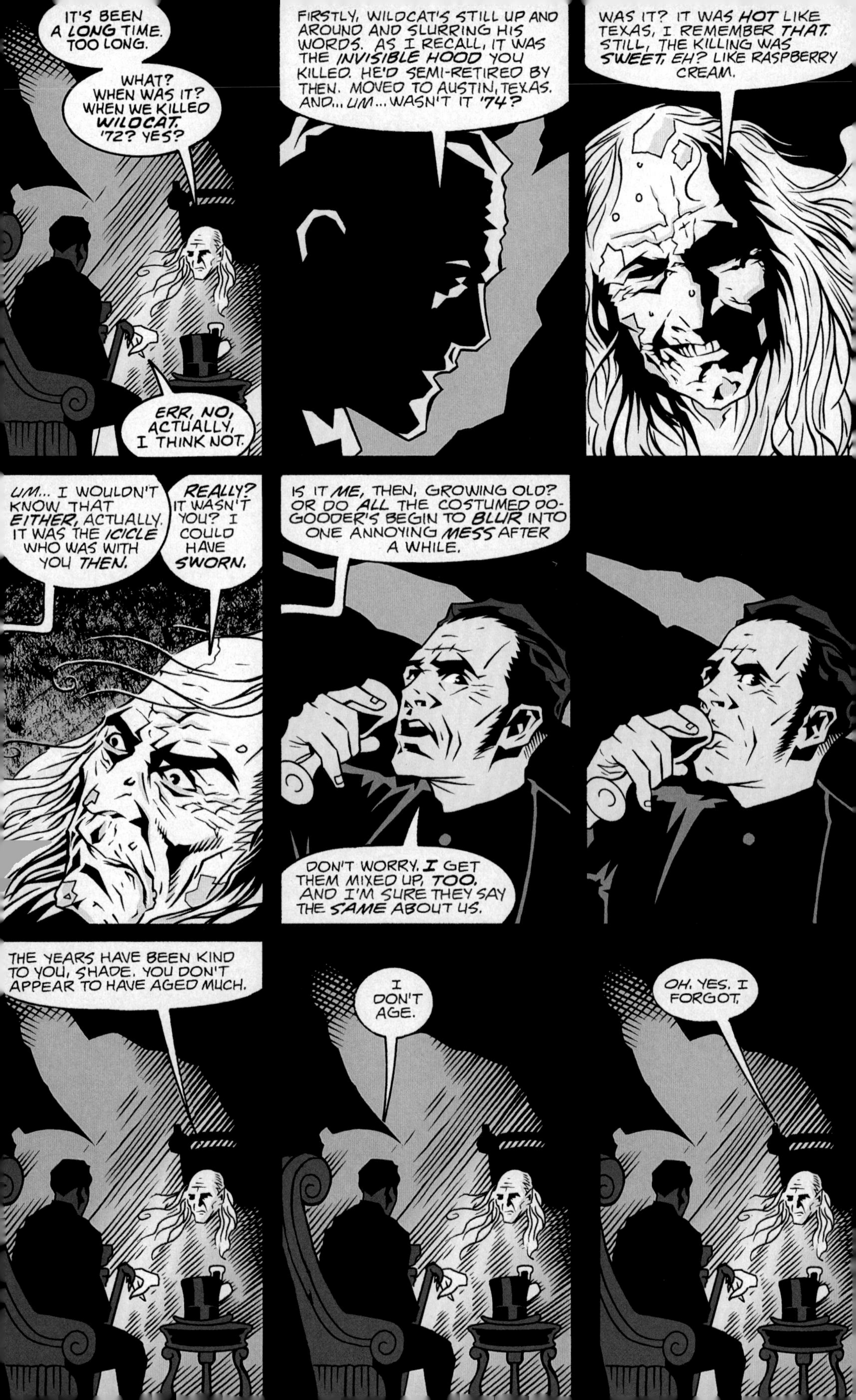
IT'S BEEN A LONG TIME. TOO LONG.
WHAT? WHEN WAS IT? WHEN WE KILLED WILDCAT. '72? YES?
ERR, NO, ACTUALLY, I THINK NOT.
FIRSTLY, WILDCAT'S STILL UP AND AROUND AND SLURRING HIS WORDS. AS I RECALL, IT WAS THE INVISIBLE HOOD YOU KILLED. HE'D SEMI-RETIRED BY THEN. MOVED TO AUSTIN, TEXAS. AND... UM... WASN'T IT '74?
WAS IT? IT WAS HOT LIKE TEXAS, I REMEMBER THAT. STILL, THE KILLING WAS SWEET, EH? LIKE RASPBERRY CREAM.
UM... I WOULDN'T KNOW THAT EITHER, ACTUALLY. IT WAS THE ICICLE WHO WAS WITH YOU THEN.
REALLY? IT WASN'T YOU? I COULD HAVE SWORN.
IS IT ME, THEN, GROWING OLD? OR DO ALL THE COSTUMED DO-GOODER'S BEGIN TO BLUR INTO ONE ANNOYING MESS AFTER A WHILE.
DON'T WORRY. I GET THEM MIXED UP, TOO. AND I'M SURE THEY SAY THE SAME ABOUT US.
THE YEARS HAVE BEEN KIND TO YOU, SHADE. YOU DON'T APPEAR TO HAVE AGED MUCH.
I DON'T AGE.
OH, YES. I FORGOT.

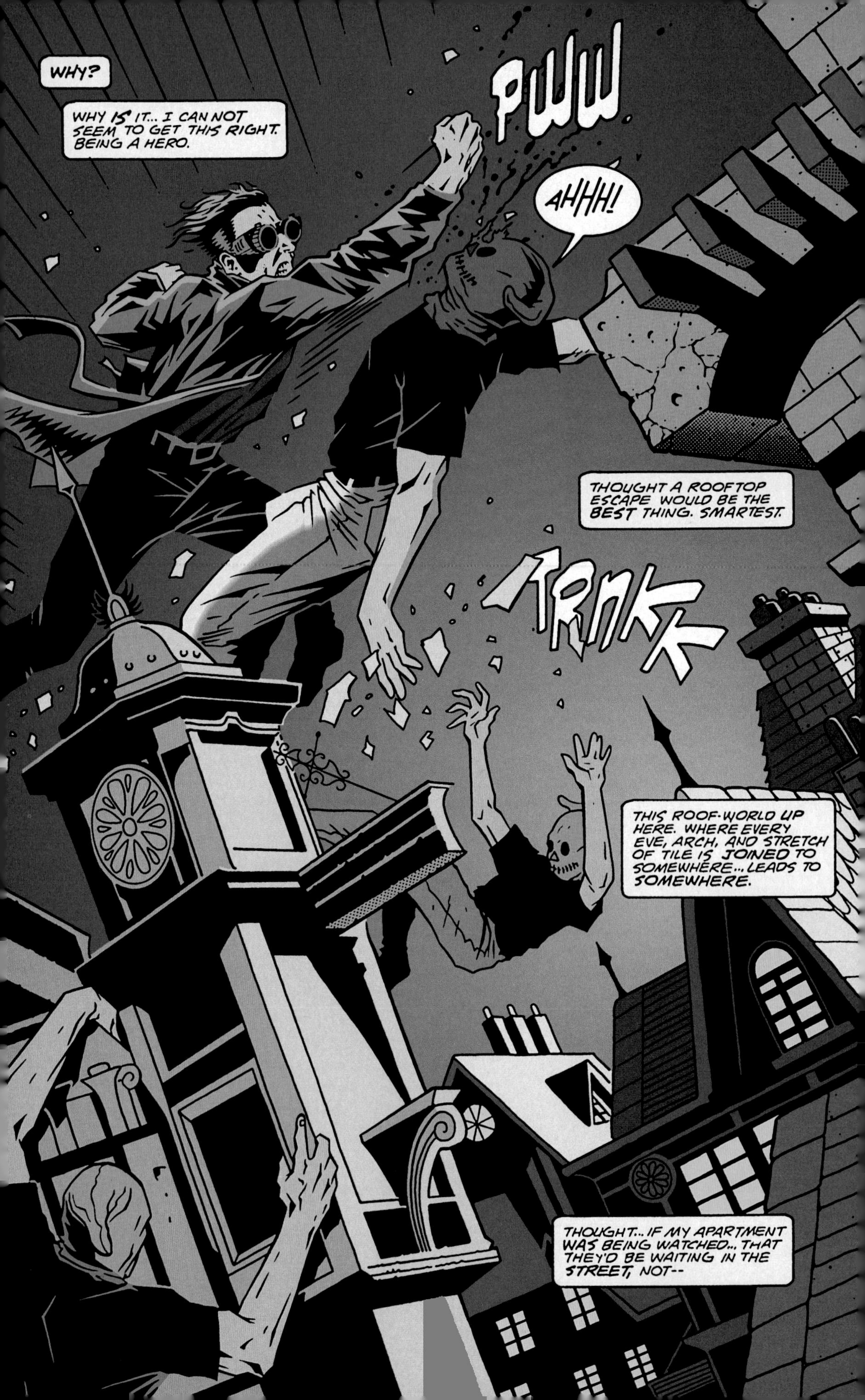
WHY?
WHY IS IT... I CAN NOT SEEM TO GET THIS RIGHT. BEING A HERO.
PWW
AHHH!
THOUGHT A ROOFTOP ESCAPE WOULD BE THE BEST THING. SMARTEST.
TRNKK
THIS ROOF-WORLD UP HERE. WHERE EVERY EVE, ARCH, AND STRETCH OF TILE IS JOINED TO SOMEWHERE... LEADS TO SOMEWHERE.
THOUGHT... IF MY APARTMENT WAS BEING WATCHED... THAT THEY'D BE WAITING IN THE STREET, NOT--

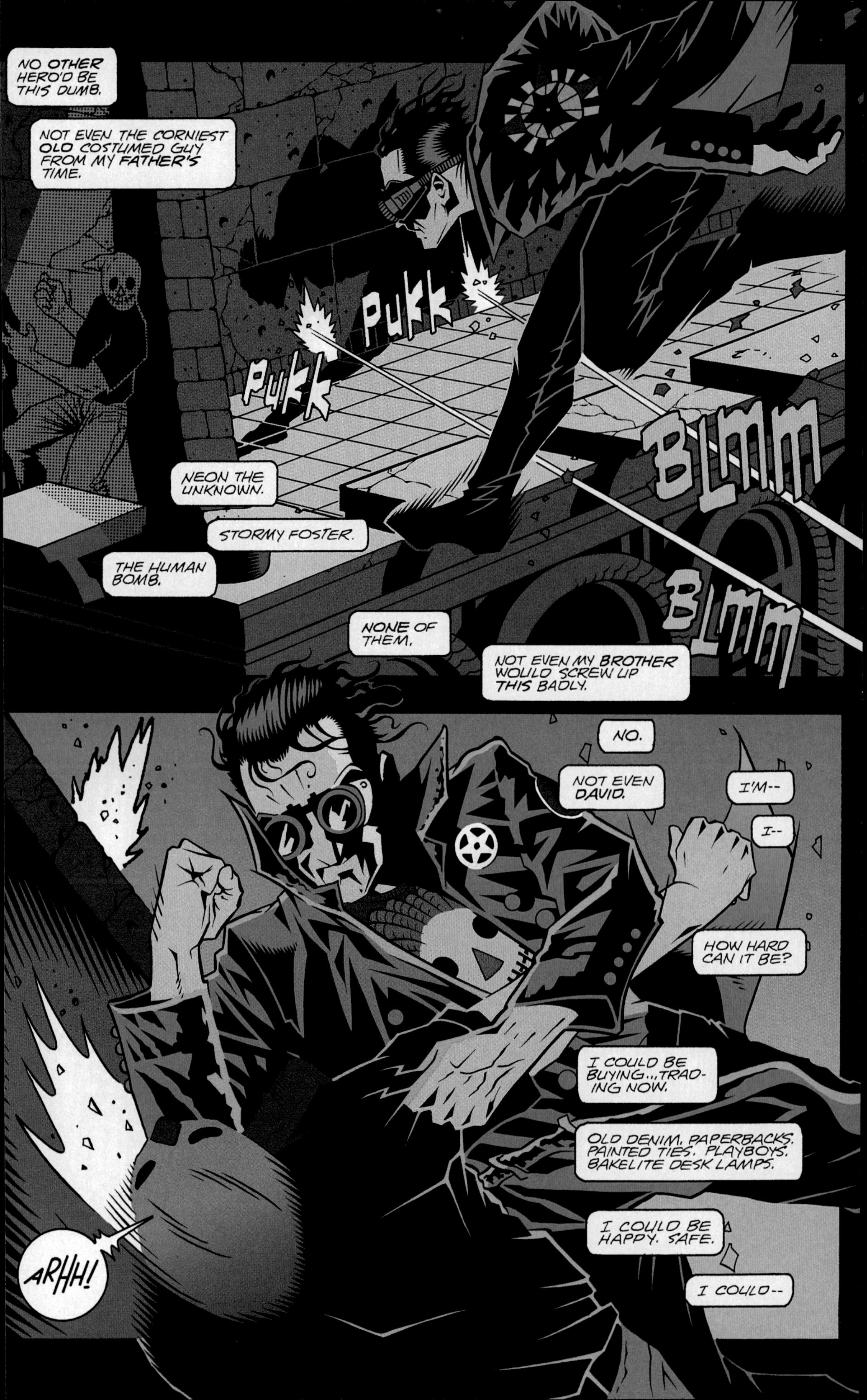
NO OTHER HERO'D BE THIS DUMB.
NOT EVEN THE CORNIEST OLD COSTUMED GUY FROM MY FATHER'S TIME.
PUKK
PUKK
NEON THE UNKNOWN.
STORMY FOSTER.
THE HUMAN BOMB.
BLMM
BLMM
NONE OF THEM.
NOT EVEN MY BROTHER WOULD SCREW UP THIS BADLY.
NO.
NOT EVEN DAVID.
I'M--
I--
HOW HARD CAN IT BE?
I COULD BE BUYING...TRADING NOW.
OLD DENIM. PAPERBACKS. PAINTED TIES. PLAYBOYS. BAKELITE DESK LAMPS.
I COULD BE HAPPY. SAFE.
I COULD--
ARHH!

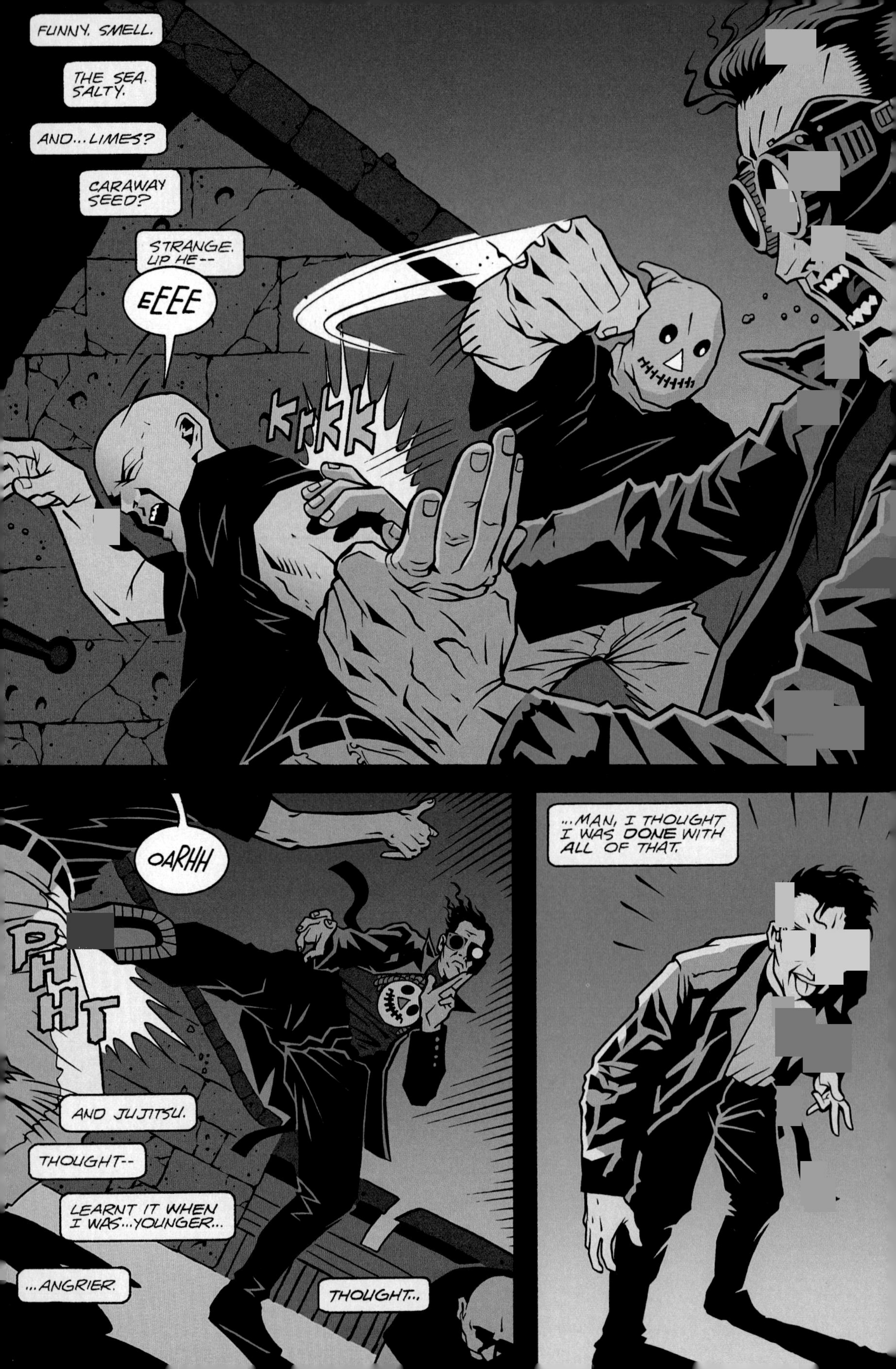
FUNNY. SMELL.
THE SEA. SALTY.
AND... LIMES?
CARAWAY SEED?
STRANGE. UP HE--
EEEE
KRKK
OARHH
PHHT
AND JUJITSU.
THOUGHT--
LEARNT IT WHEN I WAS... YOUNGER...
...ANGRIER.
THOUGHT...
...MAN, I THOUGHT I WAS DONE WITH ALL OF THAT.

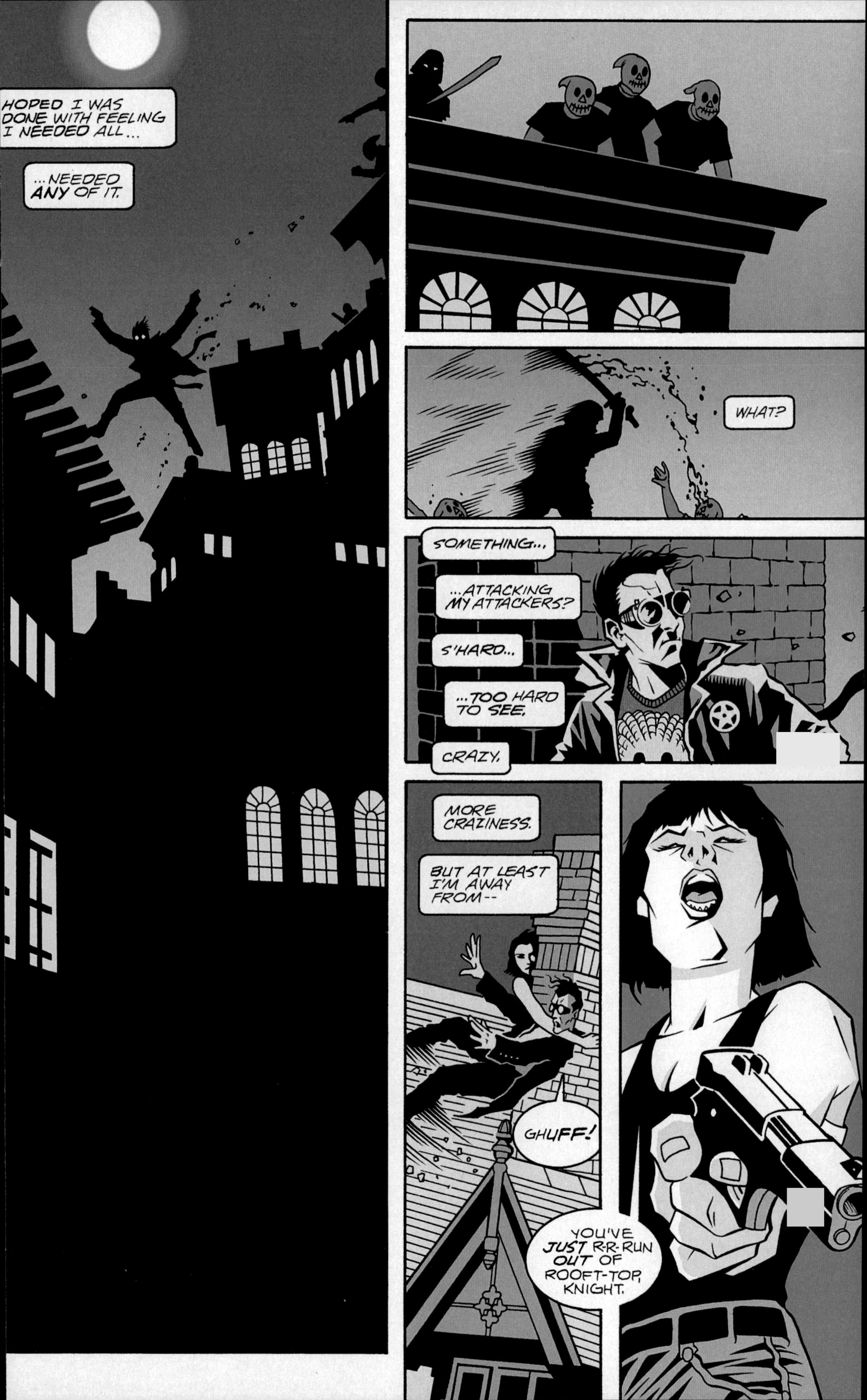
HOPED I WAS DONE WITH FEELING I NEEDED ALL...
...NEEDED ANY OF IT.
WHAT?
SOMETHING...
...ATTACKING MY ATTACKERS?
S'HARD...
...TOO HARD TO SEE.
CRAZY.
MORE CRAZINESS.
BUT AT LEAST I'M AWAY FROM--
GHUFF!
YOU'VE JUST R-R-RUN OUT OF ROOFT-TOP, KNIGHT.

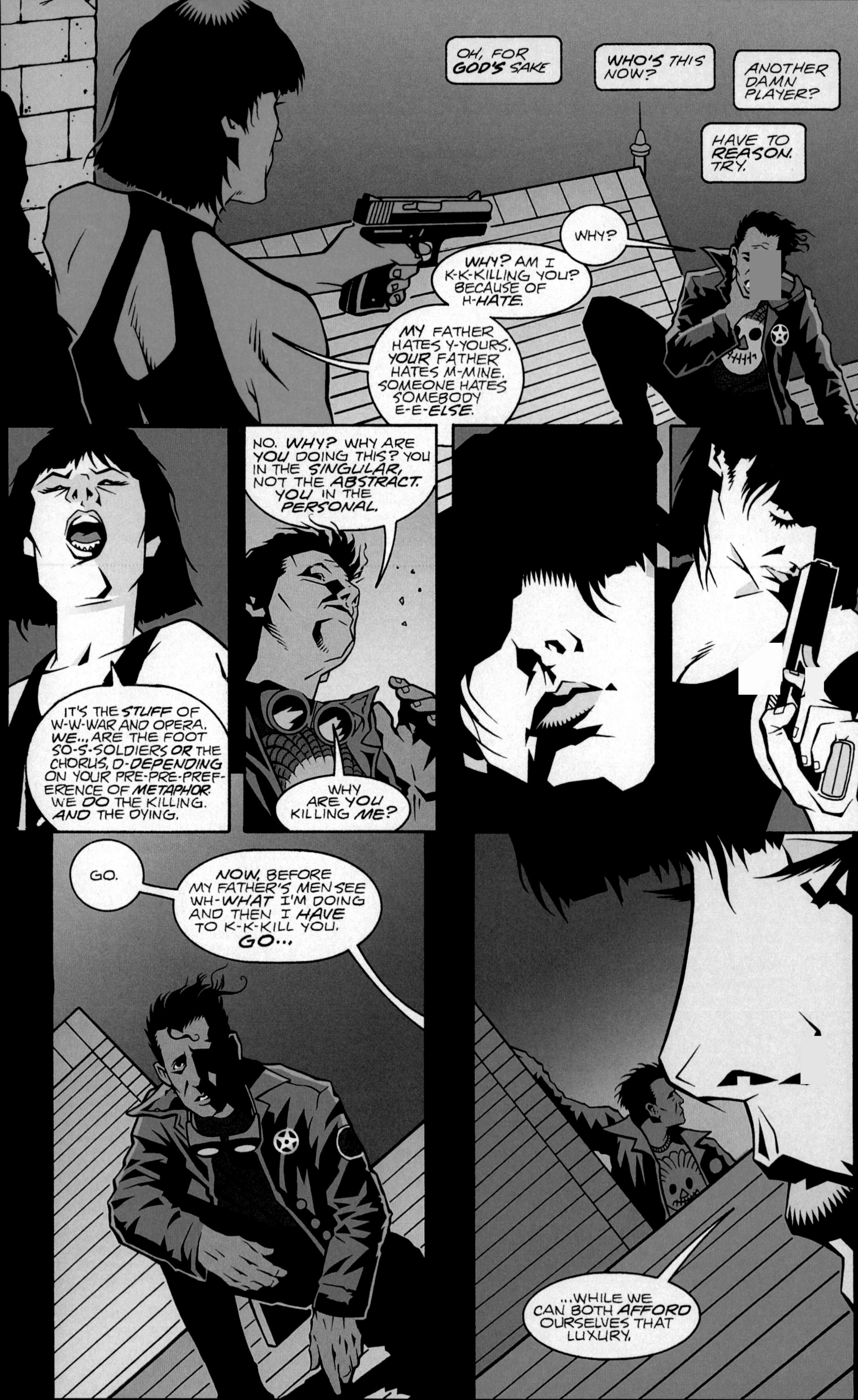
OH, FOR GOD'S SAKE
WHO'S THIS NOW?
ANOTHER DAMN PLAYER?
HAVE TO REASON. TRY.
WHY?
WHY? AM I K-K-KILLING YOU? BECAUSE OF H-HATE.
MY FATHER HATES Y-YOURS. YOUR FATHER HATES M-MINE. SOMEONE HATES SOMEBODY E-E-ELSE.
NO. WHY? WHY ARE YOU DOING THIS? YOU IN THE SINGULAR, NOT THE ABSTRACT. YOU IN THE PERSONAL.
IT'S THE STUFF OF W-W-WAR AND OPERA. WE... ARE THE FOOT SO-S-SOLDIERS OR THE CHORUS, D-DEPENDING ON YOUR PRE-PRE-PREFERENCE OF METAPHOR. WE DO THE KILLING. AND THE DYING.
WHY ARE YOU KILLING ME?
GO.
NOW, BEFORE MY FATHER'S MEN SEE WH-WHAT I'M DOING AND THEN I HAVE TO K-K-KILL YOU. GO...
...WHILE WE CAN BOTH AFFORD OURSELVES THAT LUXURY.

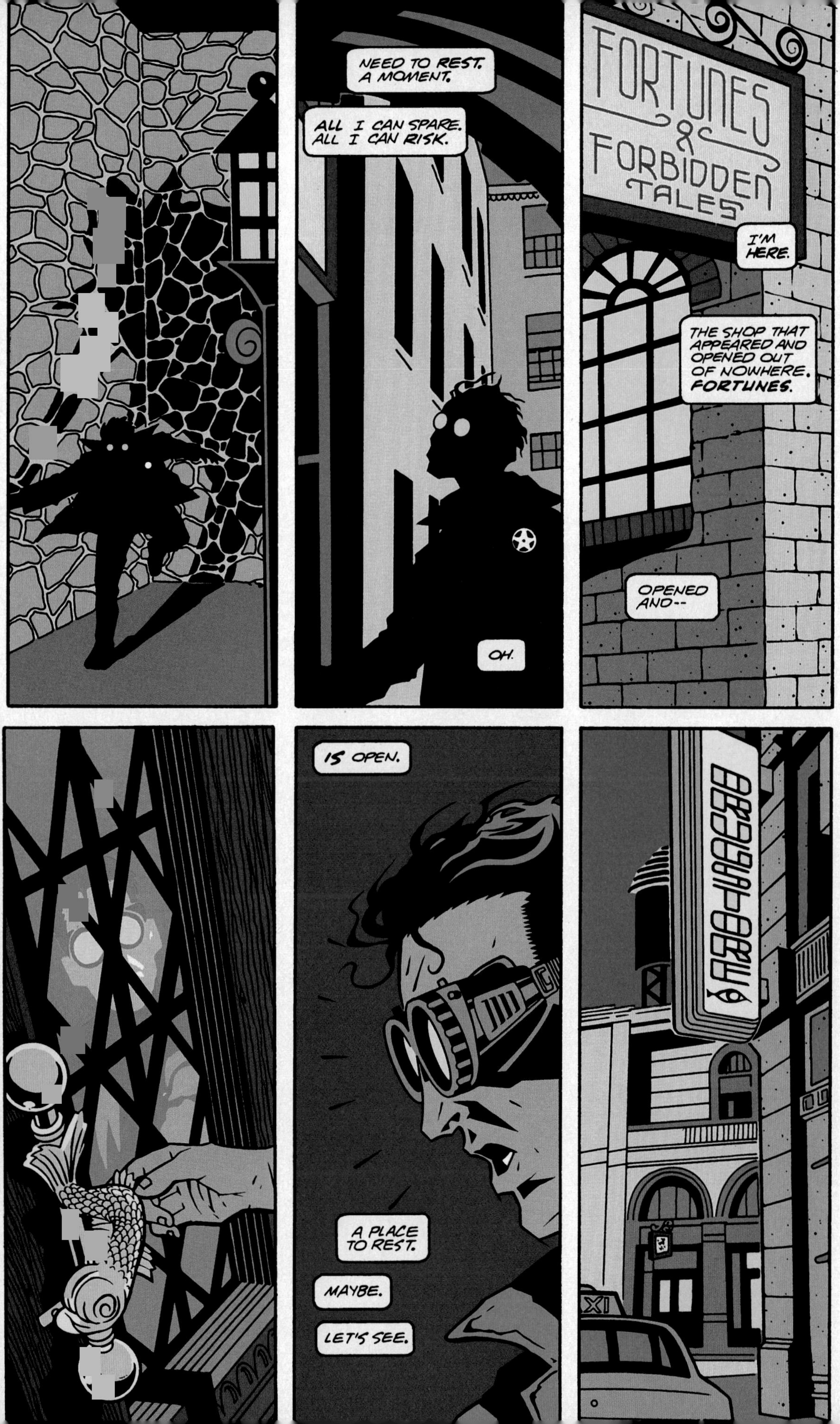
NEED TO REST. A MOMENT.
ALL I CAN SPARE. ALL I CAN RISK.
OH.
FORTUNES & FORBIDDEN TALES
I'M HERE.
THE SHOP THAT APPEARED AND OPENED OUT OF NOWHERE. FORTUNES.
OPENED AND--
IS OPEN.
A PLACE TO REST.
MAYBE.
LET'S SEE.

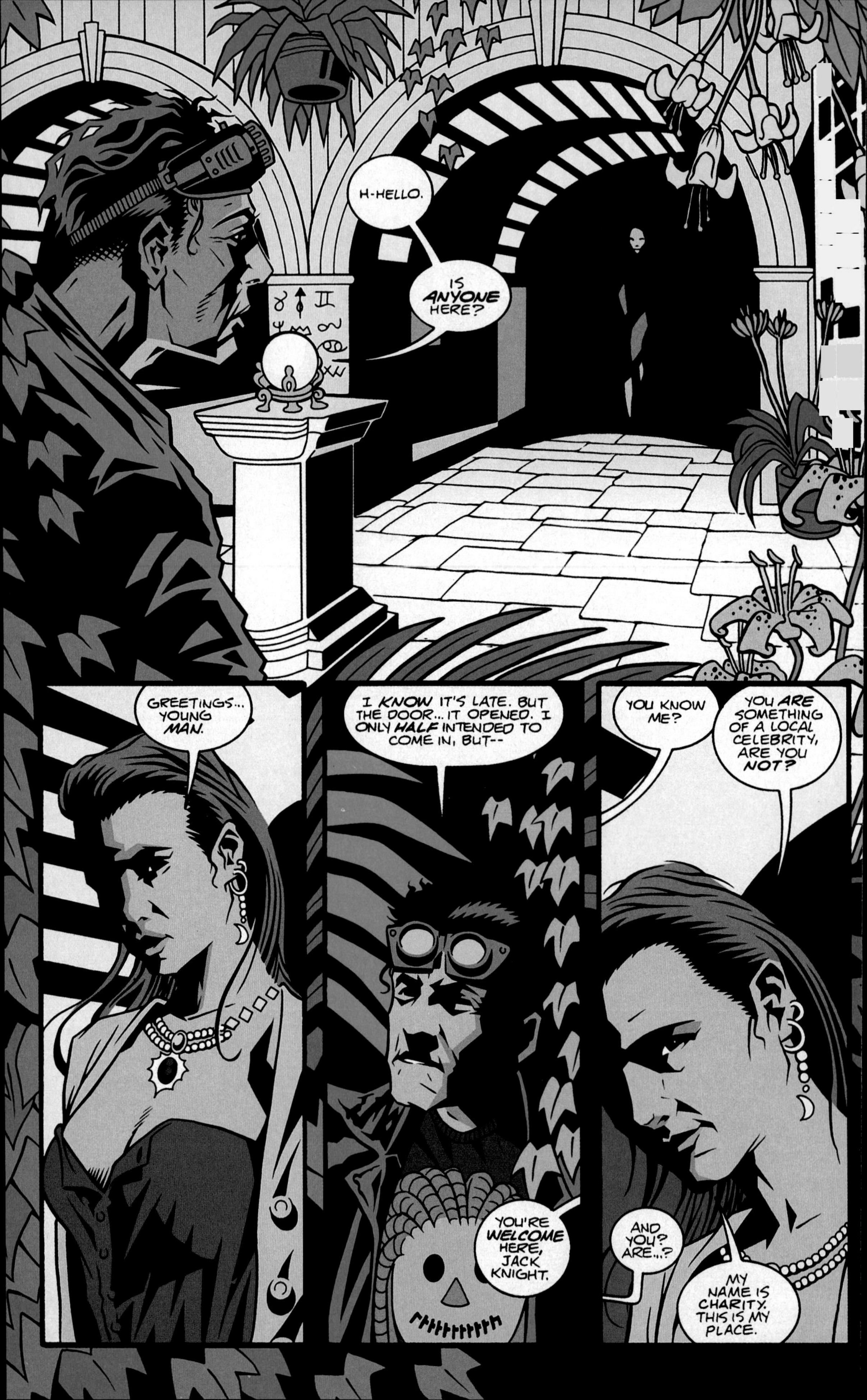
H-HELLO.
IS ANYONE HERE?
GREETINGS... YOUNG MAN.
I KNOW IT'S LATE. BUT THE DOOR... IT OPENED. I ONLY HALF INTENDED TO COME IN, BUT--
YOU'RE WELCOME HERE, JACK KNIGHT.
YOU KNOW ME?
YOU ARE SOMETHING OF A LOCAL CELEBRITY, ARE YOU NOT?
AND YOU? ARE...?
MY NAME IS CHARITY. THIS IS MY PLACE.

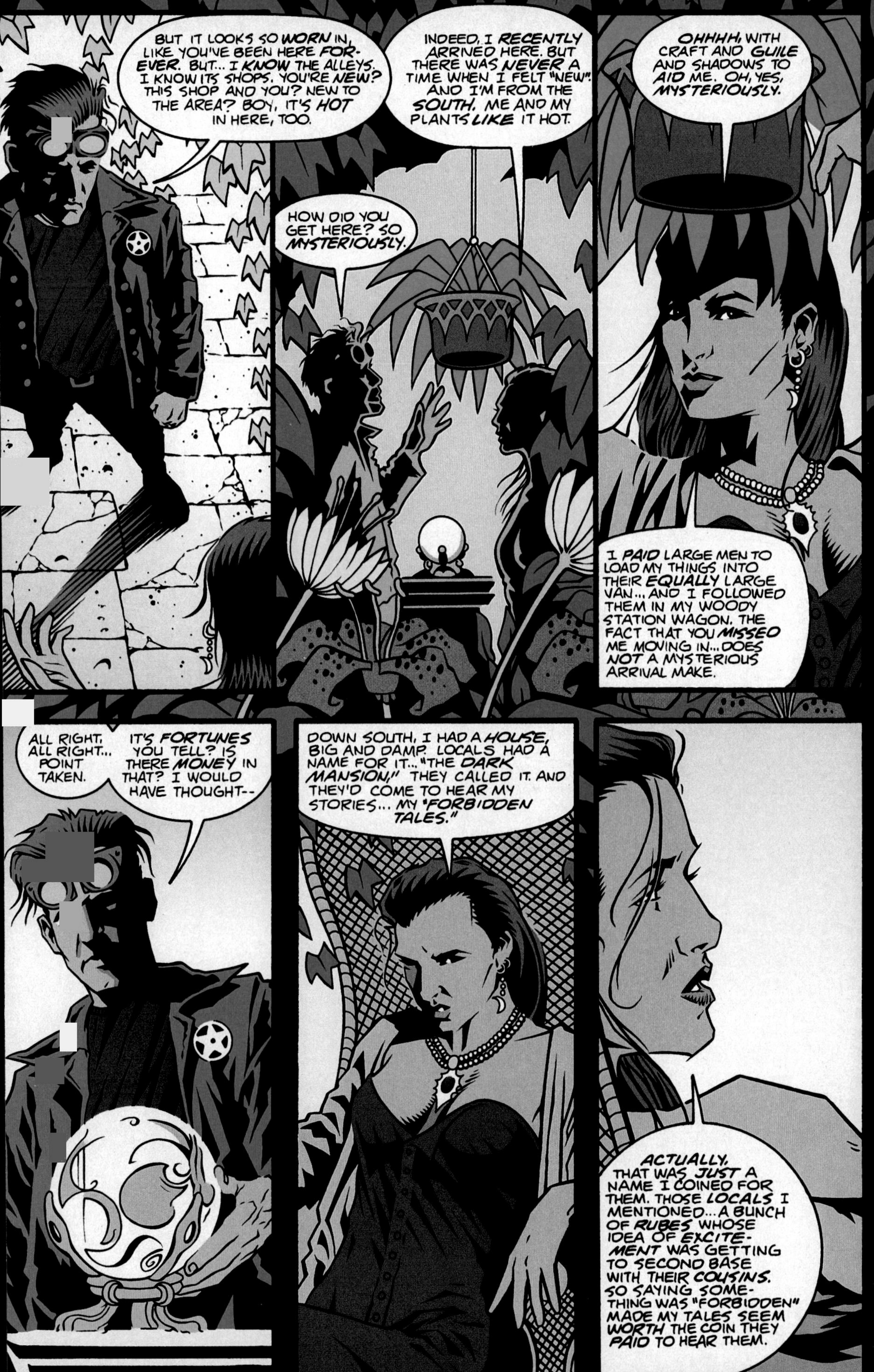
BUT IT LOOKS SO WORN IN, LIKE YOU'VE BEEN HERE FOR-EVER. BUT... I KNOW THE ALLEYS. I KNOW ITS SHOPS. YOU'RE NEW? THIS SHOP AND YOU? NEW TO THE AREA? BOY, IT'S HOT IN HERE, TOO.
INDEED, I RECENTLY ARRIVED HERE. BUT THERE WAS NEVER A TIME WHEN I FELT "NEW". AND I'M FROM THE SOUTH. ME AND MY PLANTS LIKE IT HOT.
HOW DID YOU GET HERE? SO MYSTERIOUSLY.
OHHHH, WITH CRAFT AND GUILE AND SHADOWS TO AID ME. OH, YES, MYSTERIOUSLY.
I PAID LARGE MEN TO LOAD MY THINGS INTO THEIR EQUALLY LARGE VAN... AND I FOLLOWED THEM IN MY WOODY STATION WAGON. THE FACT THAT YOU MISSED ME MOVING IN... DOES NOT A MYSTERIOUS ARRIVAL MAKE.
ALL RIGHT, ALL RIGHT... POINT TAKEN.
IT'S FORTUNES YOU TELL? IS THERE MONEY IN THAT? I WOULD HAVE THOUGHT--
DOWN SOUTH, I HAD A HOUSE, BIG AND DAMP. LOCALS HAD A NAME FOR IT... "THE DARK MANSION," THEY CALLED IT. AND THEY'D COME TO HEAR MY STORIES... MY "FORBIDDEN TALES."
ACTUALLY, THAT WAS JUST A NAME I COINED FOR THEM. THOSE LOCALS I MENTIONED... A BUNCH OF RUBES WHOSE IDEA OF EXCITE-MENT WAS GETTING TO SECOND BASE WITH THEIR COUSINS. SO SAYING SOME-THING WAS "FORBIDDEN" MADE MY TALES SEEM WORTH THE COIN THEY PAID TO HEAR THEM.

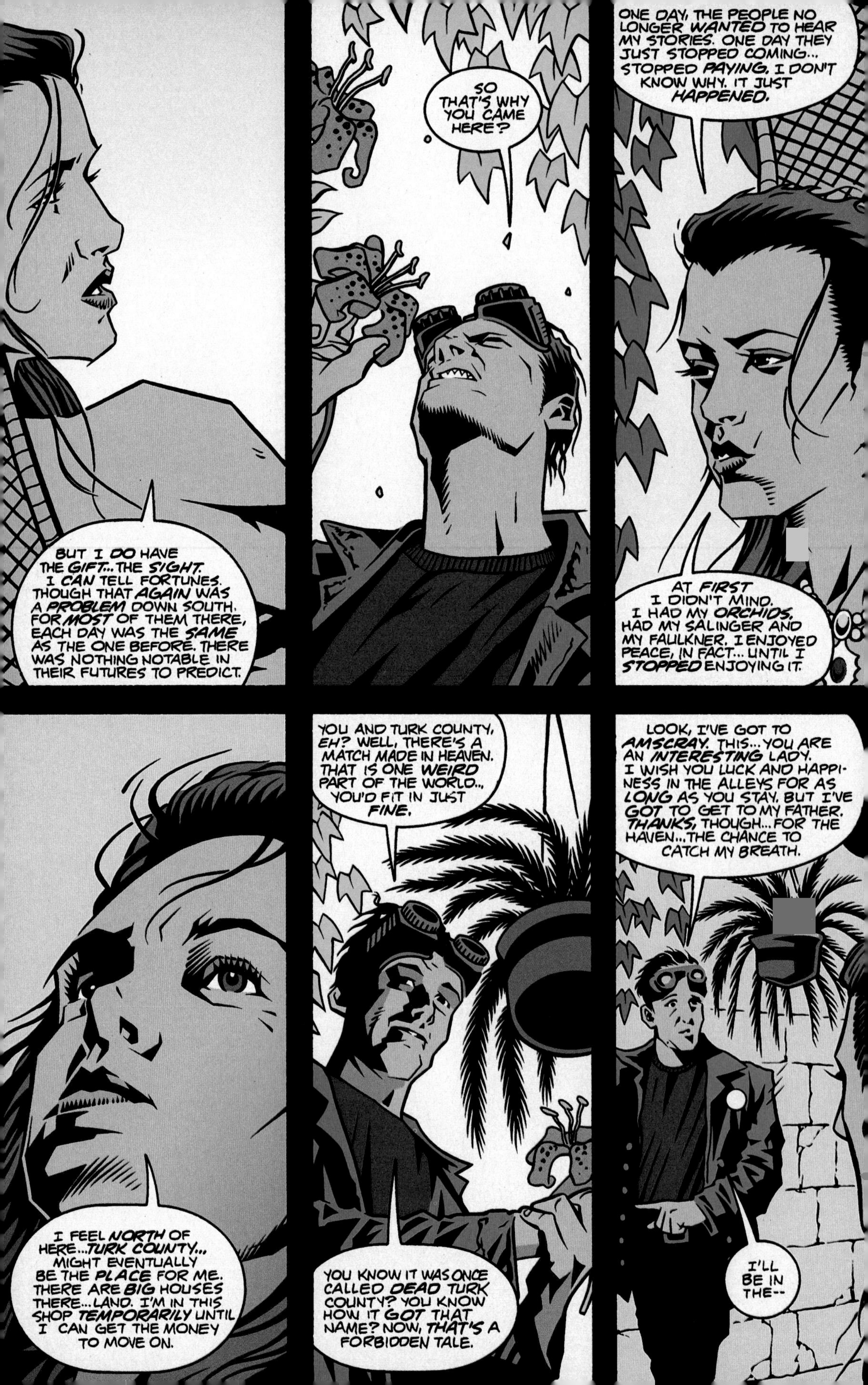
BUT I DO HAVE THE GIFT... THE SIGHT. I CAN TELL FORTUNES. THOUGH THAT AGAIN WAS A PROBLEM DOWN SOUTH. FOR MOST OF THEM THERE, EACH DAY WAS THE SAME AS THE ONE BEFORE. THERE WAS NOTHING NOTABLE IN THEIR FUTURES TO PREDICT.
SO THAT'S WHY YOU CAME HERE?
ONE DAY, THE PEOPLE NO LONGER WANTED TO HEAR MY STORIES. ONE DAY THEY JUST STOPPED COMING... STOPPED PAYING. I DON'T KNOW WHY. IT JUST HAPPENED.
AT FIRST I DIDN'T MIND. I HAD MY ORCHIDS, HAD MY SALINGER AND MY FAULKNER. I ENJOYED PEACE, IN FACT... UNTIL I STOPPED ENJOYING IT.
I FEEL NORTH OF HERE...TURK COUNTY... MIGHT EVENTUALLY BE THE PLACE FOR ME. THERE ARE BIG HOUSES THERE...LAND. I'M IN THIS SHOP TEMPORARILY UNTIL I CAN GET THE MONEY TO MOVE ON.
YOU AND TURK COUNTY, EH? WELL, THERE'S A MATCH MADE IN HEAVEN. THAT IS ONE WEIRD PART OF THE WORLD... YOU'D FIT IN JUST FINE.
YOU KNOW IT WAS ONCE CALLED DEAD TURK COUNTY? YOU KNOW HOW IT GOT THAT NAME? NOW, THAT'S A FORBIDDEN TALE.
LOOK, I'VE GOT TO AMSCRAY. THIS... YOU ARE AN INTERESTING LADY. I WISH YOU LUCK AND HAPPINESS IN THE ALLEYS FOR AS LONG AS YOU STAY. BUT I'VE GOT TO GET TO MY FATHER. THANKS, THOUGH... FOR THE HAVEN... THE CHANCE TO CATCH MY BREATH.
I'LL BE IN THE--

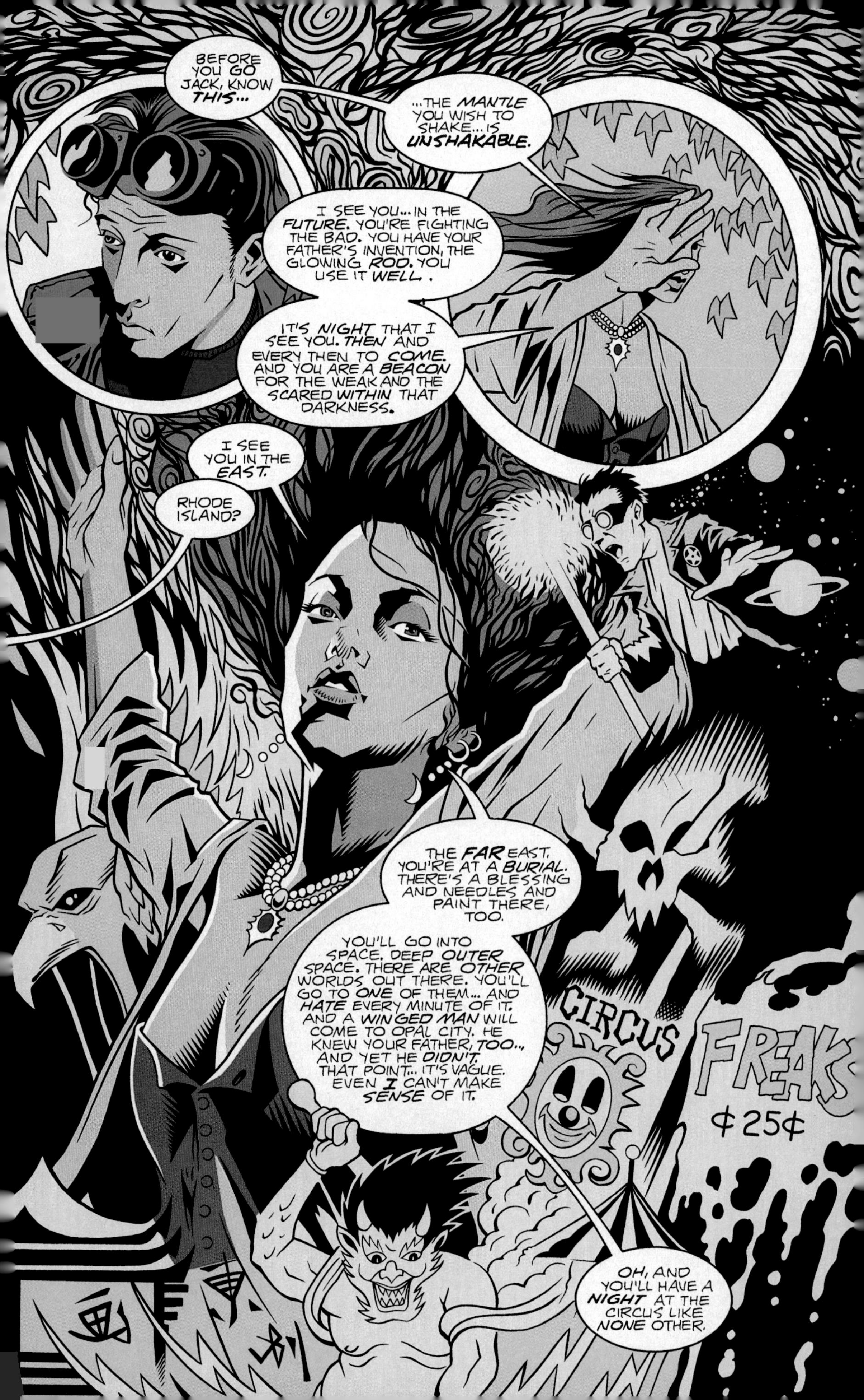
BEFORE YOU GO JACK, KNOW THIS...
...THE MANTLE YOU WISH TO SHAKE...IS UNSHAKABLE.
I SEE YOU... IN THE FUTURE. YOU'RE FIGHTING THE BAD. YOU HAVE YOUR FATHER'S INVENTION, THE GLOWING ROD. YOU USE IT WELL.
IT'S NIGHT THAT I SEE YOU. THEN AND EVERY THEN TO COME. AND YOU ARE A BEACON FOR THE WEAK AND THE SCARED WITHIN THAT DARKNESS.
I SEE YOU IN THE EAST.
RHODE ISLAND?
THE FAR EAST. YOU'RE AT A BURIAL. THERE'S A BLESSING AND NEEDLES AND PAINT THERE, TOO.
YOU'LL GO INTO SPACE. DEEP OUTER SPACE. THERE ARE OTHER WORLDS OUT THERE. YOU'LL GO TO ONE OF THEM... AND HATE EVERY MINUTE OF IT. AND A WINGED MAN WILL COME TO OPAL CITY. HE KNEW YOUR FATHER, TOO.., AND YET HE DIDN'T. THAT POINT... IT'S VAGUE. EVEN I CAN'T MAKE SENSE OF IT.
CIRCUS
FREAKS
¢25¢
OH, AND YOU'LL HAVE A NIGHT AT THE CIRCUS LIKE NONE OTHER.

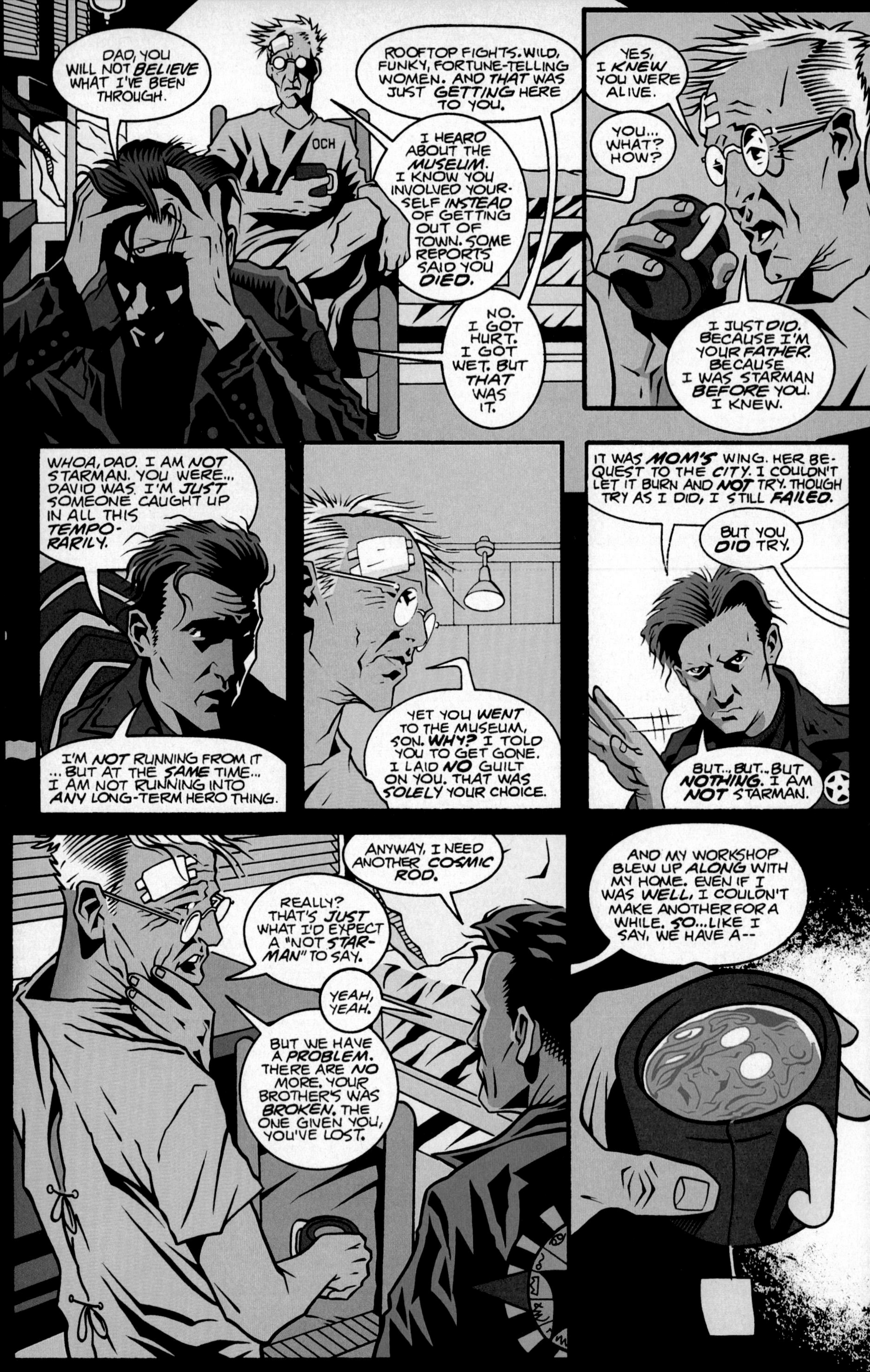
DAD, YOU WILL NOT BELIEVE WHAT I'VE BEEN THROUGH.
ROOFTOP FIGHTS. WILD, FUNKY, FORTUNE-TELLING WOMEN. AND THAT WAS JUST GETTING HERE TO YOU.
I HEARD ABOUT THE MUSEUM. I KNOW YOU INVOLVED YOURSELF INSTEAD OF GETTING OUT OF TOWN. SOME REPORTS SAID YOU DIED.
NO. I GOT HURT. I GOT WET. BUT THAT WAS IT.
YES, I KNEW YOU WERE ALIVE.
YOU... WHAT? HOW?
I JUST DID. BECAUSE I'M YOUR FATHER. BECAUSE I WAS STARMAN BEFORE YOU. I KNEW.
WHOA, DAD. I AM NOT STARMAN. YOU WERE... DAVID WAS. I'M JUST SOMEONE CAUGHT UP IN ALL THIS TEMPORARILY.
I'M NOT RUNNING FROM IT ... BUT AT THE SAME TIME... I AM NOT RUNNING INTO ANY LONG-TERM HERO THING.
YET YOU WENT TO THE MUSEUM, SON. WHY? I TOLD YOU TO GET GONE. I LAID NO GUILT ON YOU. THAT WAS SOLELY YOUR CHOICE.
IT WAS MOM'S WING. HER BEQUEST TO THE CITY. I COULDN'T LET IT BURN AND NOT TRY. THOUGH TRY AS I DID, I STILL FAILED.
BUT YOU DID TRY.
BUT.. BUT.. BUT NOTHING. I AM NOT STARMAN.
ANYWAY, I NEED ANOTHER COSMIC ROD.
REALLY? THAT'S JUST WHAT I'D EXPECT A "NOT STARMAN" TO SAY.
YEAH, YEAH.
BUT WE HAVE A PROBLEM. THERE ARE NO MORE. YOUR BROTHER'S WAS BROKEN. THE ONE GIVEN YOU, YOU'VE LOST.
AND MY WORKSHOP BLEW UP ALONG WITH MY HOME. EVEN IF I WAS WELL, I COULDN'T MAKE ANOTHER FOR A WHILE. SO...LIKE I SAY, WE HAVE A--

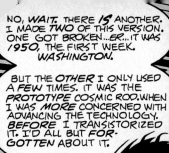

NO, *WAIT*. THERE *IS* ANOTHER. I MADE *TWO* OF THIS VERSION. ONE GOT BROKEN...*ER*... IT WAS *1950*, THE FIRST WEEK. *WASHINGTON*.

BUT THE *OTHER* I ONLY USED A *FEW* TIMES. IT WAS THE *PROTOTYPE COSMIC ROD.* WHEN I WAS *MORE* CONCERNED WITH ADVANCING THE TECHNOLOGY. *BEFORE* I TRANSISTORIZED IT. I'D ALL BUT *FOR-GOTTEN* ABOUT IT.

IT'S *BIGGER* THAN THE SMALL, HAND-HELD ONE, BUT--

IT'S *BETTER* THAN *NOTHING.* YEAH, I AGREE. WHERE IS IT?

I HAVE *THINGS* IN DEEP STORAGE. NOTES, OLD EQUIPMENT. THERE'S A COSTUME THERE, *TOO*, I THINK. YOU CAN *WEAR* IT. HERE... THE *LOCATION.* I'LL WRITE IT DOWN.

SO... IT'S *AGREED.*

HOW COULD I REFUSE? A PERCENTAGE OF THE BOOTY FROM *ALL* THE HEISTS AND CRIMES YOUR... *HELPERS* COMMIT. *QUITE* AN OFFER.

GOOD. GO, THEN. AND AS FOR *THOSE* WHO'D ALLY THEMSELVES WITH THE KNIGHTS OLD AND YOUNG...

KILL THEM *ALL.* BE CRUEL THAT MY NAME BE *FEARED* ALL THE MORE. IN THEIR *LAST* MOMENTS, HAVE THEM RUE *EVERY* MOMENT PRIOR.

AS YOU SAY.

BUT *BEFORE* ALL THAT BLOOD AND DEATH AND... *UNPLEASANT-NESS...*

I THINK ANOTHER *SHERRY* MIGHT BE IN ORDER.

I HAVE *DIED...*

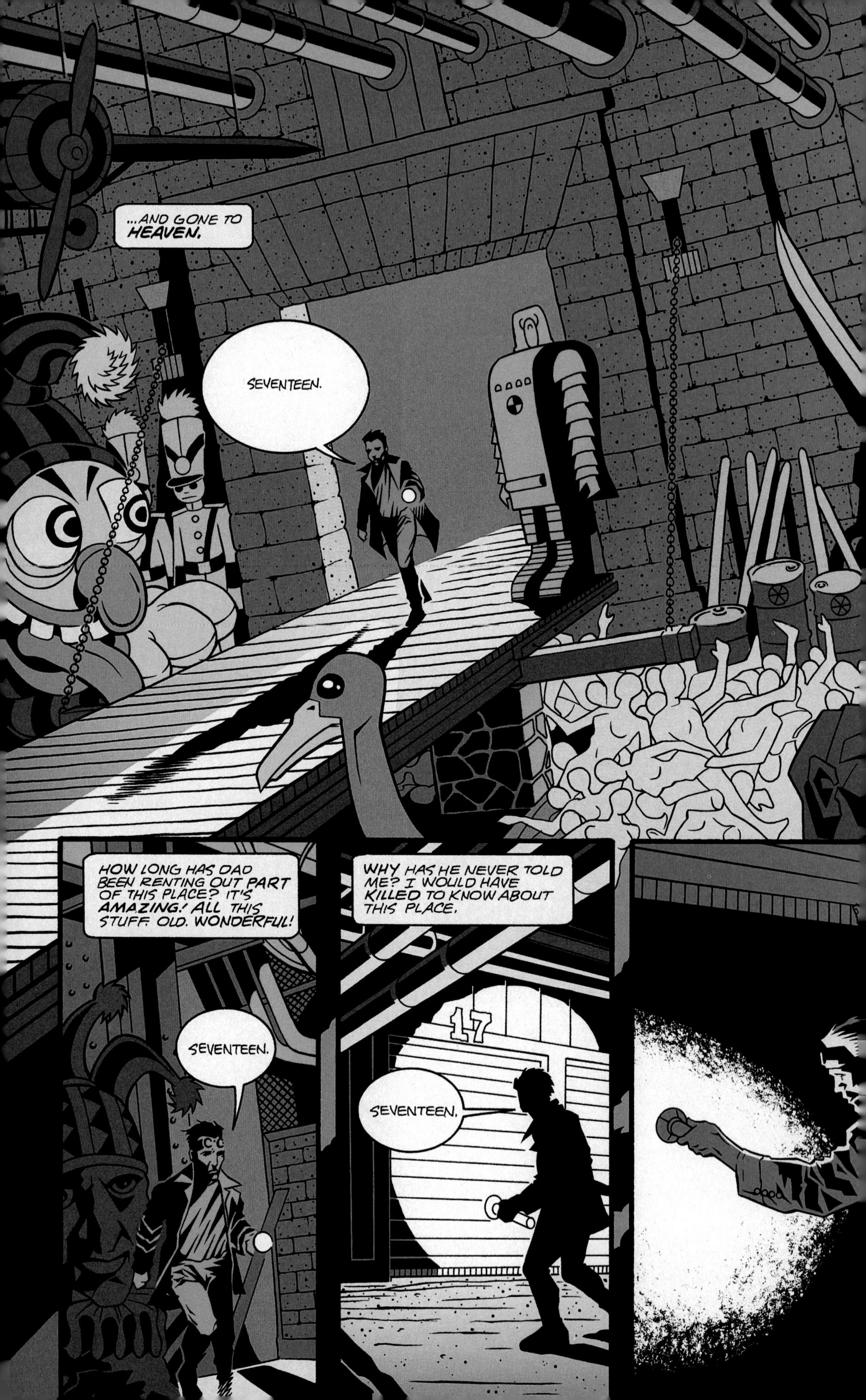
...AND GONE TO HEAVEN.
SEVENTEEN.
HOW LONG HAS DAD BEEN RENTING OUT PART OF THIS PLACE? IT'S AMAZING! ALL THIS STUFF. OLD. WONDERFUL!
SEVENTEEN.
WHY HAS HE NEVER TOLD ME? I WOULD HAVE KILLED TO KNOW ABOUT THIS PLACE.
17
SEVENTEEN.

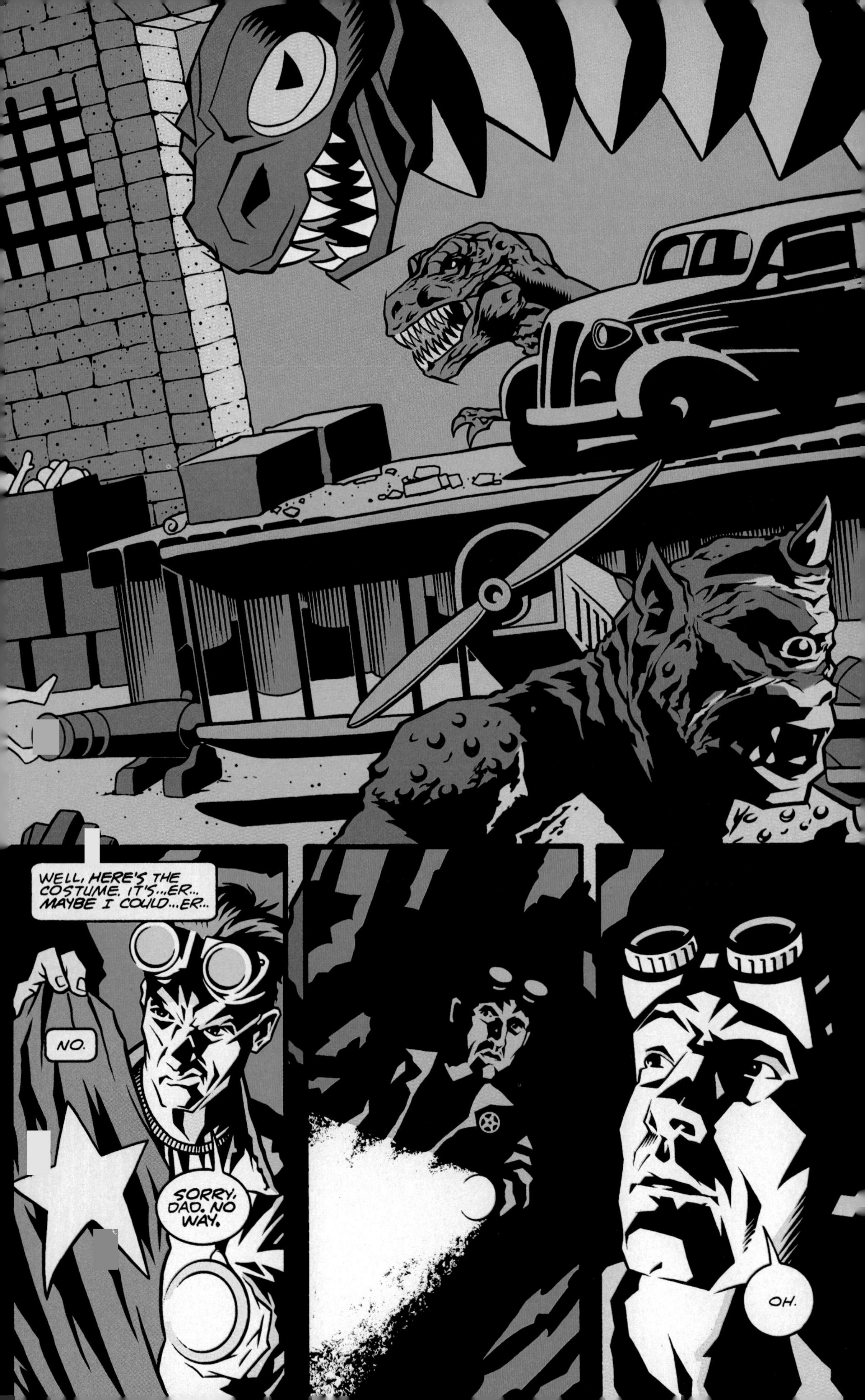
WELL, HERE'S THE COSTUME. IT'S...ER... MAYBE I COULD...ER...
NO.
SORRY, DAD. NO WAY.
OH.

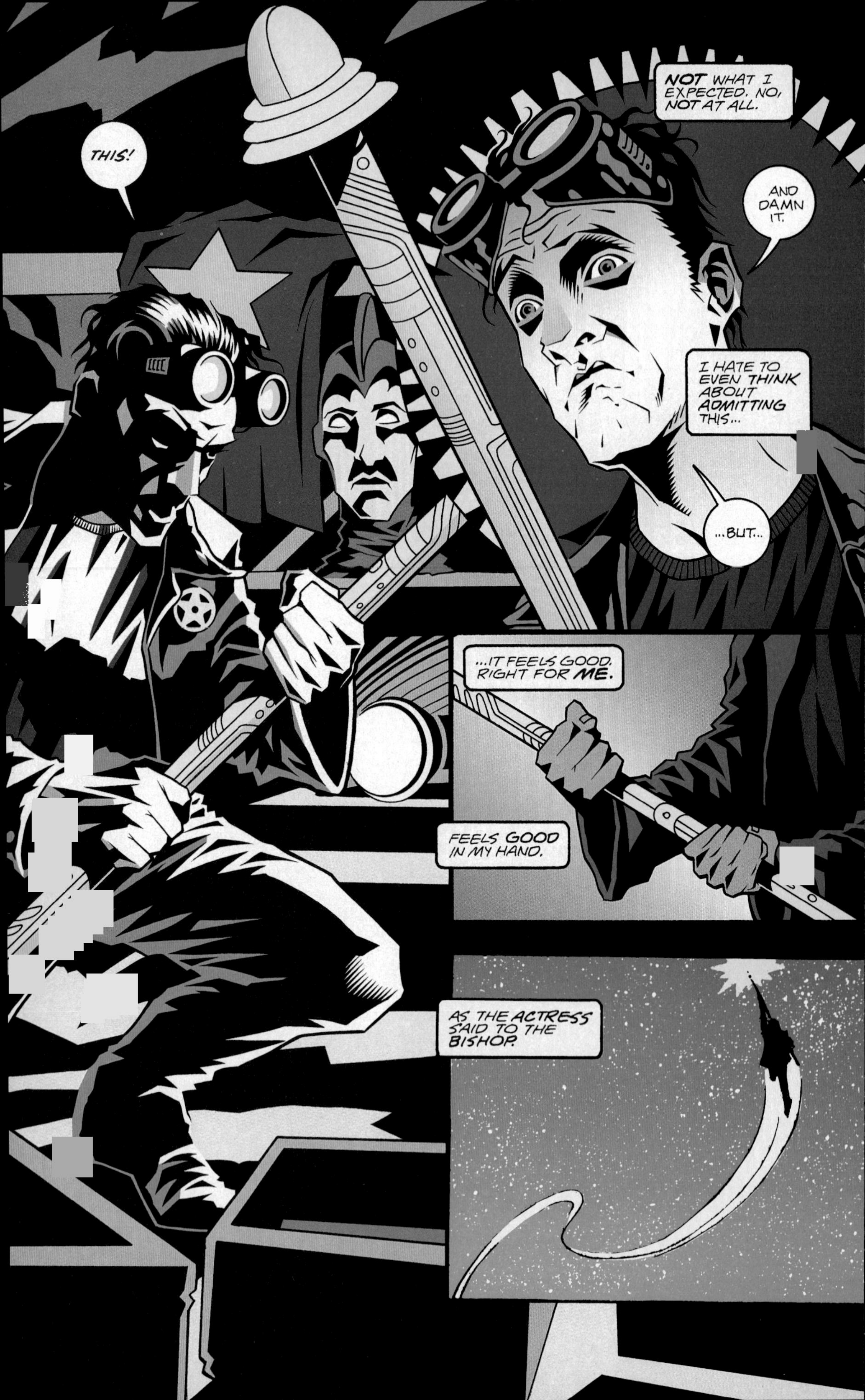
THIS!
NOT WHAT I EXPECTED. NO, NOT AT ALL.
AND DAMN IT.
I HATE TO EVEN THINK ABOUT ADMITTING THIS...
...BUT...
...IT FEELS GOOD. RIGHT FOR ME.
FEELS GOOD IN MY HAND.
AS THE ACTRESS SAID TO THE BISHOP.

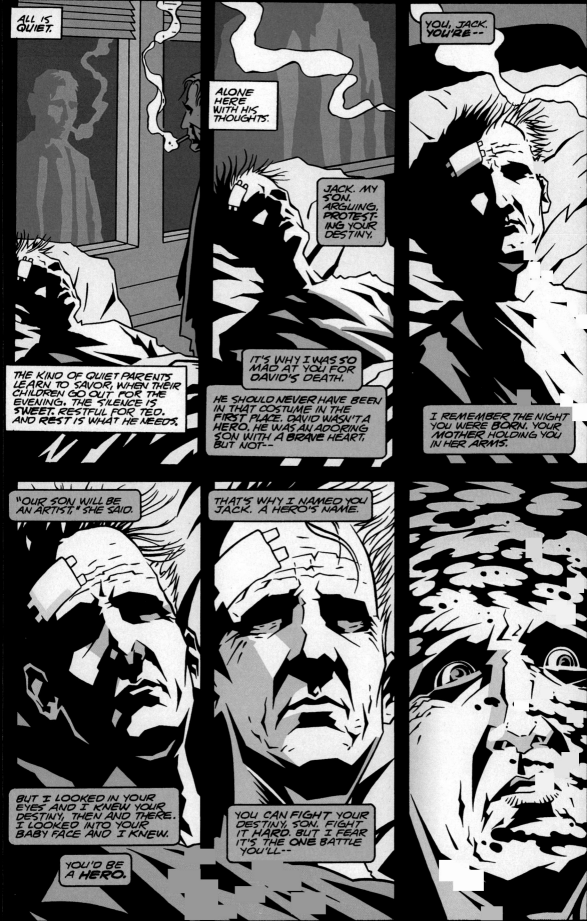

ALL IS QUIET.

ALONE HERE WITH HIS THOUGHTS.

THE KIND OF QUIET PARENTS LEARN TO SAVOR, WHEN THEIR CHILDREN GO OUT FOR THE EVENING. THE SILENCE IS SWEET. RESTFUL FOR TED. AND REST IS WHAT HE NEEDS.

JACK. MY SON. ARGUING. PROTEST-ING YOUR DESTINY.

IT'S WHY I WAS SO MAD AT YOU FOR DAVID'S DEATH.

HE SHOULD NEVER HAVE BEEN IN THAT COSTUME IN THE FIRST PLACE. DAVID WASN'T A HERO. HE WAS AN ADORING SON WITH A BRAVE HEART, BUT NOT--

YOU, JACK. YOU'RE--

I REMEMBER THE NIGHT YOU WERE BORN. YOUR MOTHER HOLDING YOU IN HER ARMS.

"OUR SON WILL BE AN ARTIST," SHE SAID.

BUT I LOOKED IN YOUR EYES AND I KNEW YOUR DESTINY, THEN AND THERE. I LOOKED INTO YOUR BABY FACE AND I KNEW.

YOU'D BE A HERO.

THAT'S WHY I NAMED YOU JACK. A HERO'S NAME.

YOU CAN FIGHT YOUR DESTINY, SON. FIGHT IT HARD. BUT I FEAR IT'S THE ONE BATTLE YOU'LL--

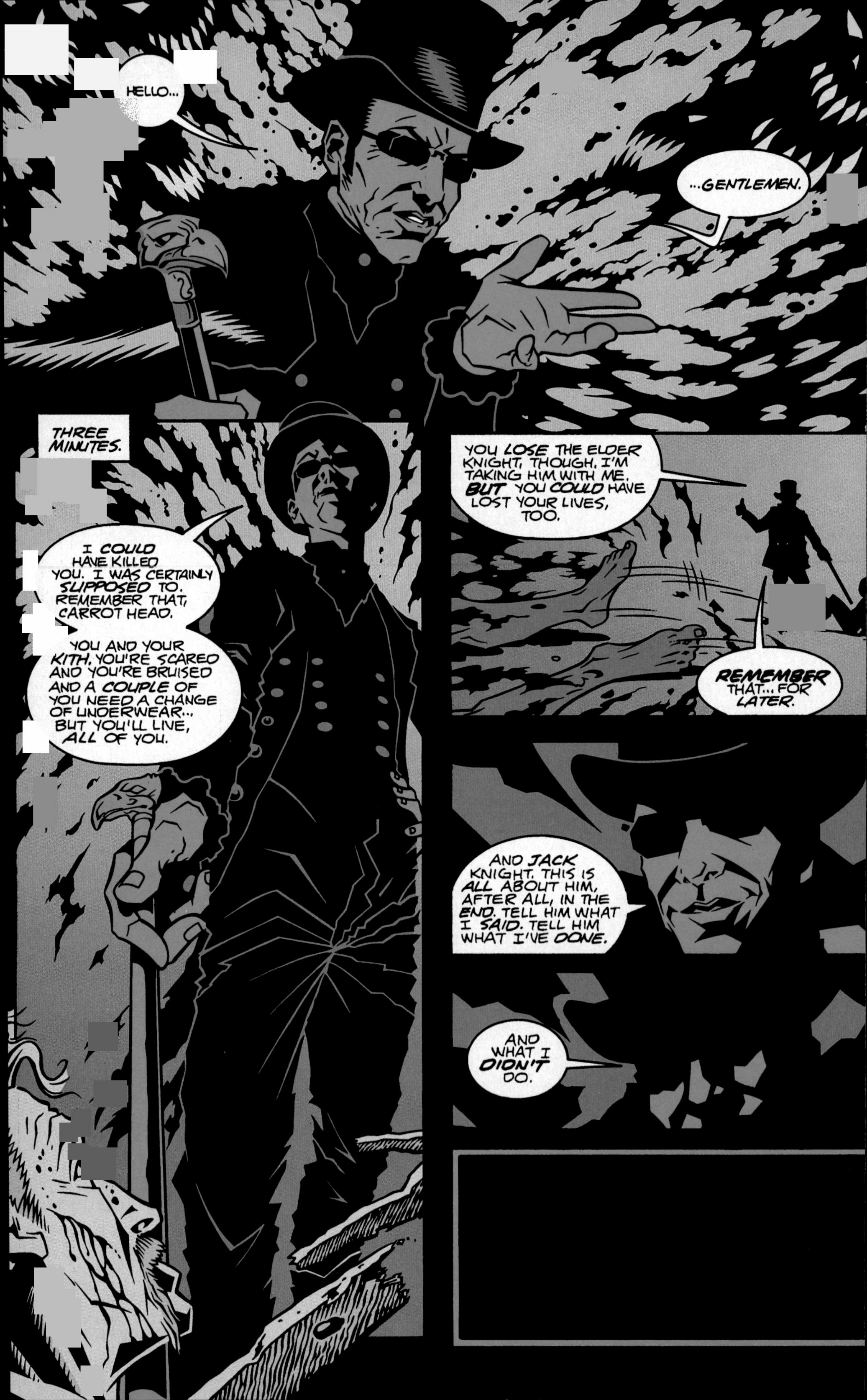
HELLO...
...GENTLEMEN.
THREE MINUTES.
I COULD HAVE KILLED YOU. I WAS CERTAINLY SUPPOSED TO. REMEMBER THAT, CARROT HEAD.
YOU AND YOUR KITH, YOU'RE SCARED AND YOU'RE BRUISED AND A COUPLE OF YOU NEED A CHANGE OF UNDERWEAR... BUT YOU'LL LIVE, ALL OF YOU.
YOU LOSE THE ELDER KNIGHT, THOUGH. I'M TAKING HIM WITH ME. BUT YOU COULD HAVE LOST YOUR LIVES, TOO.
REMEMBER THAT... FOR LATER.
AND JACK KNIGHT. THIS IS ALL ABOUT HIM, AFTER ALL, IN THE END. TELL HIM WHAT I SAID. TELL HIM WHAT I'VE DONE.
AND WHAT I DIDN'T DO.

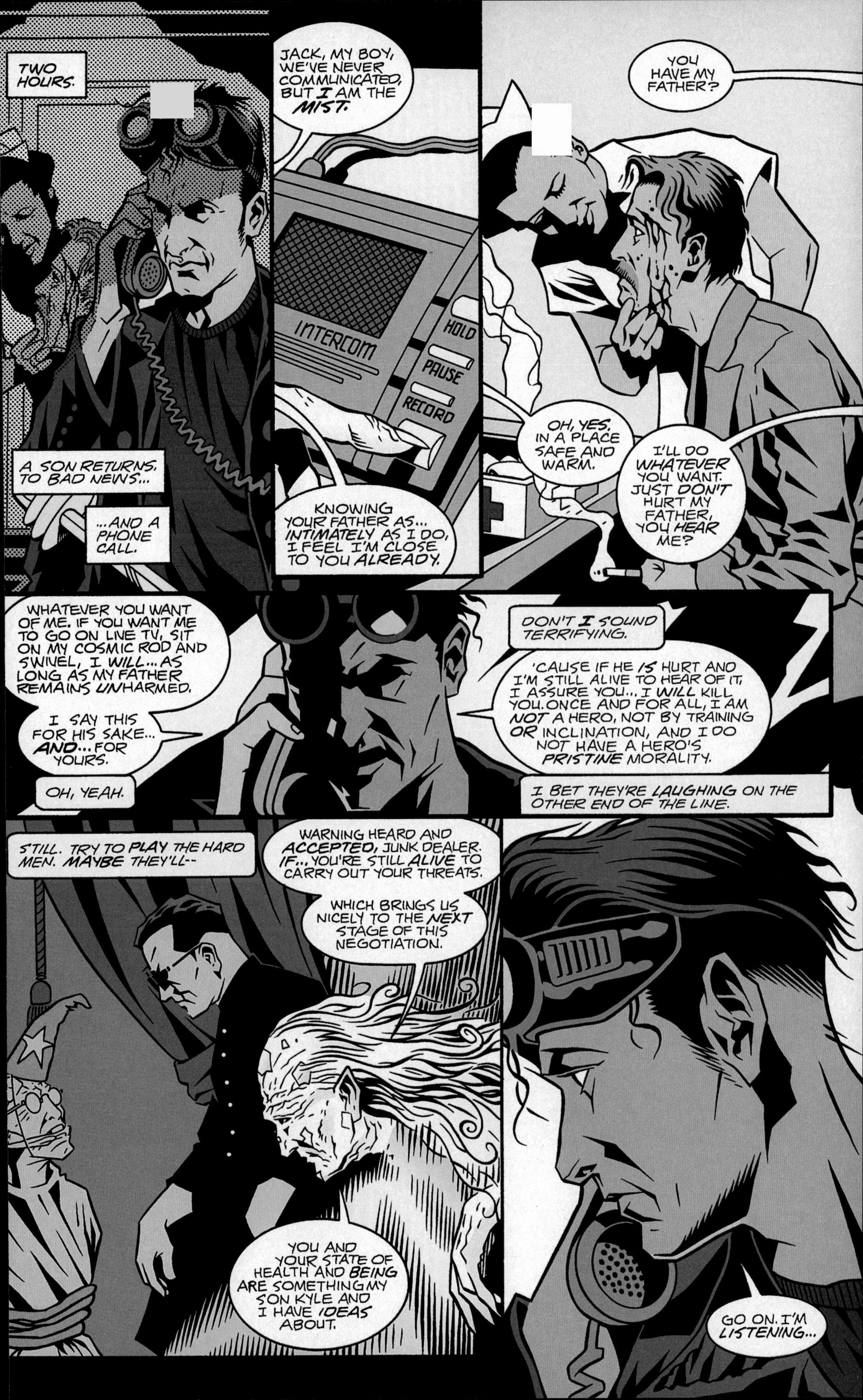
TWO HOURS.
A SON RETURNS, TO BAD NEWS...
...AND A PHONE CALL.
JACK, MY BOY, WE'VE NEVER COMMUNICATED, BUT *I* AM THE *MIST.*
INTERCOM
HOLD
PAUSE
RECORD
KNOWING YOUR FATHER AS... *INTIMATELY* AS I DO, I FEEL I'M CLOSE TO YOU *ALREADY.*
YOU HAVE MY FATHER?
OH, YES. IN A PLACE SAFE AND WARM.
I'LL DO *WHATEVER* YOU WANT. JUST *DON'T* HURT MY FATHER, YOU *HEAR* ME?
WHATEVER YOU WANT OF ME. IF YOU WANT ME TO GO ON LIVE TV, SIT ON MY COSMIC ROD AND SWIVEL, I *WILL*... AS LONG AS MY FATHER REMAINS *UN*HARMED.
I SAY THIS FOR HIS SAKE... *AND*... FOR YOURS.
OH, YEAH.
DON'T *I* SOUND TERRIFYING.
'CAUSE IF HE *IS* HURT AND I'M STILL ALIVE TO HEAR OF IT, I ASSURE YOU... I *WILL* KILL YOU. ONCE AND FOR ALL, I AM *NOT* A HERO, NOT BY TRAINING *OR* INCLINATION, AND I DO NOT HAVE A HERO'S *PRISTINE* MORALITY.
I BET THEY'RE *LAUGHING* ON THE OTHER END OF THE LINE.
STILL. TRY TO *PLAY* THE HARD MEN. *MAYBE* THEY'LL--
WARNING HEARD AND *ACCEPTED,* JUNK DEALER. *IF*... YOU'RE STILL *ALIVE* TO CARRY OUT YOUR THREATS.
WHICH BRINGS US NICELY TO THE *NEXT* STAGE OF THIS NEGOTIATION.
YOU AND YOUR STATE OF HEALTH AND *BEING* ARE SOMETHING MY SON KYLE AND I HAVE *IDEAS* ABOUT.
GO ON. I'M *LISTENING*...

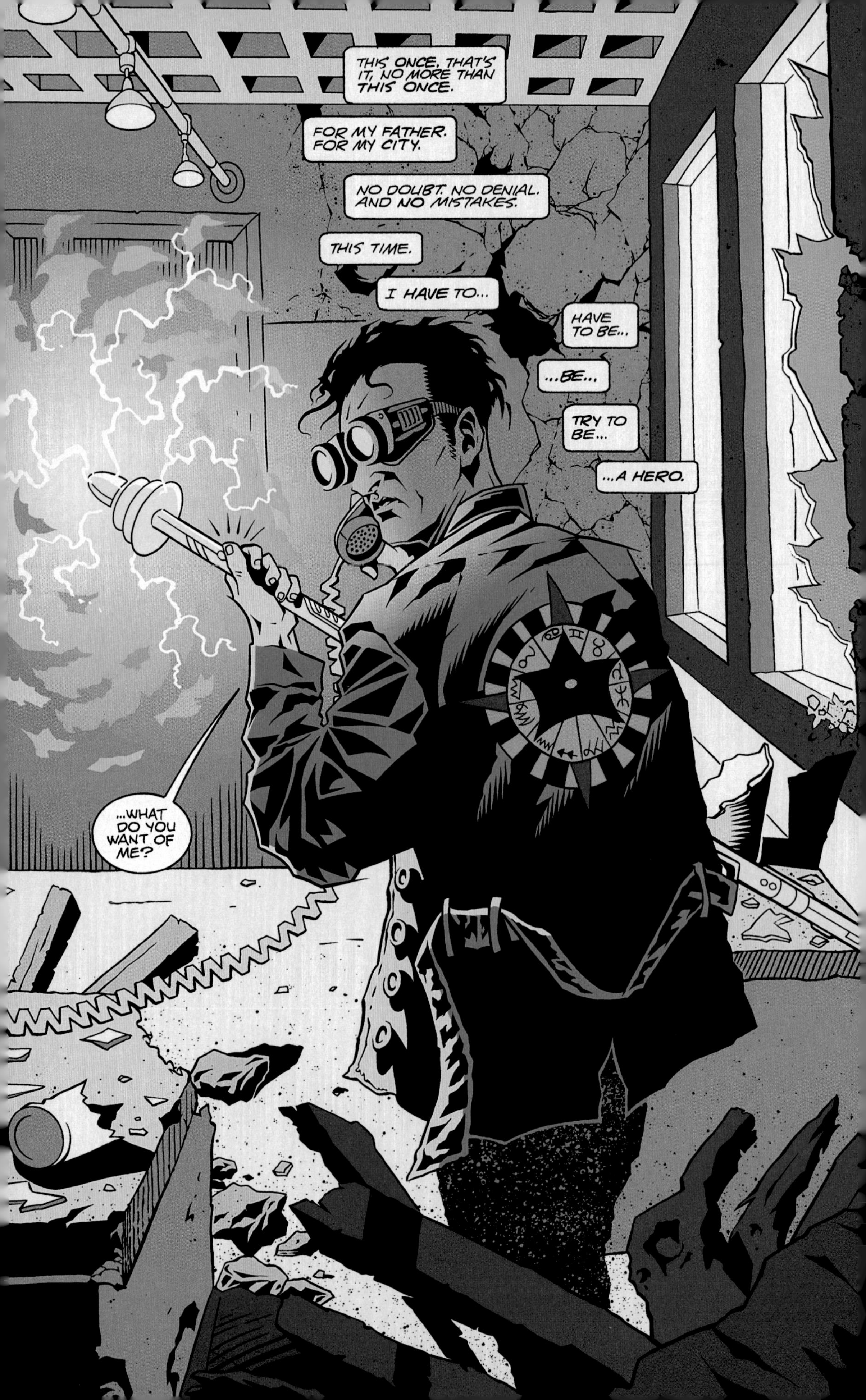
THIS ONCE. THAT'S IT, NO MORE THAN THIS ONCE.
FOR MY FATHER. FOR MY CITY.
NO DOUBT. NO DENIAL. AND NO MISTAKES.
THIS TIME.
I HAVE TO...
HAVE TO BE...
...BE...
TRY TO BE...
...A HERO.
...WHAT DO YOU WANT OF ME?

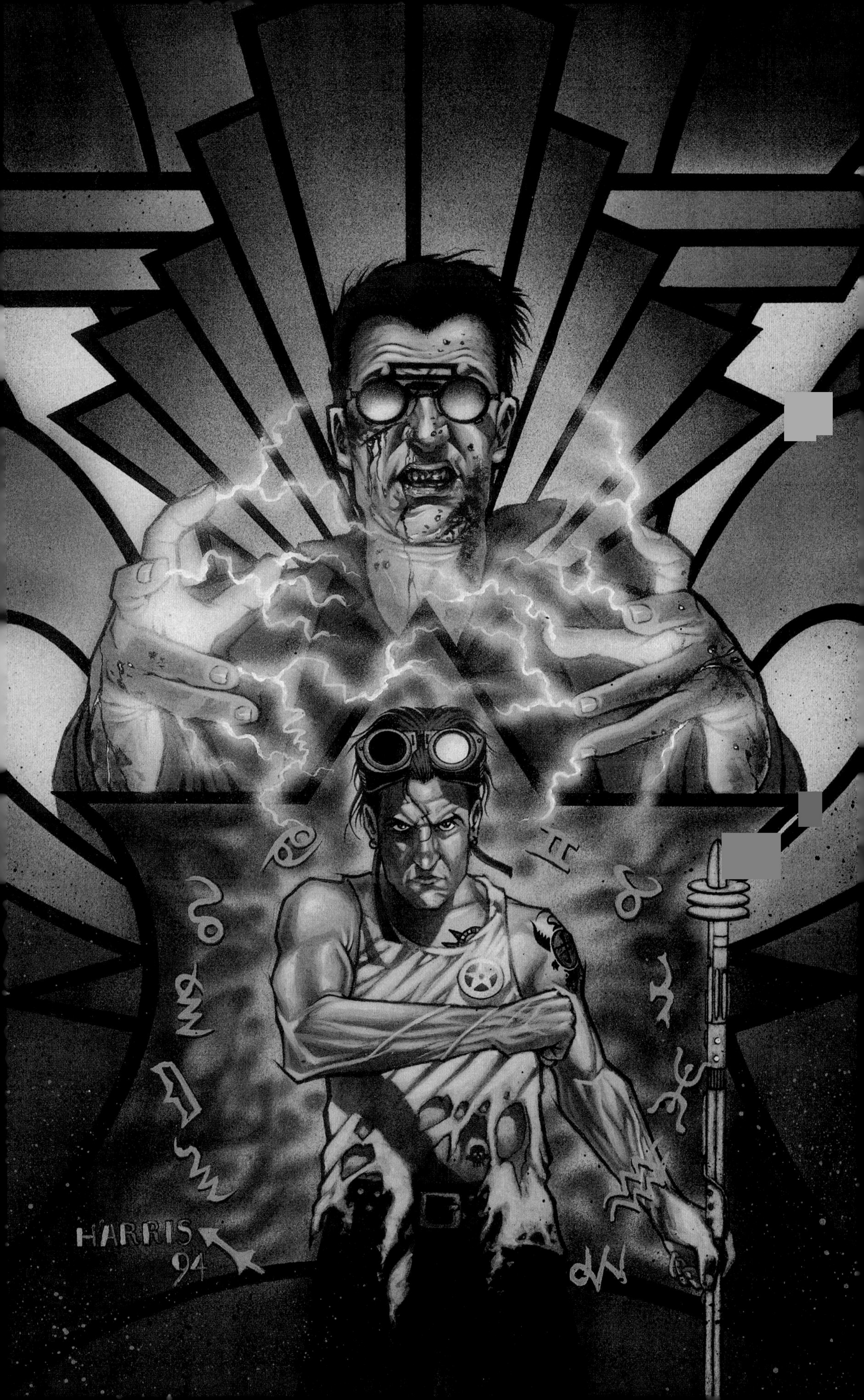
HARRIS
94

STARMAN 3

Cover by Tony Harris

Written by James Robinson

Pencils by Tony Harris,

with inks by Wade von Grawbadger

and colors by Gregory Wright

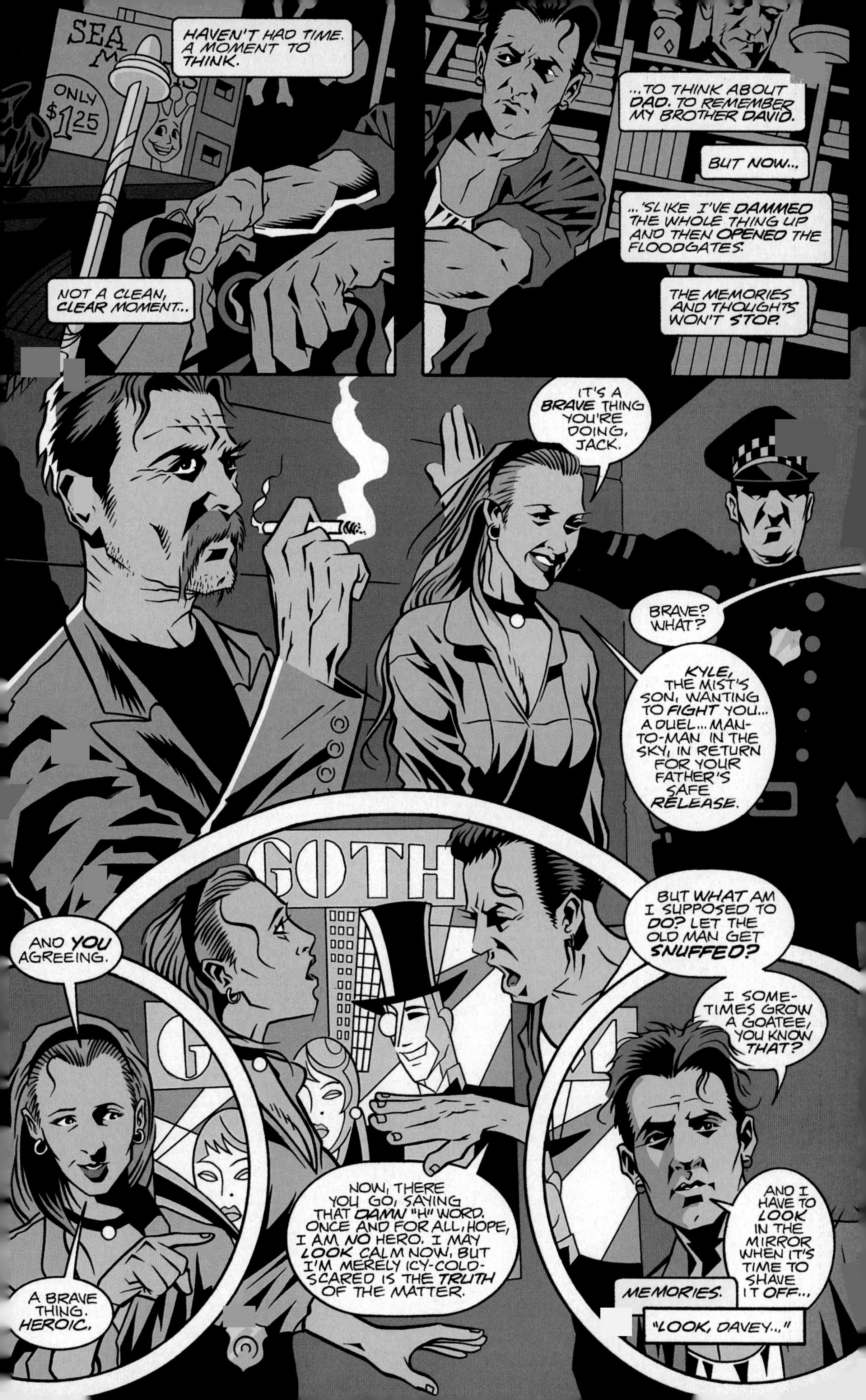
SEA
ONLY $1.25
HAVEN'T HAD TIME. A MOMENT TO THINK.
NOT A CLEAN, CLEAR MOMENT...
...TO THINK ABOUT DAD. TO REMEMBER MY BROTHER DAVID.
BUT NOW...
...'SLIKE I'VE DAMMED THE WHOLE THING UP AND THEN OPENED THE FLOODGATES.
THE MEMORIES AND THOUGHTS WON'T STOP.
IT'S A BRAVE THING YOU'RE DOING, JACK.
BRAVE? WHAT?
KYLE, THE MIST'S SON, WANTING TO FIGHT YOU... A DUEL... MAN-TO-MAN IN THE SKY, IN RETURN FOR YOUR FATHER'S SAFE RELEASE.
GOTH
AND YOU AGREEING.
A BRAVE THING. HEROIC.
BUT WHAT AM I SUPPOSED TO DO? LET THE OLD MAN GET SNUFFED?
NOW, THERE YOU GO, SAYING THAT DAMN "H" WORD. ONCE AND FOR ALL, HOPE, I AM NO HERO. I MAY LOOK CALM NOW, BUT I'M MERELY ICY-COLD-SCARED IS THE TRUTH OF THE MATTER.
I SOMETIMES GROW A GOATEE, YOU KNOW THAT?
AND I HAVE TO LOOK IN THE MIRROR WHEN IT'S TIME TO SHAVE IT OFF...
MEMORIES.
"LOOK, DAVEY..."

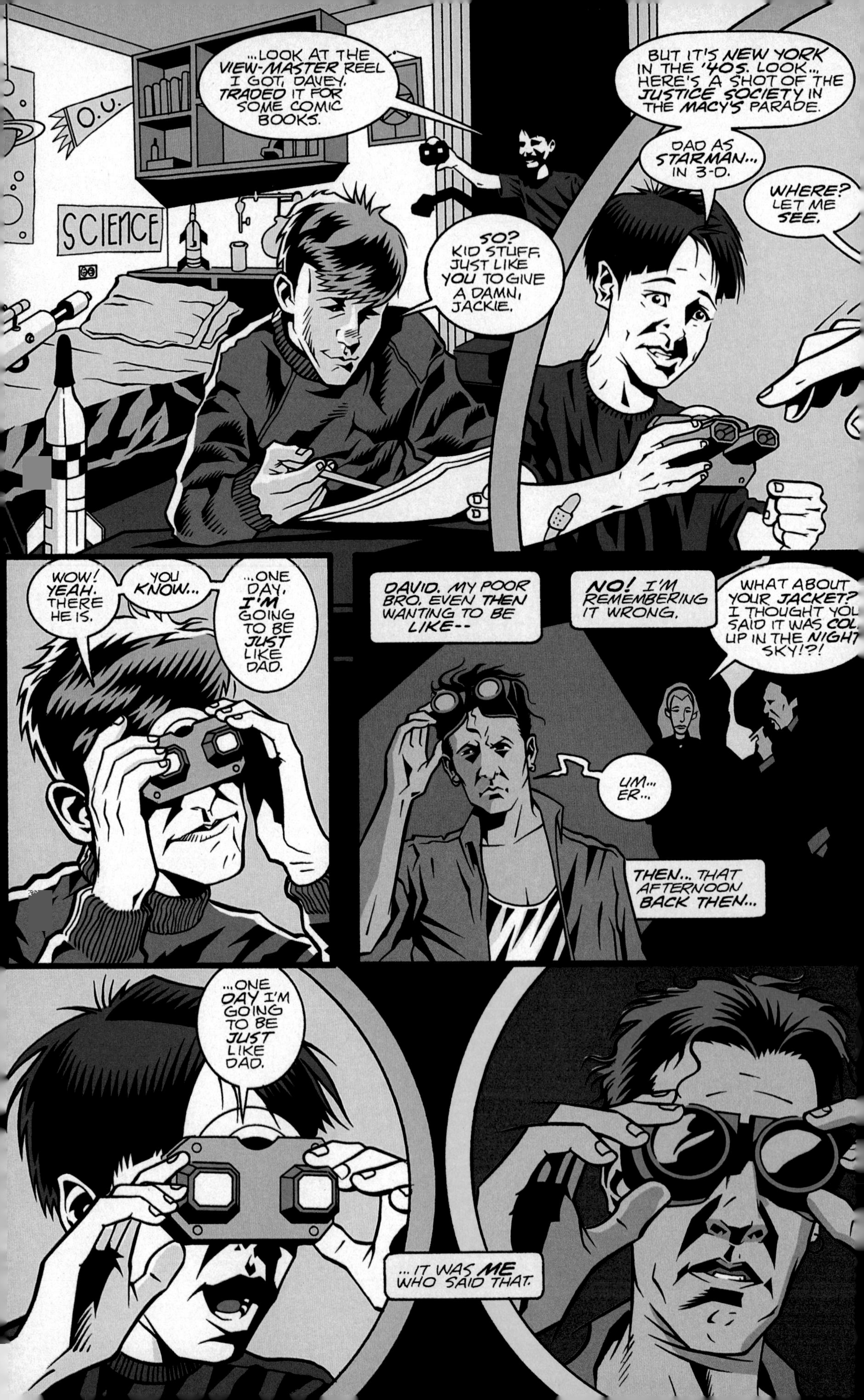
...LOOK AT THE VIEW-MASTER REEL I GOT, DAVEY. TRADED IT FOR SOME COMIC BOOKS.
SO? KID STUFF. JUST LIKE YOU TO GIVE A DAMN, JACKIE.
BUT IT'S NEW YORK IN THE '40S. LOOK... HERE'S A SHOT OF THE JUSTICE SOCIETY IN THE MACY'S PARADE.
DAD AS STARMAN... IN 3-D.
WHERE? LET ME SEE.
WOW! YEAH. THERE HE IS.
YOU KNOW...
...ONE DAY, I'M GOING TO BE JUST LIKE DAD.
DAVID. MY POOR BRO. EVEN THEN WANTING TO BE LIKE--
NO! I'M REMEMBERING IT WRONG.
WHAT ABOUT YOUR JACKET? I THOUGHT YOU SAID IT WAS COL UP IN THE NIGHT SKY!?!
UM... ER...
THEN... THAT AFTERNOON BACK THEN...
...ONE DAY I'M GOING TO BE JUST LIKE DAD.
...IT WAS ME WHO SAID THAT.

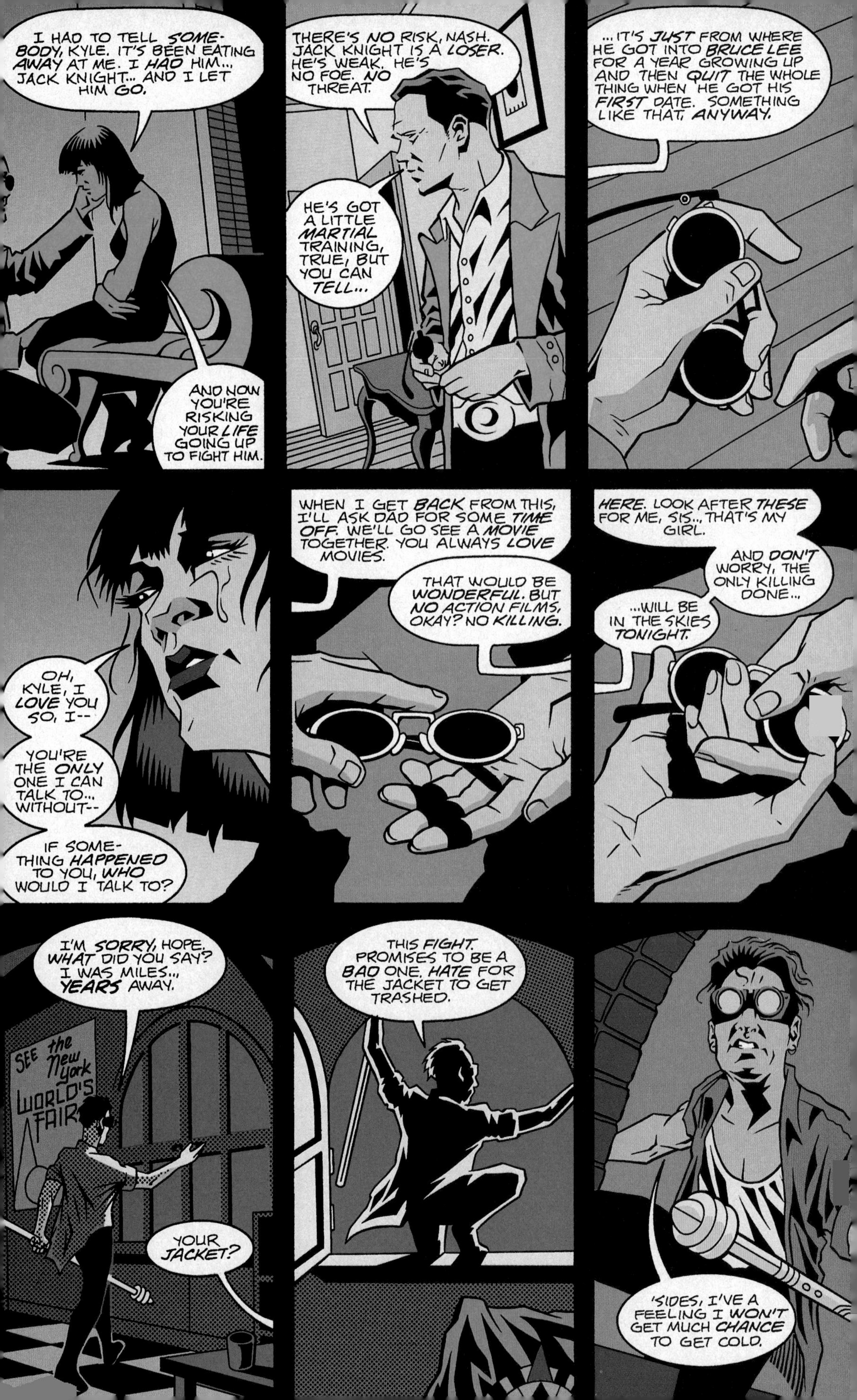
I HAD TO TELL SOMEBODY, KYLE. IT'S BEEN EATING AWAY AT ME. I HAD HIM... JACK KNIGHT... AND I LET HIM GO.
AND NOW YOU'RE RISKING YOUR LIFE GOING UP TO FIGHT HIM.
THERE'S NO RISK, NASH. JACK KNIGHT IS A LOSER. HE'S WEAK. HE'S NO FOE. NO THREAT.
HE'S GOT A LITTLE MARTIAL TRAINING, TRUE, BUT YOU CAN TELL...
...IT'S JUST FROM WHERE HE GOT INTO BRUCE LEE FOR A YEAR GROWING UP AND THEN QUIT THE WHOLE THING WHEN HE GOT HIS FIRST DATE. SOMETHING LIKE THAT, ANYWAY.
OH, KYLE, I LOVE YOU SO, I--
YOU'RE THE ONLY ONE I CAN TALK TO... WITHOUT--
IF SOMETHING HAPPENED TO YOU, WHO WOULD I TALK TO?
WHEN I GET BACK FROM THIS, I'LL ASK DAD FOR SOME TIME OFF. WE'LL GO SEE A MOVIE TOGETHER. YOU ALWAYS LOVE MOVIES.
THAT WOULD BE WONDERFUL. BUT NO ACTION FILMS, OKAY? NO KILLING.
HERE. LOOK AFTER THESE FOR ME, SIS... THAT'S MY GIRL.
AND DON'T WORRY, THE ONLY KILLING DONE...
...WILL BE IN THE SKIES TONIGHT.
I'M SORRY, HOPE. WHAT DID YOU SAY? I WAS MILES... YEARS AWAY.
SEE the New York WORLD'S FAIR
YOUR JACKET?
THIS FIGHT. PROMISES TO BE A BAD ONE. HATE FOR THE JACKET TO GET TRASHED.
'SIDES, I'VE A FEELING I WON'T GET MUCH CHANCE TO GET COLD.

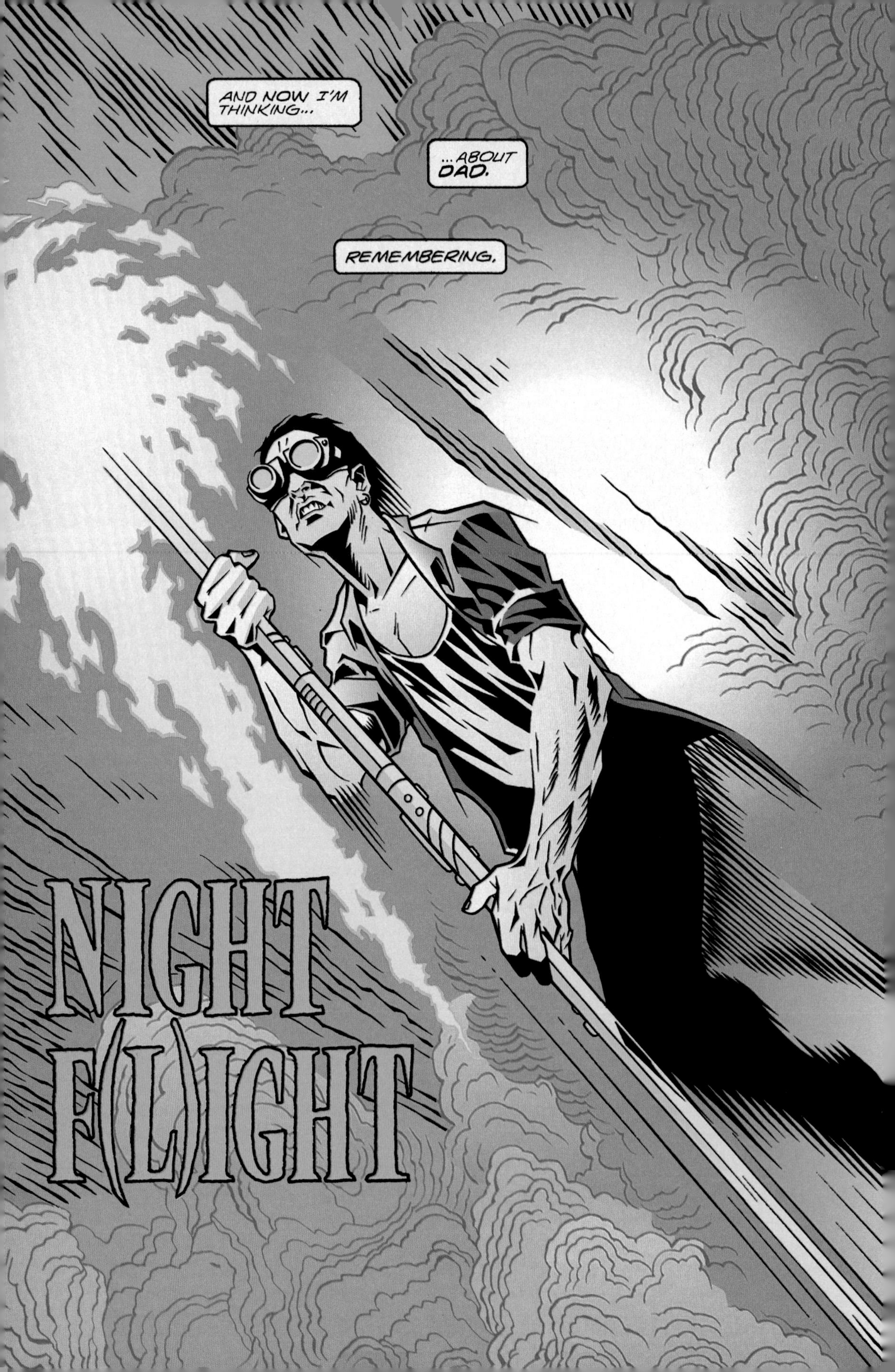
AND NOW I'M THINKING...
...ABOUT DAD.
REMEMBERING.
NIGHT F(L)IGHT

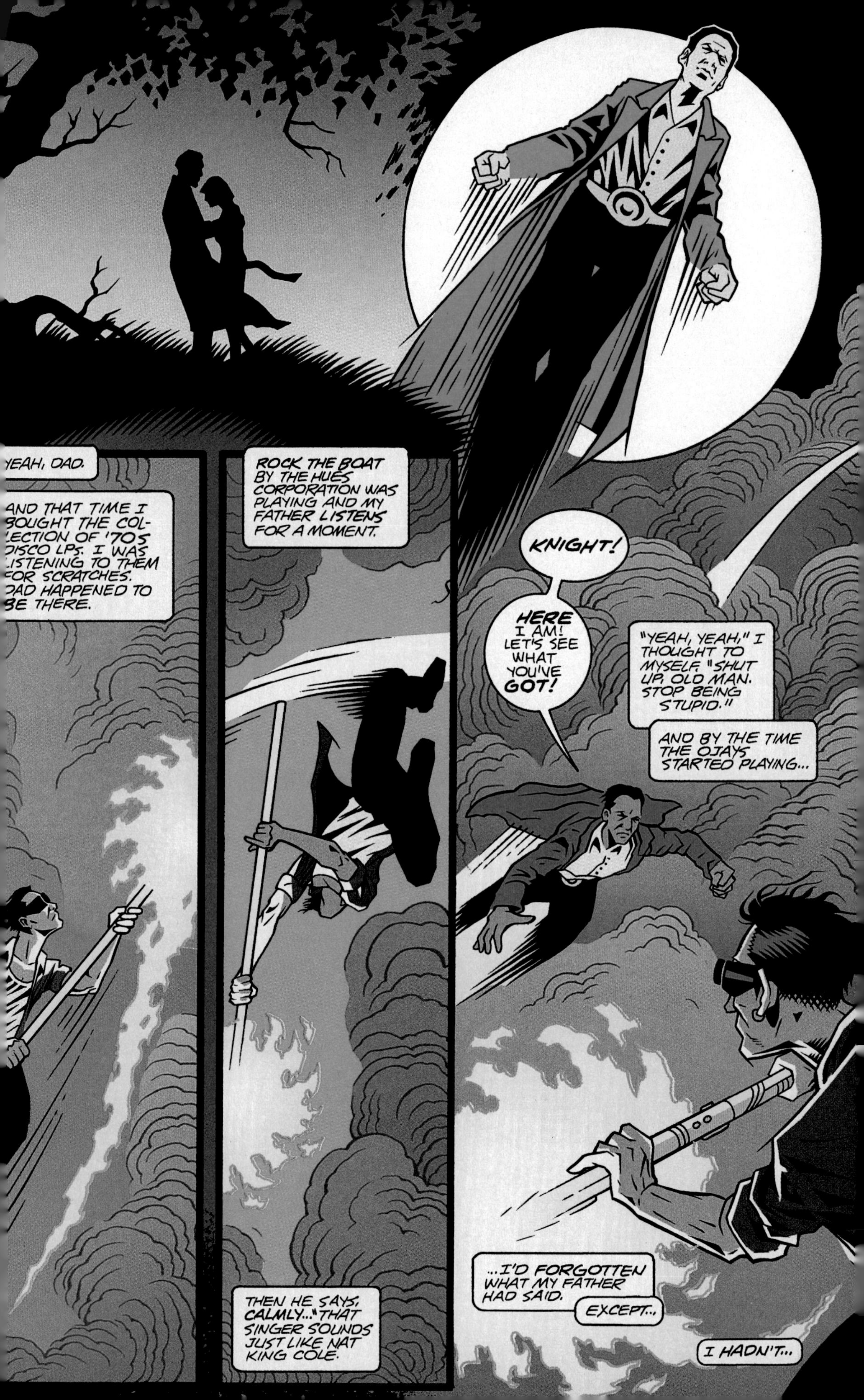

YEAH, DAD.
AND THAT TIME I BOUGHT THE COLLECTION OF '70S DISCO LPS. I WAS LISTENING TO THEM FOR SCRATCHES. DAD HAPPENED TO BE THERE.
ROCK THE BOAT BY THE HUES CORPORATION WAS PLAYING AND MY FATHER LISTENS FOR A MOMENT.
THEN HE SAYS, CALMLY..."THAT SINGER SOUNDS JUST LIKE NAT KING COLE.
KNIGHT!
HERE I AM! LET'S SEE WHAT YOU'VE GOT!
"YEAH, YEAH," I THOUGHT TO MYSELF. "SHUT UP, OLD MAN. STOP BEING STUPID."
AND BY THE TIME THE OJAYS STARTED PLAYING...
...I'D FORGOTTEN WHAT MY FATHER HAD SAID.
EXCEPT...
I HADN'T...

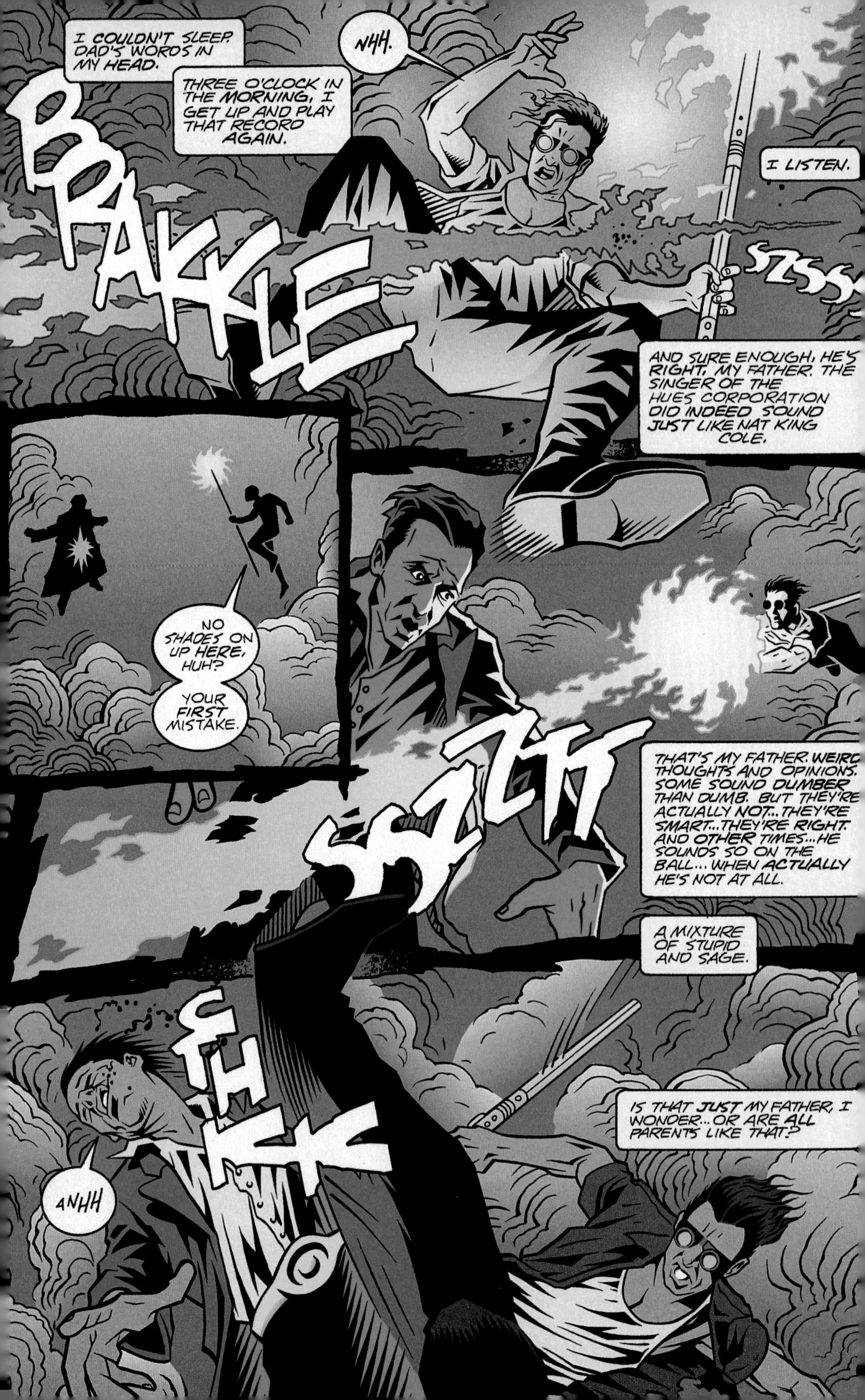
I COULDN'T SLEEP. DAD'S WORDS IN MY HEAD.
NHH.
THREE O'CLOCK IN THE MORNING, I GET UP AND PLAY THAT RECORD AGAIN.
BRAKKLE
I LISTEN.
SZSS
AND SURE ENOUGH, HE'S RIGHT, MY FATHER. THE SINGER OF THE HUES CORPORATION DID INDEED SOUND JUST LIKE NAT KING COLE.
NO SHADES ON UP HERE, HUH?
YOUR FIRST MISTAKE.
SSZZT
THAT'S MY FATHER. WEIRD THOUGHTS AND OPINIONS. SOME SOUND DUMBER THAN DUMB. BUT THEY'RE ACTUALLY NOT... THEY'RE SMART... THEY'RE RIGHT. AND OTHER TIMES... HE SOUNDS SO ON THE BALL... WHEN ACTUALLY HE'S NOT AT ALL.
A MIXTURE OF STUPID AND SAGE.
CHUK
IS THAT JUST MY FATHER, I WONDER... OR ARE ALL PARENTS LIKE THAT?
ANHH

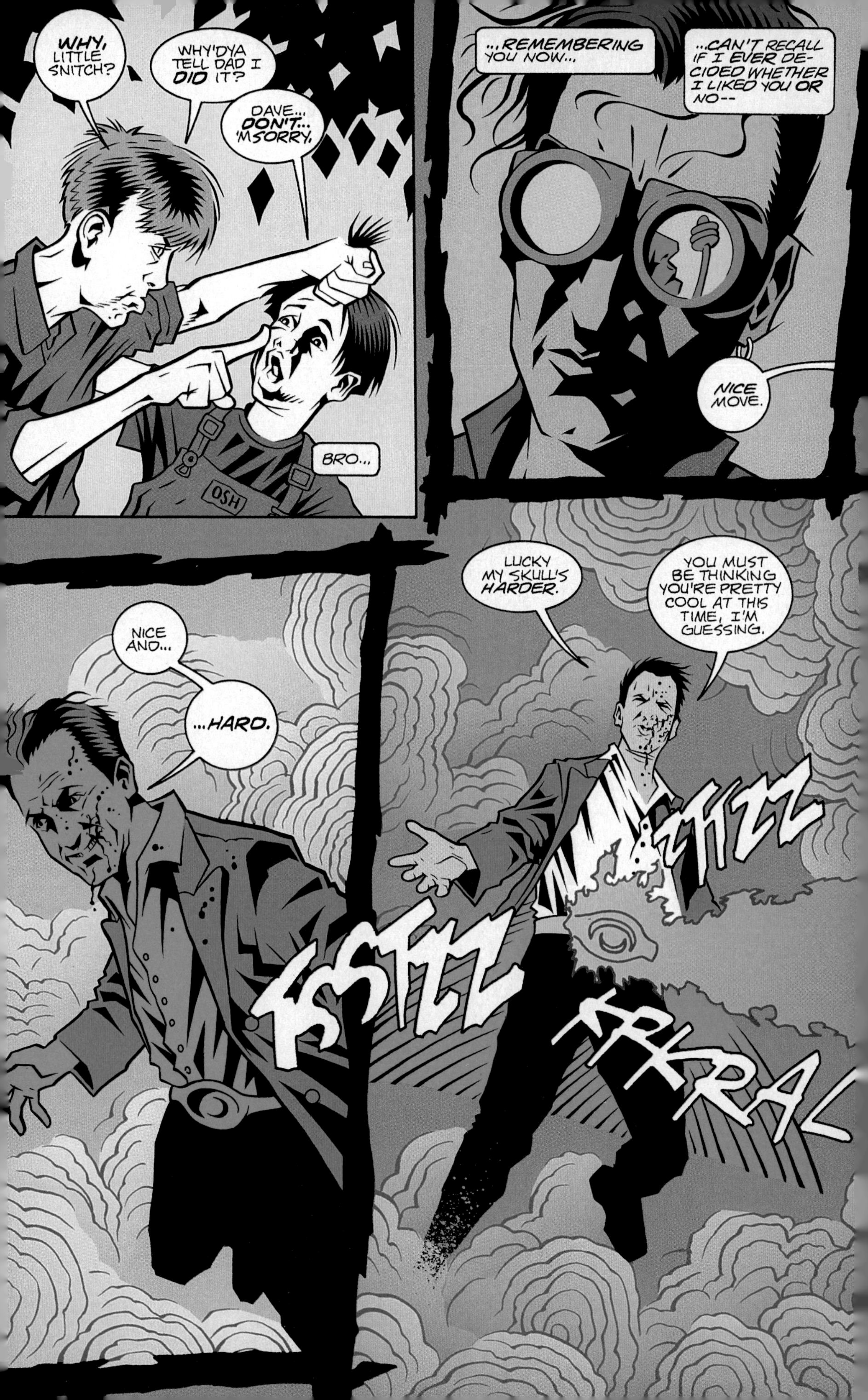

WHY, LITTLE SNITCH?
WHY'DYA TELL DAD I DID IT?
DAVE... DON'T... 'M SORRY.
BRO...
...REMEMBERING YOU NOW...
...CAN'T RECALL IF I EVER DE-CIDED WHETHER I LIKED YOU OR NO--
NICE MOVE.
NICE AND...
...HARD.
LUCKY MY SKULL'S HARDER.
YOU MUST BE THINKING YOU'RE PRETTY COOL AT THIS TIME, I'M GUESSING.
ZHZZ
FSSTZZ
KRKRAL

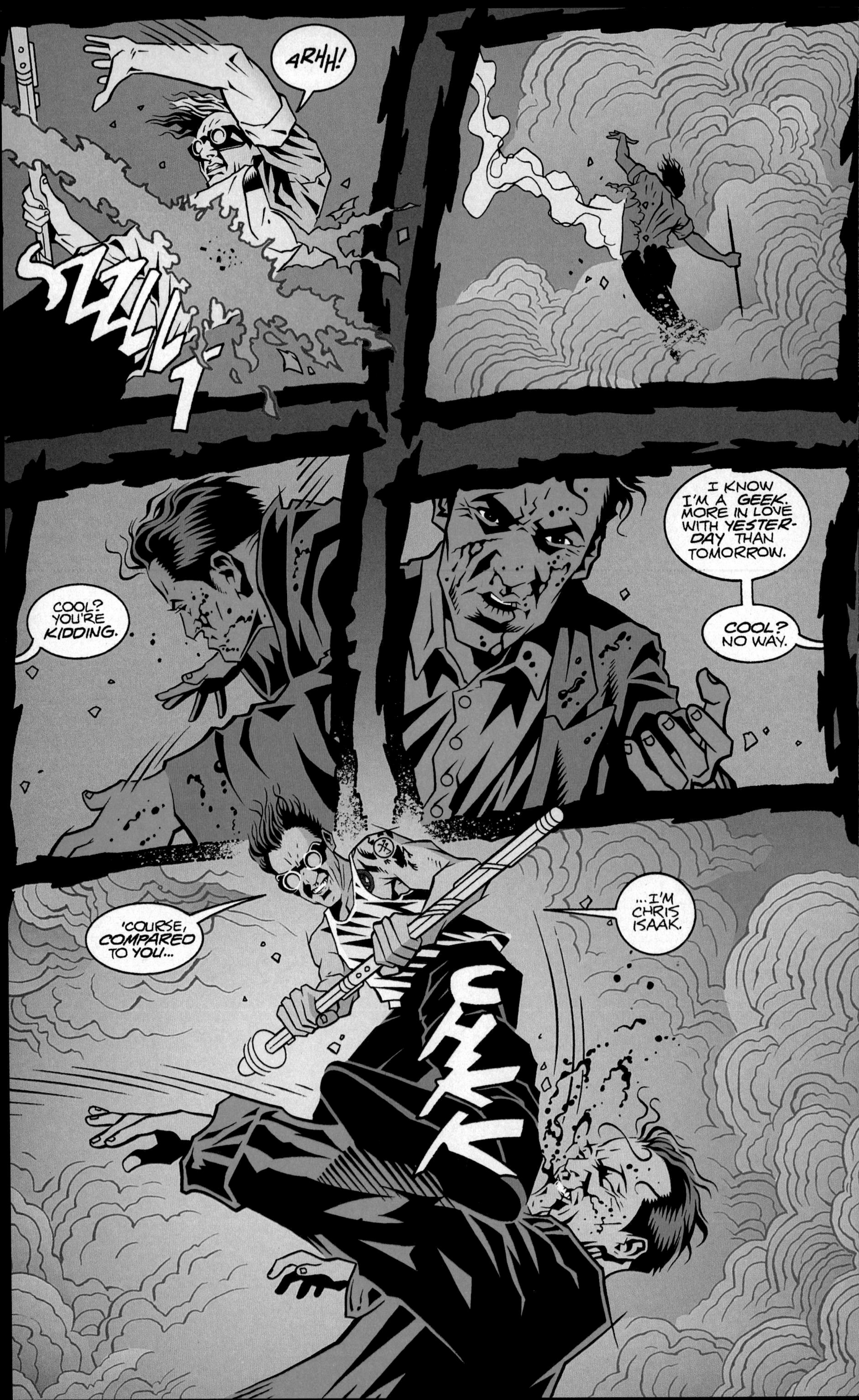
ARHH!
SZZZLL-T
I KNOW I'M A GEEK. MORE IN LOVE WITH YESTERDAY THAN TOMORROW.
COOL? NO WAY.
COOL? YOU'RE KIDDING.
'COURSE, COMPARED TO YOU...
...I'M CHRIS ISAAK.
CHKK

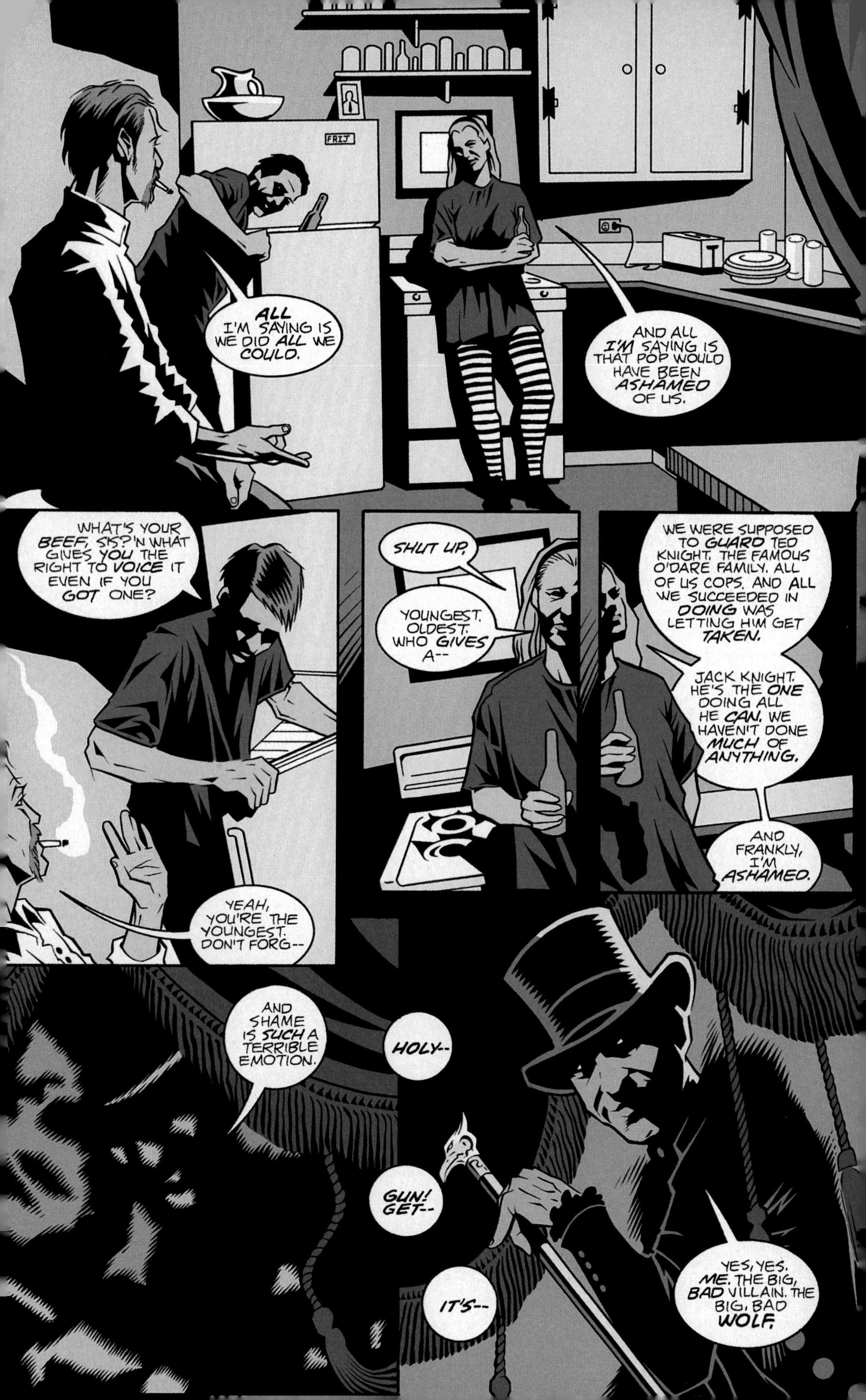
FRIJ
ALL I'M SAYING IS WE DID ALL WE COULD.
AND ALL I'M SAYING IS THAT POP WOULD HAVE BEEN ASHAMED OF US.
WHAT'S YOUR BEEF, SIS? 'N WHAT GIVES YOU THE RIGHT TO VOICE IT EVEN IF YOU GOT ONE?
YEAH, YOU'RE THE YOUNGEST. DON'T FORG--
SHUT UP.
YOUNGEST. OLDEST. WHO GIVES A--
WE WERE SUPPOSED TO GUARD TED KNIGHT. THE FAMOUS O'DARE FAMILY. ALL OF US COPS. AND ALL WE SUCCEEDED IN DOING WAS LETTING HIM GET TAKEN.
JACK KNIGHT. HE'S THE ONE DOING ALL HE CAN. WE HAVEN'T DONE MUCH OF ANYTHING.
AND FRANKLY, I'M ASHAMED.
AND SHAME IS SUCH A TERRIBLE EMOTION.
HOLY--
GUN! GET--
IT'S--
YES, YES. ME. THE BIG, BAD VILLAIN. THE BIG, BAD WOLF.

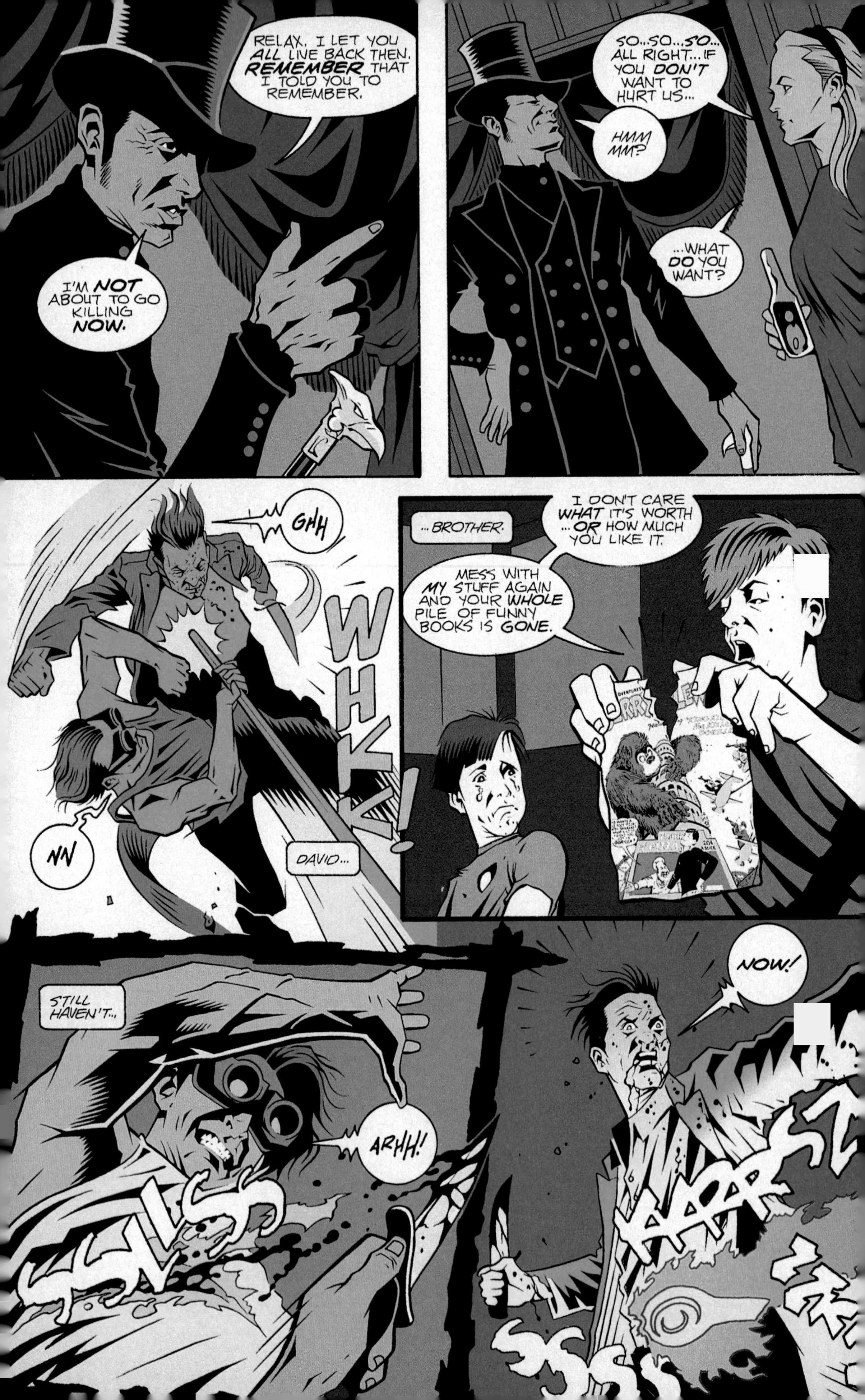
RELAX. I LET YOU ALL LIVE BACK THEN. REMEMBER THAT I TOLD YOU TO REMEMBER.
I'M NOT ABOUT TO GO KILLING NOW.
SO...SO...SO... ALL RIGHT...IF YOU DON'T WANT TO HURT US...
HMM MM?
...WHAT DO YOU WANT?
GHH
NN
DAVID...
...BROTHER.
I DON'T CARE WHAT IT'S WORTH ...OR HOW MUCH YOU LIKE IT.
MESS WITH MY STUFF AGAIN AND YOUR WHOLE PILE OF FUNNY BOOKS IS GONE.
STILL HAVEN'T...
ARHH!
NOW!

YEAH?

NOW WHAT?

ZZZ SYTT

KKRZZZZ

WHAT DO I WANT?

I WANT QUIET SUNDAY AFTERNOONS. I WANT A GOOD MEAL AND GOOD WINE, I WANT PEACE...

...IN OPAL CITY.

ALL THE LOOTING AND KILLING AND ROBBING. THAT SORT OF THING MIGHT BE FINE FOR GOTHAM CITY OR METROPOLIS. BUT NOT HERE.

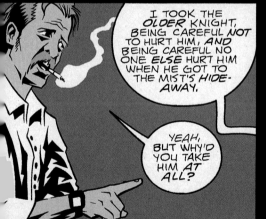

I TOOK THE OLDER KNIGHT, BEING CAREFUL NOT TO HURT HIM, AND BEING CAREFUL NO ONE ELSE HURT HIM WHEN HE GOT TO THE MIST'S HIDE-AWAY.

YEAH, BUT WHY'D YOU TAKE HIM AT ALL?

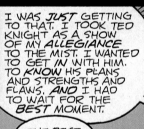

I WAS JUST GETTING TO THAT. I TOOK TED KNIGHT AS A SHOW OF MY ALLEGIANCE TO THE MIST. I WANTED TO GET IN WITH HIM. TO KNOW HIS PLANS AND STRENGTHS AND FLAWS, AND I HAD TO WAIT FOR THE BEST MOMENT.

THE BEST MOMENT?

TO STORM HIS LAIR. ARM YOURSELVES, GENTLEMEN, AND LADY, OH, AND ANY FRIENDS ON THE FORCE YOU MIGHT HAVE WHO YOU'D TRUST WITH THIS TASK.

REMEMBER A FULL-SCALE POLICE MANEUVER, ALL SIRENS AND S'WAT, MIGHT LEAD TO TED KNIGHT'S DEATH, SO YOUR FRIENDS SHOULD BE...

...SUBTLE.

THE MIST'S HIDEOUT! YOU KNOW WHERE IT IS?

NO, WE MET ON PARK BENCHES, LIKE SPIES IN A LEN DEIGHTON NOVEL.

OF COURSE I KNOW WHERE HIS HIDEOUT IS, THE LAST PLACE YOU'D THINK TO LOOK, TOO...

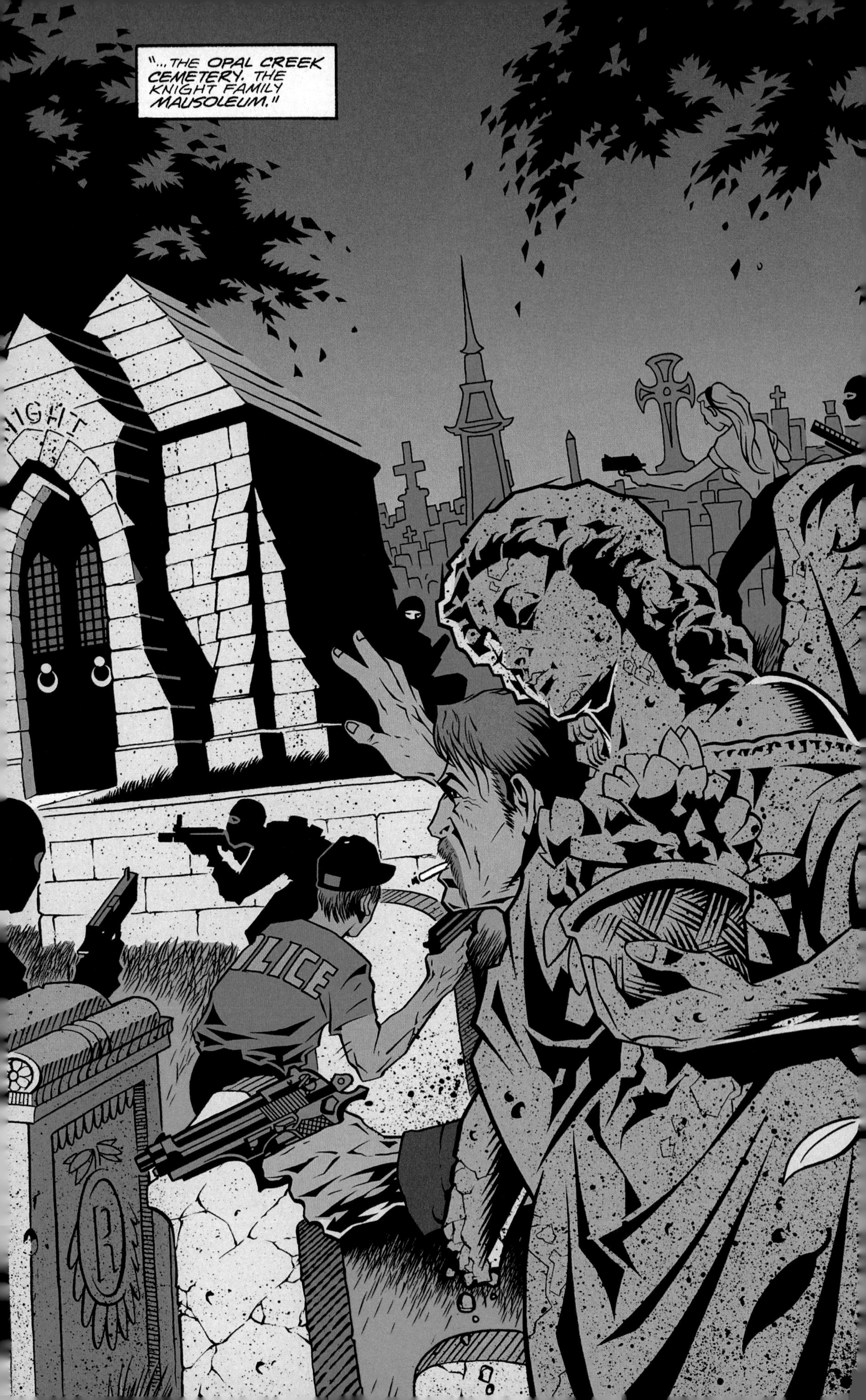
"...THE OPAL CREEK CEMETERY. THE KNIGHT FAMILY MAUSOLEUM."
NIGHT
LICE

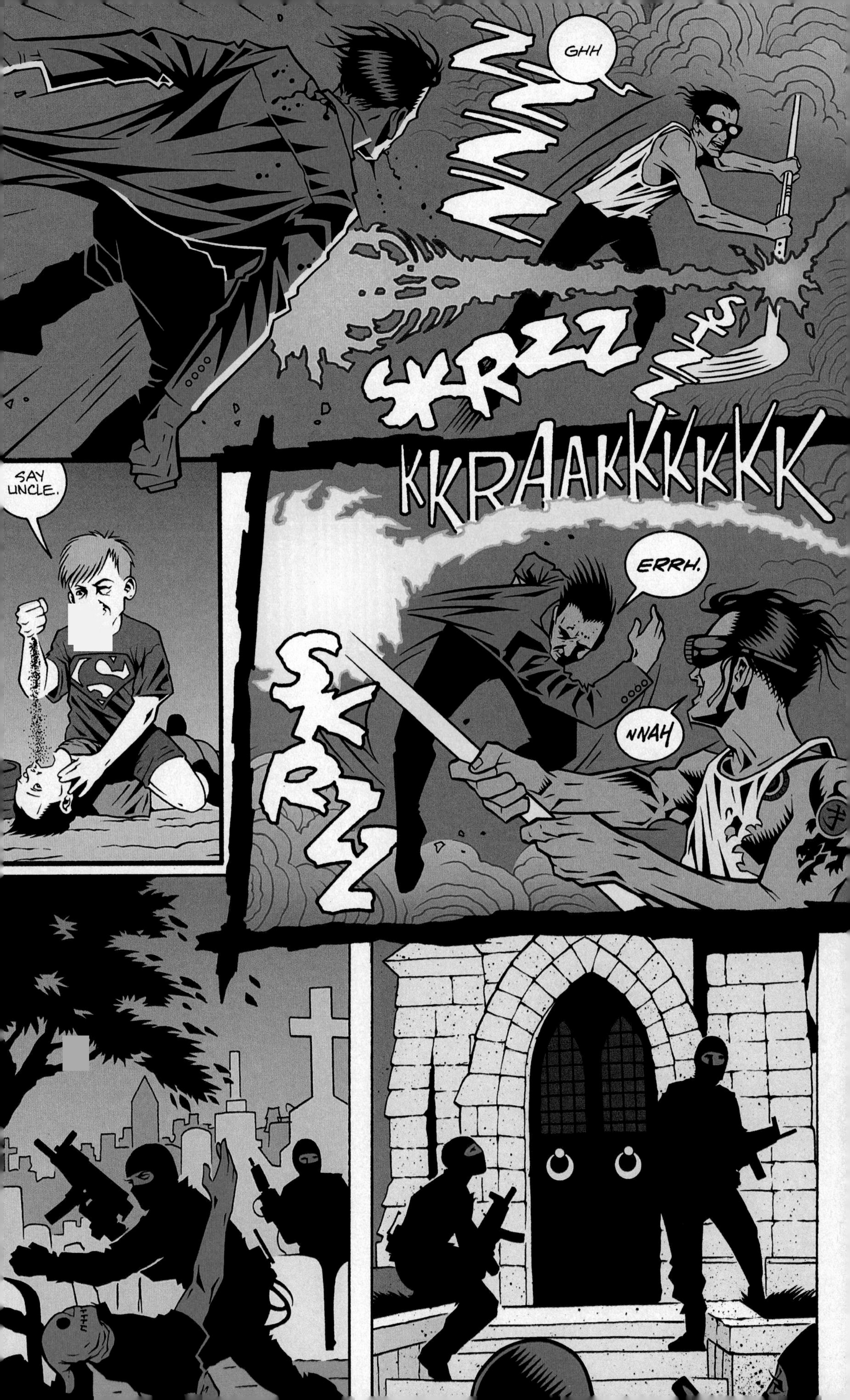
GHH
SKRZZ
SSS
KKRAAKKKKKK
SAY UNCLE.
ERRH.
NNAH
SKRZZ

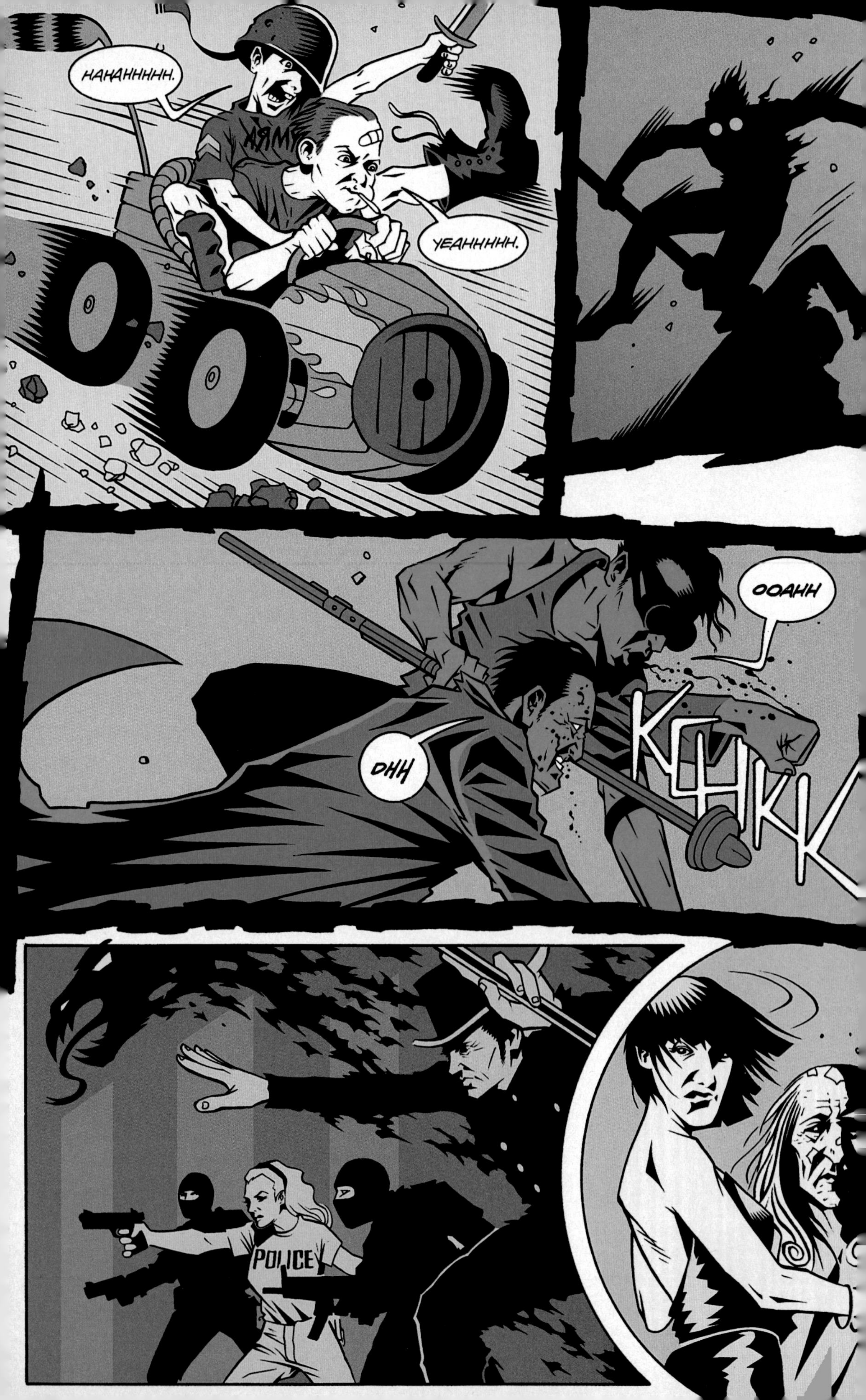
HAHAHHHHH.
YEAHHHHH.
OOAHH
OHH
KCHKK

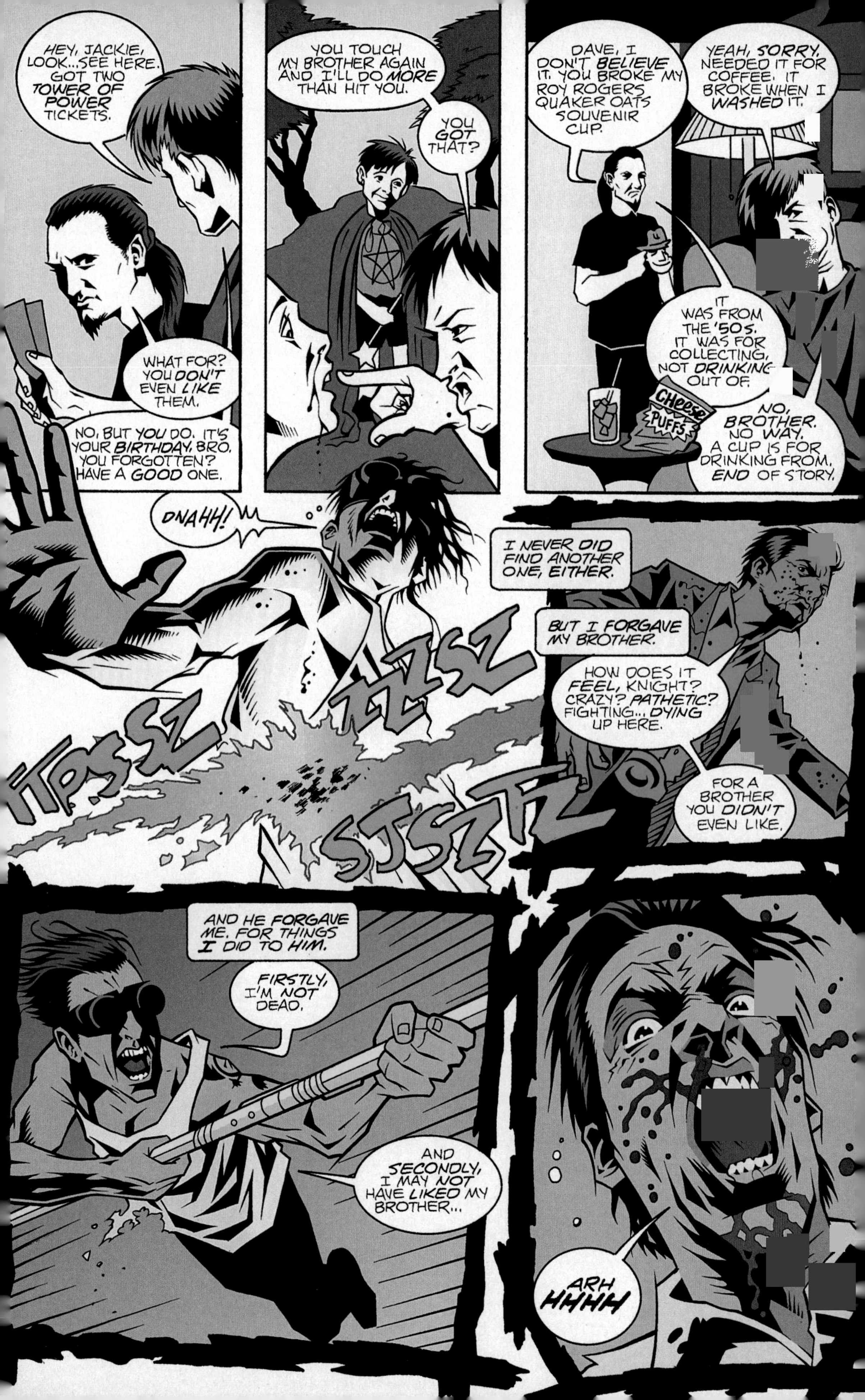
HEY, JACKIE, LOOK...SEE HERE. GOT TWO TOWER OF POWER TICKETS.
WHAT FOR? YOU DON'T EVEN LIKE THEM.
NO, BUT YOU DO. IT'S YOUR BIRTHDAY, BRO. YOU FORGOTTEN? HAVE A GOOD ONE.
YOU TOUCH MY BROTHER AGAIN AND I'LL DO MORE THAN HIT YOU.
YOU GOT THAT?
DAVE, I DON'T BELIEVE IT. YOU BROKE MY ROY ROGERS QUAKER OATS SOUVENIR CUP.
YEAH, SORRY. NEEDED IT FOR COFFEE. IT BROKE WHEN I WASHED IT.
IT WAS FROM THE '50s. IT WAS FOR COLLECTING, NOT DRINKING OUT OF.
NO, BROTHER. NO WAY. A CUP IS FOR DRINKING FROM. END OF STORY.
CHEESE PUFFS
DNAHH!
I NEVER DID FIND ANOTHER ONE, EITHER.
BUT I FORGAVE MY BROTHER.
HOW DOES IT FEEL, KNIGHT? CRAZY? PATHETIC? FIGHTING... DYING UP HERE.
FOR A BROTHER YOU DIDN'T EVEN LIKE.
ITPSSZ
ZZSZ
SJSZFZ
AND HE FORGAVE ME. FOR THINGS I DID TO HIM.
FIRSTLY, I'M NOT DEAD.
AND SECONDLY, I MAY NOT HAVE LIKED MY BROTHER...
ARH HHHH

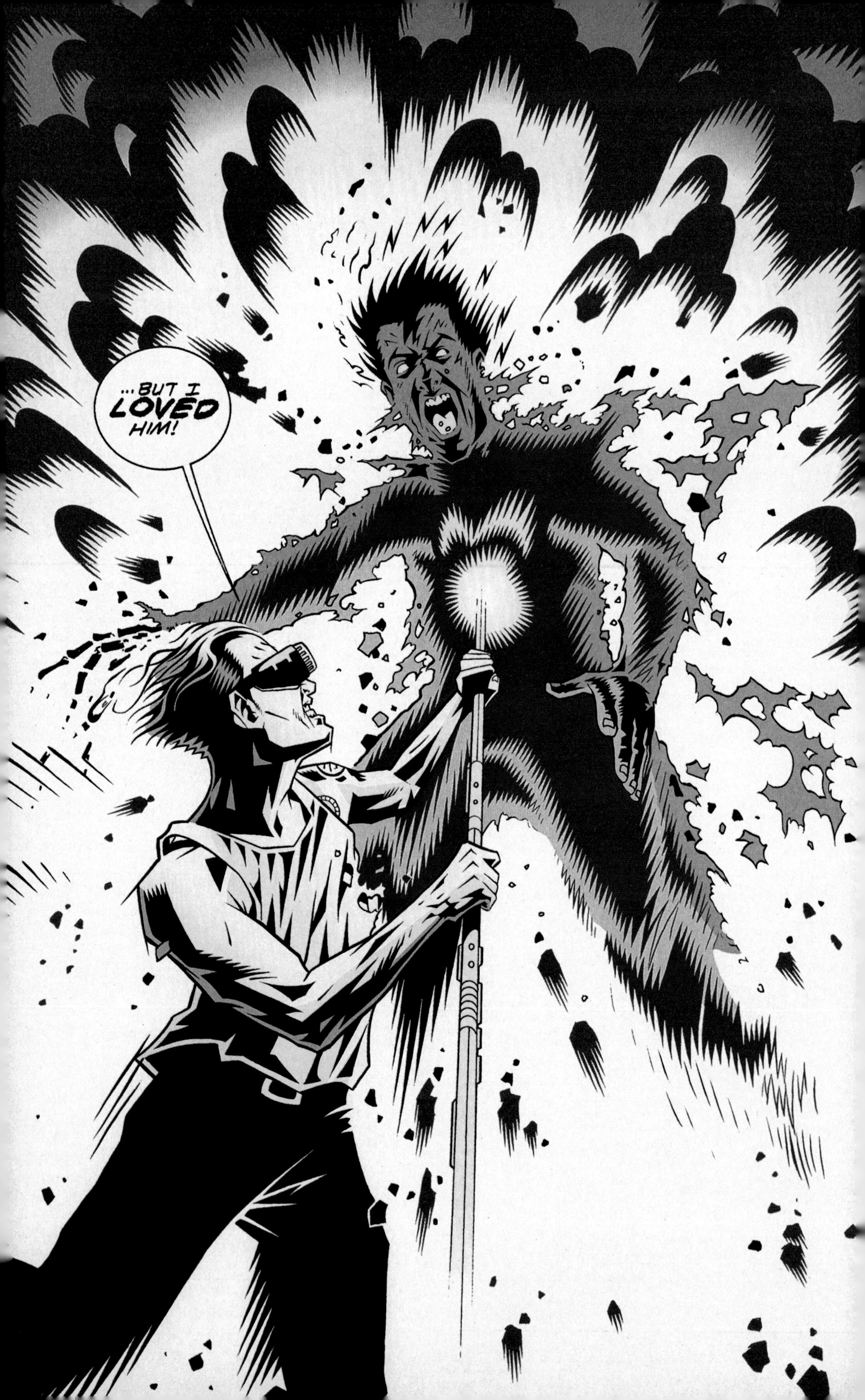
...BUT I LOVED HIM!

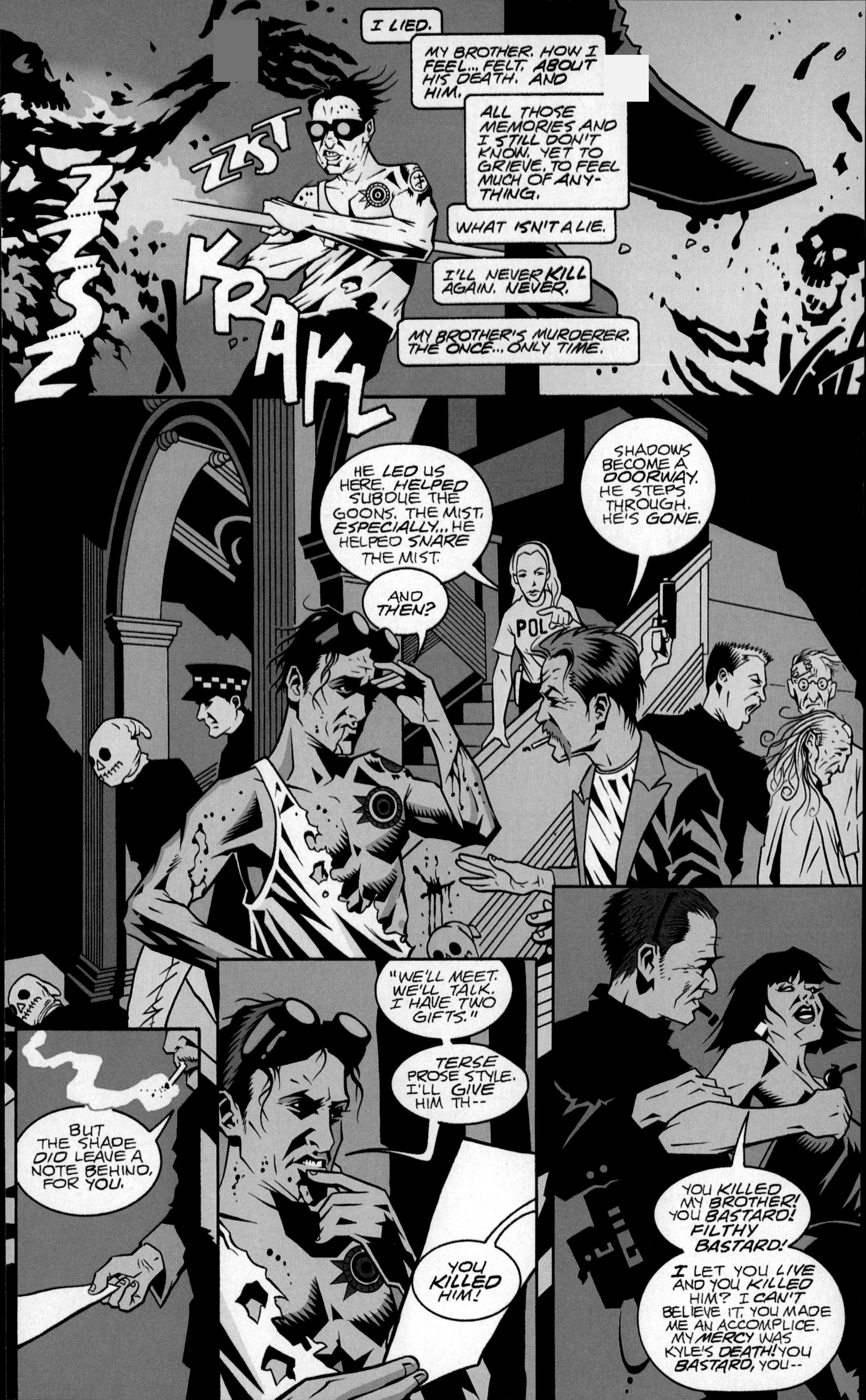

I LIED.
MY BROTHER. HOW I FEEL... FELT. ABOUT HIS DEATH. AND HIM.
ALL THOSE MEMORIES AND I STILL DON'T KNOW. YET TO GRIEVE. TO FEEL MUCH OF ANY-THING.
WHAT ISN'T A LIE.
I'LL NEVER KILL AGAIN. NEVER.
MY BROTHER'S MURDERER. THE ONCE... ONLY TIME.
ZZST
ZZZZ
KRAKL
HE LED US HERE. HELPED SUBDUE THE GOONS. THE MIST, ESPECIALLY... HE HELPED SNARE THE MIST.
AND THEN?
SHADOWS BECOME A DOORWAY. HE STEPS THROUGH. HE'S GONE.
POL
BUT THE SHADE DID LEAVE A NOTE BEHIND, FOR YOU.
"WE'LL MEET. WE'LL TALK. I HAVE TWO GIFTS."
TERSE PROSE STYLE. I'LL GIVE HIM TH--
YOU KILLED HIM!
YOU KILLED MY BROTHER! YOU BASTARD! FILTHY BASTARD!
I LET YOU LIVE AND YOU KILLED HIM? I CAN'T BELIEVE IT. YOU MADE ME AN ACCOMPLICE. MY MERCY WAS KYLE'S DEATH! YOU BASTARD, YOU--

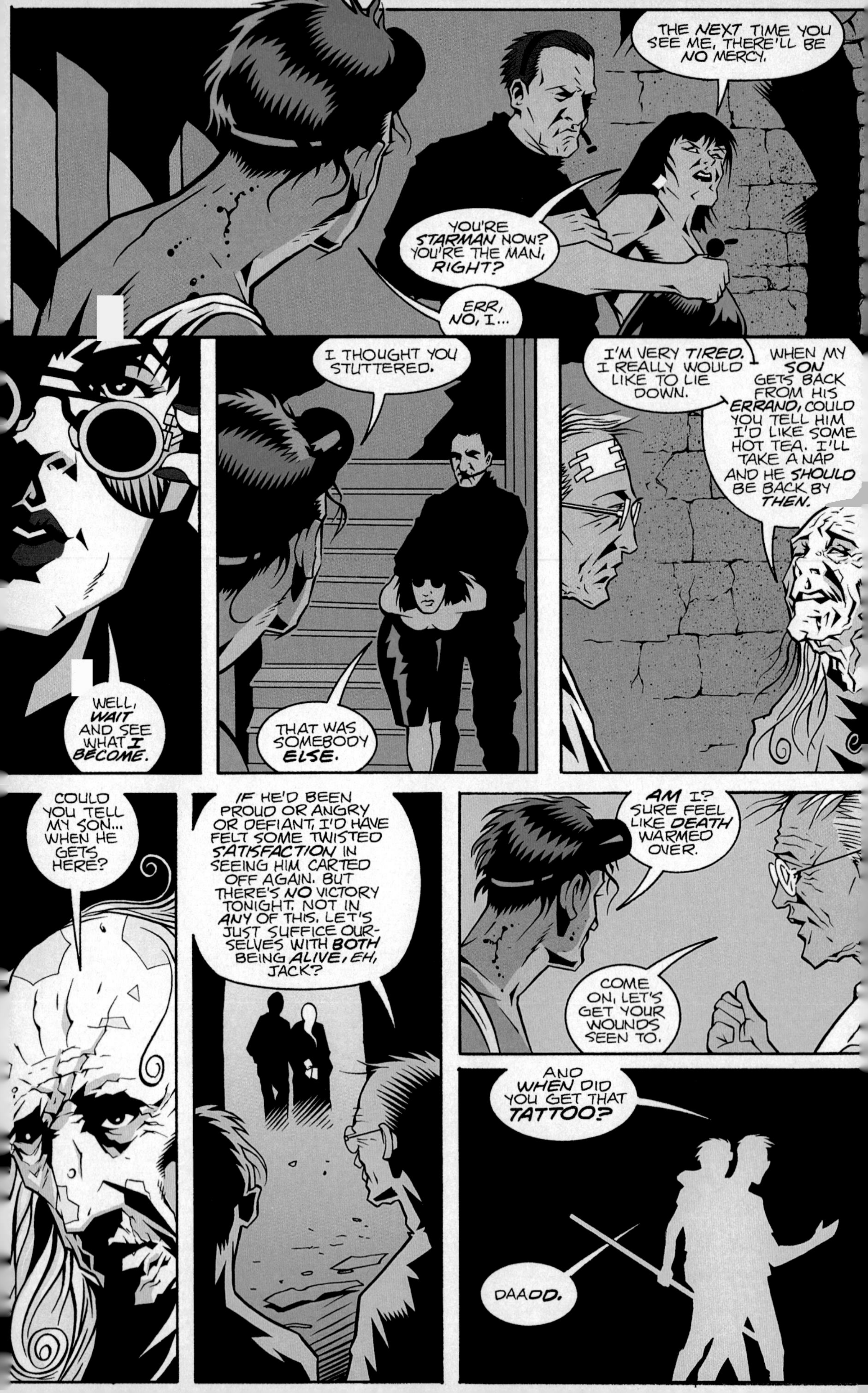
THE NEXT TIME YOU SEE ME, THERE'LL BE NO MERCY.
YOU'RE STARMAN NOW? YOU'RE THE MAN, RIGHT?
ERR, NO, I...
I THOUGHT YOU STUTTERED.
WELL, WAIT AND SEE WHAT I BECOME.
THAT WAS SOMEBODY ELSE.
I'M VERY TIRED. I REALLY WOULD LIKE TO LIE DOWN.
WHEN MY SON GETS BACK FROM HIS ERRAND, COULD YOU TELL HIM I'D LIKE SOME HOT TEA. I'LL TAKE A NAP AND HE SHOULD BE BACK BY THEN.
COULD YOU TELL MY SON... WHEN HE GETS HERE?
IF HE'D BEEN PROUD OR ANGRY OR DEFIANT, I'D HAVE FELT SOME TWISTED SATISFACTION IN SEEING HIM CARTED OFF AGAIN. BUT THERE'S NO VICTORY TONIGHT. NOT IN ANY OF THIS. LET'S JUST SUFFICE OURSELVES WITH BOTH BEING ALIVE, EH, JACK?
AM I? SURE FEEL LIKE DEATH WARMED OVER.
COME ON, LET'S GET YOUR WOUNDS SEEN TO.
AND WHEN DID YOU GET THAT TATTOO?
DAAOD.

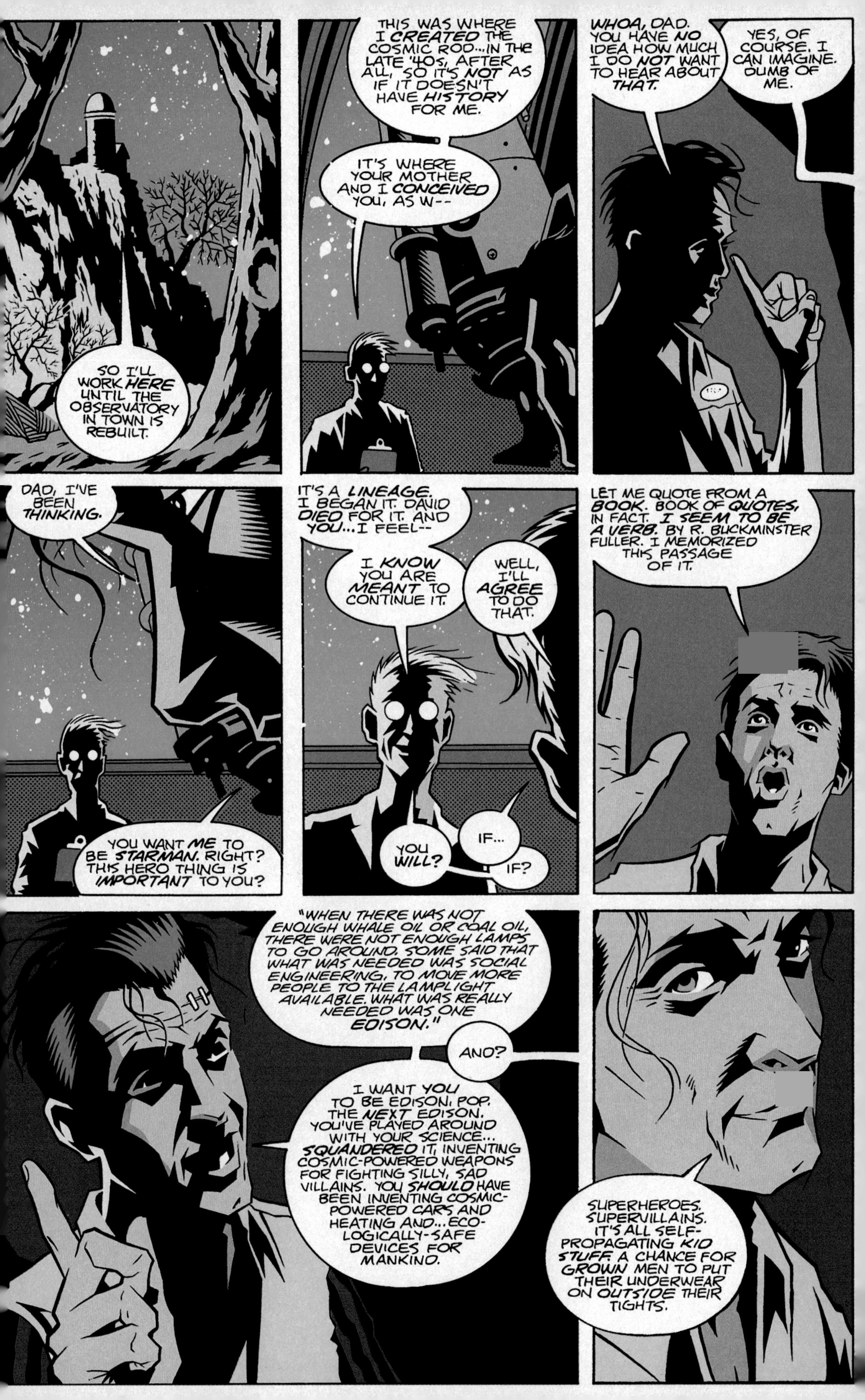
SO I'LL WORK HERE UNTIL THE OBSERVATORY IN TOWN IS REBUILT.
THIS WAS WHERE I CREATED THE COSMIC ROD...IN THE LATE '40s, AFTER ALL, SO IT'S NOT AS IF IT DOESN'T HAVE HISTORY FOR ME.
IT'S WHERE YOUR MOTHER AND I CONCEIVED YOU, AS W--
WHOA, DAD. YOU HAVE NO IDEA HOW MUCH I DO NOT WANT TO HEAR ABOUT THAT.
YES, OF COURSE. I CAN IMAGINE. DUMB OF ME.
DAD, I'VE BEEN THINKING.
YOU WANT ME TO BE STARMAN. RIGHT? THIS HERO THING IS IMPORTANT TO YOU?
IT'S A LINEAGE. I BEGAN IT. DAVID DIED FOR IT. AND YOU...I FEEL--
I KNOW YOU ARE MEANT TO CONTINUE IT.
WELL, I'LL AGREE TO DO THAT.
YOU WILL?
IF...
IF?
LET ME QUOTE FROM A BOOK. BOOK OF QUOTES, IN FACT. I SEEM TO BE A VERB. BY R. BUCKMINSTER FULLER. I MEMORIZED THIS PASSAGE OF IT.
"WHEN THERE WAS NOT ENOUGH WHALE OIL OR COAL OIL, THERE WERE NOT ENOUGH LAMPS TO GO AROUND. SOME SAID THAT WHAT WAS NEEDED WAS SOCIAL ENGINEERING, TO MOVE MORE PEOPLE TO THE LAMPLIGHT AVAILABLE. WHAT WAS REALLY NEEDED WAS ONE EDISON."
AND?
I WANT YOU TO BE EDISON, POP. THE NEXT EDISON. YOU'VE PLAYED AROUND WITH YOUR SCIENCE... SQUANDERED IT, INVENTING COSMIC-POWERED WEAPONS FOR FIGHTING SILLY, SAD VILLAINS. YOU SHOULD HAVE BEEN INVENTING COSMIC-POWERED CARS AND HEATING AND...ECO-LOGICALLY-SAFE DEVICES FOR MANKIND.
SUPERHEROES. SUPERVILLAINS. IT'S ALL SELF-PROPAGATING KID STUFF. A CHANCE FOR GROWN MEN TO PUT THEIR UNDERWEAR ON OUTSIDE THEIR TIGHTS.

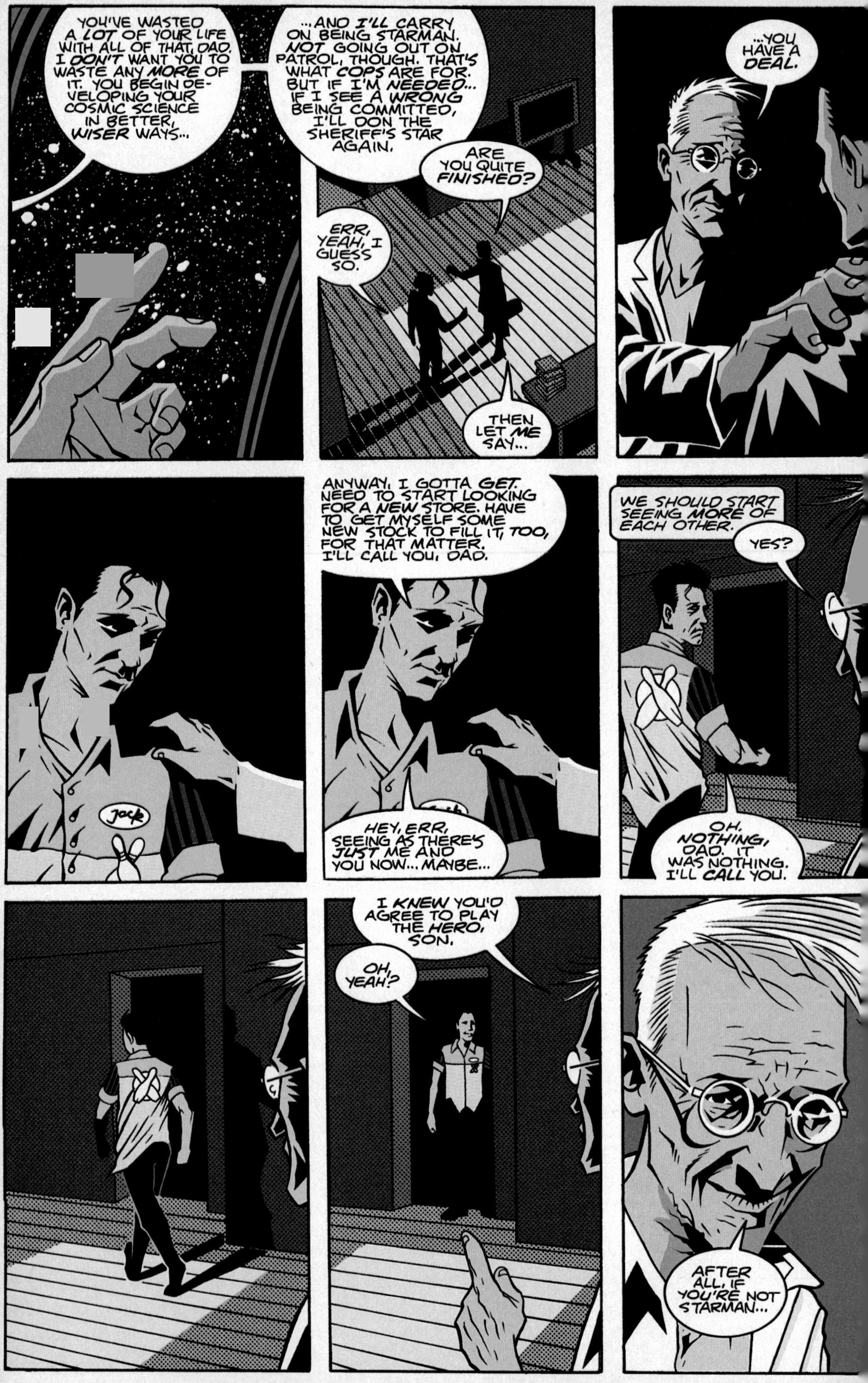
YOU'VE WASTED A LOT OF YOUR LIFE WITH ALL OF THAT, DAD. I DON'T WANT YOU TO WASTE ANY MORE OF IT. YOU BEGIN DE-VELOPING YOUR COSMIC SCIENCE IN BETTER, WISER WAYS...
...AND I'LL CARRY ON BEING STARMAN. NOT GOING OUT ON PATROL, THOUGH. THAT'S WHAT COPS ARE FOR. BUT IF I'M NEEDED... IF I SEE A WRONG BEING COMMITTED, I'LL DON THE SHERIFF'S STAR AGAIN.
ARE YOU QUITE FINISHED?
ERR, YEAH, I GUESS SO.
THEN LET ME SAY...
...YOU HAVE A DEAL.
ANYWAY, I GOTTA GET. NEED TO START LOOKING FOR A NEW STORE. HAVE TO GET MYSELF SOME NEW STOCK TO FILL IT, TOO, FOR THAT MATTER. I'LL CALL YOU, DAD.
HEY, ERR, SEEING AS THERE'S JUST ME AND YOU NOW... MAYBE...
WE SHOULD START SEEING MORE OF EACH OTHER.
YES?
OH. NOTHING, DAD. IT WAS NOTHING. I'LL CALL YOU.
I KNEW YOU'D AGREE TO PLAY THE HERO, SON.
OH, YEAH?
AFTER ALL, IF YOU'RE NOT STARMAN...

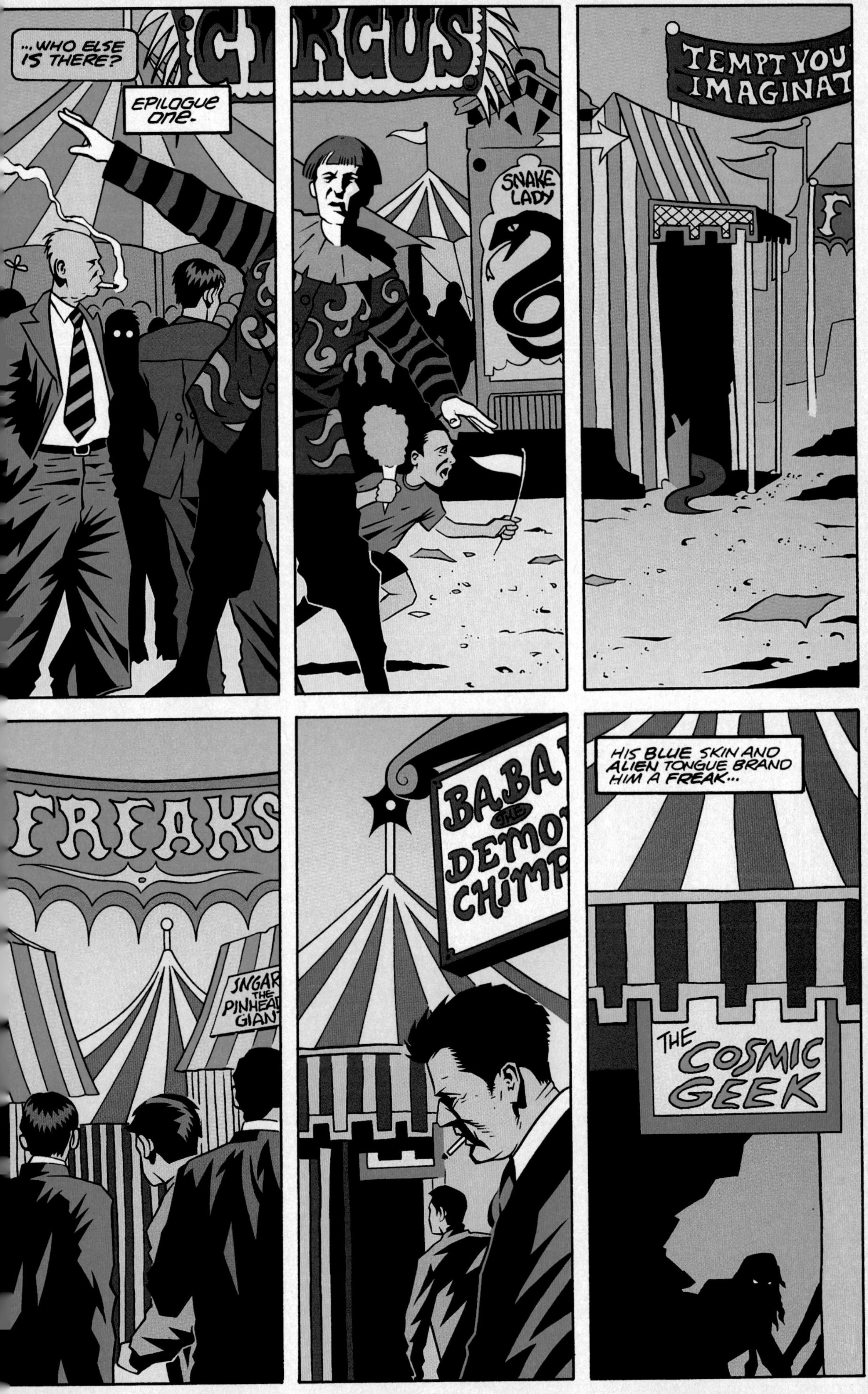
...WHO ELSE IS THERE?
EPILOGUE ONE-
CIRCUS
SNAKE LADY
TEMPT YOU
IMAGINAT
FREAKS
SNGAR THE PINHEAD GIANT
BABA THE DEMO CHIMP
HIS BLUE SKIN AND ALIEN TONGUE BRAND HIM A FREAK...
THE COSMIC GEEK

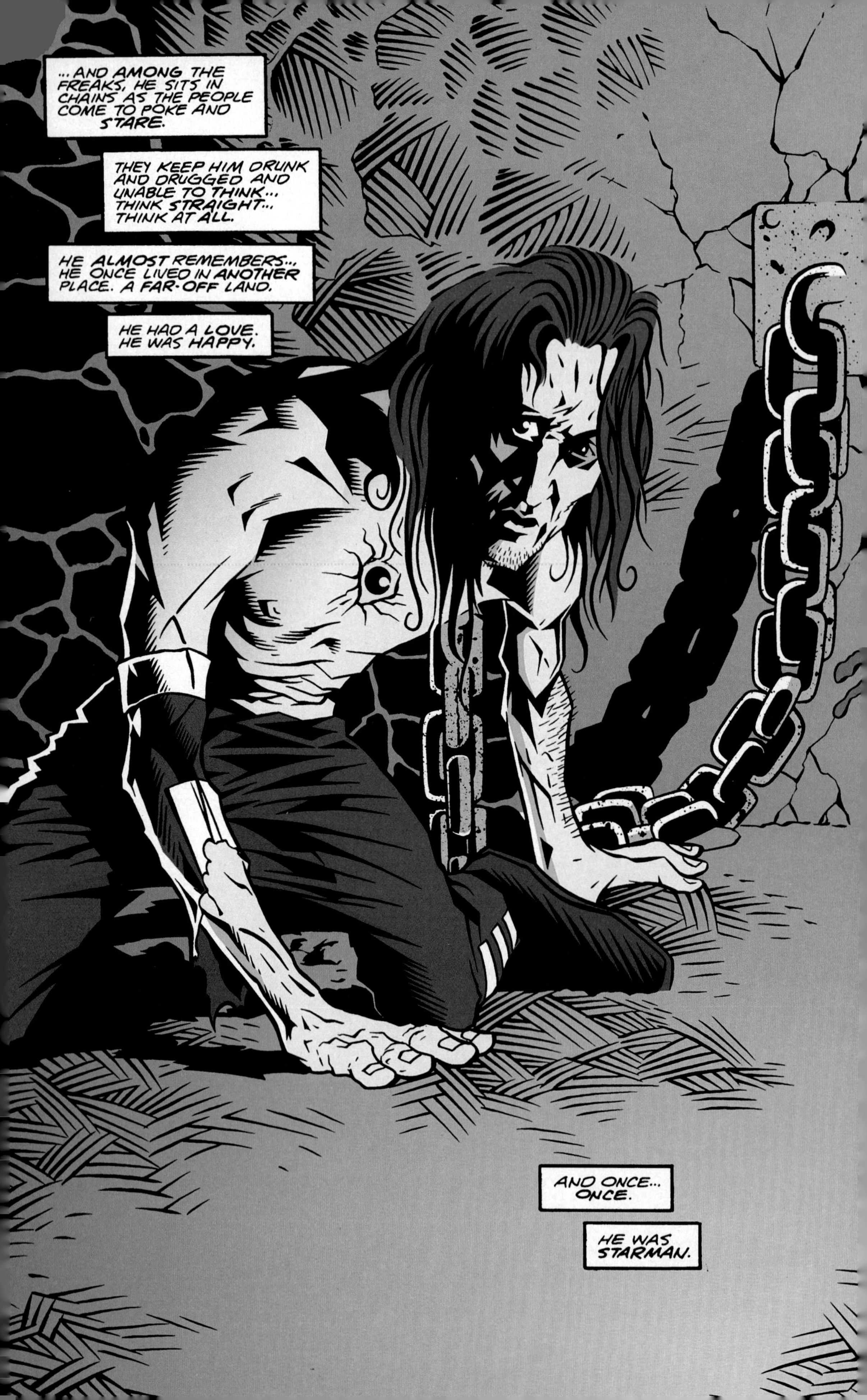
...AND AMONG THE FREAKS, HE SITS IN CHAINS AS THE PEOPLE COME TO POKE AND STARE.
THEY KEEP HIM DRUNK AND DRUGGED AND UNABLE TO THINK... THINK STRAIGHT... THINK AT ALL.
HE ALMOST REMEMBERS... HE ONCE LIVED IN ANOTHER PLACE. A FAR-OFF LAND.
HE HAD A LOVE. HE WAS HAPPY.
AND ONCE... ONCE.
HE WAS STARMAN.

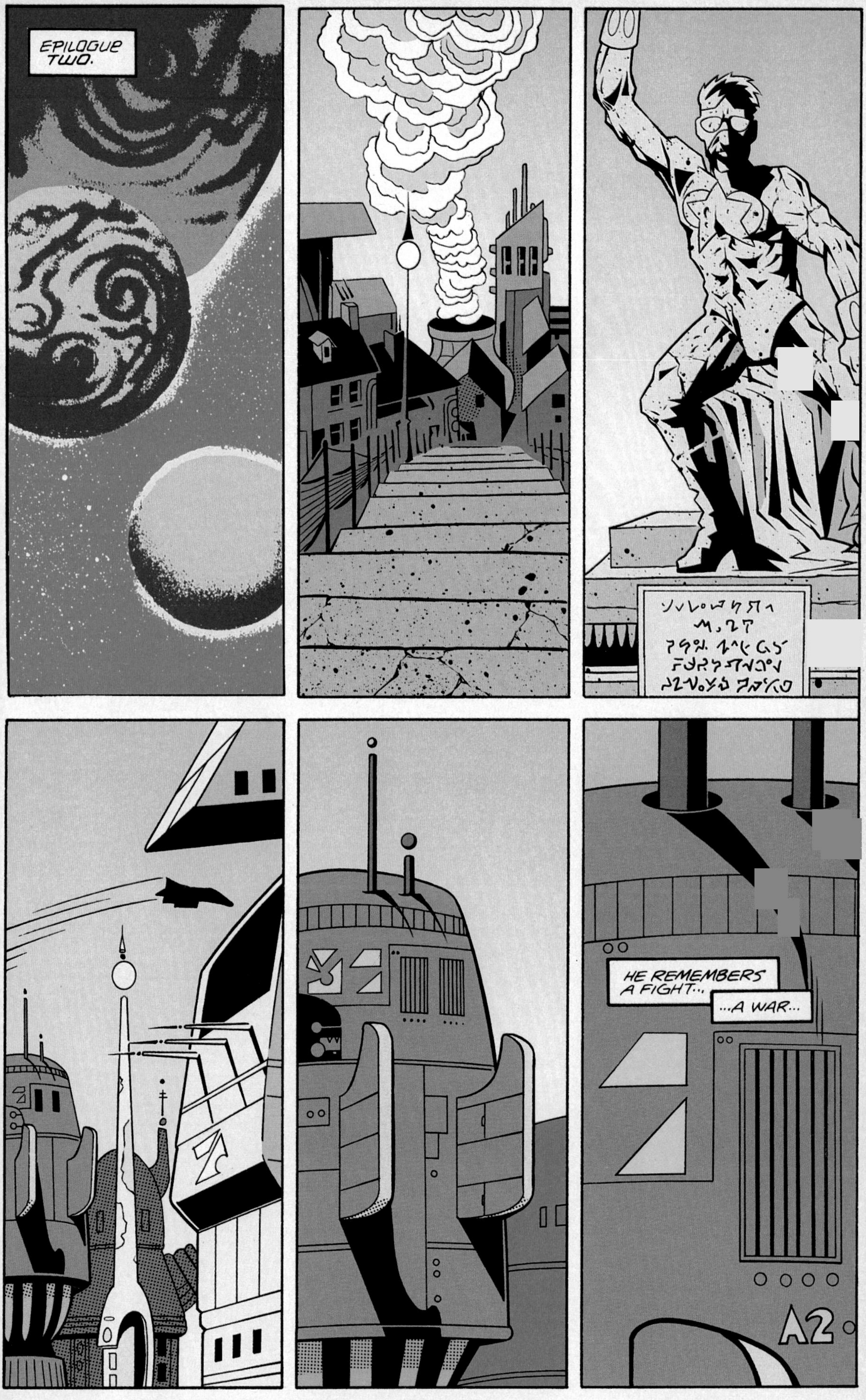
EPILOGUE TWO.
HE REMEMBERS A FIGHT...
...A WAR...
A2

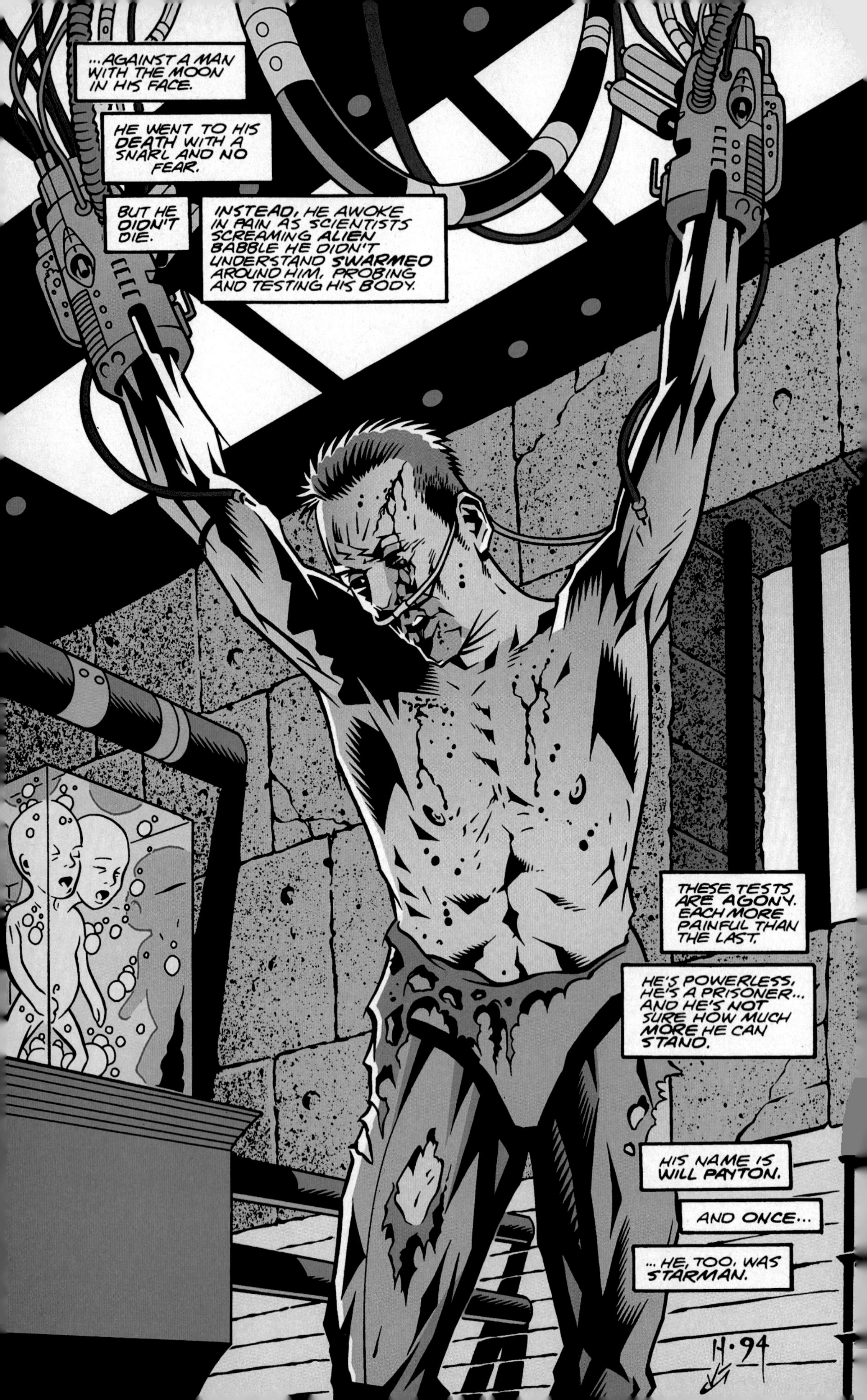
...AGAINST A MAN WITH THE MOON IN HIS FACE.
HE WENT TO HIS DEATH WITH A SNARL AND NO FEAR.
BUT HE DIDN'T DIE.
INSTEAD, HE AWOKE IN PAIN AS SCIENTISTS SCREAMING ALIEN BABBLE HE DIDN'T UNDERSTAND SWARMED AROUND HIM, PROBING AND TESTING HIS BODY.
THESE TESTS ARE AGONY. EACH MORE PAINFUL THAN THE LAST.
HE'S POWERLESS. HE'S A PRISONER... AND HE'S NOT SURE HOW MUCH MORE HE CAN STAND.
HIS NAME IS WILL PAYTON.
AND ONCE...
...HE, TOO, WAS STARMAN.
H·94

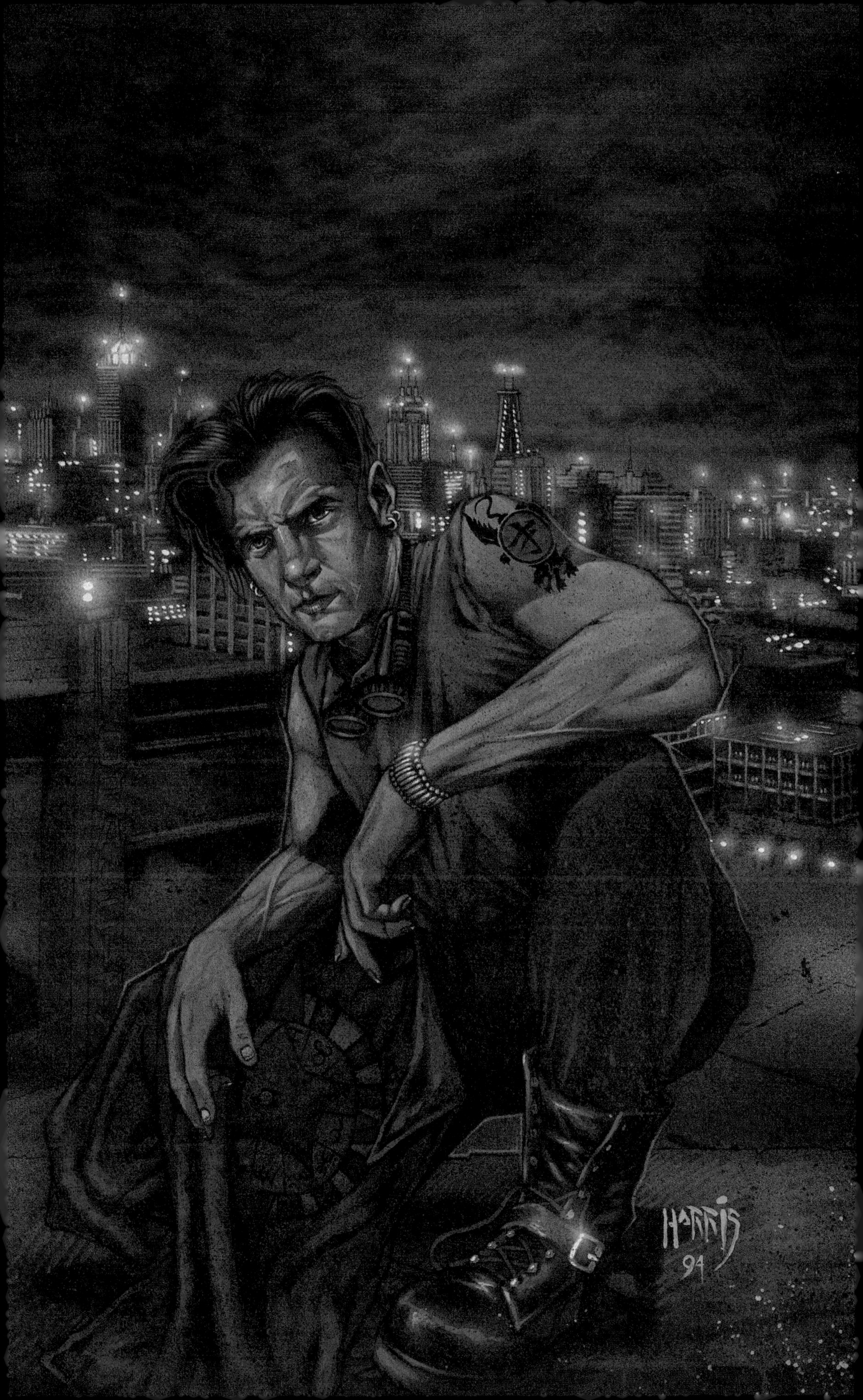
HARRIS
94

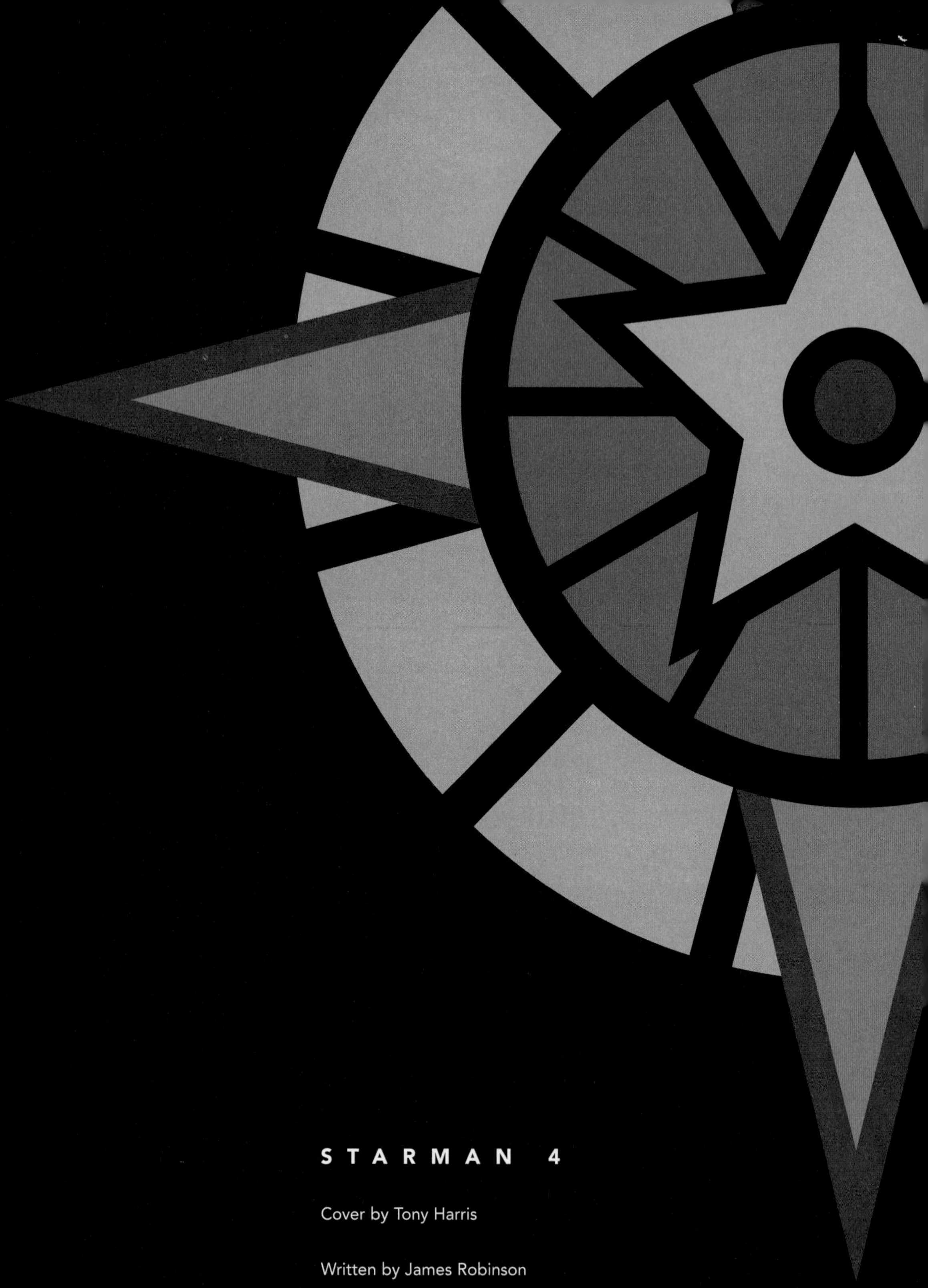

S T A R M A N 4

Cover by Tony Harris

Written by James Robinson

Pencils by Tony Harris,

with inks by Wade von Grawbadger

and colors by Gregory Wright

PROLOGUE

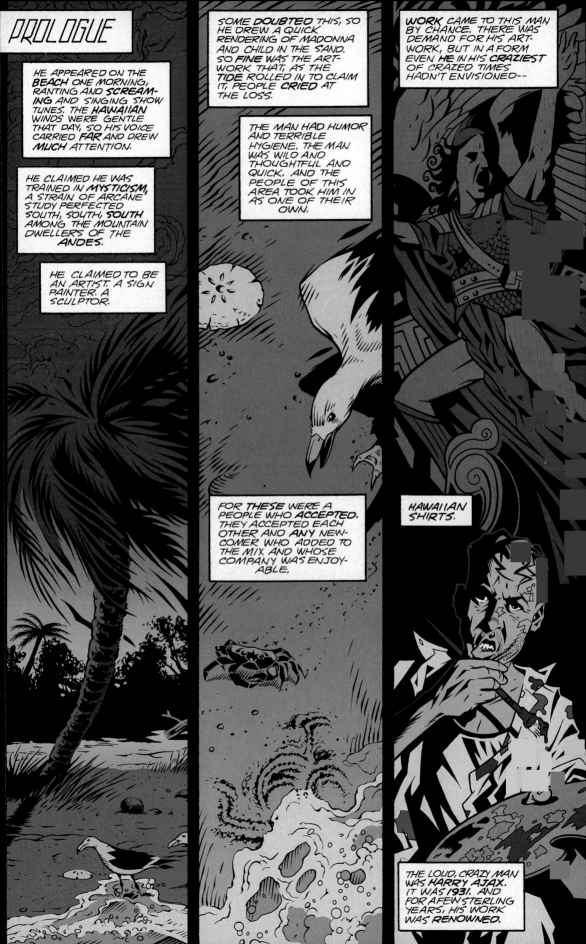

HE APPEARED ON THE **BEACH** ONE MORNING, RANTING AND **SCREAMING** AND SINGING SHOW TUNES. THE HAWAIIAN WINDS WERE GENTLE THAT DAY, SO HIS VOICE CARRIED **FAR** AND DREW **MUCH** ATTENTION.

HE CLAIMED HE WAS TRAINED IN **MYSTICISM**, A STRAIN OF ARCANE STUDY PERFECTED SOUTH, SOUTH, **SOUTH** AMONG THE MOUNTAIN DWELLERS OF THE **ANDES**.

HE CLAIMED TO BE AN ARTIST. A SIGN PAINTER. A SCULPTOR.

SOME **DOUBTED** THIS, SO HE DREW A QUICK RENDERING OF MADONNA AND CHILD IN THE SAND. SO **FINE** WAS THE ARTWORK THAT, AS THE **TIDE** ROLLED IN TO CLAIM IT, PEOPLE **CRIED** AT THE LOSS.

THE MAN HAD HUMOR AND TERRIBLE HYGIENE. THE MAN WAS WILD AND THOUGHTFUL AND QUICK. AND THE PEOPLE OF THIS AREA TOOK HIM IN AS ONE OF THEIR OWN.

FOR **THESE** WERE A PEOPLE WHO **ACCEPTED**. THEY ACCEPTED EACH OTHER AND **ANY** NEWCOMER WHO ADDED TO THE MIX AND WHOSE COMPANY WAS ENJOYABLE.

WORK CAME TO THIS MAN BY CHANCE. THERE WAS DEMAND FOR HIS ARTWORK, BUT IN A FORM EVEN **HE** IN HIS **CRAZIEST** OF CRAZED TIMES HADN'T ENVISIONED--

HAWAIIAN SHIRTS.

THE LOUD, CRAZY MAN WAS **HARRY AJAX.** IT WAS **1931**. AND FOR A FEW STERLING YEARS, HIS WORK WAS **RENOWNED**.

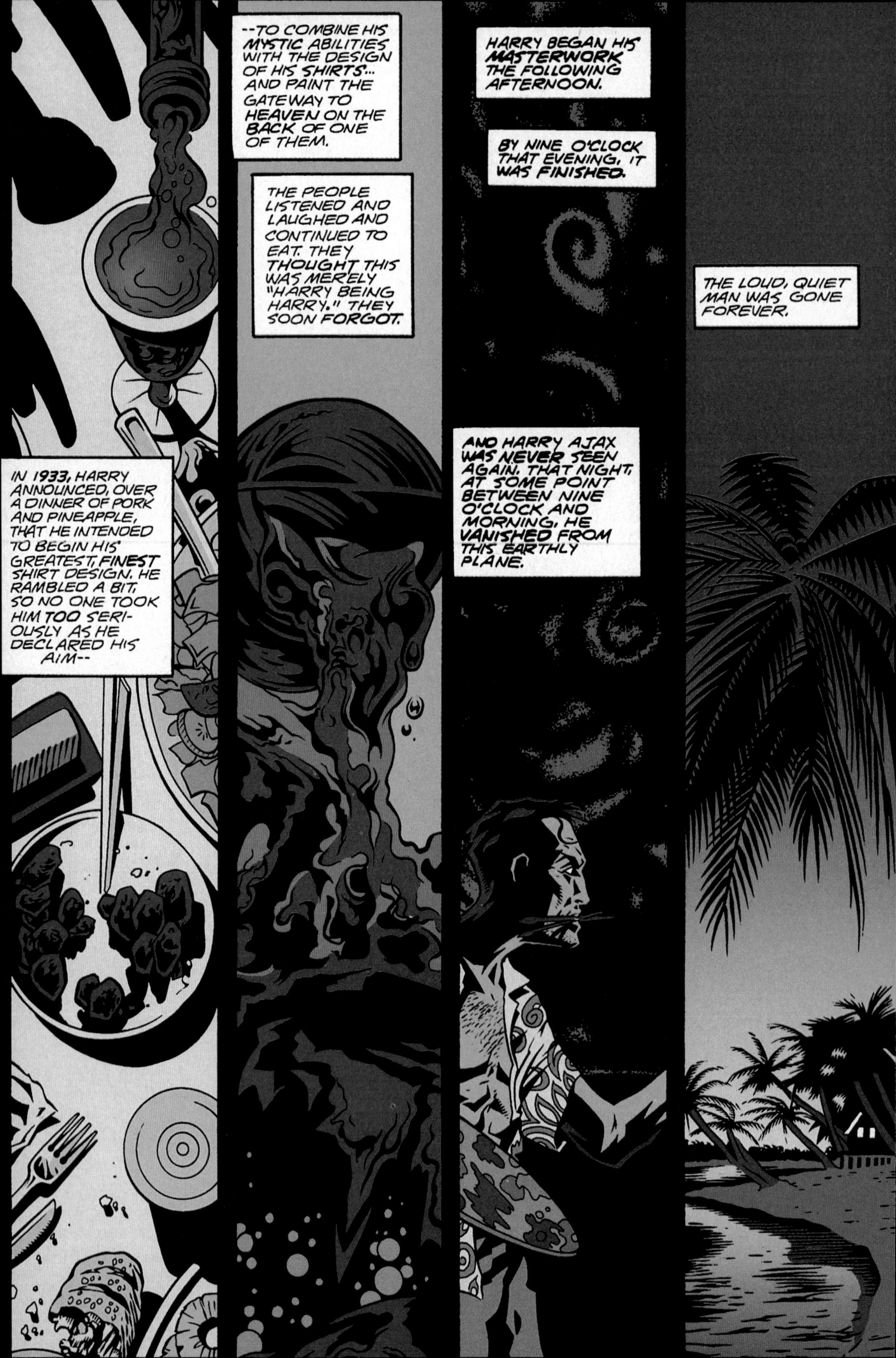
--TO COMBINE HIS MYSTIC ABILITIES WITH THE DESIGN OF HIS SHIRTS... AND PAINT THE GATEWAY TO HEAVEN ON THE BACK OF ONE OF THEM.
IN 1933, HARRY ANNOUNCED, OVER A DINNER OF PORK AND PINEAPPLE, THAT HE INTENDED TO BEGIN HIS GREATEST, FINEST SHIRT DESIGN. HE RAMBLED A BIT, SO NO ONE TOOK HIM TOO SERIOUSLY AS HE DECLARED HIS AIM--
THE PEOPLE LISTENED AND LAUGHED AND CONTINUED TO EAT. THEY THOUGHT THIS WAS MERELY "HARRY BEING HARRY." THEY SOON FORGOT.
HARRY BEGAN HIS MASTERWORK THE FOLLOWING AFTERNOON.
BY NINE O'CLOCK THAT EVENING, IT WAS FINISHED.
AND HARRY AJAX WAS NEVER SEEN AGAIN. THAT NIGHT, AT SOME POINT BETWEEN NINE O'CLOCK AND MORNING, HE VANISHED FROM THIS EARTHLY PLANE.
THE LOUD, QUIET MAN WAS GONE FOREVER.

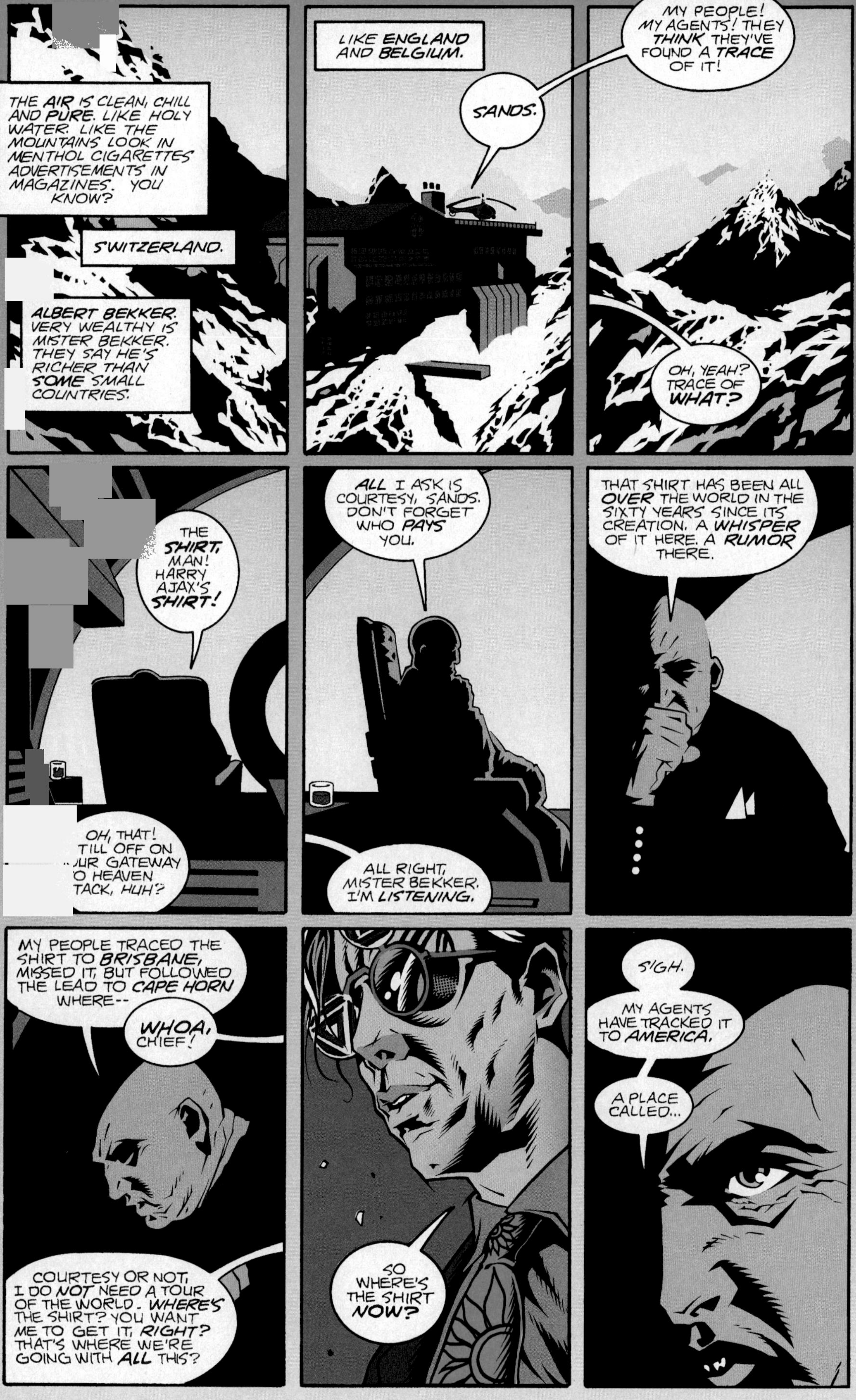
THE AIR IS CLEAN, CHILL AND PURE. LIKE HOLY WATER. LIKE THE MOUNTAINS LOOK IN MENTHOL CIGARETTES' ADVERTISEMENTS IN MAGAZINES. YOU KNOW?
SWITZERLAND.
ALBERT BEKKER. VERY WEALTHY IS MISTER BEKKER. THEY SAY HE'S RICHER THAN SOME SMALL COUNTRIES.
LIKE ENGLAND AND BELGIUM.
SANDS.
MY PEOPLE! MY AGENTS! THEY THINK THEY'VE FOUND A TRACE OF IT!
OH, YEAH? TRACE OF WHAT?
THE SHIRT, MAN! HARRY AJAX'S SHIRT!
OH, THAT! TILL OFF ON OUR GATEWAY O HEAVEN TACK, HUH?
ALL I ASK IS COURTESY, SANDS. DON'T FORGET WHO PAYS YOU.
ALL RIGHT, MISTER BEKKER. I'M LISTENING.
THAT SHIRT HAS BEEN ALL OVER THE WORLD IN THE SIXTY YEARS SINCE ITS CREATION. A WHISPER OF IT HERE. A RUMOR THERE.
MY PEOPLE TRACED THE SHIRT TO BRISBANE, MISSED IT, BUT FOLLOWED THE LEAD TO CAPE HORN WHERE--
WHOA, CHIEF!
COURTESY OR NOT, I DO NOT NEED A TOUR OF THE WORLD. WHERE'S THE SHIRT? YOU WANT ME TO GET IT, RIGHT? THAT'S WHERE WE'RE GOING WITH ALL THIS?
SO WHERE'S THE SHIRT NOW?
SIGH.
MY AGENTS HAVE TRACKED IT TO AMERICA.
A PLACE CALLED...

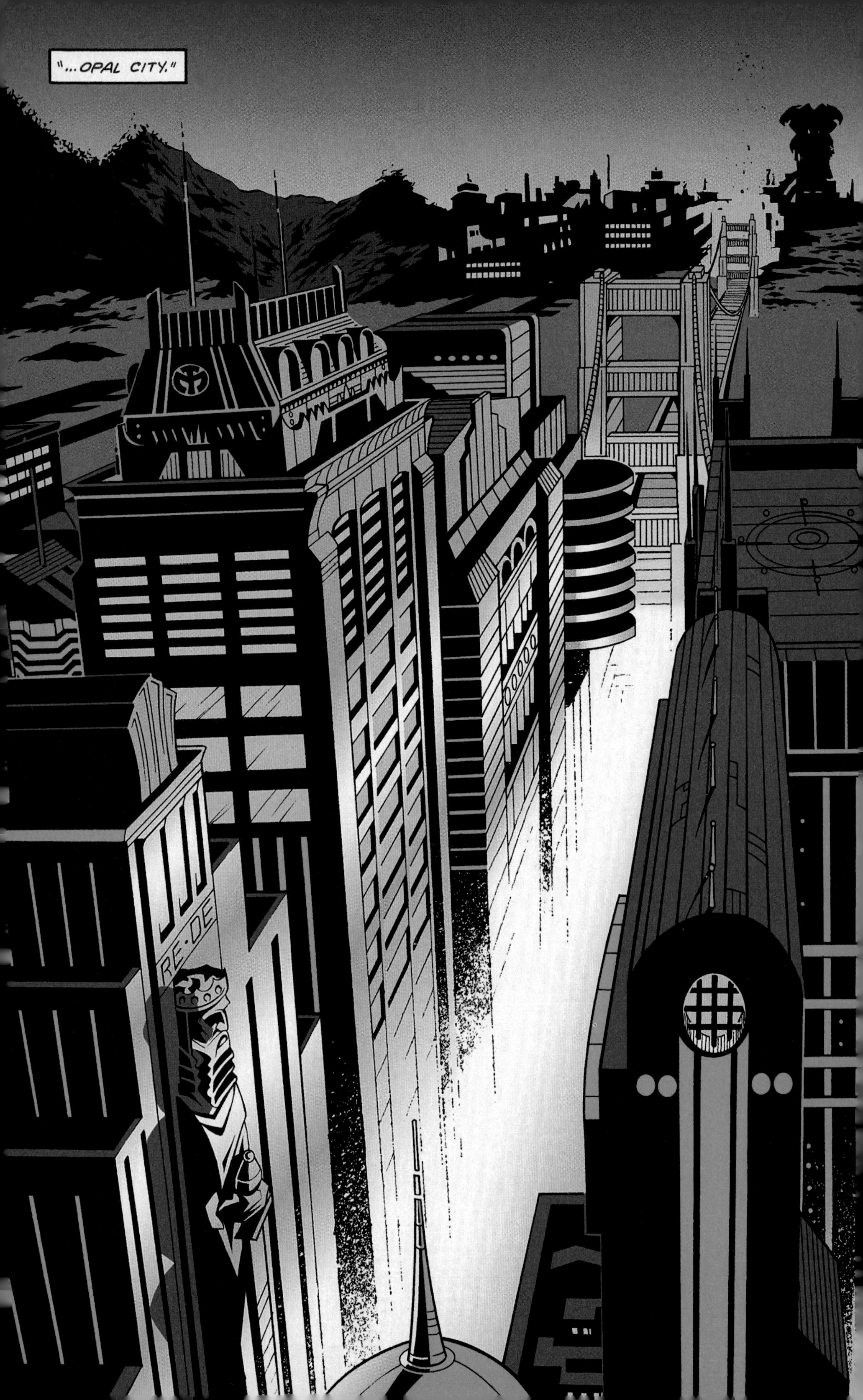
"...OPAL CITY."
RE·DE

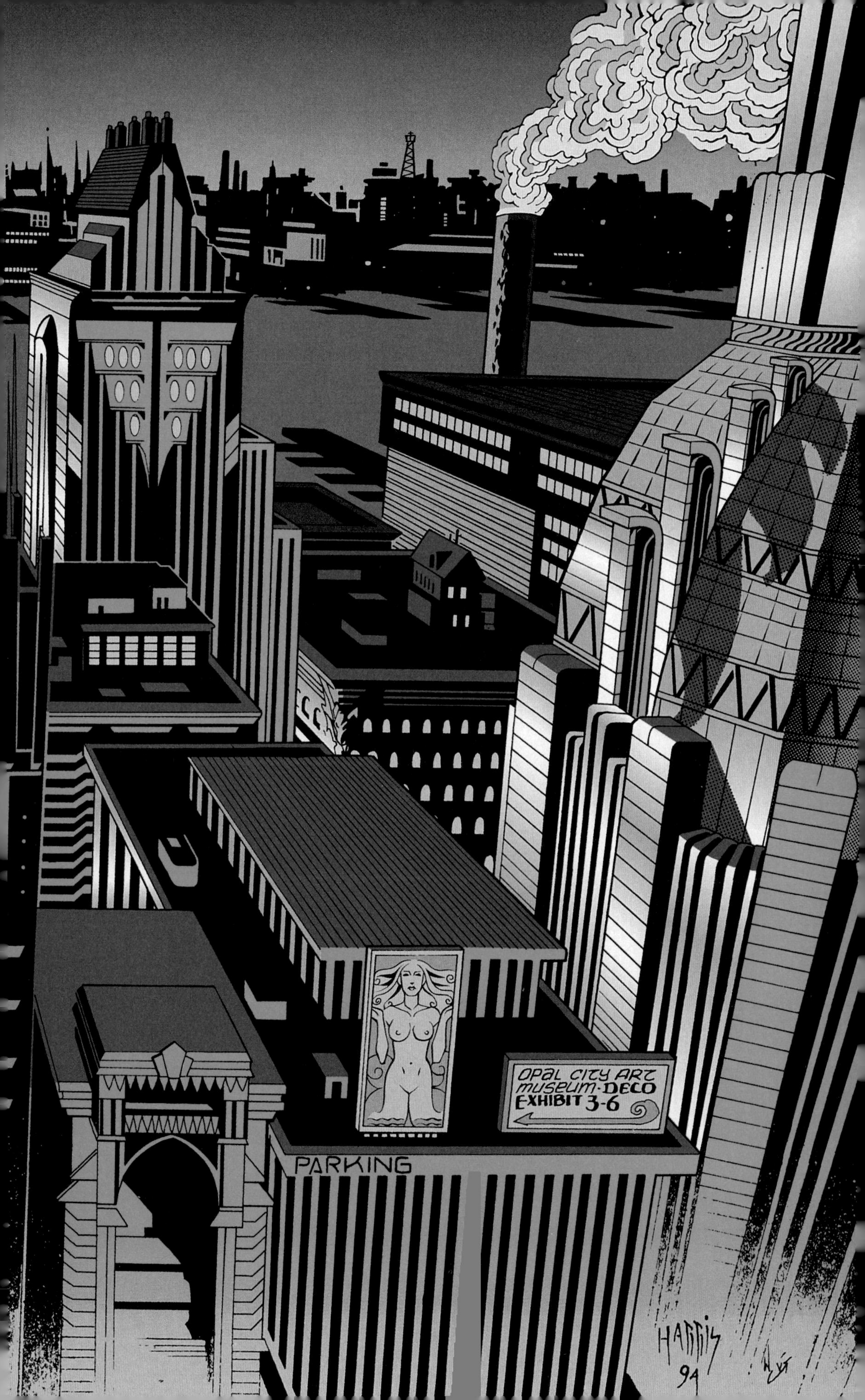
OPAL CITY ART
MUSEUM · DECO
EXHIBIT 3-6
PARKING
HARRIS
94

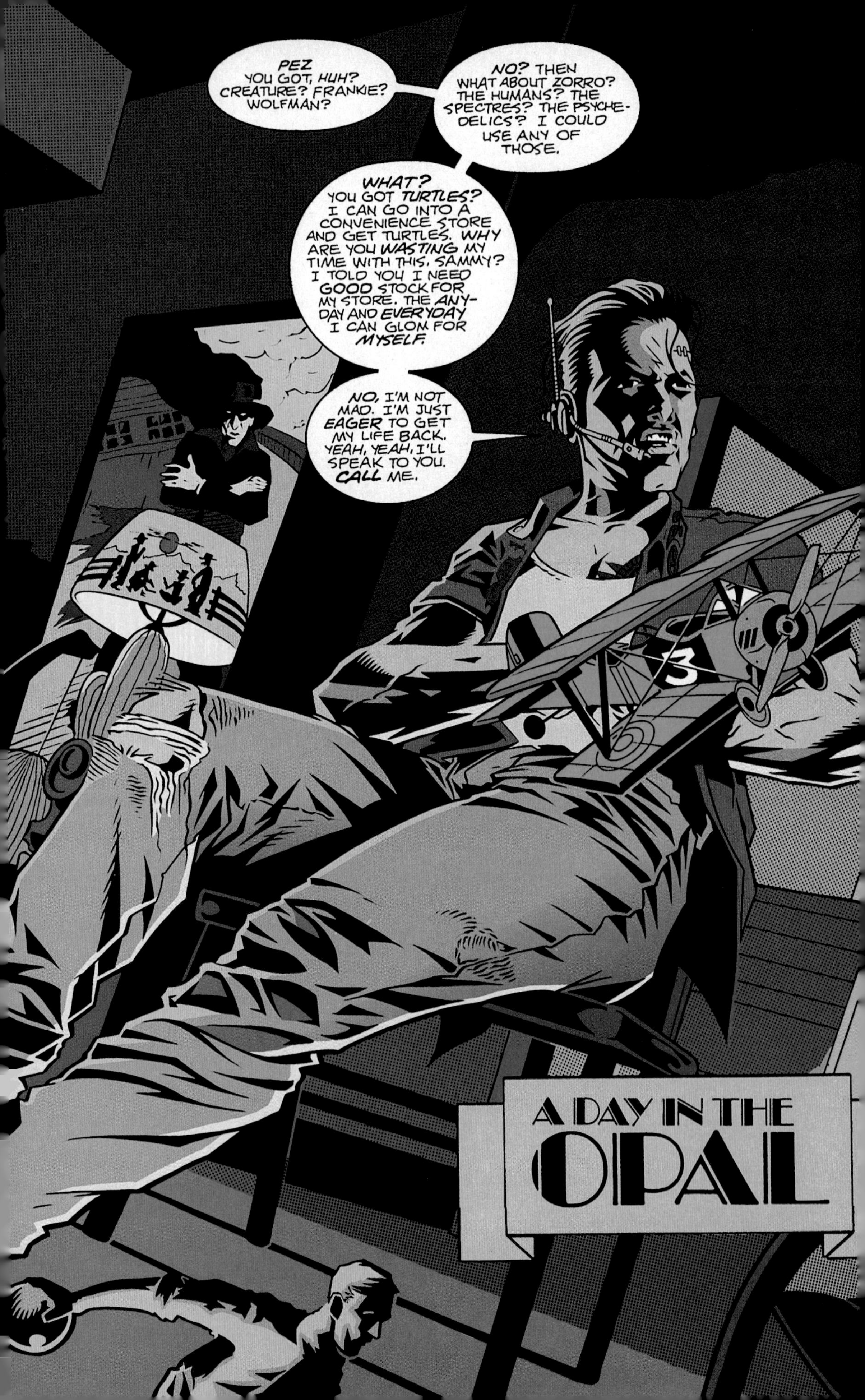
PEZ YOU GOT, HUH? CREATURE? FRANKIE? WOLFMAN?
NO? THEN WHAT ABOUT ZORRO? THE HUMANS? THE SPECTRES? THE PSYCHE-DELICS? I COULD USE ANY OF THOSE.
WHAT? YOU GOT TURTLES? I CAN GO INTO A CONVENIENCE STORE AND GET TURTLES. WHY ARE YOU WASTING MY TIME WITH THIS, SAMMY? I TOLD YOU I NEED GOOD STOCK FOR MY STORE. THE ANY-DAY AND EVERYDAY I CAN GLOM FOR MYSELF.
NO, I'M NOT MAD. I'M JUST EAGER TO GET MY LIFE BACK. YEAH, YEAH, I'LL SPEAK TO YOU. CALL ME.
A DAY IN THE OPAL

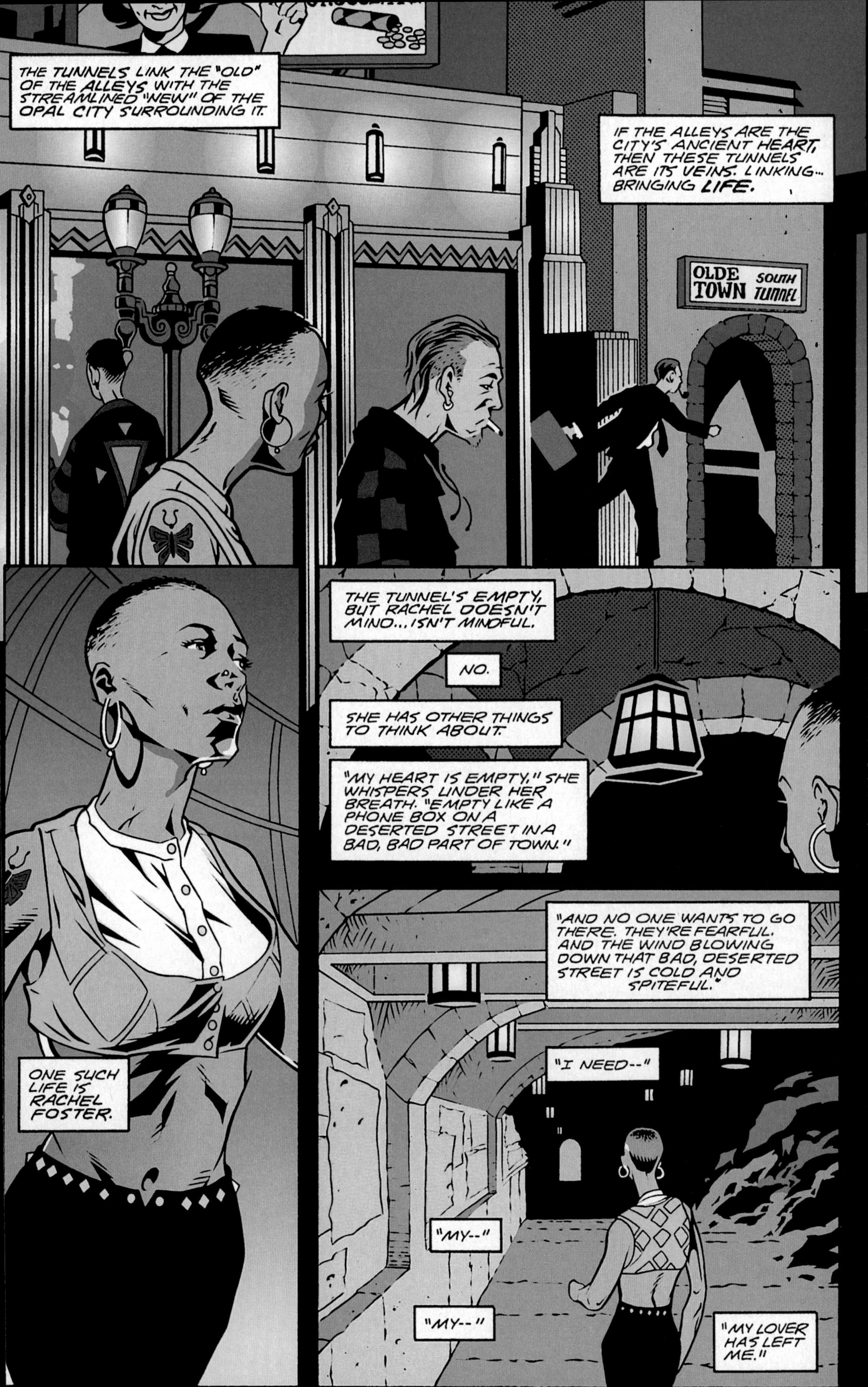
THE TUNNELS LINK THE "OLD" OF THE ALLEYS WITH THE STREAMLINED "NEW" OF THE OPAL CITY SURROUNDING IT.
IF THE ALLEYS ARE THE CITY'S ANCIENT HEART, THEN THESE TUNNELS ARE ITS VEINS. LINKING... BRINGING LIFE.
OLDE TOWN SOUTH TUNNEL
ONE SUCH LIFE IS RACHEL FOSTER.
THE TUNNEL'S EMPTY, BUT RACHEL DOESN'T MIND... ISN'T MINDFUL.
NO.
SHE HAS OTHER THINGS TO THINK ABOUT.
"MY HEART IS EMPTY," SHE WHISPERS UNDER HER BREATH. "EMPTY LIKE A PHONE BOX ON A DESERTED STREET IN A BAD, BAD PART OF TOWN."
"AND NO ONE WANTS TO GO THERE. THEY'RE FEARFUL. AND THE WIND BLOWING DOWN THAT BAD, DESERTED STREET IS COLD AND SPITEFUL."
"I NEED--"
"MY--"
"MY--"
"MY LOVER HAS LEFT ME."

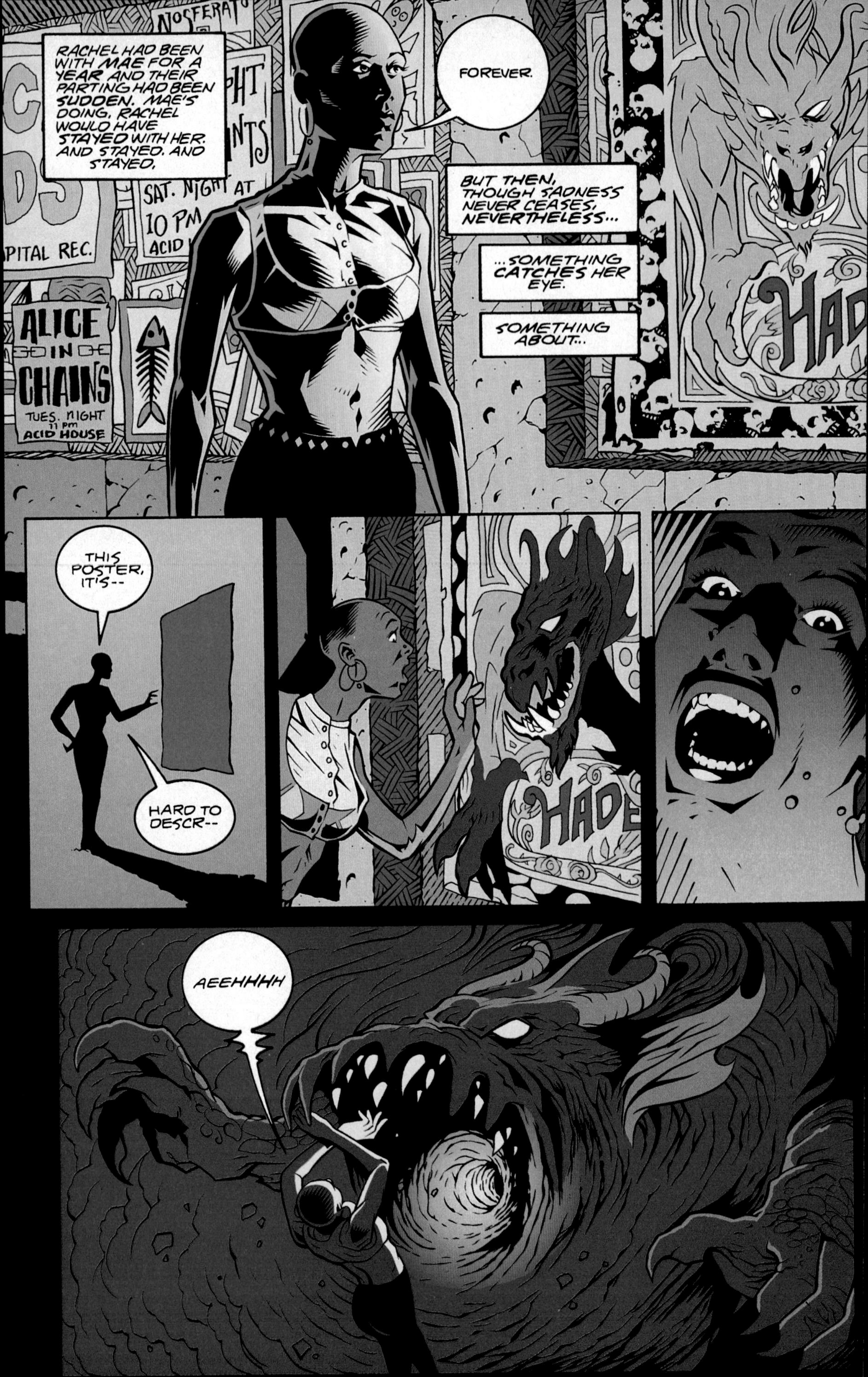
NOSFERATU
RACHEL HAD BEEN WITH MAE FOR A YEAR AND THEIR PARTING HAD BEEN SUDDEN. MAE'S DOING. RACHEL WOULD HAVE STAYED WITH HER. AND STAYED. AND STAYED.
FOREVER.
SAT. NIGHT AT 10 PM
PITAL REC.
ALICE IN CHAINS TUES. NIGHT 11 pm ACID HOUSE
BUT THEN, THOUGH SADNESS NEVER CEASES, NEVERTHELESS...
...SOMETHING CATCHES HER EYE.
SOMETHING ABOUT...
THIS POSTER, IT'S--
HARD TO DESCR--
AEEHHHH

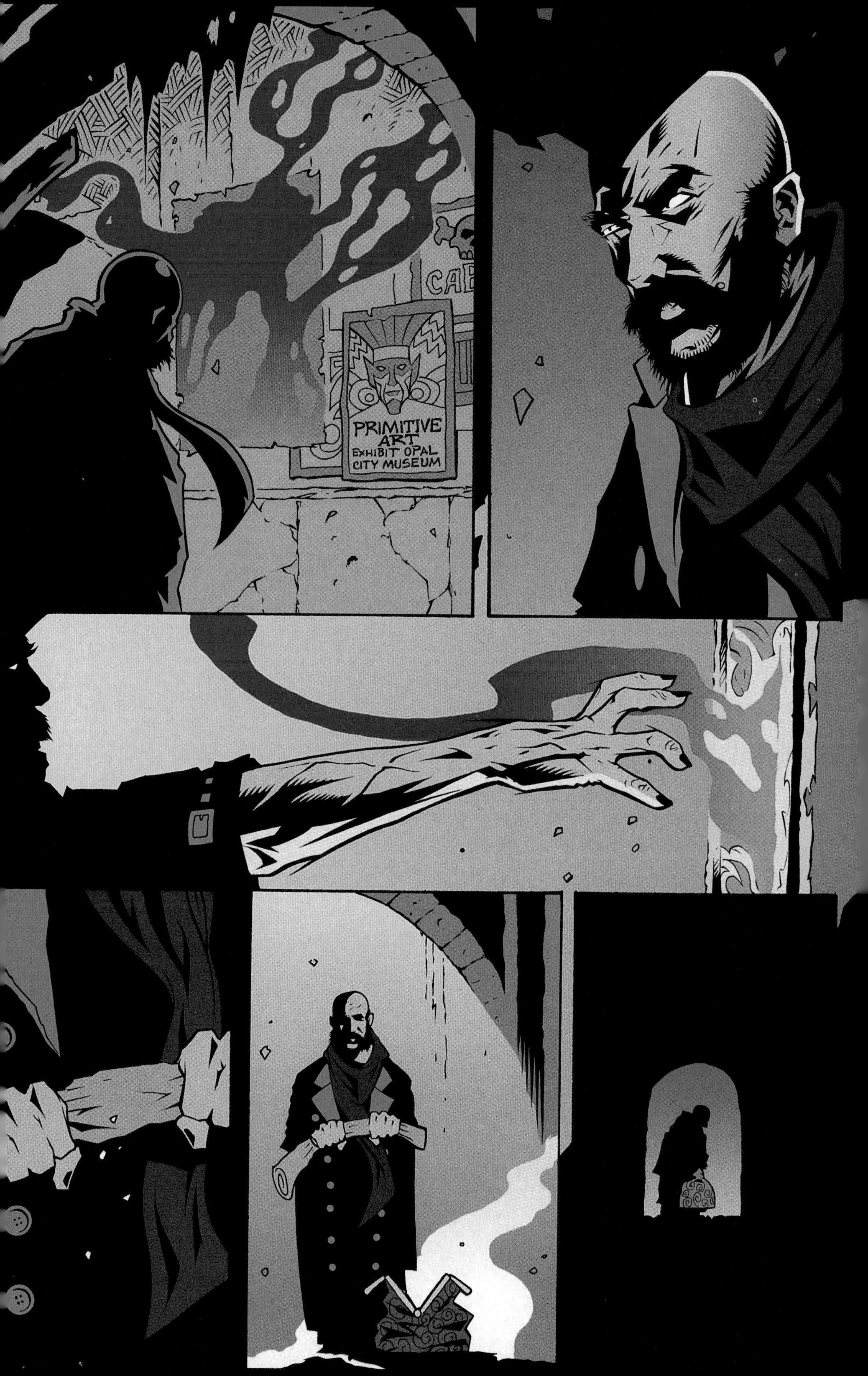

PRIMITIVE ART
EXHIBIT OPAL CITY MUSEUM

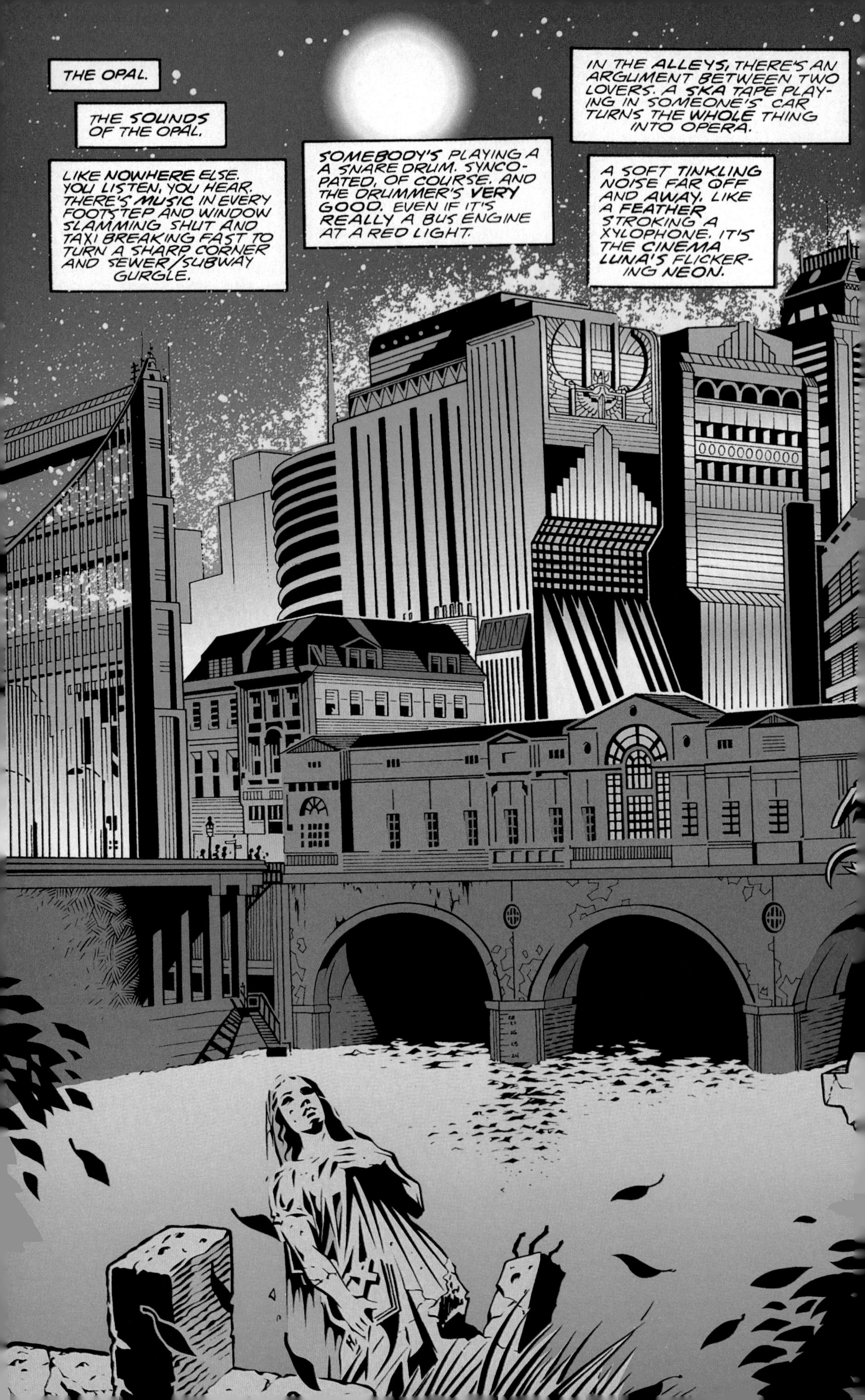
THE OPAL.
THE SOUNDS OF THE OPAL.
LIKE NOWHERE ELSE. YOU LISTEN, YOU HEAR. THERE'S MUSIC IN EVERY FOOTSTEP AND WINDOW SLAMMING SHUT AND TAXI BREAKING FAST TO TURN A SHARP CORNER AND SEWER/SUBWAY GURGLE.
SOMEBODY'S PLAYING A A SNARE DRUM. SYNCOPATED, OF COURSE. AND THE DRUMMER'S VERY GOOD. EVEN IF IT'S REALLY A BUS ENGINE AT A RED LIGHT.
IN THE ALLEYS, THERE'S AN ARGUMENT BETWEEN TWO LOVERS. A SKA TAPE PLAYING IN SOMEONE'S CAR TURNS THE WHOLE THING INTO OPERA.
A SOFT TINKLING NOISE FAR OFF AND AWAY. LIKE A FEATHER STROKING A XYLOPHONE. IT'S THE CINEMA LUNA'S FLICKERING NEON.

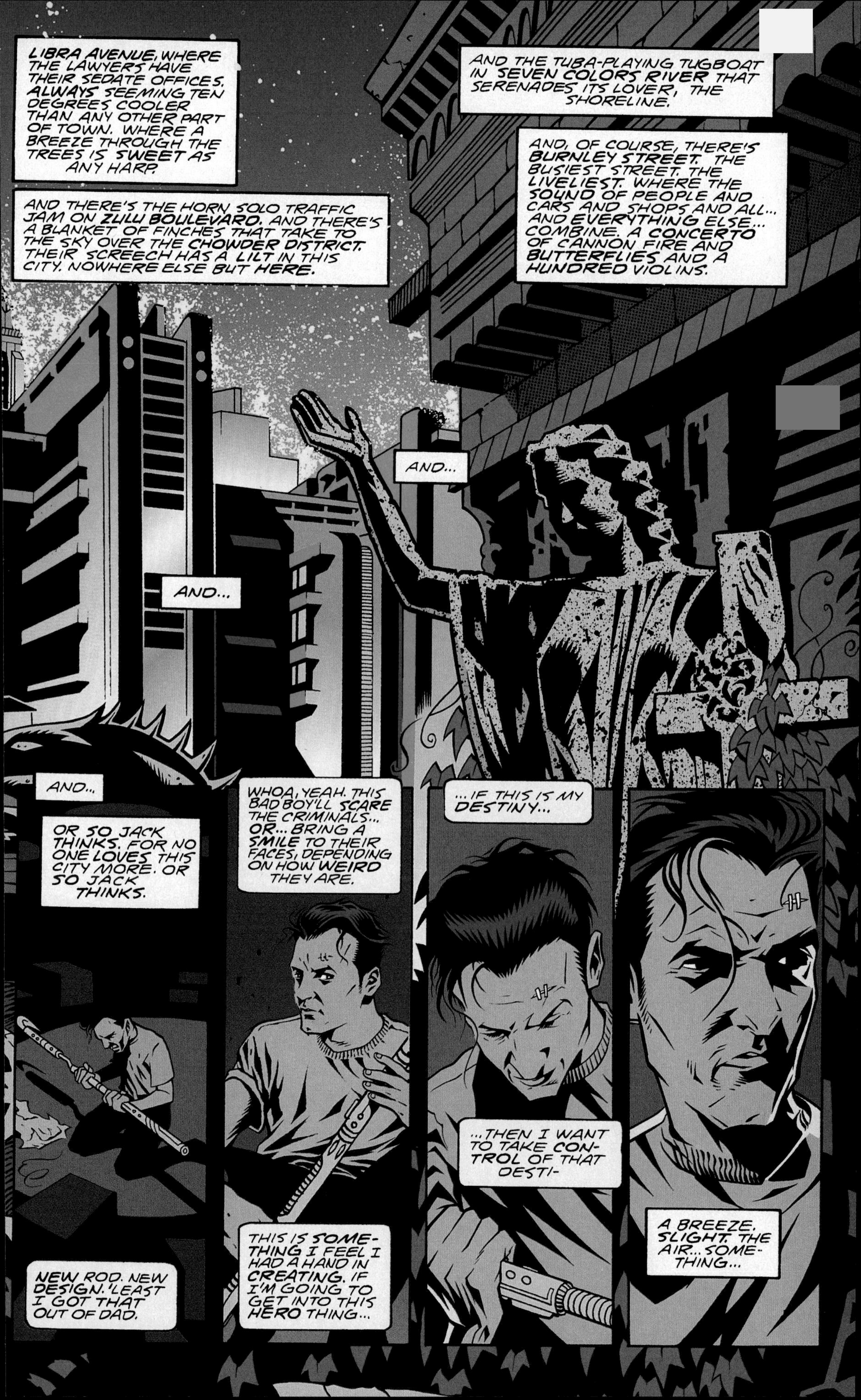

LIBRA AVENUE, WHERE THE LAWYERS HAVE THEIR SEDATE OFFICES. ALWAYS SEEMING TEN DEGREES COOLER THAN ANY OTHER PART OF TOWN. WHERE A BREEZE THROUGH THE TREES IS SWEET AS ANY HARP.
AND THERE'S THE HORN SOLO TRAFFIC JAM ON ZULU BOULEVARD. AND THERE'S A BLANKET OF FINCHES THAT TAKE TO THE SKY OVER THE CHOWDER DISTRICT. THEIR SCREECH HAS A LILT IN THIS CITY. NOWHERE ELSE BUT HERE.
AND THE TUBA-PLAYING TUGBOAT IN SEVEN COLORS RIVER THAT SERENADES ITS LOVER, THE SHORELINE.
AND, OF COURSE, THERE'S BURNLEY STREET. THE BUSIEST STREET. THE LIVELIEST. WHERE THE SOUND OF PEOPLE AND CARS AND SHOPS AND ALL... AND EVERYTHING ELSE... COMBINE. A CONCERTO OF CANNON FIRE AND BUTTERFLIES AND A HUNDRED VIOLINS.
AND...
AND...
AND...
OR SO JACK THINKS. FOR NO ONE LOVES THIS CITY MORE. OR SO JACK THINKS.
NEW ROD. NEW DESIGN. 'LEAST I GOT THAT OUT OF DAD.
WHOA, YEAH. THIS BAD BOY'LL SCARE THE CRIMINALS... OR... BRING A SMILE TO THEIR FACES, DEPENDING ON HOW WEIRD THEY ARE.
THIS IS SOMETHING I FEEL I HAD A HAND IN CREATING. IF I'M GOING TO GET INTO THIS HERO THING...
...IF THIS IS MY DESTINY...
...THEN I WANT TO TAKE CONTROL OF THAT DESTI-
A BREEZE. SLIGHT. THE AIR... SOMETHING...

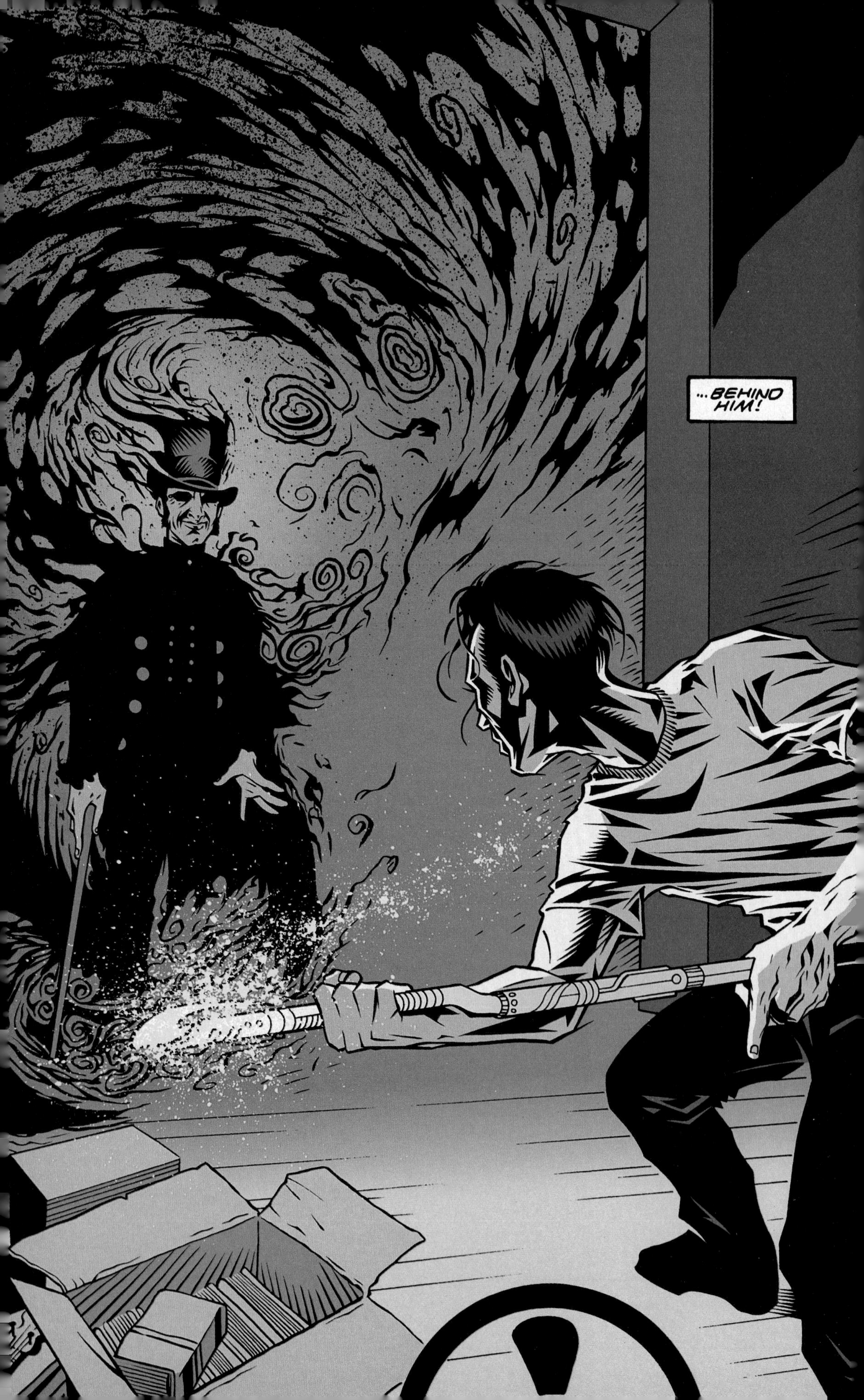
...BEHIND HIM!

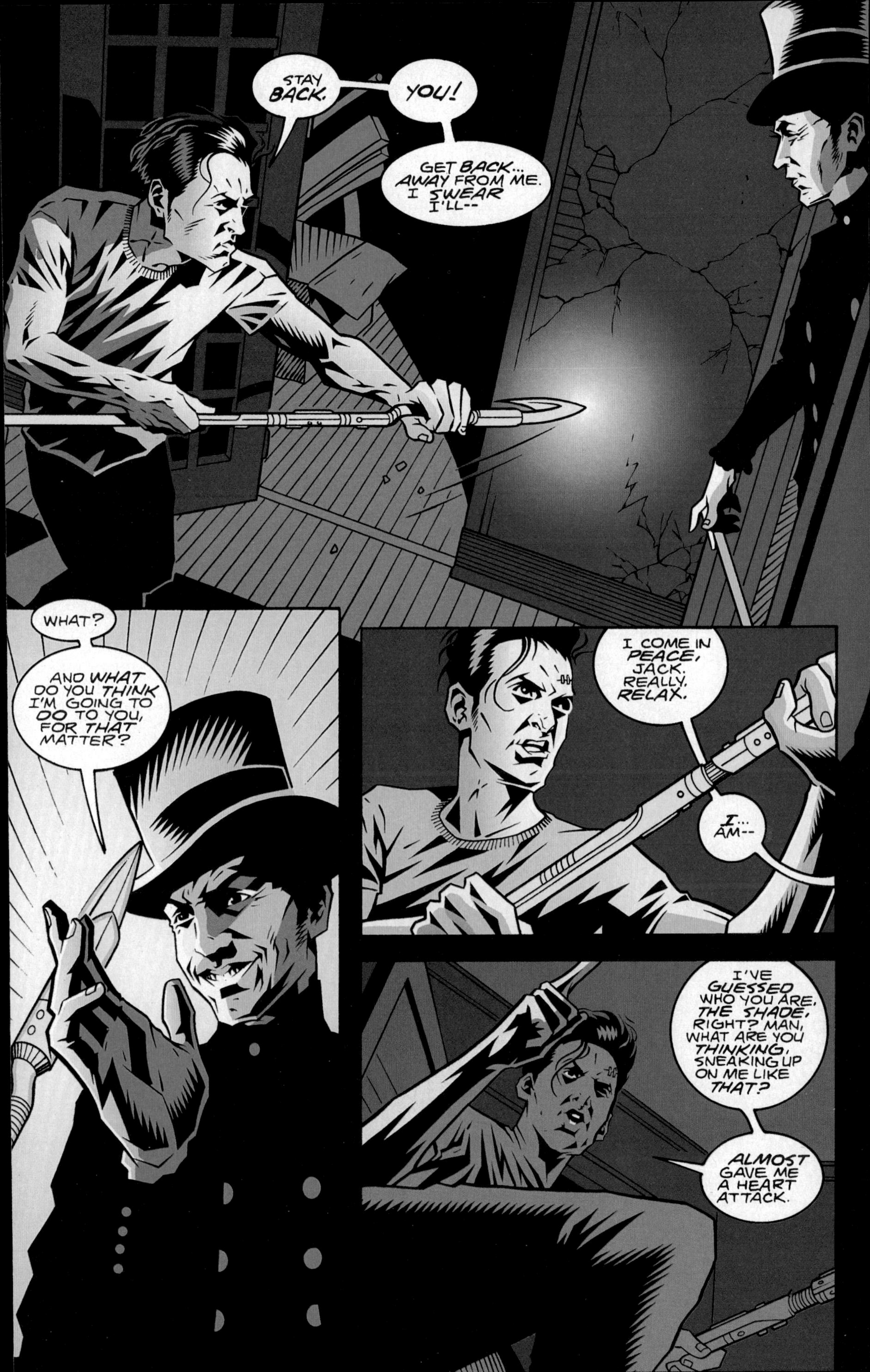
STAY BACK.
YOU!
GET BACK... AWAY FROM ME. I SWEAR I'LL--
WHAT?
AND WHAT DO YOU THINK I'M GOING TO DO TO YOU, FOR THAT MATTER?
I COME IN PEACE, JACK. REALLY. RELAX.
I... AM--
I'VE GUESSED WHO YOU ARE. THE SHADE, RIGHT? MAN, WHAT ARE YOU THINKING, SNEAKING UP ON ME LIKE THAT?
ALMOST GAVE ME A HEART ATTACK.

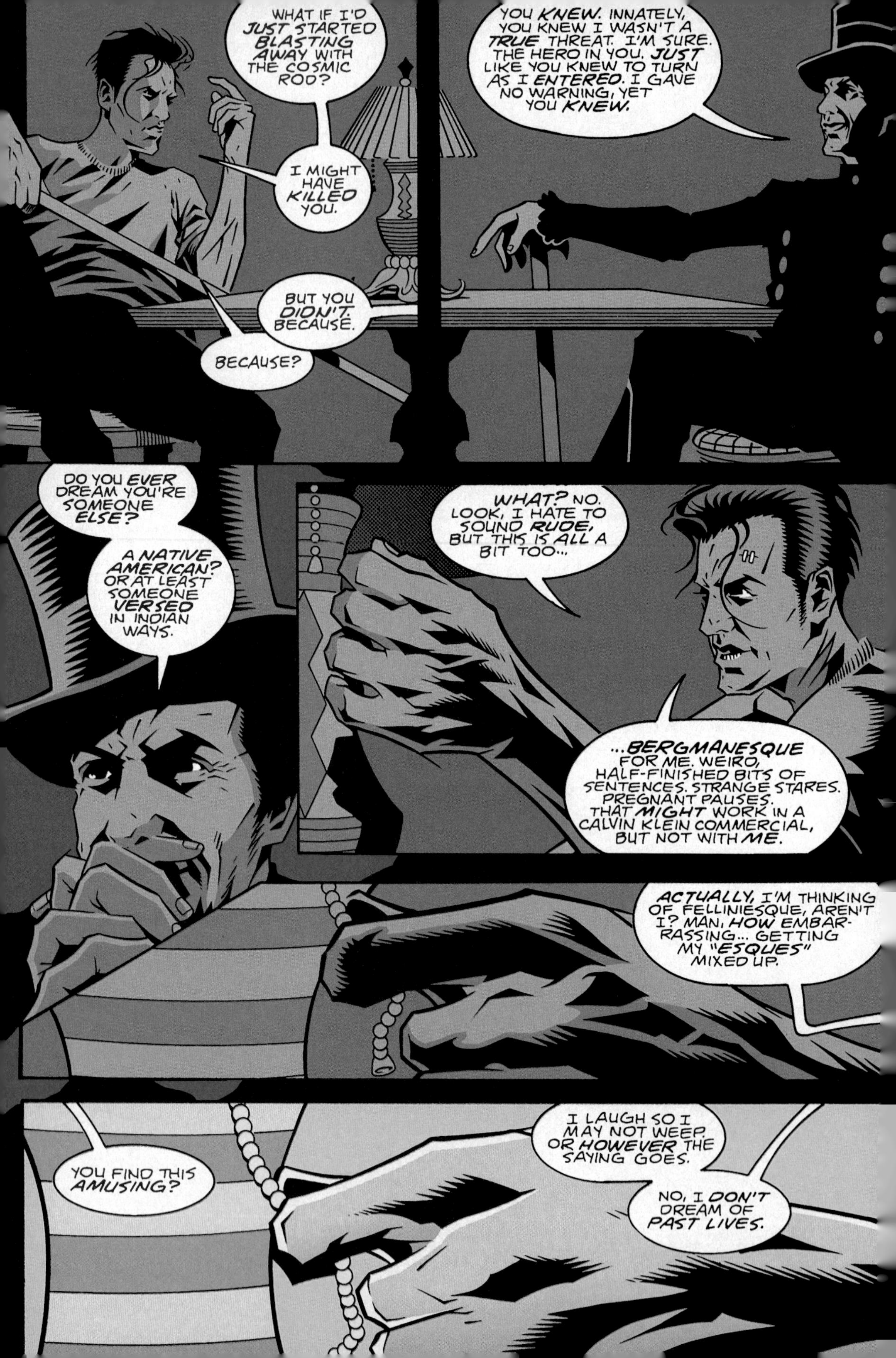
WHAT IF I'D JUST STARTED BLASTING AWAY WITH THE COSMIC ROD?
I MIGHT HAVE KILLED YOU.
BUT YOU DIDN'T. BECAUSE.
BECAUSE?
YOU KNEW. INNATELY, YOU KNEW I WASN'T A TRUE THREAT. I'M SURE. THE HERO IN YOU. JUST LIKE YOU KNEW TO TURN AS I ENTERED. I GAVE NO WARNING, YET YOU KNEW.
DO YOU EVER DREAM YOU'RE SOMEONE ELSE?
A NATIVE AMERICAN? OR AT LEAST SOMEONE VERSED IN INDIAN WAYS.
WHAT? NO. LOOK, I HATE TO SOUND RUDE, BUT THIS IS ALL A BIT TOO...
...BERGMANESQUE FOR ME. WEIRD, HALF-FINISHED BITS OF SENTENCES. STRANGE STARES. PREGNANT PAUSES. THAT MIGHT WORK IN A CALVIN KLEIN COMMERCIAL, BUT NOT WITH ME.
ACTUALLY, I'M THINKING OF FELLINIESQUE, AREN'T I? MAN, HOW EMBARRASSING... GETTING MY "ESQUES" MIXED UP.
YOU FIND THIS AMUSING?
I LAUGH SO I MAY NOT WEEP OR HOWEVER THE SAYING GOES.
NO, I DON'T DREAM OF PAST LIVES.

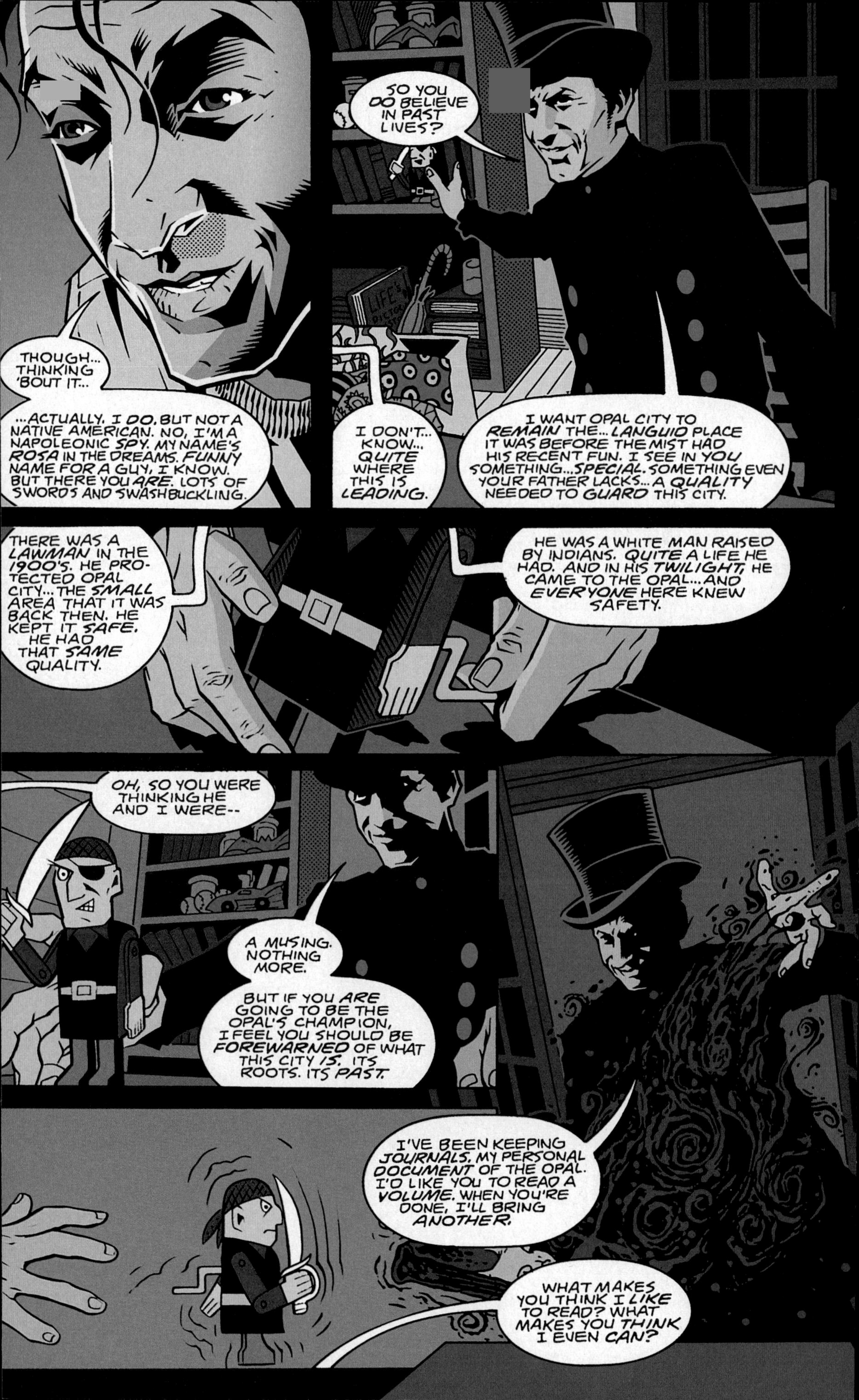
SO YOU DO BELIEVE IN PAST LIVES?
THOUGH... THINKING 'BOUT IT...
...ACTUALLY, I DO, BUT NOT A NATIVE AMERICAN. NO, I'M A NAPOLEONIC SPY. MY NAME'S ROSA IN THE DREAMS. FUNNY NAME FOR A GUY, I KNOW. BUT THERE YOU ARE. LOTS OF SWORDS AND SWASHBUCKLING.
I DON'T... KNOW... QUITE WHERE THIS IS LEADING.
I WANT OPAL CITY TO REMAIN THE... LANGUID PLACE IT WAS BEFORE THE MIST HAD HIS RECENT FUN. I SEE IN YOU SOMETHING... SPECIAL. SOMETHING EVEN YOUR FATHER LACKS... A QUALITY NEEDED TO GUARD THIS CITY.
THERE WAS A LAWMAN IN THE 1900'S. HE PROTECTED OPAL CITY... THE SMALL AREA THAT IT WAS BACK THEN. HE KEPT IT SAFE. HE HAD THAT SAME QUALITY.
HE WAS A WHITE MAN RAISED BY INDIANS. QUITE A LIFE HE HAD. AND IN HIS TWILIGHT, HE CAME TO THE OPAL... AND EVERYONE HERE KNEW SAFETY.
OH, SO YOU WERE THINKING HE AND I WERE--
A MUSING. NOTHING MORE.
BUT IF YOU ARE GOING TO BE THE OPAL'S CHAMPION, I FEEL YOU SHOULD BE FOREWARNED OF WHAT THIS CITY IS. ITS ROOTS. ITS PAST.
I'VE BEEN KEEPING JOURNALS. MY PERSONAL DOCUMENT OF THE OPAL. I'D LIKE YOU TO READ A VOLUME. WHEN YOU'RE DONE, I'LL BRING ANOTHER.
WHAT MAKES YOU THINK I LIKE TO READ? WHAT MAKES YOU THINK I EVEN CAN?

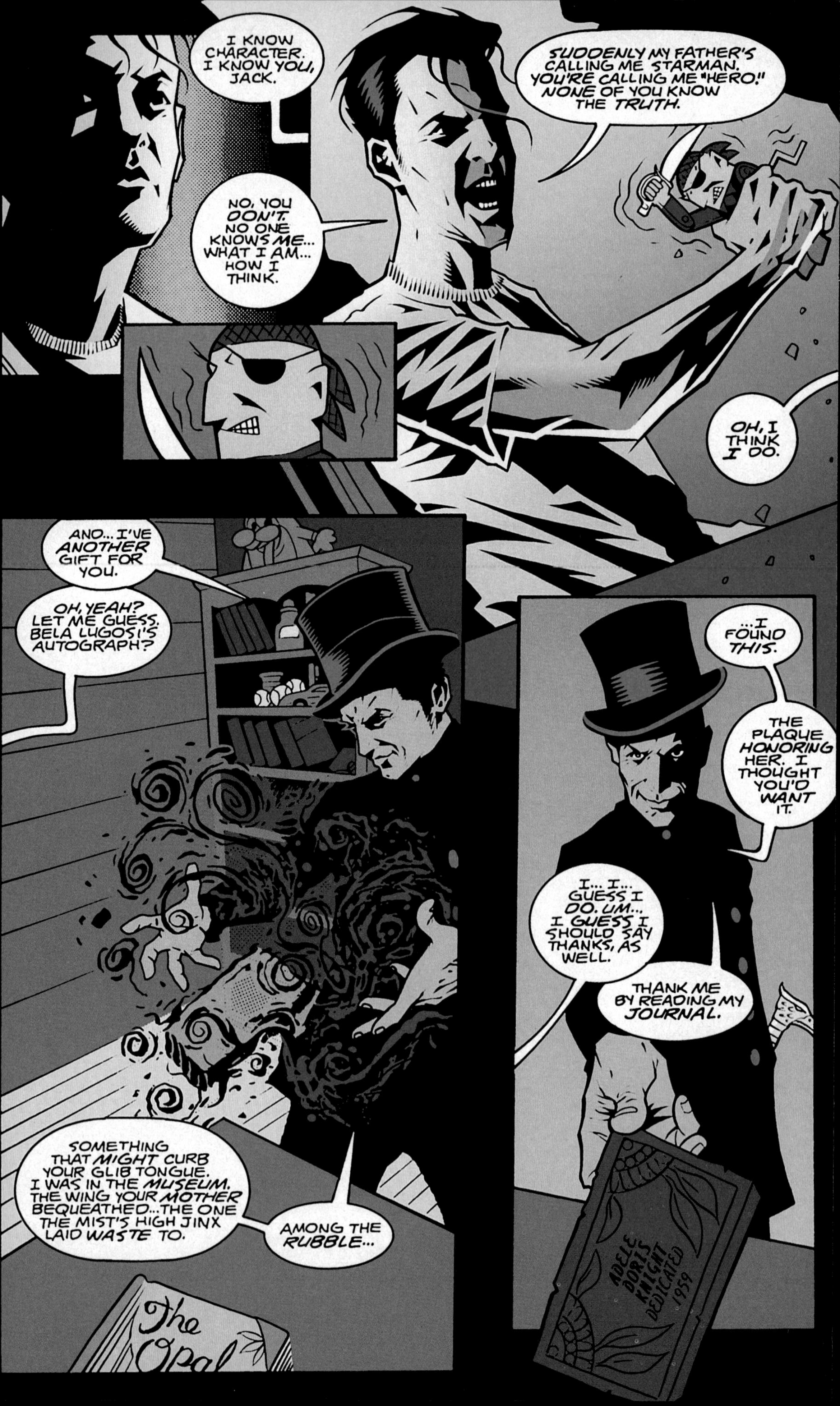

I KNOW CHARACTER. I KNOW YOU, JACK.
SUDDENLY MY FATHER'S CALLING ME STARMAN. YOU'RE CALLING ME "HERO." NONE OF YOU KNOW THE TRUTH.
NO, YOU DON'T. NO ONE KNOWS ME... WHAT I AM... HOW I THINK.
OH, I THINK I DO.
AND... I'VE ANOTHER GIFT FOR YOU.
OH, YEAH? LET ME GUESS. BELA LUGOSI'S AUTOGRAPH?
SOMETHING THAT MIGHT CURB YOUR GLIB TONGUE. I WAS IN THE MUSEUM. THE WING YOUR MOTHER BEQUEATHED...THE ONE THE MIST'S HIGH JINX LAID WASTE TO.
AMONG THE RUBBLE...
The Opal
...I FOUND THIS.
THE PLAQUE HONORING HER. I THOUGHT YOU'D WANT IT.
I... I... GUESS I DO. UM... I GUESS I SHOULD SAY THANKS, AS WELL.
THANK ME BY READING MY JOURNAL.
ADELE DORIS KNIGHT DEDICATED 1959

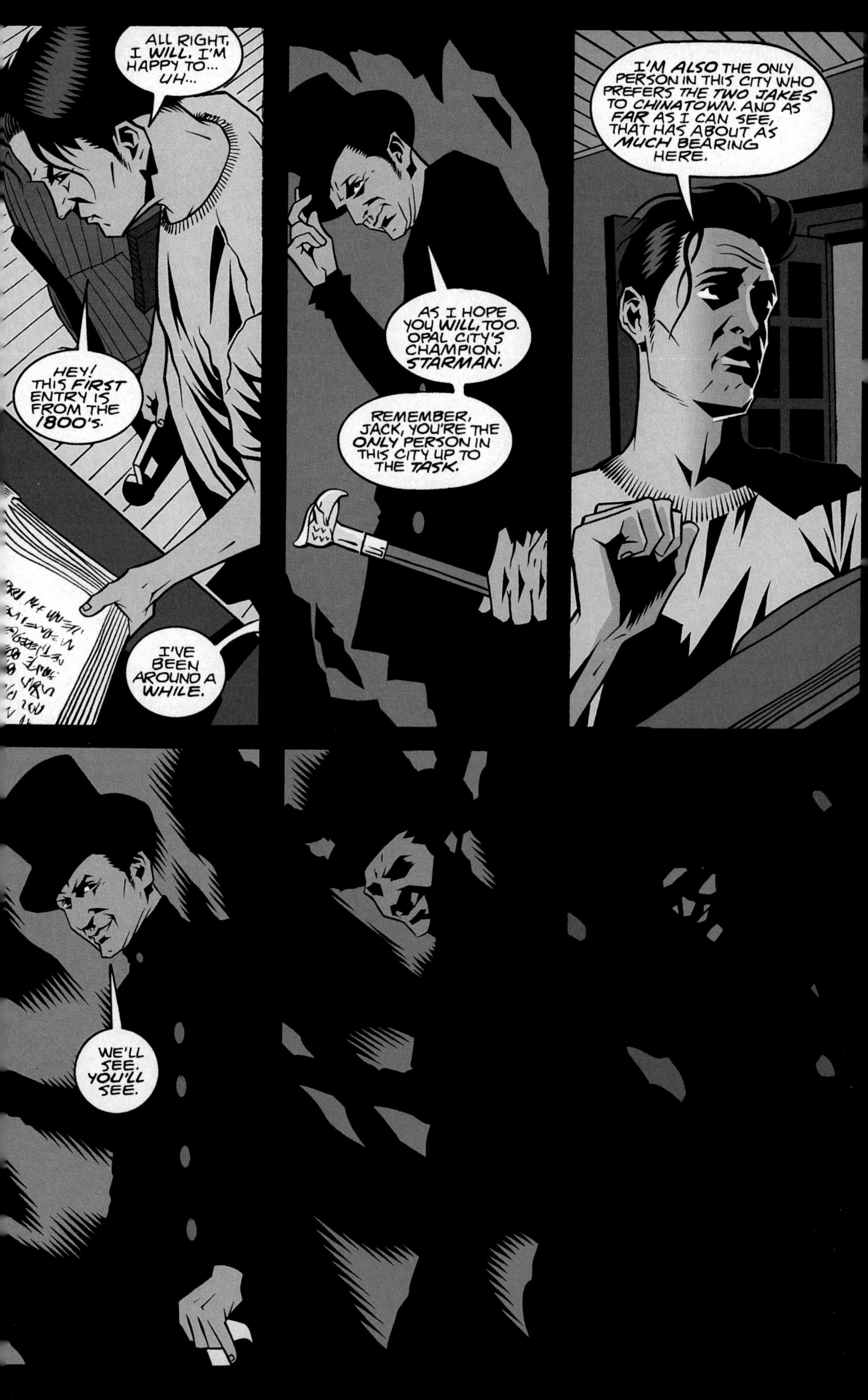
ALL RIGHT, I WILL. I'M HAPPY TO... UH...
HEY! THIS FIRST ENTRY IS FROM THE 1800'S.
I'VE BEEN AROUND A WHILE.
AS I HOPE YOU WILL, TOO. OPAL CITY'S CHAMPION. STARMAN.
REMEMBER, JACK, YOU'RE THE ONLY PERSON IN THIS CITY UP TO THE TASK.
I'M ALSO THE ONLY PERSON IN THIS CITY WHO PREFERS THE TWO JAKES TO CHINATOWN. AND AS FAR AS I CAN SEE, THAT HAS ABOUT AS MUCH BEARING HERE.
WE'LL SEE. YOU'LL SEE.

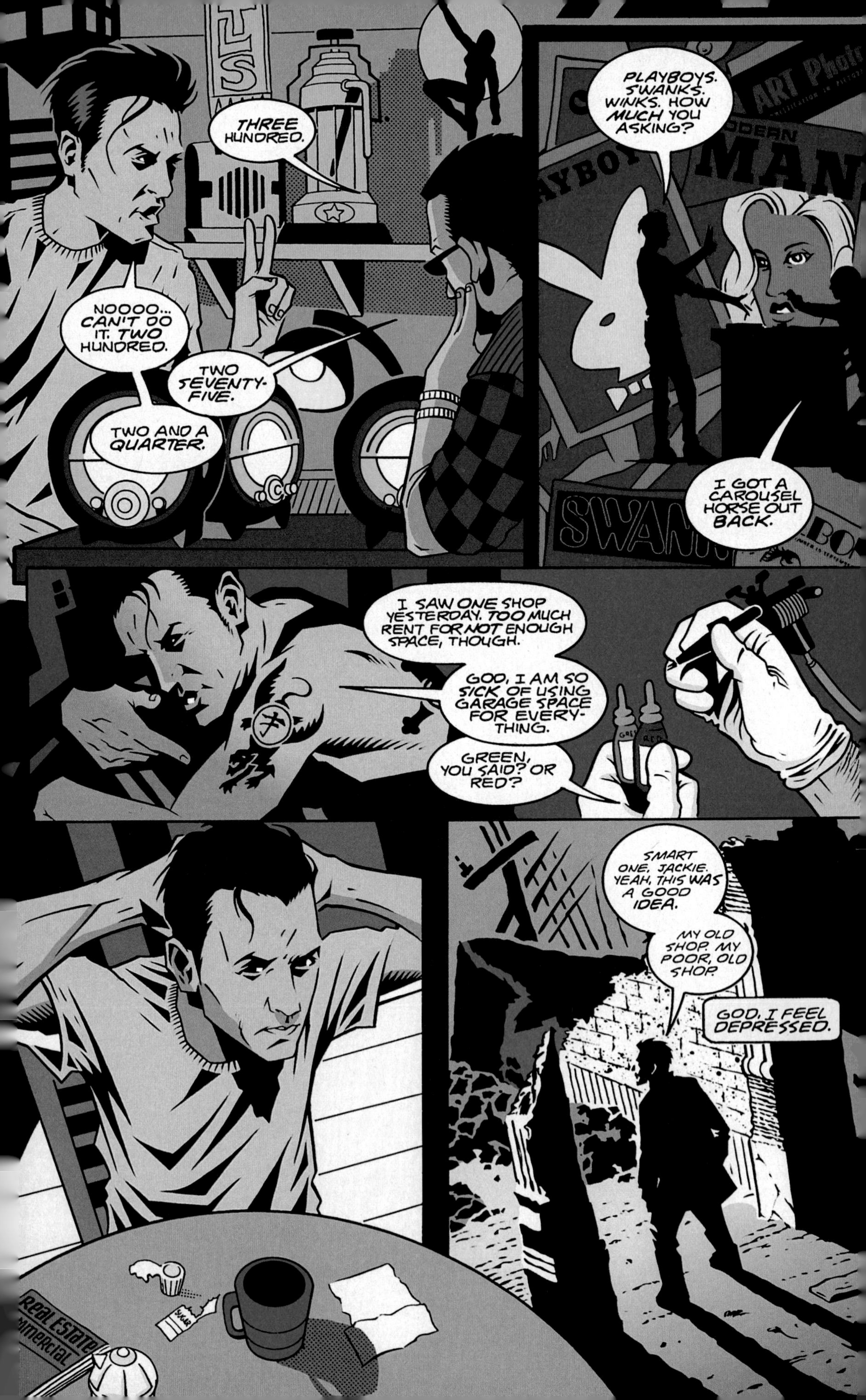
THREE HUNDRED.
NOOOO... CAN'T DO IT. TWO HUNDRED.
TWO SEVENTY-FIVE.
TWO AND A QUARTER.
PLAYBOYS. SWANKS. WINKS. HOW MUCH YOU ASKING?
I GOT A CAROUSEL HORSE OUT BACK.
I SAW ONE SHOP YESTERDAY. TOO MUCH RENT FOR NOT ENOUGH SPACE, THOUGH.
GOD, I AM SO SICK OF USING GARAGE SPACE FOR EVERY-THING.
GREEN, YOU SAID? OR RED?
SMART ONE, JACKIE. YEAH, THIS WAS A GOOD IDEA.
MY OLD SHOP. MY POOR, OLD SHOP.
GOD, I FEEL DEPRESSED.

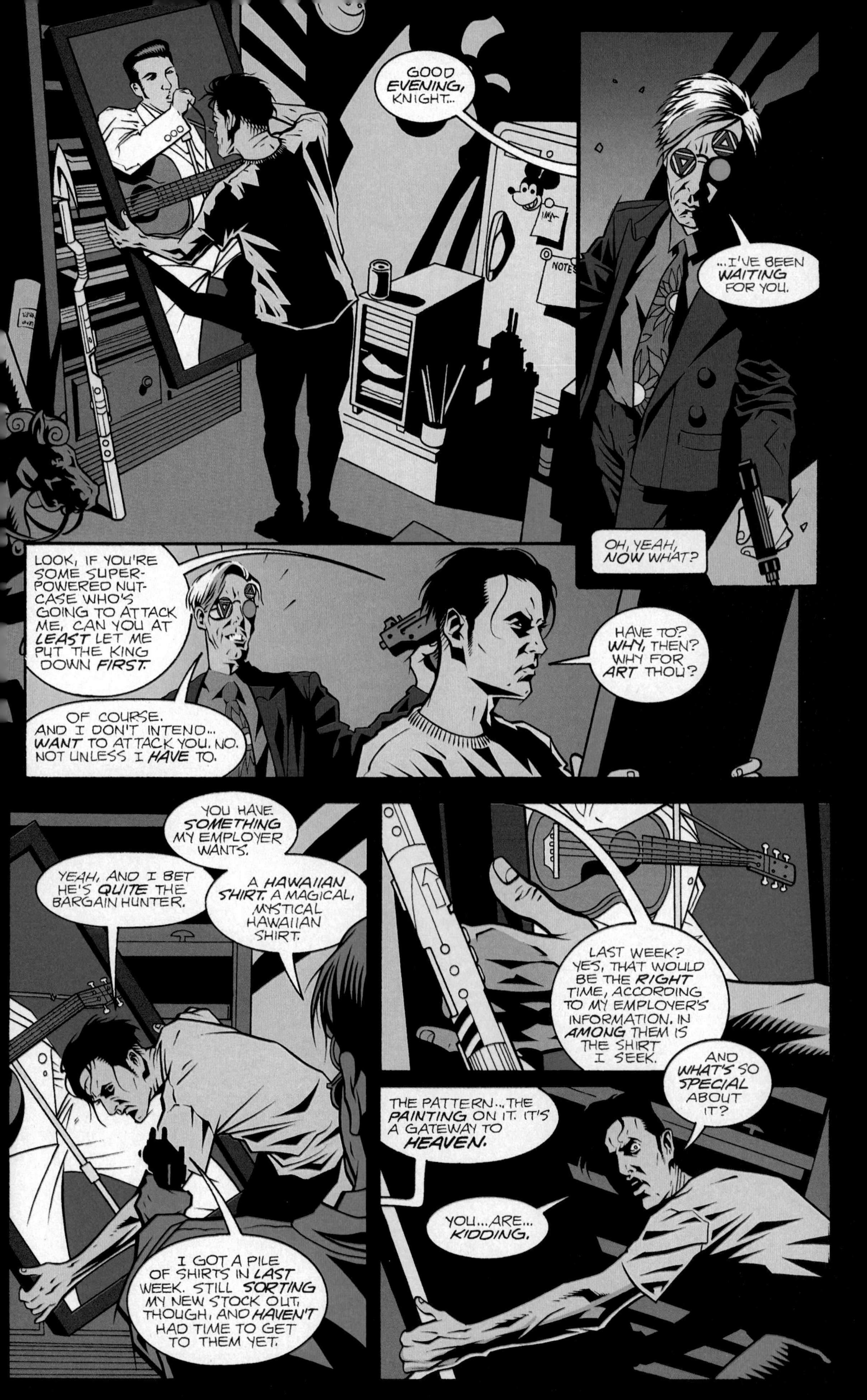
GOOD EVENING, KNIGHT...
NOTES
...I'VE BEEN WAITING FOR YOU.
OH, YEAH, NOW WHAT?
LOOK, IF YOU'RE SOME SUPER-POWERED NUT-CASE WHO'S GOING TO ATTACK ME, CAN YOU AT LEAST LET ME PUT THE KING DOWN FIRST.
OF COURSE. AND I DON'T INTEND... WANT TO ATTACK YOU. NO. NOT UNLESS I HAVE TO.
HAVE TO? WHY, THEN? WHY FOR ART THOU?
YOU HAVE. SOMETHING MY EMPLOYER WANTS.
YEAH, AND I BET HE'S QUITE THE BARGAIN HUNTER.
A HAWAIIAN SHIRT. A MAGICAL, MYSTICAL HAWAIIAN SHIRT.
I GOT A PILE OF SHIRTS IN LAST WEEK. STILL SORTING MY NEW STOCK OUT, THOUGH, AND HAVEN'T HAD TIME TO GET TO THEM YET.
LAST WEEK? YES, THAT WOULD BE THE RIGHT TIME, ACCORDING TO MY EMPLOYER'S INFORMATION. IN AMONG THEM IS THE SHIRT I SEEK.
AND WHAT'S SO SPECIAL ABOUT IT?
THE PATTERN... THE PAINTING ON IT. IT'S A GATEWAY TO HEAVEN.
YOU...ARE... KIDDING.

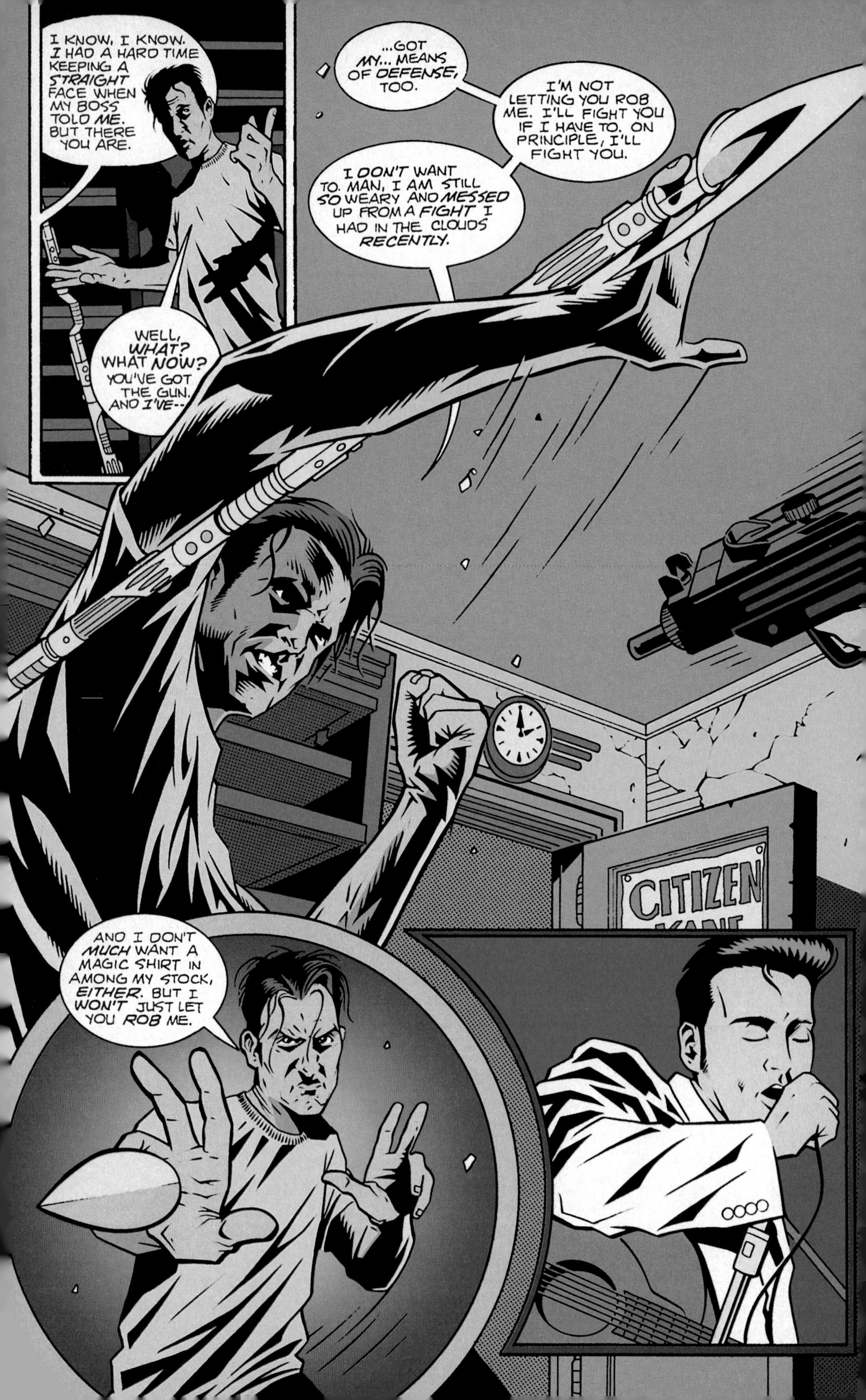
I KNOW, I KNOW. I HAD A HARD TIME KEEPING A STRAIGHT FACE WHEN MY BOSS TOLD ME. BUT THERE YOU ARE.
WELL, WHAT? WHAT NOW? YOU'VE GOT THE GUN. AND I'VE--
...GOT MY... MEANS OF DEFENSE, TOO.
I'M NOT LETTING YOU ROB ME. I'LL FIGHT YOU IF I HAVE TO. ON PRINCIPLE, I'LL FIGHT YOU.
I DON'T WANT TO. MAN, I AM STILL SO WEARY AND MESSED UP FROM A FIGHT I HAD IN THE CLOUDS RECENTLY.
CITIZEN
AND I DON'T MUCH WANT A MAGIC SHIRT IN AMONG MY STOCK, EITHER. BUT I WON'T JUST LET YOU ROB ME.

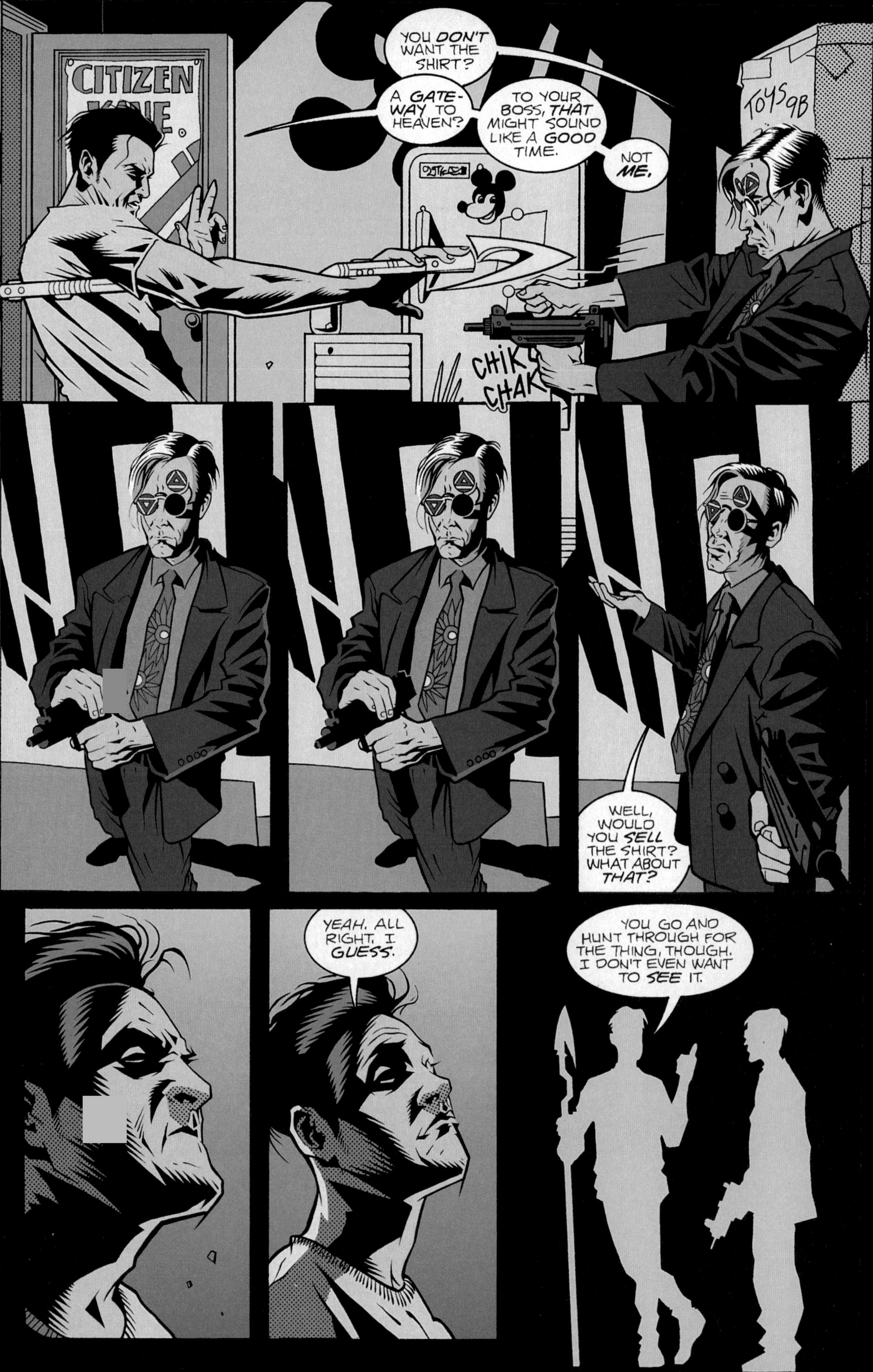
CITIZEN
TOYS 9B
YOU DON'T WANT THE SHIRT?
A GATE-WAY TO HEAVEN?
TO YOUR BOSS, THAT MIGHT SOUND LIKE A GOOD TIME.
NOT ME.
CHIK CHAK
WELL, WOULD YOU SELL THE SHIRT? WHAT ABOUT THAT?
YEAH. ALL RIGHT, I GUESS.
YOU GO AND HUNT THROUGH FOR THE THING, THOUGH. I DON'T EVEN WANT TO SEE IT.

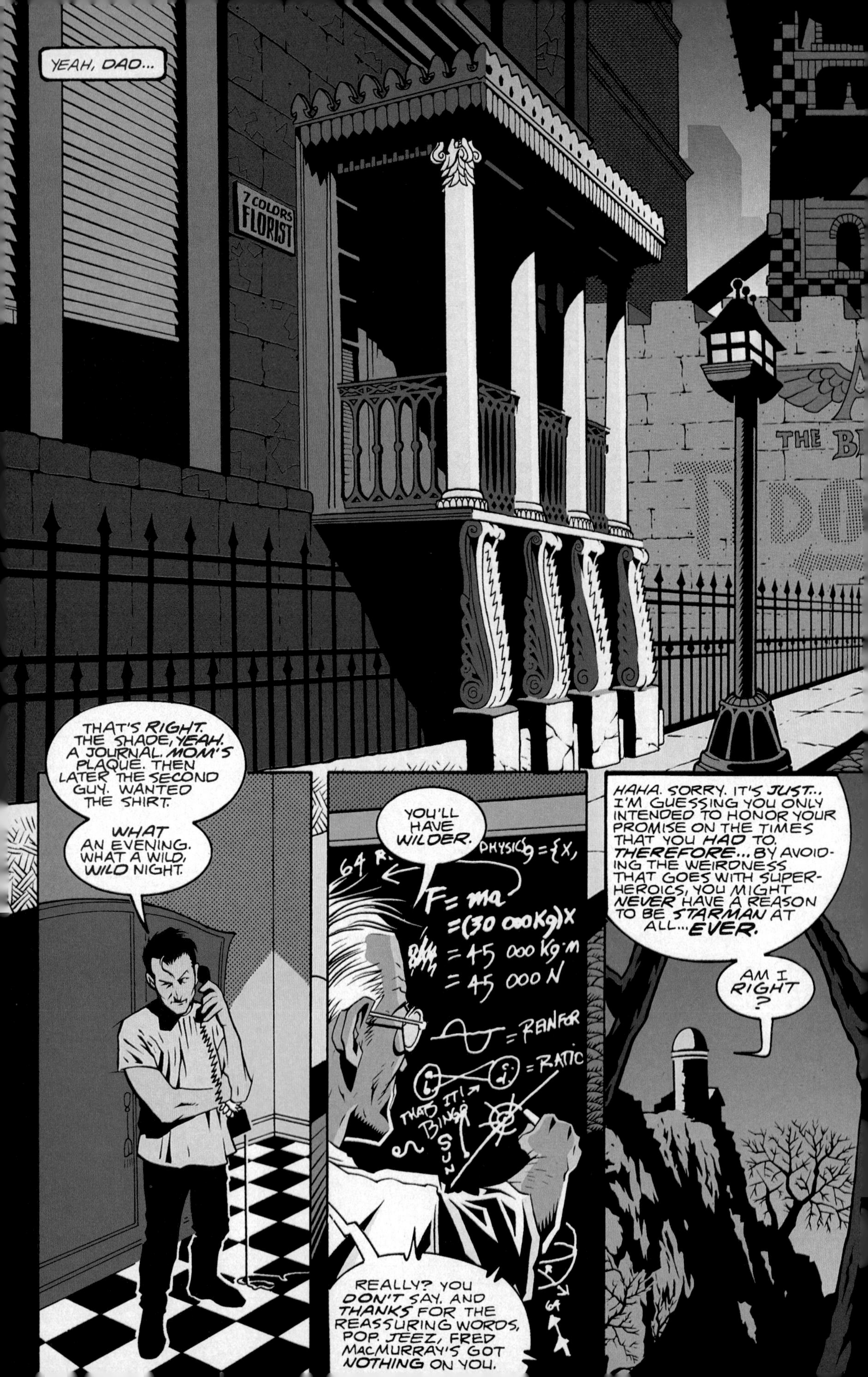

YEAH, DAD...
7 COLORS FLORIST
THE B
THAT'S RIGHT. THE SHADE, YEAH. A JOURNAL. MOM'S PLAQUE. THEN LATER THE SECOND GUY. WANTED THE SHIRT.
WHAT AN EVENING. WHAT A WILD, WILD NIGHT.
YOU'LL HAVE WILDER.
F= ma
=(30 000Kg)x
= 45 000 Kg·m
= 45 000 N
= REINFOR
= RATIC
THAT'S IT! BINGO
SUN
REALLY? YOU DON'T SAY. AND THANKS FOR THE REASSURING WORDS, POP. JEEZ, FRED MACMURRAY'S GOT NOTHING ON YOU.
HAHA. SORRY. IT'S JUST... I'M GUESSING YOU ONLY INTENDED TO HONOR YOUR PROMISE ON THE TIMES THAT YOU HAD TO. THEREFORE... BY AVOIDING THE WEIRDNESS THAT GOES WITH SUPER-HEROICS, YOU MIGHT NEVER HAVE A REASON TO BE STARMAN AT ALL... EVER.
AM I RIGHT?

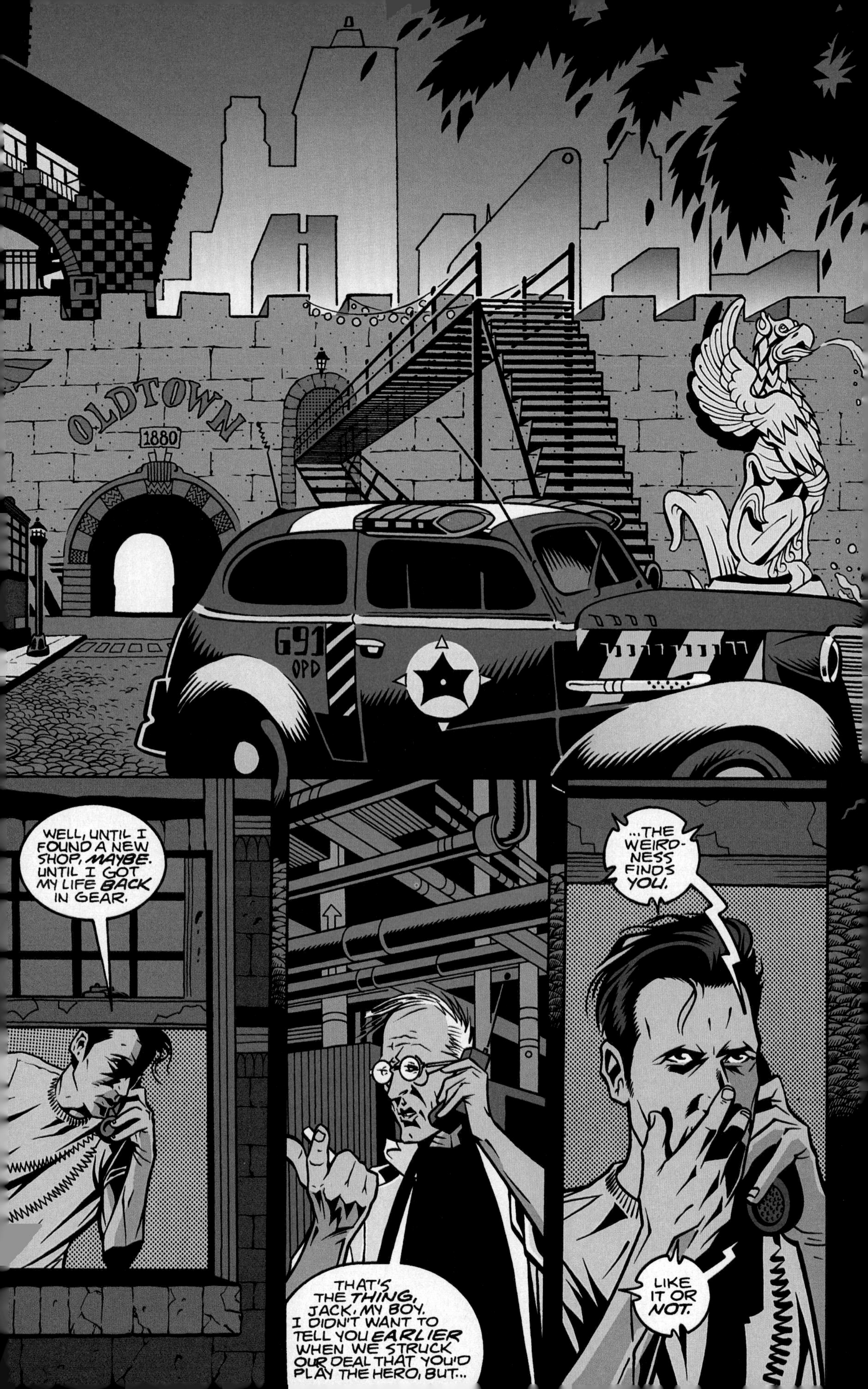
OLDTOWN
1880
G91
OPD
WELL, UNTIL I FOUND A NEW SHOP, MAYBE. UNTIL I GOT MY LIFE BACK IN GEAR.
THAT'S THE THING, JACK, MY BOY. I DIDN'T WANT TO TELL YOU EARLIER WHEN WE STRUCK OUR DEAL THAT YOU'D PLAY THE HERO, BUT...
...THE WEIRDNESS FINDS YOU.
LIKE IT OR NOT.

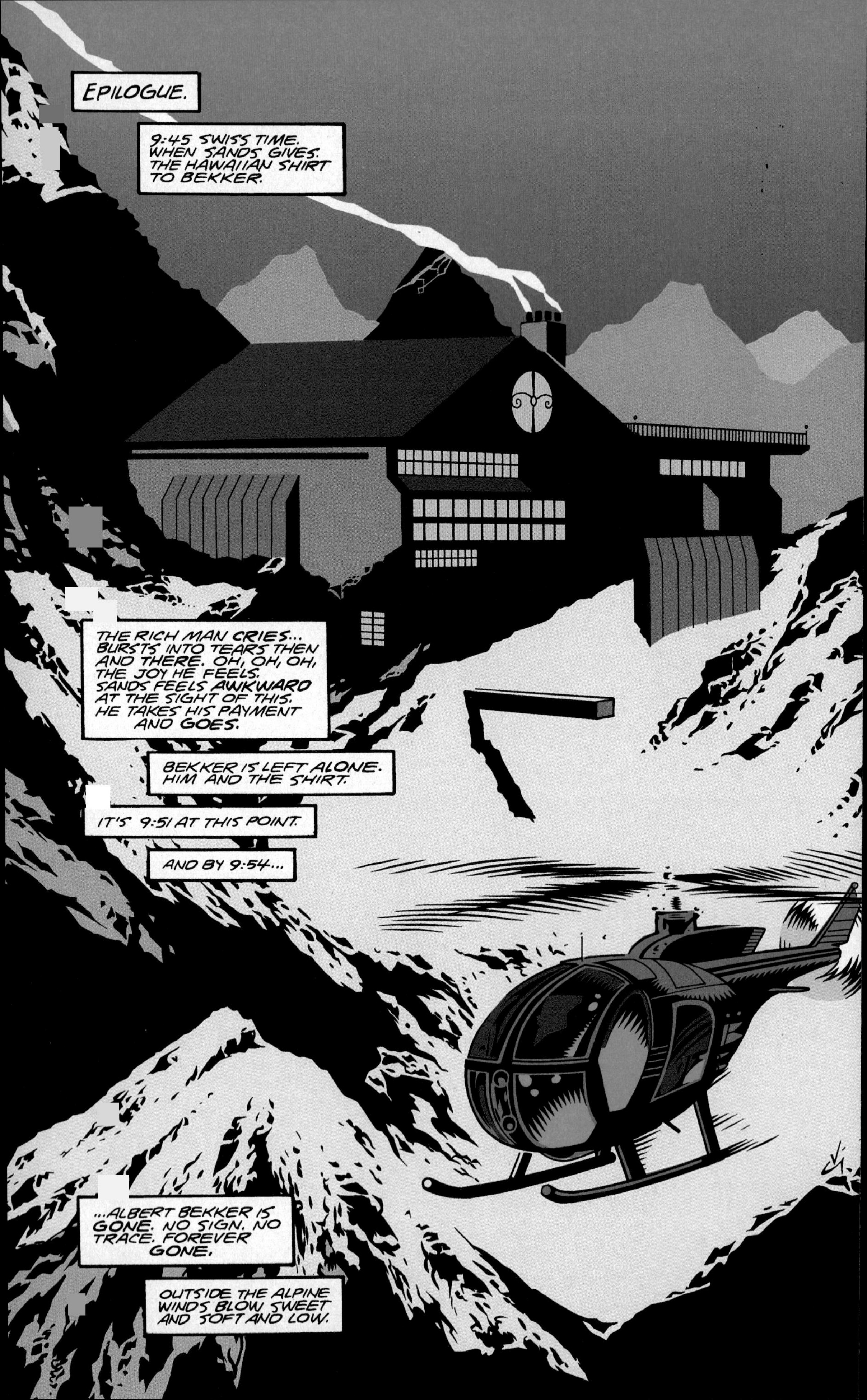
EPILOGUE.
9:45 SWISS TIME. WHEN SANDS GIVES. THE HAWAIIAN SHIRT TO BEKKER.
THE RICH MAN CRIES... BURSTS INTO TEARS THEN AND THERE. OH, OH, OH, THE JOY HE FEELS. SANDS FEELS AWKWARD AT THE SIGHT OF THIS. HE TAKES HIS PAYMENT AND GOES.
BEKKER IS LEFT ALONE. HIM AND THE SHIRT.
IT'S 9:51 AT THIS POINT.
AND BY 9:54...
...ALBERT BEKKER IS GONE. NO SIGN. NO TRACE. FOREVER GONE.
OUTSIDE THE ALPINE WINDS BLOW SWEET AND SOFT AND LOW.

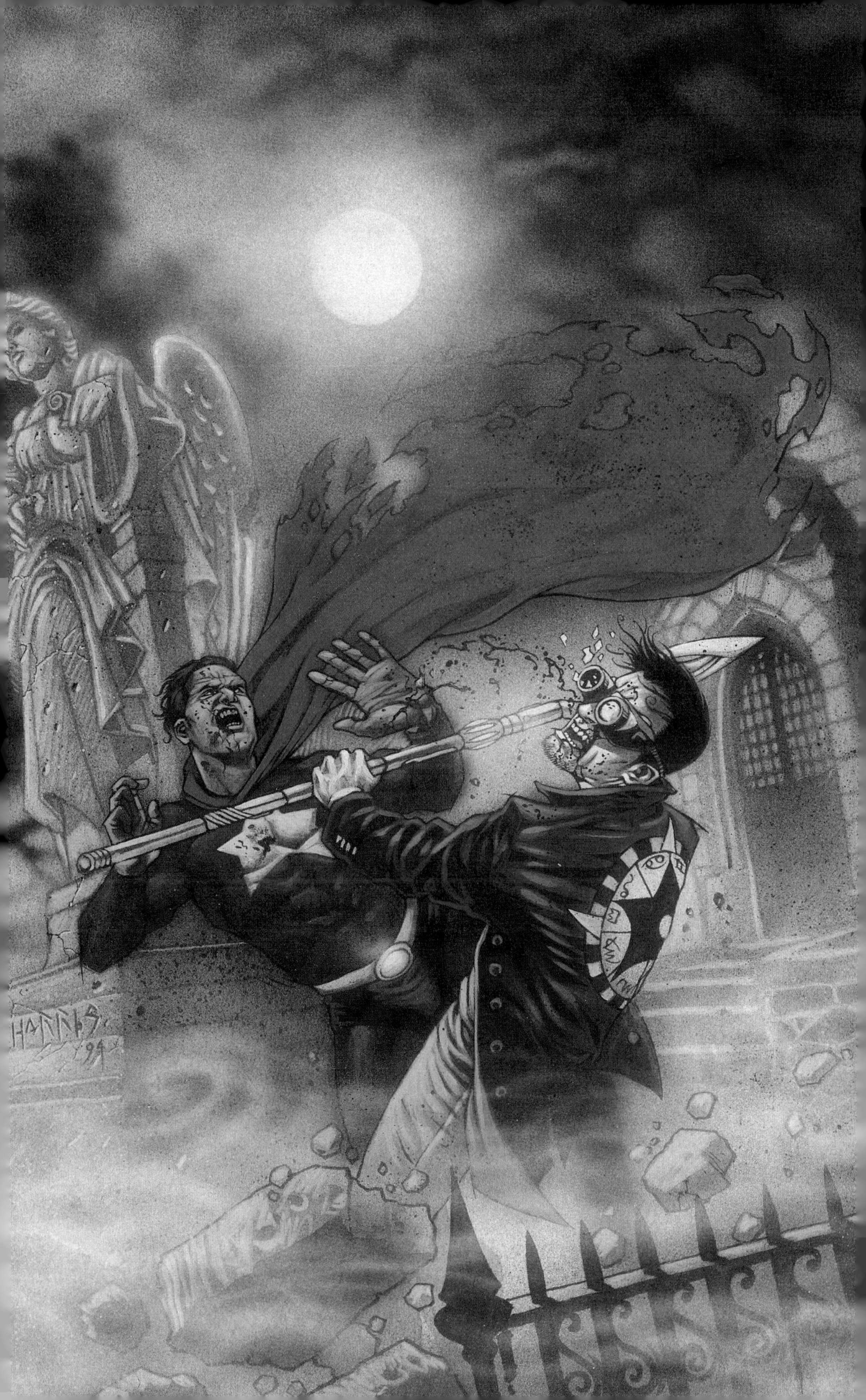

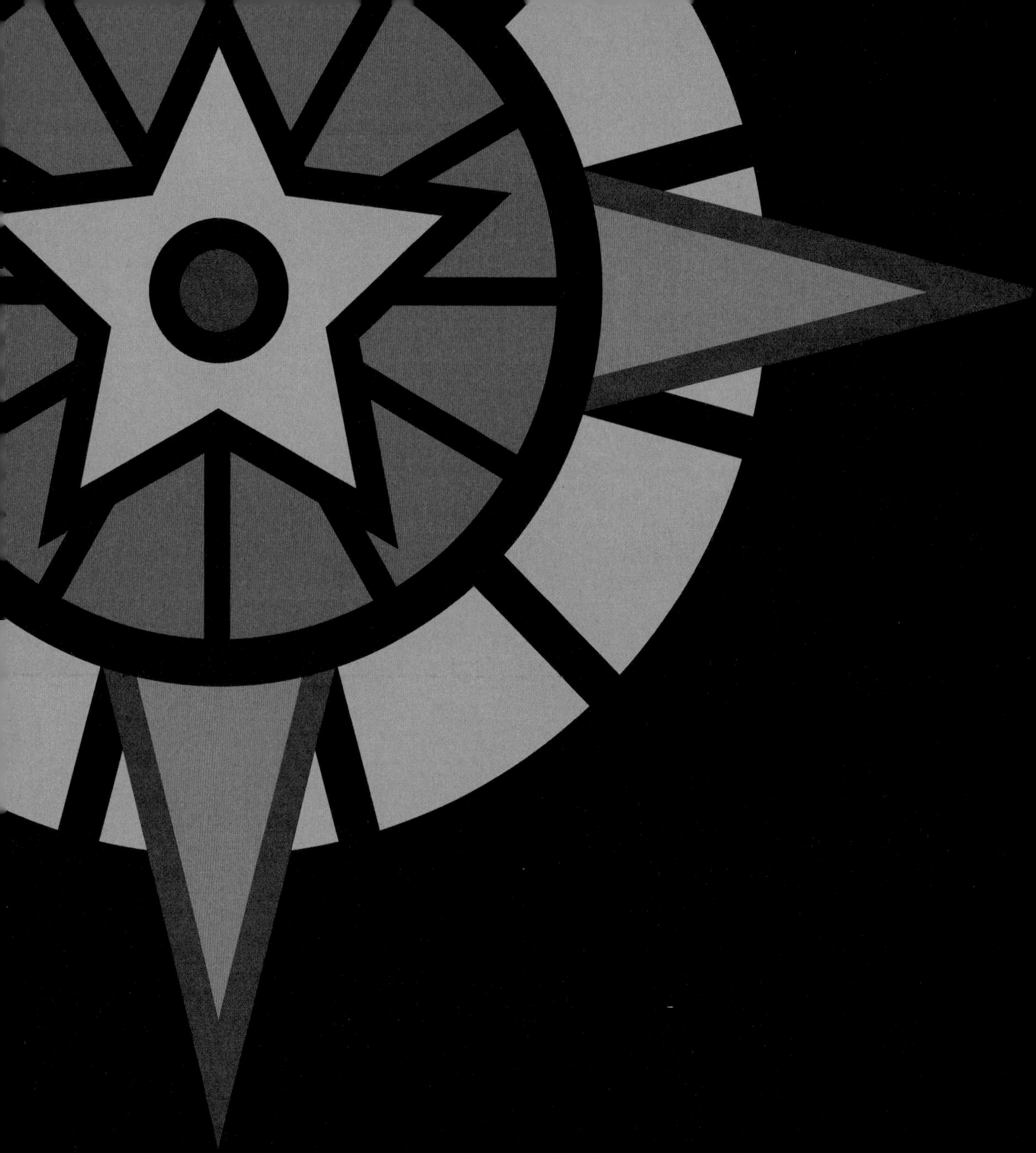

S T A R M A N   5

Cover by Tony Harris

Written by James Robinson

Pencils by Tony Harris,

with inks by Wade von Grawbadger

and colors by Gregory Wright

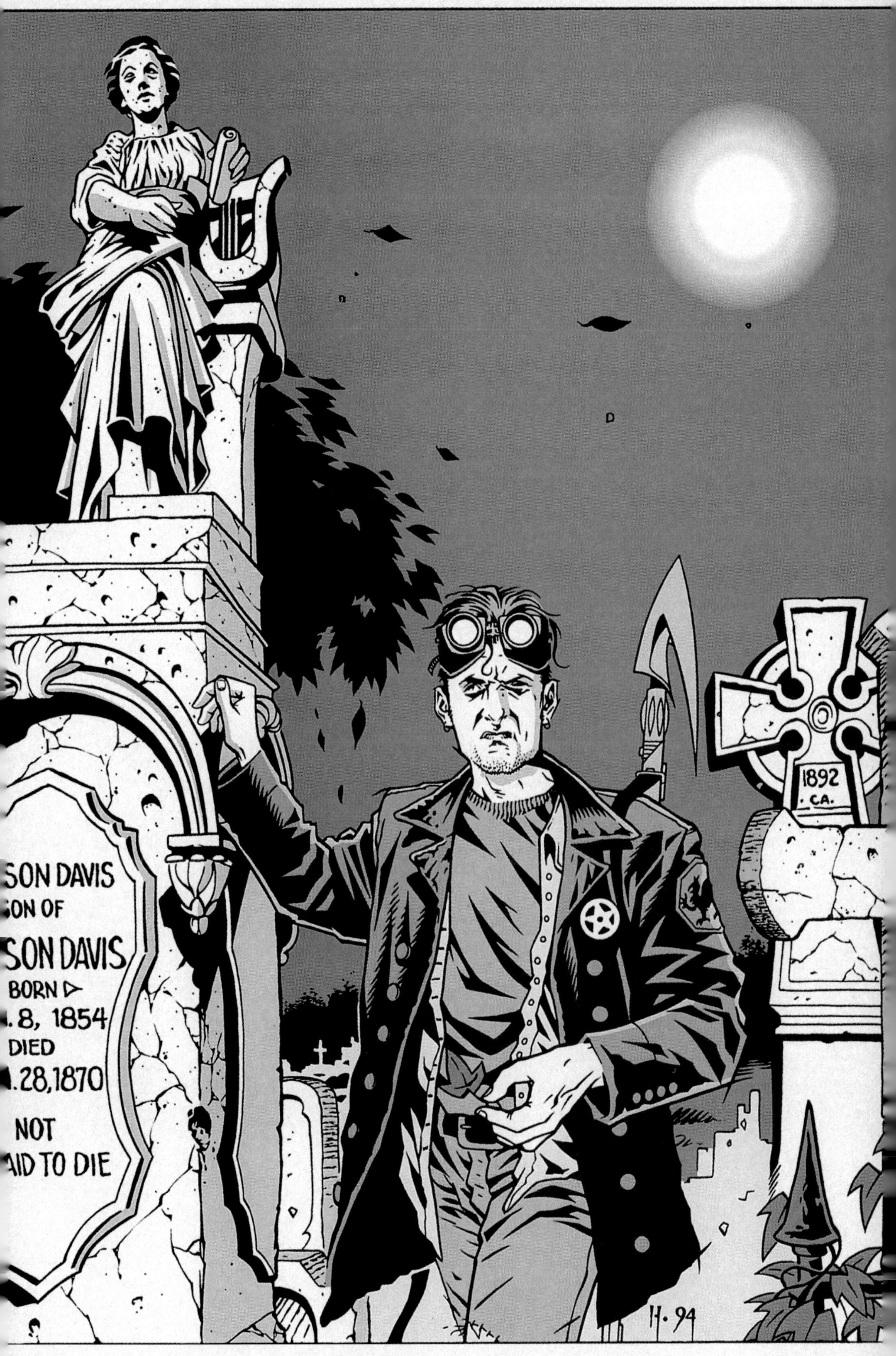

SON DAVIS
SON OF
SON DAVIS
BORN ▷
. 8, 1854
DIED
. 28,1870
NOT
AID TO DIE
1892
CA.
H. 94

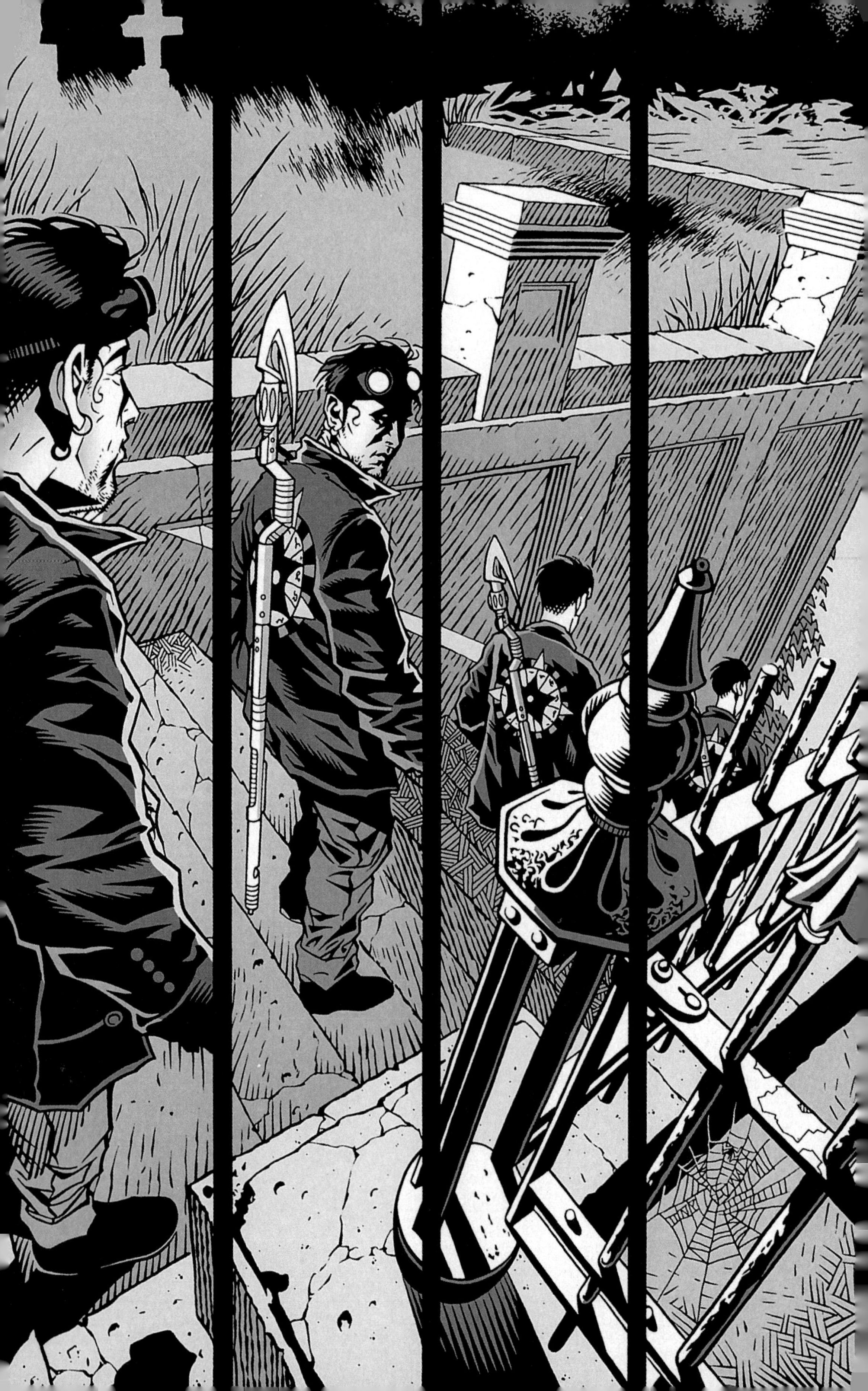

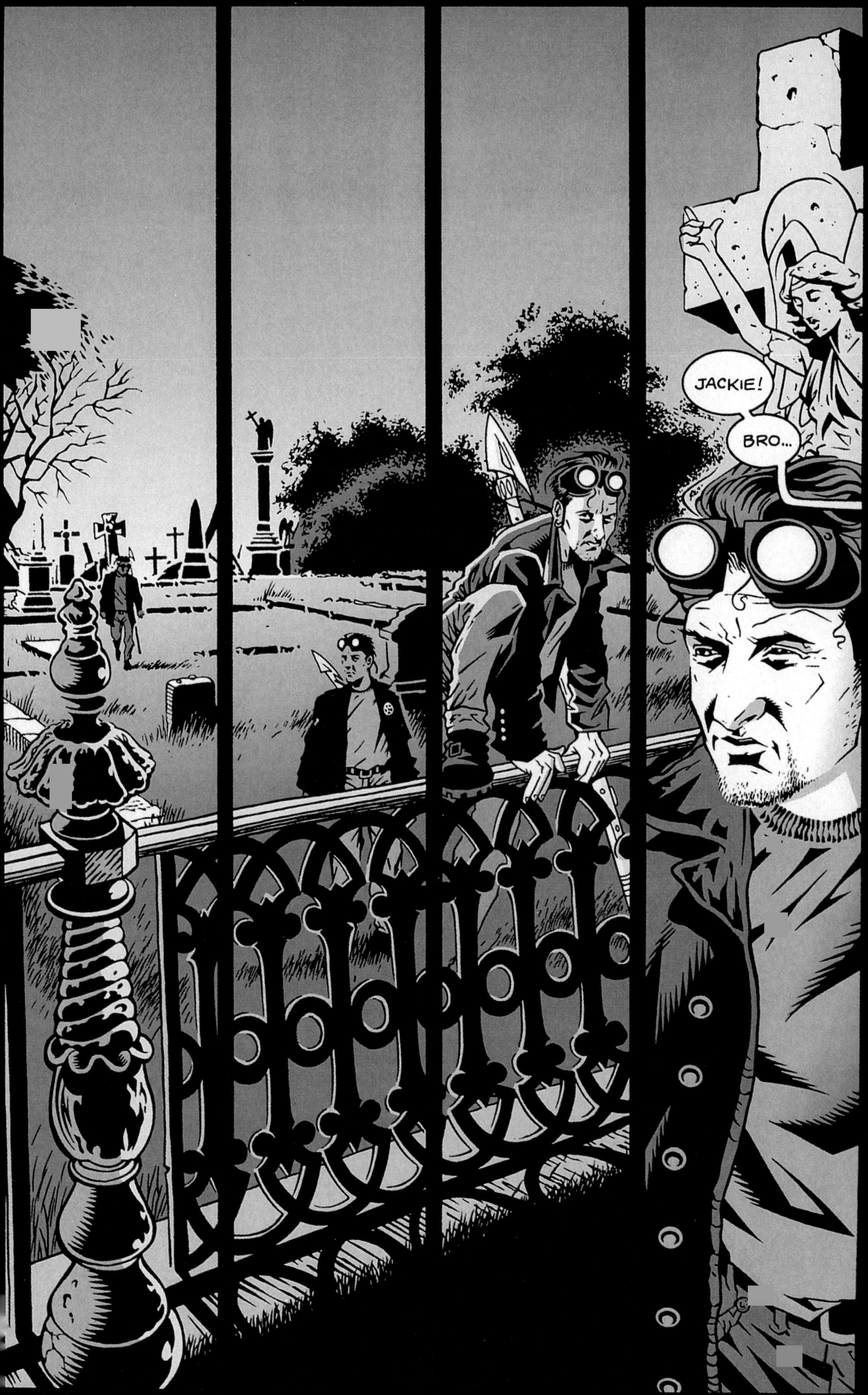
JACKIE!
BRO...

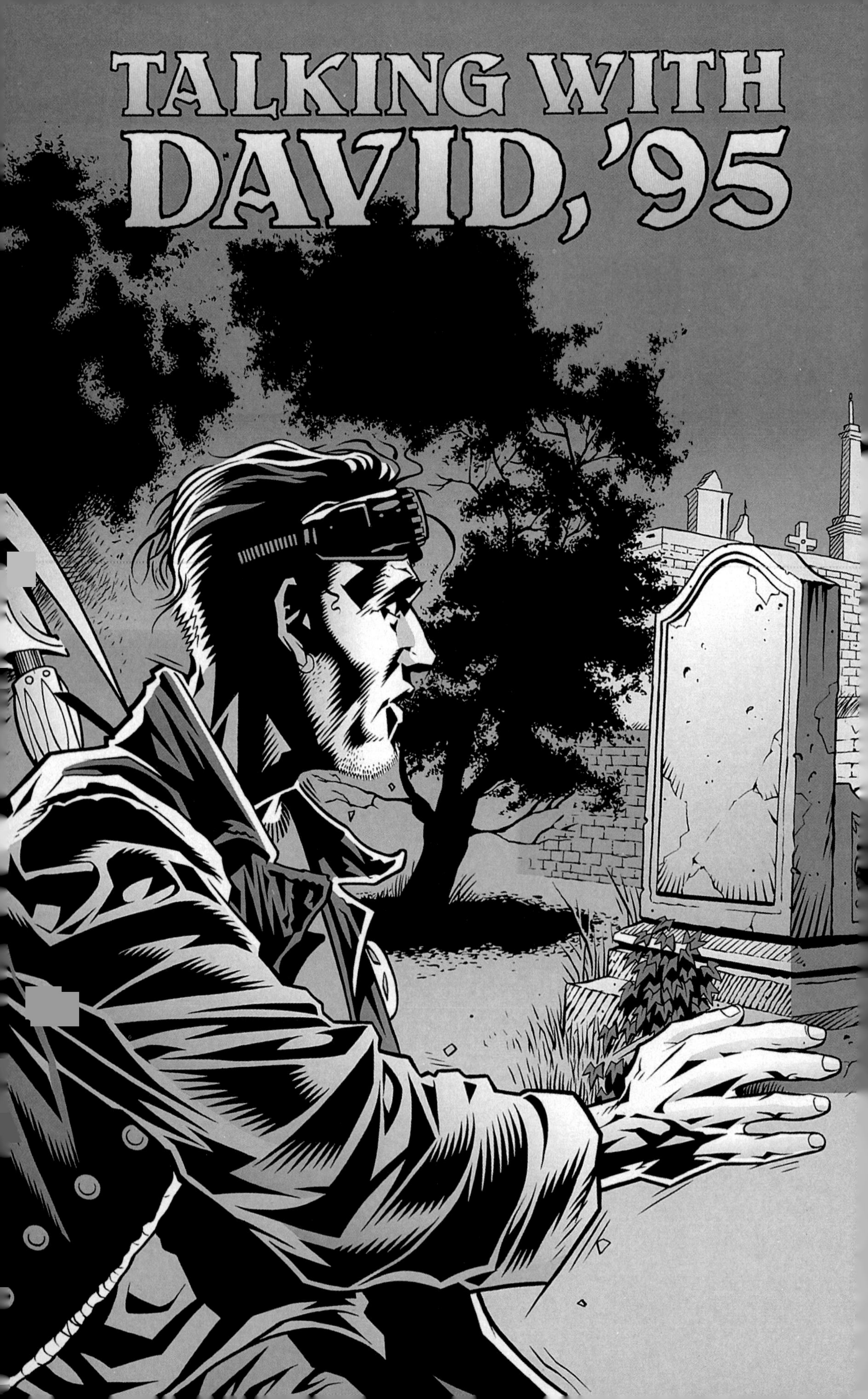
TALKING WITH
DAVID, '95

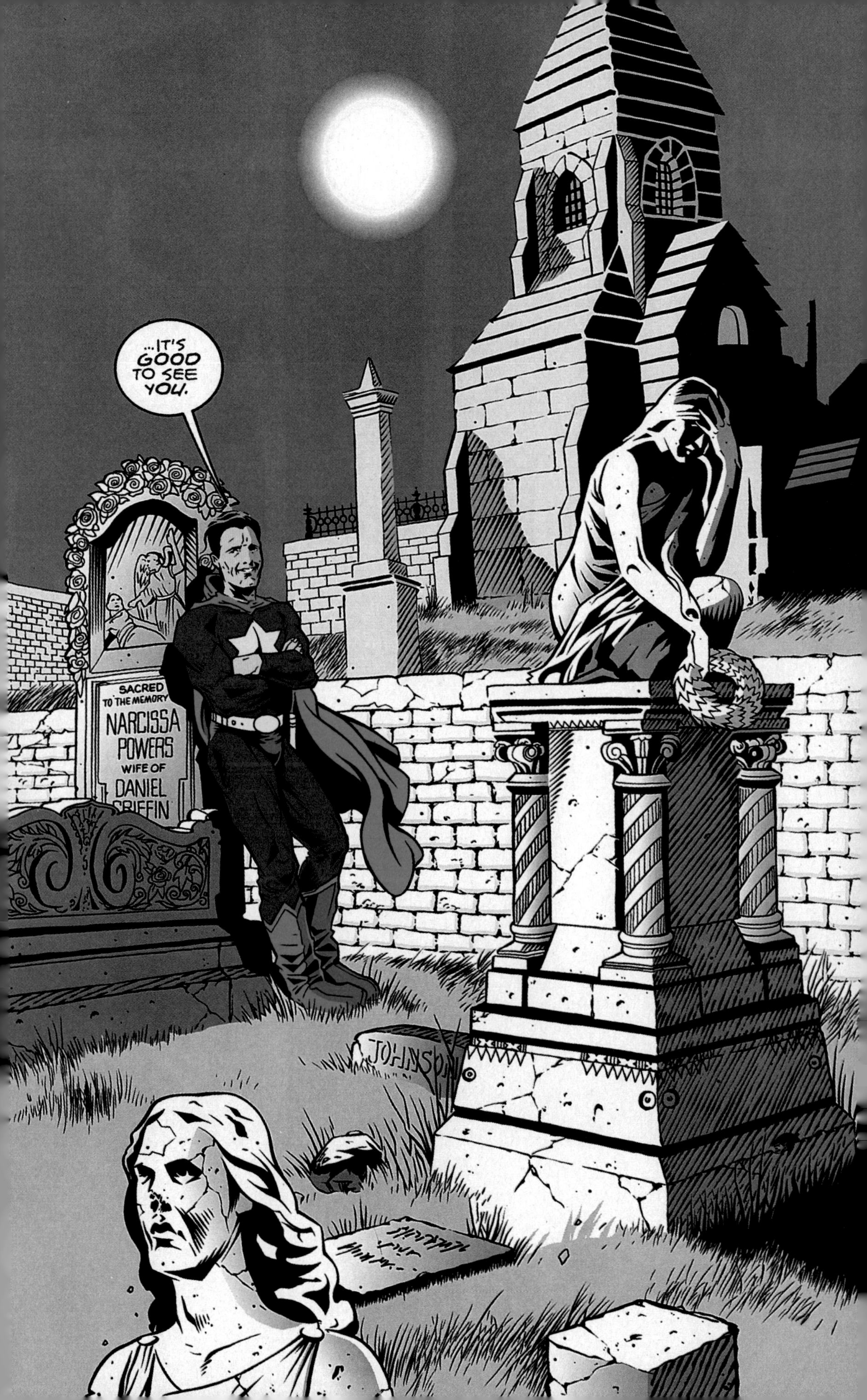
...IT'S GOOD TO SEE YOU.
SACRED TO THE MEMORY
NARCISSA POWERS
WIFE OF
DANIEL GRIFFIN
JOHNSON

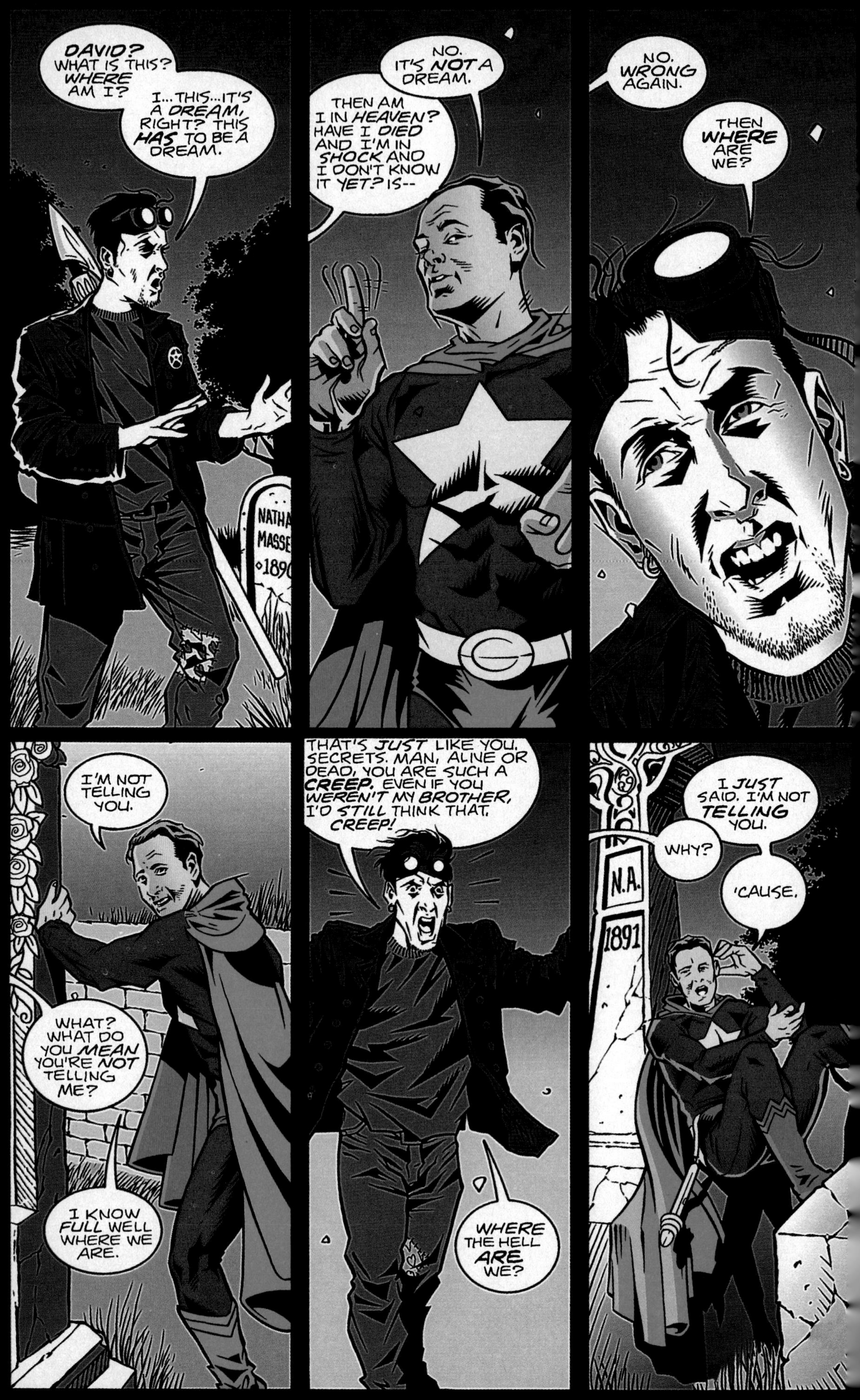
DAVID? WHAT IS THIS? WHERE AM I?
I... THIS... IT'S A DREAM, RIGHT? THIS HAS TO BE A DREAM.
NO. IT'S NOT A DREAM.
THEN AM I IN HEAVEN? HAVE I DIED AND I'M IN SHOCK AND I DON'T KNOW IT YET? IS--
NO. WRONG AGAIN.
THEN WHERE ARE WE?
I'M NOT TELLING YOU.
WHAT? WHAT DO YOU MEAN YOU'RE NOT TELLING ME?
I KNOW FULL WELL WHERE WE ARE.
THAT'S JUST LIKE YOU. SECRETS. MAN, ALIVE OR DEAD, YOU ARE SUCH A CREEP. EVEN IF YOU WEREN'T MY BROTHER, I'D STILL THINK THAT. CREEP!
WHERE THE HELL ARE WE?
I JUST SAID. I'M NOT TELLING YOU.
WHY?
'CAUSE.

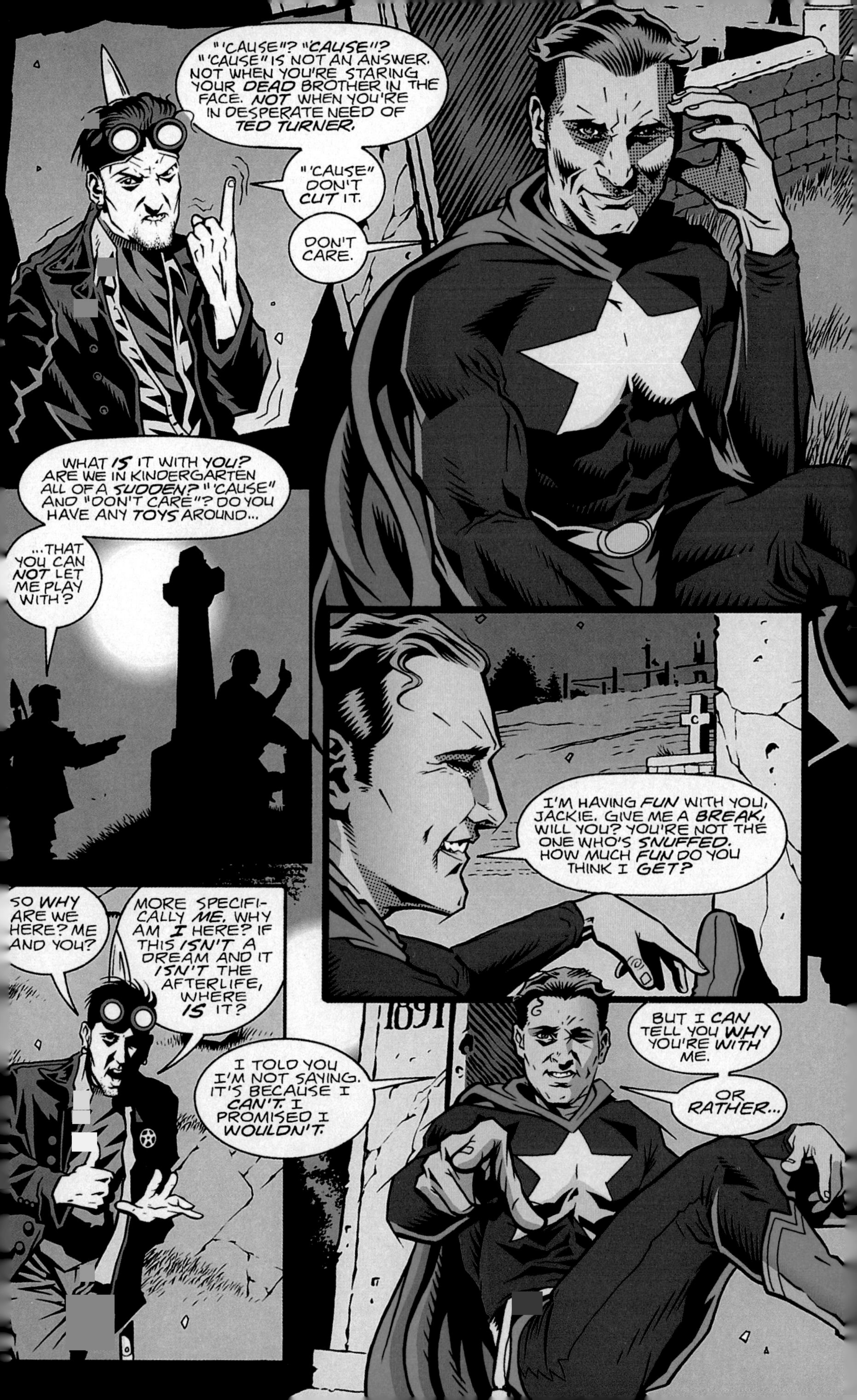

"'CAUSE"? "CAUSE"? "'CAUSE" IS NOT AN ANSWER. NOT WHEN YOU'RE STARING YOUR DEAD BROTHER IN THE FACE. NOT WHEN YOU'RE IN DESPERATE NEED OF TED TURNER.
"'CAUSE" DON'T CUT IT.
DON'T CARE.
WHAT IS IT WITH YOU? ARE WE IN KINDERGARTEN ALL OF A SUDDEN? "'CAUSE" AND "DON'T CARE"? DO YOU HAVE ANY TOYS AROUND...
...THAT YOU CAN NOT LET ME PLAY WITH?
I'M HAVING FUN WITH YOU, JACKIE. GIVE ME A BREAK, WILL YOU? YOU'RE NOT THE ONE WHO'S SNUFFED. HOW MUCH FUN DO YOU THINK I GET?
SO WHY ARE WE HERE? ME AND YOU?
MORE SPECIFICALLY ME. WHY AM I HERE? IF THIS ISN'T A DREAM AND IT ISN'T THE AFTERLIFE, WHERE IS IT?
I TOLD YOU I'M NOT SAYING. IT'S BECAUSE I CAN'T. I PROMISED I WOULDN'T.
1891
BUT I CAN TELL YOU WHY YOU'RE WITH ME.
OR RATHER...

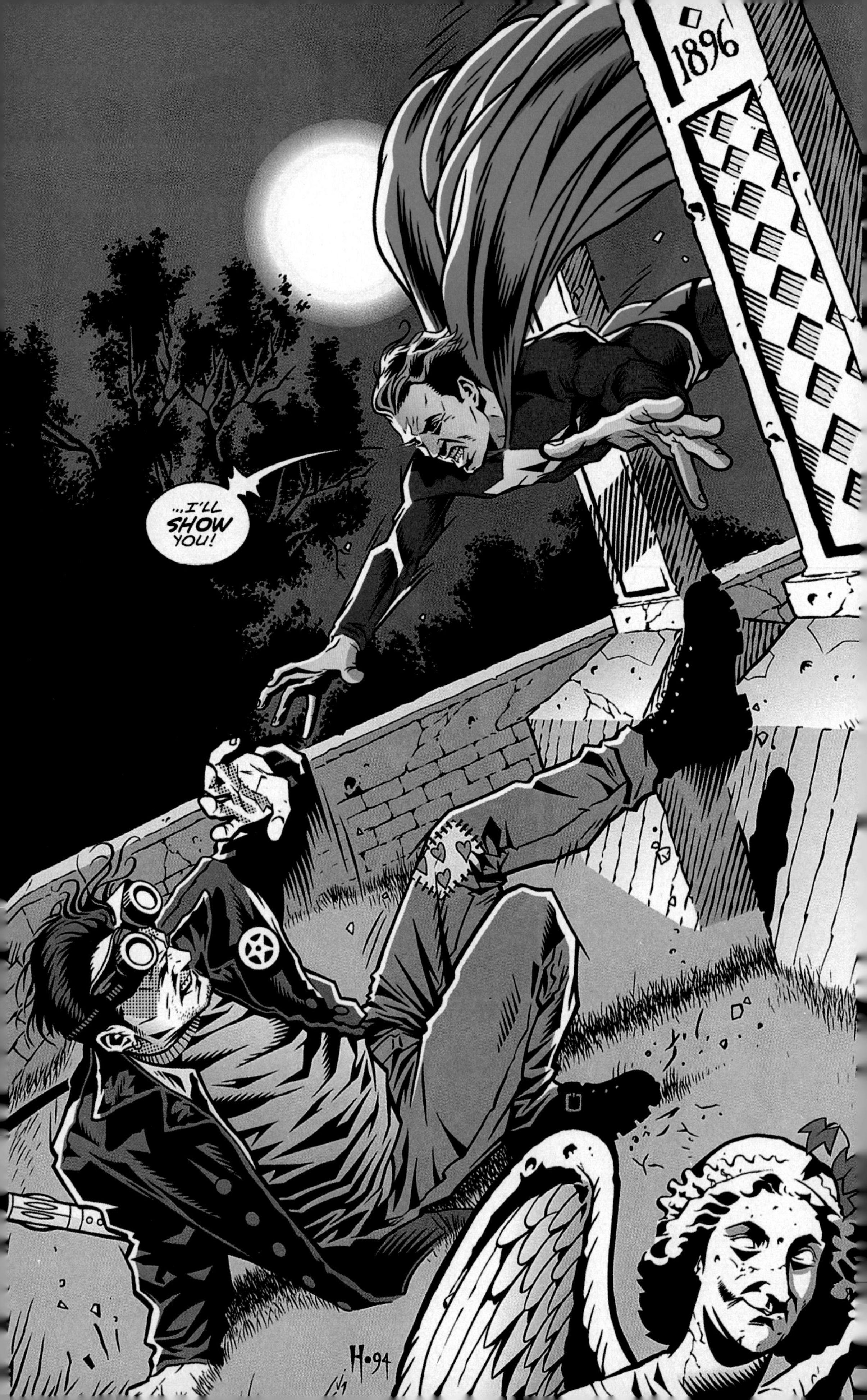
1896
...I'LL SHOW YOU!

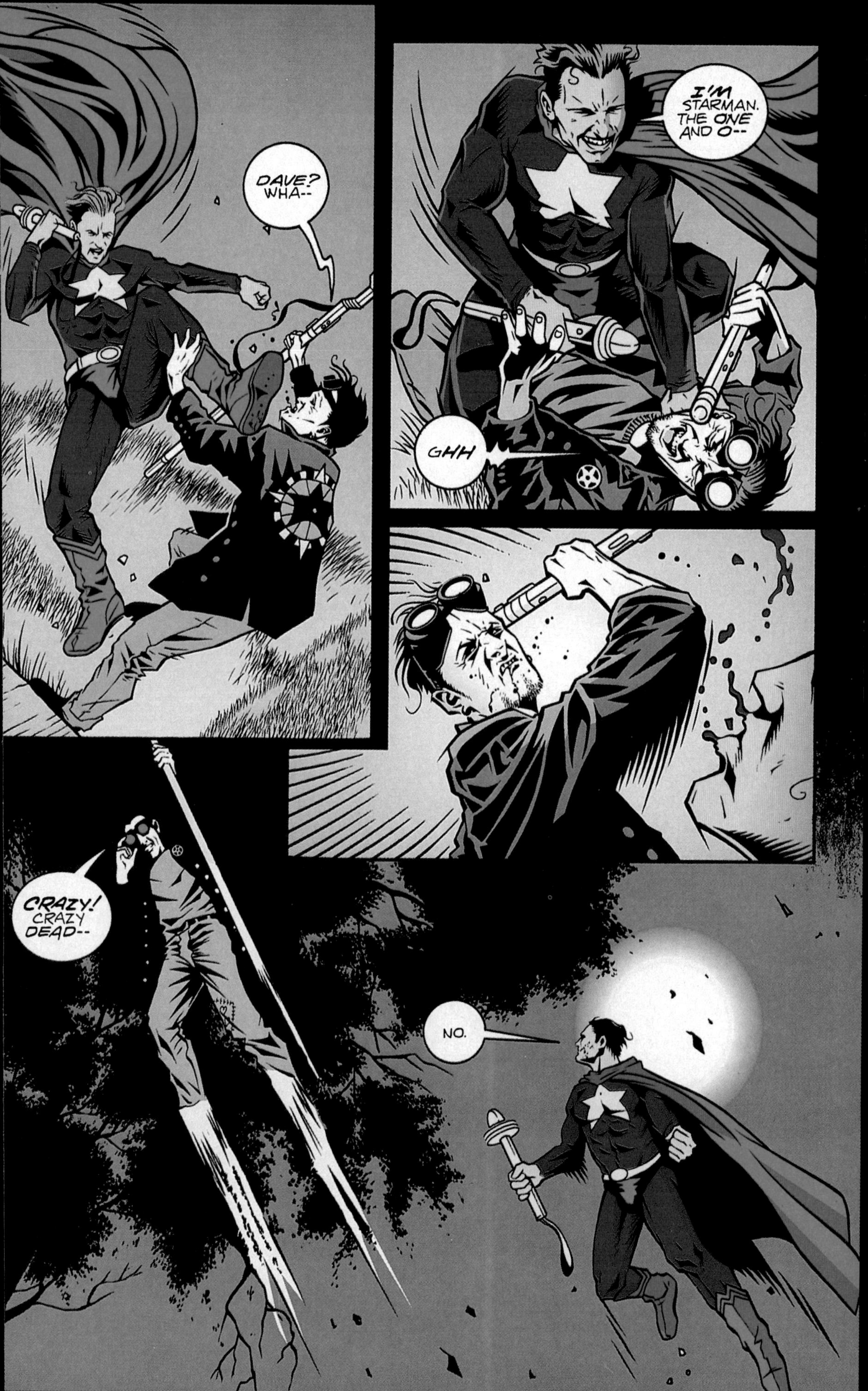
DAVE? WHA--
I'M STARMAN. THE ONE AND O--
GHH
CRAZY! CRAZY DEAD--
NO.

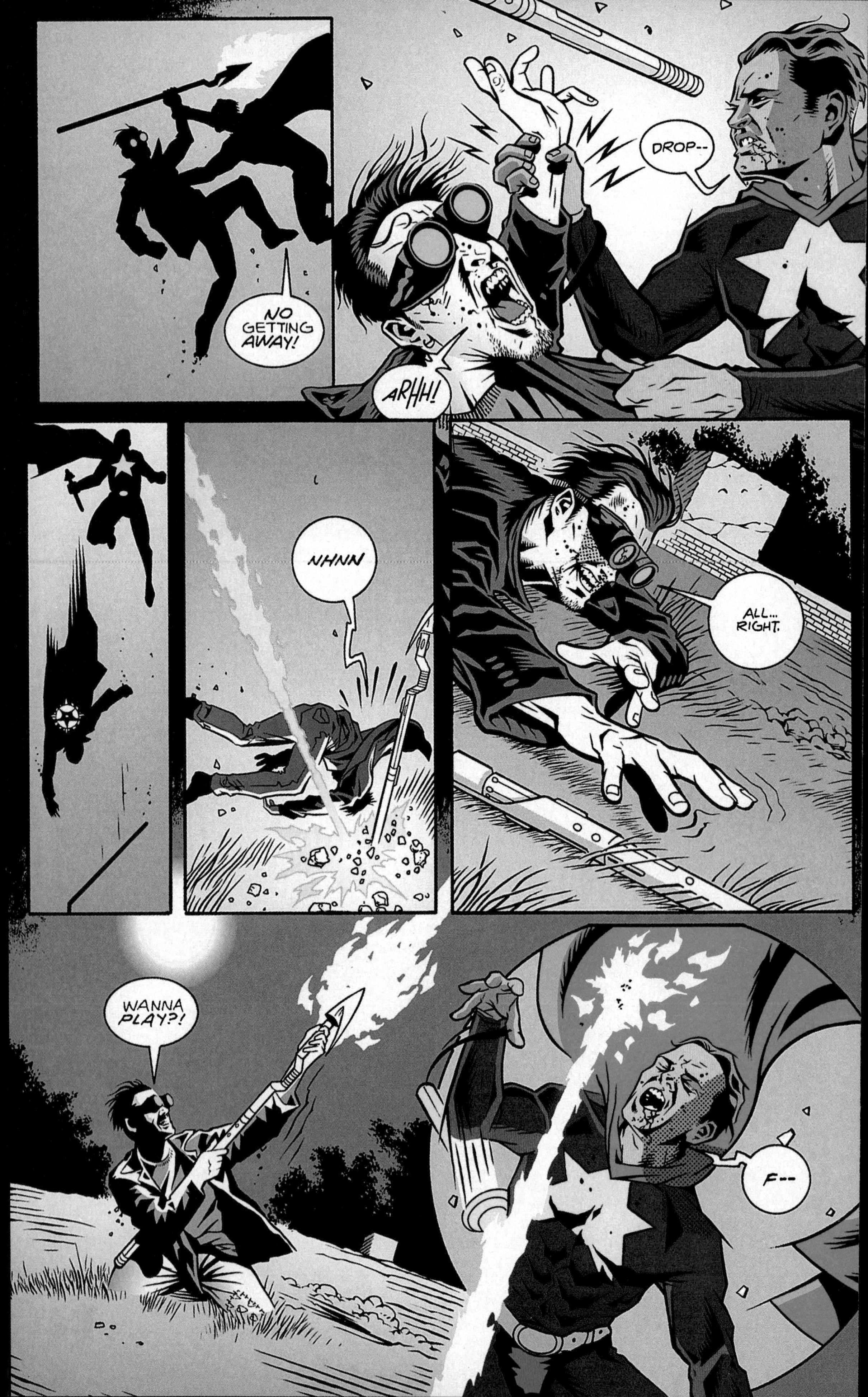
NO GETTING AWAY!
DROP--
ARHH!
NHNN
ALL... RIGHT.
WANNA PLAY?!
F--

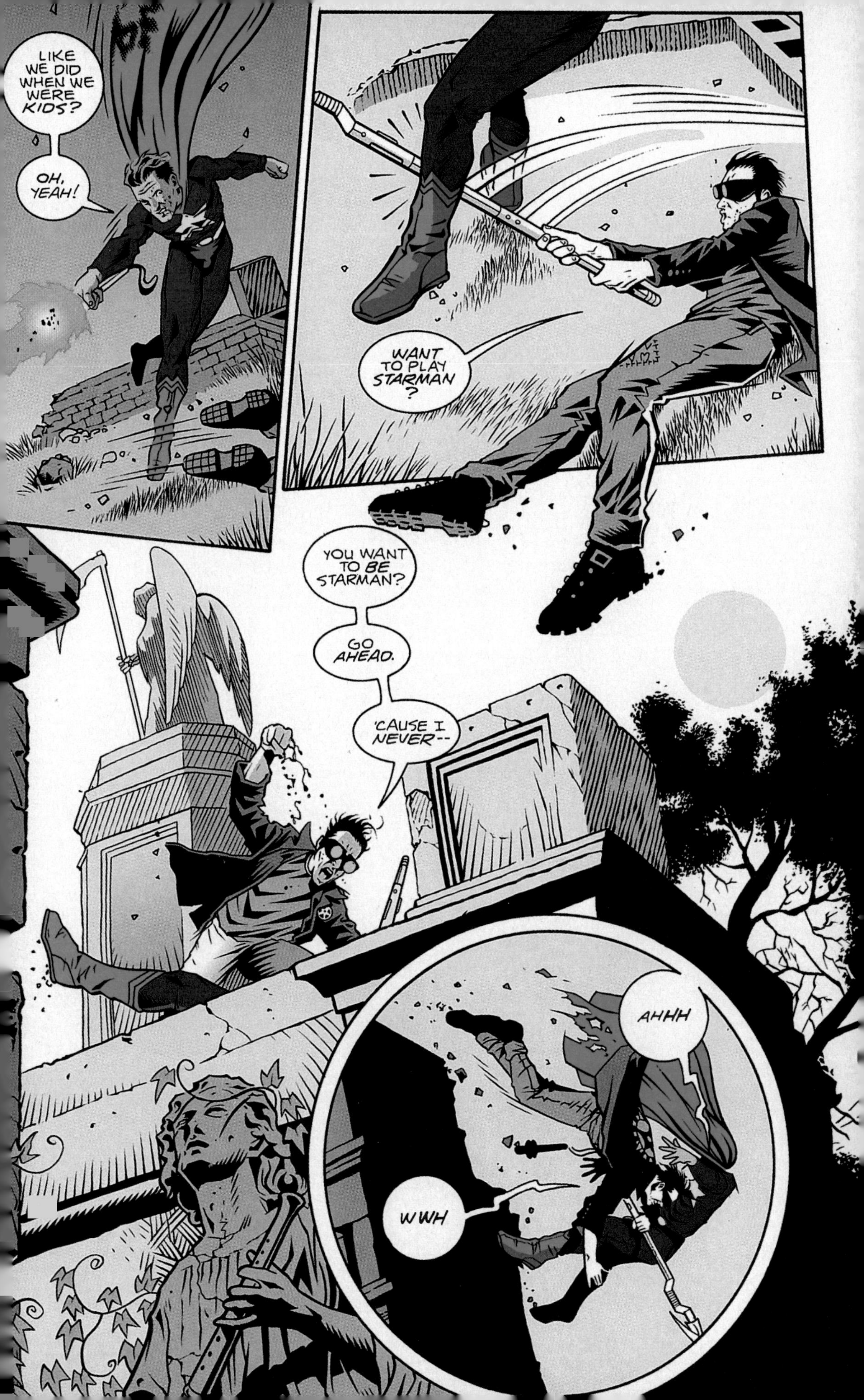
LIKE WE DID WHEN WE WERE *KIDS?*
OH, YEAH!
WANT TO PLAY STARMAN?
YOU WANT TO *BE* STARMAN?
GO *AHEAD.*
'CAUSE I *NEVER--*
AHHH
WWH

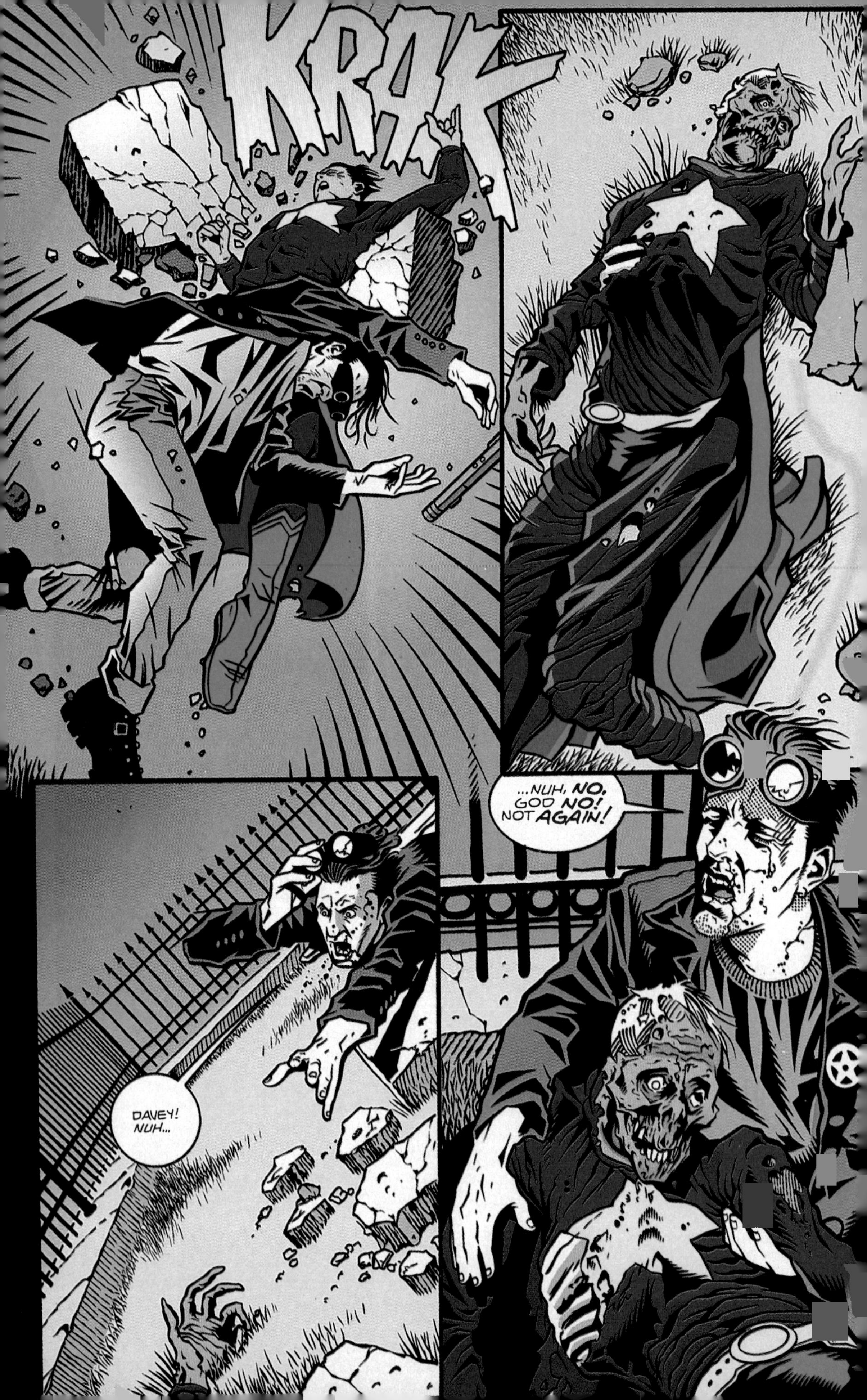
KRAK
DAVEY! NUH...
...NUH, NO. GOD NO! NOT AGAIN!

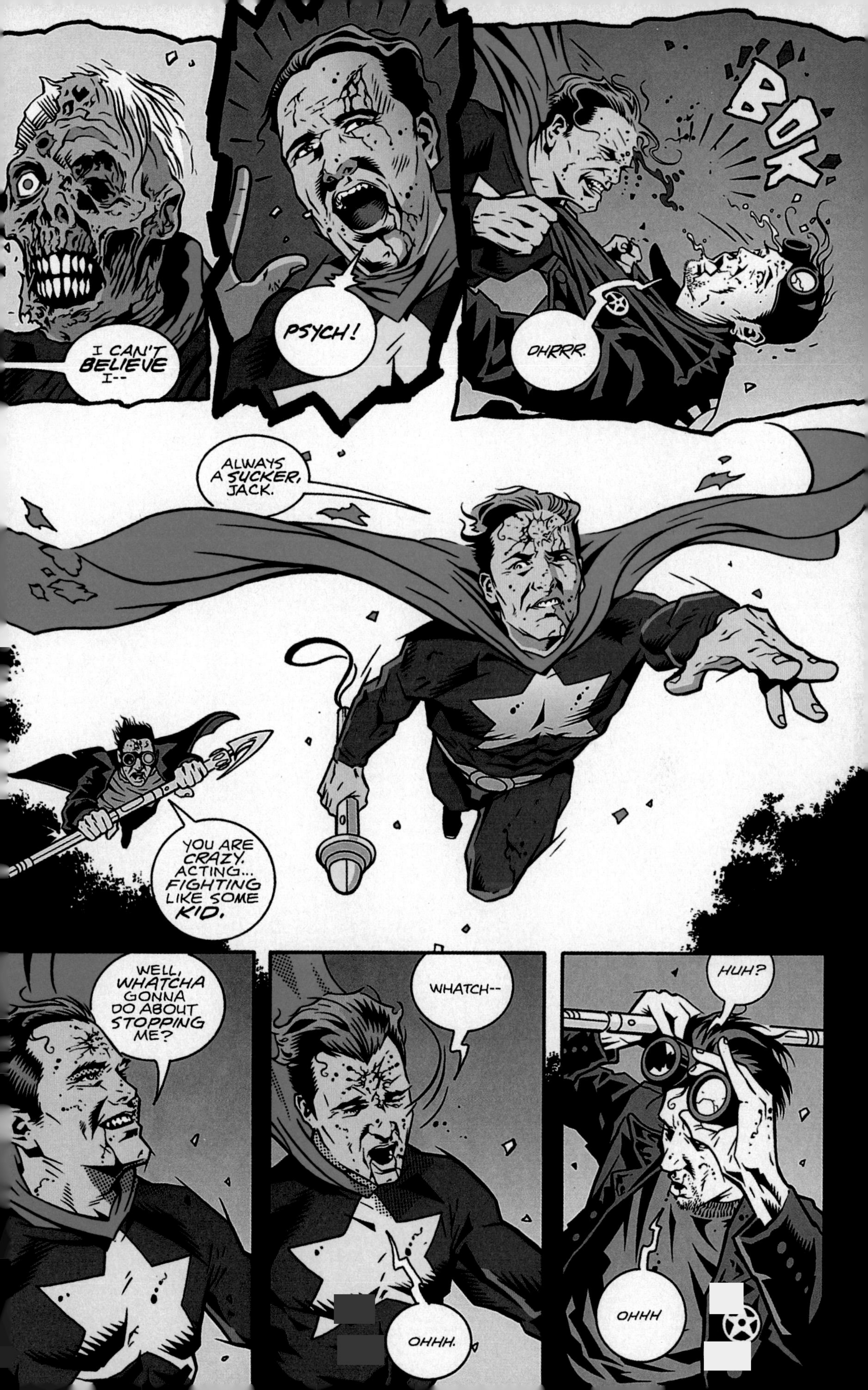
I CAN'T BELIEVE I--
PSYCH!
BOK
OHRRR.
ALWAYS A SUCKER, JACK.
YOU ARE CRAZY. ACTING... FIGHTING LIKE SOME KID.
WELL, WHATCHA GONNA DO ABOUT STOPPING ME?
WHATCH--
OHHH.
HUH?
OHHH

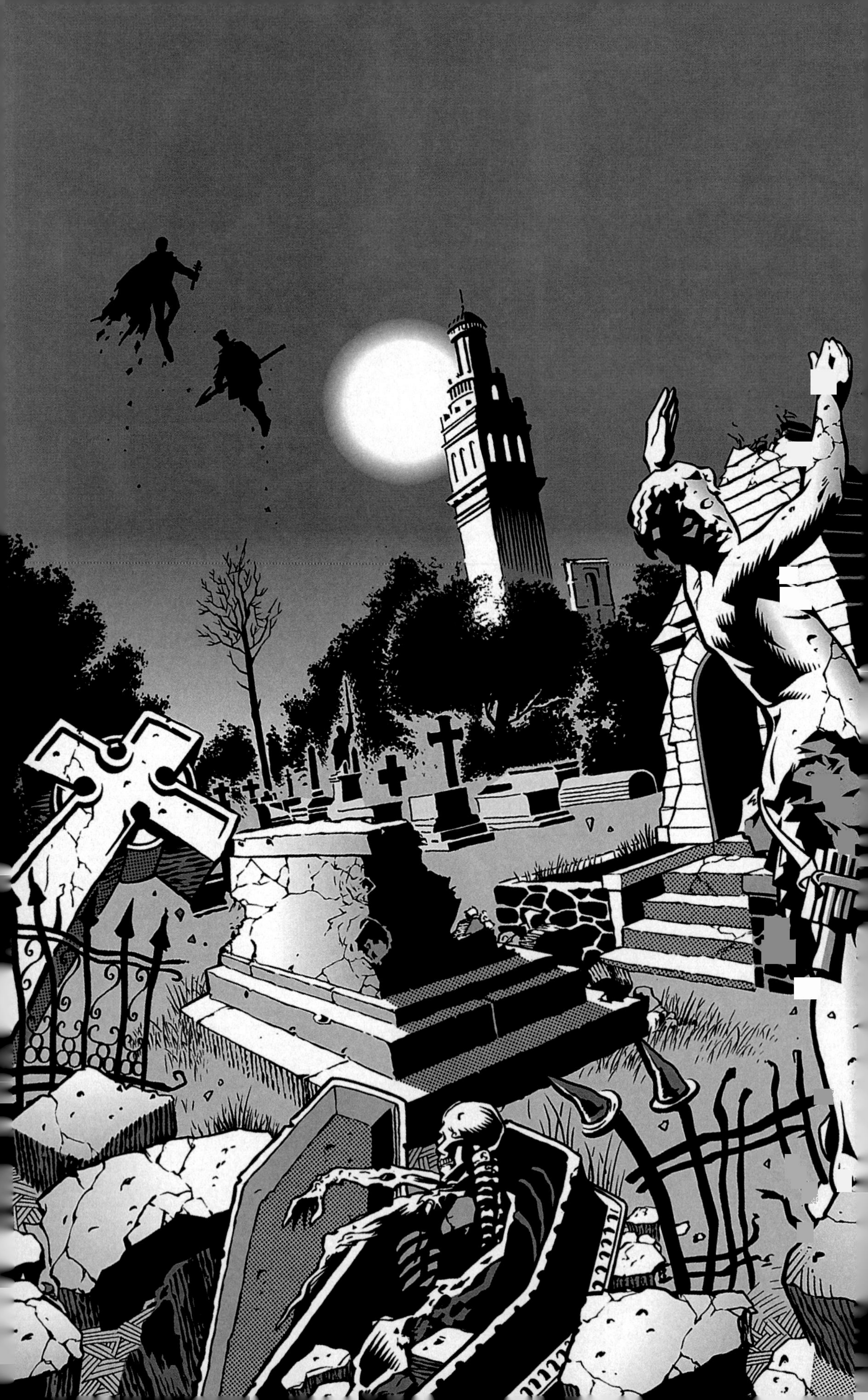

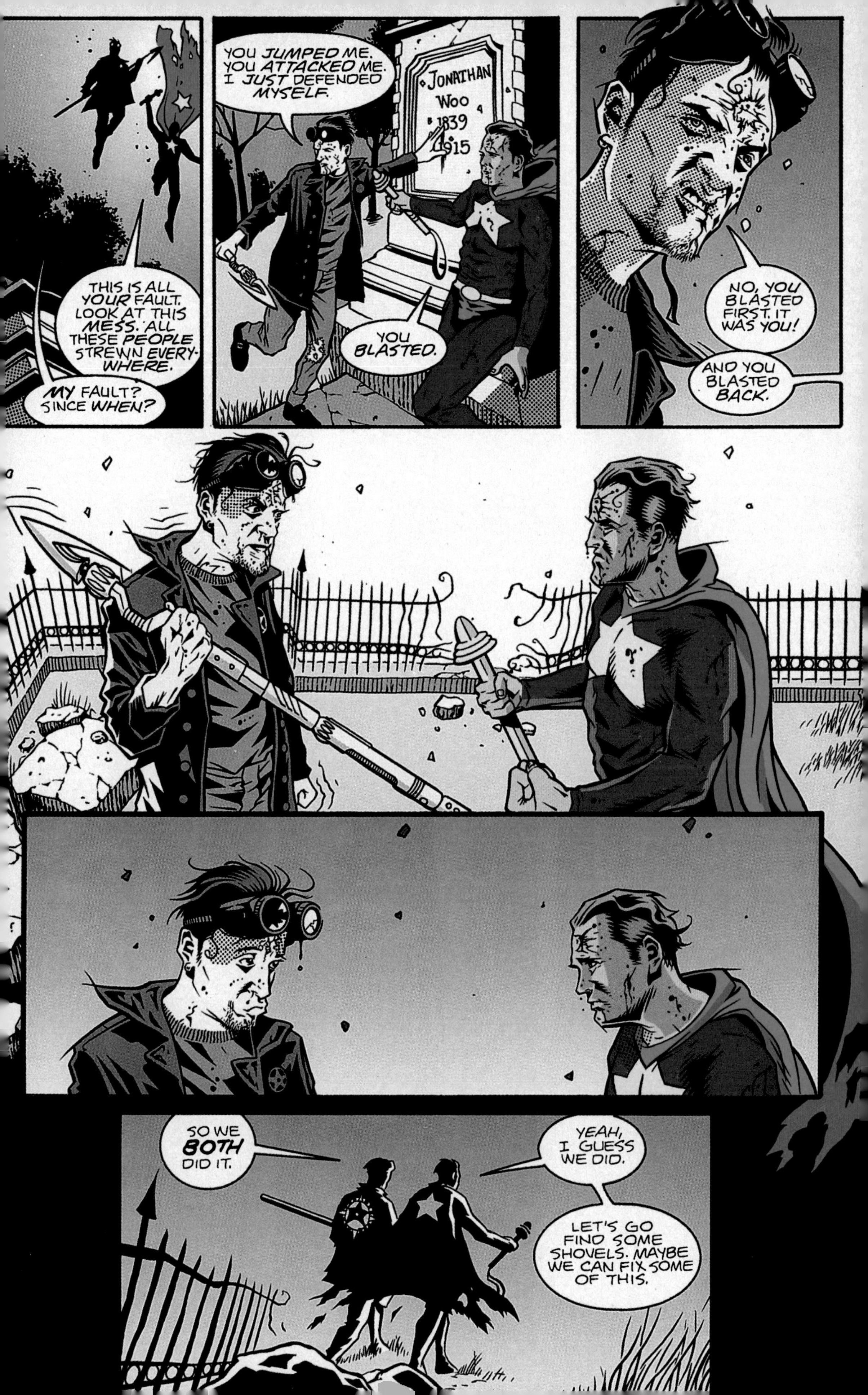
THIS IS ALL YOUR FAULT. LOOK AT THIS MESS. ALL THESE PEOPLE STREWN EVERY-WHERE.
MY FAULT? SINCE WHEN?
YOU JUMPED ME. YOU ATTACKED ME. I JUST DEFENDED MYSELF.
JONATHAN WOO 1839 1915
YOU BLASTED.
NO, YOU BLASTED FIRST. IT WAS YOU!
AND YOU BLASTED BACK.
SO WE BOTH DID IT.
YEAH, I GUESS WE DID.
LET'S GO FIND SOME SHOVELS. MAYBE WE CAN FIX SOME OF THIS.

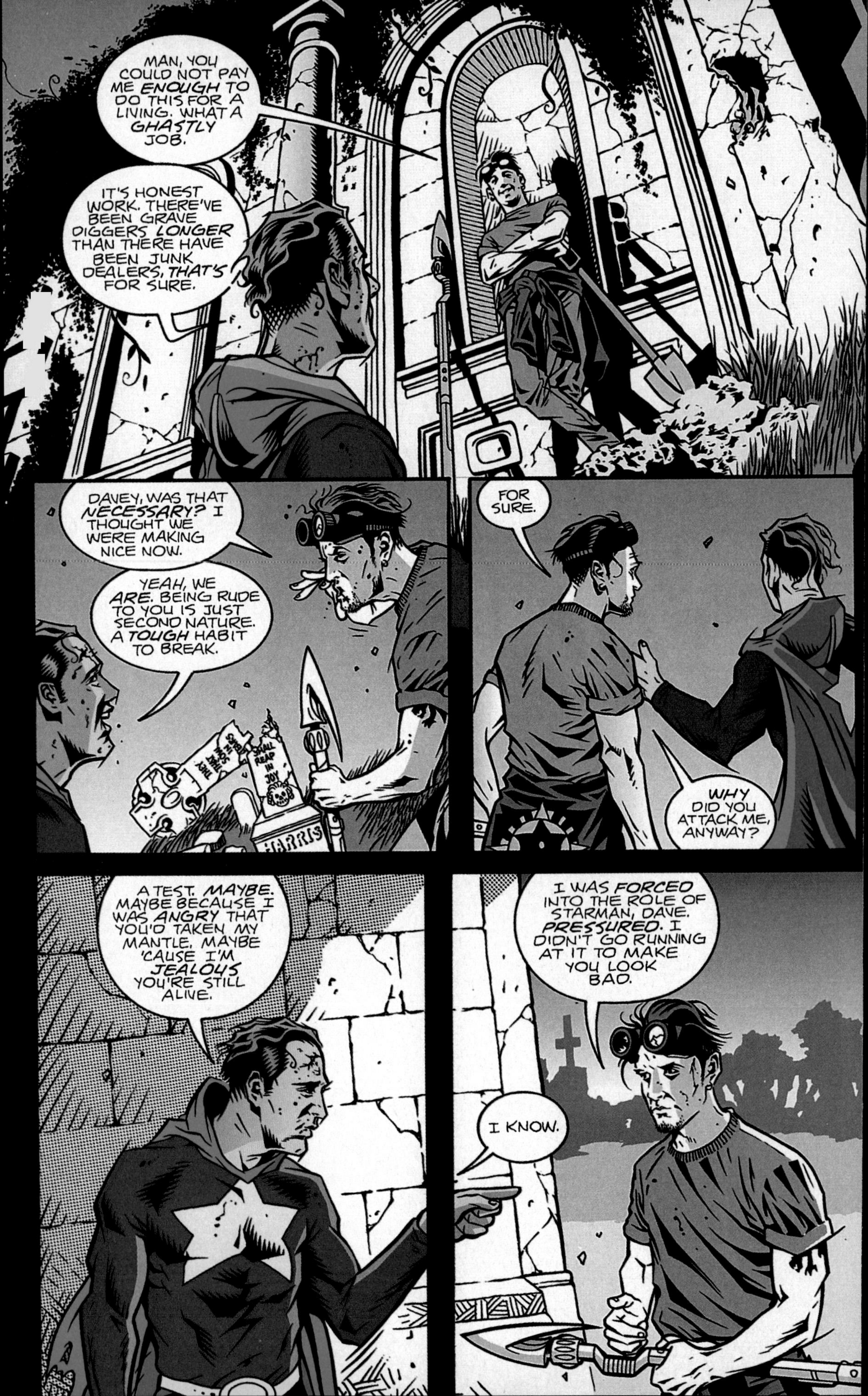
MAN, YOU COULD NOT PAY ME ENOUGH TO DO THIS FOR A LIVING. WHAT A GHASTLY JOB.
IT'S HONEST WORK. THERE'VE BEEN GRAVE DIGGERS LONGER THAN THERE HAVE BEEN JUNK DEALERS, THAT'S FOR SURE.
DAVEY, WAS THAT NECESSARY? I THOUGHT WE WERE MAKING NICE NOW.
YEAH, WE ARE. BEING RUDE TO YOU IS JUST SECOND NATURE. A TOUGH HABIT TO BREAK.
SHALL REAP IN JOY
HARRIS
FOR SURE.
WHY DID YOU ATTACK ME, ANYWAY?
A TEST. MAYBE. MAYBE BECAUSE I WAS ANGRY THAT YOU'D TAKEN MY MANTLE. MAYBE 'CAUSE I'M JEALOUS YOU'RE STILL ALIVE.
I WAS FORCED INTO THE ROLE OF STARMAN, DAVE. PRESSURED. I DIDN'T GO RUNNING AT IT TO MAKE YOU LOOK BAD.
I KNOW.

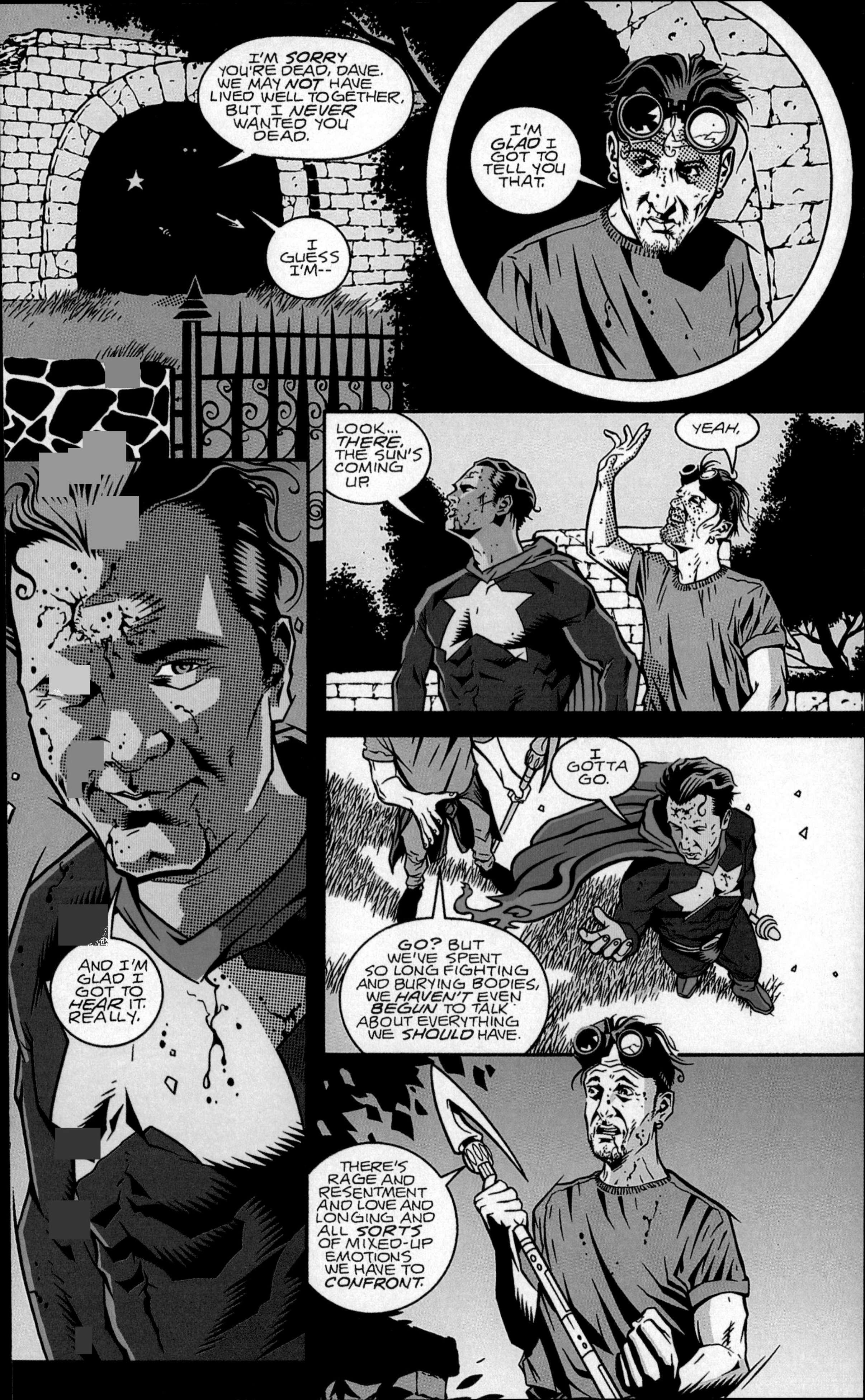
I'M SORRY YOU'RE DEAD, DAVE. WE MAY NOT HAVE LIVED WELL TOGETHER, BUT I NEVER WANTED YOU DEAD.
I GUESS I'M--
I'M GLAD I GOT TO TELL YOU THAT.
AND I'M GLAD I GOT TO HEAR IT. REALLY.
LOOK... THERE. THE SUN'S COMING UP.
YEAH.
I GOTTA GO.
GO? BUT WE'VE SPENT SO LONG FIGHTING AND BURYING BODIES, WE HAVEN'T EVEN BEGUN TO TALK ABOUT EVERYTHING WE SHOULD HAVE.
THERE'S RAGE AND RESENTMENT AND LOVE AND LONGING AND ALL SORTS OF MIXED-UP EMOTIONS WE HAVE TO CONFRONT.

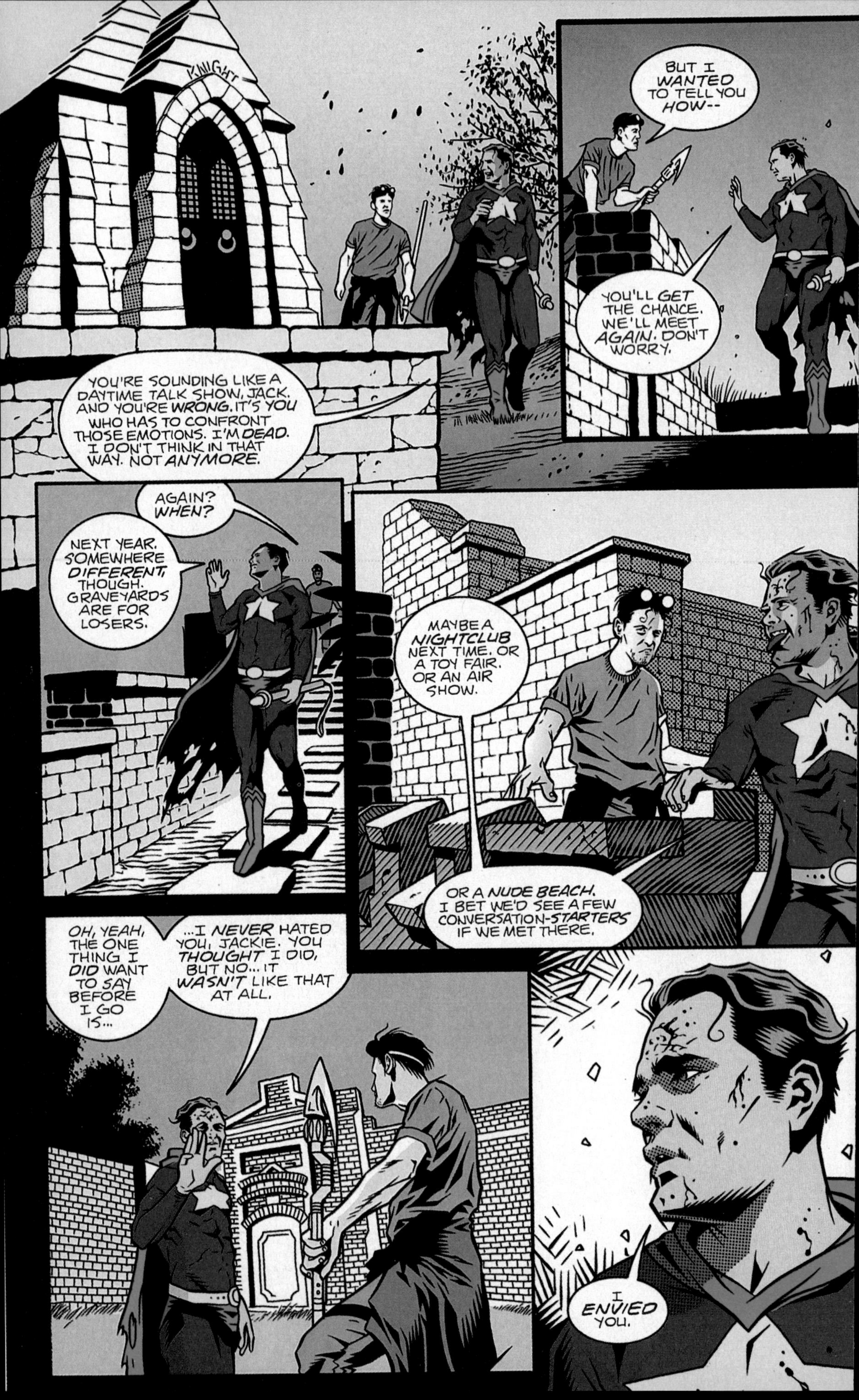
KNIGHT
YOU'RE SOUNDING LIKE A DAYTIME TALK SHOW, JACK. AND YOU'RE WRONG. IT'S YOU WHO HAS TO CONFRONT THOSE EMOTIONS. I'M DEAD. I DON'T THINK IN THAT WAY. NOT ANYMORE.
BUT I WANTED TO TELL YOU HOW--
YOU'LL GET THE CHANCE. WE'LL MEET AGAIN. DON'T WORRY.
AGAIN? WHEN?
NEXT YEAR. SOMEWHERE DIFFERENT, THOUGH. GRAVEYARDS ARE FOR LOSERS.
MAYBE A NIGHTCLUB NEXT TIME. OR A TOY FAIR. OR AN AIR SHOW.
OR A NUDE BEACH. I BET WE'D SEE A FEW CONVERSATION-STARTERS IF WE MET THERE.
OH, YEAH, THE ONE THING I DID WANT TO SAY BEFORE I GO IS...
...I NEVER HATED YOU, JACKIE. YOU THOUGHT I DID, BUT NO... IT WASN'T LIKE THAT AT ALL.
I ENVIED YOU.

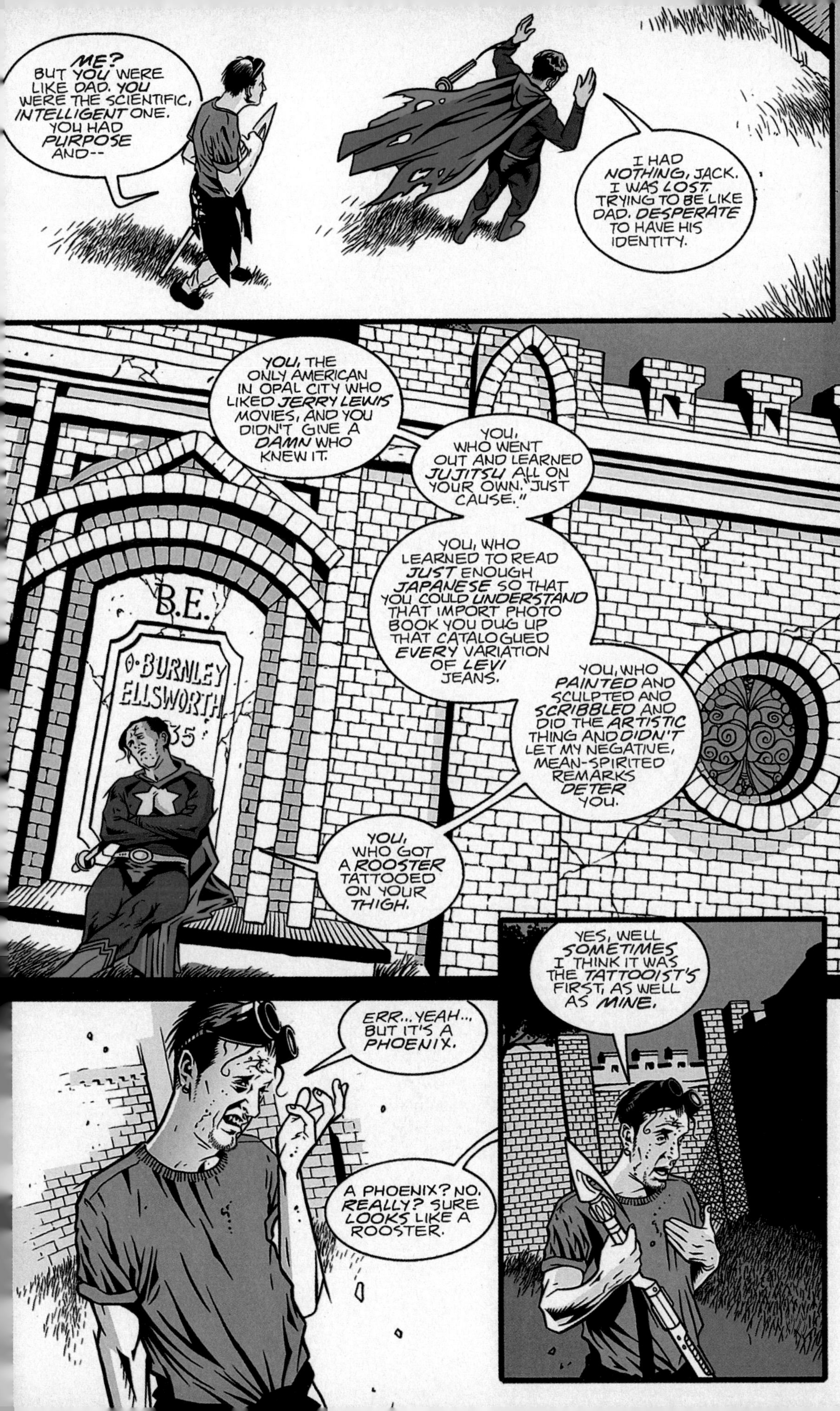
ME? BUT YOU WERE LIKE DAD. YOU WERE THE SCIENTIFIC, INTELLIGENT ONE. YOU HAD PURPOSE AND--
I HAD NOTHING, JACK. I WAS LOST. TRYING TO BE LIKE DAD. DESPERATE TO HAVE HIS IDENTITY.
YOU, THE ONLY AMERICAN IN OPAL CITY WHO LIKED JERRY LEWIS MOVIES, AND YOU DIDN'T GIVE A DAMN WHO KNEW IT.
YOU, WHO WENT OUT AND LEARNED JUJITSU ALL ON YOUR OWN. "JUST CAUSE."
YOU, WHO LEARNED TO READ JUST ENOUGH JAPANESE SO THAT YOU COULD UNDERSTAND THAT IMPORT PHOTO BOOK YOU DUG UP THAT CATALOGUED EVERY VARIATION OF LEVI JEANS.
YOU, WHO PAINTED AND SCULPTED AND SCRIBBLED AND DID THE ARTISTIC THING AND DIDN'T LET MY NEGATIVE, MEAN-SPIRITED REMARKS DETER YOU.
YOU, WHO GOT A ROOSTER TATTOOED ON YOUR THIGH.
B.E.
O. BURNLEY ELLSWORTH
YES, WELL SOMETIMES I THINK IT WAS THE TATTOOIST'S FIRST, AS WELL AS MINE.
ERR... YEAH... BUT IT'S A PHOENIX.
A PHOENIX? NO. REALLY? SURE LOOKS LIKE A ROOSTER.

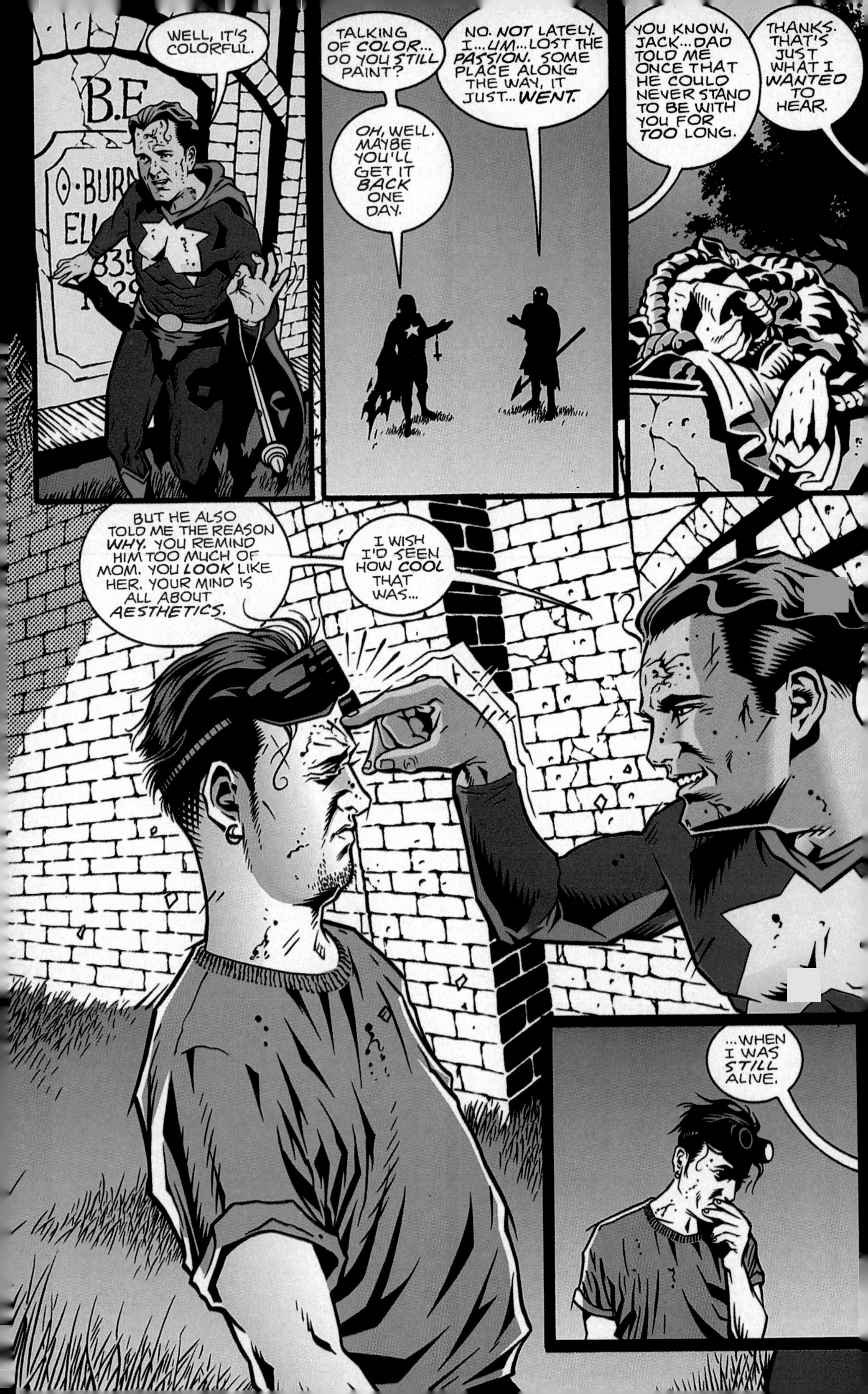
WELL, IT'S COLORFUL.
TALKING OF COLOR... DO YOU STILL PAINT?
OH, WELL. MAYBE YOU'LL GET IT BACK ONE DAY.
NO. NOT LATELY. I...UM...LOST THE PASSION. SOME PLACE ALONG THE WAY, IT JUST...WENT.
YOU KNOW, JACK...DAD TOLD ME ONCE THAT HE COULD NEVER STAND TO BE WITH YOU FOR TOO LONG.
THANKS. THAT'S JUST WHAT I WANTED TO HEAR.
BUT HE ALSO TOLD ME THE REASON WHY. YOU REMIND HIM TOO MUCH OF MOM. YOU LOOK LIKE HER. YOUR MIND IS ALL ABOUT AESTHETICS.
I WISH I'D SEEN HOW COOL THAT WAS...
...WHEN I WAS STILL ALIVE.

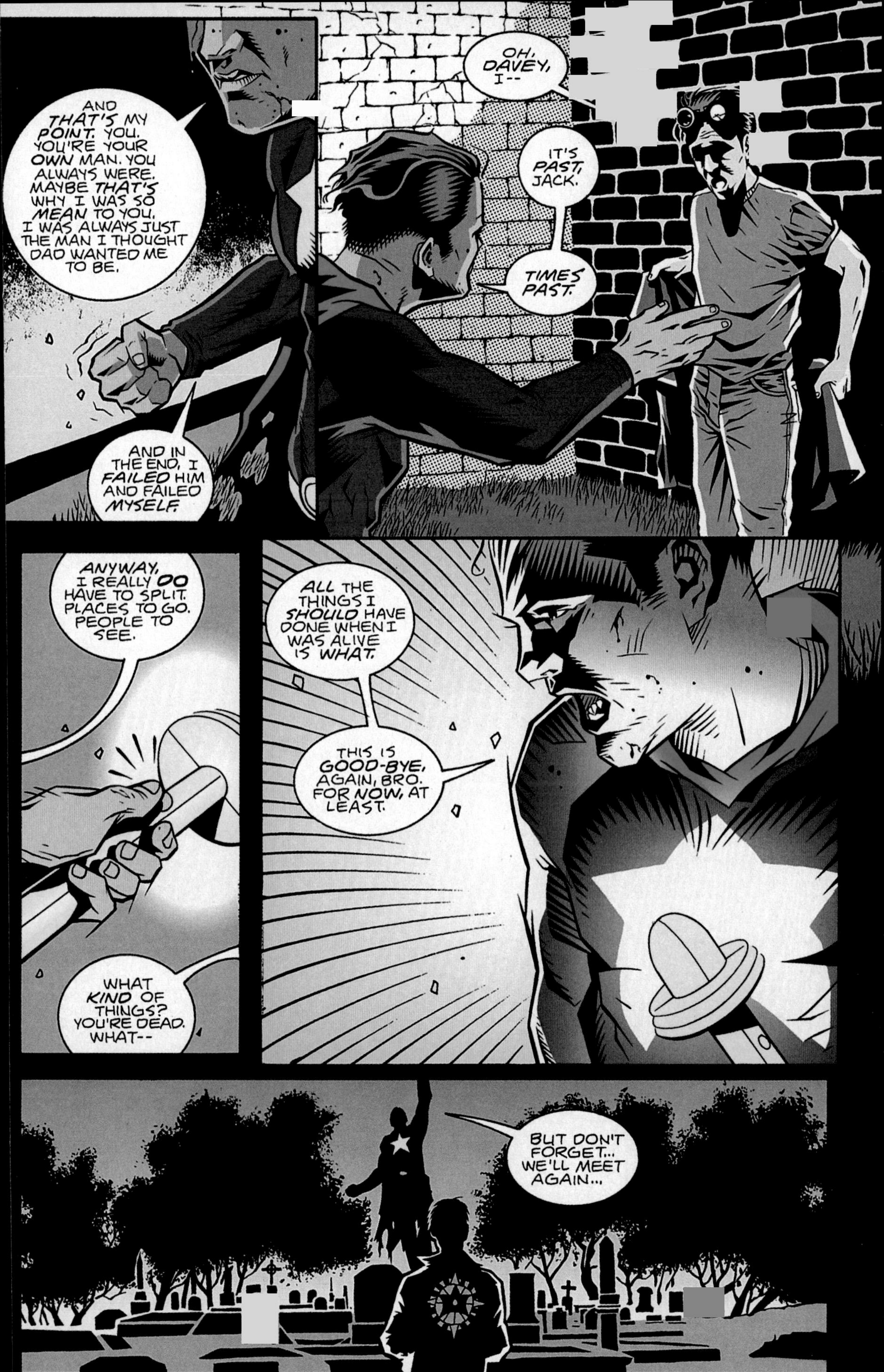
AND THAT'S MY POINT. YOU. YOU'RE YOUR OWN MAN. YOU ALWAYS WERE. MAYBE THAT'S WHY I WAS SO MEAN TO YOU. I WAS ALWAYS JUST THE MAN I THOUGHT DAD WANTED ME TO BE.
AND IN THE END, I FAILED HIM AND FAILED MYSELF.
OH, DAVEY, I--
IT'S PAST, JACK.
TIMES PAST.
ANYWAY, I REALLY DO HAVE TO SPLIT. PLACES TO GO. PEOPLE TO SEE.
WHAT KIND OF THINGS? YOU'RE DEAD. WHAT--
ALL THE THINGS I SHOULD HAVE DONE WHEN I WAS ALIVE IS WHAT.
THIS IS GOOD-BYE, AGAIN, BRO. FOR NOW, AT LEAST.
BUT DON'T FORGET... WE'LL MEET AGAIN...

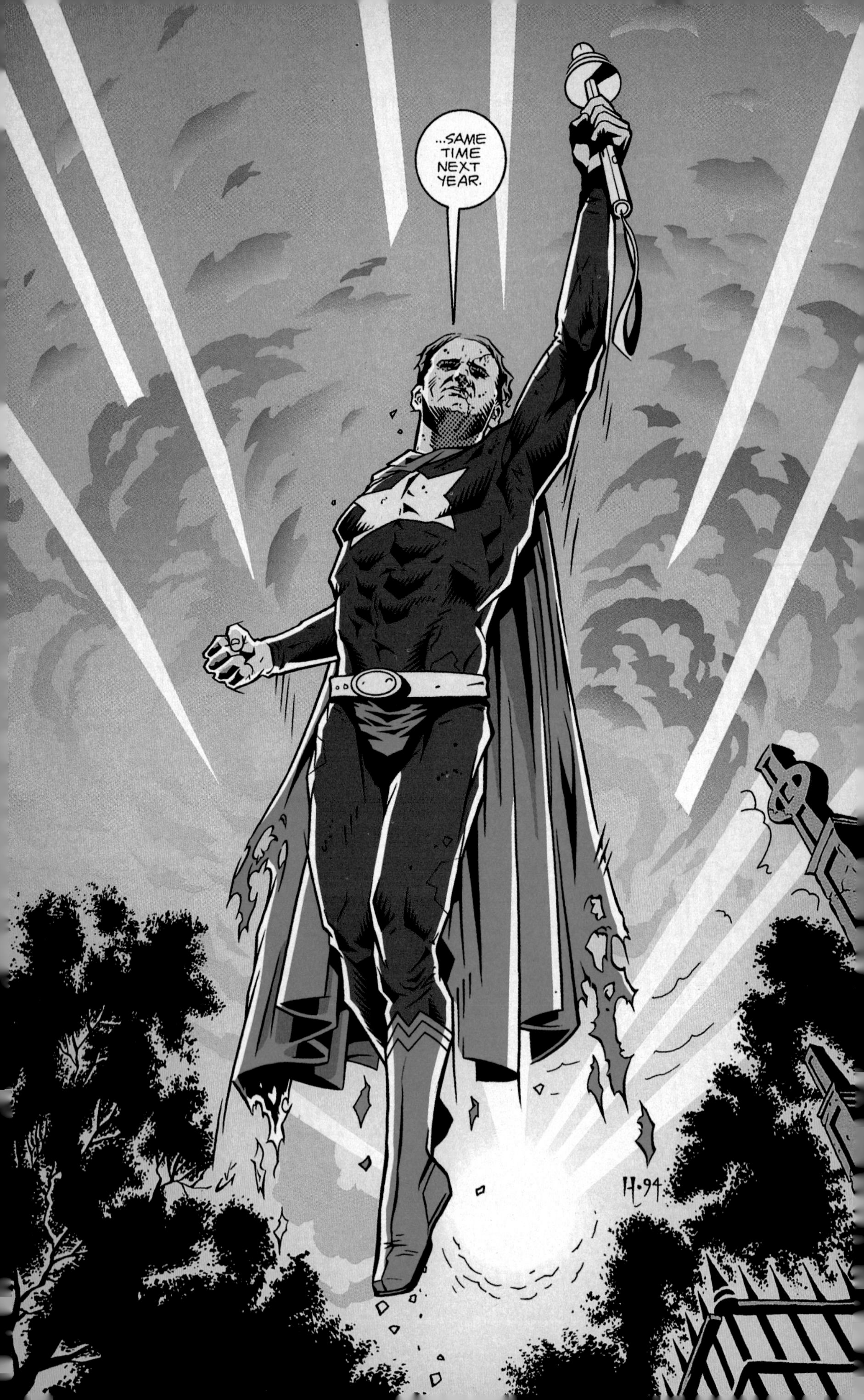
...SAME TIME NEXT YEAR.
H•94

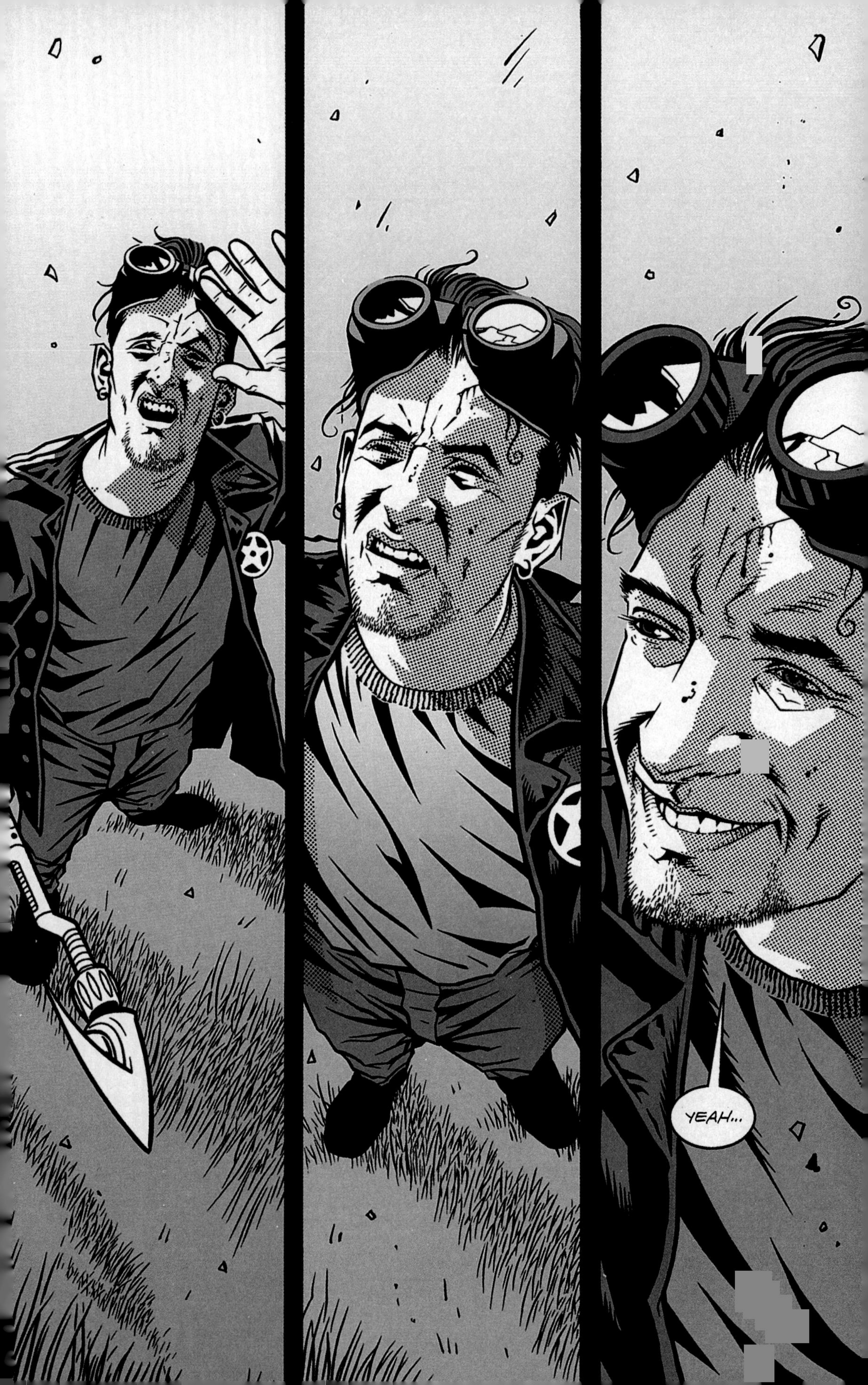
YEAH...

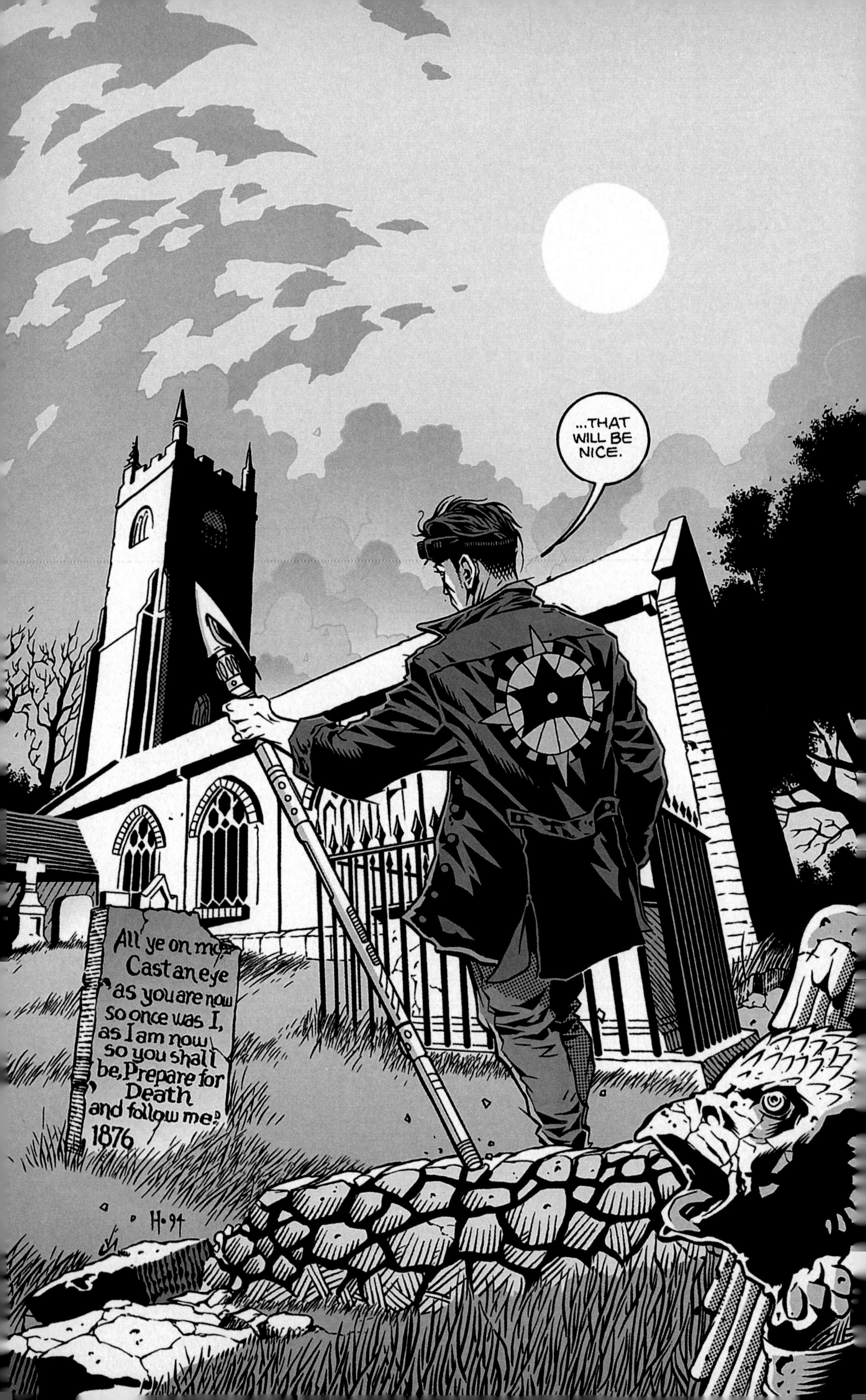
...THAT WILL BE NICE.
All ye on me
Cast an eye
as you are now
so once was I,
as I am now
so you shall
be, Prepare for
Death
and follow me.
1876
H.94

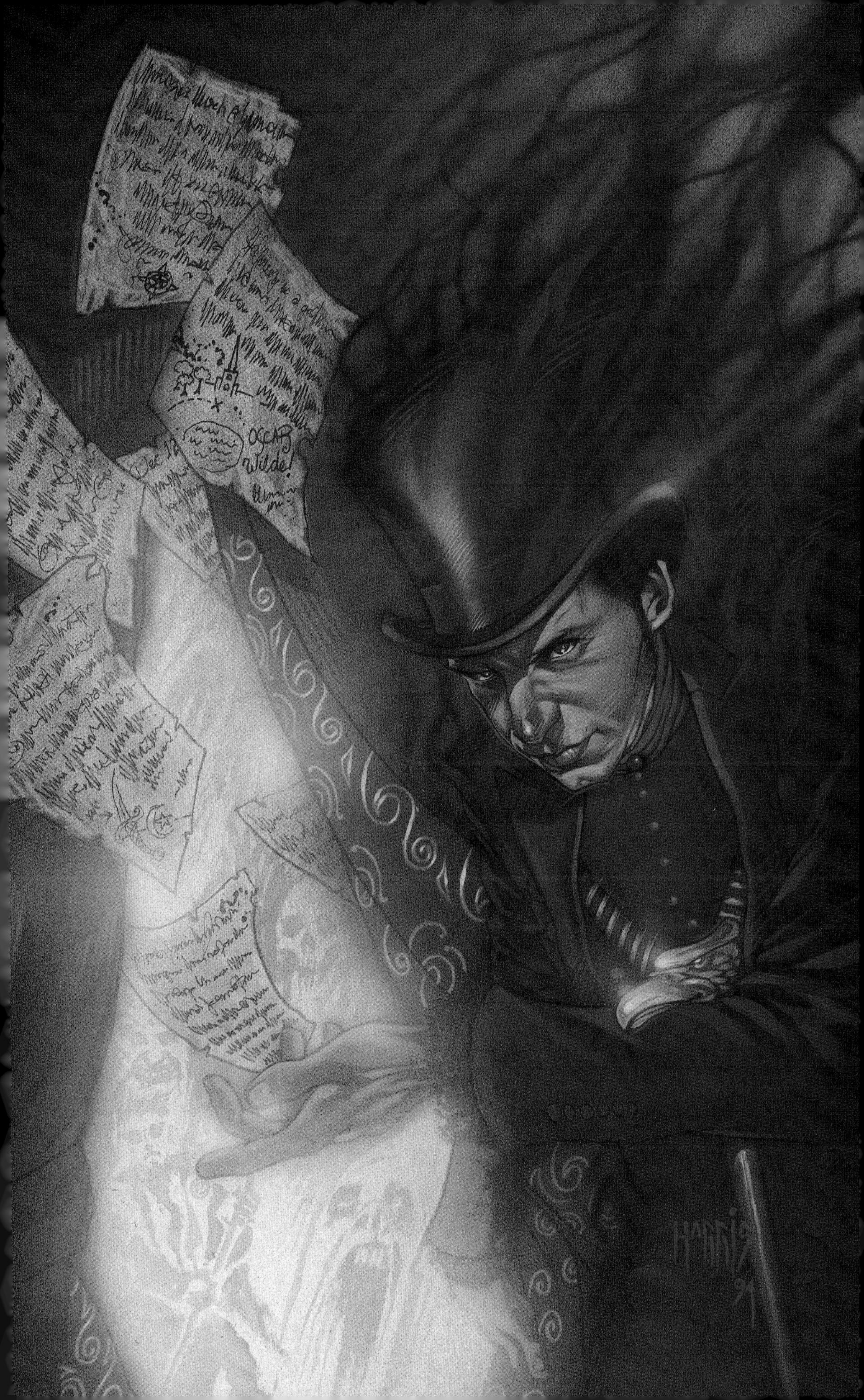
OSCAR
Wilde!

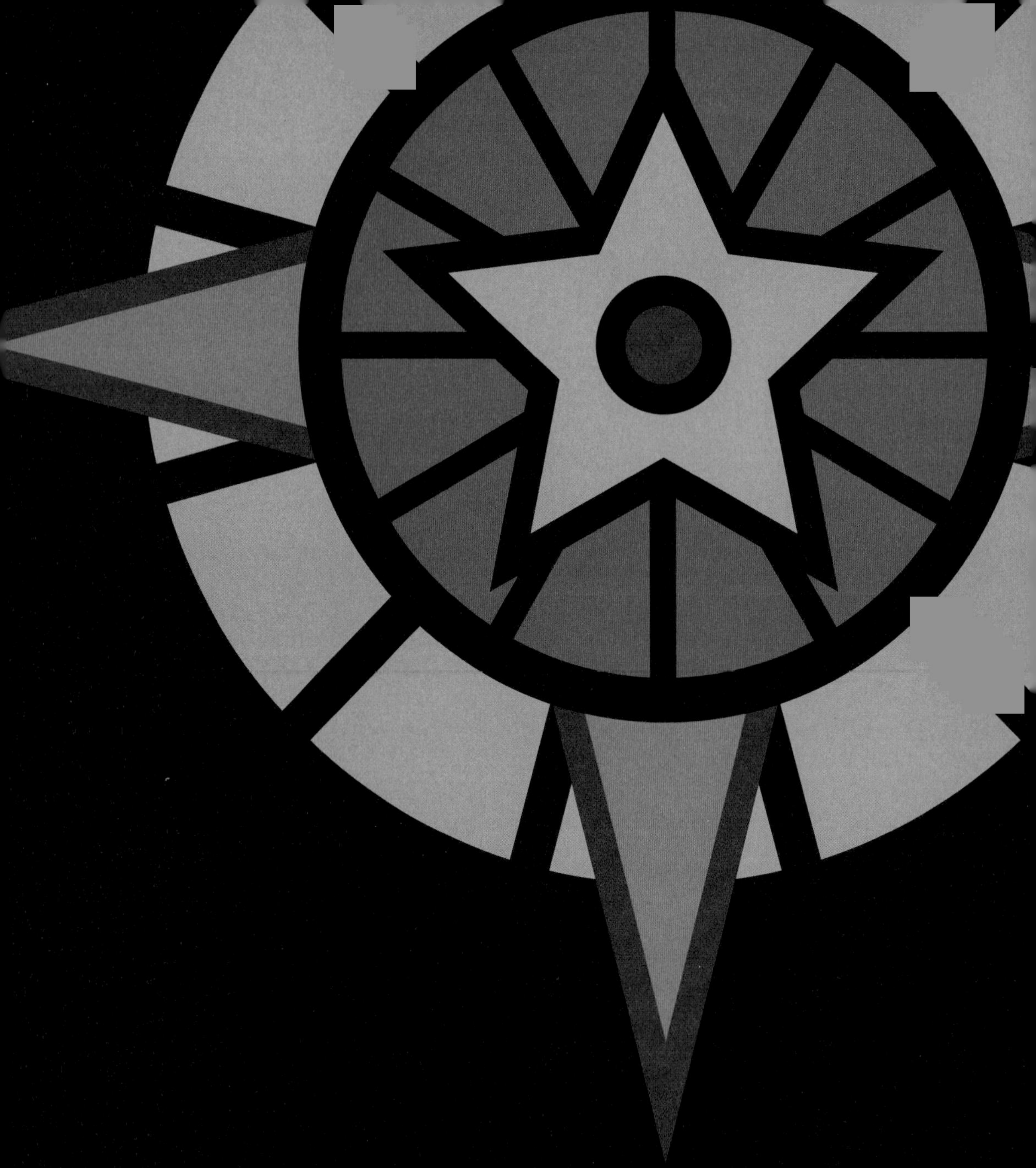

S T A R M A N 6

Cover by Tony Harris

Written by James Robinson

Pencils by Teddy Kristiansen,

with inks by Christian Højgaard, Bjarne Hansen

and Kim Hagen and colors by Gregory Wright

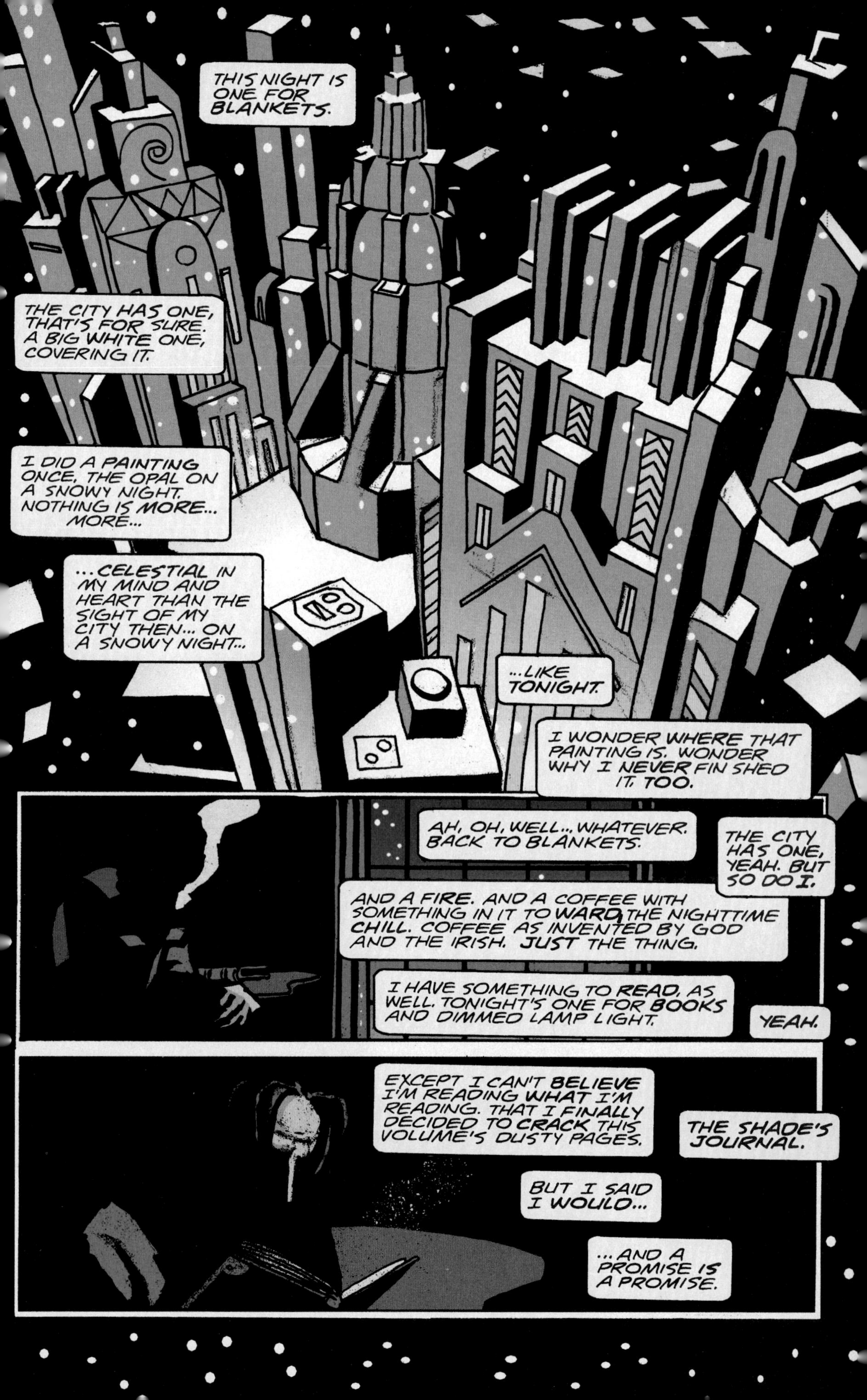

THIS NIGHT IS ONE FOR BLANKETS.
THE CITY HAS ONE, THAT'S FOR SURE. A BIG WHITE ONE, COVERING IT.
I DID A PAINTING ONCE, THE OPAL ON A SNOWY NIGHT. NOTHING IS MORE... MORE...
...CELESTIAL IN MY MIND AND HEART THAN THE SIGHT OF MY CITY THEN... ON A SNOWY NIGHT...
...LIKE TONIGHT.
I WONDER WHERE THAT PAINTING IS. WONDER WHY I NEVER FIN SHED IT, TOO.
AH, OH, WELL... WHATEVER. BACK TO BLANKETS.
THE CITY HAS ONE, YEAH. BUT SO DO I.
AND A FIRE. AND A COFFEE WITH SOMETHING IN IT TO WARD THE NIGHTTIME CHILL. COFFEE AS INVENTED BY GOD AND THE IRISH. JUST THE THING.
I HAVE SOMETHING TO READ, AS WELL. TONIGHT'S ONE FOR BOOKS AND DIMMED LAMP LIGHT.
YEAH.
EXCEPT I CAN'T BELIEVE I'M READING WHAT I'M READING. THAT I FINALLY DECIDED TO CRACK THIS VOLUME'S DUSTY PAGES.
THE SHADE'S JOURNAL.
BUT I SAID I WOULD...
...AND A PROMISE IS A PROMISE.

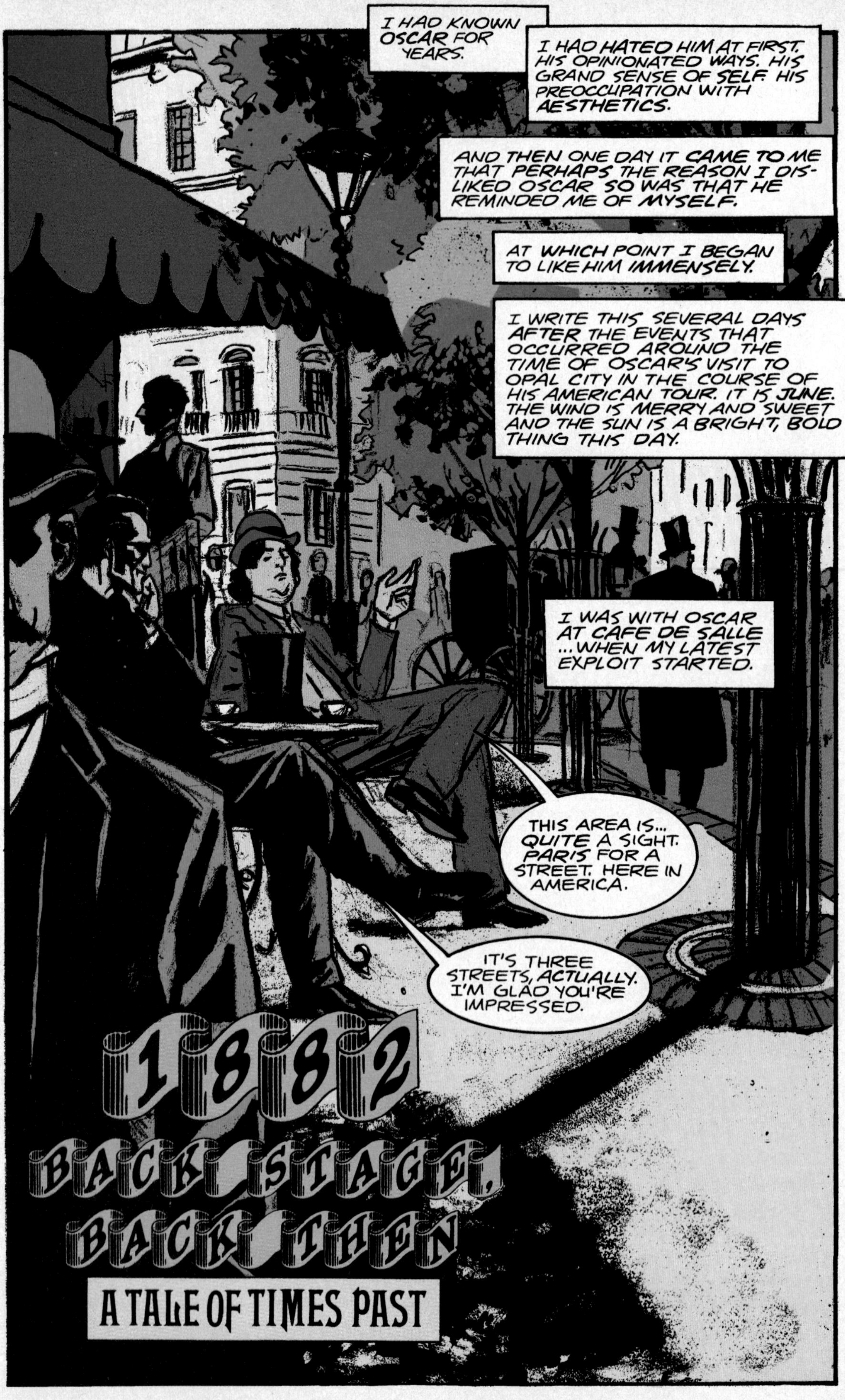
I HAD KNOWN OSCAR FOR YEARS.
I HAD HATED HIM AT FIRST. HIS OPINIONATED WAYS. HIS GRAND SENSE OF SELF. HIS PREOCCUPATION WITH AESTHETICS.
AND THEN ONE DAY IT CAME TO ME THAT PERHAPS THE REASON I DISLIKED OSCAR SO WAS THAT HE REMINDED ME OF MYSELF.
AT WHICH POINT I BEGAN TO LIKE HIM IMMENSELY.
I WRITE THIS SEVERAL DAYS AFTER THE EVENTS THAT OCCURRED AROUND THE TIME OF OSCAR'S VISIT TO OPAL CITY IN THE COURSE OF HIS AMERICAN TOUR. IT IS JUNE. THE WIND IS MERRY AND SWEET AND THE SUN IS A BRIGHT, BOLD THING THIS DAY.
I WAS WITH OSCAR AT CAFE DE SALLE ...WHEN MY LATEST EXPLOIT STARTED.
THIS AREA IS... QUITE A SIGHT. PARIS FOR A STREET. HERE IN AMERICA.
IT'S THREE STREETS, ACTUALLY. I'M GLAD YOU'RE IMPRESSED.
1882
BACK STAGE, BACK THEN
A TALE OF TIMES PAST

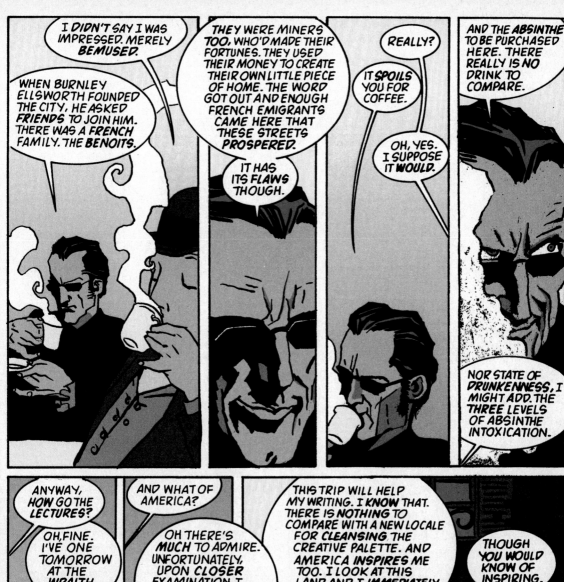

I DIDN'T SAY I WAS IMPRESSED. MERELY *BEMUSED*.

WHEN BURNLEY ELLSWORTH FOUNDED THE CITY, HE ASKED *FRIENDS* TO JOIN HIM. THERE WAS A FRENCH FAMILY. THE BENOITS.

THEY WERE MINERS *TOO*, WHO'D MADE THEIR FORTUNES. THEY USED THEIR MONEY TO CREATE THEIR OWN LITTLE PIECE OF HOME. THE WORD GOT OUT AND ENOUGH FRENCH EMIGRANTS CAME HERE THAT THESE STREETS PROSPERED.

IT HAS ITS *FLAWS* THOUGH.

REALLY?

IT *SPOILS* YOU FOR COFFEE.

OH, YES. I SUPPOSE IT *WOULD*.

AND THE *ABSINTHE* TO BE PURCHASED HERE. THERE REALLY IS *NO* DRINK TO COMPARE.

NOR STATE OF *DRUNKENNESS*, I MIGHT ADD. THE *THREE* LEVELS OF ABSINTHE INTOXICATION.

ANYWAY, HOW GO THE *LECTURES?*

OH, FINE. I'VE ONE TOMORROW AT THE WRAITH HALLS.

YES, OVER IN THE SOUTH OF TOWN. I SHALL BE THERE.

AND WHAT OF AMERICA?

OH THERE'S *MUCH* TO ADMIRE. UNFORTUNATELY, UPON *CLOSER* EXAMINATION I FIND EVERYTHING ADMIRABLE HAS BEEN *IMPORTED* FROM EUROPE.

THIS TRIP WILL HELP MY WRITING. I *KNOW* THAT. THERE IS *NOTHING* TO COMPARE WITH A NEW LOCALE FOR *CLEANSING* THE CREATIVE PALETTE. AND AMERICA *INSPIRES* ME TOO. I LOOK AT THIS LAND AND I *IMMEDIATELY* KNOW I MUST WRITE ABOUT ANYTHING *BUT*.

THOUGH YOU WOULD KNOW OF INSPIRING.

WHAT?

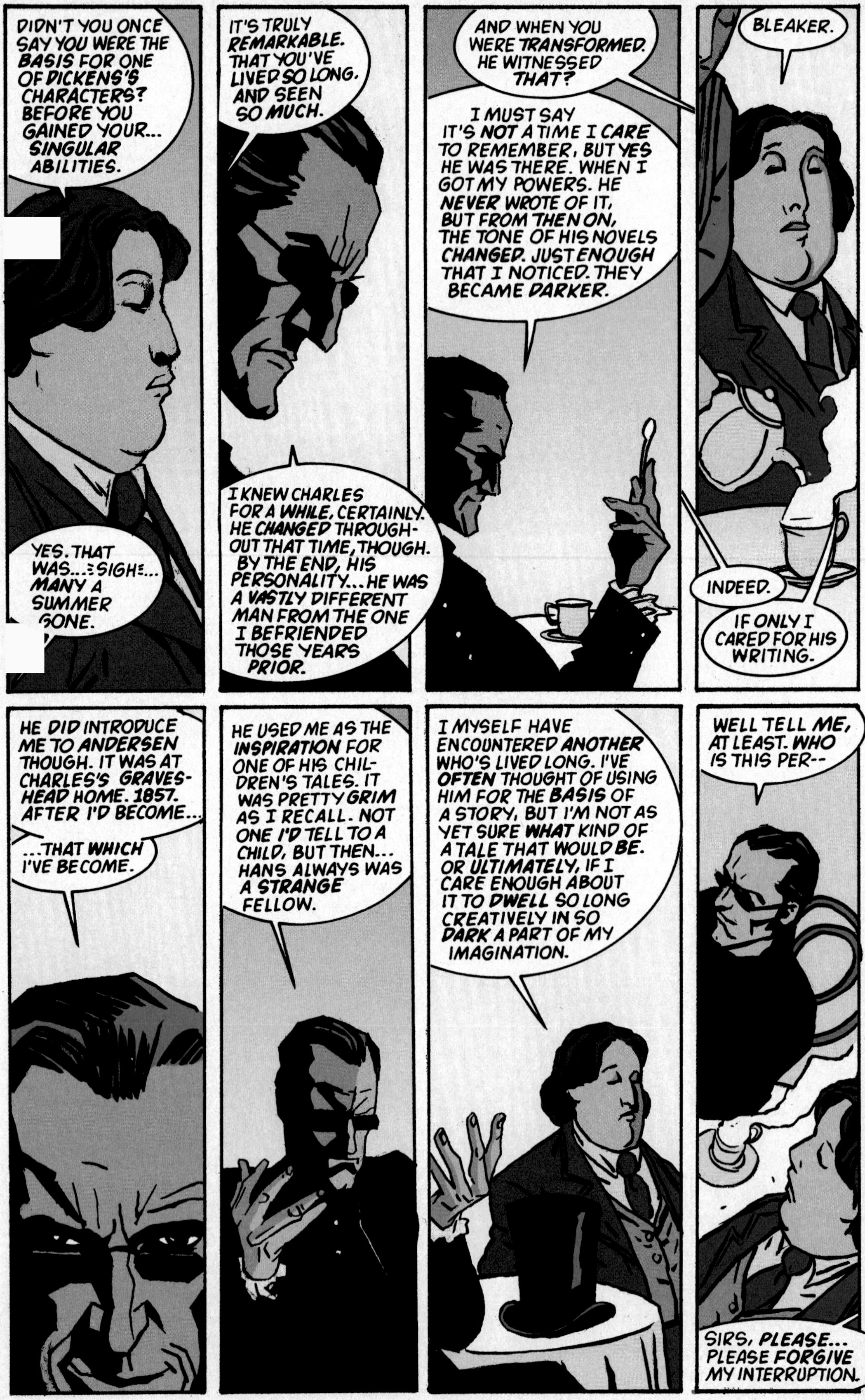
DIDN'T YOU ONCE SAY YOU WERE THE BASIS FOR ONE OF DICKENS'S CHARACTERS? BEFORE YOU GAINED YOUR... SINGULAR ABILITIES.
YES. THAT WAS... SIGH... MANY A SUMMER GONE.
IT'S TRULY REMARKABLE. THAT YOU'VE LIVED SO LONG. AND SEEN SO MUCH.
I KNEW CHARLES FOR A WHILE, CERTAINLY. HE CHANGED THROUGH-OUT THAT TIME, THOUGH. BY THE END, HIS PERSONALITY... HE WAS A VASTLY DIFFERENT MAN FROM THE ONE I BEFRIENDED THOSE YEARS PRIOR.
AND WHEN YOU WERE TRANSFORMED. HE WITNESSED THAT?
I MUST SAY IT'S NOT A TIME I CARE TO REMEMBER, BUT YES HE WAS THERE. WHEN I GOT MY POWERS. HE NEVER WROTE OF IT, BUT FROM THEN ON, THE TONE OF HIS NOVELS CHANGED. JUST ENOUGH THAT I NOTICED. THEY BECAME DARKER.
BLEAKER.
INDEED.
IF ONLY I CARED FOR HIS WRITING.
HE DID INTRODUCE ME TO ANDERSEN THOUGH. IT WAS AT CHARLES'S GRAVES-HEAD HOME. 1857. AFTER I'D BECOME...
...THAT WHICH I'VE BECOME.
HE USED ME AS THE INSPIRATION FOR ONE OF HIS CHIL-DREN'S TALES. IT WAS PRETTY GRIM AS I RECALL. NOT ONE I'D TELL TO A CHILD, BUT THEN... HANS ALWAYS WAS A STRANGE FELLOW.
I MYSELF HAVE ENCOUNTERED ANOTHER WHO'S LIVED LONG. I'VE OFTEN THOUGHT OF USING HIM FOR THE BASIS OF A STORY, BUT I'M NOT AS YET SURE WHAT KIND OF A TALE THAT WOULD BE. OR ULTIMATELY, IF I CARE ENOUGH ABOUT IT TO DWELL SO LONG CREATIVELY IN SO DARK A PART OF MY IMAGINATION.
WELL TELL ME, AT LEAST. WHO IS THIS PER--
SIRS, PLEASE... PLEASE FORGIVE MY INTERRUPTION.

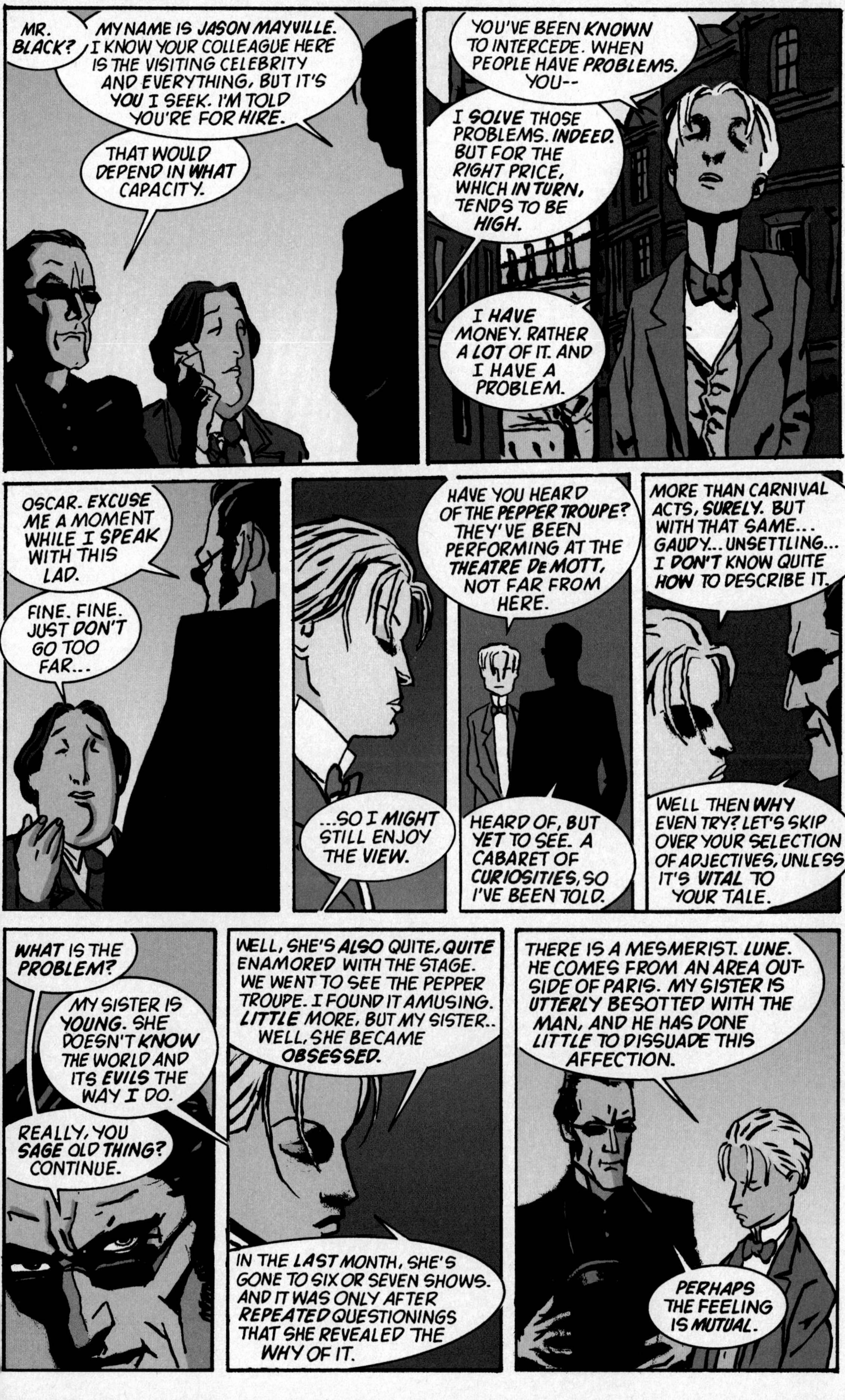
MR. BLACK?
MY NAME IS JASON MAYVILLE. I KNOW YOUR COLLEAGUE HERE IS THE VISITING CELEBRITY AND EVERYTHING, BUT IT'S YOU I SEEK. I'M TOLD YOU'RE FOR HIRE.
THAT WOULD DEPEND IN WHAT CAPACITY.
YOU'VE BEEN KNOWN TO INTERCEDE. WHEN PEOPLE HAVE PROBLEMS. YOU--
I SOLVE THOSE PROBLEMS. INDEED. BUT FOR THE RIGHT PRICE, WHICH IN TURN, TENDS TO BE HIGH.
I HAVE MONEY. RATHER A LOT OF IT. AND I HAVE A PROBLEM.
OSCAR. EXCUSE ME A MOMENT WHILE I SPEAK WITH THIS LAD.
FINE. FINE. JUST DON'T GO TOO FAR...
...SO I MIGHT STILL ENJOY THE VIEW.
HAVE YOU HEARD OF THE PEPPER TROUPE? THEY'VE BEEN PERFORMING AT THE THEATRE DE MOTT, NOT FAR FROM HERE.
HEARD OF, BUT YET TO SEE. A CABARET OF CURIOSITIES, SO I'VE BEEN TOLD.
MORE THAN CARNIVAL ACTS, SURELY. BUT WITH THAT SAME... GAUDY... UNSETTLING... I DON'T KNOW QUITE HOW TO DESCRIBE IT.
WELL THEN WHY EVEN TRY? LET'S SKIP OVER YOUR SELECTION OF ADJECTIVES, UNLESS IT'S VITAL TO YOUR TALE.
WHAT IS THE PROBLEM?
MY SISTER IS YOUNG. SHE DOESN'T KNOW THE WORLD AND ITS EVILS THE WAY I DO.
REALLY, YOU SAGE OLD THING? CONTINUE.
WELL, SHE'S ALSO QUITE, QUITE ENAMORED WITH THE STAGE. WE WENT TO SEE THE PEPPER TROUPE. I FOUND IT AMUSING. LITTLE MORE, BUT MY SISTER.. WELL, SHE BECAME OBSESSED.
IN THE LAST MONTH, SHE'S GONE TO SIX OR SEVEN SHOWS. AND IT WAS ONLY AFTER REPEATED QUESTIONINGS THAT SHE REVEALED THE WHY OF IT.
THERE IS A MESMERIST. LUNE. HE COMES FROM AN AREA OUTSIDE OF PARIS. MY SISTER IS UTTERLY BESOTTED WITH THE MAN, AND HE HAS DONE LITTLE TO DISSUADE THIS AFFECTION.
PERHAPS THE FEELING IS MUTUAL.

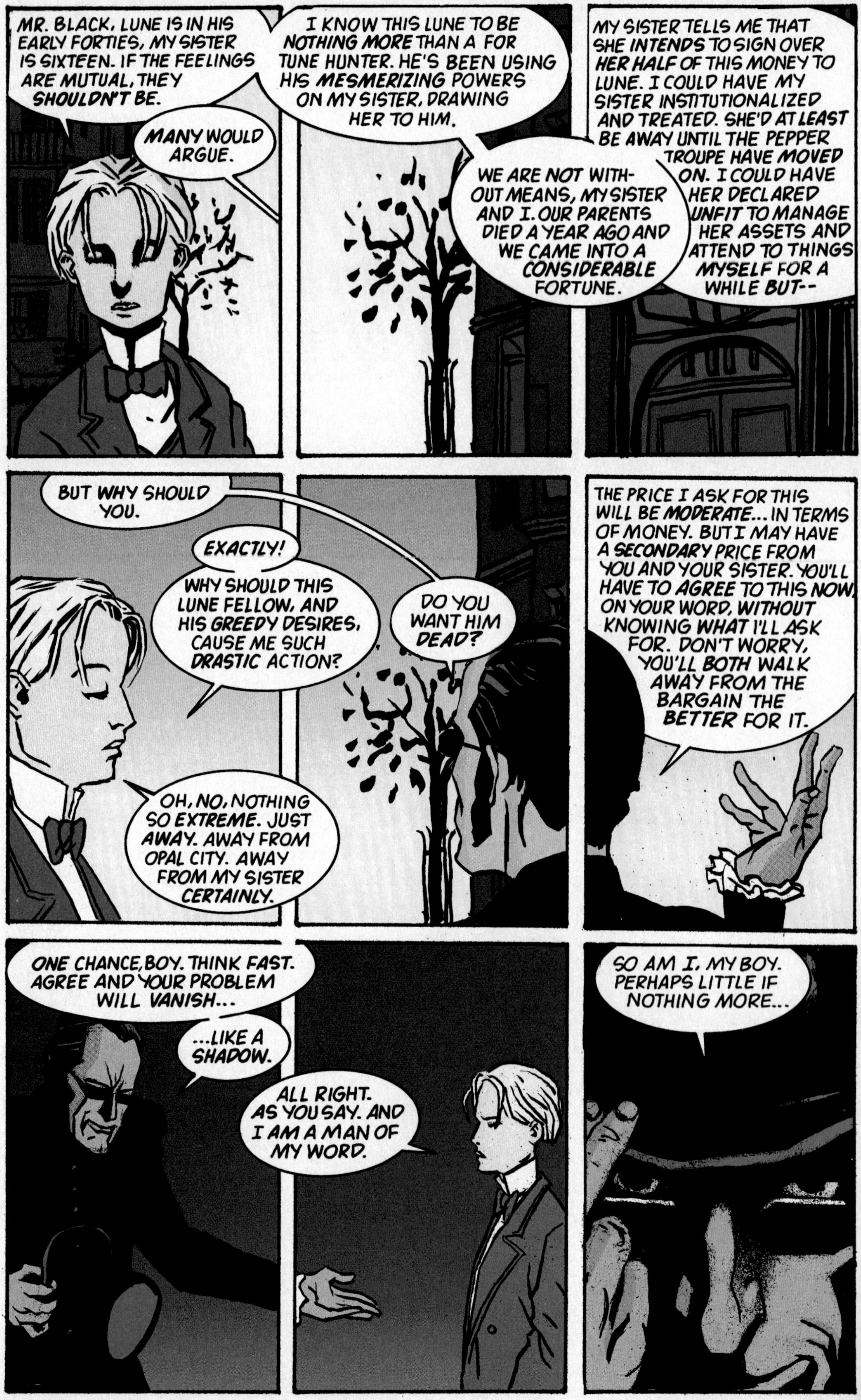
MR. BLACK, LUNE IS IN HIS EARLY FORTIES, MY SISTER IS SIXTEEN. IF THE FEELINGS ARE MUTUAL, THEY SHOULDN'T BE.
MANY WOULD ARGUE.
I KNOW THIS LUNE TO BE NOTHING MORE THAN A FOR TUNE HUNTER. HE'S BEEN USING HIS MESMERIZING POWERS ON MY SISTER, DRAWING HER TO HIM.
WE ARE NOT WITH-OUT MEANS, MY SISTER AND I. OUR PARENTS DIED A YEAR AGO AND WE CAME INTO A CONSIDERABLE FORTUNE.
MY SISTER TELLS ME THAT SHE INTENDS TO SIGN OVER HER HALF OF THIS MONEY TO LUNE. I COULD HAVE MY SISTER INSTITUTIONALIZED AND TREATED. SHE'D AT LEAST BE AWAY UNTIL THE PEPPER TROUPE HAVE MOVED ON. I COULD HAVE HER DECLARED UNFIT TO MANAGE HER ASSETS AND ATTEND TO THINGS MYSELF FOR A WHILE BUT--
BUT WHY SHOULD YOU.
EXACTLY!
WHY SHOULD THIS LUNE FELLOW, AND HIS GREEDY DESIRES, CAUSE ME SUCH DRASTIC ACTION?
OH, NO, NOTHING SO EXTREME. JUST AWAY. AWAY FROM OPAL CITY. AWAY FROM MY SISTER CERTAINLY.
DO YOU WANT HIM DEAD?
THE PRICE I ASK FOR THIS WILL BE MODERATE... IN TERMS OF MONEY. BUT I MAY HAVE A SECONDARY PRICE FROM YOU AND YOUR SISTER. YOU'LL HAVE TO AGREE TO THIS NOW, ON YOUR WORD, WITHOUT KNOWING WHAT I'LL ASK FOR. DON'T WORRY, YOU'LL BOTH WALK AWAY FROM THE BARGAIN THE BETTER FOR IT.
ONE CHANCE, BOY. THINK FAST. AGREE AND YOUR PROBLEM WILL VANISH...
...LIKE A SHADOW.
ALL RIGHT. AS YOU SAY. AND I AM A MAN OF MY WORD.
SO AM I, MY BOY. PERHAPS LITTLE IF NOTHING MORE...

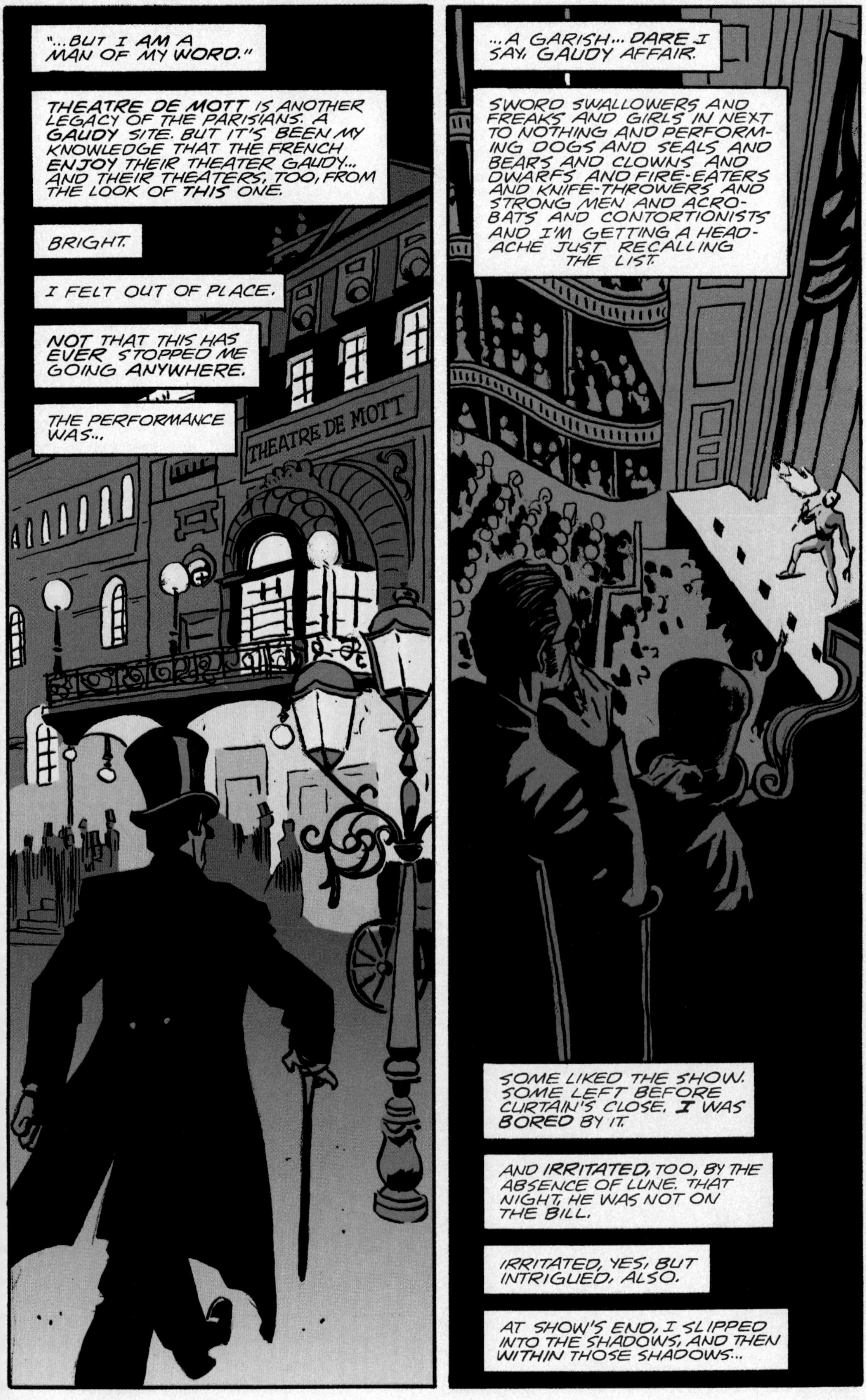
"...BUT I AM A MAN OF MY WORD."
THEATRE DE MOTT IS ANOTHER LEGACY OF THE PARISIANS. A GAUDY SITE. BUT IT'S BEEN MY KNOWLEDGE THAT THE FRENCH ENJOY THEIR THEATER GAUDY... AND THEIR THEATERS, TOO, FROM THE LOOK OF THIS ONE.
BRIGHT.
I FELT OUT OF PLACE.
NOT THAT THIS HAS EVER STOPPED ME GOING ANYWHERE.
THE PERFORMANCE WAS...
THEATRE DE MOTT
...A GARISH... DARE I SAY, GAUDY AFFAIR.
SWORD SWALLOWERS AND FREAKS AND GIRLS IN NEXT TO NOTHING AND PERFORMING DOGS AND SEALS AND BEARS AND CLOWNS AND DWARFS AND FIRE-EATERS AND KNIFE-THROWERS AND STRONG MEN AND ACROBATS AND CONTORTIONISTS AND I'M GETTING A HEADACHE JUST RECALLING THE LIST.
SOME LIKED THE SHOW. SOME LEFT BEFORE CURTAIN'S CLOSE. I WAS BORED BY IT.
AND IRRITATED, TOO, BY THE ABSENCE OF LUNE. THAT NIGHT, HE WAS NOT ON THE BILL.
IRRITATED, YES, BUT INTRIGUED, ALSO.
AT SHOW'S END, I SLIPPED INTO THE SHADOWS, AND THEN WITHIN THOSE SHADOWS...

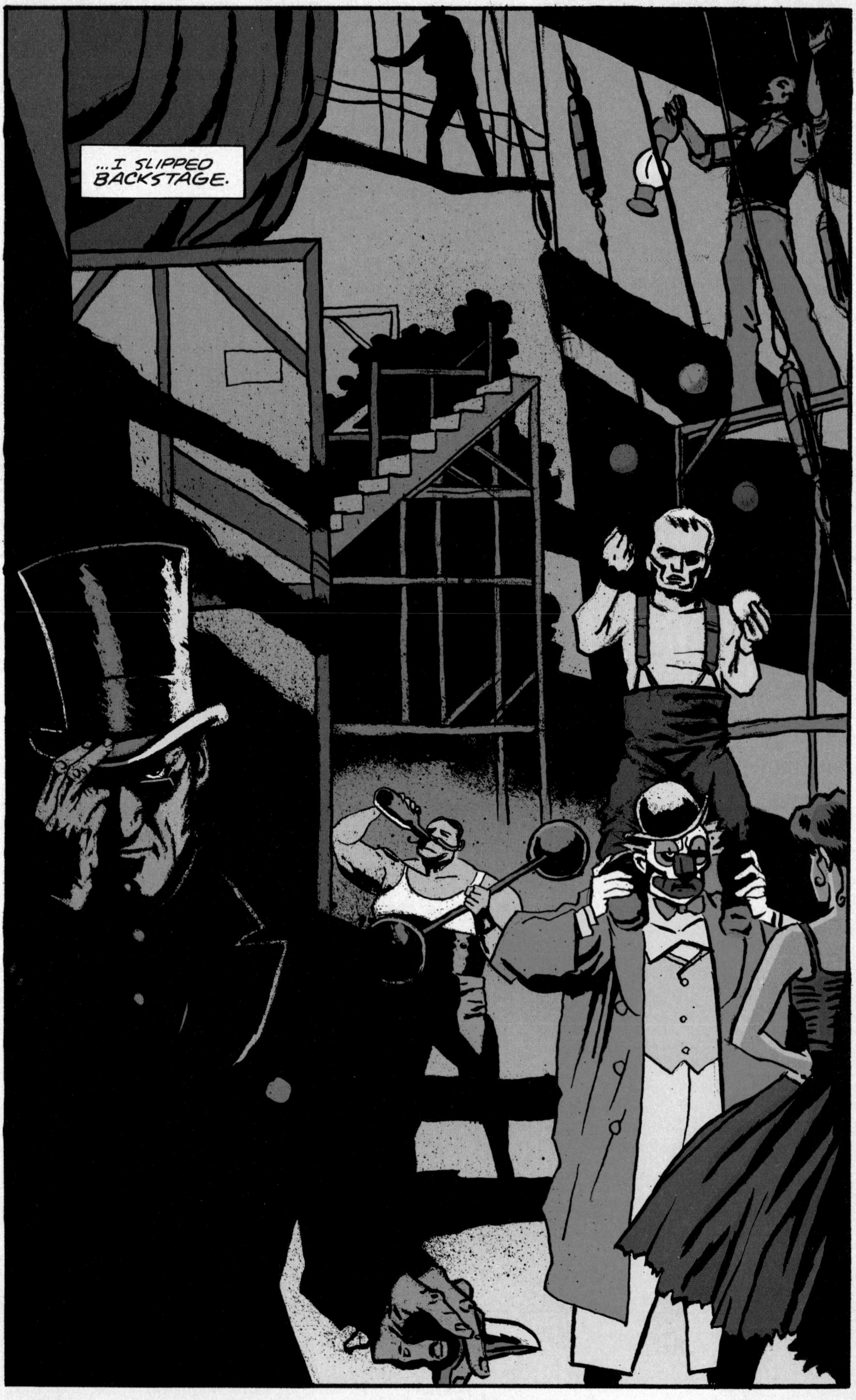
...I SLIPPED BACKSTAGE.

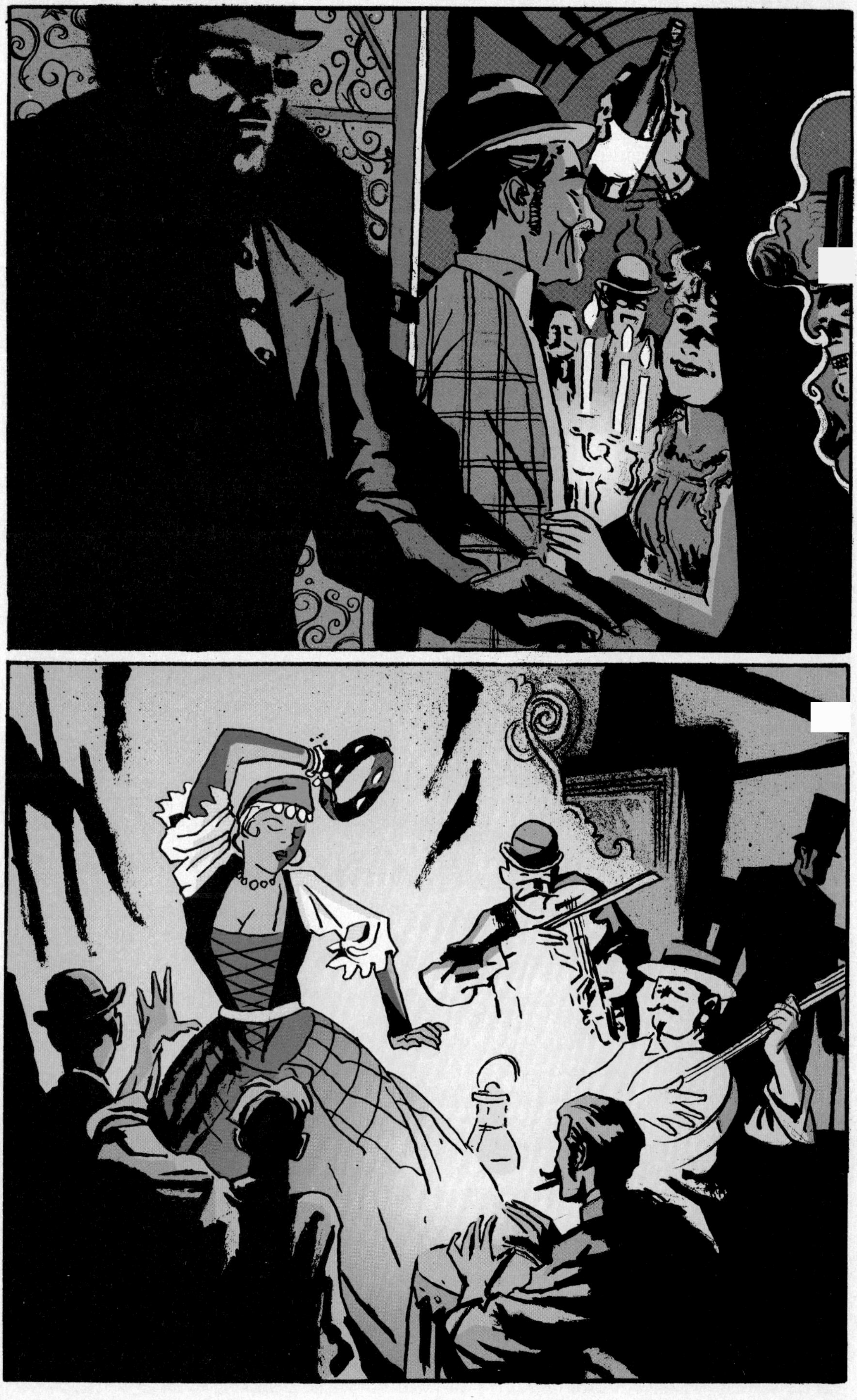

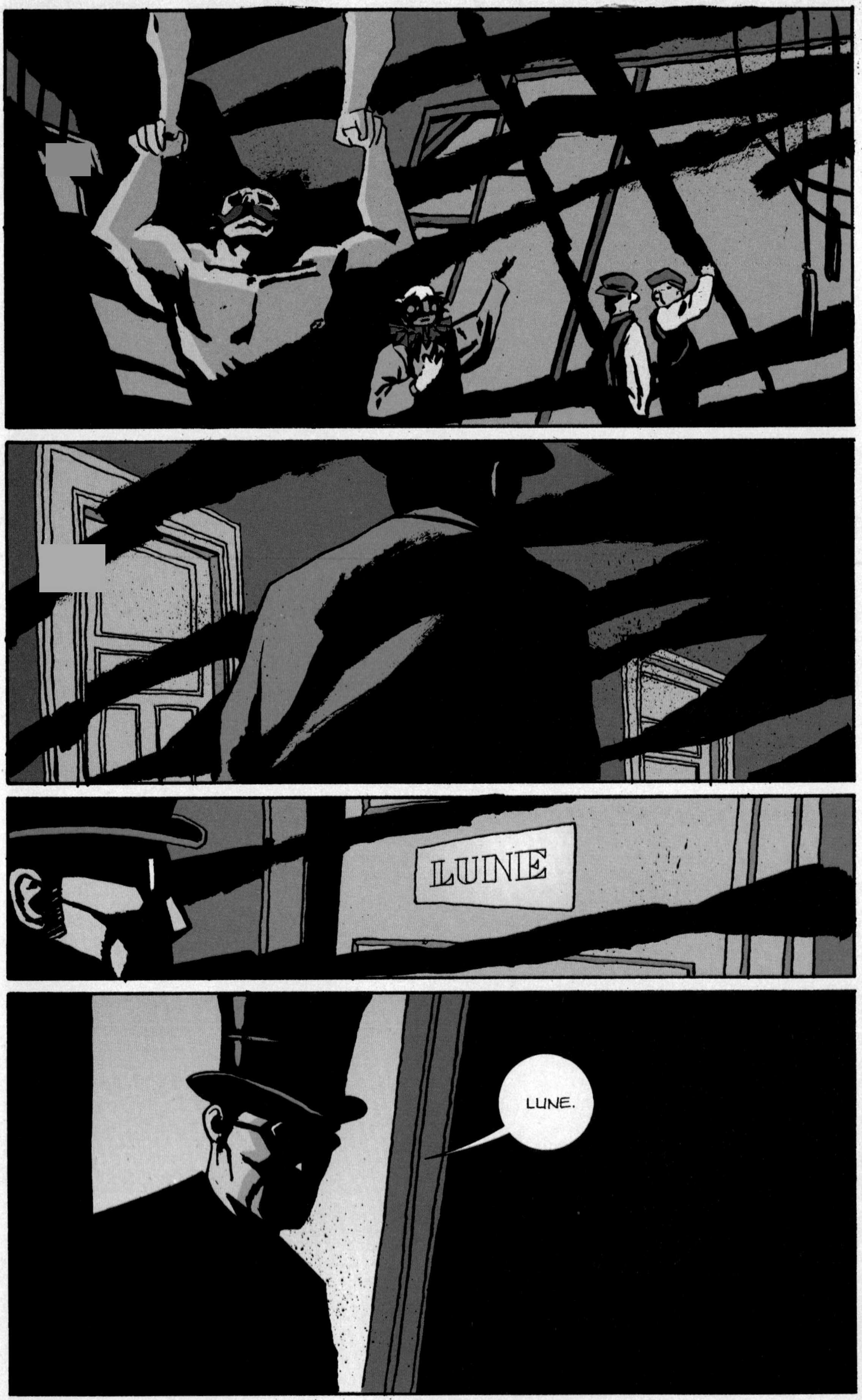
LUNE
LUNE.

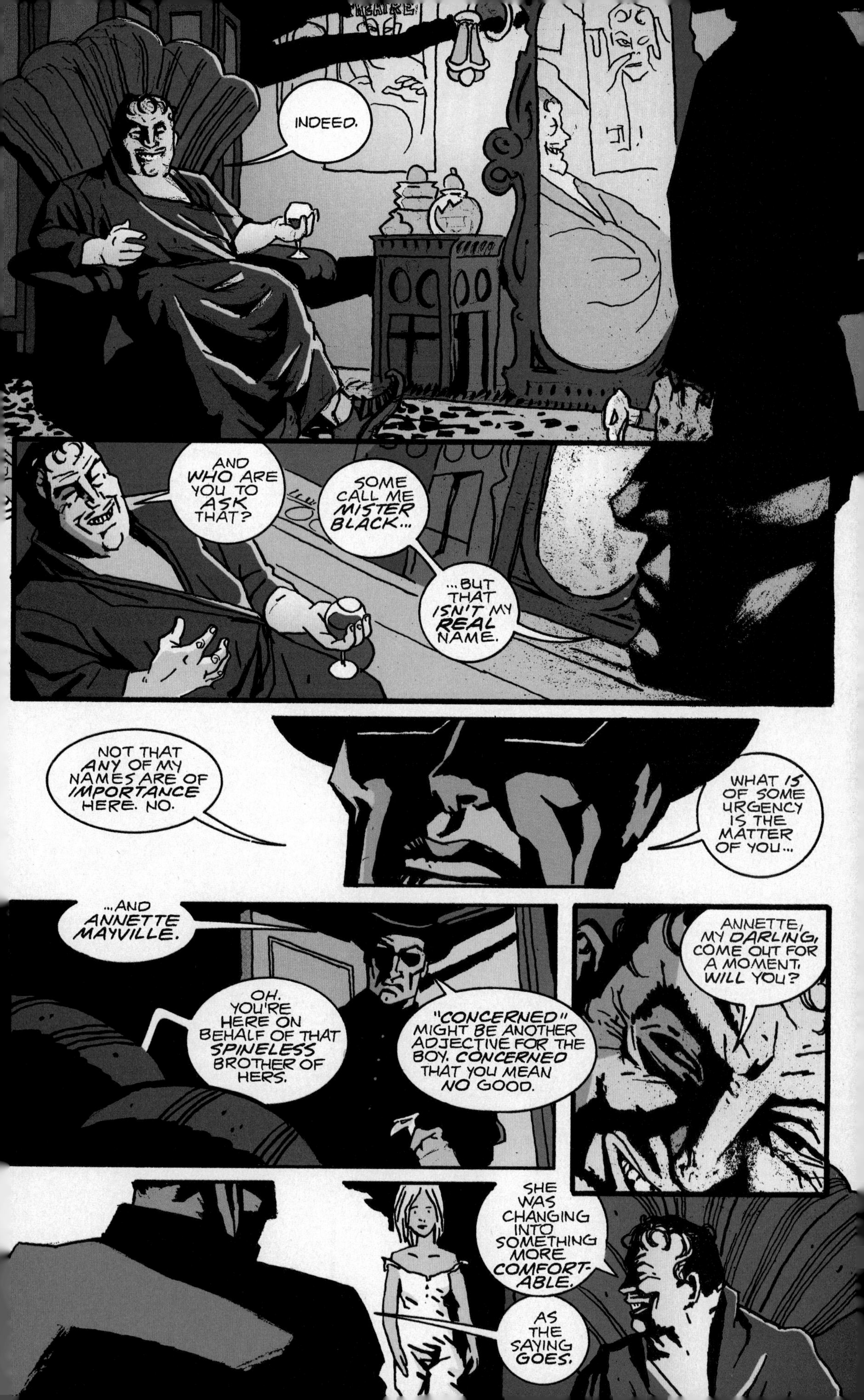
INDEED.
AND WHO ARE YOU TO ASK THAT?
SOME CALL ME MISTER BLACK...
...BUT THAT ISN'T MY REAL NAME.
NOT THAT ANY OF MY NAMES ARE OF IMPORTANCE HERE. NO.
WHAT IS OF SOME URGENCY IS THE MATTER OF YOU...
...AND ANNETTE MAYVILLE.
OH. YOU'RE HERE ON BEHALF OF THAT SPINELESS BROTHER OF HERS.
"CONCERNED" MIGHT BE ANOTHER ADJECTIVE FOR THE BOY. CONCERNED THAT YOU MEAN NO GOOD.
ANNETTE, MY DARLING, COME OUT FOR A MOMENT, WILL YOU?
SHE WAS CHANGING INTO SOMETHING MORE COMFORT-ABLE.
AS THE SAYING GOES.

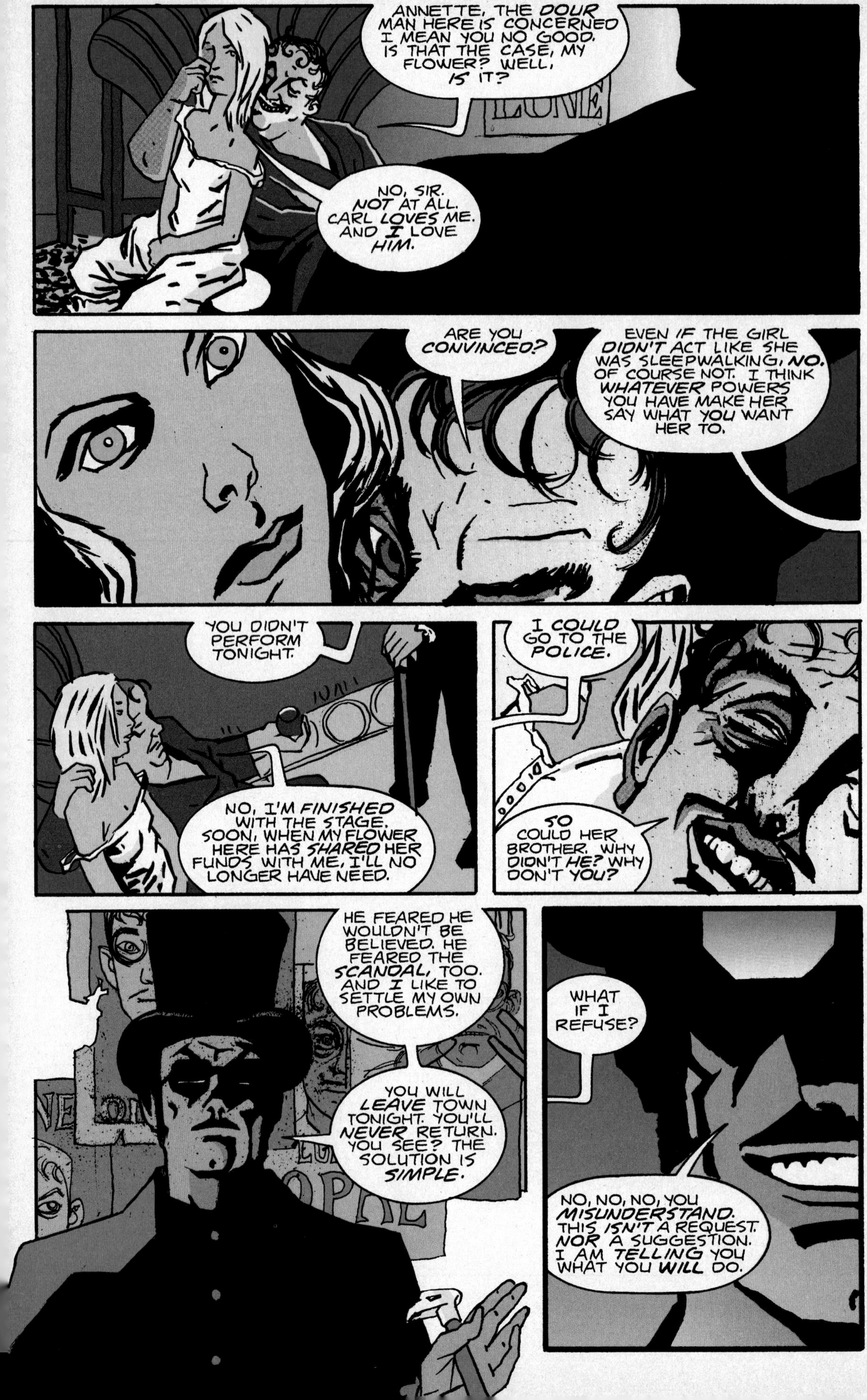
ANNETTE, THE DOUR MAN HERE IS CONCERNED I MEAN YOU NO GOOD. IS THAT THE CASE, MY FLOWER? WELL, IS IT?
NO, SIR. NOT AT ALL. CARL LOVES ME. AND I LOVE HIM.
ARE YOU CONVINCED?
EVEN IF THE GIRL DIDN'T ACT LIKE SHE WAS SLEEPWALKING, NO. OF COURSE NOT. I THINK WHATEVER POWERS YOU HAVE MAKE HER SAY WHAT YOU WANT HER TO.
YOU DIDN'T PERFORM TONIGHT.
NO, I'M FINISHED WITH THE STAGE. SOON, WHEN MY FLOWER HERE HAS SHARED HER FUNDS WITH ME, I'LL NO LONGER HAVE NEED.
I COULD GO TO THE POLICE.
SO COULD HER BROTHER. WHY DIDN'T HE? WHY DON'T YOU?
HE FEARED HE WOULDN'T BE BELIEVED. HE FEARED THE SCANDAL, TOO. AND I LIKE TO SETTLE MY OWN PROBLEMS.
YOU WILL LEAVE TOWN TONIGHT. YOU'LL NEVER RETURN. YOU SEE? THE SOLUTION IS SIMPLE.
WHAT IF I REFUSE?
NO, NO, NO, YOU MISUNDERSTAND. THIS ISN'T A REQUEST. NOR A SUGGESTION. I AM TELLING YOU WHAT YOU WILL DO.

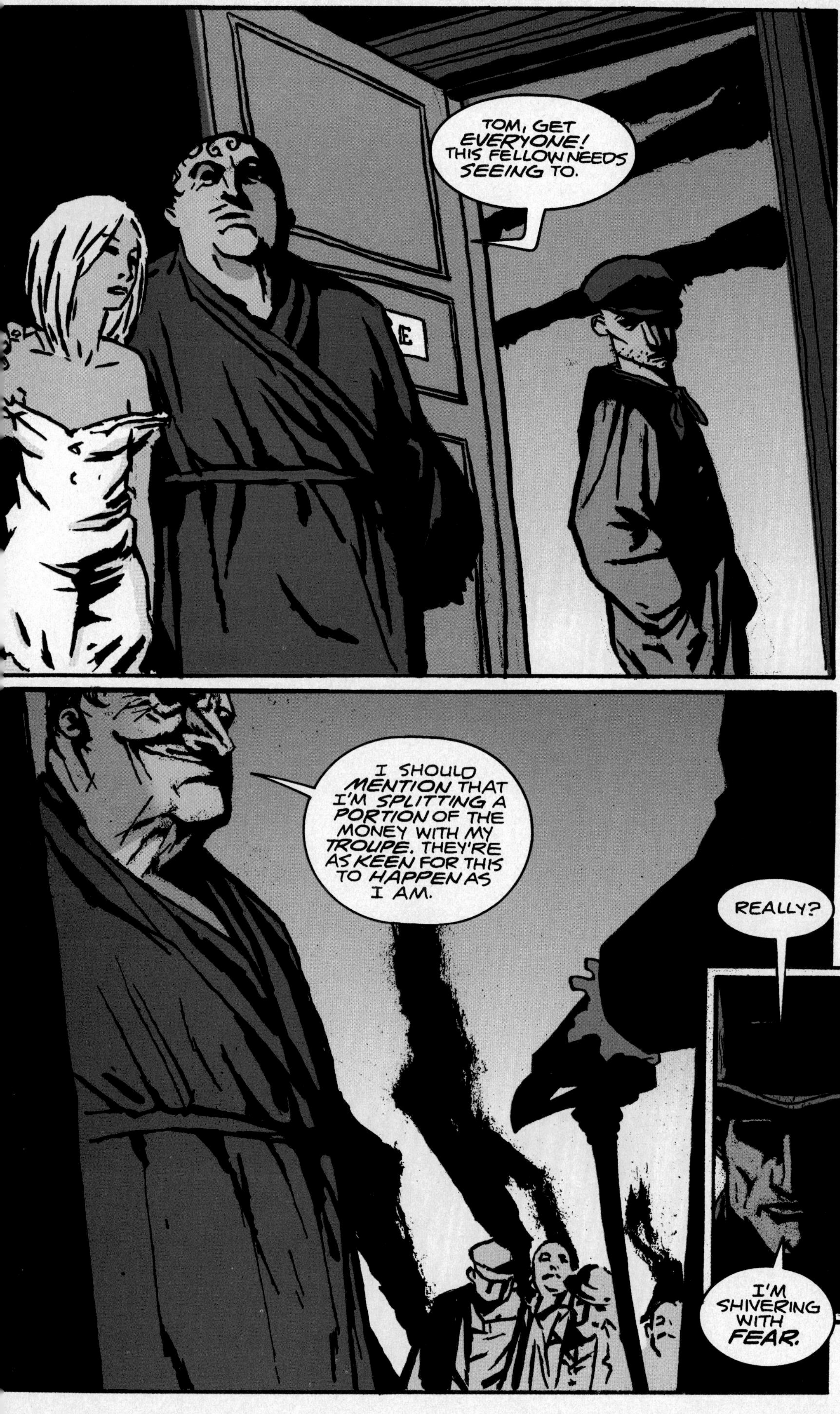
TOM, GET EVERYONE! THIS FELLOW NEEDS SEEING TO.
I SHOULD MENTION THAT I'M SPLITTING A PORTION OF THE MONEY WITH MY TROUPE. THEY'RE AS KEEN FOR THIS TO HAPPEN AS I AM.
REALLY?
I'M SHIVERING WITH FEAR.

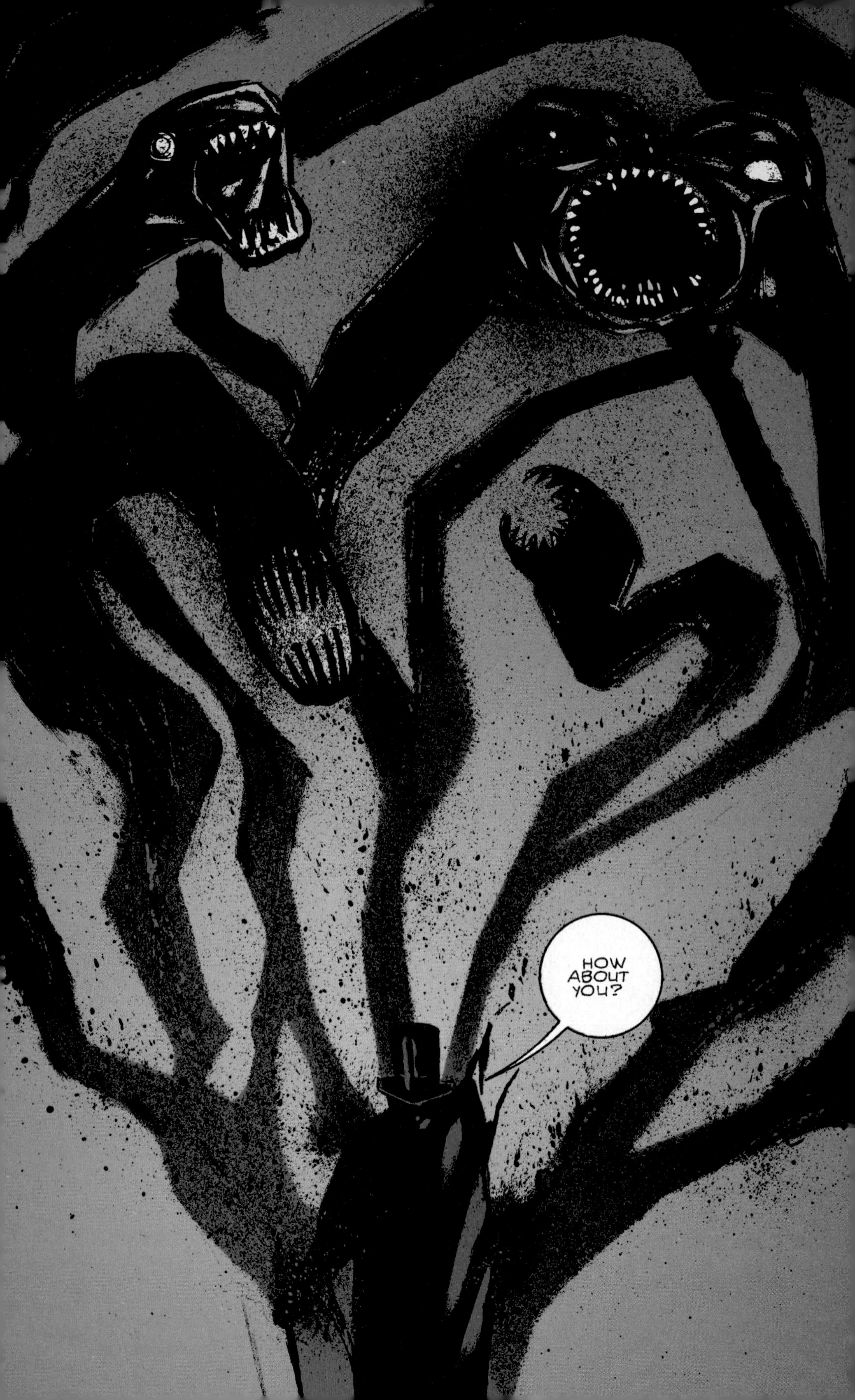
HOW ABOUT YOU?

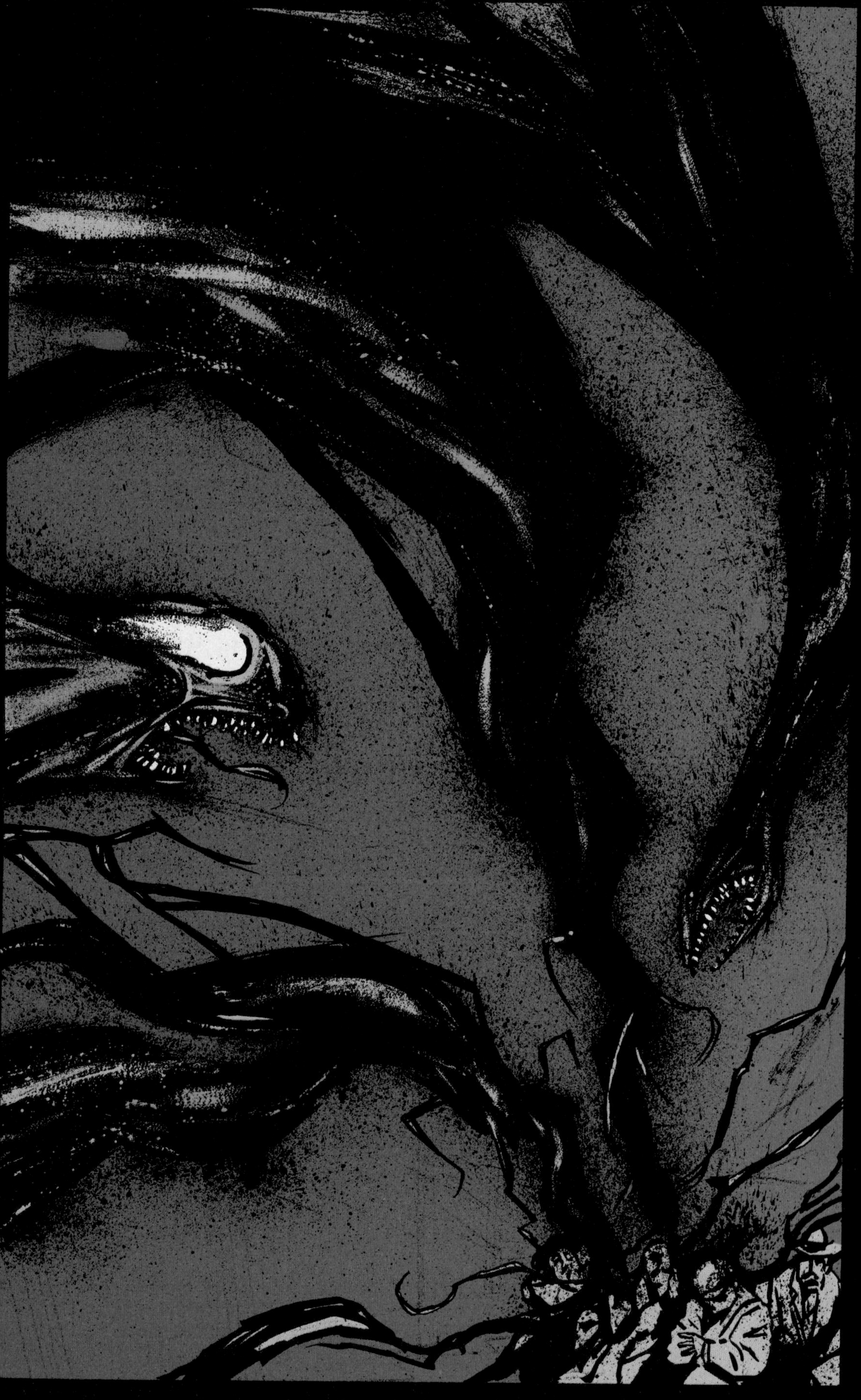

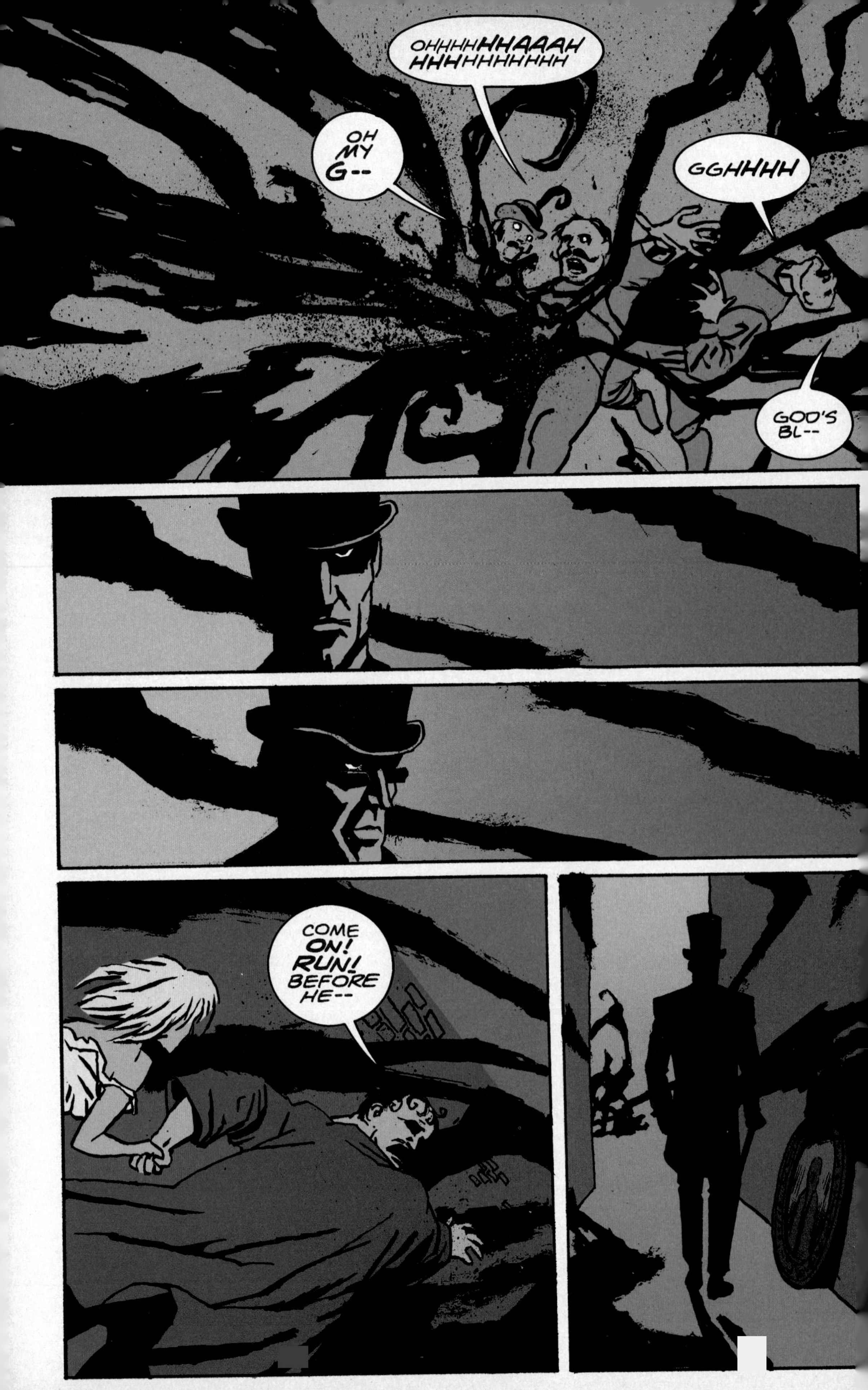
OH MY G--
OHHHHHHAAAH HHHHHHHHHH
GGHHHH
GOD'S BL--
COME ON! RUN! BEFORE HE--

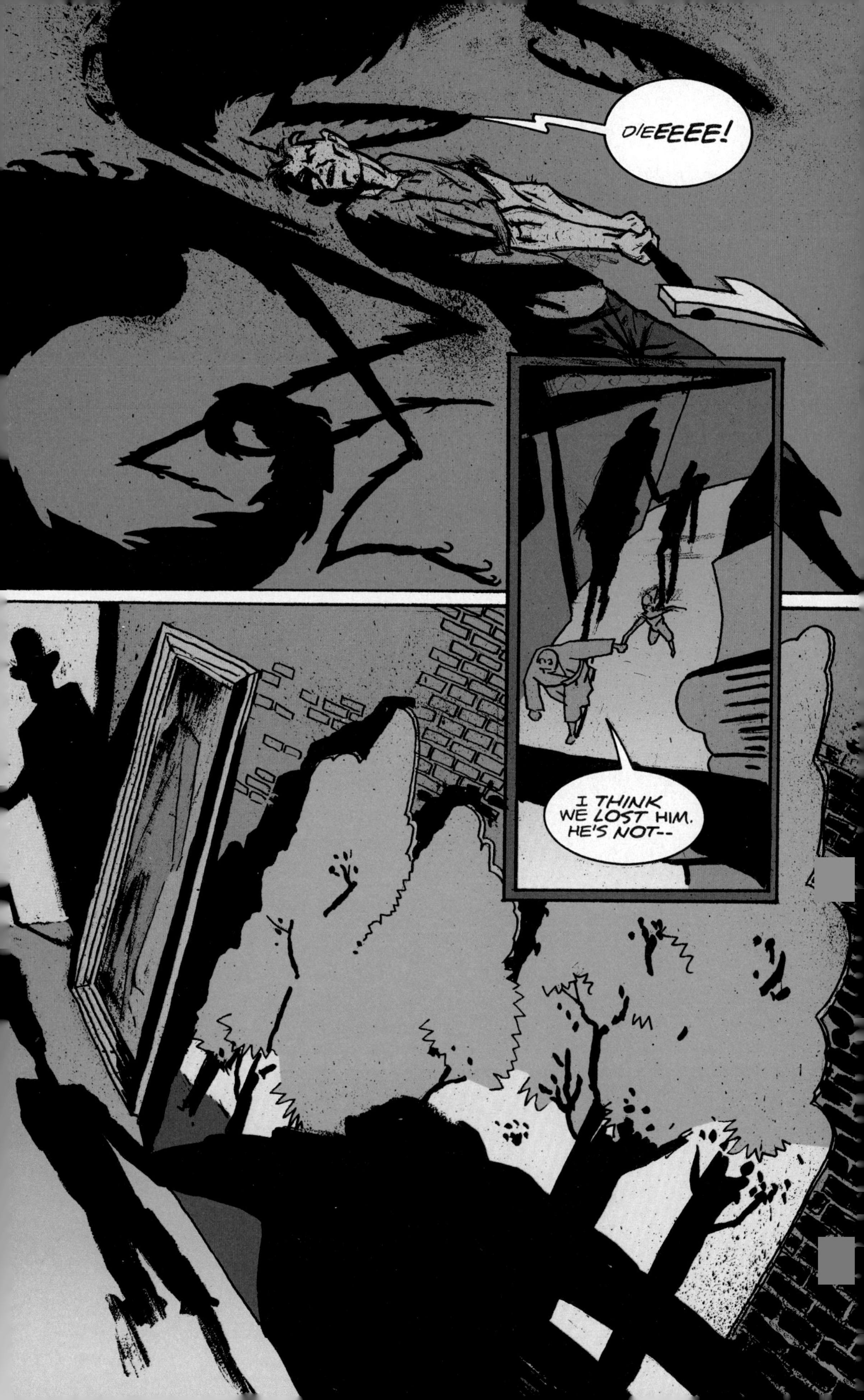
DIEEEEE!
I THINK WE LOST HIM. HE'S NOT--

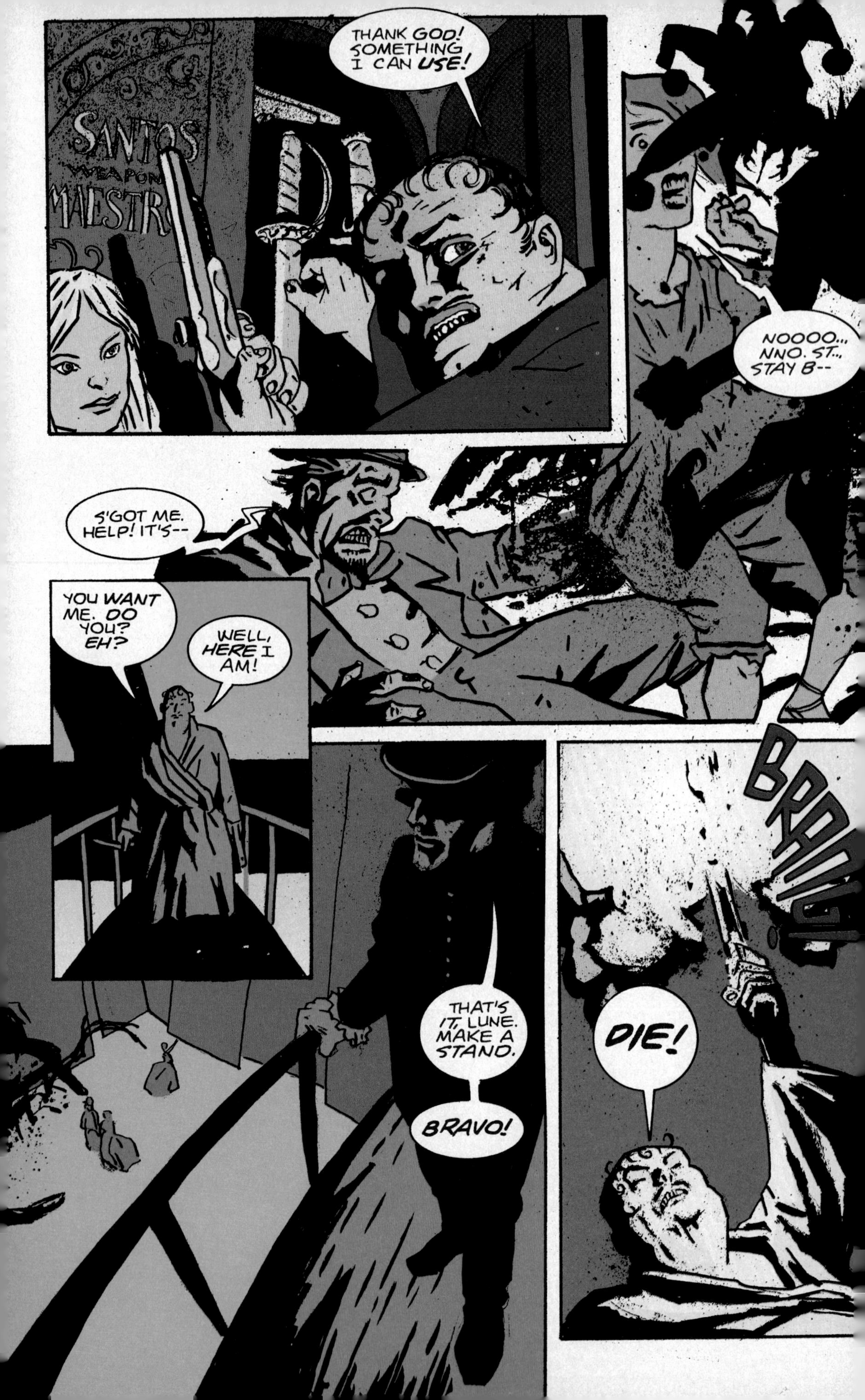

SANTOS WEAPON MAESTR
THANK GOD! SOMETHING I CAN USE!
NOOOO... NNO. ST... STAY B--
S'GOT ME. HELP! IT'S--
YOU WANT ME. DO YOU? EH?
WELL, HERE I AM!
THAT'S IT, LUNE. MAKE A STAND.
BRAVO!
BRAAG!
DIE!

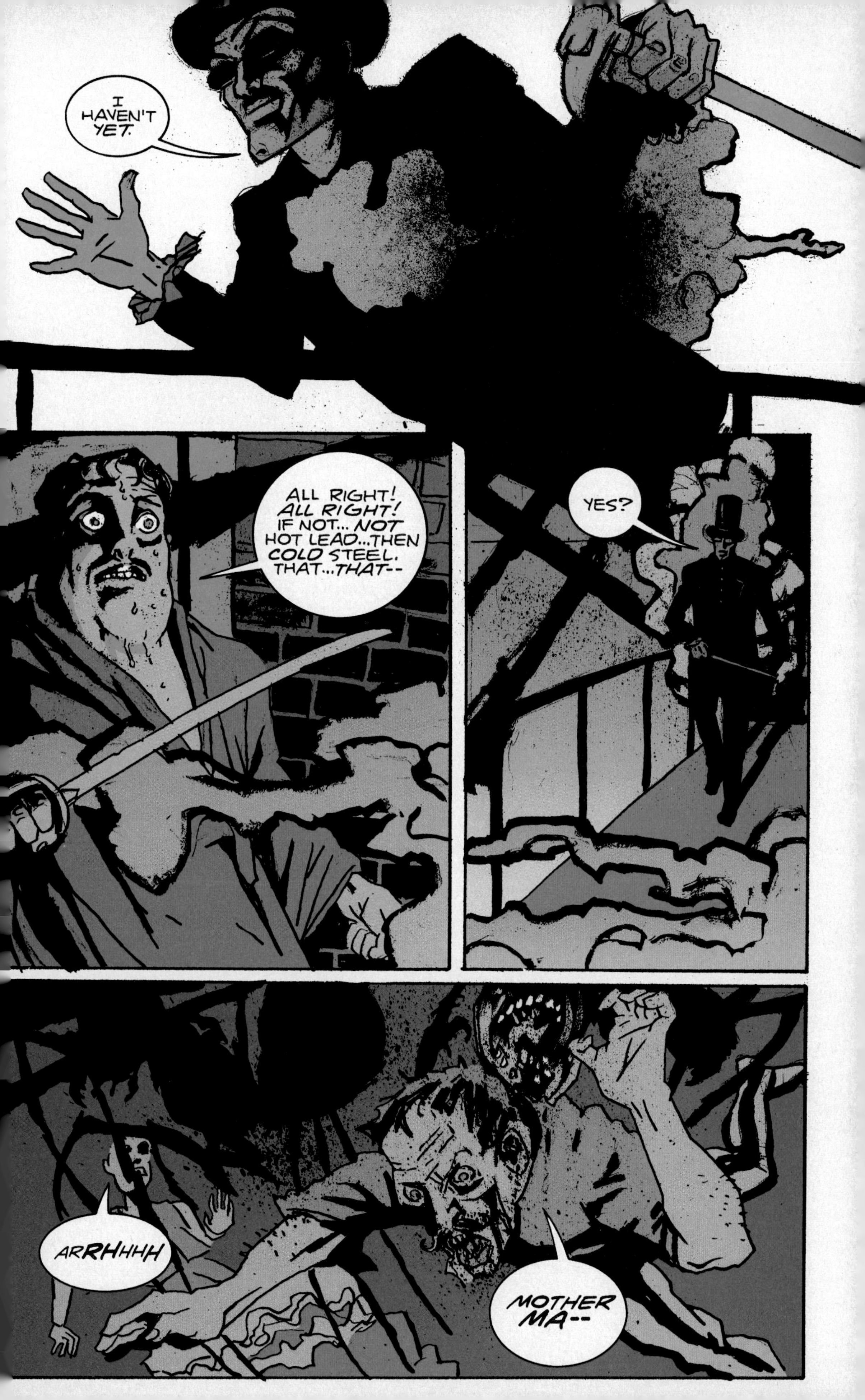
I HAVEN'T YET.
ALL RIGHT! ALL RIGHT! IF NOT... NOT HOT LEAD...THEN COLD STEEL. THAT...THAT--
YES?
ARRHHHH
MOTHER MA--

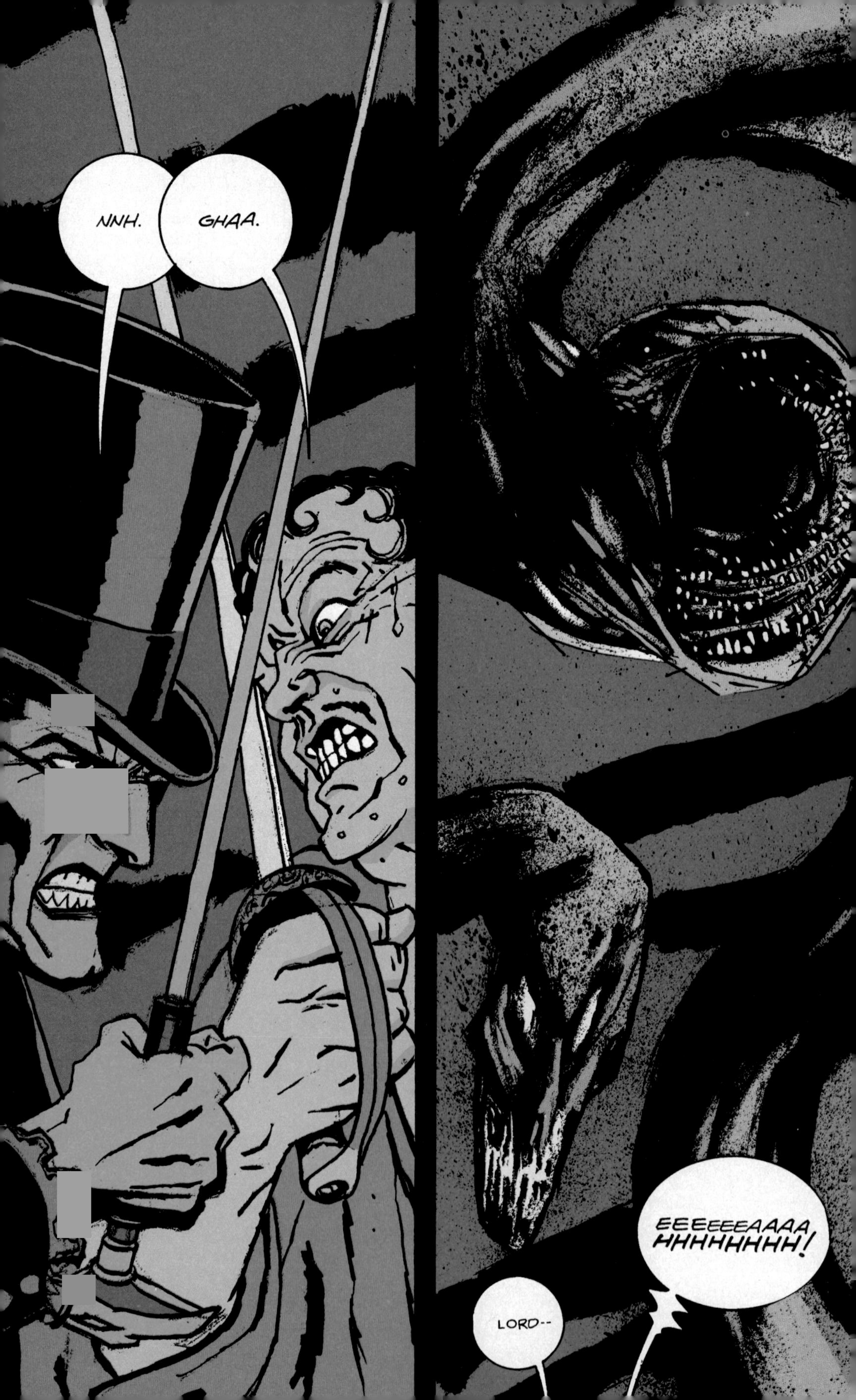
NNH.
GHAA.
EEEEEEEAAAA HHHHHHHH!
LORD--

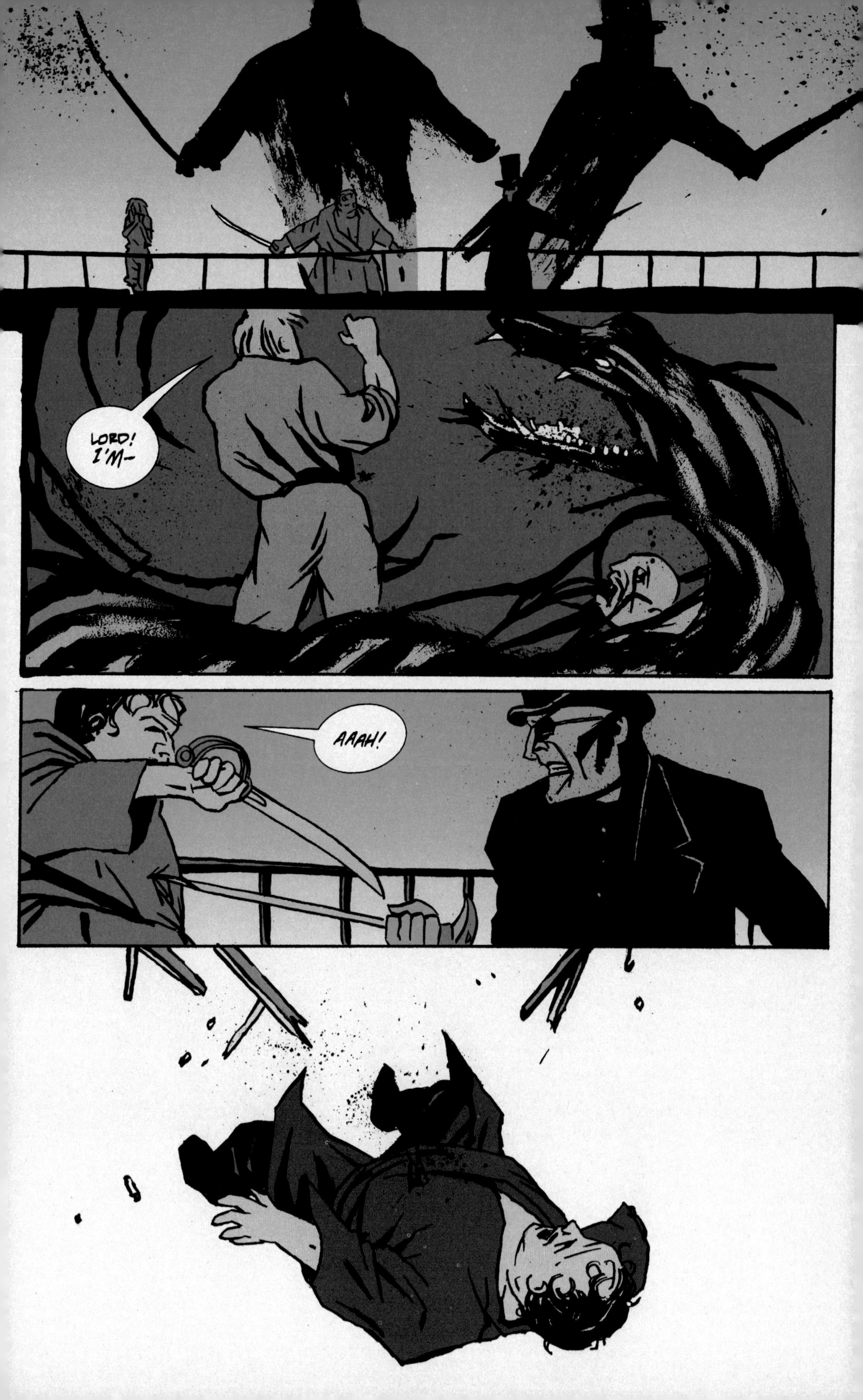
LORD! I'M-
AAAH!

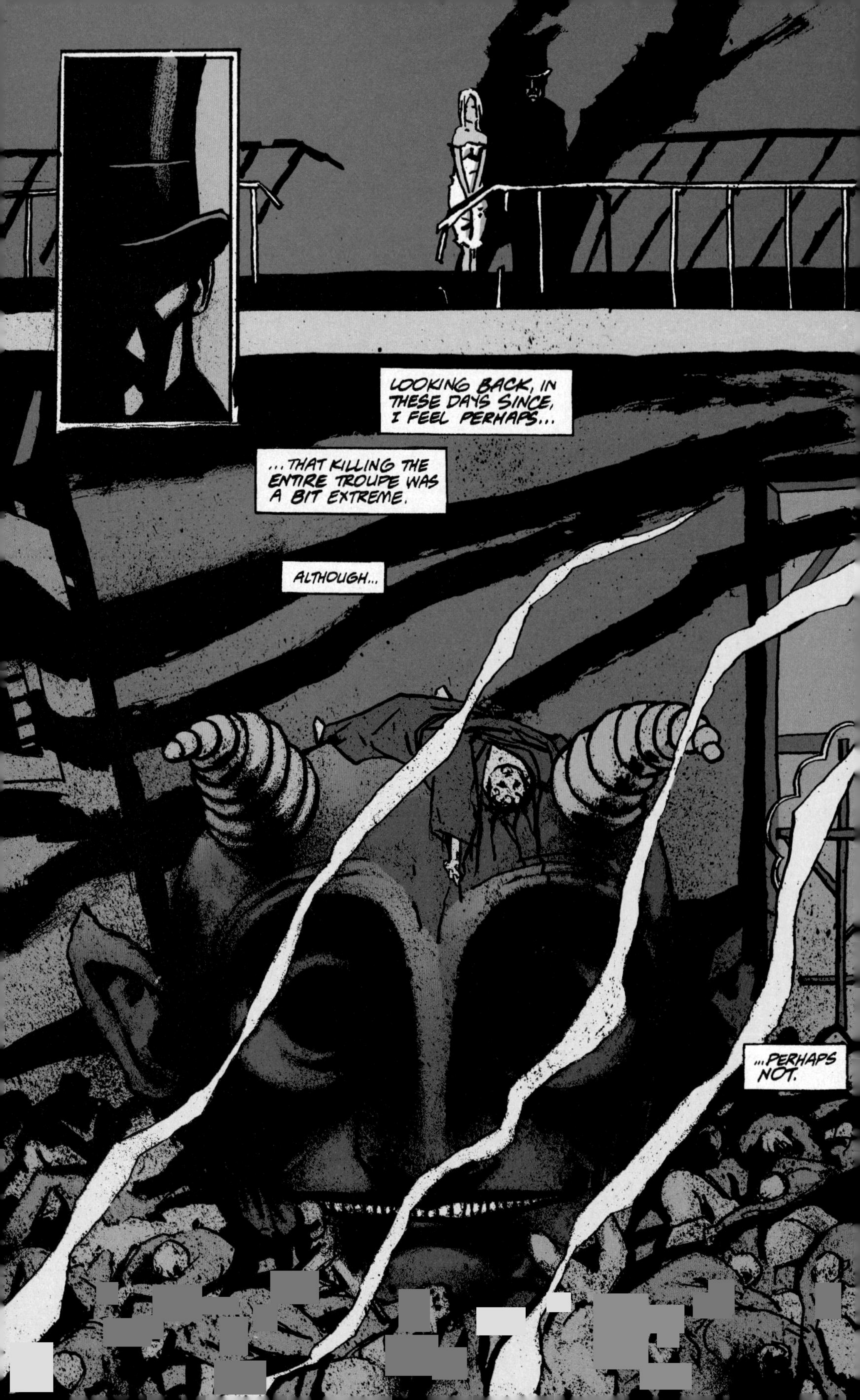
LOOKING BACK, IN THESE DAYS SINCE, I FEEL PERHAPS...
...THAT KILLING THE ENTIRE TROUPE WAS A BIT EXTREME.
ALTHOUGH...
...PERHAPS NOT.

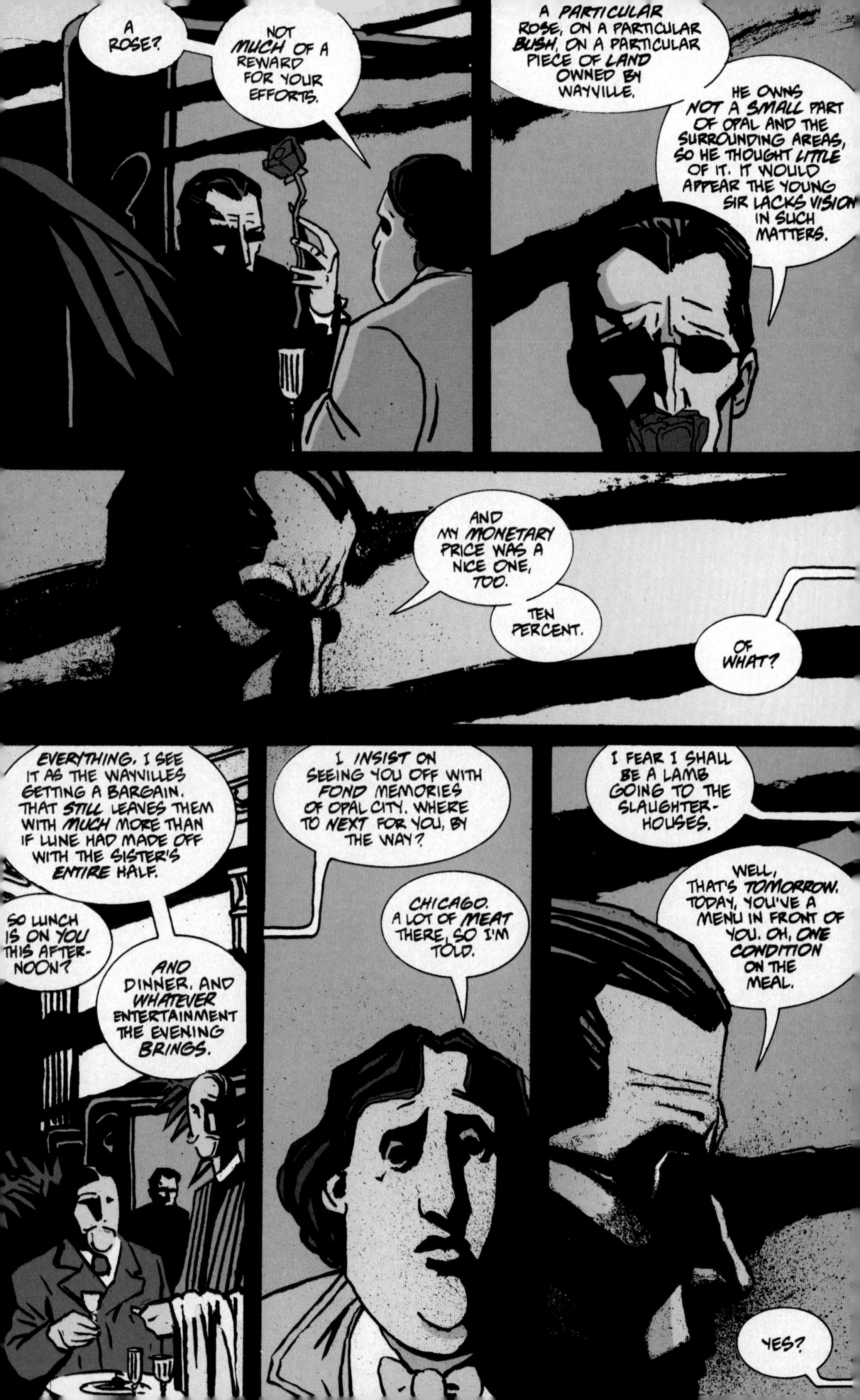
A ROSE?
NOT MUCH OF A REWARD FOR YOUR EFFORTS.
A PARTICULAR ROSE, ON A PARTICULAR BUSH, ON A PARTICULAR PIECE OF LAND OWNED BY WAYVILLE.
HE OWNS NOT A SMALL PART OF OPAL AND THE SURROUNDING AREAS, SO HE THOUGHT LITTLE OF IT. IT WOULD APPEAR THE YOUNG SIR LACKS VISION IN SUCH MATTERS.
AND MY MONETARY PRICE WAS A NICE ONE, TOO.
TEN PERCENT.
OF WHAT?
EVERYTHING. I SEE IT AS THE WAYVILLES GETTING A BARGAIN. THAT STILL LEAVES THEM WITH MUCH MORE THAN IF LUNE HAD MADE OFF WITH THE SISTER'S ENTIRE HALF.
SO LUNCH IS ON YOU THIS AFTER-NOON?
AND DINNER, AND WHATEVER ENTERTAINMENT THE EVENING BRINGS.
I INSIST ON SEEING YOU OFF WITH FOND MEMORIES OF OPAL CITY. WHERE TO NEXT FOR YOU, BY THE WAY?
CHICAGO. A LOT OF MEAT THERE, SO I'M TOLD.
I FEAR I SHALL BE A LAMB GOING TO THE SLAUGHTER-HOUSES.
WELL, THAT'S TOMORROW. TODAY, YOU'VE A MENU IN FRONT OF YOU. OH, ONE CONDITION ON THE MEAL.
YES?

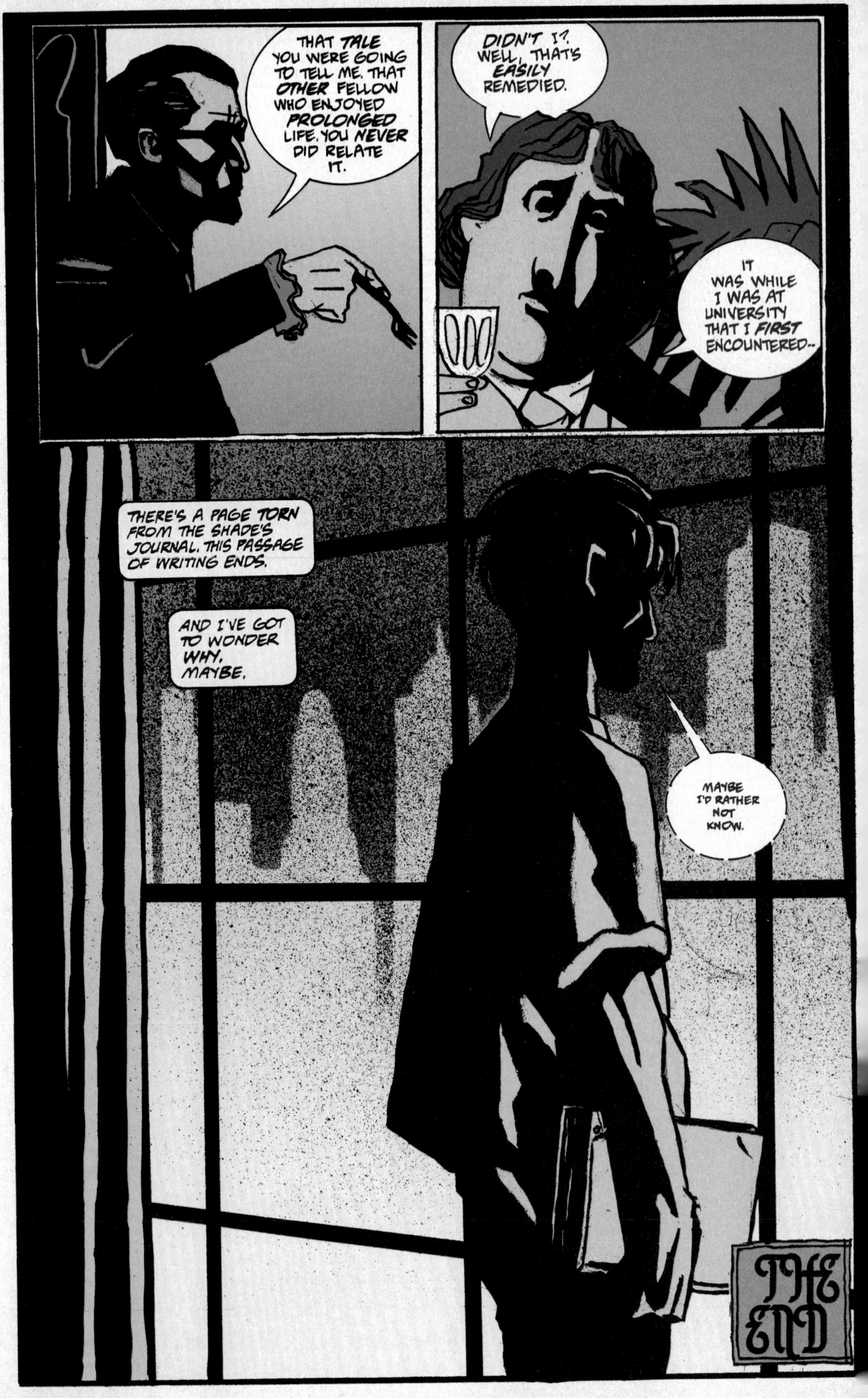
THAT TALE YOU WERE GOING TO TELL ME. THAT OTHER FELLOW WHO ENJOYED PROLONGED LIFE. YOU NEVER DID RELATE IT.
DIDN'T I? WELL, THAT'S EASILY REMEDIED.
IT WAS WHILE I WAS AT UNIVERSITY THAT I FIRST ENCOUNTERED..
THERE'S A PAGE TORN FROM THE SHADE'S JOURNAL. THIS PASSAGE OF WRITING ENDS.
AND I'VE GOT TO WONDER WHY. MAYBE.
MAYBE I'D RATHER NOT KNOW.
THE END

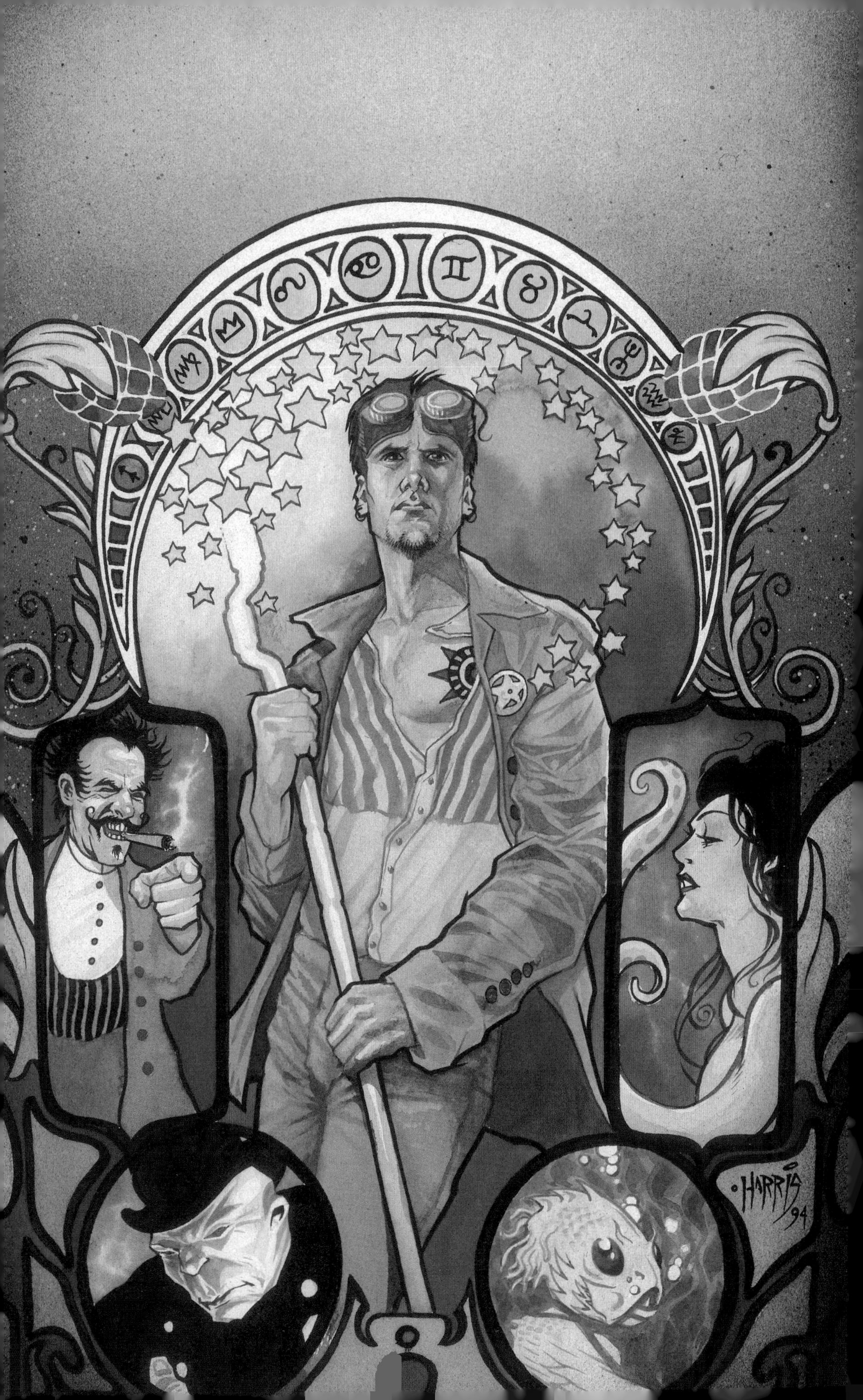
HARRIS
94

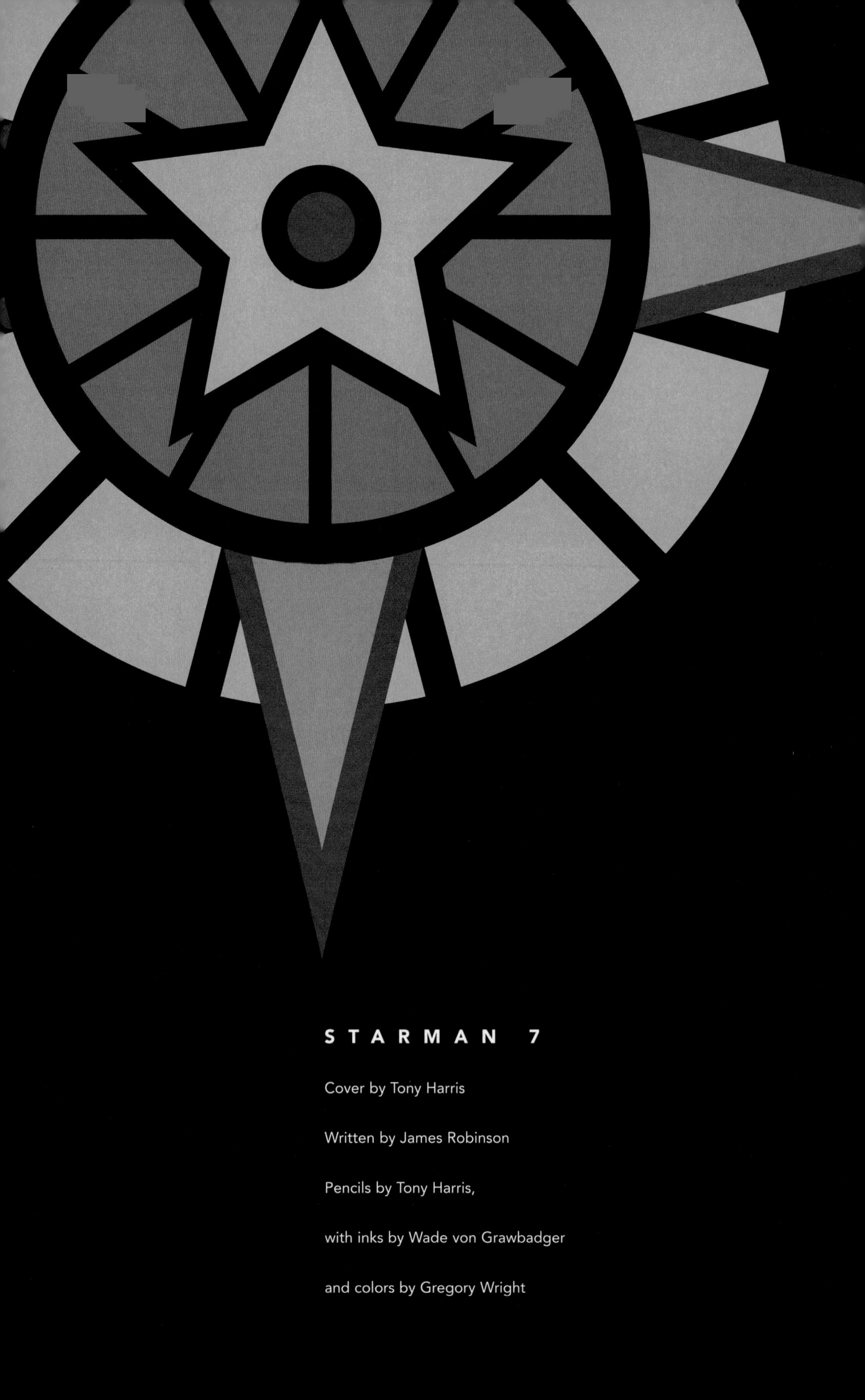

S T A R M A N 7

Cover by Tony Harris

Written by James Robinson

Pencils by Tony Harris,

with inks by Wade von Grawbadger

and colors by Gregory Wright

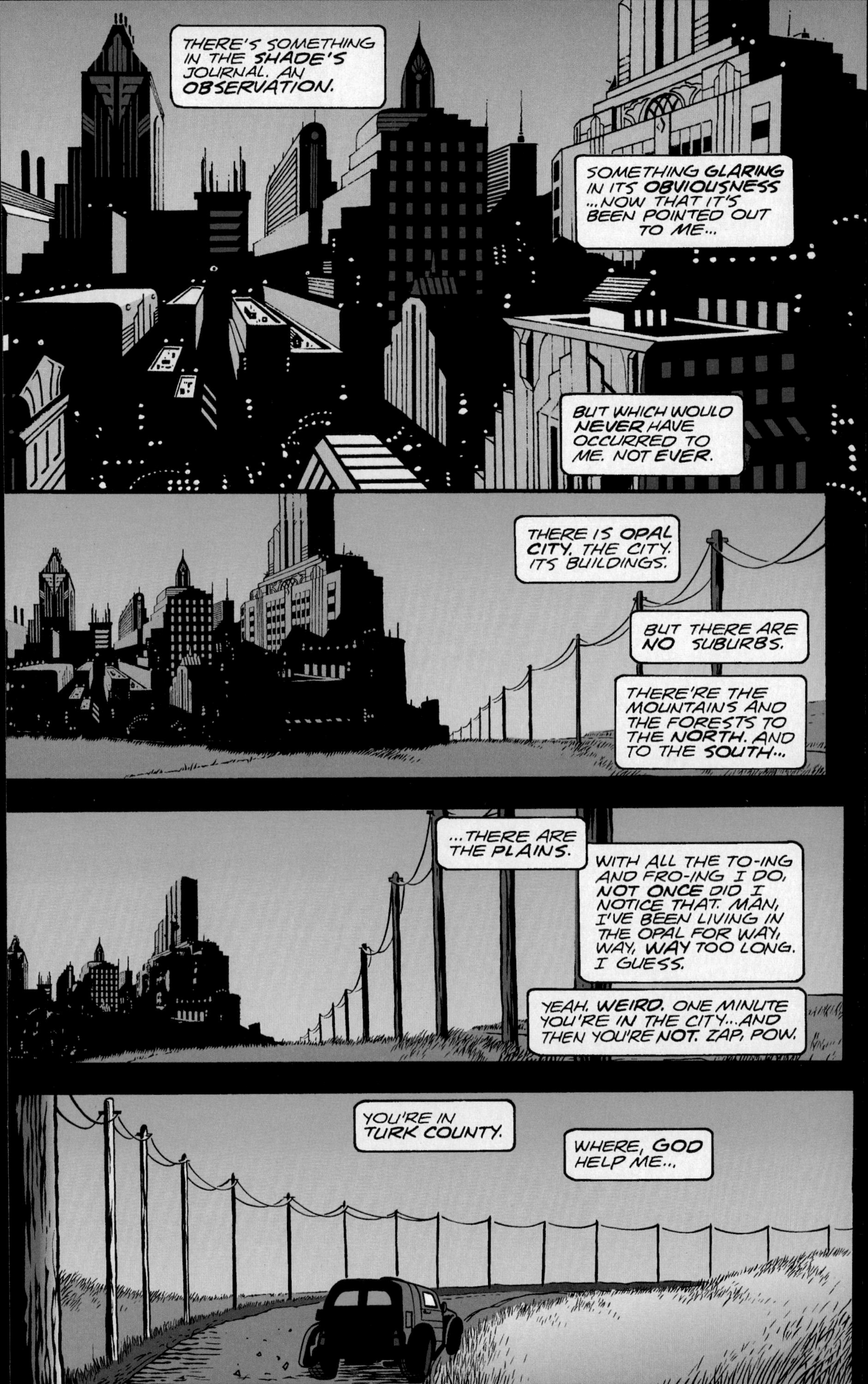
THERE'S SOMETHING IN THE SHADE'S JOURNAL. AN OBSERVATION.
SOMETHING GLARING IN ITS OBVIOUSNESS ...NOW THAT IT'S BEEN POINTED OUT TO ME...
BUT WHICH WOULD NEVER HAVE OCCURRED TO ME. NOT EVER.
THERE IS OPAL CITY. THE CITY. ITS BUILDINGS.
BUT THERE ARE NO SUBURBS.
THERE'RE THE MOUNTAINS AND THE FORESTS TO THE NORTH. AND TO THE SOUTH...
...THERE ARE THE PLAINS.
WITH ALL THE TO-ING AND FRO-ING I DO, NOT ONCE DID I NOTICE THAT. MAN, I'VE BEEN LIVING IN THE OPAL FOR WAY, WAY, WAY TOO LONG. I GUESS.
YEAH. WEIRD. ONE MINUTE YOU'RE IN THE CITY...AND THEN YOU'RE NOT. ZAP, POW.
YOU'RE IN TURK COUNTY.
WHERE, GOD HELP ME...

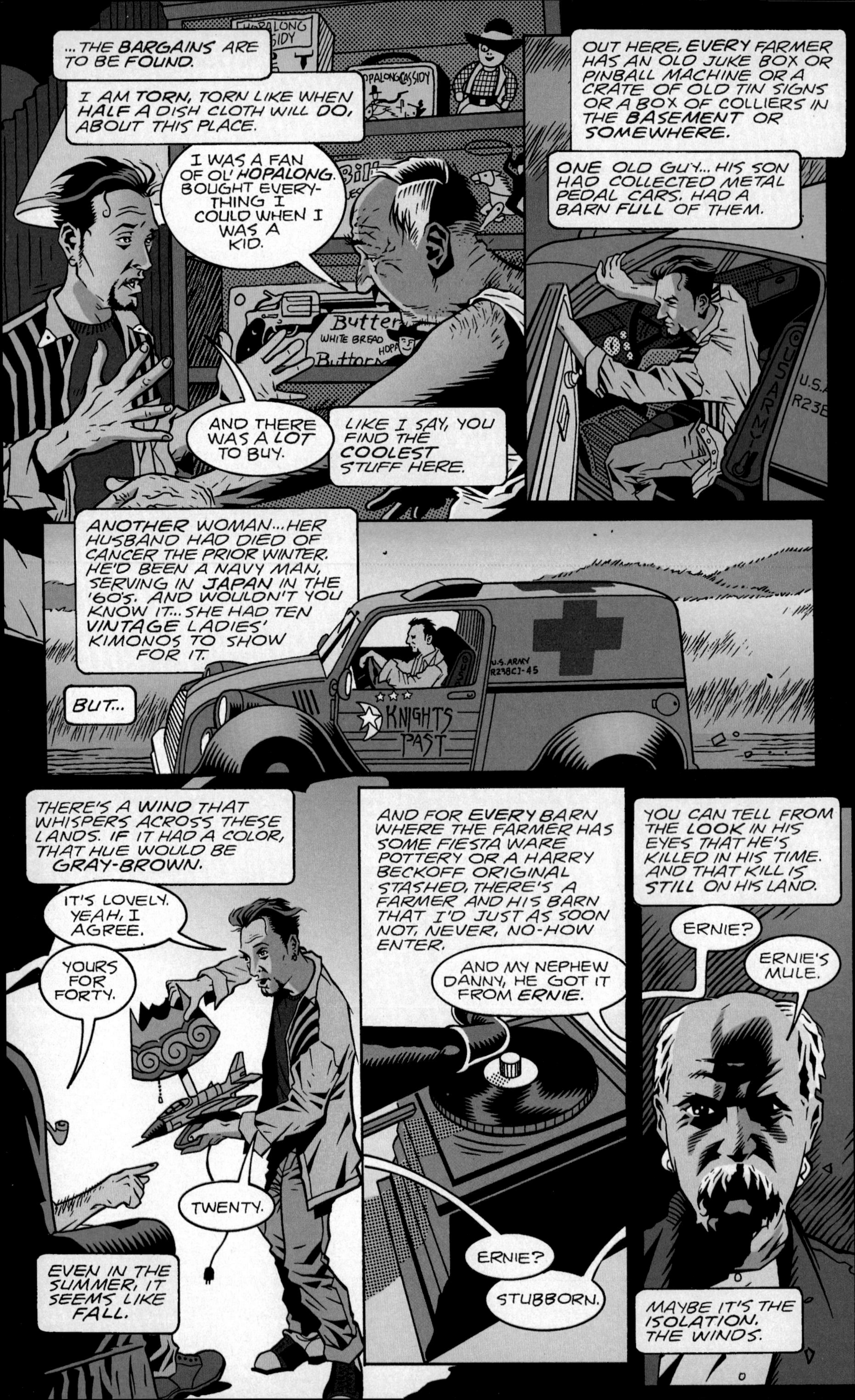

...THE BARGAINS ARE TO BE FOUND.
I AM TORN, TORN LIKE WHEN HALF A DISH CLOTH WILL DO, ABOUT THIS PLACE.
HOPALONG CASSIDY
I WAS A FAN OF OL' HOPALONG. BOUGHT EVERYTHING I COULD WHEN I WAS A KID.
Butter
WHITE BREAD
AND THERE WAS A LOT TO BUY.
LIKE I SAY, YOU FIND THE COOLEST STUFF HERE.
OUT HERE, EVERY FARMER HAS AN OLD JUKE BOX OR PINBALL MACHINE OR A CRATE OF OLD TIN SIGNS OR A BOX OF COLLIERS IN THE BASEMENT OR SOMEWHERE.
ONE OLD GUY... HIS SON HAD COLLECTED METAL PEDAL CARS. HAD A BARN FULL OF THEM.
U.S. ARMY
ANOTHER WOMAN...HER HUSBAND HAD DIED OF CANCER THE PRIOR WINTER. HE'D BEEN A NAVY MAN, SERVING IN JAPAN IN THE '60'S. AND WOULDN'T YOU KNOW IT...SHE HAD TEN VINTAGE LADIES' KIMONOS TO SHOW FOR IT.
BUT...
U.S. ARMY
R238CJ-45
KNIGHT'S PAST
THERE'S A WIND THAT WHISPERS ACROSS THESE LANDS. IF IT HAD A COLOR, THAT HUE WOULD BE GRAY-BROWN.
IT'S LOVELY. YEAH, I AGREE.
YOURS FOR FORTY.
TWENTY.
EVEN IN THE SUMMER, IT SEEMS LIKE FALL.
AND FOR EVERY BARN WHERE THE FARMER HAS SOME FIESTA WARE POTTERY OR A HARRY BECKOFF ORIGINAL STASHED, THERE'S A FARMER AND HIS BARN THAT I'D JUST AS SOON NOT, NEVER, NO-HOW ENTER.
AND MY NEPHEW DANNY, HE GOT IT FROM ERNIE.
ERNIE?
STUBBORN.
YOU CAN TELL FROM THE LOOK IN HIS EYES THAT HE'S KILLED IN HIS TIME. AND THAT KILL IS STILL ON HIS LAND.
ERNIE?
ERNIE'S MULE.
MAYBE IT'S THE ISOLATION. THE WINDS.

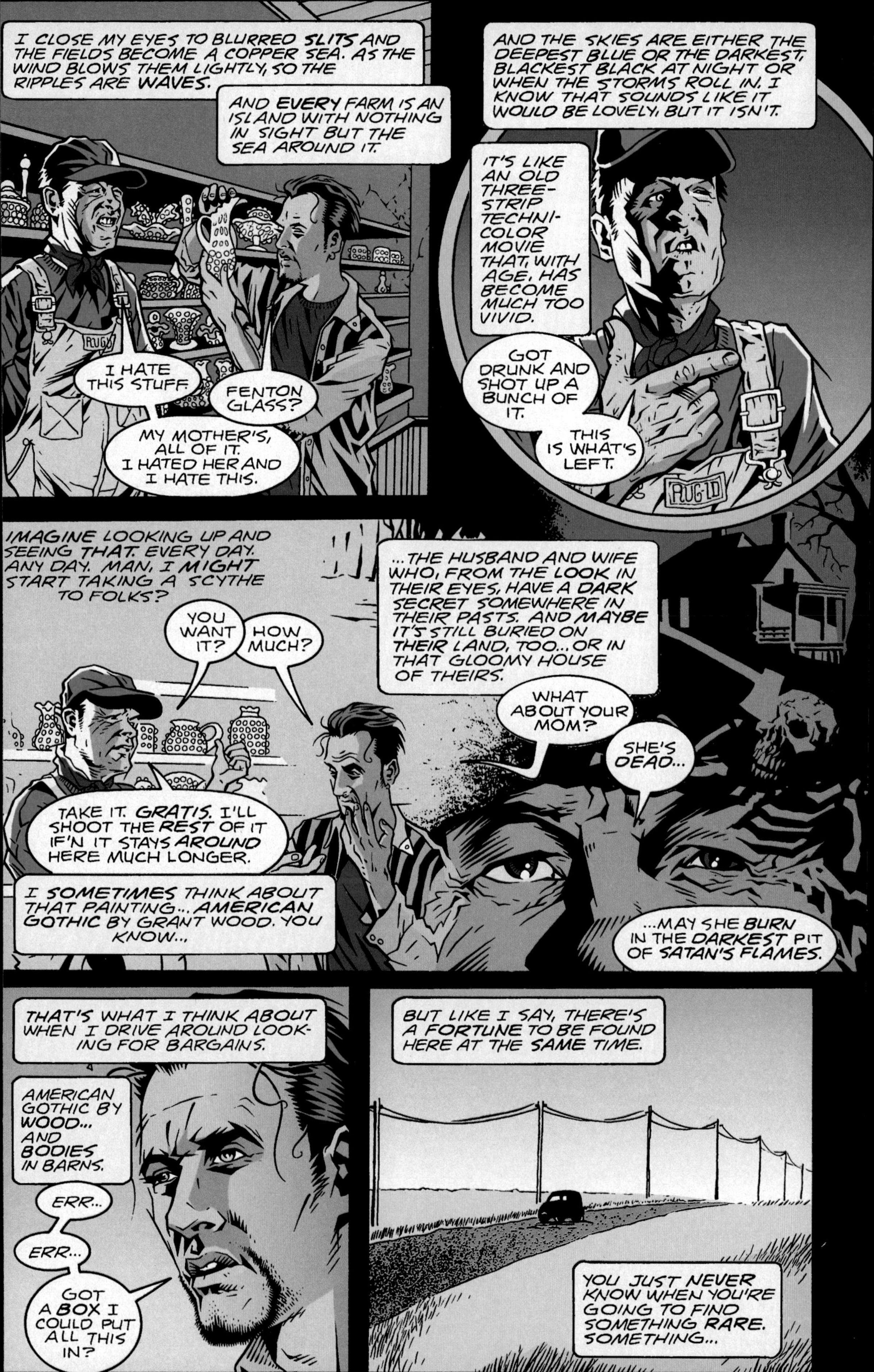
I CLOSE MY EYES TO BLURRED SLITS AND THE FIELDS BECOME A COPPER SEA. AS THE WIND BLOWS THEM LIGHTLY, SO THE RIPPLES ARE WAVES.
AND EVERY FARM IS AN ISLAND WITH NOTHING IN SIGHT BUT THE SEA AROUND IT.
I HATE THIS STUFF.
FENTON GLASS?
MY MOTHER'S, ALL OF IT. I HATED HER AND I HATE THIS.
AND THE SKIES ARE EITHER THE DEEPEST BLUE OR THE DARKEST, BLACKEST BLACK AT NIGHT OR WHEN THE STORMS ROLL IN. I KNOW THAT SOUNDS LIKE IT WOULD BE LOVELY, BUT IT ISN'T.
IT'S LIKE AN OLD THREE-STRIP TECHNI-COLOR MOVIE THAT, WITH AGE, HAS BECOME MUCH TOO VIVID.
GOT DRUNK AND SHOT UP A BUNCH OF IT.
THIS IS WHAT'S LEFT.
IMAGINE LOOKING UP AND SEEING THAT. EVERY DAY. ANY DAY. MAN, I MIGHT START TAKING A SCYTHE TO FOLKS?
YOU WANT IT?
HOW MUCH?
TAKE IT. GRATIS. I'LL SHOOT THE REST OF IT IF'N IT STAYS AROUND HERE MUCH LONGER.
I SOMETIMES THINK ABOUT THAT PAINTING... AMERICAN GOTHIC BY GRANT WOOD. YOU KNOW...,
...THE HUSBAND AND WIFE WHO, FROM THE LOOK IN THEIR EYES, HAVE A DARK SECRET SOMEWHERE IN THEIR PASTS. AND MAYBE IT'S STILL BURIED ON THEIR LAND, TOO... OR IN THAT GLOOMY HOUSE OF THEIRS.
WHAT ABOUT YOUR MOM?
SHE'S DEAD...
...MAY SHE BURN IN THE DARKEST PIT OF SATAN'S FLAMES.
THAT'S WHAT I THINK ABOUT WHEN I DRIVE AROUND LOOK-ING FOR BARGAINS.
AMERICAN GOTHIC BY WOOD... AND BODIES IN BARNS.
ERR...
ERR...
GOT A BOX I COULD PUT ALL THIS IN?
BUT LIKE I SAY, THERE'S A FORTUNE TO BE FOUND HERE AT THE SAME TIME.
YOU JUST NEVER KNOW WHEN YOU'RE GOING TO FIND SOMETHING RARE. SOMETHING...

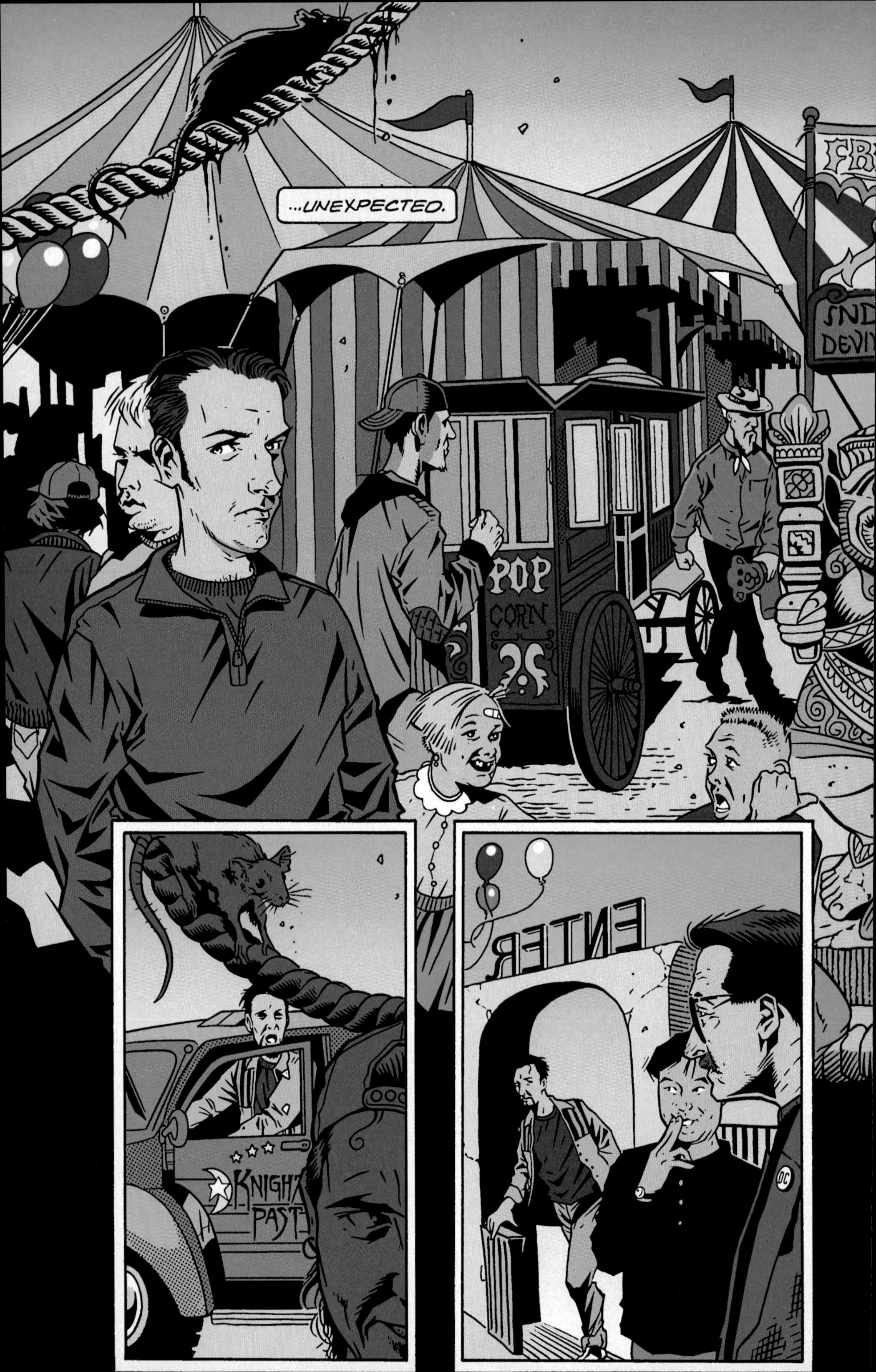
...UNEXPECTED.
POP CORN
ENTER

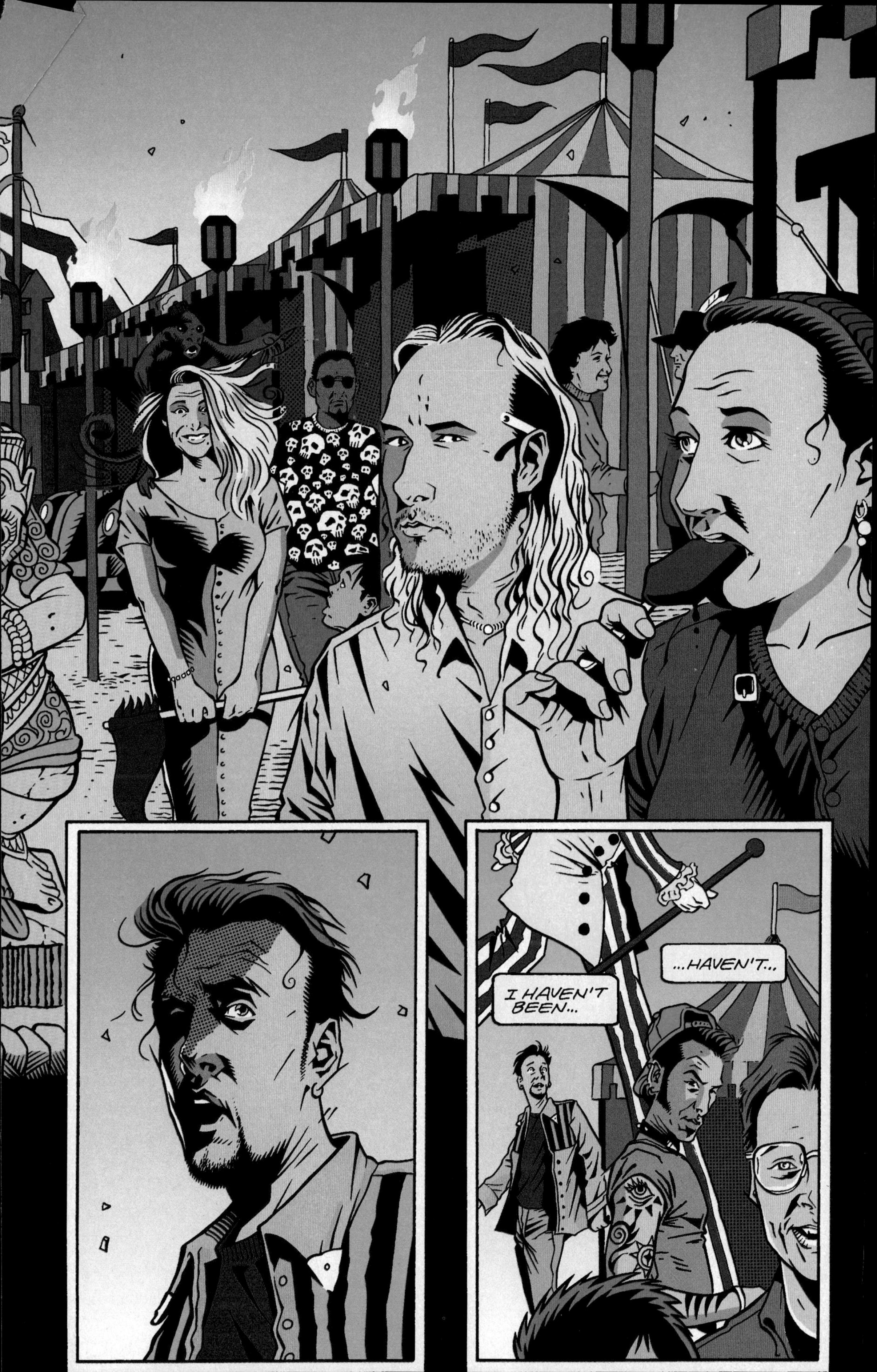
I HAVEN'T BEEN...
...HAVEN'T...

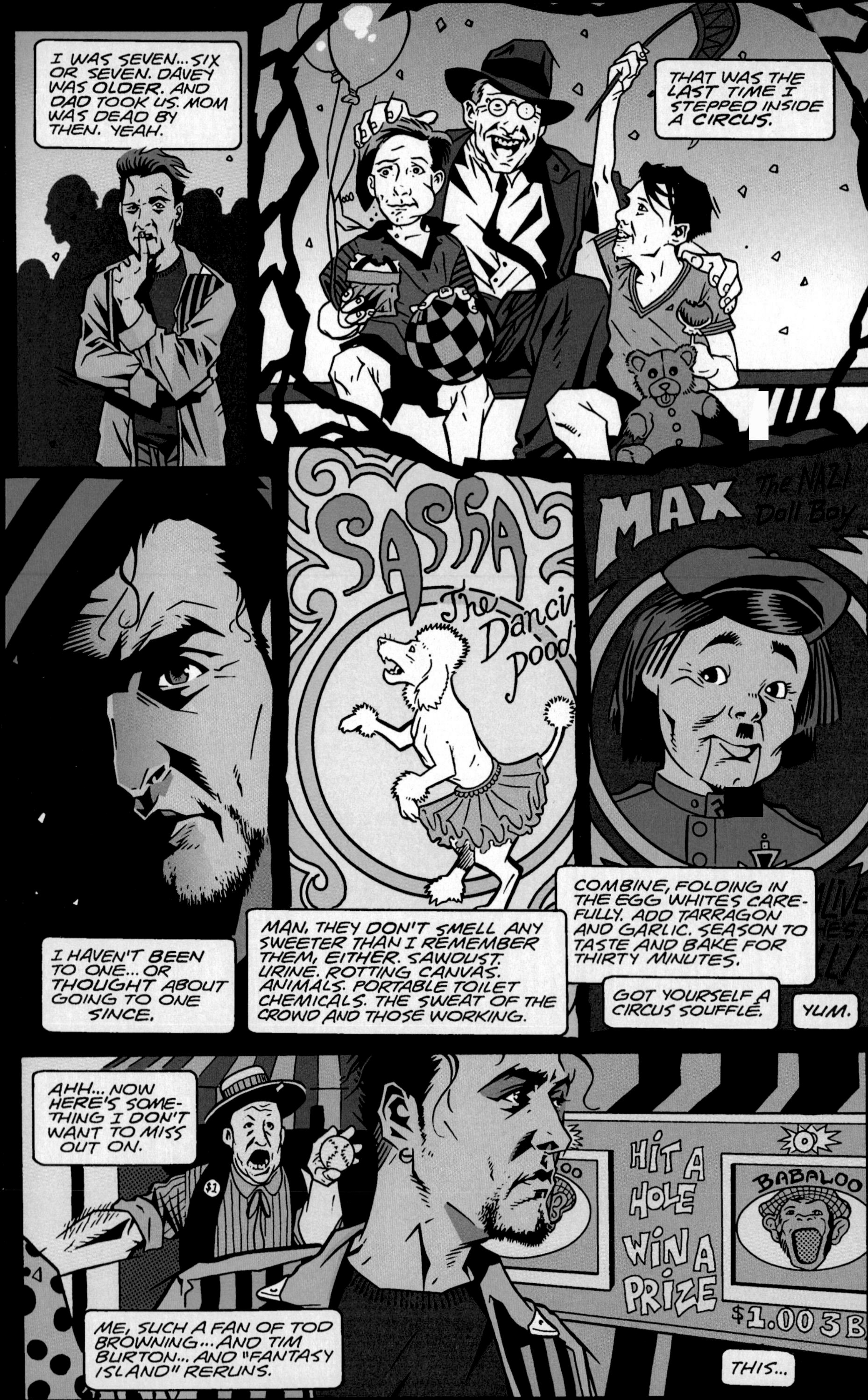
I WAS SEVEN...SIX OR SEVEN. DAVEY WAS OLDER. AND DAD TOOK US. MOM WAS DEAD BY THEN. YEAH.
THAT WAS THE LAST TIME I STEPPED INSIDE A CIRCUS.
SASHA
The
MAX
The NAZI Doll Boy
I HAVEN'T BEEN TO ONE...OR THOUGHT ABOUT GOING TO ONE SINCE.
MAN, THEY DON'T SMELL ANY SWEETER THAN I REMEMBER THEM, EITHER. SAWDUST. URINE. ROTTING CANVAS. ANIMALS. PORTABLE TOILET CHEMICALS. THE SWEAT OF THE CROWD AND THOSE WORKING.
COMBINE, FOLDING IN THE EGG WHITES CAREFULLY. ADD TARRAGON AND GARLIC. SEASON TO TASTE AND BAKE FOR THIRTY MINUTES.
GOT YOURSELF A CIRCUS SOUFFLÉ.
YUM.
AHH... NOW HERE'S SOMETHING I DON'T WANT TO MISS OUT ON.
$1
HIT A HOLE WIN A PRIZE
BABALOO
ME, SUCH A FAN OF TOD BROWNING... AND TIM BURTON... AND "FANTASY ISLAND" RERUNS.
THIS...

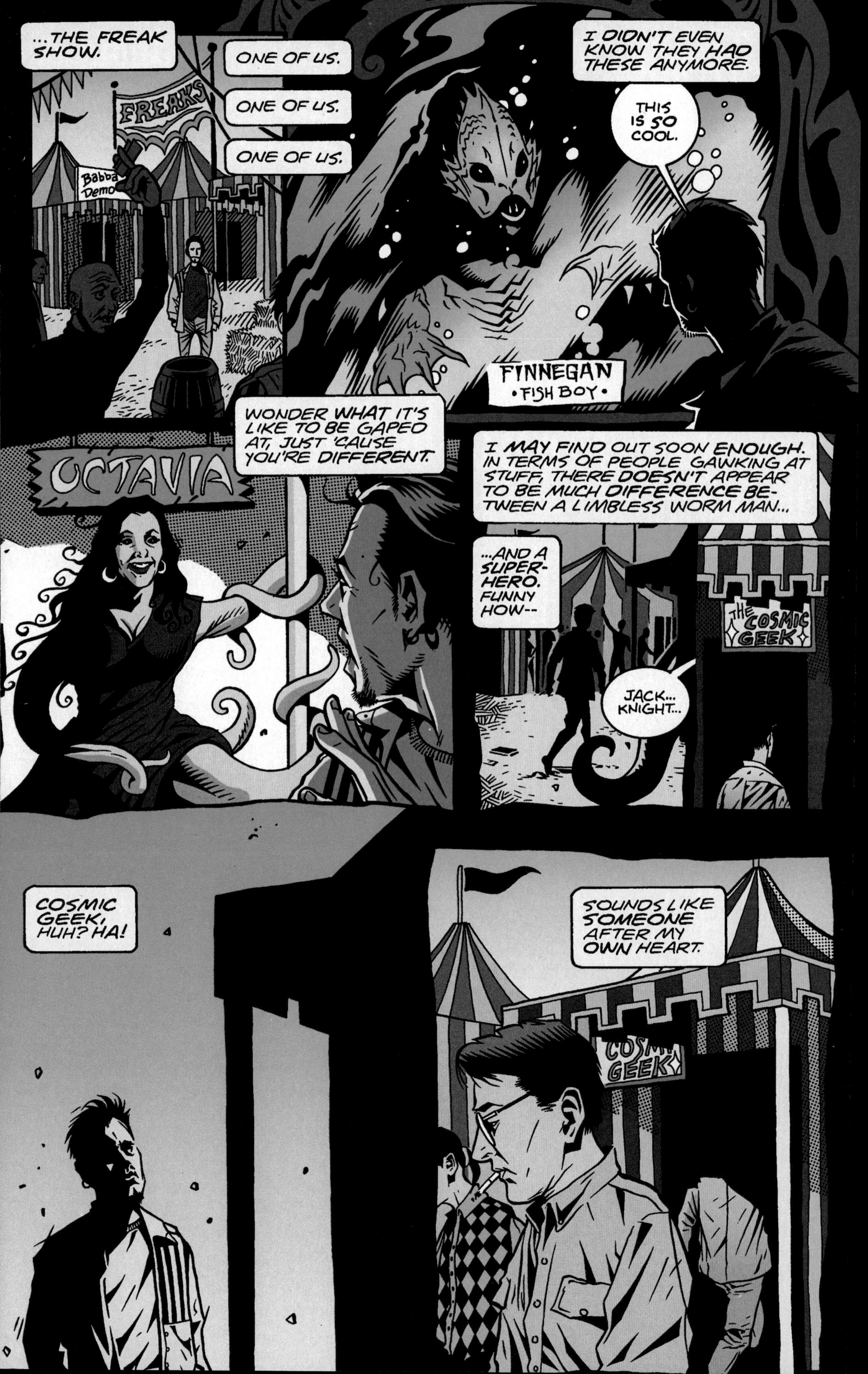
...THE FREAK SHOW.
ONE OF US.
ONE OF US.
ONE OF US.
FREAKS
I DIDN'T EVEN KNOW THEY HAD THESE ANYMORE.
THIS IS SO COOL.
FINNEGAN •FISH BOY•
OCTAVIA
WONDER WHAT IT'S LIKE TO BE GAPED AT, JUST 'CAUSE YOU'RE DIFFERENT.
I MAY FIND OUT SOON ENOUGH. IN TERMS OF PEOPLE GAWKING AT STUFF, THERE DOESN'T APPEAR TO BE MUCH DIFFERENCE BETWEEN A LIMBLESS WORM MAN...
...AND A SUPER-HERO. FUNNY HOW--
THE COSMIC GEEK
JACK... KNIGHT...
COSMIC GEEK, HUH? HA!
SOUNDS LIKE SOMEONE AFTER MY OWN HEART.

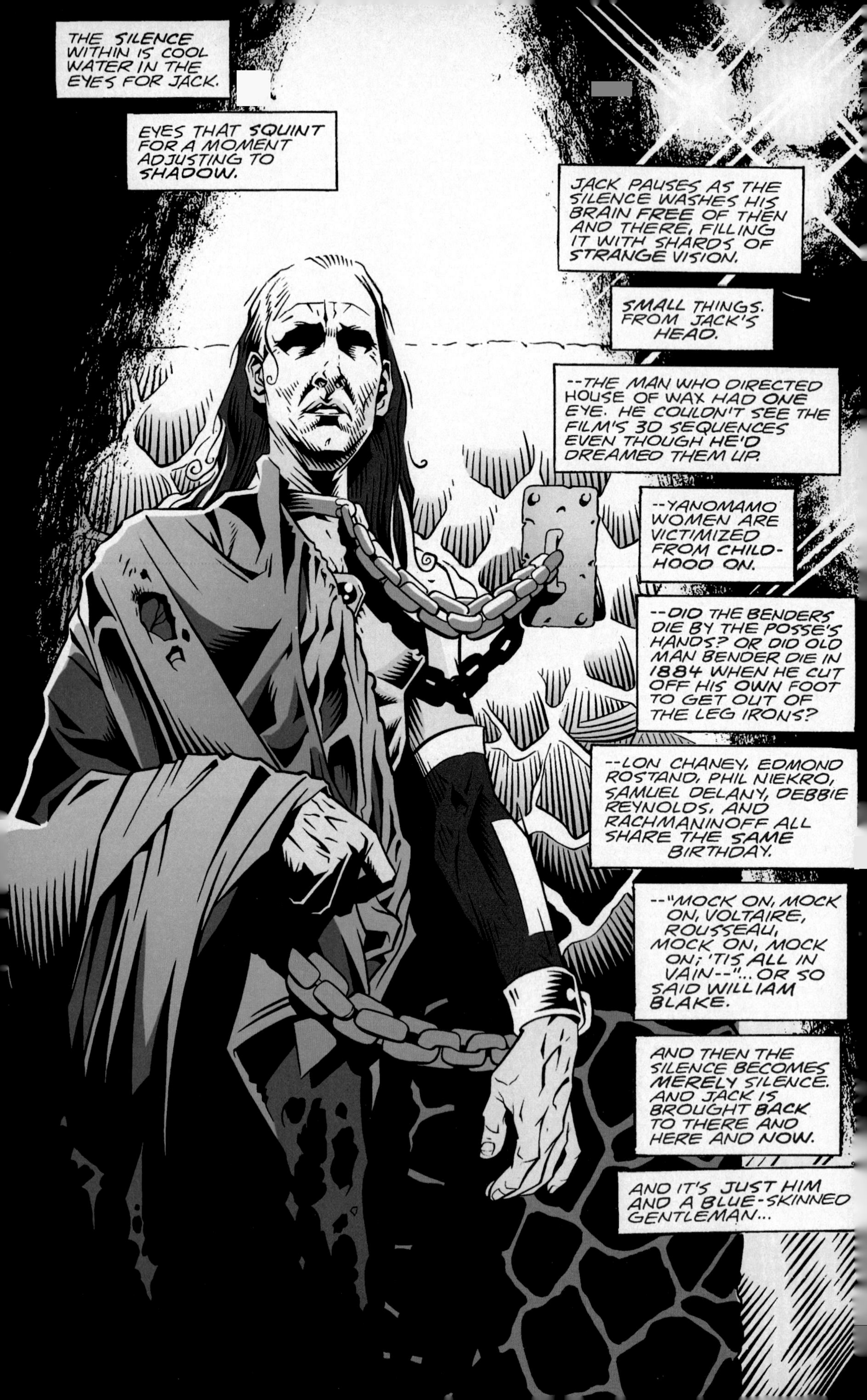
THE SILENCE WITHIN IS COOL WATER IN THE EYES FOR JACK.
EYES THAT SQUINT FOR A MOMENT ADJUSTING TO SHADOW.
JACK PAUSES AS THE SILENCE WASHES HIS BRAIN FREE OF THEN AND THERE, FILLING IT WITH SHARDS OF STRANGE VISION.
SMALL THINGS. FROM JACK'S HEAD.
--THE MAN WHO DIRECTED HOUSE OF WAX HAD ONE EYE. HE COULDN'T SEE THE FILM'S 3D SEQUENCES EVEN THOUGH HE'D DREAMED THEM UP.
--YANOMAMO WOMEN ARE VICTIMIZED FROM CHILD-HOOD ON.
--DID THE BENDERS DIE BY THE POSSE'S HANDS? OR DID OLD MAN BENDER DIE IN 1884 WHEN HE CUT OFF HIS OWN FOOT TO GET OUT OF THE LEG IRONS?
--LON CHANEY, EDMOND ROSTAND, PHIL NIEKRO, SAMUEL DELANY, DEBBIE REYNOLDS, AND RACHMANINOFF ALL SHARE THE SAME BIRTHDAY.
--"MOCK ON, MOCK ON, VOLTAIRE, ROUSSEAU, MOCK ON, MOCK ON; 'TIS ALL IN VAIN--"...OR SO SAID WILLIAM BLAKE.
AND THEN THE SILENCE BECOMES MERELY SILENCE. AND JACK IS BROUGHT BACK TO THERE AND HERE AND NOW.
AND IT'S JUST HIM AND A BLUE-SKINNED GENTLEMAN...

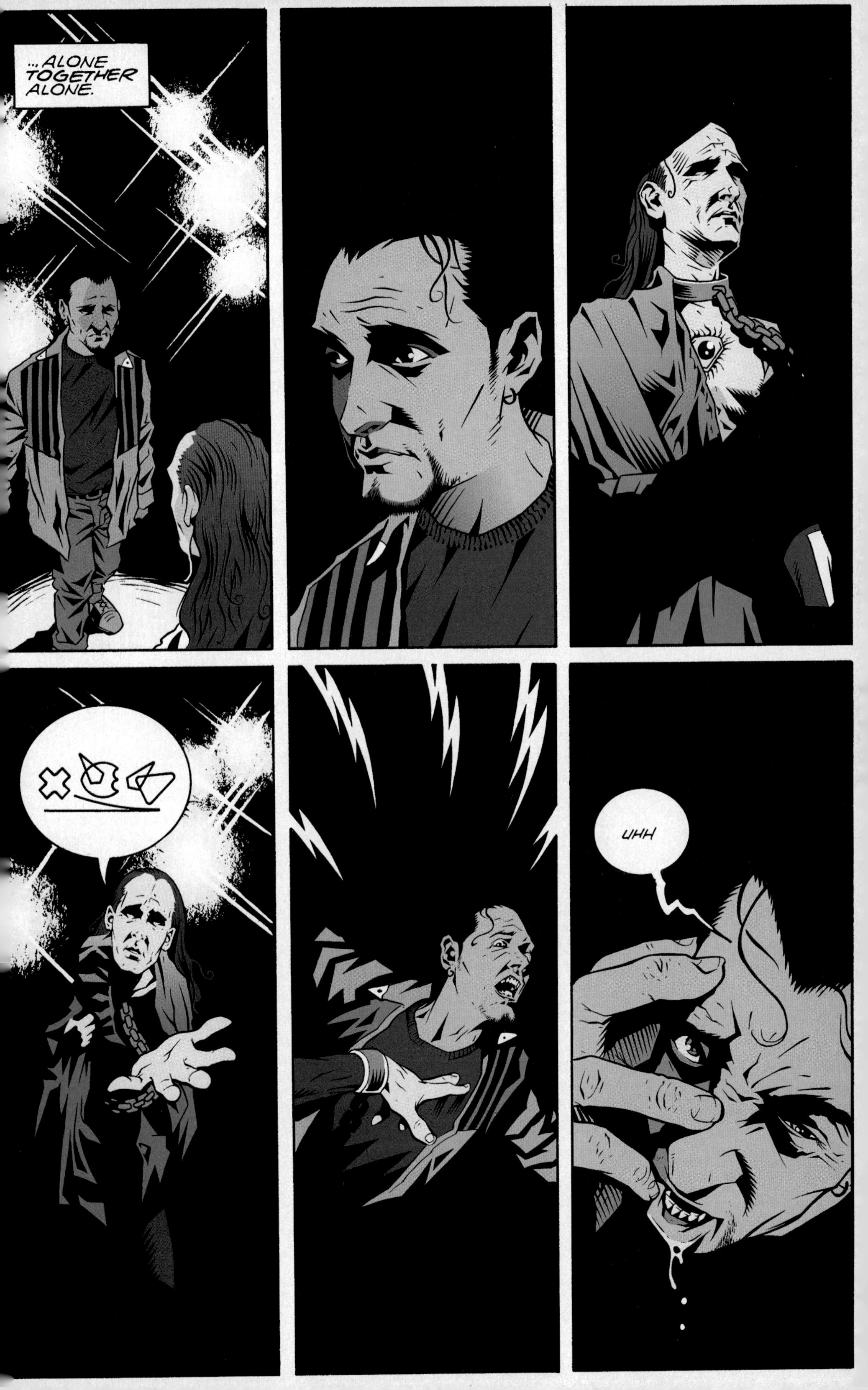
...ALONE TOGETHER ALONE.
UHH

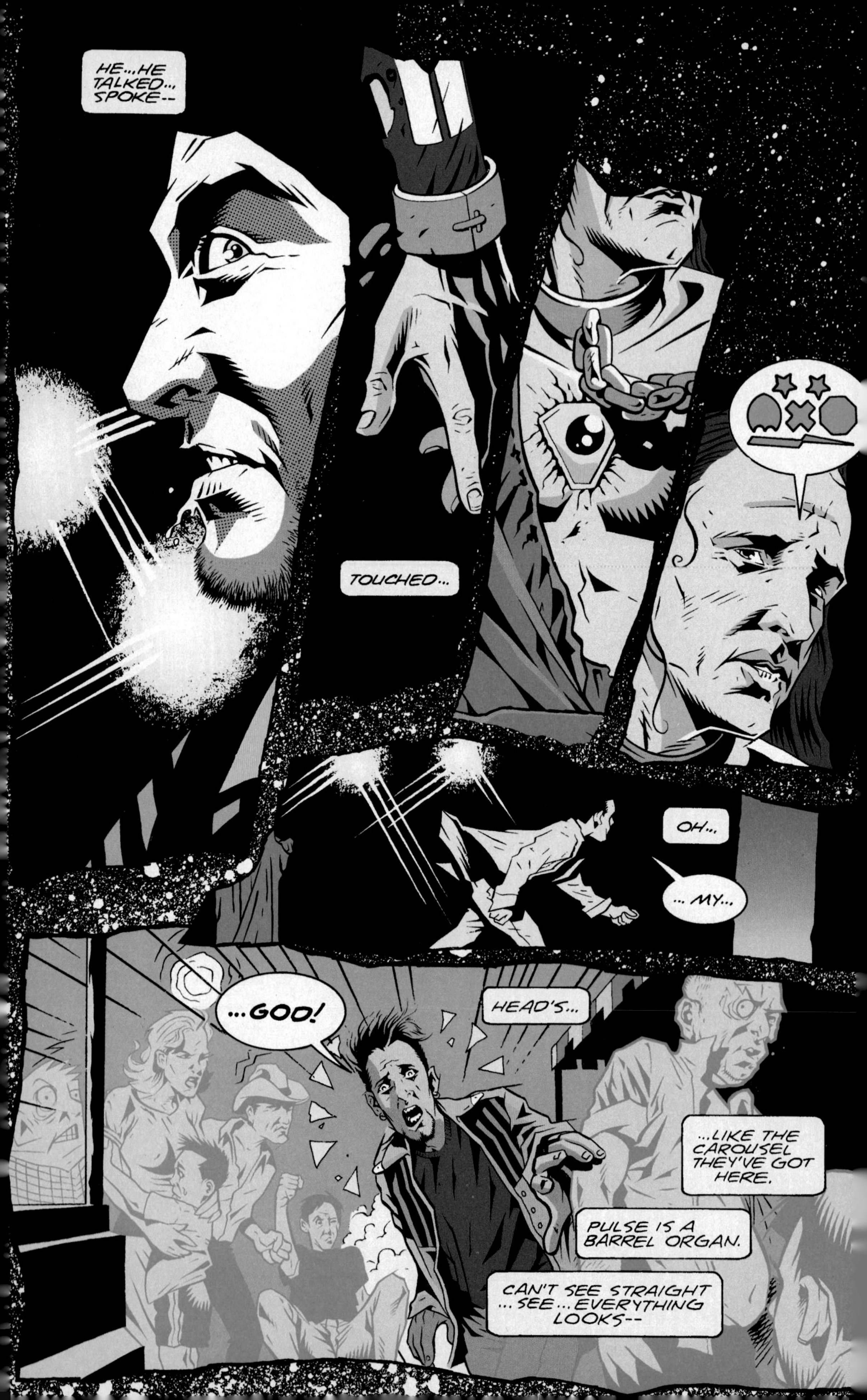

HE...HE TALKED... SPOKE--
TOUCHED...
OH...
... MY...
...GOD!
HEAD'S...
...LIKE THE CAROUSEL THEY'VE GOT HERE.
PULSE IS A BARREL ORGAN.
CAN'T SEE STRAIGHT ... SEE... EVERYTHING LOOKS--

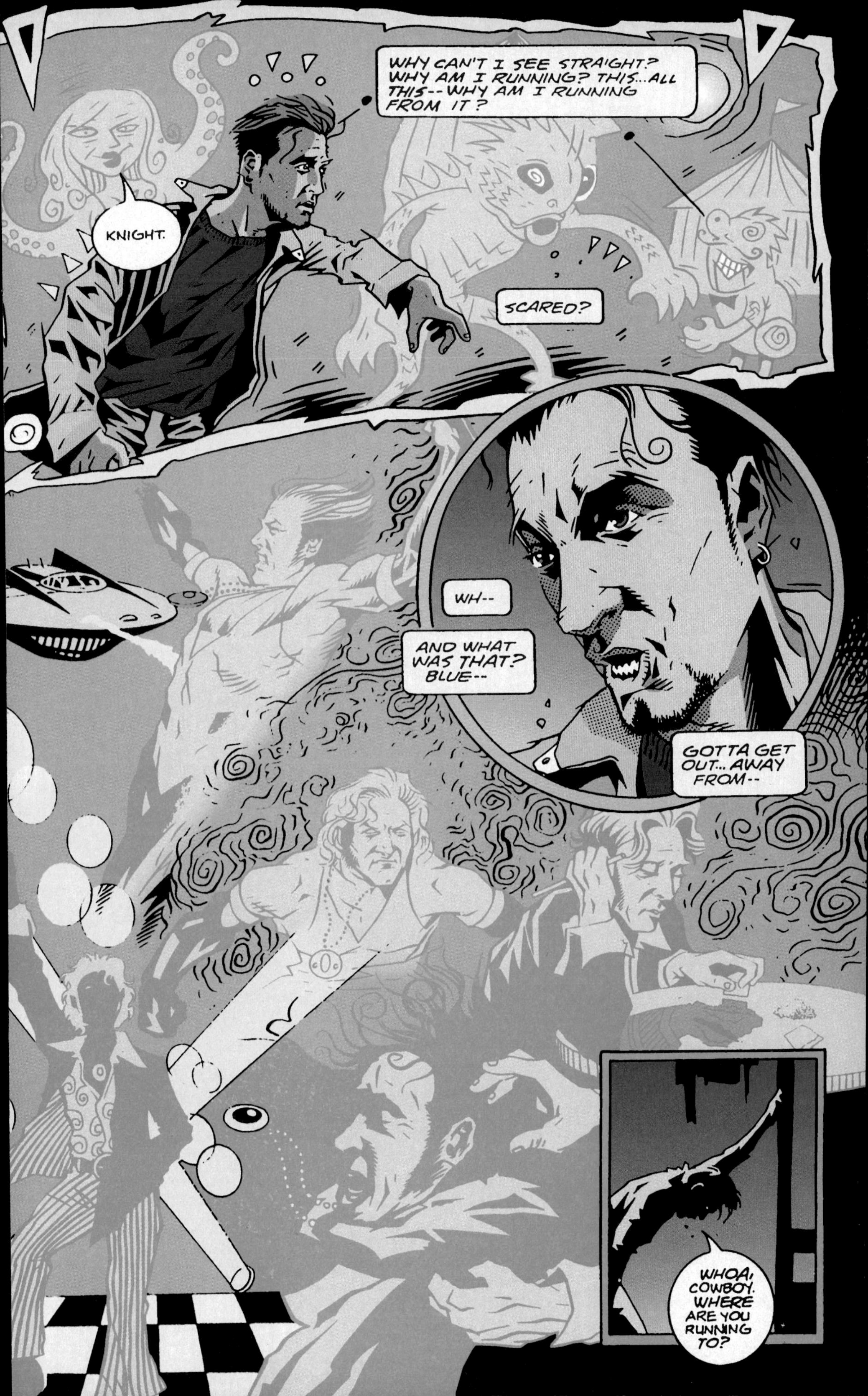
WHY CAN'T I SEE STRAIGHT? WHY AM I RUNNING? THIS...ALL THIS-- WHY AM I RUNNING FROM IT?
KNIGHT.
SCARED?
WH--
AND WHAT WAS THAT? BLUE--
GOTTA GET OUT... AWAY FROM--
WHOA, COWBOY. WHERE ARE YOU RUNNING TO?

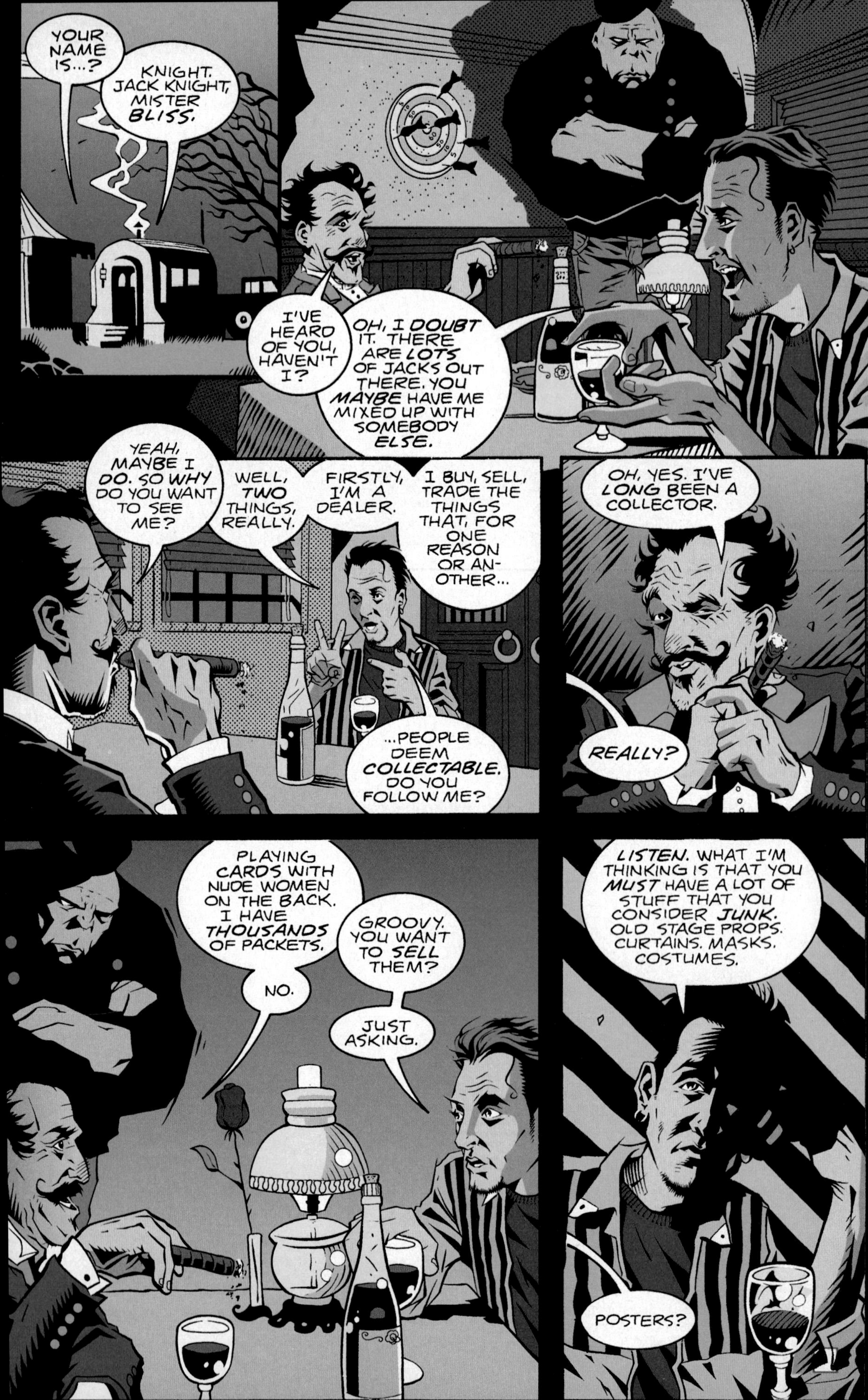
YOUR NAME IS...?
KNIGHT. JACK KNIGHT, MISTER BLISS.
I'VE HEARD OF YOU, HAVEN'T I?
OH, I DOUBT IT. THERE ARE LOTS OF JACKS OUT THERE. YOU MAYBE HAVE ME MIXED UP WITH SOMEBODY ELSE.
YEAH, MAYBE I DO. SO WHY DO YOU WANT TO SEE ME?
WELL, TWO THINGS, REALLY.
FIRSTLY, I'M A DEALER.
I BUY, SELL, TRADE THE THINGS THAT, FOR ONE REASON OR AN-OTHER...
...PEOPLE DEEM COLLECTABLE. DO YOU FOLLOW ME?
OH, YES. I'VE LONG BEEN A COLLECTOR.
REALLY?
PLAYING CARDS WITH NUDE WOMEN ON THE BACK. I HAVE THOUSANDS OF PACKETS.
GROOVY. YOU WANT TO SELL THEM?
NO.
JUST ASKING.
LISTEN. WHAT I'M THINKING IS THAT YOU MUST HAVE A LOT OF STUFF THAT YOU CONSIDER JUNK. OLD STAGE PROPS. CURTAINS. MASKS. COSTUMES.
POSTERS?

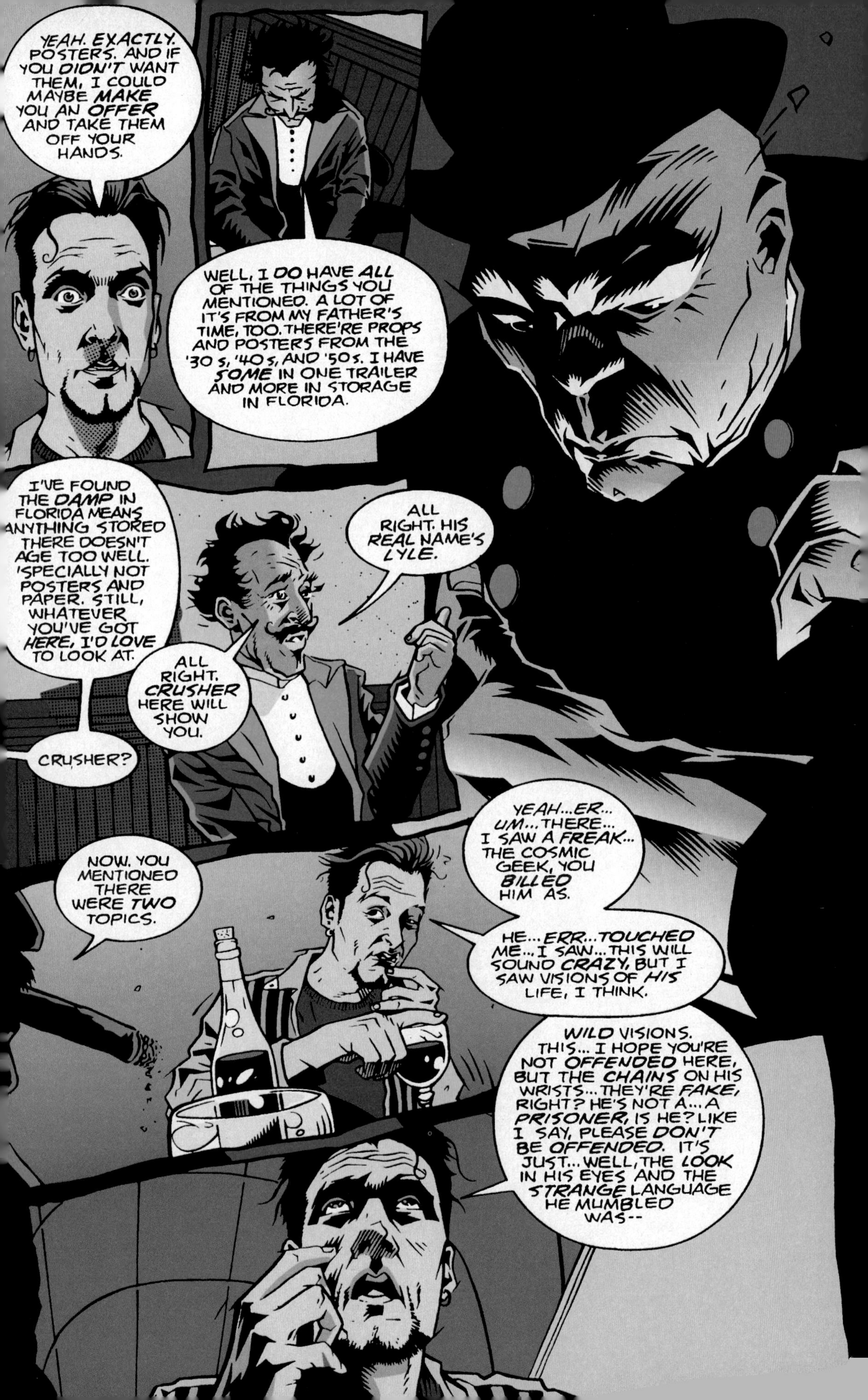
YEAH. EXACTLY. POSTERS. AND IF YOU DIDN'T WANT THEM, I COULD MAYBE MAKE YOU AN OFFER AND TAKE THEM OFF YOUR HANDS.
WELL, I DO HAVE ALL OF THE THINGS YOU MENTIONED. A LOT OF IT'S FROM MY FATHER'S TIME, TOO. THERE'RE PROPS AND POSTERS FROM THE '30s, '40s, AND '50s. I HAVE SOME IN ONE TRAILER AND MORE IN STORAGE IN FLORIDA.
I'VE FOUND THE DAMP IN FLORIDA MEANS ANYTHING STORED THERE DOESN'T AGE TOO WELL. 'SPECIALLY NOT POSTERS AND PAPER. STILL, WHATEVER YOU'VE GOT HERE, I'D LOVE TO LOOK AT.
ALL RIGHT. CRUSHER HERE WILL SHOW YOU.
CRUSHER?
ALL RIGHT. HIS REAL NAME'S LYLE.
NOW. YOU MENTIONED THERE WERE TWO TOPICS.
YEAH...ER... UM...THERE... I SAW A FREAK... THE COSMIC GEEK, YOU BILLED HIM AS.
HE...ERR...TOUCHED ME...I SAW...THIS WILL SOUND CRAZY, BUT I SAW VISIONS OF HIS LIFE, I THINK.
WILD VISIONS. THIS... I HOPE YOU'RE NOT OFFENDED HERE, BUT THE CHAINS ON HIS WRISTS...THEY'RE FAKE, RIGHT? HE'S NOT A...A PRISONER, IS HE? LIKE I SAY, PLEASE DON'T BE OFFENDED. IT'S JUST...WELL, THE LOOK IN HIS EYES AND THE STRANGE LANGUAGE HE MUMBLED WAS--

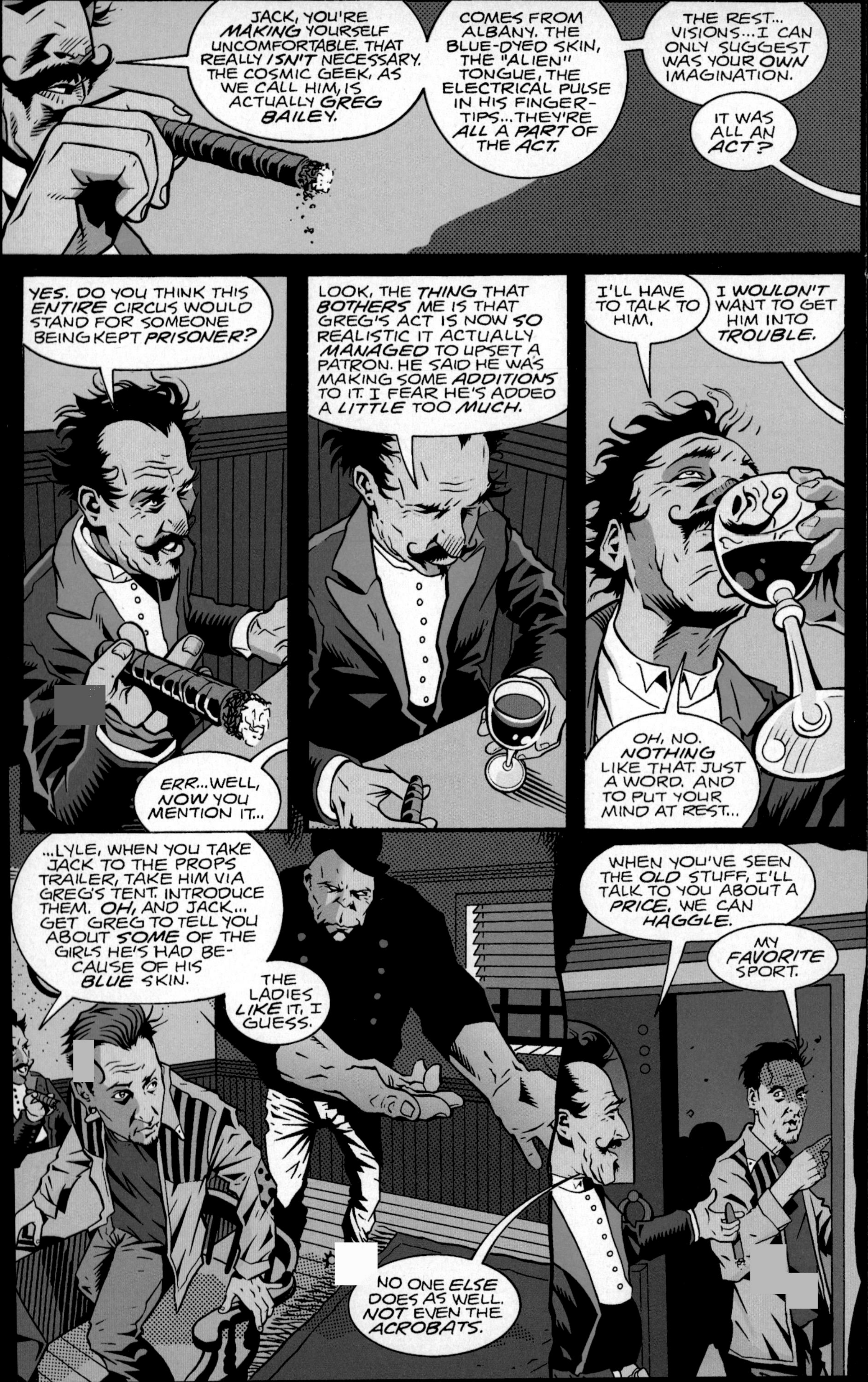

JACK, YOU'RE MAKING YOURSELF UNCOMFORTABLE. THAT REALLY ISN'T NECESSARY. THE COSMIC GEEK, AS WE CALL HIM, IS ACTUALLY GREG BAILEY.
COMES FROM ALBANY. THE BLUE-DYED SKIN, THE "ALIEN" TONGUE, THE ELECTRICAL PULSE IN HIS FINGER-TIPS... THEY'RE ALL A PART OF THE ACT.
THE REST... VISIONS... I CAN ONLY SUGGEST WAS YOUR OWN IMAGINATION.
IT WAS ALL AN ACT?
YES. DO YOU THINK THIS ENTIRE CIRCUS WOULD STAND FOR SOMEONE BEING KEPT PRISONER?
ERR... WELL, NOW YOU MENTION IT...
LOOK, THE THING THAT BOTHERS ME IS THAT GREG'S ACT IS NOW SO REALISTIC IT ACTUALLY MANAGED TO UPSET A PATRON. HE SAID HE WAS MAKING SOME ADDITIONS TO IT. I FEAR HE'S ADDED A LITTLE TOO MUCH.
I'LL HAVE TO TALK TO HIM.
I WOULDN'T WANT TO GET HIM INTO TROUBLE.
OH, NO. NOTHING LIKE THAT. JUST A WORD. AND TO PUT YOUR MIND AT REST...
...LYLE, WHEN YOU TAKE JACK TO THE PROPS TRAILER, TAKE HIM VIA GREG'S TENT. INTRODUCE THEM. OH, AND JACK... GET GREG TO TELL YOU ABOUT SOME OF THE GIRLS HE'S HAD BE-CAUSE OF HIS BLUE SKIN.
THE LADIES LIKE IT, I GUESS.
NO ONE ELSE DOES AS WELL. NOT EVEN THE ACROBATS.
WHEN YOU'VE SEEN THE OLD STUFF, I'LL TALK TO YOU ABOUT A PRICE. WE CAN HAGGLE.
MY FAVORITE SPORT.

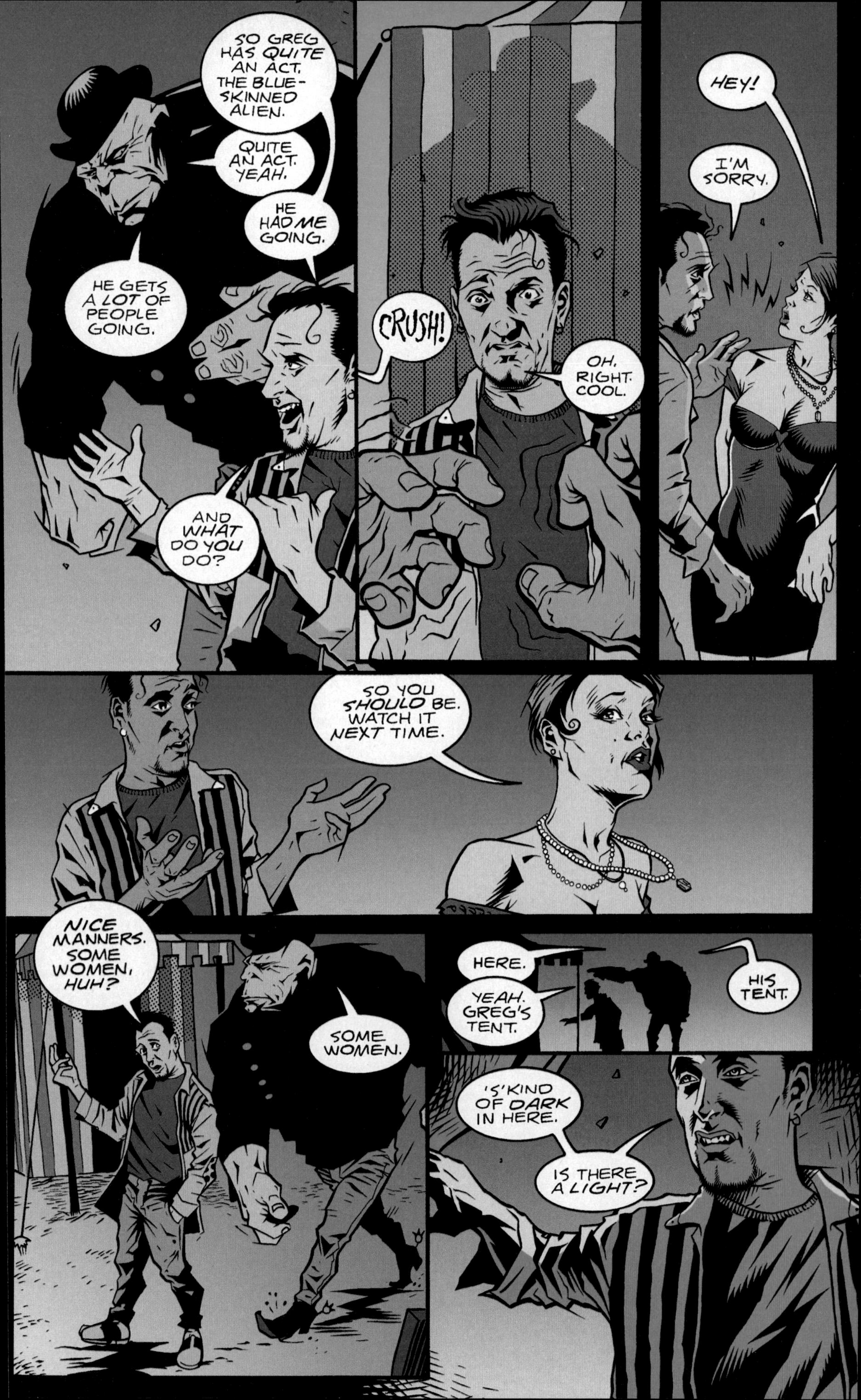
SO GREG HAS QUITE AN ACT. THE BLUE-SKINNED ALIEN.
QUITE AN ACT. YEAH.
HE HAD ME GOING.
HE GETS A LOT OF PEOPLE GOING.
AND WHAT DO YOU DO?
CRUSH!
OH. RIGHT. COOL.
HEY!
I'M SORRY.
SO YOU SHOULD BE. WATCH IT NEXT TIME.
NICE MANNERS. SOME WOMEN, HUH?
SOME WOMEN.
HERE.
YEAH. GREG'S TENT.
HIS TENT.
'S'KIND OF DARK IN HERE.
IS THERE A LIGHT?

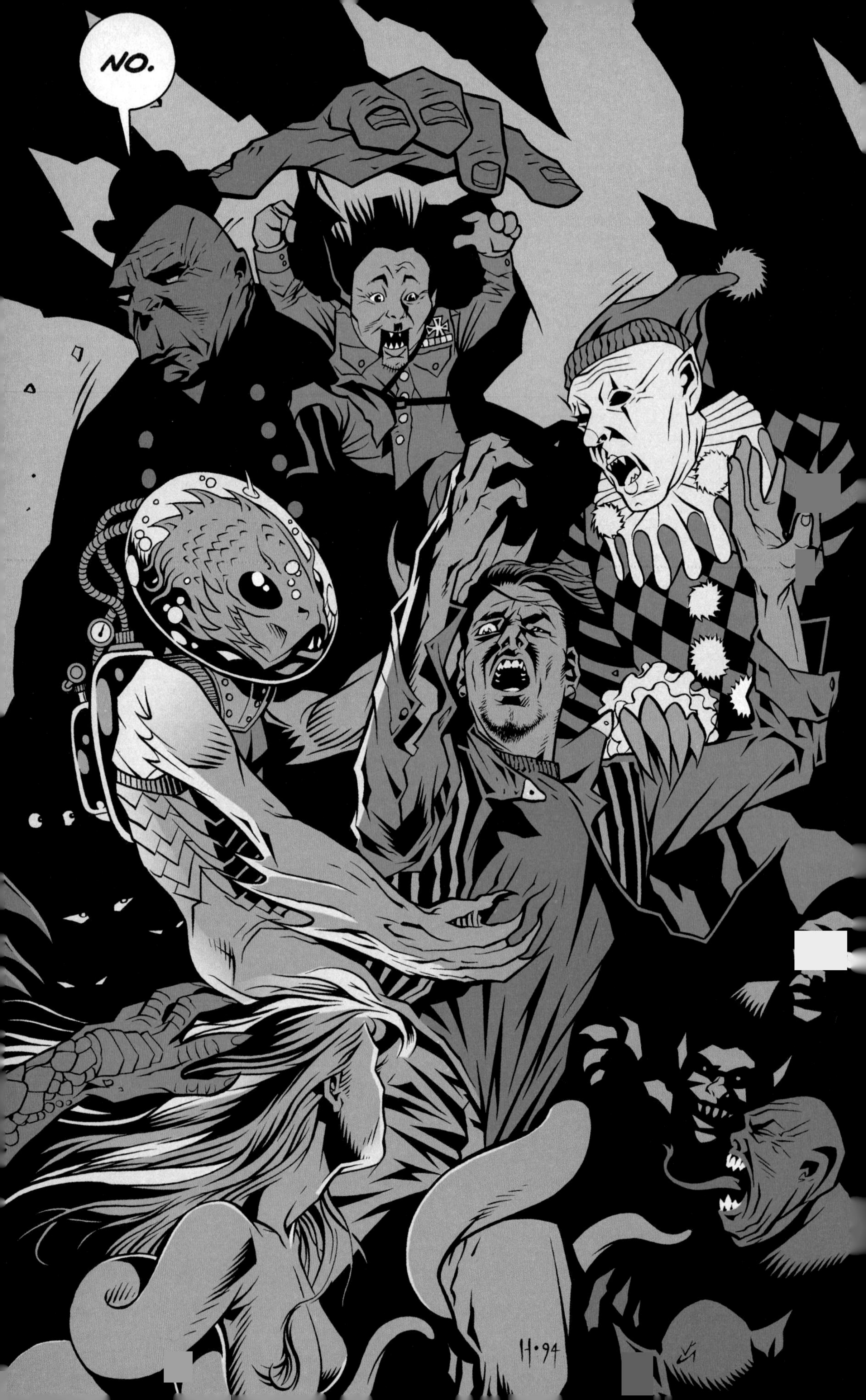
NO.
H•94

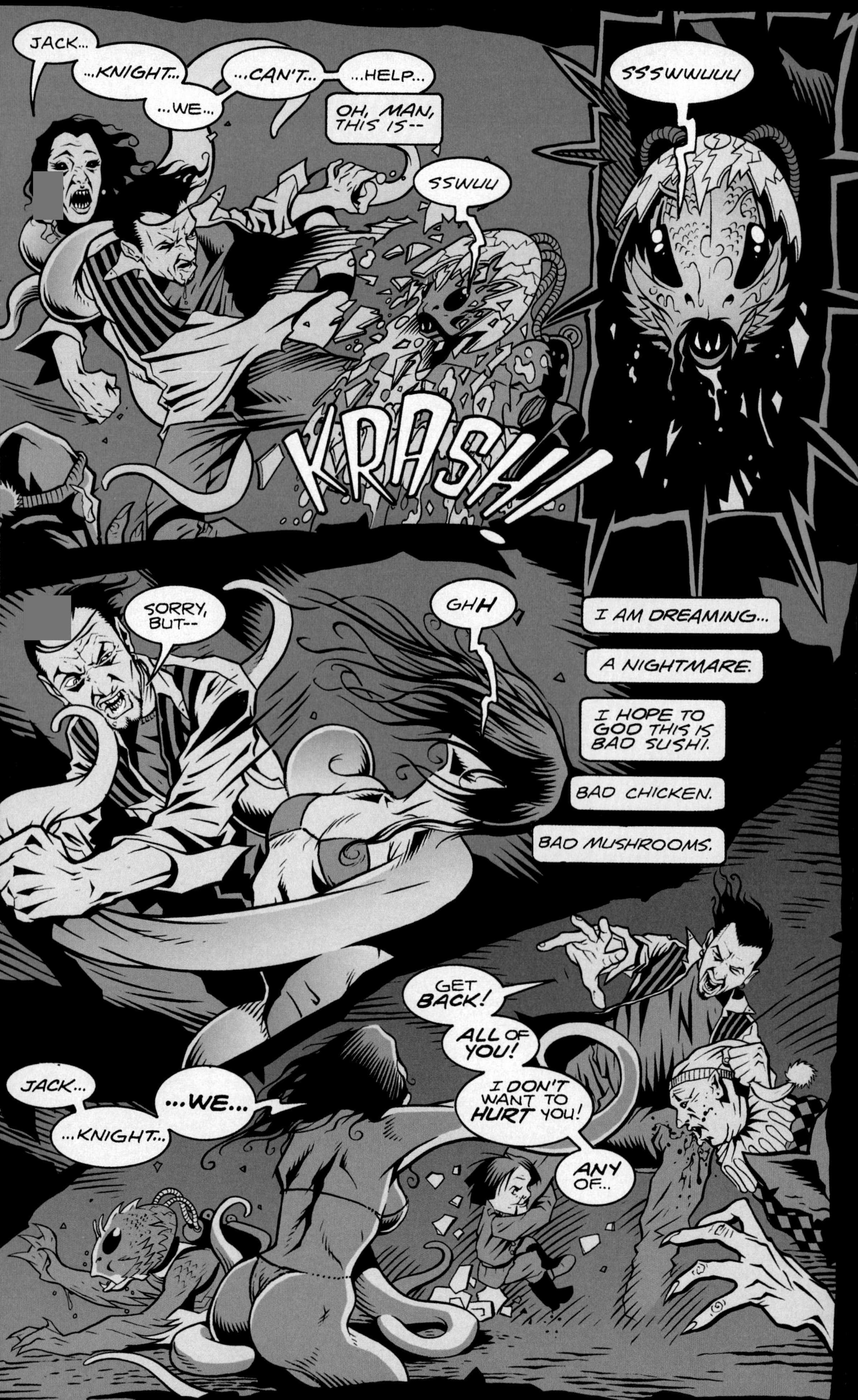
JACK...
...KNIGHT...
...WE...
...CAN'T...
...HELP...
OH, MAN, THIS IS--
SSWUU
SSSWWUUU
KRASH!!
SORRY, BUT--
GHH
I AM DREAMING...
A NIGHTMARE.
I HOPE TO GOD THIS IS BAD SUSHI.
BAD CHICKEN.
BAD MUSHROOMS.
GET BACK!
ALL OF YOU!
I DON'T WANT TO HURT YOU!
ANY OF...
JACK...
...KNIGHT...
...WE...

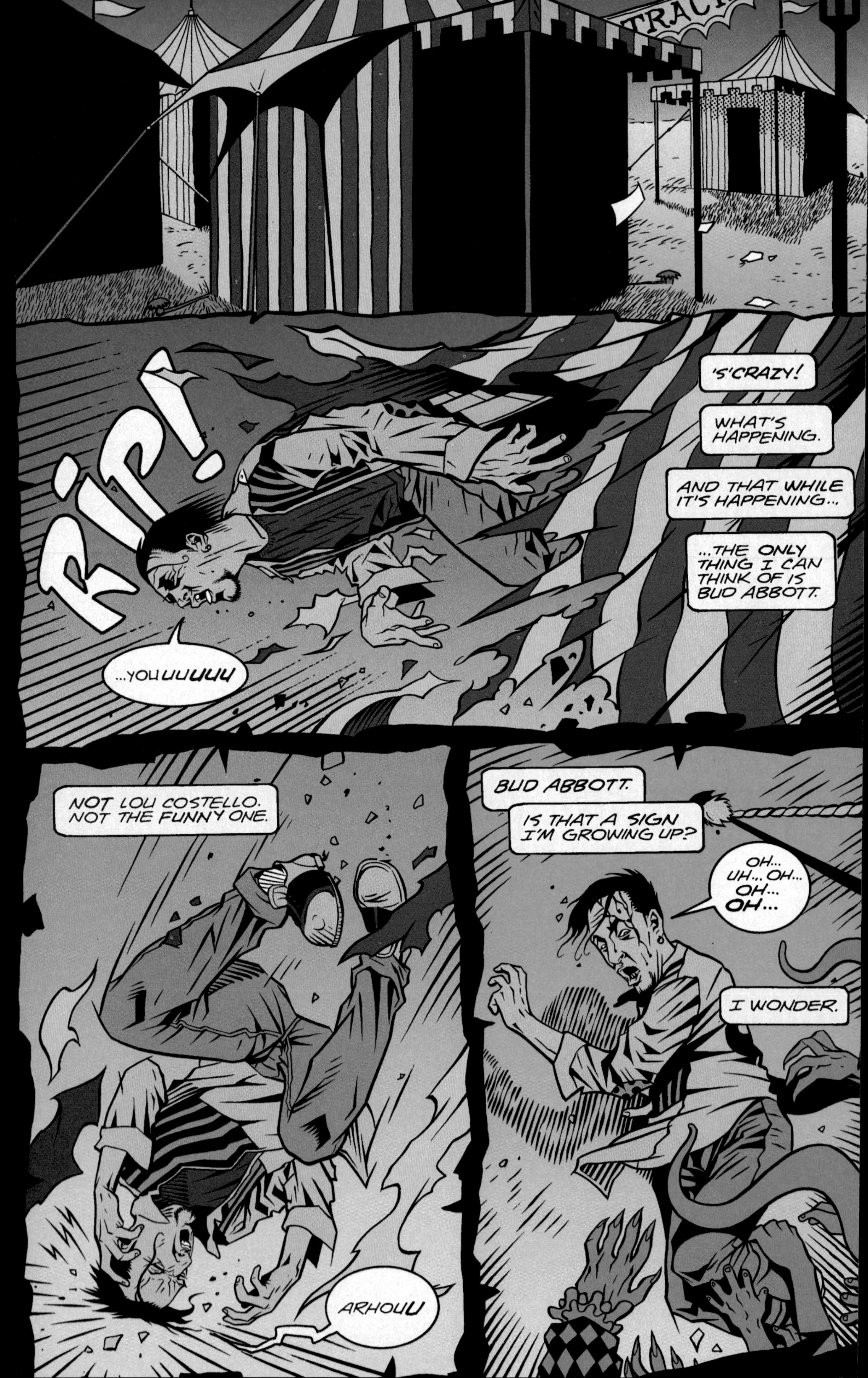
TRAC
RIP!
'S'CRAZY!
WHAT'S HAPPENING.
AND THAT WHILE IT'S HAPPENING...
...THE ONLY THING I CAN THINK OF IS BUD ABBOTT.
...YOUUUUUU
NOT LOU COSTELLO. NOT THE FUNNY ONE.
ARHOUU
BUD ABBOTT.
IS THAT A SIGN I'M GROWING UP?
OH... UH... OH... OH... OH...
I WONDER.

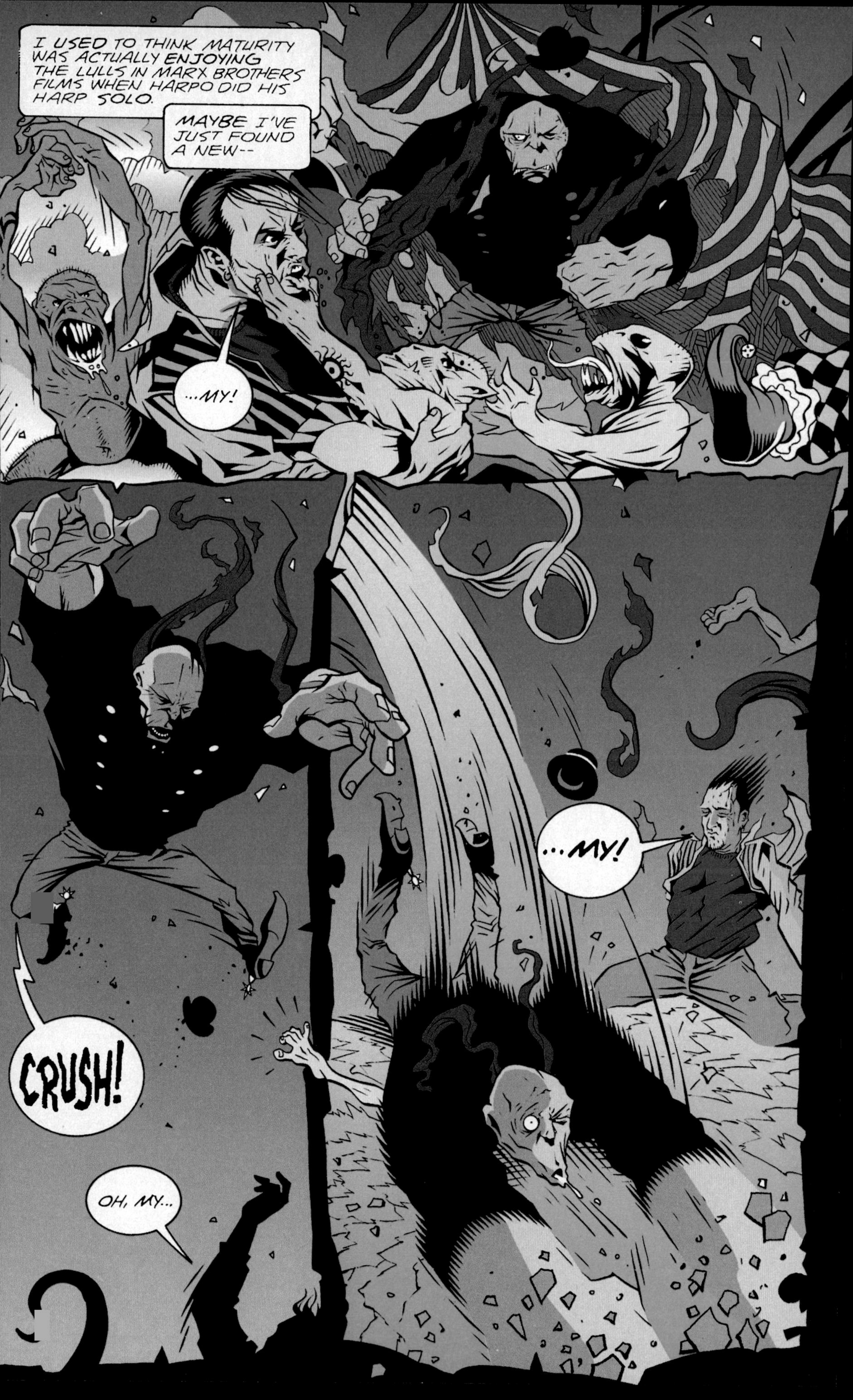
I USED TO THINK MATURITY WAS ACTUALLY ENJOYING THE LULLS IN MARX BROTHERS FILMS WHEN HARPO DID HIS HARP SOLO.
MAYBE I'VE JUST FOUND A NEW--
...MY!
...MY!
CRUSH!
OH, MY...

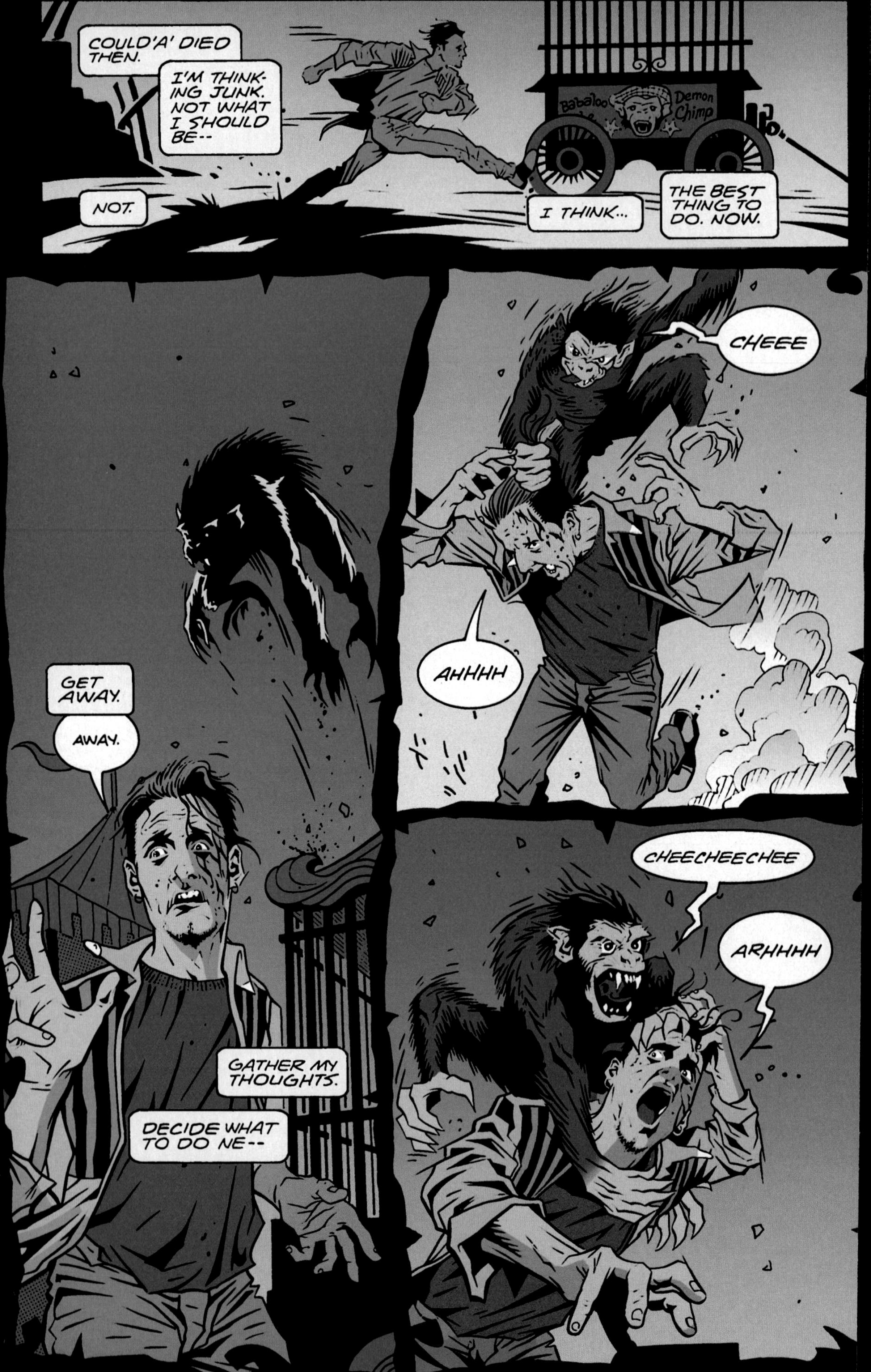
COULD'A' DIED THEN.
I'M THINKING JUNK. NOT WHAT I SHOULD BE--
NOT.
Babaloo Demon Chimp
I THINK...
THE BEST THING TO DO. NOW.
GET AWAY.
AWAY.
GATHER MY THOUGHTS.
DECIDE WHAT TO DO NE--
CHEEE
AHHHH
CHEECHEECHEE
ARHHHH

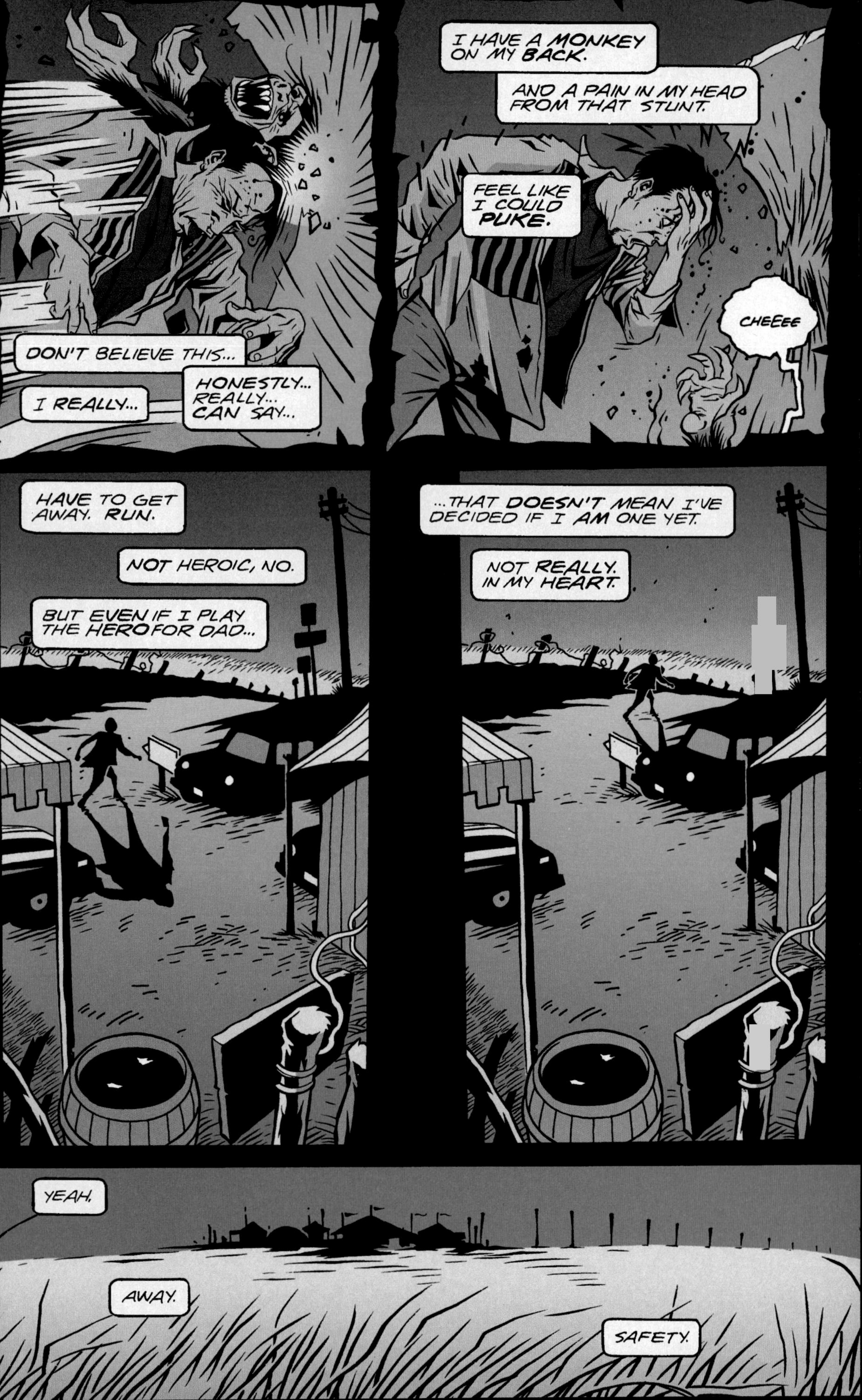
DON'T BELIEVE THIS...
I REALLY...
HONESTLY... REALLY... CAN SAY...
I HAVE A MONKEY ON MY BACK.
AND A PAIN IN MY HEAD FROM THAT STUNT.
FEEL LIKE I COULD PUKE.
CHEEEE
HAVE TO GET AWAY. RUN.
NOT HEROIC, NO.
BUT EVEN IF I PLAY THE HERO FOR DAD...
...THAT DOESN'T MEAN I'VE DECIDED IF I AM ONE YET.
NOT REALLY. IN MY HEART.
YEAH.
AWAY.
SAFETY.

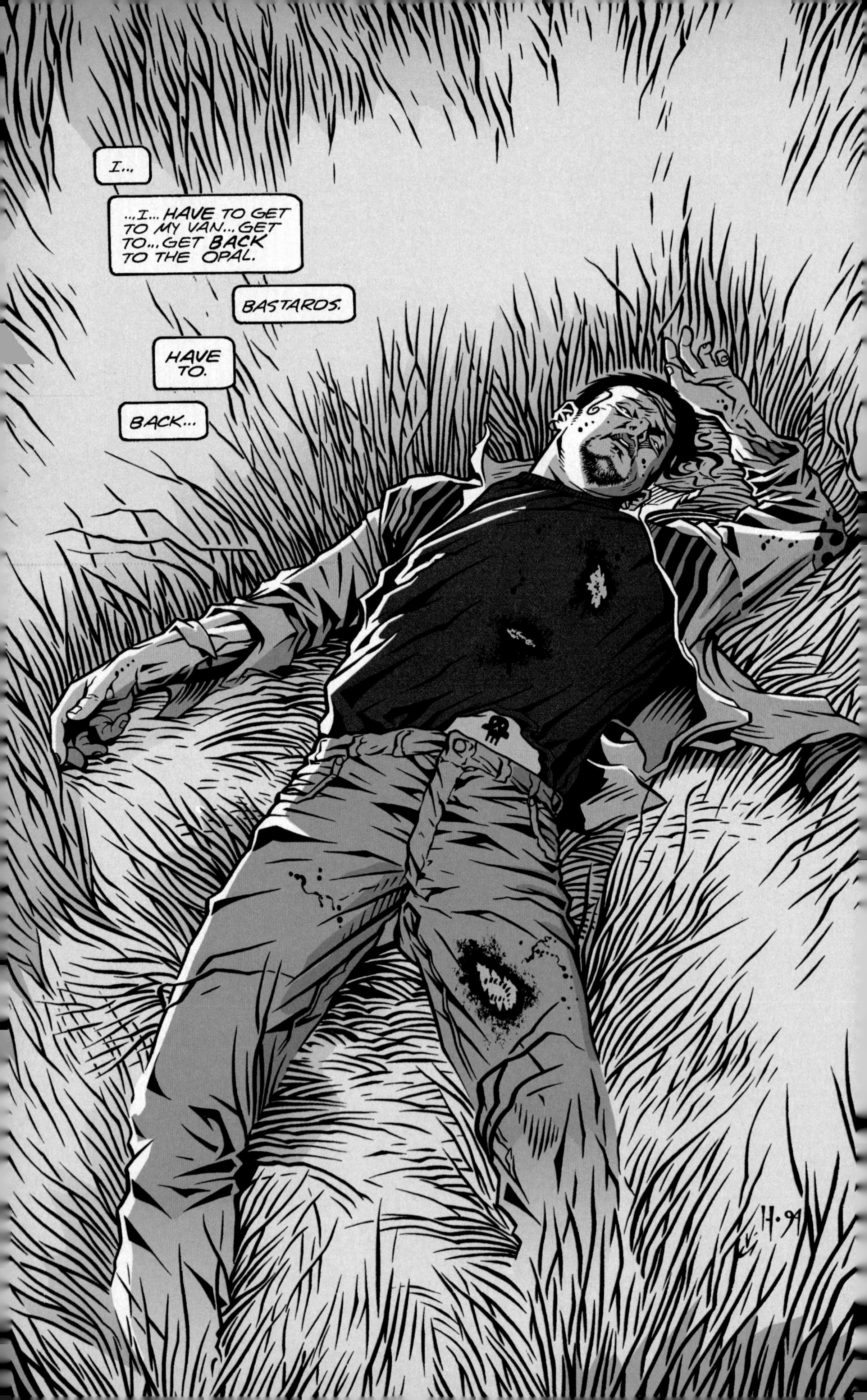
I...
...I... HAVE TO GET TO MY VAN... GET TO... GET BACK TO THE OPAL.
BASTARDS.
HAVE TO.
BACK...

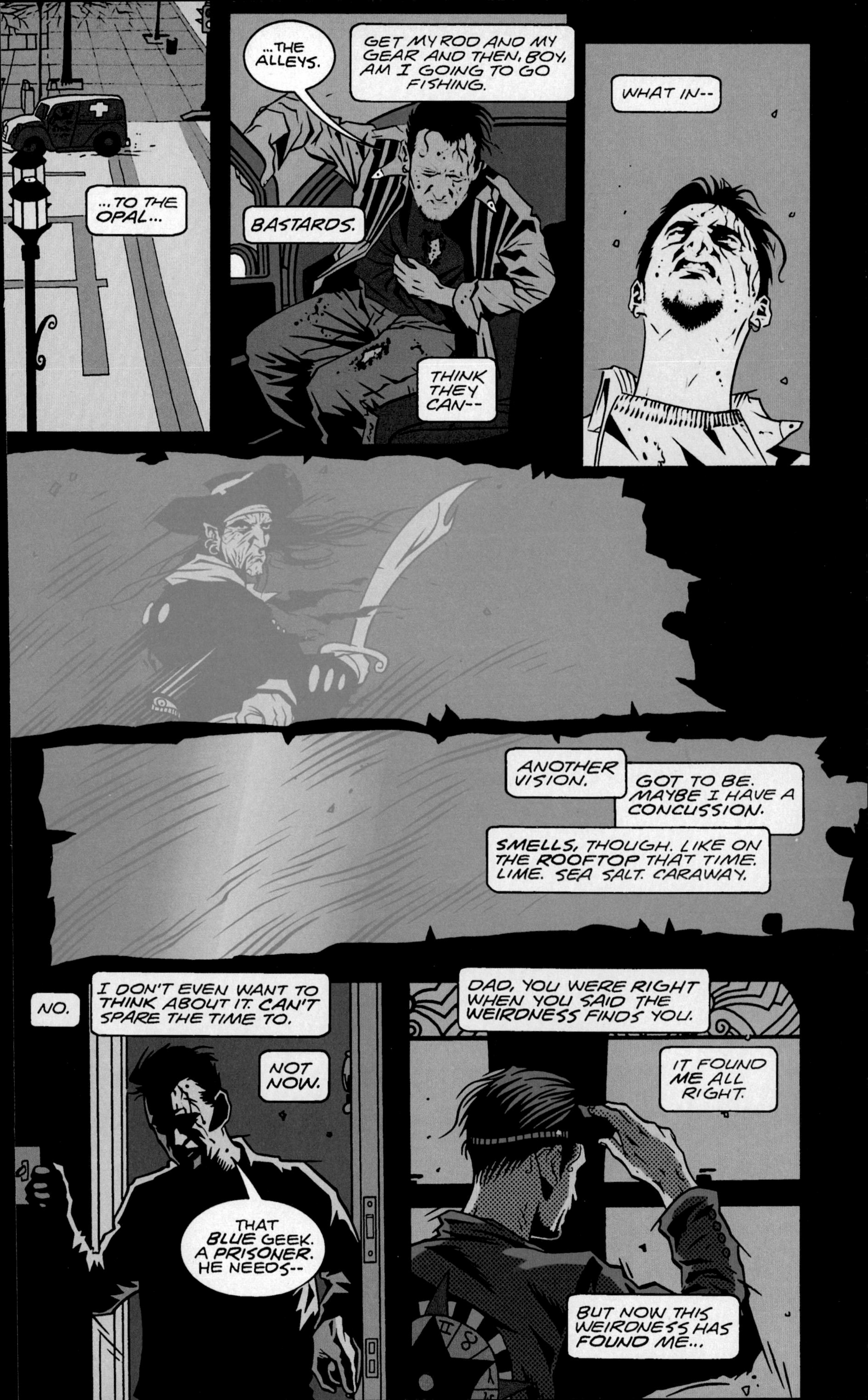
...TO THE OPAL...
...THE ALLEYS.
GET MY ROD AND MY GEAR AND THEN, BOY, AM I GOING TO GO FISHING.
BASTARDS.
THINK THEY CAN--
WHAT IN--
ANOTHER VISION.
GOT TO BE. MAYBE I HAVE A CONCUSSION.
SMELLS, THOUGH. LIKE ON THE ROOFTOP THAT TIME. LIME. SEA SALT. CARAWAY.
NO.
I DON'T EVEN WANT TO THINK ABOUT IT. CAN'T SPARE THE TIME TO.
NOT NOW.
THAT BLUE GEEK. A PRISONER. HE NEEDS--
DAD, YOU WERE RIGHT WHEN YOU SAID THE WEIRDNESS FINDS YOU.
IT FOUND ME ALL RIGHT.
BUT NOW THIS WEIRDNESS HAS FOUND ME...

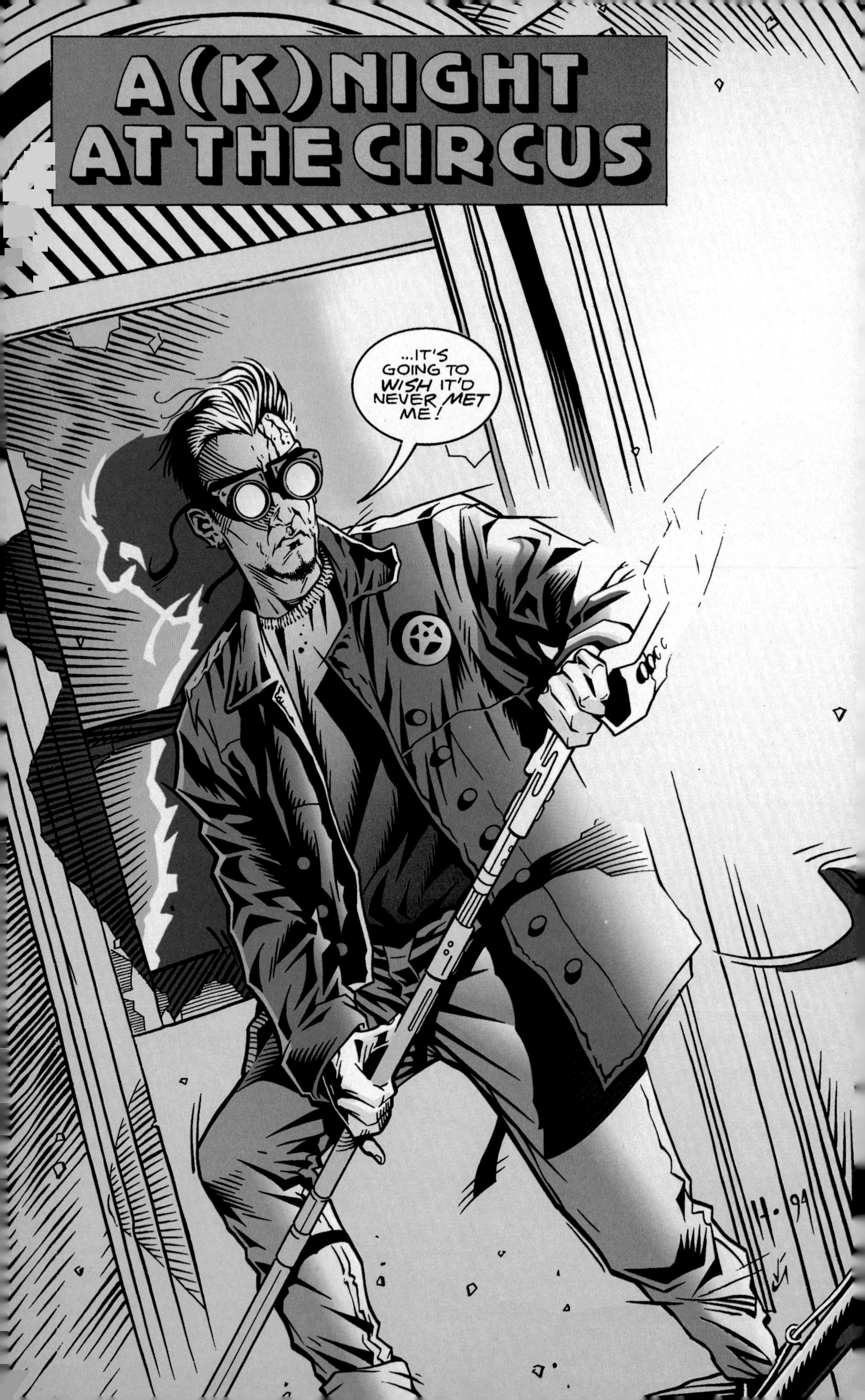
A (K) NIGHT AT THE CIRCUS
...IT'S GOING TO WISH IT'D NEVER MET ME!

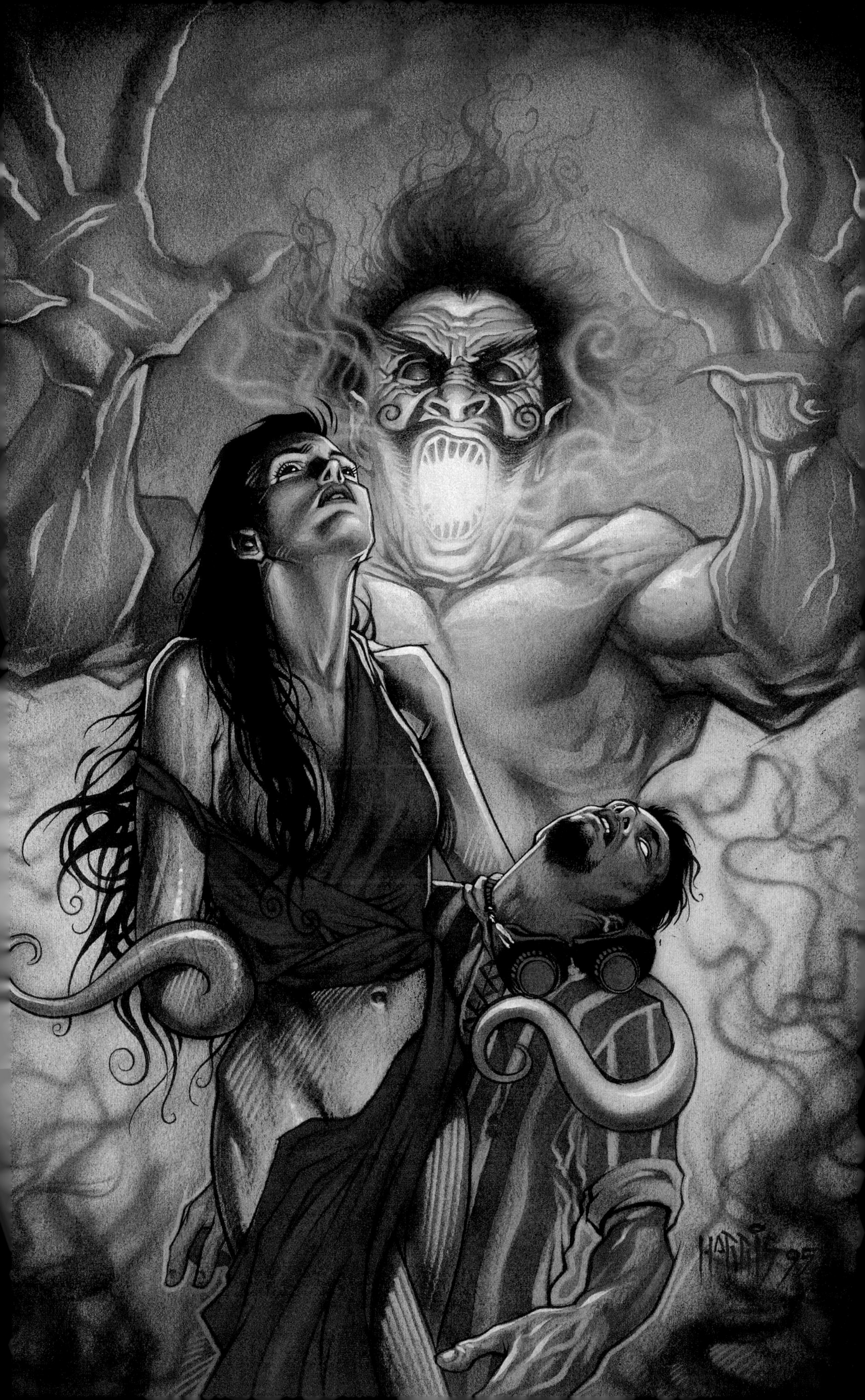

STARMAN 8

Cover by Tony Harris

Written by James Robinson

Pencils by Tony Harris,

with inks by Wade von Grawbadger

and colors by Gregory Wright

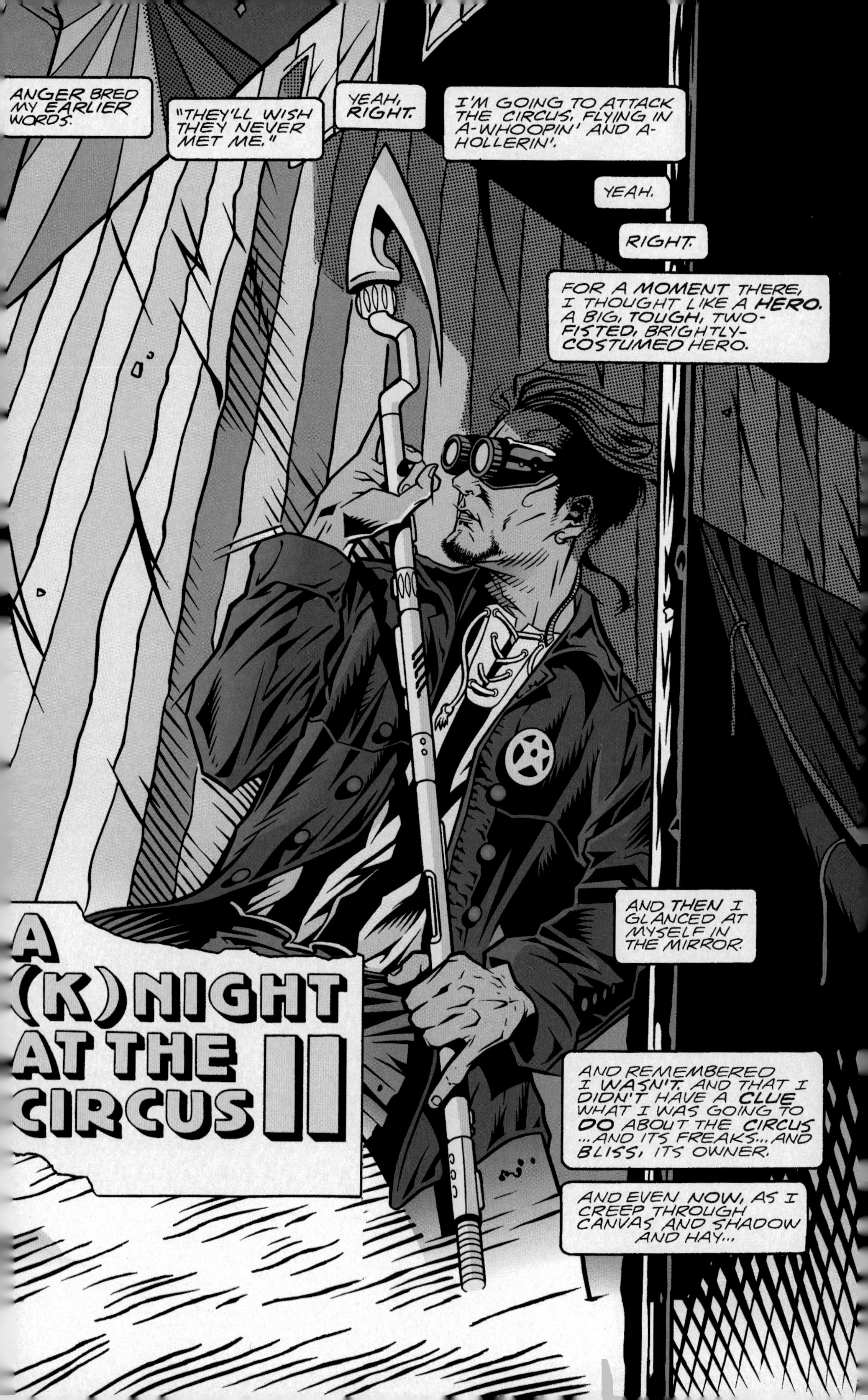

ANGER BRED MY EARLIER WORDS:
"THEY'LL WISH THEY NEVER MET ME."
YEAH, RIGHT.
I'M GOING TO ATTACK THE CIRCUS, FLYING IN A-WHOOPIN' AND A-HOLLERIN'.
YEAH.
RIGHT.
FOR A MOMENT THERE, I THOUGHT LIKE A HERO. A BIG, TOUGH, TWO-FISTED, BRIGHTLY-COSTUMED HERO.
A (K)NIGHT AT THE CIRCUS II
AND THEN I GLANCED AT MYSELF IN THE MIRROR.
AND REMEMBERED I WASN'T. AND THAT I DIDN'T HAVE A CLUE WHAT I WAS GOING TO DO ABOUT THE CIRCUS ...AND ITS FREAKS... AND BLISS, ITS OWNER.
AND EVEN NOW, AS I CREEP THROUGH CANVAS AND SHADOW AND HAY...

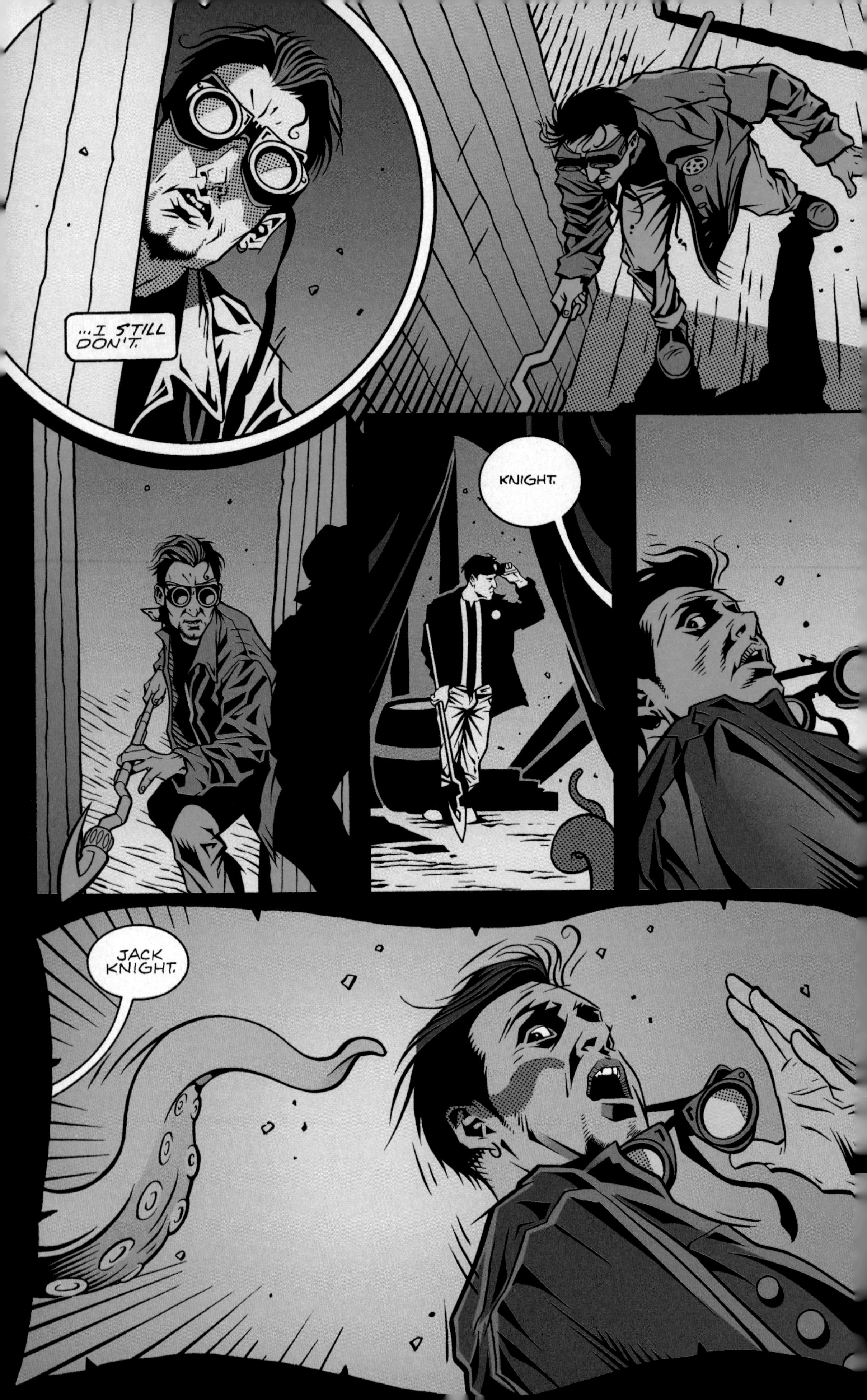
...I STILL DON'T.
KNIGHT.
JACK KNIGHT.

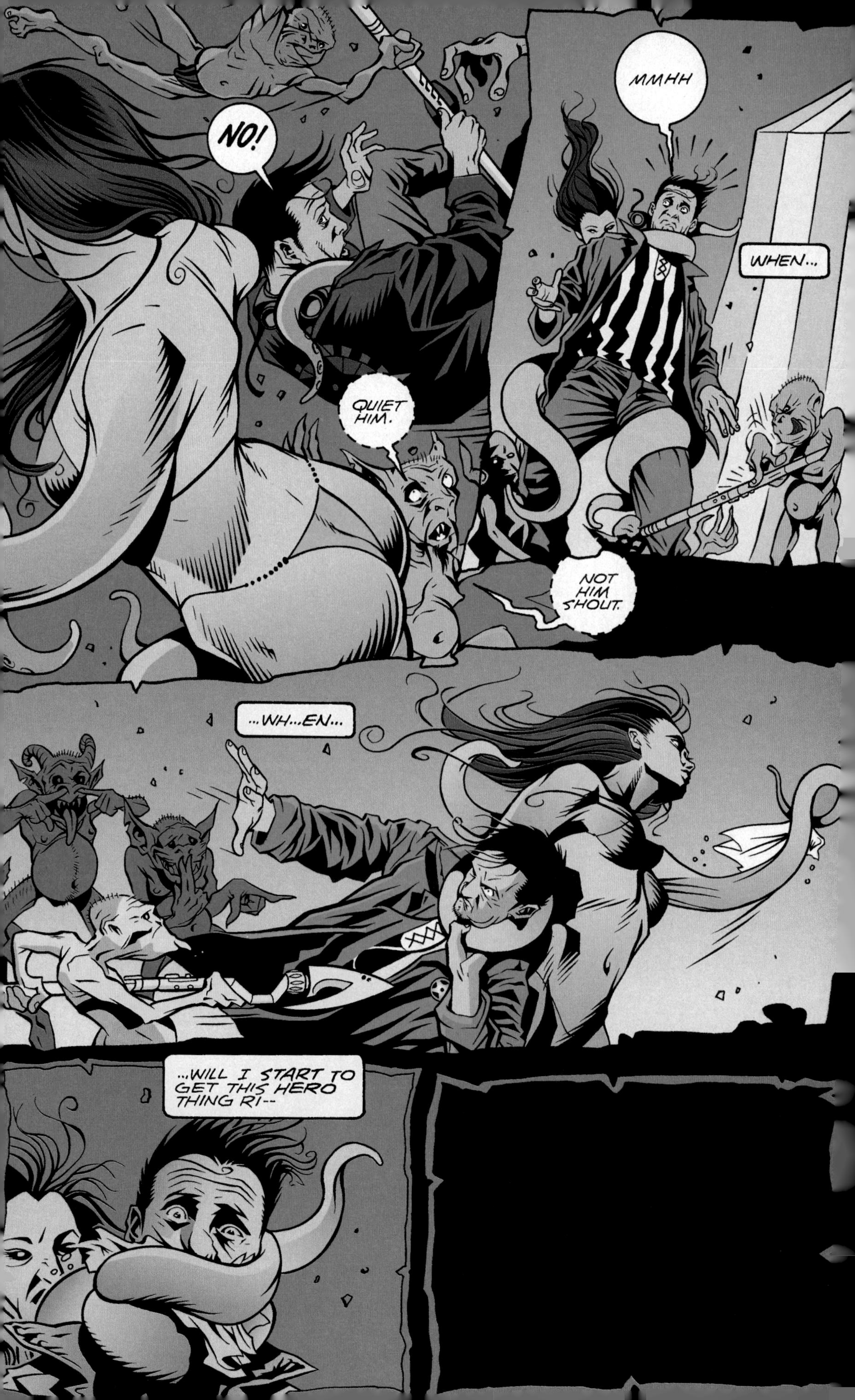
NO!
MMHH
WHEN...
QUIET HIM.
NOT HIM SHOUT.
...WH...EN...
...WILL I START TO GET THIS HERO THING RI--

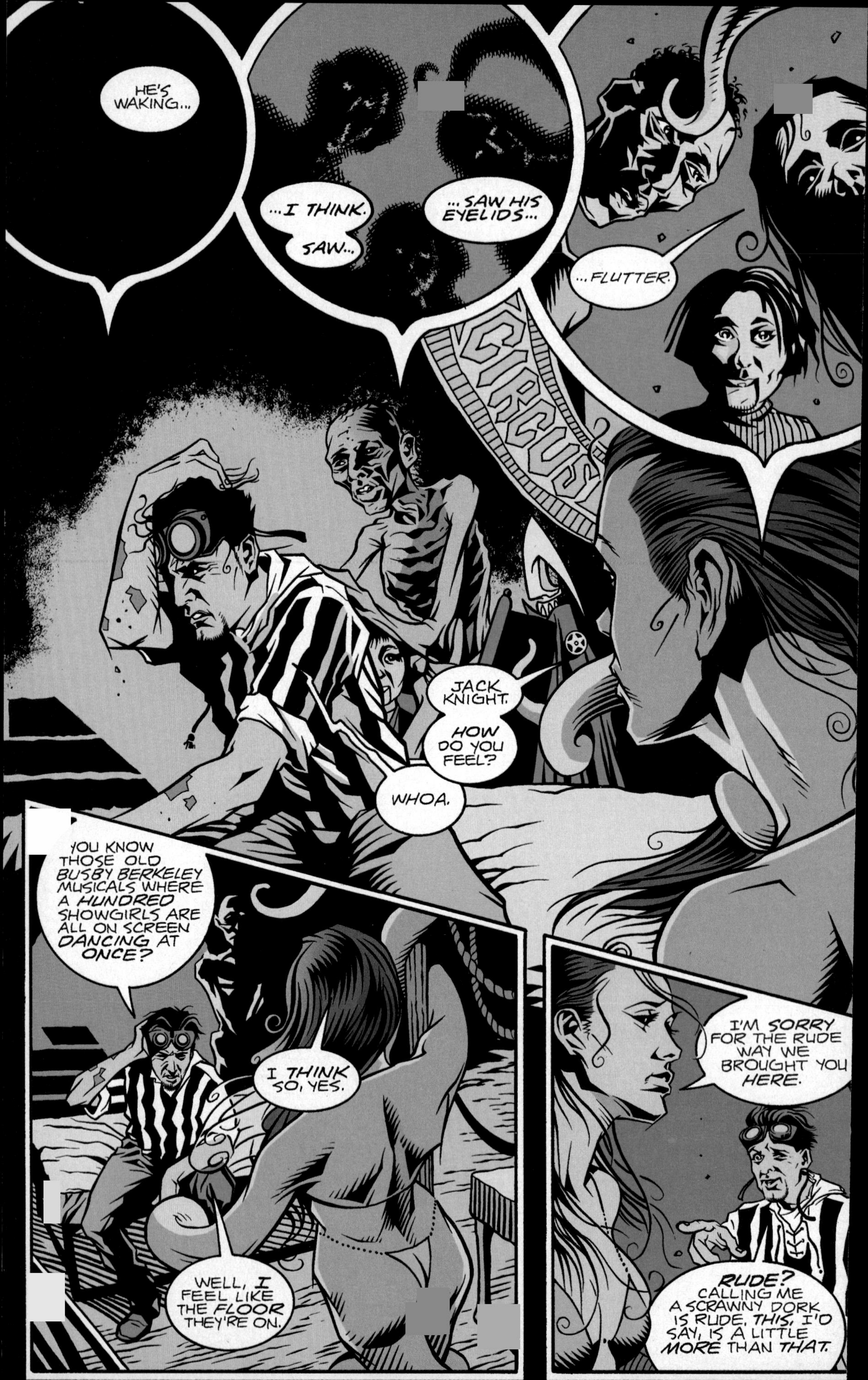
HE'S WAKING...
...I THINK.
SAW...
...SAW HIS EYELIDS...
...FLUTTER.
CIRCUS
JACK KNIGHT.
HOW DO YOU FEEL?
WHOA.
YOU KNOW THOSE OLD BUSBY BERKELEY MUSICALS WHERE A HUNDRED SHOWGIRLS ARE ALL ON SCREEN DANCING AT ONCE?
I THINK SO, YES.
WELL, I FEEL LIKE THE FLOOR THEY'RE ON.
I'M SORRY FOR THE RUDE WAY WE BROUGHT YOU HERE.
RUDE? CALLING ME A SCRAWNY DORK IS RUDE. THIS, I'D SAY, IS A LITTLE MORE THAN THAT.

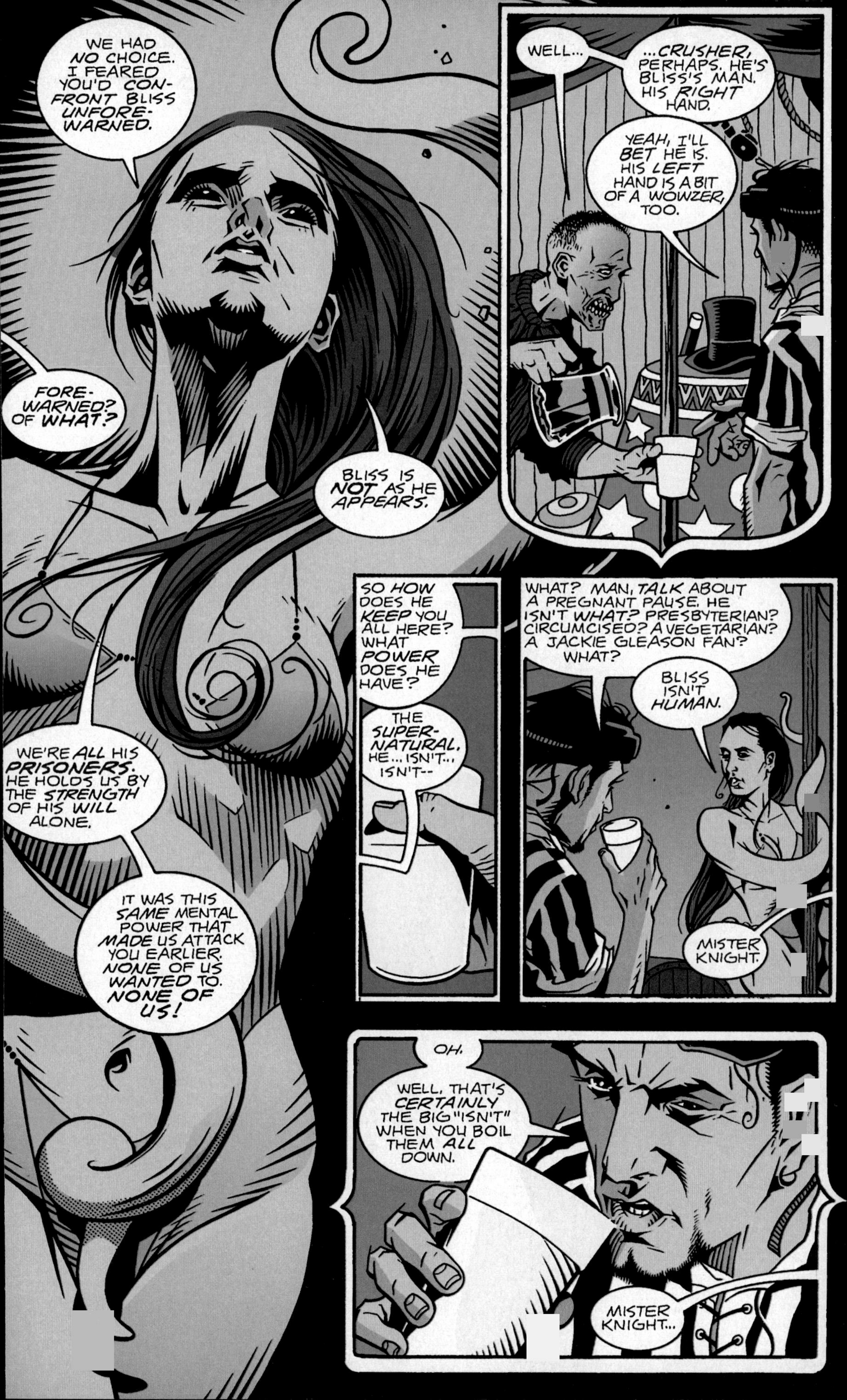
WE HAD NO CHOICE. I FEARED YOU'D CONFRONT BLISS UNFOREWARNED.
FOREWARNED? OF WHAT?
BLISS IS NOT AS HE APPEARS.
WE'RE ALL HIS PRISONERS. HE HOLDS US BY THE STRENGTH OF HIS WILL ALONE.
IT WAS THIS SAME MENTAL POWER THAT MADE US ATTACK YOU EARLIER. NONE OF US WANTED TO. NONE OF US!
WELL...
...CRUSHER, PERHAPS. HE'S BLISS'S MAN. HIS RIGHT HAND.
YEAH, I'LL BET HE IS. HIS LEFT HAND IS A BIT OF A WOWZER, TOO.
SO HOW DOES HE KEEP YOU ALL HERE? WHAT POWER DOES HE HAVE?
THE SUPERNATURAL. HE... ISN'T... ISN'T--
WHAT? MAN, TALK ABOUT A PREGNANT PAUSE. HE ISN'T WHAT? PRESBYTERIAN? CIRCUMCISED? A VEGETARIAN? A JACKIE GLEASON FAN? WHAT?
BLISS ISN'T HUMAN.
MISTER KNIGHT.
OH.
WELL, THAT'S CERTAINLY THE BIG "ISN'T" WHEN YOU BOIL THEM ALL DOWN.
MISTER KNIGHT...

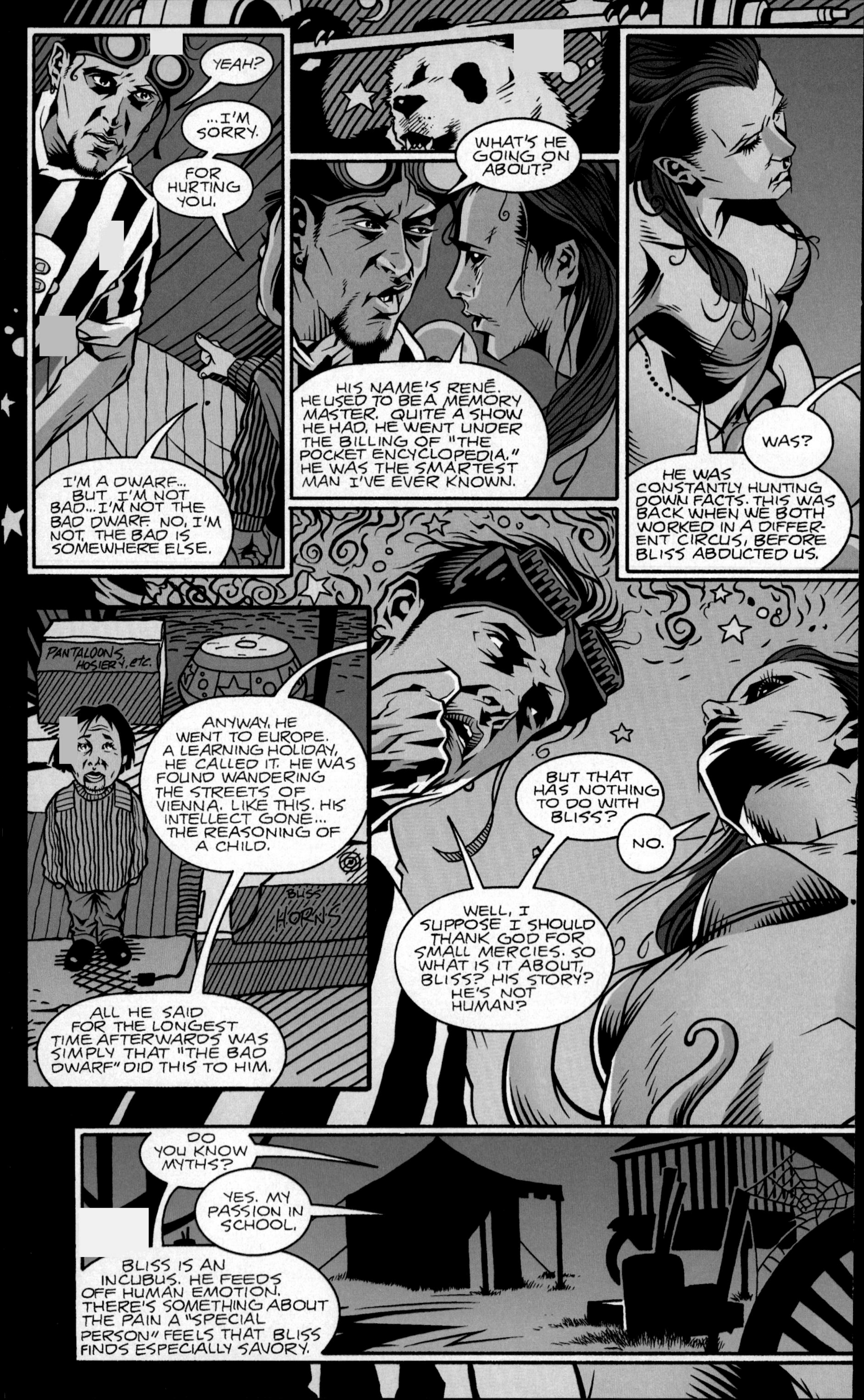
YEAH?
...I'M SORRY.
FOR HURTING YOU.
I'M A DWARF... BUT I'M NOT BAD...I'M NOT THE BAD DWARF. NO, I'M NOT. THE BAD IS SOMEWHERE ELSE.
WHAT'S HE GOING ON ABOUT?
HIS NAME'S RENÉ. HE USED TO BE A MEMORY MASTER. QUITE A SHOW HE HAD, HE WENT UNDER THE BILLING OF "THE POCKET ENCYCLOPEDIA." HE WAS THE SMARTEST MAN I'VE EVER KNOWN.
WAS?
HE WAS CONSTANTLY HUNTING DOWN FACTS. THIS WAS BACK WHEN WE BOTH WORKED IN A DIFFERENT CIRCUS, BEFORE BLISS ABDUCTED US.
PANTALOONS, HOSIERY, etc.
ANYWAY, HE WENT TO EUROPE. A LEARNING HOLIDAY, HE CALLED IT. HE WAS FOUND WANDERING THE STREETS OF VIENNA. LIKE THIS. HIS INTELLECT GONE... THE REASONING OF A CHILD.
BLISS' HORNS
ALL HE SAID FOR THE LONGEST TIME AFTERWARDS WAS SIMPLY THAT "THE BAD DWARF" DID THIS TO HIM.
BUT THAT HAS NOTHING TO DO WITH BLISS?
NO.
WELL, I SUPPOSE I SHOULD THANK GOD FOR SMALL MERCIES. SO WHAT IS IT ABOUT, BLISS? HIS STORY? HE'S NOT HUMAN?
DO YOU KNOW MYTHS?
YES. MY PASSION IN SCHOOL.
BLISS IS AN INCUBUS. HE FEEDS OFF HUMAN EMOTION. THERE'S SOMETHING ABOUT THE PAIN A "SPECIAL PERSON" FEELS THAT BLISS FINDS ESPECIALLY SAVORY.

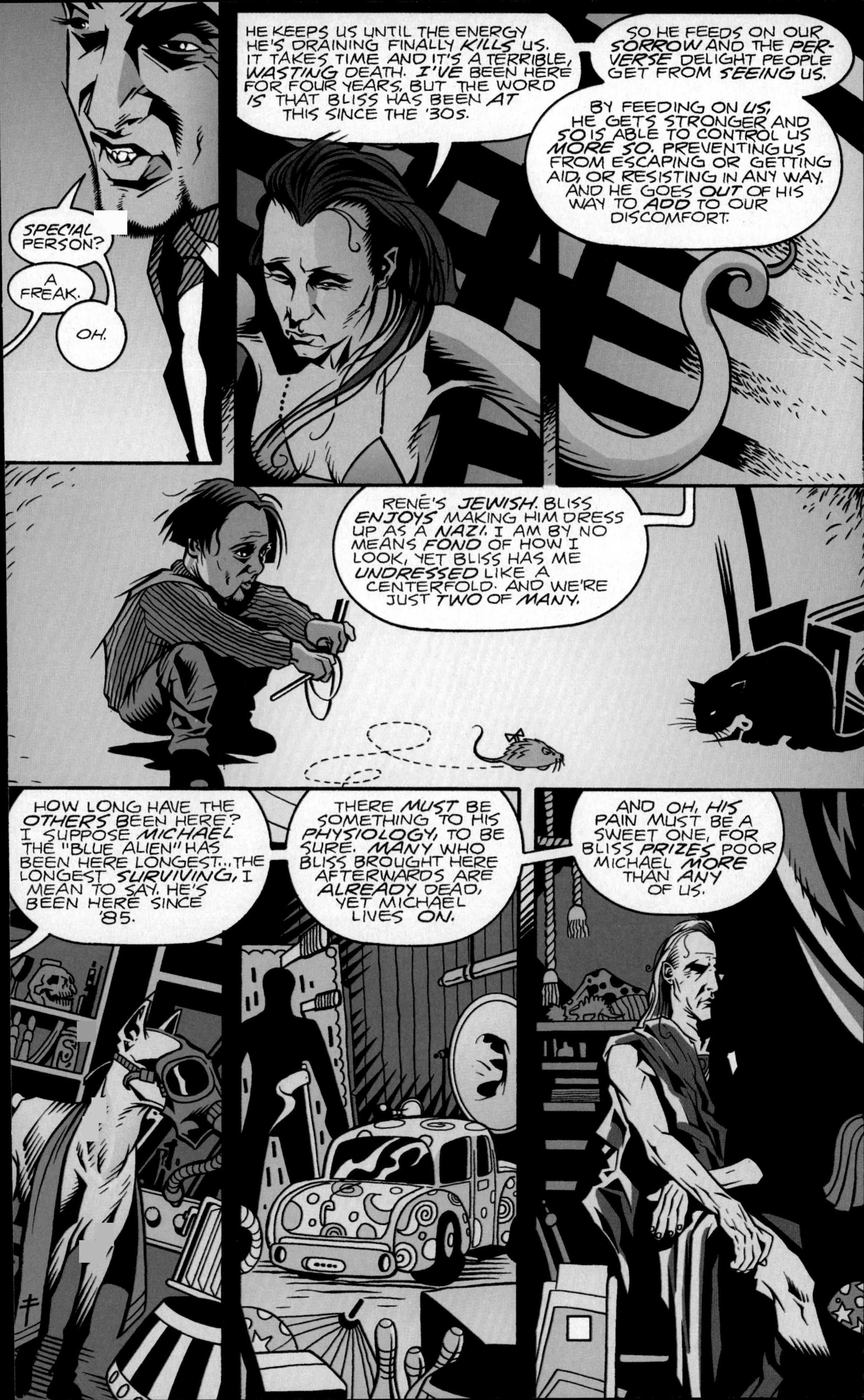
SPECIAL PERSON?
A FREAK.
OH.
HE KEEPS US UNTIL THE ENERGY HE'S DRAINING FINALLY KILLS US. IT TAKES TIME AND IT'S A TERRIBLE, WASTING DEATH. I'VE BEEN HERE FOR FOUR YEARS, BUT THE WORD IS THAT BLISS HAS BEEN AT THIS SINCE THE '30S.
SO HE FEEDS ON OUR SORROW AND THE PERVERSE DELIGHT PEOPLE GET FROM SEEING US.
BY FEEDING ON US, HE GETS STRONGER AND SO IS ABLE TO CONTROL US MORE SO, PREVENTING US FROM ESCAPING OR GETTING AID, OR RESISTING IN ANY WAY. AND HE GOES OUT OF HIS WAY TO ADD TO OUR DISCOMFORT.
RENÉ'S JEWISH. BLISS ENJOYS MAKING HIM DRESS UP AS A NAZI. I AM BY NO MEANS FOND OF HOW I LOOK, YET BLISS HAS ME UNDRESSED LIKE A CENTERFOLD. AND WE'RE JUST TWO OF MANY.
HOW LONG HAVE THE OTHERS BEEN HERE? I SUPPOSE MICHAEL THE "BLUE ALIEN" HAS BEEN HERE LONGEST... THE LONGEST SURVIVING, I MEAN TO SAY. HE'S BEEN HERE SINCE '85.
THERE MUST BE SOMETHING TO HIS PHYSIOLOGY, TO BE SURE. MANY WHO BLISS BROUGHT HERE AFTERWARDS ARE ALREADY DEAD, YET MICHAEL LIVES ON.
AND OH, HIS PAIN MUST BE A SWEET ONE, FOR BLISS PRIZES POOR MICHAEL MORE THAN ANY OF US.

BLISS *SLEEPS* NOW. *THAT'S* HOW I WAS *ABLE* TO RESIST HIS POWER ENOUGH TO *GRAB* YOU. BUT *NEVER* IS HIS HOLD SO *WEAK* THAT I...OR ANY OF MY FRIENDS HERE... COULD *ESCAPE*.

SOME ARE *FOREVER* IN A *TRANCE*, MAGGIE, THE *SAFFRON SNAIL*, IS *CLOSE* TO DEATH. AND *NONE* OF US ARE ABLE TO... TO --

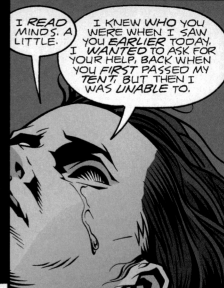

I *READ* MINDS. A LITTLE.

I KNEW *WHO* YOU WERE WHEN I *SAW* YOU *EARLIER* TODAY. I *WANTED* TO ASK FOR YOUR HELP, BACK WHEN YOU *FIRST* PASSED MY *TENT*, BUT THEN I WAS *UNABLE* TO.

I'LL BE *BACK*.

WHERE ARE YOU *GOING?* TO *BLISS?* I THINK YOU *SHOULD* GET HELP *FIRST. GO NOW...*WHILE YOU *CAN* ...AND GET THE *AUTHORITIES*.

WHAT, AND HAVE MAGGIE THE SNAIL ON MY *CONSCIENCE?* NO, THANK YOU.

I'LL BE *OKAY.* I'VE GOT MY STAR *ROD.* I GOT BREATH MINTS. WHAT *ELSE* DO I --

CRRRHHH!

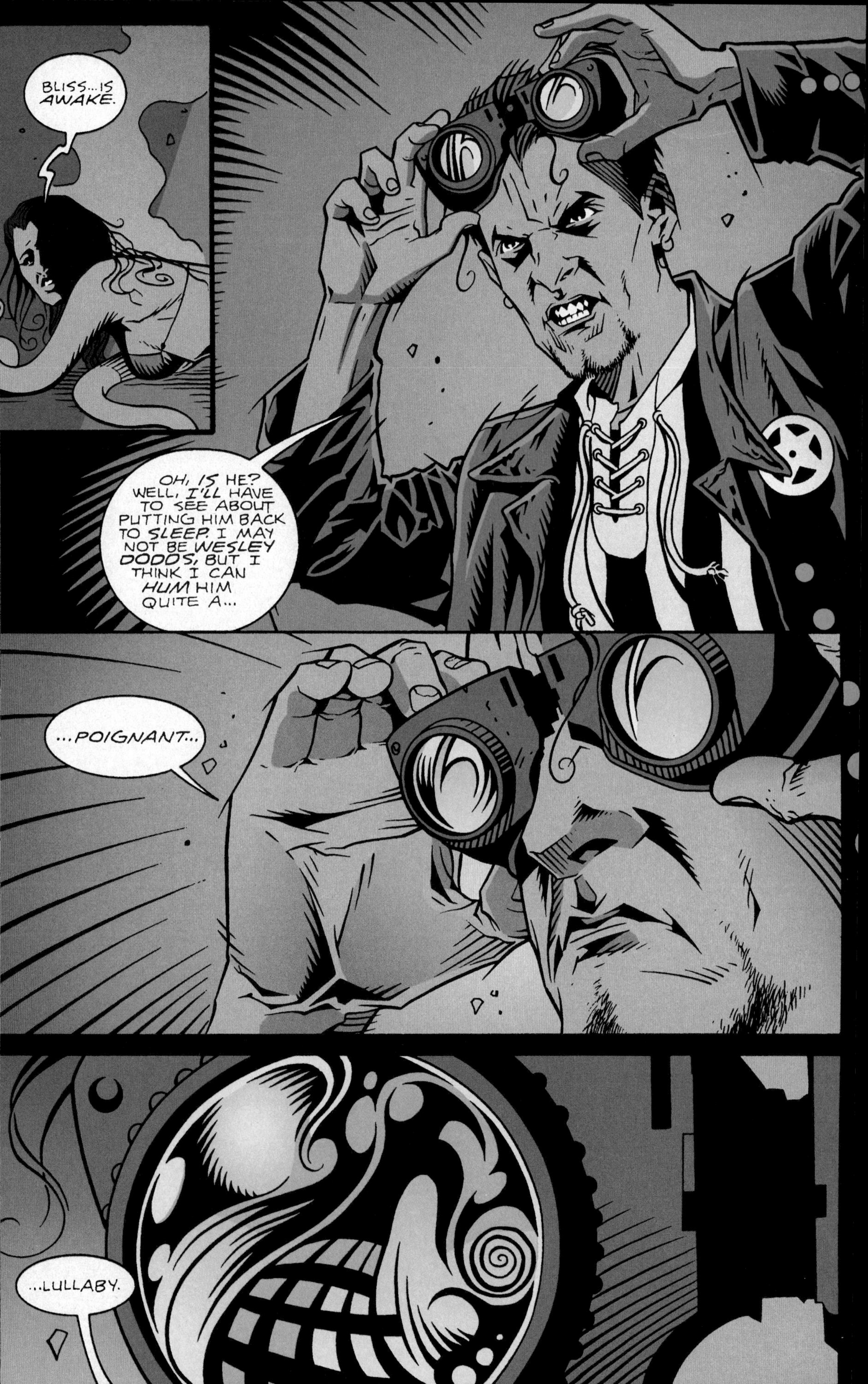
BLISS...IS AWAKE.
OH, IS HE? WELL, I'LL HAVE TO SEE ABOUT PUTTING HIM BACK TO SLEEP. I MAY NOT BE WESLEY DODDS, BUT I THINK I CAN HUM HIM QUITE A...
...POIGNANT...
...LULLABY.

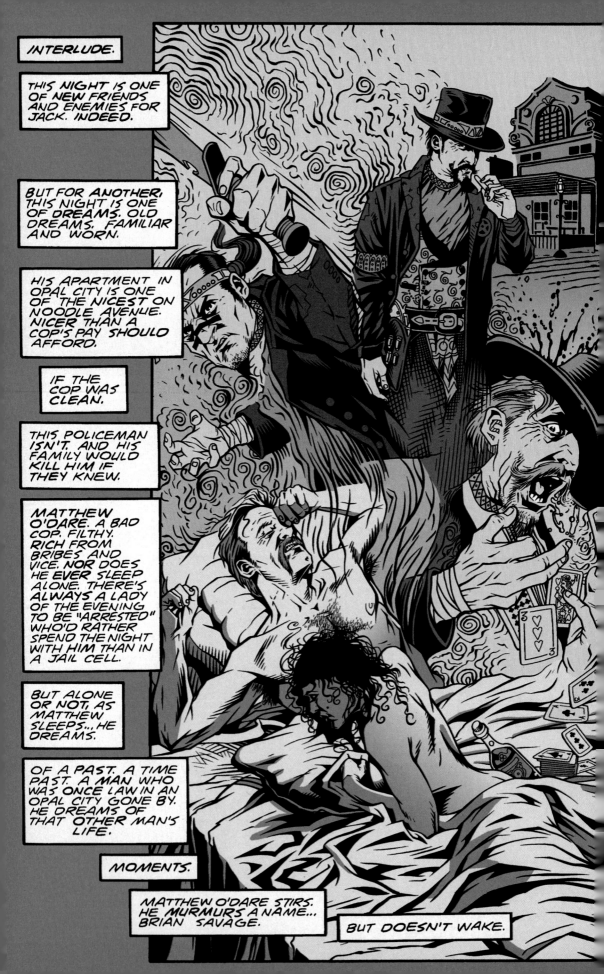

INTERLUDE.

THIS NIGHT IS ONE OF NEW FRIENDS AND ENEMIES FOR JACK. INDEED.

BUT FOR ANOTHER, THIS NIGHT IS ONE OF DREAMS. OLD DREAMS. FAMILIAR AND WORN.

HIS APARTMENT IN OPAL CITY IS ONE OF THE NICEST ON NOODLE AVENUE. NICER THAN A COP'S PAY SHOULD AFFORD.

IF THE COP WAS CLEAN.

THIS POLICEMAN ISN'T. AND HIS FAMILY WOULD KILL HIM IF THEY KNEW.

MATTHEW O'DARE. A BAD COP. FILTHY RICH FROM BRIBES AND VICE. NOR DOES HE EVER SLEEP ALONE. THERE'S ALWAYS A LADY OF THE EVENING TO BE "ARRESTED" WHO'D RATHER SPEND THE NIGHT WITH HIM THAN IN A JAIL CELL.

BUT ALONE OR NOT, AS MATTHEW SLEEPS... HE DREAMS.

OF A PAST. A TIME PAST. A MAN WHO WAS ONCE LAW IN AN OPAL CITY GONE BY. HE DREAMS OF THAT OTHER MAN'S LIFE.

MOMENTS.

MATTHEW O'DARE STIRS. HE MURMURS A NAME... BRIAN SAVAGE.

BUT DOESN'T WAKE.

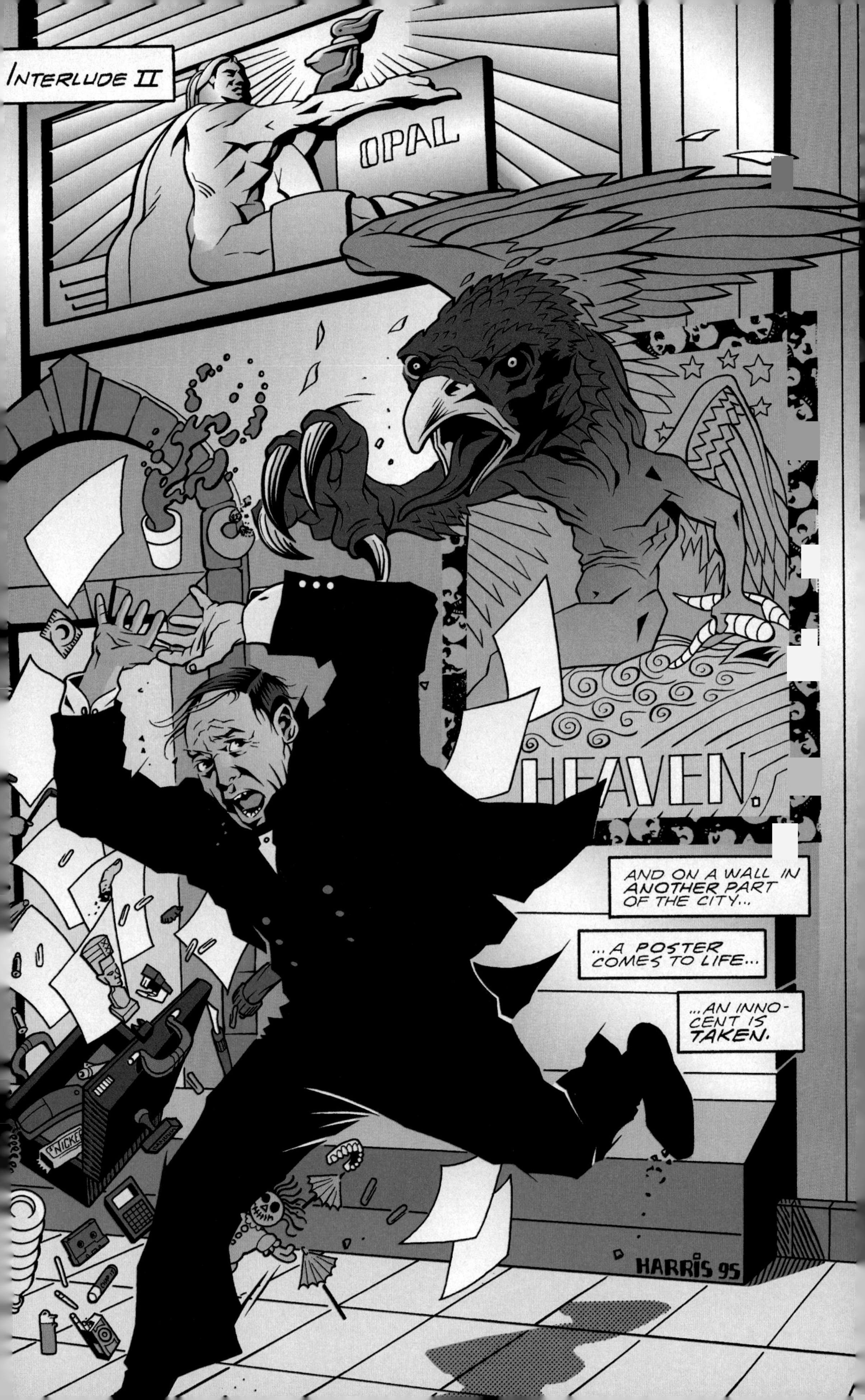

INTERLUDE II
OPAL
HEAVEN.
AND ON A WALL IN ANOTHER PART OF THE CITY...
...A POSTER COMES TO LIFE...
...AN INNOCENT IS TAKEN.
HARRIS 95

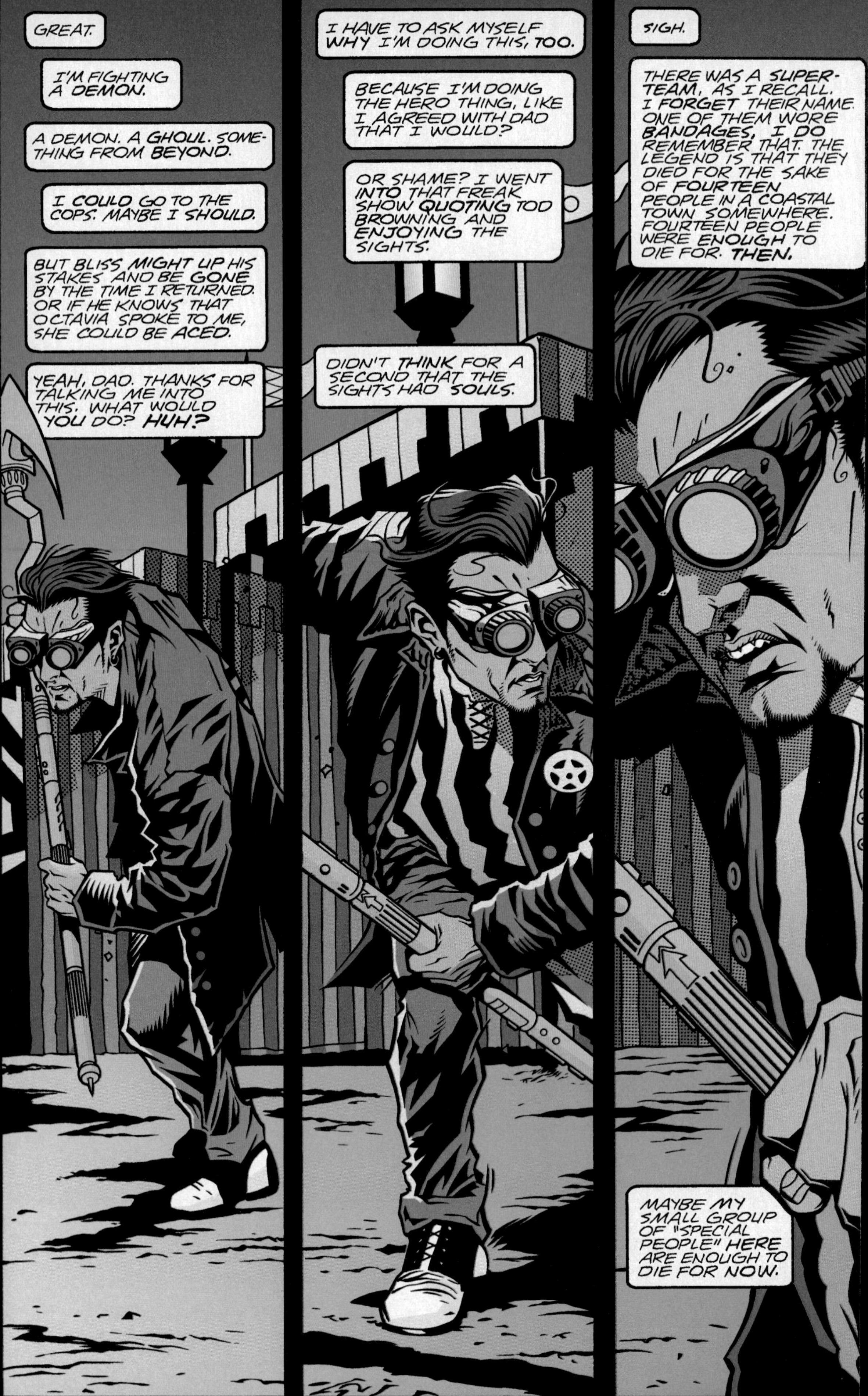
GREAT.
I'M FIGHTING A DEMON.
A DEMON. A GHOUL. SOMETHING FROM BEYOND.
I COULD GO TO THE COPS. MAYBE I SHOULD.
BUT BLISS MIGHT UP HIS STAKES AND BE GONE BY THE TIME I RETURNED. OR IF HE KNOWS THAT OCTAVIA SPOKE TO ME, SHE COULD BE ACED.
YEAH, DAD. THANKS FOR TALKING ME INTO THIS. WHAT WOULD YOU DO? HUH?
I HAVE TO ASK MYSELF WHY I'M DOING THIS, TOO.
BECAUSE I'M DOING THE HERO THING, LIKE I AGREED WITH DAD THAT I WOULD?
OR SHAME? I WENT INTO THAT FREAK SHOW QUOTING TOD BROWNING AND ENJOYING THE SIGHTS.
DIDN'T THINK FOR A SECOND THAT THE SIGHTS HAD SOULS.
SIGH.
THERE WAS A SUPER-TEAM, AS I RECALL. I FORGET THEIR NAME. ONE OF THEM WORE BANDAGES, I DO REMEMBER THAT. THE LEGEND IS THAT THEY DIED FOR THE SAKE OF FOURTEEN PEOPLE IN A COASTAL TOWN SOMEWHERE. FOURTEEN PEOPLE WERE ENOUGH TO DIE FOR. THEN.
MAYBE MY SMALL GROUP OF "SPECIAL PEOPLE" HERE ARE ENOUGH TO DIE FOR NOW.

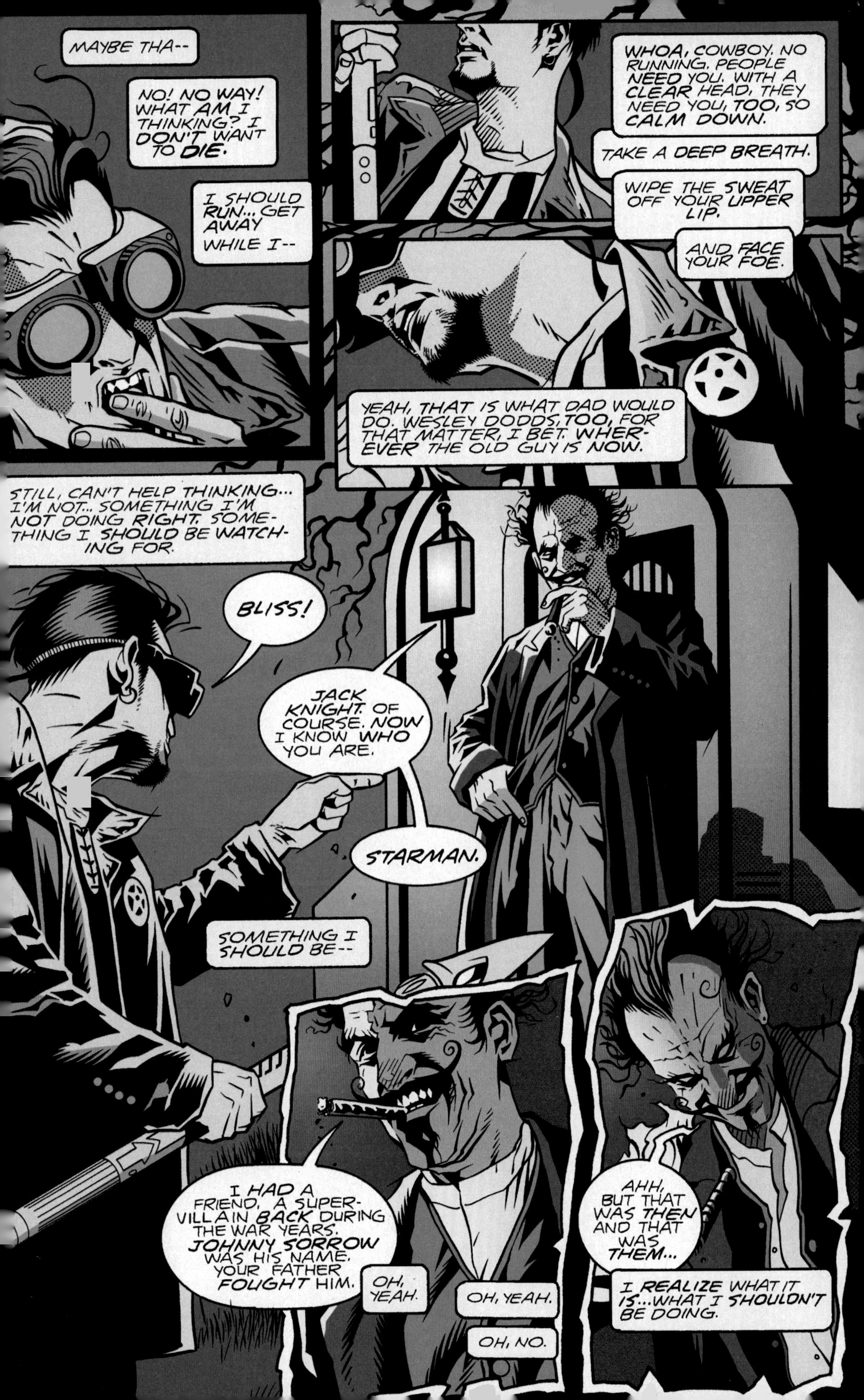
MAYBE THA--
NO! NO WAY! WHAT AM I THINKING? I DON'T WANT TO DIE.
I SHOULD RUN... GET AWAY WHILE I--
WHOA, COWBOY. NO RUNNING. PEOPLE NEED YOU. WITH A CLEAR HEAD, THEY NEED YOU, TOO, SO CALM DOWN.
TAKE A DEEP BREATH.
WIPE THE SWEAT OFF YOUR UPPER LIP.
AND FACE YOUR FOE.
YEAH, THAT IS WHAT DAD WOULD DO. WESLEY DODDS, TOO, FOR THAT MATTER, I BET. WHEREVER THE OLD GUY IS NOW.
STILL, CAN'T HELP THINKING... I'M NOT... SOMETHING I'M NOT DOING RIGHT. SOMETHING I SHOULD BE WATCHING FOR.
BLISS!
JACK KNIGHT. OF COURSE. NOW I KNOW WHO YOU ARE.
STARMAN.
SOMETHING I SHOULD BE--
I HAD A FRIEND, A SUPER-VILLAIN BACK DURING THE WAR YEARS. JOHNNY SORROW WAS HIS NAME. YOUR FATHER FOUGHT HIM.
OH, YEAH.
OH, YEAH.
OH, NO.
AHH, BUT THAT WAS THEN AND THAT WAS THEM...
I REALIZE WHAT IT IS... WHAT I SHOULDN'T BE DOING.

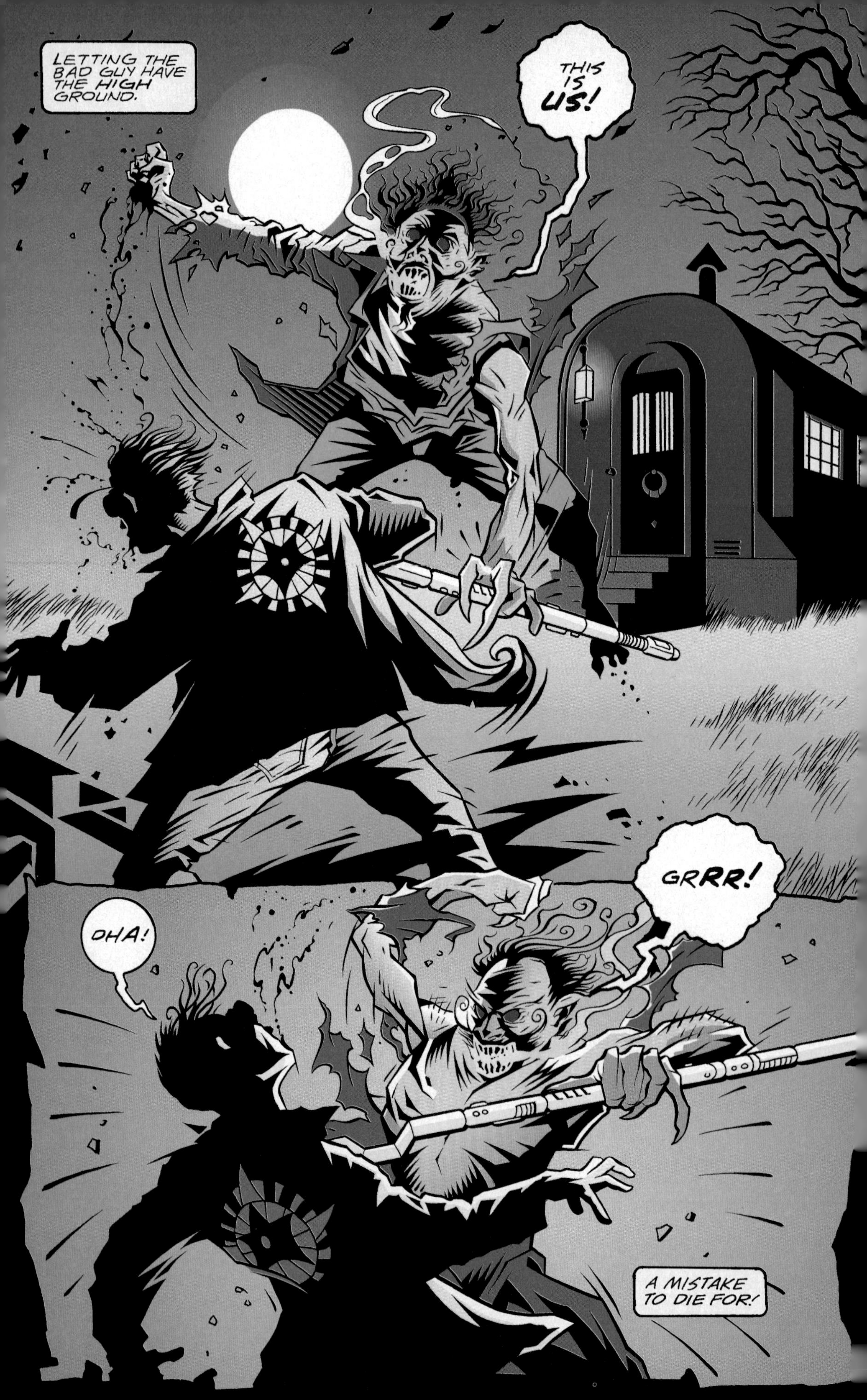
LETTING THE BAD GUY HAVE THE HIGH GROUND.
THIS IS US!
GRRR!
OHA!
A MISTAKE TO DIE FOR!

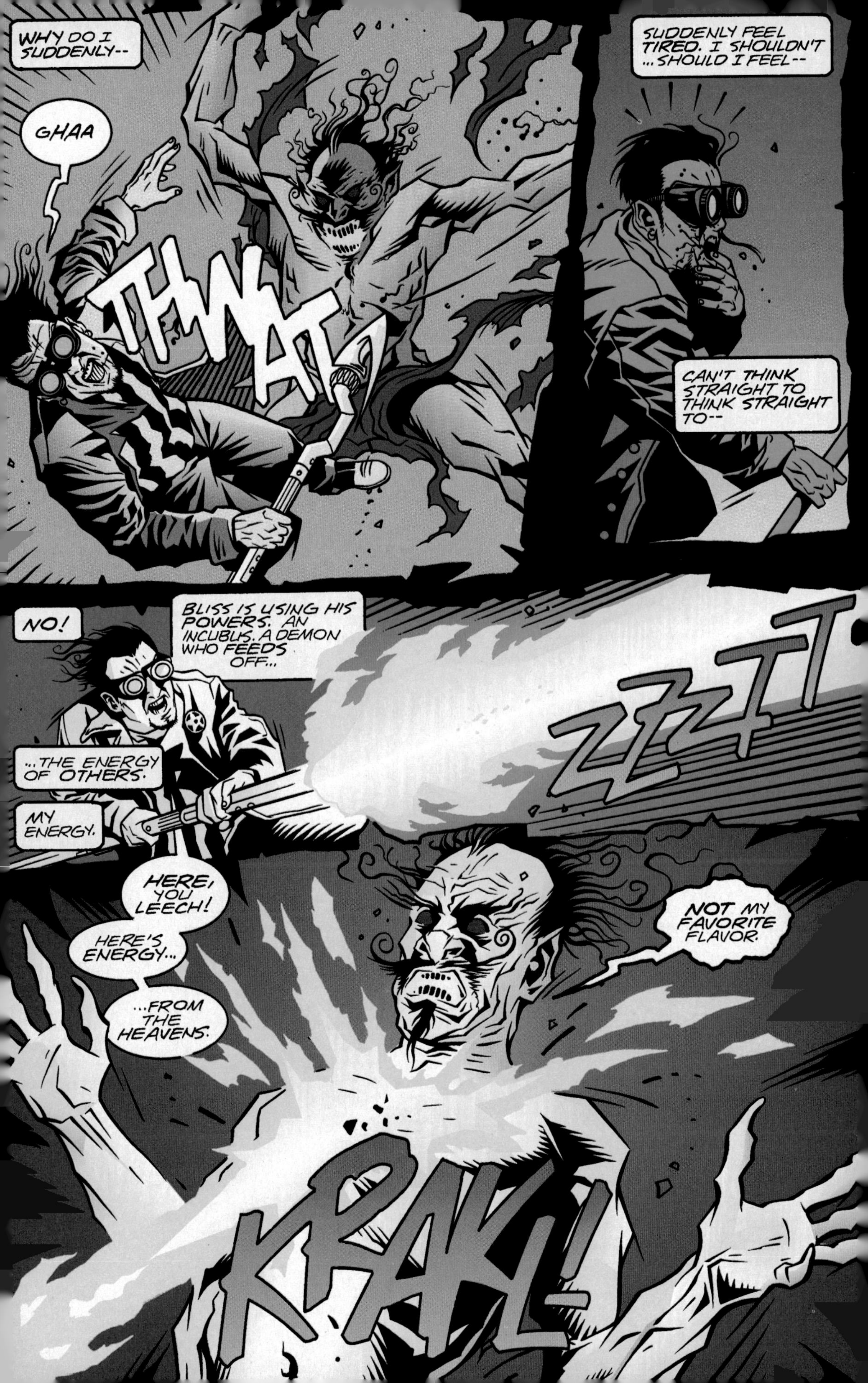
WHY DO I SUDDENLY--
GHAA
THWAT
SUDDENLY FEEL TIRED. I SHOULDN'T ...SHOULD I FEEL--
CAN'T THINK STRAIGHT TO THINK STRAIGHT TO--
NO!
BLISS IS USING HIS POWERS. AN INCUBUS. A DEMON WHO FEEDS OFF...
...THE ENERGY OF OTHERS.
MY ENERGY.
ZZZITT
HERE, YOU LEECH!
HERE'S ENERGY...
...FROM THE HEAVENS.
NOT MY FAVORITE FLAVOR.
KRAKL!

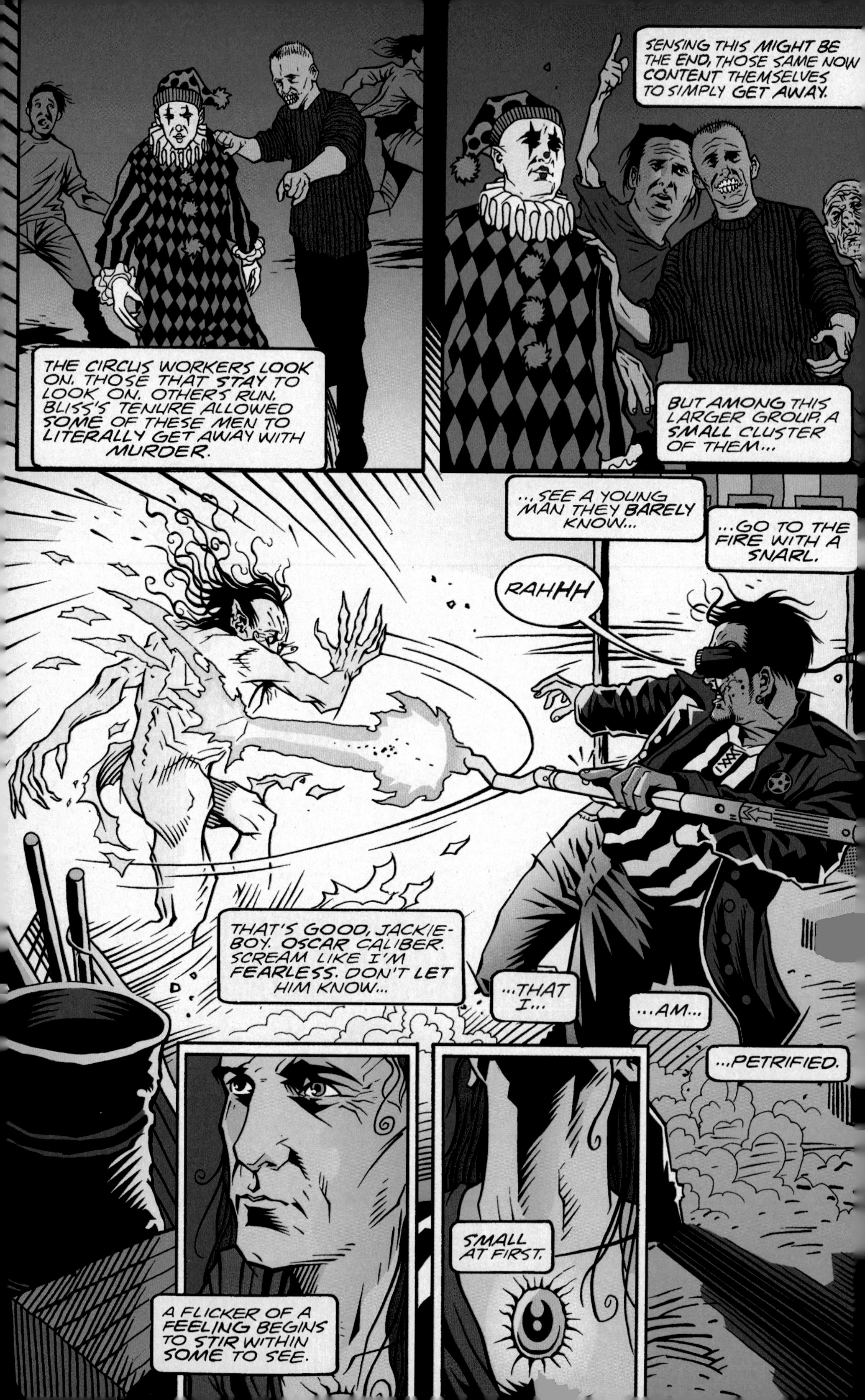
THE CIRCUS WORKERS LOOK ON. THOSE THAT STAY TO LOOK ON. OTHERS RUN. BLISS'S TENURE ALLOWED SOME OF THESE MEN TO LITERALLY GET AWAY WITH MURDER.
SENSING THIS MIGHT BE THE END, THOSE SAME NOW CONTENT THEMSELVES TO SIMPLY GET AWAY.
BUT AMONG THIS LARGER GROUP, A SMALL CLUSTER OF THEM...
...SEE A YOUNG MAN THEY BARELY KNOW...
...GO TO THE FIRE WITH A SNARL.
RAHHH
THAT'S GOOD, JACKIE-BOY. OSCAR CALIBER. SCREAM LIKE I'M FEARLESS. DON'T LET HIM KNOW...
...THAT I...
...AM...
...PETRIFIED.
A FLICKER OF A FEELING BEGINS TO STIR WITHIN SOME TO SEE.
SMALL AT FIRST.

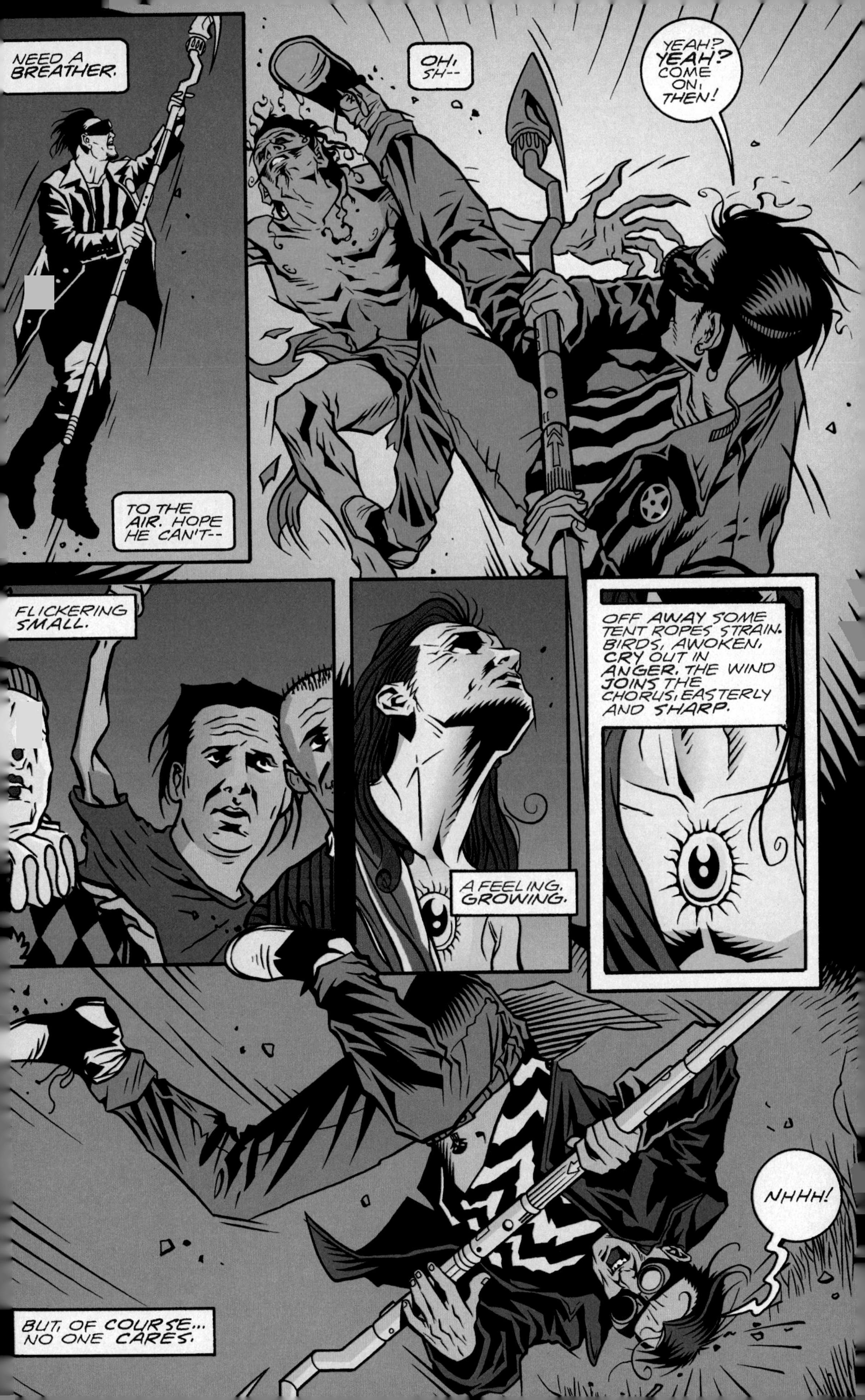
NEED A BREATHER.
TO THE AIR. HOPE HE CAN'T--
OH, SH--
YEAH? YEAH? COME ON, THEN!
FLICKERING SMALL.
A FEELING, GROWING.
OFF AWAY SOME TENT ROPES STRAIN. BIRDS, AWOKEN, CRY OUT IN ANGER. THE WIND JOINS THE CHORUS, EASTERLY AND SHARP.
BUT, OF COURSE... NO ONE CARES.
NHHH!

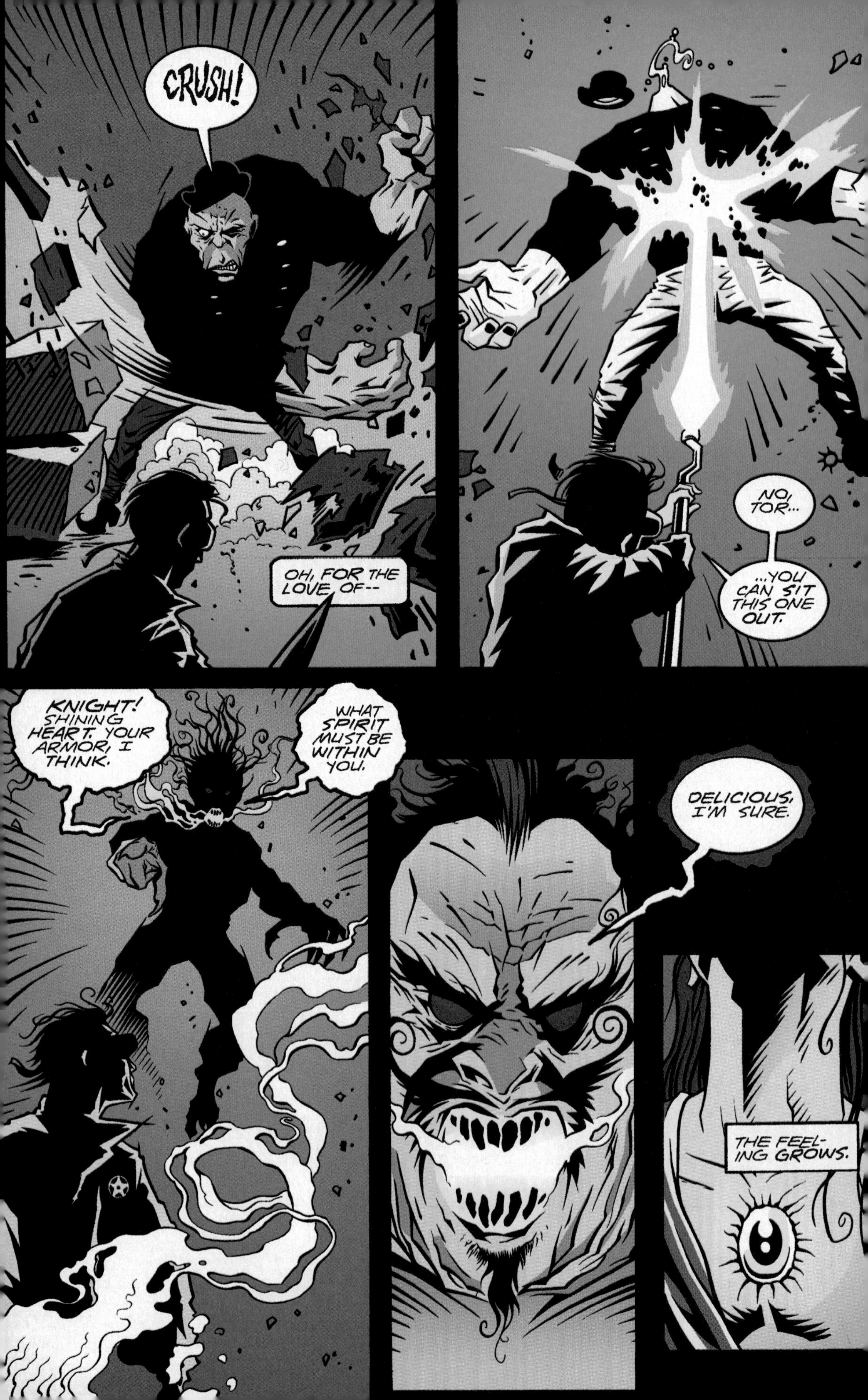
CRUSH!
OH, FOR THE LOVE OF--
NO, TOR...
...YOU CAN SIT THIS ONE OUT.
KNIGHT! SHINING HEART. YOUR ARMOR, I THINK.
WHAT SPIRIT MUST BE WITHIN YOU.
DELICIOUS, I'M SURE.
THE FEEL-ING GROWS.

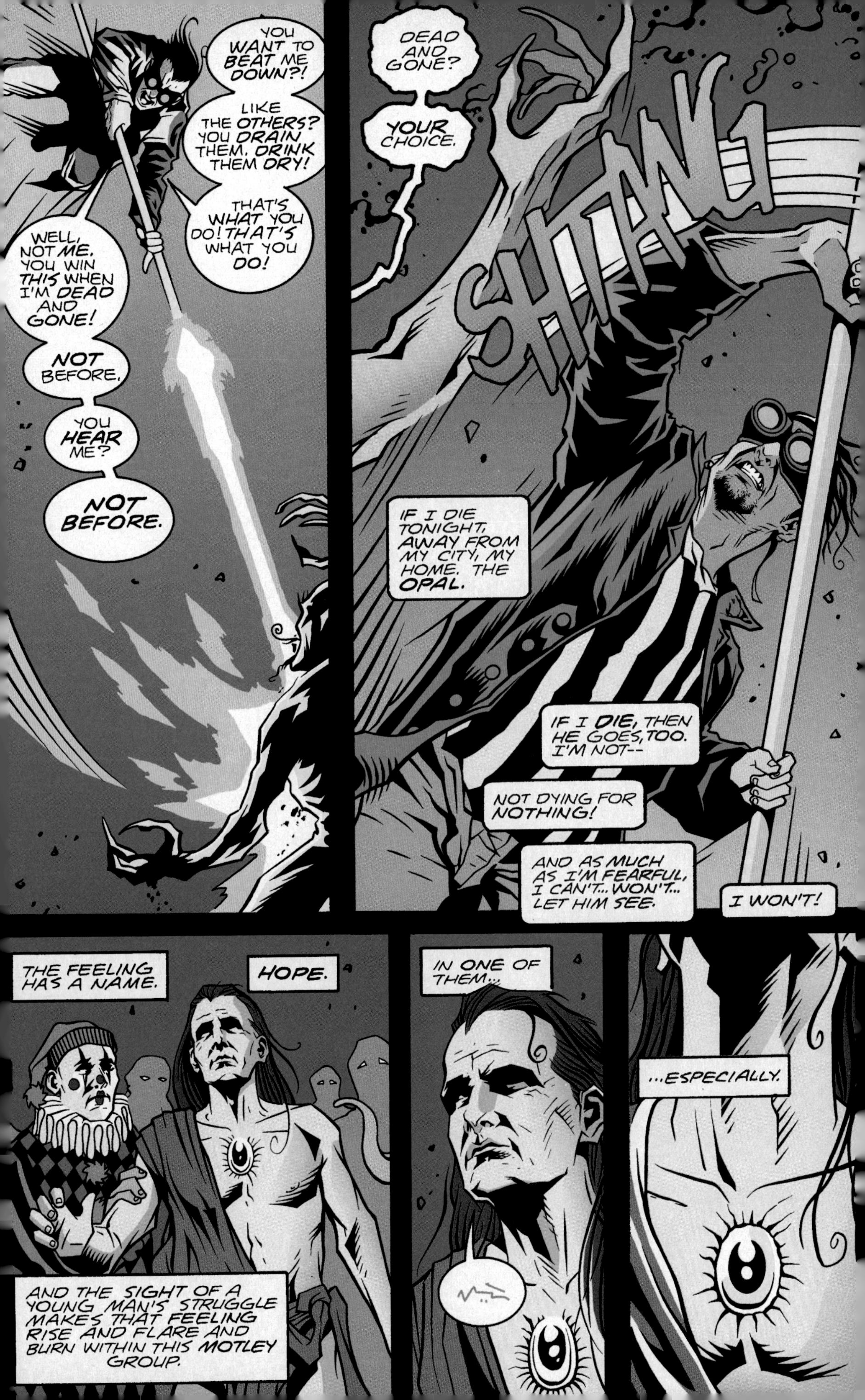
YOU WANT TO BEAT ME DOWN?!
LIKE THE OTHERS? YOU DRAIN THEM. DRINK THEM DRY!
THAT'S WHAT YOU DO! THAT'S WHAT YOU DO!
WELL, NOT ME. YOU WIN THIS WHEN I'M DEAD AND GONE!
NOT BEFORE.
YOU HEAR ME?
NOT BEFORE.
DEAD AND GONE?
YOUR CHOICE.
SHTANG
IF I DIE TONIGHT, AWAY FROM MY CITY, MY HOME. THE OPAL.
IF I DIE, THEN HE GOES, TOO. I'M NOT--
NOT DYING FOR NOTHING!
AND AS MUCH AS I'M FEARFUL, I CAN'T... WON'T... LET HIM SEE.
I WON'T!
THE FEELING HAS A NAME.
HOPE.
AND THE SIGHT OF A YOUNG MAN'S STRUGGLE MAKES THAT FEELING RISE AND FLARE AND BURN WITHIN THIS MOTLEY GROUP.
IN ONE OF THEM...
...ESPECIALLY.

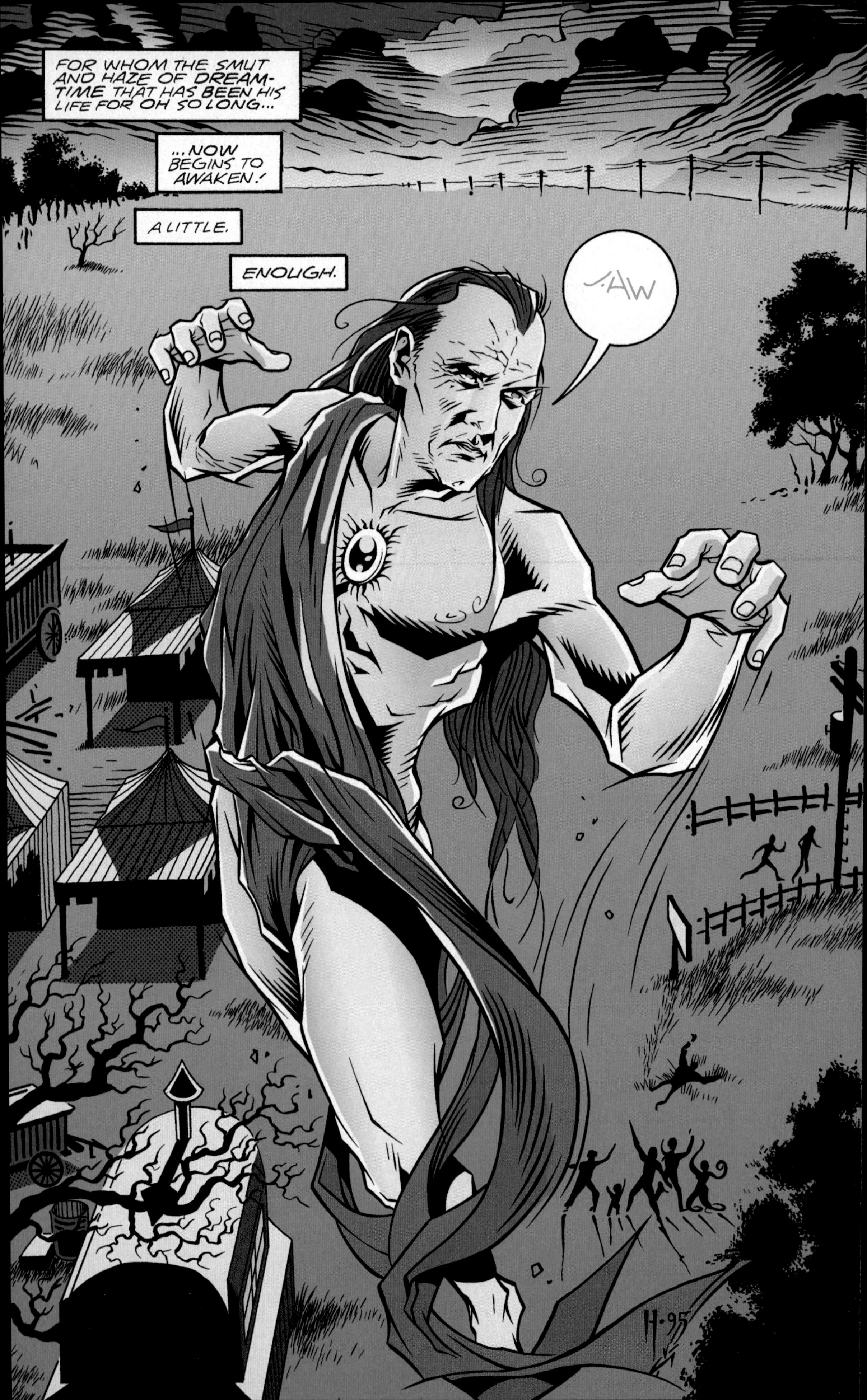
FOR WHOM THE SMUT AND HAZE OF DREAM-TIME THAT HAS BEEN HIS LIFE FOR OH SO LONG...
...NOW BEGINS TO AWAKEN!
A LITTLE.
ENOUGH.
H-95

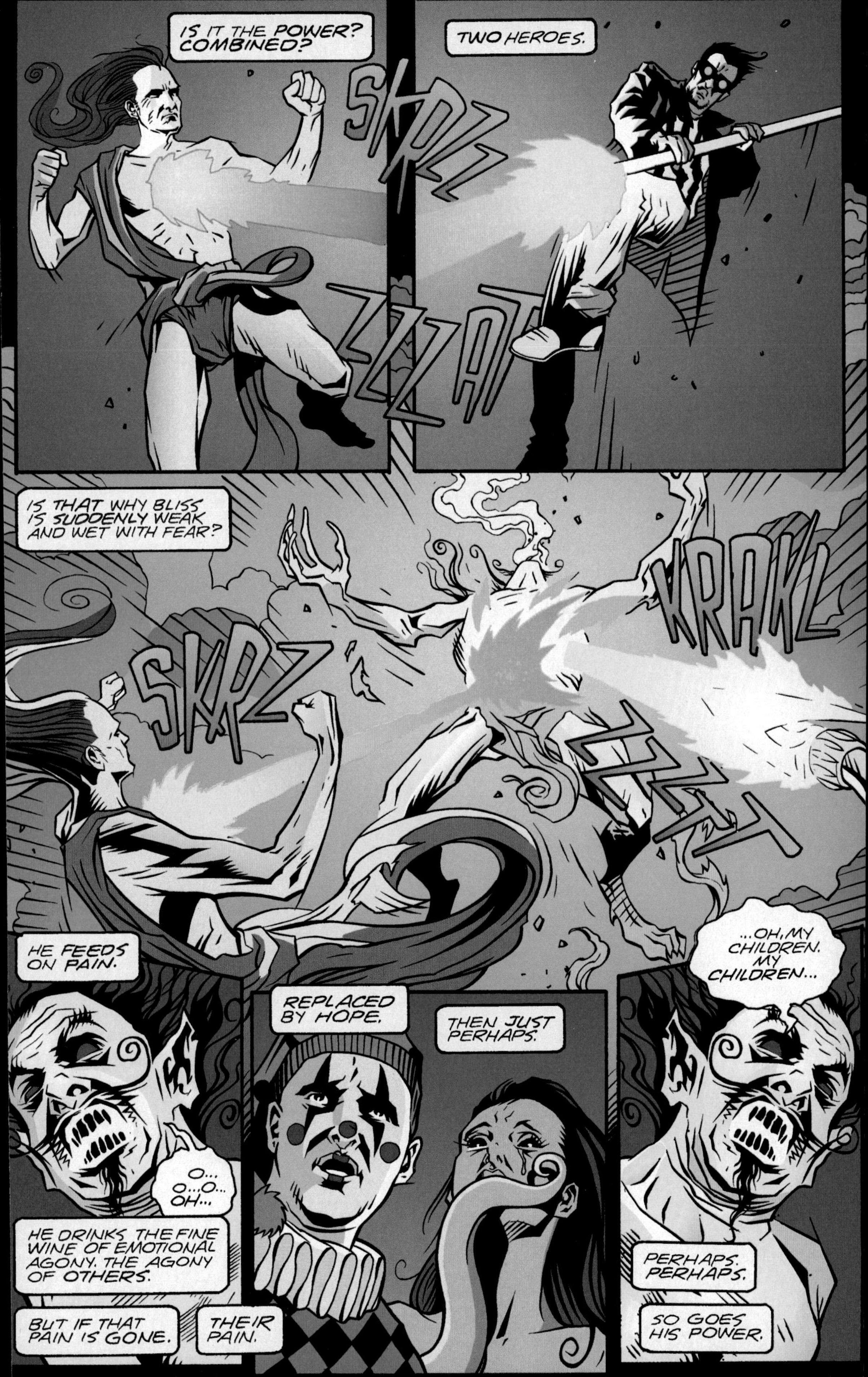
IS IT THE POWER? COMBINED?
SKRZZZ
ZZZZAT
TWO HEROES.
IS THAT WHY BLISS IS SUDDENLY WEAK AND WET WITH FEAR?
KRAKL
SKRZ
ZZZZT
HE FEEDS ON PAIN.
O... O...O... OH...
HE DRINKS THE FINE WINE OF EMOTIONAL AGONY. THE AGONY OF OTHERS.
BUT IF THAT PAIN IS GONE.
REPLACED BY HOPE.
THEN JUST PERHAPS.
THEIR PAIN.
...OH, MY CHILDREN. MY CHILDREN...
PERHAPS. PERHAPS.
SO GOES HIS POWER.

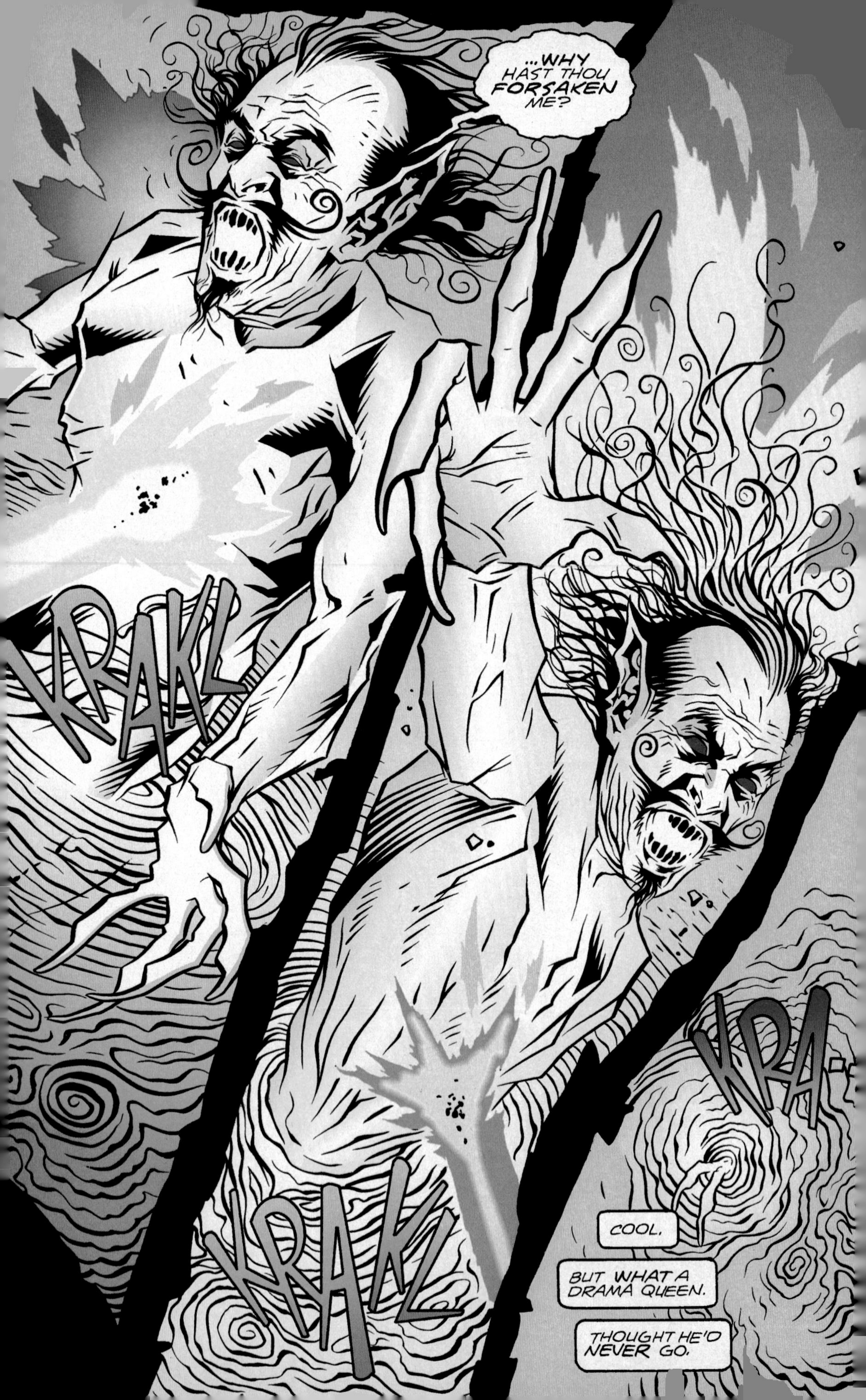
...WHY HAST THOU FORSAKEN ME?
KRAKL
KRAKL
KRA-
COOL.
BUT WHAT A DRAMA QUEEN.
THOUGHT HE'D NEVER GO.

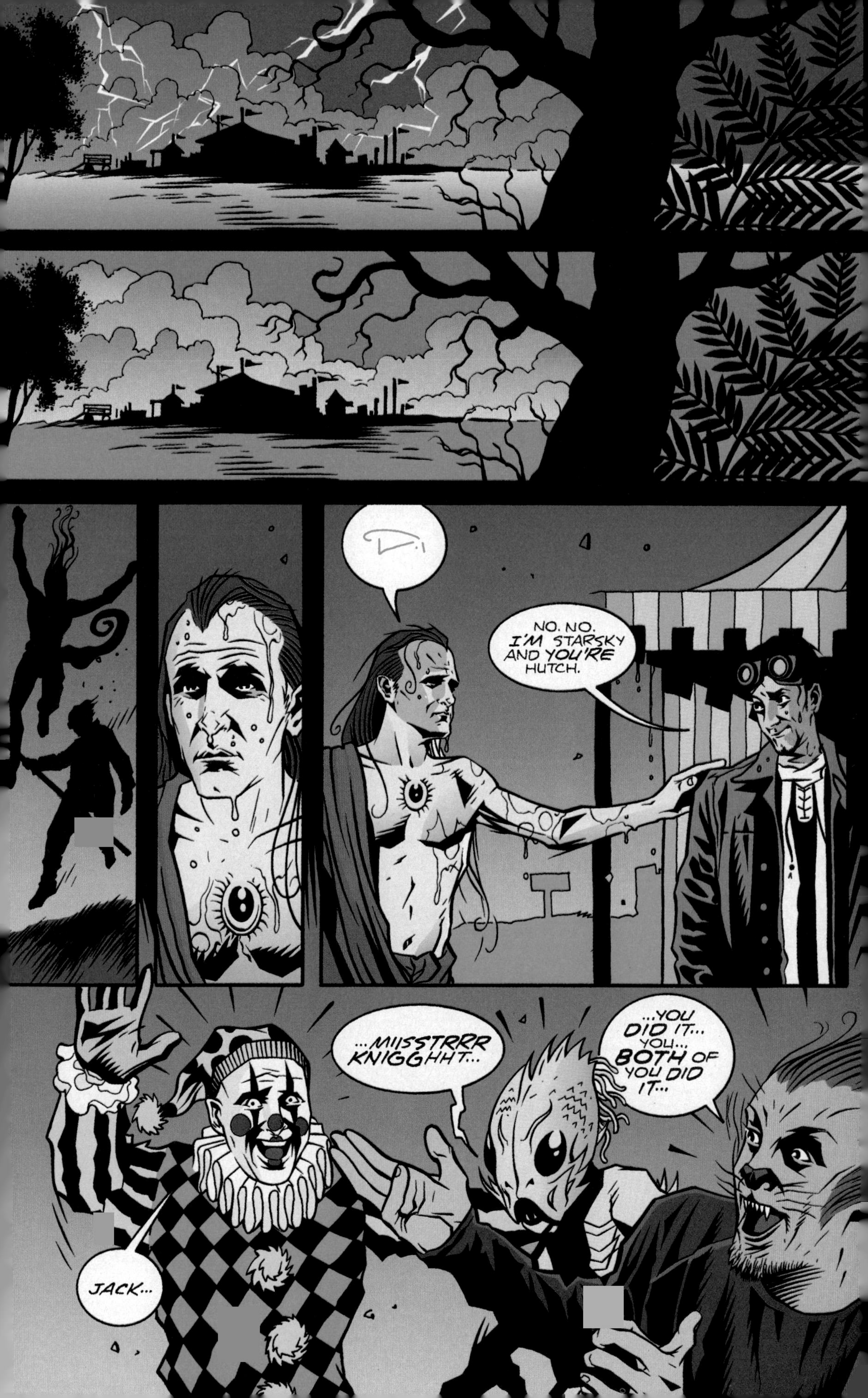
NO. NO. I'M STARSKY AND YOU'RE HUTCH.
JACK...
...MIISSTRRR KNIGGGHHT...
...YOU DID IT... YOU... BOTH OF YOU DID IT...

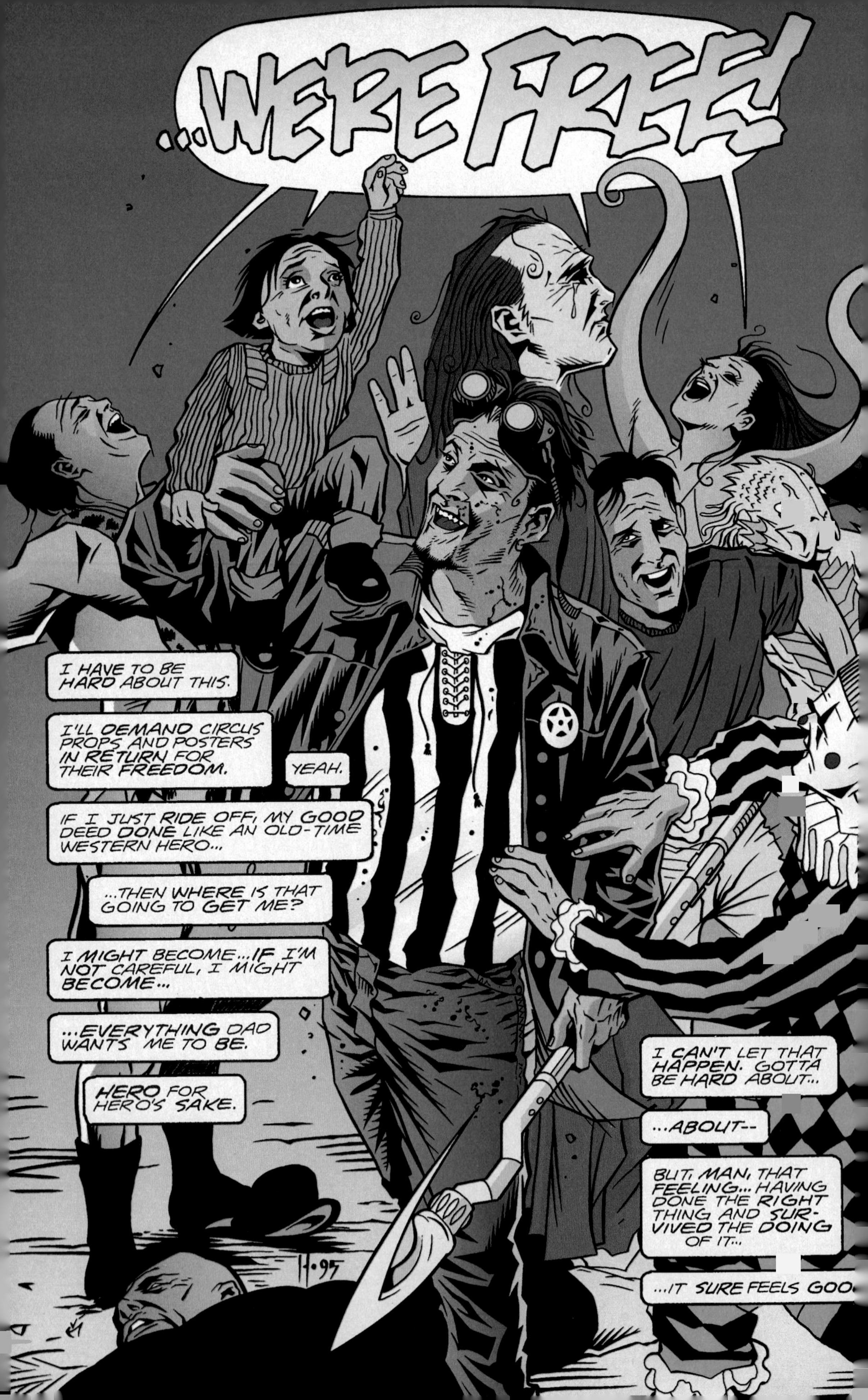
...WE'RE FREE!
I HAVE TO BE HARD ABOUT THIS.
I'LL DEMAND CIRCUS PROPS AND POSTERS IN RETURN FOR THEIR FREEDOM.
YEAH.
IF I JUST RIDE OFF, MY GOOD DEED DONE LIKE AN OLD-TIME WESTERN HERO...
...THEN WHERE IS THAT GOING TO GET ME?
I MIGHT BECOME...IF I'M NOT CAREFUL, I MIGHT BECOME...
...EVERYTHING DAD WANTS ME TO BE.
HERO FOR HERO'S SAKE.
I CAN'T LET THAT HAPPEN. GOTTA BE HARD ABOUT...
...ABOUT--
BUT, MAN, THAT FEELING... HAVING DONE THE RIGHT THING AND SURVIVED THE DOING OF IT...
...IT SURE FEELS GOO

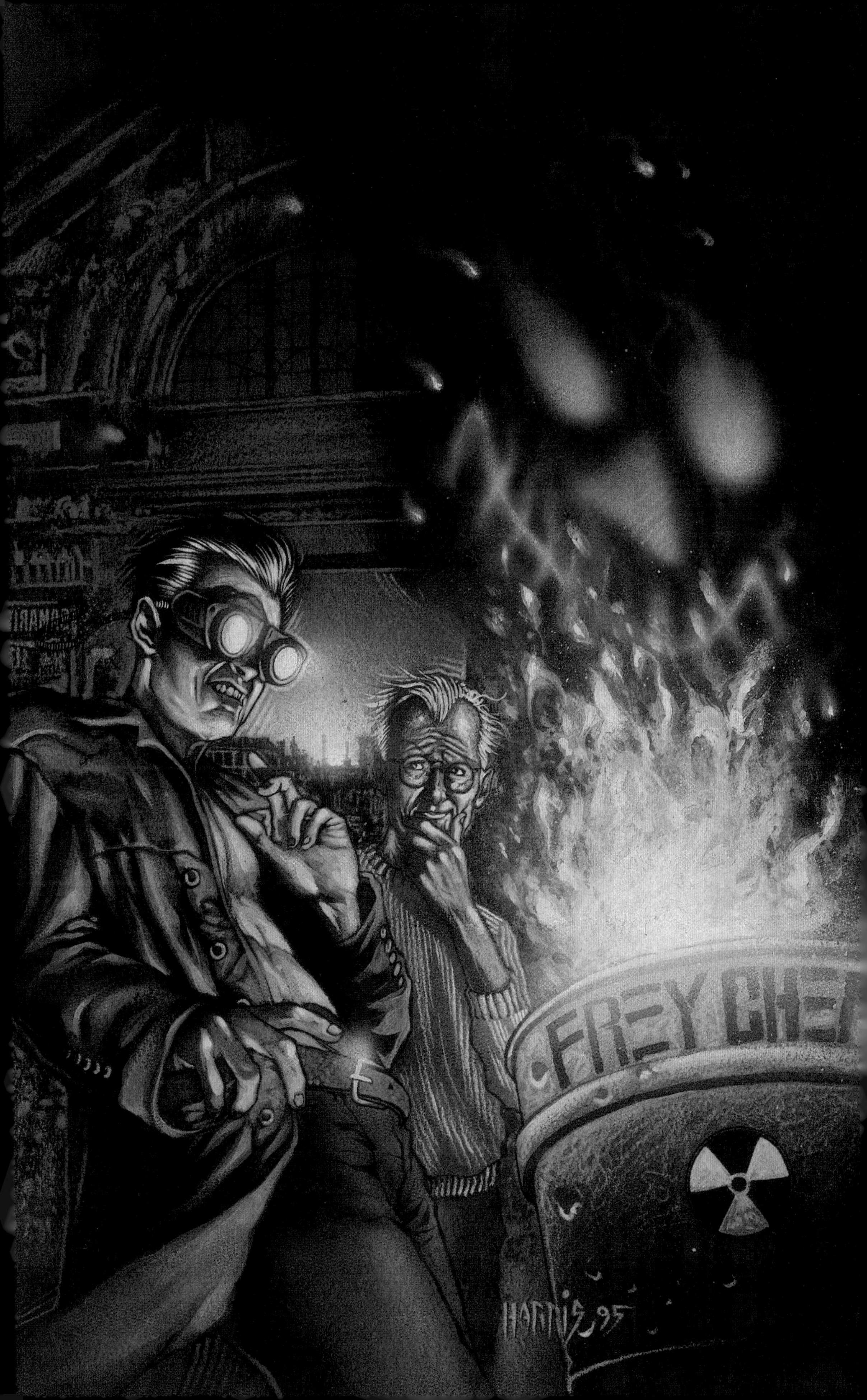

FREY CHE
HARRIS 95

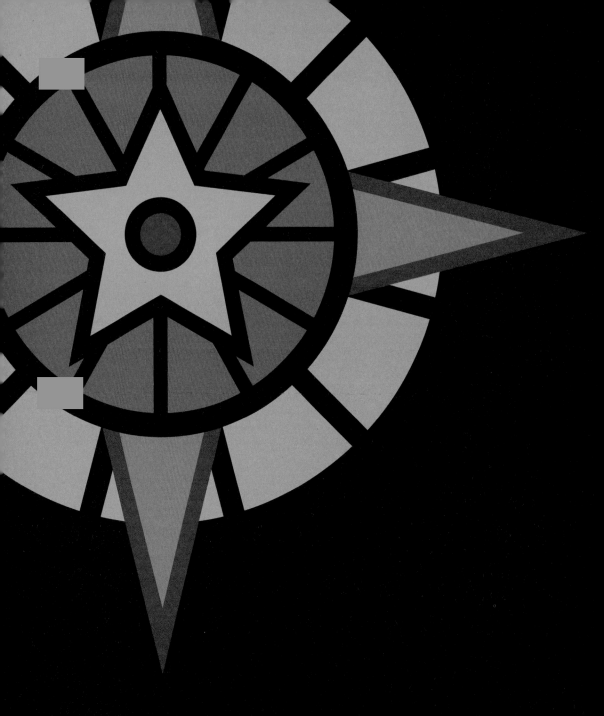

STARMAN 9

Cover by Tony Harris

Written by James Robinson

Pencils by Tony Harris,

with inks by Wade von Grawbadger

and colors by Gregory Wright

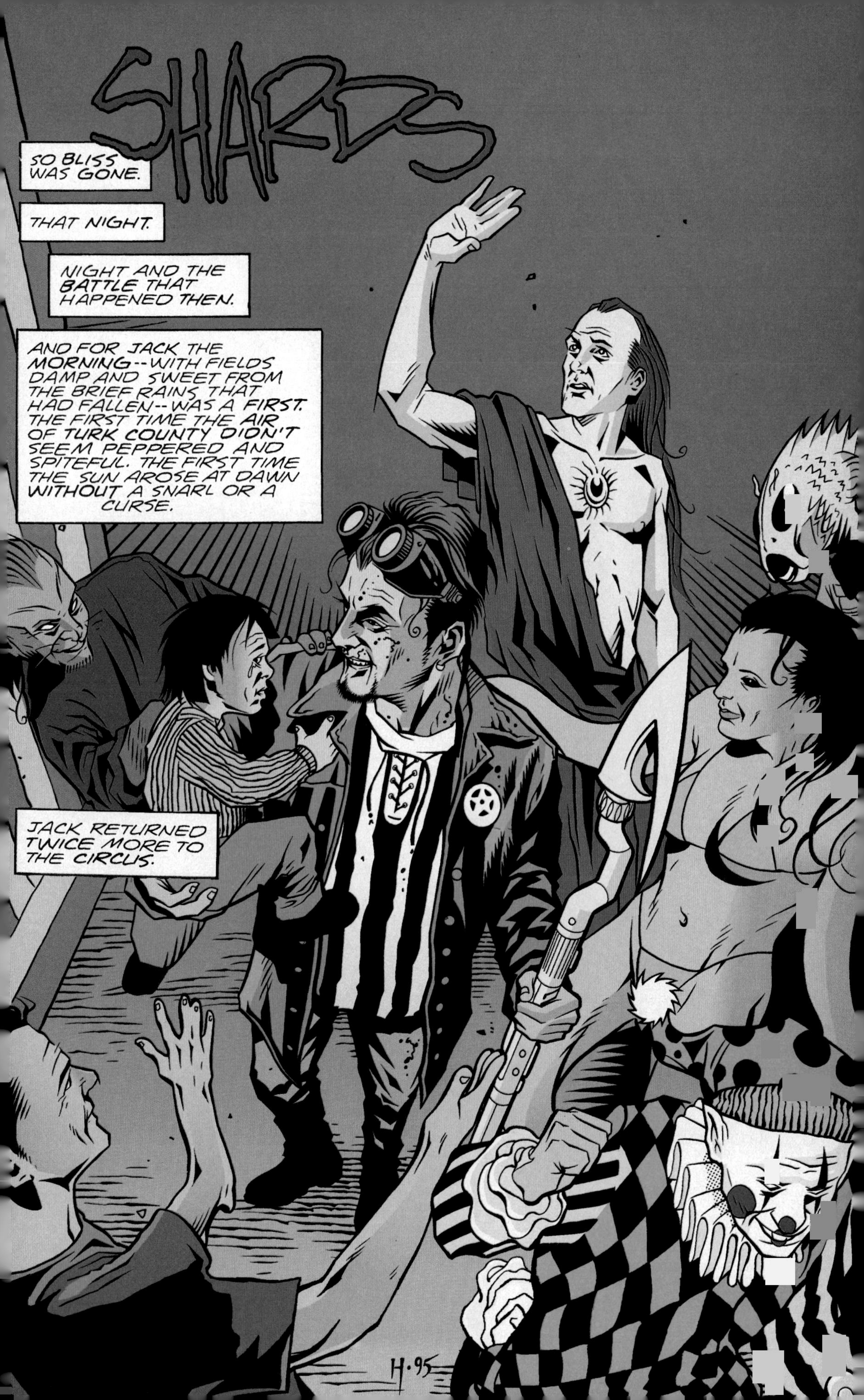
SHARDS
SO BLISS WAS GONE.
THAT NIGHT.
NIGHT AND THE BATTLE THAT HAPPENED THEN.
AND FOR JACK THE MORNING--WITH FIELDS DAMP AND SWEET FROM THE BRIEF RAINS THAT HAD FALLEN--WAS A FIRST. THE FIRST TIME THE AIR OF TURK COUNTY DIDN'T SEEM PEPPERED AND SPITEFUL. THE FIRST TIME THE SUN AROSE AT DAWN WITHOUT A SNARL OR A CURSE.
JACK RETURNED TWICE MORE TO THE CIRCUS.
H·95

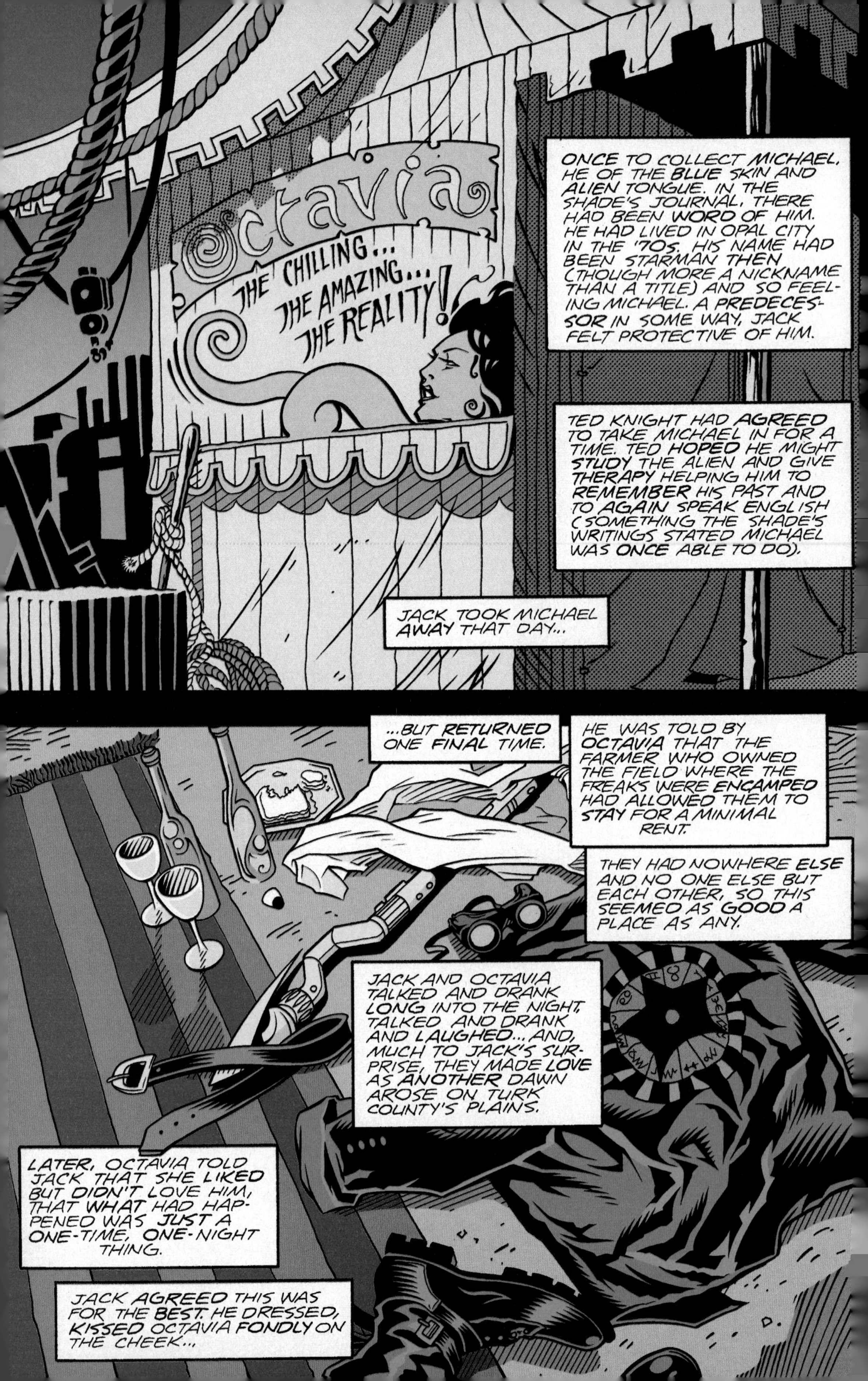
OCTAVIA
THE CHILLING... THE AMAZING... THE REALITY!
ONCE TO COLLECT MICHAEL, HE OF THE BLUE SKIN AND ALIEN TONGUE. IN THE SHADE'S JOURNAL, THERE HAD BEEN WORD OF HIM. HE HAD LIVED IN OPAL CITY IN THE '70s. HIS NAME HAD BEEN STARMAN THEN (THOUGH MORE A NICKNAME THAN A TITLE) AND SO FEELING MICHAEL A PREDECESSOR IN SOME WAY, JACK FELT PROTECTIVE OF HIM.
TED KNIGHT HAD AGREED TO TAKE MICHAEL IN FOR A TIME. TED HOPED HE MIGHT STUDY THE ALIEN AND GIVE THERAPY HELPING HIM TO REMEMBER HIS PAST AND TO AGAIN SPEAK ENGLISH (SOMETHING THE SHADE'S WRITINGS STATED MICHAEL WAS ONCE ABLE TO DO).
JACK TOOK MICHAEL AWAY THAT DAY...
...BUT RETURNED ONE FINAL TIME.
HE WAS TOLD BY OCTAVIA THAT THE FARMER WHO OWNED THE FIELD WHERE THE FREAKS WERE ENCAMPED HAD ALLOWED THEM TO STAY FOR A MINIMAL RENT.
THEY HAD NOWHERE ELSE AND NO ONE ELSE BUT EACH OTHER, SO THIS SEEMED AS GOOD A PLACE AS ANY.
JACK AND OCTAVIA TALKED AND DRANK LONG INTO THE NIGHT, TALKED AND DRANK AND LAUGHED... AND, MUCH TO JACK'S SURPRISE, THEY MADE LOVE AS ANOTHER DAWN AROSE ON TURK COUNTY'S PLAINS.
LATER, OCTAVIA TOLD JACK THAT SHE LIKED BUT DIDN'T LOVE HIM, THAT WHAT HAD HAPPENED WAS JUST A ONE-TIME, ONE-NIGHT THING.
JACK AGREED THIS WAS FOR THE BEST. HE DRESSED, KISSED OCTAVIA FONDLY ON THE CHEEK...

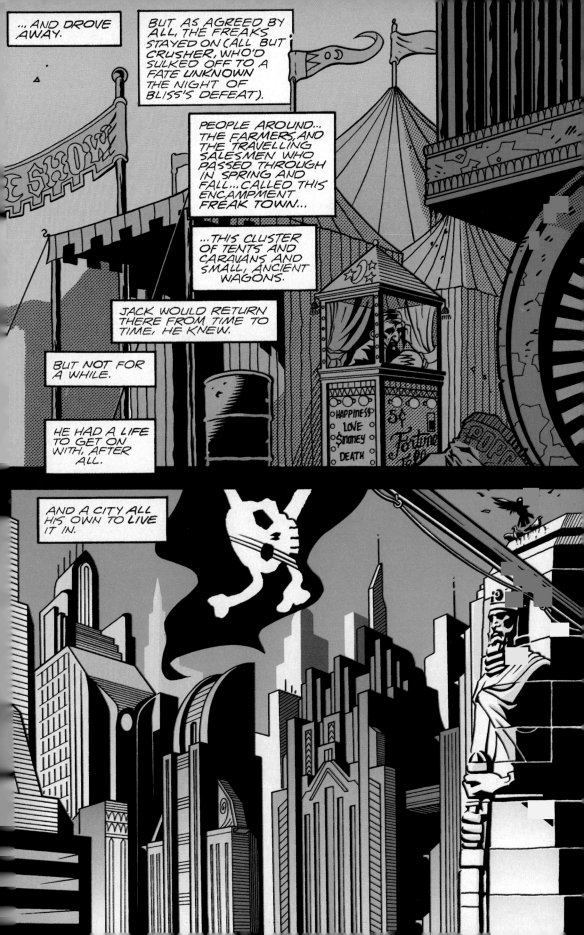

... AND DROVE AWAY.

BUT AS AGREED BY ALL, THE FREAKS STAYED ON (ALL BUT CRUSHER, WHO'D SULKED OFF TO A FATE UNKNOWN THE NIGHT OF BLISS'S DEFEAT).

PEOPLE AROUND... THE FARMERS, AND THE TRAVELLING SALESMEN WHO PASSED THROUGH IN SPRING AND FALL... CALLED THIS ENCAMPMENT FREAK TOWN...

...THIS CLUSTER OF TENTS AND CARAVANS AND SMALL, ANCIENT WAGONS.

JACK WOULD RETURN THERE FROM TIME TO TIME, HE KNEW.

BUT NOT FOR A WHILE.

HE HAD A LIFE TO GET ON WITH, AFTER ALL.

AND A CITY ALL HIS OWN TO LIVE IT IN.

HAPPINESS
LOVE
$MONEY
DEATH

5¢ Fortune

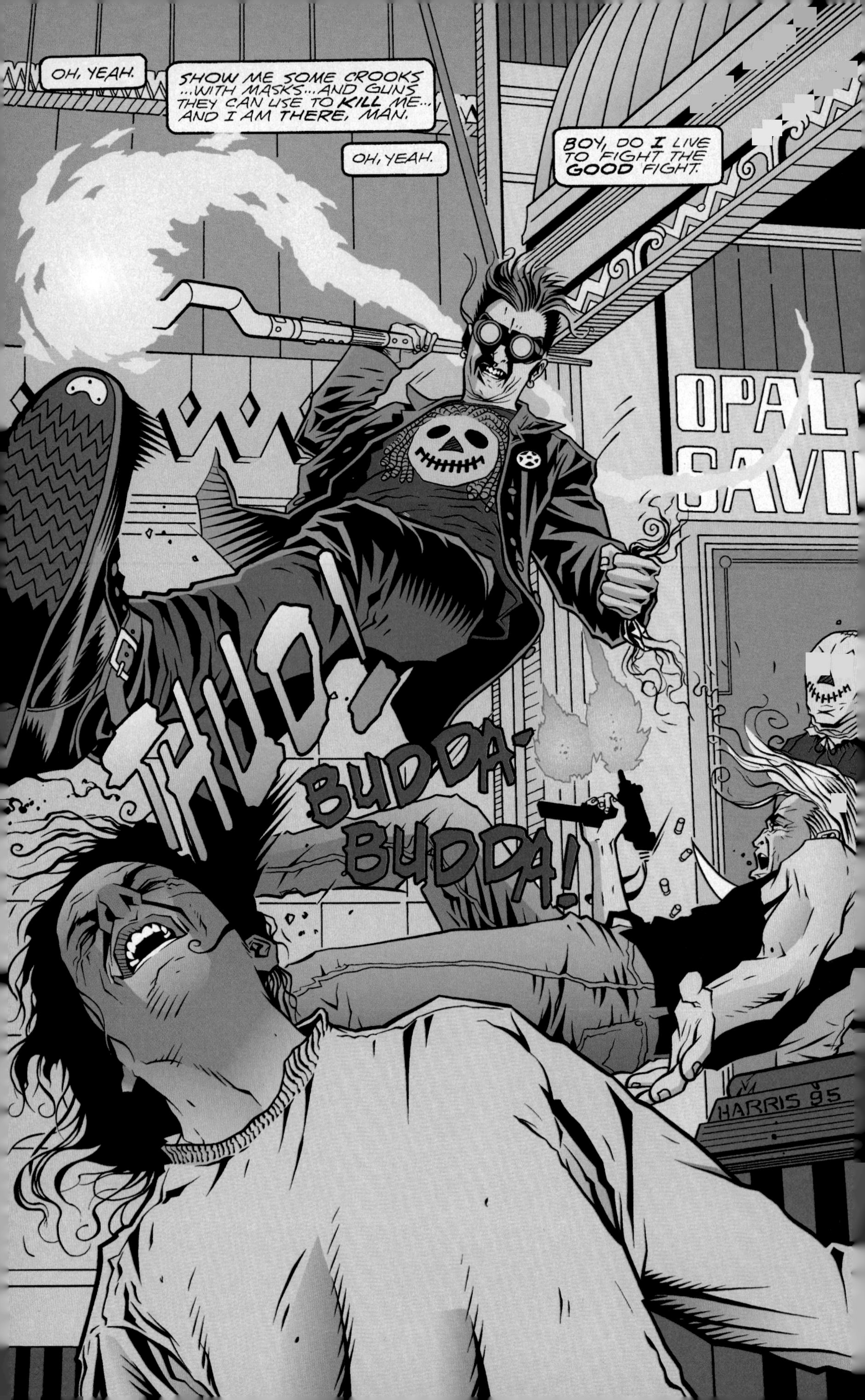
OH, YEAH.
SHOW ME SOME CROOKS ...WITH MASKS...AND GUNS THEY CAN USE TO KILL ME... AND I AM THERE, MAN.
OH, YEAH.
BOY, DO I LIVE TO FIGHT THE GOOD FIGHT.
OPAL
THUD!
BUDDA-BUDDA!
HARRIS 95

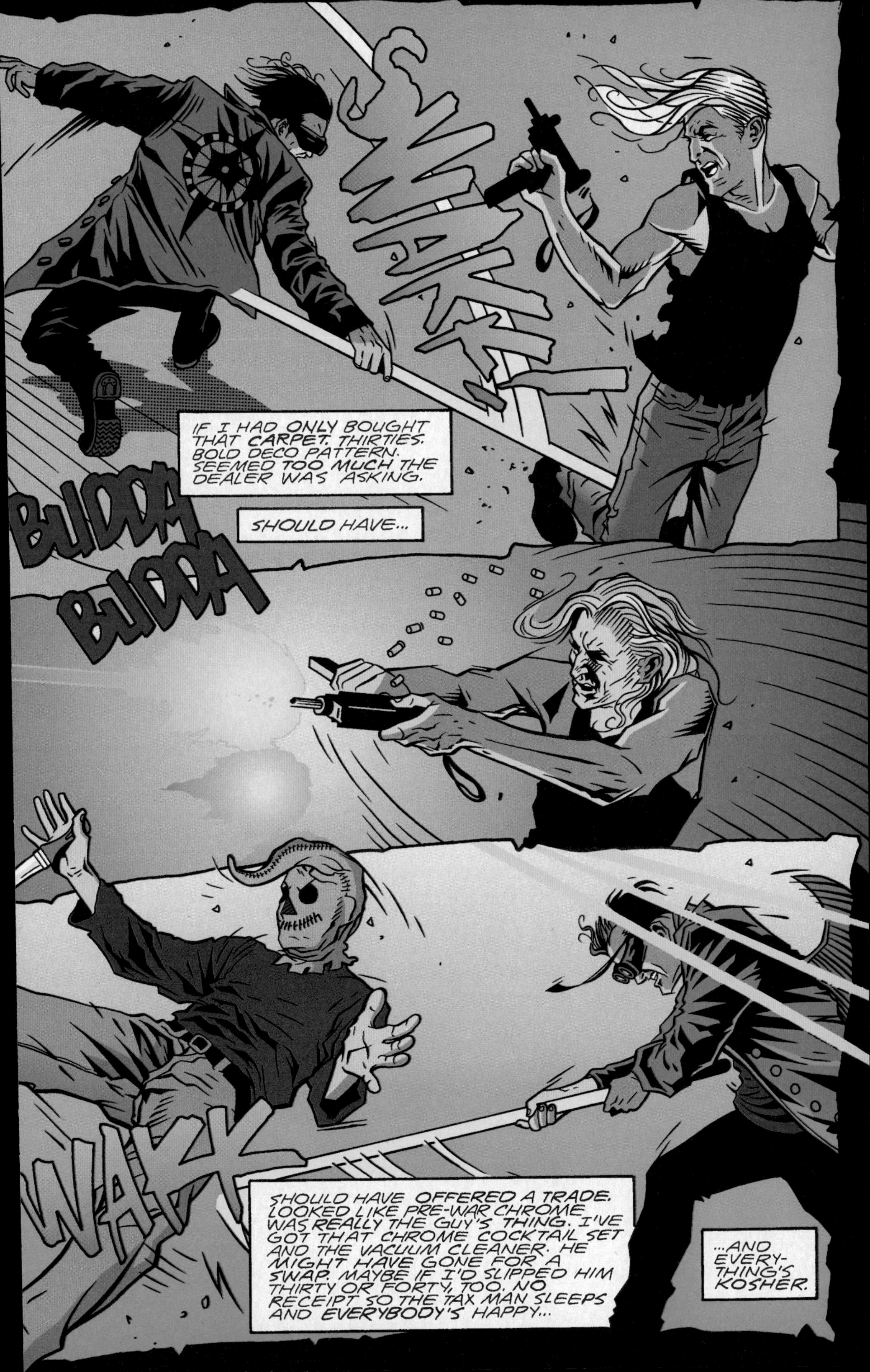

SWAKK
IF I HAD ONLY BOUGHT THAT CARPET. THIRTIES. BOLD DECO PATTERN. SEEMED TOO MUCH THE DEALER WAS ASKING.
SHOULD HAVE...
BUDDA BUDDA
WAKK
SHOULD HAVE OFFERED A TRADE. LOOKED LIKE PRE-WAR CHROME WAS REALLY THE GUY'S THING. I'VE GOT THAT CHROME COCKTAIL SET AND THE VACUUM CLEANER. HE MIGHT HAVE GONE FOR A SWAP. MAYBE IF I'D SLIPPED HIM THIRTY OR FORTY, TOO. NO RECEIPT SO THE TAX MAN SLEEPS AND EVERYBODY'S HAPPY...
...AND EVERY-THING'S KOSHER.

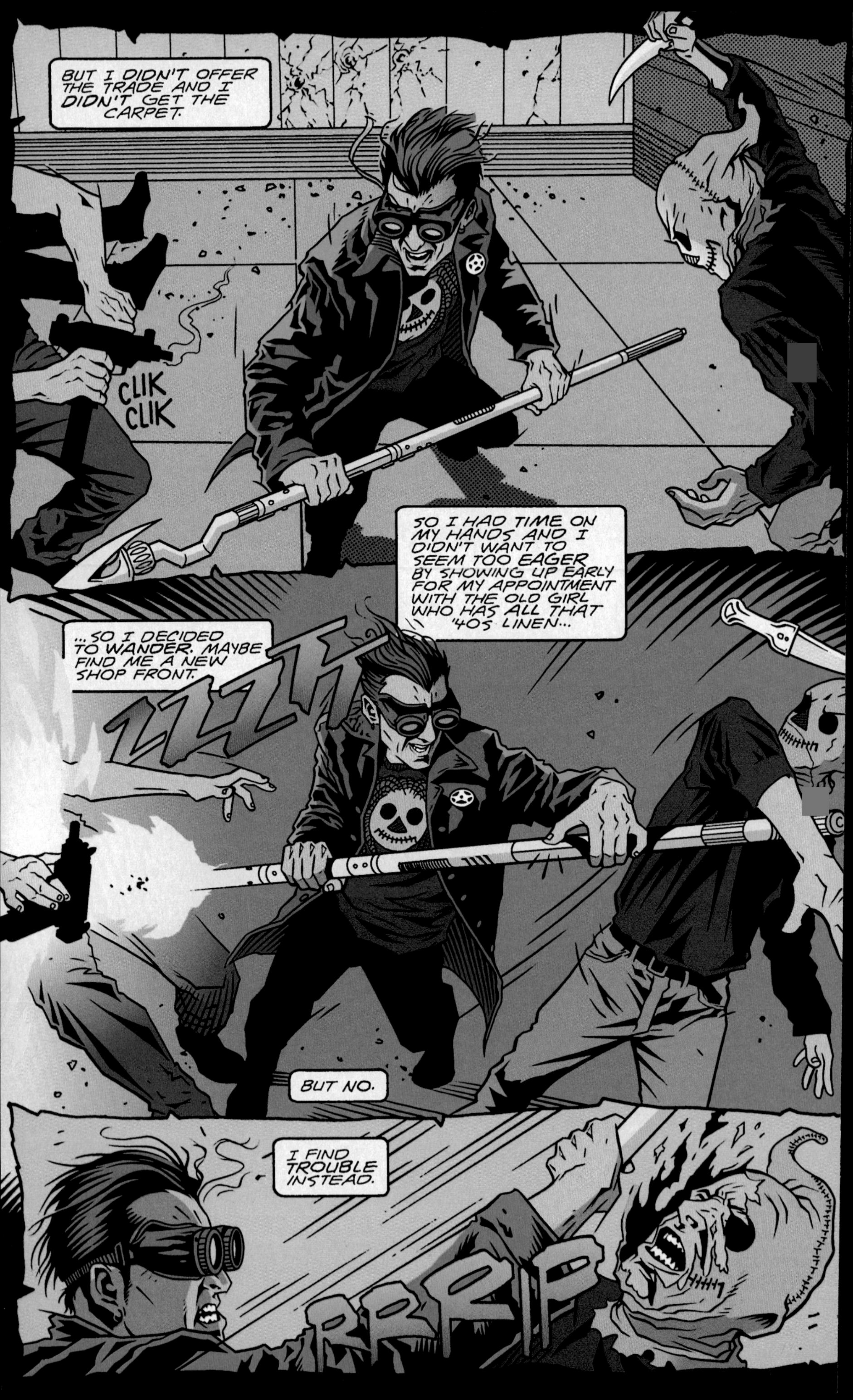

BUT I DIDN'T OFFER THE TRADE AND I DIDN'T GET THE CARPET.
CLIK CLIK
SO I HAD TIME ON MY HANDS AND I DIDN'T WANT TO SEEM TOO EAGER BY SHOWING UP EARLY FOR MY APPOINTMENT WITH THE OLD GIRL WHO HAS ALL THAT '40S LINEN...
...SO I DECIDED TO WANDER. MAYBE FIND ME A NEW SHOP FRONT.
ZZZZTT
BUT NO.
I FIND TROUBLE INSTEAD.
RRRIP

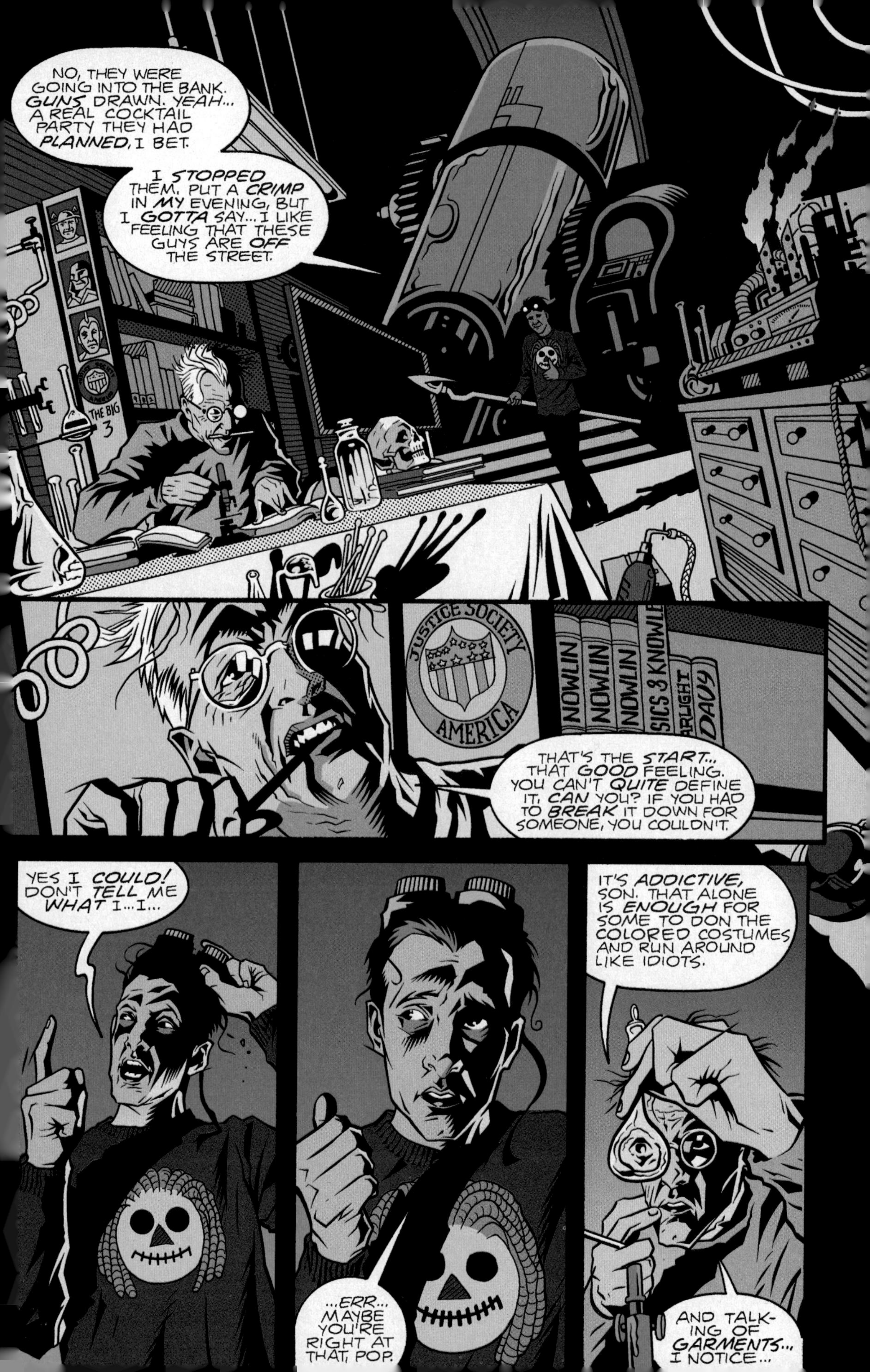
NO, THEY WERE GOING INTO THE BANK. GUNS DRAWN. YEAH... A REAL COCKTAIL PARTY THEY HAD PLANNED, I BET.
I STOPPED THEM. PUT A CRIMP IN MY EVENING, BUT I GOTTA SAY... I LIKE FEELING THAT THESE GUYS ARE OFF THE STREET.
THE BIG 3
JUSTICE SOCIETY AMERICA
NOWLIN
NOWLIN
NOWLIN
SICS & KNOWL
ARLIGHT
DAVY
THAT'S THE START... THAT GOOD FEELING. YOU CAN'T QUITE DEFINE IT, CAN YOU? IF YOU HAD TO BREAK IT DOWN FOR SOMEONE, YOU COULDN'T.
YES I COULD! DON'T TELL ME WHAT I...I...
...ERR... MAYBE YOU'RE RIGHT AT THAT, POP.
IT'S ADDICTIVE, SON. THAT ALONE IS ENOUGH FOR SOME TO DON THE COLORED COSTUMES AND RUN AROUND LIKE IDIOTS.
AND TALKING OF GARMENTS... I NOTICE...

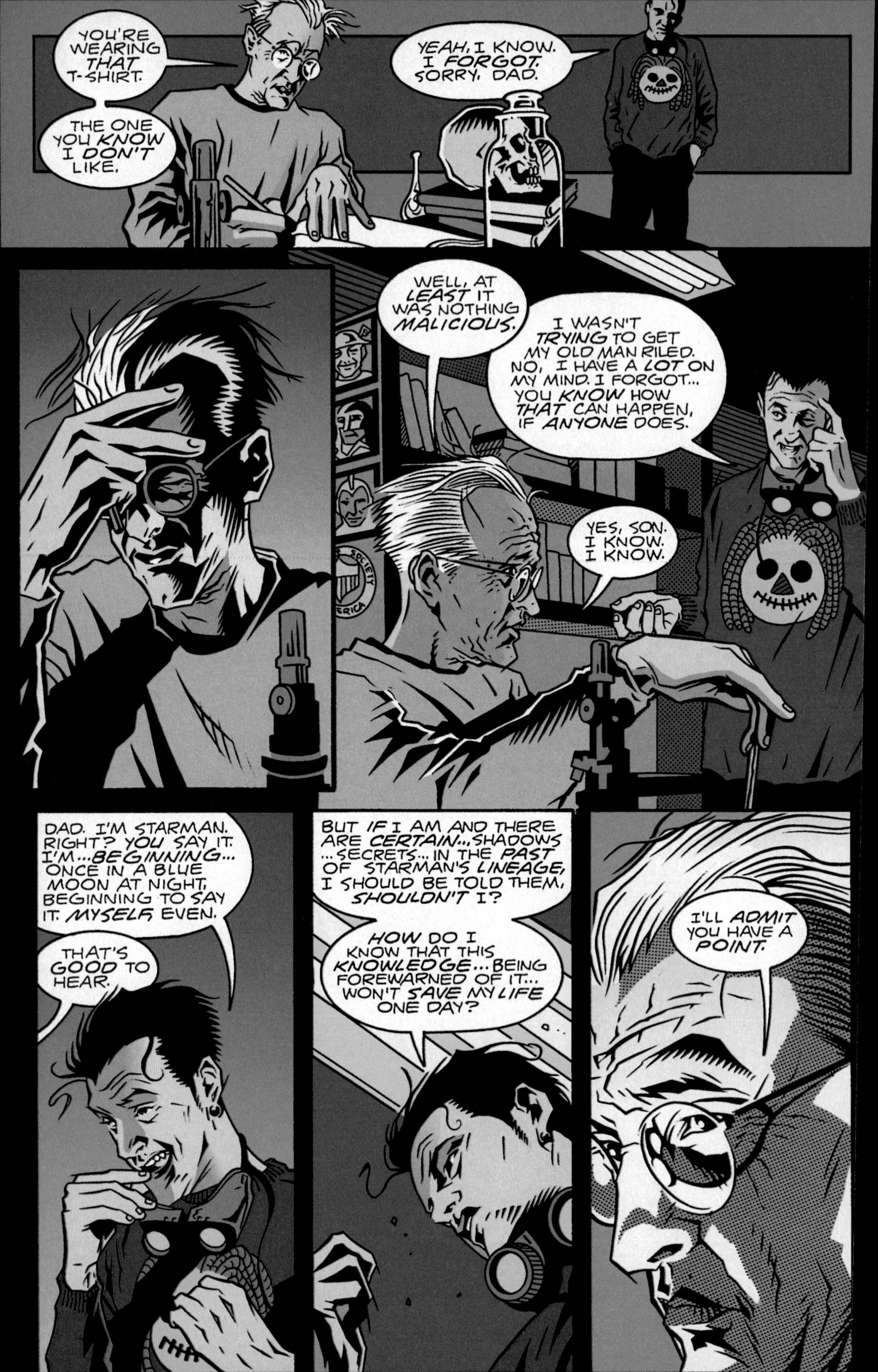

YOU'RE WEARING THAT T-SHIRT.
THE ONE YOU KNOW I DON'T LIKE.
YEAH, I KNOW. I FORGOT. SORRY, DAD.
WELL, AT LEAST IT WAS NOTHING MALICIOUS.
I WASN'T TRYING TO GET MY OLD MAN RILED. NO, I HAVE A LOT ON MY MIND. I FORGOT... YOU KNOW HOW THAT CAN HAPPEN, IF ANYONE DOES.
YES, SON. I KNOW. I KNOW.
DAD. I'M STARMAN. RIGHT? YOU SAY IT. I'M...BEGINNING... ONCE IN A BLUE MOON AT NIGHT, BEGINNING TO SAY IT. MYSELF, EVEN.
THAT'S GOOD TO HEAR.
BUT IF I AM AND THERE ARE CERTAIN...SHADOWS ...SECRETS... IN THE PAST OF STARMAN'S LINEAGE, I SHOULD BE TOLD THEM, SHOULDN'T I?
HOW DO I KNOW THAT THIS KNOWLEDGE... BEING FOREWARNED OF IT... WON'T SAVE MY LIFE ONE DAY?
I'LL ADMIT YOU HAVE A POINT.

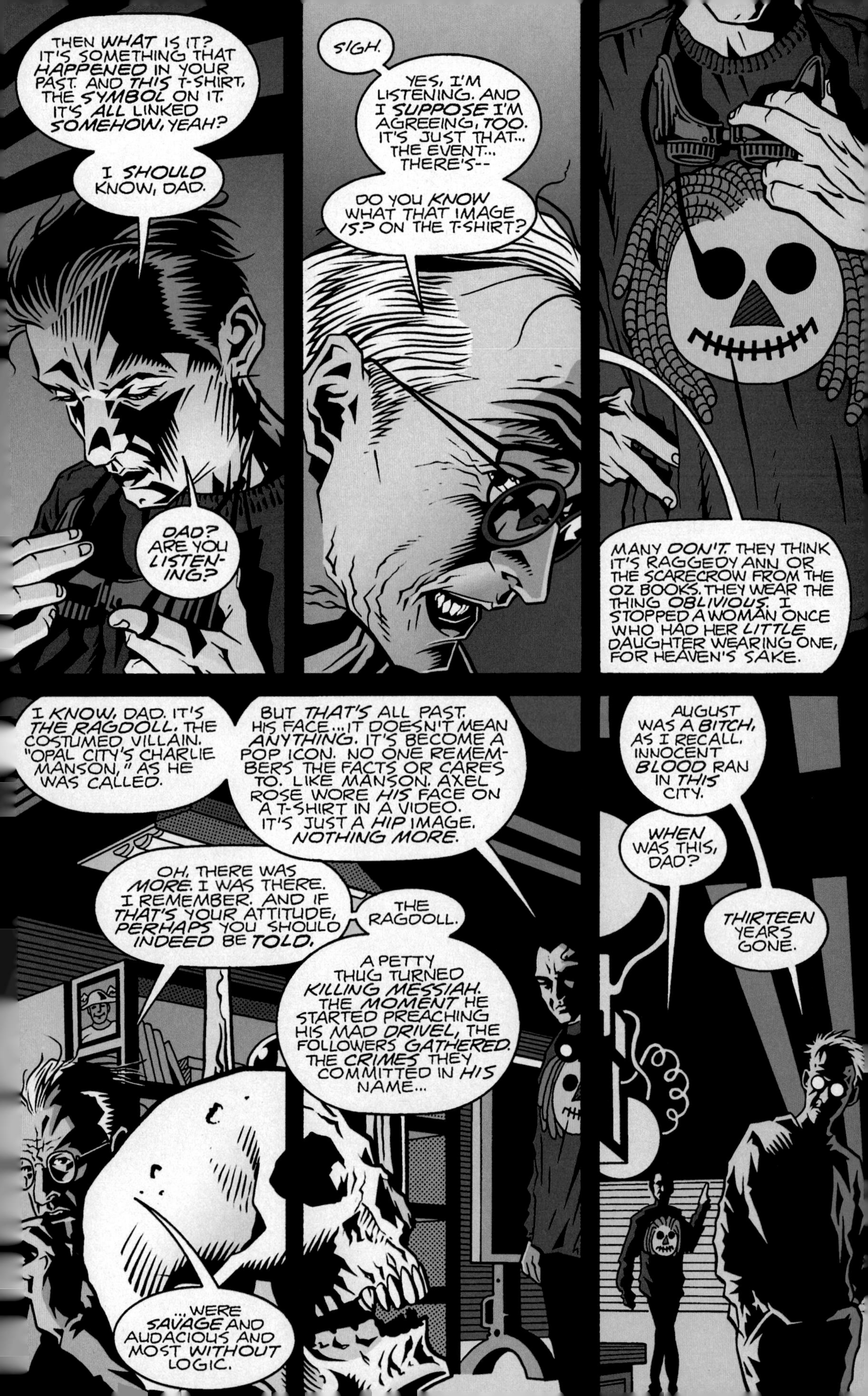
THEN WHAT IS IT? IT'S SOMETHING THAT HAPPENED IN YOUR PAST. AND THIS T-SHIRT, THE SYMBOL ON IT. IT'S ALL LINKED SOMEHOW, YEAH?
I SHOULD KNOW, DAD.
DAD? ARE YOU LISTEN-ING?
SIGH.
YES, I'M LISTENING. AND I SUPPOSE I'M AGREEING, TOO. IT'S JUST THAT... THE EVENT... THERE'S--
DO YOU KNOW WHAT THAT IMAGE IS? ON THE T-SHIRT?
MANY DON'T. THEY THINK IT'S RAGGEDY ANN OR THE SCARECROW FROM THE OZ BOOKS. THEY WEAR THE THING OBLIVIOUS. I STOPPED A WOMAN ONCE WHO HAD HER LITTLE DAUGHTER WEARING ONE, FOR HEAVEN'S SAKE.
I KNOW, DAD. IT'S THE RAGDOLL. THE COSTUMED VILLAIN. "OPAL CITY'S CHARLIE MANSON," AS HE WAS CALLED.
BUT THAT'S ALL PAST. HIS FACE... IT DOESN'T MEAN ANYTHING. IT'S BECOME A POP ICON. NO ONE REMEMBERS THE FACTS OR CARES TO. LIKE MANSON. AXEL ROSE WORE HIS FACE ON A T-SHIRT IN A VIDEO. IT'S JUST A HIP IMAGE. NOTHING MORE.
OH, THERE WAS MORE. I WAS THERE. I REMEMBER. AND IF THAT'S YOUR ATTITUDE, PERHAPS YOU SHOULD INDEED BE TOLD.
THE RAGDOLL.
A PETTY THUG TURNED KILLING MESSIAH. THE MOMENT HE STARTED PREACHING HIS MAD DRIVEL, THE FOLLOWERS GATHERED. THE CRIMES THEY COMMITTED IN HIS NAME...
...WERE SAVAGE AND AUDACIOUS AND MOST WITHOUT LOGIC.
AUGUST WAS A BITCH, AS I RECALL. INNOCENT BLOOD RAN IN THIS CITY.
WHEN WAS THIS, DAD?
THIRTEEN YEARS GONE.

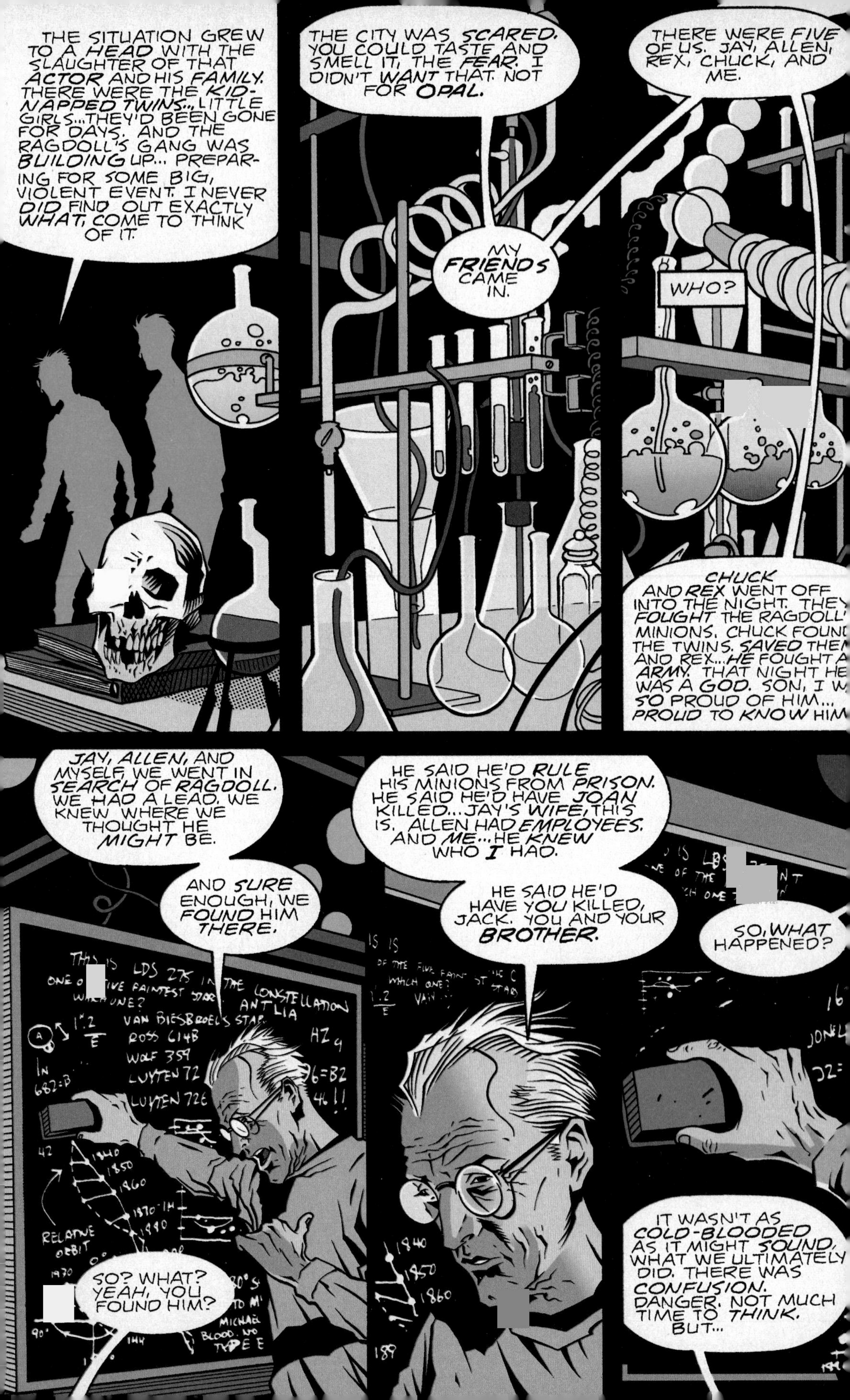

THE SITUATION GREW TO A HEAD WITH THE SLAUGHTER OF THAT ACTOR AND HIS FAMILY. THERE WERE THE KIDNAPPED TWINS... LITTLE GIRLS... THEY'D BEEN GONE FOR DAYS. AND THE RAGDOLL'S GANG WAS BUILDING UP... PREPARING FOR SOME BIG, VIOLENT EVENT. I NEVER DID FIND OUT EXACTLY WHAT, COME TO THINK OF IT.
THE CITY WAS SCARED. YOU COULD TASTE AND SMELL IT, THE FEAR. I DIDN'T WANT THAT. NOT FOR OPAL.
MY FRIENDS CAME IN.
THERE WERE FIVE OF US. JAY, ALLEN, REX, CHUCK, AND ME.
WHO?
CHUCK AND REX WENT OFF INTO THE NIGHT. THEY FOUGHT THE RAGDOLL' MINIONS. CHUCK FOUN THE TWINS. SAVED THE AND REX... HE FOUGHT A ARMY. THAT NIGHT HE WAS A GOD. SON, I W SO PROUD OF HIM... PROUD TO KNOW HIM
JAY, ALLEN, AND MYSELF, WE WENT IN SEARCH OF RAGDOLL. WE HAD A LEAD. WE KNEW WHERE WE THOUGHT HE MIGHT BE.
AND SURE ENOUGH, WE FOUND HIM THERE.
SO? WHAT? YEAH, YOU FOUND HIM?
HE SAID HE'D RULE HIS MINIONS FROM PRISON. HE SAID HE'D HAVE JOAN KILLED... JAY'S WIFE, THIS IS. ALLEN HAD EMPLOYEES. AND ME... HE KNEW WHO I HAD.
HE SAID HE'D HAVE YOU KILLED, JACK. YOU AND YOUR BROTHER.
SO, WHAT HAPPENED?
IT WASN'T AS COLD-BLOODED AS IT MIGHT SOUND, WHAT WE ULTIMATELY DID. THERE WAS CONFUSION. DANGER. NOT MUCH TIME TO THINK. BUT...

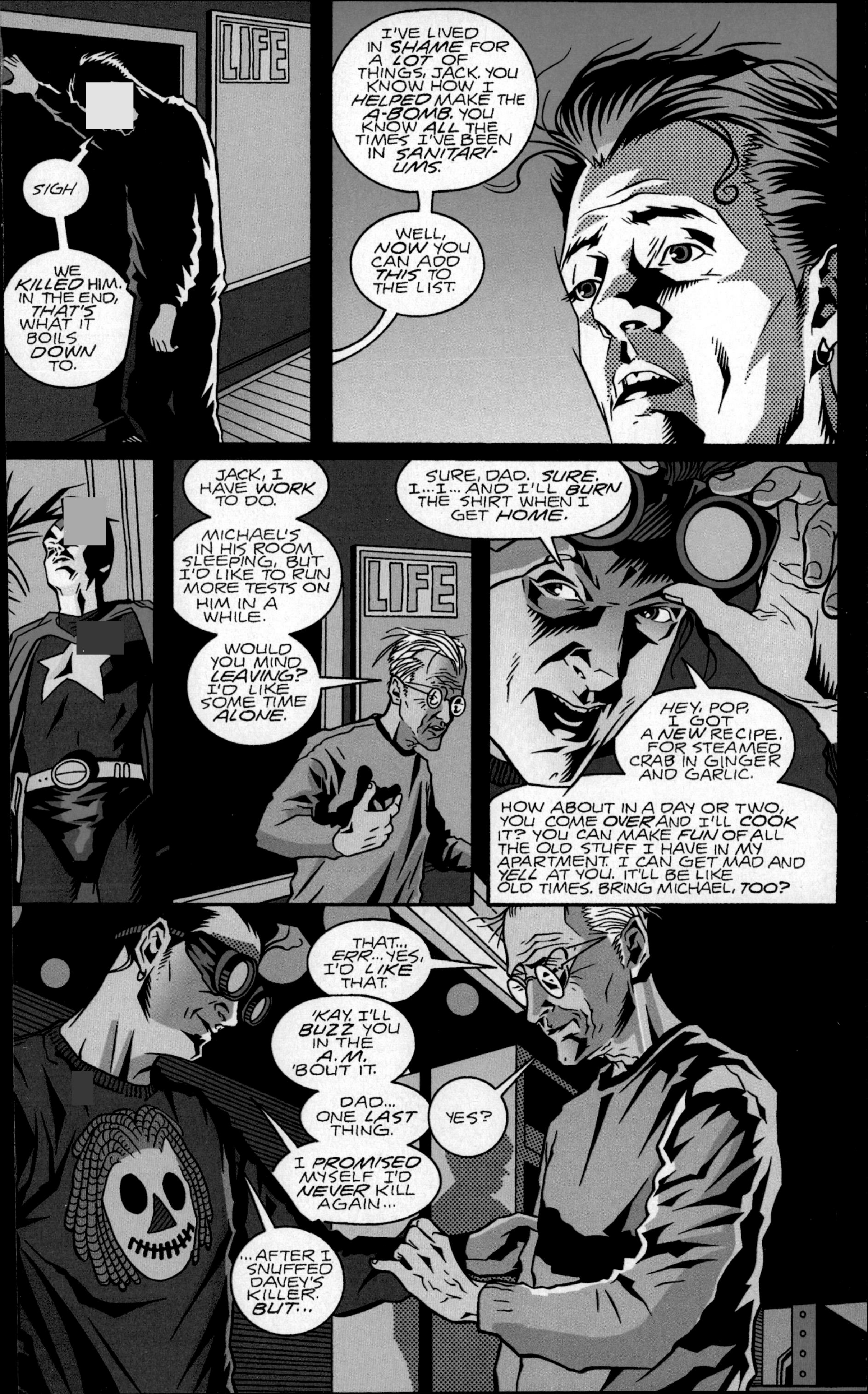
SIGH
WE KILLED HIM. IN THE END, THAT'S WHAT IT BOILS DOWN TO.
I'VE LIVED IN SHAME FOR A LOT OF THINGS, JACK. YOU KNOW HOW I HELPED MAKE THE A-BOMB. YOU KNOW ALL THE TIMES I'VE BEEN IN SANITARI-UMS.
WELL, NOW YOU CAN ADD THIS TO THE LIST.
LIFE
JACK, I HAVE WORK TO DO.
MICHAEL'S IN HIS ROOM SLEEPING, BUT I'D LIKE TO RUN MORE TESTS ON HIM IN A WHILE.
WOULD YOU MIND LEAVING? I'D LIKE SOME TIME ALONE.
LIFE
SURE, DAD. SURE. I...I... AND I'LL BURN THE SHIRT WHEN I GET HOME.
HEY, POP, I GOT A NEW RECIPE. FOR STEAMED CRAB IN GINGER AND GARLIC.
HOW ABOUT IN A DAY OR TWO, YOU COME OVER AND I'LL COOK IT? YOU CAN MAKE FUN OF ALL THE OLD STUFF I HAVE IN MY APARTMENT. I CAN GET MAD AND YELL AT YOU. IT'LL BE LIKE OLD TIMES. BRING MICHAEL, TOO?
THAT... ERR... YES, I'D LIKE THAT.
'KAY. I'LL BUZZ YOU IN THE A.M. 'BOUT IT.
DAD... ONE LAST THING.
YES?
I PROMISED MYSELF I'D NEVER KILL AGAIN...
...AFTER I SNUFFED DAVEY'S KILLER. BUT...

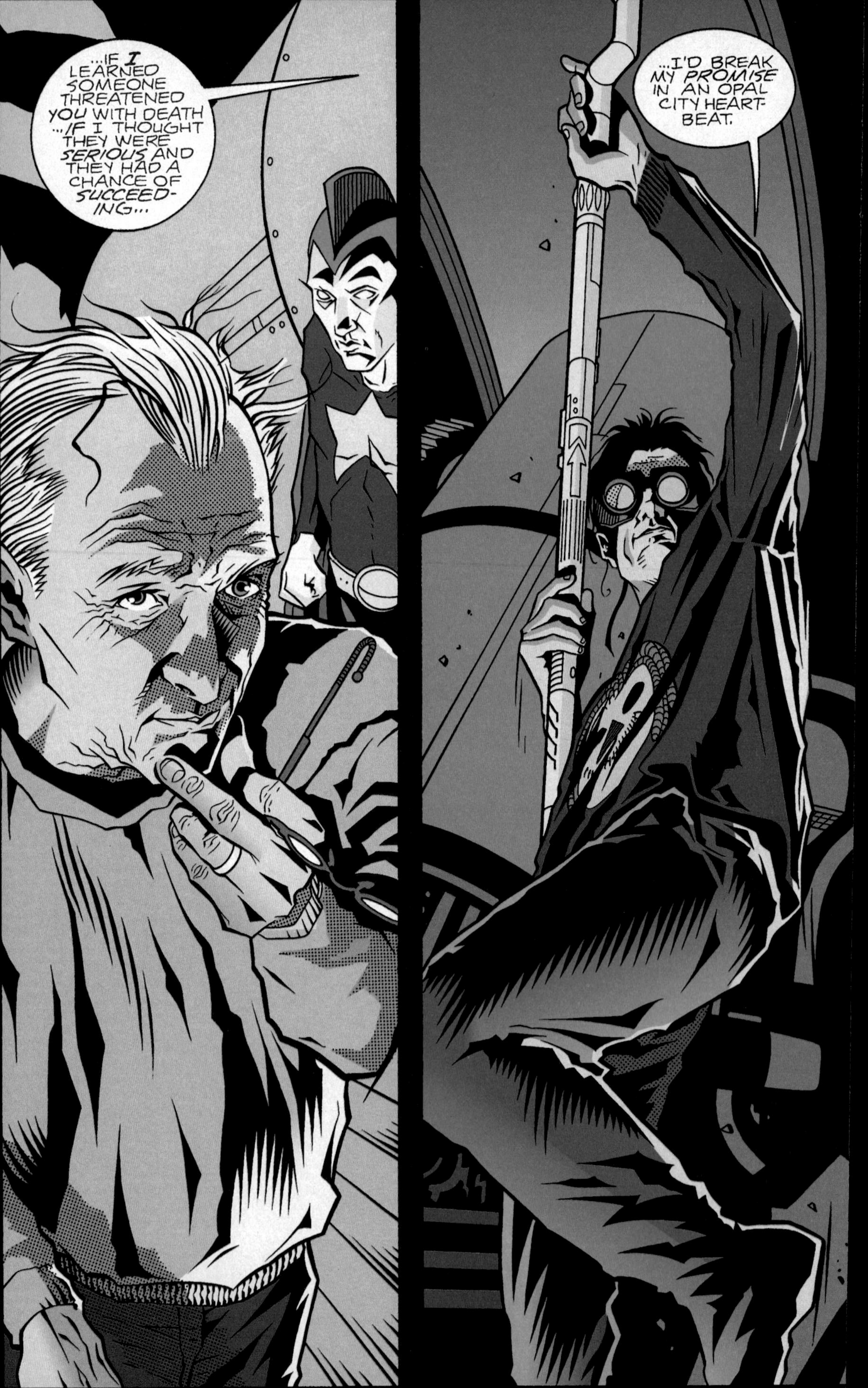
...IF I LEARNED SOMEONE THREATENED YOU WITH DEATH ...IF I THOUGHT THEY WERE SERIOUS AND THEY HAD A CHANCE OF SUCCEEDING...
...I'D BREAK MY PROMISE IN AN OPAL CITY HEART-BEAT.

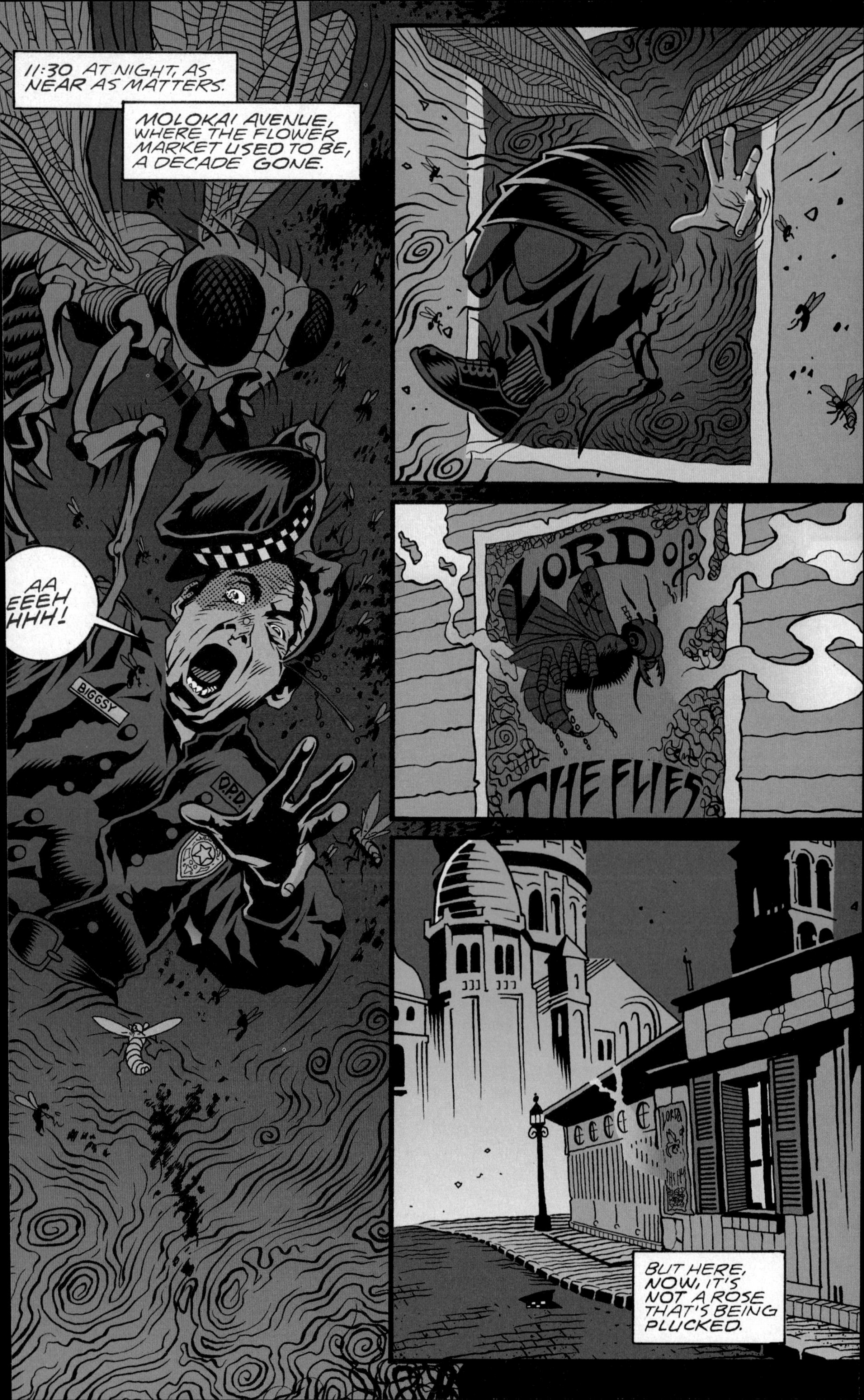
11:30 AT NIGHT, AS NEAR AS MATTERS.
MOLOKAI AVENUE, WHERE THE FLOWER MARKET USED TO BE, A DECADE GONE.
AA EEEH HHH!
BIGGSY
O.P.D.
LORD of THE FLIES
BUT HERE, NOW, IT'S NOT A ROSE THAT'S BEING PLUCKED.

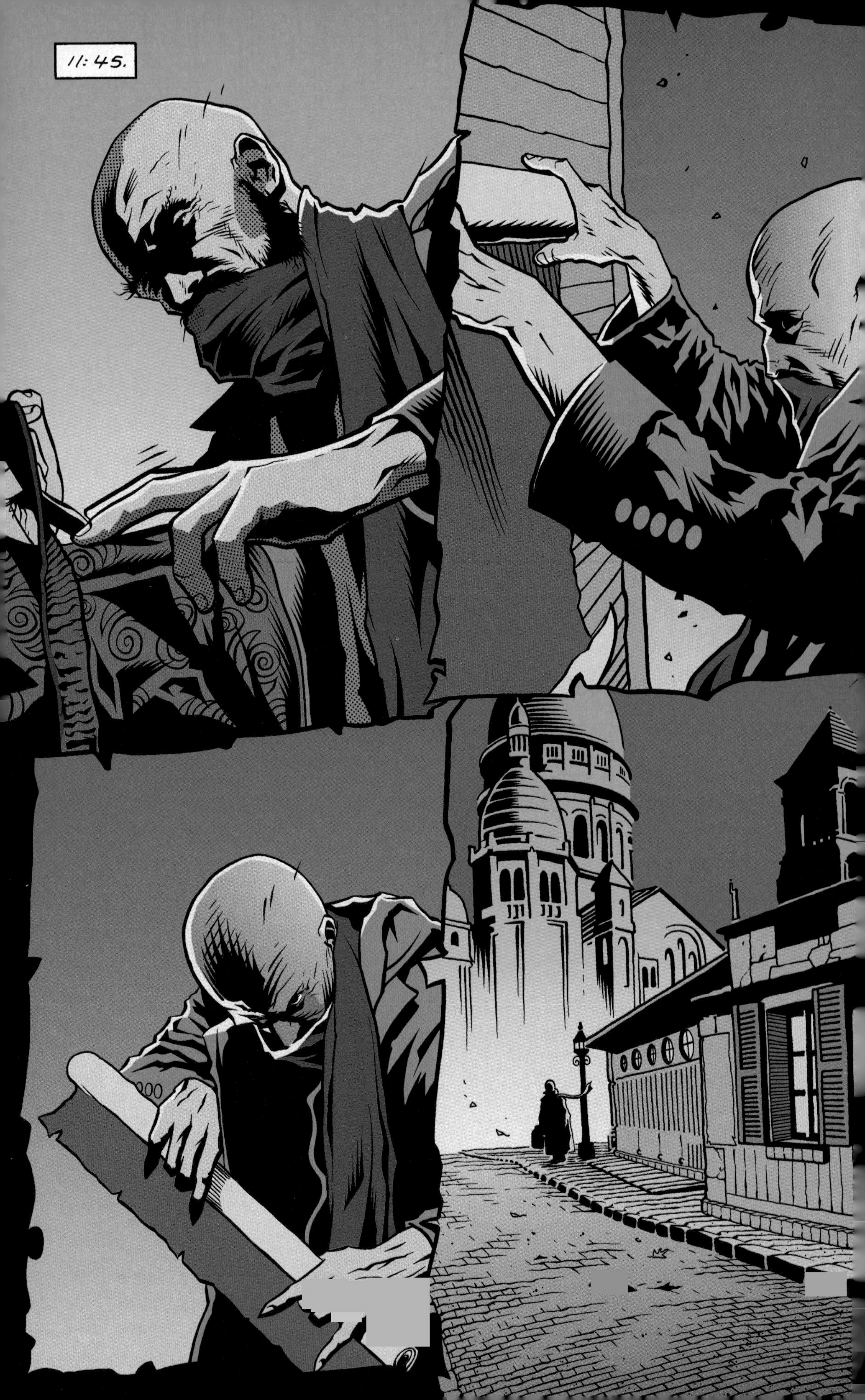
11: 45.

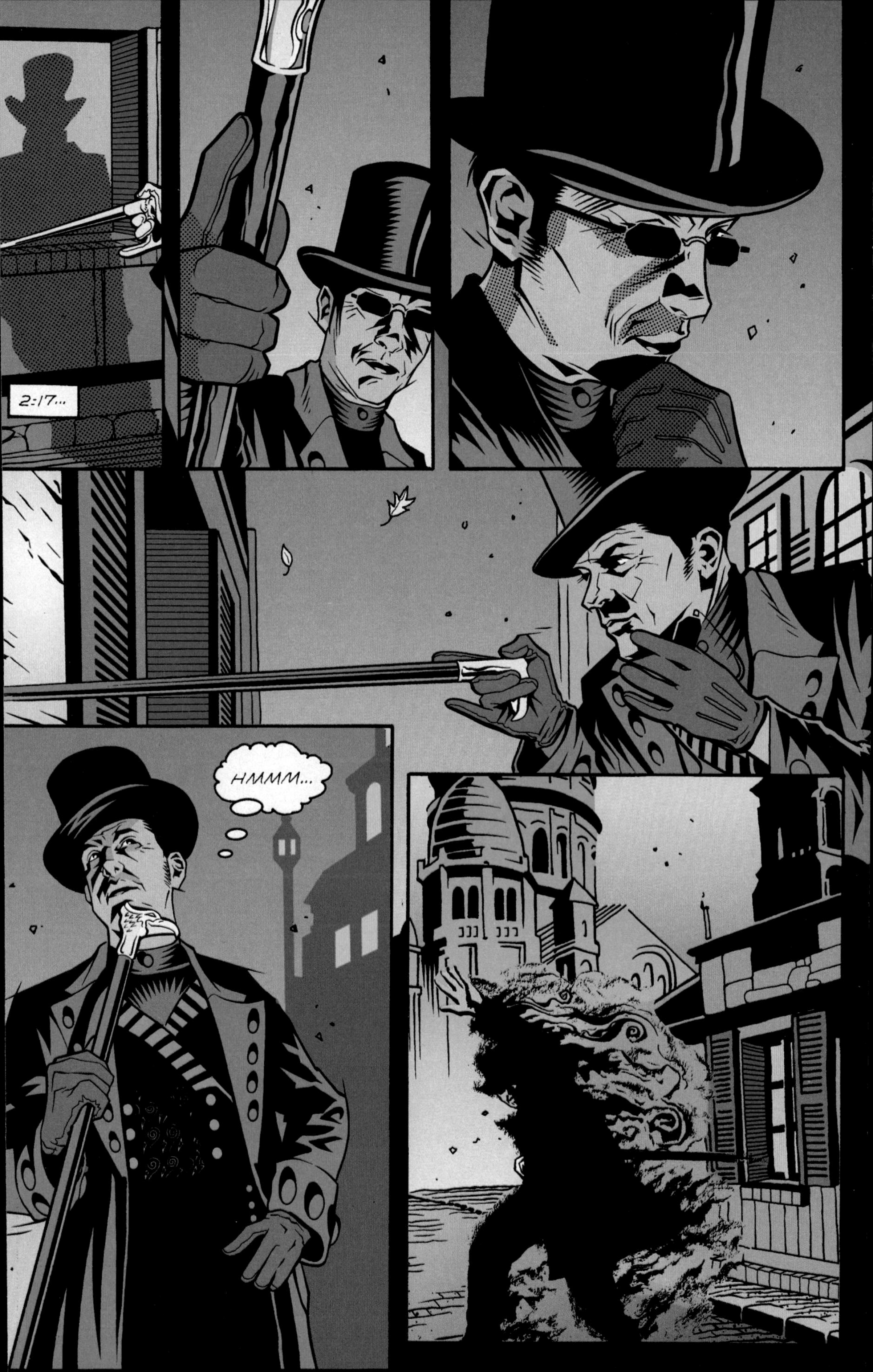
2:17...
HMMM...

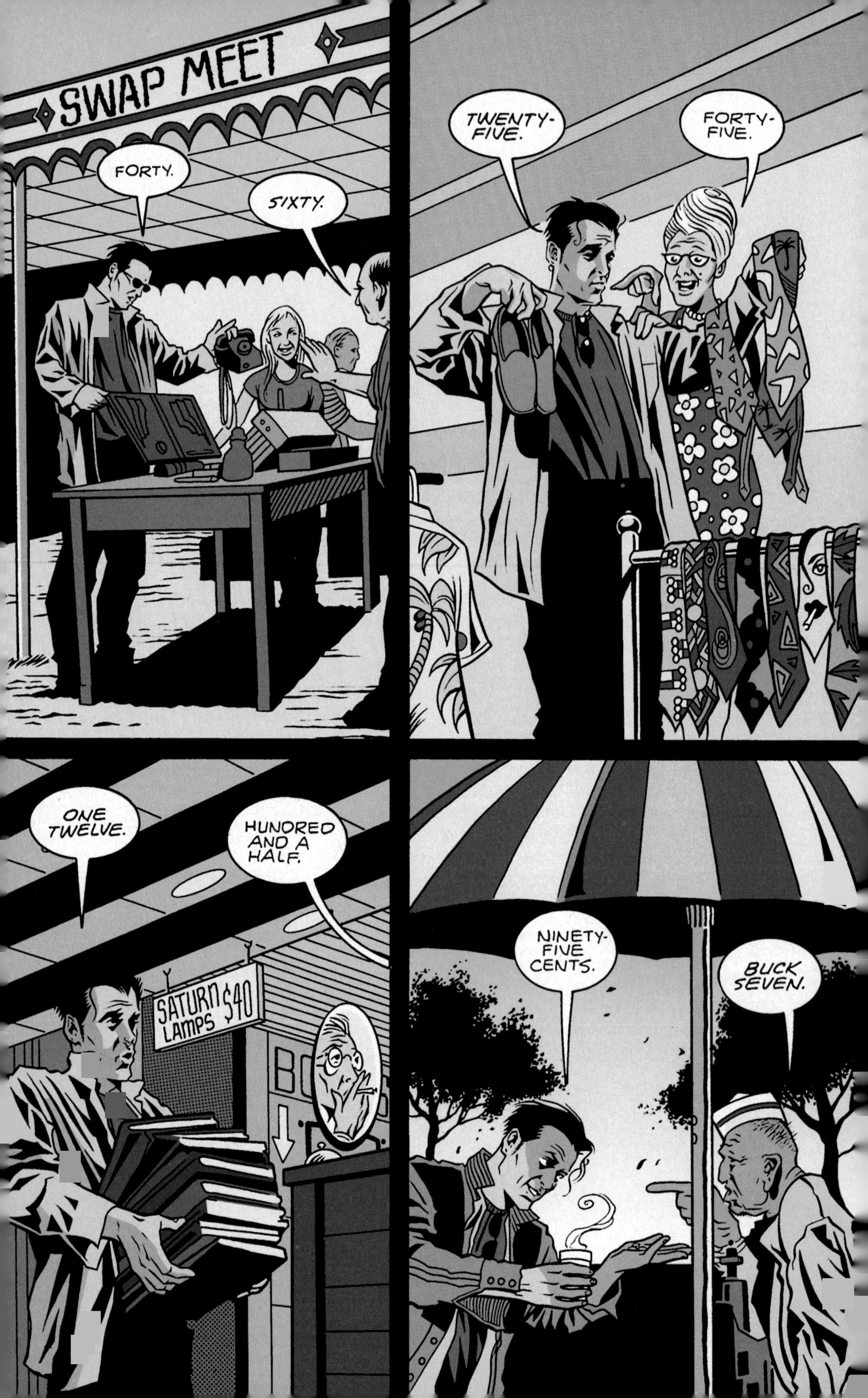
SWAP MEET
FORTY.
SIXTY.
TWENTY-FIVE.
FORTY-FIVE.
ONE TWELVE.
HUNDRED AND A HALF.
SATURN LAMPS $40
NINETY-FIVE CENTS.
BUCK SEVEN.

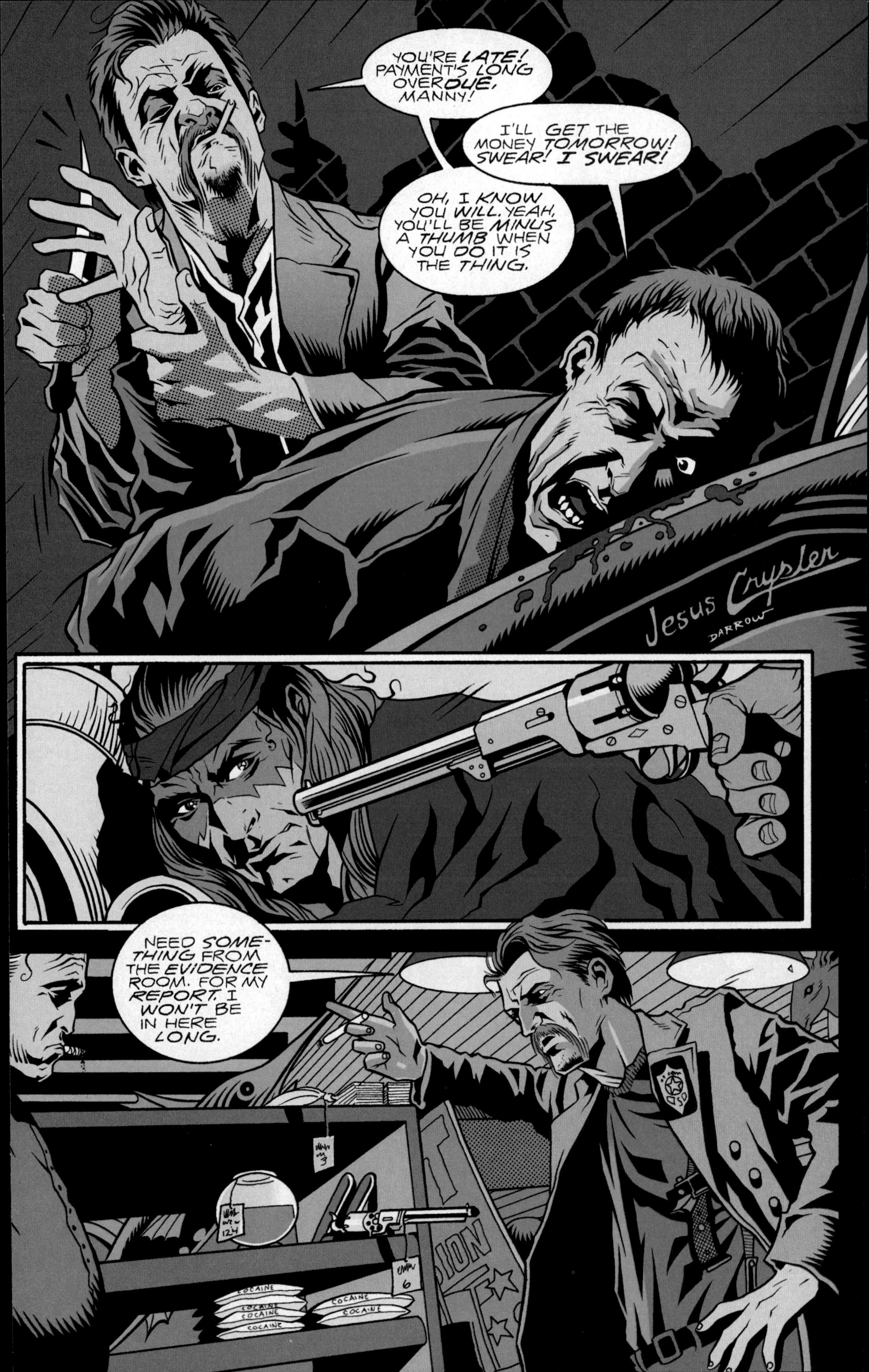
YOU'RE LATE! PAYMENT'S LONG OVERDUE, MANNY!
I'LL GET THE MONEY TOMORROW! SWEAR! I SWEAR!
OH, I KNOW YOU WILL. YEAH, YOU'LL BE MINUS A THUMB WHEN YOU DO IT IS THE THING.
Jesus Crysler
DARROW
NEED SOME-THING FROM THE EVIDENCE ROOM. FOR MY REPORT. I WON'T BE IN HERE LONG.
COCAINE
COCAINE
COCAINE
COCAINE
COCAINE
COCAINE

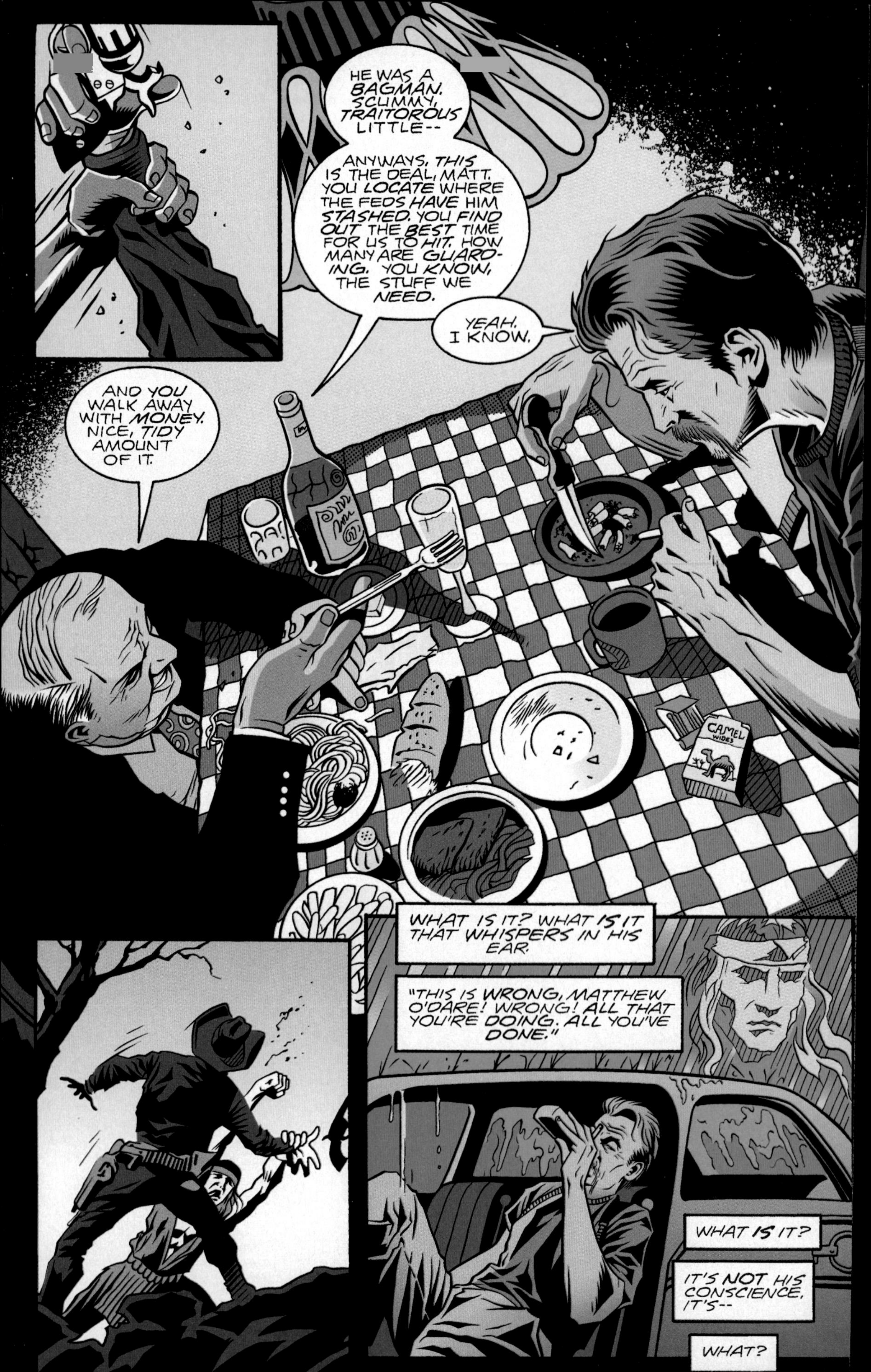
HE WAS A BAGMAN. SCUMMY, TRAITOROUS LITTLE--
ANYWAYS, THIS IS THE DEAL, MATT. YOU LOCATE WHERE THE FEDS HAVE HIM STASHED. YOU FIND OUT THE BEST TIME FOR US TO HIT. HOW MANY ARE GUARDING. YOU KNOW, THE STUFF WE NEED.
YEAH. I KNOW.
AND YOU WALK AWAY WITH MONEY. NICE, TIDY AMOUNT OF IT.
CAMEL WIDES
WHAT IS IT? WHAT IS IT THAT WHISPERS IN HIS EAR.
"THIS IS WRONG, MATTHEW O'DARE! WRONG! ALL THAT YOU'RE DOING. ALL YOU'VE DONE."
WHAT IS IT?
IT'S NOT HIS CONSCIENCE. IT'S--
WHAT?

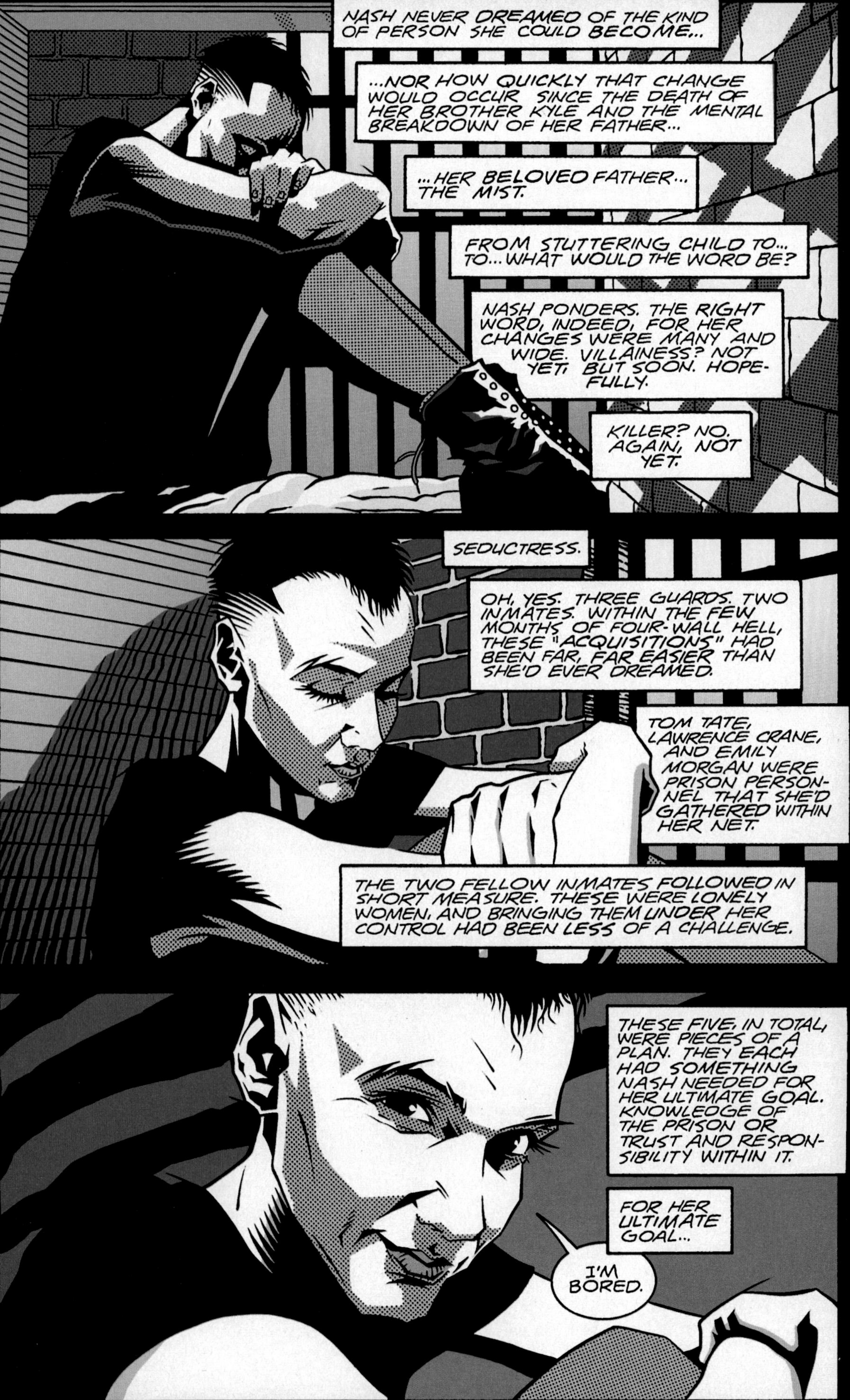

NASH NEVER DREAMED OF THE KIND OF PERSON SHE COULD BECOME...
...NOR HOW QUICKLY THAT CHANGE WOULD OCCUR SINCE THE DEATH OF HER BROTHER KYLE AND THE MENTAL BREAKDOWN OF HER FATHER...
...HER BELOVED FATHER... THE MIST.
FROM STUTTERING CHILD TO... TO... WHAT WOULD THE WORD BE?
NASH PONDERS. THE RIGHT WORD, INDEED, FOR HER CHANGES WERE MANY AND WIDE. VILLAINESS? NOT YET, BUT SOON. HOPE-FULLY.
KILLER? NO. AGAIN, NOT YET.
SEDUCTRESS.
OH, YES. THREE GUARDS. TWO INMATES. WITHIN THE FEW MONTHS OF FOUR-WALL HELL, THESE "ACQUISITIONS" HAD BEEN FAR, FAR EASIER THAN SHE'D EVER DREAMED.
TOM TATE, LAWRENCE CRANE, AND EMILY MORGAN WERE PRISON PERSON-NEL THAT SHE'D GATHERED WITHIN HER NET.
THE TWO FELLOW INMATES FOLLOWED IN SHORT MEASURE. THESE WERE LONELY WOMEN, AND BRINGING THEM UNDER HER CONTROL HAD BEEN LESS OF A CHALLENGE.
THESE FIVE, IN TOTAL, WERE PIECES OF A PLAN. THEY EACH HAD SOMETHING NASH NEEDED FOR HER ULTIMATE GOAL. KNOWLEGE OF THE PRISON OR TRUST AND RESPON-SIBILITY WITHIN IT.
FOR HER ULTIMATE GOAL...
I'M BORED.

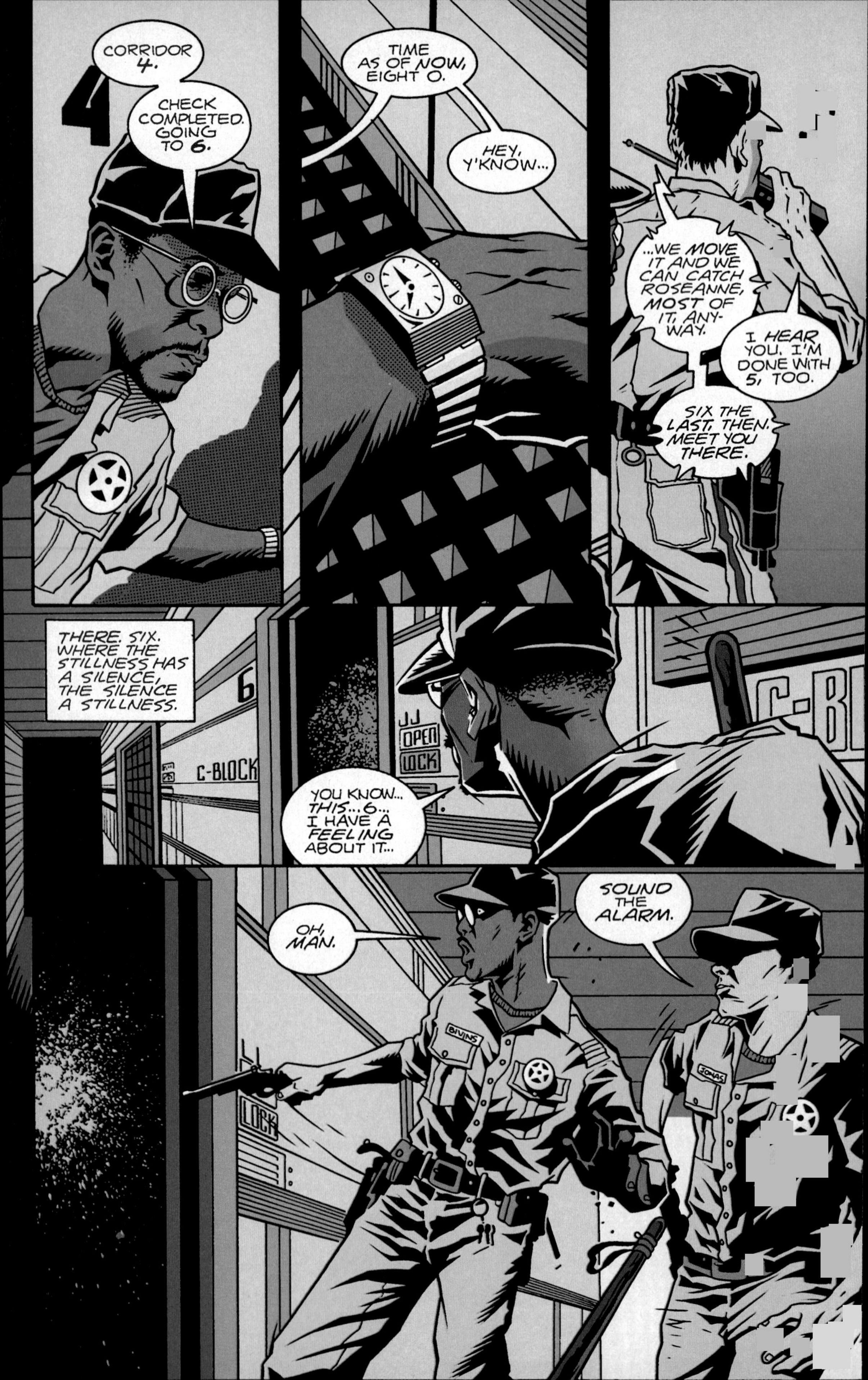
4
CORRIDOR 4.
CHECK COMPLETED. GOING TO 6.
TIME AS OF NOW, EIGHT O.
HEY, Y'KNOW...
...WE MOVE IT AND WE CAN CATCH ROSEANNE, MOST OF IT, ANYWAY.
I HEAR YOU. I'M DONE WITH 5, TOO.
SIX THE LAST, THEN. MEET YOU THERE.
THERE. SIX. WHERE THE STILLNESS HAS A SILENCE, THE SILENCE A STILLNESS.
6
C-BLOCK
JJ
OPEN
LOCK
YOU KNOW... THIS...6... I HAVE A FEELING ABOUT IT...
OH, MAN.
SOUND THE ALARM.
BIVINS
JONAS
LOCK

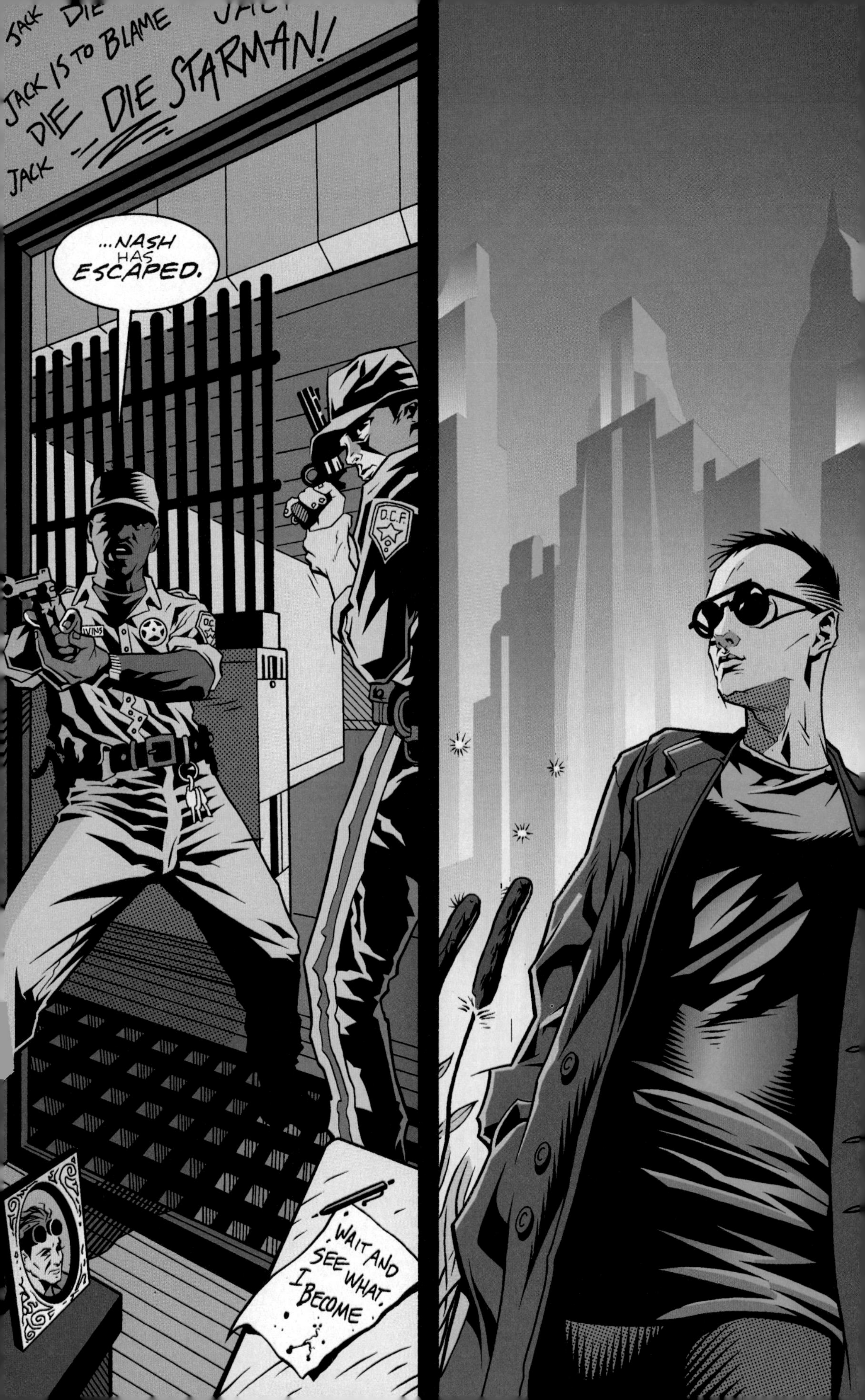
JACK DIE
JACK IS TO BLAME
JACK DIE DIE DIE STARMAN!
JACK
...NASH HAS ESCAPED.
D.C.F.
WAIT AND SEE WHAT I BECOME

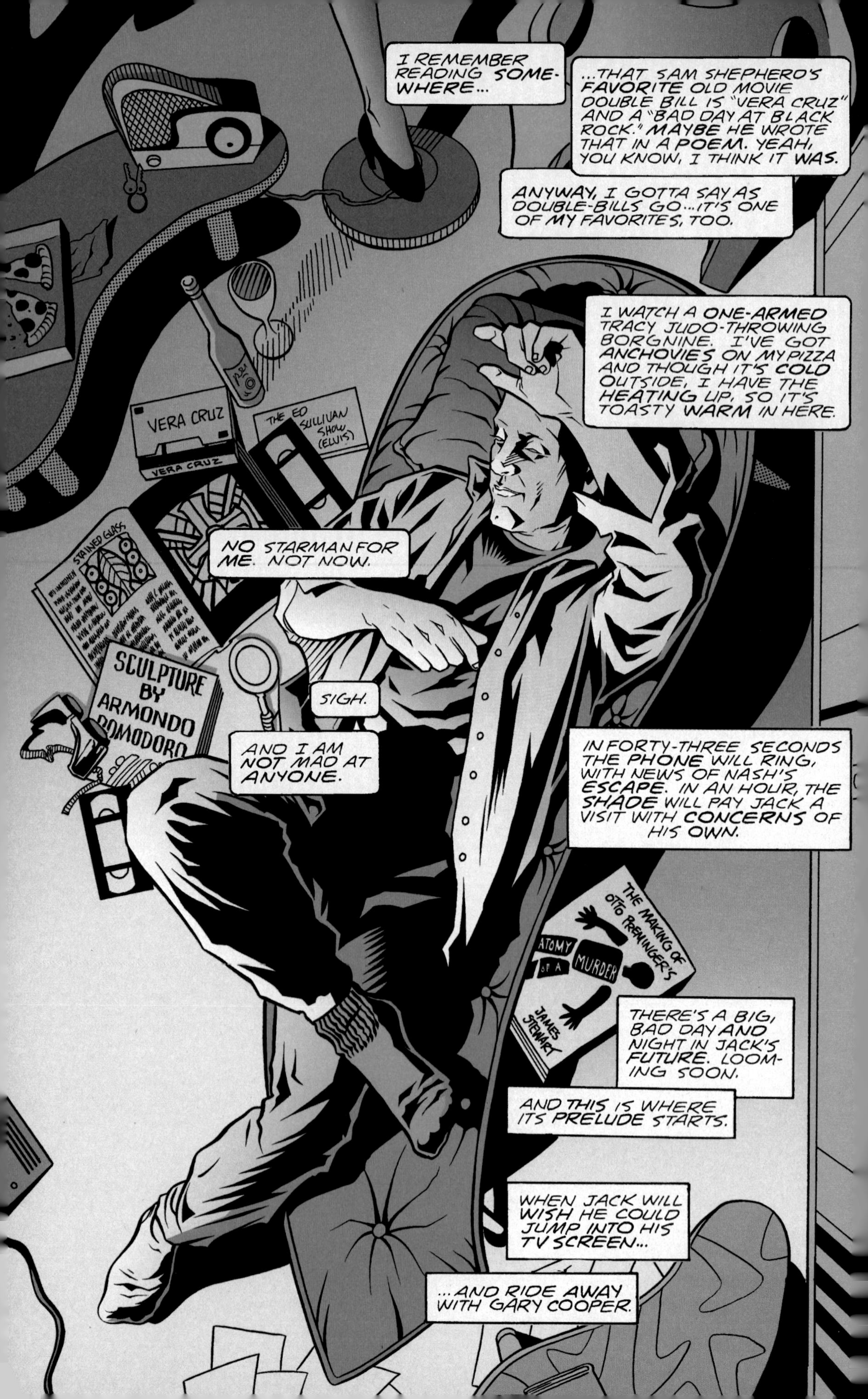

I REMEMBER READING SOME-WHERE...
...THAT SAM SHEPHERD'S FAVORITE OLD MOVIE DOUBLE BILL IS "VERA CRUZ" AND A "BAD DAY AT BLACK ROCK." MAYBE HE WROTE THAT IN A POEM. YEAH, YOU KNOW, I THINK IT WAS.
ANYWAY, I GOTTA SAY AS DOUBLE-BILLS GO...IT'S ONE OF MY FAVORITES, TOO.
I WATCH A ONE-ARMED TRACY JUDO-THROWING BORGNINE. I'VE GOT ANCHOVIES ON MY PIZZA AND THOUGH IT'S COLD OUTSIDE, I HAVE THE HEATING UP, SO IT'S TOASTY WARM IN HERE.
VERA CRUZ
VERA CRUZ
THE ED SULLIVAN SHOW (ELVIS)
STAINED GLASS
NO STARMAN FOR ME. NOT NOW.
SCULPTURE BY ARMONDO POMODORO
SIGH.
AND I AM NOT MAD AT ANYONE.
IN FORTY-THREE SECONDS THE PHONE WILL RING, WITH NEWS OF NASH'S ESCAPE. IN AN HOUR, THE SHADE WILL PAY JACK A VISIT WITH CONCERNS OF HIS OWN.
THE MAKING OF OTTO PREMINGER'S
ATOMY OF A MURDER
JAMES STEWART
THERE'S A BIG, BAD DAY AND NIGHT IN JACK'S FUTURE. LOOM-ING SOON.
AND THIS IS WHERE ITS PRELUDE STARTS.
WHEN JACK WILL WISH HE COULD JUMP INTO HIS TV SCREEN...
...AND RIDE AWAY WITH GARY COOPER.

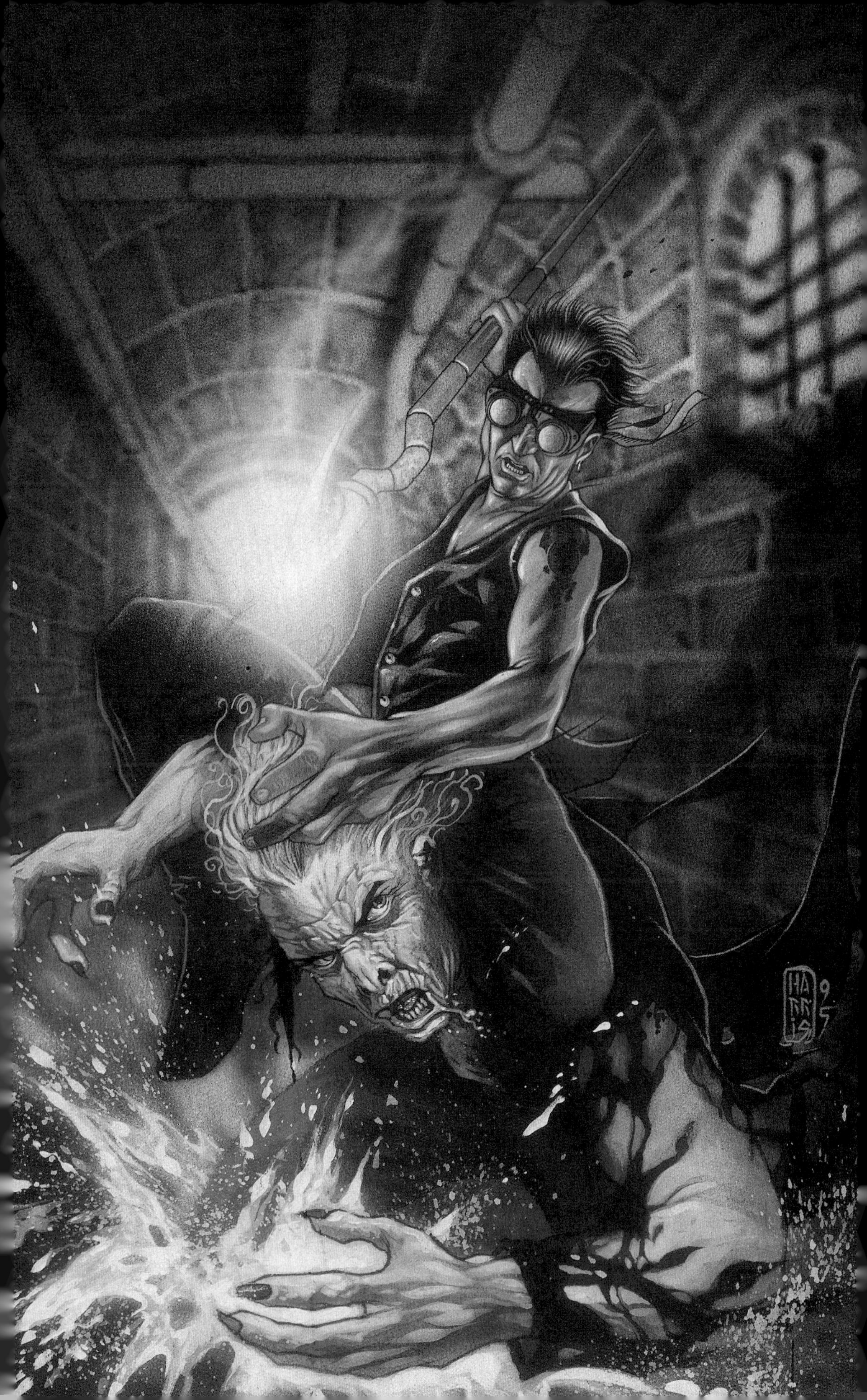

STARMAN 10

Cover by Tony Harris

Written by James Robinson

Pencils by Tony Harris,

with inks by Wade von Grawbadger

and colors by Gregory Wright

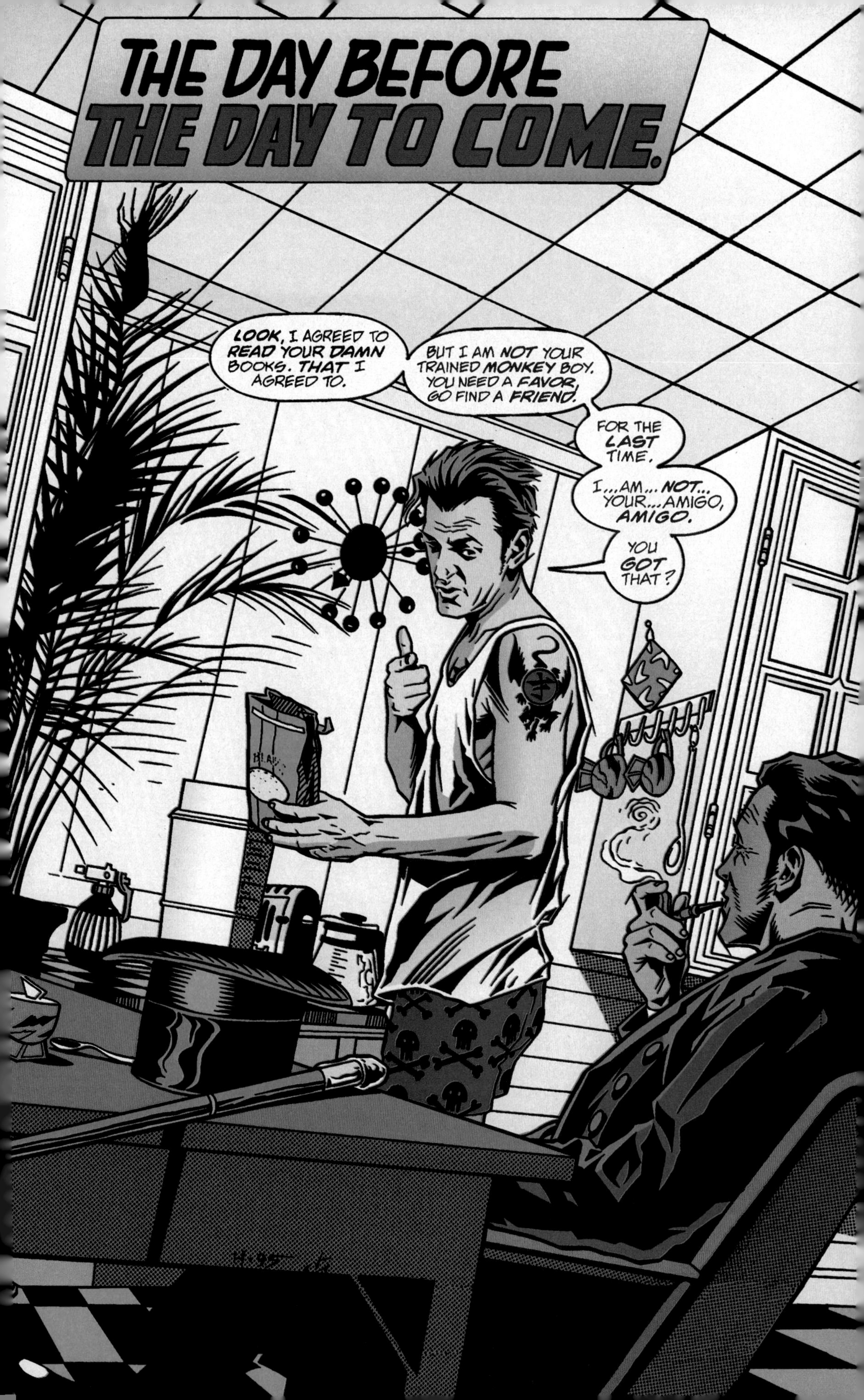
THE DAY BEFORE THE DAY TO COME.
LOOK, I AGREED TO READ YOUR DAMN BOOKS. THAT I AGREED TO.
BUT I AM NOT YOUR TRAINED MONKEY BOY. YOU NEED A FAVOR, GO FIND A FRIEND.
FOR THE LAST TIME.
I...AM...NOT... YOUR...AMIGO, AMIGO.
YOU GOT THAT?

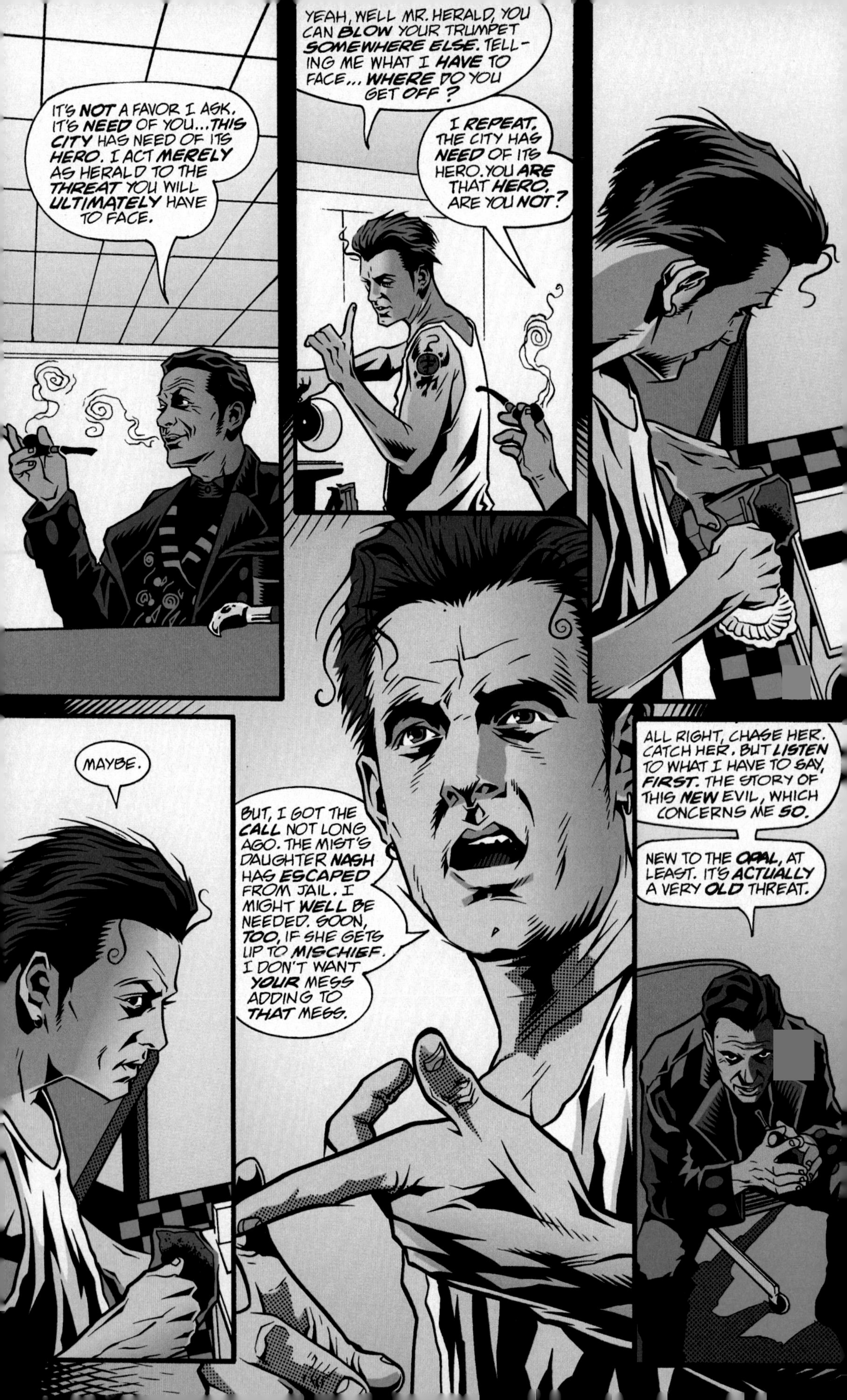
IT'S NOT A FAVOR I ASK. IT'S NEED OF YOU... THIS CITY HAS NEED OF ITS HERO. I ACT MERELY AS HERALD TO THE THREAT YOU WILL ULTIMATELY HAVE TO FACE.
YEAH, WELL MR. HERALD, YOU CAN BLOW YOUR TRUMPET SOMEWHERE ELSE. TELLING ME WHAT I HAVE TO FACE... WHERE DO YOU GET OFF?
I REPEAT. THE CITY HAS NEED OF ITS HERO. YOU ARE THAT HERO, ARE YOU NOT?
MAYBE.
BUT, I GOT THE CALL NOT LONG AGO. THE MIST'S DAUGHTER NASH HAS ESCAPED FROM JAIL. I MIGHT WELL BE NEEDED. SOON, TOO, IF SHE GETS UP TO MISCHIEF. I DON'T WANT YOUR MESS ADDING TO THAT MESS.
ALL RIGHT, CHASE HER. CATCH HER. BUT LISTEN TO WHAT I HAVE TO SAY, FIRST. THE STORY OF THIS NEW EVIL, WHICH CONCERNS ME SO.
NEW TO THE OPAL, AT LEAST. IT'S ACTUALLY A VERY OLD THREAT.

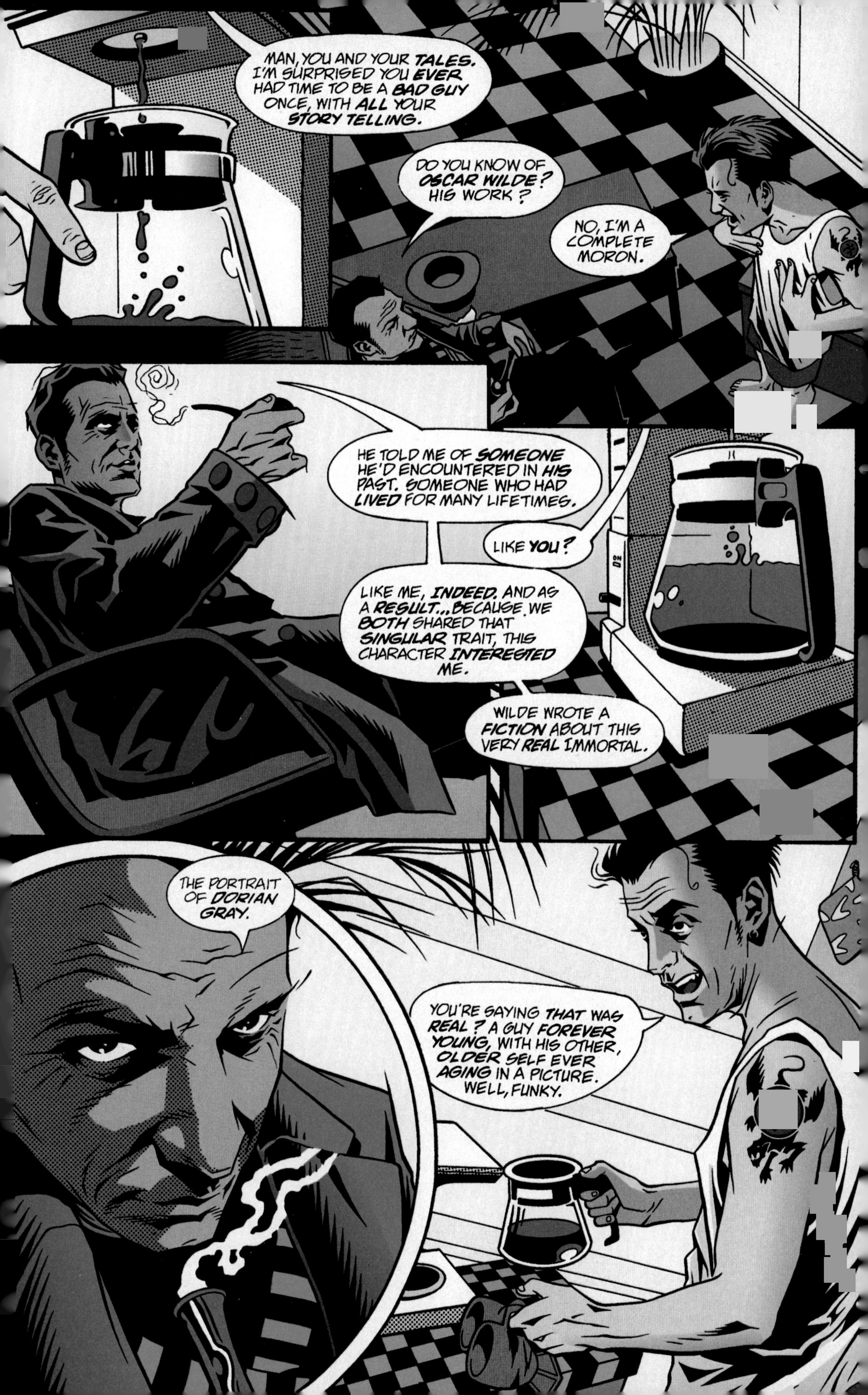
MAN, YOU AND YOUR TALES. I'M SURPRISED YOU EVER HAD TIME TO BE A BAD GUY ONCE, WITH ALL YOUR STORY TELLING.
DO YOU KNOW OF OSCAR WILDE? HIS WORK?
NO, I'M A COMPLETE MORON.
HE TOLD ME OF SOMEONE HE'D ENCOUNTERED IN HIS PAST. SOMEONE WHO HAD LIVED FOR MANY LIFETIMES.
LIKE YOU?
LIKE ME, INDEED. AND AS A RESULT... BECAUSE WE BOTH SHARED THAT SINGULAR TRAIT, THIS CHARACTER INTERESTED ME.
WILDE WROTE A FICTION ABOUT THIS VERY REAL IMMORTAL.
THE PORTRAIT OF DORIAN GRAY.
YOU'RE SAYING THAT WAS REAL? A GUY FOREVER YOUNG, WITH HIS OTHER, OLDER SELF EVER AGING IN A PICTURE. WELL, FUNKY.

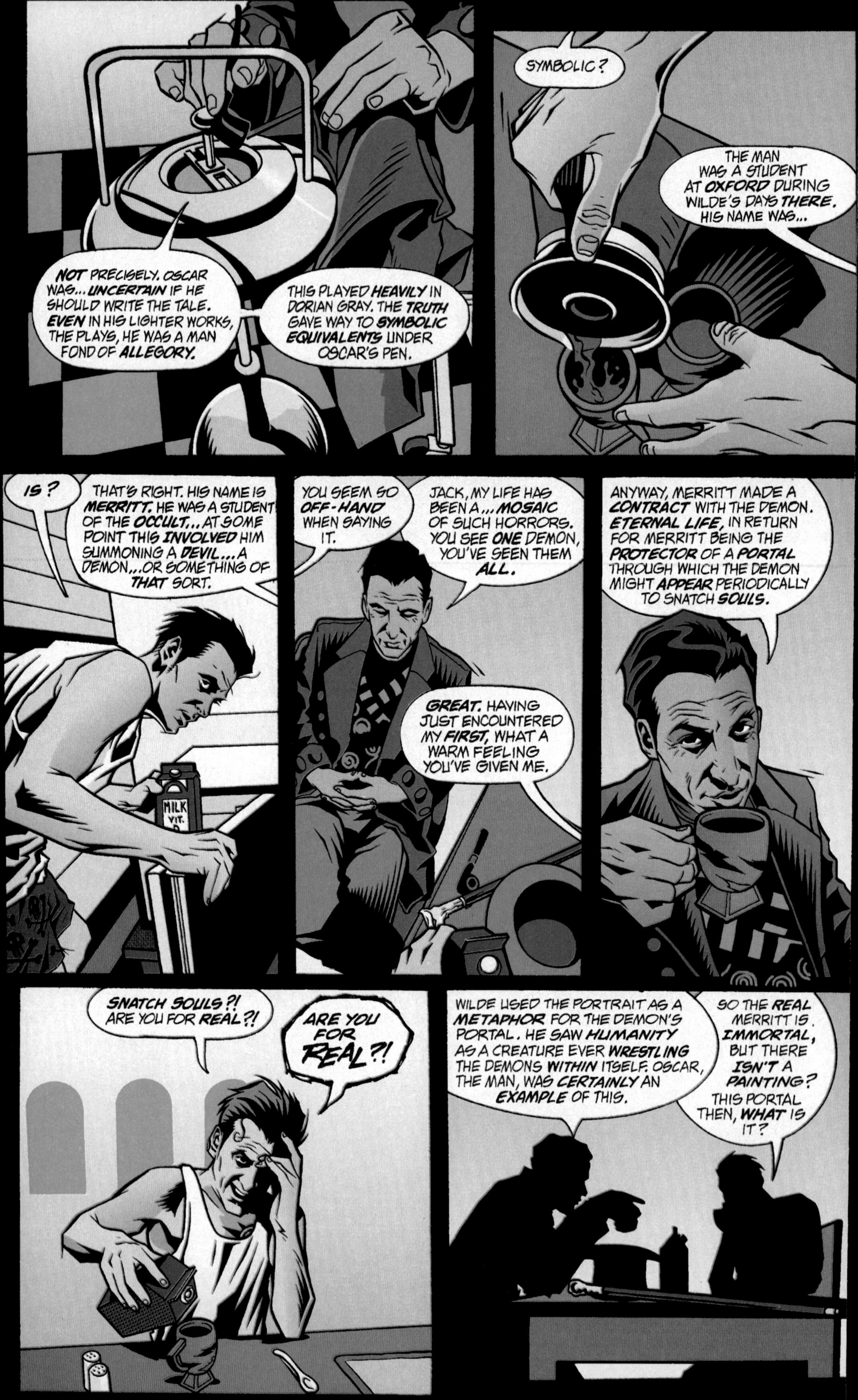
NOT PRECISELY. OSCAR WAS... UNCERTAIN IF HE SHOULD WRITE THE TALE. EVEN IN HIS LIGHTER WORKS, THE PLAYS, HE WAS A MAN FOND OF ALLEGORY.
THIS PLAYED HEAVILY IN DORIAN GRAY. THE TRUTH GAVE WAY TO SYMBOLIC EQUIVALENTS UNDER OSCAR'S PEN.
SYMBOLIC?
THE MAN WAS A STUDENT AT OXFORD DURING WILDE'S DAYS THERE. HIS NAME WAS...
IS?
THAT'S RIGHT. HIS NAME IS MERRITT. HE WAS A STUDENT OF THE OCCULT... AT SOME POINT THIS INVOLVED HIM SUMMONING A DEVIL... A DEMON... OR SOMETHING OF THAT SORT.
MILK VIT. D
YOU SEEM SO OFF-HAND WHEN SAYING IT.
JACK, MY LIFE HAS BEEN A... MOSAIC OF SUCH HORRORS. YOU SEE ONE DEMON, YOU'VE SEEN THEM ALL.
GREAT. HAVING JUST ENCOUNTERED MY FIRST, WHAT A WARM FEELING YOU'VE GIVEN ME.
ANYWAY, MERRITT MADE A CONTRACT WITH THE DEMON. ETERNAL LIFE, IN RETURN FOR MERRITT BEING THE PROTECTOR OF A PORTAL THROUGH WHICH THE DEMON MIGHT APPEAR PERIODICALLY TO SNATCH SOULS.
SNATCH SOULS?! ARE YOU FOR REAL?!
ARE YOU FOR REAL?!
WILDE USED THE PORTRAIT AS A METAPHOR FOR THE DEMON'S PORTAL. HE SAW HUMANITY AS A CREATURE EVER WRESTLING THE DEMONS WITHIN ITSELF. OSCAR, THE MAN, WAS CERTAINLY AN EXAMPLE OF THIS.
SO THE REAL MERRITT IS IMMORTAL, BUT THERE ISN'T A PAINTING? THIS PORTAL THEN, WHAT IS IT?

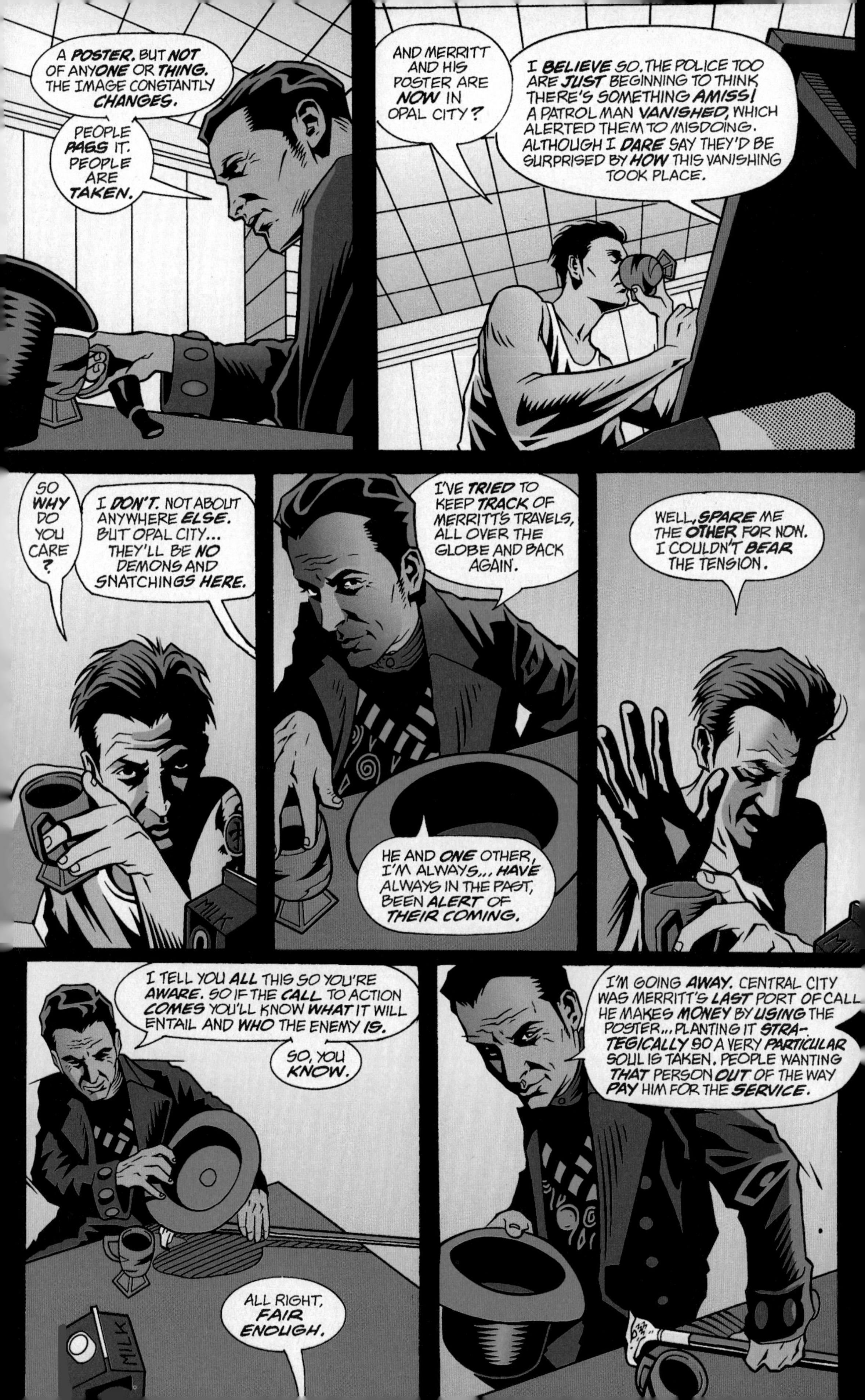

A POSTER. BUT NOT OF ANYONE OR THING. THE IMAGE CONSTANTLY CHANGES.
PEOPLE PASS IT. PEOPLE ARE TAKEN.
AND MERRITT AND HIS POSTER ARE NOW IN OPAL CITY?
I BELIEVE SO. THE POLICE TOO ARE JUST BEGINNING TO THINK THERE'S SOMETHING AMISS! A PATROL MAN VANISHED, WHICH ALERTED THEM TO MISDOING. ALTHOUGH I DARE SAY THEY'D BE SURPRISED BY HOW THIS VANISHING TOOK PLACE.
SO WHY DO YOU CARE?
I DON'T. NOT ABOUT ANYWHERE ELSE. BUT OPAL CITY... THEY'LL BE NO DEMONS AND SNATCHINGS HERE.
I'VE TRIED TO KEEP TRACK OF MERRITT'S TRAVELS, ALL OVER THE GLOBE AND BACK AGAIN.
HE AND ONE OTHER, I'M ALWAYS... HAVE ALWAYS IN THE PAST, BEEN ALERT OF THEIR COMING.
WELL, SPARE ME THE OTHER FOR NOW. I COULDN'T BEAR THE TENSION.
MILK
I TELL YOU ALL THIS SO YOU'RE AWARE. SO IF THE CALL TO ACTION COMES YOU'LL KNOW WHAT IT WILL ENTAIL AND WHO THE ENEMY IS.
SO, YOU KNOW.
ALL RIGHT, FAIR ENOUGH.
MILK
I'M GOING AWAY. CENTRAL CITY WAS MERRITT'S LAST PORT OF CALL. HE MAKES MONEY BY USING THE POSTER... PLANTING IT STRA-TEGICALLY SO A VERY PARTICULAR SOUL IS TAKEN. PEOPLE WANTING THAT PERSON OUT OF THE WAY PAY HIM FOR THE SERVICE.

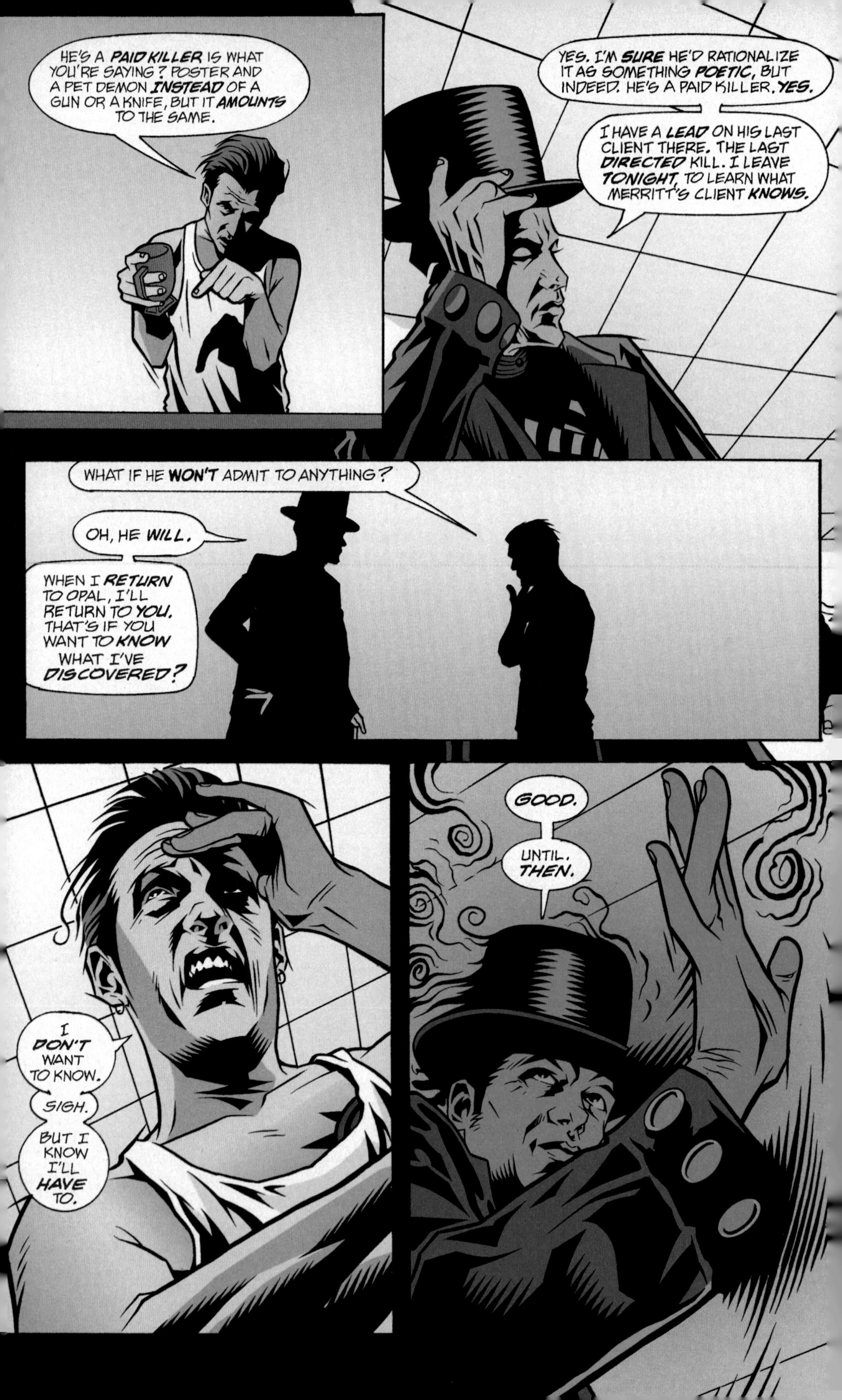
HE'S A PAID KILLER IS WHAT YOU'RE SAYING? POSTER AND A PET DEMON INSTEAD OF A GUN OR A KNIFE, BUT IT AMOUNTS TO THE SAME.
YES. I'M SURE HE'D RATIONALIZE IT AS SOMETHING POETIC, BUT INDEED. HE'S A PAID KILLER. YES.
I HAVE A LEAD ON HIS LAST CLIENT THERE. THE LAST DIRECTED KILL. I LEAVE TONIGHT, TO LEARN WHAT MERRITT'S CLIENT KNOWS.
WHAT IF HE WON'T ADMIT TO ANYTHING?
OH, HE WILL.
WHEN I RETURN TO OPAL, I'LL RETURN TO YOU. THAT'S IF YOU WANT TO KNOW WHAT I'VE DISCOVERED?
I DON'T WANT TO KNOW.
SIGH.
BUT I KNOW I'LL HAVE TO.
GOOD.
UNTIL. THEN.

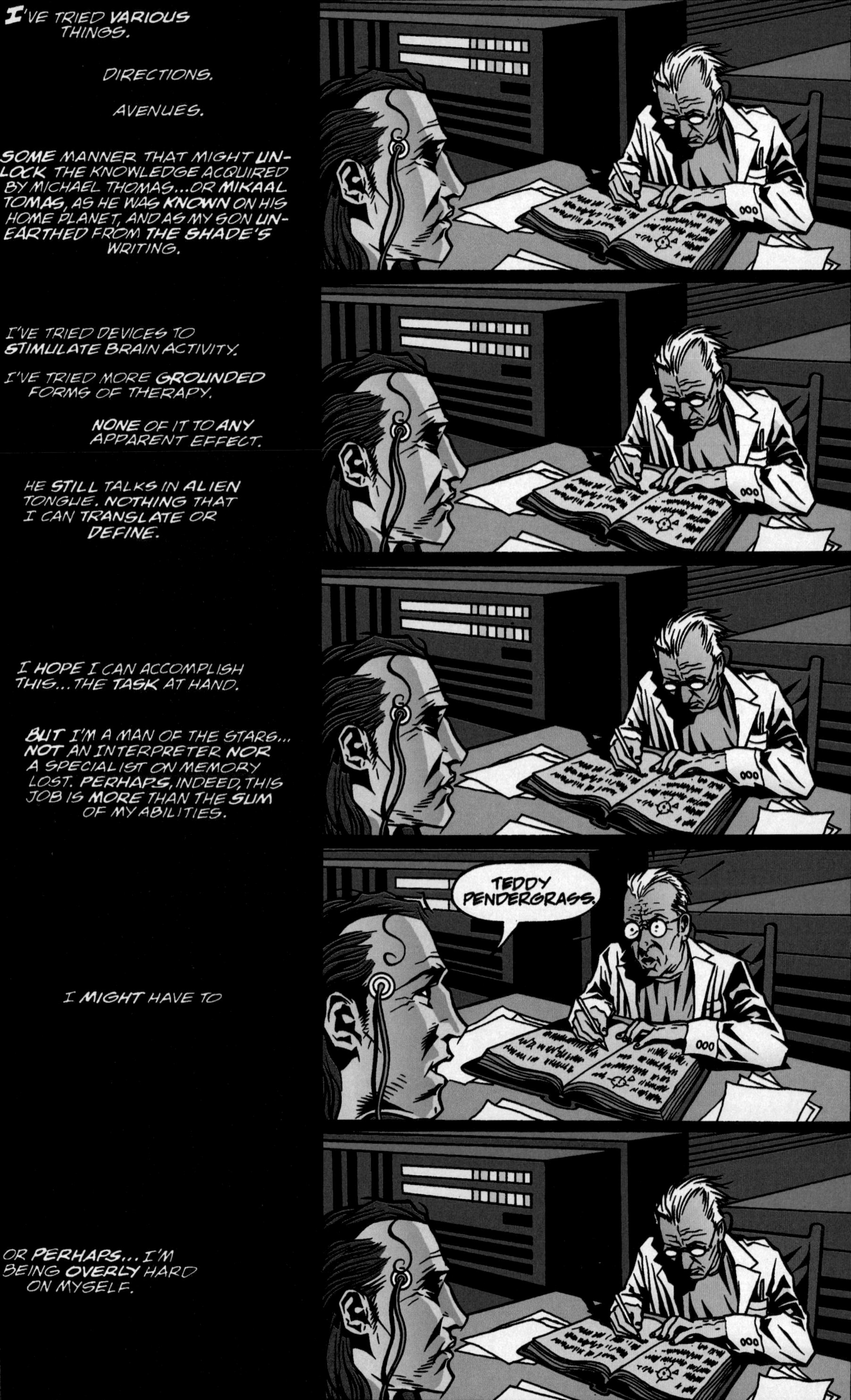
I'VE TRIED VARIOUS THINGS.
DIRECTIONS.
AVENUES.
SOME MANNER THAT MIGHT UNLOCK THE KNOWLEDGE ACQUIRED BY MICHAEL THOMAS...OR MIKAAL TOMAS, AS HE WAS KNOWN ON HIS HOME PLANET, AND AS MY SON UNEARTHED FROM THE SHADE'S WRITING.
I'VE TRIED DEVICES TO STIMULATE BRAIN ACTIVITY.
I'VE TRIED MORE GROUNDED FORMS OF THERAPY.
NONE OF IT TO ANY APPARENT EFFECT.
HE STILL TALKS IN ALIEN TONGUE. NOTHING THAT I CAN TRANSLATE OR DEFINE.
I HOPE I CAN ACCOMPLISH THIS...THE TASK AT HAND.
BUT I'M A MAN OF THE STARS... NOT AN INTERPRETER NOR A SPECIALIST ON MEMORY LOST. PERHAPS, INDEED, THIS JOB IS MORE THAN THE SUM OF MY ABILITIES.
I MIGHT HAVE TO
TEDDY PENDERGRASS.
OR PERHAPS... I'M BEING OVERLY HARD ON MYSELF.

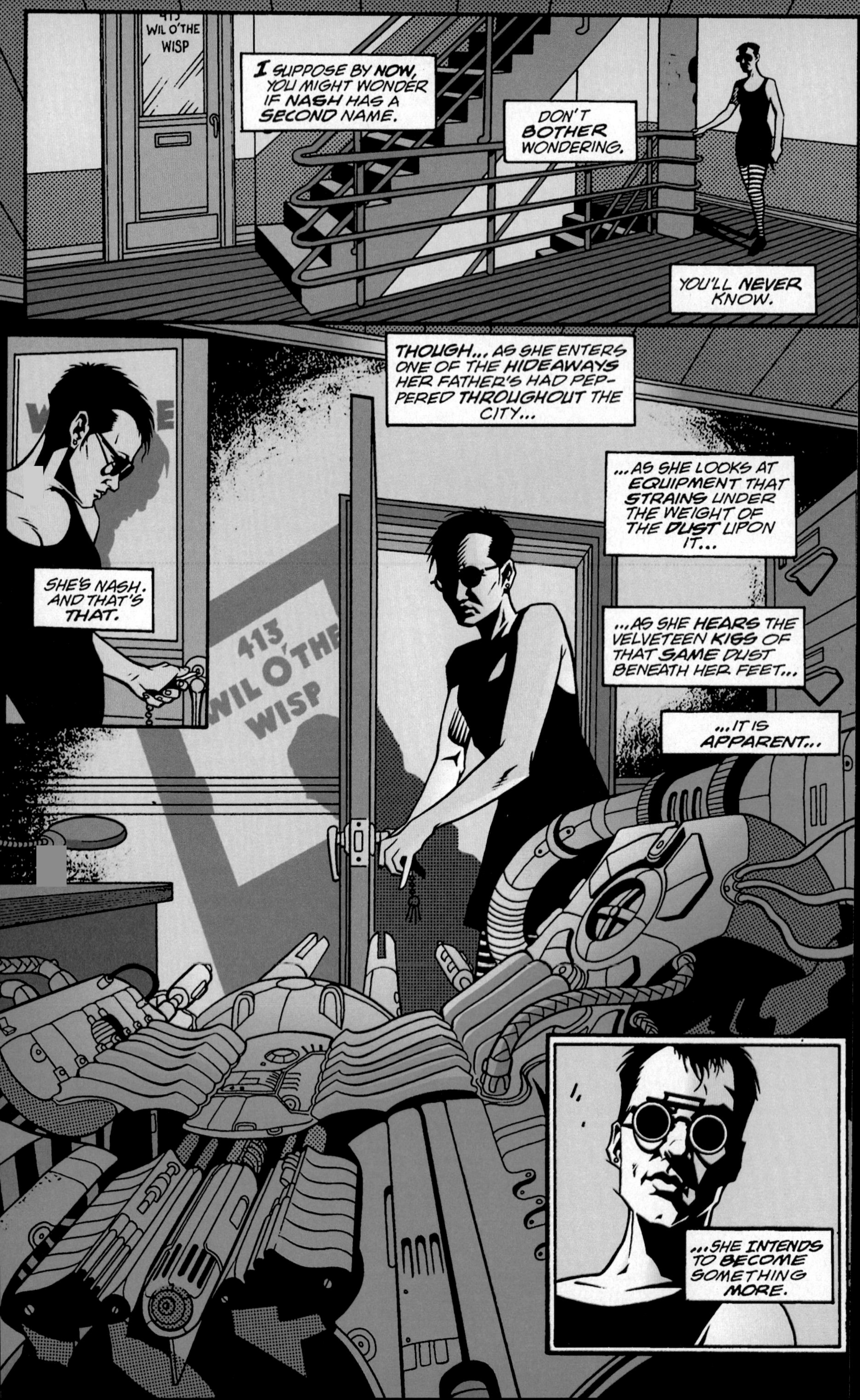
WIL O'THE WISP
I SUPPOSE BY NOW, YOU MIGHT WONDER IF NASH HAS A SECOND NAME.
DON'T BOTHER WONDERING.
YOU'LL NEVER KNOW.
SHE'S NASH. AND THAT'S THAT.
THOUGH... AS SHE ENTERS ONE OF THE HIDEAWAYS HER FATHER'S HAD PEPPERED THROUGHOUT THE CITY...
413 WIL O'THE WISP
...AS SHE LOOKS AT EQUIPMENT THAT STRAINS UNDER THE WEIGHT OF THE DUST UPON IT...
...AS SHE HEARS THE VELVETEEN KISS OF THAT SAME DUST BENEATH HER FEET...
...IT IS APPARENT...
...SHE INTENDS TO BECOME SOMETHING MORE.

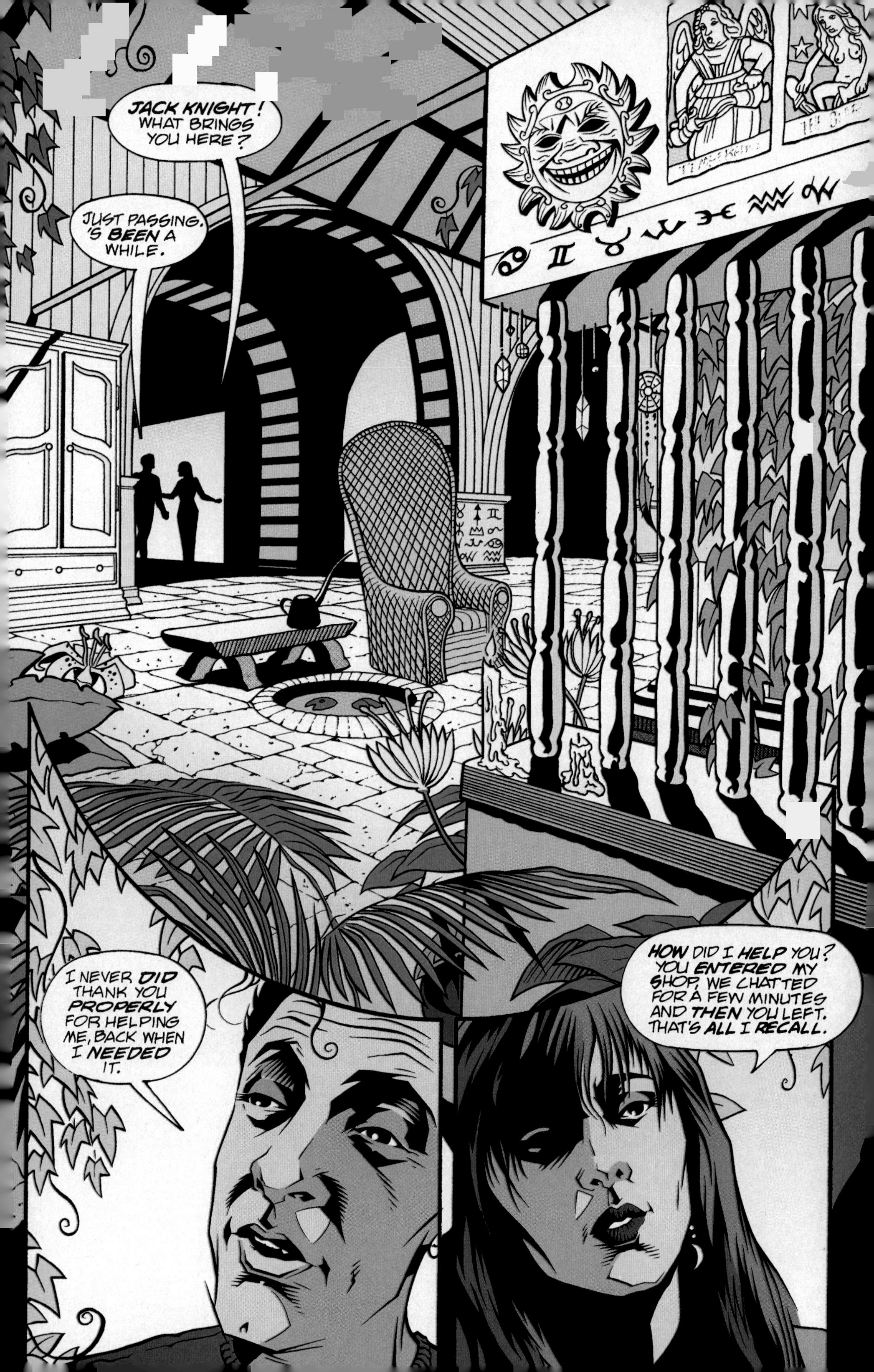
JACK KNIGHT! WHAT BRINGS YOU HERE?
JUST PASSING. 'S BEEN A WHILE.
I NEVER DID THANK YOU PROPERLY FOR HELPING ME, BACK WHEN I NEEDED IT.
HOW DID I HELP YOU? YOU ENTERED MY SHOP, WE CHATTED FOR A FEW MINUTES AND THEN YOU LEFT. THAT'S ALL I RECALL.

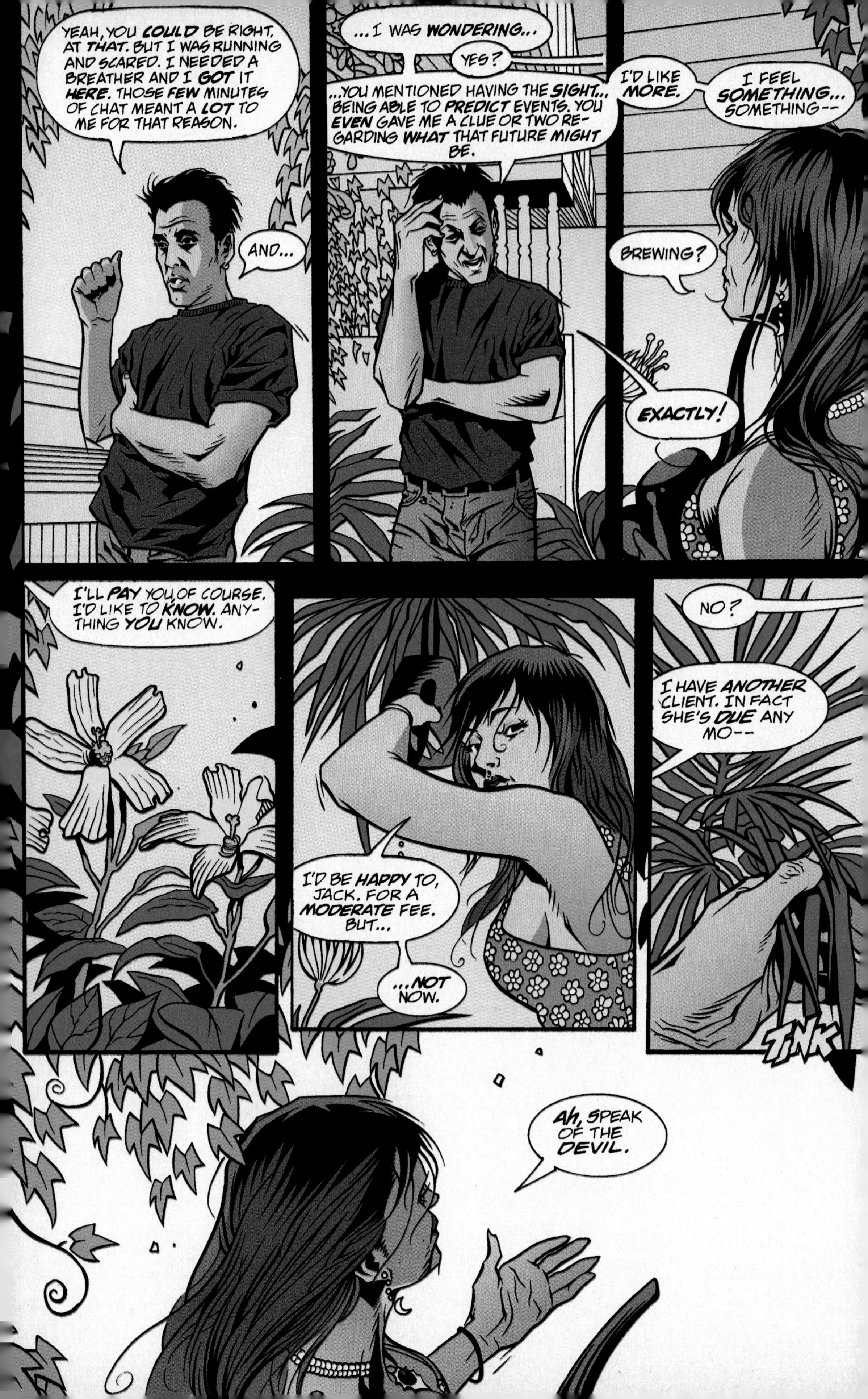
YEAH, YOU COULD BE RIGHT, AT THAT. BUT I WAS RUNNING AND SCARED. I NEEDED A BREATHER AND I GOT IT HERE. THOSE FEW MINUTES OF CHAT MEANT A LOT TO ME FOR THAT REASON.
AND...
...I WAS WONDERING...
YES?
...YOU MENTIONED HAVING THE SIGHT... BEING ABLE TO PREDICT EVENTS. YOU EVEN GAVE ME A CLUE OR TWO REGARDING WHAT THAT FUTURE MIGHT BE.
I'D LIKE MORE.
I FEEL SOMETHING... SOMETHING--
BREWING?
EXACTLY!
I'LL PAY YOU, OF COURSE. I'D LIKE TO KNOW. ANYTHING YOU KNOW.
I'D BE HAPPY TO, JACK. FOR A MODERATE FEE. BUT...
...NOT NOW.
NO?
I HAVE ANOTHER CLIENT. IN FACT SHE'S DUE ANY MO--
TNK
Ah, SPEAK OF THE DEVIL.

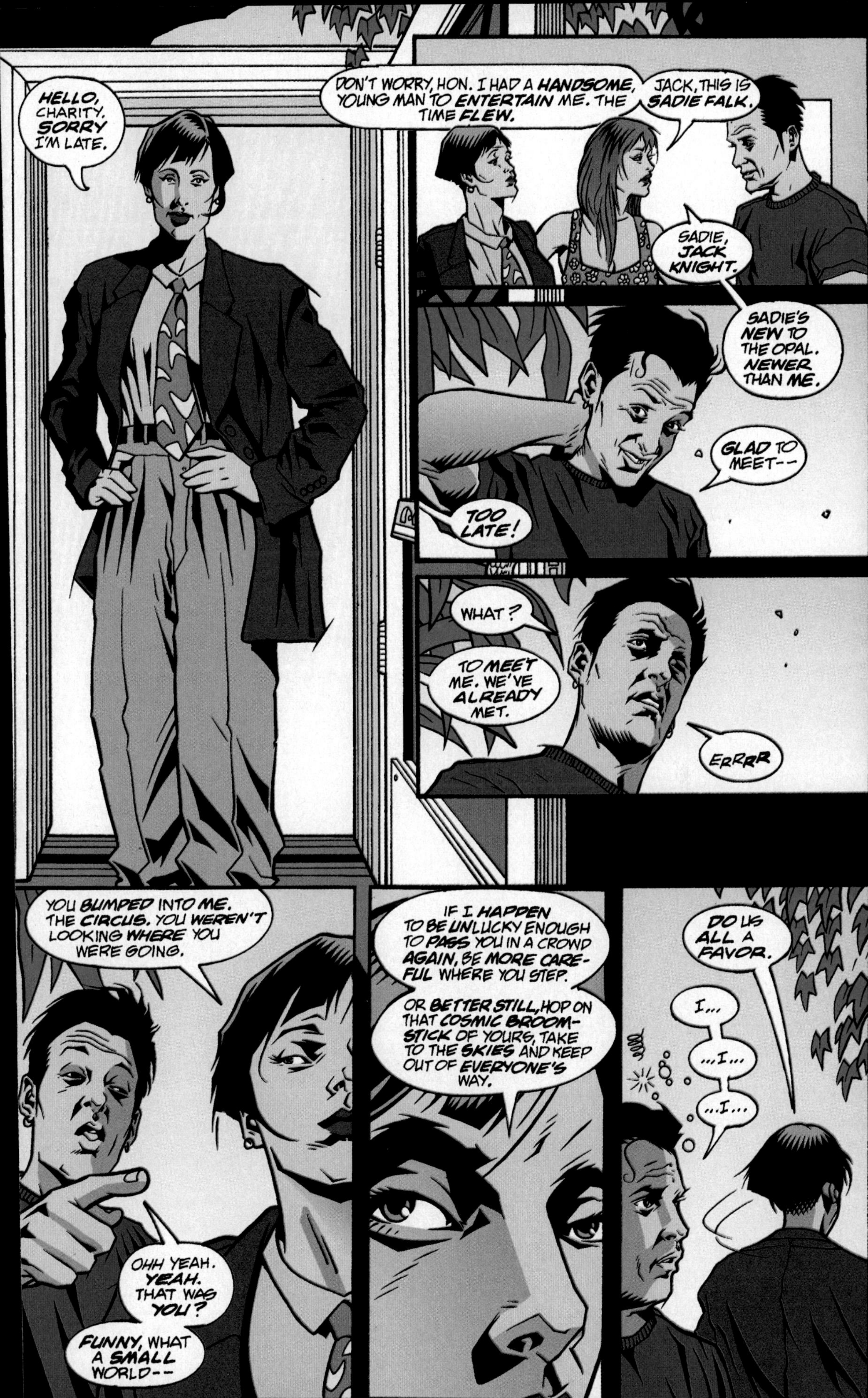
HELLO, CHARITY. SORRY I'M LATE.
DON'T WORRY, HON. I HAD A HANDSOME, YOUNG MAN TO ENTERTAIN ME. THE TIME FLEW.
JACK, THIS IS SADIE FALK.
SADIE, JACK KNIGHT.
SADIE'S NEW TO THE OPAL. NEWER THAN ME.
GLAD TO MEET--
TOO LATE!
WHAT?
TO MEET ME. WE'VE ALREADY MET.
ERRRR
YOU BUMPED INTO ME. THE CIRCUS. YOU WEREN'T LOOKING WHERE YOU WERE GOING.
OHH YEAH. YEAH. THAT WAS YOU?
FUNNY, WHAT A SMALL WORLD--
IF I HAPPEN TO BE UNLUCKY ENOUGH TO PASS YOU IN A CROWD AGAIN, BE MORE CAREFUL WHERE YOU STEP.
OR BETTER STILL, HOP ON THAT COSMIC BROOMSTICK OF YOURS, TAKE TO THE SKIES AND KEEP OUT OF EVERYONE'S WAY.
DO US ALL A FAVOR.
I...
...I...
...I...

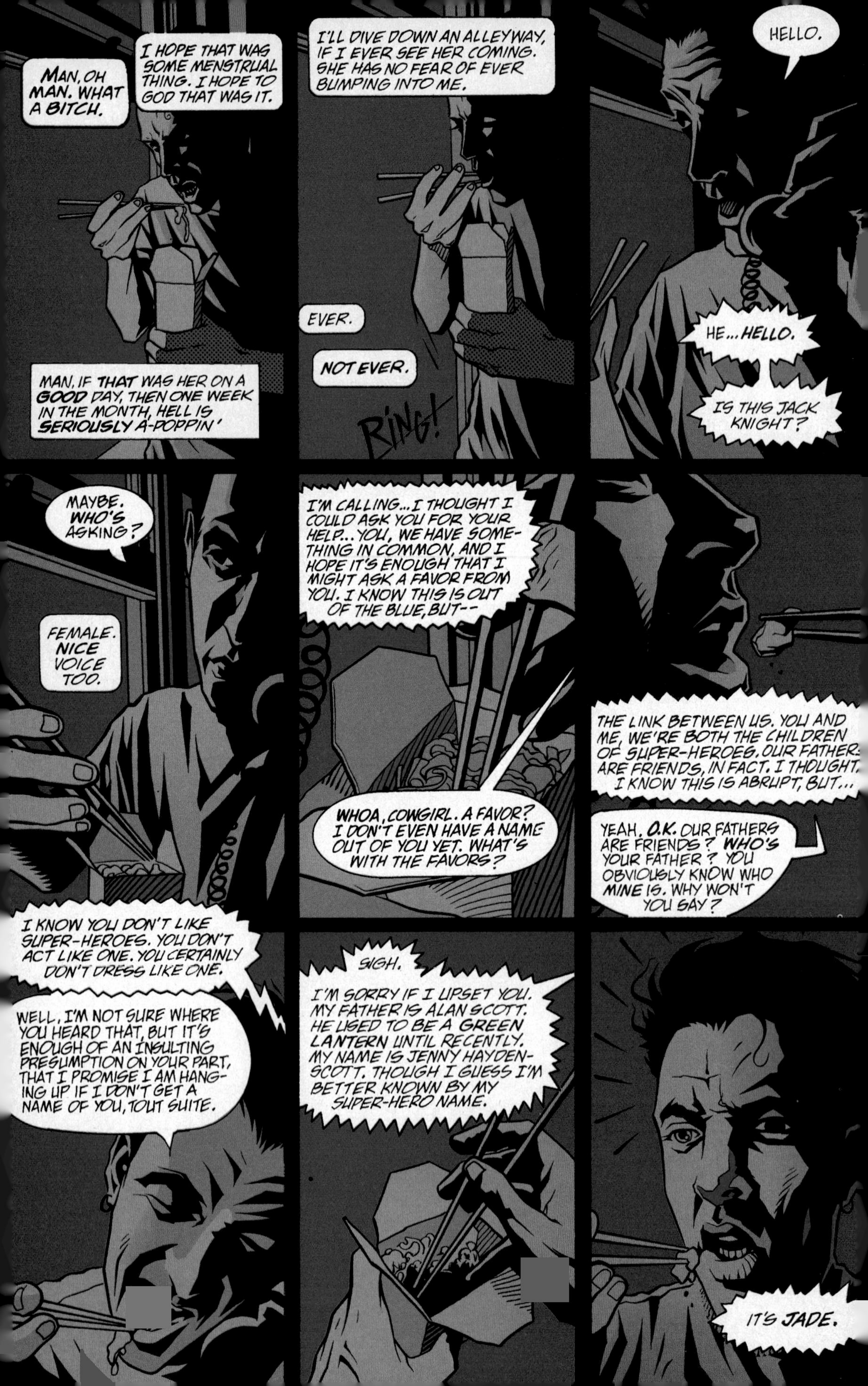
MAN, OH MAN. WHAT A BITCH.
I HOPE THAT WAS SOME MENSTRUAL THING. I HOPE TO GOD THAT WAS IT.
MAN, IF THAT WAS HER ON A GOOD DAY, THEN ONE WEEK IN THE MONTH, HELL IS SERIOUSLY A-POPPIN'
I'LL DIVE DOWN AN ALLEYWAY, IF I EVER SEE HER COMING. SHE HAS NO FEAR OF EVER BUMPING INTO ME.
EVER.
NOT EVER.
RING!
HELLO.
HE... HELLO.
IS THIS JACK KNIGHT?
MAYBE. WHO'S ASKING?
FEMALE. NICE VOICE TOO.
I'M CALLING... I THOUGHT I COULD ASK YOU FOR YOUR HELP... YOU, WE HAVE SOMETHING IN COMMON, AND I HOPE IT'S ENOUGH THAT I MIGHT ASK A FAVOR FROM YOU. I KNOW THIS IS OUT OF THE BLUE, BUT--
WHOA, COWGIRL. A FAVOR? I DON'T EVEN HAVE A NAME OUT OF YOU YET. WHAT'S WITH THE FAVORS?
THE LINK BETWEEN US. YOU AND ME, WE'RE BOTH THE CHILDREN OF SUPER-HEROES. OUR FATHERS ARE FRIENDS, IN FACT. I THOUGHT. I KNOW THIS IS ABRUPT, BUT...
YEAH. O.K. OUR FATHERS ARE FRIENDS? WHO'S YOUR FATHER? YOU OBVIOUSLY KNOW WHO MINE IS. WHY WON'T YOU SAY?
I KNOW YOU DON'T LIKE SUPER-HEROES. YOU DON'T ACT LIKE ONE. YOU CERTAINLY DON'T DRESS LIKE ONE.
WELL, I'M NOT SURE WHERE YOU HEARD THAT, BUT IT'S ENOUGH OF AN INSULTING PRESUMPTION ON YOUR PART, THAT I PROMISE I AM HANGING UP IF I DON'T GET A NAME OF YOU, TOUT SUITE.
SIGH.
I'M SORRY IF I UPSET YOU. MY FATHER IS ALAN SCOTT. HE USED TO BE A GREEN LANTERN UNTIL RECENTLY. MY NAME IS JENNY HAYDEN-SCOTT. THOUGH I GUESS I'M BETTER KNOWN BY MY SUPER-HERO NAME.
IT'S JADE.

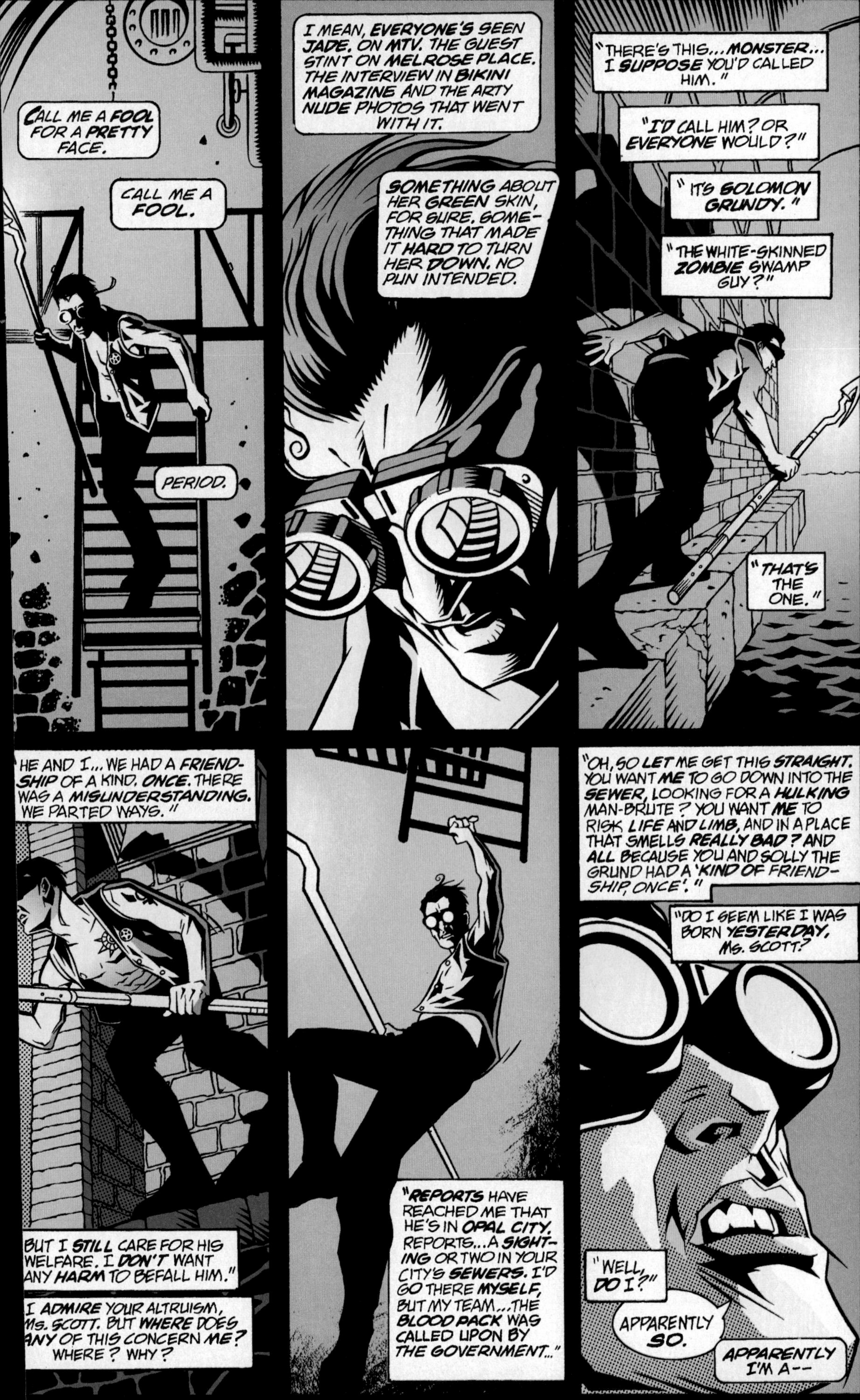
CALL ME A FOOL FOR A PRETTY FACE.
CALL ME A FOOL.
PERIOD.
I MEAN, EVERYONE'S SEEN JADE. ON MTV. THE GUEST STINT ON MELROSE PLACE. THE INTERVIEW IN BIKINI MAGAZINE AND THE ARTY NUDE PHOTOS THAT WENT WITH IT.
SOMETHING ABOUT HER GREEN SKIN, FOR SURE. SOMETHING THAT MADE IT HARD TO TURN HER DOWN. NO PUN INTENDED.
"THERE'S THIS... MONSTER... I SUPPOSE YOU'D CALLED HIM."
"I'D CALL HIM? OR EVERYONE WOULD?"
"IT'S SOLOMON GRUNDY."
"THE WHITE-SKINNED ZOMBIE SWAMP GUY?"
"THAT'S THE ONE."
"HE AND I... WE HAD A FRIENDSHIP OF A KIND, ONCE. THERE WAS A MISUNDERSTANDING. WE PARTED WAYS."
BUT I STILL CARE FOR HIS WELFARE. I DON'T WANT ANY HARM TO BEFALL HIM."
I ADMIRE YOUR ALTRUISM, MS. SCOTT. BUT WHERE DOES ANY OF THIS CONCERN ME? WHERE? WHY?
"REPORTS HAVE REACHED ME THAT HE'S IN OPAL CITY. REPORTS... A SIGHTING OR TWO IN YOUR CITY'S SEWERS. I'D GO THERE MYSELF, BUT MY TEAM... THE BLOOD PACK WAS CALLED UPON BY THE GOVERNMENT..."
"OH, SO LET ME GET THIS STRAIGHT. YOU WANT ME TO GO DOWN INTO THE SEWER, LOOKING FOR A HULKING MAN-BRUTE? YOU WANT ME TO RISK LIFE AND LIMB, AND IN A PLACE THAT SMELLS REALLY BAD? AND ALL BECAUSE YOU AND SOLLY THE GRUND HAD A 'KIND OF FRIENDSHIP, ONCE'."
"DO I SEEM LIKE I WAS BORN YESTERDAY, MS. SCOTT?
"WELL, DO I?"
APPARENTLY SO.
APPARENTLY I'M A--

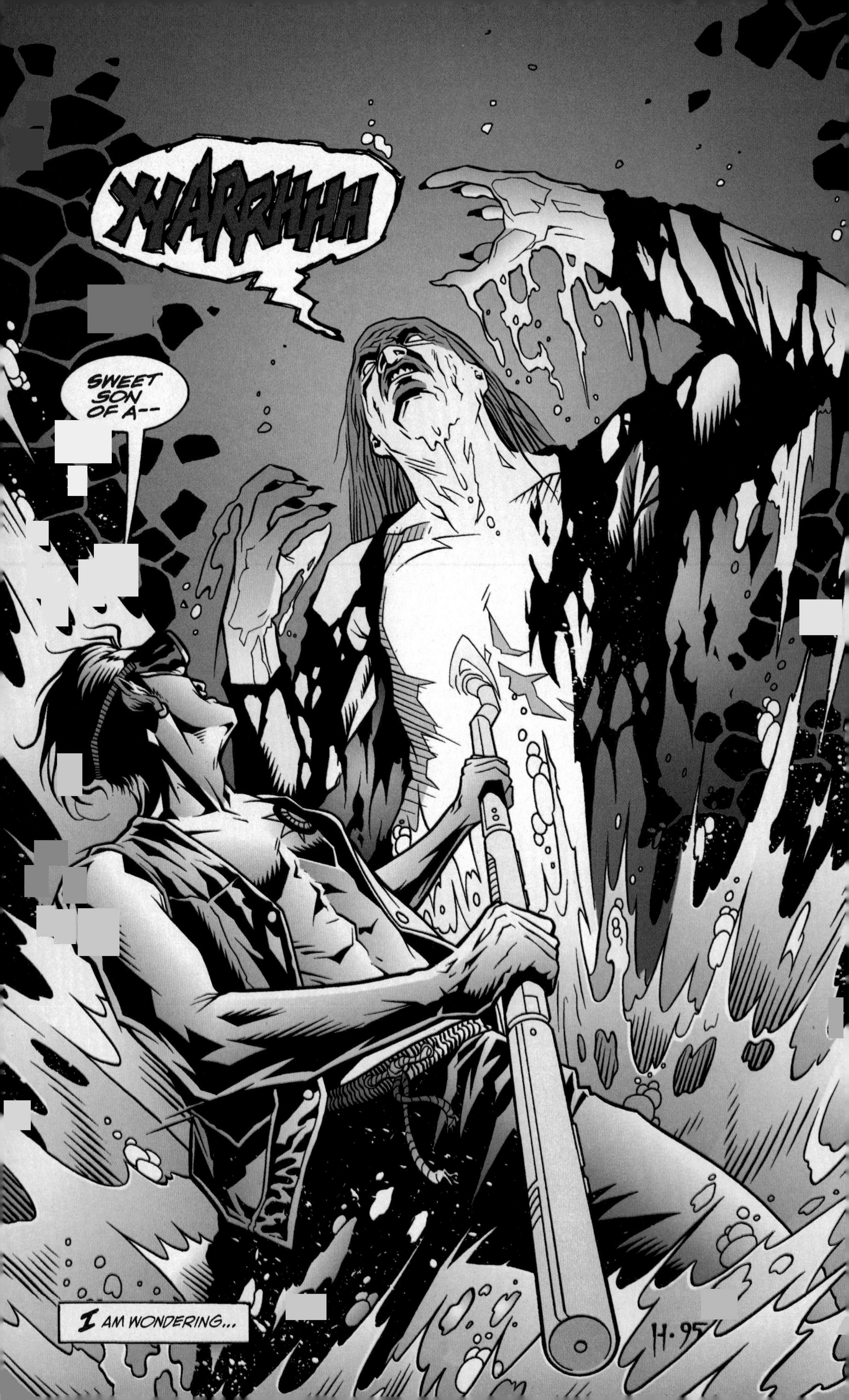
YYARRHHH
SWEET SON OF A--
I AM WONDERING...
H·95

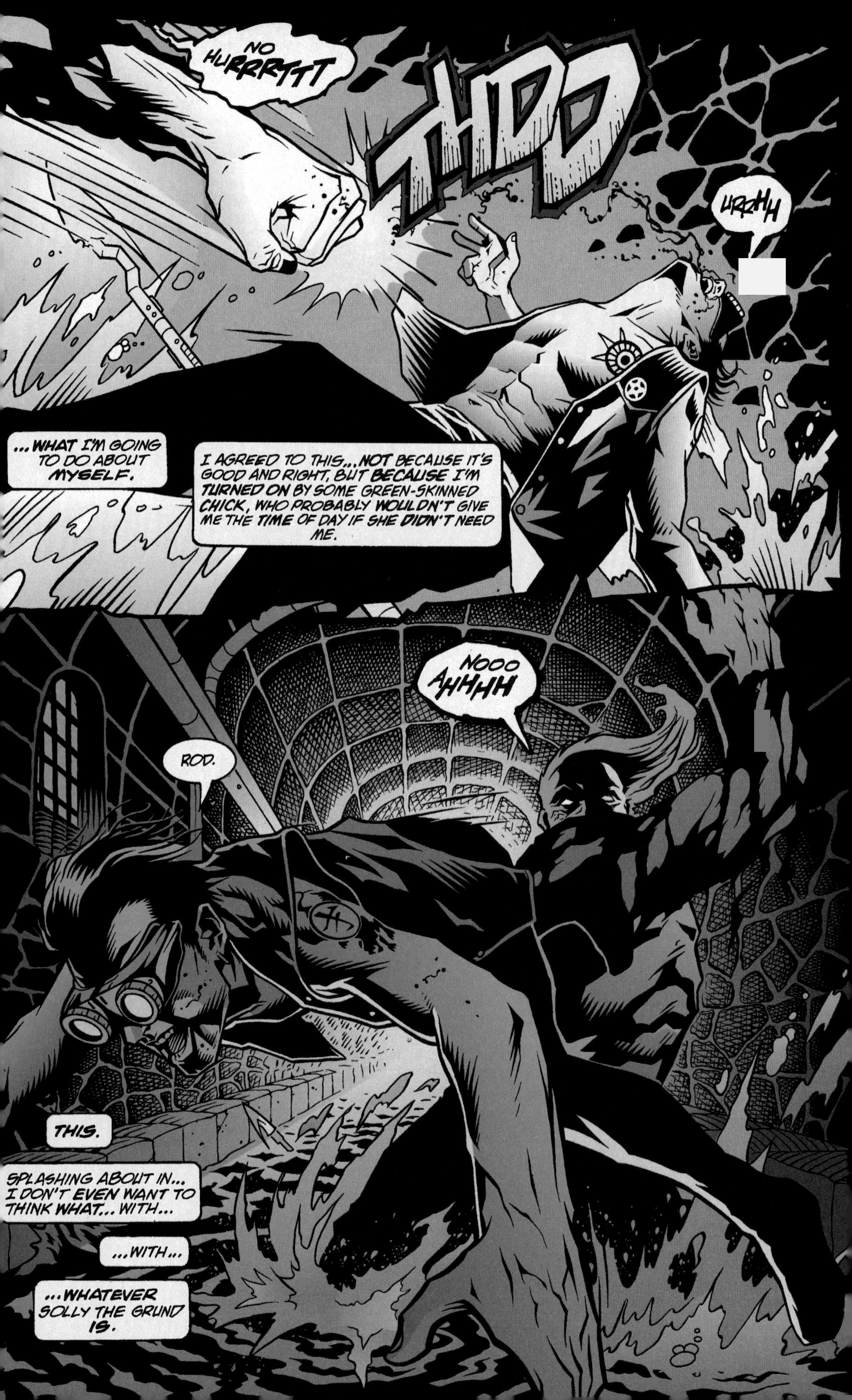
NO HURRRTTT
THDD
URRHH
...WHAT I'M GOING TO DO ABOUT MYSELF.
I AGREED TO THIS... NOT BECAUSE IT'S GOOD AND RIGHT, BUT BECAUSE I'M TURNED ON BY SOME GREEN-SKINNED CHICK, WHO PROBABLY WOULDN'T GIVE ME THE TIME OF DAY IF SHE DIDN'T NEED ME.
NOOO AHHHH
ROD.
THIS.
SPLASHING ABOUT IN... I DON'T EVEN WANT TO THINK WHAT... WITH...
...WITH...
...WHATEVER SOLLY THE GRUND IS.

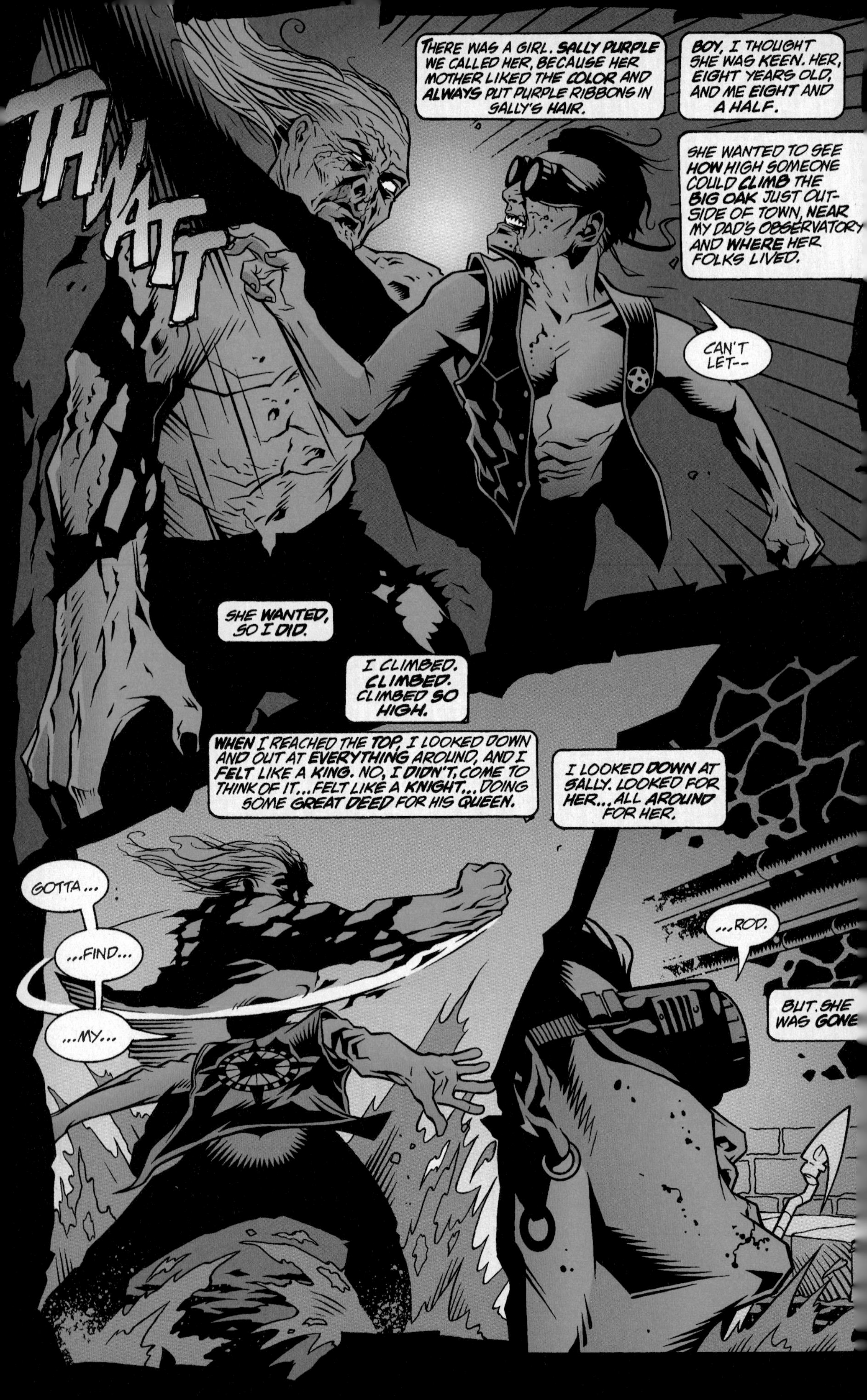
THWATT
THERE WAS A GIRL. SALLY PURPLE WE CALLED HER, BECAUSE HER MOTHER LIKED THE COLOR AND ALWAYS PUT PURPLE RIBBONS IN SALLY'S HAIR.
BOY, I THOUGHT SHE WAS KEEN. HER, EIGHT YEARS OLD, AND ME EIGHT AND A HALF.
SHE WANTED TO SEE HOW HIGH SOMEONE COULD CLIMB THE BIG OAK JUST OUTSIDE OF TOWN, NEAR MY DAD'S OBSERVATORY AND WHERE HER FOLKS LIVED.
CAN'T LET--
SHE WANTED, SO I DID.
I CLIMBED. CLIMBED. CLIMBED SO HIGH.
WHEN I REACHED THE TOP, I LOOKED DOWN AND OUT AT EVERYTHING AROUND, AND I FELT LIKE A KING. NO, I DIDN'T, COME TO THINK OF IT... FELT LIKE A KNIGHT... DOING SOME GREAT DEED FOR HIS QUEEN.
I LOOKED DOWN AT SALLY. LOOKED FOR HER... ALL AROUND FOR HER.
GOTTA...
...FIND...
...MY...
...ROD.
BUT. SHE WAS GONE

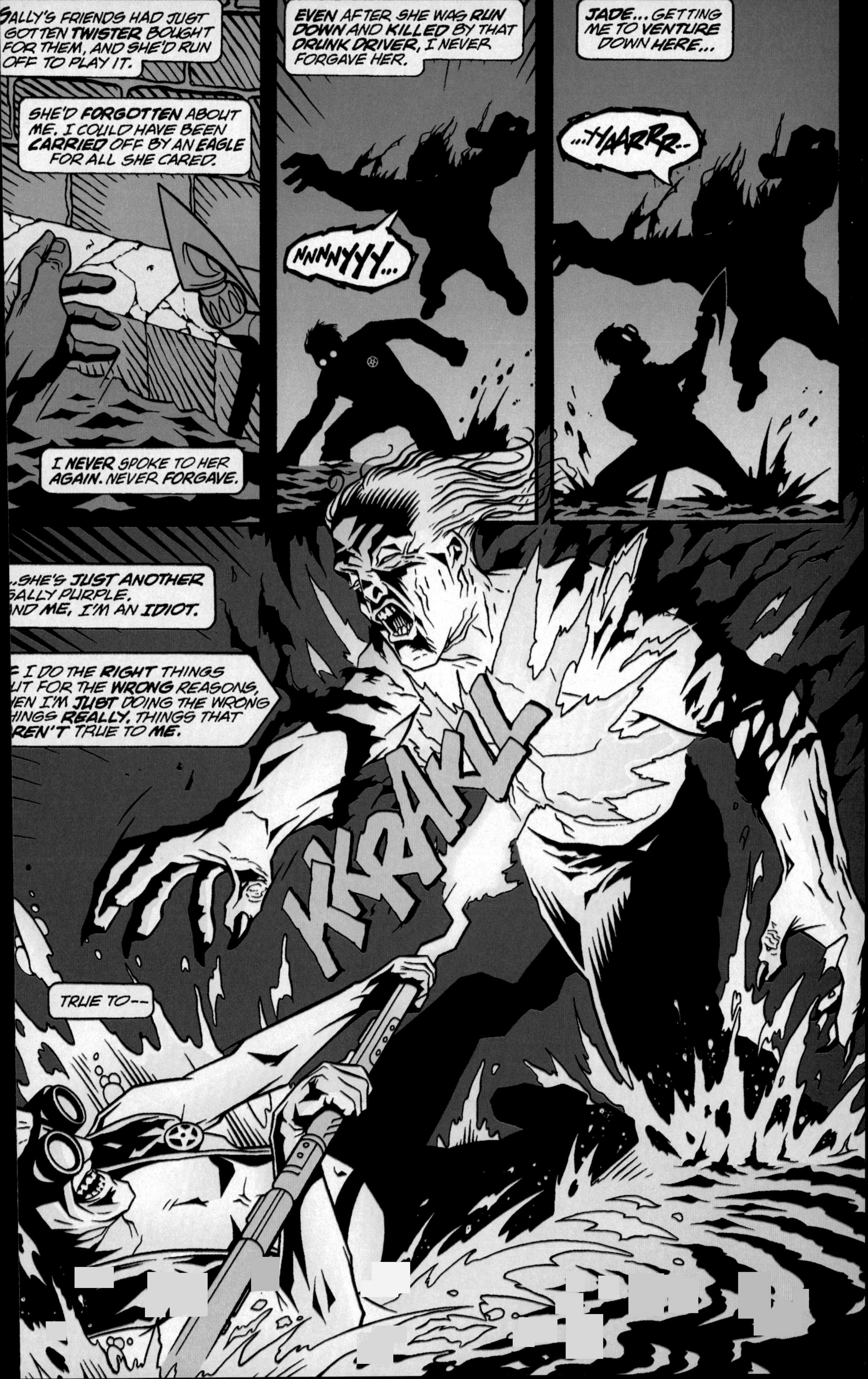

SALLY'S FRIENDS HAD JUST GOTTEN TWISTER BOUGHT FOR THEM, AND SHE'D RUN OFF TO PLAY IT.
SHE'D FORGOTTEN ABOUT ME. I COULD HAVE BEEN CARRIED OFF BY AN EAGLE FOR ALL SHE CARED.
I NEVER SPOKE TO HER AGAIN. NEVER FORGAVE.
EVEN AFTER SHE WAS RUN DOWN AND KILLED BY THAT DRUNK DRIVER, I NEVER FORGAVE HER.
NNNNYYY...
JADE... GETTING ME TO VENTURE DOWN HERE...
...YAARRR...
..SHE'S JUST ANOTHER SALLY PURPLE. ND ME, I'M AN IDIOT.
I DO THE RIGHT THINGS UT FOR THE WRONG REASONS, EN I'M JUST DOING THE WRONG HINGS REALLY. THINGS THAT REN'T TRUE TO ME.
KKRAKL
TRUE TO--

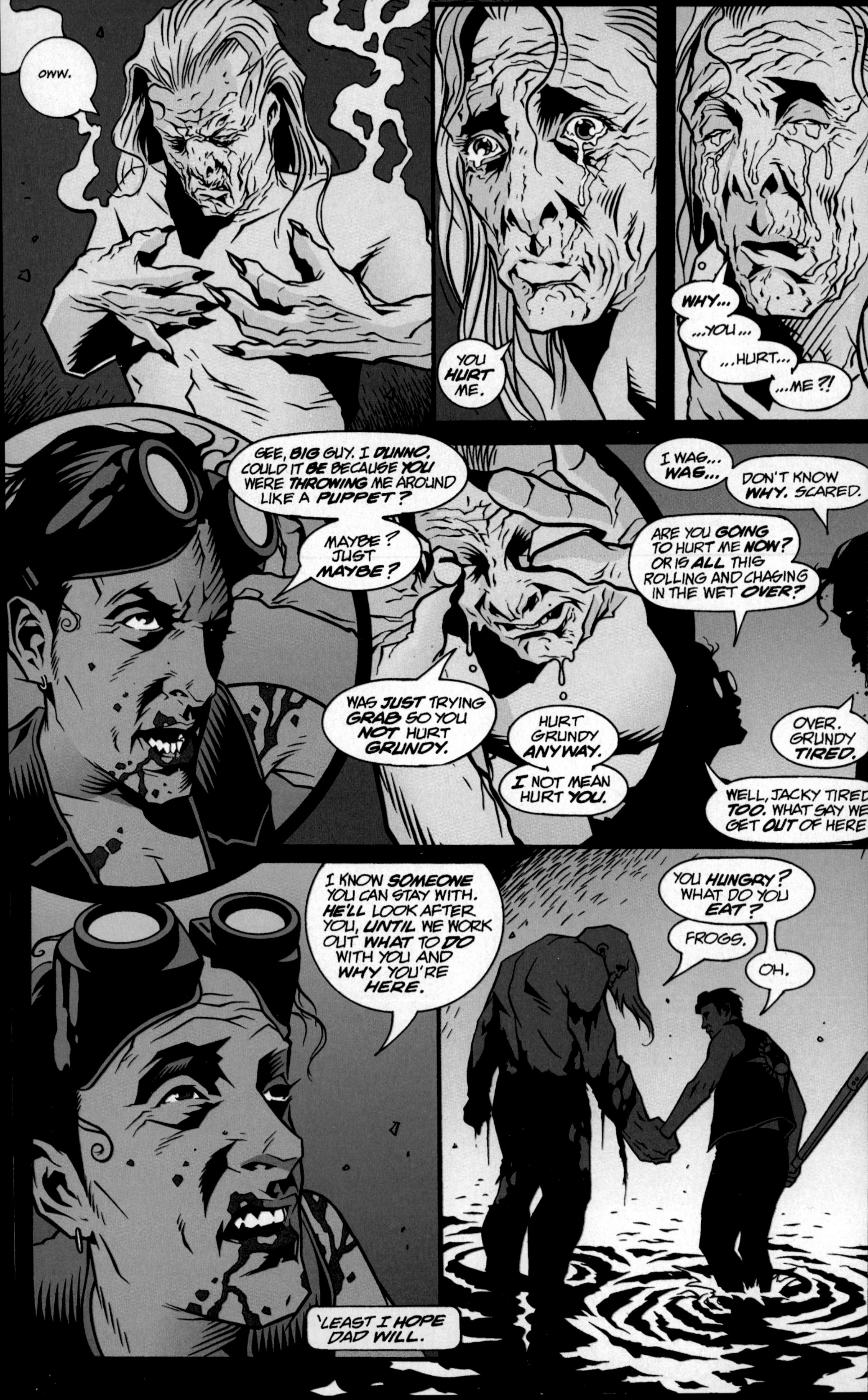

OWW.
YOU HURT ME.
WHY...
...YOU...
...HURT...
...ME?!
GEE, BIG GUY. I DUNNO. COULD IT BE BECAUSE YOU WERE THROWING ME AROUND LIKE A PUPPET?
MAYBE? JUST MAYBE?
I WAS... WAS...
DON'T KNOW WHY. SCARED.
ARE YOU GOING TO HURT ME NOW? OR IS ALL THIS ROLLING AND CHASING IN THE WET OVER?
WAS JUST TRYING GRAB SO YOU NOT HURT GRUNDY.
HURT GRUNDY ANYWAY.
I NOT MEAN HURT YOU.
OVER. GRUNDY TIRED.
WELL, JACKY TIRED TOO. WHAT SAY WE GET OUT OF HERE
I KNOW SOMEONE YOU CAN STAY WITH. HE'LL LOOK AFTER YOU, UNTIL WE WORK OUT WHAT TO DO WITH YOU AND WHY YOU'RE HERE.
'LEAST I HOPE DAD WILL.
YOU HUNGRY? WHAT DO YOU EAT?
FROGS.
OH.

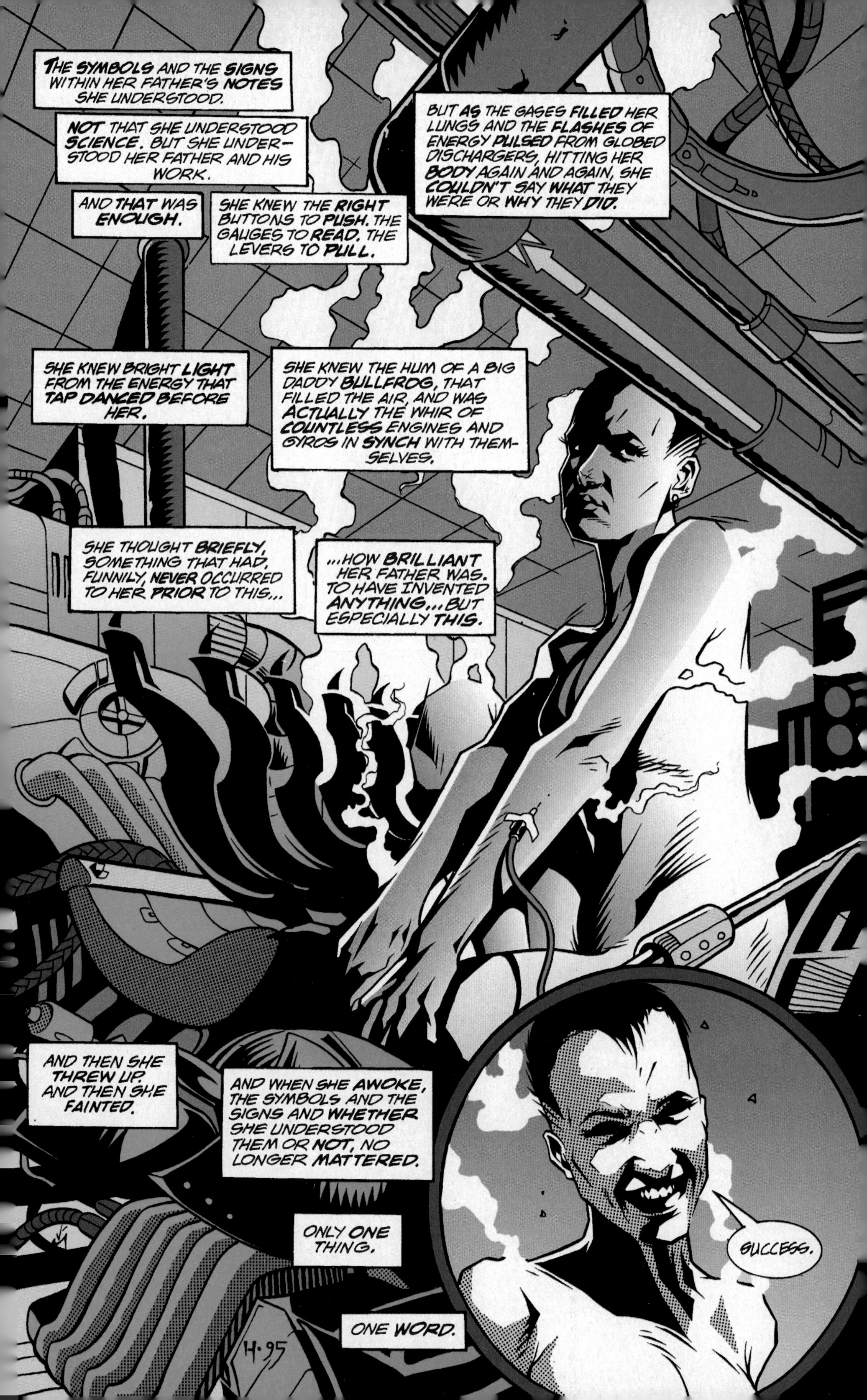
THE SYMBOLS AND THE SIGNS WITHIN HER FATHER'S NOTES SHE UNDERSTOOD.
NOT THAT SHE UNDERSTOOD SCIENCE. BUT SHE UNDER-STOOD HER FATHER AND HIS WORK.
AND THAT WAS ENOUGH.
SHE KNEW THE RIGHT BUTTONS TO PUSH. THE GAUGES TO READ. THE LEVERS TO PULL.
BUT AS THE GASES FILLED HER LUNGS AND THE FLASHES OF ENERGY PULSED FROM GLOBED DISCHARGERS, HITTING HER BODY AGAIN AND AGAIN, SHE COULDN'T SAY WHAT THEY WERE OR WHY THEY DID.
SHE KNEW BRIGHT LIGHT FROM THE ENERGY THAT TAP DANCED BEFORE HER.
SHE KNEW THE HUM OF A BIG DADDY BULLFROG, THAT FILLED THE AIR, AND WAS ACTUALLY THE WHIR OF COUNTLESS ENGINES AND GYROS IN SYNCH WITH THEM-SELVES.
SHE THOUGHT BRIEFLY, SOMETHING THAT HAD, FUNNILY, NEVER OCCURRED TO HER PRIOR TO THIS...
...HOW BRILLIANT HER FATHER WAS. TO HAVE INVENTED ANYTHING... BUT ESPECIALLY THIS.
AND THEN SHE THREW UP. AND THEN SHE FAINTED.
AND WHEN SHE AWOKE, THE SYMBOLS AND THE SIGNS AND WHETHER SHE UNDERSTOOD THEM OR NOT, NO LONGER MATTERED.
ONLY ONE THING.
SUCCESS.
ONE WORD.
H·95

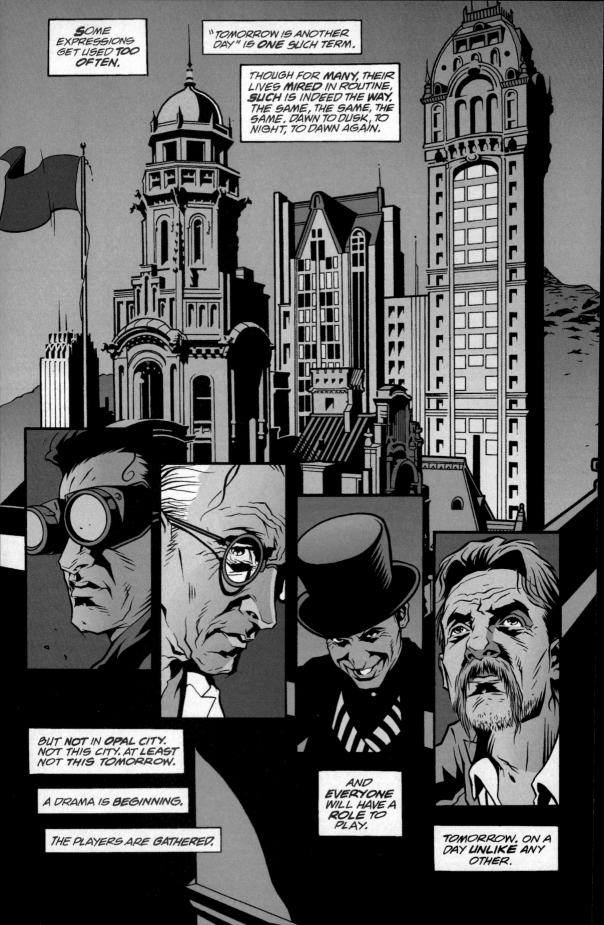

SOME EXPRESSIONS GET USED *TOO* OFTEN.

"*TOMORROW IS ANOTHER DAY*" IS *ONE* SUCH TERM.

THOUGH FOR *MANY*, THEIR LIVES *MIRED* IN ROUTINE, *SUCH* IS INDEED THE *WAY*. THE SAME, THE SAME, THE SAME. DAWN TO DUSK, TO NIGHT, TO DAWN AGAIN.

BUT NOT IN *OPAL CITY*. NOT THIS CITY. AT LEAST NOT THIS TOMORROW.

A DRAMA IS BEGINNING.

THE PLAYERS ARE GATHERED.

AND EVERYONE WILL HAVE A ROLE TO PLAY.

TOMORROW. ON A DAY *UNLIKE* ANY OTHER.

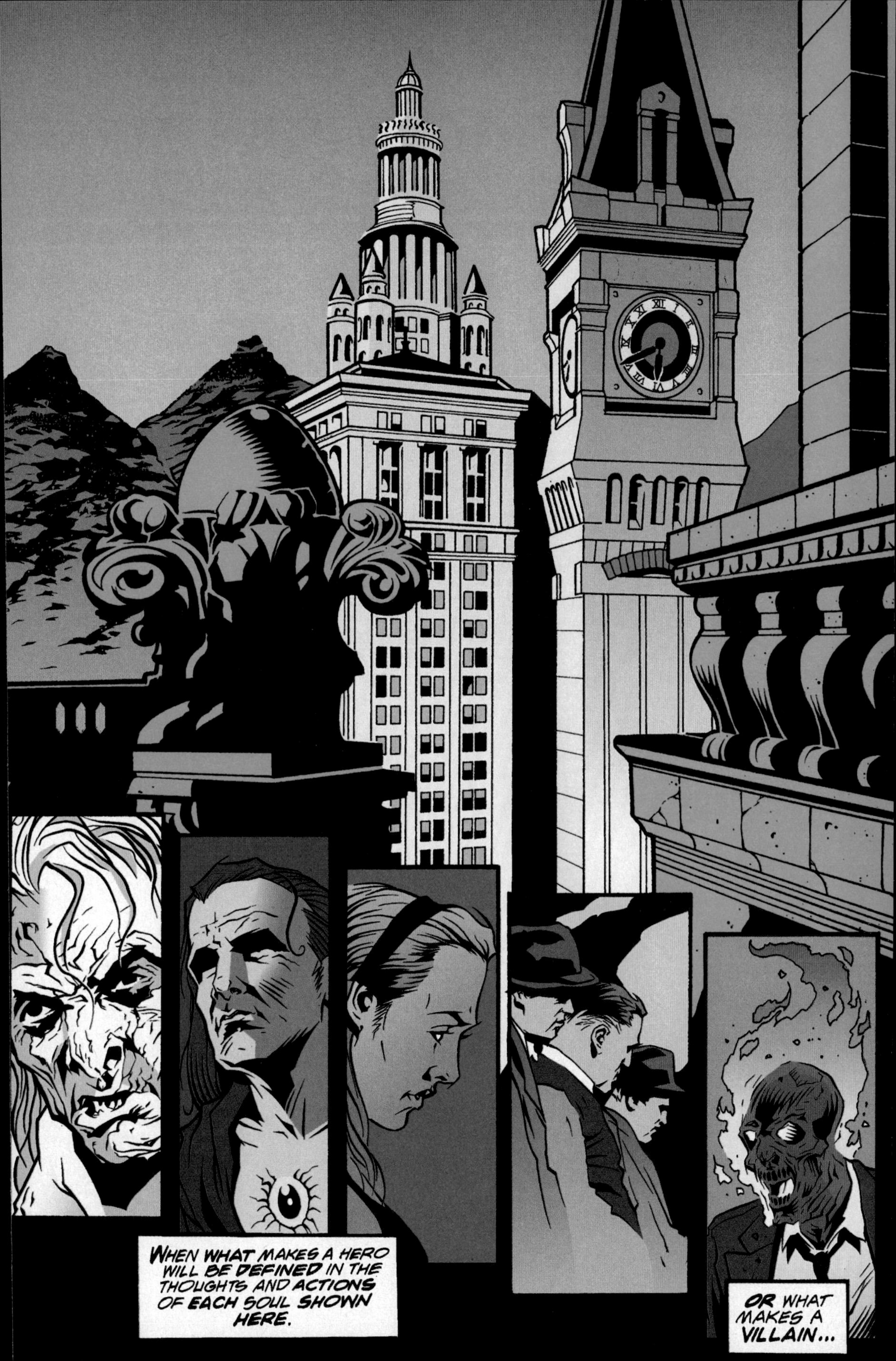
WHEN WHAT MAKES A HERO WILL BE DEFINED IN THE THOUGHTS AND ACTIONS OF EACH SOUL SHOWN HERE.
OR WHAT MAKES A VILLAIN...

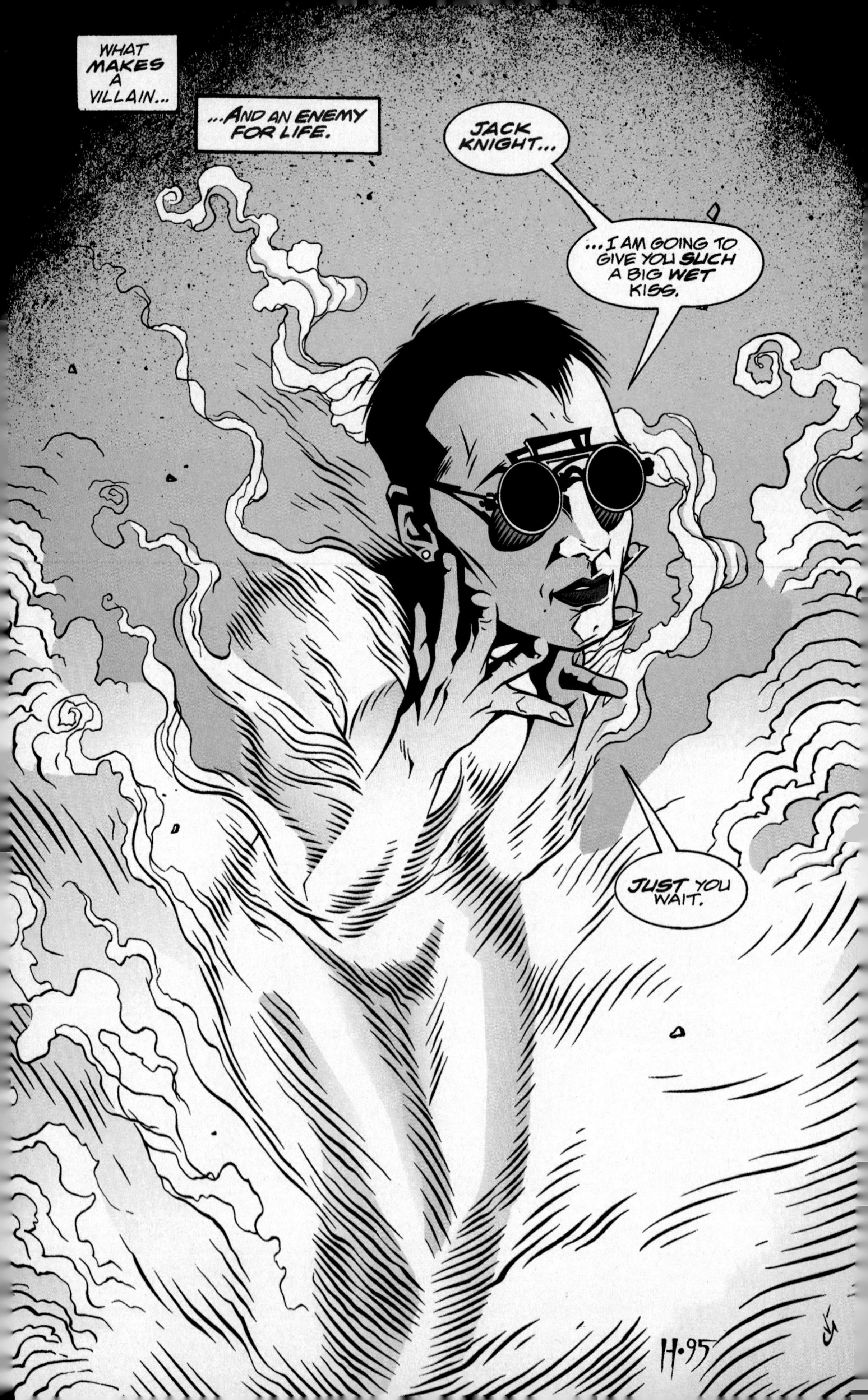
WHAT MAKES A VILLAIN...
...AND AN ENEMY FOR LIFE.
JACK KNIGHT...
...I AM GOING TO GIVE YOU SUCH A BIG WET KISS.
JUST YOU WAIT.
H•95

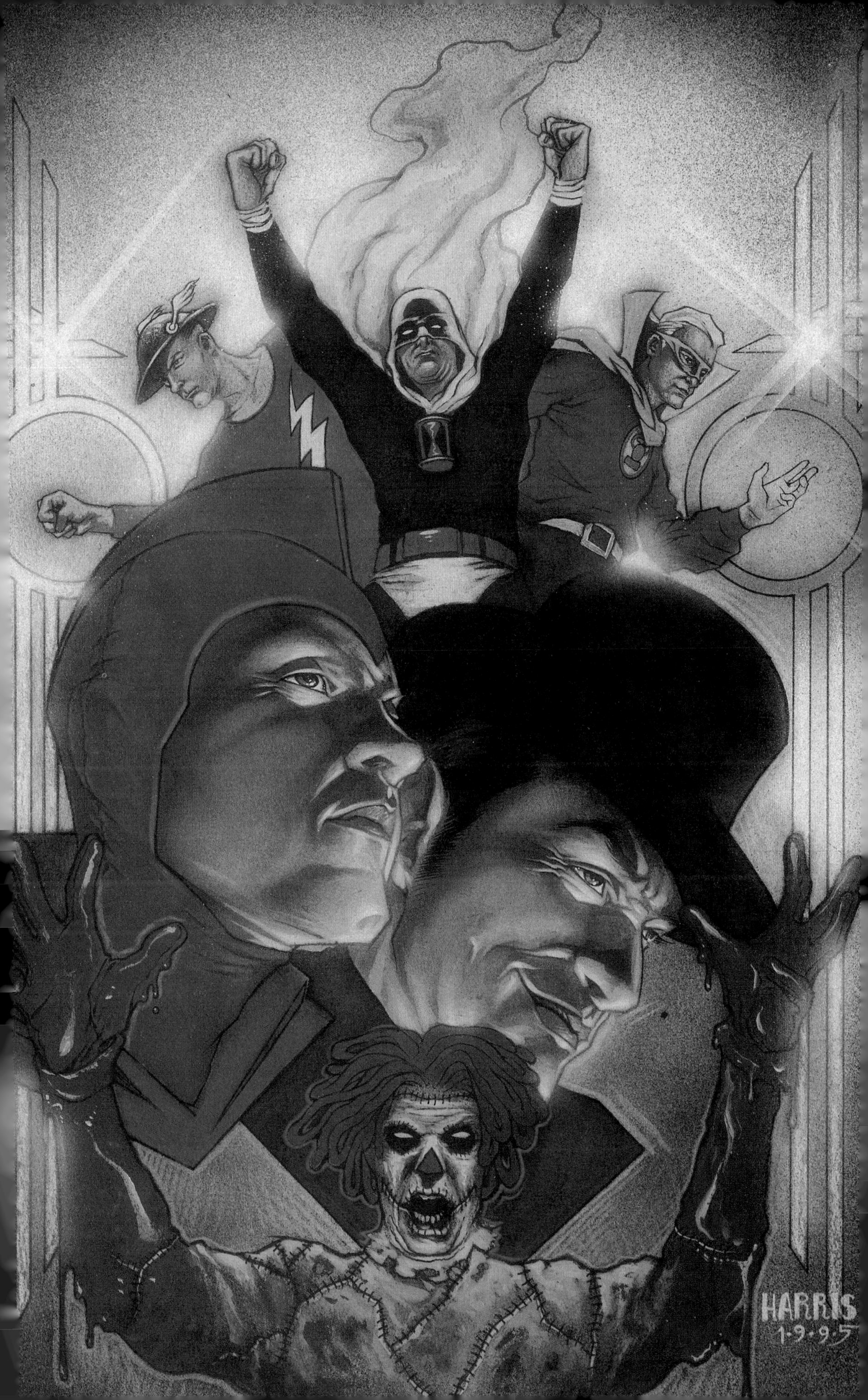
HARRIS
1·9·9·5

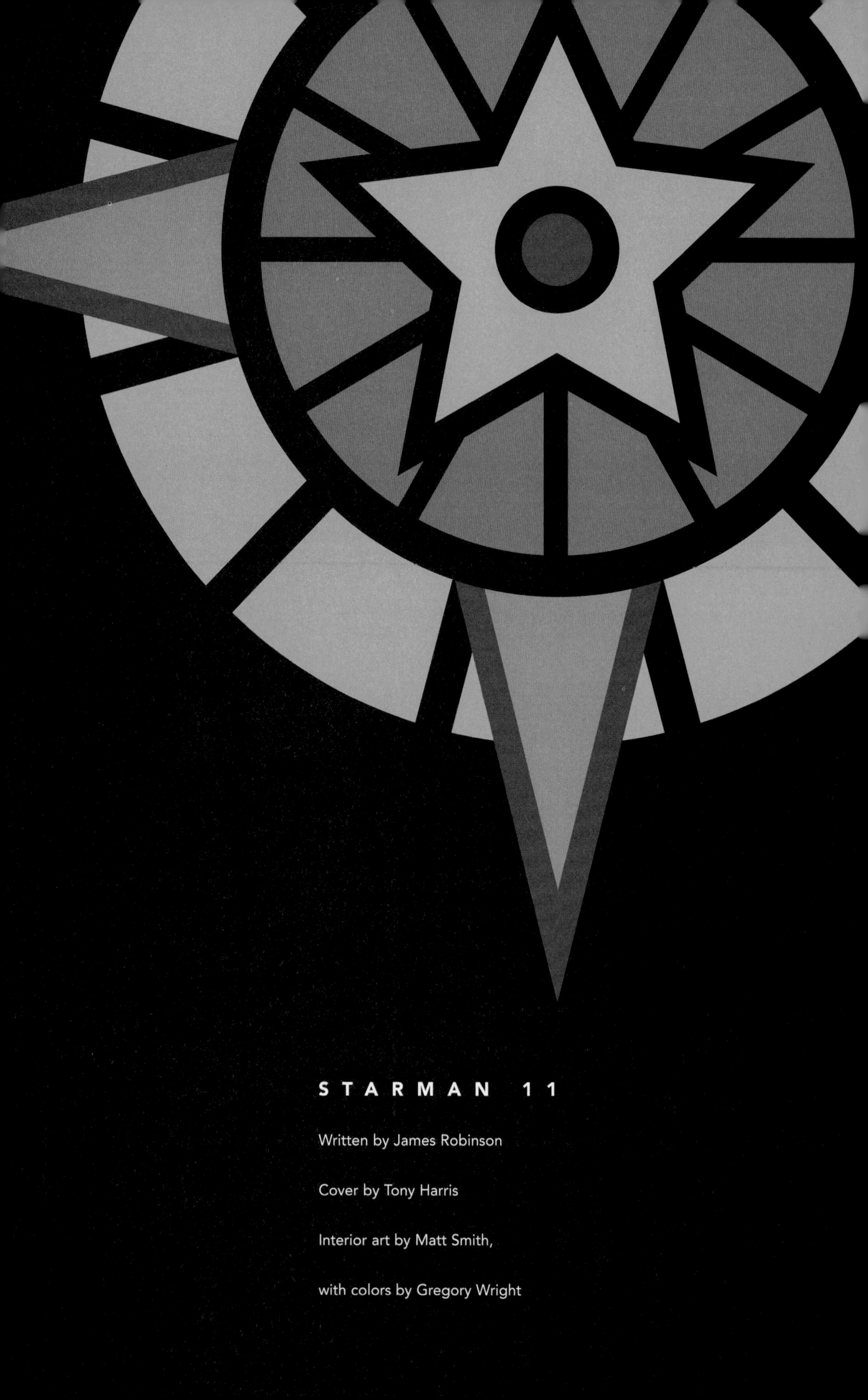

S T A R M A N 1 1

Written by James Robinson

Cover by Tony Harris

Interior art by Matt Smith,

with colors by Gregory Wright

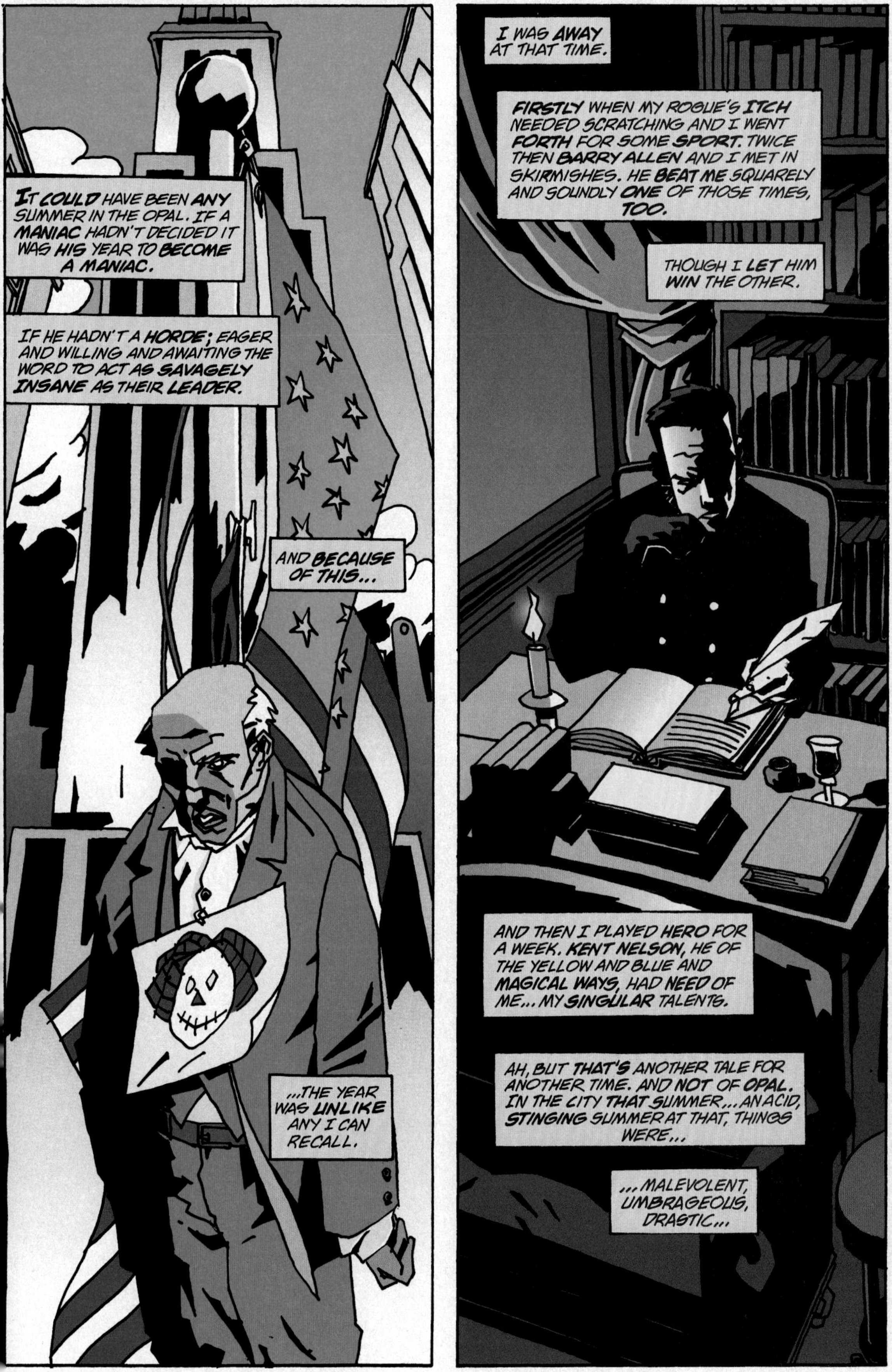
IT COULD HAVE BEEN ANY SUMMER IN THE OPAL. IF A MANIAC HADN'T DECIDED IT WAS HIS YEAR TO BECOME A MANIAC.
IF HE HADN'T A HORDE; EAGER AND WILLING AND AWAITING THE WORD TO ACT AS SAVAGELY INSANE AS THEIR LEADER.
AND BECAUSE OF THIS...
...THE YEAR WAS UNLIKE ANY I CAN RECALL.
I WAS AWAY AT THAT TIME.
FIRSTLY WHEN MY ROGUE'S ITCH NEEDED SCRATCHING AND I WENT FORTH FOR SOME SPORT. TWICE THEN BARRY ALLEN AND I MET IN SKIRMISHES. HE BEAT ME SQUARELY AND SOUNDLY ONE OF THOSE TIMES, TOO.
THOUGH I LET HIM WIN THE OTHER.
AND THEN I PLAYED HERO FOR A WEEK. KENT NELSON, HE OF THE YELLOW AND BLUE AND MAGICAL WAYS, HAD NEED OF ME... MY SINGULAR TALENTS.
AH, BUT THAT'S ANOTHER TALE FOR ANOTHER TIME. AND NOT OF OPAL. IN THE CITY THAT SUMMER... AN ACID, STINGING SUMMER AT THAT, THINGS WERE...
...MALEVOLENT, UMBRAGEOUS, DRASTIC...

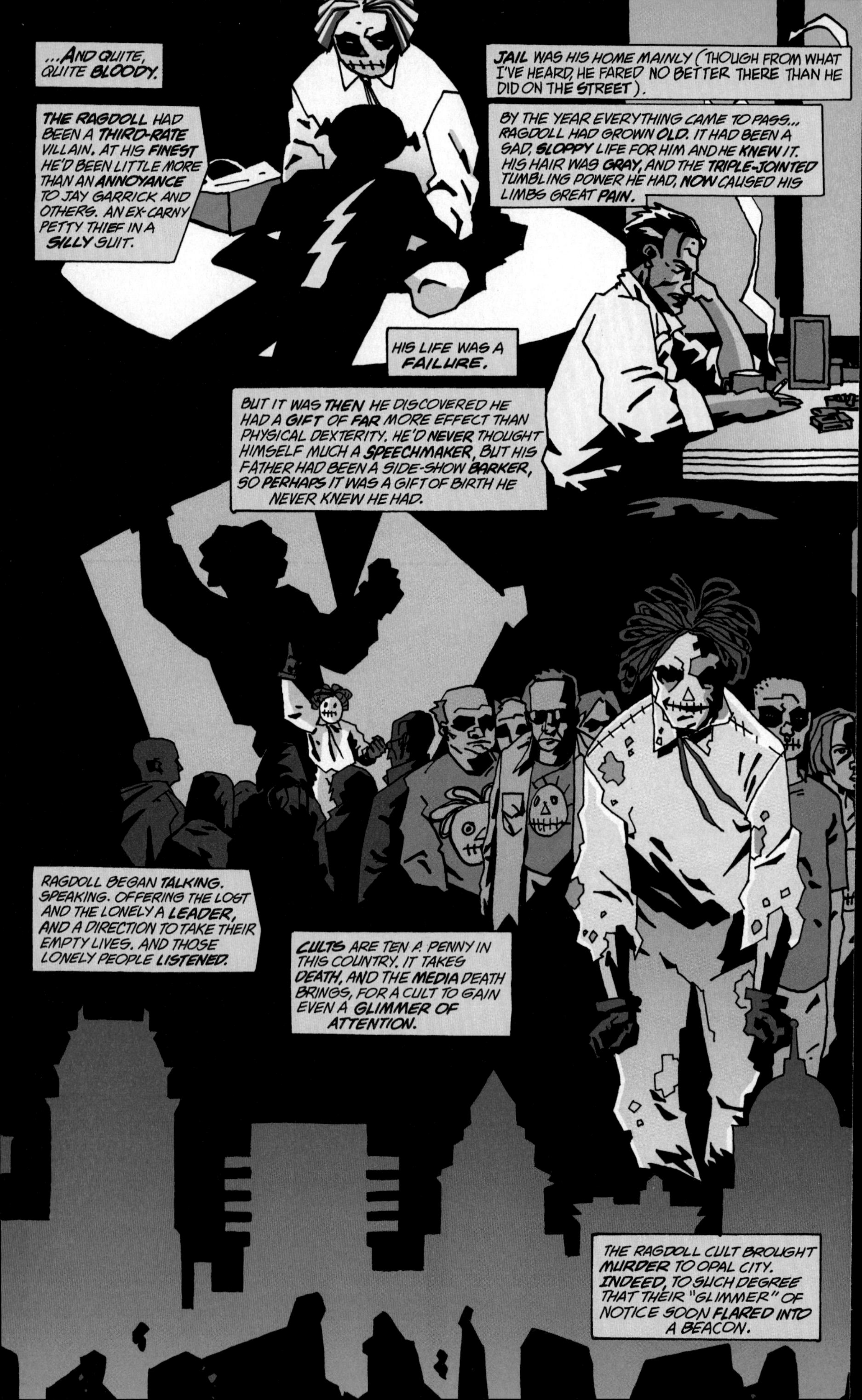
...AND QUITE, QUITE BLOODY.
THE RAGDOLL HAD BEEN A THIRD-RATE VILLAIN. AT HIS FINEST HE'D BEEN LITTLE MORE THAN AN ANNOYANCE TO JAY GARRICK AND OTHERS. AN EX-CARNY PETTY THIEF IN A SILLY SUIT.
JAIL WAS HIS HOME MAINLY (THOUGH FROM WHAT I'VE HEARD, HE FARED NO BETTER THERE THAN HE DID ON THE STREET).
BY THE YEAR EVERYTHING CAME TO PASS... RAGDOLL HAD GROWN OLD. IT HAD BEEN A SAD, SLOPPY LIFE FOR HIM AND HE KNEW IT. HIS HAIR WAS GRAY, AND THE TRIPLE-JOINTED TUMBLING POWER HE HAD, NOW CAUSED HIS LIMBS GREAT PAIN.
HIS LIFE WAS A FAILURE.
BUT IT WAS THEN HE DISCOVERED HE HAD A GIFT OF FAR MORE EFFECT THAN PHYSICAL DEXTERITY. HE'D NEVER THOUGHT HIMSELF MUCH A SPEECHMAKER, BUT HIS FATHER HAD BEEN A SIDE-SHOW BARKER, SO PERHAPS IT WAS A GIFT OF BIRTH HE NEVER KNEW HE HAD.
RAGDOLL BEGAN TALKING. SPEAKING. OFFERING THE LOST AND THE LONELY A LEADER, AND A DIRECTION TO TAKE THEIR EMPTY LIVES. AND THOSE LONELY PEOPLE LISTENED.
CULTS ARE TEN A PENNY IN THIS COUNTRY. IT TAKES DEATH, AND THE MEDIA DEATH BRINGS, FOR A CULT TO GAIN EVEN A GLIMMER OF ATTENTION.
THE RAGDOLL CULT BROUGHT MURDER TO OPAL CITY. INDEED, TO SUCH DEGREE THAT THEIR "GLIMMER" OF NOTICE SOON FLARED INTO A BEACON.

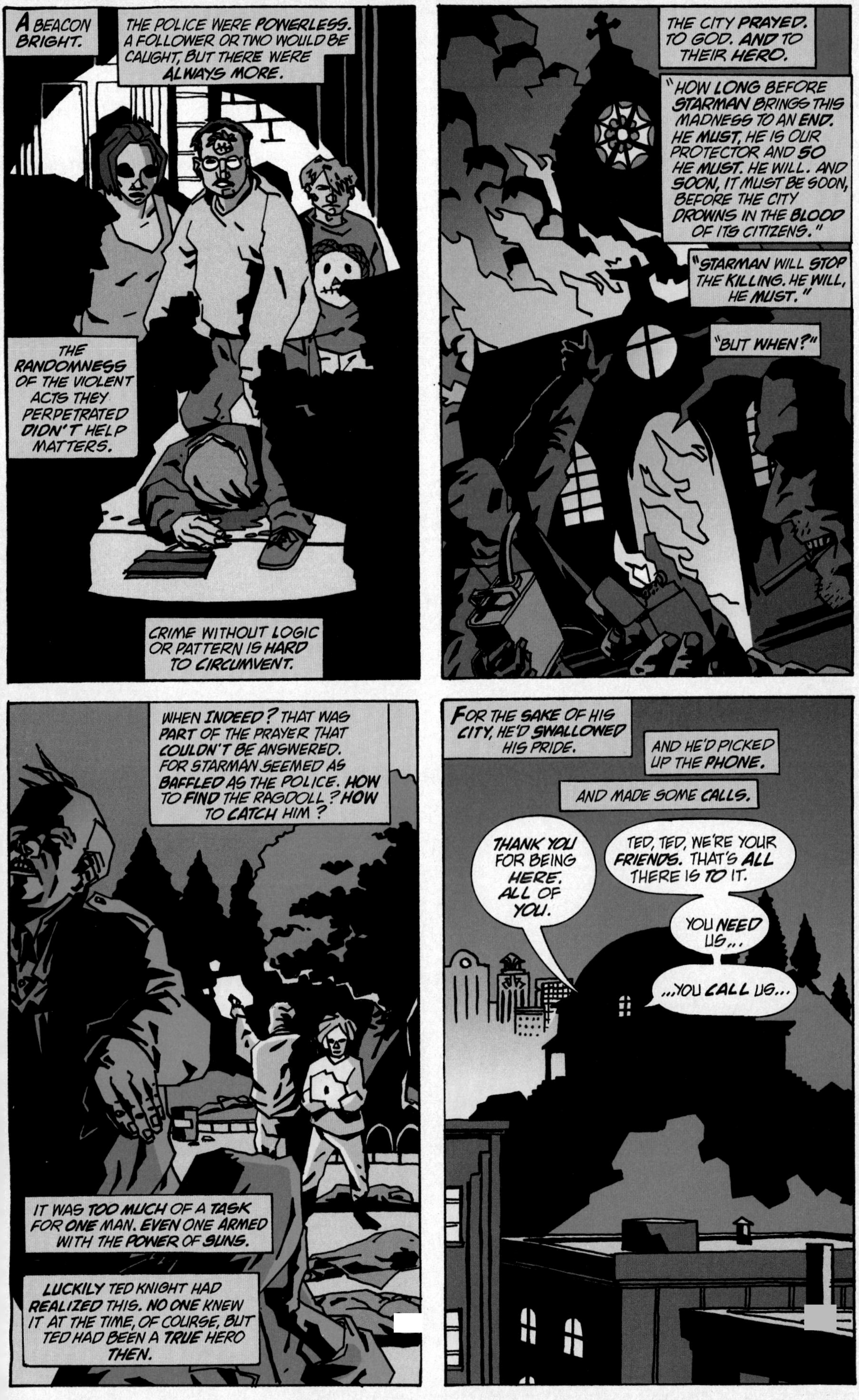
A BEACON BRIGHT.
THE POLICE WERE POWERLESS. A FOLLOWER OR TWO WOULD BE CAUGHT, BUT THERE WERE ALWAYS MORE.
THE RANDOMNESS OF THE VIOLENT ACTS THEY PERPETRATED DIDN'T HELP MATTERS.
CRIME WITHOUT LOGIC OR PATTERN IS HARD TO CIRCUMVENT.
THE CITY PRAYED. TO GOD. AND TO THEIR HERO.
"HOW LONG BEFORE STARMAN BRINGS THIS MADNESS TO AN END. HE MUST, HE IS OUR PROTECTOR AND SO HE MUST. HE WILL. AND SOON, IT MUST BE SOON, BEFORE THE CITY DROWNS IN THE BLOOD OF ITS CITIZENS."
"STARMAN WILL STOP THE KILLING. HE WILL, HE MUST."
"BUT WHEN?"
WHEN INDEED? THAT WAS PART OF THE PRAYER THAT COULDN'T BE ANSWERED. FOR STARMAN SEEMED AS BAFFLED AS THE POLICE. HOW TO FIND THE RAGDOLL? HOW TO CATCH HIM?
IT WAS TOO MUCH OF A TASK FOR ONE MAN. EVEN ONE ARMED WITH THE POWER OF SUNS.
LUCKILY TED KNIGHT HAD REALIZED THIS. NO ONE KNEW IT AT THE TIME, OF COURSE, BUT TED HAD BEEN A TRUE HERO THEN.
FOR THE SAKE OF HIS CITY, HE'D SWALLOWED HIS PRIDE.
AND HE'D PICKED UP THE PHONE.
AND MADE SOME CALLS.
THANK YOU FOR BEING HERE. ALL OF YOU.
TED, TED, WE'RE YOUR FRIENDS. THAT'S ALL THERE IS TO IT.
YOU NEED US...
...YOU CALL US...

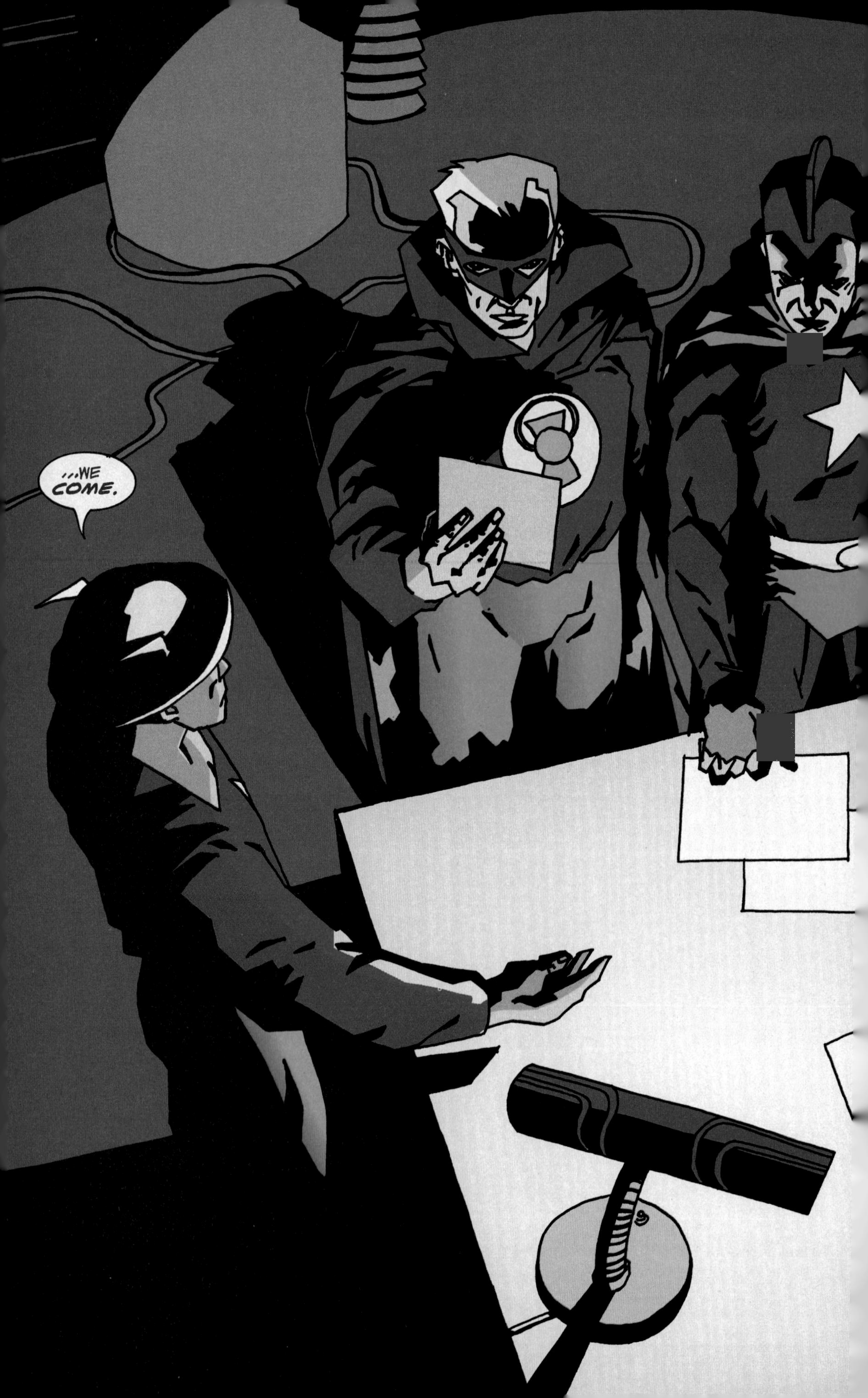
...WE COME.

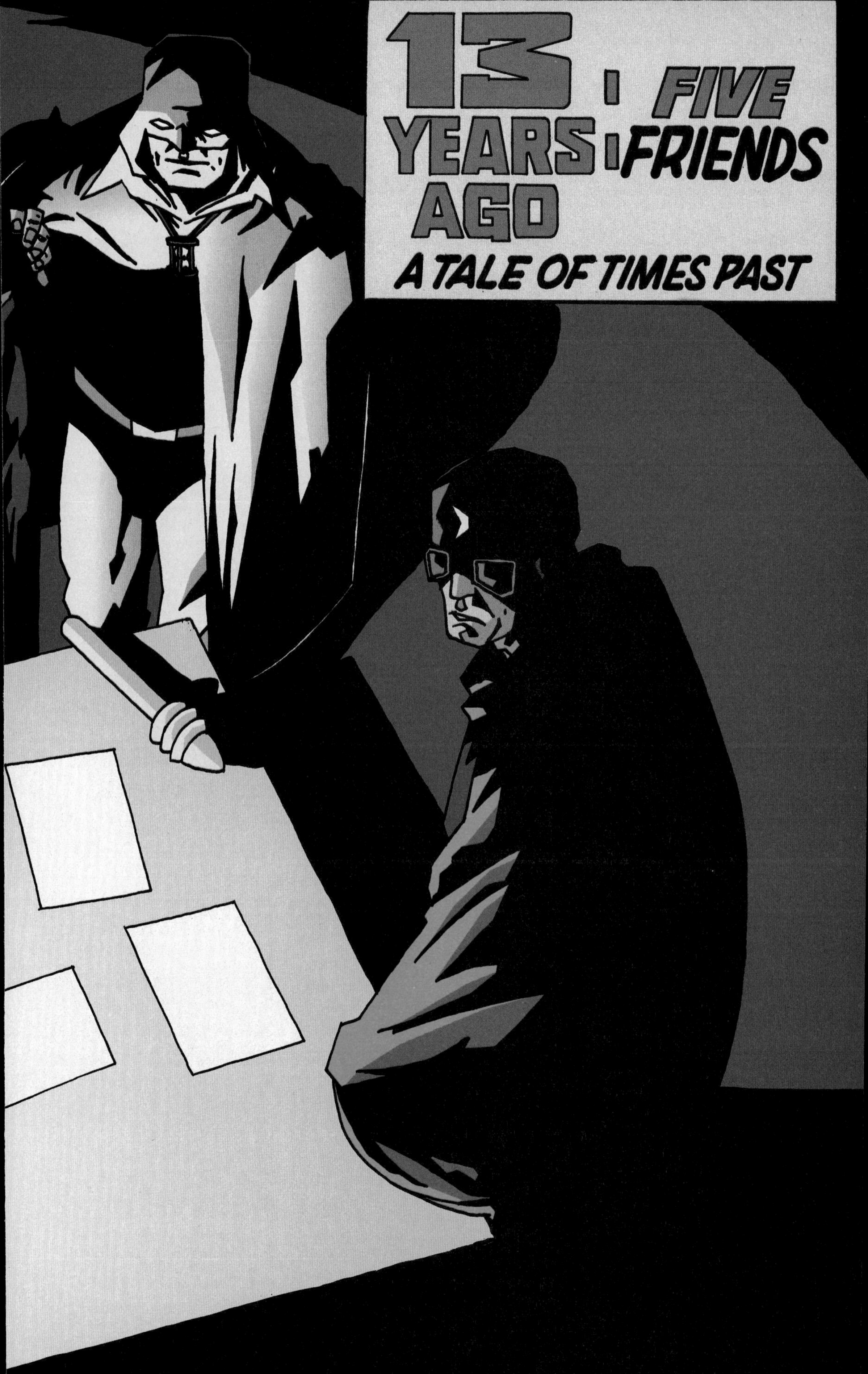

13 YEARS AGO
FIVE FRIENDS
A TALE OF TIMES PAST

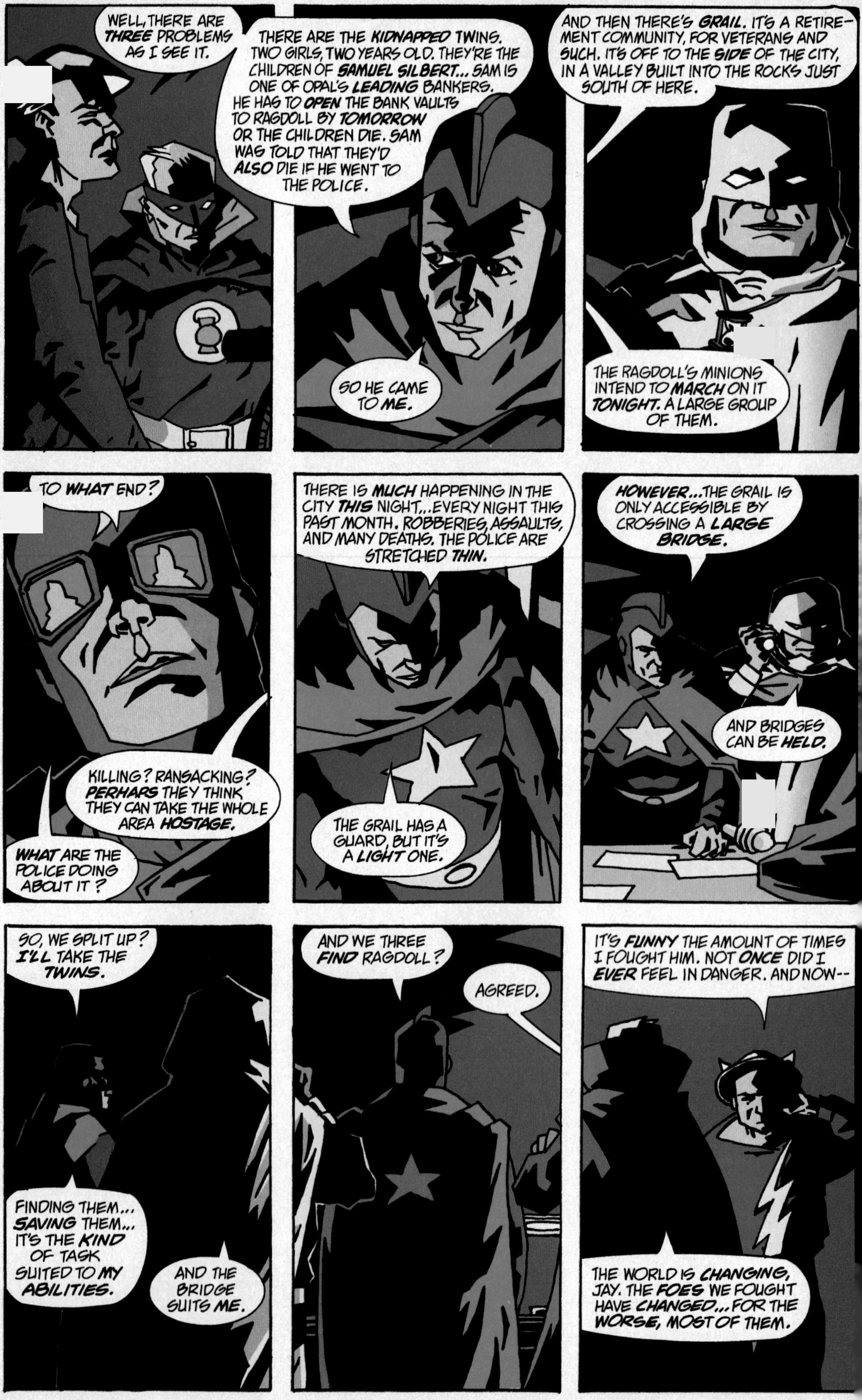
WELL, THERE ARE THREE PROBLEMS AS I SEE IT.
THERE ARE THE KIDNAPPED TWINS. TWO GIRLS, TWO YEARS OLD. THEY'RE THE CHILDREN OF SAMUEL SILBERT... SAM IS ONE OF OPAL'S LEADING BANKERS. HE HAS TO OPEN THE BANK VAULTS TO RAGDOLL BY TOMORROW OR THE CHILDREN DIE. SAM WAS TOLD THAT THEY'D ALSO DIE IF HE WENT TO THE POLICE.
SO HE CAME TO ME.
AND THEN THERE'S GRAIL. IT'S A RETIREMENT COMMUNITY, FOR VETERANS AND SUCH. IT'S OFF TO THE SIDE OF THE CITY, IN A VALLEY BUILT INTO THE ROCKS JUST SOUTH OF HERE.
THE RAGDOLL'S MINIONS INTEND TO MARCH ON IT TONIGHT. A LARGE GROUP OF THEM.
TO WHAT END?
KILLING? RANSACKING? PERHAPS THEY THINK THEY CAN TAKE THE WHOLE AREA HOSTAGE.
WHAT ARE THE POLICE DOING ABOUT IT?
THERE IS MUCH HAPPENING IN THE CITY THIS NIGHT... EVERY NIGHT THIS PAST MONTH. ROBBERIES, ASSAULTS, AND MANY DEATHS. THE POLICE ARE STRETCHED THIN.
THE GRAIL HAS A GUARD, BUT IT'S A LIGHT ONE.
HOWEVER... THE GRAIL IS ONLY ACCESSIBLE BY CROSSING A LARGE BRIDGE.
AND BRIDGES CAN BE HELD.
SO, WE SPLIT UP? I'LL TAKE THE TWINS.
FINDING THEM... SAVING THEM... IT'S THE KIND OF TASK SUITED TO MY ABILITIES.
AND THE BRIDGE SUITS ME.
AND WE THREE FIND RAGDOLL?
AGREED.
IT'S FUNNY THE AMOUNT OF TIMES I FOUGHT HIM. NOT ONCE DID I EVER FEEL IN DANGER. AND NOW--
THE WORLD IS CHANGING, JAY. THE FOES WE FOUGHT HAVE CHANGED... FOR THE WORSE, MOST OF THEM.

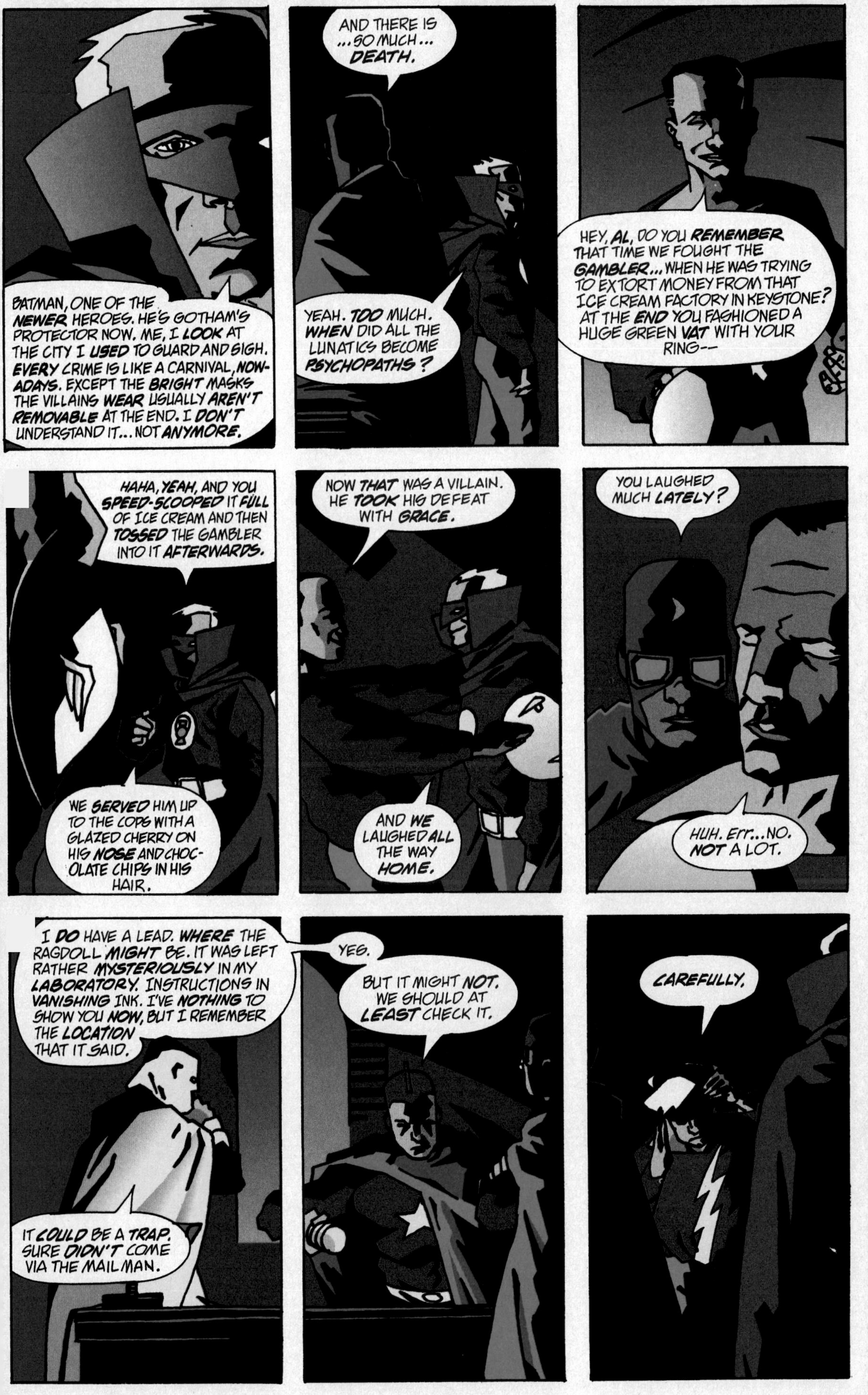
BATMAN, ONE OF THE NEWER HEROES. HE'S GOTHAM'S PROTECTOR NOW. ME, I LOOK AT THE CITY I USED TO GUARD AND SIGH. EVERY CRIME IS LIKE A CARNIVAL, NOW-ADAYS. EXCEPT THE BRIGHT MASKS THE VILLAINS WEAR USUALLY AREN'T REMOVABLE AT THE END. I DON'T UNDERSTAND IT... NOT ANYMORE.
AND THERE IS ...SO MUCH... DEATH.
YEAH. TOO MUCH. WHEN DID ALL THE LUNATICS BECOME PSYCHOPATHS?
HEY, AL, DO YOU REMEMBER THAT TIME WE FOUGHT THE GAMBLER... WHEN HE WAS TRYING TO EXTORT MONEY FROM THAT ICE CREAM FACTORY IN KEYSTONE? AT THE END YOU FASHIONED A HUGE GREEN VAT WITH YOUR RING--
HAHA, YEAH, AND YOU SPEED-SCOOPED IT FULL OF ICE CREAM AND THEN TOSSED THE GAMBLER INTO IT AFTERWARDS.
WE SERVED HIM UP TO THE COPS WITH A GLAZED CHERRY ON HIS NOSE AND CHOC-OLATE CHIPS IN HIS HAIR.
NOW THAT WAS A VILLAIN. HE TOOK HIS DEFEAT WITH GRACE.
AND WE LAUGHED ALL THE WAY HOME.
YOU LAUGHED MUCH LATELY?
HUH. Err...NO. NOT A LOT.
I DO HAVE A LEAD. WHERE THE RAGDOLL MIGHT BE. IT WAS LEFT RATHER MYSTERIOUSLY IN MY LABORATORY. INSTRUCTIONS IN VANISHING INK. I'VE NOTHING TO SHOW YOU NOW, BUT I REMEMBER THE LOCATION THAT IT SAID.
IT COULD BE A TRAP. SURE DIDN'T COME VIA THE MAILMAN.
YES.
BUT IT MIGHT NOT. WE SHOULD AT LEAST CHECK IT.
CAREFULLY.

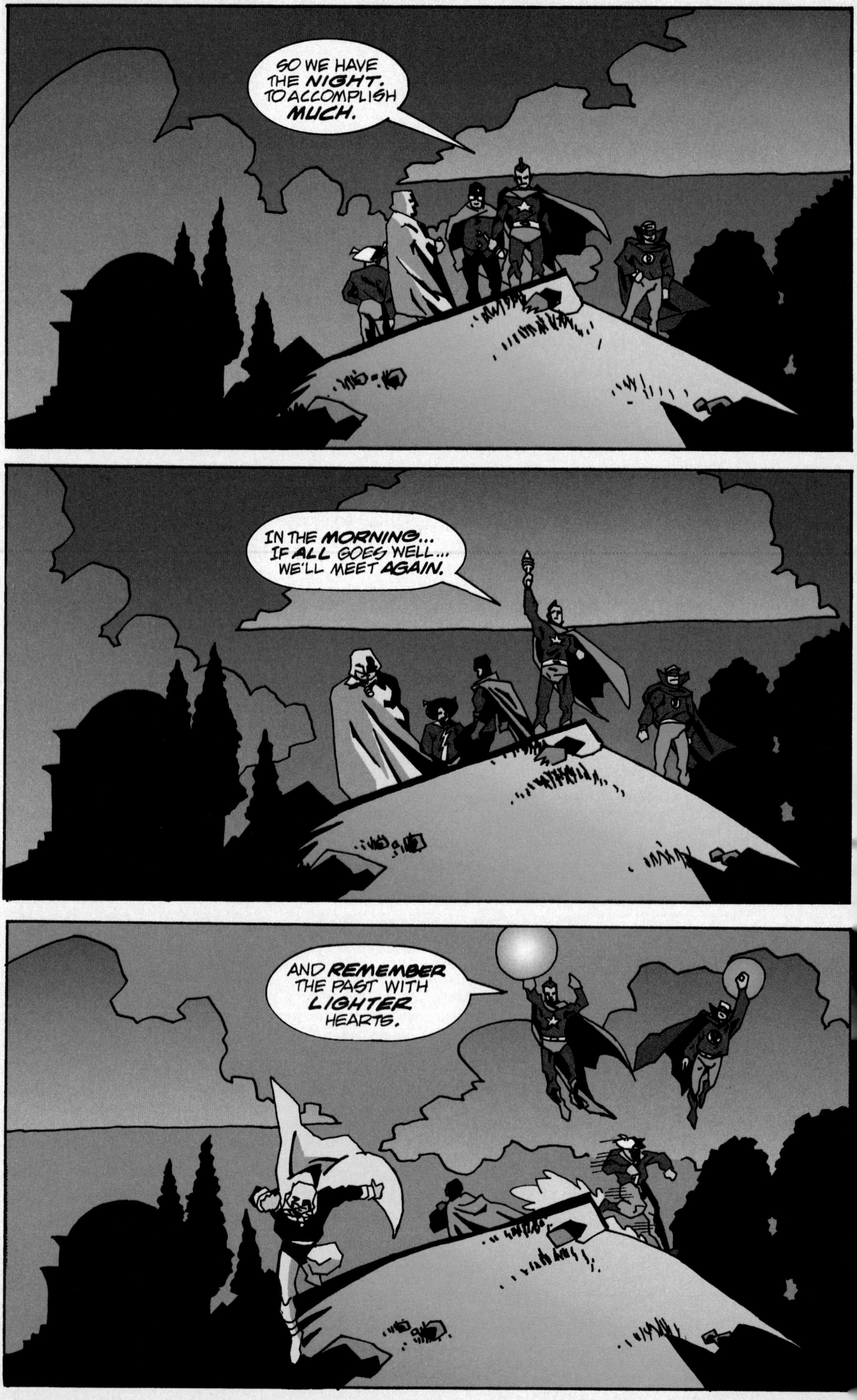
SO WE HAVE THE NIGHT. TO ACCOMPLISH MUCH.
IN THE MORNING... IF ALL GOES WELL... WE'LL MEET AGAIN.
AND REMEMBER THE PAST WITH LIGHTER HEARTS.

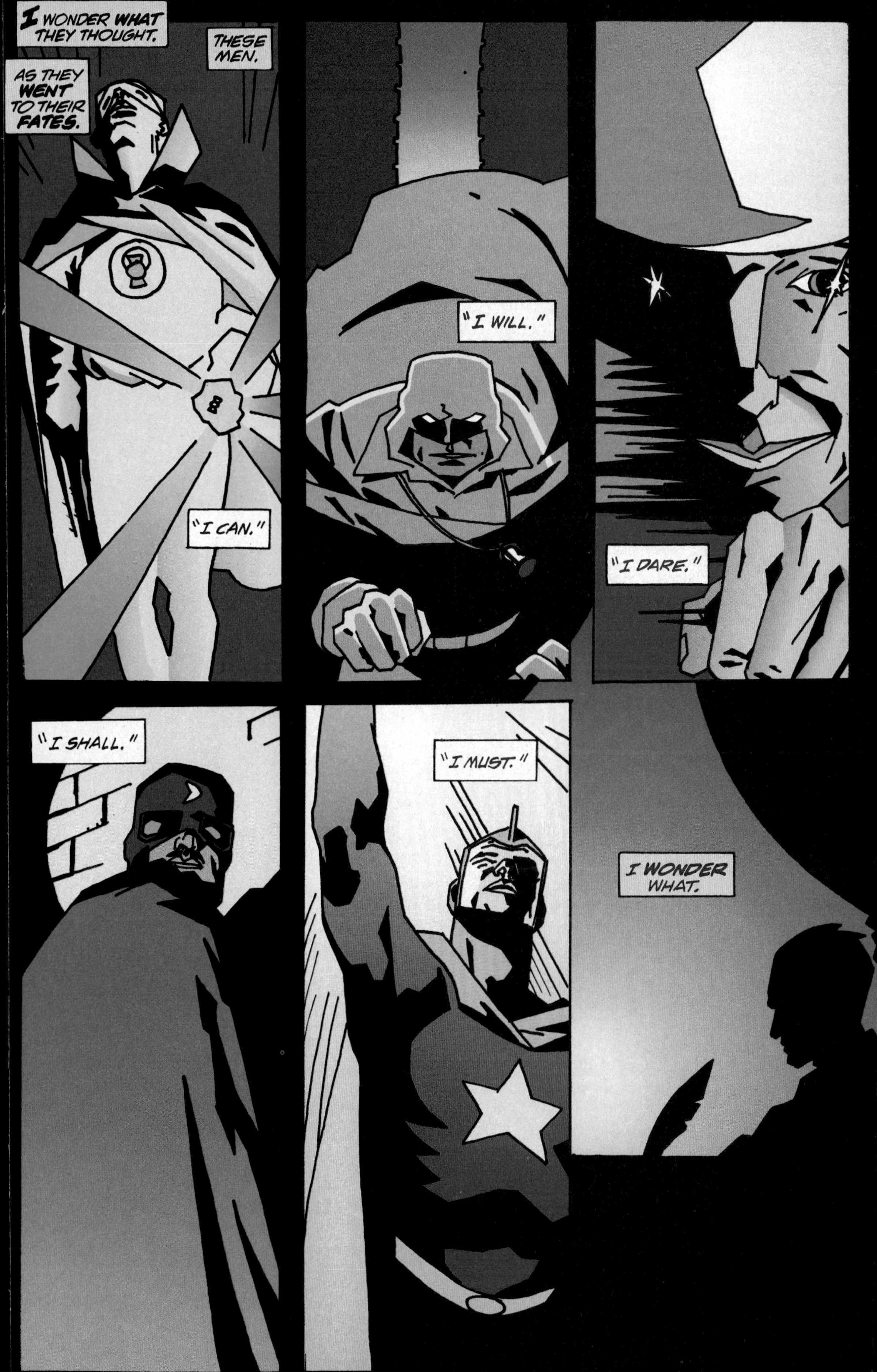
I WONDER WHAT THEY THOUGHT.
THESE MEN.
AS THEY WENT TO THEIR FATES.
"I CAN."
"I WILL."
"I DARE."
"I SHALL."
"I MUST."
I WONDER WHAT.

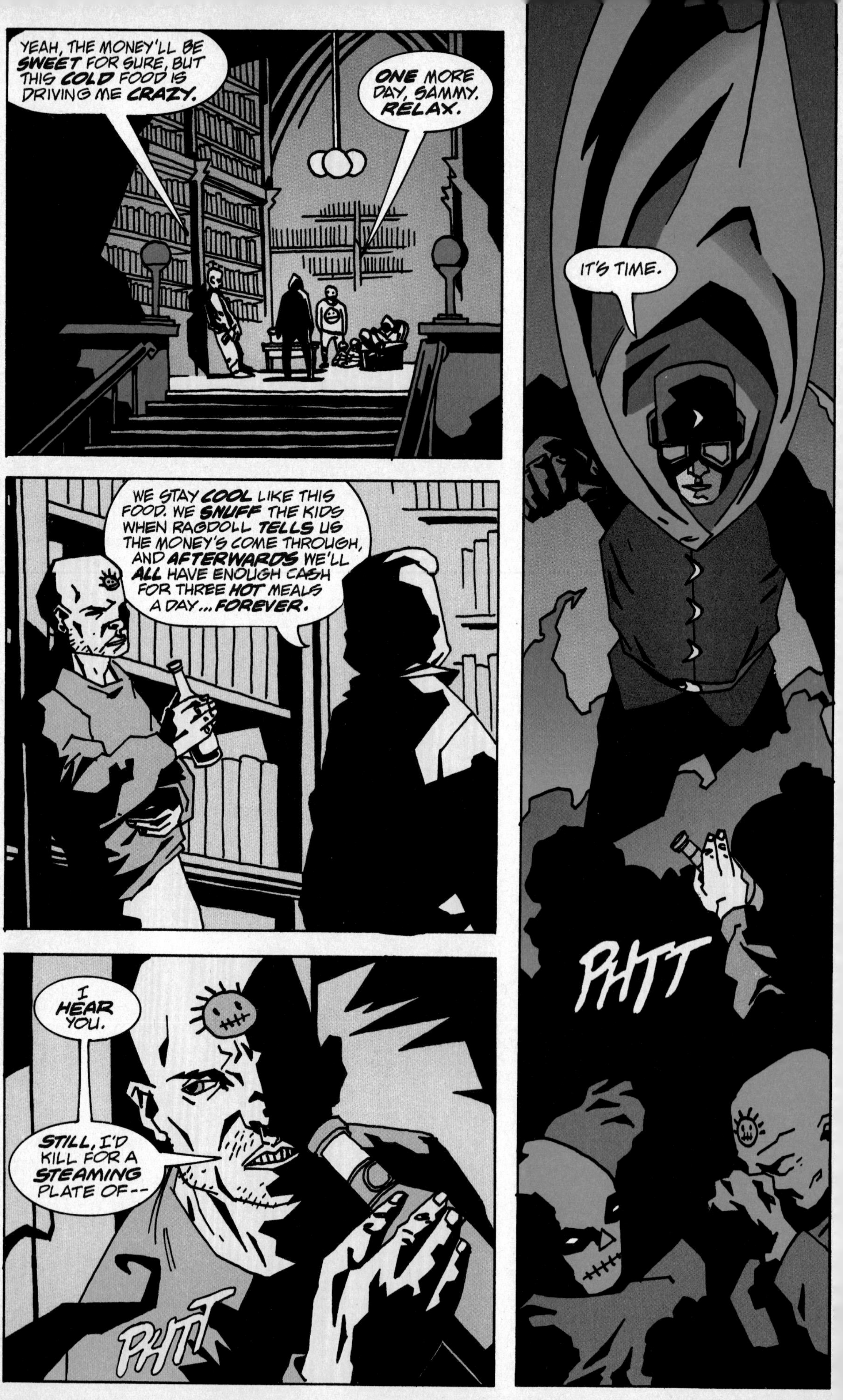
YEAH, THE MONEY'LL BE SWEET FOR SURE, BUT THIS COLD FOOD IS DRIVING ME CRAZY.
ONE MORE DAY, SAMMY. RELAX.
WE STAY COOL LIKE THIS FOOD. WE SNUFF THE KIDS WHEN RAGDOLL TELLS US THE MONEY'S COME THROUGH, AND AFTERWARDS WE'LL ALL HAVE ENOUGH CASH FOR THREE HOT MEALS A DAY... FOREVER.
I HEAR YOU.
STILL, I'D KILL FOR A STEAMING PLATE OF--
PHTT
IT'S TIME.
PHTT

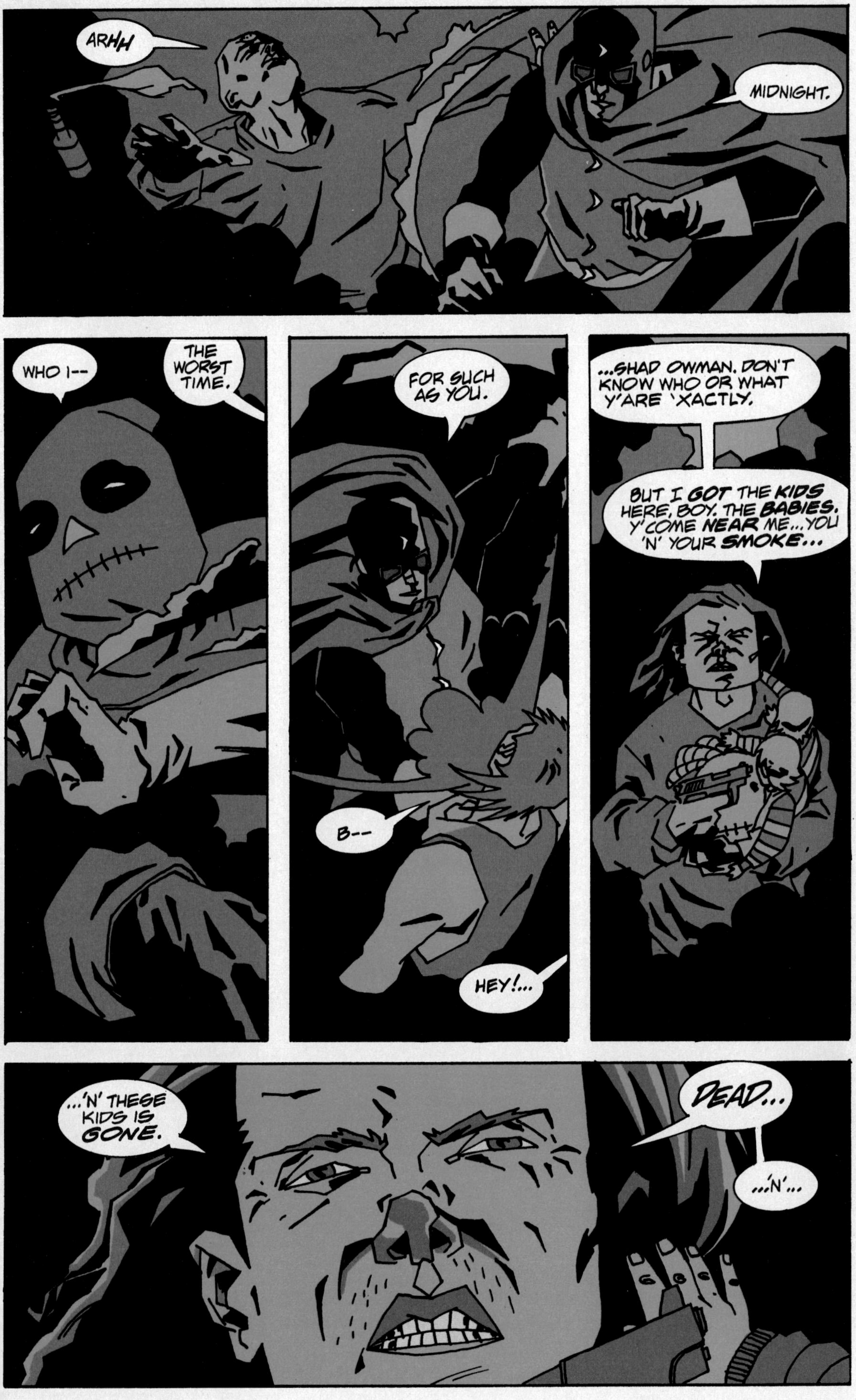
ARHH
MIDNIGHT.
WHO I--
THE WORST TIME.
FOR SUCH AS YOU.
B--
HEY!...
...SHAD OWMAN. DON'T KNOW WHO OR WHAT Y'ARE 'XACTLY.
BUT I GOT THE KIDS HERE, BOY. THE BABIES. Y'COME NEAR ME... YOU 'N' YOUR SMOKE...
...'N' THESE KIDS IS GONE.
DEAD...
...'N'...

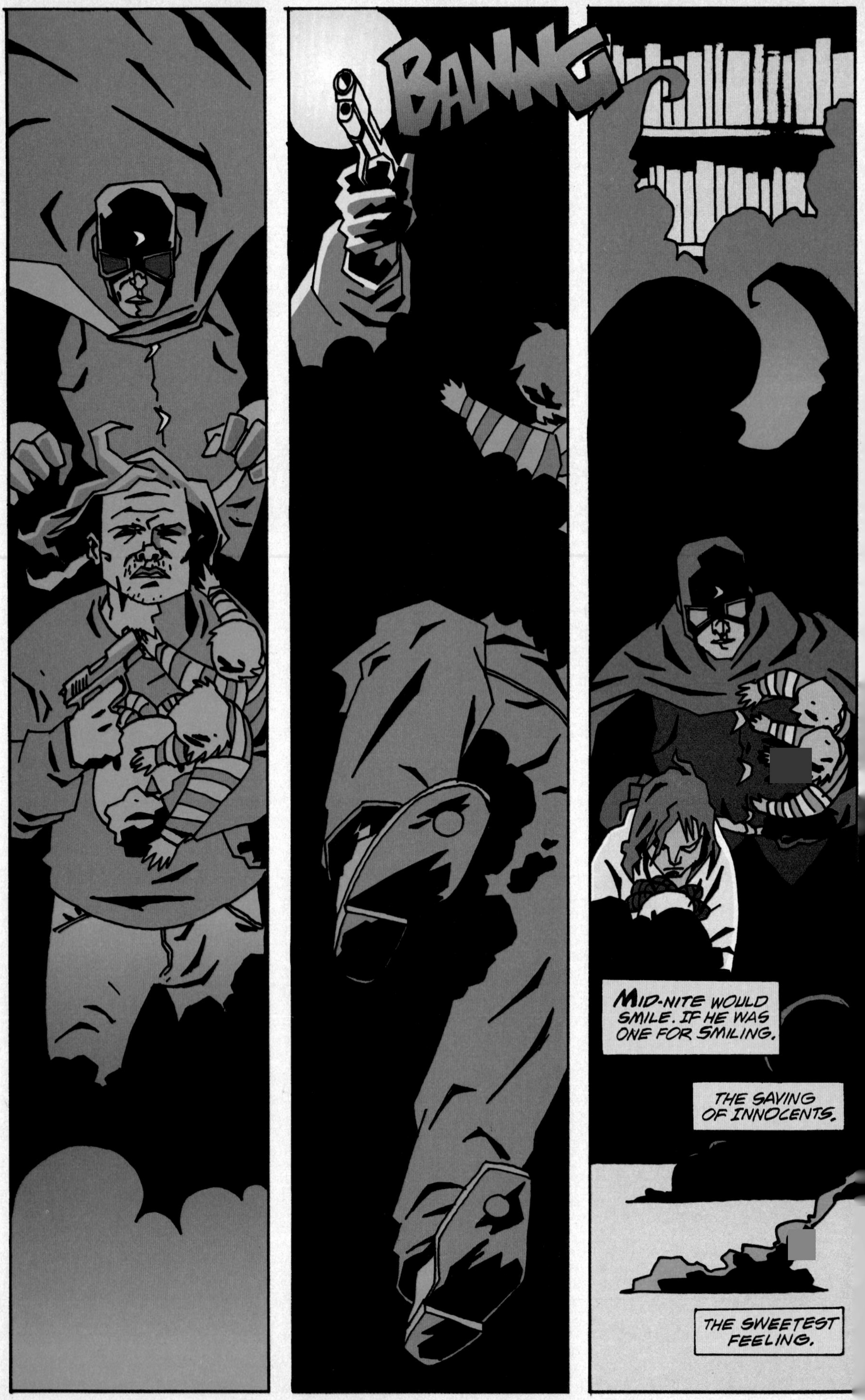
BANNG
MID-NITE WOULD SMILE. IF HE WAS ONE FOR SMILING.
THE SAVING OF INNOCENTS.
THE SWEETEST FEELING.

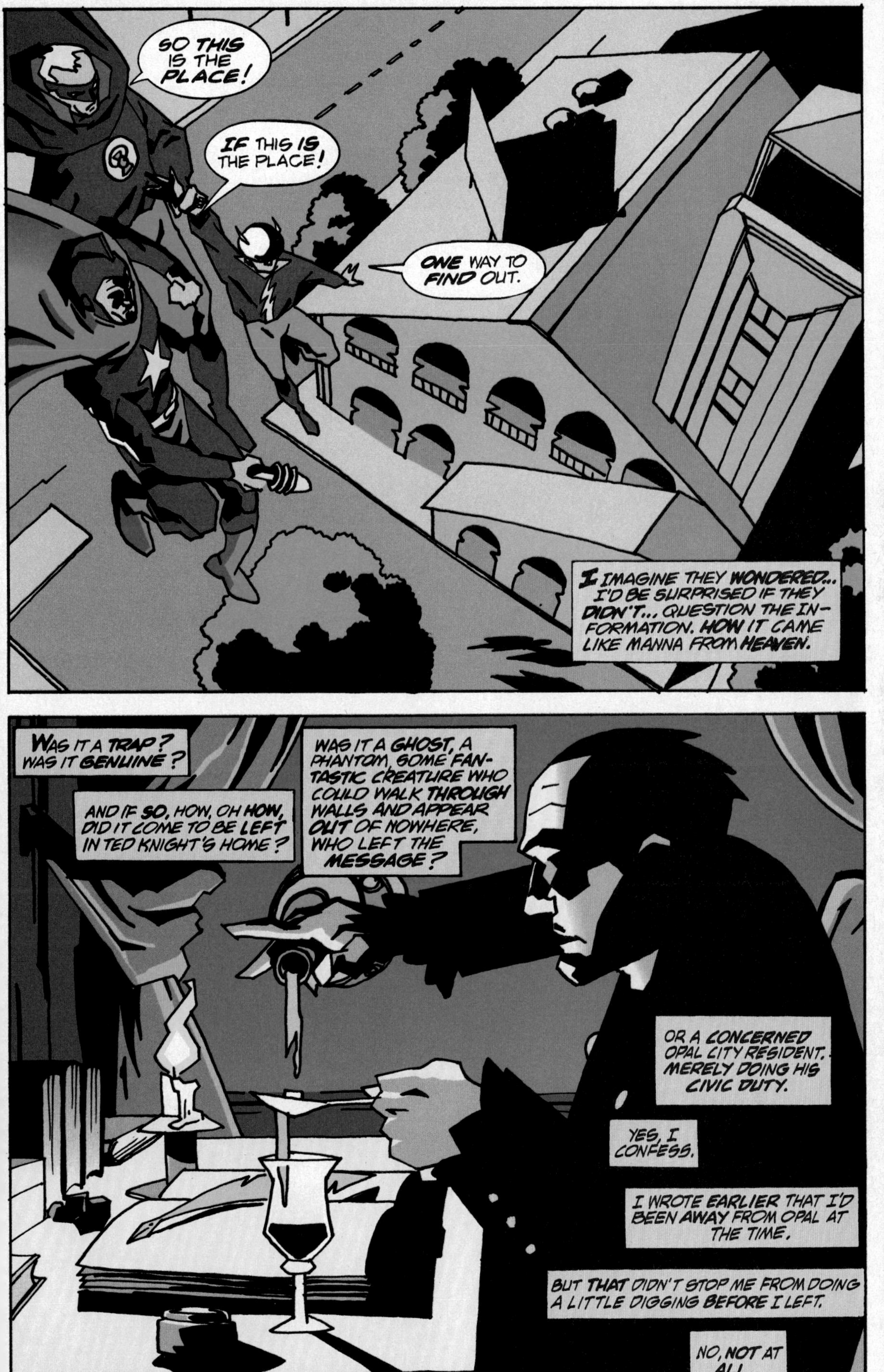
SO THIS IS THE PLACE!
IF THIS IS THE PLACE!
ONE WAY TO FIND OUT.
I IMAGINE THEY WONDERED... I'D BE SURPRISED IF THEY DIDN'T... QUESTION THE INFORMATION. HOW IT CAME LIKE MANNA FROM HEAVEN.
WAS IT A TRAP? WAS IT GENUINE?
AND IF SO, HOW, OH HOW, DID IT COME TO BE LEFT IN TED KNIGHT'S HOME?
WAS IT A GHOST, A PHANTOM, SOME FANTASTIC CREATURE WHO COULD WALK THROUGH WALLS AND APPEAR OUT OF NOWHERE, WHO LEFT THE MESSAGE?
OR A CONCERNED OPAL CITY RESIDENT. MERELY DOING HIS CIVIC DUTY.
YES, I CONFESS.
I WROTE EARLIER THAT I'D BEEN AWAY FROM OPAL AT THE TIME.
BUT THAT DIDN'T STOP ME FROM DOING A LITTLE DIGGING BEFORE I LEFT.
NO, NOT AT ALL.

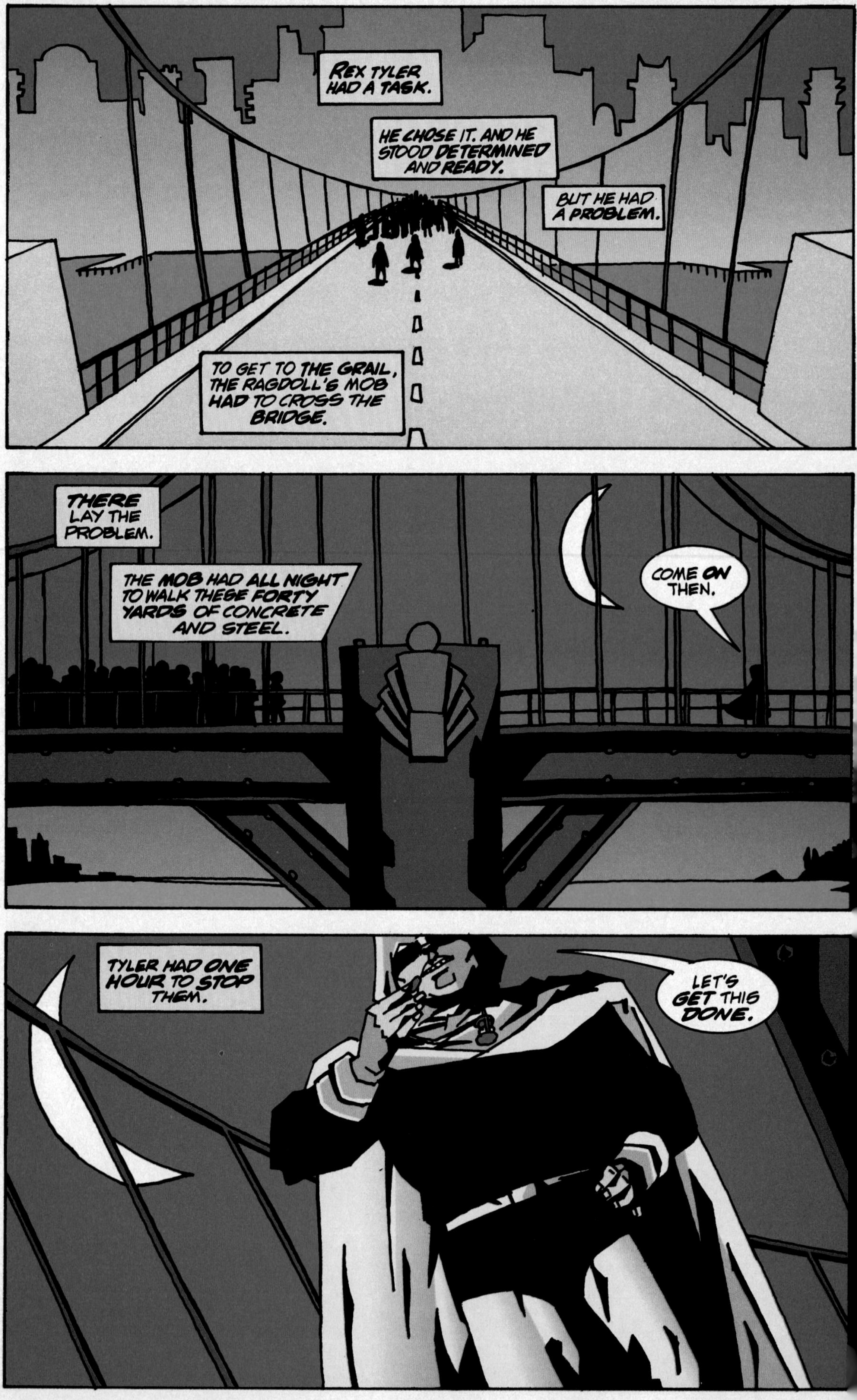
REX TYLER HAD A TASK.
HE CHOSE IT. AND HE STOOD DETERMINED AND READY.
BUT HE HAD A PROBLEM.
TO GET TO THE GRAIL, THE RAGDOLL'S MOB HAD TO CROSS THE BRIDGE.
THERE LAY THE PROBLEM.
THE MOB HAD ALL NIGHT TO WALK THESE FORTY YARDS OF CONCRETE AND STEEL.
COME ON THEN.
TYLER HAD ONE HOUR TO STOP THEM.
LET'S GET THIS DONE.

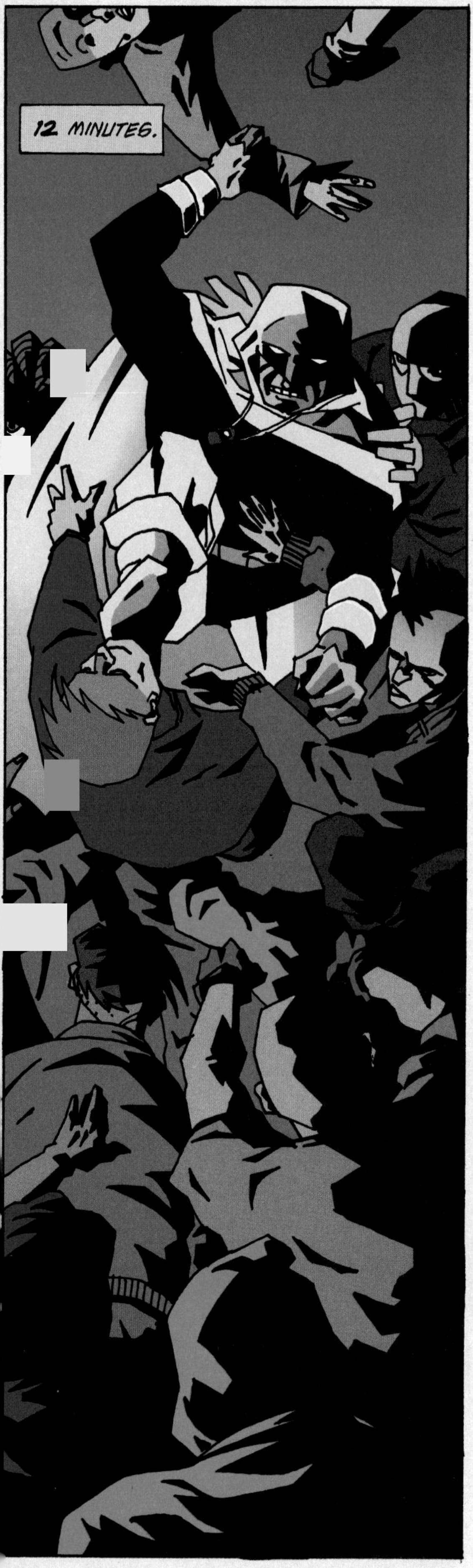
12 MINUTES.
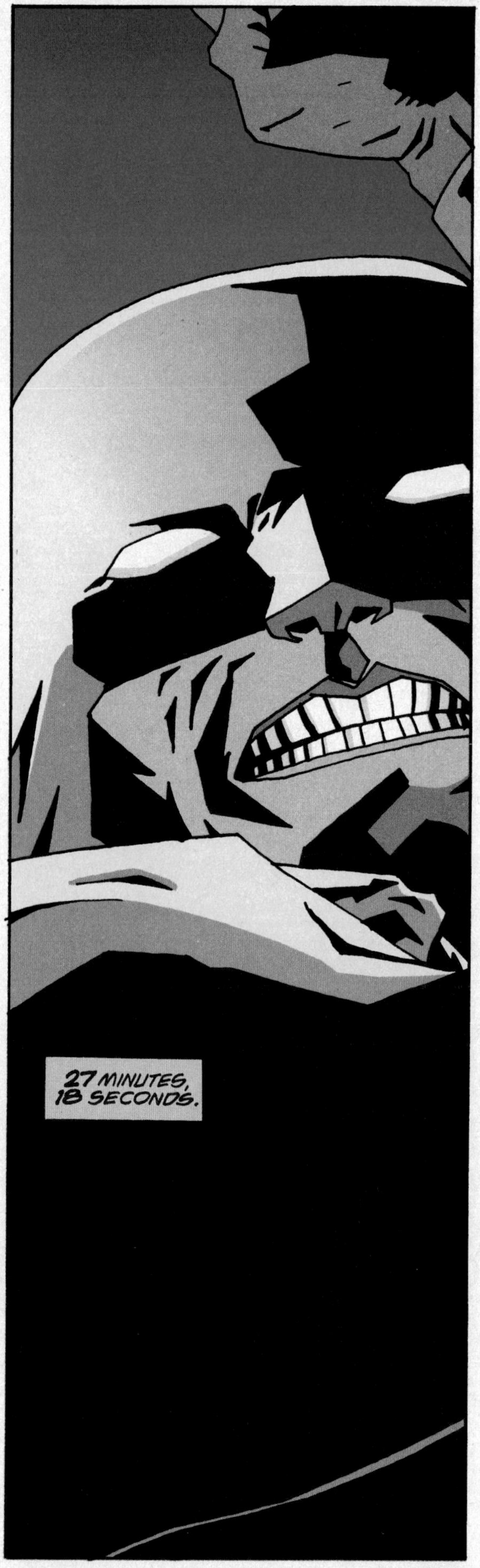
27 MINUTES,
18 SECONDS.

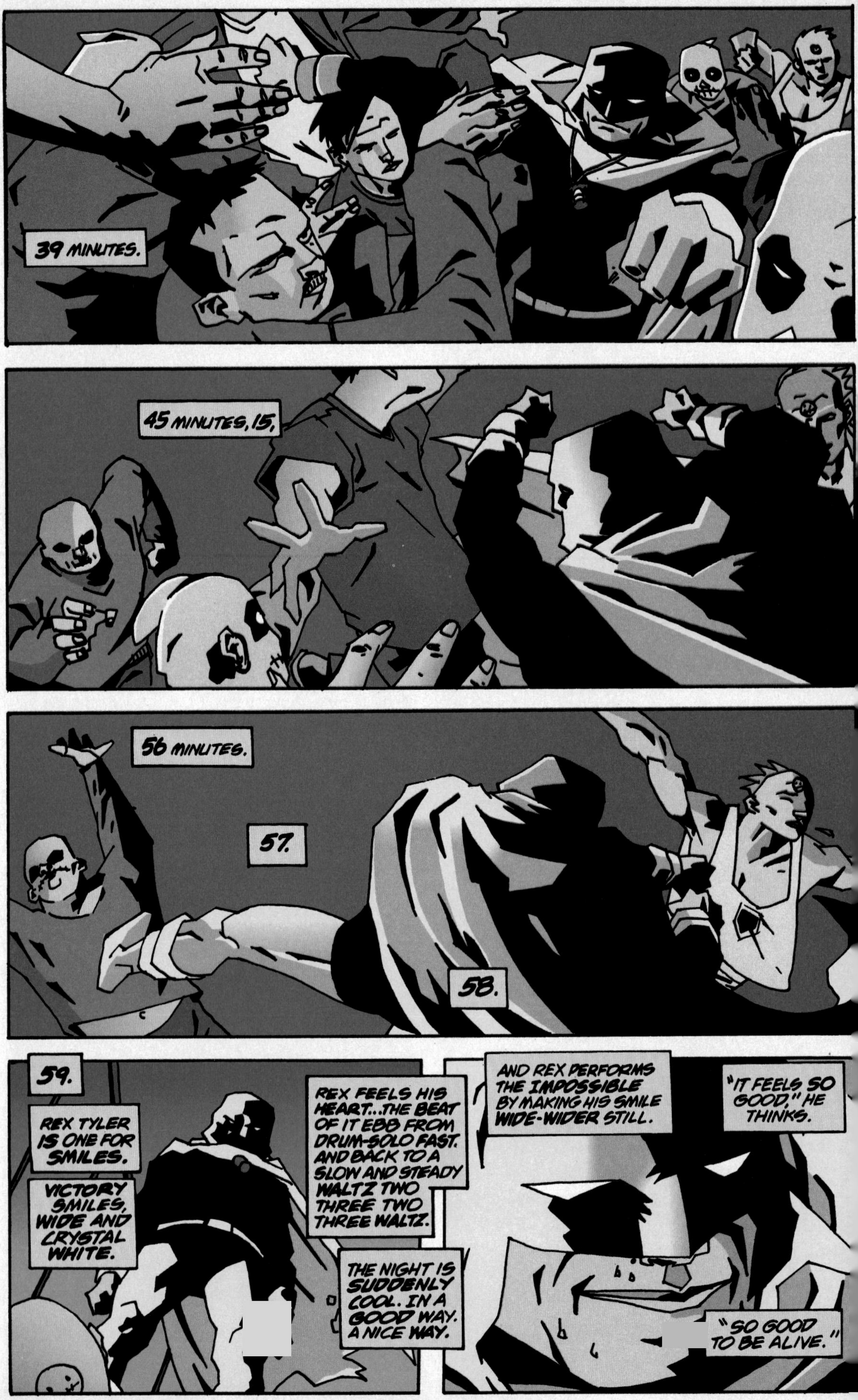
39 MINUTES.
45 MINUTES, 15,
56 MINUTES.
57.
58.
59.
REX TYLER IS ONE FOR SMILES.
VICTORY SMILES, WIDE AND CRYSTAL WHITE.
REX FEELS HIS HEART... THE BEAT OF IT EBB FROM DRUM-SOLO FAST. AND BACK TO A SLOW AND STEADY WALTZ TWO THREE TWO THREE WALTZ.
THE NIGHT IS SUDDENLY COOL. IN A GOOD WAY. A NICE WAY.
AND REX PERFORMS THE IMPOSSIBLE BY MAKING HIS SMILE WIDE-WIDER STILL.
"IT FEELS SO GOOD," HE THINKS.
"SO GOOD TO BE ALIVE."

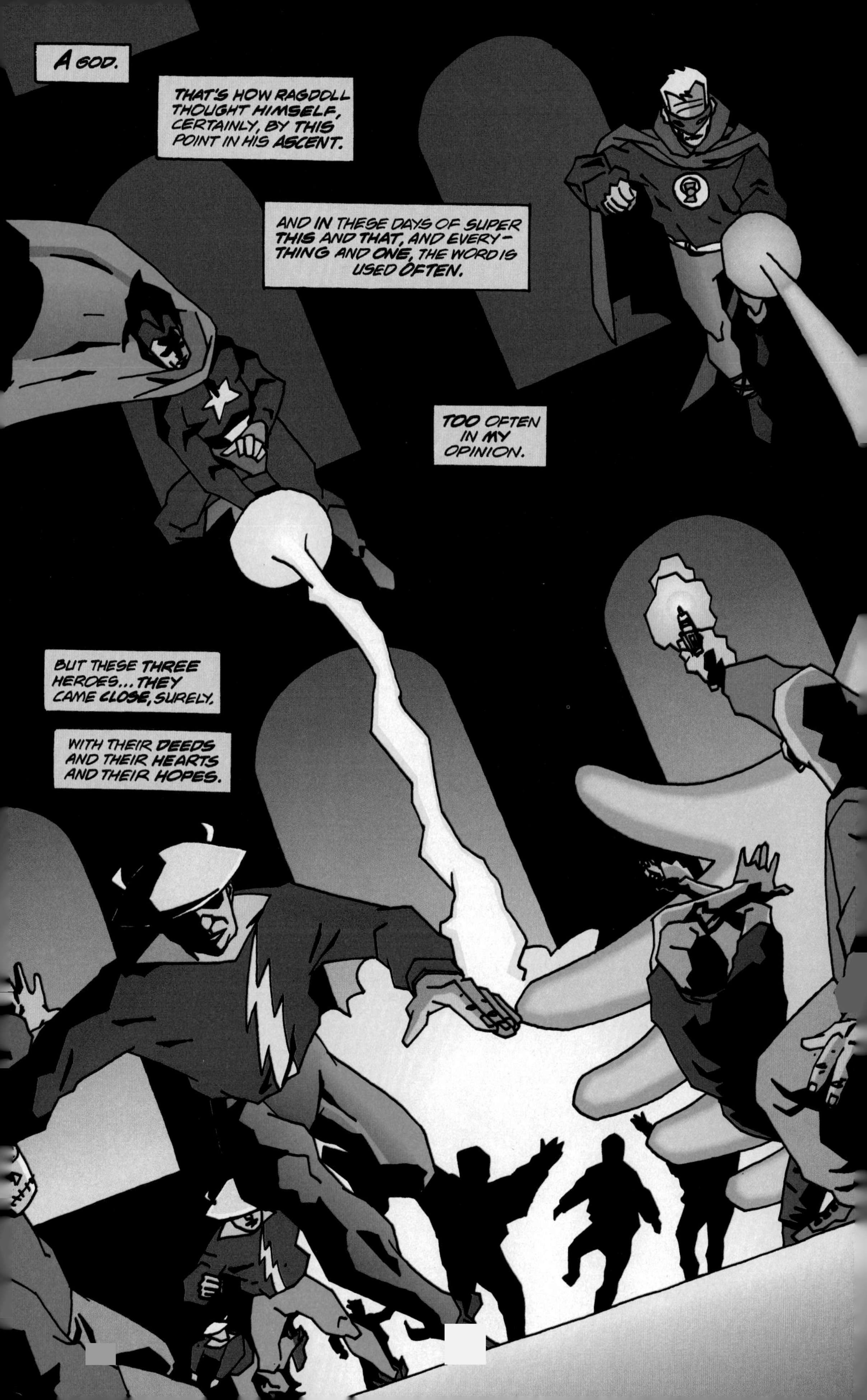
A GOD.
THAT'S HOW RAGDOLL THOUGHT HIMSELF, CERTAINLY, BY THIS POINT IN HIS ASCENT.
AND IN THESE DAYS OF SUPER THIS AND THAT, AND EVERYTHING AND ONE, THE WORD IS USED OFTEN.
TOO OFTEN IN MY OPINION.
BUT THESE THREE HEROES... THEY CAME CLOSE, SURELY.
WITH THEIR DEEDS AND THEIR HEARTS AND THEIR HOPES.

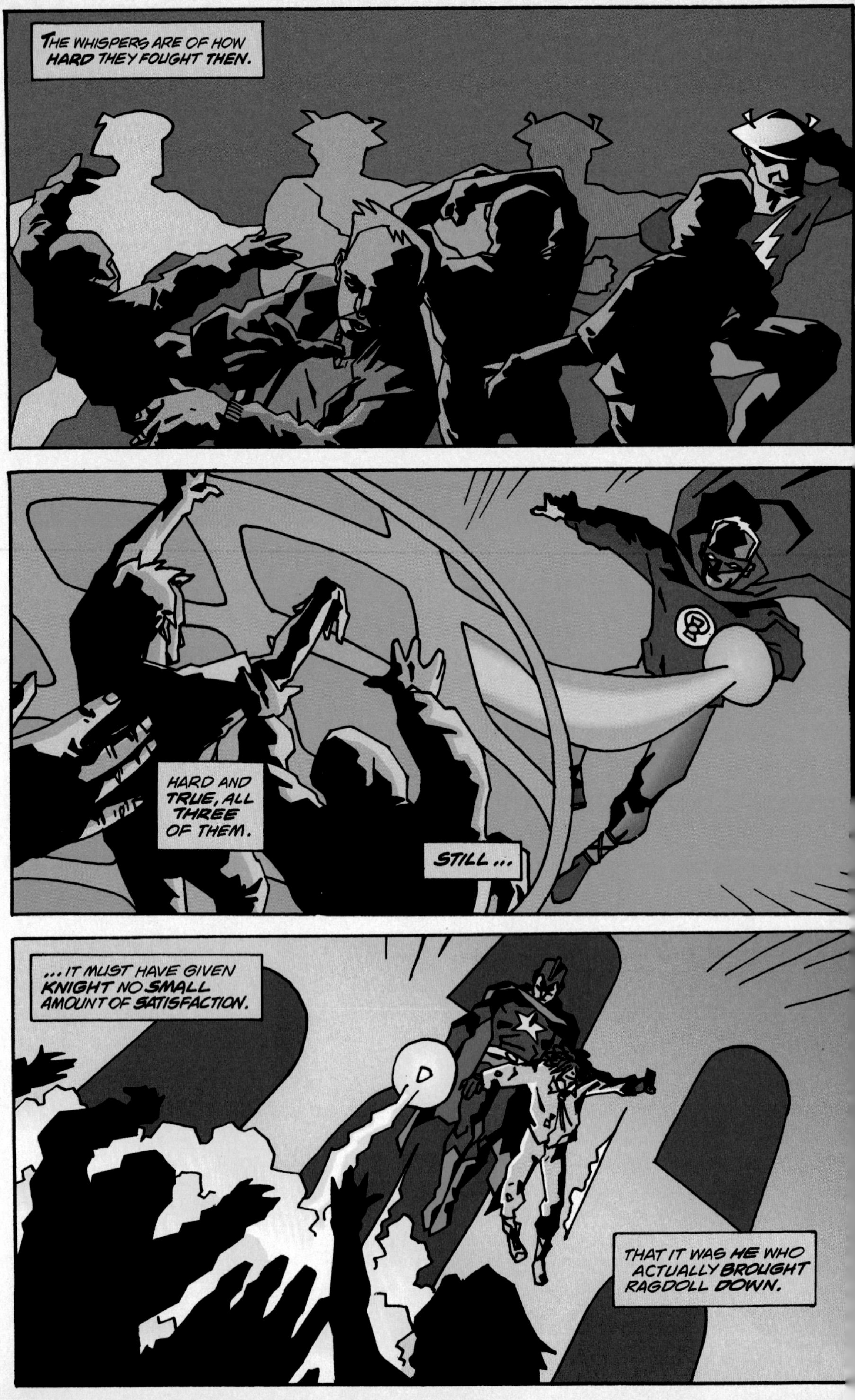

THE WHISPERS ARE OF HOW HARD THEY FOUGHT THEN.
HARD AND TRUE, ALL THREE OF THEM.
STILL ...
... IT MUST HAVE GIVEN KNIGHT NO SMALL AMOUNT OF SATISFACTION.
THAT IT WAS HE WHO ACTUALLY BROUGHT RAGDOLL DOWN.

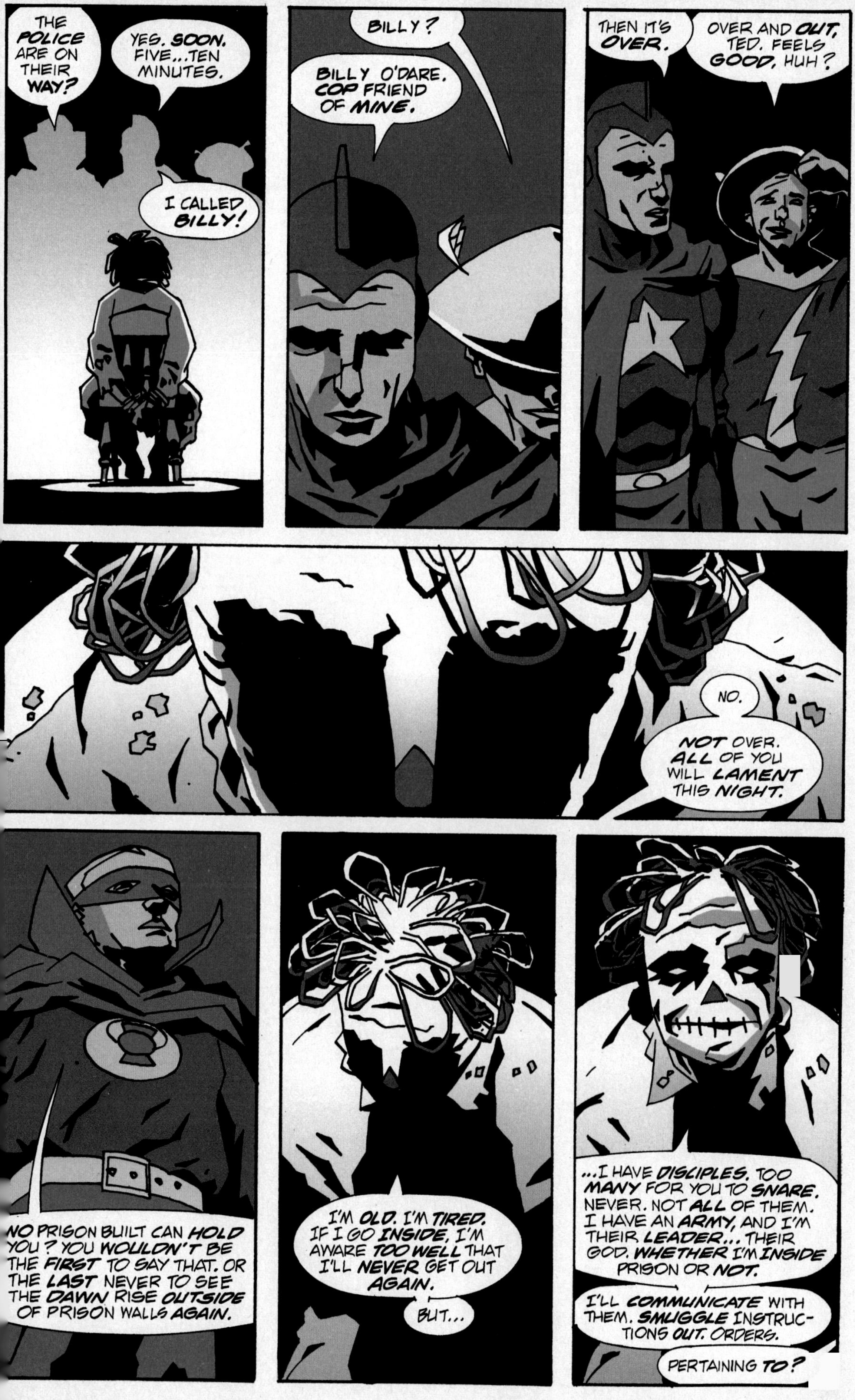
THE POLICE ARE ON THEIR WAY?
YES. SOON. FIVE...TEN MINUTES.
I CALLED BILLY!
BILLY?
BILLY O'DARE. COP FRIEND OF MINE.
THEN IT'S OVER.
OVER AND OUT, TED. FEELS GOOD, HUH?
NO.
NOT OVER. ALL OF YOU WILL LAMENT THIS NIGHT.
NO PRISON BUILT CAN HOLD YOU? YOU WOULDN'T BE THE FIRST TO SAY THAT. OR THE LAST NEVER TO SEE THE DAWN RISE OUTSIDE OF PRISON WALLS AGAIN.
I'M OLD. I'M TIRED. IF I GO INSIDE, I'M AWARE TOO WELL THAT I'LL NEVER GET OUT AGAIN.
BUT...
...I HAVE DISCIPLES. TOO MANY FOR YOU TO SNARE. NEVER. NOT ALL OF THEM. I HAVE AN ARMY, AND I'M THEIR LEADER... THEIR GOD. WHETHER I'M INSIDE PRISON OR NOT.
I'LL COMMUNICATE WITH THEM. SMUGGLE INSTRUCTIONS OUT. ORDERS.
PERTAINING TO?

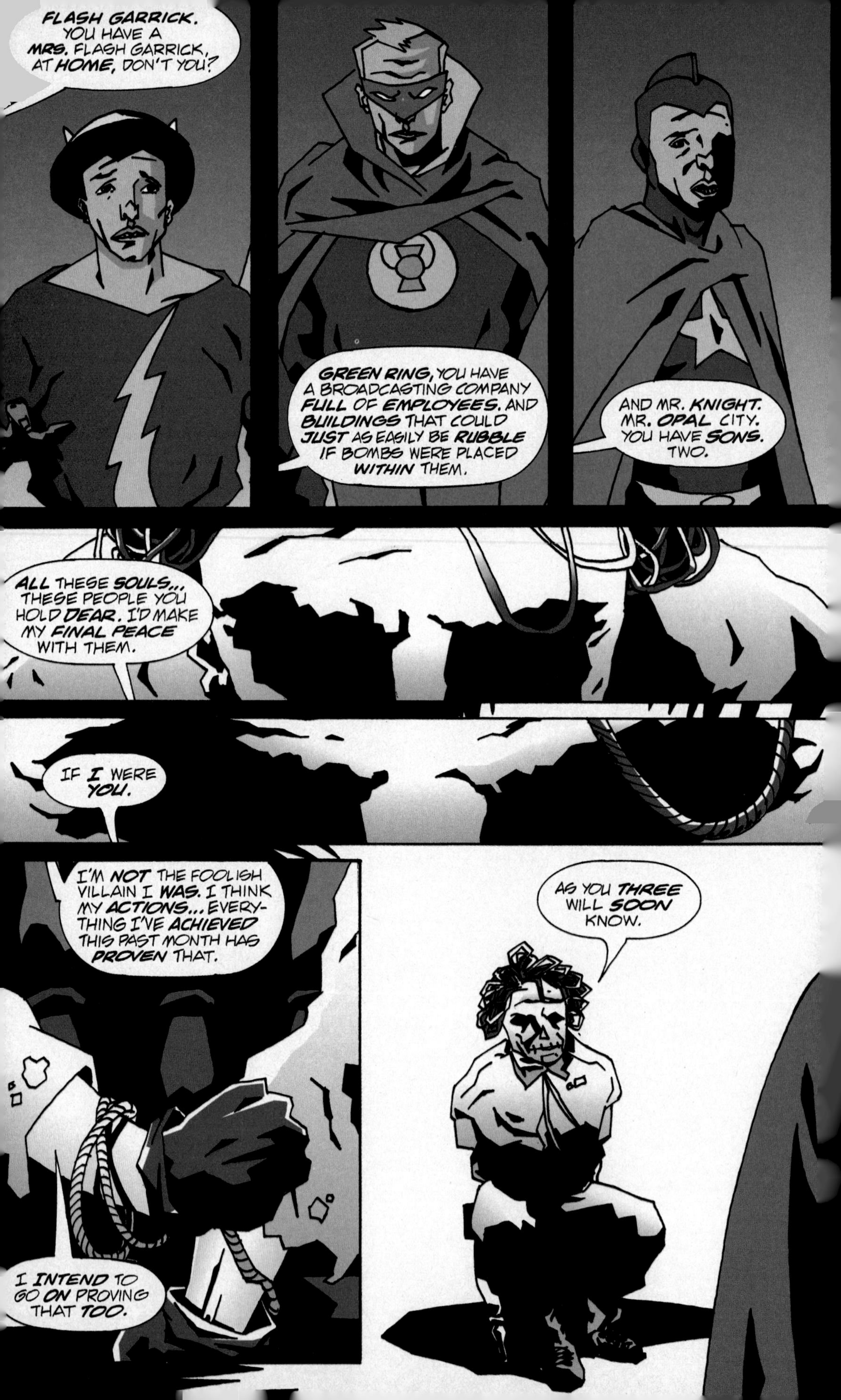
FLASH GARRICK. YOU HAVE A MRS. FLASH GARRICK, AT HOME, DON'T YOU?
GREEN RING, YOU HAVE A BROADCASTING COMPANY FULL OF EMPLOYEES. AND BUILDINGS THAT COULD JUST AS EASILY BE RUBBLE IF BOMBS WERE PLACED WITHIN THEM.
AND MR. KNIGHT. MR. OPAL CITY. YOU HAVE SONS. TWO.
ALL THESE SOULS... THESE PEOPLE YOU HOLD DEAR. I'D MAKE MY FINAL PEACE WITH THEM.
IF I WERE YOU.
I'M NOT THE FOOLISH VILLAIN I WAS. I THINK MY ACTIONS... EVERYTHING I'VE ACHIEVED THIS PAST MONTH HAS PROVEN THAT.
I INTEND TO GO ON PROVING THAT TOO.
AS YOU THREE WILL SOON KNOW.

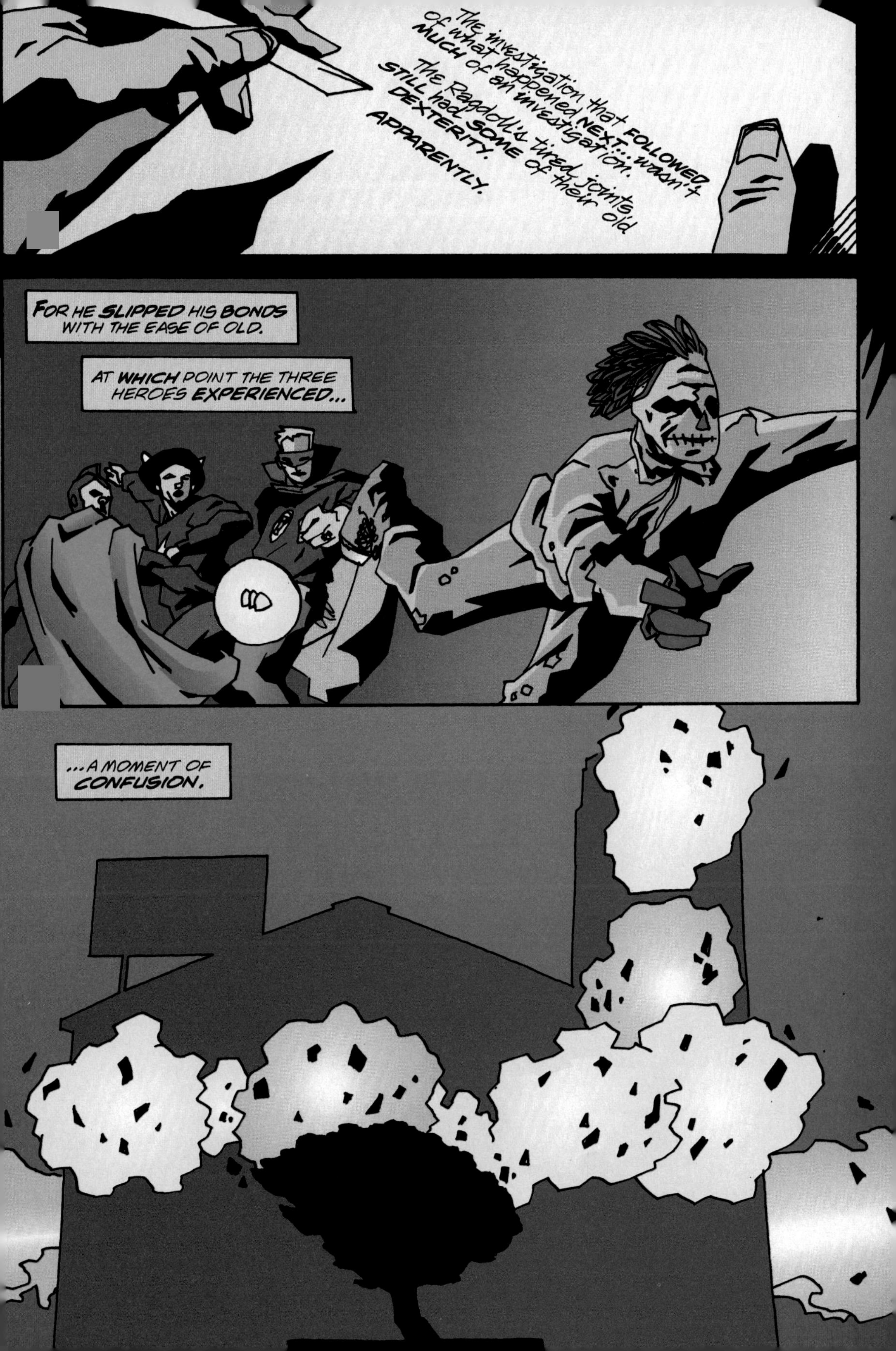
The investigation that FOLLOWED of what happened NEXT... wasn't MUCH of an investigation.
The Ragdoll's tired joints STILL had SOME of their old DEXTERITY.
APPARENTLY.
FOR HE SLIPPED HIS BONDS WITH THE EASE OF OLD.
AT WHICH POINT THE THREE HEROES EXPERIENCED...
...A MOMENT OF CONFUSION.

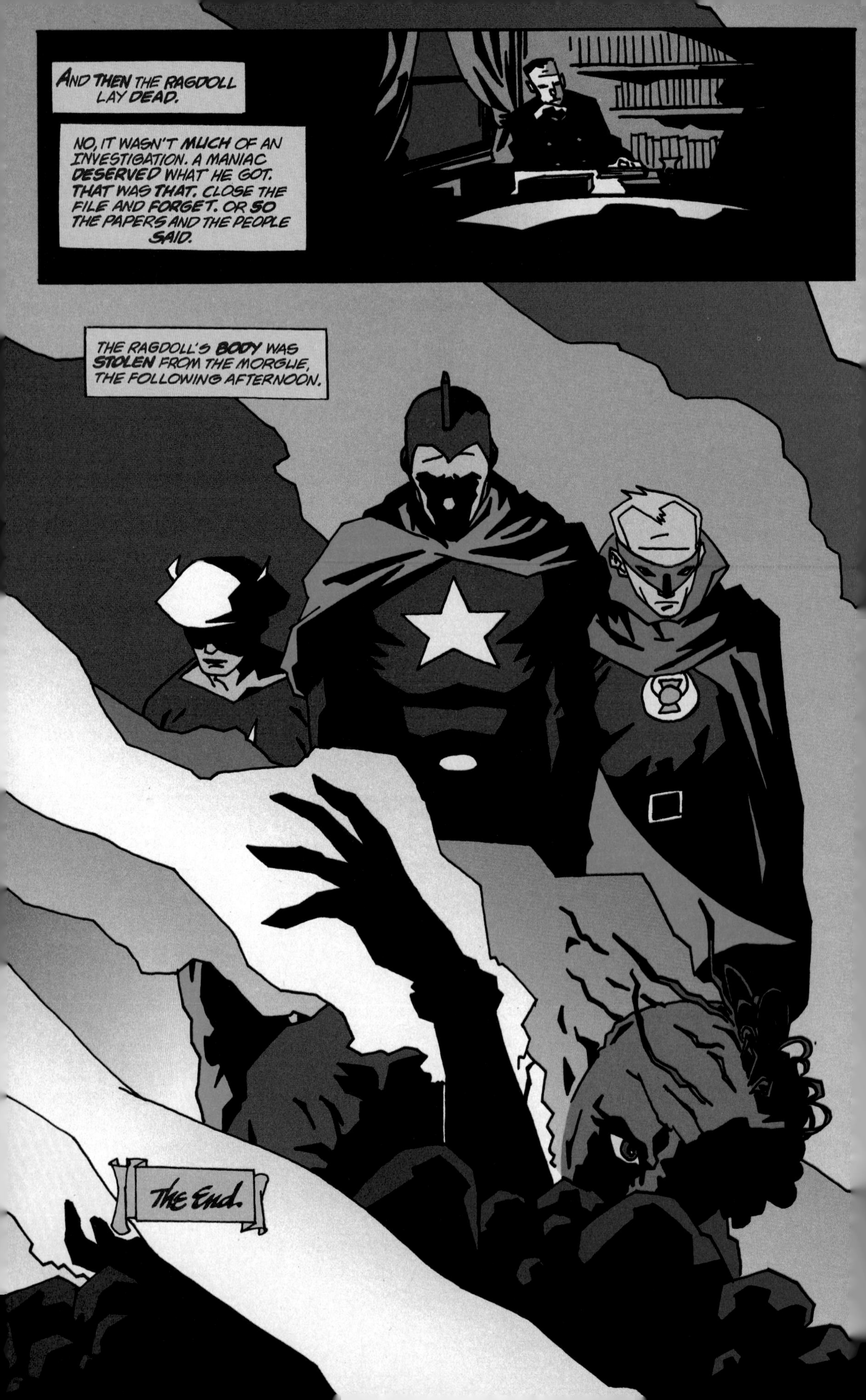
AND THEN THE RAGDOLL LAY DEAD.
NO, IT WASN'T MUCH OF AN INVESTIGATION. A MANIAC DESERVED WHAT HE GOT. THAT WAS THAT. CLOSE THE FILE AND FORGET. OR SO THE PAPERS AND THE PEOPLE SAID.
THE RAGDOLL'S BODY WAS STOLEN FROM THE MORGUE, THE FOLLOWING AFTERNOON.
THE END.

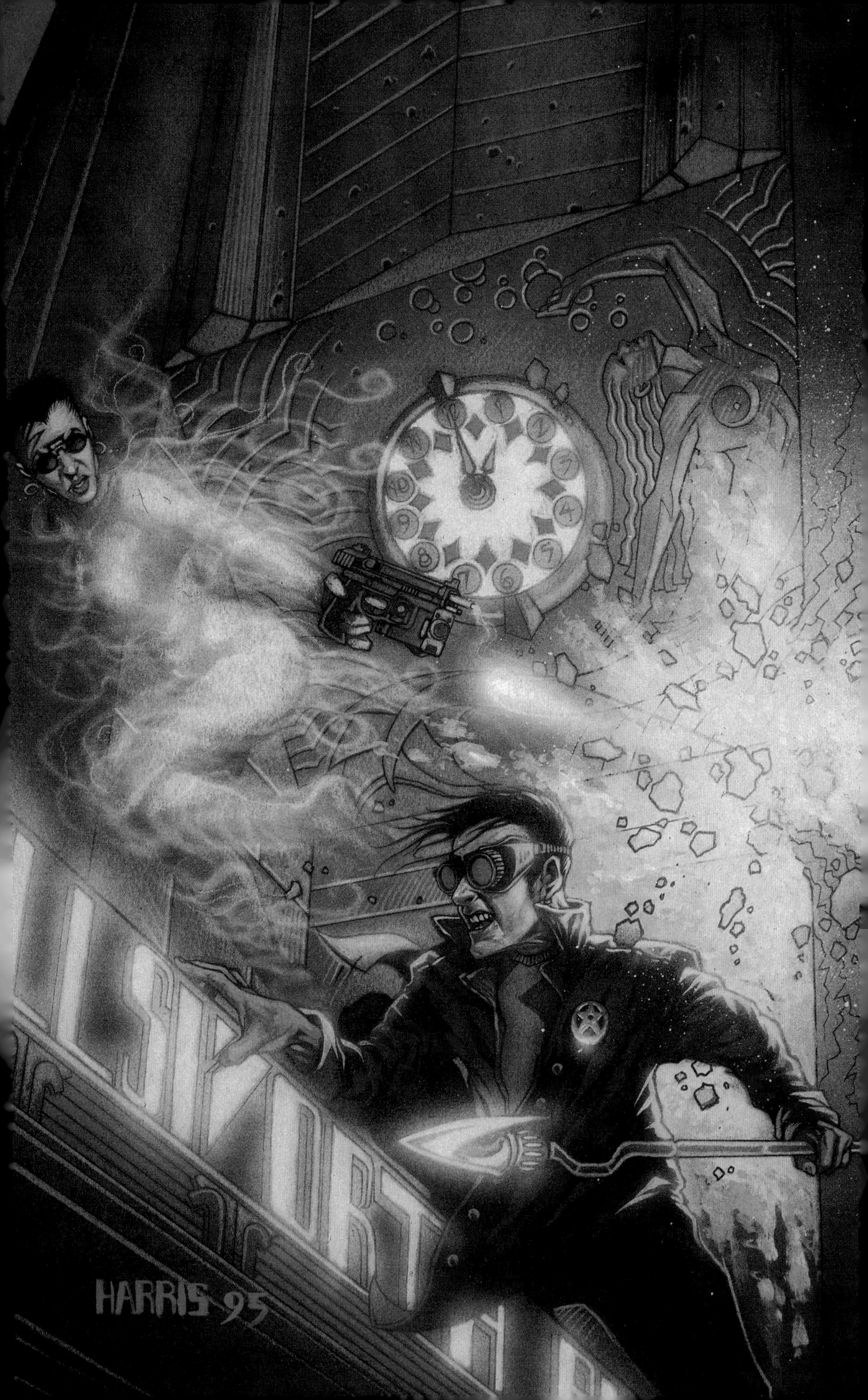
HARRIS 95

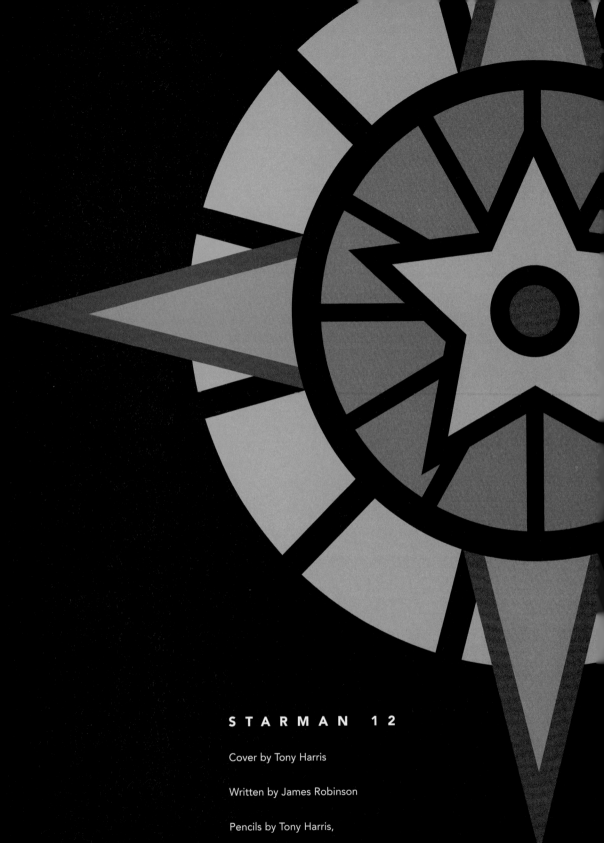

STARMAN 12

Cover by Tony Harris

Written by James Robinson

Pencils by Tony Harris,

with inks by Wade von Grawbadger

and colors by Gregory Wright

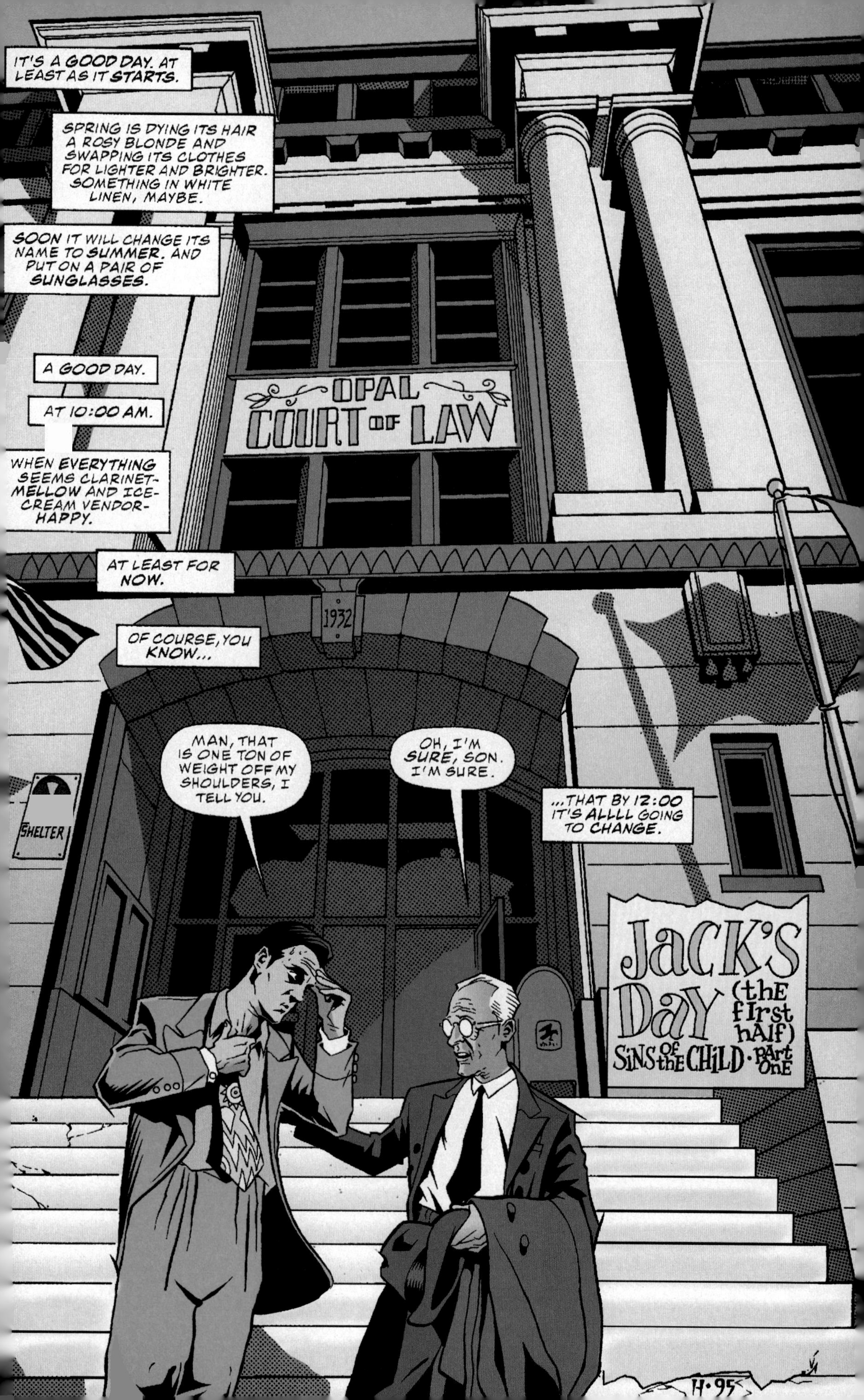
IT'S A GOOD DAY. AT LEAST AS IT STARTS.
SPRING IS DYING ITS HAIR A ROSY BLONDE AND SWAPPING ITS CLOTHES FOR LIGHTER AND BRIGHTER. SOMETHING IN WHITE LINEN, MAYBE.
SOON IT WILL CHANGE ITS NAME TO SUMMER. AND PUT ON A PAIR OF SUNGLASSES.
A GOOD DAY.
AT 10:00 AM.
WHEN EVERYTHING SEEMS CLARINET-MELLOW AND ICE-CREAM VENDOR-HAPPY.
OPAL COURT OF LAW
AT LEAST FOR NOW.
1932
OF COURSE, YOU KNOW...
MAN, THAT IS ONE TON OF WEIGHT OFF MY SHOULDERS, I TELL YOU.
OH, I'M SURE, SON. I'M SURE.
...THAT BY 12:00 IT'S ALLLL GOING TO CHANGE.
SHELTER
JACK'S DAY (the first half)
SINS OF THE CHILD · PART ONE
H·95

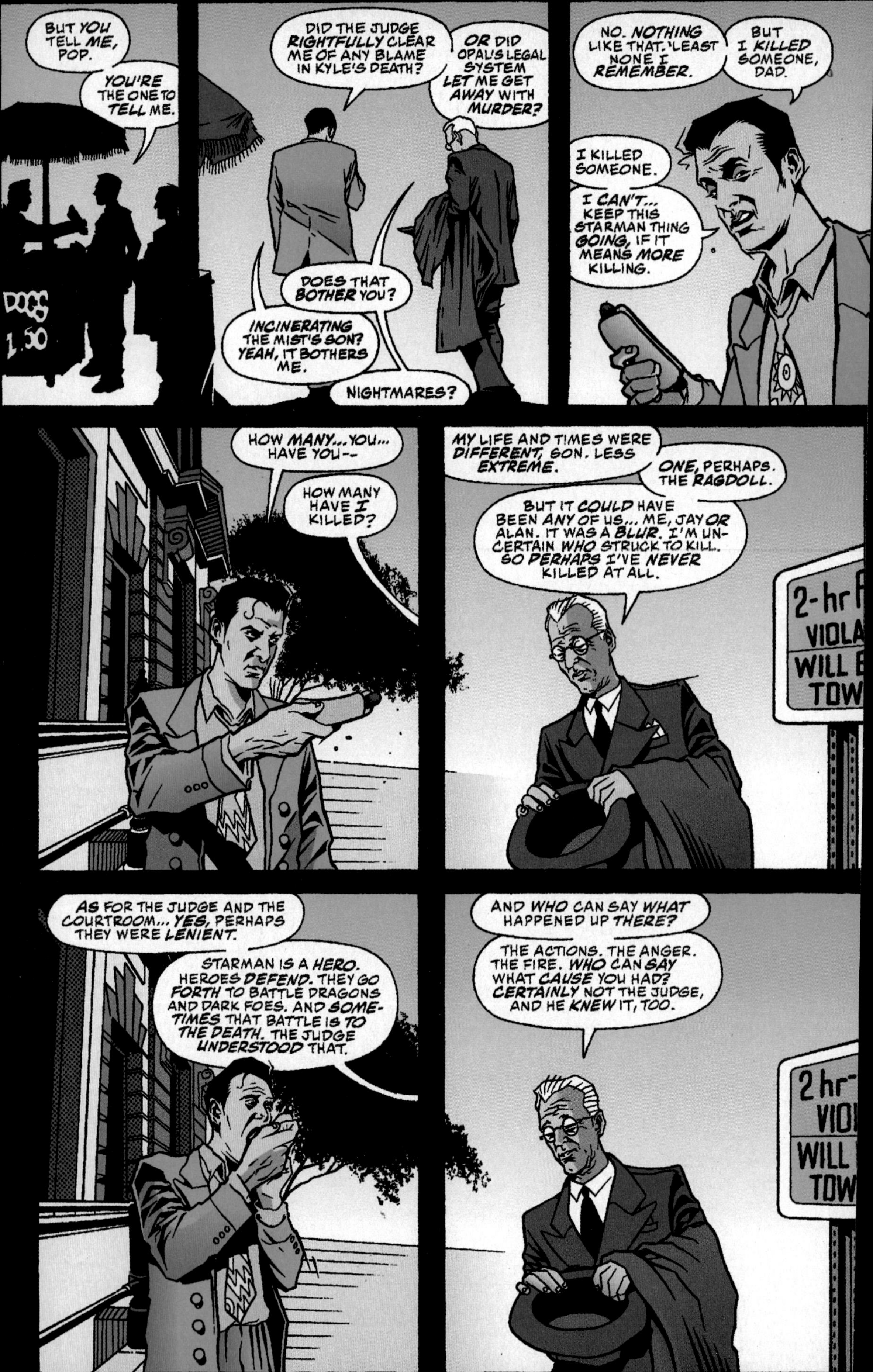
BUT YOU TELL ME, POP.
YOU'RE THE ONE TO TELL ME.
DOGS 1.50
DID THE JUDGE RIGHTFULLY CLEAR ME OF ANY BLAME IN KYLE'S DEATH?
OR DID OPAL'S LEGAL SYSTEM LET ME GET AWAY WITH MURDER?
DOES THAT BOTHER YOU?
INCINERATING THE MIST'S SON? YEAH, IT BOTHERS ME.
NIGHTMARES?
NO. NOTHING LIKE THAT. 'LEAST NONE I REMEMBER.
BUT I KILLED SOMEONE, DAD.
I KILLED SOMEONE.
I CAN'T... KEEP THIS STARMAN THING GOING, IF IT MEANS MORE KILLING.
HOW MANY... YOU... HAVE YOU--
HOW MANY HAVE I KILLED?
MY LIFE AND TIMES WERE DIFFERENT, SON. LESS EXTREME.
ONE, PERHAPS. THE RAGDOLL.
BUT IT COULD HAVE BEEN ANY OF US... ME, JAY OR ALAN. IT WAS A BLUR. I'M UNCERTAIN WHO STRUCK TO KILL. SO PERHAPS I'VE NEVER KILLED AT ALL.
AS FOR THE JUDGE AND THE COURTROOM... YES, PERHAPS THEY WERE LENIENT.
STARMAN IS A HERO. HEROES DEFEND. THEY GO FORTH TO BATTLE DRAGONS AND DARK FOES. AND SOMETIMES THAT BATTLE IS TO THE DEATH. THE JUDGE UNDERSTOOD THAT.
AND WHO CAN SAY WHAT HAPPENED UP THERE?
THE ACTIONS. THE ANGER. THE FIRE. WHO CAN SAY WHAT CAUSE YOU HAD? CERTAINLY NOT THE JUDGE, AND HE KNEW IT, TOO.

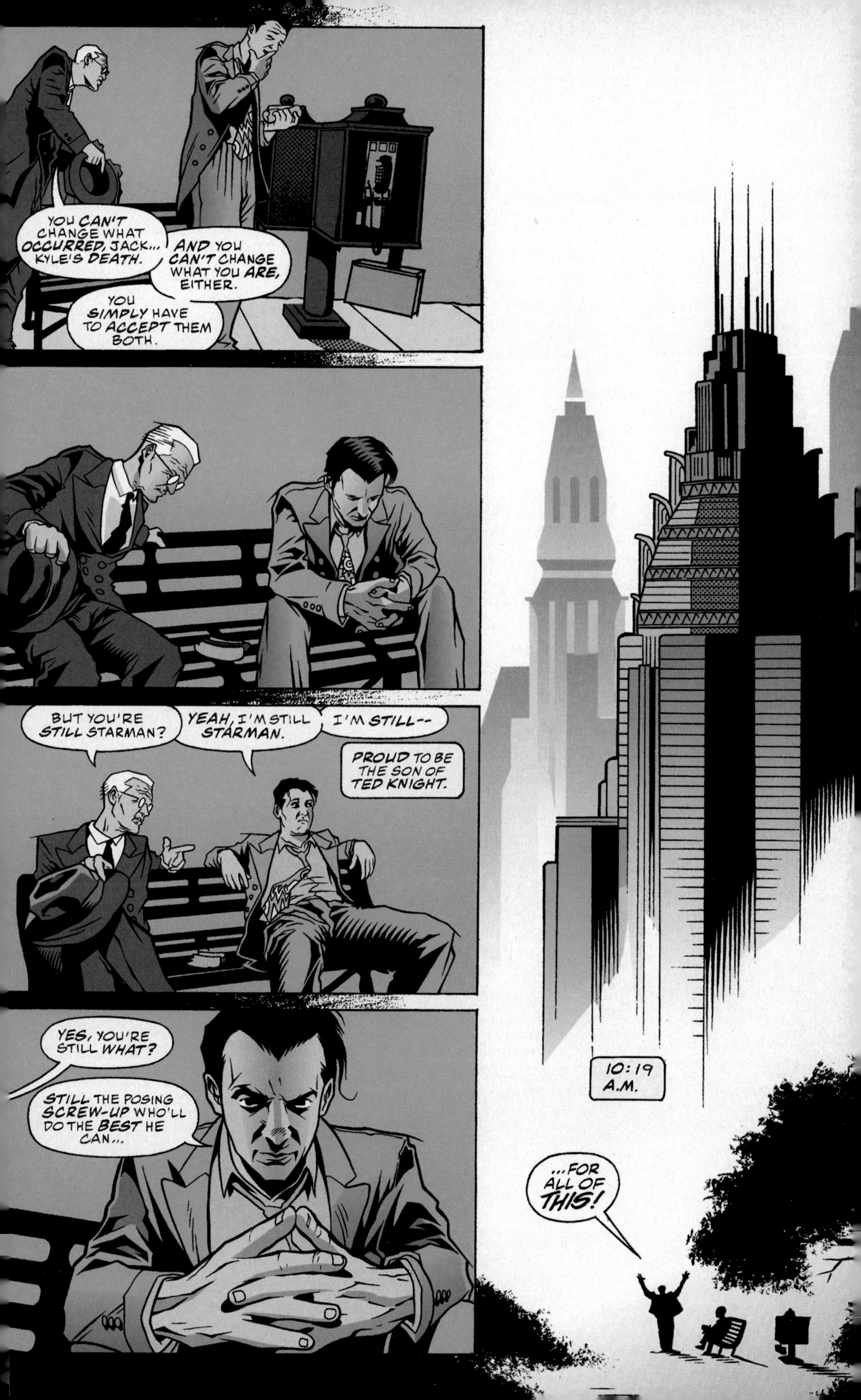
YOU CAN'T CHANGE WHAT OCCURRED, JACK... KYLE'S DEATH.
AND YOU CAN'T CHANGE WHAT YOU ARE, EITHER.
YOU SIMPLY HAVE TO ACCEPT THEM BOTH.
BUT YOU'RE STILL STARMAN?
YEAH, I'M STILL STARMAN.
I'M STILL--
PROUD TO BE THE SON OF TED KNIGHT.
YES, YOU'RE STILL WHAT?
STILL THE POSING SCREW-UP WHO'LL DO THE BEST HE CAN...
10:19 A.M.
...FOR ALL OF THIS!

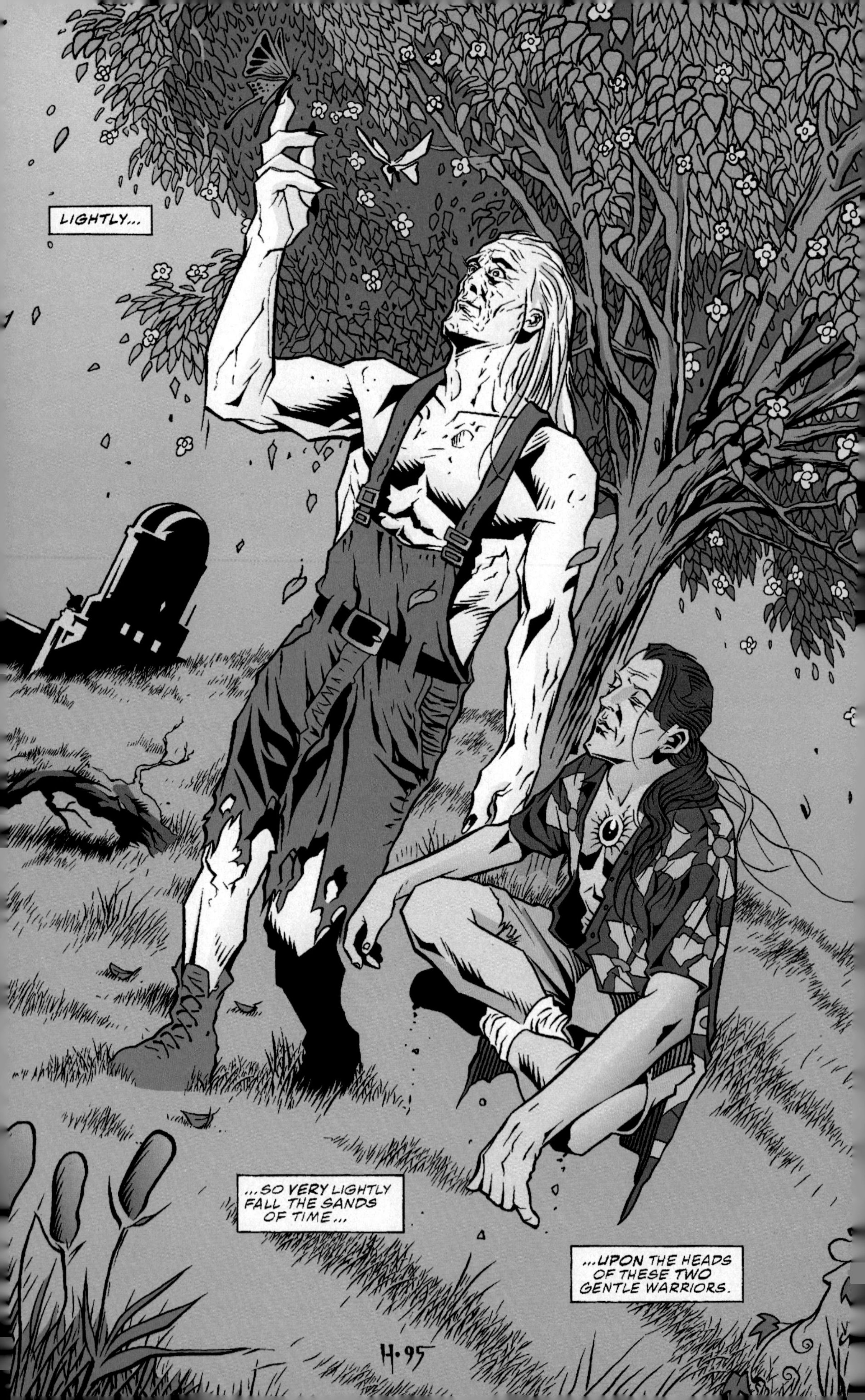
LIGHTLY...
...SO VERY LIGHTLY FALL THE SANDS OF TIME...
...UPON THE HEADS OF THESE TWO GENTLE WARRIORS.
H•95

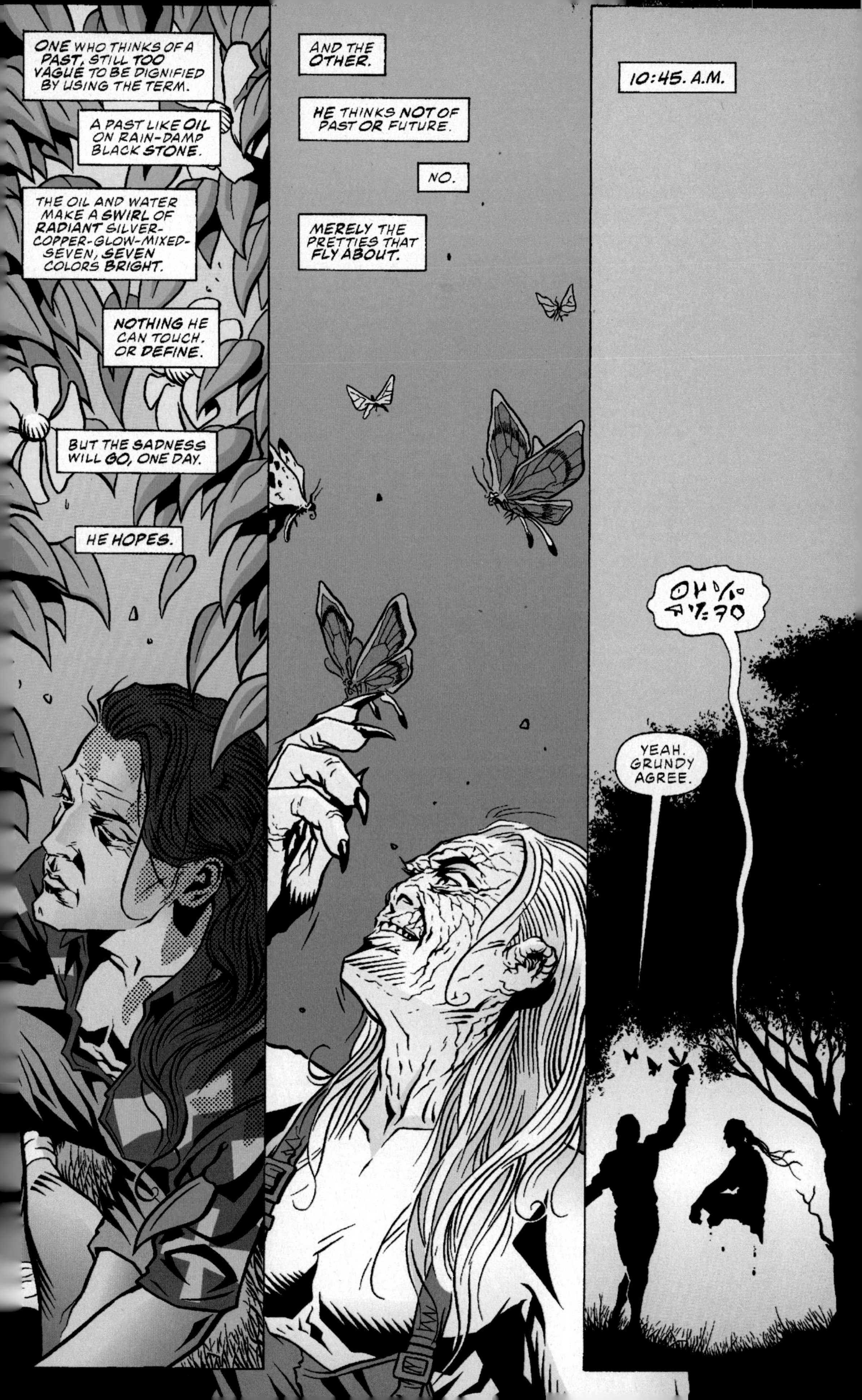
ONE WHO THINKS OF A PAST, STILL TOO VAGUE TO BE DIGNIFIED BY USING THE TERM.
A PAST LIKE OIL ON RAIN-DAMP BLACK STONE.
THE OIL AND WATER MAKE A SWIRL OF RADIANT SILVER-COPPER-GLOW-MIXED-SEVEN, SEVEN COLORS BRIGHT.
NOTHING HE CAN TOUCH. OR DEFINE.
BUT THE SADNESS WILL GO, ONE DAY.
HE HOPES.
AND THE OTHER.
HE THINKS NOT OF PAST OR FUTURE.
NO.
MERELY THE PRETTIES THAT FLY ABOUT.
10:45. A.M.
YEAH. GRUNDY AGREE.

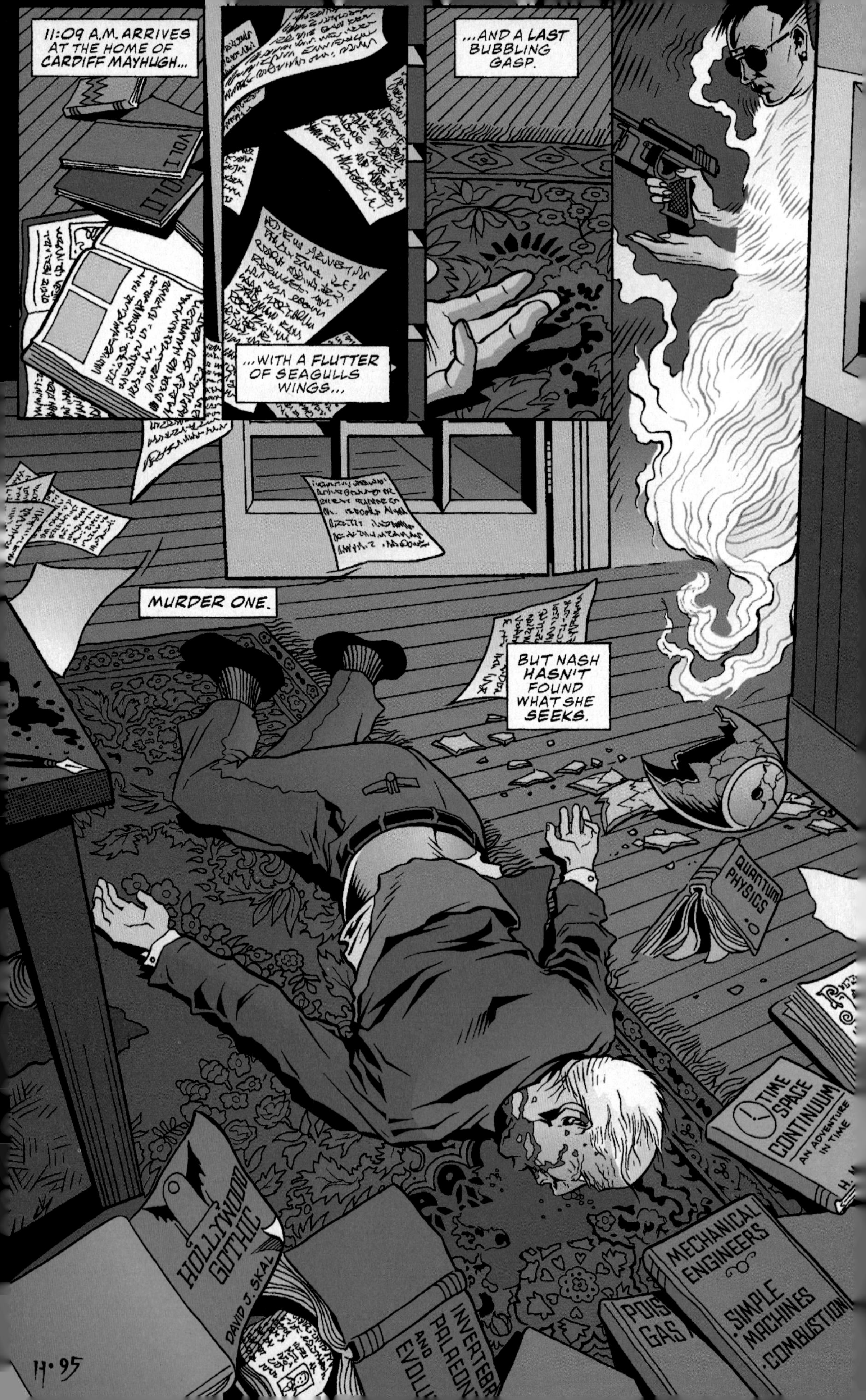
11:09 A.M. ARRIVES AT THE HOME OF CARDIFF MAYHUGH...
...WITH A FLUTTER OF SEAGULLS WINGS...
...AND A LAST BUBBLING GASP.
MURDER ONE.
BUT NASH HASN'T FOUND WHAT SHE SEEKS.
QUANTUM PHYSICS
TIME SPACE CONTINUUM
AN ADVENTURE IN TIME
HOLLYWOOD GOTHIC
DAVID J. SKAL
INVERTEBR PALAEONT AND EVOLU
POIS GAS
MECHANICAL ENGINEERS
SIMPLE MACHINES
COMBUSTION

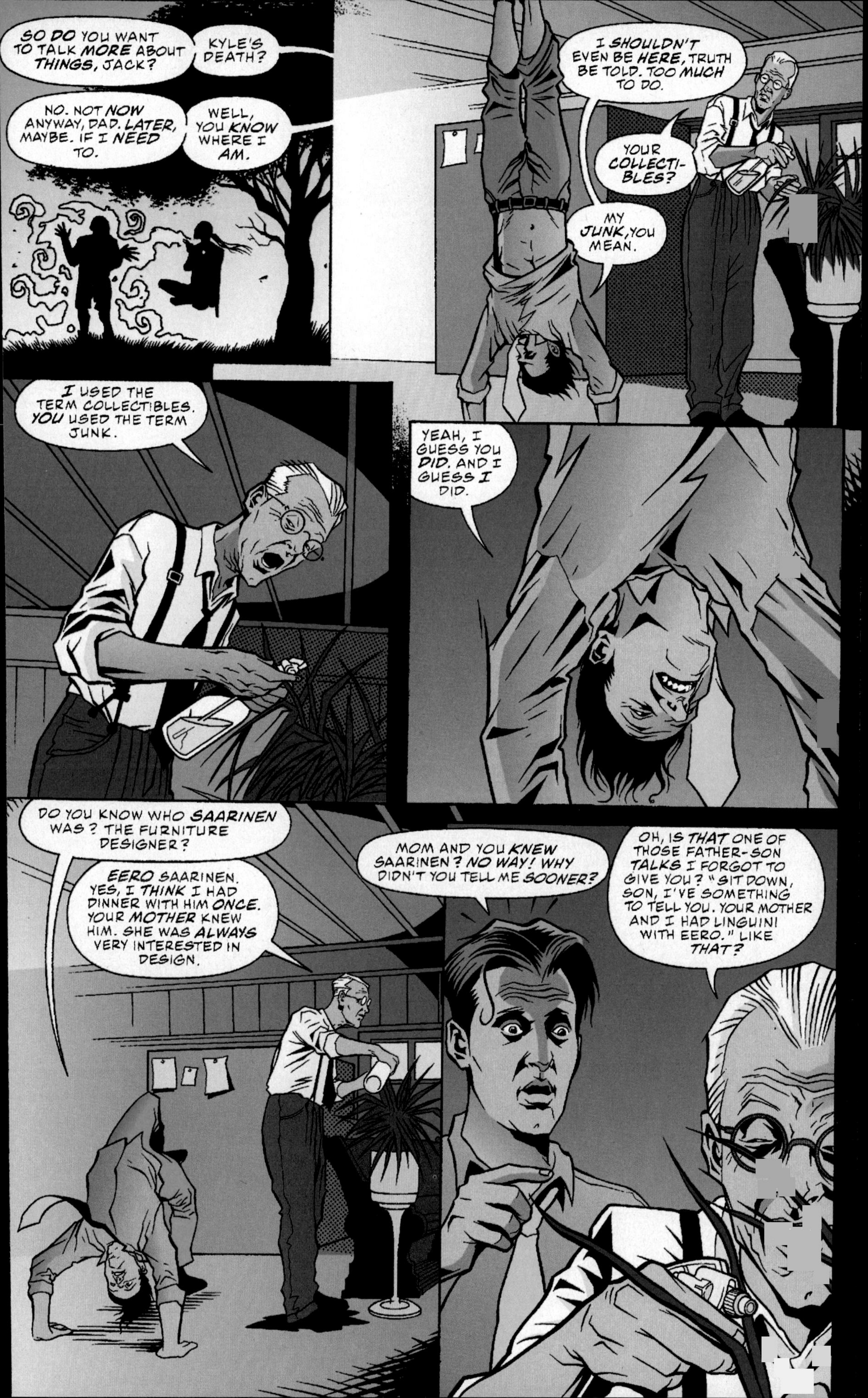
SO DO YOU WANT TO TALK MORE ABOUT THINGS, JACK?
KYLE'S DEATH?
NO. NOT NOW ANYWAY, DAD. LATER, MAYBE. IF I NEED TO.
WELL, YOU KNOW WHERE I AM.
I SHOULDN'T EVEN BE HERE, TRUTH BE TOLD. TOO MUCH TO DO.
YOUR COLLECTI-BLES?
MY JUNK, YOU MEAN.
I USED THE TERM COLLECTIBLES. YOU USED THE TERM JUNK.
YEAH, I GUESS YOU DID. AND I GUESS I DID.
DO YOU KNOW WHO SAARINEN WAS? THE FURNITURE DESIGNER?
EERO SAARINEN. YES, I THINK I HAD DINNER WITH HIM ONCE. YOUR MOTHER KNEW HIM. SHE WAS ALWAYS VERY INTERESTED IN DESIGN.
MOM AND YOU KNEW SAARINEN? NO WAY! WHY DIDN'T YOU TELL ME SOONER?
OH, IS THAT ONE OF THOSE FATHER-SON TALKS I FORGOT TO GIVE YOU? "SIT DOWN, SON, I'VE SOMETHING TO TELL YOU. YOUR MOTHER AND I HAD LINGUINI WITH EERO." LIKE THAT?

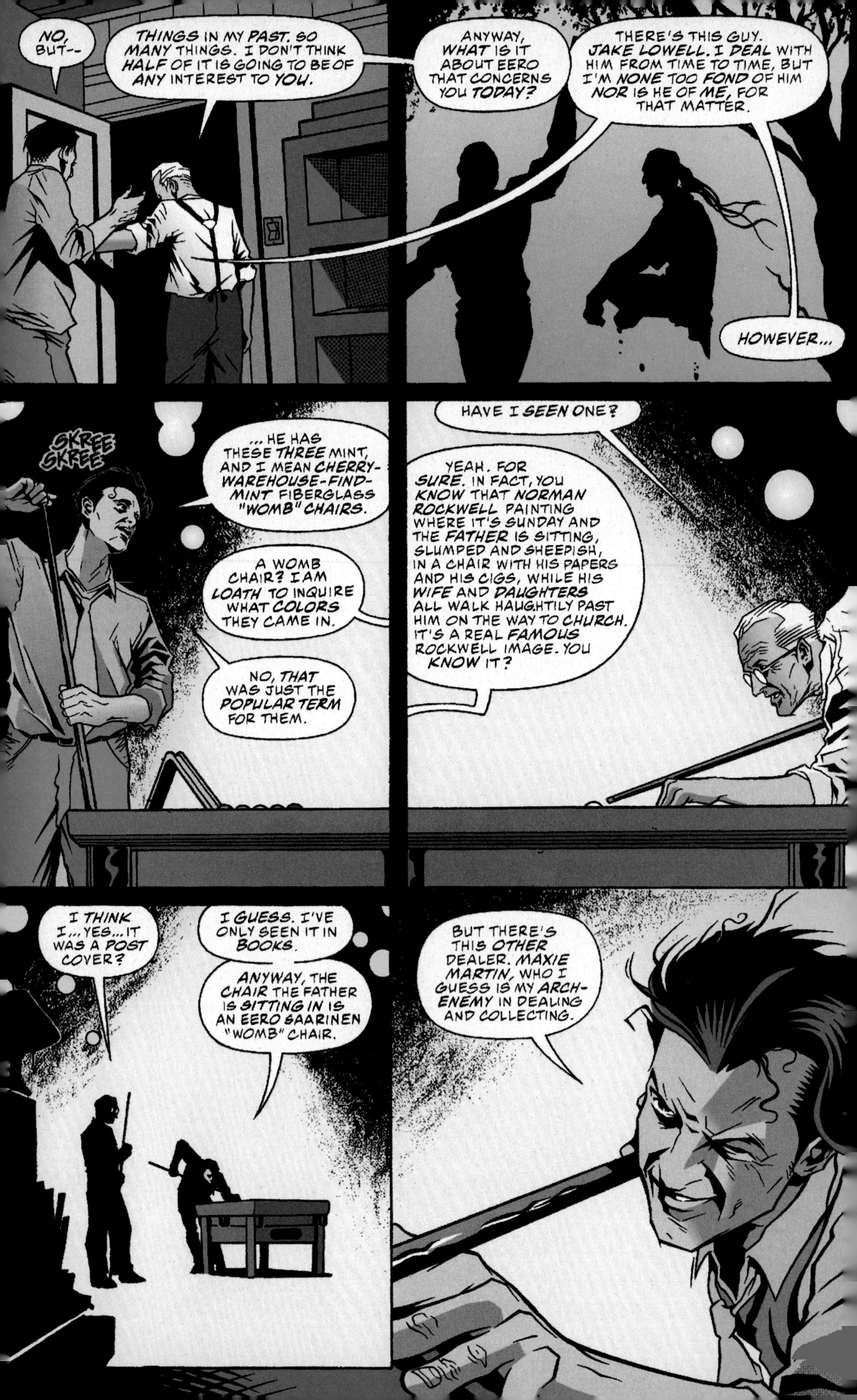
NO, BUT--
THINGS IN MY PAST. SO MANY THINGS. I DON'T THINK HALF OF IT IS GOING TO BE OF ANY INTEREST TO YOU.
ANYWAY, WHAT IS IT ABOUT EERO THAT CONCERNS YOU TODAY?
THERE'S THIS GUY. JAKE LOWELL. I DEAL WITH HIM FROM TIME TO TIME, BUT I'M NONE TOO FOND OF HIM NOR IS HE OF ME, FOR THAT MATTER.
HOWEVER...
SKREE SKREE
...HE HAS THESE THREE MINT, AND I MEAN CHERRY-WAREHOUSE-FIND-MINT FIBERGLASS "WOMB" CHAIRS.
A WOMB CHAIR? I AM LOATH TO INQUIRE WHAT COLORS THEY CAME IN.
NO, THAT WAS JUST THE POPULAR TERM FOR THEM.
HAVE I SEEN ONE?
YEAH. FOR SURE. IN FACT, YOU KNOW THAT NORMAN ROCKWELL PAINTING WHERE IT'S SUNDAY AND THE FATHER IS SITTING, SLUMPED AND SHEEPISH, IN A CHAIR WITH HIS PAPERS AND HIS CIGS, WHILE HIS WIFE AND DAUGHTERS ALL WALK HAUGHTILY PAST HIM ON THE WAY TO CHURCH. IT'S A REAL FAMOUS ROCKWELL IMAGE. YOU KNOW IT?
I THINK I...YES...IT WAS A POST COVER?
I GUESS. I'VE ONLY SEEN IT IN BOOKS.
ANYWAY, THE CHAIR THE FATHER IS SITTING IN IS AN EERO SAARINEN "WOMB" CHAIR.
BUT THERE'S THIS OTHER DEALER. MAXIE MARTIN, WHO I GUESS IS MY ARCH-ENEMY IN DEALING AND COLLECTING.

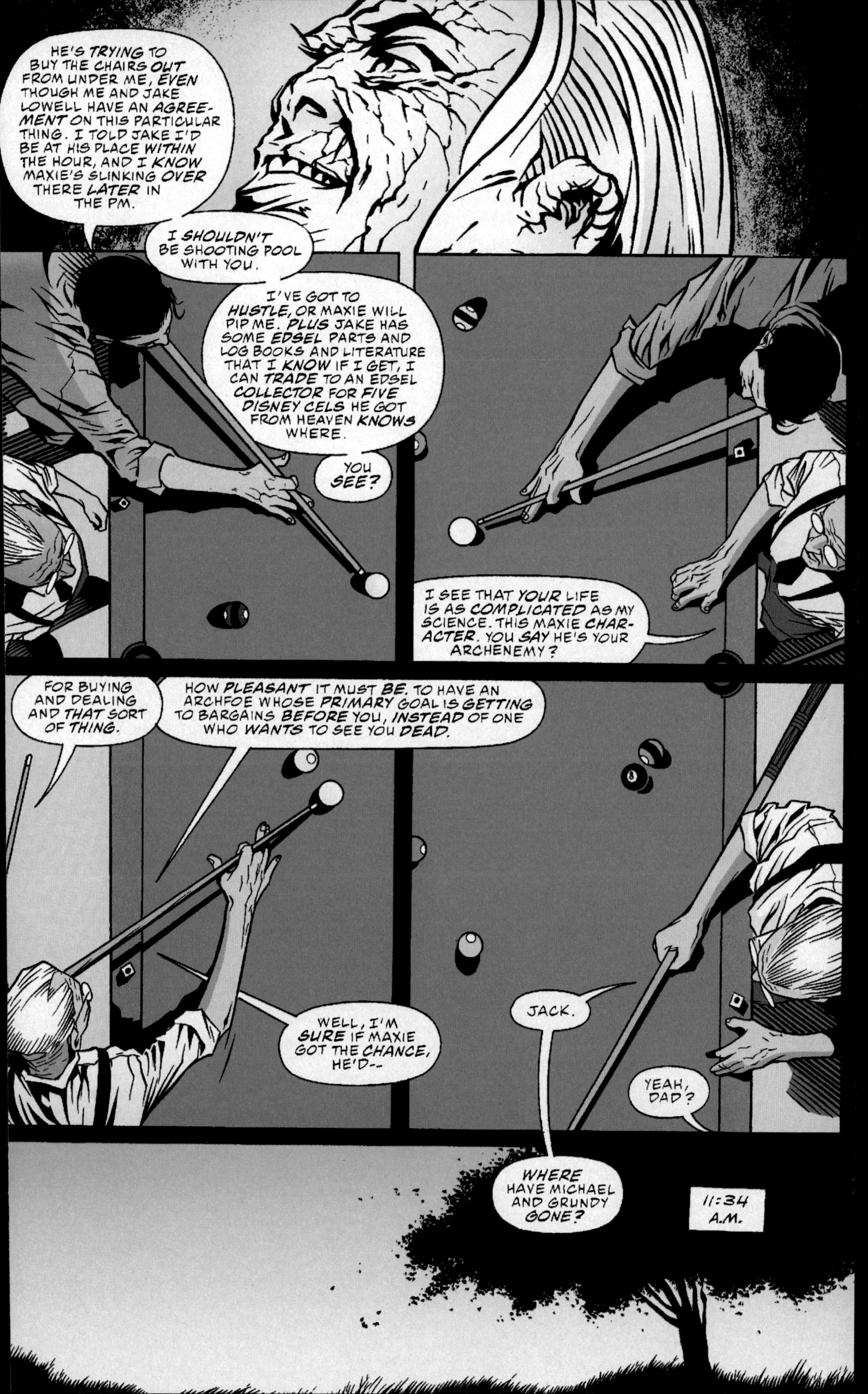

HE'S TRYING TO BUY THE CHAIRS OUT FROM UNDER ME, EVEN THOUGH ME AND JAKE LOWELL HAVE AN AGREEMENT ON THIS PARTICULAR THING. I TOLD JAKE I'D BE AT HIS PLACE WITHIN THE HOUR, AND I KNOW MAXIE'S SLINKING OVER THERE LATER IN THE PM.
I SHOULDN'T BE SHOOTING POOL WITH YOU.
I'VE GOT TO HUSTLE, OR MAXIE WILL PIP ME. PLUS JAKE HAS SOME EDSEL PARTS AND LOG BOOKS AND LITERATURE THAT I KNOW IF I GET, I CAN TRADE TO AN EDSEL COLLECTOR FOR FIVE DISNEY CELS HE GOT FROM HEAVEN KNOWS WHERE.
YOU SEE?
I SEE THAT YOUR LIFE IS AS COMPLICATED AS MY SCIENCE. THIS MAXIE CHARACTER. YOU SAY HE'S YOUR ARCHENEMY?
FOR BUYING AND DEALING AND THAT SORT OF THING.
HOW PLEASANT IT MUST BE. TO HAVE AN ARCHFOE WHOSE PRIMARY GOAL IS GETTING TO BARGAINS BEFORE YOU, INSTEAD OF ONE WHO WANTS TO SEE YOU DEAD.
WELL, I'M SURE IF MAXIE GOT THE CHANCE, HE'D--
JACK.
YEAH, DAD?
WHERE HAVE MICHAEL AND GRUNDY GONE?
11:34 A.M.

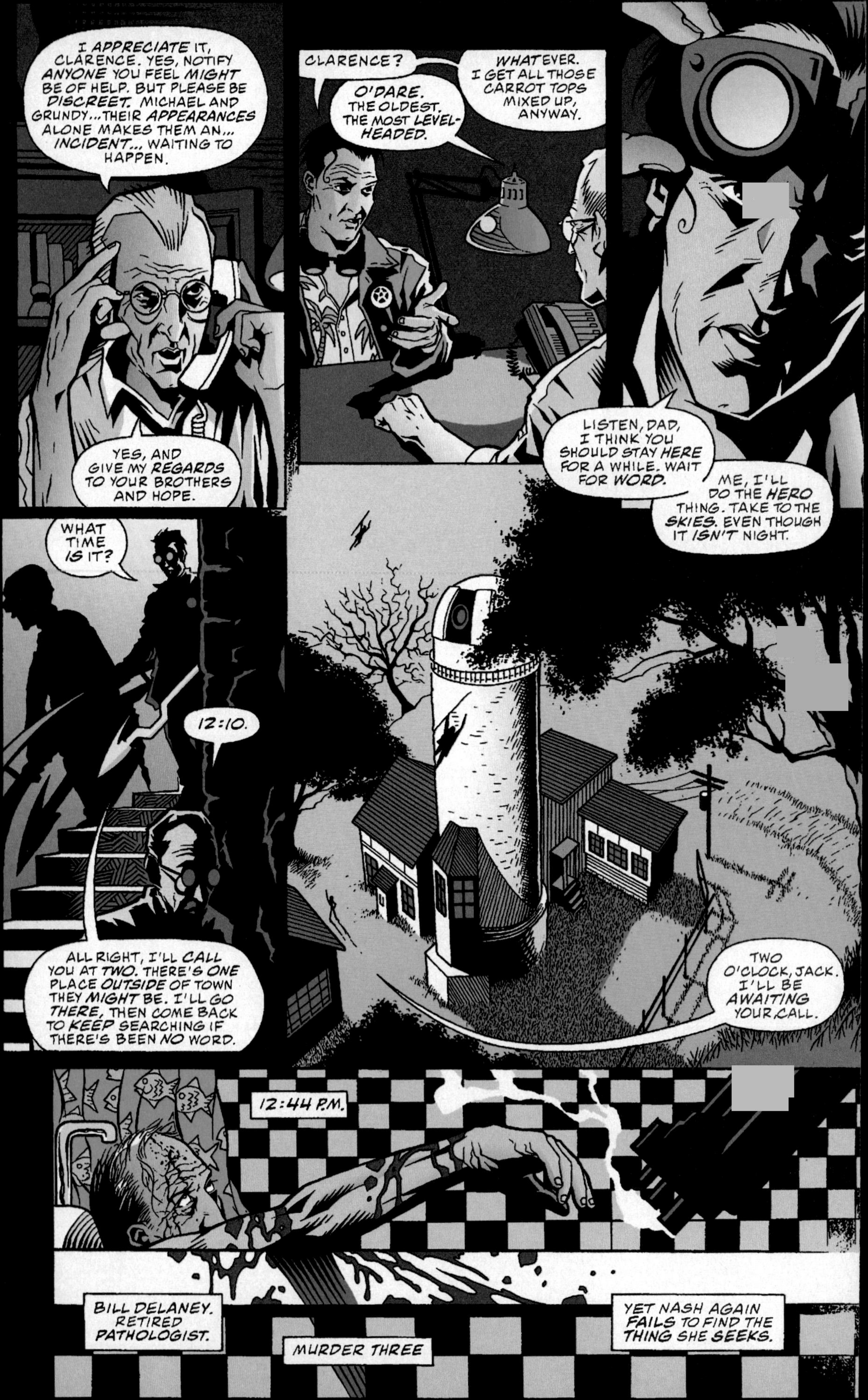

I APPRECIATE IT, CLARENCE. YES, NOTIFY ANYONE YOU FEEL MIGHT BE OF HELP. BUT PLEASE BE DISCREET. MICHAEL AND GRUNDY... THEIR APPEARANCES ALONE MAKES THEM AN... INCIDENT... WAITING TO HAPPEN.
YES, AND GIVE MY REGARDS TO YOUR BROTHERS AND HOPE.
CLARENCE?
O'DARE. THE OLDEST. THE MOST LEVEL-HEADED.
WHATEVER. I GET ALL THOSE CARROT TOPS MIXED UP, ANYWAY.
LISTEN, DAD, I THINK YOU SHOULD STAY HERE FOR A WHILE. WAIT FOR WORD.
ME, I'LL DO THE HERO THING. TAKE TO THE SKIES. EVEN THOUGH IT ISN'T NIGHT.
WHAT TIME IS IT?
12:10.
ALL RIGHT, I'LL CALL YOU AT TWO. THERE'S ONE PLACE OUTSIDE OF TOWN THEY MIGHT BE. I'LL GO THERE, THEN COME BACK TO KEEP SEARCHING IF THERE'S BEEN NO WORD.
TWO O'CLOCK, JACK. I'LL BE AWAITING YOUR CALL.
12:44 P.M.
BILL DELANEY. RETIRED PATHOLOGIST.
MURDER THREE
YET NASH AGAIN FAILS TO FIND THE THING SHE SEEKS.

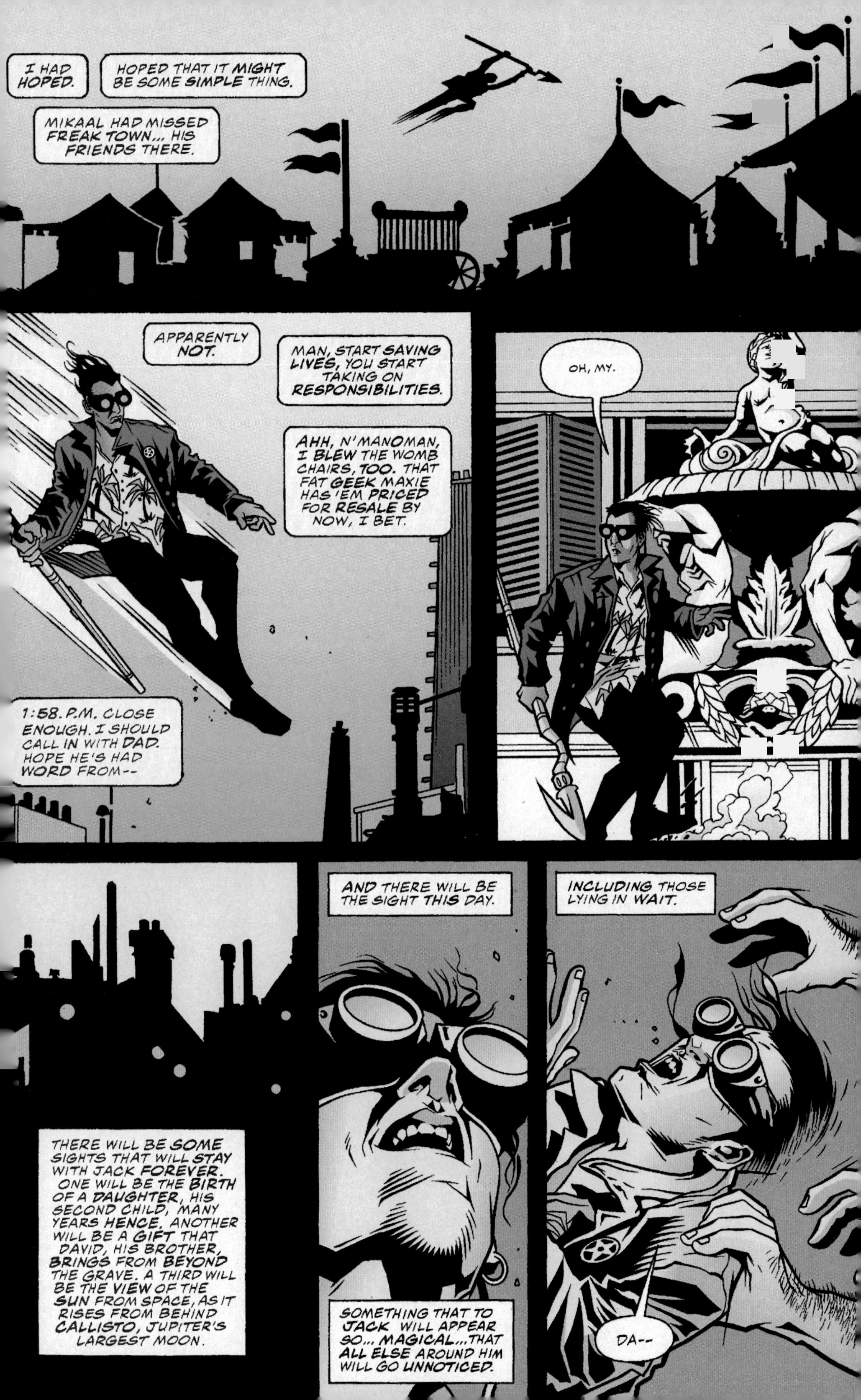
I HAD HOPED.
HOPED THAT IT MIGHT BE SOME SIMPLE THING.
MIKAAL HAD MISSED FREAK TOWN... HIS FRIENDS THERE.
APPARENTLY NOT.
MAN, START SAVING LIVES, YOU START TAKING ON RESPONSIBILITIES.
AHH, N'MANOMAN, I BLEW THE WOMB CHAIRS, TOO. THAT FAT GEEK MAXIE HAS 'EM PRICED FOR RESALE BY NOW, I BET.
1:58 P.M. CLOSE ENOUGH. I SHOULD CALL IN WITH DAD. HOPE HE'S HAD WORD FROM--
OH, MY.
THERE WILL BE SOME SIGHTS THAT WILL STAY WITH JACK FOREVER. ONE WILL BE THE BIRTH OF A DAUGHTER, HIS SECOND CHILD, MANY YEARS HENCE. ANOTHER WILL BE A GIFT THAT DAVID, HIS BROTHER, BRINGS FROM BEYOND THE GRAVE. A THIRD WILL BE THE VIEW OF THE SUN FROM SPACE, AS IT RISES FROM BEHIND CALLISTO, JUPITER'S LARGEST MOON.
AND THERE WILL BE THE SIGHT THIS DAY.
SOMETHING THAT TO JACK WILL APPEAR SO... MAGICAL... THAT ALL ELSE AROUND HIM WILL GO UNNOTICED.
INCLUDING THOSE LYING IN WAIT.
DA--

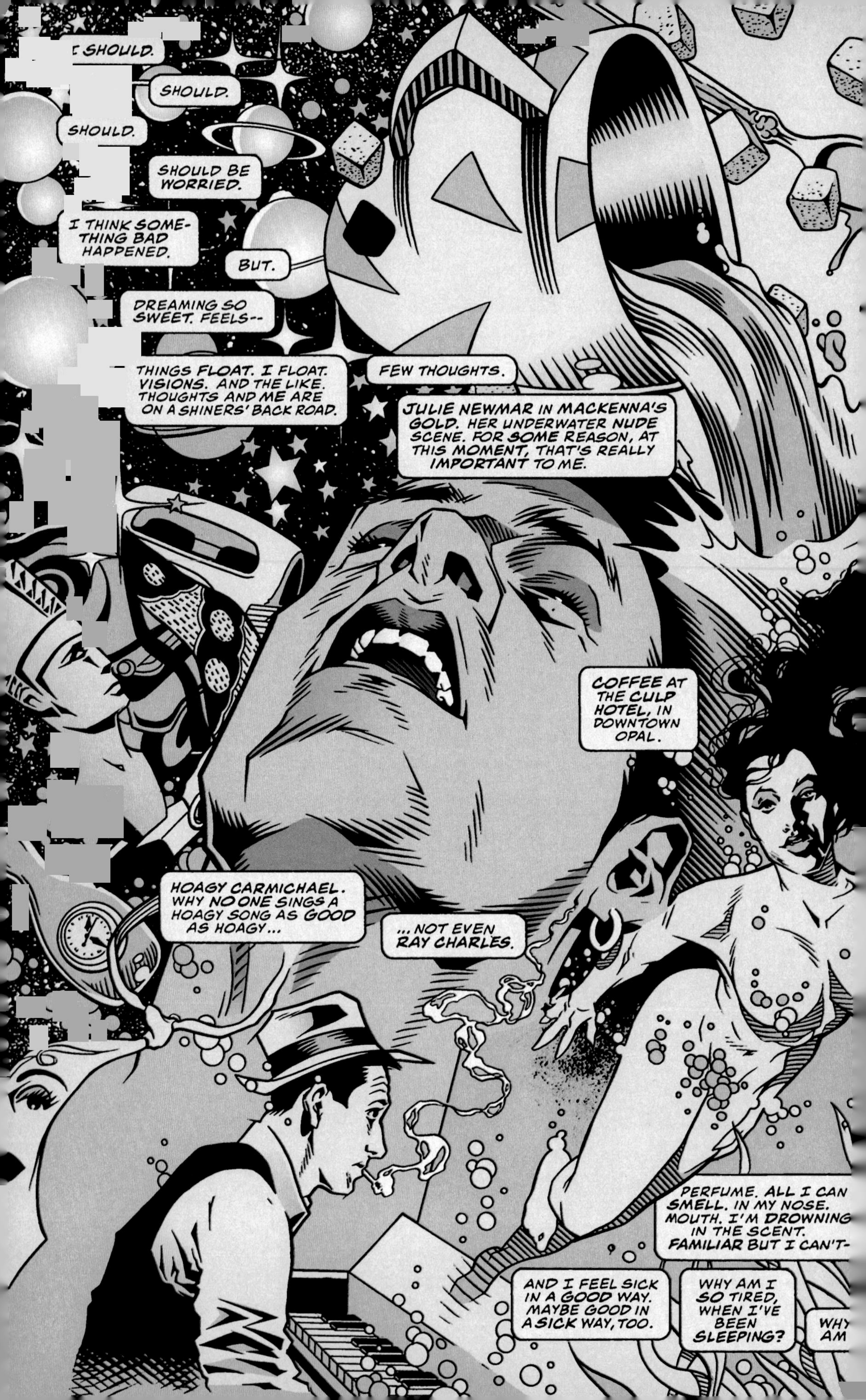
I SHOULD.
SHOULD.
SHOULD.
SHOULD BE WORRIED.
I THINK SOME-THING BAD HAPPENED.
BUT.
DREAMING SO SWEET. FEELS--
THINGS FLOAT. I FLOAT. VISIONS. AND THE LIKE. THOUGHTS AND ME ARE ON A SHINERS' BACK ROAD.
FEW THOUGHTS.
JULIE NEWMAR IN MACKENNA'S GOLD. HER UNDERWATER NUDE SCENE. FOR SOME REASON, AT THIS MOMENT, THAT'S REALLY IMPORTANT TO ME.
COFFEE AT THE CULP HOTEL, IN DOWNTOWN OPAL.
HOAGY CARMICHAEL. WHY NO ONE SINGS A HOAGY SONG AS GOOD AS HOAGY...
...NOT EVEN RAY CHARLES.
PERFUME. ALL I CAN SMELL. IN MY NOSE. MOUTH. I'M DROWNING IN THE SCENT. FAMILIAR BUT I CAN'T-
AND I FEEL SICK IN A GOOD WAY. MAYBE GOOD IN A SICK WAY, TOO.
WHY AM I SO TIRED, WHEN I'VE BEEN SLEEPING?
WHY AM

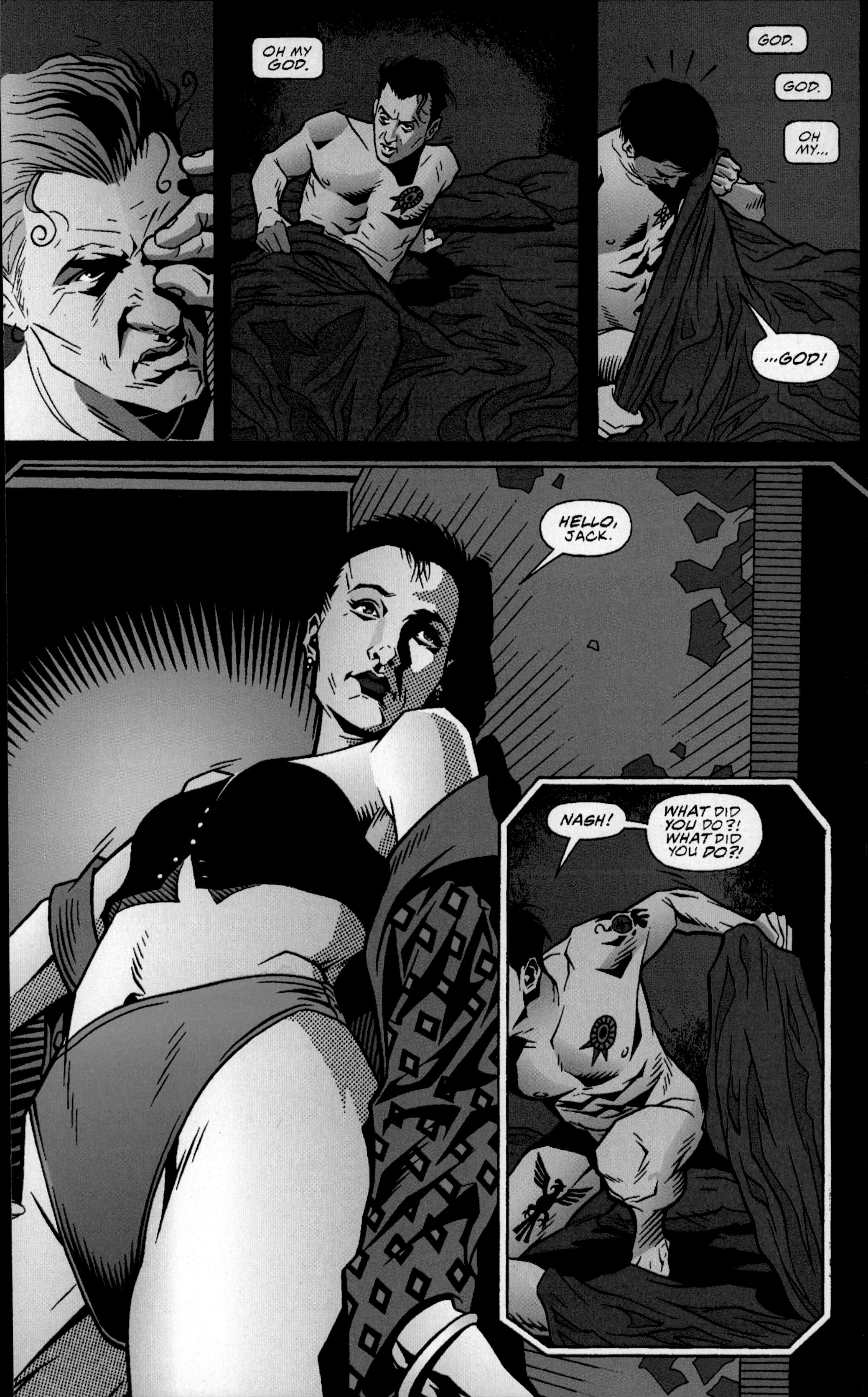
OH MY GOD.
GOD.
GOD.
OH MY...
...GOD!
HELLO, JACK.
NASH!
WHAT DID YOU DO?! WHAT DID YOU DO?!

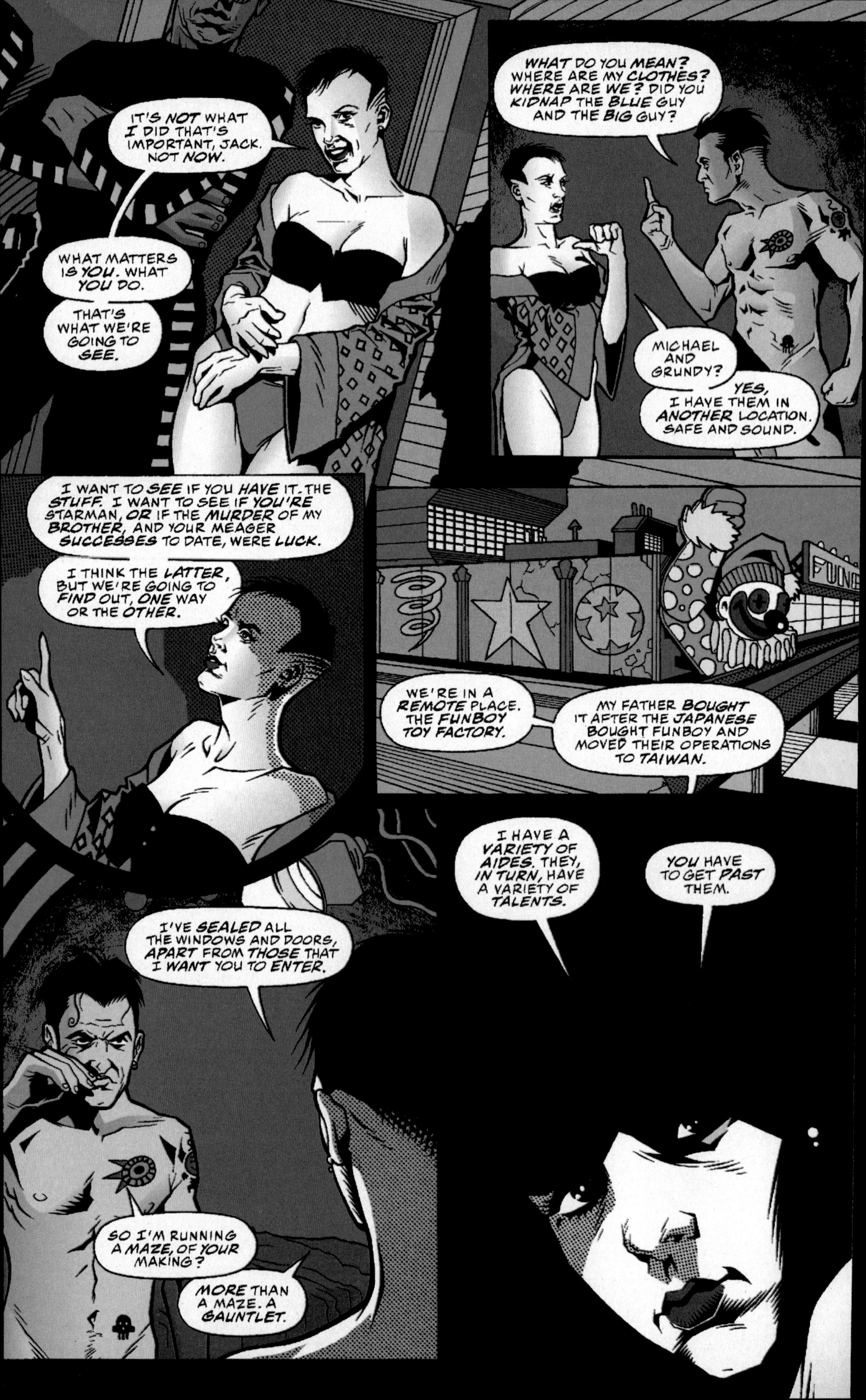
IT'S NOT WHAT I DID THAT'S IMPORTANT, JACK. NOT NOW.
WHAT MATTERS IS YOU. WHAT YOU DO.
THAT'S WHAT WE'RE GOING TO SEE.
WHAT DO YOU MEAN? WHERE ARE MY CLOTHES? WHERE ARE WE? DID YOU KIDNAP THE BLUE GUY AND THE BIG GUY?
MICHAEL AND GRUNDY?
YES, I HAVE THEM IN ANOTHER LOCATION. SAFE AND SOUND.
I WANT TO SEE IF YOU HAVE IT. THE STUFF. I WANT TO SEE IF YOU'RE STARMAN, OR IF THE MURDER OF MY BROTHER, AND YOUR MEAGER SUCCESSES TO DATE, WERE LUCK.
I THINK THE LATTER, BUT WE'RE GOING TO FIND OUT, ONE WAY OR THE OTHER.
FUNB
WE'RE IN A REMOTE PLACE. THE FUNBOY TOY FACTORY.
MY FATHER BOUGHT IT AFTER THE JAPANESE BOUGHT FUNBOY AND MOVED THEIR OPERATIONS TO TAIWAN.
I'VE SEALED ALL THE WINDOWS AND DOORS, APART FROM THOSE THAT I WANT YOU TO ENTER.
I HAVE A VARIETY OF AIDES. THEY, IN TURN, HAVE A VARIETY OF TALENTS.
YOU HAVE TO GET PAST THEM.
SO I'M RUNNING A MAZE, OF YOUR MAKING?
MORE THAN A MAZE. A GAUNTLET.

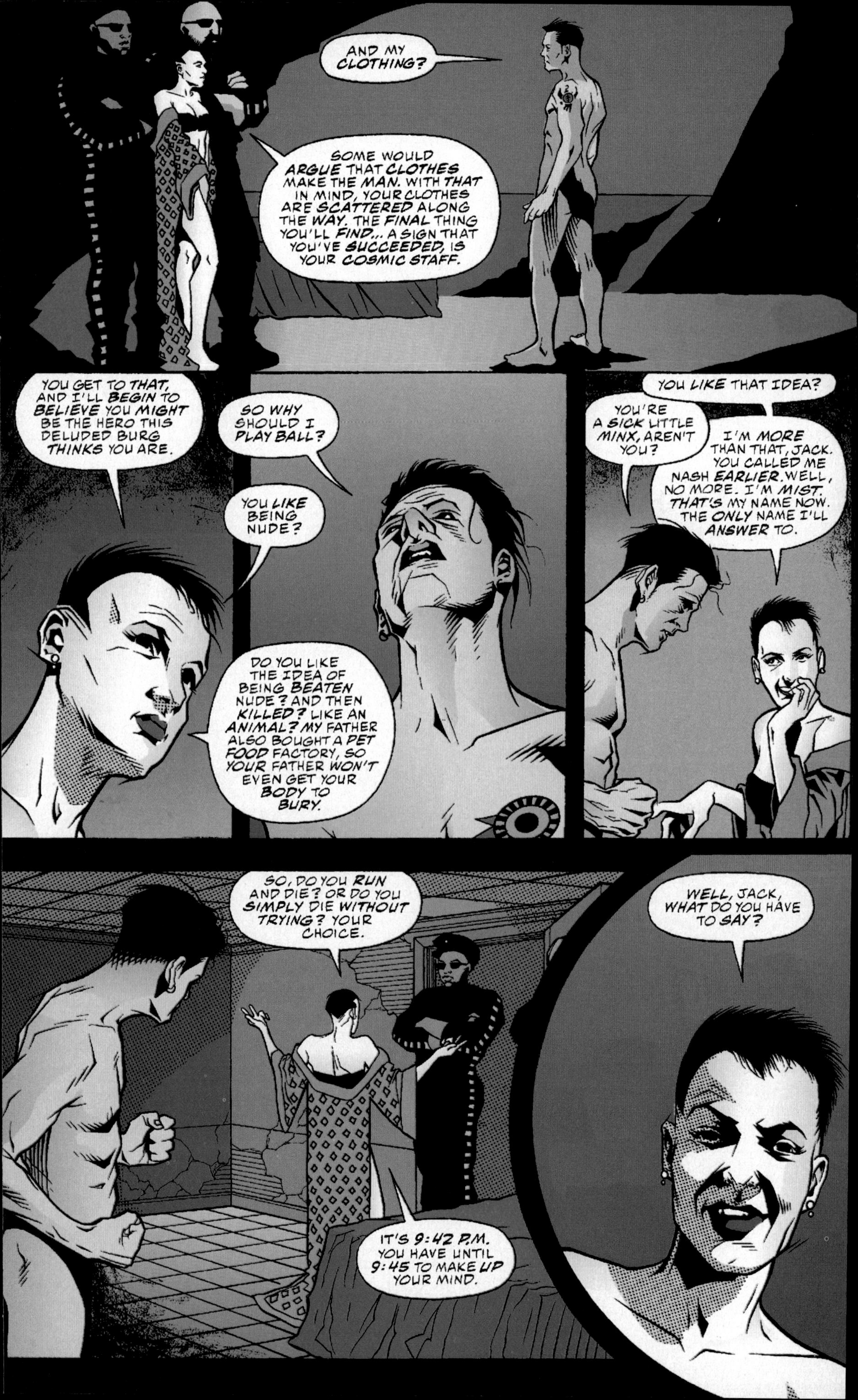
AND MY CLOTHING?
SOME WOULD ARGUE THAT CLOTHES MAKE THE MAN. WITH THAT IN MIND, YOUR CLOTHES ARE SCATTERED ALONG THE WAY. THE FINAL THING YOU'LL FIND... A SIGN THAT YOU'VE SUCCEEDED, IS YOUR COSMIC STAFF.
YOU GET TO THAT, AND I'LL BEGIN TO BELIEVE YOU MIGHT BE THE HERO THIS DELUDED BURG THINKS YOU ARE.
SO WHY SHOULD I PLAY BALL?
YOU LIKE BEING NUDE?
DO YOU LIKE THE IDEA OF BEING BEATEN NUDE? AND THEN KILLED? LIKE AN ANIMAL? MY FATHER ALSO BOUGHT A PET FOOD FACTORY, SO YOUR FATHER WON'T EVEN GET YOUR BODY TO BURY.
YOU LIKE THAT IDEA?
YOU'RE A SICK LITTLE MINX, AREN'T YOU?
I'M MORE THAN THAT, JACK. YOU CALLED ME NASH EARLIER. WELL, NO MORE. I'M MIST. THAT'S MY NAME NOW. THE ONLY NAME I'LL ANSWER TO.
SO, DO YOU RUN AND DIE? OR DO YOU SIMPLY DIE WITHOUT TRYING? YOUR CHOICE.
IT'S 9:42 P.M. YOU HAVE UNTIL 9:45 TO MAKE UP YOUR MIND.
WELL, JACK, WHAT DO YOU HAVE TO SAY?

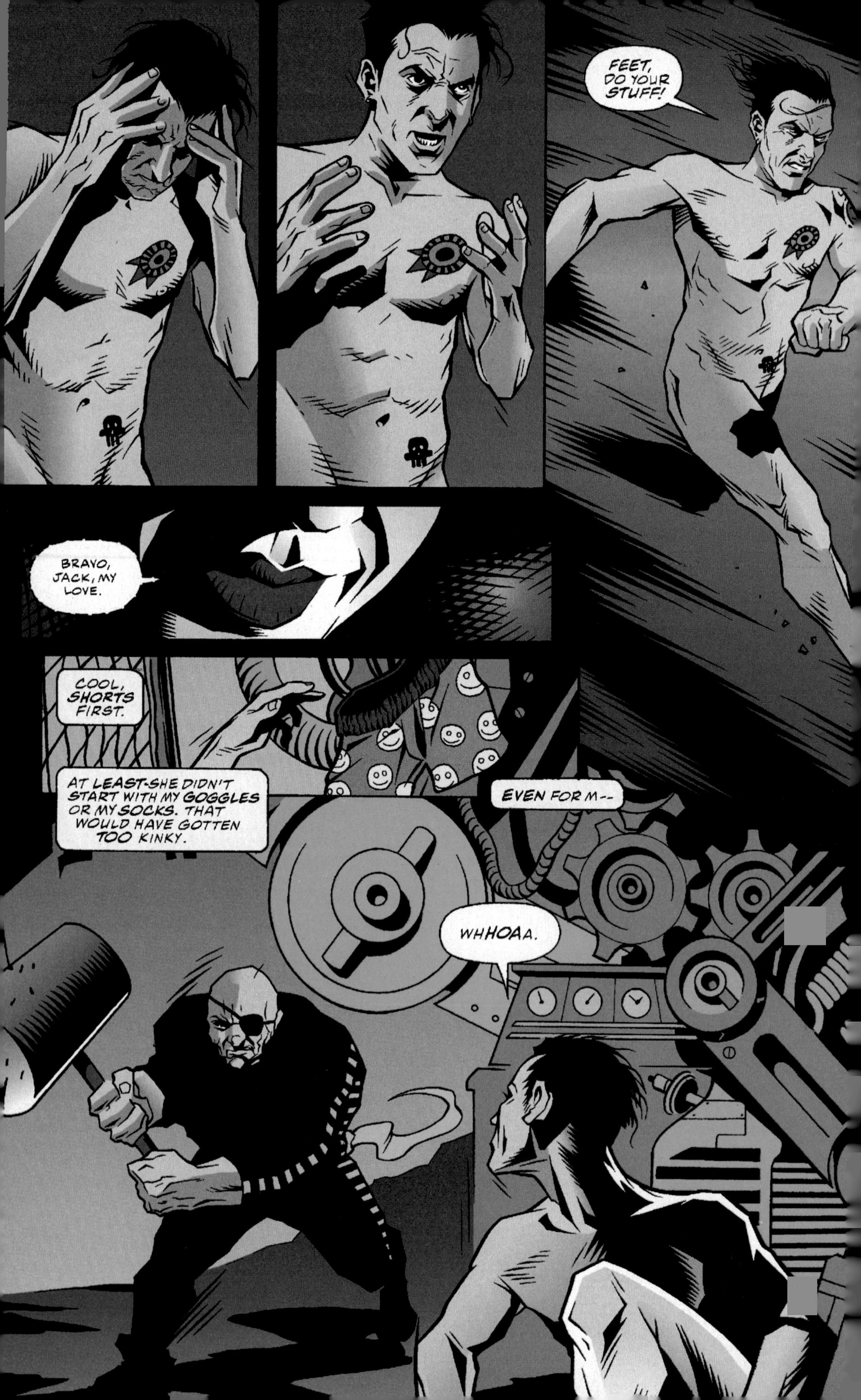
FEET, DO YOUR STUFF!
BRAVO, JACK, MY LOVE.
COOL, SHORTS FIRST.
AT LEAST SHE DIDN'T START WITH MY GOGGLES OR MY SOCKS. THAT WOULD HAVE GOTTEN TOO KINKY.
EVEN FOR M--
WHHOAA.

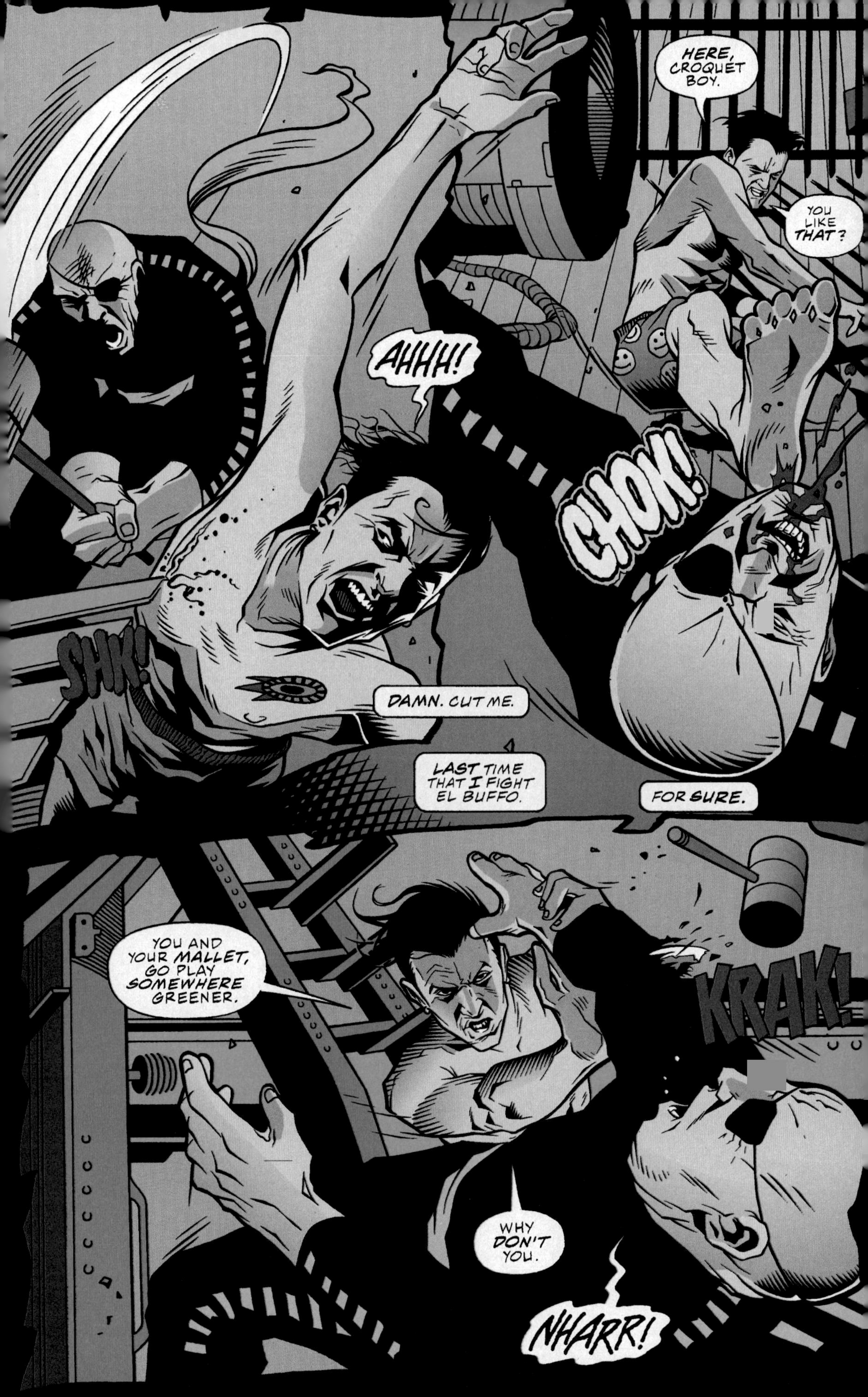
HERE, CROQUET BOY.
YOU LIKE THAT?
AHHH!
CHOK!
SHK!
DAMN. CUT ME.
LAST TIME THAT I FIGHT EL BUFFO.
FOR SURE.
YOU AND YOUR MALLET, GO PLAY SOMEWHERE GREENER.
KRAK!
WHY DON'T YOU.
NHARR!

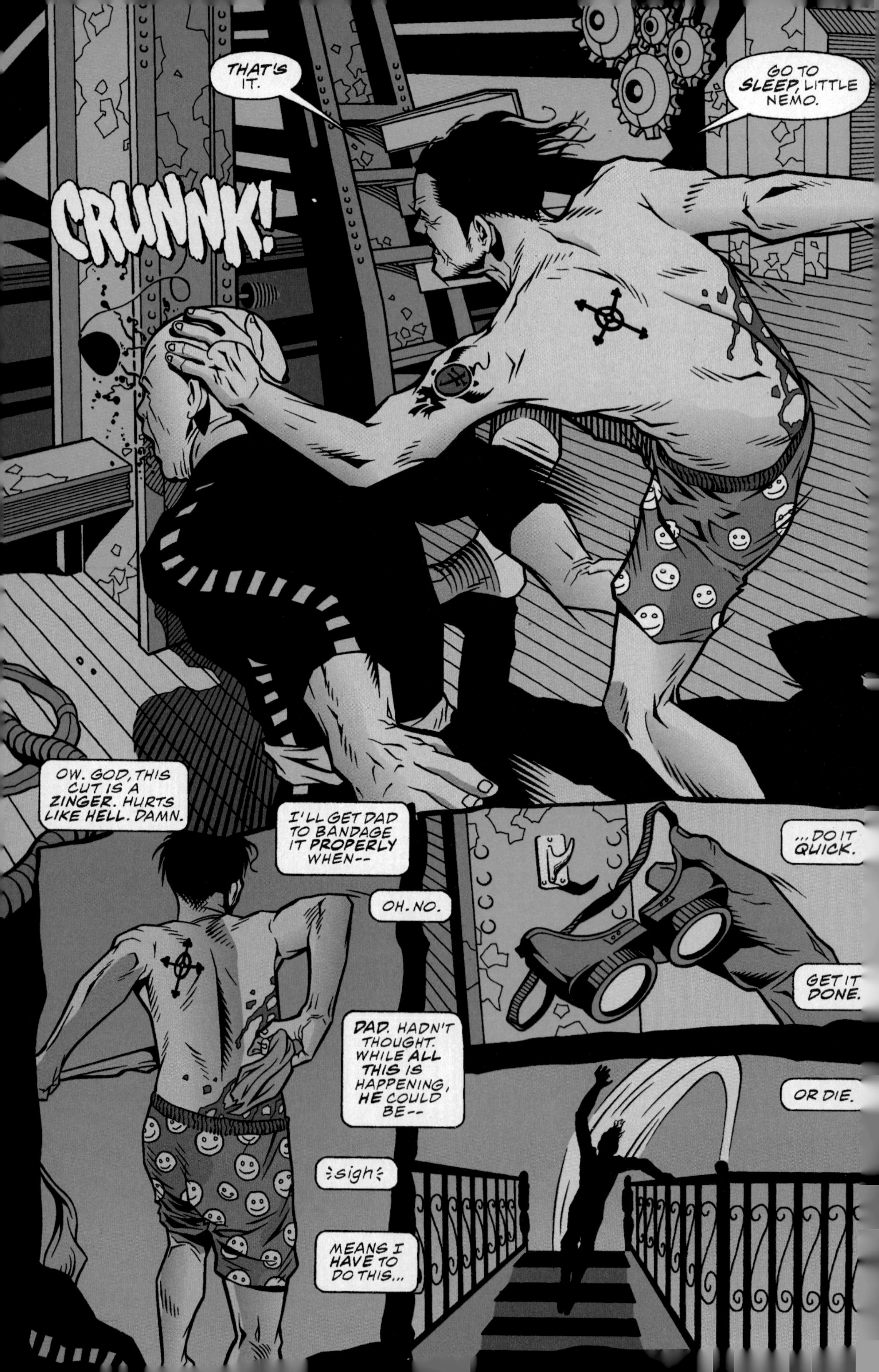
THAT'S IT.
GO TO SLEEP, LITTLE NEMO.
CRUNNK!
OW. GOD, THIS CUT IS A ZINGER. HURTS LIKE HELL. DAMN.
I'LL GET DAD TO BANDAGE IT PROPERLY WHEN--
OH. NO.
DAD. HADN'T THOUGHT. WHILE ALL THIS IS HAPPENING, HE COULD BE--
sigh
MEANS I HAVE TO DO THIS...
...DO IT QUICK.
GET IT DONE.
OR DIE.

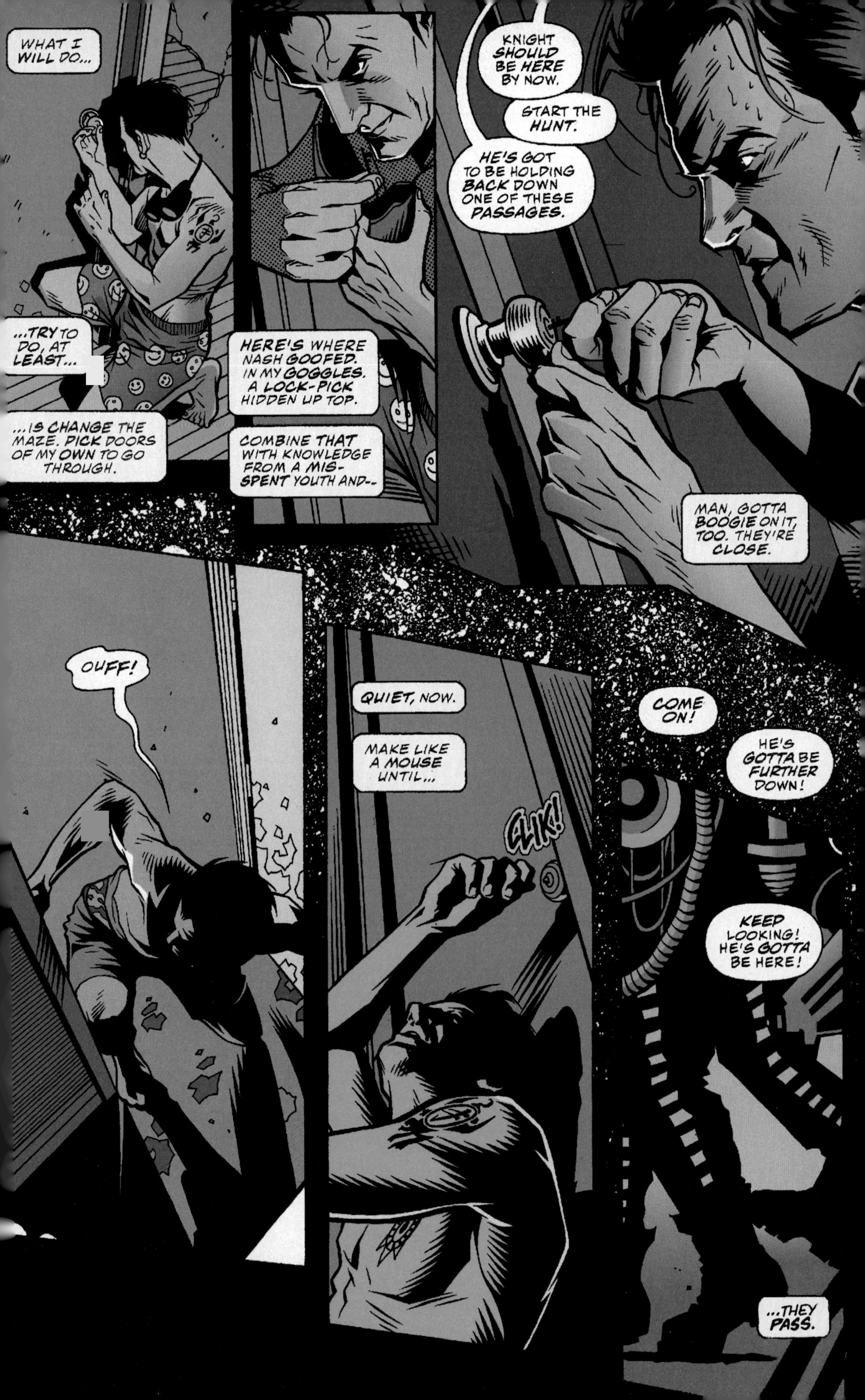

WHAT I WILL DO...
...TRY TO DO, AT LEAST...
...IS CHANGE THE MAZE. PICK DOORS OF MY OWN TO GO THROUGH.
HERE'S WHERE NASH GOOFED. IN MY GOGGLES. A LOCK-PICK HIDDEN UP TOP.
COMBINE THAT WITH KNOWLEDGE FROM A MIS-SPENT YOUTH AND--
KNIGHT SHOULD BE HERE BY NOW.
START THE HUNT.
HE'S GOT TO BE HOLDING BACK DOWN ONE OF THESE PASSAGES.
MAN, GOTTA BOOGIE ON IT, TOO. THEY'RE CLOSE.
OUFF!
QUIET, NOW.
MAKE LIKE A MOUSE UNTIL...
CLIK!
COME ON!
HE'S GOTTA BE FURTHER DOWN!
KEEP LOOKING! HE'S GOTTA BE HERE!
...THEY PASS.

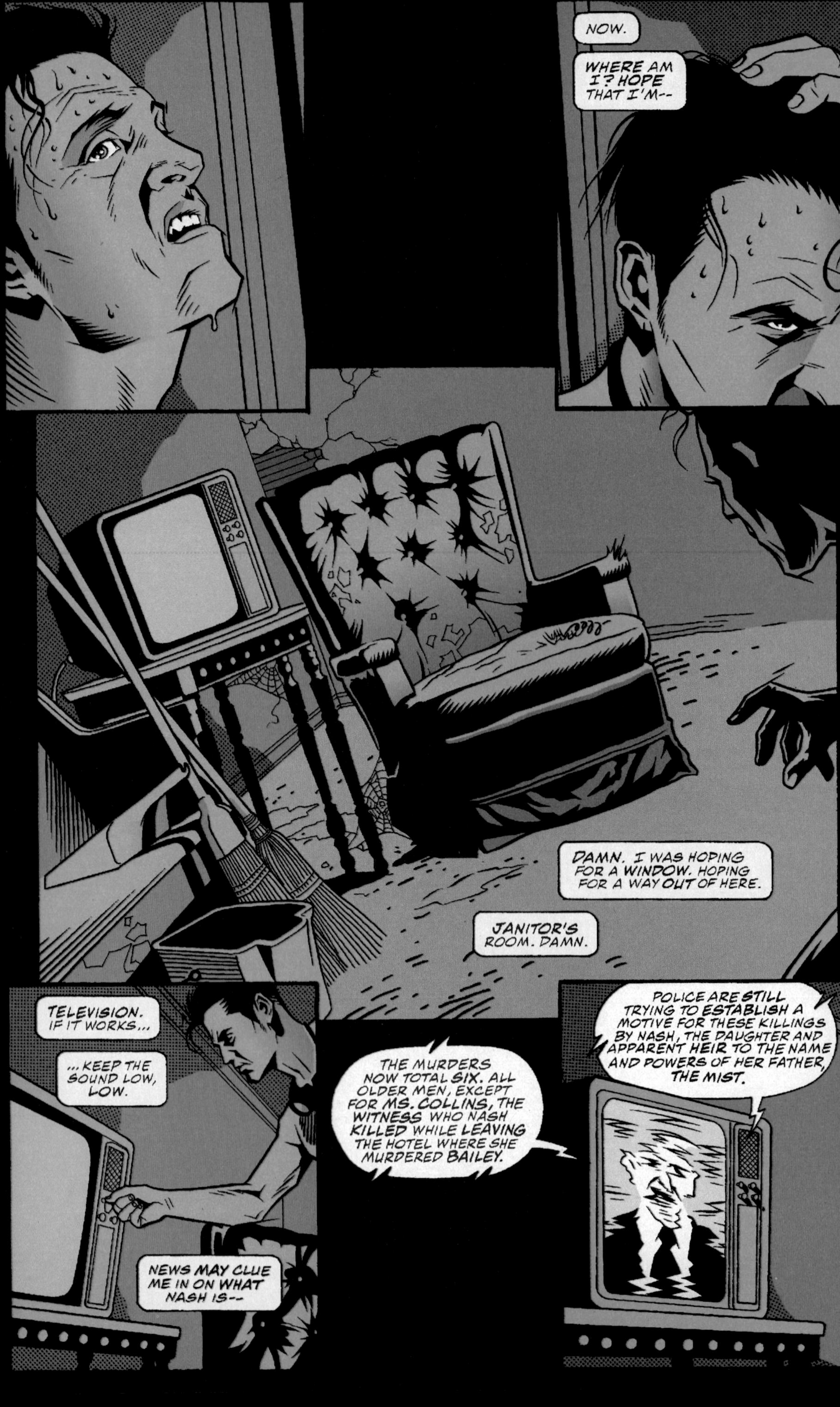
NOW.
WHERE AM I? HOPE THAT I'M--
DAMN. I WAS HOPING FOR A WINDOW. HOPING FOR A WAY OUT OF HERE.
JANITOR'S ROOM. DAMN.
TELEVISION. IF IT WORKS...
...KEEP THE SOUND LOW, LOW.
NEWS MAY CLUE ME IN ON WHAT NASH IS--
THE MURDERS NOW TOTAL SIX. ALL OLDER MEN, EXCEPT FOR MS. COLLINS, THE WITNESS WHO NASH KILLED WHILE LEAVING THE HOTEL WHERE SHE MURDERED BAILEY.
POLICE ARE STILL TRYING TO ESTABLISH A MOTIVE FOR THESE KILLINGS BY NASH, THE DAUGHTER AND APPARENT HEIR TO THE NAME AND POWERS OF HER FATHER, THE MIST.

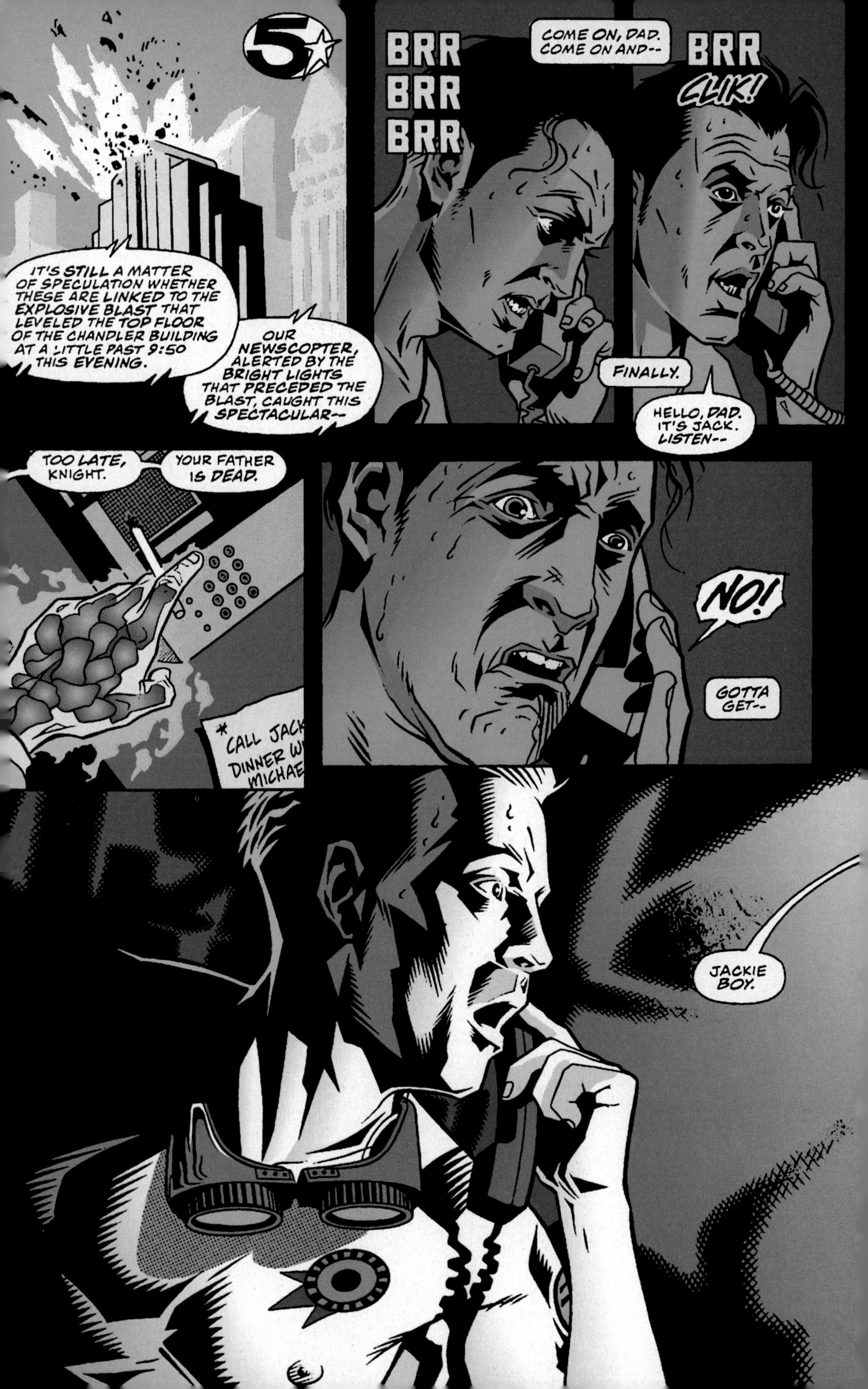
IT'S STILL A MATTER OF SPECULATION WHETHER THESE ARE LINKED TO THE EXPLOSIVE BLAST THAT LEVELED THE TOP FLOOR OF THE CHANDLER BUILDING AT A LITTLE PAST 9:50 THIS EVENING.
OUR NEWSCOPTER, ALERTED BY THE BRIGHT LIGHTS THAT PRECEDED THE BLAST, CAUGHT THIS SPECTACULAR--
BRR
BRR
BRR
COME ON, DAD. COME ON AND--
FINALLY.
BRR
CLIK!
HELLO, DAD. IT'S JACK. LISTEN--
TOO LATE, KNIGHT.
YOUR FATHER IS DEAD.
* CALL JACK
DINNER W
MICHAE
NO!
GOTTA GET--
JACKIE BOY.

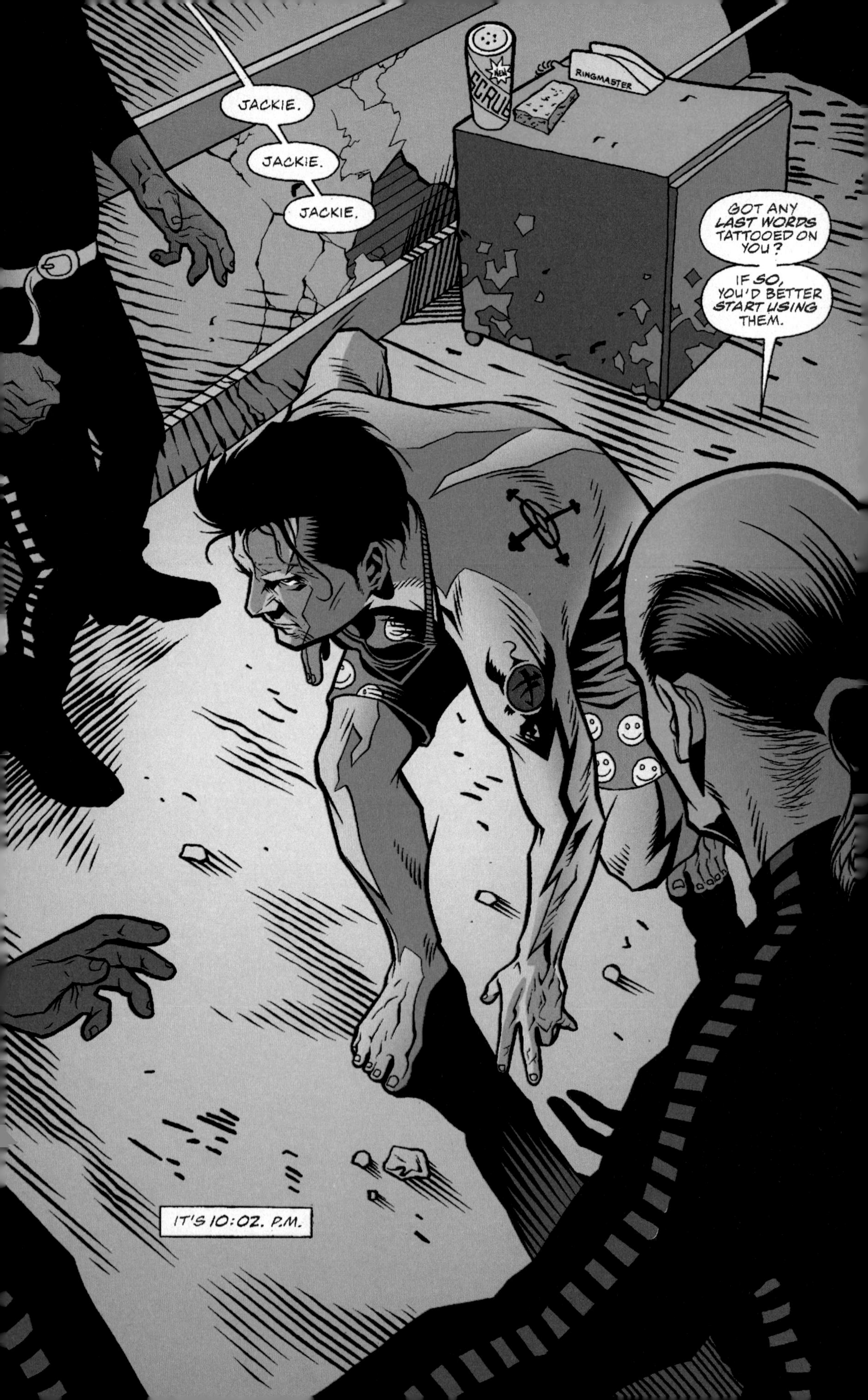
SCRUB
RINGMASTER
JACKIE.
JACKIE.
JACKIE.
GOT ANY LAST WORDS TATTOOED ON YOU?
IF SO, YOU'D BETTER START USING THEM.
IT'S 10:02. P.M.

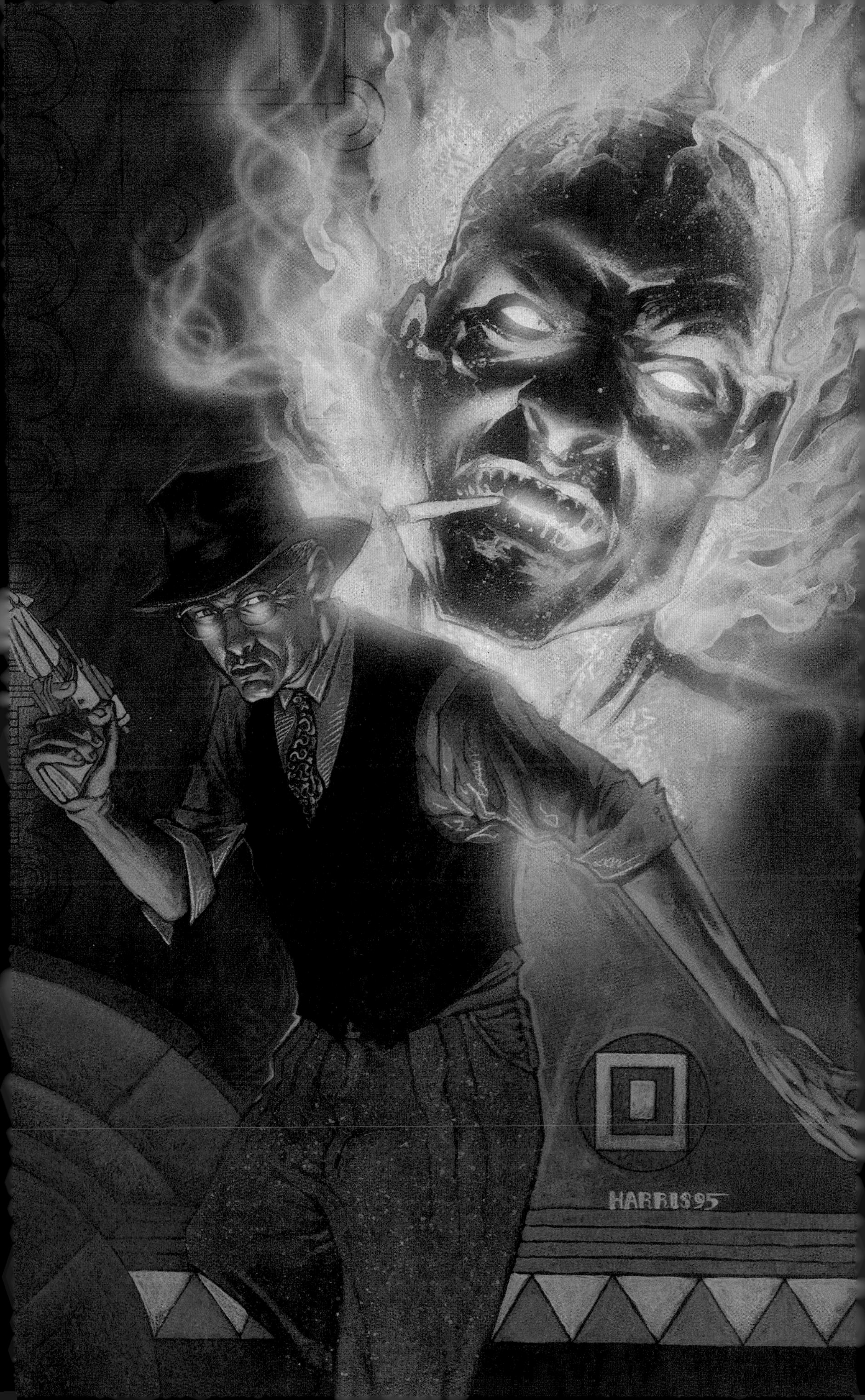
HARRIS95

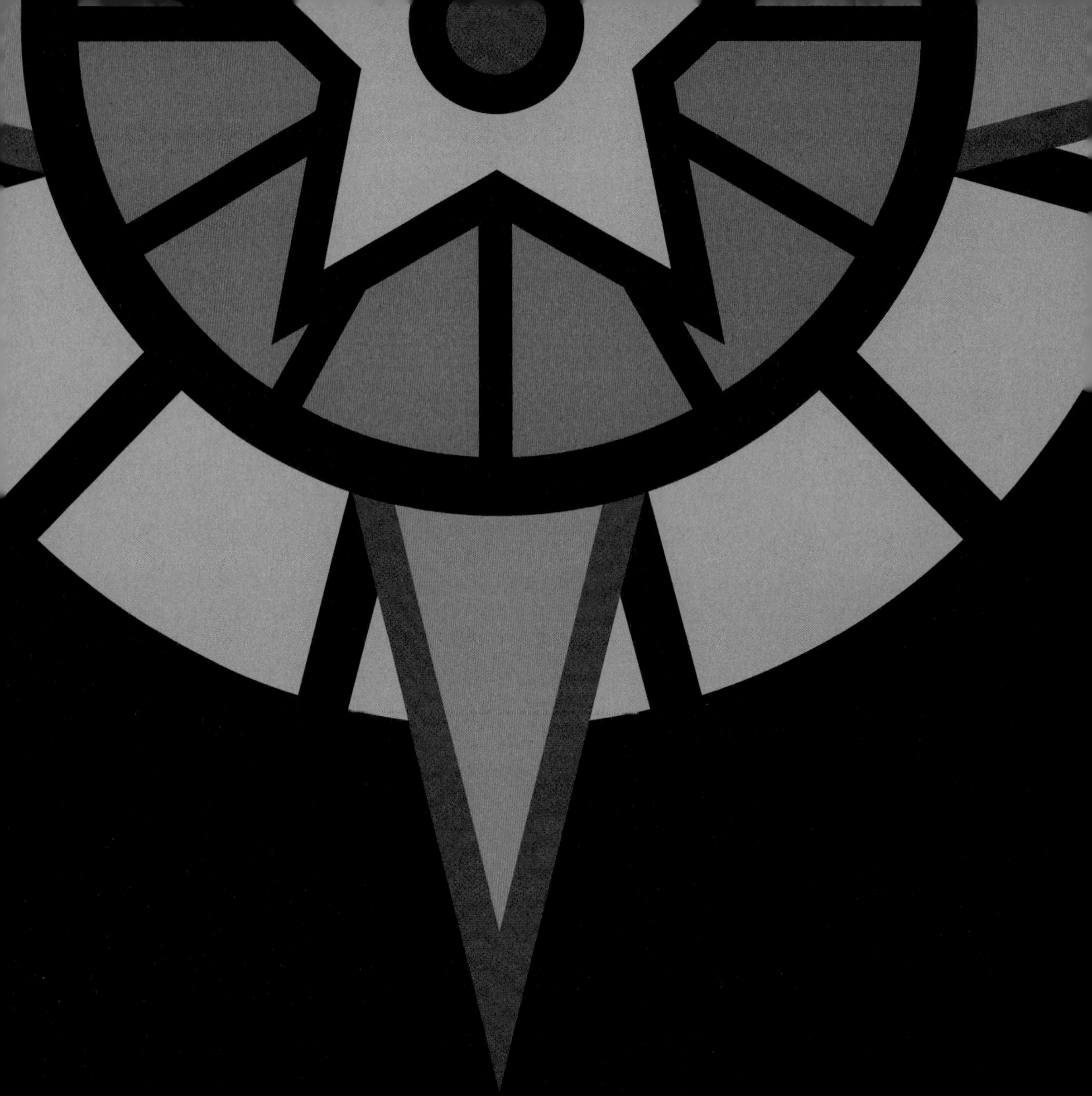

STARMAN 13

Cover by Tony Harris

Written by James Robinson

Pencils by Tony Harris,

with inks by Wade von Grawbadger

and colors by Gregory Wright

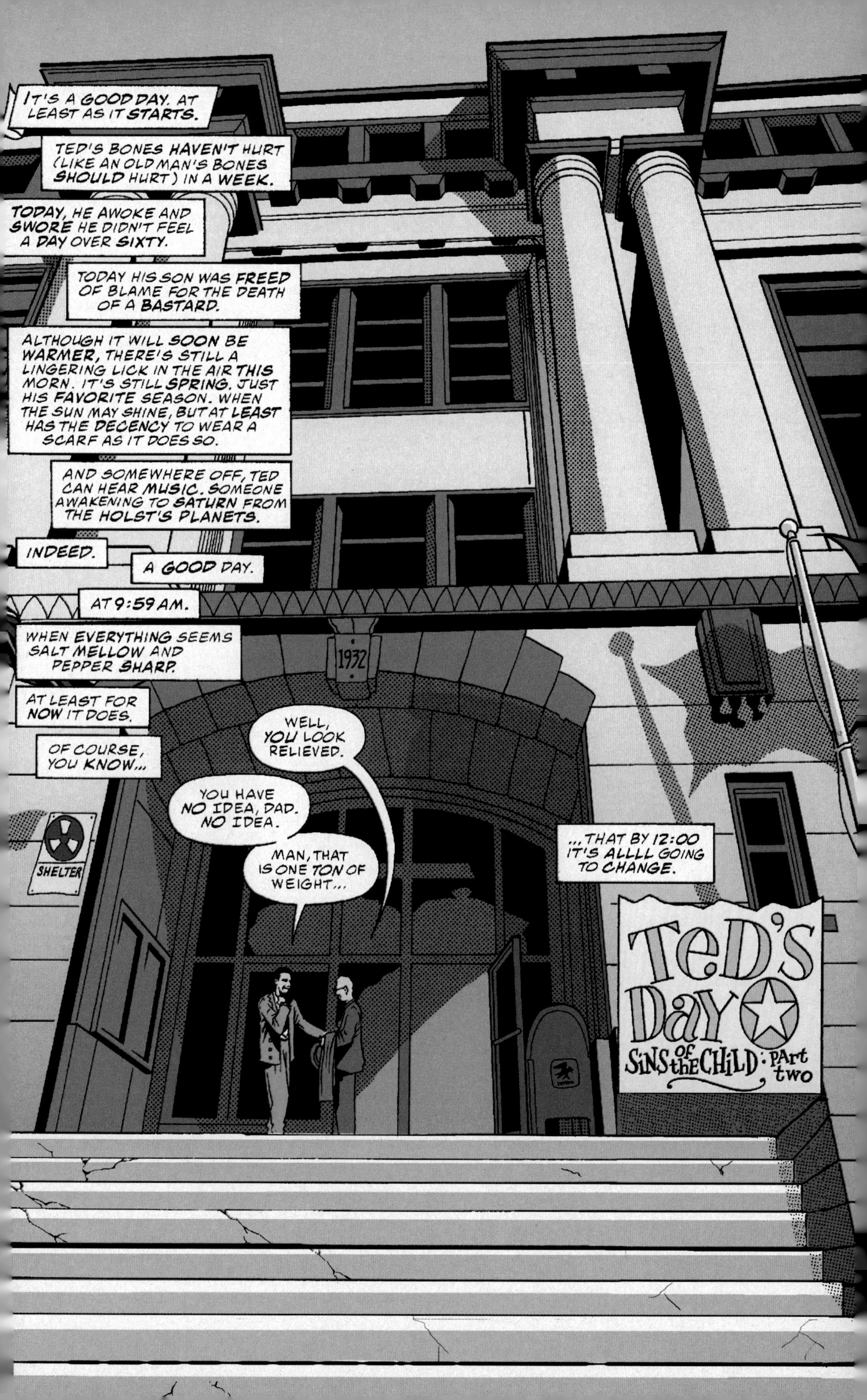
IT'S A GOOD DAY. AT LEAST AS IT STARTS.
TED'S BONES HAVEN'T HURT (LIKE AN OLD MAN'S BONES SHOULD HURT) IN A WEEK.
TODAY, HE AWOKE AND SWORE HE DIDN'T FEEL A DAY OVER SIXTY.
TODAY HIS SON WAS FREED OF BLAME FOR THE DEATH OF A BASTARD.
ALTHOUGH IT WILL SOON BE WARMER, THERE'S STILL A LINGERING LICK IN THE AIR THIS MORN. IT'S STILL SPRING. JUST HIS FAVORITE SEASON. WHEN THE SUN MAY SHINE, BUT AT LEAST HAS THE DECENCY TO WEAR A SCARF AS IT DOES SO.
AND SOMEWHERE OFF, TED CAN HEAR MUSIC. SOMEONE AWAKENING TO SATURN FROM THE HOLST'S PLANETS.
INDEED.
A GOOD DAY.
AT 9:59 AM.
WHEN EVERYTHING SEEMS SALT MELLOW AND PEPPER SHARP.
AT LEAST FOR NOW IT DOES.
OF COURSE, YOU KNOW...
1932
WELL, YOU LOOK RELIEVED.
YOU HAVE NO IDEA, DAD. NO IDEA.
MAN, THAT IS ONE TON OF WEIGHT...
SHELTER
...THAT BY 12:00 IT'S ALLLL GOING TO CHANGE.
TeD's Day
SiNS of the CHiLD: Part two

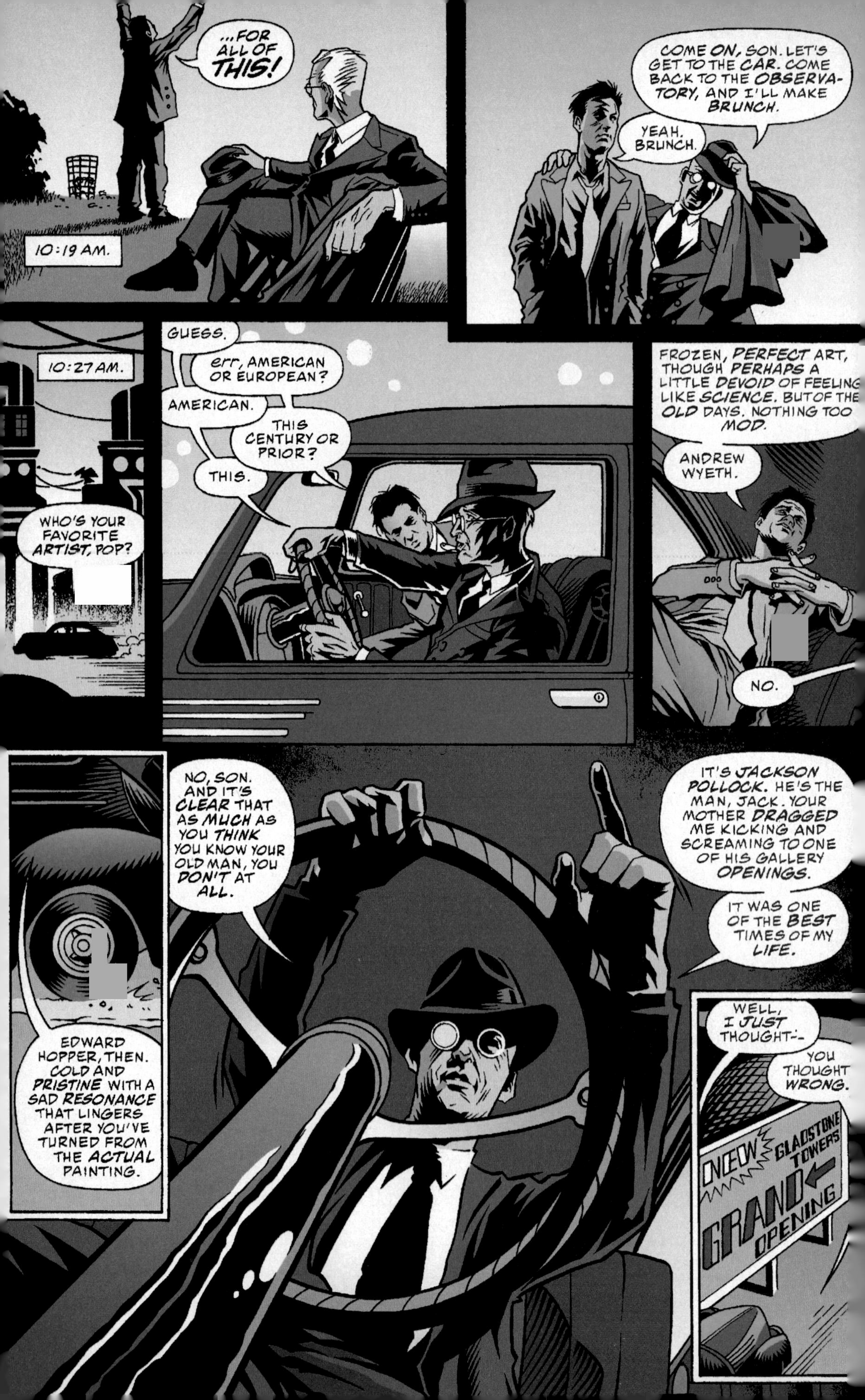
...FOR ALL OF THIS!
10:19 AM.
COME ON, SON. LET'S GET TO THE CAR. COME BACK TO THE OBSERVATORY, AND I'LL MAKE BRUNCH.
YEAH. BRUNCH.
10:27 AM.
WHO'S YOUR FAVORITE ARTIST, POP?
GUESS.
err, AMERICAN OR EUROPEAN?
AMERICAN.
THIS CENTURY OR PRIOR?
THIS.
FROZEN, PERFECT ART, THOUGH PERHAPS A LITTLE DEVOID OF FEELING LIKE SCIENCE. BUT OF THE OLD DAYS. NOTHING TOO MOD.
ANDREW WYETH.
NO.
EDWARD HOPPER, THEN. COLD AND PRISTINE WITH A SAD RESONANCE THAT LINGERS AFTER YOU'VE TURNED FROM THE ACTUAL PAINTING.
NO, SON. AND IT'S CLEAR THAT AS MUCH AS YOU THINK YOU KNOW YOUR OLD MAN, YOU DON'T AT ALL.
IT'S JACKSON POLLOCK. HE'S THE MAN, JACK. YOUR MOTHER DRAGGED ME KICKING AND SCREAMING TO ONE OF HIS GALLERY OPENINGS.
IT WAS ONE OF THE BEST TIMES OF MY LIFE.
WELL, I JUST THOUGHT--
YOU THOUGHT WRONG.
GLADSTONE TOWERS
GRAND OPENING

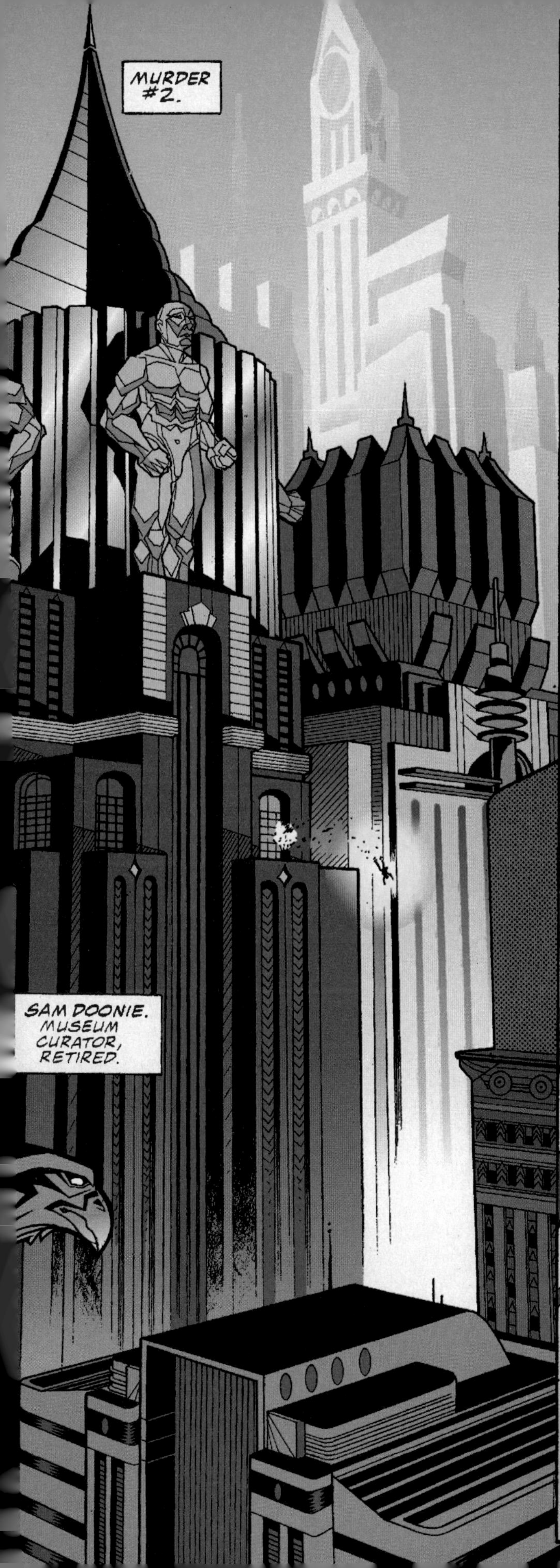
MURDER #2.
SAM DOONIE. MUSEUM CURATOR, RETIRED.

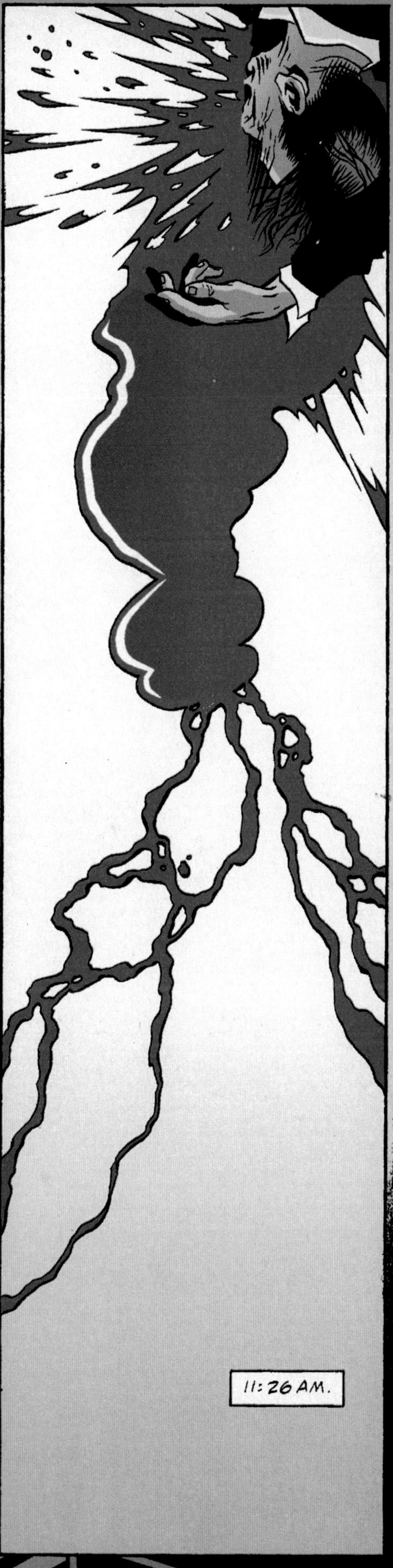
11:26 AM.

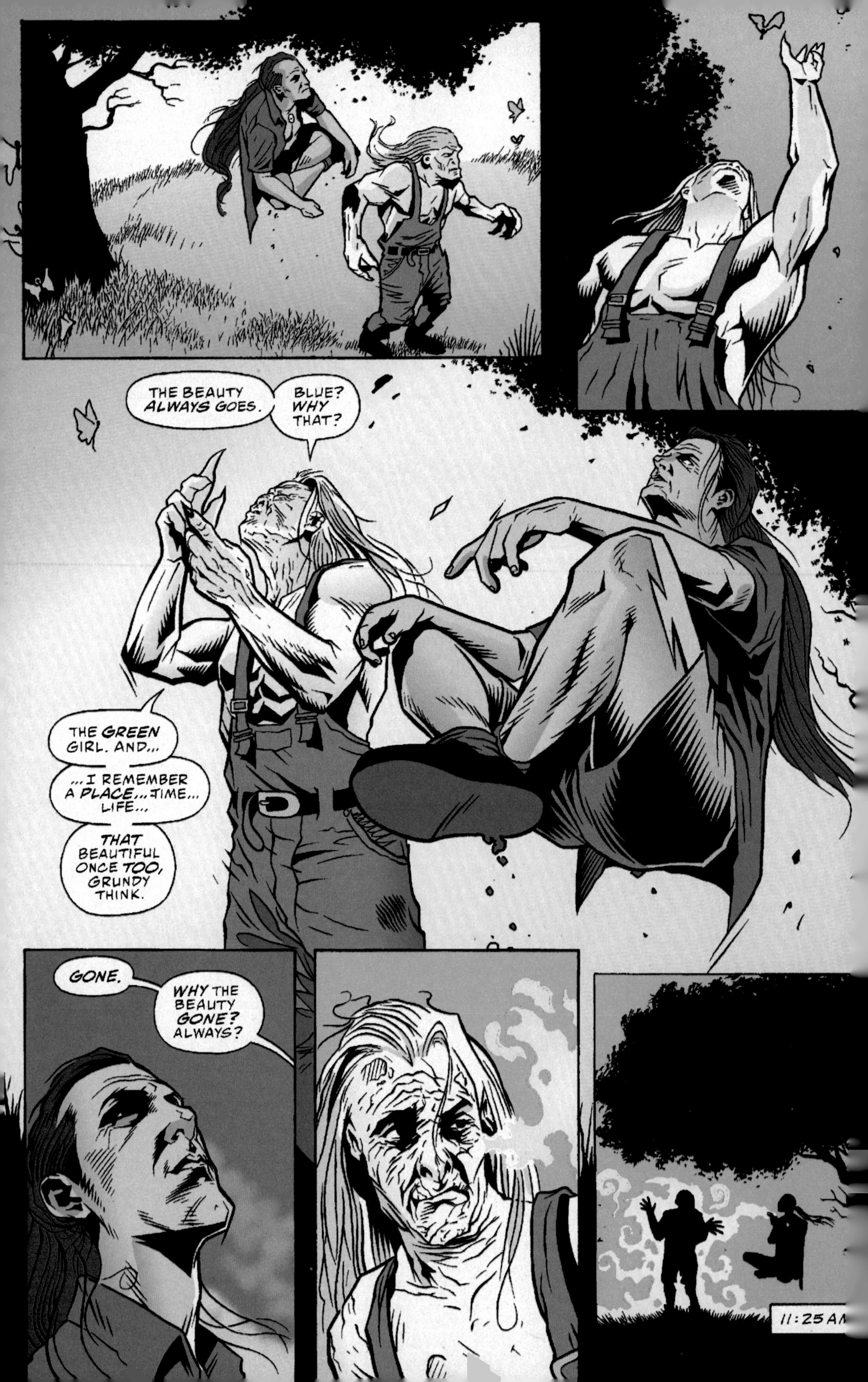
THE BEAUTY ALWAYS GOES.
BLUE? WHY THAT?
THE GREEN GIRL. AND...
...I REMEMBER A PLACE... TIME... LIFE...
THAT BEAUTIFUL ONCE TOO, GRUNDY THINK.
GONE.
WHY THE BEAUTY GONE? ALWAYS?
11:25 AM

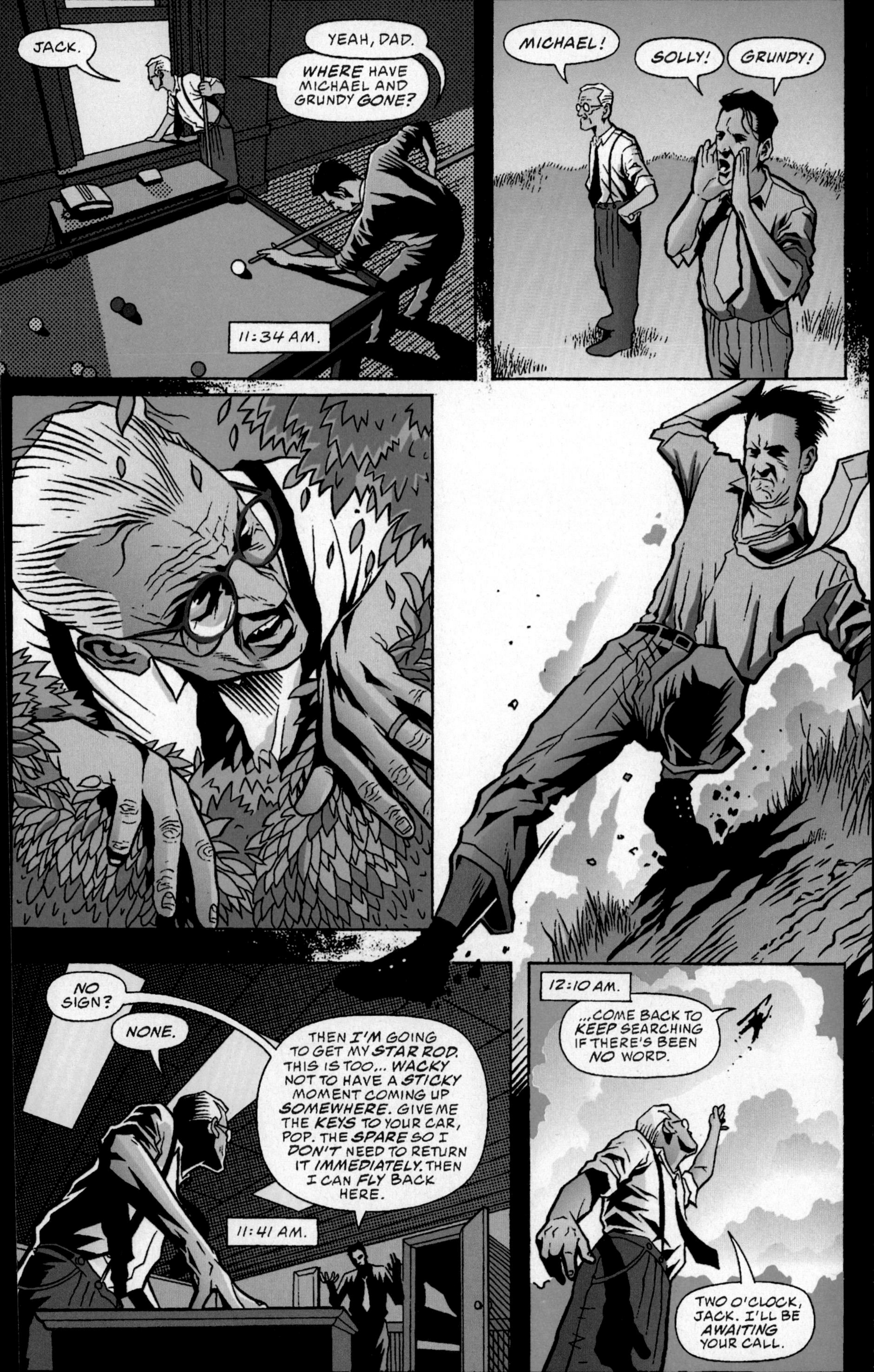
JACK.
YEAH, DAD.
WHERE HAVE MICHAEL AND GRUNDY GONE?
11:34 AM.
MICHAEL!
SOLLY!
GRUNDY!
NO SIGN?
NONE.
THEN I'M GOING TO GET MY STAR ROD. THIS IS TOO... WACKY NOT TO HAVE A STICKY MOMENT COMING UP SOMEWHERE. GIVE ME THE KEYS TO YOUR CAR, POP. THE SPARE SO I DON'T NEED TO RETURN IT IMMEDIATELY. THEN I CAN FLY BACK HERE.
11:41 AM.
12:10 AM.
...COME BACK TO KEEP SEARCHING IF THERE'S BEEN NO WORD.
TWO O'CLOCK, JACK. I'LL BE AWAITING YOUR CALL.

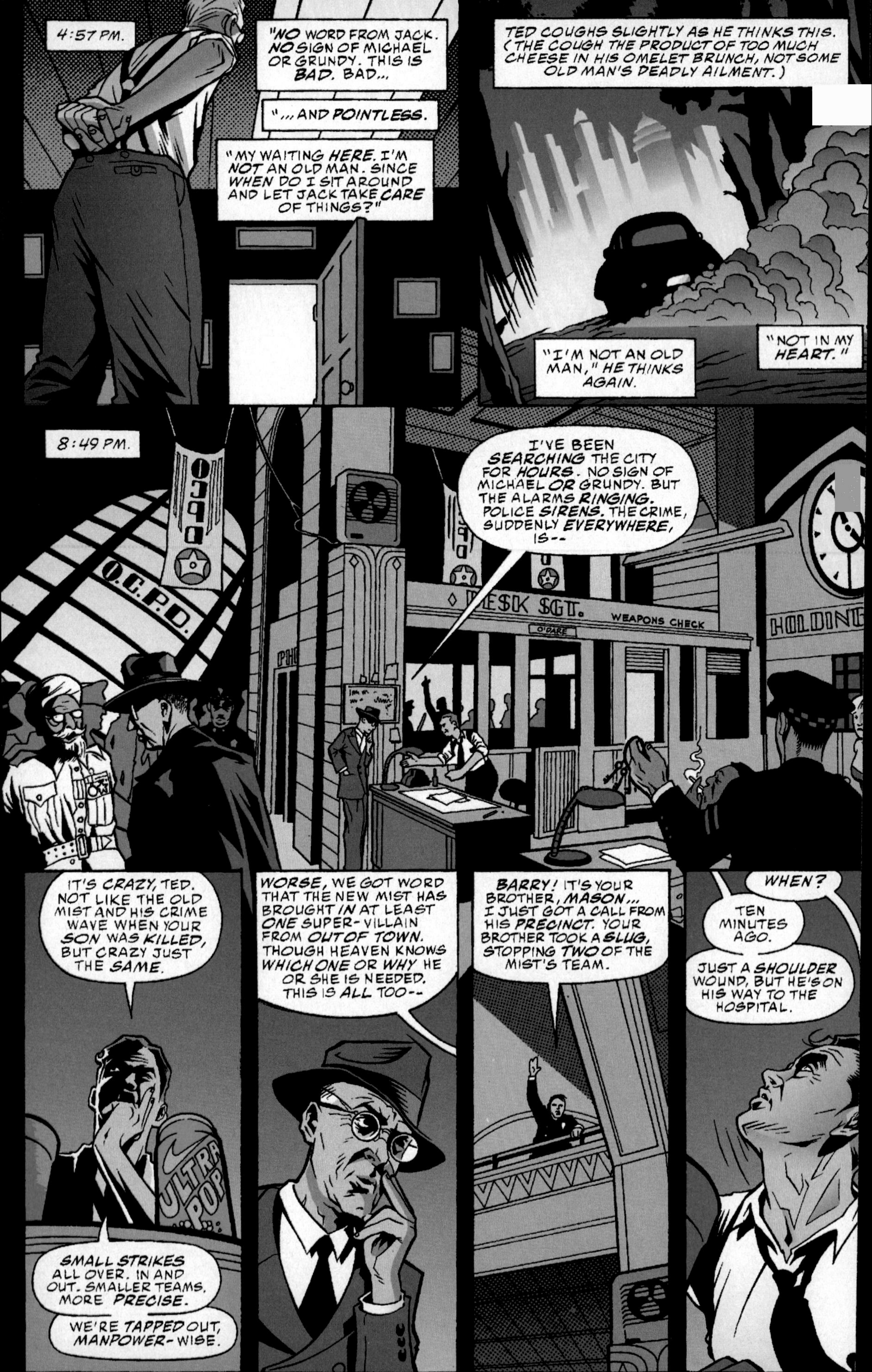
4:57 PM.
"NO WORD FROM JACK. NO SIGN OF MICHAEL OR GRUNDY. THIS IS BAD. BAD...
"...AND POINTLESS.
"MY WAITING HERE. I'M NOT AN OLD MAN. SINCE WHEN DO I SIT AROUND AND LET JACK TAKE CARE OF THINGS?"
TED COUGHS SLIGHTLY AS HE THINKS THIS. (THE COUGH THE PRODUCT OF TOO MUCH CHEESE IN HIS OMELET BRUNCH, NOT SOME OLD MAN'S DEADLY AILMENT.)
"I'M NOT AN OLD MAN," HE THINKS AGAIN.
"NOT IN MY HEART."
8:49 PM.
O.C.P.D.
DESK SGT.
WEAPONS CHECK
O'DARE
HOLDING
I'VE BEEN SEARCHING THE CITY FOR HOURS. NO SIGN OF MICHAEL OR GRUNDY. BUT THE ALARMS RINGING. POLICE SIRENS. THE CRIME, SUDDENLY EVERYWHERE, IS--
IT'S CRAZY, TED. NOT LIKE THE OLD MIST AND HIS CRIME WAVE WHEN YOUR SON WAS KILLED, BUT CRAZY JUST THE SAME.
SMALL STRIKES ALL OVER. IN AND OUT. SMALLER TEAMS, MORE PRECISE.
WE'RE TAPPED OUT, MANPOWER-WISE.
WORSE, WE GOT WORD THAT THE NEW MIST HAS BROUGHT IN AT LEAST ONE SUPER-VILLAIN FROM OUT OF TOWN. THOUGH HEAVEN KNOWS WHICH ONE OR WHY HE OR SHE IS NEEDED. THIS IS ALL TOO--
BARRY! IT'S YOUR BROTHER, MASON... I JUST GOT A CALL FROM HIS PRECINCT. YOUR BROTHER TOOK A SLUG, STOPPING TWO OF THE MIST'S TEAM.
WHEN?
TEN MINUTES AGO.
JUST A SHOULDER WOUND, BUT HE'S ON HIS WAY TO THE HOSPITAL.

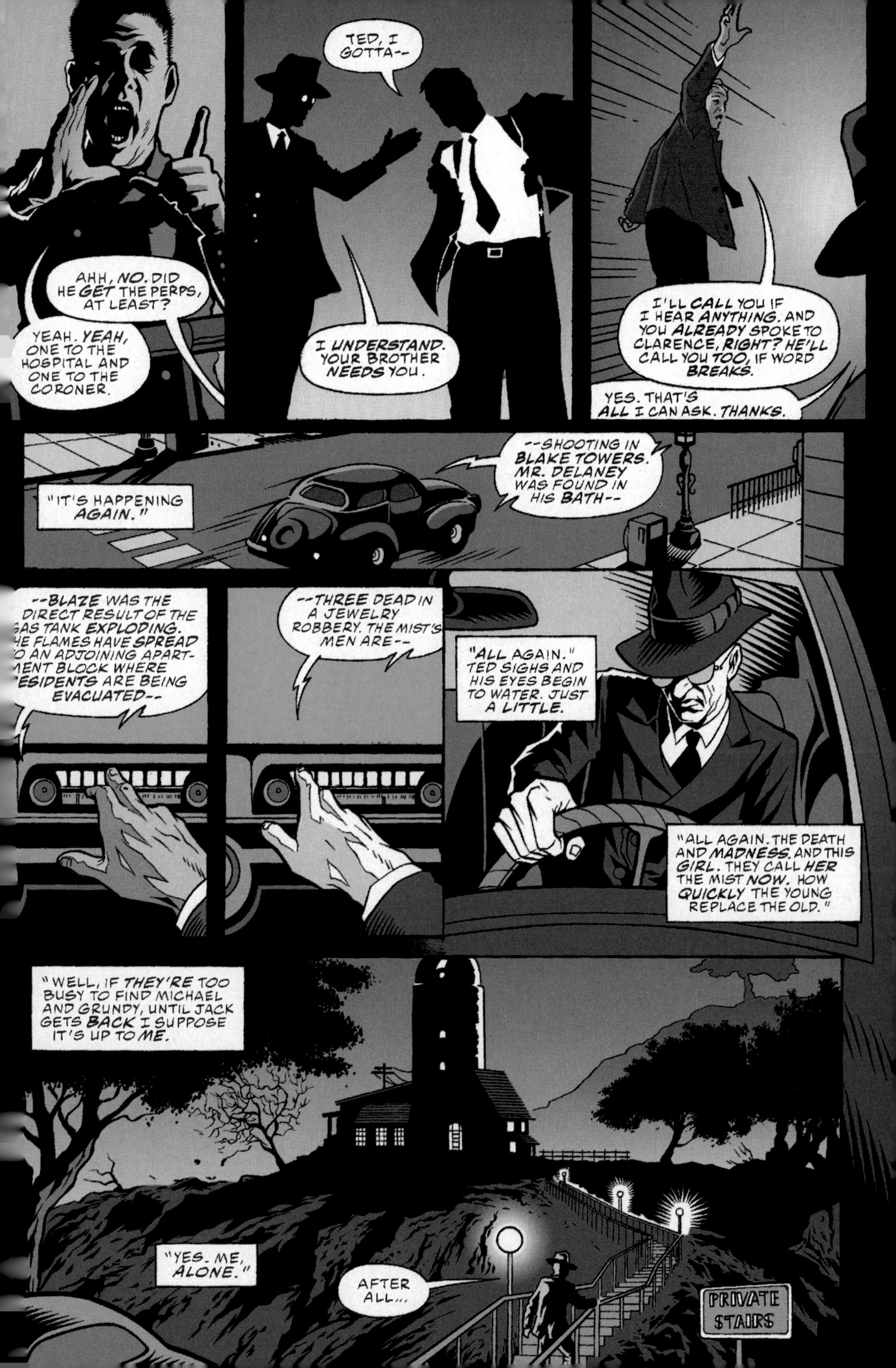
TED, I GOTTA--
AHH, NO. DID HE GET THE PERPS, AT LEAST?
YEAH. YEAH, ONE TO THE HOSPITAL AND ONE TO THE CORONER.
I UNDERSTAND. YOUR BROTHER NEEDS YOU.
I'LL CALL YOU IF I HEAR ANYTHING. AND YOU ALREADY SPOKE TO CLARENCE, RIGHT? HE'LL CALL YOU TOO, IF WORD BREAKS.
YES. THAT'S ALL I CAN ASK. THANKS.
"IT'S HAPPENING AGAIN."
--SHOOTING IN BLAKE TOWERS. MR. DELANEY WAS FOUND IN HIS BATH--
--BLAZE WAS THE DIRECT RESULT OF THE GAS TANK EXPLODING. THE FLAMES HAVE SPREAD TO AN ADJOINING APARTMENT BLOCK WHERE RESIDENTS ARE BEING EVACUATED--
--THREE DEAD IN A JEWELRY ROBBERY. THE MIST'S MEN ARE--
"ALL AGAIN." TED SIGHS AND HIS EYES BEGIN TO WATER. JUST A LITTLE.
"ALL AGAIN. THE DEATH AND MADNESS. AND THIS GIRL. THEY CALL HER THE MIST NOW. HOW QUICKLY THE YOUNG REPLACE THE OLD."
"WELL, IF THEY'RE TOO BUSY TO FIND MICHAEL AND GRUNDY, UNTIL JACK GETS BACK I SUPPOSE IT'S UP TO ME.
"YES. ME, ALONE."
AFTER ALL...
PRIVATE STAIRS

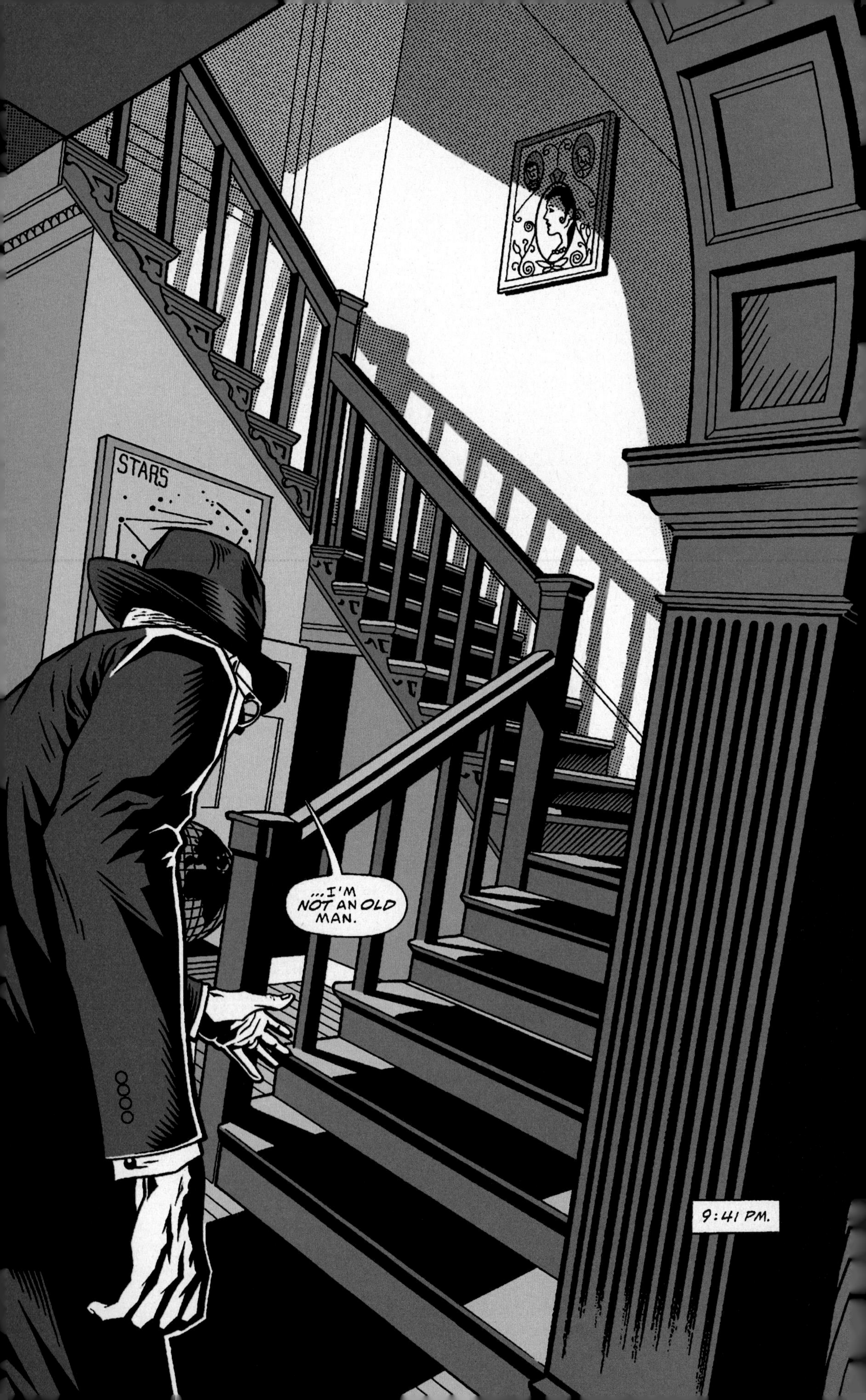
STARS
...I'M NOT AN OLD MAN.
9:41 PM.

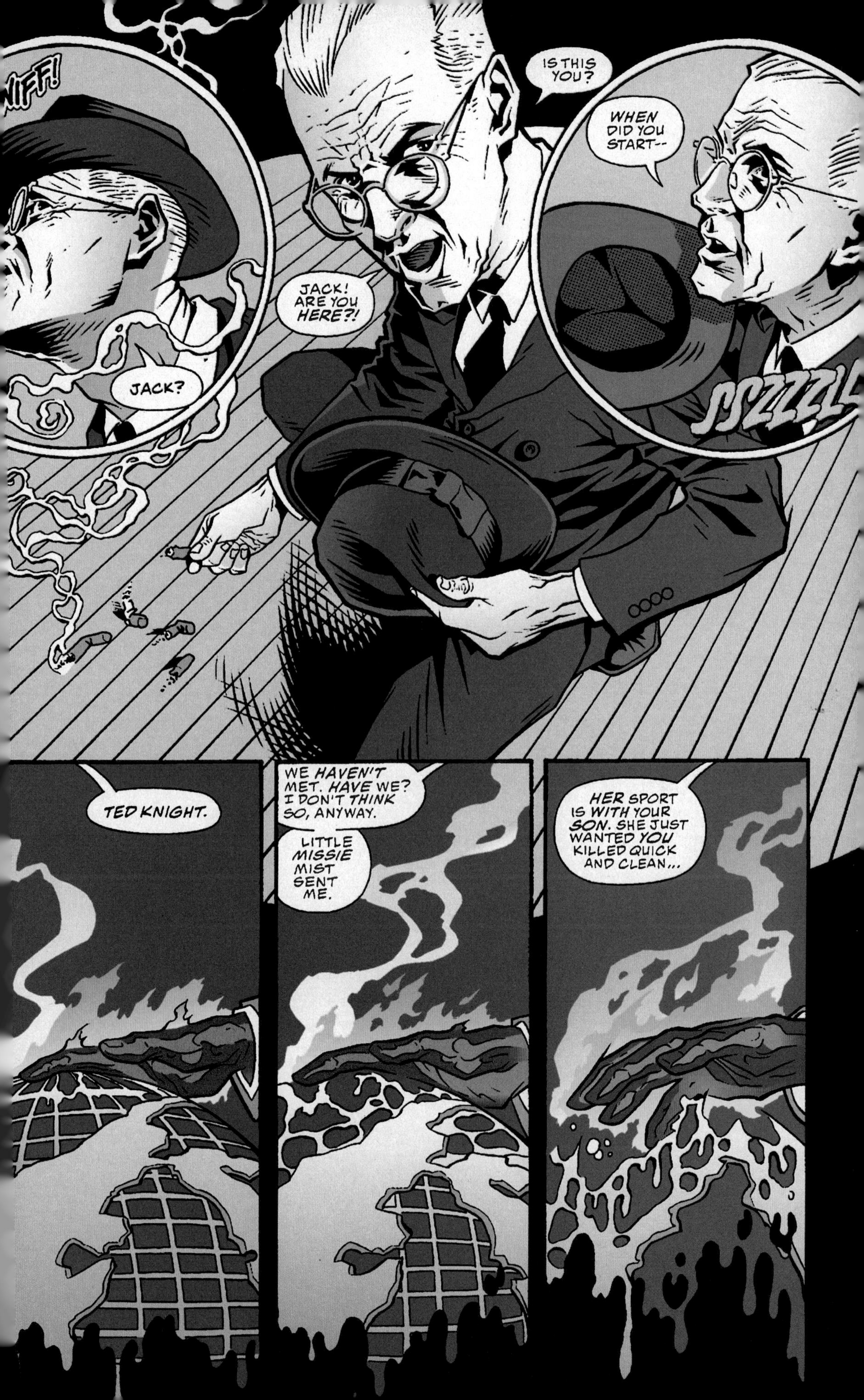

SNIFF!
JACK?
JACK! ARE YOU HERE?!
IS THIS YOU?
WHEN DID YOU START--
SSZZZLE
TED KNIGHT.
WE HAVEN'T MET. HAVE WE? I DON'T THINK SO, ANYWAY.
LITTLE MISSIE MIST SENT ME.
HER SPORT IS WITH YOUR SON. SHE JUST WANTED YOU KILLED QUICK AND CLEAN...

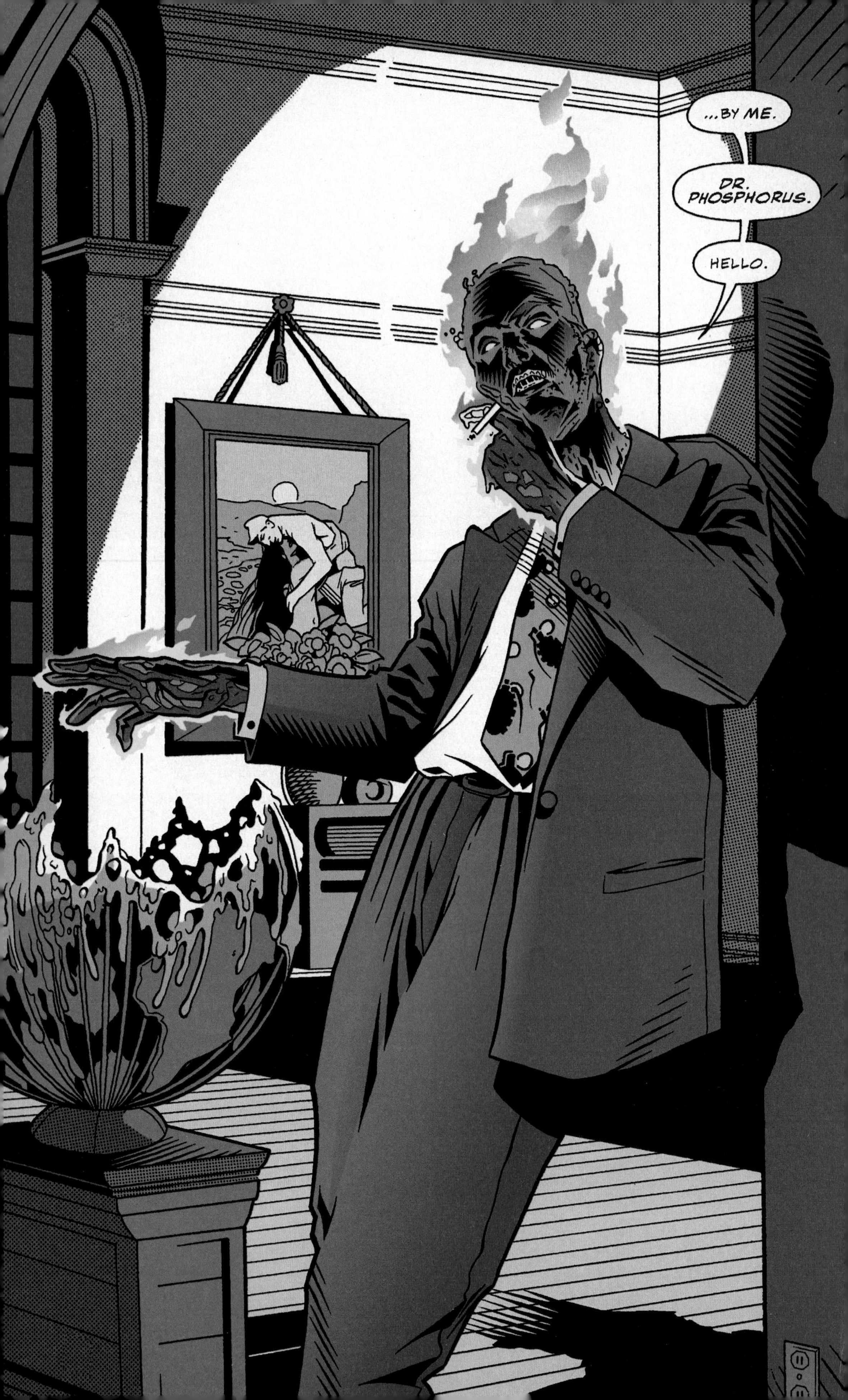
...BY ME.
DR. PHOSPHORUS.
HELLO.

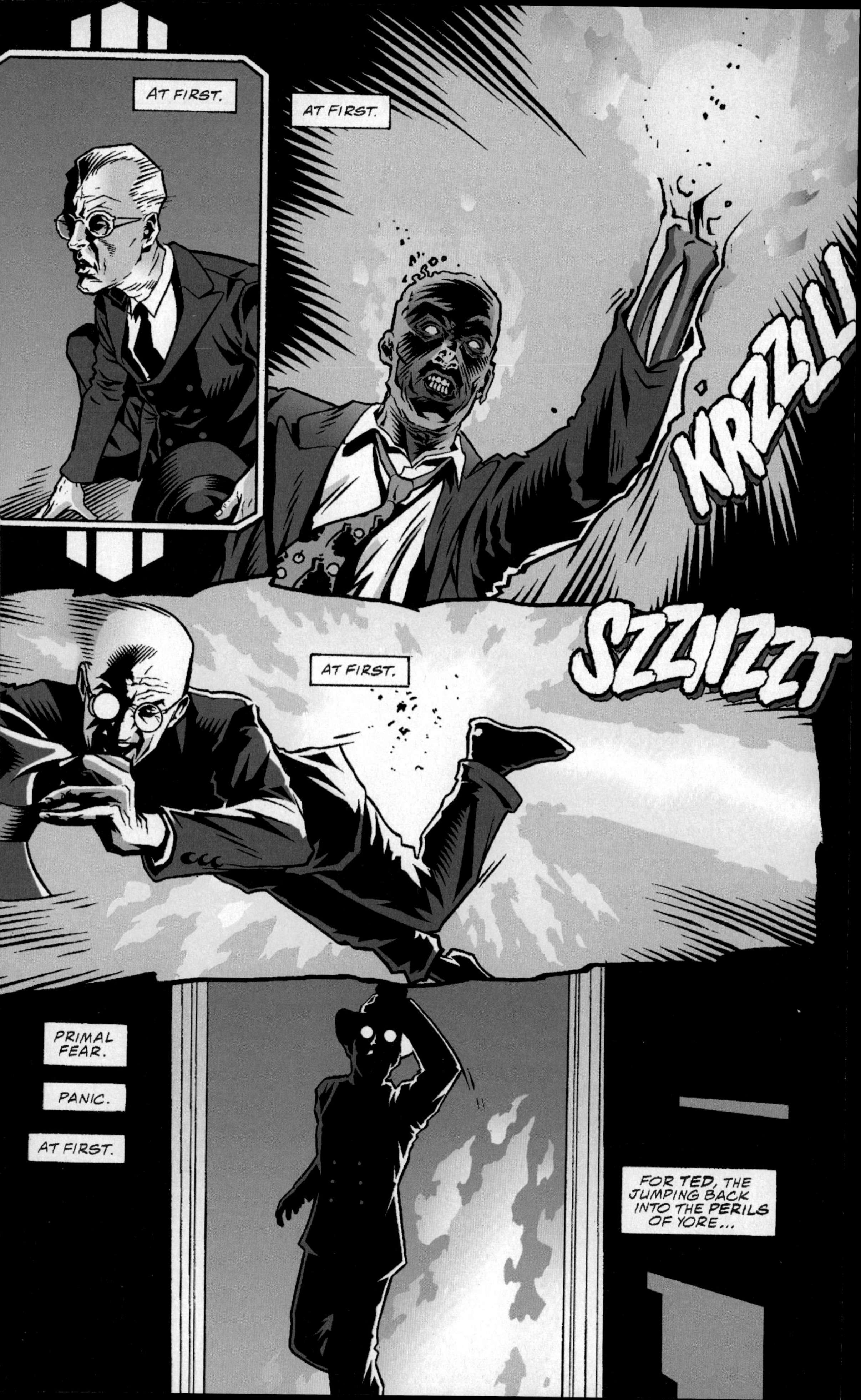
AT FIRST.
AT FIRST.
KRZZLL
SZZIIZZT
AT FIRST.
PRIMAL FEAR.
PANIC.
AT FIRST.
FOR TED, THE JUMPING BACK INTO THE PERILS OF YORE...

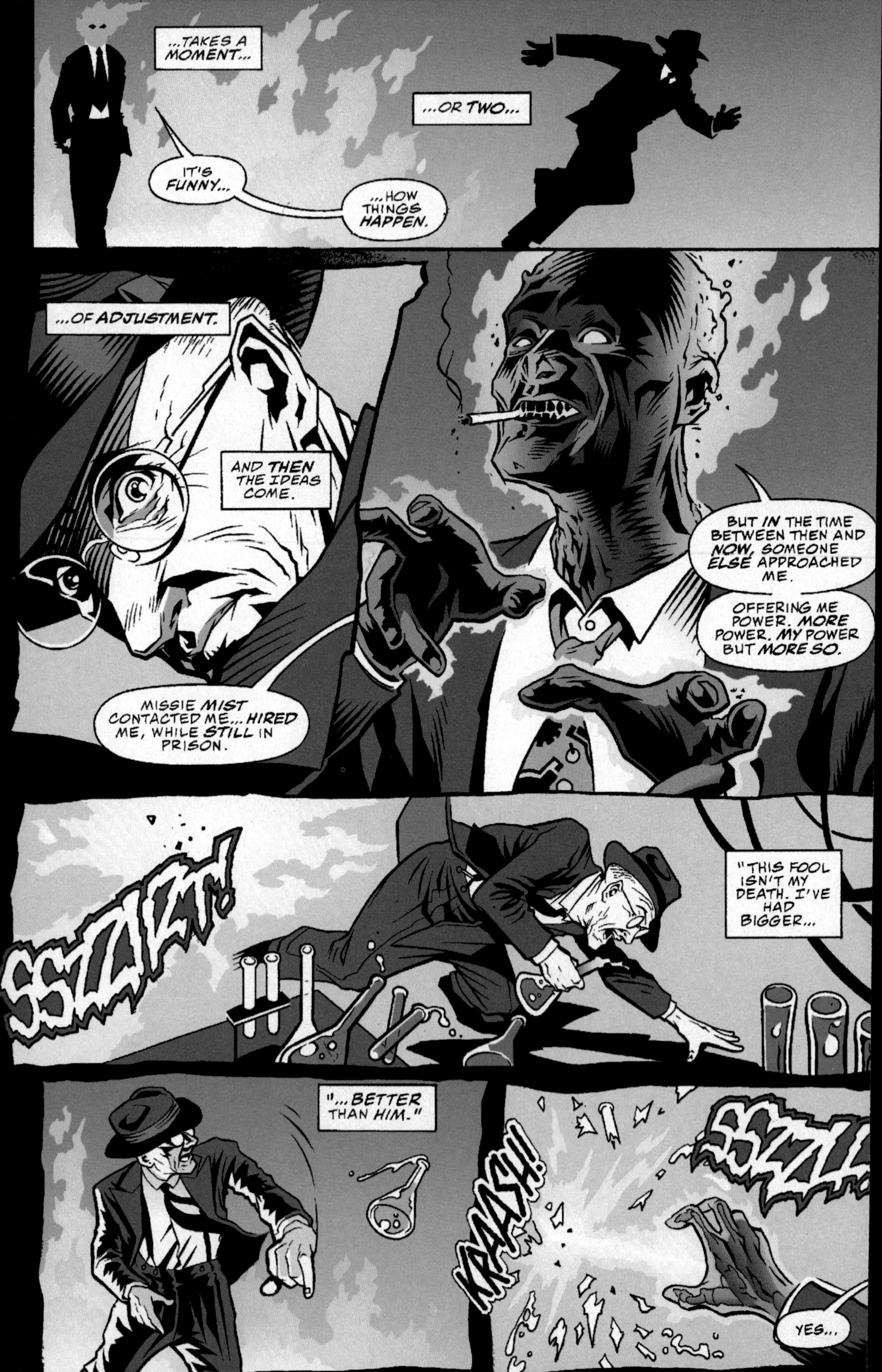

...TAKES A MOMENT...
...OR TWO...
IT'S FUNNY...
...HOW THINGS HAPPEN.
...OF ADJUSTMENT.
AND THEN THE IDEAS COME.
BUT IN THE TIME BETWEEN THEN AND NOW, SOMEONE ELSE APPROACHED ME.
OFFERING ME POWER. MORE POWER. MY POWER BUT MORE SO.
MISSIE MIST CONTACTED ME... HIRED ME, WHILE STILL IN PRISON.
SSZZZZT!
"THIS FOOL ISN'T MY DEATH. I'VE HAD BIGGER...
"...BETTER THAN HIM."
KRAASH!
SSZZ
YES...

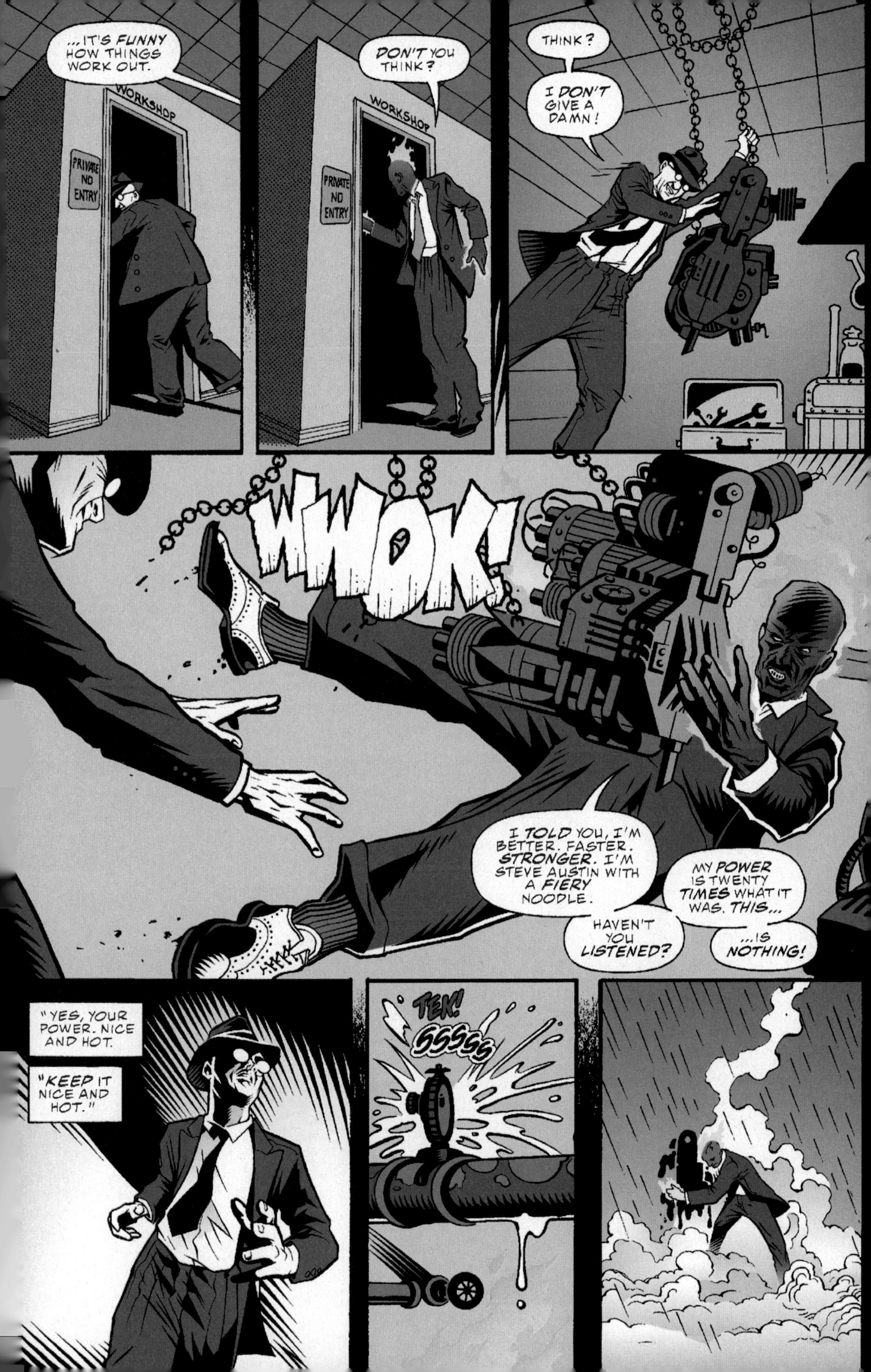
...IT'S FUNNY HOW THINGS WORK OUT.
WORKSHOP
PRIVATE NO ENTRY
DON'T YOU THINK?
WORKSHOP
PRIVATE NO ENTRY
THINK?
I DON'T GIVE A DAMN!
WWOK!
I TOLD YOU, I'M BETTER. FASTER. STRONGER. I'M STEVE AUSTIN WITH A FIERY NOODLE.
HAVEN'T YOU LISTENED?
MY POWER IS TWENTY TIMES WHAT IT WAS. THIS...
...IS NOTHING!
"YES, YOUR POWER. NICE AND HOT.
"KEEP IT NICE AND HOT."
TEK!
SSSSS

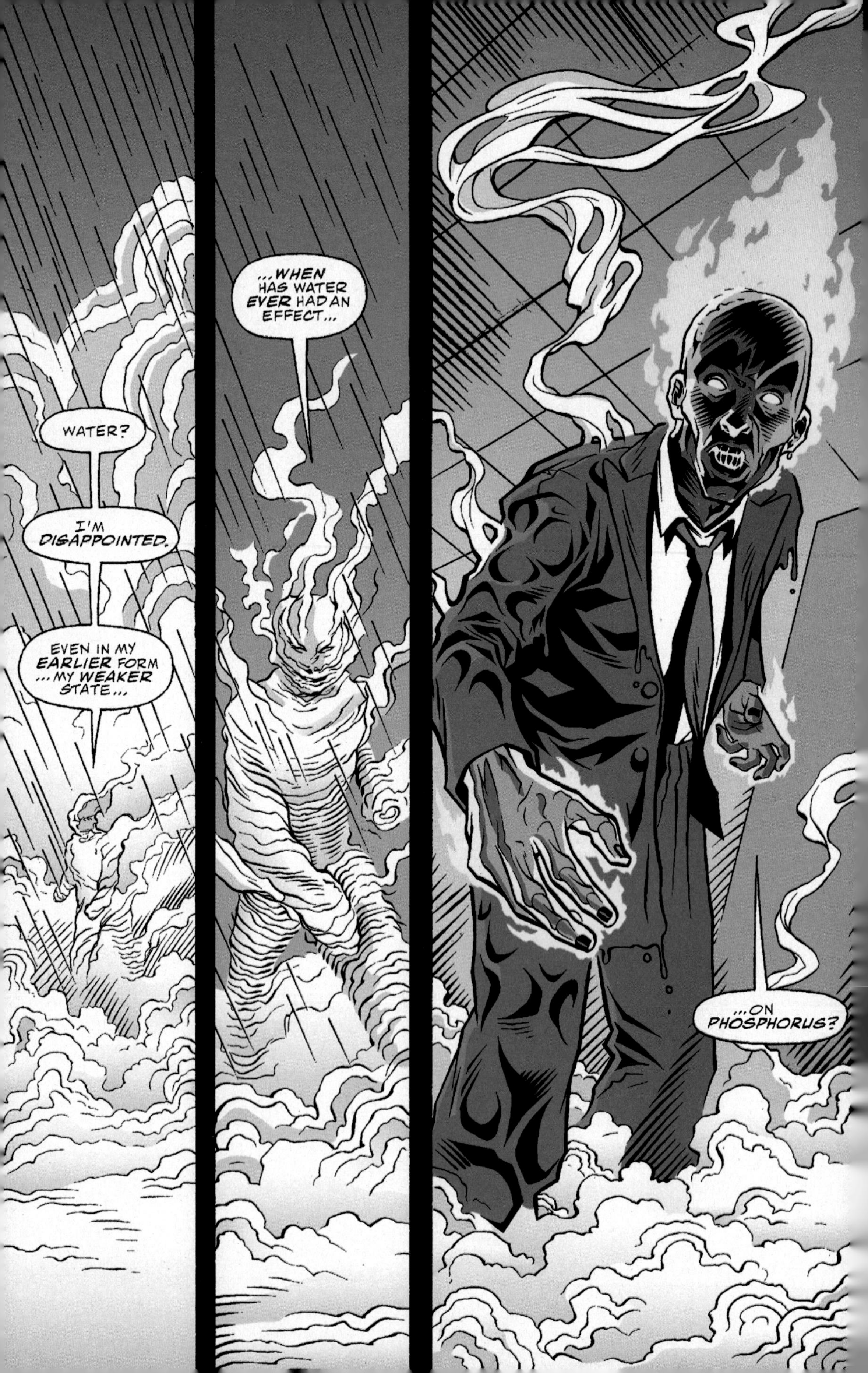
WATER?
I'M DISAPPOINTED.
EVEN IN MY EARLIER FORM ...MY WEAKER STATE...
...WHEN HAS WATER EVER HAD AN EFFECT...
...ON PHOSPHORUS?

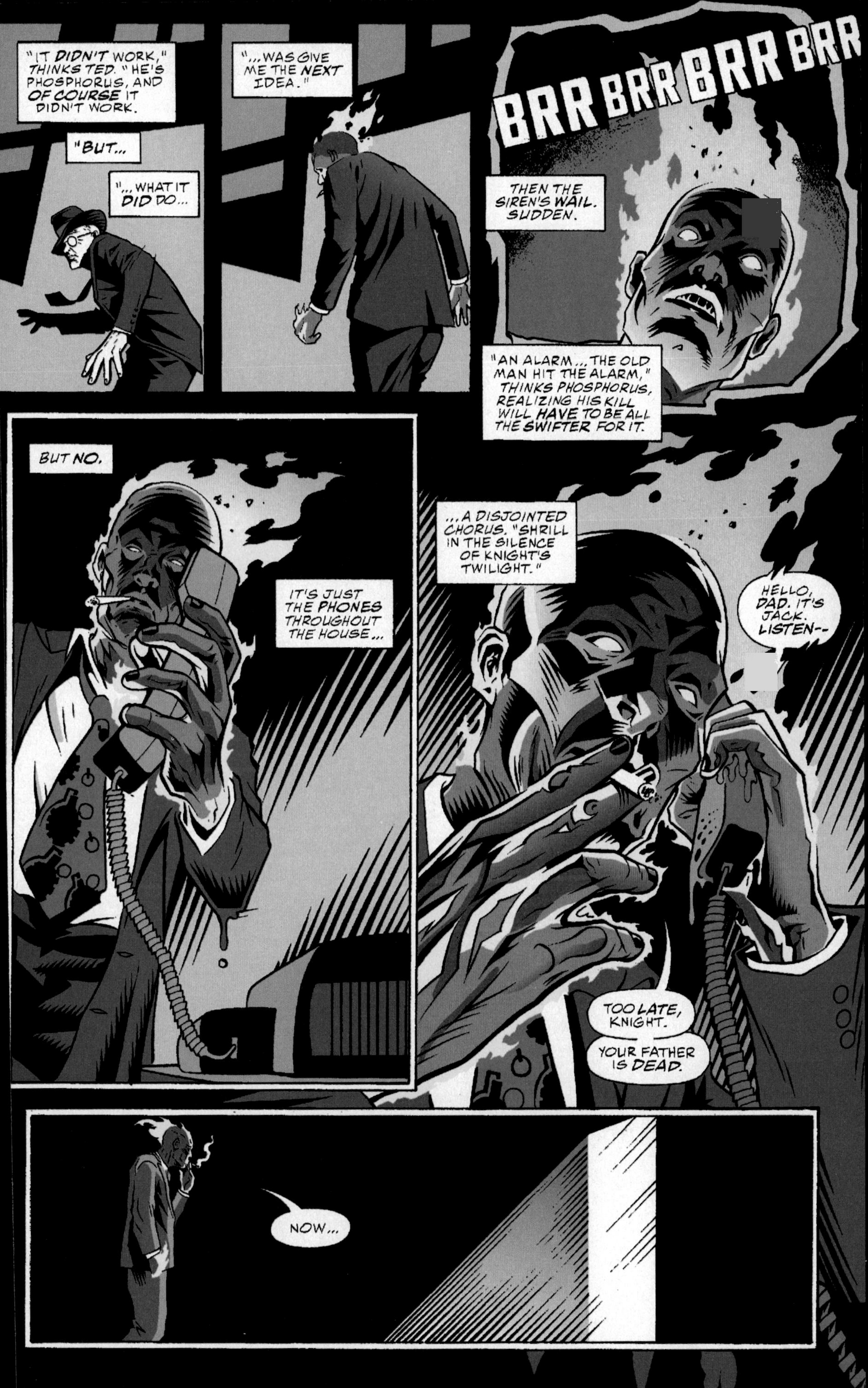
"IT DIDN'T WORK," THINKS TED. "HE'S PHOSPHORUS, AND OF COURSE IT DIDN'T WORK.
"BUT...
"...WHAT IT DID DO...
"...WAS GIVE ME THE NEXT IDEA."
BRR BRR BRR BRR
THEN THE SIREN'S WAIL. SUDDEN.
"AN ALARM... THE OLD MAN HIT THE ALARM," THINKS PHOSPHORUS, REALIZING HIS KILL WILL HAVE TO BE ALL THE SWIFTER FOR IT.
BUT NO.
IT'S JUST THE PHONES THROUGHOUT THE HOUSE...
...A DISJOINTED CHORUS. "SHRILL IN THE SILENCE OF KNIGHT'S TWILIGHT."
HELLO, DAD. IT'S JACK. LISTEN--
TOO LATE, KNIGHT.
YOUR FATHER IS DEAD.
NOW...

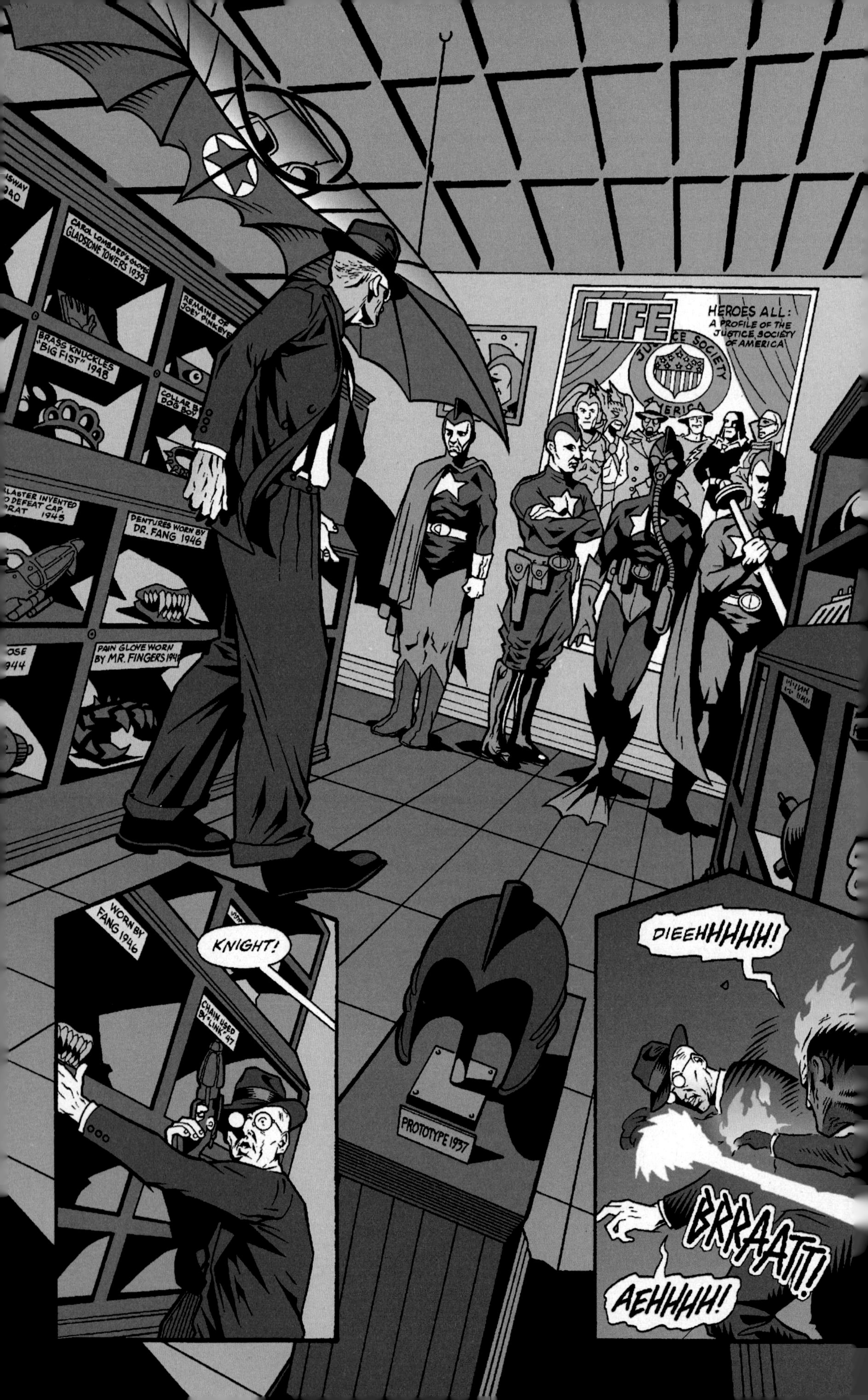

CAROL LOMBARD'S GLOVES GLADSONE TOWERS 1939
BRASS KNUCKLES "BIG FIST" 1948
DENTURES WORN BY DR. FANG 1946
LIFE
HEROES ALL: A PROFILE OF THE JUSTICE SOCIETY OF AMERICA
WORN BY FANG 1946
CHAIN USED BY "LINK" '47
KNIGHT!
PROTOTYPE 1937
DIEEHHHHH!
BRRAATT!
AEHHHH!

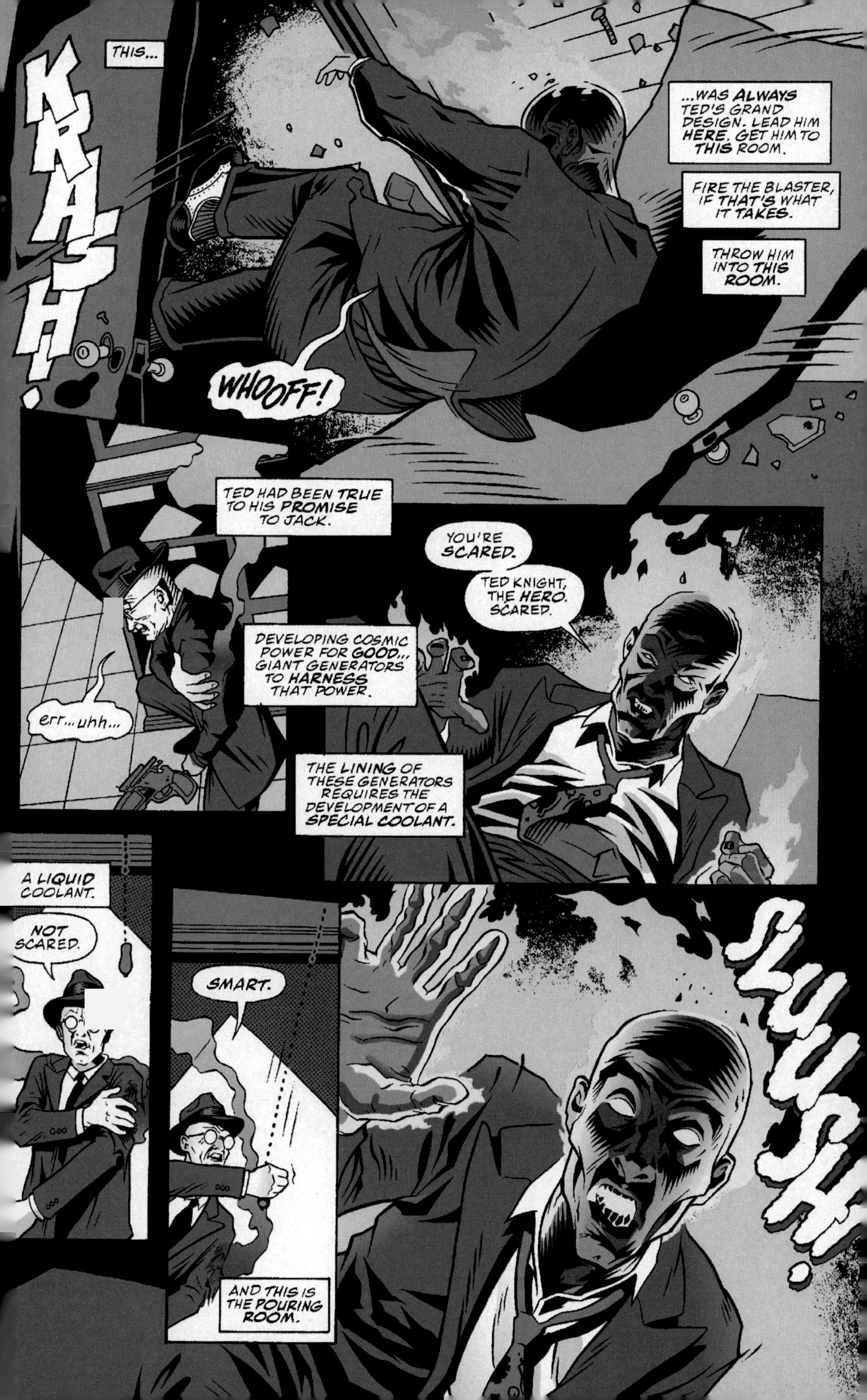
THIS...
KRASH!
...WAS ALWAYS TED'S GRAND DESIGN. LEAD HIM HERE. GET HIM TO THIS ROOM.
FIRE THE BLASTER, IF THAT'S WHAT IT TAKES.
THROW HIM INTO THIS ROOM.
WHOOFF!
TED HAD BEEN TRUE TO HIS PROMISE TO JACK.
err...uhh...
DEVELOPING COSMIC POWER FOR GOOD... GIANT GENERATORS TO HARNESS THAT POWER.
YOU'RE SCARED.
TED KNIGHT, THE HERO. SCARED.
THE LINING OF THESE GENERATORS REQUIRES THE DEVELOPMENT OF A SPECIAL COOLANT.
A LIQUID COOLANT.
NOT SCARED.
SMART.
AND THIS IS THE POURING ROOM.
SLUUSH!

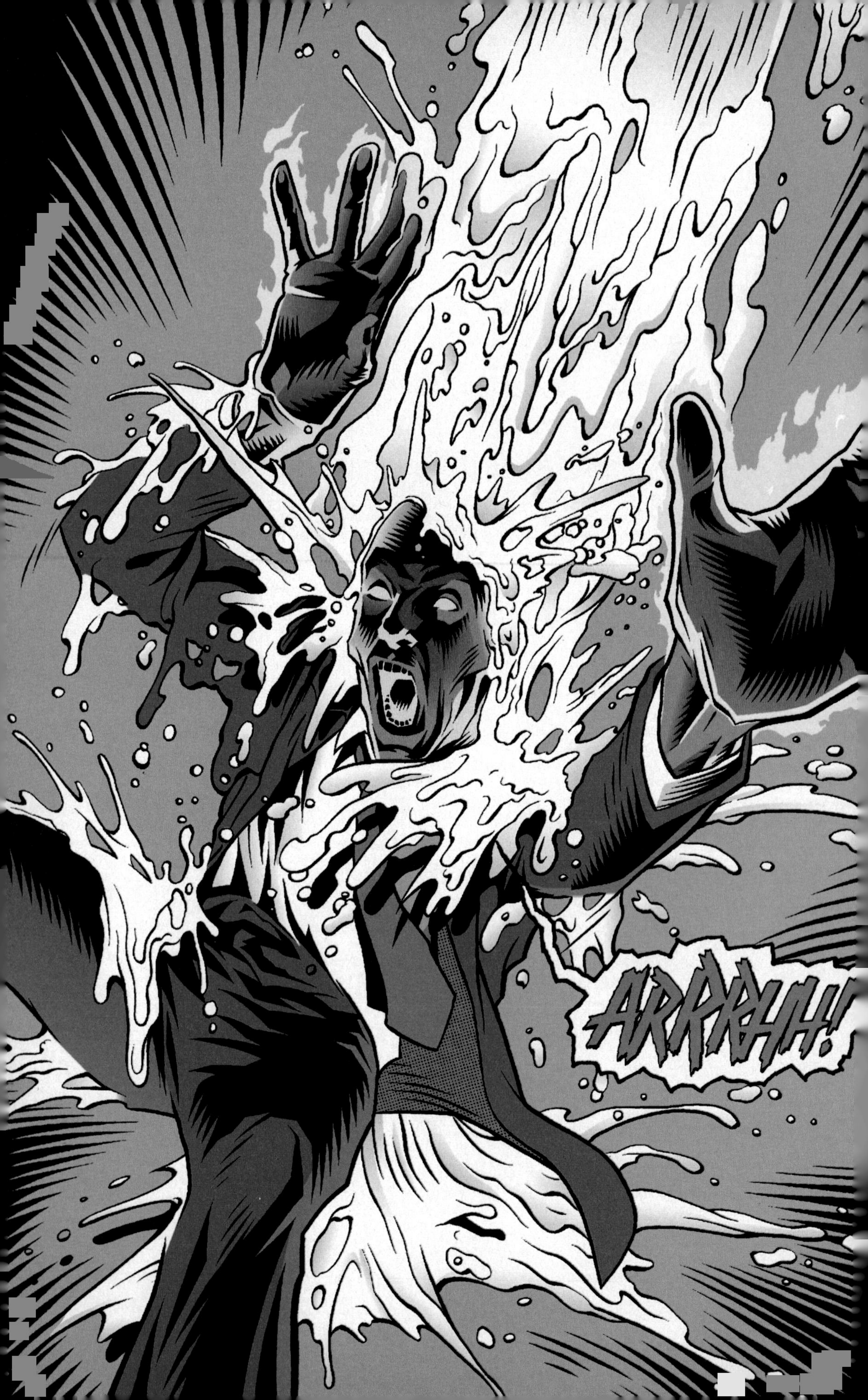
ARRRHH!

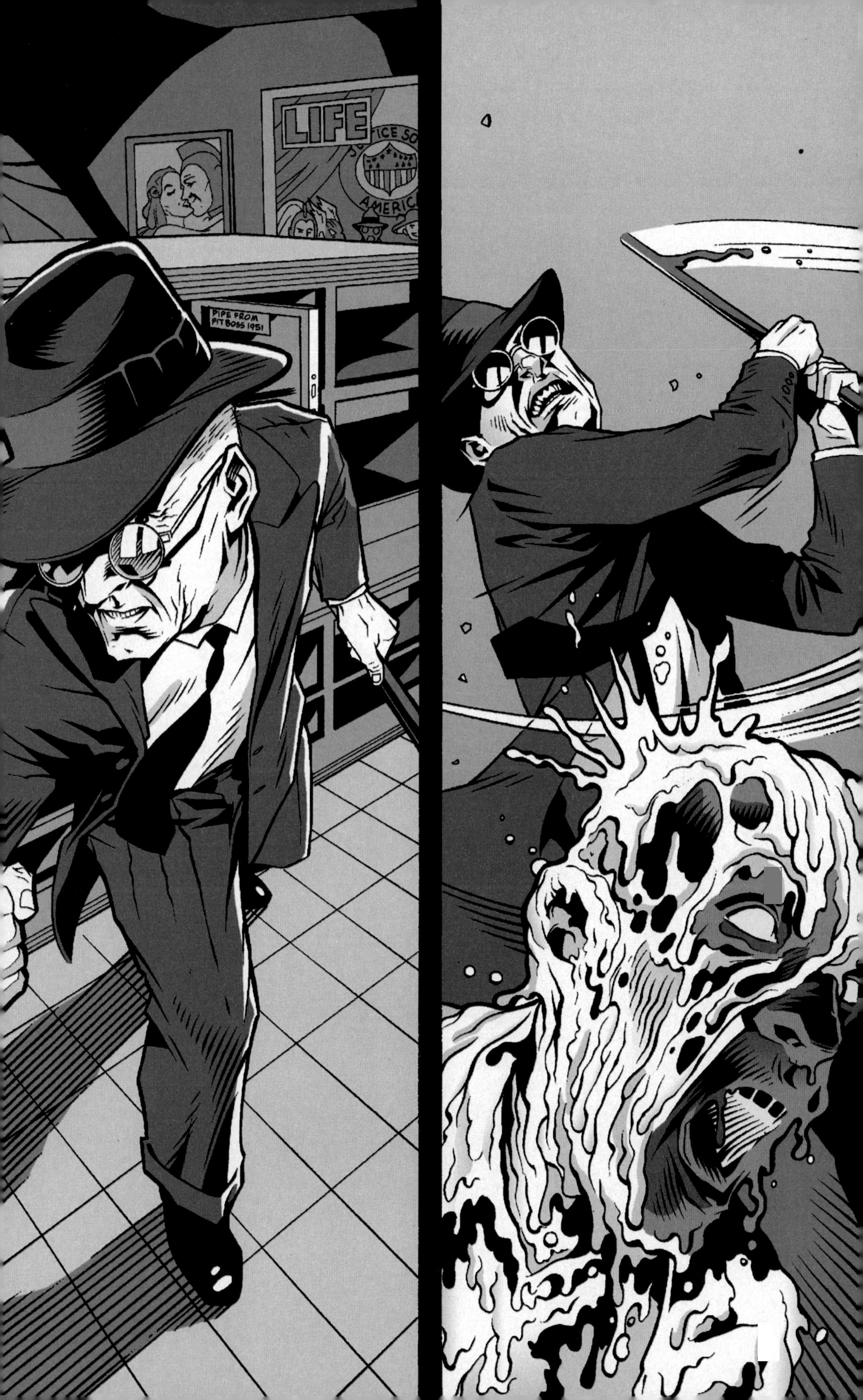
LIFE
PIPE FROM
PIT BOSS 1951

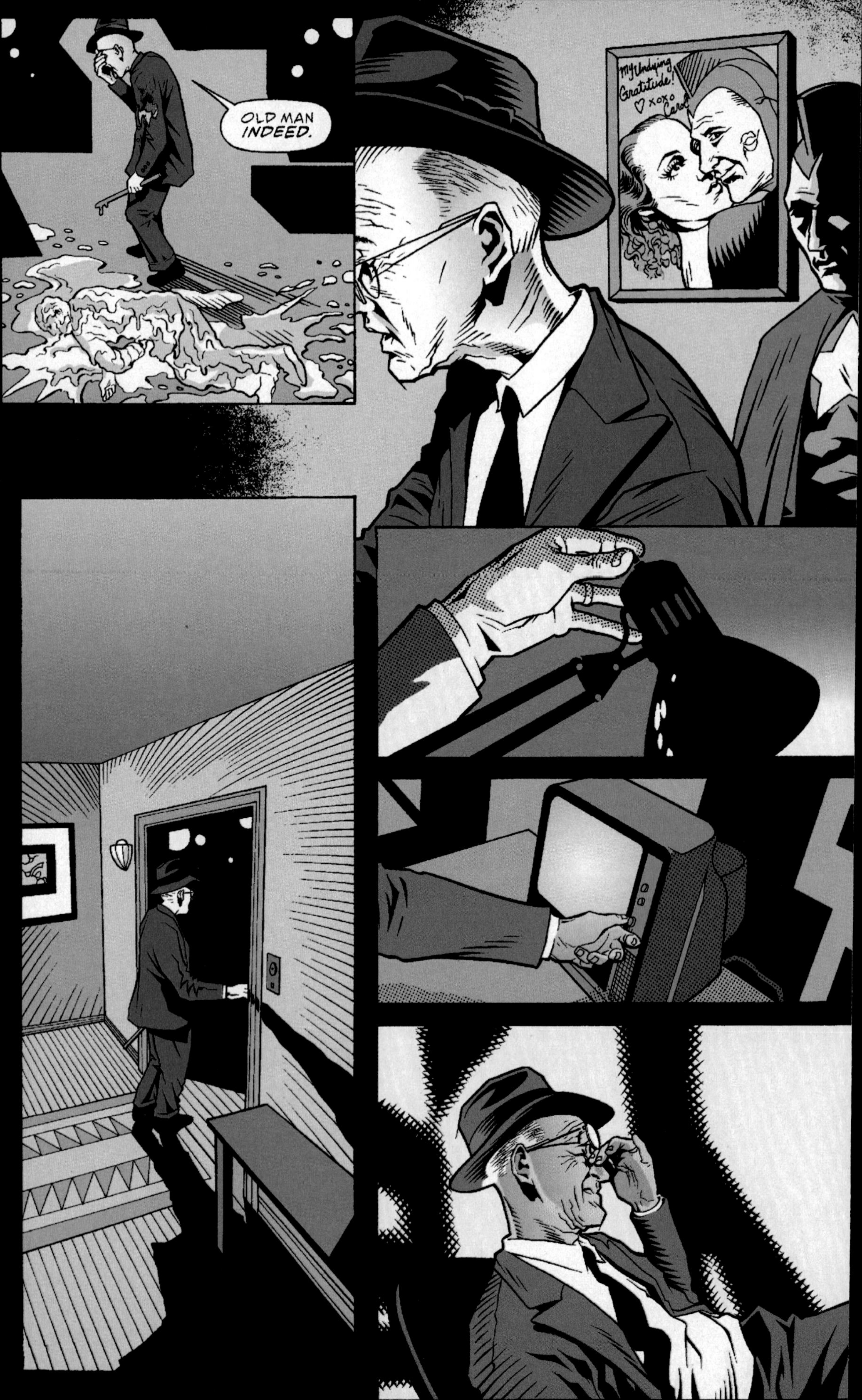
OLD MAN INDEED.
My Undying Gratitude! ♡ xoxo Carol

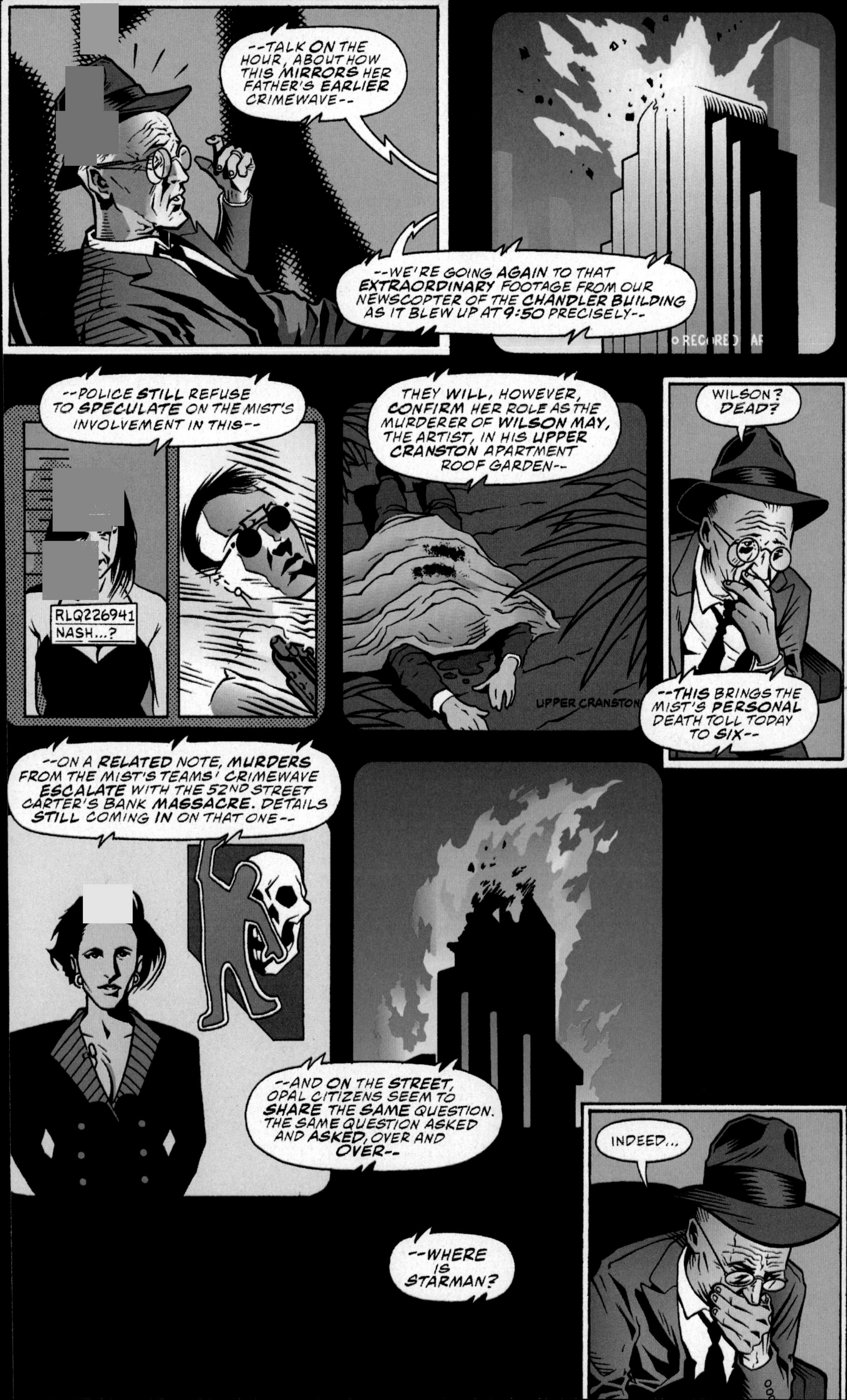
--TALK ON THE HOUR, ABOUT HOW THIS MIRRORS HER FATHER'S EARLIER CRIMEWAVE--
--WE'RE GOING AGAIN TO THAT EXTRAORDINARY FOOTAGE FROM OUR NEWSCOPTER OF THE CHANDLER BUILDING AS IT BLEW UP AT 9:50 PRECISELY--
--POLICE STILL REFUSE TO SPECULATE ON THE MIST'S INVOLVEMENT IN THIS--
RLQ226941
NASH...?
THEY WILL, HOWEVER, CONFIRM HER ROLE AS THE MURDERER OF WILSON MAY, THE ARTIST, IN HIS UPPER CRANSTON APARTMENT ROOF GARDEN--
UPPER CRANSTON
WILSON? DEAD?
--THIS BRINGS THE MIST'S PERSONAL DEATH TOLL TODAY TO SIX--
--ON A RELATED NOTE, MURDERS FROM THE MIST'S TEAMS' CRIMEWAVE ESCALATE WITH THE 52ND STREET CARTER'S BANK MASSACRE. DETAILS STILL COMING IN ON THAT ONE--
--AND ON THE STREET, OPAL CITIZENS SEEM TO SHARE THE SAME QUESTION. THE SAME QUESTION ASKED AND ASKED, OVER AND OVER--
INDEED...
--WHERE IS STARMAN?

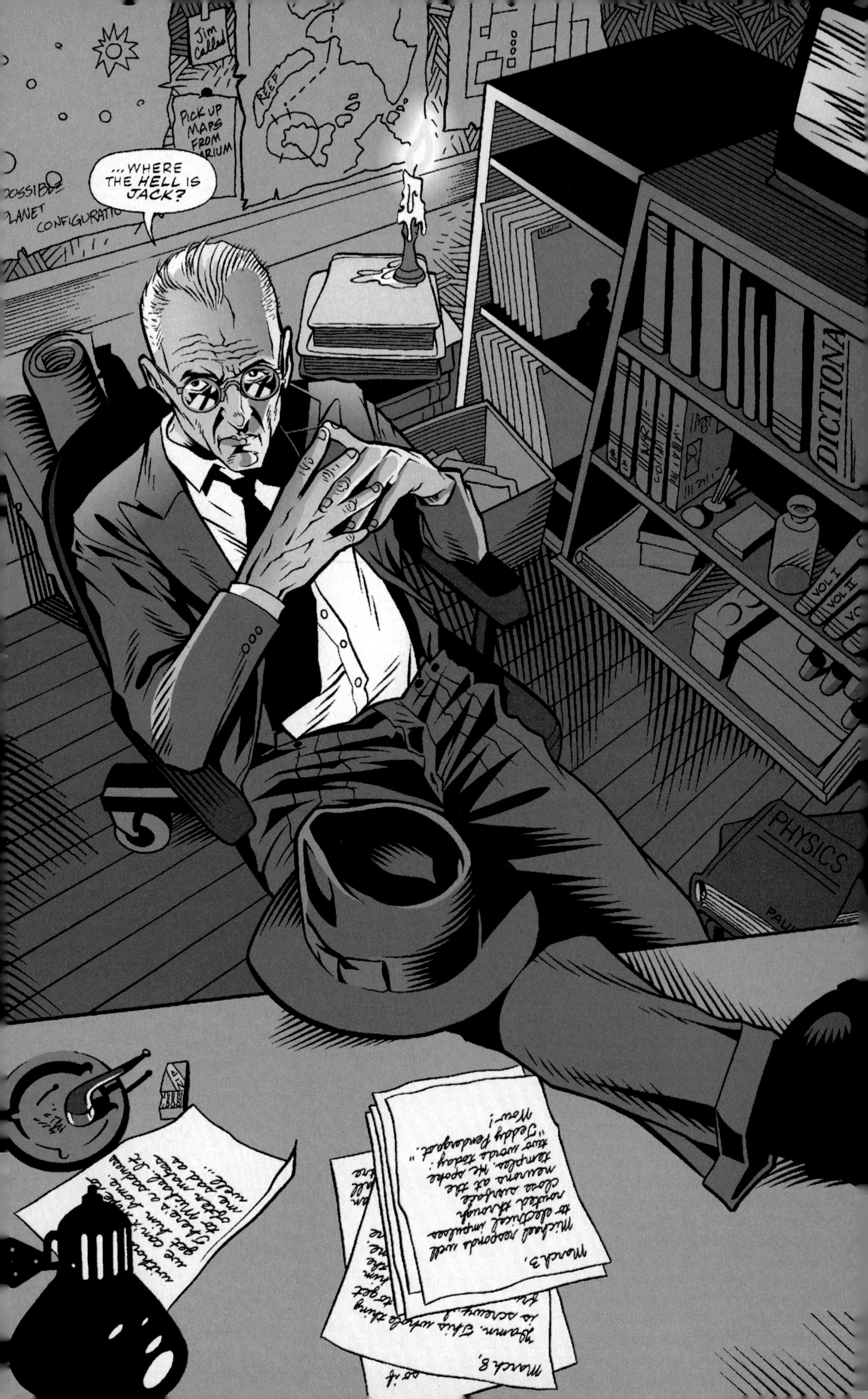
...WHERE THE HELL IS JACK?
Jim Called
PICK UP MAPS FROM
REEF
PLANET CONFIGURATIO
DICTIONA
PHYSICS
VOL I
VOL II

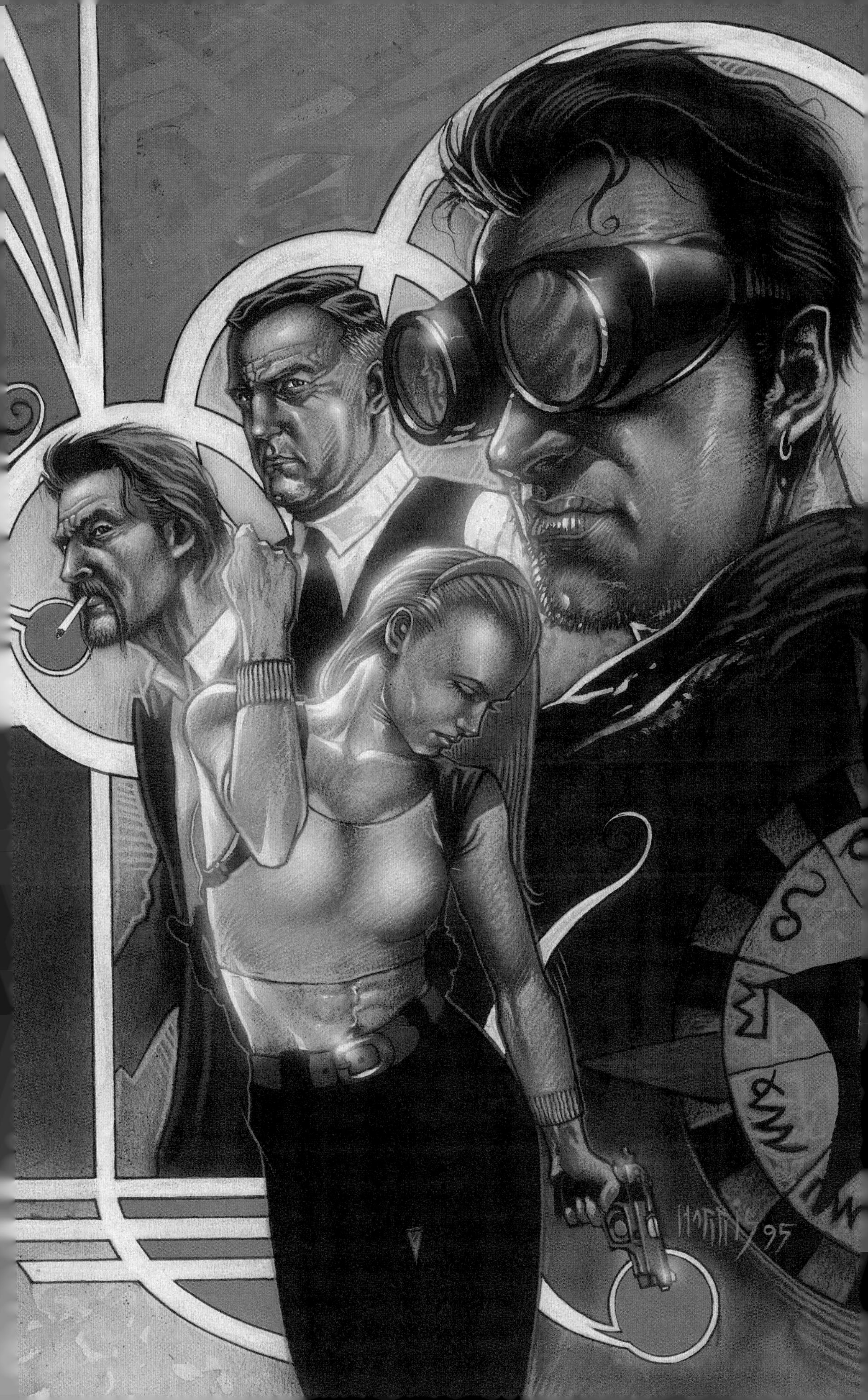

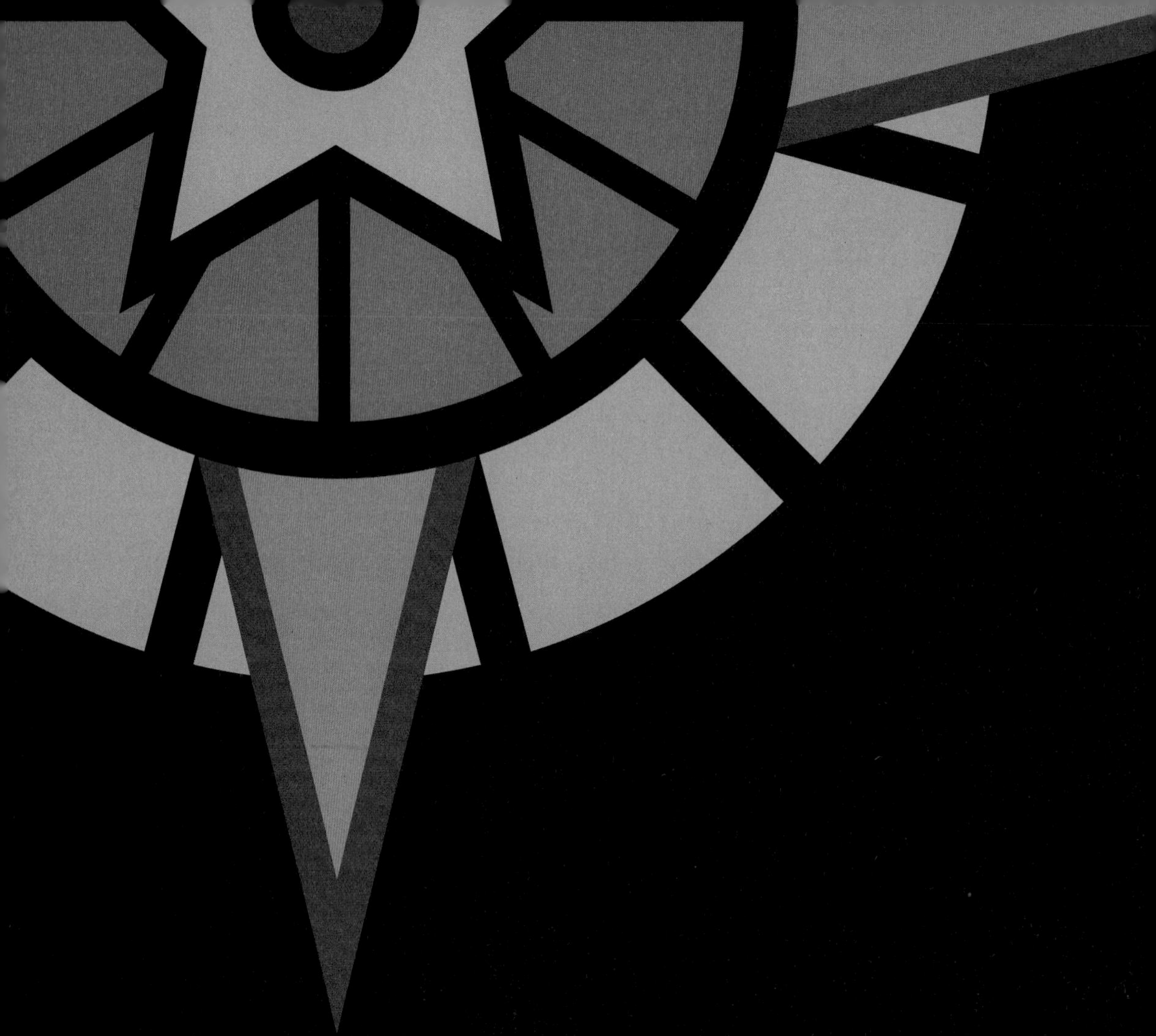

S T A R M A N   1 4

Cover by Tony Harris

Written by James Robinson

Pencils by Tommy Lee Edwards, Stuart Immonen,

Tony Harris, Chris Sprouse, Andrew Robinson,

Gary Erskine, and Amanda Conner,

with inks by Wade von Grawbadger and Gary Erskine,

and colors by Gregory Wright

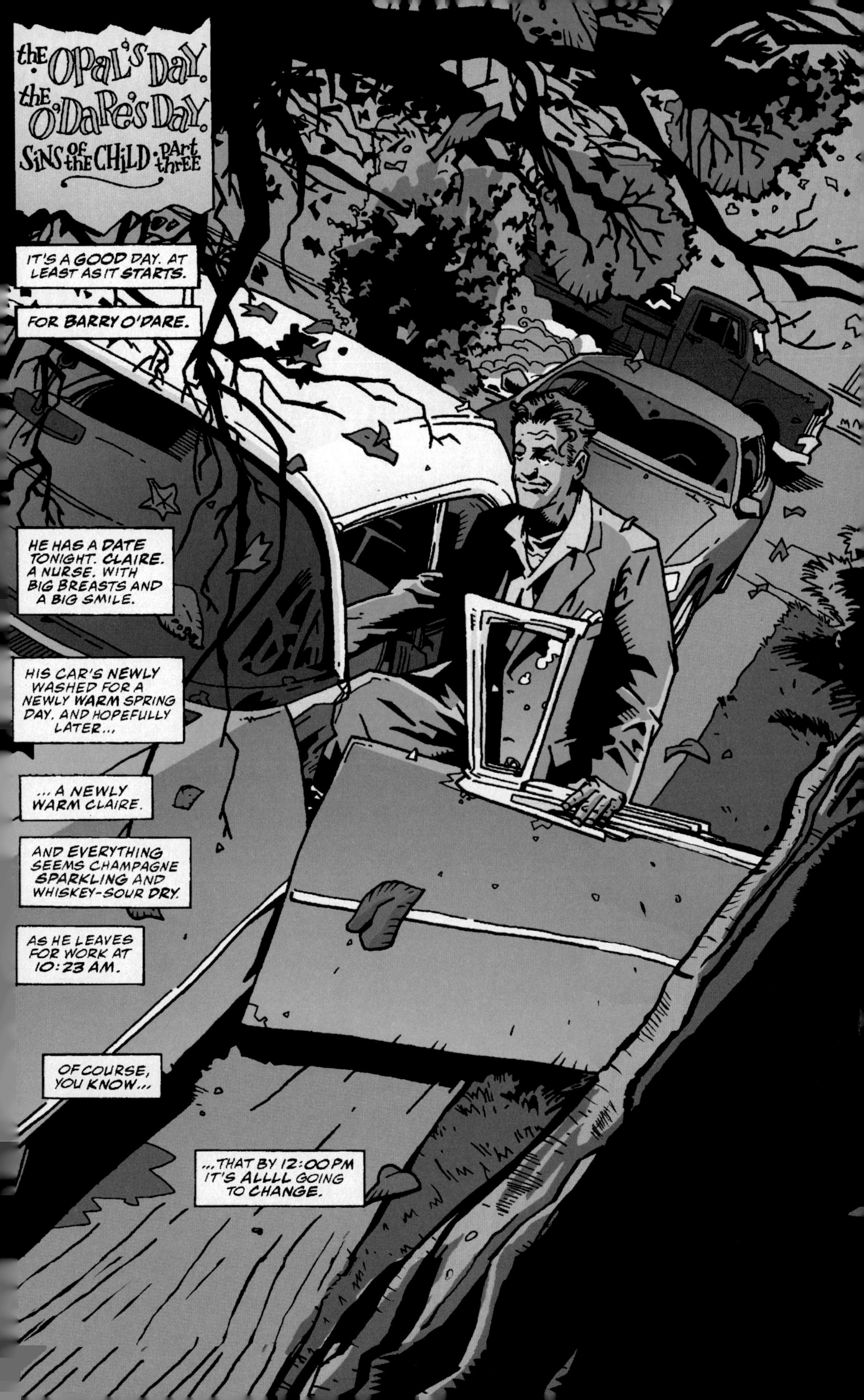
THE OPAL'S DAY. THE O'DARE'S DAY.
SINS OF THE CHILD · PART THREE
IT'S A GOOD DAY. AT LEAST AS IT STARTS.
FOR BARRY O'DARE.
HE HAS A DATE TONIGHT. CLAIRE. A NURSE. WITH BIG BREASTS AND A BIG SMILE.
HIS CAR'S NEWLY WASHED FOR A NEWLY WARM SPRING DAY. AND HOPEFULLY LATER...
... A NEWLY WARM CLAIRE.
AND EVERYTHING SEEMS CHAMPAGNE SPARKLING AND WHISKEY-SOUR DRY.
AS HE LEAVES FOR WORK AT 10:23 AM.
OF COURSE, YOU KNOW...
...THAT BY 12:00 PM IT'S ALLLL GOING TO CHANGE.

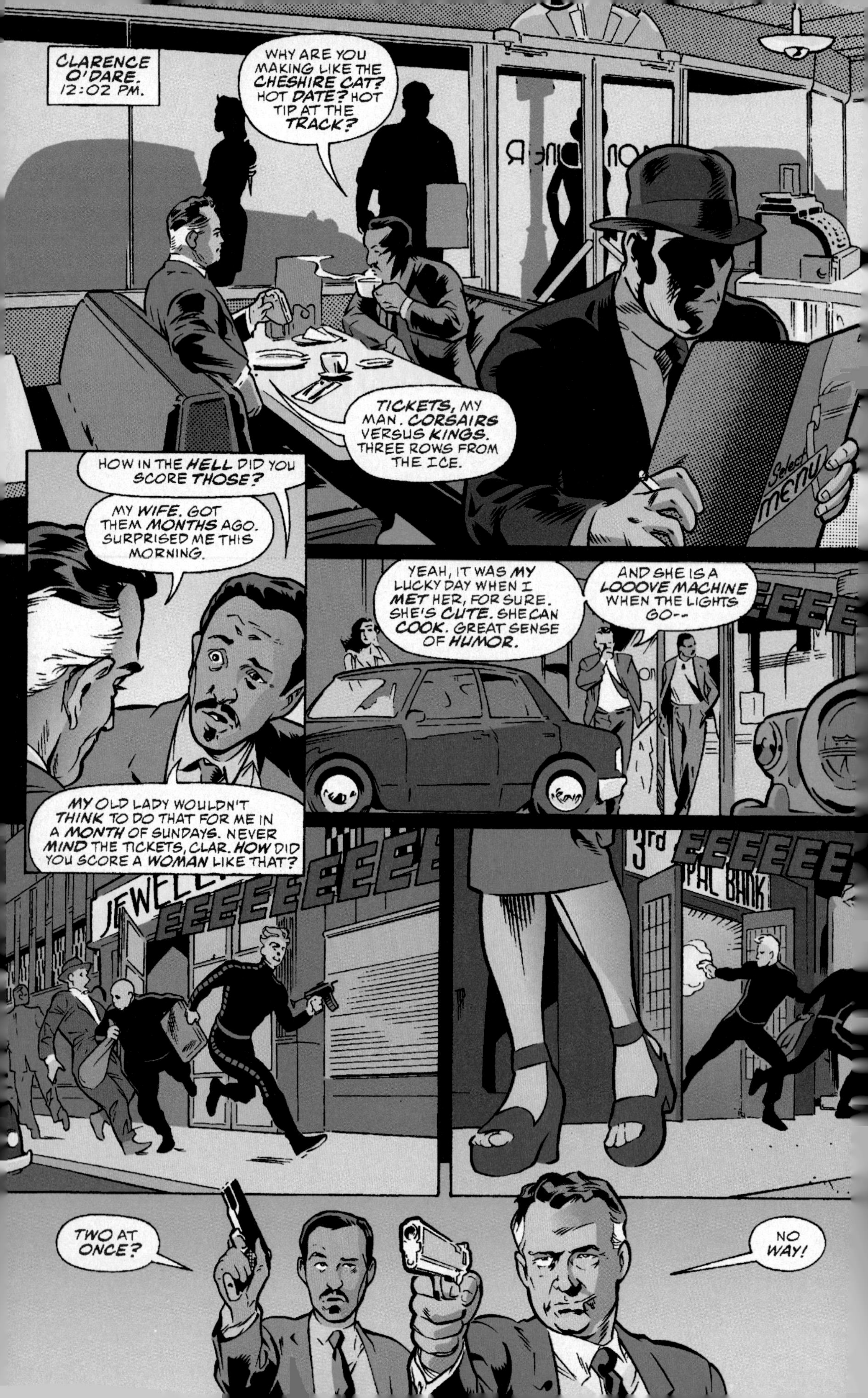
CLARENCE O'DARE. 12:02 PM.
WHY ARE YOU MAKING LIKE THE CHESHIRE CAT? HOT DATE? HOT TIP AT THE TRACK?
TICKETS, MY MAN. CORSAIRS VERSUS KINGS. THREE ROWS FROM THE ICE.
Select menu
HOW IN THE HELL DID YOU SCORE THOSE?
MY WIFE. GOT THEM MONTHS AGO. SURPRISED ME THIS MORNING.
YEAH, IT WAS MY LUCKY DAY WHEN I MET HER, FOR SURE. SHE'S CUTE. SHE CAN COOK. GREAT SENSE OF HUMOR.
AND SHE IS A LOOOVE MACHINE WHEN THE LIGHTS GO--
EEEE
MY OLD LADY WOULDN'T THINK TO DO THAT FOR ME IN A MONTH OF SUNDAYS. NEVER MIND THE TICKETS, CLAR. HOW DID YOU SCORE A WOMAN LIKE THAT?
EEEEEEEEEEEE
3rd
EEEEEE
TWO AT ONCE?
NO WAY!

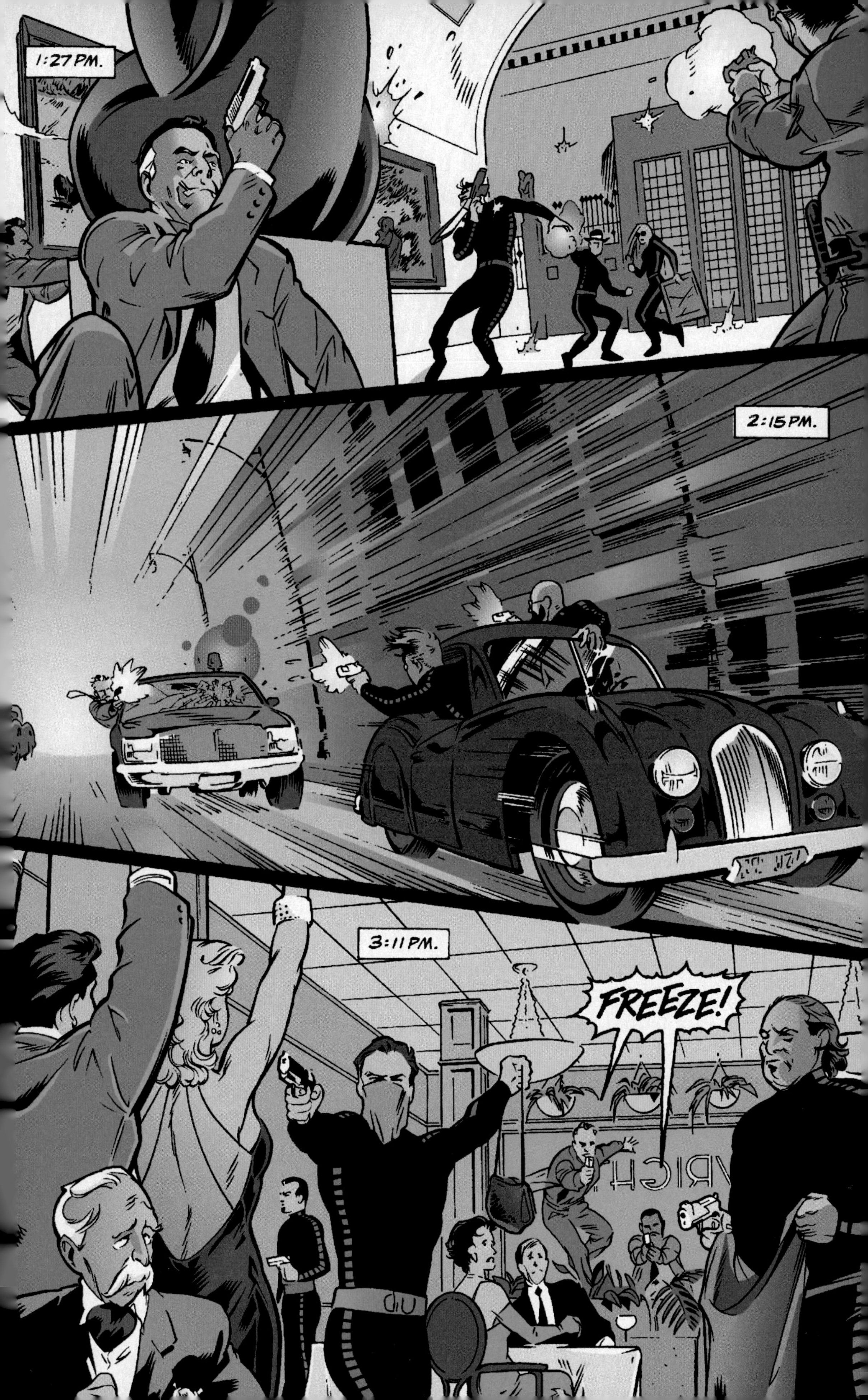
1:27 PM.
2:15 PM.
3:11 PM.
FREEZE!

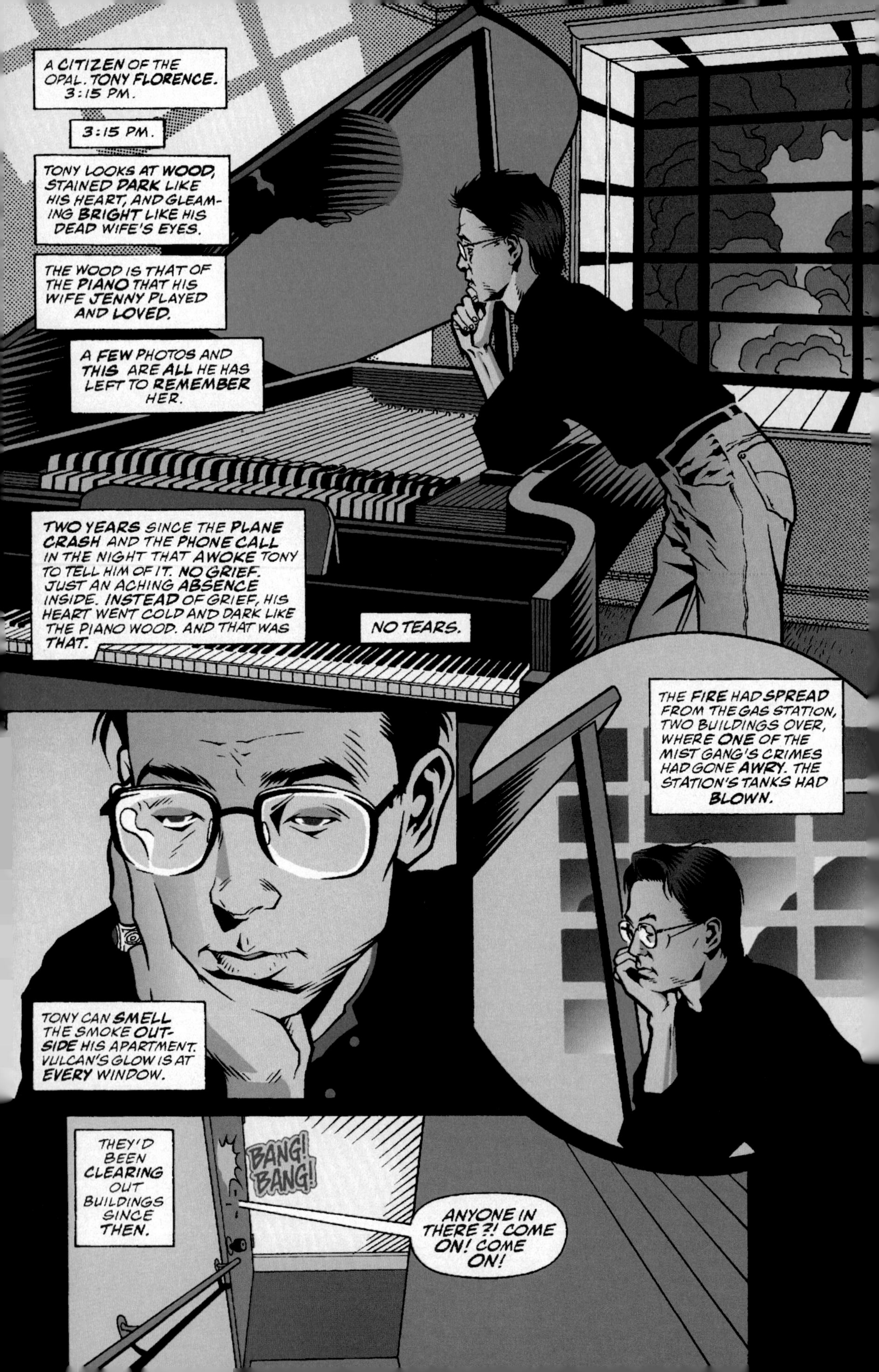

A CITIZEN OF THE OPAL. TONY FLORENCE. 3:15 PM.
3:15 PM.
TONY LOOKS AT WOOD, STAINED DARK LIKE HIS HEART, AND GLEAMING BRIGHT LIKE HIS DEAD WIFE'S EYES.
THE WOOD IS THAT OF THE PIANO THAT HIS WIFE JENNY PLAYED AND LOVED.
A FEW PHOTOS AND THIS ARE ALL HE HAS LEFT TO REMEMBER HER.
TWO YEARS SINCE THE PLANE CRASH AND THE PHONE CALL IN THE NIGHT THAT AWOKE TONY TO TELL HIM OF IT. NO GRIEF. JUST AN ACHING ABSENCE INSIDE. INSTEAD OF GRIEF, HIS HEART WENT COLD AND DARK LIKE THE PIANO WOOD. AND THAT WAS THAT.
NO TEARS.
TONY CAN SMELL THE SMOKE OUTSIDE HIS APARTMENT. VULCAN'S GLOW IS AT EVERY WINDOW.
THE FIRE HAD SPREAD FROM THE GAS STATION, TWO BUILDINGS OVER, WHERE ONE OF THE MIST GANG'S CRIMES HAD GONE AWRY. THE STATION'S TANKS HAD BLOWN.
THEY'D BEEN CLEARING OUT BUILDINGS SINCE THEN.
BANG! BANG!
ANYONE IN THERE?! COME ON! COME ON!

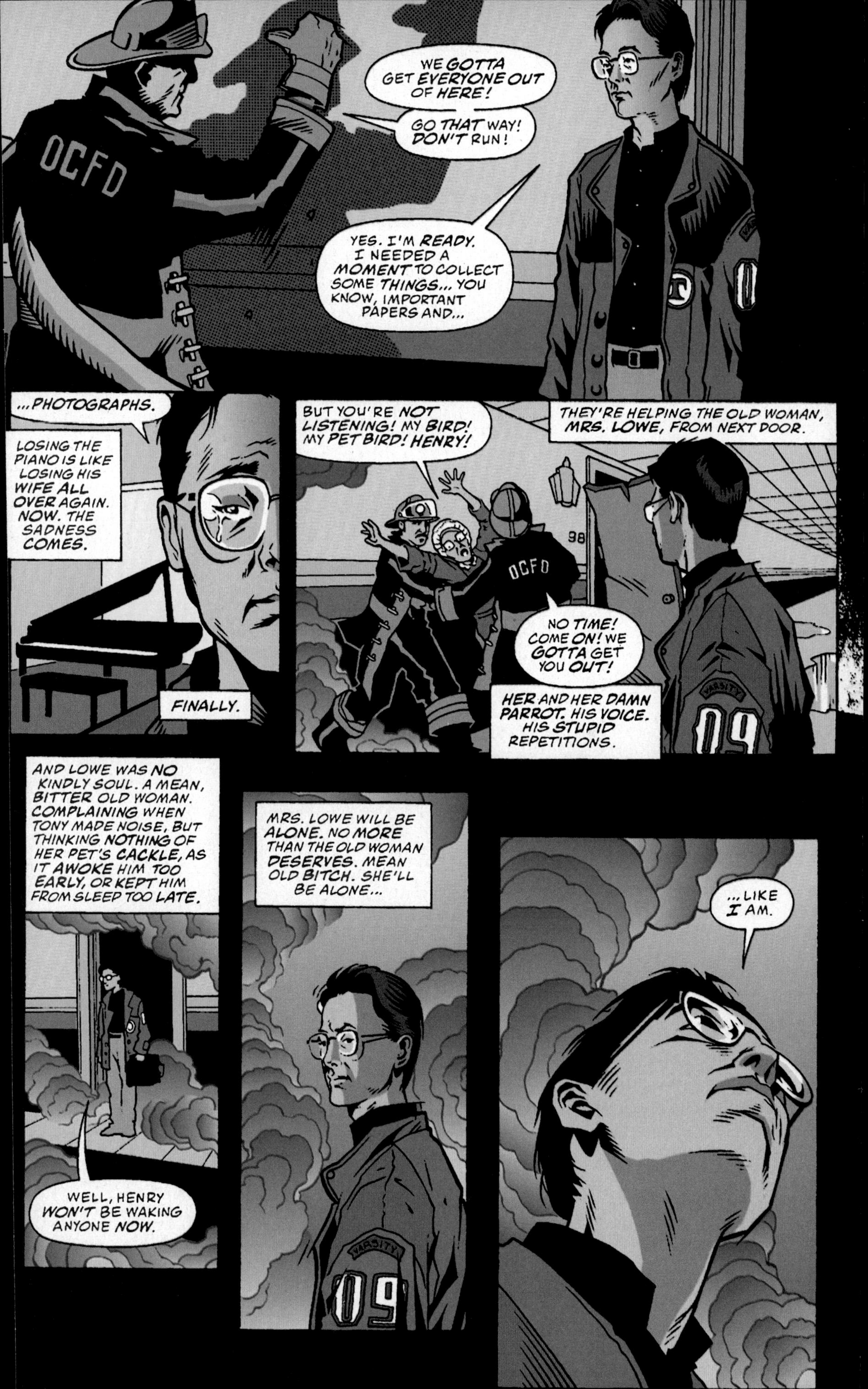
WE GOTTA GET EVERYONE OUT OF HERE!
GO THAT WAY! DON'T RUN!
YES. I'M READY. I NEEDED A MOMENT TO COLLECT SOME THINGS... YOU KNOW, IMPORTANT PAPERS AND...
...PHOTOGRAPHS.
LOSING THE PIANO IS LIKE LOSING HIS WIFE ALL OVER AGAIN. NOW. THE SADNESS COMES.
FINALLY.
BUT YOU'RE NOT LISTENING! MY BIRD! MY PET BIRD! HENRY!
THEY'RE HELPING THE OLD WOMAN, MRS. LOWE, FROM NEXT DOOR.
NO TIME! COME ON! WE GOTTA GET YOU OUT!
HER AND HER DAMN PARROT. HIS VOICE. HIS STUPID REPETITIONS.
AND LOWE WAS NO KINDLY SOUL. A MEAN, BITTER OLD WOMAN. COMPLAINING WHEN TONY MADE NOISE, BUT THINKING NOTHING OF HER PET'S CACKLE, AS IT AWOKE HIM TOO EARLY, OR KEPT HIM FROM SLEEP TOO LATE.
WELL, HENRY WON'T BE WAKING ANYONE NOW.
MRS. LOWE WILL BE ALONE. NO MORE THAN THE OLD WOMAN DESERVES. MEAN OLD BITCH. SHE'LL BE ALONE...
...LIKE I AM.

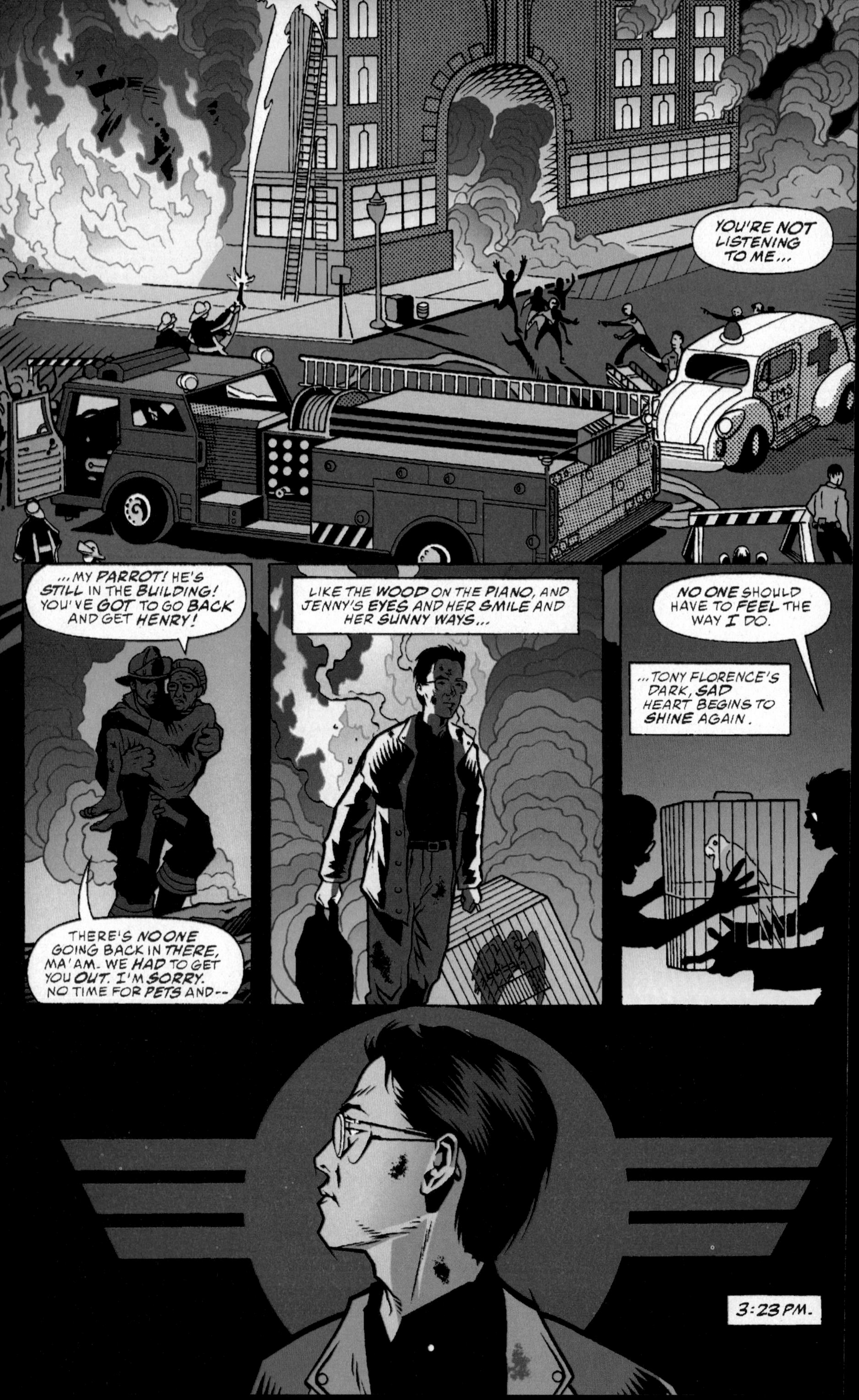
YOU'RE NOT LISTENING TO ME...
...MY PARROT! HE'S STILL IN THE BUILDING! YOU'VE GOT TO GO BACK AND GET HENRY!
THERE'S NO ONE GOING BACK IN THERE, MA'AM. WE HAD TO GET YOU OUT. I'M SORRY. NO TIME FOR PETS AND--
LIKE THE WOOD ON THE PIANO, AND JENNY'S EYES AND HER SMILE AND HER SUNNY WAYS...
NO ONE SHOULD HAVE TO FEEL THE WAY I DO.
...TONY FLORENCE'S DARK, SAD HEART BEGINS TO SHINE AGAIN.
3:23 PM.

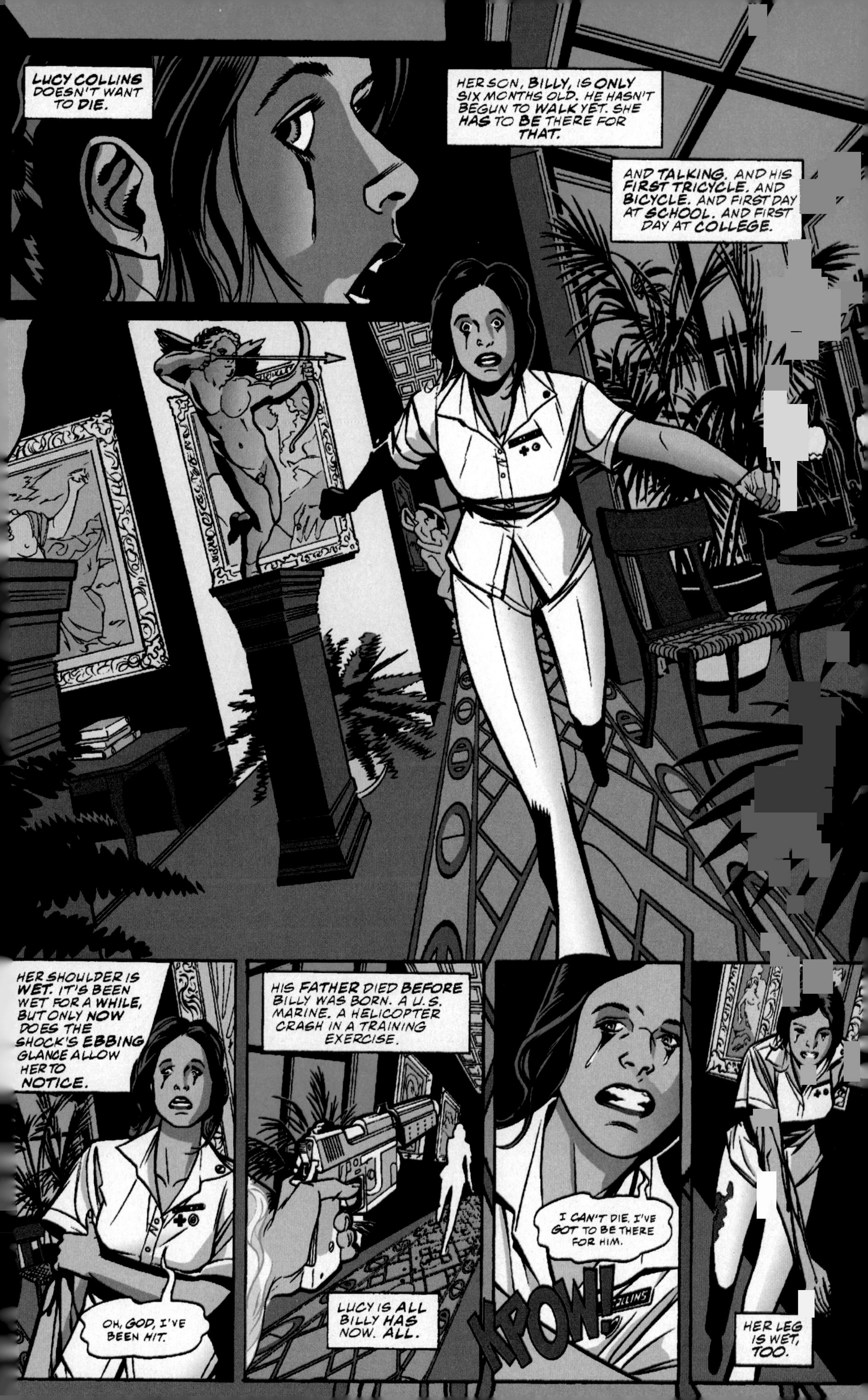
LUCY COLLINS DOESN'T WANT TO DIE.
HER SON, BILLY, IS ONLY SIX MONTHS OLD. HE HASN'T BEGUN TO WALK YET. SHE HAS TO BE THERE FOR THAT.
AND TALKING. AND HIS FIRST TRICYCLE. AND BICYCLE. AND FIRST DAY AT SCHOOL. AND FIRST DAY AT COLLEGE.
HER SHOULDER IS WET. IT'S BEEN WET FOR A WHILE, BUT ONLY NOW DOES THE SHOCK'S EBBING GLANCE ALLOW HER TO NOTICE.
OH, GOD, I'VE BEEN HIT.
HIS FATHER DIED BEFORE BILLY WAS BORN. A U.S. MARINE. A HELICOPTER CRASH IN A TRAINING EXERCISE.
LUCY IS ALL BILLY HAS NOW. ALL.
I CAN'T DIE. I'VE GOT TO BE THERE FOR HIM.
KPOW!
HER LEG IS WET, TOO.

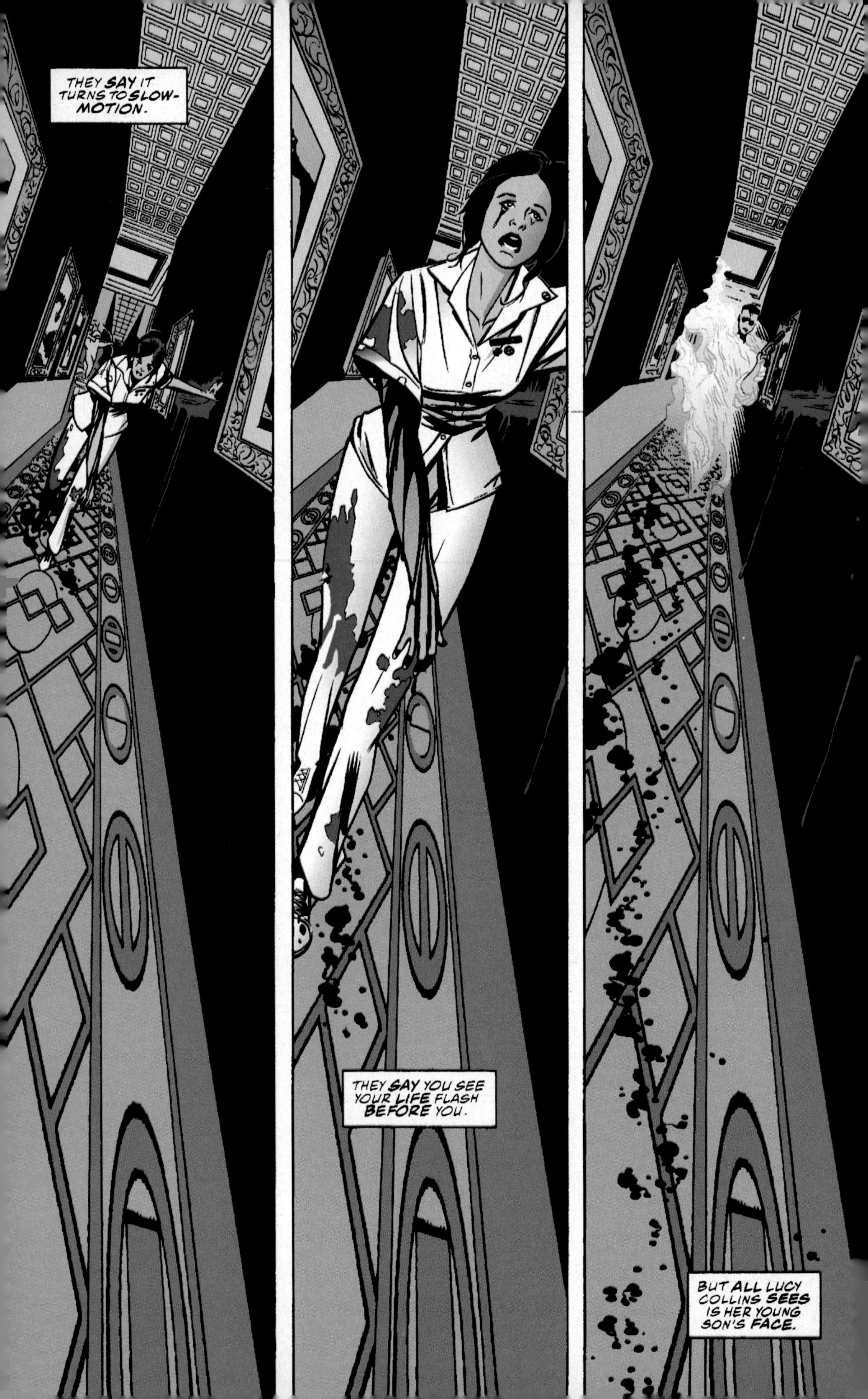
THEY SAY IT TURNS TO SLOW-MOTION.
THEY SAY YOU SEE YOUR LIFE FLASH BEFORE YOU.
BUT ALL LUCY COLLINS SEES IS HER YOUNG SON'S FACE.

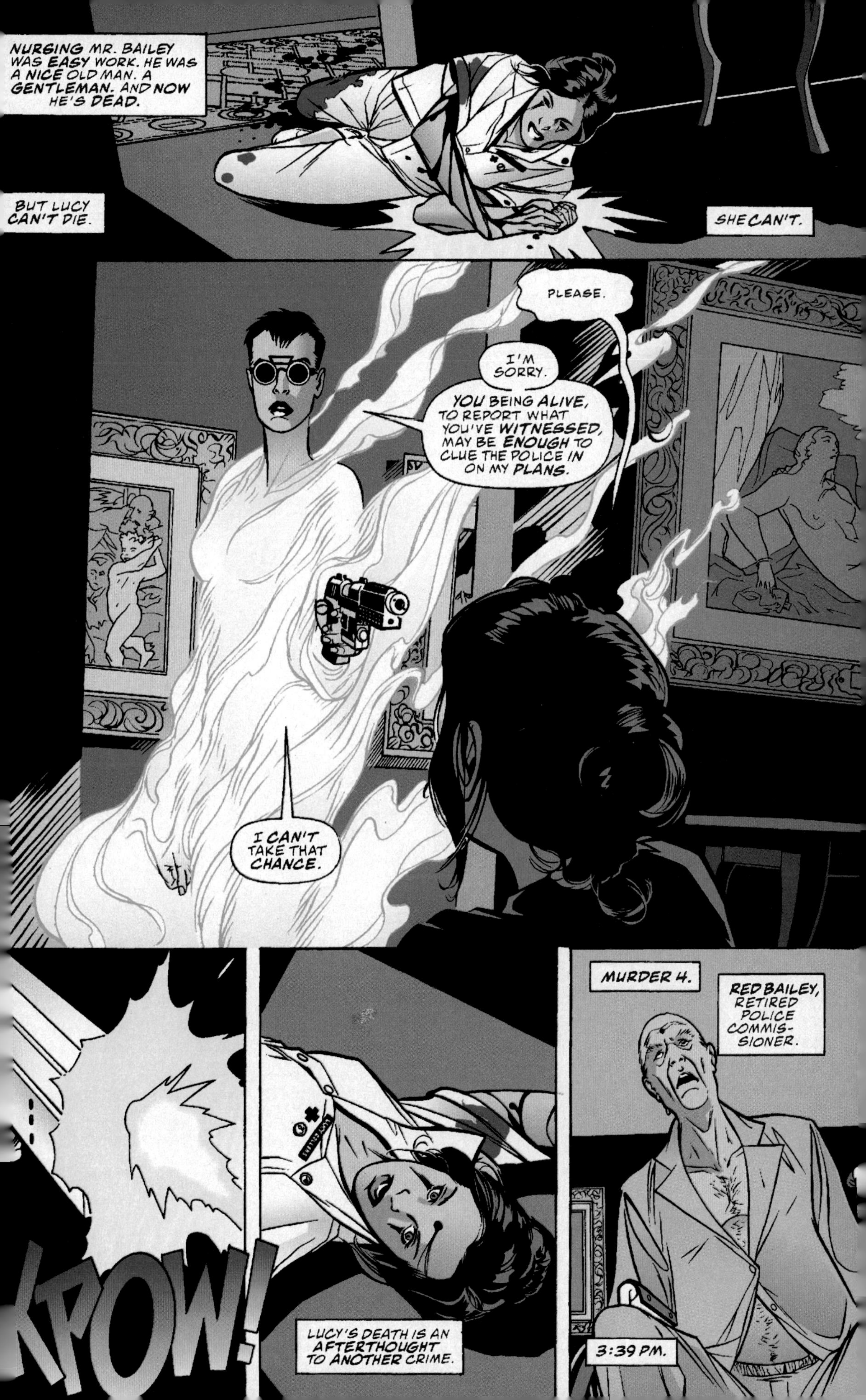
NURGING MR. BAILEY WAS EASY WORK. HE WAS A NICE OLD MAN. A GENTLEMAN. AND NOW HE'S DEAD.
BUT LUCY CAN'T DIE.
SHE CAN'T.
PLEASE.
I'M SORRY.
YOU BEING ALIVE, TO REPORT WHAT YOU'VE WITNESSED, MAY BE ENOUGH TO CLUE THE POLICE IN ON MY PLANS.
I CAN'T TAKE THAT CHANCE.
...
KPOW!
LUCY'S DEATH IS AN AFTERTHOUGHT TO ANOTHER CRIME.
MURDER 4.
RED BAILEY, RETIRED POLICE COMMIS-SIONER.
3:39 PM.

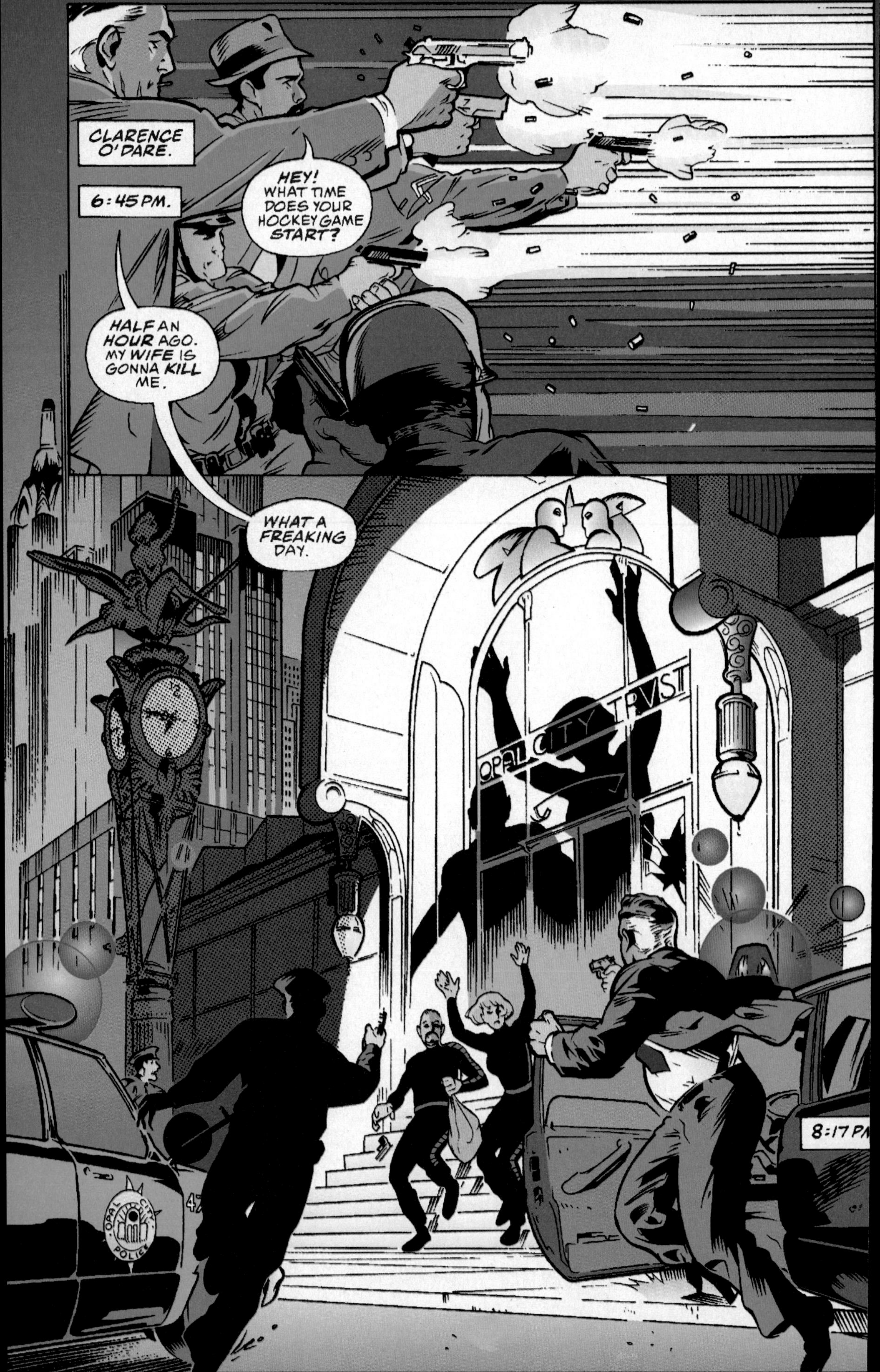
CLARENCE O'DARE.
6:45 PM.
HEY! WHAT TIME DOES YOUR HOCKEY GAME START?
HALF AN HOUR AGO. MY WIFE IS GONNA KILL ME.
WHAT A FREAKING DAY.
OPAL CITY TRUST
8:17 PM
OPAL CITY POLICE

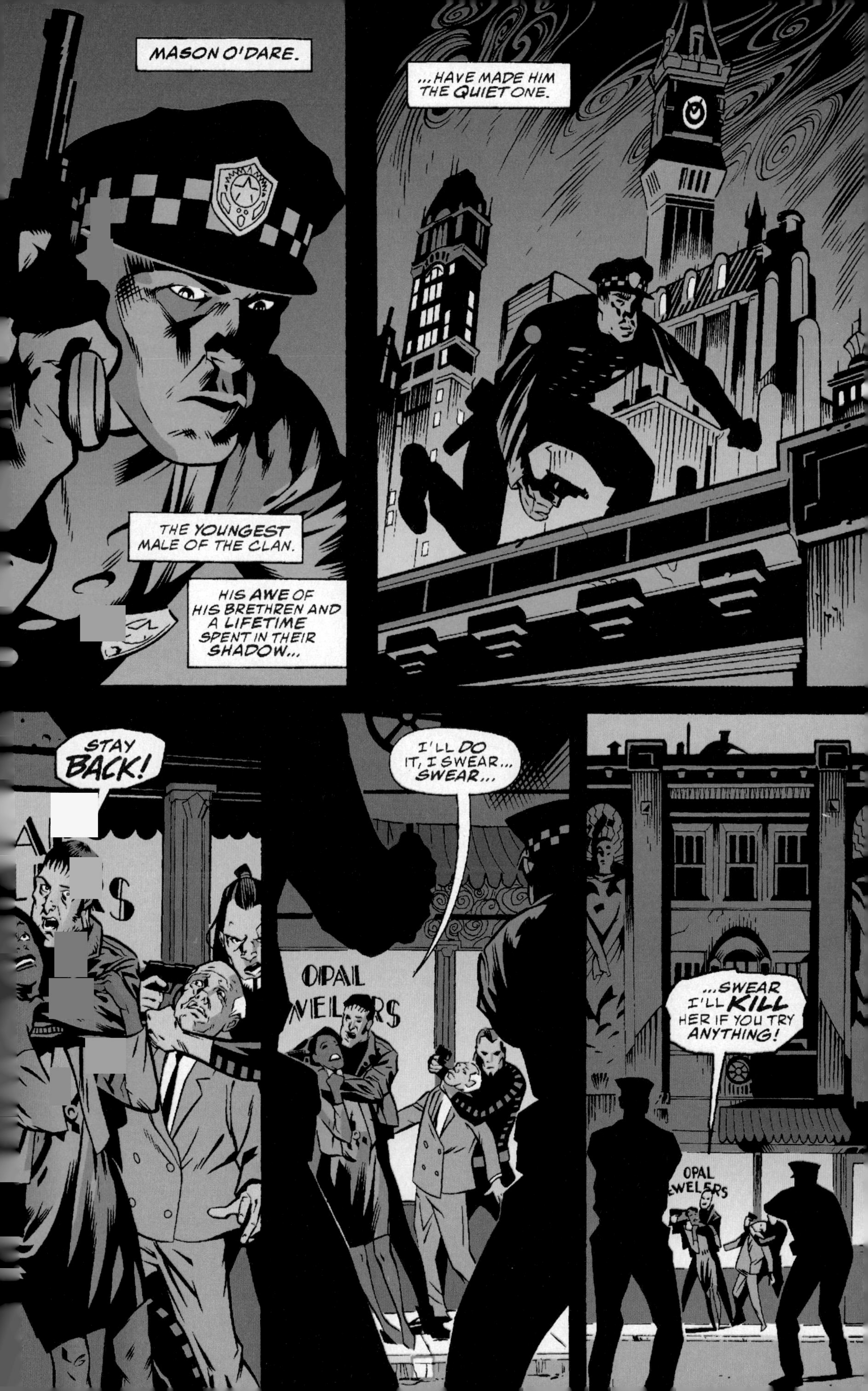
MASON O'DARE.
...HAVE MADE HIM THE QUIET ONE.
THE YOUNGEST MALE OF THE CLAN.
HIS AWE OF HIS BRETHREN AND A LIFETIME SPENT IN THEIR SHADOW...
STAY BACK!
I'LL DO IT, I SWEAR... SWEAR...
OPAL
...SWEAR I'LL KILL HER IF YOU TRY ANYTHING!
OPAL

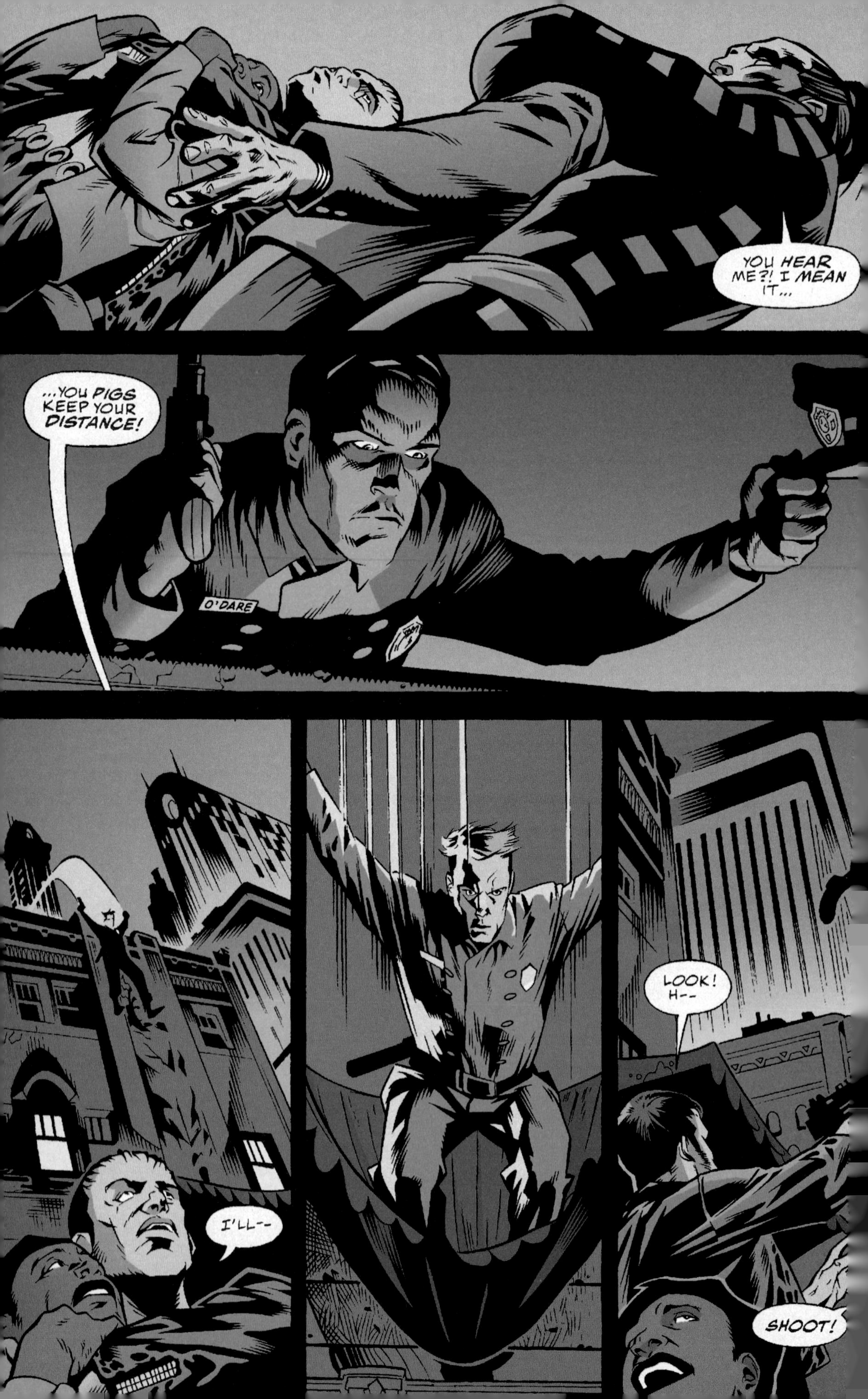
YOU HEAR ME?! I MEAN IT...
...YOU PIGS KEEP YOUR DISTANCE!
O'DARE
I'LL--
LOOK! H--
SHOOT!

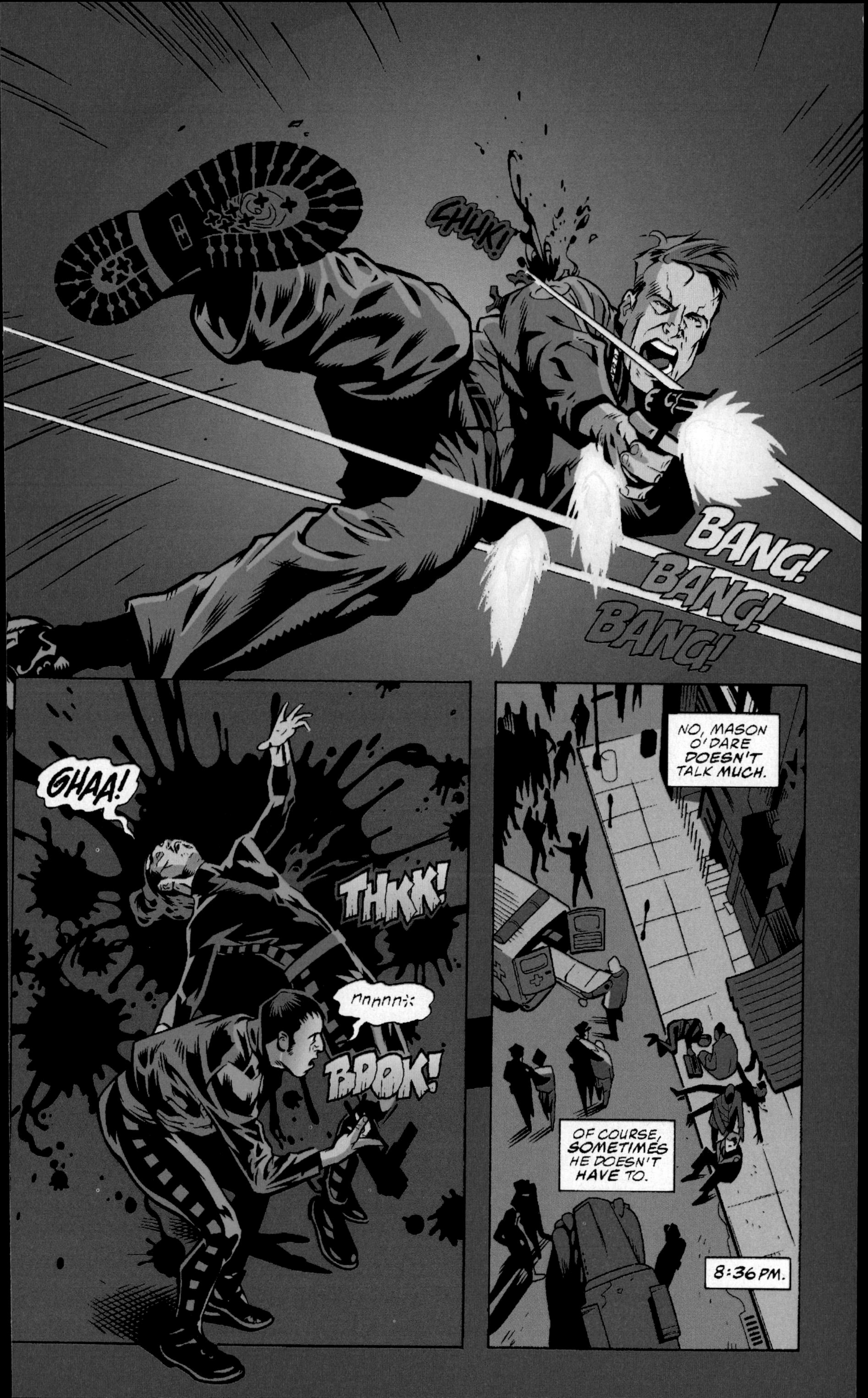
CHUK!
BANG!
BANG!
BANG!
GHAA!
THKK!
nnnnn
BOOK!
NO, MASON O'DARE DOESN'T TALK MUCH.
OF COURSE, SOMETIMES HE DOESN'T HAVE TO.
8:36 PM.

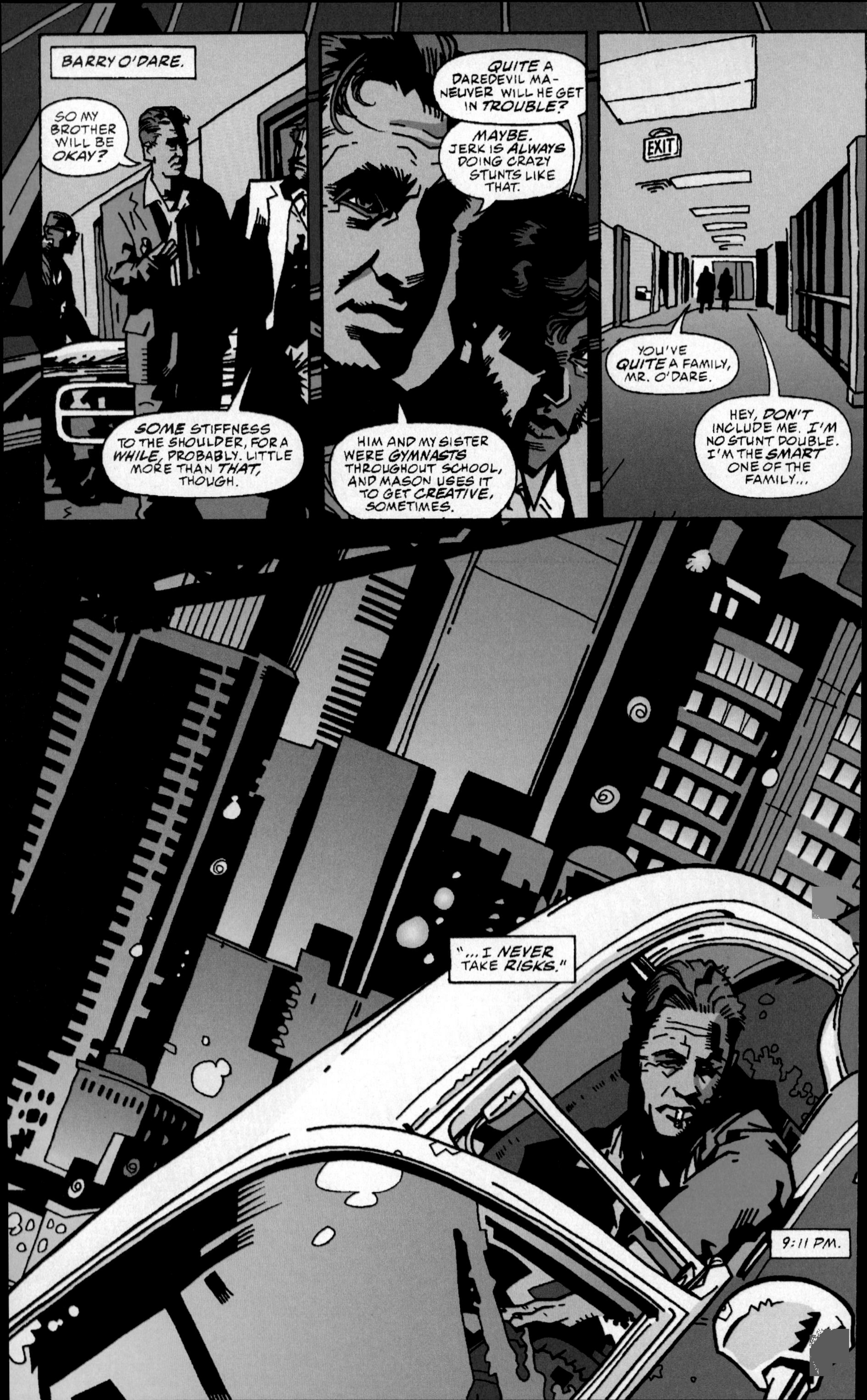
BARRY O'DARE.
SO MY BROTHER WILL BE OKAY?
SOME STIFFNESS TO THE SHOULDER, FOR A WHILE, PROBABLY. LITTLE MORE THAN THAT, THOUGH.
QUITE A DAREDEVIL MA-NEUVER. WILL HE GET IN TROUBLE?
MAYBE. JERK IS ALWAYS DOING CRAZY STUNTS LIKE THAT.
HIM AND MY SISTER WERE GYMNASTS THROUGHOUT SCHOOL, AND MASON USES IT TO GET CREATIVE, SOMETIMES.
EXIT
YOU'VE QUITE A FAMILY, MR. O'DARE.
HEY, DON'T INCLUDE ME. I'M NO STUNT DOUBLE. I'M THE SMART ONE OF THE FAMILY...
"...I NEVER TAKE RISKS."
9:11 PM.

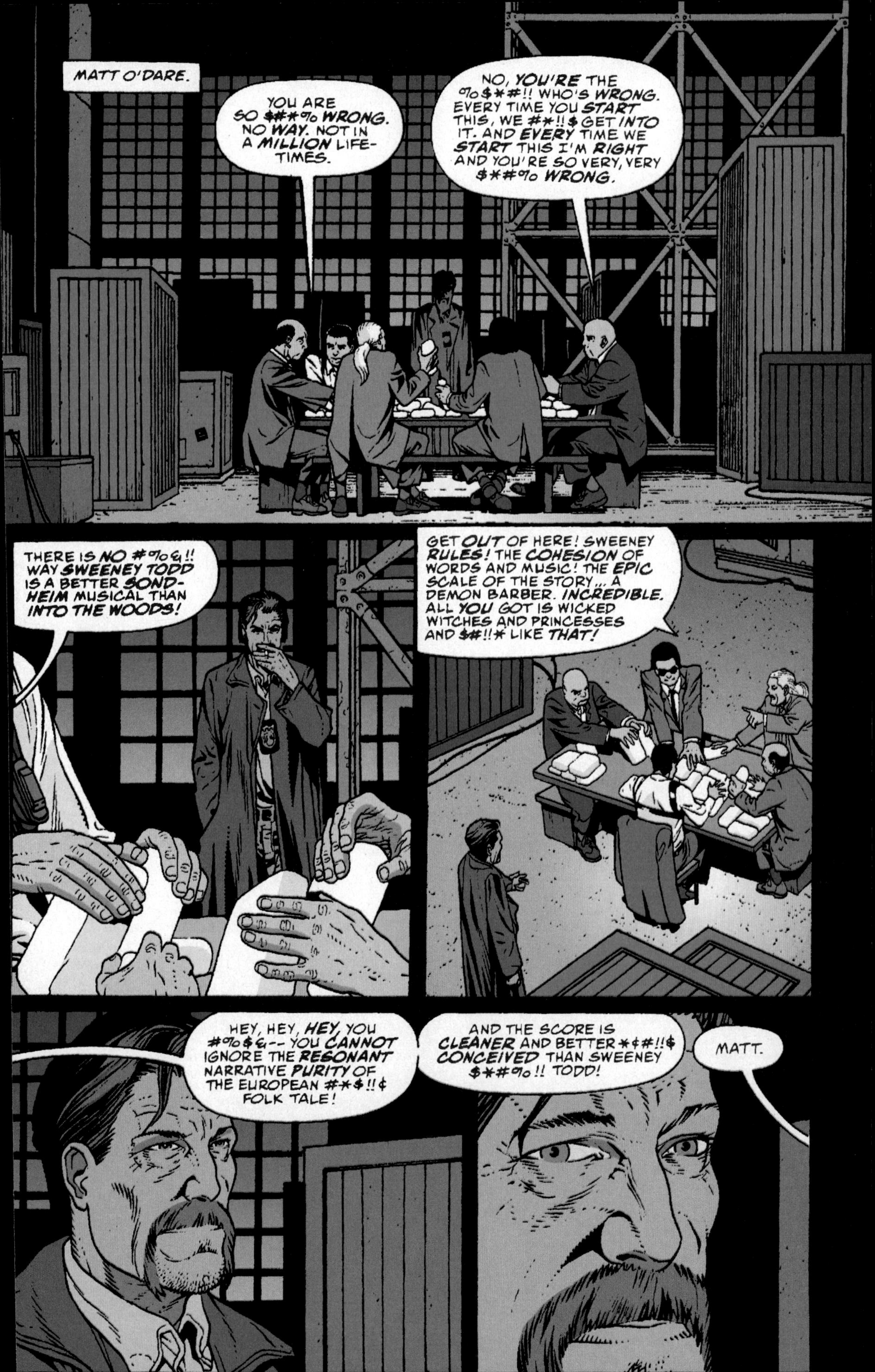
MATT O'DARE.
YOU ARE SO $#*% WRONG. NO WAY. NOT IN A MILLION LIFE-TIMES.
NO, YOU'RE THE %$**!! WHO'S WRONG. EVERY TIME YOU START THIS, WE #*!!$ GET INTO IT. AND EVERY TIME WE START THIS I'M RIGHT AND YOU'RE SO VERY, VERY $*#% WRONG.
THERE IS NO #%&!! WAY SWEENEY TODD IS A BETTER SONDHEIM MUSICAL THAN INTO THE WOODS!
GET OUT OF HERE! SWEENEY RULES! THE COHESION OF WORDS AND MUSIC! THE EPIC SCALE OF THE STORY... A DEMON BARBER. INCREDIBLE. ALL YOU GOT IS WICKED WITCHES AND PRINCESSES AND $#!!* LIKE THAT!
HEY, HEY, HEY, YOU #%$&-- YOU CANNOT IGNORE THE RESONANT NARRATIVE PURITY OF THE EUROPEAN #*$!!¢ FOLK TALE!
AND THE SCORE IS CLEANER AND BETTER *¢#!!$ CONCEIVED THAN SWEENEY $*#%!! TODD!
MATT.

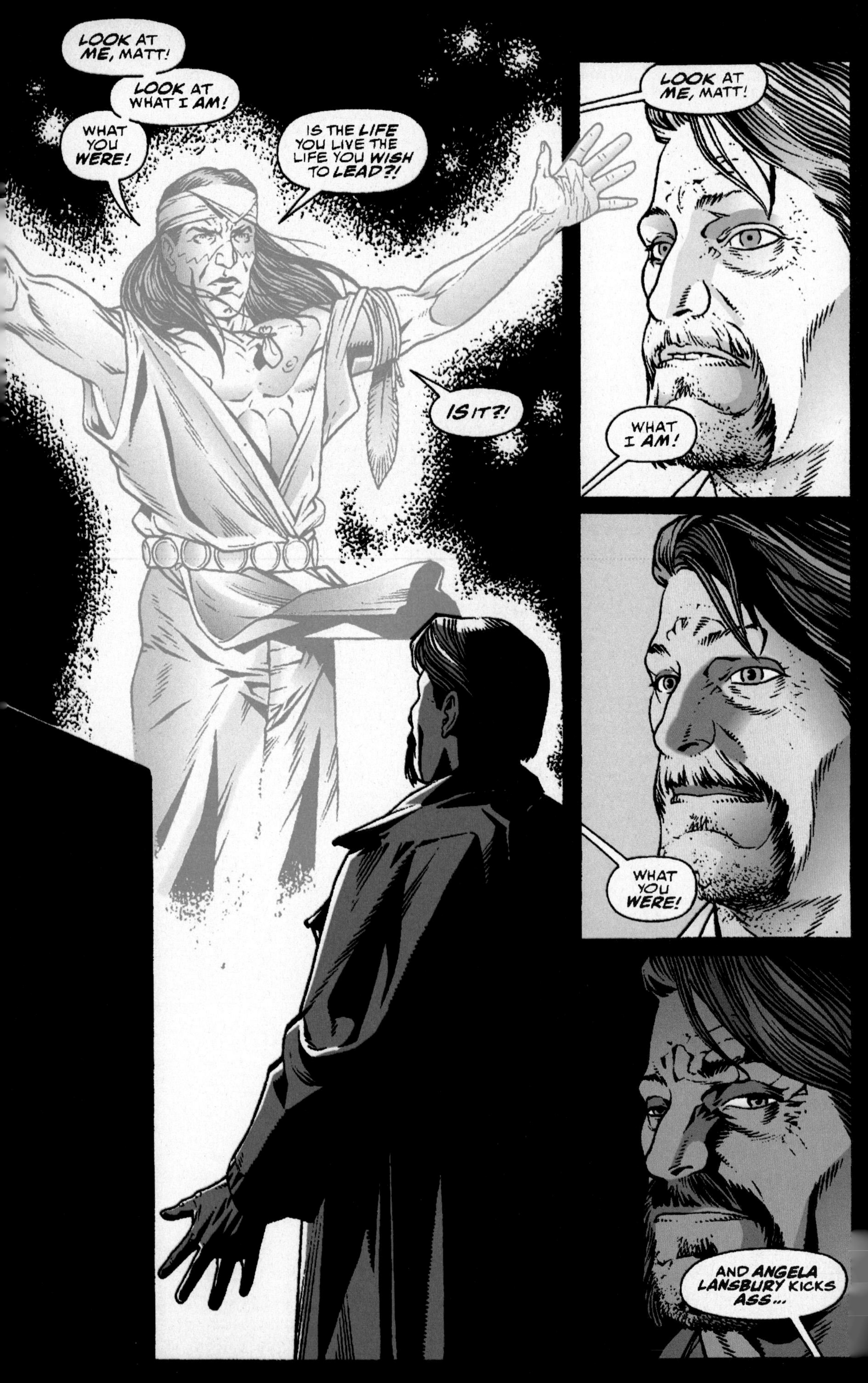
LOOK AT ME, MATT!
LOOK AT WHAT I AM!
WHAT YOU WERE!
IS THE LIFE YOU LIVE THE LIFE YOU WISH TO LEAD?!
IS IT?!
LOOK AT ME, MATT!
WHAT I AM!
WHAT YOU WERE!
AND ANGELA LANSBURY KICKS ASS...

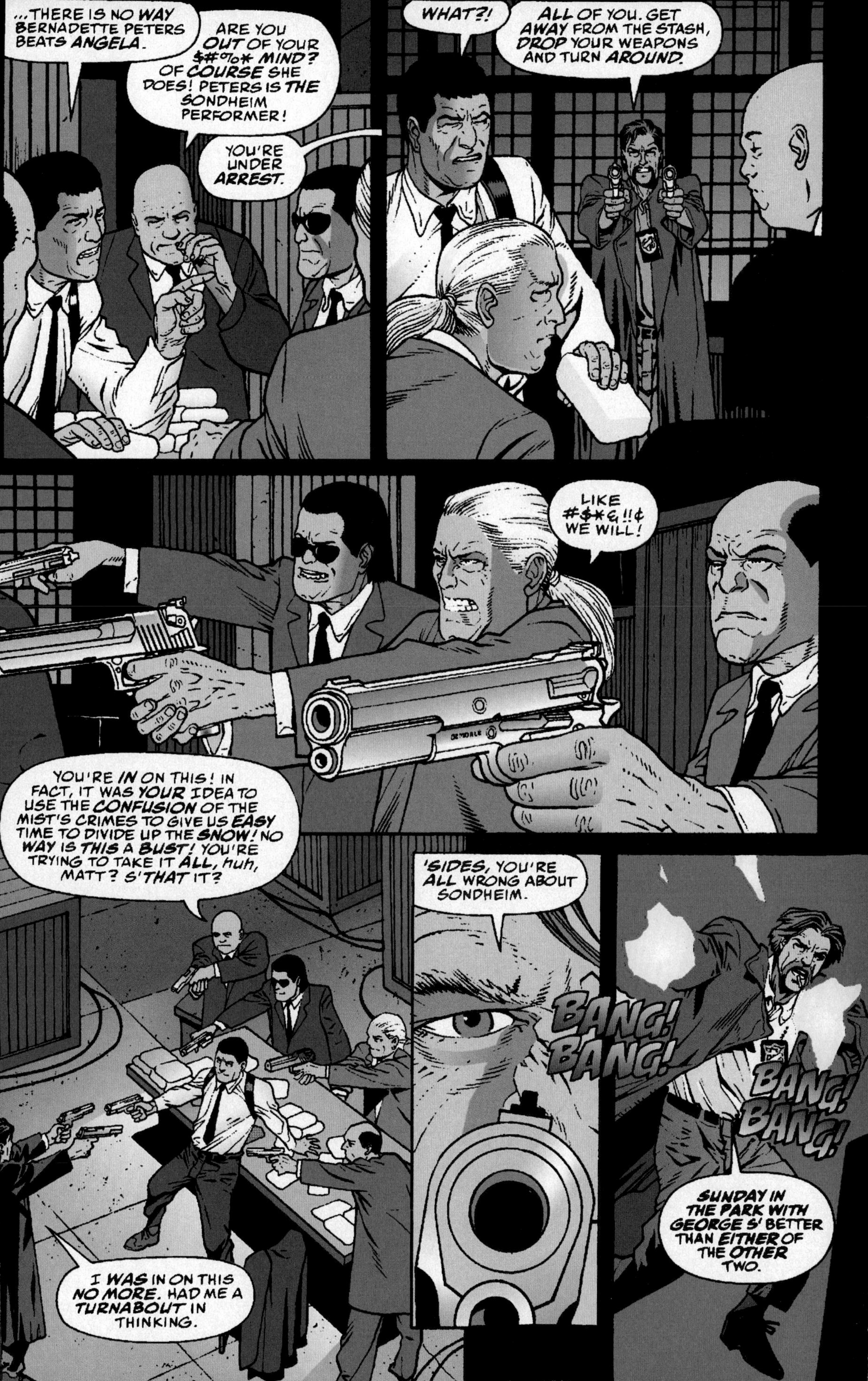
...THERE IS NO WAY BERNADETTE PETERS BEATS ANGELA.
ARE YOU OUT OF YOUR $#%* MIND? OF COURSE SHE DOES! PETERS IS THE SONDHEIM PERFORMER!
YOU'RE UNDER ARREST.
WHAT?!
ALL OF YOU. GET AWAY FROM THE STASH, DROP YOUR WEAPONS AND TURN AROUND.
LIKE #$*&!!¢ WE WILL!
YOU'RE IN ON THIS! IN FACT, IT WAS YOUR IDEA TO USE THE CONFUSION OF THE MIST'S CRIMES TO GIVE US EASY TIME TO DIVIDE UP THE SNOW! NO WAY IS THIS A BUST! YOU'RE TRYING TO TAKE IT ALL, huh, MATT? S'THAT IT?
I WAS IN ON THIS NO MORE. HAD ME A TURNABOUT IN THINKING.
'SIDES, YOU'RE ALL WRONG ABOUT SONDHEIM.
BANG! BANG!
BANG! BANG!
SUNDAY IN THE PARK WITH GEORGE S' BETTER THAN EITHER OF THE OTHER TWO.

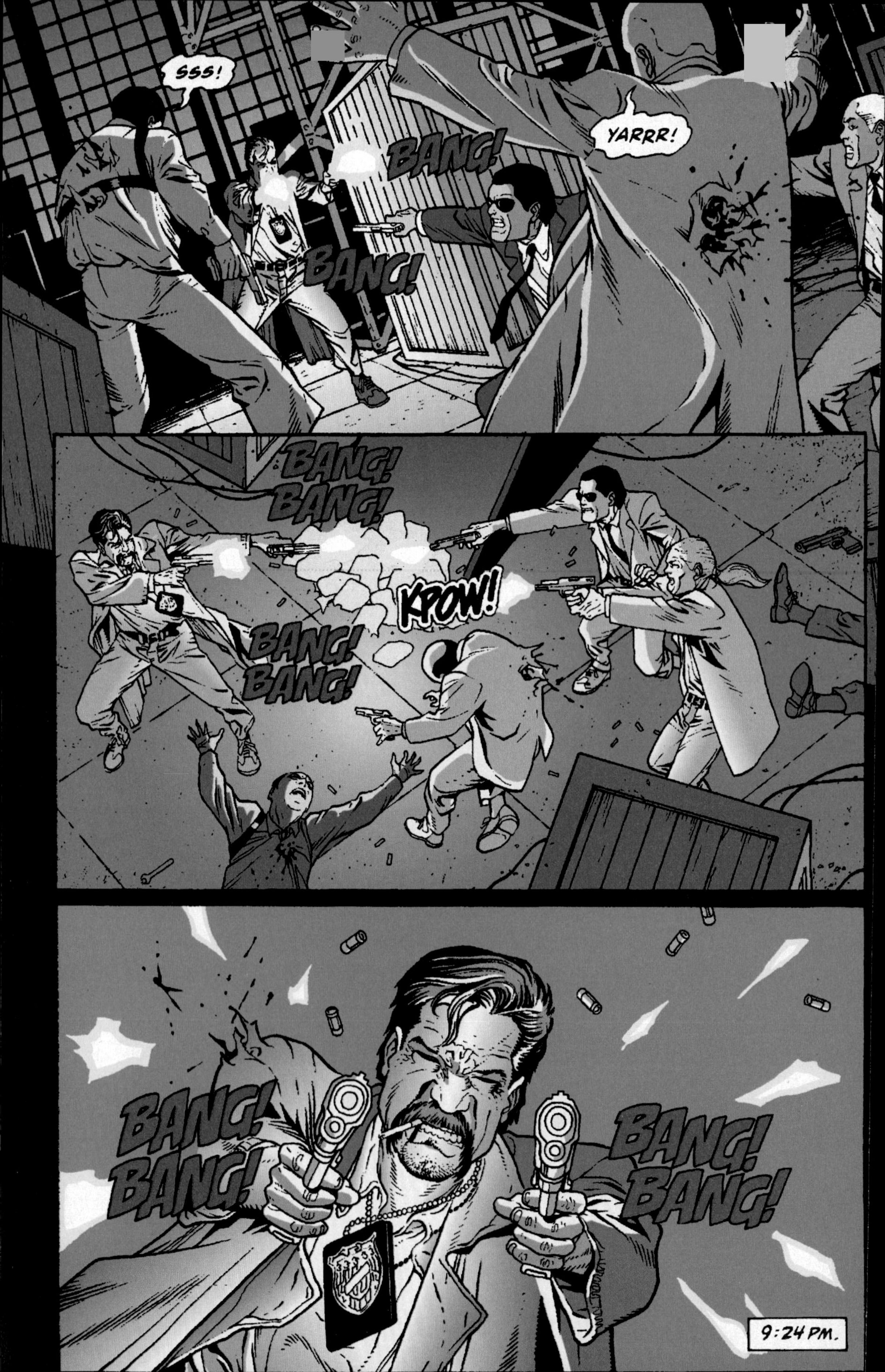

SSS!
YARRR!
BANG!
BANG!
BANG!
BANG!
KPOW!
BANG!
BANG!
BANG!
BANG!
BANG!
BANG!
9:24 PM.

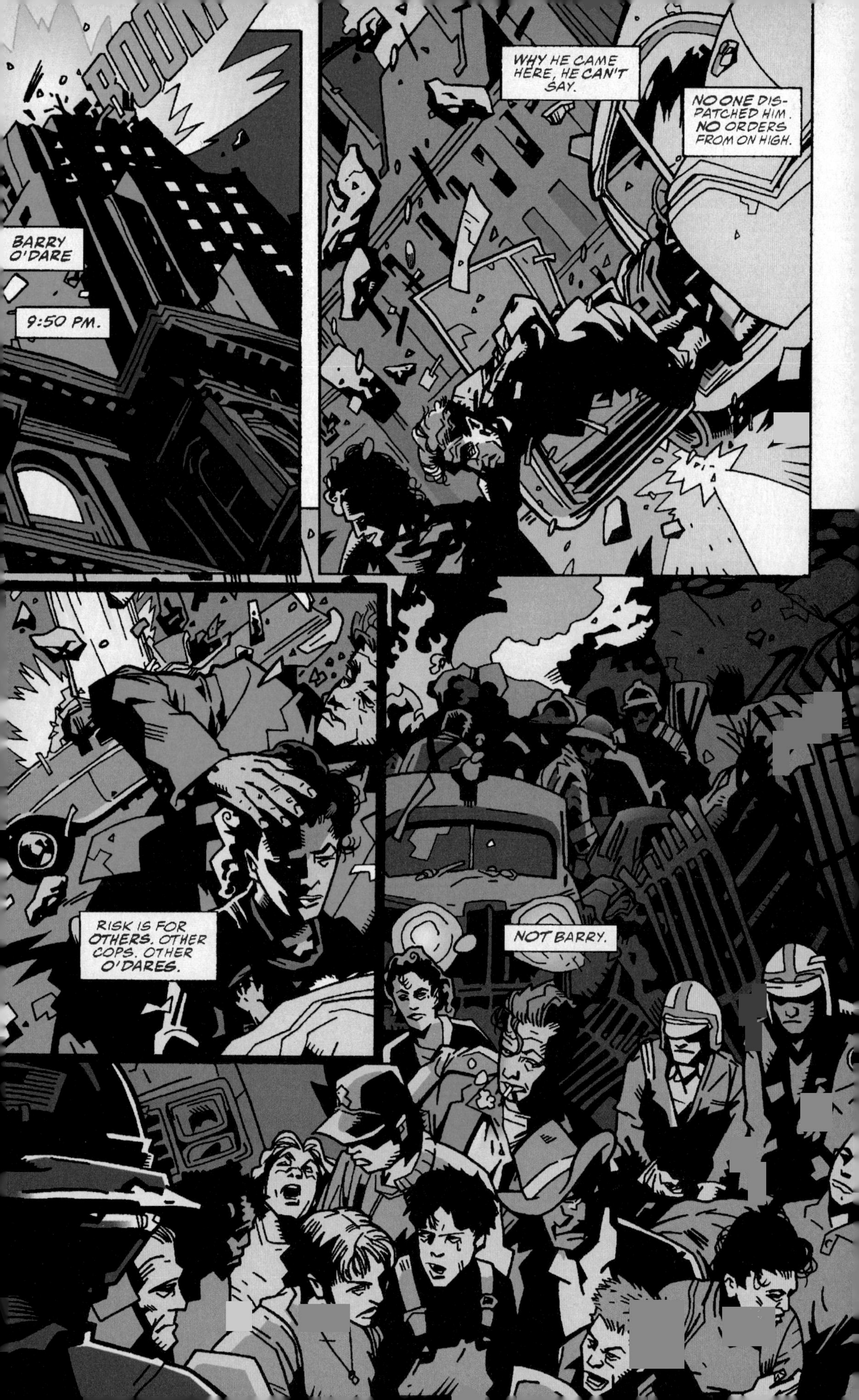
BOOM
BARRY O'DARE
9:50 PM.
WHY HE CAME HERE, HE CAN'T SAY.
NO ONE DISPATCHED HIM. NO ORDERS FROM ON HIGH.
RISK IS FOR OTHERS. OTHER COPS. OTHER O'DARES.
NOT BARRY.

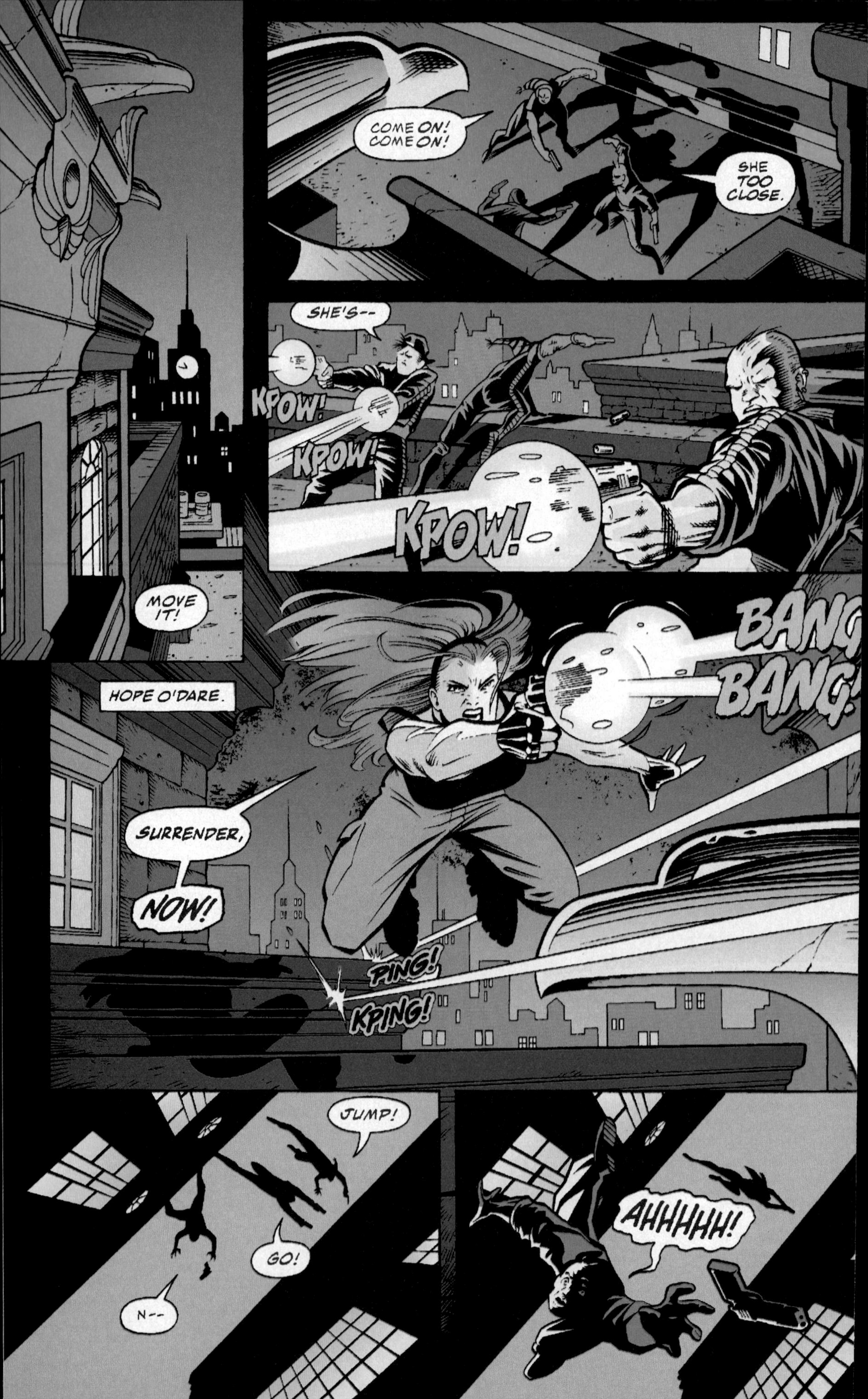
MOVE IT!
COME ON! COME ON!
SHE TOO CLOSE.
SHE'S--
KPOW!
KPOW!
KPOW!
HOPE O'DARE.
BANG!
BANG!
SURRENDER, NOW!
PING!
KPING!
JUMP!
GO!
N--
AHHHHH!

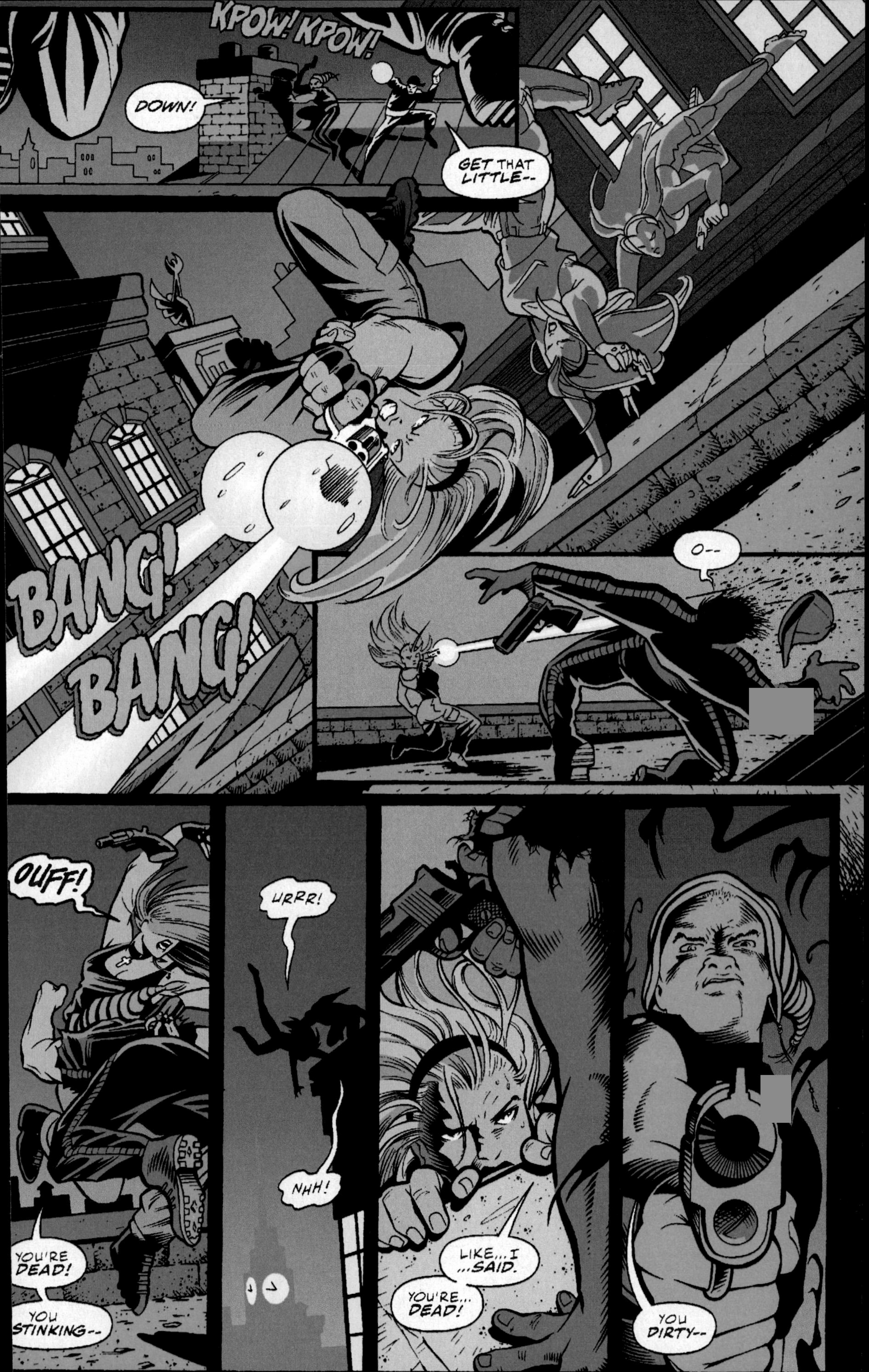
KPOW! KPOW!
DOWN!
GET THAT LITTLE--
BANG!
BANG!
O--
OUFF!
YOU'RE DEAD!
YOU STINKING--
URRR!
NHH!
LIKE... I ...SAID.
YOU'RE... DEAD!
YOU DIRTY--

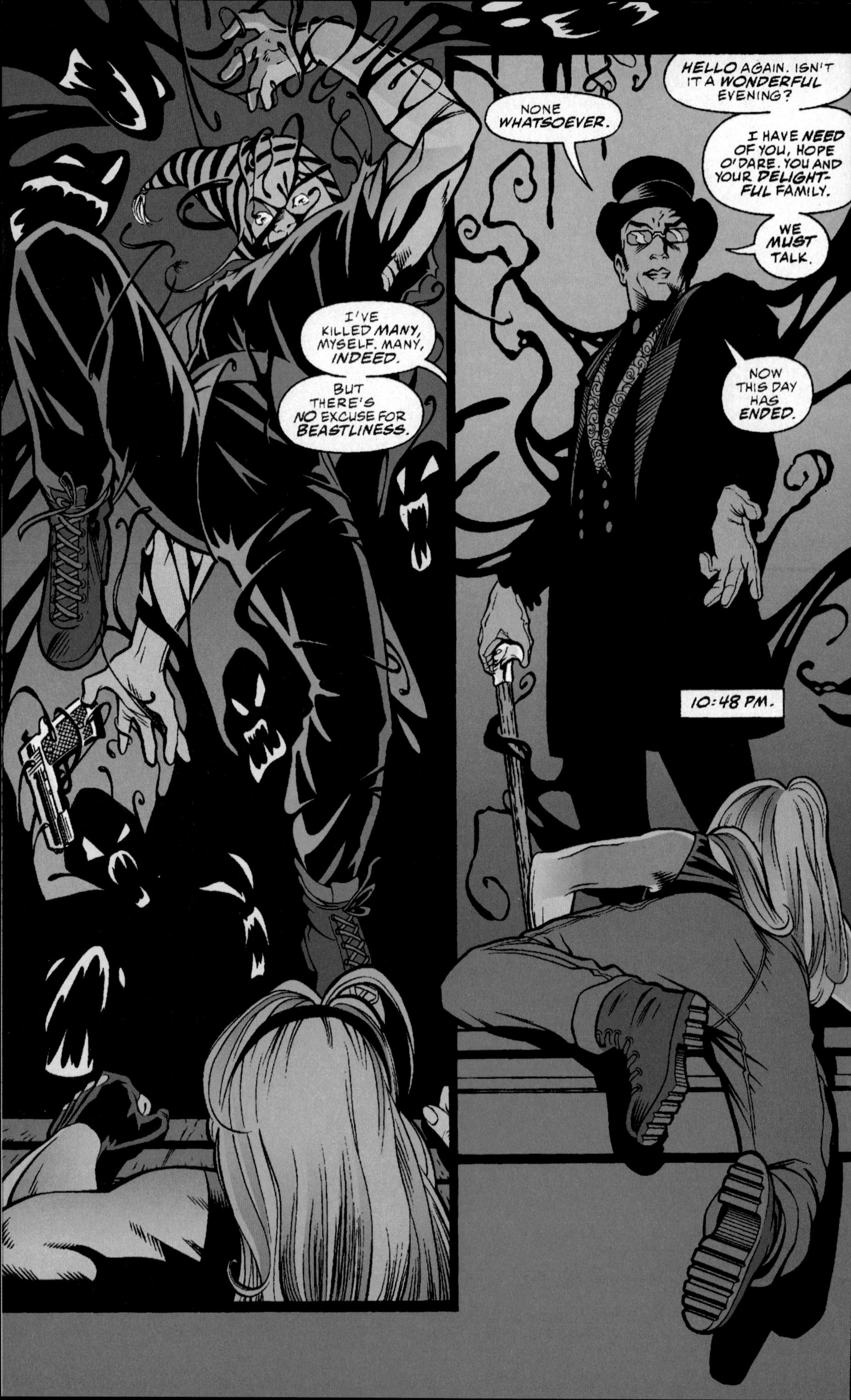
I'VE KILLED MANY, MYSELF. MANY, INDEED.
BUT THERE'S NO EXCUSE FOR BEASTLINESS.
NONE WHATSOEVER.
HELLO AGAIN. ISN'T IT A WONDERFUL EVENING?
I HAVE NEED OF YOU, HOPE O'DARE. YOU AND YOUR DELIGHTFUL FAMILY.
WE MUST TALK.
NOW THIS DAY HAS ENDED.
10:48 PM.

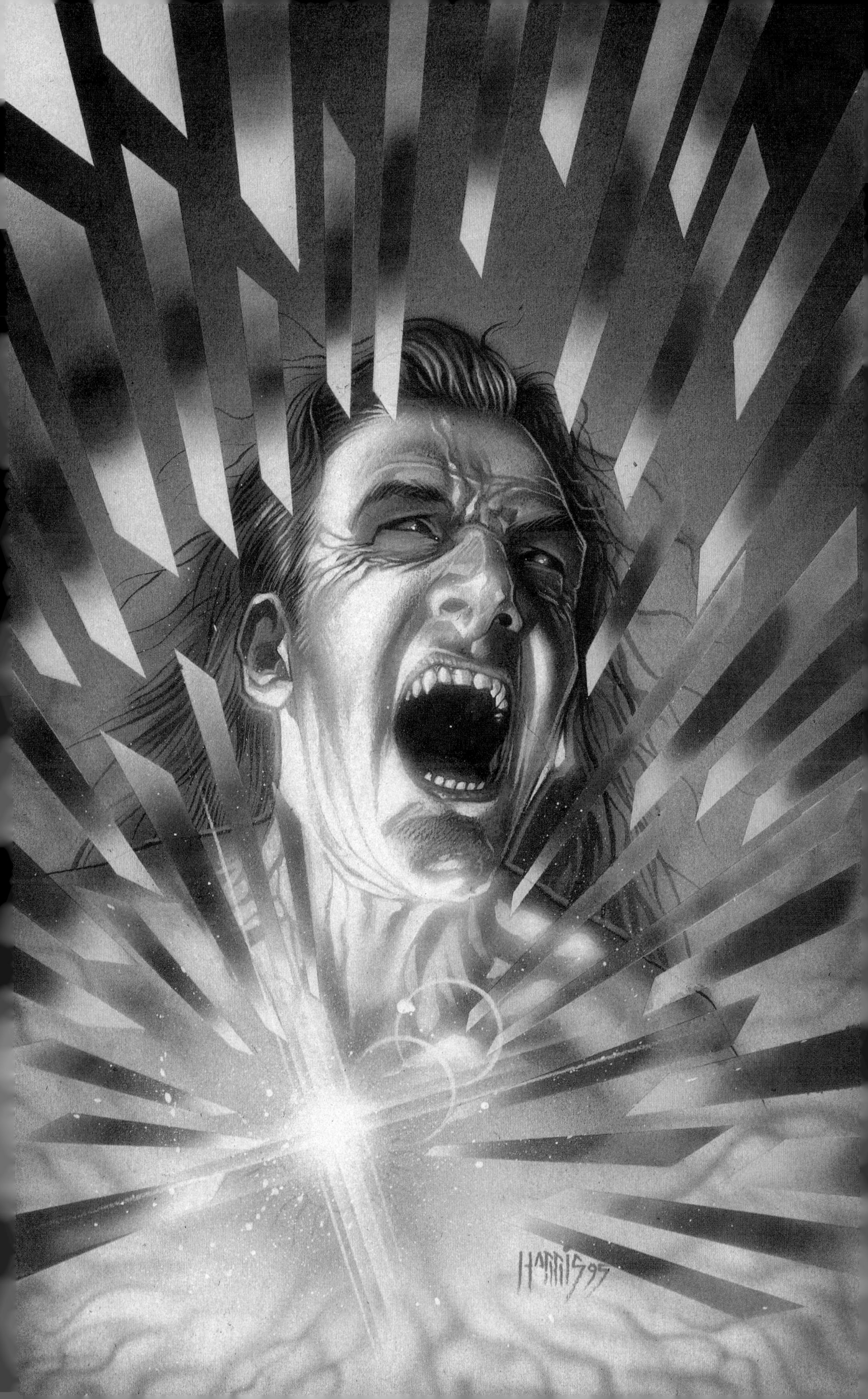
HARRIS 95

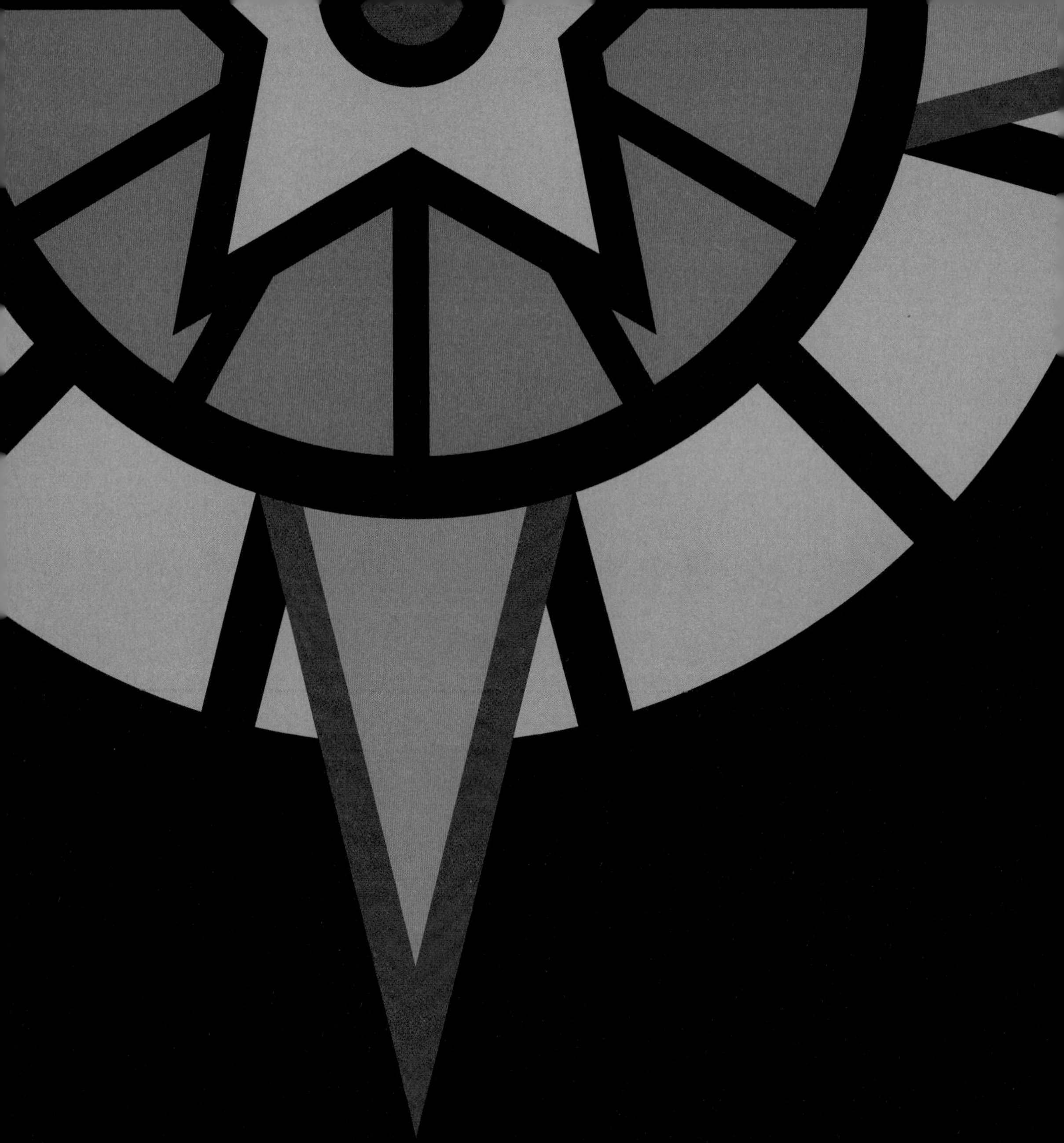

S T A R M A N   1 5

Cover by Tony Harris

Written by James Robinson

Pencils by Tony Harris,

with inks by Wade von Grawbadger

and colors by Ted McKeever

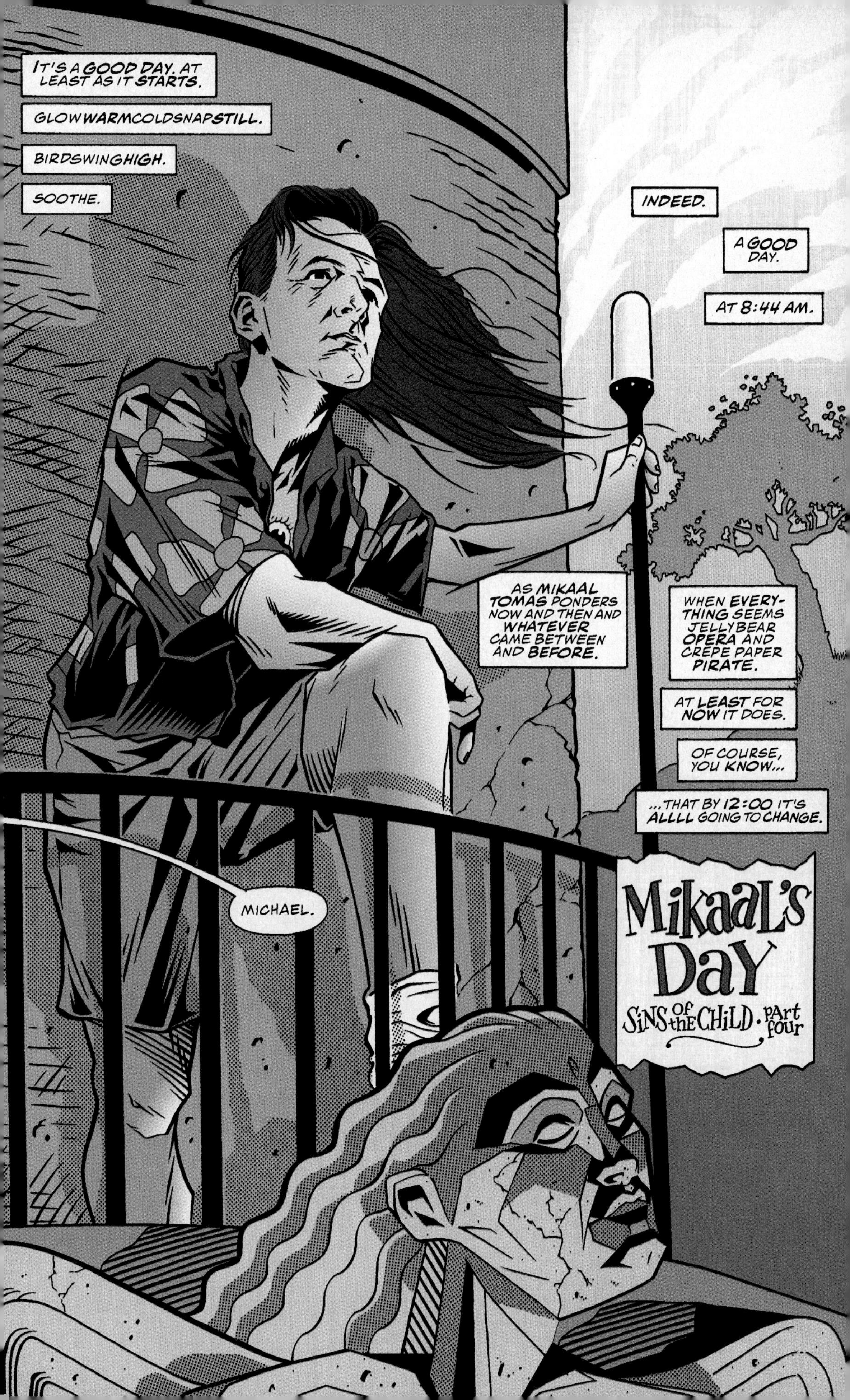
IT'S A GOOD DAY. AT LEAST AS IT STARTS.
GLOWWARMCOLDSNAPSTILL.
BIRDSWINGHIGH.
SOOTHE.
INDEED.
A GOOD DAY.
AT 8:44 AM.
AS MIKAAL TOMAS PONDERS NOW AND THEN AND WHATEVER CAME BETWEEN AND BEFORE.
WHEN EVERYTHING SEEMS JELLYBEAR OPERA AND CREPE PAPER PIRATE.
AT LEAST FOR NOW IT DOES.
OF COURSE, YOU KNOW...
...THAT BY 12:00 IT'S ALLLL GOING TO CHANGE.
MIKAAL'S DAY
SINS OF THE CHILD • PART FOUR
MICHAEL.

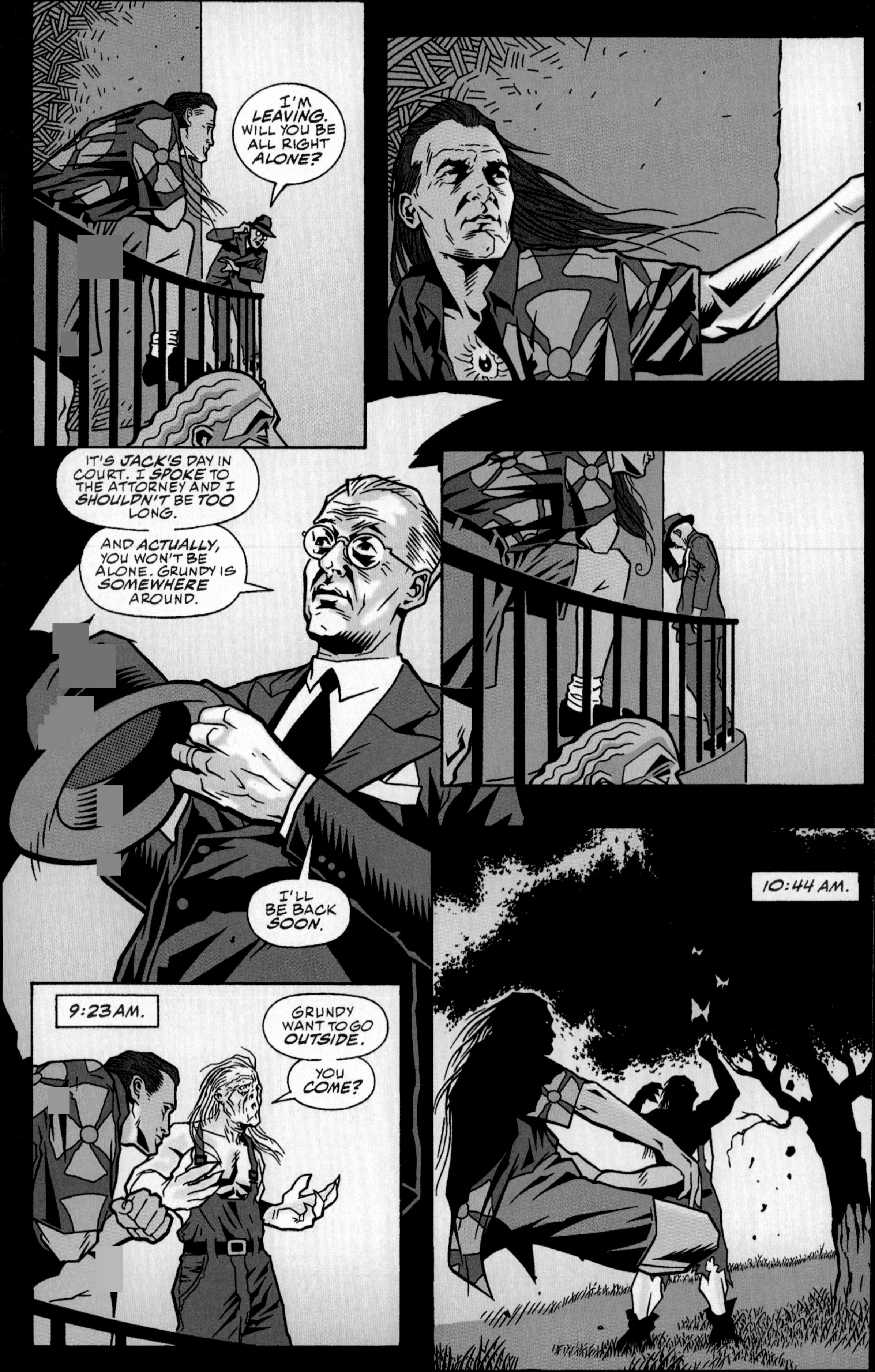

I'M LEAVING. WILL YOU BE ALL RIGHT ALONE?
IT'S JACK'S DAY IN COURT. I SPOKE TO THE ATTORNEY AND I SHOULDN'T BE TOO LONG.
AND ACTUALLY, YOU WON'T BE ALONE. GRUNDY IS SOMEWHERE AROUND.
I'LL BE BACK SOON.
9:23 AM.
GRUNDY WANT TO GO OUTSIDE.
YOU COME?
10:44 AM.

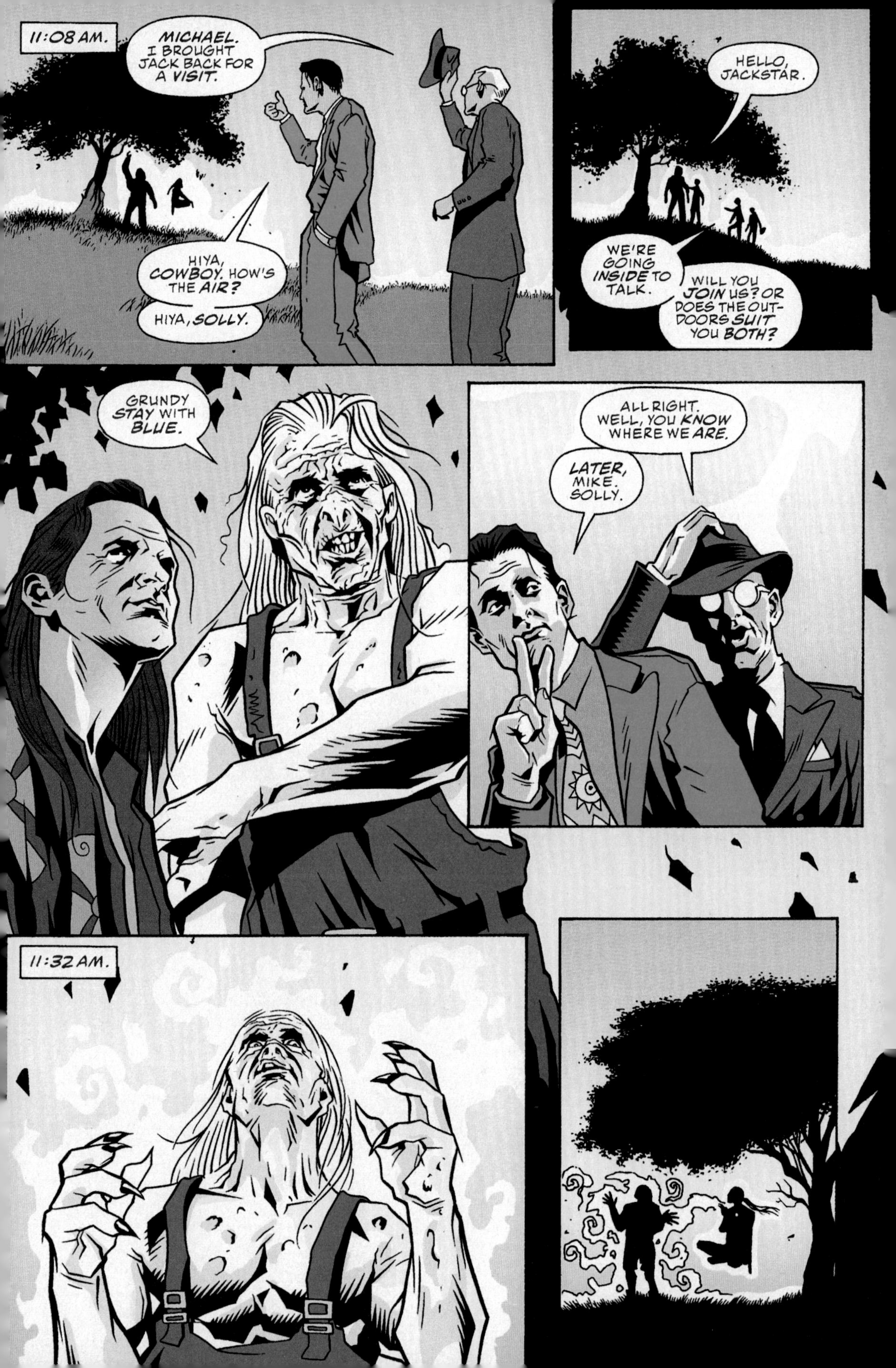
11:08 AM.
MICHAEL. I BROUGHT JACK BACK FOR A VISIT.
HIYA, COWBOY. HOW'S THE AIR?
HIYA, SOLLY.
HELLO, JACKSTAR.
WE'RE GOING INSIDE TO TALK.
WILL YOU JOIN US? OR DOES THE OUTDOORS SUIT YOU BOTH?
GRUNDY STAY WITH BLUE.
ALL RIGHT. WELL, YOU KNOW WHERE WE ARE.
LATER, MIKE. SOLLY.
11:32 AM.

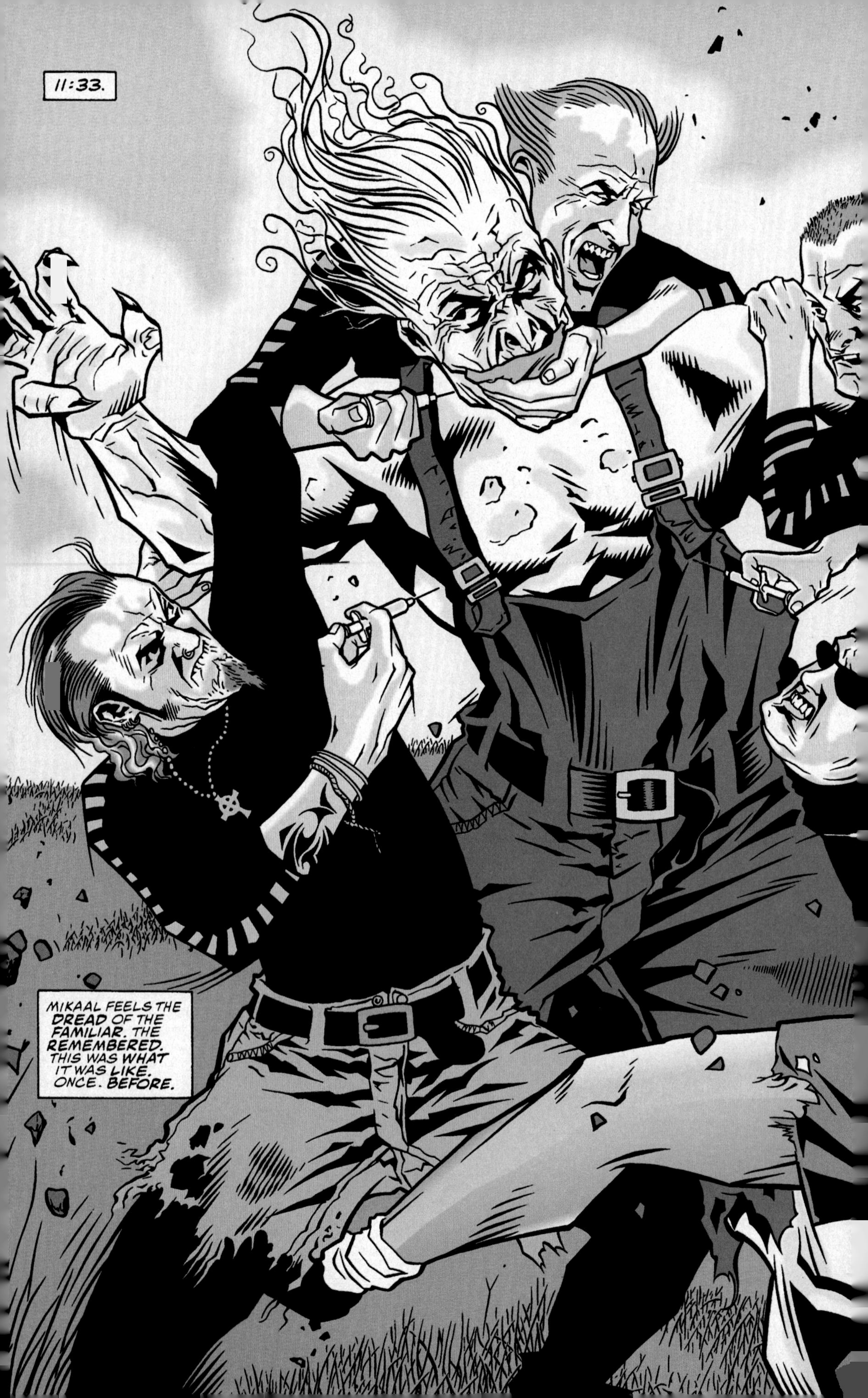
11:33.
MIKAAL FEELS THE DREAD OF THE FAMILIAR. THE REMEMBERED. THIS WAS WHAT IT WAS LIKE. ONCE. BEFORE.

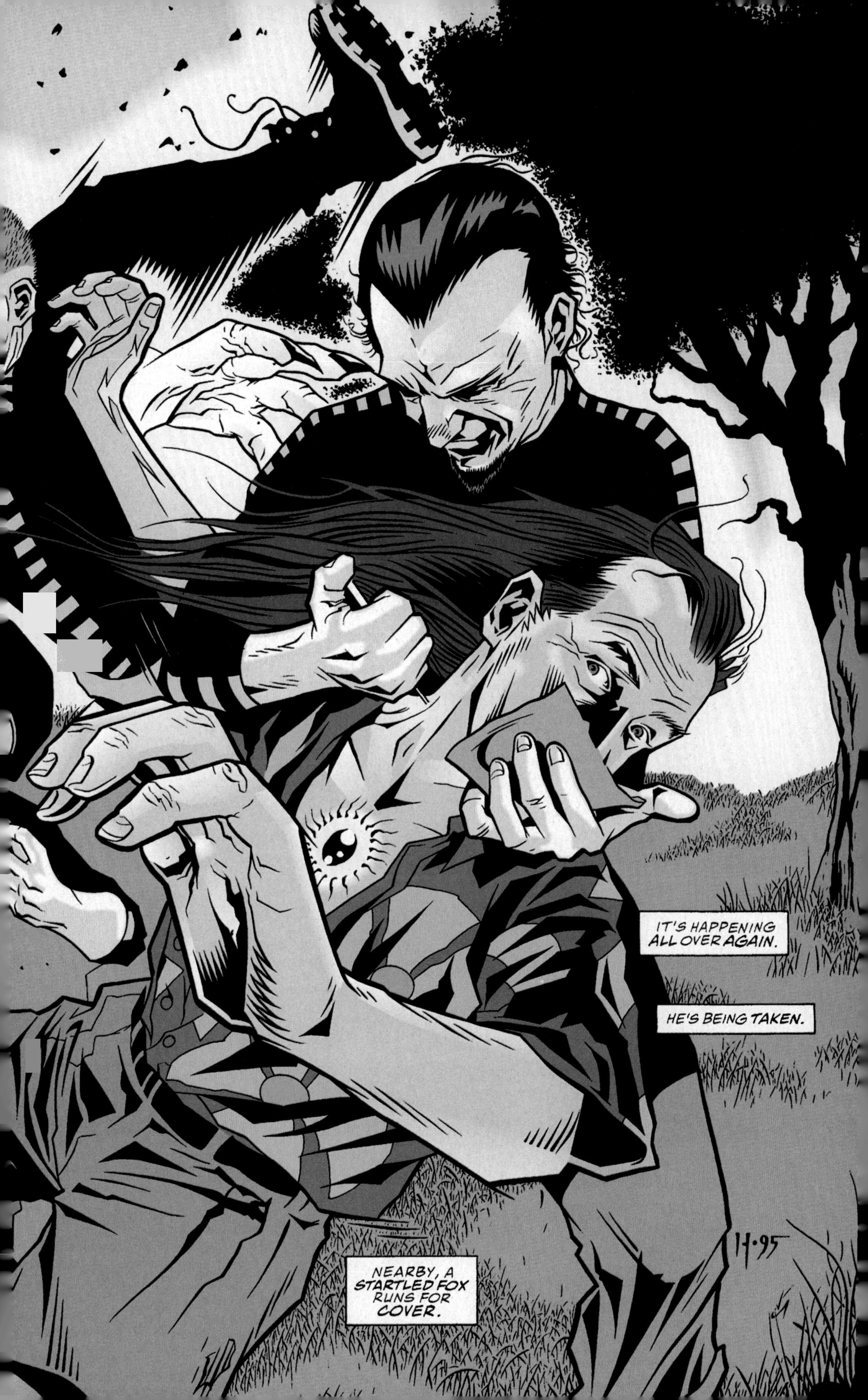
IT'S HAPPENING ALL OVER AGAIN.
HE'S BEING TAKEN.
NEARBY, A STARTLED FOX RUNS FOR COVER.

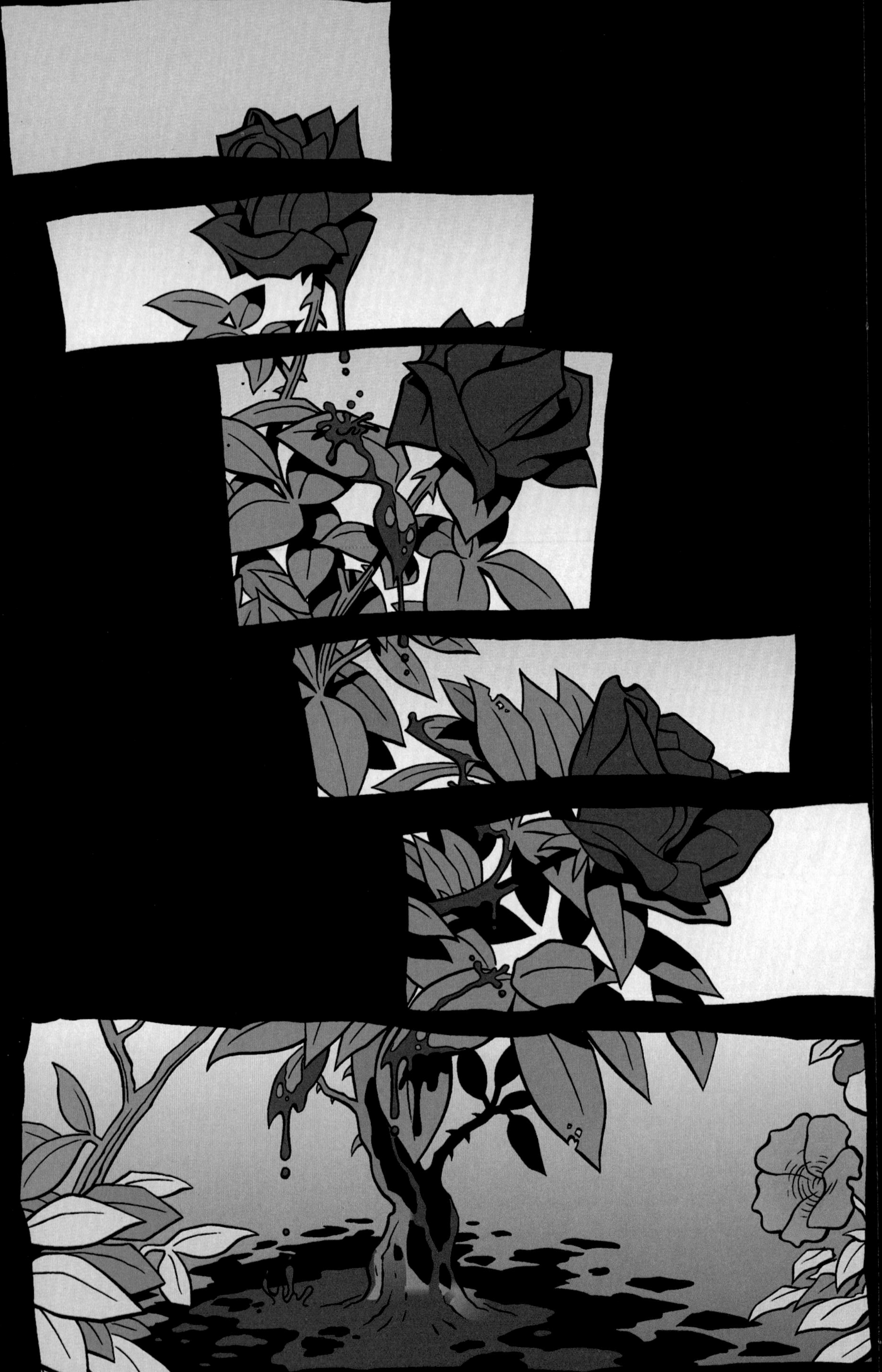

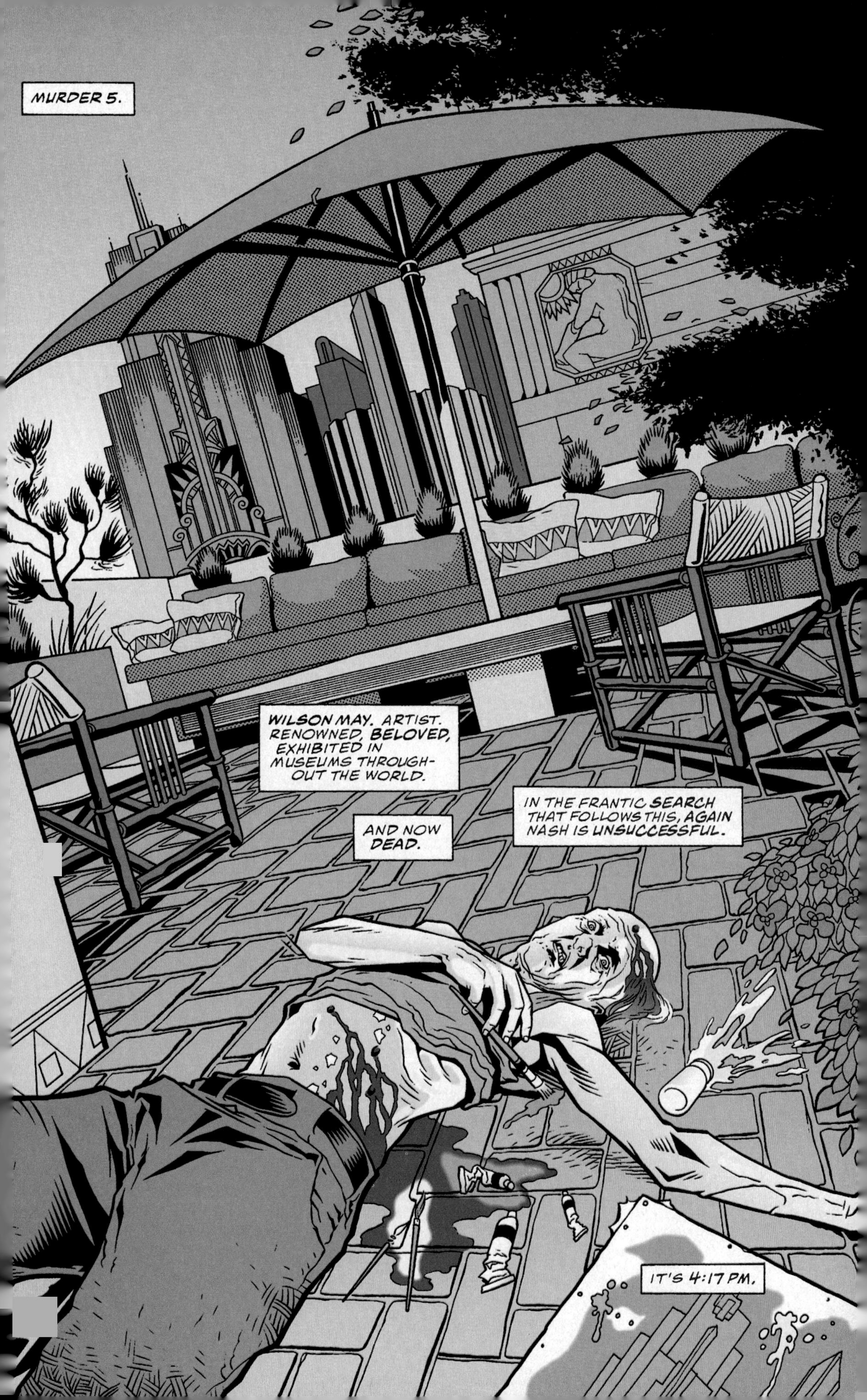
MURDER 5.
WILSON MAY. ARTIST. RENOWNED, BELOVED, EXHIBITED IN MUSEUMS THROUGH-OUT THE WORLD.
AND NOW DEAD.
IN THE FRANTIC SEARCH THAT FOLLOWS THIS, AGAIN NASH IS UNSUCCESSFUL.
IT'S 4:17 PM.

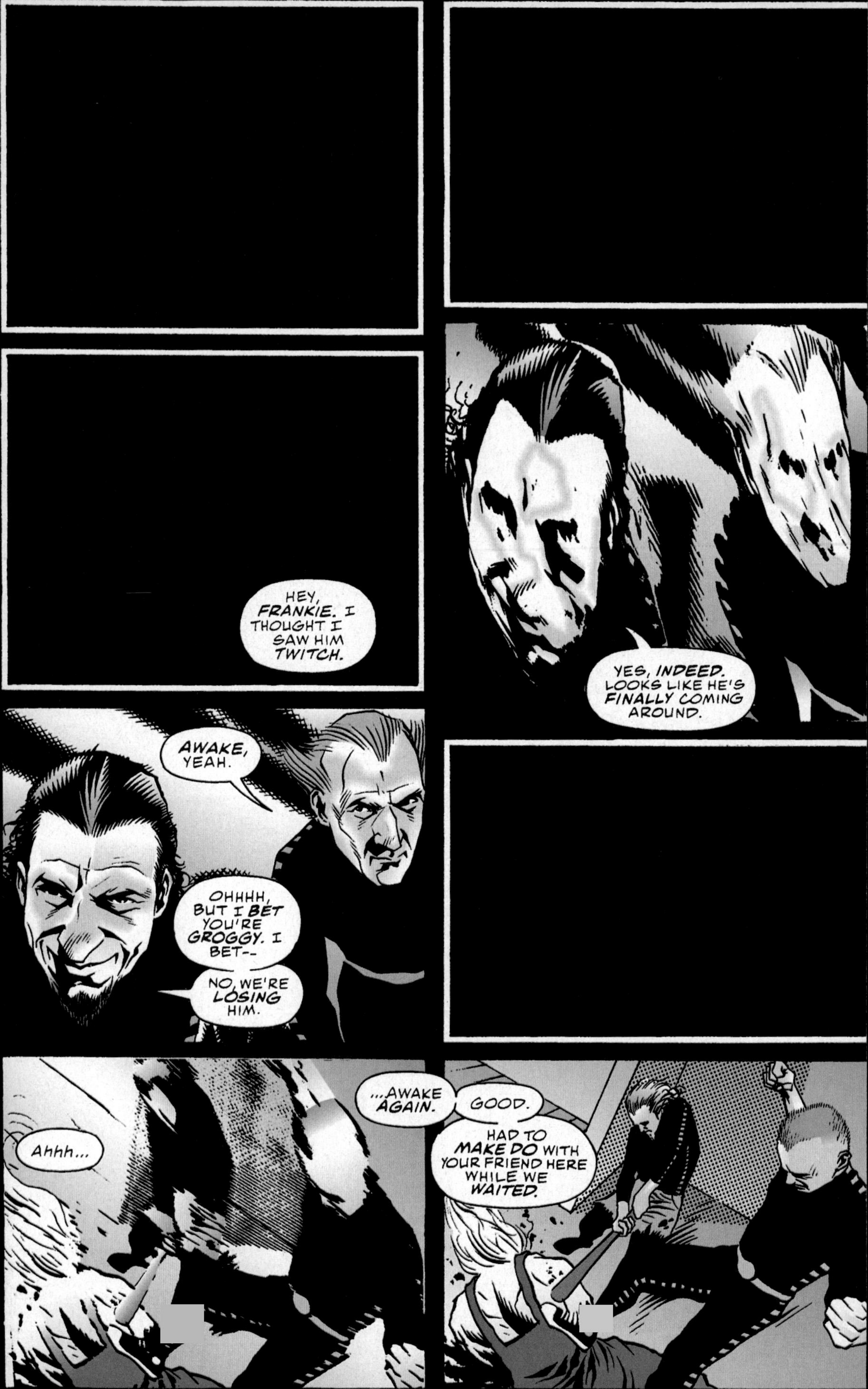
HEY, FRANKIE. I THOUGHT I SAW HIM TWITCH.
YES, INDEED. LOOKS LIKE HE'S FINALLY COMING AROUND.
AWAKE, YEAH.
OHHHH, BUT I BET YOU'RE GROGGY. I BET--
NO, WE'RE LOSING HIM.
Ahhh...
...AWAKE AGAIN.
GOOD.
HAD TO MAKE DO WITH YOUR FRIEND HERE WHILE WE WAITED.

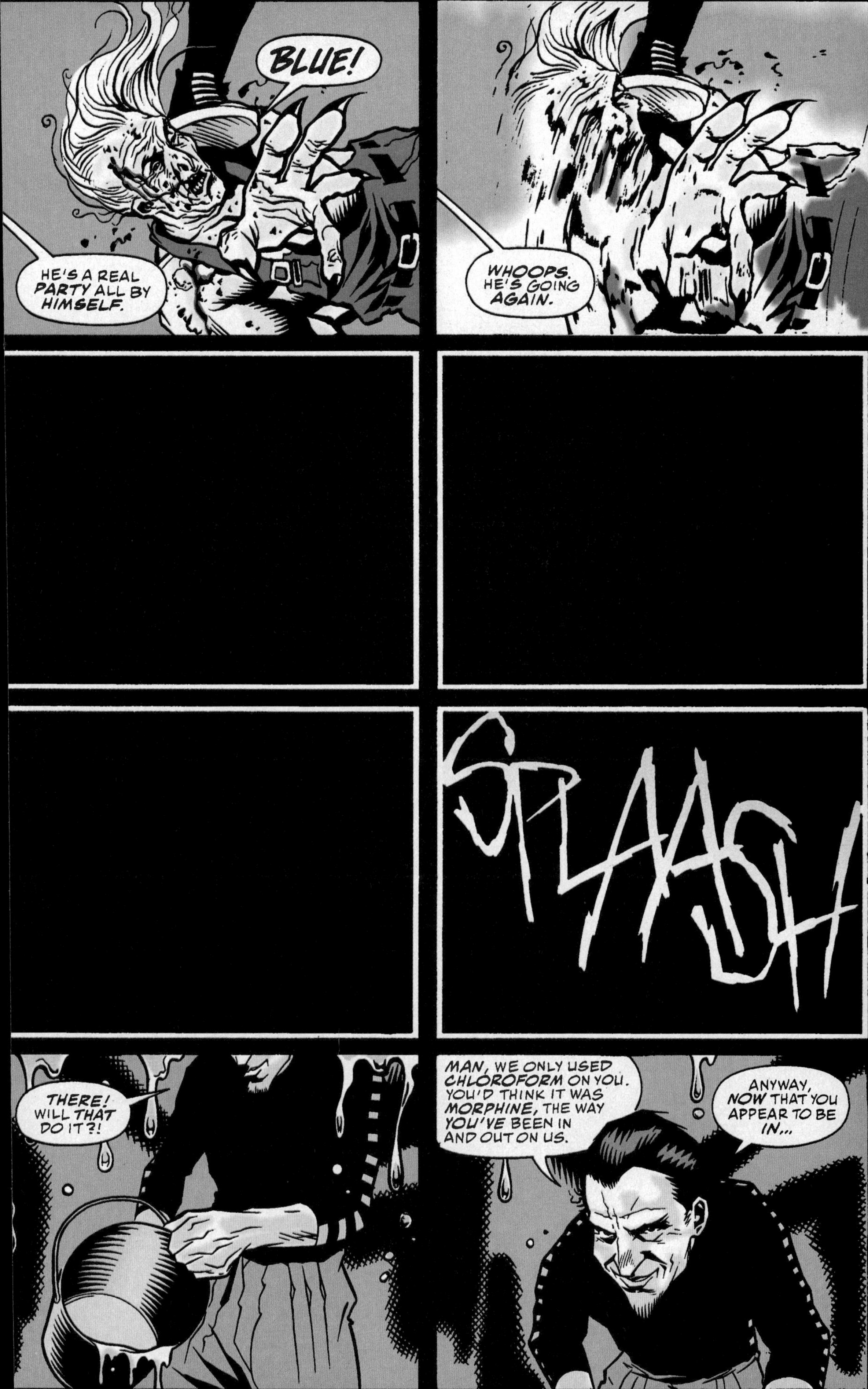
BLUE!
HE'S A REAL PARTY ALL BY HIMSELF.
WHOOPS. HE'S GOING AGAIN.
SPLAASH!
THERE! WILL THAT DO IT?!
MAN, WE ONLY USED CHLOROFORM ON YOU. YOU'D THINK IT WAS MORPHINE, THE WAY YOU'VE BEEN IN AND OUT ON US.
ANYWAY, NOW THAT YOU APPEAR TO BE IN...

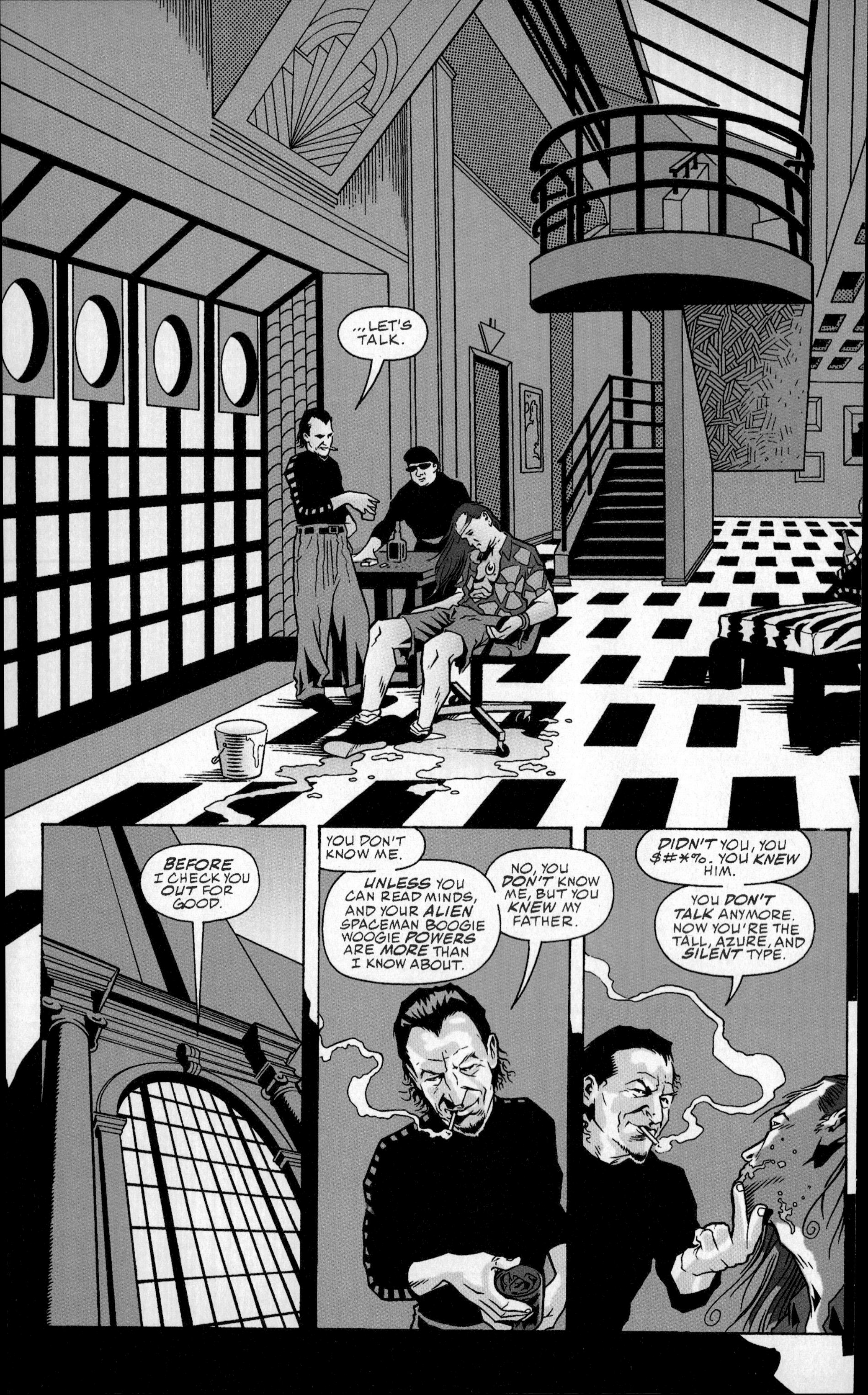
...LET'S TALK.
BEFORE I CHECK YOU OUT FOR GOOD.
YOU DON'T KNOW ME.
UNLESS YOU CAN READ MINDS, AND YOUR ALIEN SPACEMAN BOOGIE WOOGIE POWERS ARE MORE THAN I KNOW ABOUT.
NO, YOU DON'T KNOW ME, BUT YOU KNEW MY FATHER.
DIDN'T YOU, YOU $#*%. YOU KNEW HIM.
YOU DON'T TALK ANYMORE. NOW YOU'RE THE TALL, AZURE, AND SILENT TYPE.

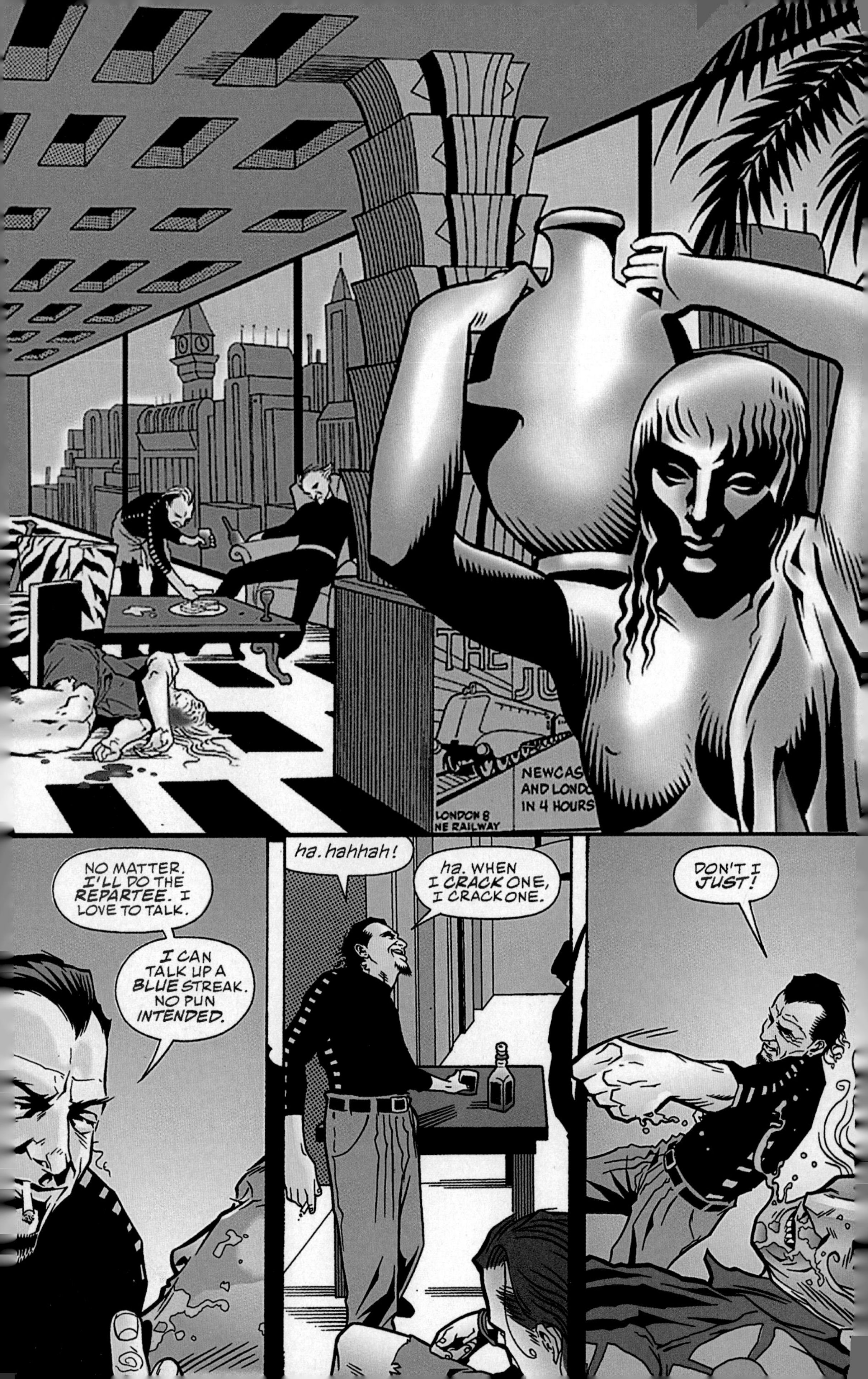
THE
NEWCAS
AND LONDO
IN 4 HOURS
LONDON &
NE RAILWAY
NO MATTER. I'LL DO THE REPARTEE. I LOVE TO TALK.
I CAN TALK UP A BLUE STREAK. NO PUN INTENDED.
ha. hahhah!
ha. WHEN I CRACK ONE, I CRACK ONE.
DON'T I JUST!

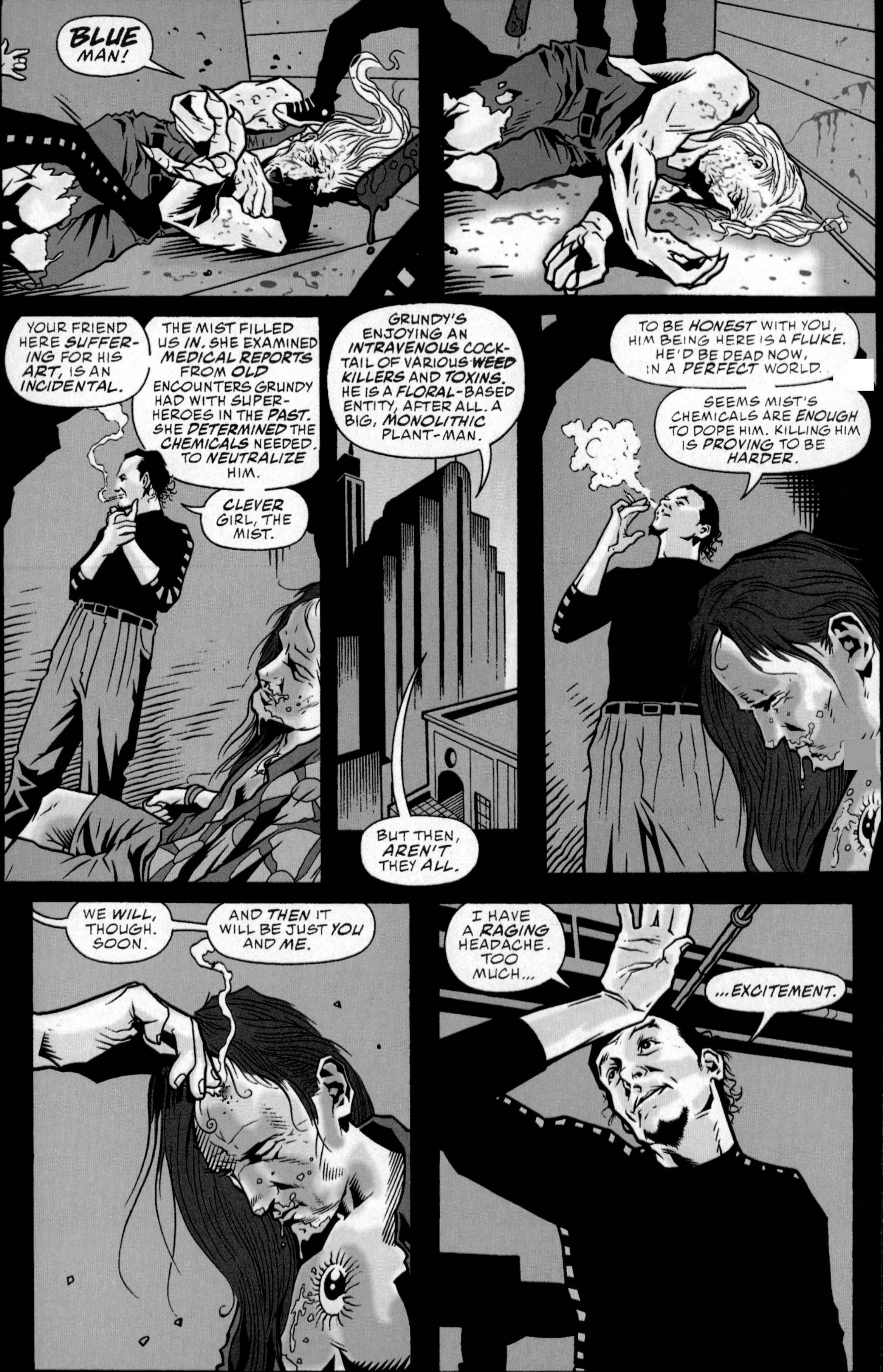
BLUE MAN!
YOUR FRIEND HERE SUFFERING FOR HIS ART, IS AN INCIDENTAL.
THE MIST FILLED US IN. SHE EXAMINED MEDICAL REPORTS FROM OLD ENCOUNTERS GRUNDY HAD WITH SUPER-HEROES IN THE PAST. SHE DETERMINED THE CHEMICALS NEEDED TO NEUTRALIZE HIM.
CLEVER GIRL, THE MIST.
GRUNDY'S ENJOYING AN INTRAVENOUS COCKTAIL OF VARIOUS WEED KILLERS AND TOXINS. HE IS A FLORAL-BASED ENTITY, AFTER ALL. A BIG, MONOLITHIC PLANT-MAN.
BUT THEN, AREN'T THEY ALL.
TO BE HONEST WITH YOU, HIM BEING HERE IS A FLUKE. HE'D BE DEAD NOW, IN A PERFECT WORLD.
SEEMS MIST'S CHEMICALS ARE ENOUGH TO DOPE HIM. KILLING HIM IS PROVING TO BE HARDER.
WE WILL, THOUGH. SOON.
AND THEN IT WILL BE JUST YOU AND ME.
I HAVE A RAGING HEADACHE. TOO MUCH...
...EXCITEMENT.

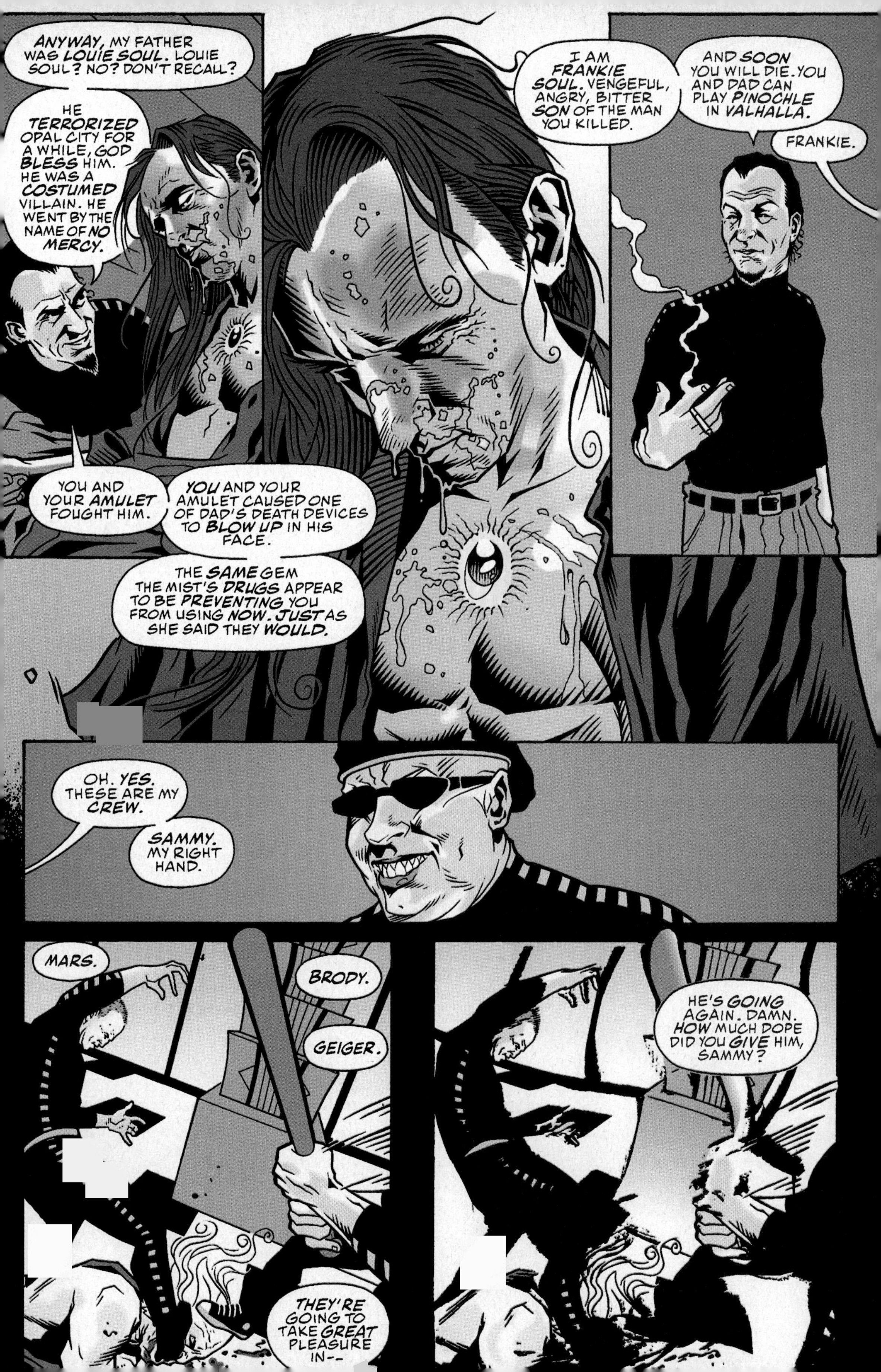
ANYWAY, MY FATHER WAS LOUIE SOUL. LOUIE SOUL? NO? DON'T RECALL?
HE TERRORIZED OPAL CITY FOR A WHILE, GOD BLESS HIM. HE WAS A COSTUMED VILLAIN. HE WENT BY THE NAME OF NO MERCY.
YOU AND YOUR AMULET FOUGHT HIM.
YOU AND YOUR AMULET CAUSED ONE OF DAD'S DEATH DEVICES TO BLOW UP IN HIS FACE.
THE SAME GEM THE MIST'S DRUGS APPEAR TO BE PREVENTING YOU FROM USING NOW. JUST AS SHE SAID THEY WOULD.
I AM FRANKIE SOUL. VENGEFUL, ANGRY, BITTER SON OF THE MAN YOU KILLED.
AND SOON YOU WILL DIE. YOU AND DAD CAN PLAY PINOCHLE IN VALHALLA.
FRANKIE.
OH. YES. THESE ARE MY CREW.
SAMMY. MY RIGHT HAND.
MARS.
BRODY.
GEIGER.
THEY'RE GOING TO TAKE GREAT PLEASURE IN--
HE'S GOING AGAIN. DAMN. HOW MUCH DOPE DID YOU GIVE HIM, SAMMY?

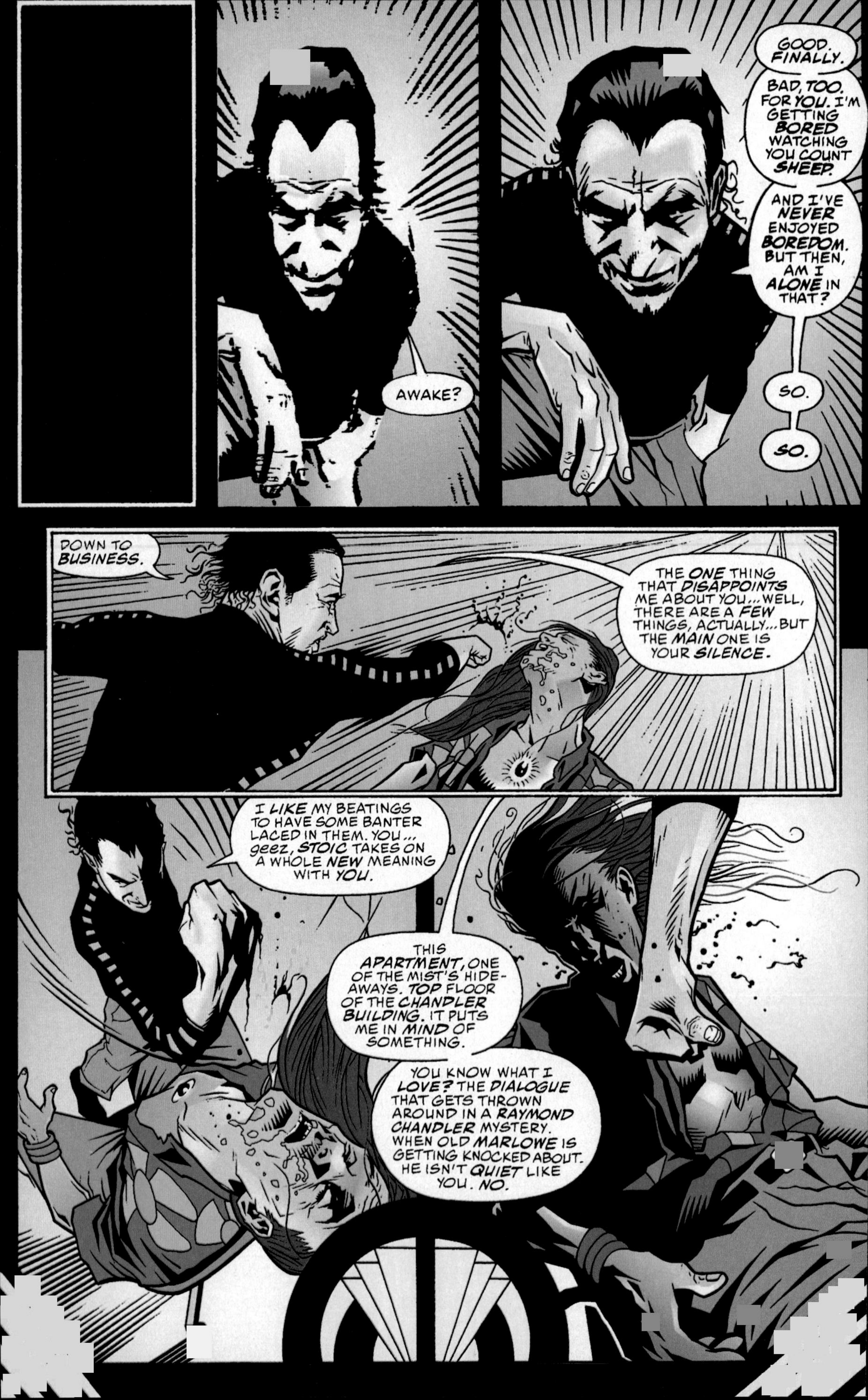
AWAKE?
GOOD. FINALLY.
BAD, TOO. FOR YOU. I'M GETTING BORED WATCHING YOU COUNT SHEEP.
AND I'VE NEVER ENJOYED BOREDOM. BUT THEN, AM I ALONE IN THAT?
SO.
SO.
DOWN TO BUSINESS.
THE ONE THING THAT DISAPPOINTS ME ABOUT YOU... WELL, THERE ARE A FEW THINGS, ACTUALLY... BUT THE MAIN ONE IS YOUR SILENCE.
I LIKE MY BEATINGS TO HAVE SOME BANTER LACED IN THEM. YOU... geez, STOIC TAKES ON A WHOLE NEW MEANING WITH YOU.
THIS APARTMENT, ONE OF THE MIST'S HIDE-AWAYS. TOP FLOOR OF THE CHANDLER BUILDING. IT PUTS ME IN MIND OF SOMETHING.
YOU KNOW WHAT I LOVE? THE DIALOGUE THAT GETS THROWN AROUND IN A RAYMOND CHANDLER MYSTERY. WHEN OLD MARLOWE IS GETTING KNOCKED ABOUT. HE ISN'T QUIET LIKE YOU. NO.

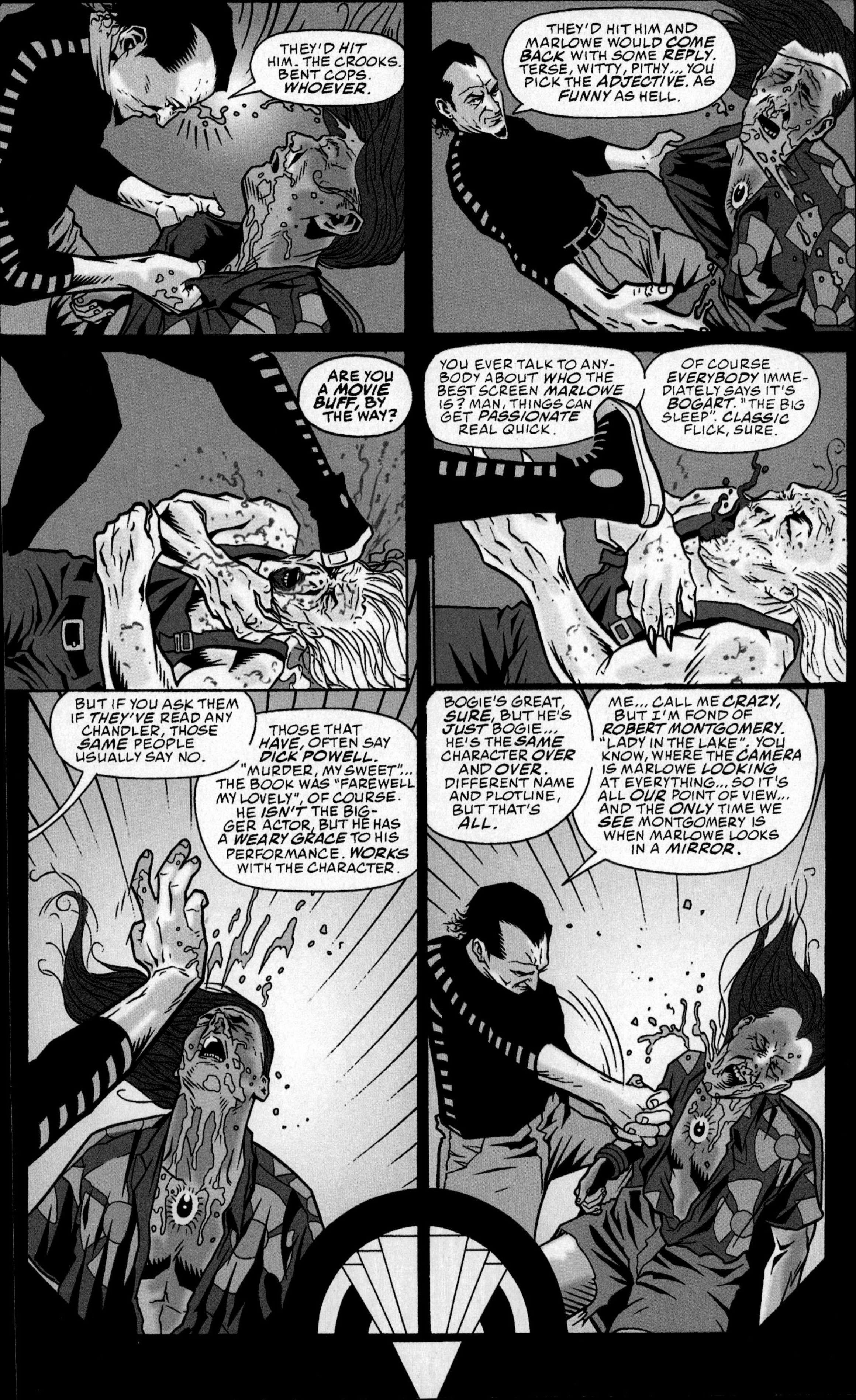
THEY'D *HIT* HIM. THE CROOKS. BENT COPS. *WHOEVER.*
THEY'D HIT HIM AND MARLOWE WOULD *COME BACK* WITH SOME *REPLY*. TERSE, WITTY, PITHY... YOU PICK THE *ADJECTIVE*. AS *FUNNY* AS HELL.
ARE YOU A *MOVIE BUFF*, BY THE WAY?
YOU EVER TALK TO ANYBODY ABOUT *WHO* THE BEST SCREEN *MARLOWE* IS? MAN, THINGS CAN GET *PASSIONATE* REAL QUICK.
OF COURSE *EVERYBODY* IMMEDIATELY SAYS IT'S *BOGART*. "THE BIG SLEEP". *CLASSIC* FLICK, SURE.
BUT IF YOU ASK THEM IF *THEY'VE* READ ANY CHANDLER, THOSE *SAME* PEOPLE USUALLY SAY NO.
THOSE THAT *HAVE*, OFTEN SAY *DICK POWELL*. "MURDER, MY SWEET"... THE BOOK WAS "FAREWELL MY LOVELY", OF COURSE. HE *ISN'T* THE BIGGER ACTOR, BUT HE HAS A *WEARY GRACE* TO HIS PERFORMANCE. *WORKS* WITH THE CHARACTER.
BOGIE'S GREAT, *SURE*, BUT HE'S *JUST* BOGIE... HE'S THE *SAME* CHARACTER *OVER* AND *OVER*. DIFFERENT NAME AND PLOTLINE, BUT THAT'S *ALL*.
ME... CALL ME *CRAZY*, BUT I'M FOND OF *ROBERT MONTGOMERY*. "LADY IN THE LAKE". YOU KNOW, WHERE THE *CAMERA* IS MARLOWE *LOOKING* AT EVERYTHING... SO IT'S ALL *OUR* POINT OF VIEW... AND THE *ONLY* TIME WE *SEE* MONTGOMERY IS WHEN MARLOWE LOOKS IN A *MIRROR*.

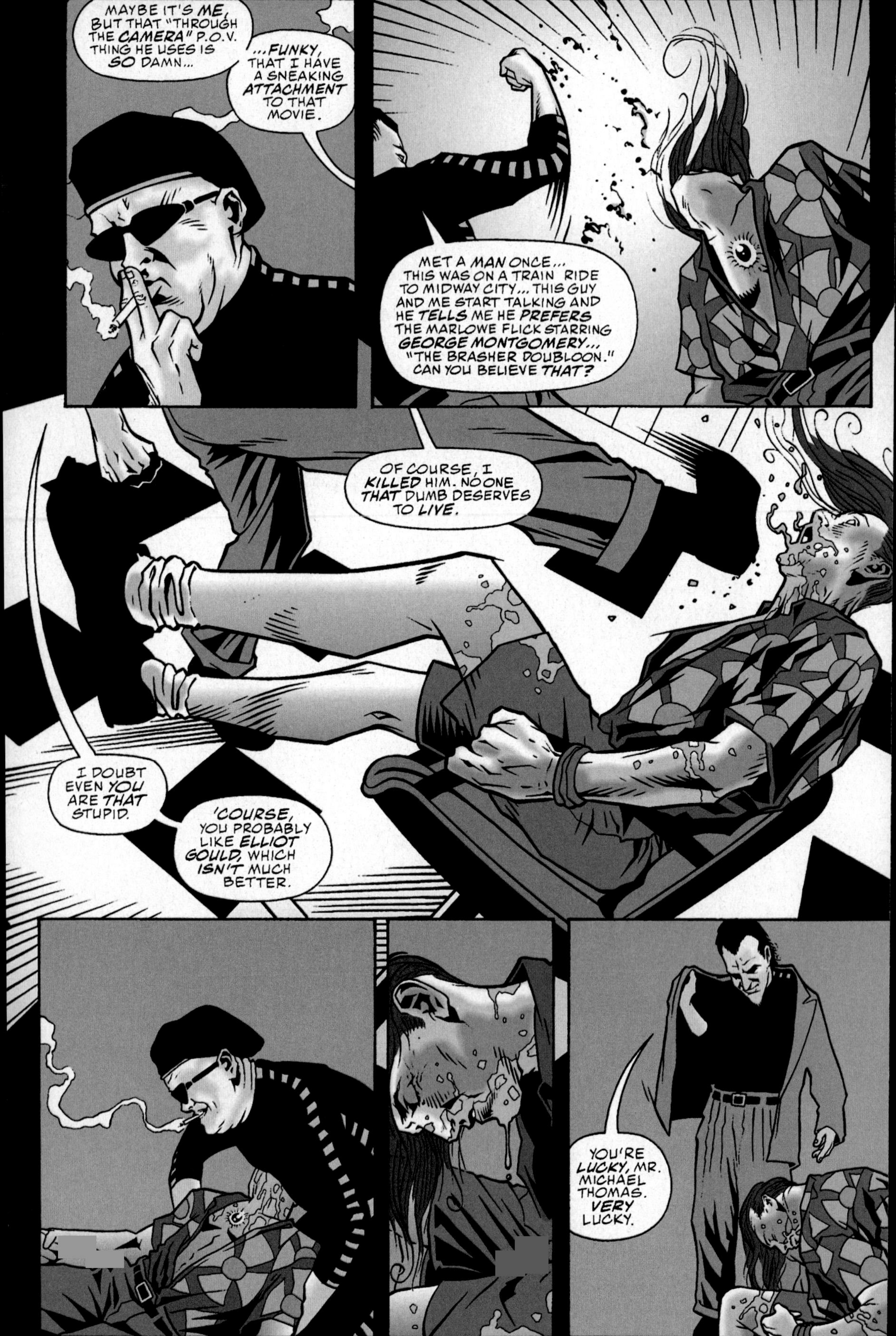

MAYBE IT'S ME, BUT THAT "THROUGH THE CAMERA" P.O.V. THING HE USES IS SO DAMN...
...FUNKY, THAT I HAVE A SNEAKING ATTACHMENT TO THAT MOVIE.
MET A MAN ONCE... THIS WAS ON A TRAIN RIDE TO MIDWAY CITY... THIS GUY AND ME START TALKING AND HE TELLS ME HE PREFERS THE MARLOWE FLICK STARRING GEORGE MONTGOMERY... "THE BRASHER DOUBLOON." CAN YOU BELIEVE THAT?
OF COURSE, I KILLED HIM. NO ONE THAT DUMB DESERVES TO LIVE.
I DOUBT EVEN YOU ARE THAT STUPID.
'COURSE, YOU PROBABLY LIKE ELLIOT GOULD, WHICH ISN'T MUCH BETTER.
YOU'RE LUCKY, MR. MICHAEL THOMAS. VERY LUCKY.

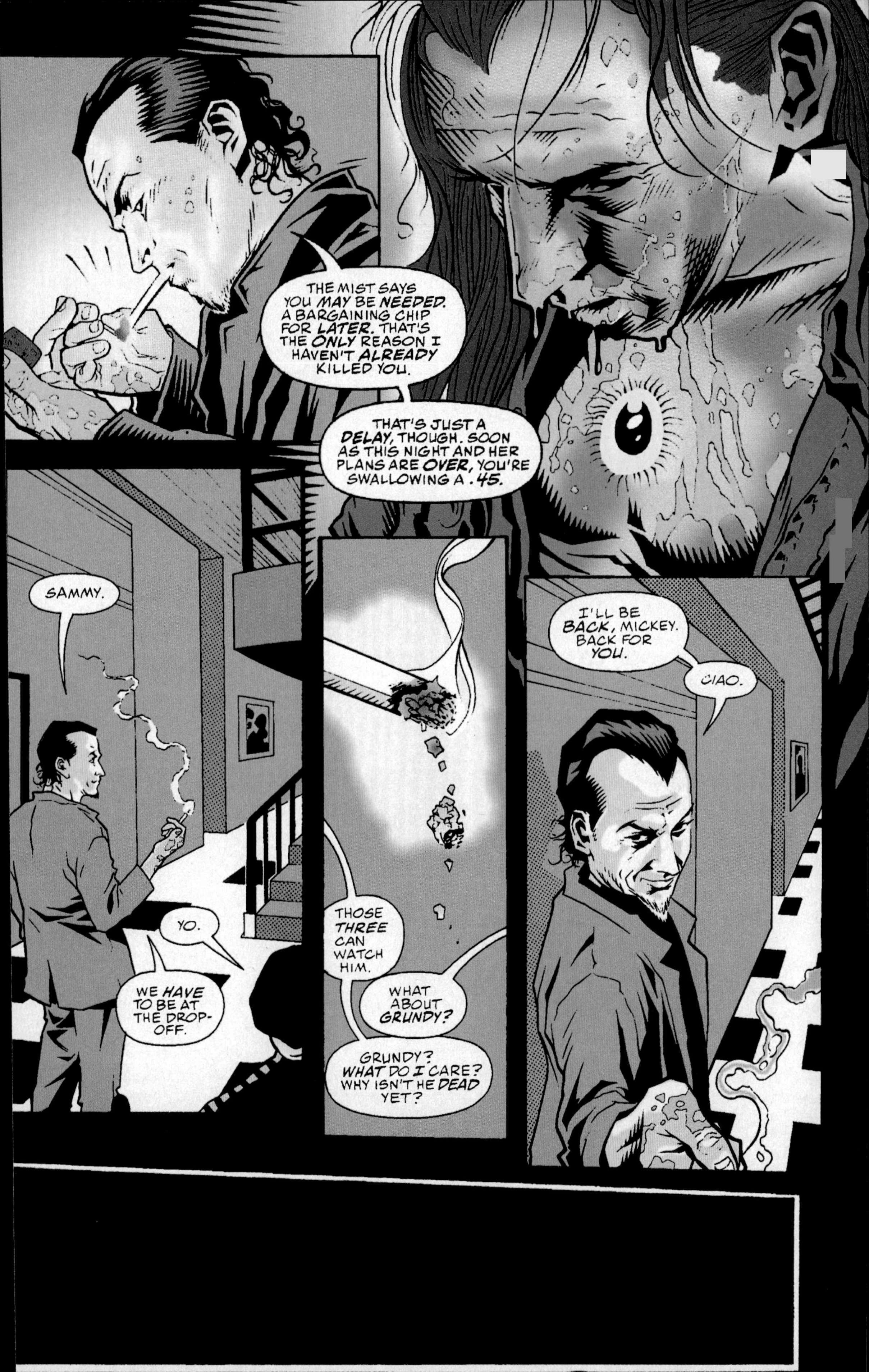
THE MIST SAYS YOU MAY BE NEEDED. A BARGAINING CHIP FOR LATER. THAT'S THE ONLY REASON I HAVEN'T ALREADY KILLED YOU.
THAT'S JUST A DELAY, THOUGH. SOON AS THIS NIGHT AND HER PLANS ARE OVER, YOU'RE SWALLOWING A .45.
SAMMY.
YO.
WE HAVE TO BE AT THE DROP-OFF.
THOSE THREE CAN WATCH HIM.
WHAT ABOUT GRUNDY?
GRUNDY? WHAT DO I CARE? WHY ISN'T HE DEAD YET?
I'LL BE BACK, MICKEY. BACK FOR YOU.
CIAO.

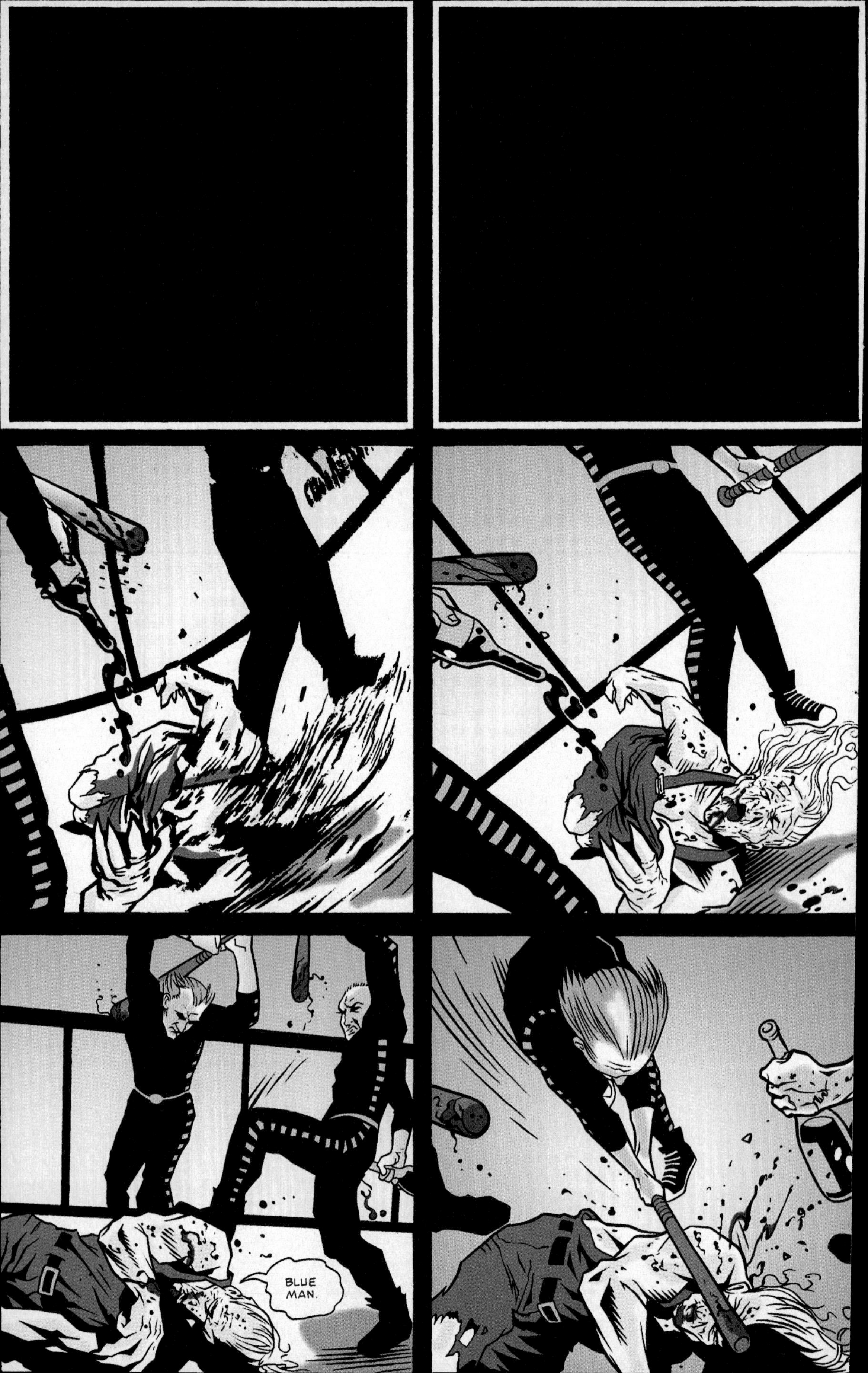
BLUE MAN.

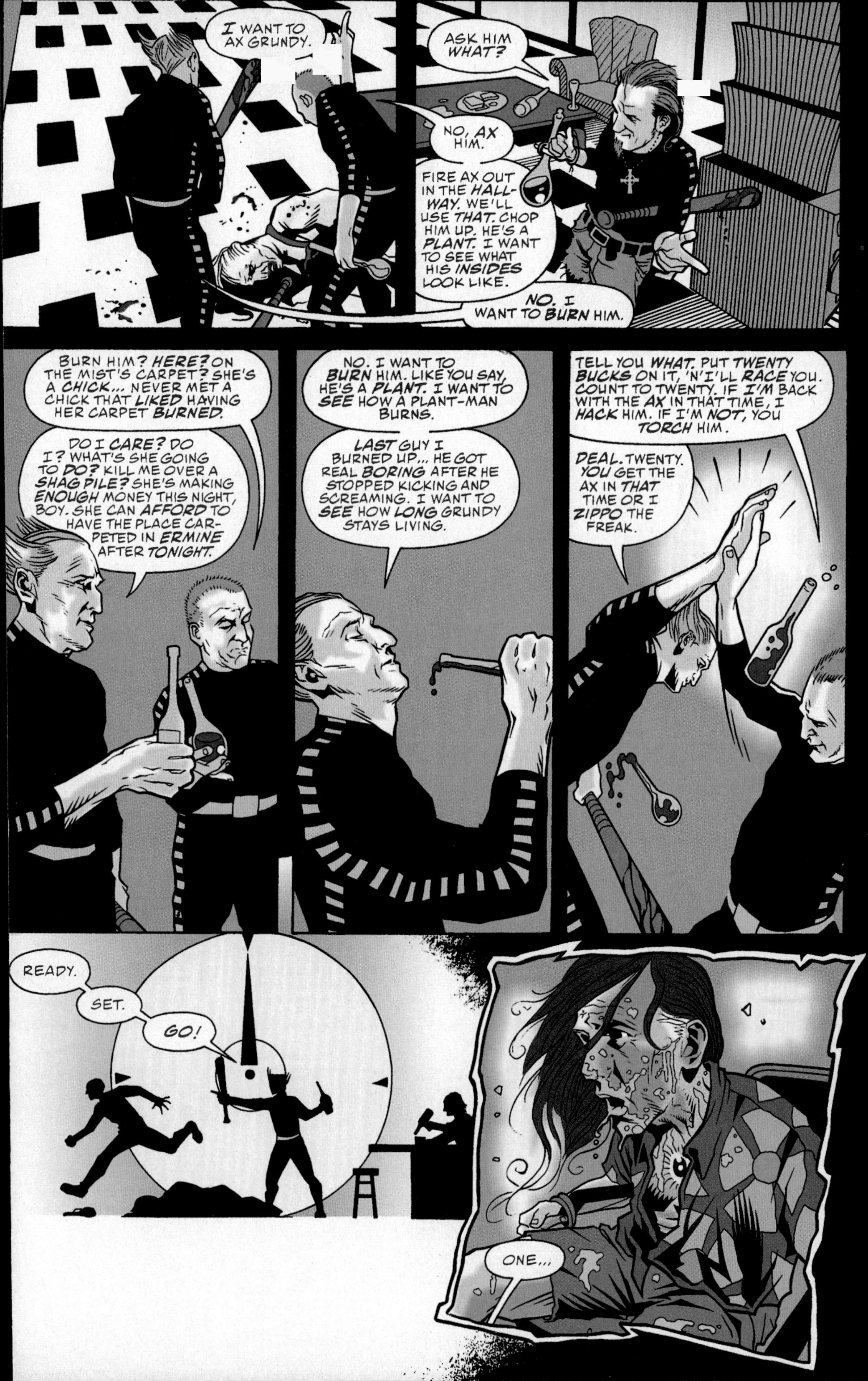
I WANT TO AX GRUNDY.
ASK HIM WHAT?
NO, AX HIM.
FIRE AX OUT IN THE HALLWAY. WE'LL USE THAT. CHOP HIM UP. HE'S A PLANT. I WANT TO SEE WHAT HIS INSIDES LOOK LIKE.
NO. I WANT TO BURN HIM.
BURN HIM? HERE? ON THE MIST'S CARPET? SHE'S A CHICK... NEVER MET A CHICK THAT LIKED HAVING HER CARPET BURNED.
DO I CARE? DO I? WHAT'S SHE GOING TO DO? KILL ME OVER A SHAG PILE? SHE'S MAKING ENOUGH MONEY THIS NIGHT, BOY. SHE CAN AFFORD TO HAVE THE PLACE CARPETED IN ERMINE AFTER TONIGHT.
NO. I WANT TO BURN HIM. LIKE YOU SAY, HE'S A PLANT. I WANT TO SEE HOW A PLANT-MAN BURNS.
LAST GUY I BURNED UP... HE GOT REAL BORING AFTER HE STOPPED KICKING AND SCREAMING. I WANT TO SEE HOW LONG GRUNDY STAYS LIVING.
TELL YOU WHAT. PUT TWENTY BUCKS ON IT, 'N' I'LL RACE YOU. COUNT TO TWENTY. IF I'M BACK WITH THE AX IN THAT TIME, I HACK HIM. IF I'M NOT, YOU TORCH HIM.
DEAL. TWENTY. YOU GET THE AX IN THAT TIME OR I ZIPPO THE FREAK.
READY.
SET.
GO!
ONE...

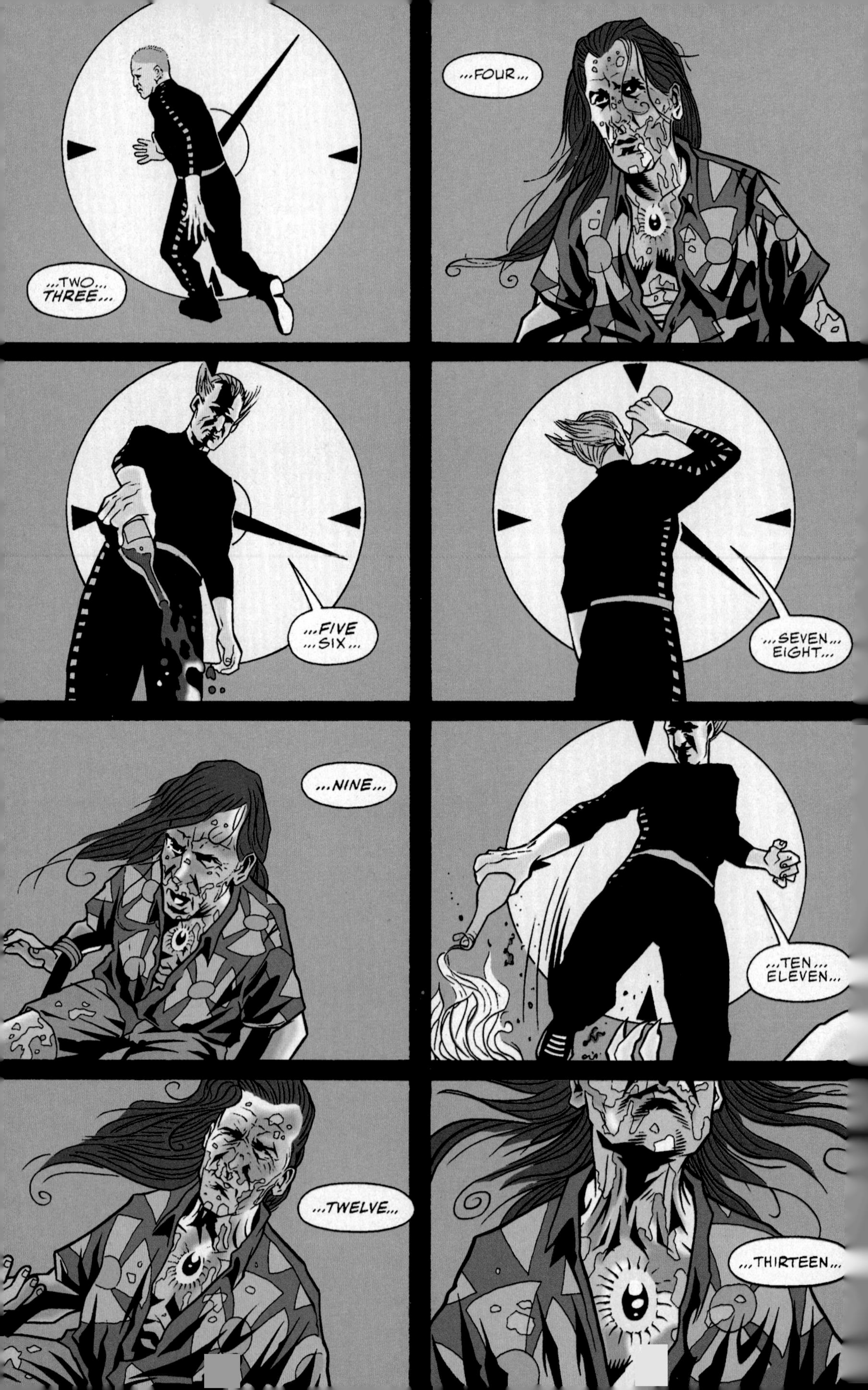
...TWO...
THREE...
...FOUR...
...FIVE
...SIX...
...SEVEN...
EIGHT...
...NINE...
...TEN...
ELEVEN...
...TWELVE...
...THIRTEEN...

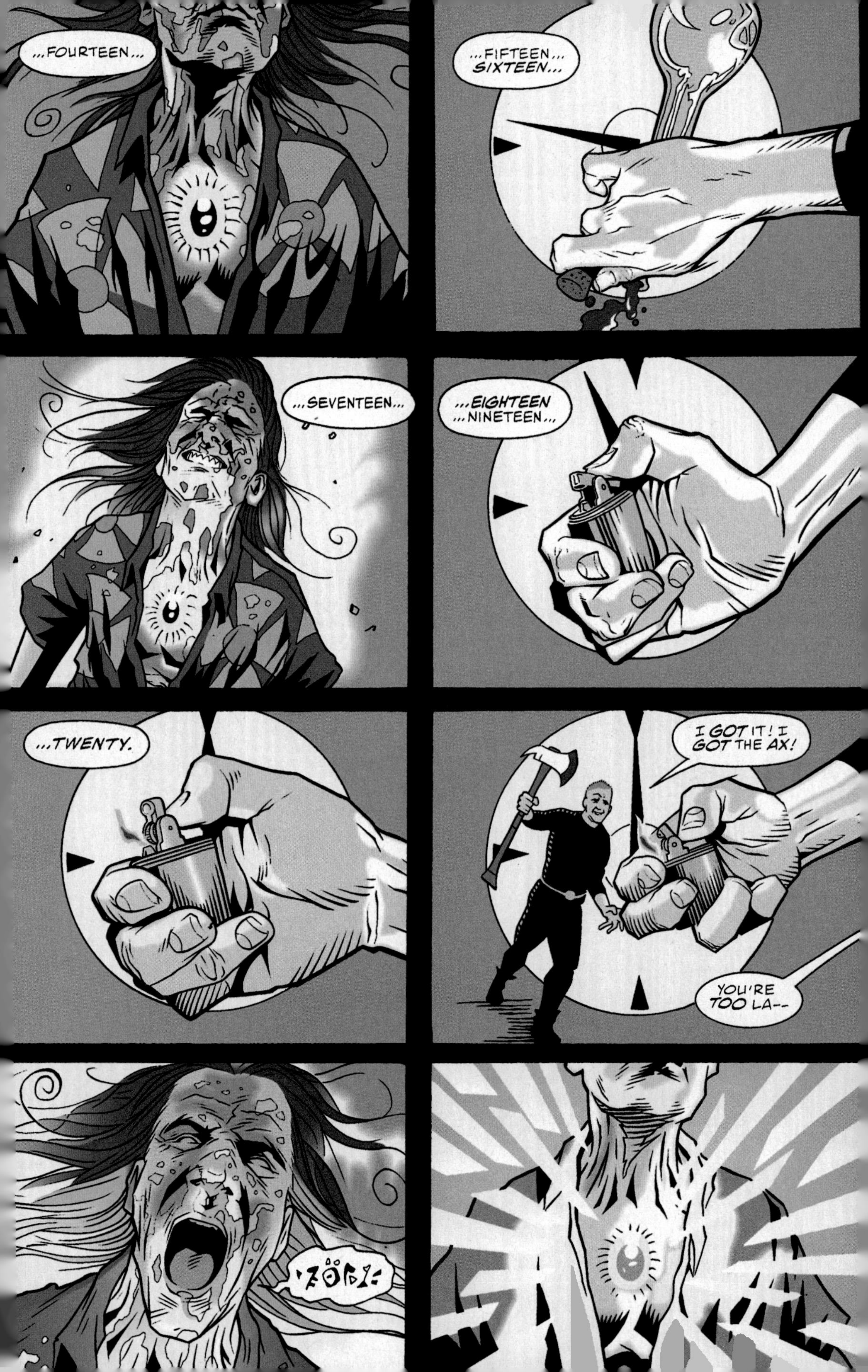
...FOURTEEN...
...FIFTEEN... SIXTEEN...
...SEVENTEEN...
...EIGHTEEN ...NINETEEN...
...TWENTY.
I GOT IT! I GOT THE AX!
YOU'RE TOO LA--

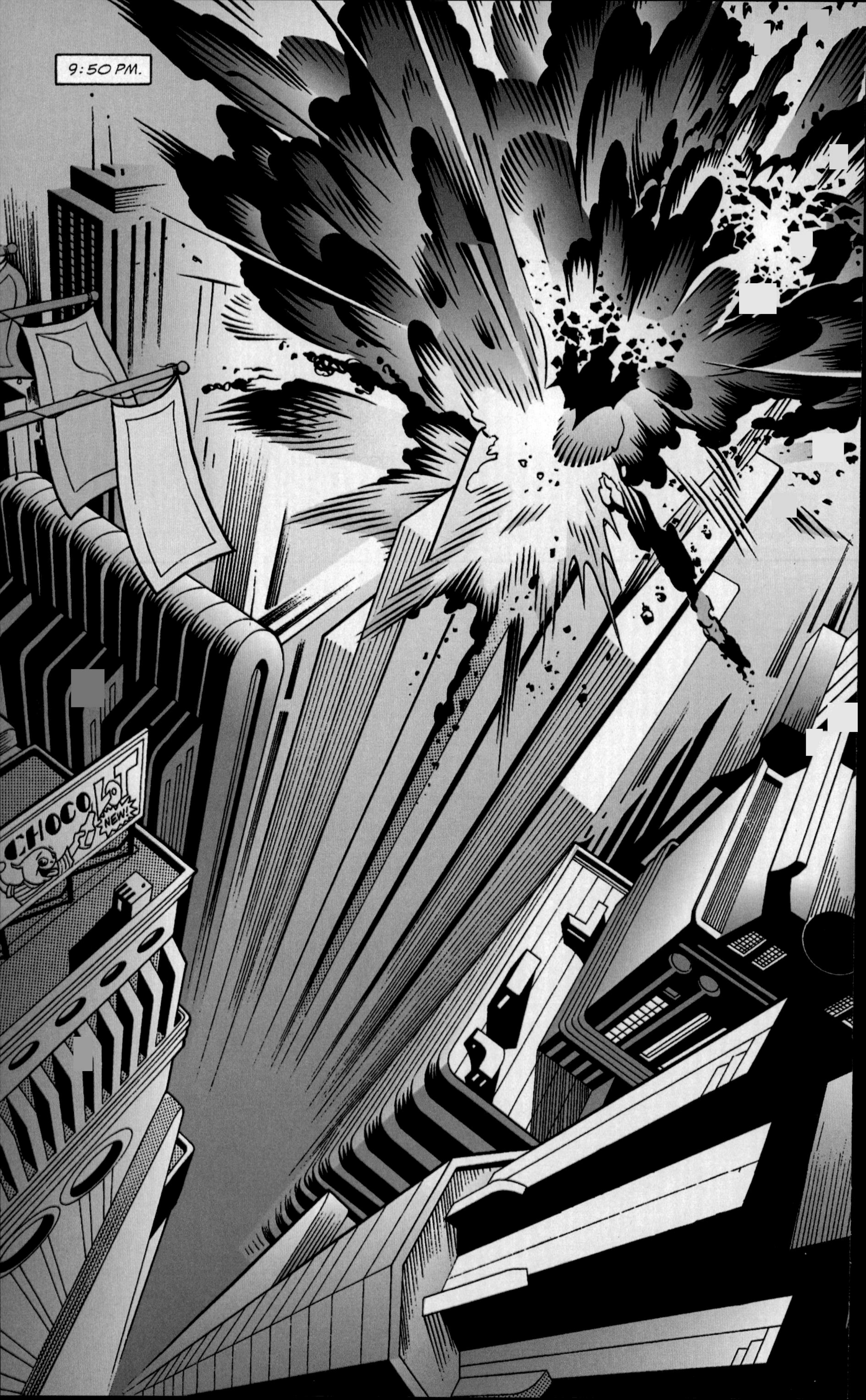
9:50 PM.
CHOCOLOT
NEW!!

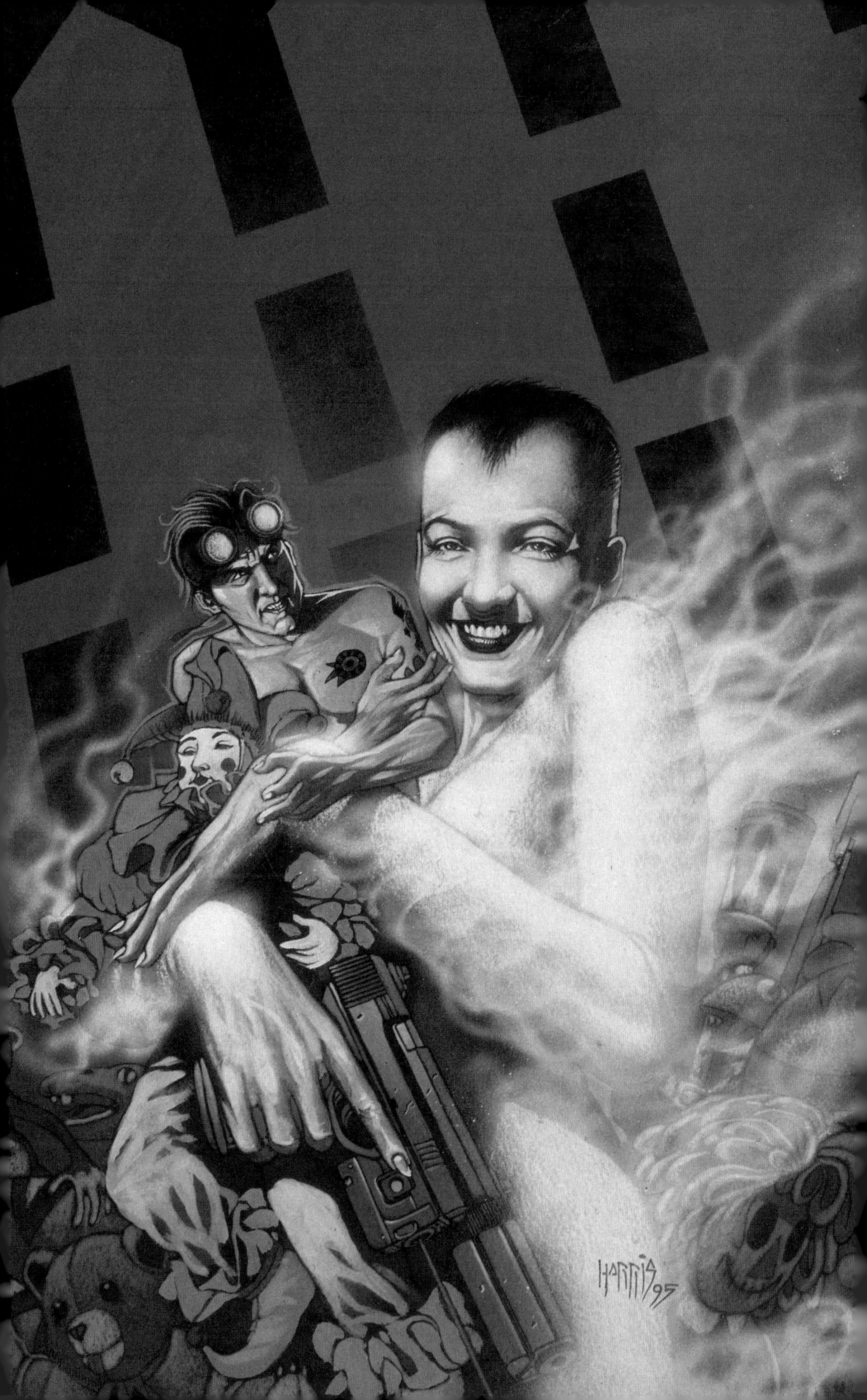
HARRIS 95

STARMAN 16

Cover by Tony Harris

Written by James Robinson

Pencils by Tony Harris,

with inks by Wade von Grawbadger

and colors by Ted McKeever

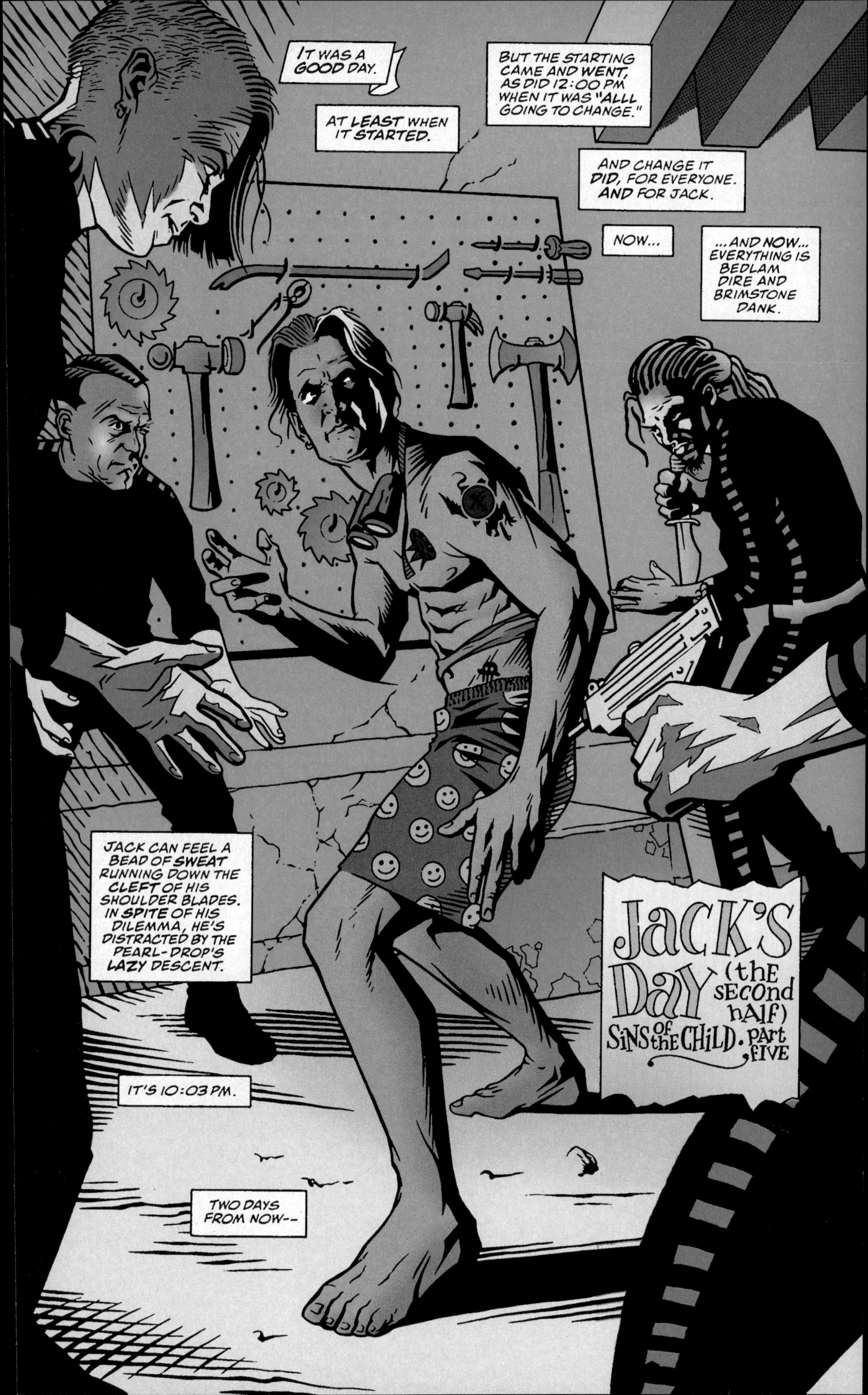
IT WAS A GOOD DAY.
AT LEAST WHEN IT STARTED.
BUT THE STARTING CAME AND WENT, AS DID 12:00 PM WHEN IT WAS "ALLL GOING TO CHANGE."
AND CHANGE IT DID, FOR EVERYONE. AND FOR JACK.
NOW...
...AND NOW... EVERYTHING IS BEDLAM DIRE AND BRIMSTONE DANK.
JACK CAN FEEL A BEAD OF SWEAT RUNNING DOWN THE CLEFT OF HIS SHOULDER BLADES. IN SPITE OF HIS DILEMMA, HE'S DISTRACTED BY THE PEARL-DROP'S LAZY DESCENT.
JACK'S DAY (the SECOND half)
SINS OF the CHILD. PART FIVE
IT'S 10:03 PM.
TWO DAYS FROM NOW--

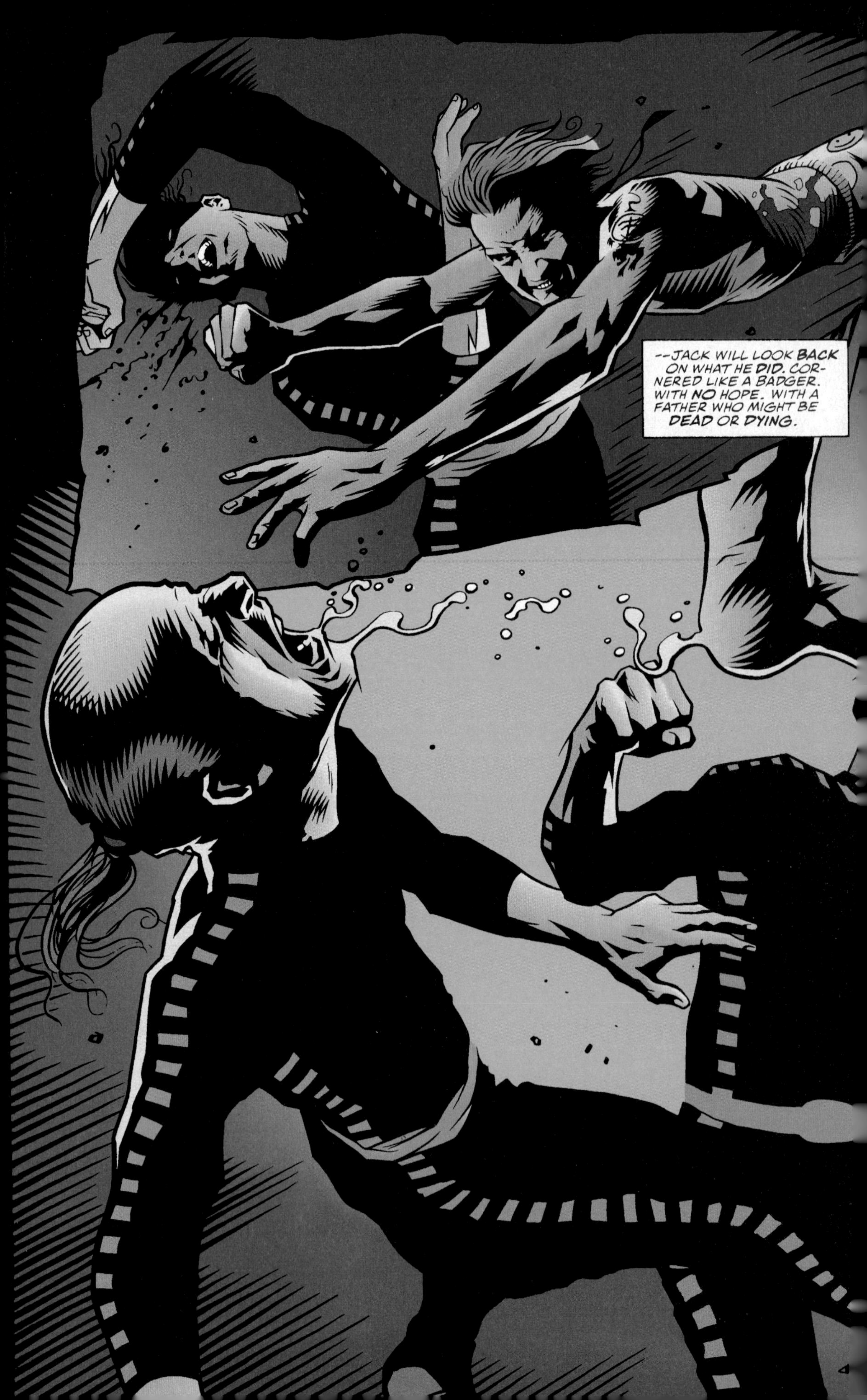
--JACK WILL LOOK BACK ON WHAT HE DID. CORNERED LIKE A BADGER. WITH NO HOPE. WITH A FATHER WHO MIGHT BE DEAD OR DYING.

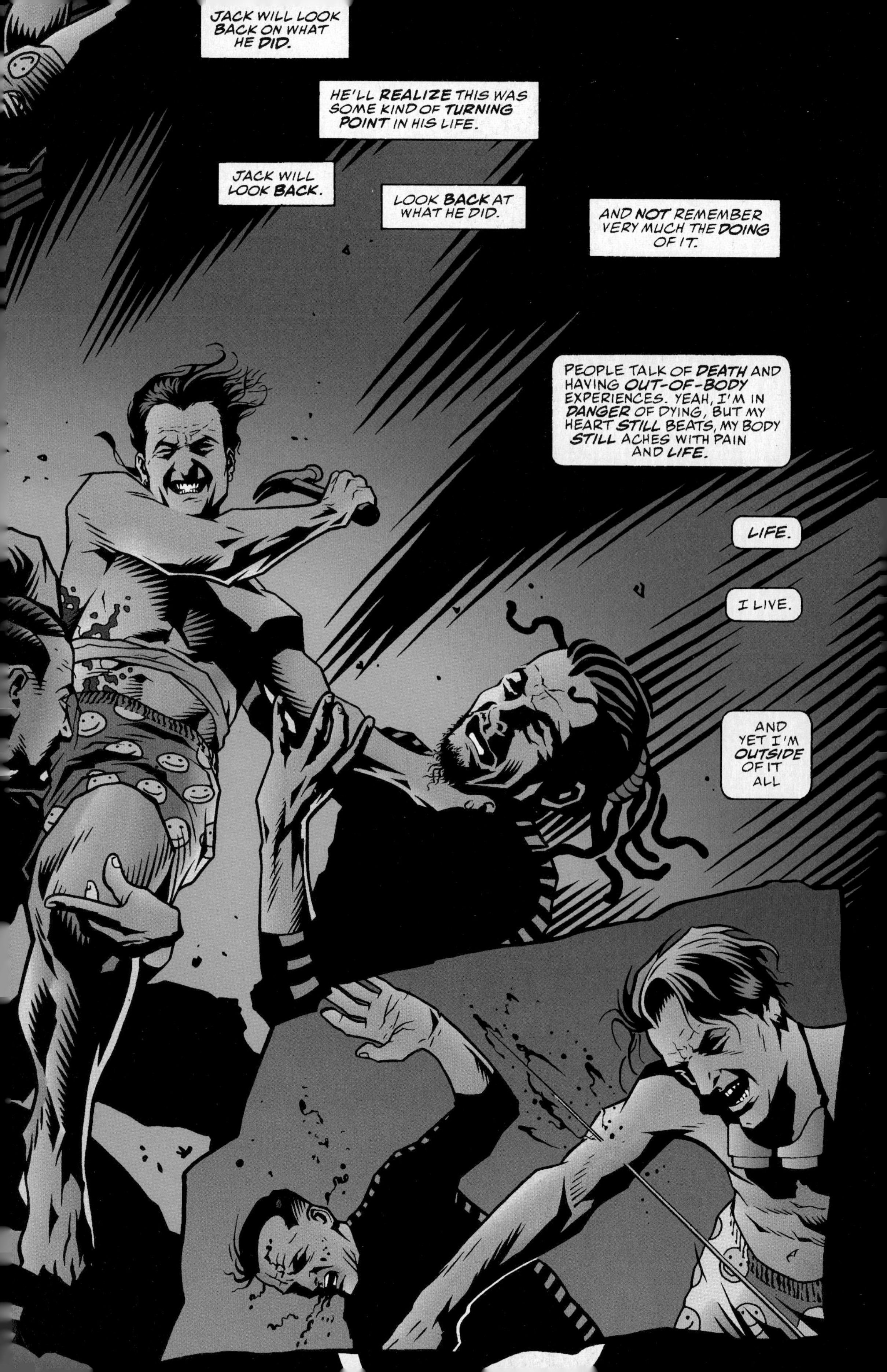
JACK WILL LOOK BACK ON WHAT HE DID.
HE'LL REALIZE THIS WAS SOME KIND OF TURNING POINT IN HIS LIFE.
JACK WILL LOOK BACK.
LOOK BACK AT WHAT HE DID.
AND NOT REMEMBER VERY MUCH THE DOING OF IT.
PEOPLE TALK OF DEATH AND HAVING OUT-OF-BODY EXPERIENCES. YEAH, I'M IN DANGER OF DYING, BUT MY HEART STILL BEATS, MY BODY STILL ACHES WITH PAIN AND LIFE.
LIFE.
I LIVE.
AND YET I'M OUTSIDE OF IT ALL

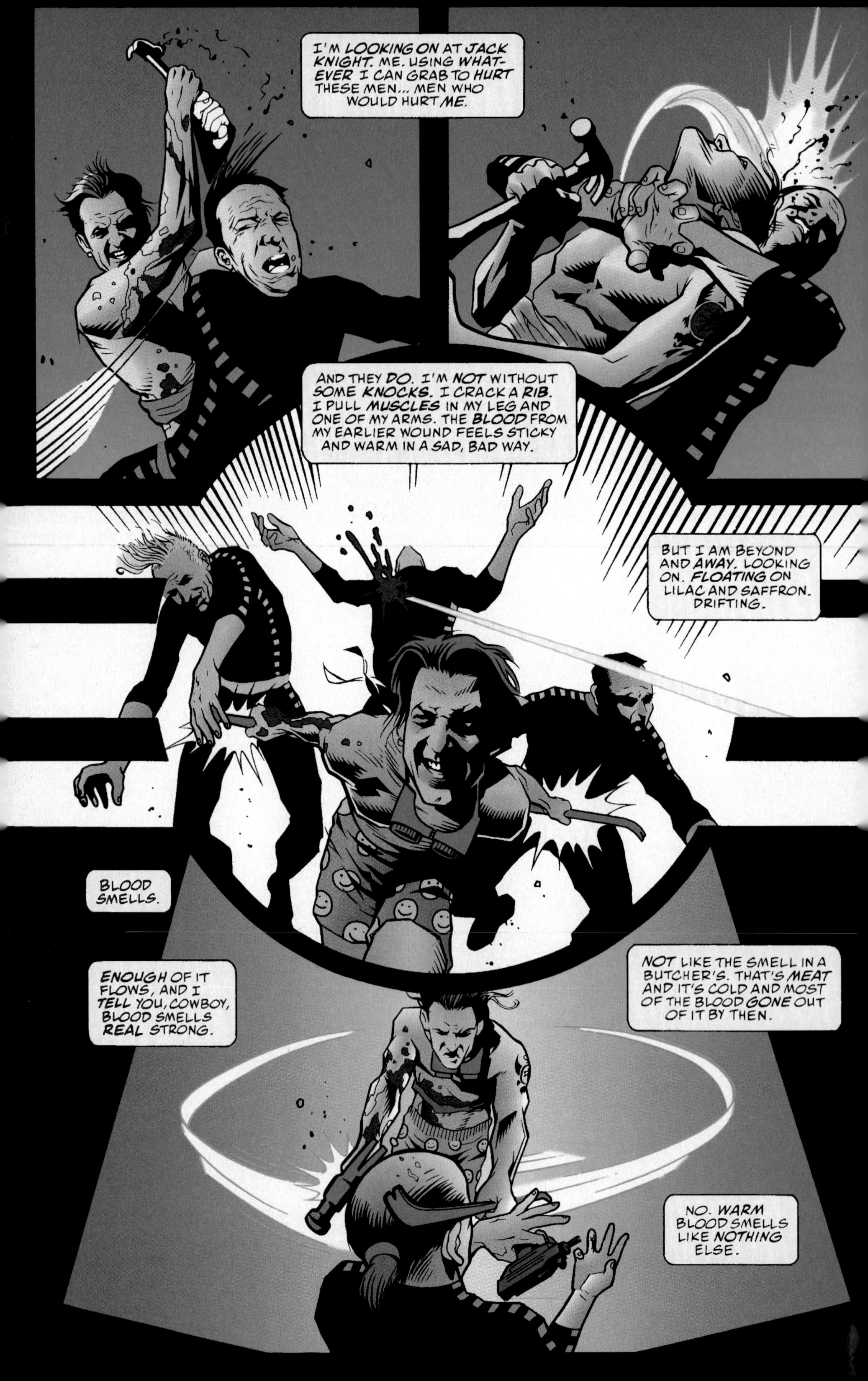
I'M LOOKING ON AT JACK KNIGHT. ME. USING WHATEVER I CAN GRAB TO HURT THESE MEN... MEN WHO WOULD HURT ME.
AND THEY DO. I'M NOT WITHOUT SOME KNOCKS. I CRACK A RIB. I PULL MUSCLES IN MY LEG AND ONE OF MY ARMS. THE BLOOD FROM MY EARLIER WOUND FEELS STICKY AND WARM IN A SAD, BAD WAY.
BUT I AM BEYOND AND AWAY. LOOKING ON. FLOATING ON LILAC AND SAFFRON. DRIFTING.
BLOOD SMELLS.
ENOUGH OF IT FLOWS, AND I TELL YOU, COWBOY, BLOOD SMELLS REAL STRONG.
NOT LIKE THE SMELL IN A BUTCHER'S. THAT'S MEAT AND IT'S COLD AND MOST OF THE BLOOD GONE OUT OF IT BY THEN.
NO. WARM BLOOD SMELLS LIKE NOTHING ELSE.

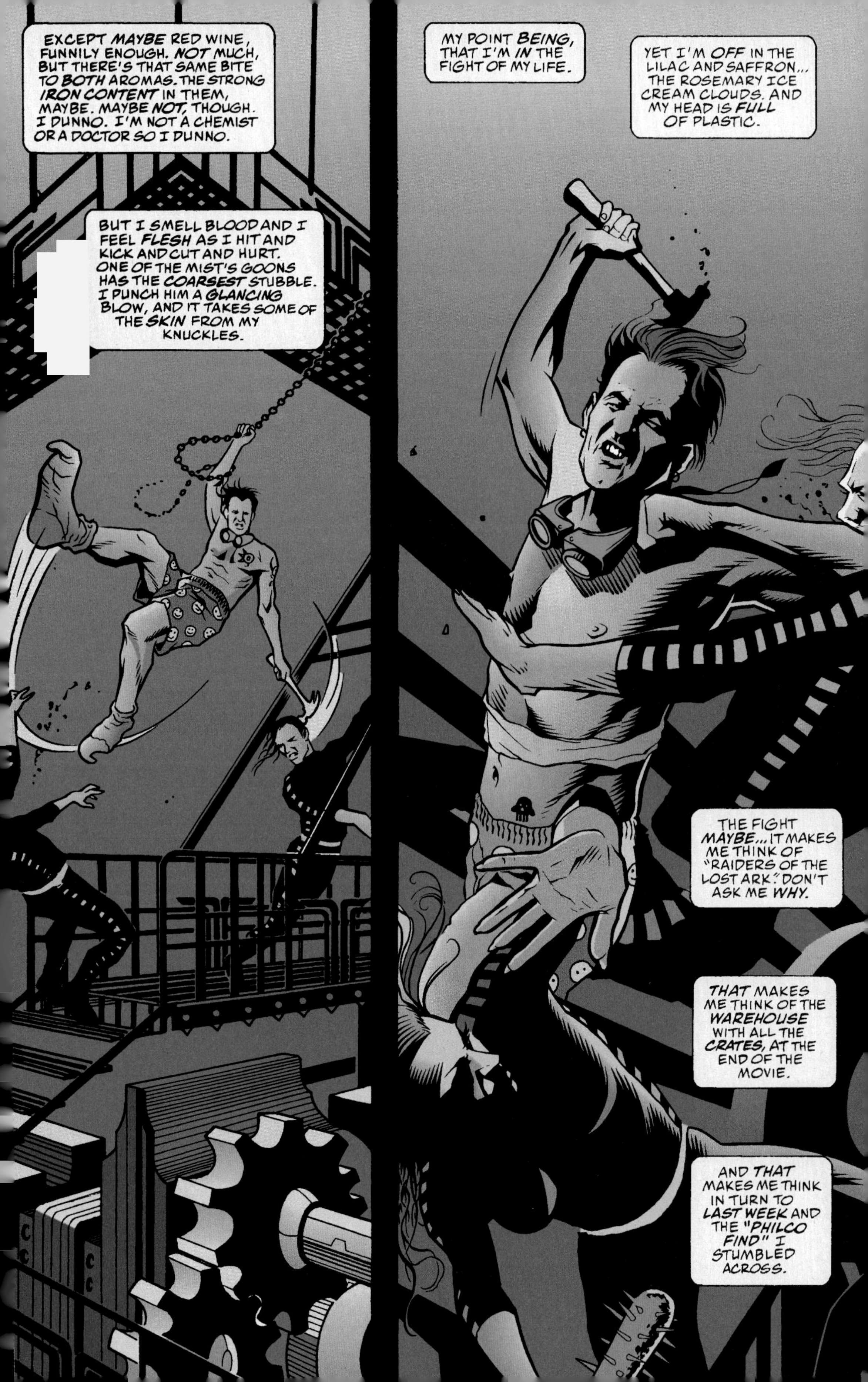
EXCEPT MAYBE RED WINE, FUNNILY ENOUGH. NOT MUCH, BUT THERE'S THAT SAME BITE TO BOTH AROMAS. THE STRONG IRON CONTENT IN THEM, MAYBE. MAYBE NOT, THOUGH. I DUNNO. I'M NOT A CHEMIST OR A DOCTOR SO I DUNNO.
BUT I SMELL BLOOD AND I FEEL FLESH AS I HIT AND KICK AND CUT AND HURT. ONE OF THE MIST'S GOONS HAS THE COARSEST STUBBLE. I PUNCH HIM A GLANCING BLOW, AND IT TAKES SOME OF THE SKIN FROM MY KNUCKLES.
MY POINT BEING, THAT I'M IN THE FIGHT OF MY LIFE.
YET I'M OFF IN THE LILAC AND SAFFRON... THE ROSEMARY ICE CREAM CLOUDS. AND MY HEAD IS FULL OF PLASTIC.
THE FIGHT MAYBE... IT MAKES ME THINK OF "RAIDERS OF THE LOST ARK." DON'T ASK ME WHY.
THAT MAKES ME THINK OF THE WAREHOUSE WITH ALL THE CRATES, AT THE END OF THE MOVIE.
AND THAT MAKES ME THINK IN TURN TO LAST WEEK AND THE "PHILCO FIND" I STUMBLED ACROSS.

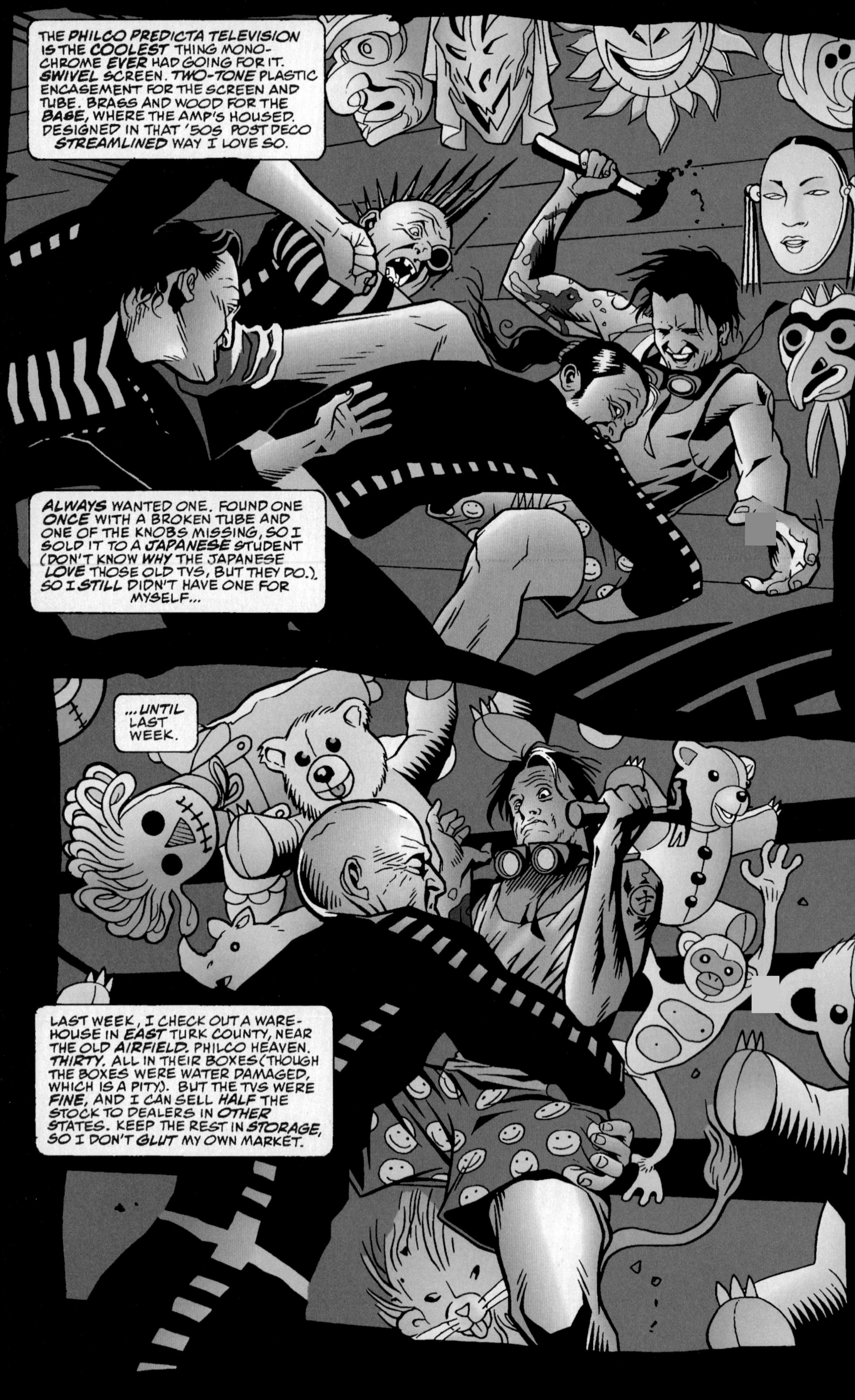
THE PHILCO PREDICTA TELEVISION IS THE COOLEST THING MONOCHROME EVER HAD GOING FOR IT. SWIVEL SCREEN. TWO-TONE PLASTIC ENCASEMENT FOR THE SCREEN AND TUBE. BRASS AND WOOD FOR THE BASE, WHERE THE AMP'S HOUSED. DESIGNED IN THAT '50S POST DECO STREAMLINED WAY I LOVE SO.
ALWAYS WANTED ONE. FOUND ONE ONCE WITH A BROKEN TUBE AND ONE OF THE KNOBS MISSING, SO I SOLD IT TO A JAPANESE STUDENT (DON'T KNOW WHY THE JAPANESE LOVE THOSE OLD TVS, BUT THEY DO.). SO I STILL DIDN'T HAVE ONE FOR MYSELF...
...UNTIL LAST WEEK.
LAST WEEK, I CHECK OUT A WAREHOUSE IN EAST TURK COUNTY, NEAR THE OLD AIRFIELD. PHILCO HEAVEN. THIRTY. ALL IN THEIR BOXES (THOUGH THE BOXES WERE WATER DAMAGED, WHICH IS A PITY). BUT THE TVS WERE FINE, AND I CAN SELL HALF THE STOCK TO DEALERS IN OTHER STATES. KEEP THE REST IN STORAGE, SO I DON'T GLUT MY OWN MARKET.

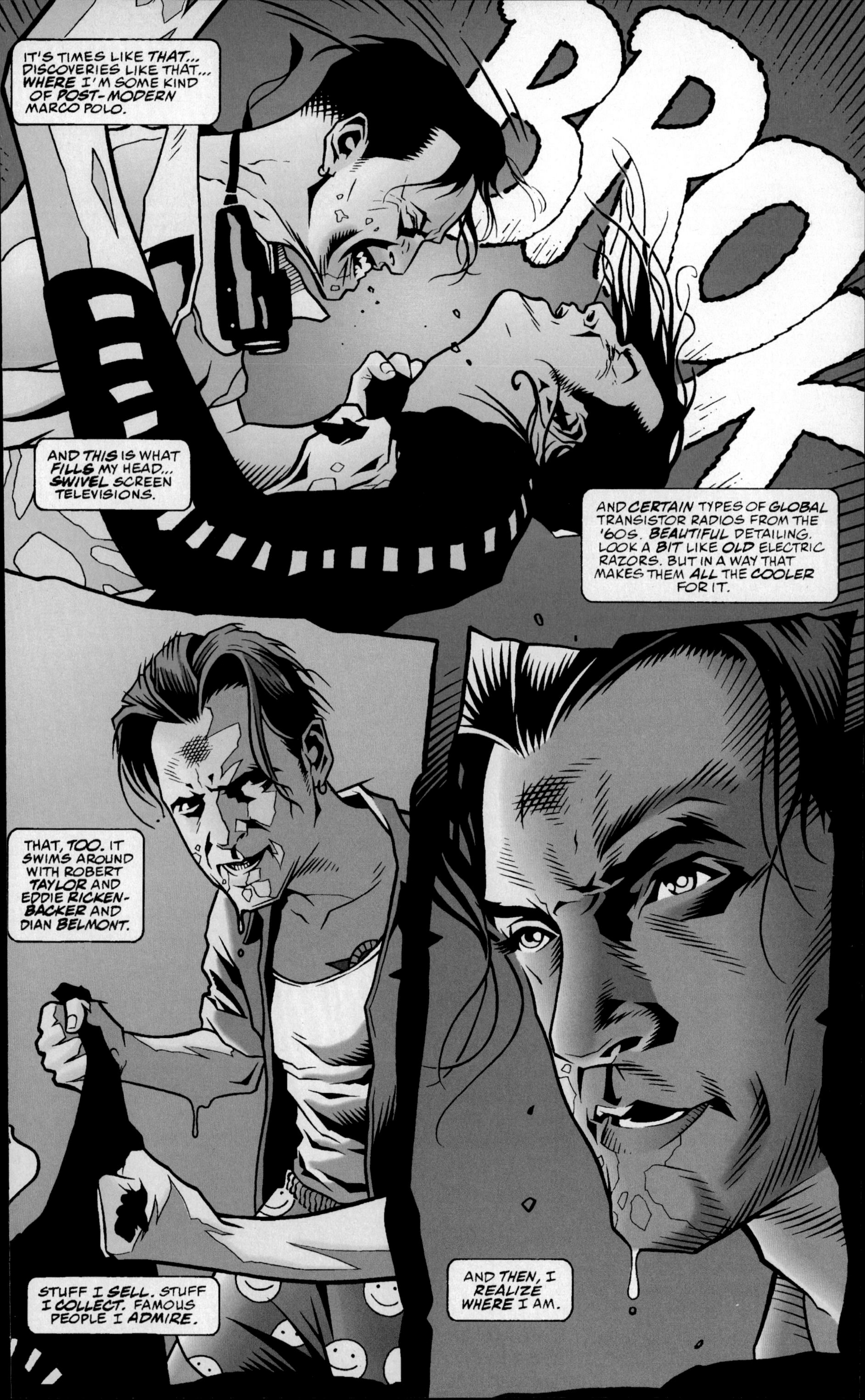
IT'S TIMES LIKE THAT... DISCOVERIES LIKE THAT... WHERE I'M SOME KIND OF POST-MODERN MARCO POLO.
BRRO
AND THIS IS WHAT FILLS MY HEAD... SWIVEL SCREEN TELEVISIONS.
AND CERTAIN TYPES OF GLOBAL TRANSISTOR RADIOS FROM THE '60S. BEAUTIFUL DETAILING. LOOK A BIT LIKE OLD ELECTRIC RAZORS. BUT IN A WAY THAT MAKES THEM ALL THE COOLER FOR IT.
THAT, TOO. IT SWIMS AROUND WITH ROBERT TAYLOR AND EDDIE RICKEN-BACKER AND DIAN BELMONT.
STUFF I SELL. STUFF I COLLECT. FAMOUS PEOPLE I ADMIRE.
AND THEN, I REALIZE WHERE I AM.

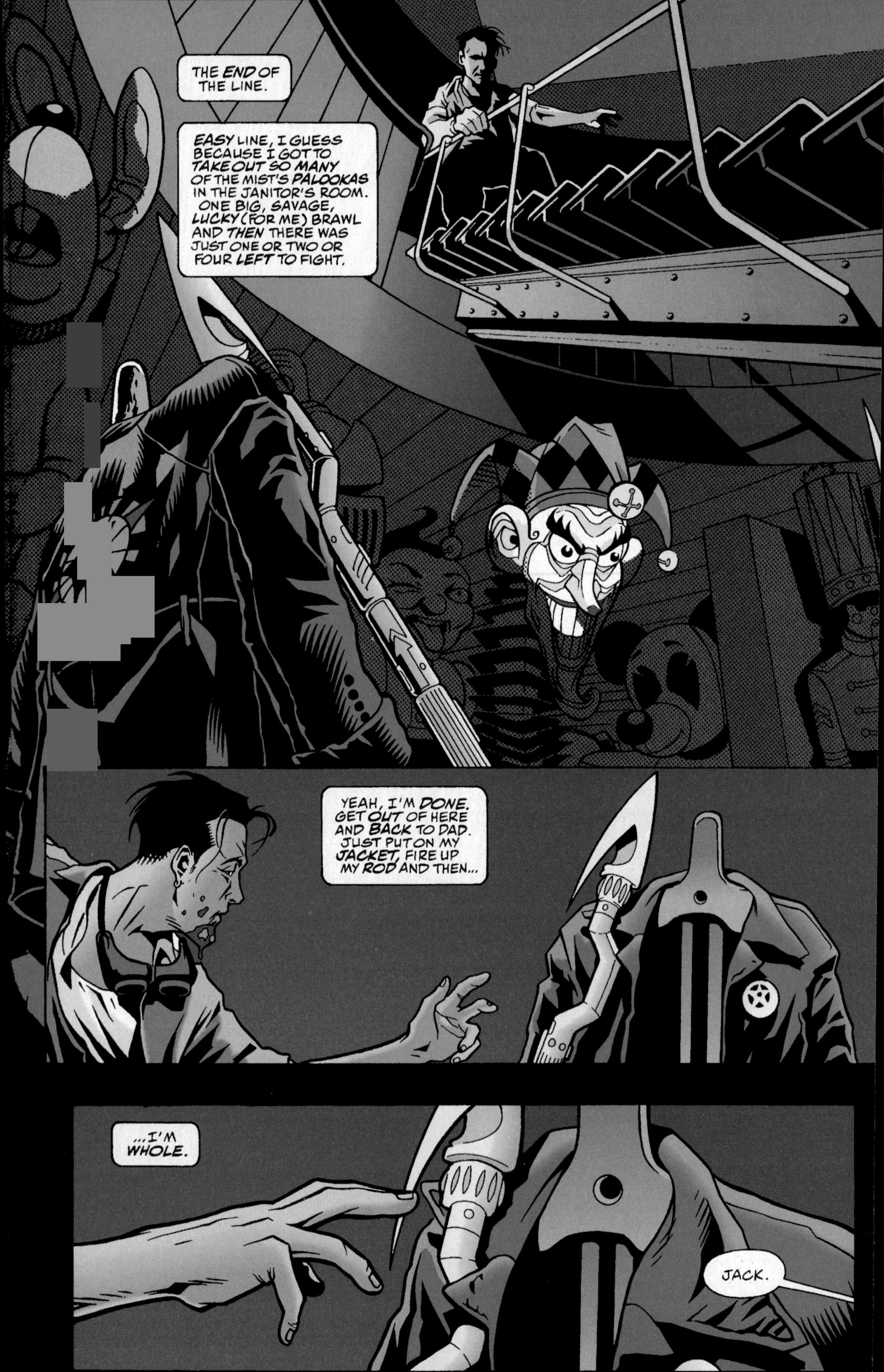
THE END OF THE LINE.
EASY LINE, I GUESS BECAUSE I GOT TO TAKE OUT SO MANY OF THE MIST'S PALOOKAS IN THE JANITOR'S ROOM. ONE BIG, SAVAGE, LUCKY (FOR ME) BRAWL AND THEN THERE WAS JUST ONE OR TWO OR FOUR LEFT TO FIGHT.
YEAH, I'M DONE. GET OUT OF HERE AND BACK TO DAD. JUST PUT ON MY JACKET, FIRE UP MY ROD AND THEN...
...I'M WHOLE.
JACK.

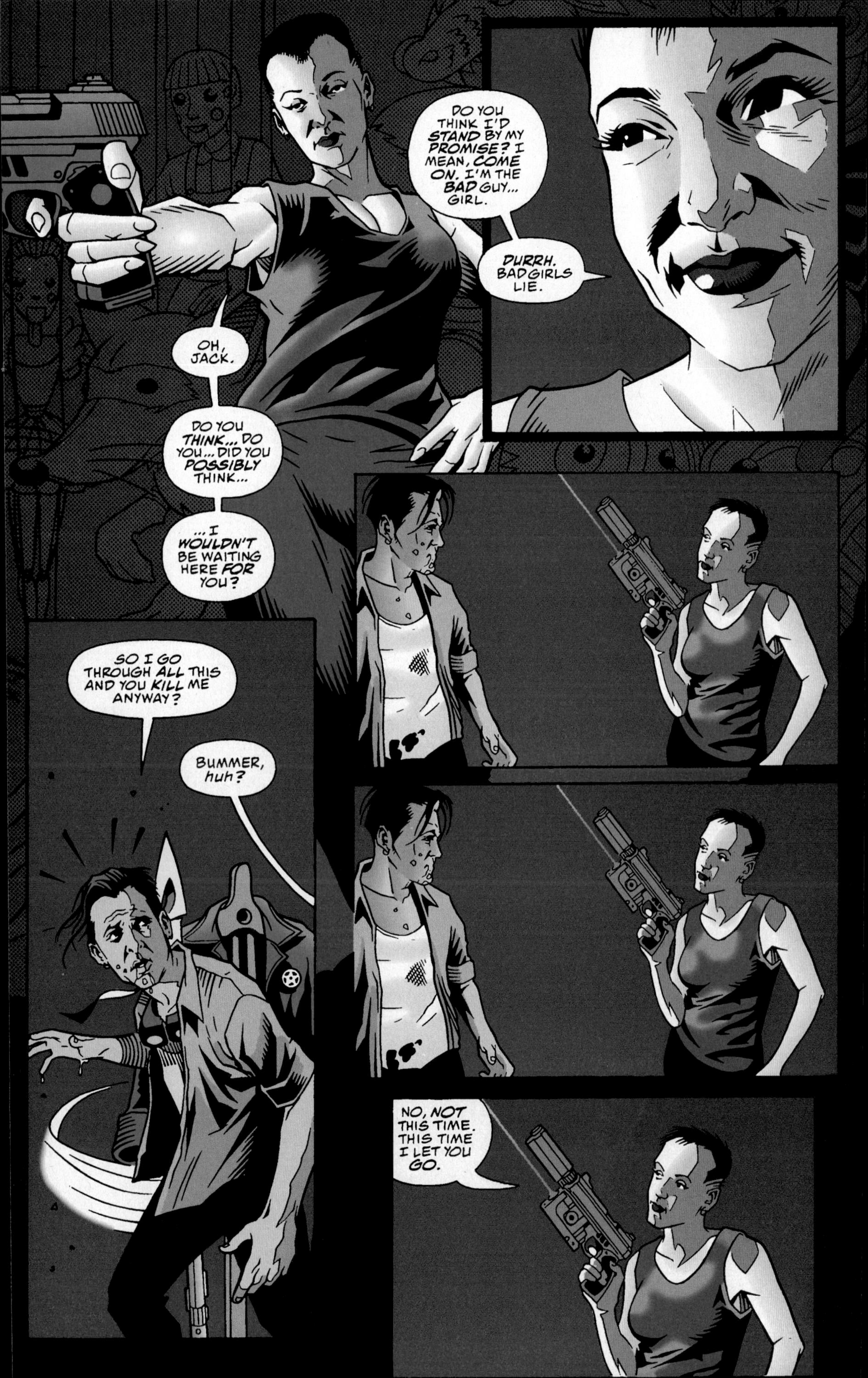

DO YOU THINK I'D STAND BY MY PROMISE? I MEAN, COME ON. I'M THE BAD GUY... GIRL.
DURRH. BAD GIRLS LIE.
OH, JACK.
DO YOU THINK... DO YOU... DID YOU POSSIBLY THINK...
...I WOULDN'T BE WAITING HERE FOR YOU?
SO I GO THROUGH ALL THIS AND YOU KILL ME ANYWAY?
BUMMER, huh?
NO, NOT THIS TIME. THIS TIME I LET YOU GO.

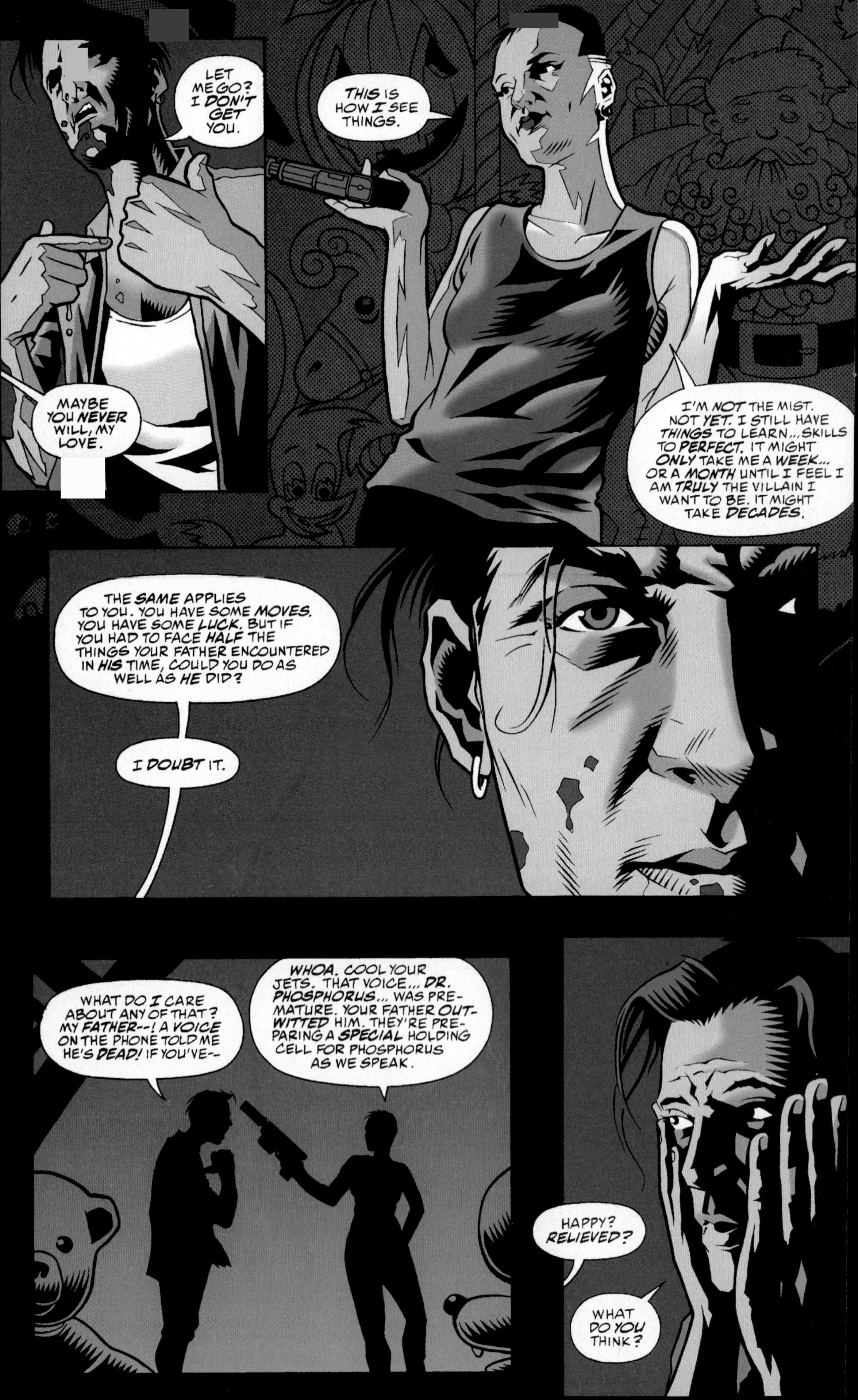
LET ME GO? I DON'T GET YOU.
THIS IS HOW I SEE THINGS.
MAYBE YOU NEVER WILL, MY LOVE.
I'M NOT THE MIST. NOT YET. I STILL HAVE THINGS TO LEARN... SKILLS TO PERFECT. IT MIGHT ONLY TAKE ME A WEEK... OR A MONTH UNTIL I FEEL I AM TRULY THE VILLAIN I WANT TO BE. IT MIGHT TAKE DECADES.
THE SAME APPLIES TO YOU. YOU HAVE SOME MOVES. YOU HAVE SOME LUCK. BUT IF YOU HAD TO FACE HALF THE THINGS YOUR FATHER ENCOUNTERED IN HIS TIME, COULD YOU DO AS WELL AS HE DID?
I DOUBT IT.
WHAT DO I CARE ABOUT ANY OF THAT? MY FATHER--! A VOICE ON THE PHONE TOLD ME HE'S DEAD! IF YOU'VE--
WHOA. COOL YOUR JETS. THAT VOICE... DR. PHOSPHORUS... WAS PRE-MATURE. YOUR FATHER OUT-WITTED HIM. THEY'RE PRE-PARING A SPECIAL HOLDING CELL FOR PHOSPHORUS AS WE SPEAK.
HAPPY? RELIEVED?
WHAT DO YOU THINK?

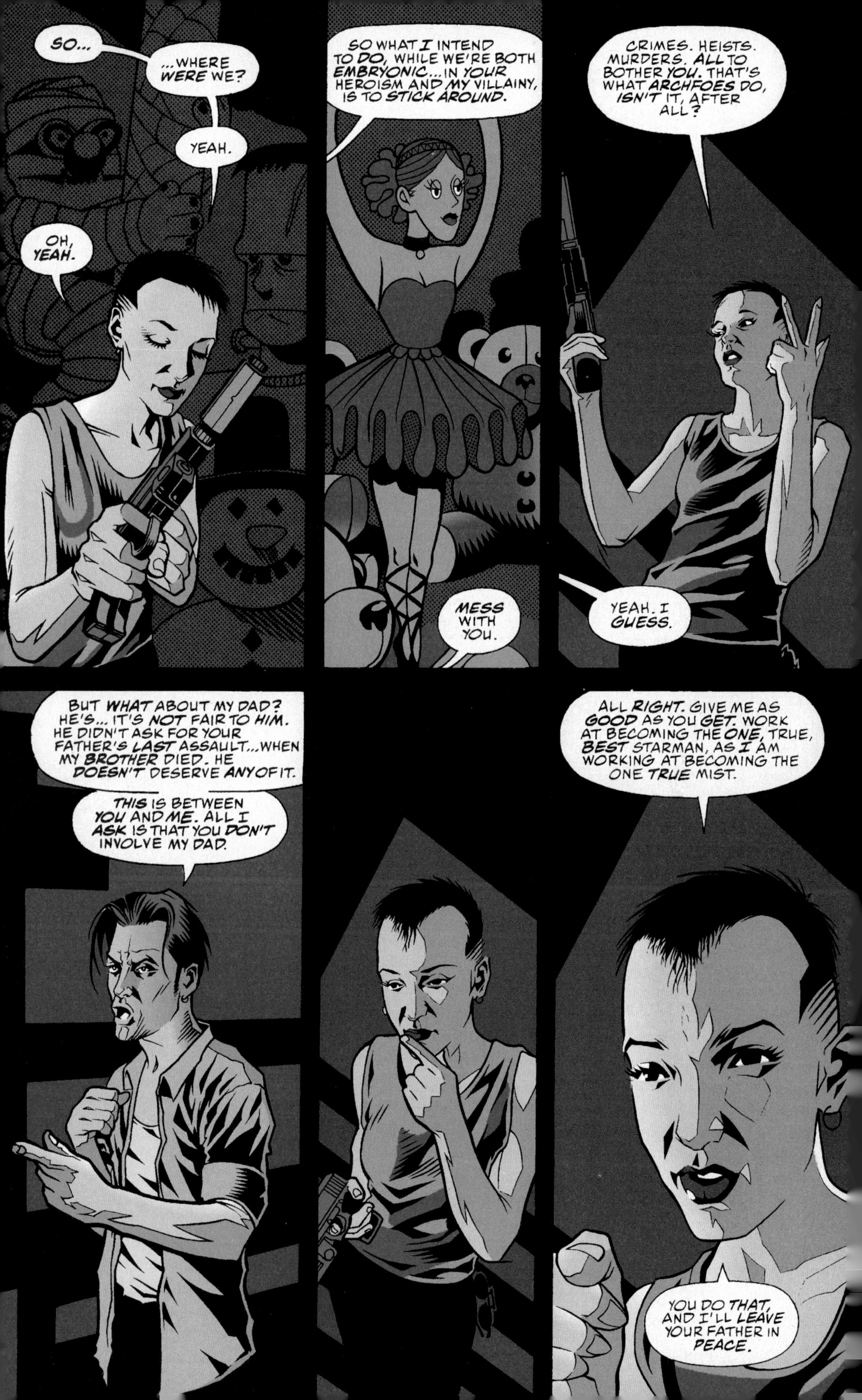
SO...
...WHERE WERE WE?
YEAH.
OH, YEAH.
SO WHAT I INTEND TO DO, WHILE WE'RE BOTH EMBRYONIC... IN YOUR HEROISM AND MY VILLAINY, IS TO STICK AROUND.
MESS WITH YOU.
CRIMES. HEISTS. MURDERS. ALL TO BOTHER YOU. THAT'S WHAT ARCHFOES DO, ISN'T IT, AFTER ALL?
YEAH. I GUESS.
BUT WHAT ABOUT MY DAD? HE'S... IT'S NOT FAIR TO HIM. HE DIDN'T ASK FOR YOUR FATHER'S LAST ASSAULT... WHEN MY BROTHER DIED. HE DOESN'T DESERVE ANY OF IT.
THIS IS BETWEEN YOU AND ME. ALL I ASK IS THAT YOU DON'T INVOLVE MY DAD.
ALL RIGHT. GIVE ME AS GOOD AS YOU GET. WORK AT BECOMING THE ONE, TRUE, BEST STARMAN, AS I AM WORKING AT BECOMING THE ONE TRUE MIST.
YOU DO THAT, AND I'LL LEAVE YOUR FATHER IN PEACE.

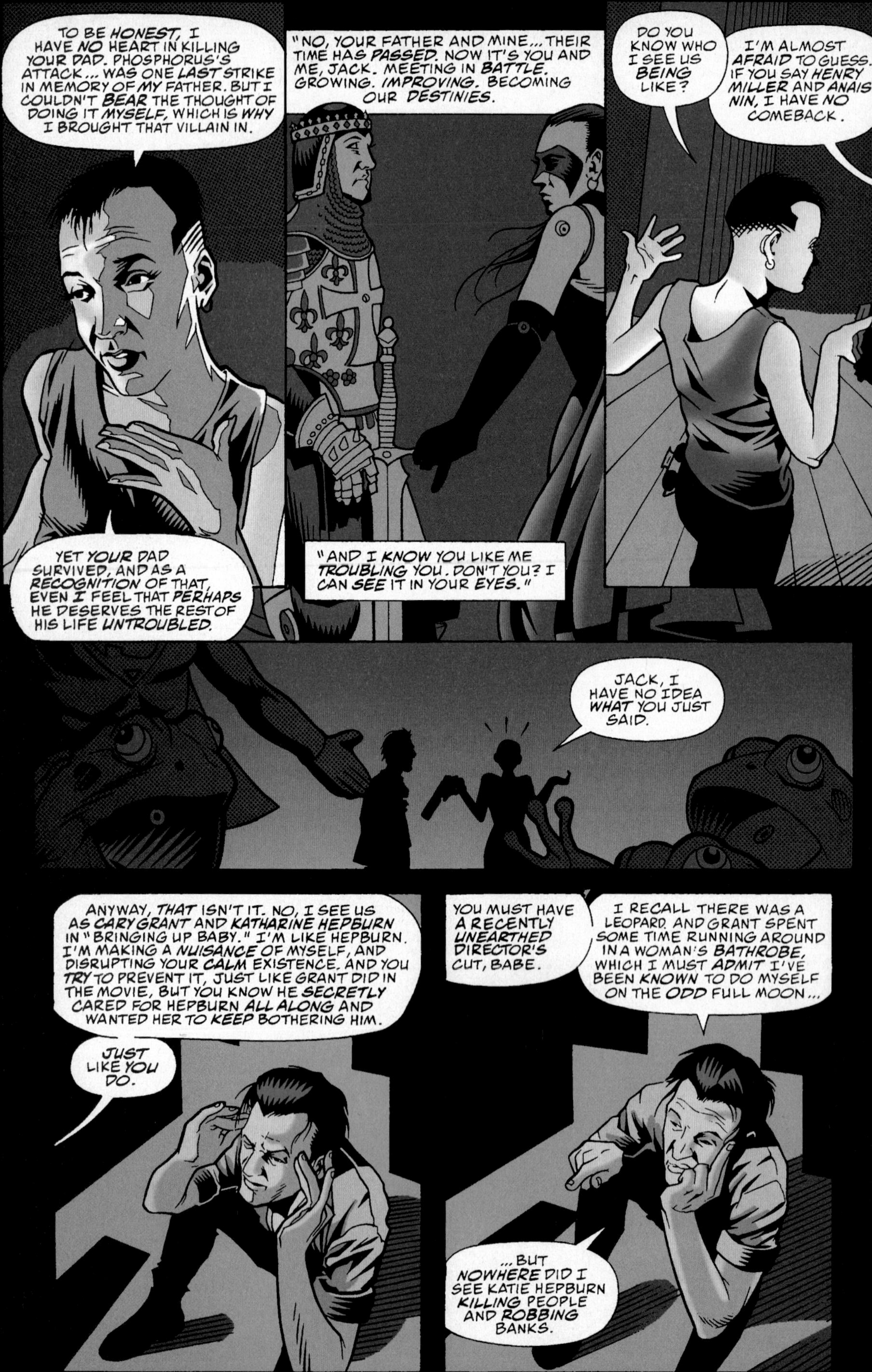
TO BE HONEST, I HAVE NO HEART IN KILLING YOUR DAD. PHOSPHORUS'S ATTACK... WAS ONE LAST STRIKE IN MEMORY OF MY FATHER. BUT I COULDN'T BEAR THE THOUGHT OF DOING IT MYSELF, WHICH IS WHY I BROUGHT THAT VILLAIN IN.
YET YOUR DAD SURVIVED, AND AS A RECOGNITION OF THAT, EVEN I FEEL THAT PERHAPS HE DESERVES THE REST OF HIS LIFE UNTROUBLED.
"NO, YOUR FATHER AND MINE... THEIR TIME HAS PASSED. NOW IT'S YOU AND ME, JACK. MEETING IN BATTLE. GROWING. IMPROVING. BECOMING OUR DESTINIES.
"AND I KNOW YOU LIKE ME TROUBLING YOU. DON'T YOU? I CAN SEE IT IN YOUR EYES."
DO YOU KNOW WHO I SEE US BEING LIKE?
I'M ALMOST AFRAID TO GUESS. IF YOU SAY HENRY MILLER AND ANAIS NIN, I HAVE NO COMEBACK.
JACK, I HAVE NO IDEA WHAT YOU JUST SAID.
ANYWAY, THAT ISN'T IT. NO, I SEE US AS CARY GRANT AND KATHARINE HEPBURN IN "BRINGING UP BABY." I'M LIKE HEPBURN. I'M MAKING A NUISANCE OF MYSELF, AND DISRUPTING YOUR CALM EXISTENCE. AND YOU TRY TO PREVENT IT, JUST LIKE GRANT DID IN THE MOVIE, BUT YOU KNOW HE SECRETLY CARED FOR HEPBURN ALL ALONG AND WANTED HER TO KEEP BOTHERING HIM.
JUST LIKE YOU DO.
YOU MUST HAVE A RECENTLY UNEARTHED DIRECTOR'S CUT, BABE.
I RECALL THERE WAS A LEOPARD. AND GRANT SPENT SOME TIME RUNNING AROUND IN A WOMAN'S BATHROBE, WHICH I MUST ADMIT I'VE BEEN KNOWN TO DO MYSELF ON THE ODD FULL MOON...
...BUT NOWHERE DID I SEE KATIE HEPBURN KILLING PEOPLE AND ROBBING BANKS.

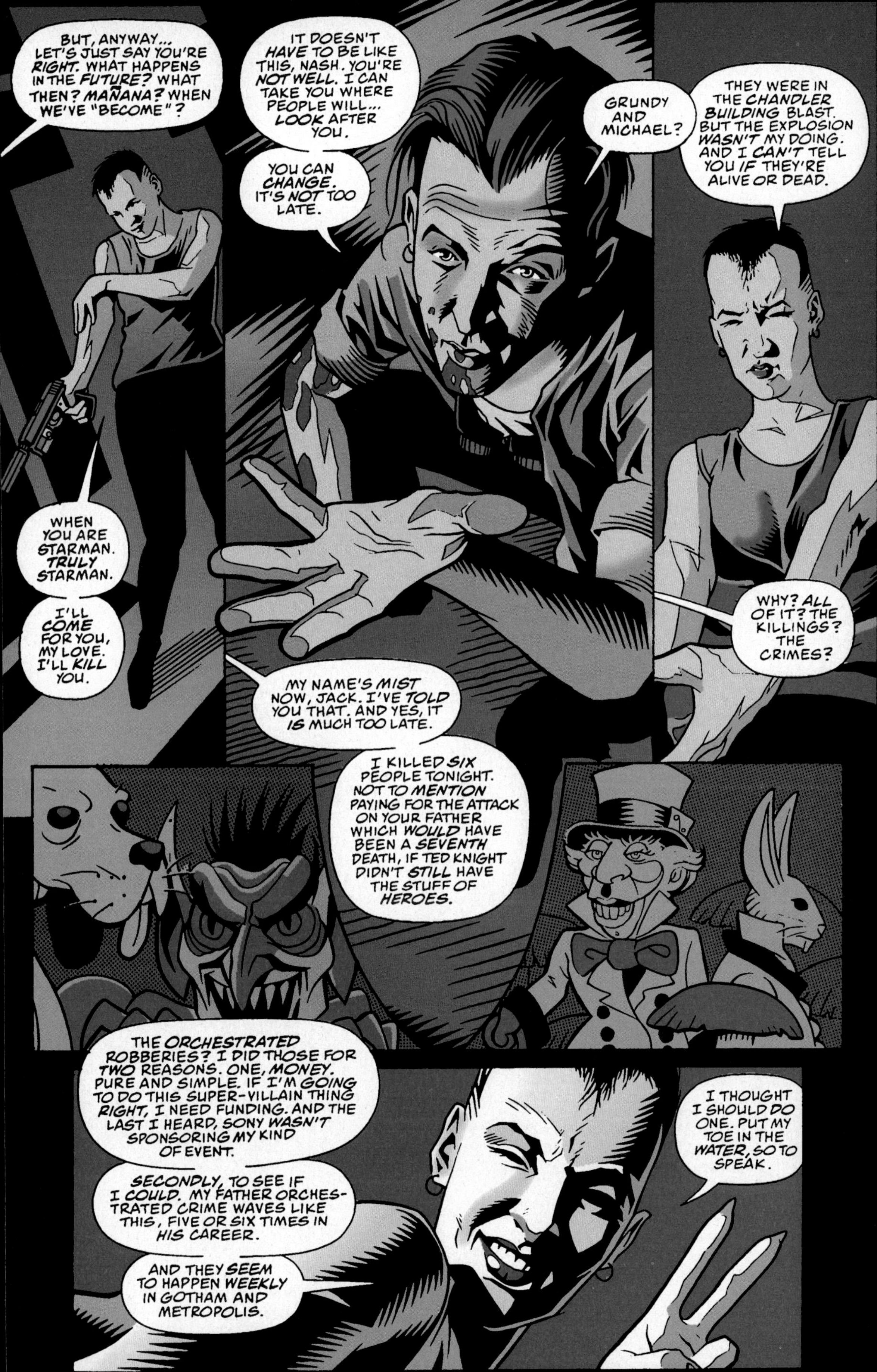
BUT, ANYWAY... LET'S JUST SAY YOU'RE RIGHT. WHAT HAPPENS IN THE FUTURE? WHAT THEN? MAÑANA? WHEN WE'VE "BECOME"?
IT DOESN'T HAVE TO BE LIKE THIS, NASH. YOU'RE NOT WELL. I CAN TAKE YOU WHERE PEOPLE WILL... LOOK AFTER YOU.
YOU CAN CHANGE. IT'S NOT TOO LATE.
WHEN YOU ARE STARMAN. TRULY STARMAN.
I'LL COME FOR YOU, MY LOVE. I'LL KILL YOU.
MY NAME'S MIST NOW, JACK. I'VE TOLD YOU THAT. AND YES, IT IS MUCH TOO LATE.
GRUNDY AND MICHAEL?
THEY WERE IN THE CHANDLER BUILDING BLAST. BUT THE EXPLOSION WASN'T MY DOING. AND I CAN'T TELL YOU IF THEY'RE ALIVE OR DEAD.
WHY? ALL OF IT? THE KILLINGS? THE CRIMES?
I KILLED SIX PEOPLE TONIGHT. NOT TO MENTION PAYING FOR THE ATTACK ON YOUR FATHER WHICH WOULD HAVE BEEN A SEVENTH DEATH, IF TED KNIGHT DIDN'T STILL HAVE THE STUFF OF HEROES.
THE ORCHESTRATED ROBBERIES? I DID THOSE FOR TWO REASONS. ONE, MONEY. PURE AND SIMPLE. IF I'M GOING TO DO THIS SUPER-VILLAIN THING RIGHT, I NEED FUNDING. AND THE LAST I HEARD, SONY WASN'T SPONSORING MY KIND OF EVENT.
SECONDLY, TO SEE IF I COULD. MY FATHER ORCHESTRATED CRIME WAVES LIKE THIS, FIVE OR SIX TIMES IN HIS CAREER.
AND THEY SEEM TO HAPPEN WEEKLY IN GOTHAM AND METROPOLIS.
I THOUGHT I SHOULD DO ONE. PUT MY TOE IN THE WATER, SO TO SPEAK.

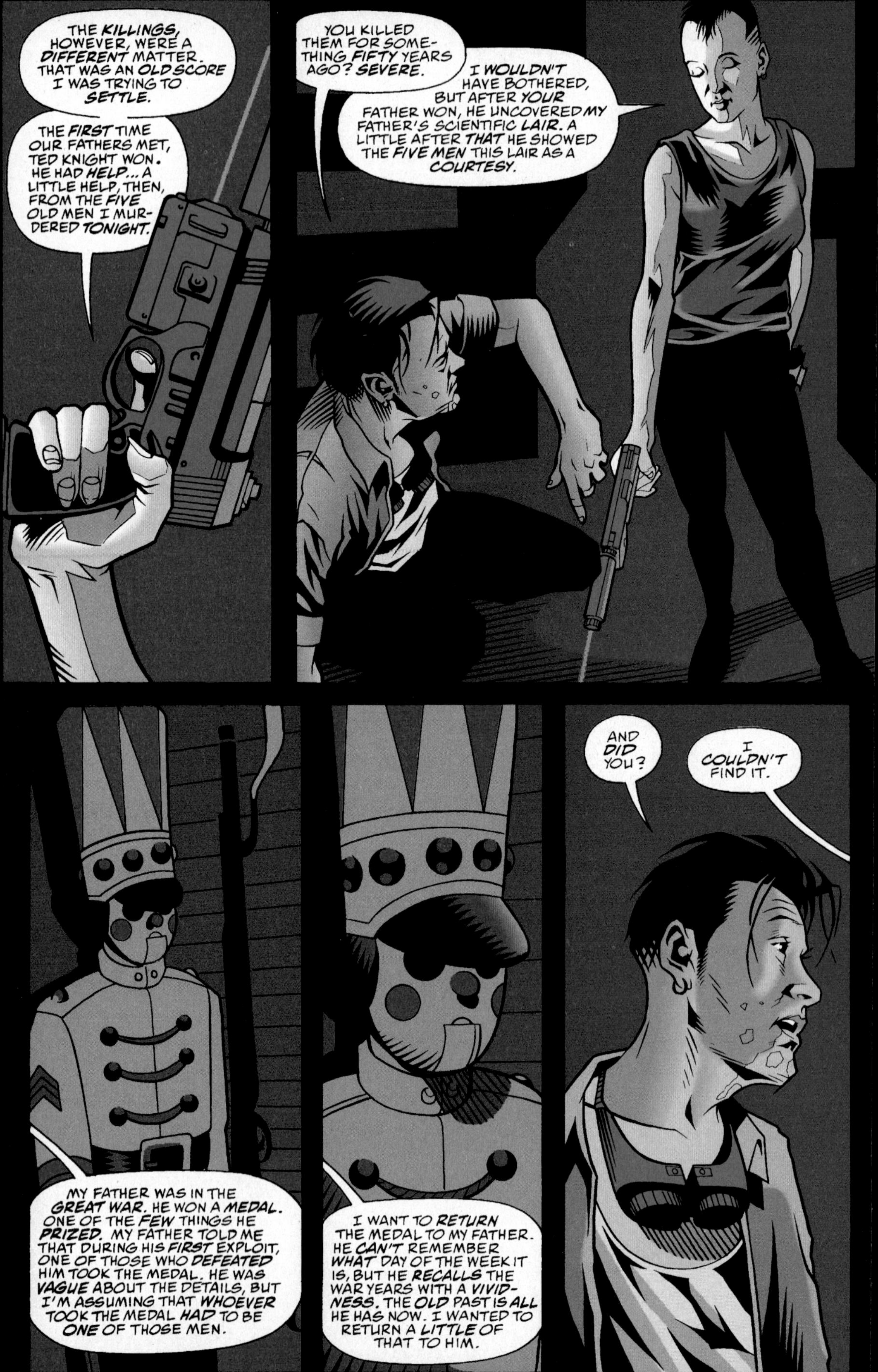
THE KILLINGS, HOWEVER, WERE A DIFFERENT MATTER. THAT WAS AN OLD SCORE I WAS TRYING TO SETTLE.
THE FIRST TIME OUR FATHERS MET, TED KNIGHT WON. HE HAD HELP... A LITTLE HELP, THEN, FROM THE FIVE OLD MEN I MURDERED TONIGHT.
YOU KILLED THEM FOR SOMETHING FIFTY YEARS AGO? SEVERE.
I WOULDN'T HAVE BOTHERED, BUT AFTER YOUR FATHER WON, HE UNCOVERED MY FATHER'S SCIENTIFIC LAIR. A LITTLE AFTER THAT HE SHOWED THE FIVE MEN THIS LAIR AS A COURTESY.
MY FATHER WAS IN THE GREAT WAR. HE WON A MEDAL. ONE OF THE FEW THINGS HE PRIZED. MY FATHER TOLD ME THAT DURING HIS FIRST EXPLOIT, ONE OF THOSE WHO DEFEATED HIM TOOK THE MEDAL. HE WAS VAGUE ABOUT THE DETAILS, BUT I'M ASSUMING THAT WHOEVER TOOK THE MEDAL HAD TO BE ONE OF THOSE MEN.
I WANT TO RETURN THE MEDAL TO MY FATHER. HE CAN'T REMEMBER WHAT DAY OF THE WEEK IT IS, BUT HE RECALLS THE WAR YEARS WITH A VIVIDNESS. THE OLD PAST IS ALL HE HAS NOW. I WANTED TO RETURN A LITTLE OF THAT TO HIM.
AND DID YOU?
I COULDN'T FIND IT.

WHAT ABOUT MY FATHER? DIDN'T *HE* HAVE IT?

I SEARCHED *BOTH* HIS OBSERVATORIES *LAST YEAR* BEFORE PLANTING THE *EXPLOSIVES* AT THE ONE IN TOWN. NO, HE *DOESN'T* HAVE IT.

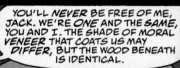

SO AT *LEAST* IN TERMS OF *THAT* PART OF THE DAY'S EVENTS...

...I FAILED.

SO YOU'VE EXPLAINED *EVERYTHING,* MORE OR LESS.

NOW YOU *VANISH* TO REENTER MY LIFE WHEN YOU *NEXT* FEEL INCLINED?

BINGO.

YOU'LL *NEVER* BE FREE OF ME, JACK. WE'RE *ONE* AND THE *SAME,* YOU AND I. THE SHADE OF MORAL *VENEER* THAT COATS US MAY *DIFFER,* BUT THE WOOD BENEATH IS IDENTICAL.

WE'RE THE *CHILDREN* OF THE SUPER-POWERED *CRAZINESS* THAT INFESTS THE PLANET. AND WE ARE *DESTINED* TO PERPETUATE IT.

WE'RE *NOT* THE SAME.

YES WE ARE. LOOK HARD AT YOURSELF. LOOK *INTO* THE SOUL OF *EVERYTHING* YOU'RE BECOMING...

...AND I'LL BE THERE LOOKING BACK.

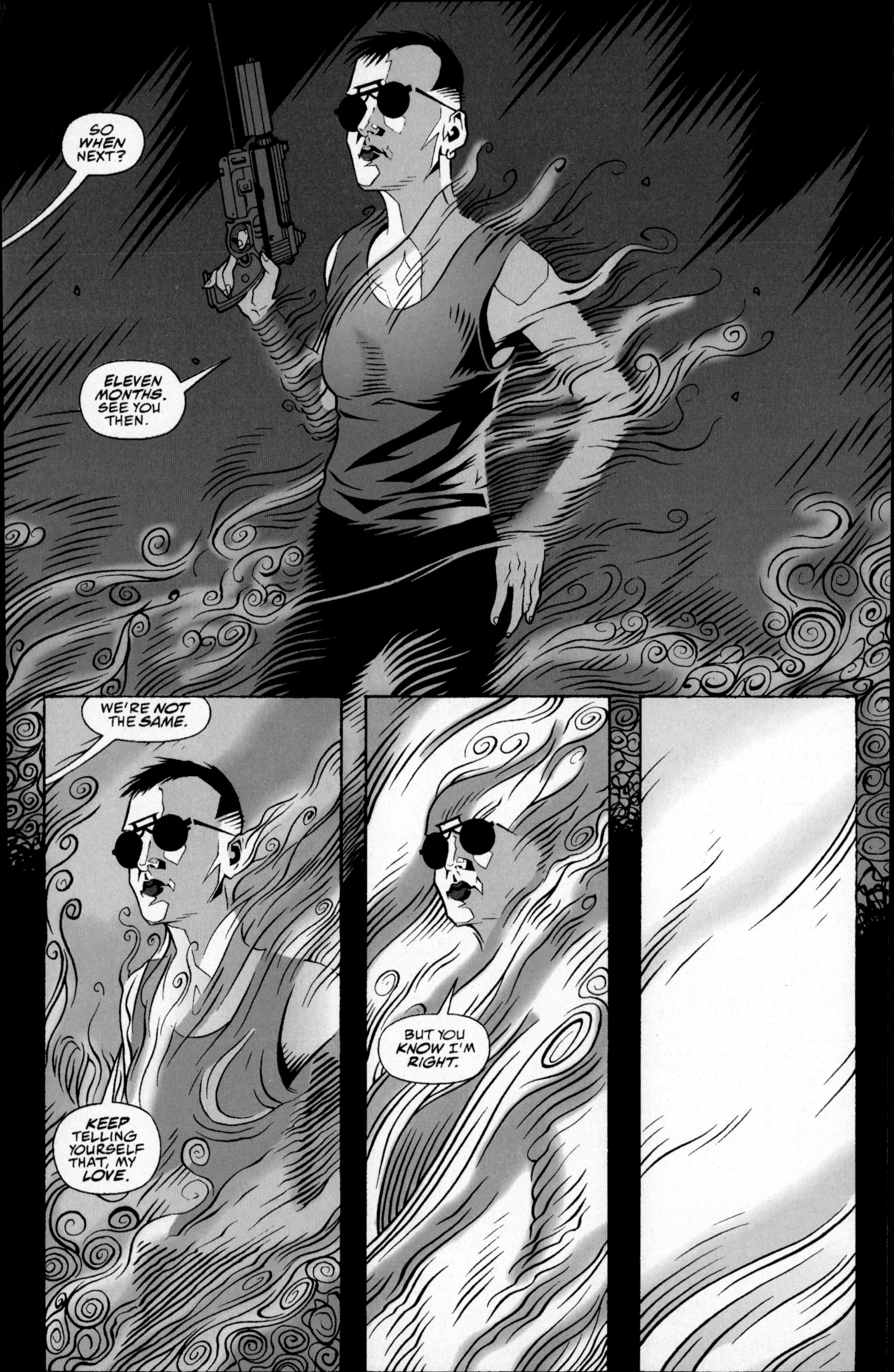
SO WHEN NEXT?
ELEVEN MONTHS. SEE YOU THEN.
WE'RE NOT THE SAME.
KEEP TELLING YOURSELF THAT, MY LOVE.
BUT YOU KNOW I'M RIGHT.

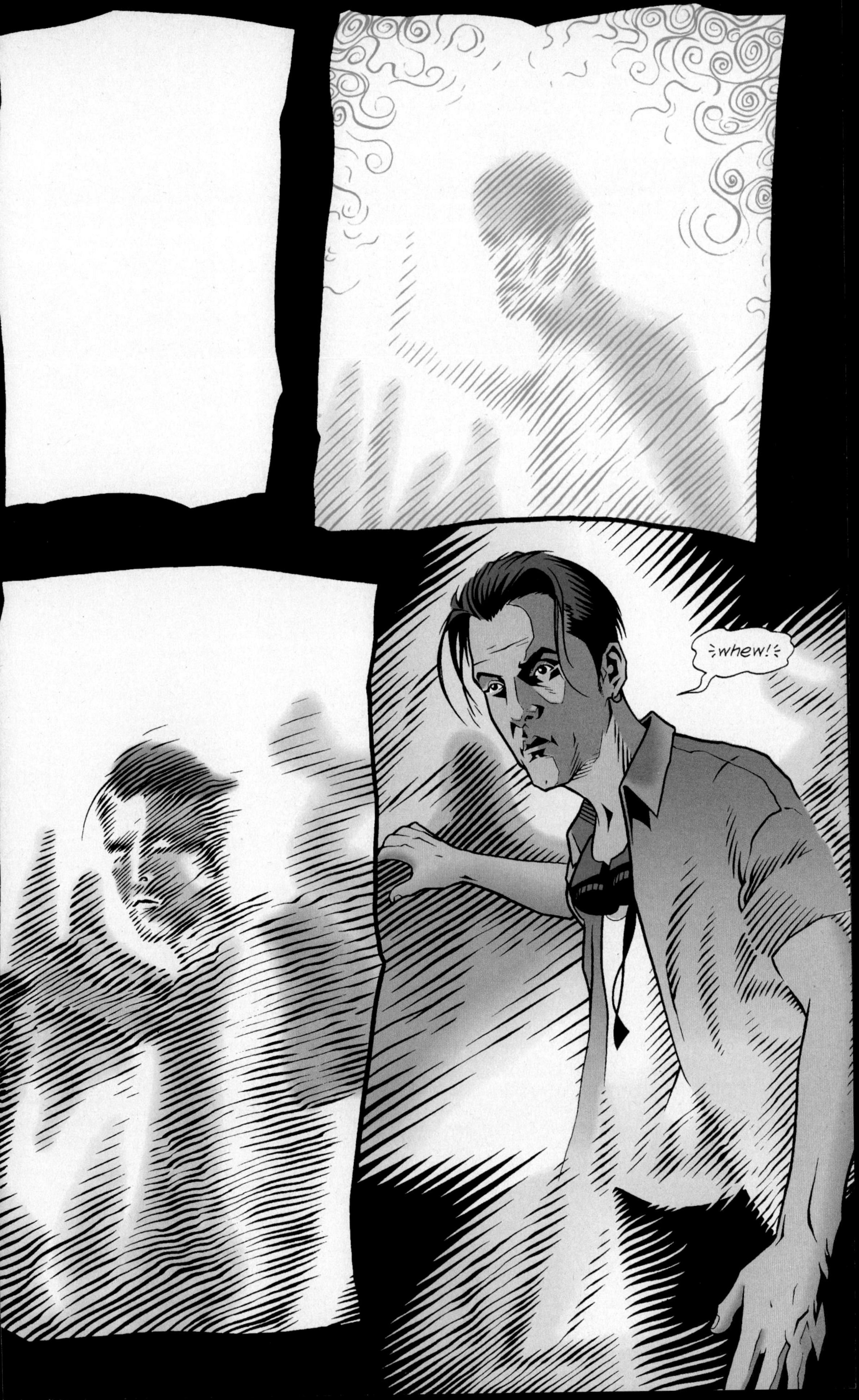
whew!

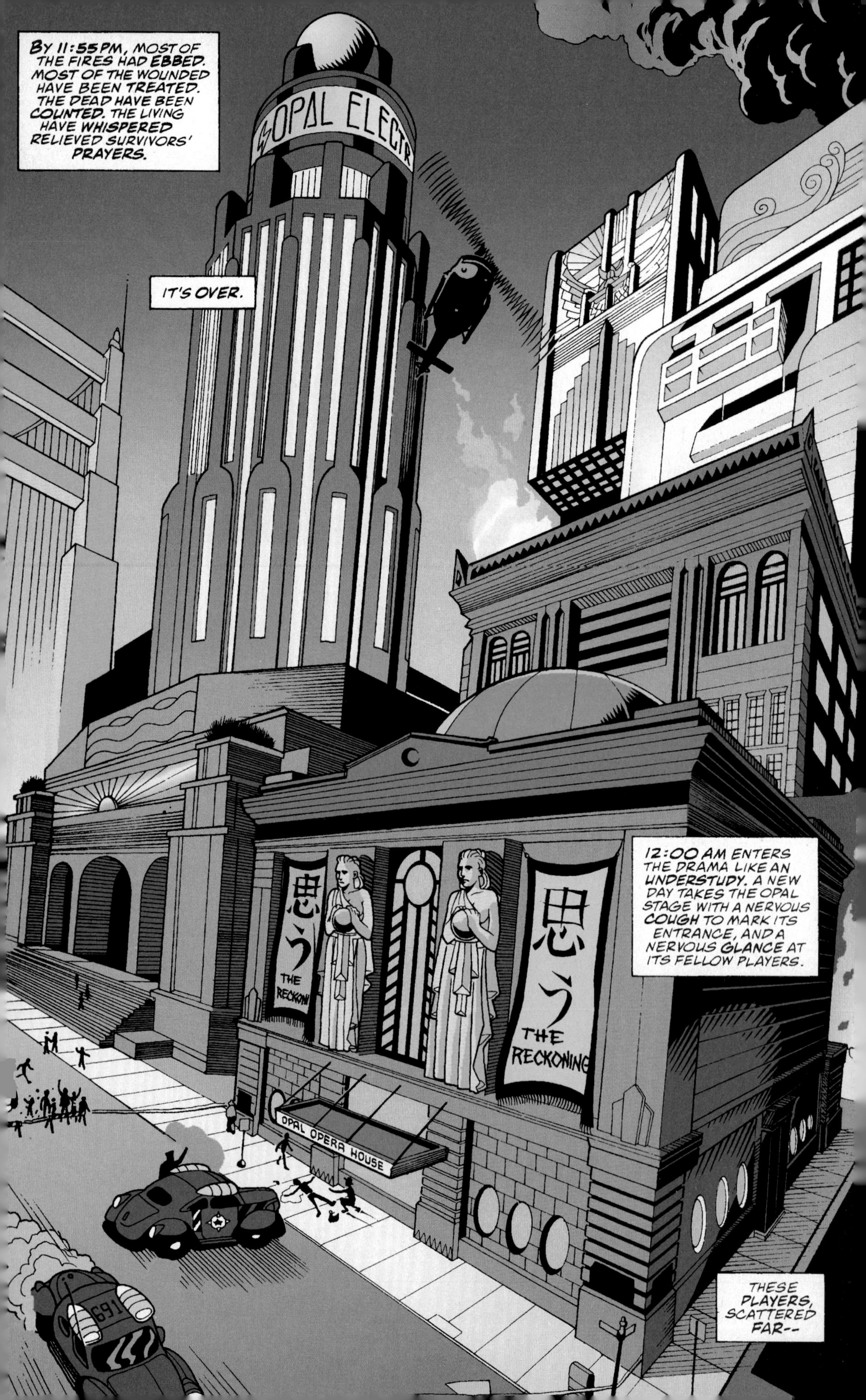

BY 11:55 PM, MOST OF THE FIRES HAD EBBED. MOST OF THE WOUNDED HAVE BEEN TREATED. THE DEAD HAVE BEEN COUNTED. THE LIVING HAVE WHISPERED RELIEVED SURVIVORS' PRAYERS.
OPAL ELECTR
IT'S OVER.
12:00 AM ENTERS THE DRAMA LIKE AN UNDERSTUDY. A NEW DAY TAKES THE OPAL STAGE WITH A NERVOUS COUGH TO MARK ITS ENTRANCE, AND A NERVOUS GLANCE AT ITS FELLOW PLAYERS.
思う THE RECKONING
思う THE RECKONING
OPAL OPERA HOUSE
691
THESE PLAYERS, SCATTERED FAR--

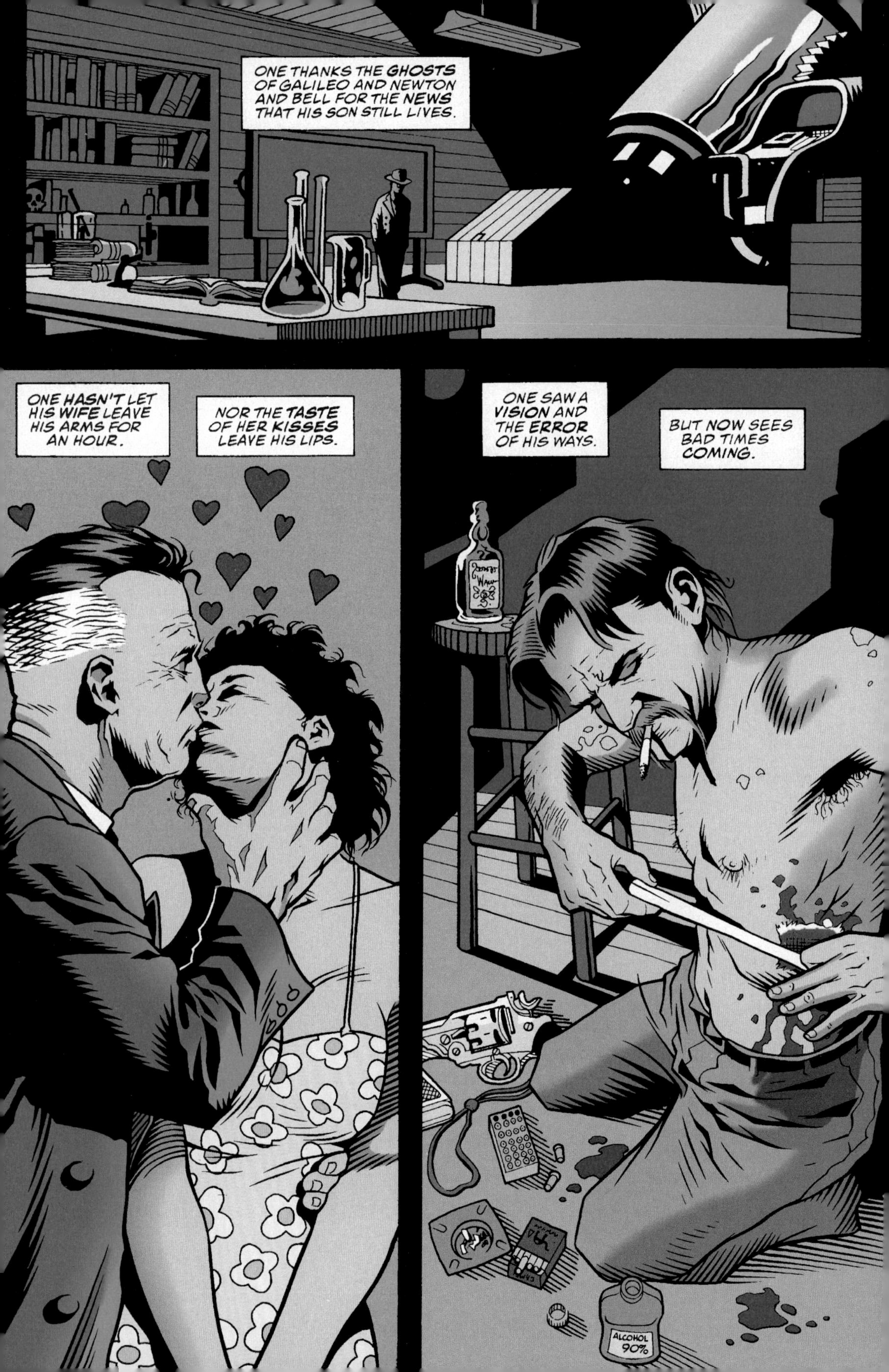
ONE THANKS THE GHOSTS OF GALILEO AND NEWTON AND BELL FOR THE NEWS THAT HIS SON STILL LIVES.
ONE HASN'T LET HIS WIFE LEAVE HIS ARMS FOR AN HOUR.
NOR THE TASTE OF HER KISSES LEAVE HIS LIPS.
ONE SAW A VISION AND THE ERROR OF HIS WAYS.
BUT NOW SEES BAD TIMES COMING.
ALCOHOL 90%

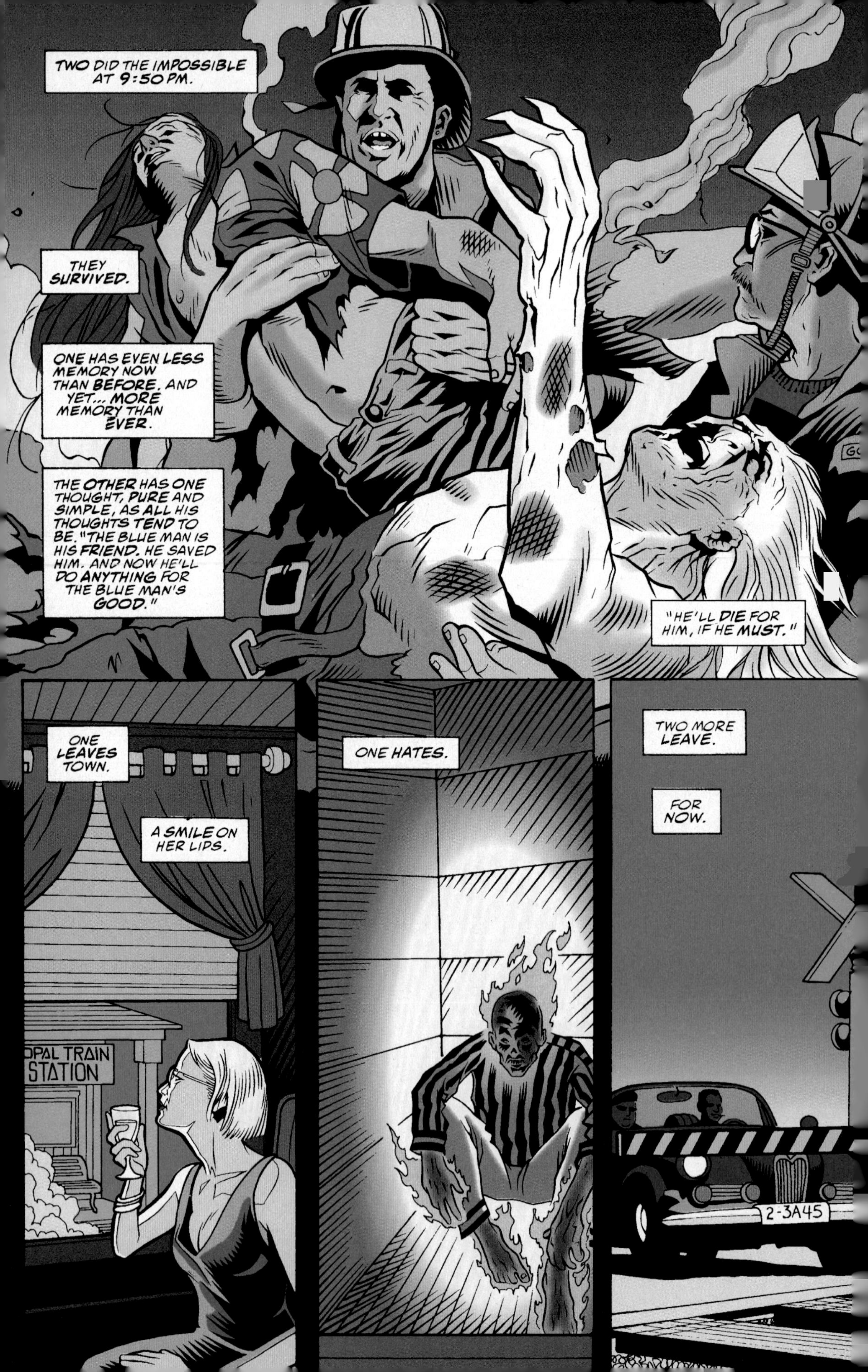

TWO DID THE IMPOSSIBLE AT 9:50 PM.
THEY SURVIVED.
ONE HAS EVEN LESS MEMORY NOW THAN BEFORE. AND YET... MORE MEMORY THAN EVER.
THE OTHER HAS ONE THOUGHT, PURE AND SIMPLE, AS ALL HIS THOUGHTS TEND TO BE. "THE BLUE MAN IS HIS FRIEND. HE SAVED HIM. AND NOW HE'LL DO ANYTHING FOR THE BLUE MAN'S GOOD."
"HE'LL DIE FOR HIM, IF HE MUST."
ONE LEAVES TOWN.
A SMILE ON HER LIPS.
OPAL TRAIN STATION
ONE HATES.
TWO MORE LEAVE.
FOR NOW.
2-3A45

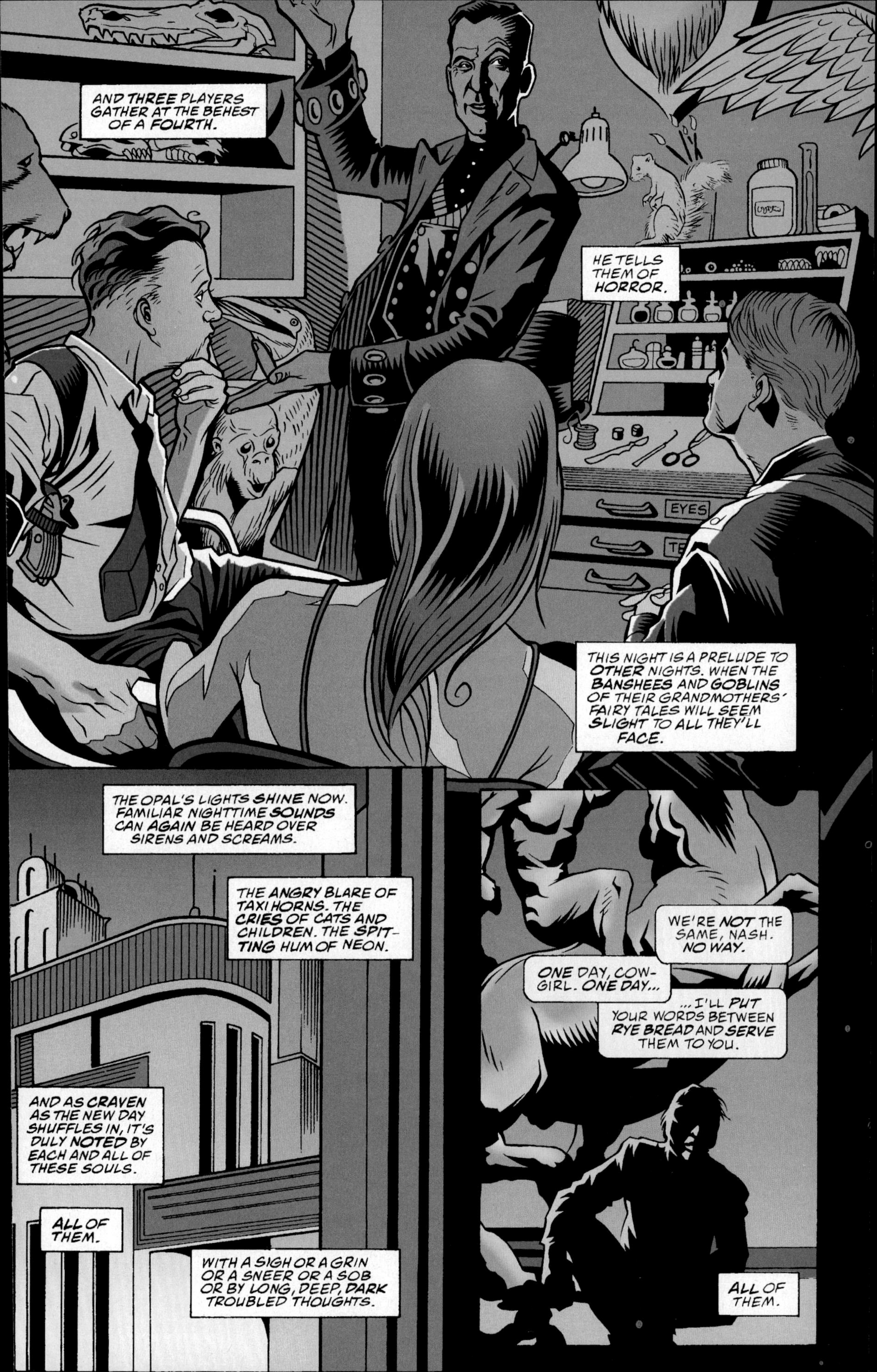
AND THREE PLAYERS GATHER AT THE BEHEST OF A FOURTH.
HE TELLS THEM OF HORROR.
EYES
THIS NIGHT IS A PRELUDE TO OTHER NIGHTS. WHEN THE BANSHEES AND GOBLINS OF THEIR GRANDMOTHERS' FAIRY TALES WILL SEEM SLIGHT TO ALL THEY'LL FACE.
THE OPAL'S LIGHTS SHINE NOW. FAMILIAR NIGHTTIME SOUNDS CAN AGAIN BE HEARD OVER SIRENS AND SCREAMS.
THE ANGRY BLARE OF TAXI HORNS. THE CRIES OF CATS AND CHILDREN. THE SPITTING HUM OF NEON.
WE'RE NOT THE SAME, NASH. NO WAY.
ONE DAY, COWGIRL. ONE DAY...
...I'LL PUT YOUR WORDS BETWEEN RYE BREAD AND SERVE THEM TO YOU.
AND AS CRAVEN AS THE NEW DAY SHUFFLES IN, IT'S DULY NOTED BY EACH AND ALL OF THESE SOULS.
ALL OF THEM.
WITH A SIGH OR A GRIN OR A SNEER OR A SOB OR BY LONG, DEEP, DARK TROUBLED THOUGHTS.
ALL OF THEM.

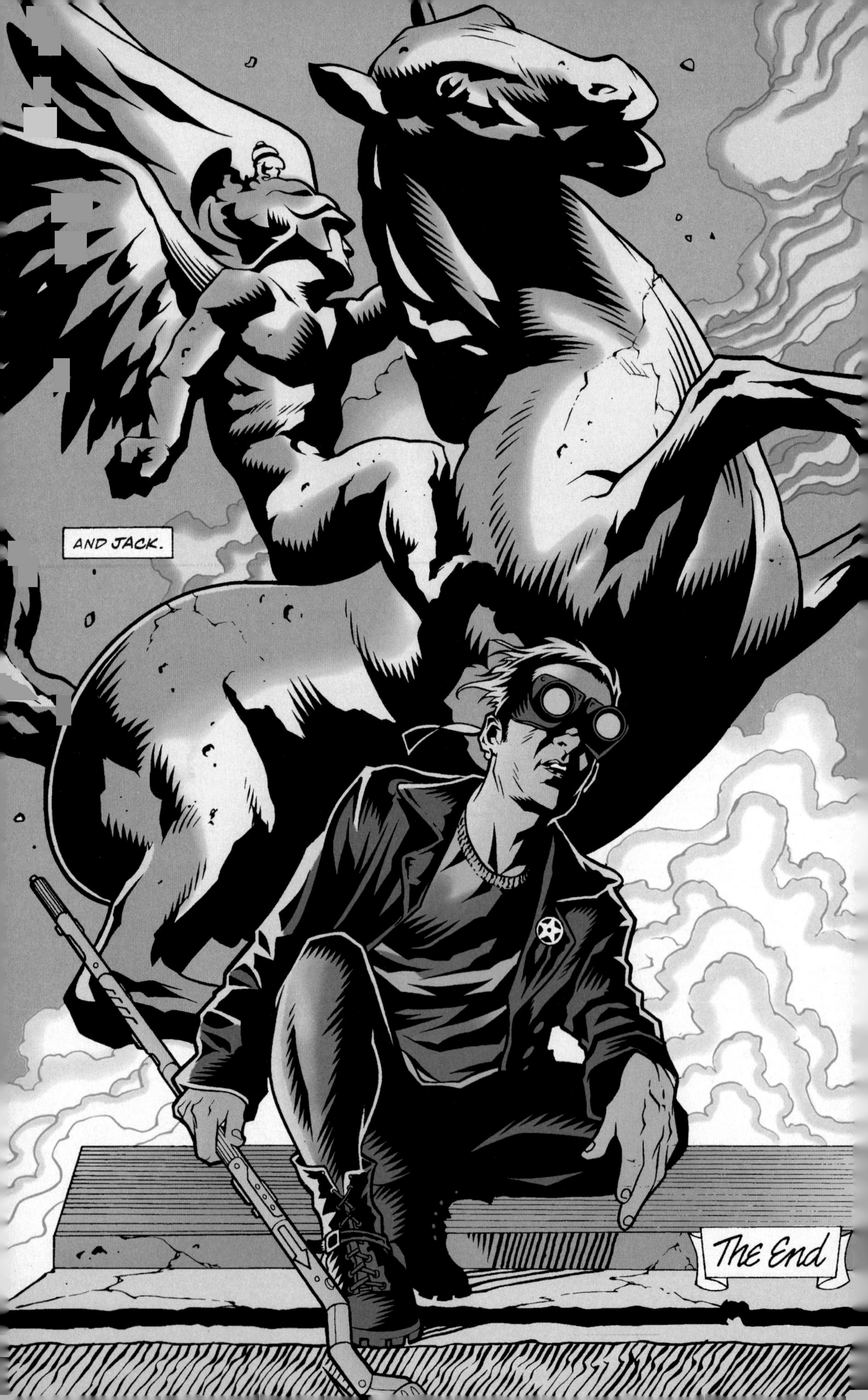
AND JACK.
THE End

TIMES PAST An (ongoing) afterword

The birth of STARMAN seems so long ago and far away from the man I am now.

The time has flown by, it seems so recent, the first issue, life then, all of it — and yet, as I try to recall any one aspect of it, the memories are so vague and far-flung it's hard to know where to begin when it comes to how the comic got started.

To begin with I guess I should say that I was a far different person *then* than I am *now*. I was vain and stupid and blindly ambitious. I was hungry for some sort of recognition within the field of comics and, as a result, jealous of anyone who seemed to be having a more successful time of it than me. I was far from nice. I see that now. The only redemptive quality I had to my career at that time was the patronage of Archie Goodwin, of which more will be said presently. I didn't deserve his support, but I was lucky and I got it anyway.

STARMAN began, as I recall now, not from any overwhelming desire to write this character, but more a desire to write a kind of comic. The *kind* that I felt used to exist and which excited me, and for a variety of factors seemed to no longer be.

I have always read comics, loving them — as I'm sure all of you reading this also love them — as a unique

form of storytelling. However, loving the medium though I did, I still came up against the fact that as I grew up a lot of the superhero fare was starting to seem stale. I mean that to in no way reflect on the work being done or the creators doing it; I'm sure it was just a young man turning to wine and women.

And then, seemingly synchronistically across the medium, different creators, different publishers were beginning to publish books that all had somewhat the same feel — that being a marriage of the fantasy and action of the standard fare coupled with a neo-realistic edge that gave the stuff a freshness and coolness — which of course was especially important for any young man foolhardy enough to tell the date he was with that he still read comics. Some books were more mature than others. Some were from the mainstream, some from the rapidly burgeoning (at that time) world of the independents. I guess it's easiest to use examples to explain what I mean.

(A word of warning: I'm English. Grew up in London. Moved to Los Angeles in 1990. God help all of us.)

I guess the first thing anyone in England was aware of was *Warrior Magazine*, published by Dez Skinn — featuring Alan Moore's first notable work on "Marvel Man" and "V for Vendetta." At the same time Frank Miller was first coming onto the radar with *Daredevil.* Moore's "Captain Britain" soon followed. Then SWAMP THING. All of this, bear in mind, with the exception of the *Warrior* material, was PG — intended for the mainstream. Other stuff followed, some more mature than others but all with that same marriage of the real and the fantastic. Wagner's *Mage* and *Grendel.* Chaykin's *American Flagg* and BLACKHAWK. *Love and Rockets* and *Mister X* by the Hernandez Brothers. The work of Matt Howarth and Bernie Mireault. *Cerebus* by Sim, an obvious inclusion. I'm sure I'm missing a few things at that time. I'm sure. But you get the idea. It was the beginning of something different and exciting, and God help me, it kept me in comics as a fan at a time when I was trying to get out.

And as we know it got worse, or better, with creators — especially Miller and Moore adding to their catalogue of work in correlation to their growing talent. The former raised the stakes with RONIN, THE DARK KNIGHT RETURNS, *Elektra: Assassin,* BATMAN: YEAR ONE. The latter did WATCHMEN, as well as uniquely wonderful Superman stories.

★ Cover sketch for first trade paperback.

I'm sure there were more things. Treasures. And I apologize for all those who might be offended by their omission.

Meanwhile, I'm straight out of film school, full of piss, vinegar and rank arrogance. I think I'm a genius. I'm an idiot. I get a job as a freelance editor at Titan Books in London, distributor of American reprints DC/Marvel/Fantagraphics — basically a lot of the cool stuff I listed above. They also reprint stuff from *2000AD*. And also the odd original work. One such piece is the graphic novel *Violent Cases* written by the obscure scribe Neil Gaiman, drawn by the equally little-known artist Dave McKean. I thought then/think today that the work is great, admire the shit out of what they did, but to my shame (the man I am today) was so full of hubris from nothing at all that I don't think I ever let them know how highly I regarded them. In fact, like the little boy with the crush on the girl in kindergarten, who, liking her, pulls her hair instead of telling her how he feels, I recall I went out of my way to be rude to McKean whenever our paths crossed. Regrets. This is the thing with writing about projects so long ago, they unlock a vault of memories — more bad than good, at least in my case.

So on we go, me arrogantly thinking I could do as good. I meet an artist, Paul Johnson (*Espers*, BOOKS OF MAGIC #4) who I'm lucky enough to discover wants to work with me, and we fashion a graphic novel based on my mother's memories of the Eastend of London during wartime coupled with a healthy dose of mainstream English spiritualism. It's called *London's Dark*. My first work. Published due to the patronage of Titan Books owners Nick Landau and his partner Mike Lake.

This is my afterword, so let me take it wherever it goes — and so it goes — Mike Lake. Mike Lake. There is a book to be written about this guy. Lover of comics (especially Jack Kirby), comic art, dogs and beautiful women. And at that time a believer in me. He got *London's Dark* published, God bless him. And my life in this wonderful, dire, up and down, fantastic, four-color wasteland began. His fault.

For those who know my work intimately, an issue of the *Firearm* comic I did back in the day involved a husky hi-bred named Kirby. This was a tribute to Mike's husky hi-bred Kirby who had recently died, as a way of thanking a man I owe a lot to. Mike is a lot like a dog in that he likes/loves people first and asks little/nothing in return. As a result he's helped/cared for many people and has been forgotten, overlooked by many people. Including me. I am not nice. I see that as I grow older and view Jack Knight

"SHADE"

then and the man I am now. And Mike Lake deserves a hell of a lot more than that.

Mike, if you read this, I am truly sorry for the person I was. I wish I could go back in time and shake myself by the collar. Unfortunately that sort of thing only happens in comic books.

Anyway, back to the here and now, back and then — *London's Dark* is read by two people who further help me.

One, it takes a while. The other is more immediate.

Matt Wagner reads a rough of *London's Dark* while visiting in London and asks me to write a run of *Grendel Tales* when he gives the title over.

Let's take another sidebar here —

Matt Wagner. A wide-eyed, big-hearted fellow. A smart, deep, probing fellow. Quick to think. Quick to like. If you meet him and don't like him, there's something wrong with you. I don't know what he saw in my work (really, I'm not being coy), but he

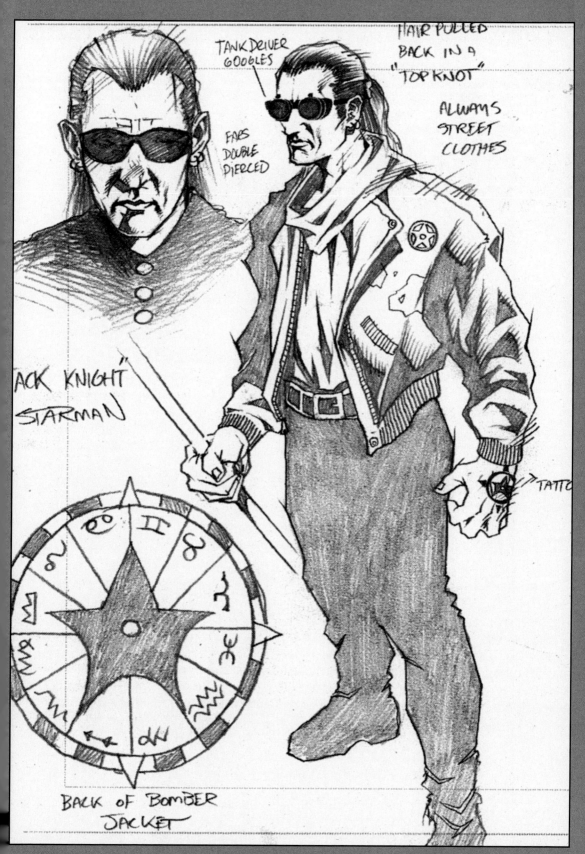

TANK DRIVER GOGGLES

HAIR PULLED BACK IN A "TOP KNOT"

EARS DOUBLE PIERCED

ALWAYS STREET CLOTHES

"JACK KNIGHT" STARMAN

TATTOO

BACK OF BOMBER JACKET

★ An early design for Jack Knight.

EDITOR:
ARTIST:
INKER:
DC COVER STOCK
COVER TITLE
MONTH
NO.
IDENTIFICATION
5·90
STARMAN
ALTERNATE COVER "TRADE"
LOGO AREA
LOGO AREA
YELLOW TS
RED TS
BLACK TS
BLUE TS
BI-PAD:
© TM DC Comics Inc. © 1990 All Rights Reserved.

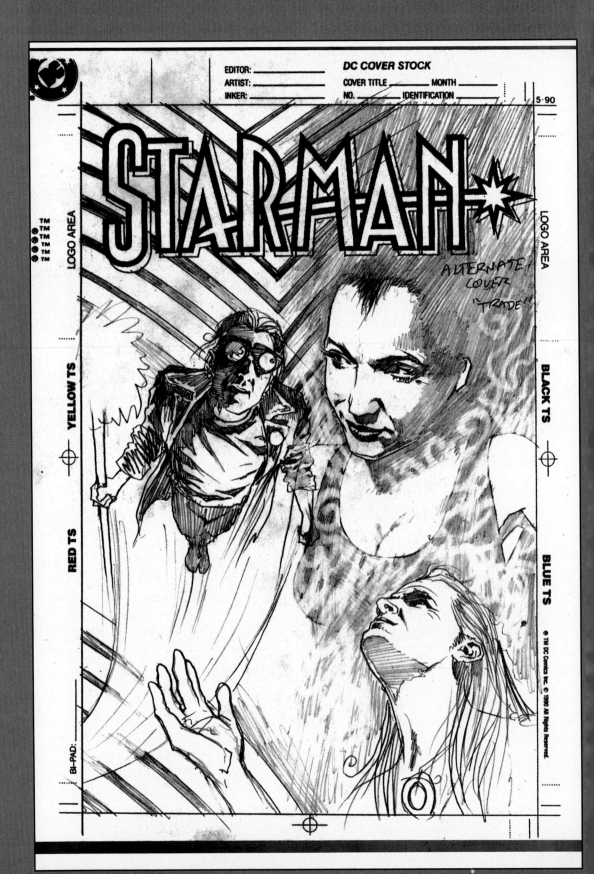

★ An alternate cover sketch for the second trade paperback.

offered me the gig writing *Grendel Tales* after him, and the quixotic world of American comics began forever.

And at the same time the other, less immediate element to my future (and the work you hold in your hands) presented itself in the need for back-cover copy for *London's Dark* prior to it being published. Archie Goodwin read it, liked it enough to give me a quote, and liked me and my work enough to stay in contact.

Where are we now? So many names and pieces of the puzzle I'm getting confused. Oh, yeah, one more. Mark Badger. He was another big heart, fresh from doing Marvel's *Gargoyle* miniseries. Big-heart, sure and big style. Wild. Seriously like nothing else in mainstream comics at that time (and maybe not ever since, seriously, call me wrong). I met him at the same UKAC, made friends with him and hung out with him when he decided to stay on in London longer than the convention. These are the relevant aspects to that — vis-à-vis me and Starman and you reading this rambling text. Mark and I, drunk in Notting Hill, staggering into an art-house movie theater to watch Tom Waits' performance movie *Big Time*. People who know me, know my divine worship of Waits, but this is the moment, watching vision along with his words —

— Megaphones and fleabag motels and the poetry in the bottom of a shot glass and John Fante being a genius and the warm pulse of a burlesque organ and the sudden crescendo of a string section and all that — that something fell into place.

And that was Mark, drunk and a good guy and not knowing the crazy stuff going on in my head. It was also Mark, when I ventured from England on a brief visit to New York, who stepped up and introduced me to an editor at DC. Mark Waid. Back in the day. Mark Waid. Who seemed full of a secret knowledge no one else knew — that being he was a brilliant writer in his own right. Like I say, who knew? All I do know is, he was the editor of SECRET ORIGINS, and while allowing Roy Thomas as a writer to then chart the pre-Crisis history of the DC Universe character by character (half of each issue) he seemed to allow all and sundry to do their thing in the present day DC Universe — including me. Based on Mark B's recommendation, Mark W took a jump into the abyss and gave me my first mainstream gig — "The Secret Origin of Dinosaur Island."

Back in London, I wrote it with the glee of someone knowing he was doing perfection. (I'm lying — the reality is I overwrote the script — full of piss and vinegar and none — not one bit — of the creative guile that a true master of words of the page pulls into play.) Despite this, the story got an artist — Tim Burgard — who pencilled his heart out and made my crap look half decent on the page. Was it the beginning of something great? I can tell you, Tim's pencils were certainly wonderful. My script? I dunno. It's moot. During DC's move from 666 Fifth Avenue to its next location, everything was lost. Oh well.

Meanwhile Mike Lake (remember him?) offers me a brief job helping to open a comic book store in Los Angeles. I accept the job and here I am — America. I never really go back, and before I know it this is home.

— WAIT. Back up. There's a big piece here — a big person — I almost forget to mention. How could I? The person? Grant Morrison. Everyone has a hero in the field they choose to call their own — many heroes — influences — people to aspire to. I've listed a few above. The one I've yet to acknowledge is Grant.

I consider Grant a truly unique figure. Truth be told, I can't figure him out. Every creator has some flaw, and I've yet to find his. He does standard superhero fare brilliantly (his run on BATMAN being a fine example). He does narrative at the far reaches of the abstract equally brilliantly. Each way, all in all, I think he's a genius. Back in the day, *Zenith, The New Adventures of Hitler*, amazing. And then there was DOOM PATROL.

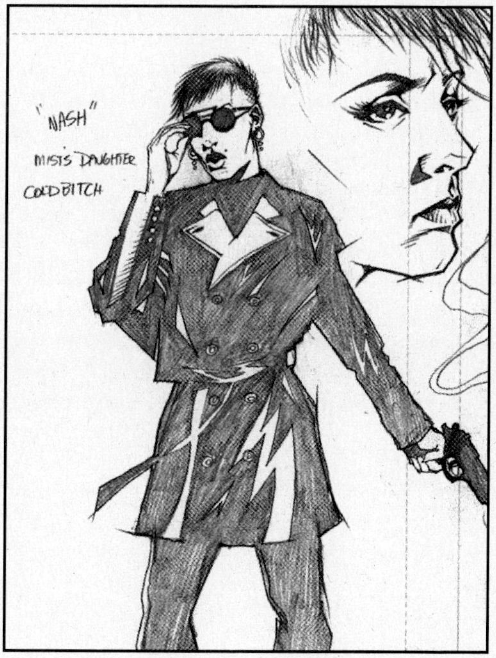
"NASH"
MIST'S DAUGHTER
COLD BITCH

"KYLE" WYSTS SON

KYLES WEAPON
.44 MAGNUM
AUTOMATIC 8 ROUND MAGAZINE
WITH OPTIONAL
MINI FLAMETHROWER
16 OZ. CAPACITY
LIQUID PLASMA FLAME

Before Vertigo, the Doom Patrol's "rebirth" lay at the helm of editor Robert Greenberger. Eighteen issues had been published as a DC title. Grant began with #19.

Sidebar here — back in the day before mega conventions, when fan and pro could walk and talk alike at the local bar as long as they enjoyed alcohol on their lips, England was a much happier place. This was where I first met Gibbons and Bolland and shared brandies with Kaluta and Vess. And later still, with my professional career about to begin, at a convention in Birmingham, I nervously approached Grant and first spoke about my appreciation of his *2000AD* work (*Zenith*) and my hopes for his work on DOOM PATROL.

He told me his hopes were thus — fact — that Arnold Drake's run on the original DOOM PATROL is one of the weirdest, most wonderful things ever published. "Negative Man" alone. "Robot Man" alone. "Monsieur Mallah," a talking ape with a beret and a French accent, "the Brain" — a, well…a brain, in a trolley. "The Animal-Vegetable-Mineral Man." And on and on. Grant listed an array of elements that made this book the most surreal thing published under the banner of mainstream comics, and it was his intention to keep that going, marrying the world of Superman and superheroics now with the crazy fantasy of then — Arnold Drake and Bruno

Premiani. And, as Grant was eager to point out, all that surreal wonder was available for kids, the same kids reading Superman Red and Superman Blue.

And so he did for the first arc, and then something happened. Seemingly overnight, comics grew up.

DC launched their Vertigo line. Comics at the mature end of the spectrum were swept up. They became what they became. Some overwrought. Some brilliant. Out-of-the-gate brilliant was THE SANDMAN by Gaiman. A masterpiece. Another masterpiece — Grant's DOOM PATROL. Grant's ANIMAL MAN, for that matter. Given complete freedom, he turned the book into a hallucinogenic wonderland of characters and situations. A French-speaking transvestite street(?) called Danny — a nod to the brilliant British tranny comic Danny La Rue. Forgive me, but Morrison is a genius. But. The thing I was hoping for. Arnold Drake meets the mainstream. Was lost.

(I think I should take a break here between paragraphs about Grant M and Archie G to apologize for my overuse of the words "genius" and "brilliant.")

At the same time DC wasn't the "anything goes" place it is now. It was a world of editorial domains and everything "almost" and "not quite" and me, hungry, prowling like a caged lion, wanting to get in.

Back to Archie Goodwin. I'd met him. He'd liked me. (Like Matt Wagner, if you didn't like him back, there's something wrong with you — times, like, a billion.) Plus he created the mythology for

"BLACK PIRATE" MAYBE LOSE THE PUPILS IN EYES (JUST WHITES)

Vampirella. Plus he single-handedly started/wrote all the amazing horror and war stories at Warren, editing as he was writing — with the artistic cream of creativity at that time: Craig, Crandell, Ditko, Colan and Toth (Alex Toth, crazy genius, the Orson Welles of comics, these two — Archie and Alex — created majesty. At Warren and later at DC — for all you collectors — "Burma Sky" [OUR FIGHTING FORCES #146] is one of the greatest short pieces ever created.) Plus Archie (re)created Manhunter as a backup in the 100-page DETECTIVE COMICS. Never mind that the Batman stories in DETECTIVE by Archie were amazing (yeah, I know I said he was the editor, but he wrote too, bear with me...the man was a genius). "Manhunter" was beyond comics at that time. Archie saw the future — Bruce Lee, martial arts, 1970s paranoia, the intimate savagery of Peckinpah's "The Killer Elite." Plus he brought Walt Simonson to the public's attention with this arc (now, not so singular — *then*, nothing like him in comics). And on. And on. And — Archie was the nicest, funniest, most inspiring fellow you might ever hope to meet.

Who I met. Who I to this day thank God that I met.

Archie was in transit, between Marvel and DC. Then at DC, at that time of editorial hierarchy unable to offer much work, we kicked about this or that (non-superhero) idea. Then, as the floodgates started to

open, he began editing non-continuity DC character miniseries. And that is when Archie, Paul Smith and I came up with THE GOLDEN AGE.

It remains one of my greatest feats, but — this isn't about that. In terms of this afterword THE GOLDEN AGE is merely another step. It took an age to get that four-parter out, and in that time Archie was given provisional entry into the mainstream DC Universe through LEGENDS OF THE DARK KNIGHT (DCU, but before present day). Through Matt Wagner I'd met Tim Sale — artist of a *Grendel* arc. Archie suggested I make some dough — while THE GOLDEN AGE took its rusty, slow-turning age to get completed — by writing an arc. Archie loved Tim Sale's work. I loved the fact that Basil Rathbone was a legitimate swordsman — and there begat LEGENDS OF THE DARK KNIGHT: BLADES.

At the same time the work of mainstream comics (at DC where I'd decided to hang my hat and frankly where I felt most comfortable — for no other reason that for every Kree/Skrull appearance I loved the albeit hokier Earth X/Earth S appearance) was slipping into two distinct paths. Superheroes. Vertigo. Neither better nor worse. Just different. Gaiman's SANDMAN. Gerard Jones's JUSTICE LEAGUE. Good luck comparing either one/all.

And yet, I missed what had been. That moment. When the mature comic met the gleam and color and surreal mayhem of the comic book fantastic. To this day, I recall the end of the first true arc of SWAMP THING by Moore. When cleaning up after Woodrue's mayhem, Superman called Green Lantern "Hal" and GL called Supes "Kal," and the dialogue, like weary cops doing what they do with no end in sight, they fell from the sky, collected the ne'er-do-well (Woodrue) and were gone again. Tired. Colorful. Tired. Heroes.

As come-what-may as it sounds now, I recall people calling that the greatest Justice League moment of all time. Alan Moore. What a guy.

So, where were we? I forget with all these sidebars and what-have-yous. I read through this and I'm torn — part of me feels this is an opportunity to give you a running play-by-play of what was going on in my head during the run-up to/and as Starman came to be. Part of me thinks this is a load of cobblers.

So where were we? (Mainstream) comics were polarized — mature and not. The mid-ground I loved seemed on hold. Meanwhile I'm hovering in space, hoping I can finally get the monthly gig that all fledgling writers hope for.

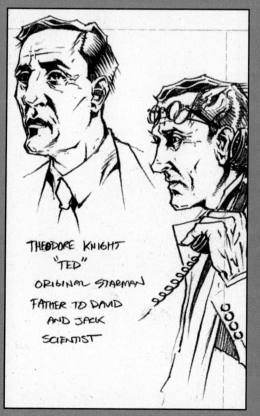

THEODORE KNIGHT
"TED"
ORIGINAL STARMAN
FATHER TO DAVID
AND JACK
SCIENTIST

I have a feeling. A tone. A need to return to the superhero and the real/the Miller/the Moore.

At this point in time it could be interchangeable, based on characters, based on companies. I pitch a character called "Mr. Jones" to Karen Berger at Vertigo. It would be Vertigo continuing to dip its foot in the DCU, with references to the Haunted Tank, Jason Woodrue (who now, reformed, would be a Louisiana version of the Shade/anti-hero arche-type) and a bunch of other obscure elements from DCU's illustrious past. Karen passes.

At the same time Marvel approaches me to do a re-vamp of "Doc Samson," taking him away from his Hulk roots and making him a character in his own right. I come up with a take set in San Francisco (no fictional cities in Marvelverse) involving more arcane Marvel lore and The Ringmaster from the Circus of Crime as the anti-hero archetype. The editor of the Hulk passed on that too.

Oh well.

At the same time I looked at the books from times past that had made something of an impact. *Daredevil* was a bimonthly, close to cancellation, when Miller took it over. SWAMP THING was on the ropes. DOOM PATROL wasn't looking the best before Grant touched it with his greatness.

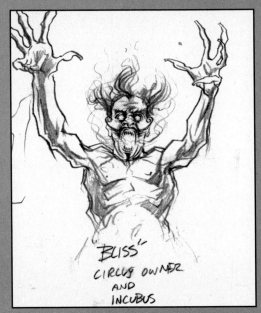

"BLISS"
CIRCUS OWNER
AND
INCUBUS

I looked at STARMAN. Will Payton. A version of the character that to all and sundry among readers of comics was reviled. I don't completely understand why. It just was.

I could tell this book was close to cancellation. I mentioned it to Archie, who listened and took it in his stride as any sane fellow would.

Oh, but Archie didn't get it. I had plans for Will Payton. I would create a lineage of Starmen. I would begin with Ted Knight and bring each subse-quent Starman into the fold. That, I saw, was the problem. Jay Garrick and Barry Allen and Wally West all run together. Hal Jordan and Alan Scott shine good green light in unison. Al Pratt and Ray Palmer do — whatever it is they do individually — together. Where was the passing of the cosmic torch with Starman, even at that point with more heroes having that mantle than any of them?

So I had plans. Will Payton meets/bonds with the Knights, at the same time relocating to a city where he could become (for want of a better terminology) the cosmic "Tom Waits" of comics. I admit the plan needed work. But I tell the idea to Archie who, I assume, based on my wistful mist of an idea, forgets about it immediately.

Weeks, months pass. And then they cancel the book and then they kill Will Payton. Good and bad. A lot of stuff needs shifting around, but now I was free and clear.

I call up Archie, flush with excitement. I should mention that by now, Archie's assistant is one Chuck

FAX 4 ARCHIE
"INGAR"
THE PINHEAD
GIANT
LATER
BECOMES
"CRUSHER"

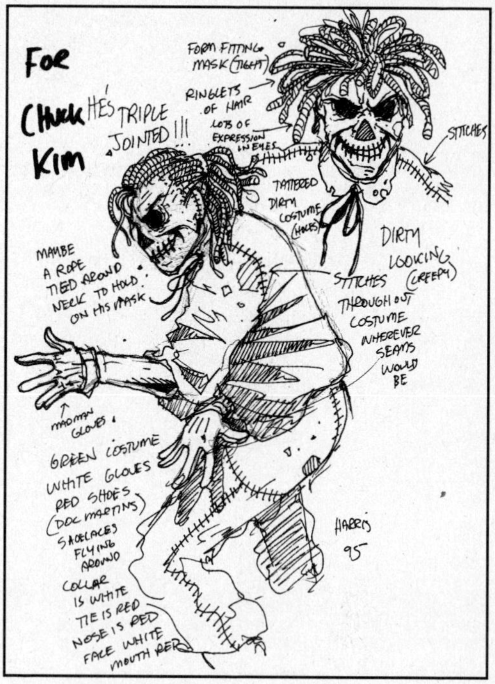
For Chuck Kim
HE'S TRIPLE JOINTED!!!
FORM FITTING MASK (TIGHT)
RINGLETS OF HAIR
LOTS OF EXPRESSION IN EYES
STITCHES
TATTERED DIRTY COSTUME (HOLES)
DIRTY LOOKING (CREEPY)
MAYBE A ROPE TIED AROUND NECK TO HOLD ON HIS MASK
STITCHES THROUGHOUT COSTUME WHEREVER SEAMS WOULD BE
MADMAN GLOVES
GREEN COSTUME
WHITE GLOVES
RED SHOES (DOC MARTINS)
SHOELACES FLYING AROUND
COLLAR IS WHITE
TIE IS RED
NOSE IS RED
FACE WHITE
MOUTH RED
HARRIS 95

Kim, a young man who became a hero in my eyes later in our narrative — another day, another time when Archie became ill. That's later. Sadder.

Now. At this moment in time Chuck is bright eyed, bushy tailed, young and eager and not quite everything he would become. And there I am on the phone with Archie, breathless —

"STARMAN is cancelled, Archie. Starman is dead. Reserve the character for us, Archie! Archie, aren't you listening?"

Archie responds with all the humor and sarcasm and joy that he was known for, yelling off-telephone —

"Chuck! It's the Starman call! Reserve, Chuck! Run! Chuck! Fly!!"

So once I stopped laughing and realized what an idiot I sounded like, Archie informed me that he had never forgotten my thoughts on the character and he'd already reserved Starman for me (and him, and as it turned out, for a fantastic artist named Tony Harris).

I came up with the initial idea for Jack Knight quicker than I can believe. I think I was always meant to write this character. I had to have been. Once the idea began to form, so much of it cascaded from me, elements that didn't manifest themselves until the final arcs — that's the only way I can explain it. I was told that this would be a miniseries, four issues — that if they went well might lead to an ongoing series, no promises.

Archie (a group editor) needed another group editor to sign off on the project (that was how they did it at that time). He went to Mike Carlin. Carlin is a man I've never worked with, but since that time I've met and enjoyed his company every time we've had a drink or a bite. Some people say he's tough. I saw immediately that the guy simply cared about stuff — not in the saving his ass/his job kind of way. Rather, the guy genuinely cared about the lore of these characters. And not in a geeky, uncomfortable way — if Carlin had been a guy doing wheel alignments in a Brooklyn garage or working at a games company designing a version of Monopoly around the presidency of Woodrow Wilson, you'd still want to hang with him and hear what he had to say. And what he'd say would be funny. In fact, in the world of comics, as far as I'm concerned, Carlin is second to Archie in my book in terms of his humor.

Anyway, back before I knew this about Mike — when he was just this "hard-assed" Superman group editor, he signed off on STARMAN, not just as a miniseries, but as an ongoing. (Come to think of it — I've never thanked him for that. Another example of my being a knucklehead. Mike, you know I think you're amazing. Thanks. Thank you. Helping me then, and the way each time we shake hands at a convention, and it feels like the other day, not last year, it means the world to me. You really are one in a million.)

So now where are we — good God, I love a drink so by this point, several tequilas into this, even I'm losing track —

— Oh yeah. I honed my first arc. Basically "Sins of the Father" — issues #0 to 3. Enjoy. And we needed an artist. I didn't know who exactly. All I knew was we needed two things:

1. We needed someone who was comfortable with shadow and darkness. One of the light, bright superhero artists wasn't going to cut it. I based this both on my ideas for the characters in this first arc and the cloudy ideas, slowly coming real for future arcs. On top of that, I saw that two of my favorite Golden Age artists to draw Starman — Jack Burnley and Mort Meskin (a king — one of the greats in my eyes) — always depicted the character as a hero of the night. (Thinking about it now, as I write, maybe that's why Will Payton didn't resonate with readers. I think Payton, and I think "sun" and "bright" and nothing like the original character. Yeah, I know the sun is a star but — Burnley, especially, was adept at

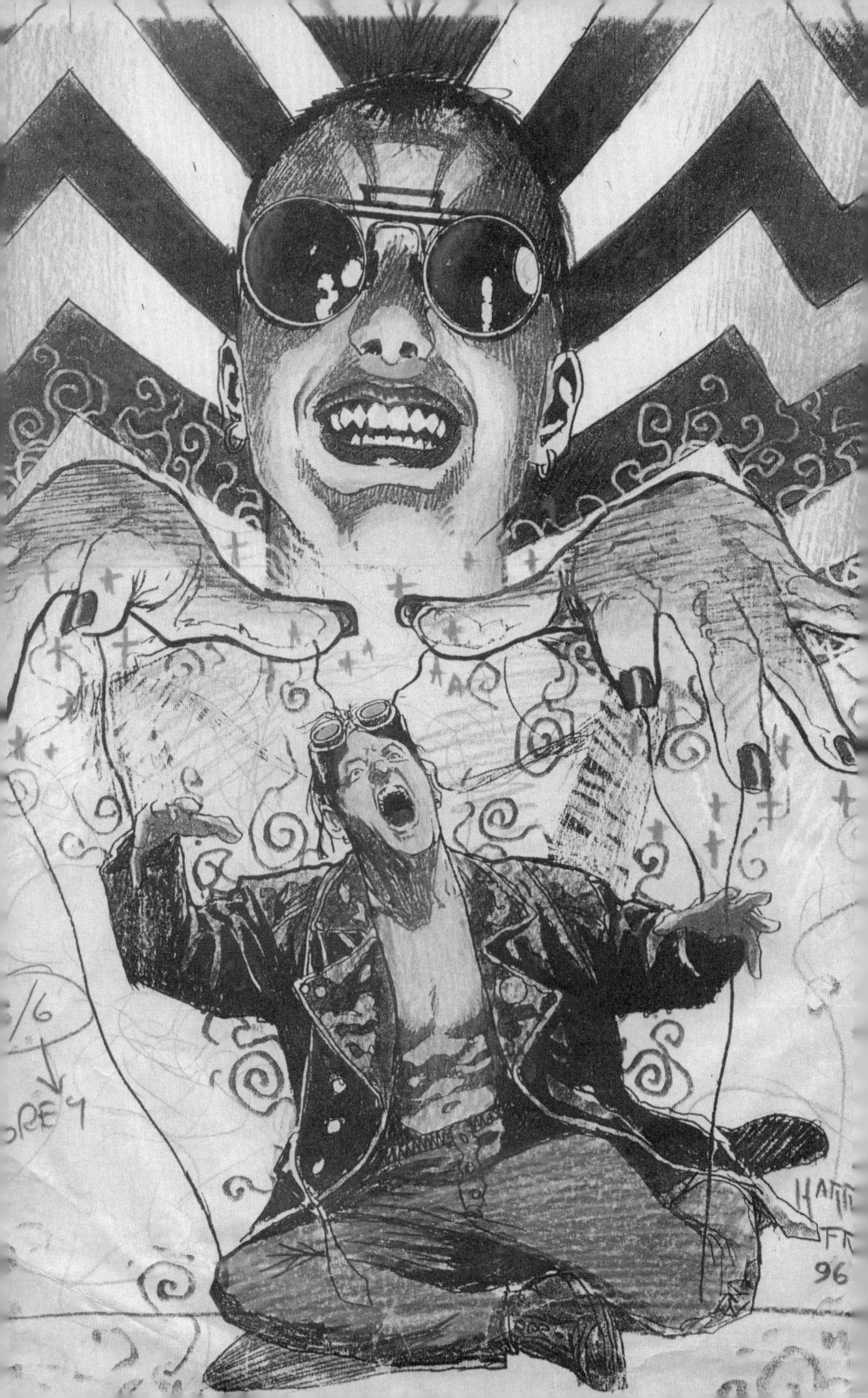
/6
96

"BABALOO" THE DEMON CHIMP

H·94

Superman, the brightest, sunniest character of them all. And yet Burnley took pains to make Starman a hero of the night.)

Jeez, I'm lost again. Oh yeah —

2. For a monthly book to catch hold and keep hold, it needs a regular artistic vision that can make the deadline month after month.

I had a feeling that someone from one of the "studios" that were popping up might give us what we needed. "Studios?" No. One studio in particular. Gaijin Studios in Georgia. All of them had that marriage of light and shadow, real and fantastic, down. And I, as a person, had met them all, liked them all. The one problem —

— At that time none of them seemed up to a monthly gig. They were all way cool as artists, but they all seemed a part of that three-issue-and-bail syndrome. But they were all brilliant. Don't get me wrong. And they all knew light and dark, shadow and light. And. And. And…

One guy stood out. He did not have the best reputation for deadlines or being easy to work with. And yet. He had a quality.

Tony Harris. God, I've known this guy for so long. Are we friends? I don't know. I know we've argued

like friends. I know I like him like a friend should, but we live so far apart, I confess I've never really gotten a handle on the guy.

My concern working with him was that he was too reliant on photos. That's great for a cover or a page of conversation, but if we have a page of Darkseid's Hunger Dogs attacking the Justice League, God help you. Plus, I heard he had an attitude. I have an attitude. The two of us would be a nightmare.

What I found — Tony did indeed have an attitude. He cared about his work. He cared. We argued, sure, but always for the right reasons and so the book was better for the conflict. Plus, Archie, apple-pie Archie, could be a tiger when crossed. He showed me no quarter when push came to shove and I think Tony got the same stern taskmaster when he needed it.

I built in the "Times Past" device as a way for me to have fun with Opal City and Jack and all the historical things I liked. I also knew it was a way to give Tony breathing room. Archie and I, at first, thought he might only do the first arc of four issues and leave. And yet he stayed. He stayed and stayed and became completely invested in Jack Knight.

With a regular artist nowadays, you're lucky if you get nine issues a year. With Tony we got ten, and with a hiccup here or there, he stayed pretty consistent through his tenure.

You have the book in front of you, so you can see for yourself, but the art on the first few issues is a little suspect. (Quite frankly, so is the writing.) But with issue #4, you see the beginning of something special beginning to manifest in Tony's art.

Then Issue #5, the first "Talking with David." Tony called me, excited, aware he had creatively crossed a hurdle. I saw his work, his pencils, and I could have cried with pride. Tony was everything I'd hoped for and hoped he would be. I still have the original art for the first page of that issue. It's everything I ever wanted for Jack Knight.

And so you have it. Everything in this meandering afterword — this is the book I wanted to write, the book I thought in my arrogance DC needed — a return to that marriage of maturity and wonder, superheroes and everyday chats about nothing at all. On top of that I wanted a little Tom Waits and John Fante and Charles Dickens. And although I didn't know it then — in hindsight I wanted to speak to my dead mother and father and let them know I was doing okay and that I loved them. I was vain

★ Left: Approved cover sketch for second trade paperback.

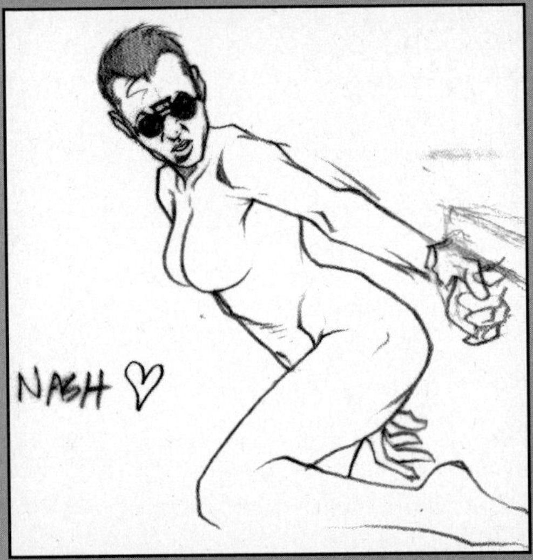
NASH ♡

enough to want people to know how much I loved Hoagy Carmichael and Robert Ryan and black velvet painted portraits of Elvis Presley.

There's one other aspect of this book I take singular pride in. Some may beg to differ, but I think I revived a dying aspect of comics (DC comics in particular). This being the fictional city, clearly based on a real one. How these metropolises were meant to coexist in roughly the same space as the real cities is beyond me, but that sense of unreality, guessing where the city was meant to be, was fun. Fun that DC comics of late had failed to embrace. Metropolis, yeah. Gotham, yeah. Supes, Bats, whatever. Apart from that, everything had taken the Marvel route, living in a real city. Lot of New York. Whole lot of New York.

I loved Central City, Midway City, Happy Harbor, Ivy Town. Creating Opal City was the most fun creatively I think I've ever had.

Oh, and how soon after do Morrison and Millar create a fictional city for Aztek? Just the start. Before you know it, everyone's got a fresh city with a fresh name. Gentlemen, you know who you are. Bow down to the one who came first.

I'll wrap this up. I thought you might enjoy a DC Comics version of *War and Peace*, word for word, but I think that will keep until the next volume.

The point is, the point I am trying to get across is how all these people — big-hearted people — can, in small ways, make something bigger. In this case, my life — at that time.

How all these people can be acknowledged and loved in hindsight. They all were a part of it, and I was so quick to assume that it was the divine right of my talent as a writer. In light of time spent living, I see I was a fool and all these people were jewels only the luckiest of souls gets to hold to the sun and in them see the wonder of everything. Again, I apologize to one and all.

Now before I convince you all to kill yourselves, let's lighten up, remember that "Hey, it's only funny books." I hope you enjoyed this, the first of Tony Harris's and my fledgling attempts at immortality.

Of which more will be told in our next installment.

James Robinson
Hollywood, California
March, 2008

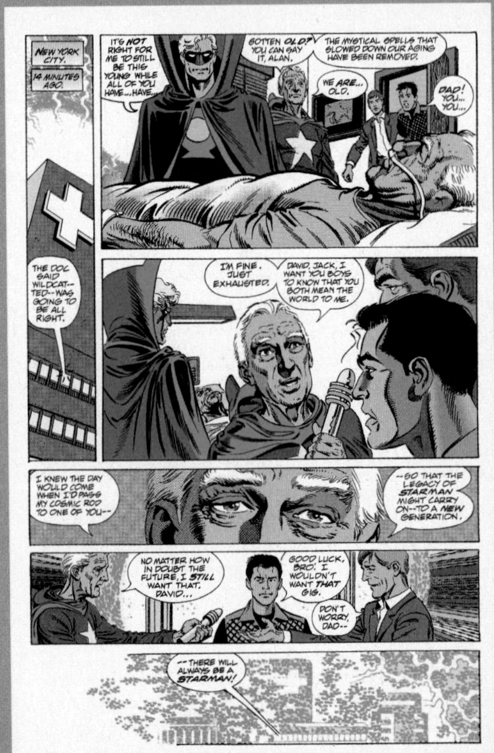
NEW YORK CITY.
14 MINUTES AGO.
IT'S NOT RIGHT FOR ME TO STILL BE THIS YOUNG WHILE ALL OF YOU HAVE... HAVE...
GOTTEN OLD? YOU CAN SAY IT, ALAN.
THE MYSTICAL SPELLS THAT SLOWED DOWN OUR AGING HAVE BEEN REMOVED.
WE ARE... OLD.
DAD! YOU... YOU...
THE DOC SAID WILDCAT--TED--WAS GOING TO BE ALL RIGHT.
I'M FINE. JUST EXHAUSTED.
DAVID, JACK, I WANT YOU BOYS TO KNOW THAT YOU BOTH MEAN THE WORLD TO ME.
I KNEW THE DAY WOULD COME WHEN I'D PASS MY COSMIC ROD TO ONE OF YOU--
--SO THAT THE LEGACY OF STARMAN MIGHT CARRY ON--TO A NEW GENERATION.
NO MATTER HOW IN DOUBT THE FUTURE, I STILL WANT THAT. DAVID...
GOOD LUCK, BRO! I WOULDN'T WANT THAT GIG.
DON'T WORRY, DAD--
--THERE WILL ALWAYS BE A STARMAN!
Jack Knight's first appearance, in **ZERO HOUR #1** (1994). Written and pencilled by Dan Jurgens, with inks by Jerry Ordway, colors by Gregory Wright and letters by Gaspar Saladino.